AUTOCOURSE™

THE WORLD'S LEADING GRAND PRIX ANNUAL

icon
PUBLISHING LIMITED

SINGHA
Red Bull racing
FORMULA ONE TEAM
TEAM PARTNER
A GLOBAL PARTNER
Mark
Webber
Sebastian
Vettel
RISING
A NEW ERA
SINGHA
LG
www.singhabeer.com

AUTOCOURSE
2010–2011
is published by:
Icon Publishing Limited
Regent Lodge
4 Hanley Road
Malvern
Worcestershire
WR14 4PQ
United Kingdom

Tel: +44 (0)1684 564511

Email: info@autocourse.com
Website: www.autocourse.com

Printed in the United Kingdom by
Butler Tanner and Dennis Ltd
Caxton Road, Frome
Somerset BA11 1NF

ISBN: 978-1905334-57-5

DISTRIBUTORS
Gardners Books
1 Whittle Drive, Eastbourne,
East Sussex, BN23 6QH
Tel: +44 (0)1323 521555
email: sales@gardners.com

Chaters Wholesale Ltd
10B Doman Road
Camberley
Surrey GU15 3DF
Telephone: +44 (0)1276 686639
email: sales@gardners.com

NORTH AMERICA
Quayside Distribution Services
400 First Avenue North, Suite 300
Minneapolis, MN 55401 USA
Telephone: 612 344 8100
Fax: 612 344 8691

Dust jacket: 2010 World Champion Red Bull's Sebastian Vettel.

Title page: Hail the new champion! Sebastian Vettel is given a liberal dousing by Lewis Hamilton and Jenson Button.
Photographs: Peter J Fox

CONTENTS

Acknowledgements

The Editor of AUTOCOURSE wishes to thank the following for their assistance in compiling the 2010-11 edition. **France:** ACO; Federation Francaise du Sport Automobile; FIA (Jean Todt, Matteo Bonciani, Richard Woods, Alexandra Scherin, Charlie Whiting, Herbie Blash and Pat Behar). Renault F1 (Eric Bouiller, Bradley Lord, Clarisse Hoffmann and Will Hings) World Series by Renault); **Germany:** Formula 3 Vereinigung; Mercedes-Benz (Ross Brawn, Norbert Haug, Wolfgang Schattling and Nicola Armstrong); Sabine Kehm; Michael Schmidt; **Great Britain:** *Autocar;* Mark Blundell; Martin Brundle; Bob Constanduros; Maurice Hamilton; Jules Goux; Peter Windsor; Lotus (Tom Webb, Tony Fernandes and Mike Gascoyne); McLaren (Ron Dennis, Martin Whitmarsh, Jonathan Neale, Matt Bishop, Steve Cooper, Silvia Hoffer Frangipane, Justine Bowen, Clare Robertson, Sarah Shortt, Lyndy Redding, Simon Points, Paddy Lowe and Neil Oatley); Red Bull Racing (Christian Horner, Adrian Newey, Helmut Marko, Katie Tweedle, Britta Roeske and Amelia Hooper); Force India (Lucy Genon); Nigel Roebuck; Sir Stirling Moss; Sir Jackie Stewart; Williams F1 (Sir Frank Williams, Patrick Head, Sam Michael, Jonathan Williams, Claire Williams and Liam Clogger); VirgIn Racing (John Booth and Tracy Novak); **Italy:** Commissione Sportiva Automobilistica Italiana; Scuderia Ferrari (Stefano Domenicali, Luca Colajanni and Stefania BoccI); Scuderia Toro Rosso (Franz Tost, Giorgio Ascanelli, Eric Silberman, Fabiana Valenti and Marieluise Mammitsch); **Japan:** Bridgestone (Rachel Ingham and Andy Stobart); **Spain:** HRT (Colin Kolles, Alba Saiz and Julia Spacek); **Switzerland:** BMW Sauber (Peter Sauber, Hanspeter Brack and Heikke Hinnitsch); USA: ALMS Media Service; Speed TV; Indy Racing League; Indianapolis Motor Speedway; Daytona International Speedway; NASCAR, Roger Penske, *SportsCar.*

Photographs published in AUTOCOURSE 2010–2011 have been contributed by:

Chief photographer: Peter J Fox. **Chief contributing photographers:** Bernard Asset; Paul-Henri Cahier; Lucas Gorys; Peter Nygaard of GP Photo; Jad Sherif and Jean François-Galeron of WRi2.

Other photographs contributed by: GP2 Media; GP3 Media; F3 Euroseries; World Series by Renault; HRT F1 Team; Lotus Racing; Renault F1 Team; Red Bull Racing; Sauber F1 Team; Shell Motorsport; Vodafone McLaren Mercedes; Luca Bassini, Dieter Mathis and Studio Colombo for WRi2; LAT Photographic: Phil Abbott, Jeff Bloxham, Dan R. Boyd, Charles Coates, Brian Czobat, Jakob Ebrey, Drew Gibson, Nigel Kinrade, Walt Kuhn, Michael Levitt, Lesley Ann Miller, Alastair Staley and Kevin Wood.

publisher
STEVE SMALL
steve.small@iconpublishinglimited.com

commercial director
BRYN WILLIAMS
bryn.williams@iconpublishinglimited.com

editor
ALAN HENRY

f1 correspondent
SIMON ARRON

f1 technical editor
MARK HUGHES

text editor
IAN PENBERTHY

results and statistics
DAVID HAYHOE

chief photographer
PETER J FOX
www.peterjfox.com

chief contributing photographers
BERNARD ASSET
PAUL-HENRI CAHIER
JEAN-FRANÇOIS GALERON
LUKAS GORYS
PETER NYGAARD
JAD SHERIF

f1 car and circuit illustrations
ADRIAN DEAN
f1artwork@blueyonder.co.uk

AUTOCOURSE™
www.autocourse.com

FOREWORD by

SEBASTIAN VETTEL

Firstly, I would like to thank all of Red Bull's supporters in the UK and around the world. When I stood on the podium in Abu Dhabi and realised that we had done it, seeing the Red Bull Racing boys waving and shouting, I had a lot of mixed emotions. I thought for a moment, "Is this real or just a dream?" Then I was so proud of us and everyone who had always believed in our mission, especially after races like Spa and Korea. It is not over until it's over!

In the end, it was an extraordinary battle and one of the most competitive championships of all time. From racing karts around my parents' back garden at the age of six, to crossing the finish line in Abu Dhabi, all I have ever wanted to do is race cars. Now I am just so proud of my team and myself. It's important not to look back and to always have a target, and my goal for 2011 is clear – to repeat what we have done. It won't be easy, but first it starts with the belief!

Sebastian Vettel

Photo: Peter J Fox

The Home of Business
The Bahrain International Circuit is setting new standards in the world of business. Set against a stunning desert landscape, BIC provides a unique and exclusive setting to host conferences, stage seminars, hold media events and organise private functions.
حلبة البحرين الدولية
Bahrain International Circuit
بابكو
Bapco
بتلكو
Batelco
ARCAPITA
ابراهيم خليل كانو
EBRAHIM K. KANOO

and Motorsport

EDITOR'S INTRODUCTION

AN EPIC SEASON

By any standards, 2010 delivered an epic grand prix season. You might say that tinkering with the points system opened up the possibility of more contenders being in play for the championship for longer than usual, but there was still a premium on consistency and dependability, as Fernando Alonso and Mark Webber found to their cost when the shadows lengthened and the track lighting came on in Abu Dhabi, and the final race of the season edged towards its spine-tingling conclusion.

Despite rule changes that further restricted the number of tyres competitors could use, and the initially controversial decision to dispense with in-race refuelling, the racing was generally pretty good. The doomsayers predictably wrote the whole thing off as a bad job after the year opened on a depressingly processional note in Bahrain, but the competition soon took off, and it's fair to say that F1 never looked back from that point on, even though some of the newer circuits on the schedule did not do much by way of enhancing a reputation for close racing.

At the end of the day, Sebastian Vettel stood astride the F1 globe as the youngest champion that the sport has ever produced. He won five of Red Bull Racing's nine grand prix victories, the other four deservedly – and brilliantly – garnered by his dogged team-mate, Mark Webber. If there was any criticism, it would be that, given the technical superiority displayed by Adrian Newey's superb Red Bull RB6, the team could reasonably have been expected to deliver significantly more race wins during the record 19-race contest.

Yet in so many ways, the RB6 was a classic grand prix car: edgy, brittle and operating right on the margins. Truly it embodied Newey's uncompromising commitment to wring every ounce of performance from its specification, and if sometimes that meant tipping it over the brink into a bout of unreliability, then that was a risk that he and the team were prepared to take in this high-stakes battle.

Red Bull again used Renault engines, which, by common consensus, were not quite on a par with the rival Mercedes V8s employed by McLaren, the factory Merc squad (née Brawn) and the occasionally impressive Force Indias, but they were certainly good enough in the high-performance environment created by the Milton Keynes-based squad.

The two Red Bull drivers stormed into the 2010 season on the crest of a wave of optimism. With good reason. Vettel had finished runner-up in the previous year's title chase, in a season when Webber had recovered from leg injuries to cement his reputation as a potential grand prix winner. Now they were ready to use that crucial experience as a springboard to even more sustained success. And they did just that.

Not that it was an easy ride for Red Bull team principal Christian Horner, whose innate diplomacy and political skills were sometimes stretched close to breaking point as he worked to prevent the rivalry between his charges from bubbling over. The most fraught moment of the year came at Istanbul Park, where the two Red Bull drivers collided while battling for the lead. But the intensity of their rivalry was what drove both men to push the envelope as relentlessly as they did. When the dust settled on Red Bull's successful clinching of the constructors' championship after the penultimate race at Interlagos, followed a week later by Vettel's wrapping up of the drivers' crown, you would be hard put to argue that this rivalry was a bad thing.

Ferrari and McLaren shared the winning game with Red Bull, Jenson Button taking the very logical decision to sign up to an offer from McLaren, where he joined sitting tenant Lewis Hamilton. While Hamilton stayed in play – albeit as a rank outsider – right up to the final race of the season, Button had a less-consistent year. When he got his McLaren set up to his personal preference, he was certainly a formidable contender, but when he drifted away from the 'sweet spot', he could deliver disappointing form. Nevertheless, McLaren continued to be a force in pretty much every race on the calendar, even if it was unable to thwart the Red Bull victory bandwagon.

At Ferrari, Fernando Alonso duly rolled up at Maranello to take over from Kimi Räikkönen. The Ferrari F1.10 was not the most competitive car on the starting grid, but Alonso's driving genius ensured that it could be pushed the final mile, to the point where it was always in contention for a podium finish. Unfortunately for the Prancing Horse, its challenge fell apart strategically in the final race of the year, so even the imposition of team orders at Hockenheim, where Felipe Massa was controversially 'invited' to concede the lead to his team-mate, did not save the day.

If Vettel starred on the F1 stage as the youngest ever world champion, so the oldest man on the grid, at 41, made a game effort to reinvent himself after three years away from the cockpit of an F1 machine. Michael Schumacher strapped himself into the the newly branded Mercedes, but the re-learning process was far more difficult than most of his supporters anticipated. Taken as a whole across the season, he was blown away by his young team-mate, Nico Rosberg, and although he was supported by weighty technical explanations to the effect that he found the current generation of Bridgestone tyres difficult to work to best effect – and that things would likely be better in 2011 – there was no way that Schumacher's return to F1 could be argued as anything but an acute disappointment.

At the opposite end of the starting grid, there were three

As ever, Mr E was the real winner in the five-way driver battle for the 2010 World Championship.

Photo: Peter J Fox

Above: Ferrari fell at the final hurdle in Abu Dhabi. With both Massa *(above)* and Alonso covering Webber, Vettel took the win – and the title.
Photo: Peter J Fox

Left: Sir Jackie Stewart, who continues to be a vibrant and eloquent force on the F1 scene, in discussion with FIA steward Danny Sullivan in Singapore.
Photo: Jad Sherif/WRi2

Below: My flexible friend? Adrian Newey and his team oversee every detail of the championship winning Red Bull RB6 chassis at Suzuka.
Photo: Peter J Fox

new teams – Lotus, Virgin and HRT – who arrived on the scene prompted by a raft of regulation changes agreed with the established entrants. The deep-seated complexity involved in trying to get a fledgling F1 operation off the ground in the current commercial climate was highlighted by the fact that none of these Cosworth-propelled teams managed to score a single championship point all year. On the other hand, Williams showcased what could be done with a Cosworth engine package, and Nico Hülkenberg planted one of Sir Frank's cars on pole in Brazil, more than five years after they had last registered such a worthy achievement.

Of course, this was the 60th anniversary of the start of the official F1 world championship, which had kicked off in 1950 at Silverstone, so it was appropriate that the self-styled home of British motor racing was spruced up for the occasion with a superbly re-vamped track developed by its owner, the British Racing Drivers' Club. The administration and imposition of penalties at the races also had a fresh consistency to it, thanks to the FIA's decision to appoint a retired driver to the stewards' panel at each of the world championship rounds. This also helped to consolidate what many insiders discerned as a less confrontational and more tranquil environment under Jean Todt's FIA presidency compared to that under the regime of his predecessor, Max Mosley.

In addition to offering the reader a detailed chronicle of the 2010 FIA F1 world championship, we have cast our editorial net rather wider than usual, with penetrating interviews with Sir Stirling Moss and Sir Jackie Stewart to offer a perspective on the sport's development, which serve as graphic reminders of how the sport has evolved over those action packed 60 years.

Elsewhere on the international racing scene, Audi excelled to win at Le Mans for the ninth time, equalling the second-place tally of wins achieved by Ferrari and now only headed by Porsche, which has won the French endurance classic on 16 occasions. Meanwhile, on the opposite side of the Atlantic, Scot Dario Franchitti continued to be one of the leading lights on the IRL scene, winning the Indianapolis 500 for the second time in his career.

Looking ahead, the F1 championship is set to expand to 20 races in 2011 with the planned arrival of India on the schedule to succeed 2010 fixture Korea as the most recent country to embrace the world championship business. Although commercially the sport is still under pressure, as can be seen from the fact that there is vacant advertising space on even the most established front running cars, the long-term outlook looks brighter than some might reasonably have expected a couple of years ago, with television viewing figures holding up pretty well considering the economic pressure in the wider world.

Germany's RTL channel, whihc had not attracted viewing figures in excess of ten million since before Schumacher retired in 2006, peaked at 12.1 million viewers during Vettel's title clinching run at Abu Dhabi, and even though there was no celebration this time for a British world champion, the UK figures only dipped to 5.3 million, from the 6.6 million who had switched on to watch Jenson clinch the title at Interlagos 12 months ago. Not bad, given all the circumstances.

Alan Henry,
Tillingham, Essex, UK
November 2010

THE DRIVER'S WATCH
No other watch is engineered quite like a Rolex. The Cosmograph Daytona, introduced in 1963, was designed to meet the demands of professional race-car drivers and quickly earned its iconic status. With its patented chronograph mechanism and bezel with tachometric scale, it allows drivers to perfectly measure elapsed circuit time and calculate average speed. The Cosmograph Daytona is presented here in Rolex-patented Everose gold.
THE COSMOGRAPH DAYTONA
ROLEX
ROLEX.COM

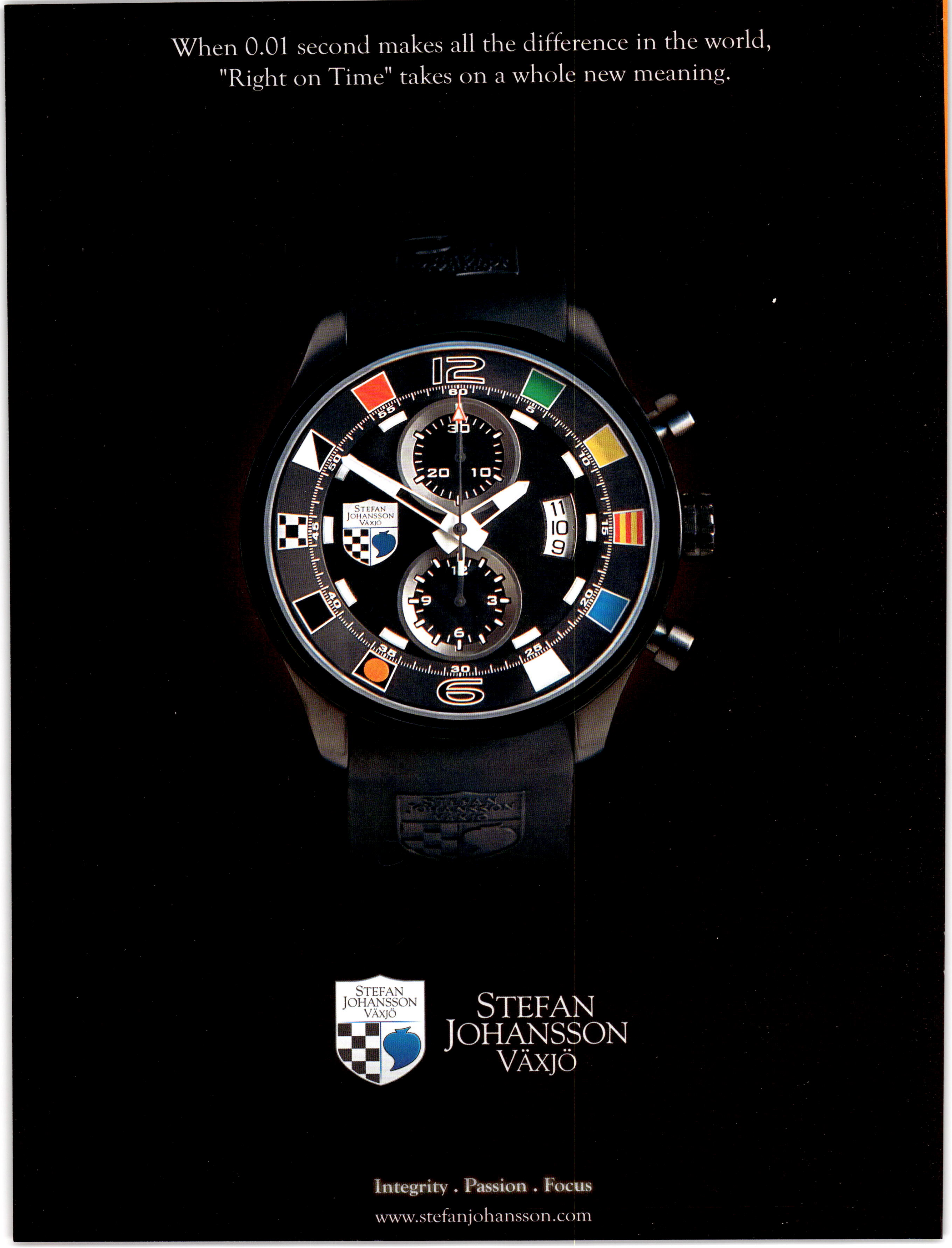
When 0.01 second makes all the difference in the world,
"Right on Time" takes on a whole new meaning.
STEFAN
JOHANSSON
VÄXJÖ
Integrity . Passion . Focus
www.stefanjohansson.com

FIA F1 WORLD CHAMPIONSHIP 2010

TOP TEN DRIVERS

THE EDITOR'S CHOICE

Photo: Peter J Fox

Driver Portraits by Peter J Fox

SEBASTIAN VETTEL

1

ROUNDING off the season with flawless wins at Interlagos and Abu Dhabi, Sebastian Vettel became the sport's youngest champion, and deservedly so. He won five races in 2010 and should have won eight. At least.

Almost certainly he was the best driver out there if one quantifies driving skill blended with raw racing savvy. That said, Vettel struggled initially to shrug aside the perception that he was Red Bull's chosen one, despite the soothing efforts of team principal Christian Horner, particularly in the wake of his collision with Webber at Istanbul. In summary, it was very much a bruising and instructive start to the season for the bright young talent who surely will bestride the F1 community much like Michael Schumacher did a decade ago.

For all that, sometimes it was difficult to remember Vettel as the polished outsider who drove so brilliantly to win the 2008 Italian GP at Monza for the Toro Rosso squad. That golden memory was somewhat tarnished by Seb's part in the Turkish fiasco, his penalty for being tardy at the restart in Hungary and his collision with Button at Spa.

Wins in Malaysia, Valencia and Suzuka nonetheless were top-drawer performances, particularly at Sepang, where he was outqualified by Webber, but then outgunned his Australian rival from the moment the starting light went out, surging off the grid into an immediate lead that he never relinquished. But there were moments of inexperience as well, most notably at Spa-Francorchamps, where a fumbled overtaking manoeuvre saw him ram Jenson Button's McLaren off the road and out of the race.

One should also recall that technical problems with a sparking plug in Bahrain, and a major engine failure after a dominant run in Korea almost certainly deprived Vettel of two more grand prix victories and significantly reduced his championship points tally.

Yet, make no mistake, if you scratch the surface of that disappointment, you will still find a steely and motivated personality unwavering in his self-belief. Taken in the round, it was a brilliant season for Vettel, who finished the championship campaign much tougher than he started it.

2

LEWIS HAMILTON

LEWIS Hamilton started the season coming off the back of a difficult 2009 campaign as reigning world champion and finding his life further complicated by the challenge of squaring up to Jenson Button as his new team-mate. Although he had to watch Jenson take victories in Melbourne and Shanghai before getting his own tally off the ground, generally he did an outstanding job of fighting his corner and defending his reputation.

If Hamilton felt in any way ruffled by the arrival of another British world champion as his team-mate, he concealed it for most of the season. His first victory of the year came at the Turkish GP, where the internecine rivalry between the Red Bull boys handed him the win on a plate, even though Button overtook him in the closing stages, only for Lewis to pass him back in a move that was as decisive as it was symbolic. For a couple of corners, the two McLarens ran side by side before Hamilton reasserted his position. It was a telling demonstration of the two men's maturity and their understanding that ending up with both cars off the road would help nobody.

Lewis racked up his next victory in the following race at Montreal, followed by a fine success at Spa-Francorchamps, where he successfully rescued an off-track moment across a gravel trap that looked certain to end with his McLaren buried in the safety wall.

Yet there were moments when Lewis's exuberance – or his determination to outperform his machine – tempted him to push a little too hard. On the opening lap at Monza, he was a little too audacious when it came to challenging Felipe Massa's Ferrari under braking for the second chicane mid-way around the opening lap. He paid the price with broken right front suspension and an instant retirement.

A fortnight later in Singapore, he retired with a punctured tyre after snagging Webber's Red Bull during a fight for track position. This time, it was a legitimate racing incident that could be attributed to neither driver, but the fact was that a potential 50 points had gone out of Hamilton's window in two consecutive races, and from then on it always looked as though a second world championship crown was unlikely to come his way in the near future.

Thankfully, he put things back on track with second places in Korea and Abu Dhabi, remaining an outside hope for the championship right up to the final race of the year. Lewis never gave up right to the bitter end, even when his McLaren was being comprehensively outgunned by the opposition.

3

FERNANDO ALONSO

THERE is no doubt that Fernando Alonso is one of the finest drivers of the current F1 generation. Whether he can be categorised as a truly *great* driver is another matter altogether, and the essence of this debate is crystallised by the tempo of his 2010 campaign. Certainly, his long-awaited arrival in the Ferrari squad reinvigorated the Maranello brigade in the wake of Felipe Massa's accident in Hungary in 2009 and the departure of the curiously semi-detached Kimi Räikkönen who, it could be argued, never quite fully integrated himself with the Scuderia in the manner expected of its chosen ones.

Alonso may have won as many races as the eventual champion, although one is entitled to say that only two of those victories were achieved in the manner that is really the stuff of which legends are made. That said, in retrospect, perhaps too much was made of Ferrari's imposition of team orders, which yielded his victory over Massa at Hockenheim. Undoubtedly, his wins in Bahrain and Korea came as a result of Vettel encountering technical problems, but his successes at Monza and Singapore were absolutely outstanding, the Spanish ace seeing off Button and Vettel respectively after race-long chases that saw him under intense pressure all the way to the chequered flag.

In addition, Alonso had a lot of bad luck with safety cars and so-on, which meant the dice didn't always roll his way. Getting bogged down in traffic as the title crown slipped away from him in Abu Dhabi was a rare low moment and essentially not one of his making. The team that gained him those valuable extra points at Hockenheim cost him many more at Abu Dhabi and ultimately the chance of a third world championship title.

On balance, it was a good year, but not a great one, for Alonso, who continues to be one of the great enigmas of contemporary F1. After two seasons marking time with Renault, he started the year with a huge sense of anticipation surrounding his switch to Ferrari. He will be expected to deliver more in 2011. Much more.

MARK WEBBER

THE Australian tough nut built brilliantly on his 2009 achievements to make the very best of what most would agree was the late afternoon of his F1 career, and launch a credible and highly impressive world championship challenge. Dynamic, determined and charismatic, Webber was sufficiently shrewd to know that this was also his final opportunity to give the precocious young Sebastian Vettel a figurative clip around the ear before the German driver fully matures into the rounded and accomplished future title challenger that quite clearly he is.

Never one to be intimidated, either on or off the track, Webber didn't allow himself to be flustered by a late-race collision with Lewis Hamilton in Melbourne or a thrashing by Vettel in Malaysia, finally getting his own winning challenge off the deck with brilliant consecutive victories at Barcelona and Monaco. By any standards, both these successes were absolutely outstanding, but then came the low spot of his year when he tangled with Vettel as they battled for the lead at Istanbul Park, an unfortunate derailment for both Red Bull drivers from which he was lucky to rescue third place. Some blamed Webber for holding up the leading train for too long, others rightly thought that Sebastian simply moved across his team-mate long before he was clear of his left front wheel.

After a disappointing fifth in Canada, he was lucky to walk away unscathed from a huge shunt in Valencia, surviving a 160mph backward flip after running into the back of Heikki Kovalainen as he came up to lap the Lotus-Cosworth. The British GP at Silverstone left Mark boiling with indignation after the one remaining 'new spec' uprated front wing was given to Vettel for qualifying, but come race day, the Aussie bounced back to register his third win of the year and arguably the one that psychologically was the most difficult.

One more race win followed in Hungary, after which Mark found himself heading the title chase, a lead that he nurtured successfully all the way to Korea, where he crashed out spectacularly after allowing his RB6 to slide wide up a rain-slicked kerb early in the race. Sir Jack Brabham, Australia's retired triple world champion, adjudged that Mark had blown his title chances by this mistake. It proved to be so.

4

ROBERT KUBICA

5

IT seems a long time since the lanky Pole won the 2008 Canadian GP for BMW, but a series of strong performances in the below-par Renault successfully kept his reputation in play, and rumours that one day he will find his way to Ferrari intensified rather than cooled during the season.

Second place to Button in Australia was a great start to the season, followed by fourth in Malaysia and fifth in China. Monaco yielded a superb third, which was as good a drive as delivered by any of his rivals throughout the season.

The introduction of Renault's long-overdue F-duct in time for the Belgian GP also gave Kubica's fortunes a worthwhile boost, and if he had not overshot his pit slightly coming in for a tyre change, he might well have beaten Webber's Red Bull for second place.

Certainly the high-speed environment of Spa-Francorchamps served to showcase Robert's talent and precision, and he finished the season having further enhanced his position as one of the most seasoned and accomplished performers on the starting grid. As it was, Robert had to settle for third on the Belgian track, the same spot in which he had qualified.

Later he qualified fourth with high expectations at Suzuka, only for his Renault to shed a rear wheel a couple of laps into what he had hoped would be an extremely rewarding performance. His season may have ended in a somewhat subdued manner, but there is a continuing feeling within F1 ranks that 'Bobby K' could be a serial race winner if he gets his hands on the right car.

6

JENSON BUTTON

JENSON Button's decision to join the McLaren team at the start of the season left the F1 community divided as to the wisdom of trying to gatecrash what some felt was looking increasingly like Lewis Hamilton's personal domain. On the face of it, the logic in turning his back on the Brawn squad, which had carried him to his world championship crown, seemed strangely perverse, particularly as the Brackley-based squad was on the verge of a major boost after being taken over by Mercedes-Benz. Surely he was missing a golden opportunity for his career to surge onwards and upwards.

Yet this was only one side of the coin. Button had reasoned that when McLaren came knocking on a driver's door, it was not a proposition to be brushed aside lightly. Assessing all the possibilities, he came to the totally rational decision to make the move. And while he did not quite achieve the level of success he was hoping for, being thwarted in his ambition to take a second title crown, he certainly did better than he would have done had he stayed on in the Mercedes line-up.

Button quickly meshed into the McLaren way of doing things like the great team player he has always been, and he continued to conduct himself with the relaxed, unruffled good nature that has always made him such a popular personality in the F1 community. If there is a downside to Button's repertoire, it is that he can handle any opposition when the car set-up is to his liking, but on the other hand can appear quite average if the car isn't working in the way he wants it to. His two early-season victories were certainly impressive, and he was slightly unlucky not to have added a third at Monza, where Alonso just squeezed out of the pits ahead of him in the closing stages.

Key setbacks included Monaco, where a radiator cover designed to bring the engine up to temperature while it was being warmed up prior to the race, was mistakenly left on for the first out-lap, and Spa where he fell victim to Vettel's unexpected assault. But taken in the round, Button had a pretty reasonable campaign in 2010.

TO a certain extent, Nico Rosberg was damned if he did beat Michael Schumacher and damned if he did not. From the start of the season, some observers expected him to easily outshine the veteran 41-year-old, while others smugly predicted that the young German would be the recipient of a season-long driving lesson from his senior colleague.

As things transpired, the cards fell convincingly in Rosberg's favour, commandingly so. On no fewer than 15 occasions in 19 races, Nico outqualified the seven-times world champion and achieved two podium finishes in third place from the first four races of the year. It was difficult for him to field some of the waspish flak that was aimed in his direction by some journalists, who seemed to revel in deliberately making his life uncomfortable with barbed inquiries seemingly designed to unsettle his relationship with Schumacher. In fairness to those members of the fourth estate, they did not stint themselves when it came to grilling Schumacher in much the same fashion, although probably he was more inured to it.

All in all, Rosberg delivered respectable results consistently and conscientiously, despite all the pre-season hype suggesting that he would be destroyed by Schumacher. This was the year in which Nico finally grew to maturity and rounded credibility. In a better car, surely he would have won races. It was a shame that Mark Webber's unfortunate pirouette in Korea deprived him of what could well have been second place. At least.

NICO ROSBERG

7

8

RUBENS BARRICHELLO

DESPITE Rubens Barrichello achieving two victories for the Brawn squad in 2009, it was clear that there would be no room for him in the Mercedes team for 2010, so the Brazilian veteran, at 37 the second oldest man on the grid after Schumacher, opened talks with Frank Williams and Patrick Head with the aim of spearheading what all concerned hoped would be a Cosworth propelled revival of the famous British team.

At first glance, it seemed a rather unlikely alliance. Whispering soothing words of encouragement with a reassuring arm around the shoulder has never really been the Williams way of responding to its hired hands behind the wheel. But once they realised just what worthwhile and wide-ranging technical input Barrichello could offer the team, they seemed prepared to offer all the encouragement they could muster.

It certainly proved to be a challenging season for this new alliance, with Rubens languishing just on the lower fringes of the top ten for the opening races of the season. But a fourth in Valencia, followed immediately by a fifth at Silverstone, demonstrated the latent potential beneath the skin of the Williams FW32, which, as expected, was easily the most impressive among the new generation of Cosworth runners. Barrichello also seemed to fit well and comfortably within the team: later he confided that it had been his ambition to drive for Williams ever since he had started in F1 in 1993.

Rubens is basically a passionate motor racing enthusiast and a significantly underrated performer. One can only hope that, having built a solid and worthwhile foundation on which to progress his relationship with Williams, that he is re-signed for 2011 and sustains the momentum we witnessed in 2010.

9

FELIPE MASSA

THE pleasant and gregarious Brazilian driver made a complete and very welcome physical recovery from the serious head injuries sustained from his accident during qualifying at the Hungaroring in 2009, but it took him perhaps slightly longer than expected to get back into the racing rhythm after seven months away from the cockpit. Ironically, when Felipe fully clicked, it was in the German GP, where there were other political considerations to blur the quality of his drive.

His body language after the race, during which his engineer, Rob Smedley, was given the embarrassing job of relaying the radio message "Fernando is faster than you" held nothing back in terms of sheer indignation and disappointment. The issue was further compounded by some observations from Luca di Montezemolo, reminding the world that Ferrari drivers drove first and foremost for the Scuderia, implying that they should subjugate their own personal ambition to the greater good of the Prancing Horse. Not quite the *raison de'être* that motivated Michael Schumacher, let's remember, but perhaps it would be churlish to dwell on this issue.

Germany apart, Felipe looked as though he had lost the fine edge of his racing talent. He started the year with a second place in Bahrain, then a third in Australia, but another nine races would pass before he reappeared on the podium at Hockenheim. Third place at Monza gave the pleasant Brazilian a helpful boost, but this was followed by a first-corner pile-up at Suzuka, which did little for his self-confidence. His customary mastery of Interlagos failed to materialise, and Abu Dhabi saw him once again mired in the midfield pack, ending his season on a somewhat downbeat note.

Massa has always been a popular member of the Ferrari family and officially should continue in the team until 2012. That will be fine with Alonso, who has always indicated a preference for compliant team-mates, as his stint with McLaren serves to remind us.

MICHAEL SCHUMACHER

10

THE much anticipated return of the seven-times world champion warrants a potted biography of his individual season alone. No matter how you slice it, Schumacher's return to the cockpit after a three-year lay-off was a significant disappointment, despite the sustained and self-conscious efforts by Mercedes to shoulder the majority of the blame by admitting it had not given him a very good car. But that, and efforts to rationalise his poor show by blaming tyre characteristics, did not alter the fact that he was roundly eclipsed by team-mate Nico Rosberg. And that's all you really need to know.

The first sign that Schumacher might be getting restless in retirement came in the aftermath of Massa's Hungarian GP shunt, when the veteran German ace expressed a willingness to stand in for his former team-mate, possibly for the balance of the season. Schumacher duly tested an outdated Ferrari at Mugello, quickly getting back into the swing of things, only for the project to founder due to a lingering neck injury that he had sustained in a motorcycle testing accident earlier in the year.

Eventually, Ross Brawn and the newly rebranded Mercedes squad picked up on the idea and duly did a deal for Schumacher to partner Nico Rosberg. But those who imagined that somehow he would magically re-create the glory days of his Ferrari era were being excessively optimistic. Restrictions on testing meant that he did not cover as many pre-season miles as he would have liked; it took him some time to get the feel for the latest generation of Bridgestone tyres; and the Mercedes chassis was difficult to set up for his own personal preference. He kicked off with a sixth place in Bahrain, and although he improved to the point where he was fourth in Barcelona, it took him until Korea before he could match that position again.

The only real glimpse of the old Schumacher was his unpleasant effort in trying to drive his former team-mate, Rubens Barrichello, into the pit wall in Hungary. Some things never change.

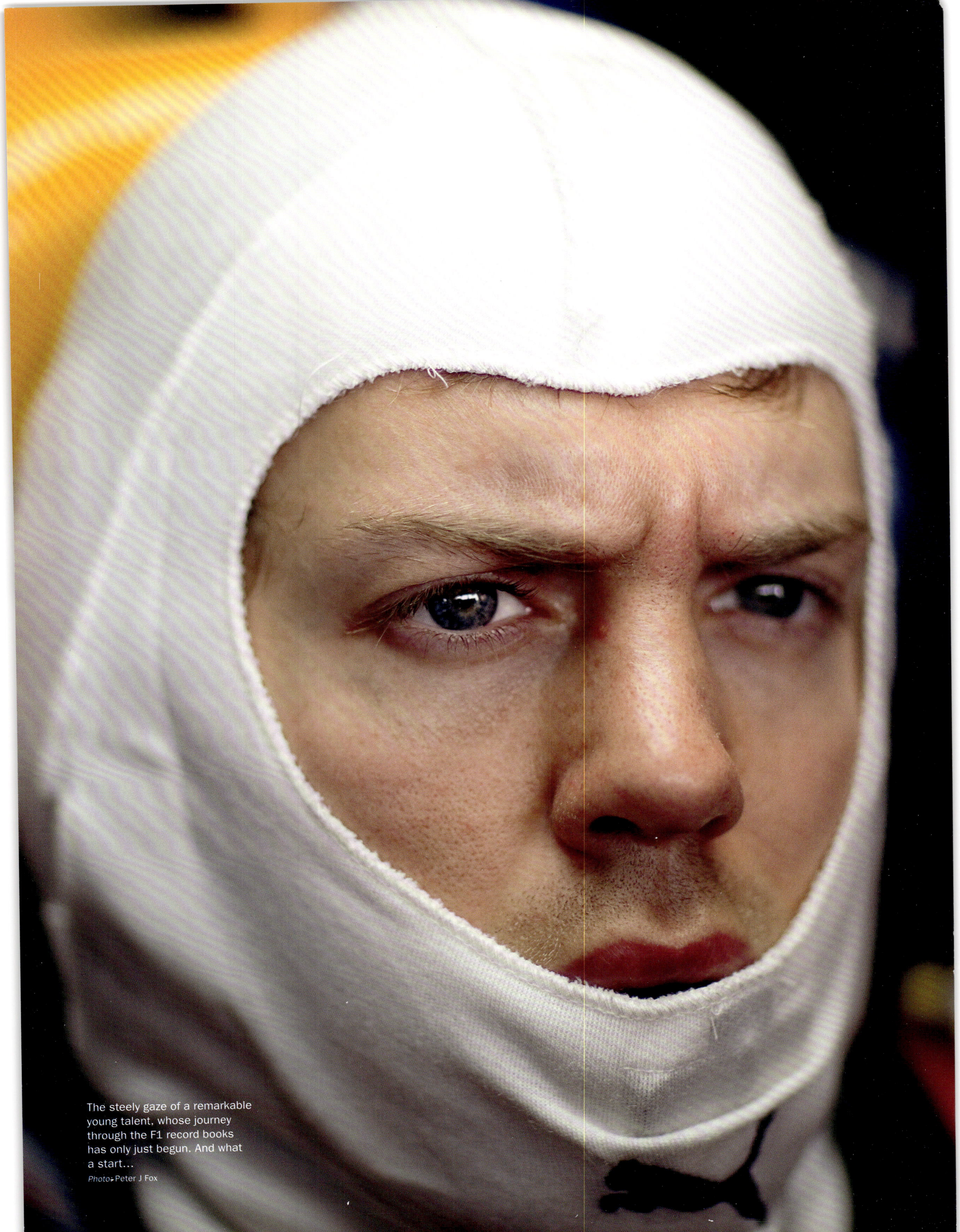

The steely gaze of a remarkable young talent, whose journey through the F1 record books has only just begun. And what a start...

Photo Peter J Fox

SEBASTIAN VETTEL

MAN OF THE FUTURE

WORLD CHAMPION PROFILE by MAURICE HAMILTON

SEBASTIAN Vettel is the first German driver since Michael Schumacher to win the world championship. Schumacher broke every record in the book, but Vettel has already established a benchmark that suggests he might actually surpass the exceptional achievements of his fellow countryman.

Vettel started at the other end of the scale. He is the youngest driver to have taken part in a grand prix weekend (Friday practice, Turkey 2006, for BMW), to have scored points (United States 2007, for BMW), to have led a race (Japan 2007, for Toro Rosso), to have taken pole position and to have won a grand prix (both in Italy 2008, for Toro Rosso).

On 14th November, 2010, he achieved the greatest accolade of them all: at the age of 23 years and 135 days, Sebastian Vettel became the youngest world champion when he won the last race of the season in Abu Dhabi.

It was a surprise only insofar as championship points pre-race dictated that Vettel was the outsider when compared with his Red Bull team-mate, Mark Webber, and Ferrari's Fernando Alonso. On the other hand, there were one or two in motor sport – most notably Bernie Ecclestone – who had earmarked Vettel as F1's man of the future.

Appropriately enough, Vettel's first official appearance in Turkey as the Friday test driver for BMW came towards the end of Schumacher's reign. By the time the seven-times world champion had returned in March 2010, Vettel was established not only as a winner, but also a favourite to win the title. Whether the youngster was actually capable of going the final glorious mile remained open to question.

Vettel may be small in stature, but he is cocky by nature: too cocky for some during his early days in F1. He admits to being intimidated just once on the race track when, at the age of eight, the spectre of a 12-year-old almost twice his size caused young Sebastian to think twice about making a pass when karting: "Other than that, I've never been frightened by another car."

That self-assurance, coupled with obvious natural talent, led to the German Formula BMW title in 2004, and competitive results in F3 and World Series by Renault before he received the call from BMW.

Elevation to a race seat came courtesy of Robert Kubica's massive accident during the 2007 Canadian Grand Prix. Kubica was unhurt, but, as a precaution, stood down for the next race a week later at Indianapolis. Vettel qualified seventh and finished eighth to score a point on his debut.

A few months later, BMW released Vettel to join Red Bull's Scuderia Toro Rosso as a replacement for Scott Speed from the Hungarian Grand Prix. Lowly finishes reflected both his inexperience and an uncompetitive car, although a wet Japanese Grand Prix promised to change all that. Working his way into third place on the streaming Fuji track, Vettel collided with, of all things, a Red Bull driven by Mark Webber as they ran behind the safety car. Webber was not slow in coming forward with his thoughts.

"It's kids, isn't it," said Webber. "Kids with not enough experience: they do a good job and then they fuck it all up."

Vettel was distraught over losing the possibility of a podium finish and taking out a Red Bull at the same time, although he would be vindicated by a spectator's video showing that the leader, Lewis Hamilton, may have sparked the chain reaction. Nonetheless, it was an unfortunate beginning to an uneasy relationship with his future team-mate.

Vettel made amends and produced a significant signpost to the future by finishing fourth a week later during wet conditions at Shanghai. Initially, 2008 would be marked by nothing more than incidents and mechanical failures. But all of that would be wiped clean in the most magnificent way at a rain soaked Monza, where he took his first pole and led the race with barely a single error.

"I always liked racing in the wet," Vettel told *F1 Racing*. "When I was karting, rain tyres were very expensive, and to save money I used to drive a lot in the wet using slick tyres. That was very difficult, but I learnt a lot, and it meant that the kart felt much nicer when I put on wet tyres."

David Coulthard's retirement meant that Vettel was the obvious replacement at Red Bull. The 2009 season saw a shaky start in every sense, thanks to a collision in Melbourne, but Sebastian finished with four wins to move into second place in the championship and place his name in the frame for 2010. Yet the nagging doubts continued.

The received wisdom was that Vettel was not yet ready to become champion. The evidence from early in the season indicated that he may have been happy-go-lucky, but beneath that boyish charm was a 23-year-old who was fragile and likely to crack under pressure. That impression was consolidated in Turkey, where he collided with Webber while disputing the lead and then compounded the felony by acting in a petulant manner. This seemed to be the result of Webber having won two races on the bounce, while Vettel, with just a single victory (in Malaysia) to his name, was sliding down the points table.

There was a commanding win a month later in Valencia, but then his season took another dive, thanks to misjudging the gap to the safety car while leading in Hungary, a basic mistake that brought a drive-through penalty. Then came a collision at Spa that took out Jenson Button's second-place McLaren.

The signs of a new, improved Vettel surfaced in Korea. The race was bought and paid for, but then his engine failed unexpectedly with a few laps to go. Instead of leading the championship, the German was back among the supporting cast, particularly as a grateful and lucky Alonso stepped forward to claim the win.

As Vettel returned to the Red Bull garage, everyone ducked for cover. Stand by for outrage and the stamping of feet. Not a bit of it. "These things happen," he said as he shook hands with his crew and recognised that they were just as disappointed as he was. "It's not over yet. Two more races to go. Let's do it."

That was all very well, but, assuming Vettel did win the title, would he be mature enough to act as the sport's ambassador? The answer to that would come in the winner's (and world champion's) press conference in Abu Dhabi.

Vettel's thoughtful, compassionate and impressively honest answers ranked among the best we had heard as he summed up his season. His reflection on Spa was particularly telling.

"I tried to pass. I lost the car and took him [Button] out, took both of us out. I got a lot of bad press. It wasn't easy at that time, with a lot of people talking bad things and trying to knock us down, but that's when you realise who your friends are, who belongs to you and who is supporting you.

"In the end, the whole paddock is a group full of people, and it was important to invest my energy into them, in order to get it back until today. At some point, I accepted the fact that sometimes things don't go your way, but in the long term, I think there's something called justice, and today, at least in my calculation, it turned out to be right. Sometimes it goes that way, sometimes it goes the other way."

And then his thoughts on Korea:

"I kept believing in myself, in the team, and I got a lot of positive energy from the people around me, tapping on my shoulder, and I could see that they were believing in me as well, so obviously then it's a bit easier. When you have things like Korea, when what happened you cannot change any more, but you know you can still change what will happen. We were in a good position and then boom, the engine went, so of course that's disappointing. But, immediately, I said the positive is the most important.

"I had to go through situations like Hungary and Spa. I think it's important to be who you are and not try to be someone else. Many times, in sports, when you ask people what is most important, they answer something like 'to be in balance', but it's actually sometimes not that easy to keep your head cool when everyone is panicking around you. It makes sense to invest your energy because you know that you will get it back. You might make experiences that you don't like, but that's part of life. I think that's not only in F1 or in sport, I think that's for all of us.

"We have occasions like that, and I think that was one of the main lessons this year, because in the end, I do believe that guys like Jenson, Lewis, Fernando, Mark and others in F1, they are the best drivers in the world, and to be one of them is fantastic, it's a great feeling.

"In the end, you just enjoy yourself. Being happy to be able to do what you do, reminds you of who you are."

Which is to say, the youngest ever world champion. And the potential winner of many more.

PRIME MOVERS

Drivers are the visible heroes of racing, but F1 owes much to many others who have shaped it from beyond the limelight. ALAN HENRY looks at 12 influential men who, in their unique ways, have exerted a profound influence on the sport's history.

Photo: Autocourse archive

BERNIE ECCLESTONE

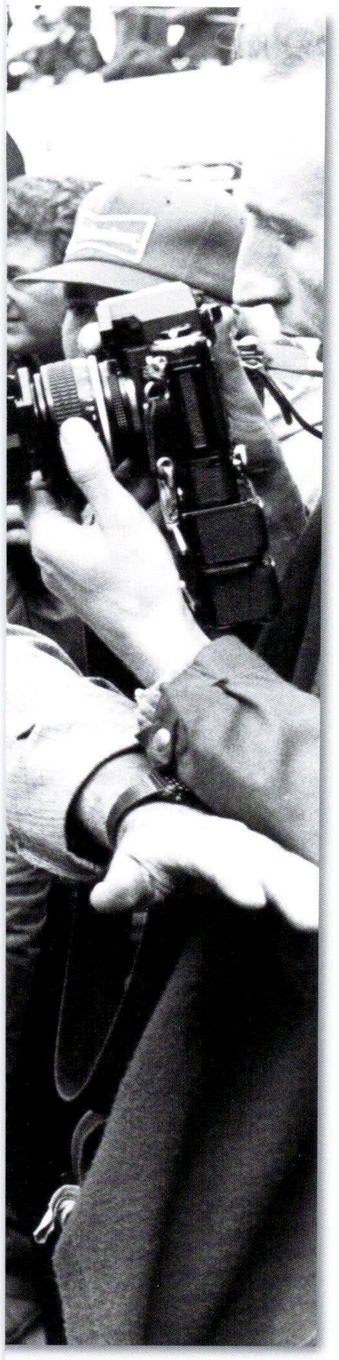

BERNIE ECCLESTONE reached the remarkable age of 80 on 31st October, 2010, and was still working the sort of punishing schedule that some people half his age would find downright exhausting. Like so many driven and highly motivated individuals, F1's commercial rights holder seems to be keeping his business foot more tightly welded to the throttle pedal than ever before, at a time when the stereotypical pensioner is supposedly reaching for their slippers and a late evening cup of Horlicks.

Walk into any F1 paddock today and you will see lines of perfectly parked transporters in immaculate formation. It is a far cry from the gravel and roughly laid tarmac that – if they were lucky – would have greeted the teams back in the 1960s. Bernie has been responsible for this remarkable transformation. To those who worked for the Brabham F1 team in the 1970s – and were driven mad by Bernie's insistence that advertising decals on the rear wing endplates were a couple of millimetres out of line – it was no surprise. "Delegation," he would memorably announce, "is the art of accepting second best."

'Mr E' can be one of the boys, but during his ownership of the Brabham squad – from 1971 to 1989 – he was definitely the man in charge. Many people who worked for him discovered to their cost that it was 'his way or the highway'. He kept a tight coterie of loyal insiders, many of whom are still in the F1 business in senior positions. Some remember just how difficult he could be on the pit wall.

"Oh God, yes, he could be an interfering so-and-so," recalled Charlie Whiting, the FIA race director and safety delegate, who was chief mechanic at Brabham when Ecclestone owned the team.

"He was always standing on the pit wall with a couple of stop watches that he did not know how to work. Then he would lose track, mutter, 'Damned stopwatches!' and throw them down. But yes, he did like to be involved.

"So I think perhaps Bernie got a little more deeply immersed in it than he should have done, but at the end of the day, it was his bat, his ball and he wanted to play the game exactly as he saw it."

Ask Bernie just how many people worked at Brabham and he will reply, "About half of them." He is master of the one-liner.

But he has always been a racer. Tough with the esteemed Brabham F1 technical director Gordon Murray, he respected him and approved of his 'on the edge' engineering, which was probably best encapsulated by the Brabham 'fan car'. As the years rolled by, ostensibly he may have changed from a team owner to the sport's all-powerful commercial rights holder, but he is still a racer.

Yet he also knew when it was best to make a tactical retreat to emerge victorious in the longer term. After the 'fan car' won the 1978 Swedish GP in the hands of Niki Lauda, there was an outcry from Brabham's rivals. Sensibly, Bernie withdrew the car on the spot and it never raced again. The solidarity of the F1 Constructors' Association, his emergent power base on the long journey to becoming the most powerful man in the sport, was far more important to him than short-term success on the circuit.

Photo: Autocourse archive

Photo: Autocourse archive

Photo: LAT Photographic

Photo: Autocourse archive

Photo: LAT Photographic

RON DENNIS

ATTENTION to detail, the ability to think through problems to their exhaustive conclusion and an acceptance that the very best is only just good enough have become the key guiding principles behind the career of Ron Dennis, a man whom some people in the F1 pit lane believe ranks second only to Bernie Ecclestone in terms of his contribution to accelerating the growth of the sport over the past 30 years.

Perfectionists are not always the easiest of personalities to deal with, and Dennis is first to admit that his workforce at McLaren find him exacting and demanding to work for. But in the 30 years since he took control of the British F1 team, he has crafted it into a cutting-edge organisation where engineering excellence and immaculate presentation have achieved huge success on the racetrack. More recently, he has shifted his managerial emphasis to take full responsibility for the emergent McLaren Automotive organization, which will release the first of a range of high-performance road cars in 2011.

Dennis made his name in F2 during the early 1970s with the Rondel Racing operation, which proved that you didn't have to be involved in F1 to field immaculately prepared racing cars. But his big breakthrough came in 1980, when Philip Morris, whose Marlboro cigarette brand had been title sponsor of McLaren since 1974, brokered an amalgamation between Dennis's Project-3 organisation and the existing McLaren management. The team had been sliding downhill for several years, and the new partnership was ordained as a pre-requisite to retaining that financial support.

Dennis helped create the environment of technical excellence in which John Barnard could develop his radical carbon-fibre composite chassis technology, and worked meticulously to get the best out of a succession of engine supply partnerships. With investment from TAG, he put McLaren in a position to commission Porsche to build a bespoke, state-of-the-art 1.5-litre V6 turbo that won a hat trick of world championships from 1984. Then the team won four straight titles using Honda power, and in 1985 began an engine supply partnership with Mercedes-Benz that endures to this day.

Yet some of Dennis's most outstanding achievements have been registered away from the rasping roar of F1 exhausts. Most notably, his vision for a new corporate headquarters, built on a green-field site in Surrey, came to fruition when the McLaren Technology Centre, designed by noted architect Norman Foster, was formally opened by Queen Elizabeth in 2004.

Dennis also had the vision and perspicacity to support and help nurture the career of young Lewis Hamilton, from teenage kart racer through to F1 champion. And he survived a controversial episode when McLaren was found guilty of what amounted to technical espionage by the FIA, after it was alleged that the team had benefited from leaked Ferrari data during 2008, although many within the F1 community believe there was more to this episode than was made public at the time.

COLIN CHAPMAN

ORIGINALITY of technical thought in F1 has become progressively more difficult to achieve in recent years as engineers have become increasingly hemmed in by restrictive regulations: to a very large extent, the rule book dictates the configuration of today's generation of grand prix machines. Extra performance is squeezed out of the packages by attention to detail and fine-tuning. It is a far cry from the 'blinding flash' technical revolutions instigated by Lotus boss Colin Chapman who, at the zenith of his career, would regularly come up with ideas that comprehensively redrew the parameters of F1 car design.

Born the son of a publican in Richmond, Surrey, in 1928, Anthony Colin Bruce Chapman graduated in engineering from London University and was called up to spend his National Service in the Royal Air Force, just as he was becoming involved with that powerhouse of enthusiasm and mechanical ingenuity, the 750 Motor Club. He was a man always well in harmony with his era, almost anticipating the mood of the times with an endearing and breezy confidence.

A host of tiny, lightweight, agile and affordable sports racing cars flowed from the Lotus factories during the 1950s, and on the racing front, Chapman shrugged aside many prevailing design conventions. In 1956, his profile was given something of a major boost when he was asked to re-engineer the chassis of the Vanwall F1 car. The autocratic Tony Vandervell was impressed with his frank and outspoken views on the original Cooper designed frame and gave him carte blanche to revamp it. Two years later, Chapman and Lotus were in F1 on their own account.

Although the long-established Cooper organisation had pioneered the central-engined revolution in F1, Chapman picked up the theme, crafting and refining it to a level far beyond anything Cooper was able to achieve. Lotus finally hit the big time in 1960 when Rob Walker bought one of its new type 18s for Stirling Moss, who won the marque's maiden Grand Épreuve victory at Monaco.

Yet it was Chapman's partnership with the dynamic Jim Clark that could be said to have defined the 1960s F1 generation. Clark won the 1963 and 1965 world championships at the wheel of Chapman's radical monocoque Lotus F1 challengers, and came within an ace of winning in 1962 and 1964 as well. His Lotus 38 shook the foundations at Indianapolis and brought an end to the front-engined roadsters at the 'Brickyard', culminating in Clark's 1965 win.

Off track, Chapman simply thrived on the competitive pressure of the F1 business. Only Jim Clark's death at Hockenheim in 1968 caused him to consider withdrawing, but only fleetingly. Graham Hill helped regroup the team and took the championship that year; Jochen Rindt, Emerson Fittipaldi and Mario Andretti would win more world championships, but none would form the personal bond that Clark had enjoyed with his employer. There were new technical furrows to plough, most notably the harnessing of under-car aerodynamics to generate ground effect, although Chapman was aghast when the FIA banned the radical 'twin chassis' Lotus 86 and 88 designs in 1981, and never quite felt the same about the F1 business in the little over a year he had left to live.

KEITH DUCKWORTH

WHEN the first of Keith Duckworth's magnificent Cosworth DFV V8 engines propelled Jimmy Clark's Lotus 49 to a debut victory in the 1967 Dutch Grand Prix, it was almost impossible to foresee the implications of its arrival on the F1 scene. Within a year, it would be freely available to customers with the necessary financial wherewithal, spawning a whole new generation of F1 teams, all anxious to prove that, given the chance, they could take on and beat the established top guns of the day.

David Keith Duckworth was born in 1933 to a prosperous family in Blackburn, Lancashire. He trained as a pilot with the RAF during his National Service, but was ejected from the course for "dangerous and incompetent night flying" after dozing off in the cockpit on one occasion. But such lapses were uncharacteristic for the confident young man who later trained with distinction as an engineer.

Duckworth and his business partner, Mike Costin, advanced the cause of British motor racing in the early 1960s with a succession of brilliant small-capacity engines. But it was when Colin Chapman approached Ford with the idea of funding Cosworth's development of what evolved into the DFV that Duckworth really hit the big time. He had grown into a confident young man and would, in later life, become rather smugly tiresome in the way he advanced his trenchant and deeply believed technical philosophies. Trouble was for his critics, he was generally on the right side of the argument.

He could also work at a prodigious pace. To progress the DFV project, he set up a design studio at his home, well away from the day-to-day bustle of the Cosworth factory in Northampton. The task took just under two years from the moment that Ken put pen to paper for the first time to the moment when the first completed Cosworth DFV was handed over to Ford in April 1967. Sixteen years later, Michele Alboreto's Tyrrell-Cosworth DFR would post the final victory for the engine whose bloodline stretched back to the first DFV, when he won the Detroit GP.

Yet there was no doubt that the effort expended on the DFV project took a toll on Duckworth's health. He worked for up to 16 hours a day during the height of the initial nine-month design process, during which he lost 40 pounds in weight. Later he would reward himself for his endeavours by treating himself to a Brantley helicopter, but following a heart attack in 1973, he would have to give up his pilot's licence. After a second heart attack, it was absolutely clear that he regarded his body as a deficient machine that had let him down, and he submitted to open-heart surgery. His acerbic wit endured to the very end of his life.

Photo: Autocourse archive

NOBUHIKO KAWAMOTO

Photo: Paul-Henri Cahier

Nobuhiko Kawamoto was one of the profound driving forces behind the evolution of the Honda company, both in terms of F1 involvement and the evolution of a range of road cars that found particular favour in Europe. A great Anglophile, Kawamoto was first and foremost an engineer, regarded with respect by his peers as one of the first high fliers from that background to reach the very top of Honda's management.

After graduating from Tohoku university in 1963, he joined the fledgling Honda F1 programme as a design engineer, later working on the Brabham-Honda F2 cars raced by Jack Brabham and Denny Hulme in 1965 and 1966, when he gained the irreverent nickname 'Hong Kong mechanic' from his European colleagues. When Honda withdrew from F1 at the end of the 1968 season, he returned to Japan and rose through the ranks, contributing to the development of the Honda Civic in 1972 as well as the radical CVCC road car engine.

Eventually, Kawamoto became head of Honda's research and design department, and much of his influence was behind Honda's return to F1 in 1983 with the Williams team. This proved an extremely steep technical learning curve for the Japanese car maker, for while McLaren had commissioned Porsche to build it the neatly conceived and compact TAG turbo V6, the first Honda V6 arrived at Williams in a crate with a couple of turbochargers lying beside it. Crucial ancillaries, such as radiators and plumbing for both the turbos and the exhaust system, had to be worked out by Williams.

The early Honda V6s were also horrifyingly unreliable, and while Frank Williams remembers that Honda was "thrilled to bits" when Keke Rosberg gave the partnership its first win at Dallas in 1984, Kawamoto came to appreciate that a wholesale revamp of Honda's F1 engine programme would be required after that year's Dutch GP, where Rosberg ran as high as third, only to roll silently to a halt in the pits, out of fuel, with two laps to go. That came on top of three broken engines in practice. Williams's Japanese guests were suitably embarrassed.

Later Kawamoto would be deeply concerned about the effects on Williams of Frank's road accident, which left him paralysed in 1986. There was a feeling in the Honda ranks that any company needed a figurehead leader, and although the team won constructors' world championships with Honda power in 1986 and 1987 – after Frank's accident – the lure of Ayrton Senna in a Honda propelled McLaren was just too tempting and the manufacturer duly made the switch of team in 1988.

In 1990, Kawamoto was appointed as Honda's chief executive officer, and two years later he brought Honda's F1 programme to an end, blaming high costs and the need to create a more environmentally friendly image for the company. As CEO, he reorganised the business into three areas – cars, motorcycles and power – while splitting the company's geographical focus into four regions: Japan, North America, Europe and the rest of the world.

Although he was ousted from power in 1998, Kawamoto's earlier commitment to grand prix racing sparked a massive interest in the sport in Japan. Despite the recent withdrawals of Toyota and Honda due to the global recession, Japan, which boasts some of the most passionate fans in the world, is still seen as a vital and important target in F1's seemingly unquenchable sprint for expansion.

ENZO FERRARI

ENZO FERRARI played on the emotional charisma surrounding his cars and company almost from the moment Froilán González won the 1951 British Grand Prix at Silverstone, a success that brought to an end a long spell of success for rival Alfa Romeo, whose racing manager Ferrari had been before the Second World War.

Despite the fact that Ferrari was, to some extent, a myth-maker, happy to adapt the course of history in his own recollections to paint his company in the best possible light, that cannot alter the fact that he was the last of the automotive giants, whose influence shaped and steered the very fabric of the sport across no fewer than seven decades.

Ferrari came from the humblest of backgrounds, but he became a volatile and unpredictable autocrat, who ruled his racing team on almost a day-to-day basis until he died in 1988, at the age of 90. The first V12-engined sports car to carry the Ferrari name raced in June 1947, and over the decades that followed the company would build its reputation through competition success and the sales of a succession of mouthwatering road cars to what might best be described as 'cafe society'.

Nevertheless, by the late 1960s, the economics of the Ferrari business model were in free fall. It was only through the discreet intervention of Fiat patriarch Gianni Agnelli, who approached the old autocrat with tact and graciousness, that the Ferrari company was rescued from impending bankruptcy in 1969.

However, the defining event in Enzo Ferrari's life was the death of his son, Dino, from nephritis, a kidney ailment, in the summer of 1955. Thereafter, he withdrew increasingly into his Maranello fortress and seldom left it during the last 30 years of his life. Ferrari's cars may have raced all around the globe, but he relied heavily on television coverage to keep himself abreast of racing events, and also his nervous lieutenants on the spot, some of whom could not be relied upon to report impartially if the cars' performance was below par.

Ferrari also gained a perverse sense of satisfaction from fostering internal rivalry between his drivers. He seldom nominated a number one, instead preferring them to race each other to establish a pecking order. It was often a destructive and counter-productive strategy. Yet, on the other hand, he could be warm and sympathetic to those drivers to whom he took a shine, notably Peter Collins, Chris Amon and Gilles Villeneuve. To the likes of Eugenio Castellotti and Phil Hill, he remained strangely cool and unsympathetic.

Within his domain, Enzo Ferrari's word was law. Although Fiat took the road car side of the business fully under its wing from 1969, the racing department remained under Enzo's control until the end of his life. And right to the end, the employees of this giant personality went in fear and trepidation of his disapproval. By any standards, Enzo Ferrari was a one-off.

Photo: LAT Photographic

Photo: LAT Photographic

Photo: LAT Photographic

Photo: Autocourse archive

MAX MOSLEY

INFLUENTIAL, certainly, but not always universally popular, Max Mosley rounded off his 19-year tenure as president of the FIA at the end of 2009 with a vigorous campaign to support the election of former Ferrari sporting director Jean Todt as his successor. Todt duly won the vote, beating off a challenge from former world rally champion Ari Vatanen, much to Mosley's satisfaction.

Just under two decades earlier, the charismatic Mosley had seen off sitting tenant Jean-Marie Balestre to gain motorsport's top job, a challenge that in many ways was Mosley's personal substitute for a conventional career in British politics. Max's father, Sir Oswald Mosley, had been one of Britain's most able politicians in the 1920s, before his career took something of a wrong turn and he established the British League of Fascists.

Educated in France and Germany, Max gained a university place at Christ Church, Oxford, where he read physics and law. He got as far as secretary of the Oxford Union before the shadow of his father's extreme political views prevented him from running for president. Soon after being called to the Bar, he tried his hand at motor racing, first in clubman's sports cars and subsequently in F2. He was driving a Brabham BT23C in the rain soaked race at Hockenheim that claimed Jim Clark's life on 7th April, 1968. He learned a lot about the dangers of motor racing first hand, which later fuelled his various safety initiatives during his time as FIA president.

After his Lotus 59 F2 car dumped him into the scenery at Nürburgring while practising for the 1969 Eifelrennen, Mosley called it a day, joining Robin Herd, Alan Rees and Graham Coaker in setting up March Engineering, an ambitious new constructor that built cars for pretty much every category in the motor racing business, from F1 down. Max did a fine job of creating the illusion that March had private backing from a so-called 'secret sponsor', but, as he confessed later, much of this was smoke and mirrors, aided by a very sympathetic banker.

Max stayed loyal to March for seven years before severing his links with the company, by which time he was edging towards a position of power and influence in the sport, initially gaining the presidency of the Manufacturers' Commission, which represented the interests of global motor manufacturers on the World Motor Sport Council. More important still, he had become an informal legal advisor to Bernie Ecclestone, and that relationship would prove absolutely central to the manner in which he handled the 19-year stint as one of the sport's most powerful movers and shakers. From the outset, he was a supremely well-connected member of the F1 fraternity, and he made the most of that advantage.

LEO MEHL

Photo: Paul-Henri Cahier

GOODYEAR heads the record books as easily the most successful of tyre companies ever involved in F1, posting no fewer than 368 grand prix victories between 1965 and 1998. Much of the company's achievement in this highly political sport can be credited to the firm and sure management touch displayed by Leo Mehl in his role as Goodyear's director of international racing.

Mehl joined Goodyear straight from university in 1959 and quickly became involved with the chemical aspect of racing tyre development, before gaining his first practical experience in the field working on NASCAR programmes. Later he worked on Shelby Cobras in US national sports car events, and he first crossed the Atlantic as part of the tyre support group for the Ford GT40s racing at Le Mans in 1964 and 1965.

In 1967, Mehl was appointed head of Goodyear's European F1 operations. It was a time of great commercial expansion for motor racing in general, and Mehl's relaxed no-nonsense dealings with both teams and drivers balanced cordiality with just the right amount of commercial pressure when necessary. For the 1971 season, he helped engineers do the deal that led to Jackie Stewart and the Tyrrell team running on Goodyears, an achievement that not only saw the Scot win the second of his three championships that year, but also enabled Akron to harness his fluent and outgoing personality as a very effective public relations tool.

Mehl was also very shrewd politically when it came to managing Goodyear's relationships with the F1 team principals. Towards the end of 1984, a season when his McLaren-TAGs won 12 of the 16 races, Ron Dennis approached Mehl to ask about switching from Michelin to Goodyear in 1985. Mehl jumped at the chance and the deal was signed; shortly afterwards, Michelin announced that it would be withdrawing from F1. Cynics suggested that Dennis had been forewarned, but he was far too shrewd to have misled Goodyear – and Mehl too clever to be taken in.

In 1996, Mehl retired from Goodyear, having successfully maintained a good-natured public face on the competition activities of the giant US tyre company for more than two decades. There was also no doubt that the company had derived huge commercial benefit from its racing activities, as Leo would repeatedly claim.

"We found it impossible to get an equal 'bang for the buck'as we derived from racing in any other activity," was his continuing mantra.

After his Goodyear career ended, Mehl spent a period as executive director of the Indy Racing League and vice-president of Indianapolis Motor Speedway. He retired in 1999, after a lifetime of service dedicated to the sport he loved.

ADRIAN NEWEY

IN many ways the dazzling star of F1 design during the first decade of the new millennium, Adrian Newey has made a significant contribution towards some of the most high-profile winning spells for the Williams, McLaren and Red Bull teams. He graduated from Southampton University with a first-class honours degree in astronautics and aeronautics, and then immediately began working for the fading Fittipaldi F1 squad under the late Harvey Postlethwaite.

From there, he spent a period as race engineer for Johnny Cecotto in the European F2 championship, after which he designed his first car, the highly successful March GTP, which won the IMSA GTP title two years running.

From 1983 through to 1986, Adrian worked on the March Indycar project, assisting Al Unser and Bobby Rahal to the CART championships in 1985 and 1986 respectively. During that time, Newey formed a close friendship with Rahal, which would have consequences for their respective careers some 15 years later.

After a brief spell with the fleeting FORCE F1 organisation, he was rehired by March to work on its F1 project as chief designer. This was very much a period when F1 aerodynamics were, by the standards of today, relatively poorly understood. But after March became Leyton House, the promising form displayed by Newey's cars indicated that he knew more than most about this specialised area, something he proved in dramatic style by his contribution to the Williams FW14 and 14B, which dominated the world championship in 1991 and 1992, triggering a run of success for the Grove-based cars that lasted until 1997

By then, Adrian had made the switch to McLaren, where he masterminded the design of the cars that took Mika Häkkinen to the title crown in 1998 and 1999. By the summer of 2001, Bobby Rahal was working in a new role as the principal for the newly rebranded Jaguar squad, and audaciously he tried to steal Newey from McLaren in a bid to catapult the Ford owned team to the front of the field. Ron Dennis proved more than a match for Rahal, however, and managed to persuade Adrian to stay put, a decision that had dire consequences for Bobby, who was dropped from his role at Jaguar shortly afterwards.

It was supremely ironic that in 2007 Newey accepted an invitation to head up the technical operation at Red Bull Racing, the former Jaguar team that had been sold by Ford to the Austrian sports drinks company. By 2010, its two drivers, Sebastian Vettel and Mark Webber, would be fighting McLaren and Ferrari for the world championship as Newey, ever impassive and under control, watched the triumphant progress of his latest supercar, the Red Bull RB6, from the pit wall.

Photo: Peter J Fox

FRANK WILLIAMS

Photo: Autocourse archive

IN a very real sense, Frank Williams has defined the character of contemporary F1 for the past 40 years, first elevating himself and his team to the sport's upper reaches in 1969, when he fielded a single Brabham BT26-Cosworth for his close friend, brewing heir Piers Courage. The partnership proved that it was possible to make a worthwhile impact on the world championship on a frugal budget, Piers taking second place in the Monaco and US GPs. Tragically, however, their burgeoning partnership was brutally ripped apart in the following year when the British driver was killed in a fiery smash at Zandvoort.

It was an experience that hardened Frank Williams to the rigour and perilous nature of his chosen sport. He had grown up with a fiercely independent streak, developing an early interest in cars and motor racing, which was fuelled by an arduous programme of hitch-hiking around the UK to attend a variety of race meetings. Eventually he achieved his aim, first in saloon cars and later in single-seaters – actually winning a minor-league international F3 race in Finland during 1966 – but it was as a race entrant, who also dealt in secondhand racing cars, that he made his reputation over the next few years.

Recovering from Piers's death took several years from the viewpoint of his team's competitiveness. He struggled with poor machinery at the back of the grid, the lowest point coming in 1975 when he decided to sell control to Austro-Canadian oil millionaire Walter Wolf. But working for others had never been part of Frank's business rationale. By the summer of 1977, he had started up a new team of his own. And this time it achieved all the success he could crave.

With a succession of brilliant designs from the pen of talented young engineer Patrick Head, the Williams team quickly climbed the ladder. Clay Regazzoni took its first GP victory at Silverstone in 1970, while Alan Jones and Keke Rosberg followed with world championship titles in 1980 and 1982. Constructors and drivers titles followed in abundance, with Nelson Piquet, Alain Prost, Nigel Mansell, Damon Hill and Jacques Villeneuve all achieving lifelong ambitions behind the wheels of Williams machines. Sadly, there was also more tragedy, with Ayrton Senna's death in a Williams at Imola in 1994 coming eight years after Frank himself had been paralysed in a road accident.

Yet this tragic lack of mobility has in no way impinged on Frank Williams's all-consuming determination that his team should not only remain a vibrant presence on the F1 grid, but also fight its way back to success and respectability at the front of the field. Six years have passed since Juan Pablo Montoya won the team's most recent GP success at Interlagos. For Frank – now Sir Frank, of course – it has been far too long.

Photo: Autocourse archive

GORDON MURRAY

ONE of Bernie Ecclestone's favourite stories about his early years as owner of the Brabham F1 team involved his first meeting with its chief designer, Gordon Murray. "When I arrived, I found him under a drawing board," said Bernie. "Ron Tauranac told me that I should get rid of him and keep everybody else, so I kept Gordon and got rid of everybody else."

Born in Durban, South Africa, in 1946, Ian Gordon Murray studied on a part-time basis at Natal Technical College while working at the same institution as a mechanical design draughtsman. His enthusiasm for cars and motor racing had been fired by his father, Bill, who originally raced motorcycles and later prepared cars for a local racer.

He arrived in England in December 1969, his rather dreamy nature causing him to forget to pack as much as a pullover. For the same reason, on a journey to Lotus in Norfolk, seeking employment, he travelled by coach from London. He was under the impression that coaches were quicker than trains, a notion of which he was quickly disabused. Eventually, however, he got a job with the Brabham squad, where Bernie was happy to indulge his creative technical aspirations.

Throughout the 1970s, a succession of technically advanced and radical F1 machines flowed from Murray's drawing board. There were the BT44s, with their distinctive pyramid-shaped monocoques, one of which Carlos Reutemann very nearly took to victory in the 1974 Argentine GP at Buenos Aires before it ran out of petrol. But the two most novel of Murray's Brabhams were created as a result of Ecclestone's decision to use Alfa Romeo engines from the start of 1976. Heavier, more thirsty and less compact than the Cosworth DFV, packaging the Alfa flat-12 into a chassis was a task that considerably stretched Murray's design flair and ingenuity.

The engine coolant and oil temperatures were kept under control on the 1978 Brabham BT46 by means of a surface cooling systems, with heat exchangers set into the monocoque flanks. Trouble was, it didn't work, so Murray had to think again as he toyed with possible solutions to beat the pace setting, ground-effect Lotus 79s.

The result of his deliberations was the Brabham BT46B 'fan car', which used a gearbox driven fan fitted over the back of the engine to cool it. The fact that the fan also created a low-pressure area below the car, sucking it down towards the tarmac, gave the crucial benefit to performance. But after Niki Lauda drove one to victory in the Swedish GP at Anderstorp, Ecclestone took the politically astute decision that it should never race again.

Subsequently, Murray designed the Brabham BT49C and Brabham BT52, which carried Nelson Piquet to the 1981 and 1983 world championships, and showed great ingenuity in reviving tactical refuelling in 1982, although this was prohibited from the end of 1983.

Later Murray moved to McLaren, where he directed the design of the 'lowline' MP4-4, which was driven by Prost and Senna to 15 wins out of 16 races during the high summer of 1988. Then he turned the focus of his technical ingenuity on to road cars, creating the original McLaren F1, which remains a coveted collector's piece. More recently, Murray's restless and exploring mind has been concentrating on the development of a new generation of 'city cars', compact, efficient and ecologically frugal.

LOUIS T. STANLEY

Photo: Autocourse archive

WHEN working on the editorial staff of *Motoring News* during the early 1970s, I was given the opportunity to interview Louis T. Stanley during his days as chairman of the BRM team. Stanley, who had married industrialist Sir Alfred Owen's sister, Jean, in 1955, operated in some style and kept a suite at the Dorchester Hotel on Park Lane. It was to that elegant venue that I was invited with another colleague, to be given what amounted to a 'state of the nation' address by this large and imposing individual.

Although well worth hearing, Stanley's observations amounted to a monologue that one was not invited to interrupt. At one point, for theatrical effect, he threw his spectacles on to one of the plumped-up sofas and a few moments later flopped down in the same place. There was a crack like a rifle shot as the spectacles broke under his weight.

In a sense, that tells you a lot about Louis T. Stanley. On first acquaintance, he seemed to be a pompous and rather vacuous individual. But there was more to him than that – much more.

Truth be told, Stanley was also a man ahead of his time. There is no question that Jackie Stewart made a huge contribution to making F1 safer during his wide ranging crusade in the 1960s and 1970s, but it could be argued that Stanley, who got to know Stewart well during the Scot's tenure at BRM, was an equally significant advocate of the safety movement during that period when drivers were killed with frightening regularity.

Stewart recalled him with respect bordering on affection: "Louis was brutally frank, but I think that anyone of mature years who has lived through a period like that is allowed to be," said the triple world champion. "I rather liked him."

Stanley experienced first hand the aftermath of Jochen Rindt's fatal accident at Monza in 1970, so it was no surprise that, as honorary secretary of the original Grand Prix Drivers' Association (GPDA), he also became a trustee of the Jim Clark Foundation and the founder of the Jo Siffert Advisory Council, all persuasive and influential bodies lobbying for improved track facilities at the time.

One of his greatest achievements was to create the International Grand Prix Medical Service in 1967, whose mobile hospital was intended to provide a consistently adequate level of care for drivers at a time when safety, for the most part, was a low priority among race organisers and promoters. Later, perhaps ironically, he brought Marlboro into F1 as BRM title sponsor, something he lived to regret. To this day, Philip Morris remains a powerful and influential member of the F1 community.

Overwhelmingly, Louis Stanley brought a touch of old-school elegance to the F1 pit lane. He was usually dressed in a double-breasted blue blazer, light flannels and an old school tie, radiating sufficient presence and gravitas to take the wind out of the most difficult and obstructive of race official's sails. He and his wife attended almost every grand prix contested by the BRM team for over 20 years and were established fixtures in the racing community. Behind the pomposity, Louis Stanley was a well-intentioned man who genuinely cared for those he attempted to help, and he had a shrewd regard for his peers.

SIR Jackie Stewart's enduring iconic status was built on the achievements of a career that spanned just nine seasons contesting the F1 World Championship, which yielded three title crowns and 27 grand prix victories, a record at the time that he held for 14 years. Yet who could have imagined when he climbed from the cockpit of his Tyrrell-Ford at Watkins Glen for the last time after final practice for the 1973 United States Grand Prix that he would remain one of the sport's most influential personalities and opinion formers more than 37 years later?

Like the sport in which he became famous, Jackie has evolved over the years. Apart from his respected racing record, his track safety initiatives were both radical and controversial, as well as ahead of their time. Amazing as it may seem today that anybody should be less than totally receptive to motor racing safety initiatives, Stewart even received death threats after he played a leading role in getting the 1970 German Grand Prix moved from the too-dangerous Nürburgring to Hockenheim.

"There were a lot of small companies, hotels and guest houses in the Eifel region, who depended on what regularly turned into a week-long motor racing festival for the thousands of campers, sometimes as many as 375,000-strong, who lined the 14-mile track," he recalled.

"And here was I, president of the GPDA, fresh from a meeting in Louis Stanley's suite at the Dorchester Hotel, coming along to close down their beloved Nürburgring for GP racing. I mean, can you *imagine* it? I was not flavour of the month in that part of the world for quite some time. But the organisers were absolutely opposed to meeting our demands, even when we sent Jochen [Rindt] as an emissary to speak to them."

Yet Jackie wasn't out to win a popularity contest. Ever since he'd been trapped in the wreckage of his BRM V8, with fuel gushing all over him, after crashing on the Masta straight during the rain soaked 1966 Belgian GP at Spa-Francorchamps, track safety enhancements became an abiding priority alongside his racing. Yet it says much for the Scot, and the BRM and Tyrrell team management – he only drove for those F1 operations during his career – that he was able to separate his priorities so meticulously. Jackie may have had his critics when it came to his safety campaigns, but you would have to search far and wide – and possibly in vain – to find anybody who would say he was anything less than one of the all-time great grand prix drivers.

In that respect, just as the FIA Formula 1 World Championship reaches its 60th anniversary, it seems equally important to celebrate Jackie's contribution to the sport as that of Sir Stirling Moss, a feature on whom can also be found within these pages. Between them, these two men projected very different personalities, but behind the wheel they were bound together by an unquenchable will to win and a meticulously unflurried driving style.

Their racing careers overlapped albeit briefly. In 1961, when Stirling was busy winning at Monaco and the Nürburgring, the young Jackie was showing his fledgling potential at the wheel of Scottish enthusiast Barry Filer's Marcos. In 1962 came the crash that

INTERVIEW

THE FLYING SCOT

ALAN HENRY talks to motor racing icon SIR JACKIE STEWART, OBE

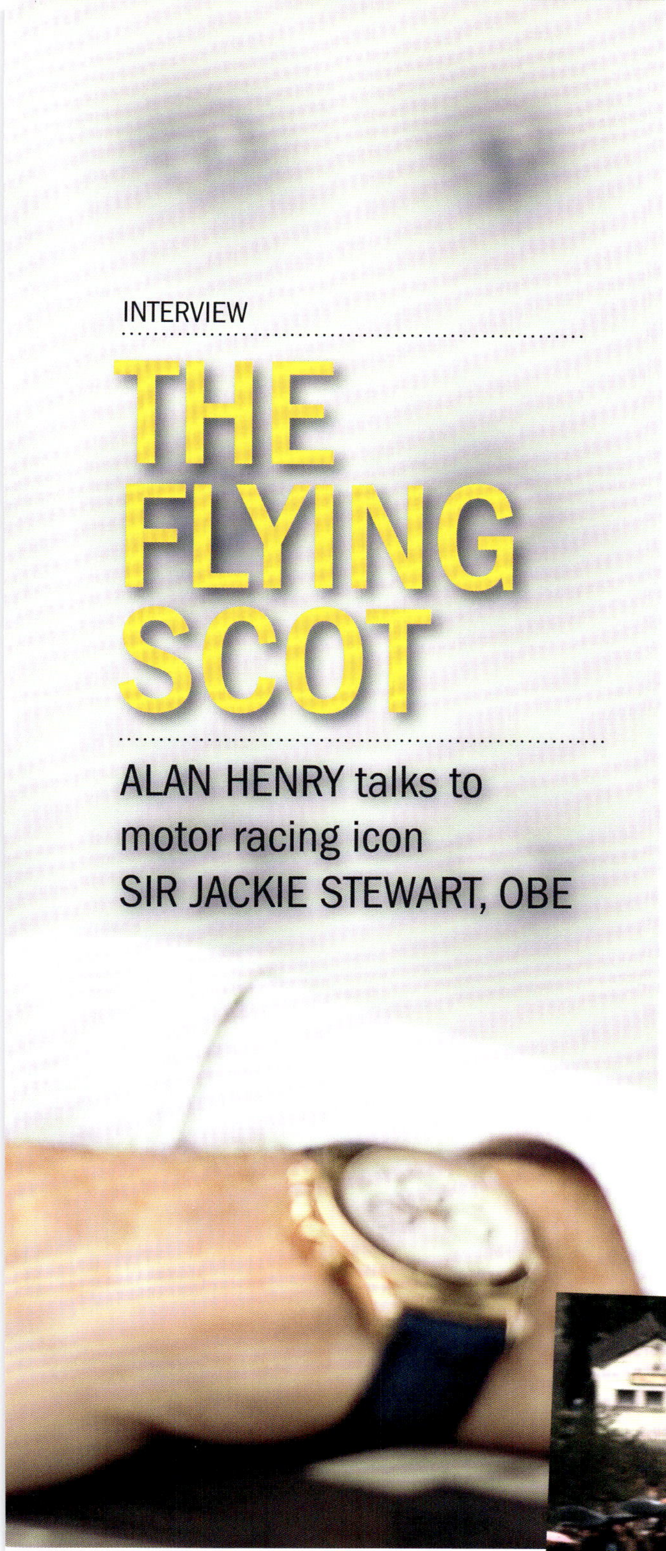

ended Stirling's career, and Jackie began to think in terms of going professional.

Yet at this early stage in his career, he would be the first to admit that the concept of motor racing as an overtly dangerous sport was something that was completely eclipsed by the sheer pleasure and elation he experienced from participating.

"I simply had no awareness of the potential downside risks of driving a racing car at that time," he confessed. "I was so intoxicated by the experience of suddenly being able to drive on the limit, not only of myself, but also the car. All the emotions – frustration, satisfaction, elation – all blended into an all-time high in terms of personal experience. So whether it was a case of skimming around the oil drums or straw bales which delineated the edge of the circuit at places like Charterhall or Rufforth, this was how it was.

"That's what you accepted, that's what you drove around. There was no peripheral 'what if' awareness of the very serious consequences of an accident. That, for me, developed very much later. To be honest, it did not really develop until I had the accident at Spa in 1966."

But surely the experience of chasing Jimmy Clark's Lotus 33 all the way to second place in 1965 at Spa must have triggered an awareness of the risks involved? "No, at that stage in my career, I wasn't thinking in terms of anything which might involve huge risk. I just wasn't thinking in those terms at that stage in my development.

"I was just intoxicated to be there up on the podium with Jim. Just think about it. Three times during the 1965 season, my first year in F1, I was on the rostrum alongside Jim, who was unquestionably the finest driver I ever raced against and the one I respected the most.

"And yet here I was on the podium at Spa, and Jimmy turns to say to me, 'Oh, I was really worried about you.' He was worried that the conditions might have been too bad and too dangerous for me, because he had already passed that window of experience in his own career. And what I couldn't quite understand at the time was the fact that he didn't pull away from me all the time. There were periods when he seemed to steady his lead and keep a fixed distance ahead.

"The conditions were so bad, but I was so young and fresh, lacking in maturity, so I just drove the car to the best of my mental and physical ability. I did not have the experience to accurately assess the conditions and conclude, 'Hey, this is silly,' and back off. I know that this was on the old eight-mile road circuit which had a lap speed faster than Monza. Can you imagine?

"But Jimmy was in total command. When I pushed a little harder, he slapped my wrists and I pulled away."

Jackie likens the racing relationship – or the counterpoint – between himself and Jim Clark as similar to the one between Red Bull team-mates Sebastian Vettel and Mark Webber. "There is Sebastian at 23 and Lewis Hamilton at 26, and Mark at 34, and their experiences make me think back to how I was in my mid-twenties, a raw, bright-eyed, bushy-tailed kid, if you like, and the man I had turned into by the time I reached my early and mid-thirties."

So when it comes to assessing the safety mindset that he championed so fervently four decades ago, he can understand that the younger drivers might suspect he was exaggerating the dangers involved.

"I could understand it if Sebastian and Lewis, let's say, felt, 'What's Jackie talking about? Surely Jackie is laying this on a little bit thick,' but then

Above: Sir Jackie Stewart at the 2010 Brazilian Grand Prix.
Photo: Peter J Fox

Right: Driving his BRM to second in the 1965 Belgian Grand Prix on the old Spa-Francorchamps circuit.
Photo: LAT Photographic

Right: A dangerous club. Just a few months before Jackie would make his grand prix debut, this photograph was taken of the participants in the 1964 British Grand Prix. Of the 18 drivers pictured, half would lose their lives in accidents.
Standing, l to r: Tony Maggs, Jim Clark, Jo Bonnier, Giancarlo Baghetti, Dan Gurney, Phil Hill, Jack Brabham, Jo Siffert, Lorenzo Bandini (hidden), Mike Spence, Bruce McLaren, Peter Revson, Chris Amon and Graham Hill. *Seated:* Richie Ginther, Bob Anderson, John Taylor and Mike Hailwood.
Photo: Autocourse archive

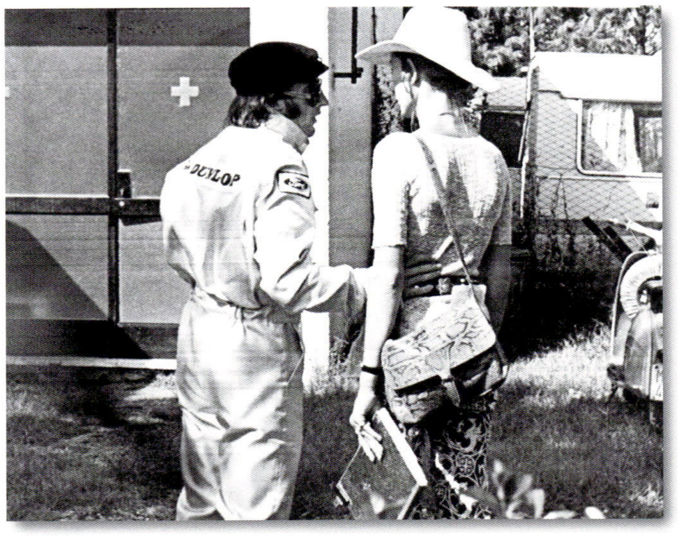

Above: Stewart on his way to victory in the 1971 Monaco Grand Prix with the Tyrrell-Ford.

Above right: Monza, 1970. Jackie offers support to Nina Rindt after her husband, Jochen, was fatally injured in a practice crash.

Right: Tragedy was ever present during Stewart's era. Jo Schlesser perished in an inferno at Rouen in 1968 after he crashed his Honda. As was the convention, the race continued without interuption.
Photos: Autocourse archive

there is Mark: older, more mature and seasoned, who walked away from that huge shunt at Valencia." In fact, Webber later observed to the press that if Jackie had not done all that safety work so many years ago, he would not have survived the shunt.

"How you perceive these things is obviously a matter of where you are at a particular moment in your career or your own wisdom and maturity," said the Scot.

Having taken such a trenchant and uncompromising stance on the matter of circuit safety, Jackie admits that his position hardened as his career advanced. Moreover, added weight was given to his stance by the fact that he brought more financial investment into the sport than any other driver before or since. Yet by the turn of the 1970s, it was not just the fans and journalists who were criticising him, but circuit promoters who found themselves facing the potential of hefty bills for updating their tracks.

"It was very clear to me that I was being paid to display and showcase my skill, not wantonly to risk my life," he said very directly. "This was a view which certainly did not find favour with the traditionalists, but the world was changing. I never made any apologies for the way I felt or what I did to support the safety cause.

"Race organisers and promoters were giving me a hard time, but to an extent that served to harden my resolve. I thought people were paying me to demonstrate my ability, not submit to unreasonable risks."

Of course, foremost of his critics was Denis Jenkinson, the legendary Continental Correspondent of *Motor Sport* magazine. At the time, before the internet age had arrived, this publication sold well over 100,000 copies a month. It was one of the sport's most influential media outlets and required reading for the entire motor racing fraternity.

Jenks was a hard-line right-winger when it came to safety, and some of his critical attacks on Jackie Stewart in print seem extraordinary when viewed from a distance of 40 years. Yet the little bearded chap spoke from a position of some experience, having navigated Stirling Moss to his historic victory in the 1955 Mille Miglia in the Mercedes-Benz 300SLR. And Jackie was shrewd enough to take that reality on board. Jenks may have been crackers to some people, but Stewart knew that many readers hung on every word he wrote. He was not a man to be dismissed lightly. He was regarded as the doyen.

"I have to say that we were not arguing with each other all the time," said Jackie, "but he sometimes took my breath away. I asked him if he couldn't understand the potential dangers of the unprotected pit lanes at Spa and Monaco. How, if somebody got it wrong coming out of the old Gasometer hairpin at Monaco, or lost it at any point between there and Ste Devote, then there was the potential for a fire storm as the car was likely to crash into all the people and the cars in the pits, spilling all the open fuel churns and likely killing a lot of people.

"In response to that, Jenks replied, 'I trust you. You are the world's top drivers. I have confidence in your ability not to make such a mistake.' I have to confess this rather took my breath away. I told him that I was grateful for that confidence, but that it might be misplaced."

None of this criticism prevented Jackie from keeping up the pressure for serious change. His voice softened as he highlighted some of the tragedies he had witnessed. "I'm not just talking about Piers Courage, in Frank's Brabham, kicking up a section of kerbing at 150mph at Woodcote during practice for the 1969 British Grand Prix and ripping the left rear tyre off the rim of my Matra," he said.

"I'm talking about driving through the fires which killed Piers and Roger Williamson at Zandvoort, Jo Siffert at Brands Hatch, Jo Schlesser at Rouen. Then the horrible circumstances of Jochen [Rindt] and Francois [Cevert]..." His voice momentarily wavered. "I'm telling you that I've seen things that no man should ever have seen." I know he is talking about the graphic and painful immediate aftermath of the Rindt and Cevert disasters. But he is not going to elaborate. Even after four decades, the detail is too painful. Still starkly etched in his mind. "We just all felt that these things should not be permitted to continue," he said rather wistfully.

"We were a group of young people who'd been to so many funerals and memorial services, had to support wives, girlfriends and children in their grief, and in the case of the surviving wives, like Helen, Bette Hill and many others, knowing that they were going to experience their husband still going racing, doing the same thing, tomorrow, next week, next month, next year. And have to endure it."

Yet, by the same token, talking of Cevert inevitably brings a smile to his face. To recap, the charismatic Frenchman was set to be Jackie's successor as Tyrrell team leader in 1974, and Jackie believes there is no doubt that he was world championship material. "In my final season, I made sure that Francois had everything I knew in terms of data and information about how the car performed," he said. "I didn't hold anything back. By the summer of 1973, Francois was pretty much as fast as I was on occasion and had developed into a fine driver."

Mention of Francois inevitably raises that 2010 *cause célèbre*, the issue of team orders and whether or not they should be acceptable. Jackie believes that such strategic orders have always been an integral part of grand prix racing, and the rule forbidding them should be rescinded.

"I think if big teams are going to invest in F1, then they need to be able to influence the outcome of their own team's performance. Look back in history, and whether it's Auto Union and Mercedes in the 1930s, Ferrari versus Alfa Romeo, or Lotus versus Tyrrell, there have always been team strategies involved. And I firmly believe that is the way it ought to be. We had a system in place at Tyrrell that if I should build up more than a 30-second window over the rest of the field, then he would stop trying to push me. That seems a perfectly logical way to conduct oneself in what, as I previously emphasised, is a team sport.

"And remember, the constructors' world championship is commercially the most important contest which will

Below: A touching image of François Cevert and Helen Stewart taking a nap on a long-haul flight.

Photo: Autocourse archive

Bottom: New and old worlds meet in Bahrain 2010. To celebrate 60 years of the world championship, great cars and drivers from the past were assembled. Jackie and David Coulthard confer.

Photo: Bernard Asset

Above: Jackie is greeted by Roger Penske at Indianapolis in 2005. Both men developed hugely successful business careers after retiring from driving.
Photo: Lesley Ann Miller/LAT Photographic

Above right: Always on the move. Jackie arrives at the Bahrain circuit for the first race of the 2010 season. His schedule never seems to ease up.
Photo: Bernard Asset

Top: A magical moment for Jackie as he demonstrates Jimmy Clark's Lotus 38 at Goodwood. The beautifully prepared car had been retired to a museum for decades.
Photo: Jeff Bloxham/LAT Photographic

determine the percentage of income earned by the team under the Concorde agreement. So the teams need the operational freedom to maximise these opportunities."

Yet for all the bruising experiences he has been through during his racing years, Jackie remains fascinated and absorbed by how the sport is developing and looks likely to evolve over the next few years.

"Well, I think it is important to note that, at a time when we are celebrating 60 years of the world championship, for at least 30 of those years, F1 has turned into the most commercial and financially intensive of all professional global sports in the world," said Jackie.

"For that, it requires enormous financial backing. So when Bernie created FOCA, as it was then, he was on a percentage of the commercial rights income, but subsequently the business side grew considerably, which meant that the teams had to obtain outside investment to put them in a position where they could start earning income to invest in their own futures. In that respect, you can see how far the sport has come from Ken Tyrrell's wooden shed at Ripley to the McLaren Technology Centre at Woking.

"By the same token, that's why I sold Stewart Grand Prix ten years ago, because F1 was growing at such a rate that, even with the excellent backing we had, I just could not see any way in which we could compete with teams like Ferrari or McLaren going forward.

"We've almost got to the point where the financial river, if you like, can no longer keep up the required flow of funding required for F1. So going forward, this has to be managed with considerable care to permit all the parties in F1 to have an affordable business future and the sport [to] continue to survive.

"For F1 to continue to thrive, it has to be governed with care. A little more of the feel-good factor for all concerned would not be amiss. I'm totally confident that F1 has a very strong long-term future. The global population are going to be travelling on wheels for a long time. They are coming out of the desert, down from the hills, seeking the personal mobility which many of us have taken for granted. And therefore it logically follows that people will still be mesmerised and attracted by the finest machines in the world driven by the finest drivers.

"That's what F1 has achieved over the last 60 years, and the next 60 years promises to bring more of the same."

MOËT
CHAMPAGNE
MOËT & CHANDON
IMPÉRIAL
Please enjoy responsibly. www.moet.com
MOËT

ENGINE DEVELOPMENT

BACK TO THE FUTURE

IAN BAMSEY discovers that the future of F1 engine development lies in the past...

Above: State of the art. The Alfa Romeo T159 on the grid for the 1951 British Grand Prix at Silversone. Apart from the engine being mounted in the front of the car, essentially the same power principles remain in use today.
Photo: LAT Photographic

Above right: The Toyota RVX-09 has valve operation from twin overhead camshafts via finger cam followers. DLC coating on follower and camshaft keeps this system alive to 20,000rpm.

Right: The heart of the Toyota RVX-09 is an aluminium-alloy piston driving a titanium con-rod. Titanium con-rods weren't exploited in 1950, but wartime aircraft such as the Spitfire had established the benefits of RR58 alloy for the piston.

Far right: The Toyota RVX-09 is unconventional in respect of its cooling provision. Coolant not only travels through the block and heads, but also passes through the lower crankcase, underneath the main bearing journals.
Photos: Race Engine Technology magazine

Opening spread: Heart of the matter – the Renault RS27 engine buried deep in the Red Bull chassis.
Photo: Jad Sherif/WRi2

SADLY, it is too late to ask him now, but I suspect that as the Alfa Romeo 158/9 swept to victory in the first world championship Formula One race, engine designer Gioacchino Colombo would have foreseen a 21st-century grand prix winner as something far more radical than we know today. In 1950, the world was still reeling from a nuclear attack, the computer had just been invented and the development of all manner of technologies, such as television and rocket motors, had accelerated as a spin-off from the excessive demands of war. In 1950, most people had a futuristic view of the following century, quite at odds with today's Formula One cars.

You can argue that the likes of mid-mounted engines, slicks and wings are consistent with that futurist vision, but under the carbon-fibre skin (arguably the most futuristic development of all), there isn't some form of CVT transmission, let alone anything as radical as a rotary or gas-turbine engine. In fact, in most respects, today's engine is disappointingly traditional, aside from a crankshaft speed that is mind boggling from the 1950 perspective.

This might change in the near future if, as expected, Formula One reverts to something like Colombo's supercharged 1.5-litre engine. Where the Alfa Romeo had eight cylinders, four is expected to be the maximum (together with 1.6 litres), and the supercharging will come not from a mechanically driven blower, but from a turbo, since that is a means of recovering energy from the exhaust. Granted, Formula One has been down the 1.5-litre turbocharged route before, in the 1980s, when restrictions on fuel consumption and (later) boost pressure were so lenient that 1000bhp could be exploited over a race distance.

As it was in 1950, the emphasis to date has always been on attaining an ever higher level of boost or running a naturally-aspirated engine ever faster to the same end: that of handling more air and with it more fuel, to make more power. Ultimately (at the end of 1951), Colombo's V8 didn't make more than about 400bhp at 9,000rpm on unrestricted fuel, unrestricted fuel type and unrestricted supercharging, since at that time the resources, the materials and the knowledge weren't available to do better. On the other hand, that was a hugely impressive output by the standard of the day.

We've gone on to see a naturally-aspirated 3.0-litre V10 using unleaded petrol exceed 19,000rpm to make close to 1,000bhp, a figure left out of reach only by the enforced cut to 2.4 litres for 2006. That year, the new V8s were pushing 20,000rpm, but that is as far as development went thanks to an increasingly restrictive engine specification freeze that continues to this day (together with a rev limit, initially of 19,000rpm, now 18,000).

The reason that the next generation of Formula One might be more 1950s science fiction than what we have today is that almost certainly the emphasis will be upon making more from a given quantity of fuel, rather than simply trying to exploit more of the stuff. Faced with a fuel flow meter and/or maximum fuel tank size, engine designers will be forced to strive for the maximum thermal efficiency, and (assuming the regulations allow) their efforts will incorporate development of ever more complex turbocharging systems and other forms of energy recovery, including kinetic energy recovery.

Of course, we had a sneak preview of kinetic energy recovery systems (KERS) in 2009, when the technology was highly restrained by the regulations (as it will be when it returns in 2011). We should see more powerful electrical and mechanical KERS supporting the next generation of small-displacement Formula One engines, which may well exploit the likes of two-stage turbocharging or even turbo-compounding (whereby residual exhaust gas downstream of the turbo unit drives another turbine, the output of which is fed mechanically to the crankshaft).

But the internal-combustion engine at the core of this more futuristic power unit, at least initially, is likely to be a straightforward derivative of the current V8s, carrying forward some of the lessons of the past six decades. Not all of them, however, for some of the lessons of high boost and of high rpm will be made irrelevant by actual or logistical limits on plenum pressure and crankshaft speed.

We know what is inside today's naturally-aspirated 2.4-litre V8s, since, having quit Formula One at the end of the 2009 season, Toyota revealed the internals of its (2009 pole and rostrum achieving) RVX-09 to *Race Engine Technology* magazine. Those uncloaked internals wouldn't have surprised Colombo, for they represent a very clear evolution from the technology of 1950, aside from the advent of computer-based electronic controls. Even that he saw in his retirement (born in 1903, he died in 1988).

Exploited since 1984, the engine management system is the biggest departure from 1950s technology, offering ultra-precise fuelling and ignition timing that respond to real-time sensing of engine requirements, and allied to traction and launch control. Or at least it was, until the advent of the Standard Electronic Control Unit (SECU) put paid to the last remaining 'driver aids'.

Fuel has come under a clamp-down, too. While it isn't standardised and is an ongoing area of development, today's regulations don't provide much scope to diverge from the characteristics of roadside pump unleaded. It is a far cry from the early 1950s, when even nitromethane was legal and the Alfa Romeo engine was awash with an exotic blend,

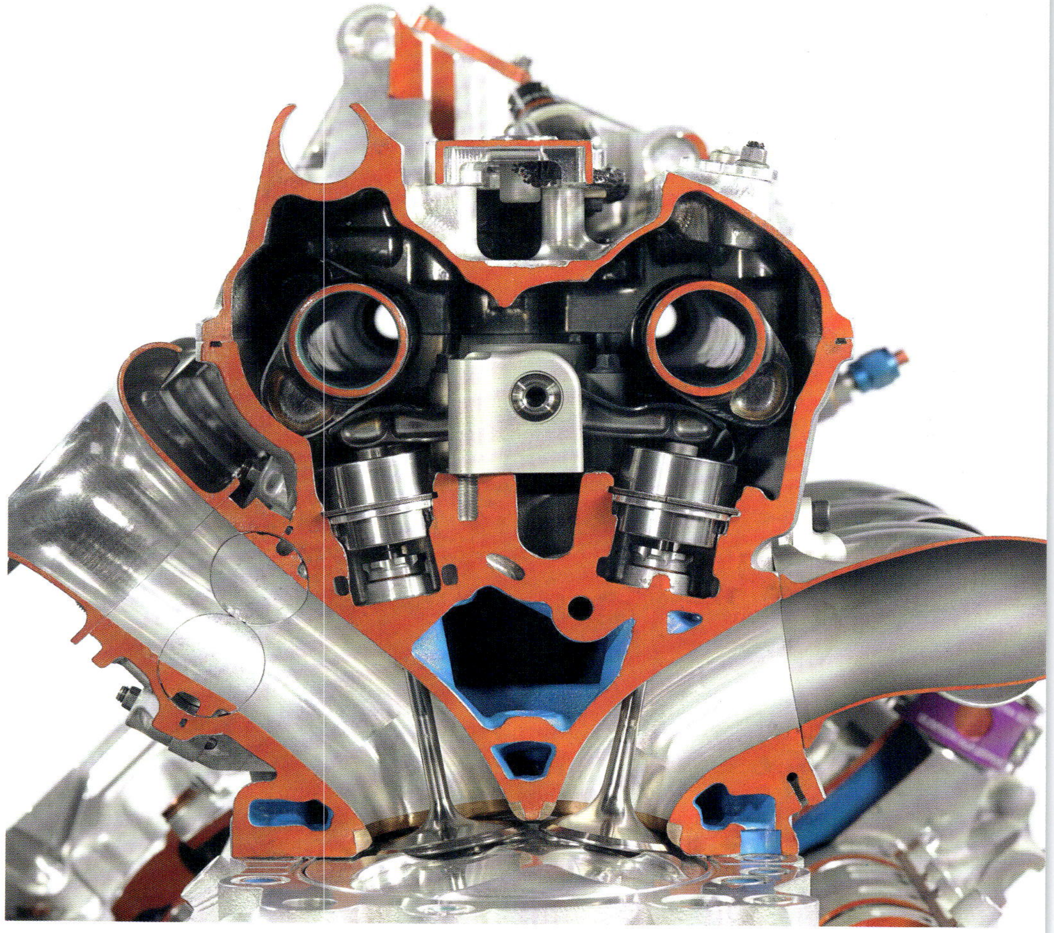

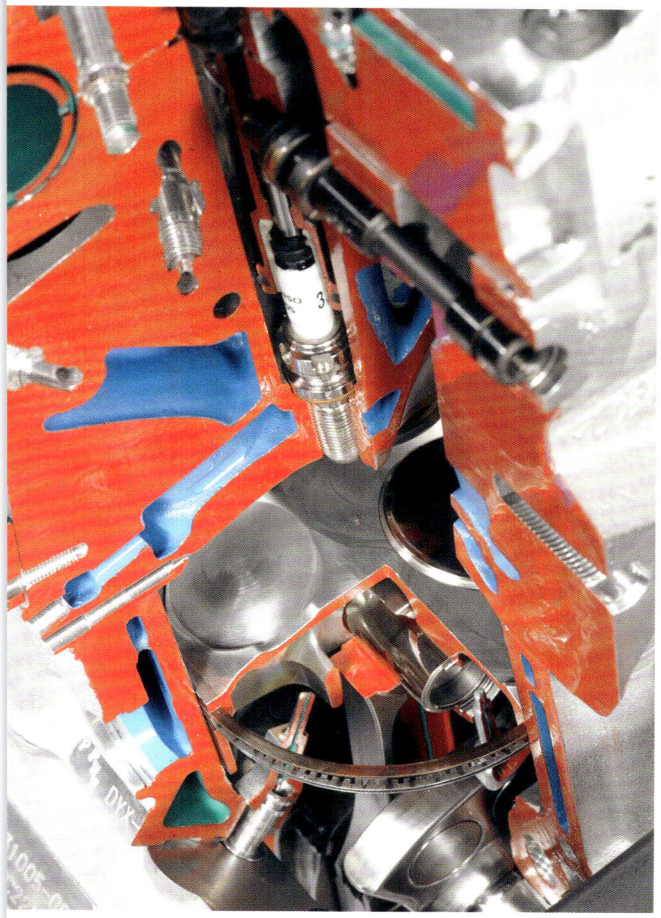

Above: Cosworth returned to Formula 1 for the first time since 2006 with its CA2010V8 engine. This powerplant enabled new teams, such as Virgin Racing and Hispania, to enter the world championship for the first time.

Right: The Renault R27, which powered Red Bull Racing to the 2010 title.

Above right: The Mercedes-Benz F0108X engine was widely regarded as the most powerful on the grid in 2010.

Photos: Race Engine Technology magazine

more to cool it, however, than was needed for power production.

In terms of packaging, by the standard of 1950, the current Toyota (which remains available to customer teams, unlike the rival BMW, which has been scrapped along with the marque's Formula One programme) is hugely impressive. Since Colin Chapman and Keith Duckworth collaborated on the design of the Lotus-Cosworth DFV for 1967, invariably any bespoke engine will have been designed as a fully stressed member of the chassis, and through the post-turbo-era V8, V10 and V12 engines, designers have strived tirelessly to obtain smaller lighter units.

Design optimisation, taking advantage of computer-based tools such as Finite Element Analysis, plus improving material specifications and upgraded casting techniques have all helped. A notable step came with the 1999 Cosworth V10, which dispensed with cylinder liners to set a new standard in compactness and weight reduction.

In fact, the current V8s were designed to FIA specified criteria, including minimum weight, minimum centre of gravity height and minimum bore spacing, which impacted on the overall package. The 2005 Toyota V10 weighed slightly less than 95kg, which was set as the minimum for the new V8s, even though a V8 is inherently 10kg lighter than a V10 of the same 300cc cylinder displacement.

The minimum bore spacing left room for a 98mm bore, the maximum permitted from 2006. That didn't stop engines reaching 20,000rpm, which (given the corresponding 39.77mm stroke to obtain a 300cc cylinder displacement) implied a mean piston speed of 26.5m/sec. Mind you, that isn't a particularly impressive figure – a 2006 NASCAR Cup V8 saw an mps of 27.5m/sec at half the crankshaft speed. What is telling is the maximum piston acceleration of 10,622g, which even with a lightweight piston and (titanium) con-rod assembly put a load of no less than 6,045kg on to the big end.

It took very clever component design to produce an engine capable of such loading at such a high speed, the like of which won't be seen again. Once more, advanced tools, and the development of materials and manufacturing techniques assisted. On the other side of the coin, the rule makers stopped the exploitation of some advanced materials that came along in the last couple of decades, most notably MMC and aluminium-beryllium.

In fact, given its compatibility with the aluminium cylinder, and the fact that it outperformed both regular aluminium and MMC in terms of heat rejection, heat resistance and strength, aluminium-beryllium was the ideal piston material as Formula One engine speed first crept over 17,500rpm. It was introduced by Ilmor/Mercedes in 1998, but by 2000 it had been effectively outlawed.

Come 2006 and the rules forced everyone to use straightforward aluminium alloys for pistons. The state of the art then was Rolls-Royce alloy RR58, developed during the Second World War, when it was used for the pistons in Merlin aircraft engines. Mind you, the manufacturing and heat-treatment technologies applied to 2006 pistons would hugely impress a time traveller from 1950. So would the design of the piston and its two steel rings, the top ring made from nothing more exotic than steel, but tiny in comparison with the standard of the 1950s, largely due to improved manufacturing techniques.

On top of that, the piston used by Toyota (in conjunction with a plasma sprayed, ceramic-based cylinder bore coating) has a DLC skirt coating. DLC stands for Diamond-Like Carbon: in simple terms, it is a coating that is extremely hard and slippery, which offers a significant reduction in friction compared to polishing the substrate material.

DLC arrived in Formula One around 1992, when engine speed really started to take off from the 12,000/13,000rpm baseline of the pre-turbo era. In the quest for 14,000rpm-plus, two major hurdles were the traditional wire-coil valve spring and the cam/tappet interface. Finger cam followers replaced direct operation of a tappet atop the valve by the overhead camshaft, but they needed DLC to keep them alive. The Toyota engine has DLC coating on both its camshafts and its finger followers.

The Toyota also has a pneumatic valve return system (PVRS), which overcomes the challenge of keeping coil springs under control at 20,000rpm. Mind you, forced to run coils, the Toyota CART engine evolved to attain 18,000rpm before its programme was terminated. Doubtless, with enough development effort, coils could operate within a 20,000rpm Formula One engine, but that is now academic. A PVRS creates more friction than coils, so new-generation, high-efficiency Formula One engines may well bring coils back.

Whatever form the new-generation power train takes, initially at least there is likely to be little in the internal-combustion engine at its heart to shock a time traveller from the first ever world championship Formula One race. But the surrounding energy-recovery systems should impress.

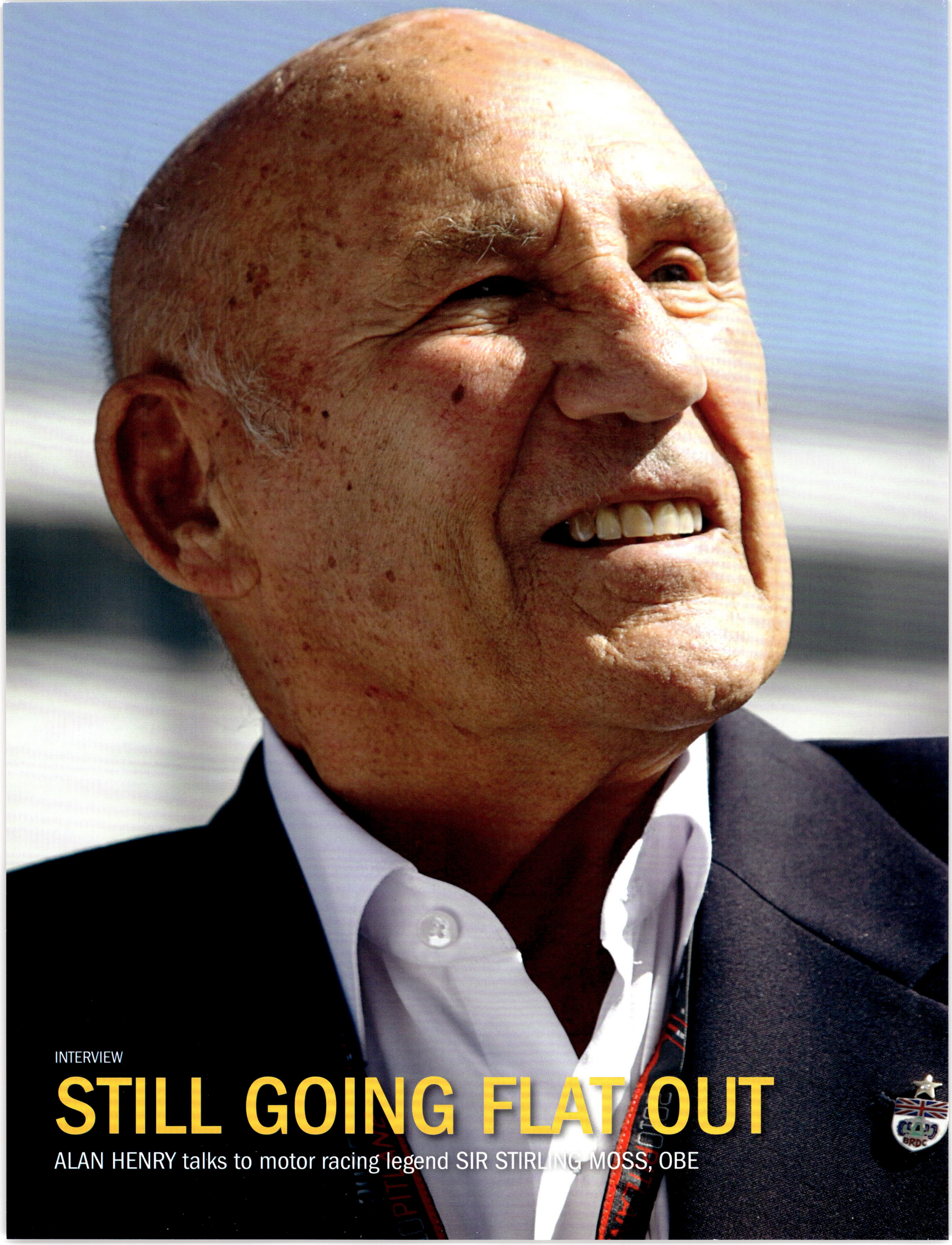

INTERVIEW

STILL GOING FLAT OUT

ALAN HENRY talks to motor racing legend SIR STIRLING MOSS, OBE

SIXTY years have passed since Sir Stirling Moss, OBE, as he is now, stood between Duncan Hamilton and Peter Collins on the starting grid at Silverstone, shaking hands with King George VI and Queen Elizabeth at the inaugural round of the official F1 world championship. Although Stirling did not compete in the main race, he won the first heat of the 500cc F3 race and went on to finish second in the final. As a proud and longstanding member of the British Racing Drivers' Club, whose distinctive lapel badge he never fails to wear each time he leaves his home, Stirling is the last survivor of those men who competed on the Northamptonshire aerodrome circuit on that sunny afternoon back in 1950.

At the end of a season in which the sport celebrated the 60th anniversary of the world championship, we asked Sir Stirling to share his thoughts about how the sport has developed, during both his own career and the 48 years since he stopped racing at a professional level. Lest we forget, Stirling's racing heyday was at a time of immense diversity at the highest level. He drove in 585 motorsport events between March 1947 and April 1962. These included 66 world championship grands prix, of which he won 16 and started the same number from pole position. Four times he was runner-up in the world championship and three times he was third.

He grew up in a family already suffused with an interest in motorsport. His father, Alfred, a successful dentist, competed at Indianapolis in 1924, while his mother, Aileen, drove in rallies and sporting trials during the 1930s. Stirling recalled a family holiday in 1947 at Menton on the Côte d'Azur, during which they attended the street race at Nice, which was won by Luigi Villoresi's Maserati. Alfred Moss topped up the family funds for the trip by selling a spare tyre from their elderly Rolls-Royce for £50, which must have seemed like a fortune in those austere immediate post-war days.

To this day, Stirling retains a keen interest in contemporary F1 developments and has strong feelings about the way the sport has evolved. Yet when one speaks to him, he never gives the impression that he is consumed by nostalgia and craves for the sport to be as it was at the height of his racing career. He has a sharply tuned sense of perspective and appreciates just what today's breed of professional sportsmen achieve behind the wheel, even though he believes he had much more fun than today's drivers.

"After I won a race, I could go off and chase crumpet," he said with a sly grin. "Lewis Hamilton has to go and talk to Vodafone."

Of course, that is only a small part of the story. Stirling raced at a time when the sport was seriously dangerous. Lapping a slower car in his HWM-Alta at Naples in 1950, he was pitched into a spin and hit a tree. His face slammed into the rear-view mirror on the side of the cockpit, knocking out four teeth in the process. At the same time, his left knee was broken as it hit the dashboard.

When he was practising in a Lotus 18 at Spa-Francorchamps in 1960, the notoriously frail machine shed a rear wheel on the Masta straight. Cryptically, he wrote in his diary on the page for 18th June that year, "Shunt. Nose. Back. Legs. Bruises. Bugger!"

Above: High jinks with Jenks.

Above left: Stirling with Fangio after his win in the 1955 British Grand Prix at Aintree.

Centre right: One of his greatest drives occurred at Monaco in 1961, when his Lotus beat the more powerful Ferraris.

Top left: A well-earned cigarette for the young Stirling after winning a race in Dundrod, Northern Ireland, in 1951.
Photos: LAT Photographic

Top right: A 'cuppa' is just the ticket at Goodwood with Jackie Stewart.
Photo: Jeff Bloxham/LAT Photographic

Left: Still going flat out at 81 years young.
Photo: Charles Coates/LAT Photographic

Those words spoke for themselves. Finally, of course, there was the massive accident at Goodwood on Easter Monday, 1962, which brought his professional front-line career to a premature end at the age of 32.

Considering the physical suffering he has experienced because of his chosen sport, you might have expected it to have shaped his attitude toward motor racing safety, and that he might be an unreserved supporter of the safety campaign initiated by Jackie Stewart throughout the 1960s. But Stirling has different terms of reference.

On Stewart's attitude toward safety, he said, "I can see absolutely what he's about and totally respect his viewpoint. Let's just say that we see things from a different perspective. When we formed the UPPI, the forerunner of the Grand Prix Drivers' Association, back in the 1950s, we all agreed that the overriding priority was that the marshals and spectators were kept absolutely as safe as possible. UPPI stood for Union Pilotes Professional Internationale, but we felt the word 'union' should be avoided.

"We, the drivers, were the ones who were paid to take the risks. I know Jackie has a different interpretation, that he was paid to demonstrate his skill rather than risk his life, but I just see things differently. Of course, that doesn't prevent us getting along okay together, and I obviously respect the amount of energy he has put into the cause of circuit safety. We just have different views.

"The possibility of death, or being killed while you were racing, was something you accepted. You got used to losing friends. And you had to realise that it could be you, or it could be someone else. It was simply the risk you took." He made the dispassionate point that if you dropped a wheel off the track on a high-speed circuit like Spa-Francorchamps, then you might well hit a tree and be killed. It was all a question of positioning yourself in the correct place on the circuit. Peter Collins, he pointed out, was killed at Nürburgring in 1958 in what was little more than a 60mph accident. But he was on the wrong place on the circuit, said Stirling.

"Having said that," he continued, "I'm amazed that some of today's drivers have not got the urge to try some of the epic old circuits on which we raced during my time at the wheel. And I'm really slightly aghast when I see the rumble strips on corners at modern-day tracks, which the current breed of F1 driver simply takes for granted as an extension of the circuit itself.

"If I had my way, I would have a small brick wall, perhaps less than a foot high, instead of these rumble strips on the apex of these corners, a bit like there used to be at Silverstone up to the late 1960s. I'd also insist that the walls were painted white, like the kerbs at Monaco, so that anybody's contact with the wall was on public display for all to see, and the spectators could really appreciate the drivers' skills."

The 1967 Monaco GP, of course, was marred by the tragic fiery accident that cost the life of Ferrari driver Lorenzo Bandini. It was one of the catalysts that triggered the steady forward march in making the sport much safer.

Moss agreed that fire held the most terror for competitors in his era: "That's why we never wore seat belts, because it seemed safer to be thrown out than burned to death. But now, of course, with the possibility of fire much reduced, it's a totally different ball game, and I can quite see why you want to stay tightly strapped into what is effectively a survival cell." He felt that Mark Webber's spectacular escape from the huge accident at Valencia in 2010 was an obvious illustration of this.

He was impressed with the way in which Webber rose to the occasion during the season, but thought that Sebastian Vettel's over-ambitious manoeuvres in search of the championship led him into collisions and other costly errors that undermined his quest. Even so, he admired the young German for the "true racing spirit" he exhibited.

It is a measure of Moss's high status and long-standing credibility that one's instinctive reaction is to listen and consider what he is saying, rather than dismissing it as misty-eyed nostalgia. But that's the whole point about Stirling: while he has his own deep-rooted philosophy and long-held views, he is also receptive to other peoples' viewpoints. Paradoxically, this makes it easier to assimilate and consider his own views.

Like Jackie Stewart with Ken Tyrrell, Stirling enjoyed a very close personal friendship with Rob Walker, for whom he drove from 1959 through to the end of his career in that terrible crash at Goodwood in 1962. "We never had a contract, or indeed anything written down," he recalled. "We just did business on the basis

Left: Stirling whiles away the time with a game of dice with his great friend, Peter Collins. He was one of many colleagues who paid the ultimate price.
Photo: Autocourse archive

Far left: Stirling and his victorious Mercedes at the 1955 British Grand Prix at Aintree.
Photo: LAT Photographic

Below left: Jim Clark drifts around the low brick wall on the inside of Woodcote Corner in the 1963 British Grand Prix,
Photo: Autocourse archive

Below: No margin for error in taming the Pescara road circuit. Such was his dominance that Stirling finished the 1957 Pescara Grand Prix more than two minutes ahead of second-placed Fangio.
Photo: LAT Photographic

Left: Valentino Rossi and Stirling Moss during the Australian Grand Prix, 2004.
Photo: Jean-François Galeron/WRi2

Below: Stirling demonstrates the Mercedes W196 at Goodwood in July 2009.
Photo: Jeff Bloxham/LAT Photographic

of a handshake, nothing more was needed. To give you an indication of just how close our relationship really was, when I asked Rob whether we could take his Cooper-Climax to the 1958 Argentine Grand Prix, he just replied, 'Ask Alf [Francis, the chief mechanic]. If he's up for it, then that's fine.'"

As history relates, Moss drove brilliantly at that race, nursing his one set of tyres through the entire distance while at the same time double-bluffing the Ferrari team into thinking he would be stopping after all. He admitted that it was one of his most satisfying Grand Épreuve successes, if not quite as good as his victory at Monaco in 1961 with Rob Walker's underpowered Lotus 18.

Asked if he felt he could have been comfortable driving a factory Lotus, he responded, "I reckon I could have worked with Colin Chapman, but I didn't really warm to him as a person."

In general terms, he is respectful and moderate in his comments about other drivers, but on Michael Schumacher's driving methods, and in particular what he did to Rubens Barrichello in the 2010 Hungarian GP, Stirling had extremely strong views. "I think it was absolutely terrible what he tried to do to Barrichello, and trying to excuse it on the basis that he was 'inviting' Rubens to pass him on the left is adding insult to injury.

"That's one of the problems of a safe sport. All the run-off areas and barriers can breed that sort of dangerous driving. People begin to think that they can take all sorts of liberties and get away with it."

Stirling respects Schumacher's level of achievement, but with the caveat that he has never really had to prove himself against an equal team-mate in identical cars. "I think Rubens showed up very well against him on occasions, but you always felt that the team loaded the dice in Michael's favour to a large extent.

"For that reason, I think it's difficult to judge just how good Schumacher really is. I certainly don't think that the fact he has won seven world championships puts him in the same league as Ayrton Senna and Jim Clark, for example."

As far as the evolution of the F1 world championship is concerned, Stirling had some very clear-cut and structured thoughts that he delivered in an analytical and objective fashion, even though some might expect him to rail against a system that never delivered him this ultimate accolade. Put simply, he understands the need for a championship system as part of the sport's attraction and appeal to the public, but in his own mind it is a rather overrated distinction.

"The problem with a world championship system is that you get a situation where drivers are competing with an eye on their overall points tally rather than on simply winning the race on that particular day. I particularly remember Emerson Fittipaldi driving strategically to finish fourth in the 1974 US GP at Watkins Glen because that position would be good enough to clinch his second world championship.

"I couldn't approach racing in that way. To me, it was always a case of a race is a race is a race, and 'today's race' was always the most important in my mind, not last week's or next week's. But I think Bernie Ecclestone correctly judged if F1 was going to have a world championship, then it needed to be as well organised and slickly run as possible, and he has done a great job in that respect."

Stirling retains a wide-ranging interest in all forms of motorsport, whether on two wheels or four: "I should also put on record just how much respect I have always had for motorcycle racers, and in particular a high regard for just how much Valentino Rossi has contributed to the success of MotoGP. I think it would almost be a shame if he switched to four-wheels because he is such an integral part of MotoGP and the motorcycle racing community."

As for his own career, Moss doesn't dwell on lost opportunities. He does not trade in might-have-beens. Pressed on the matter, he ventured that he might well have raced through to the mid-1970s had he not made the admittedly premature decision to retire after the Goodwood shunt.

"It meant that I had to go out and get a job rather than having fun racing," he twinkled mischievously, "but I'm still here, still going flat out, so on balance I think I'm well ahead!"

A Daimler brand
Like at the Louvre. Only with 21,000 hp.
The Mercedes-Benz Museum. Works of art from nearly 125 years of automotive history. www.mercedes-benz-classic.com
Mercedes-Benz
The best or nothing.

APPRECIATIONS 2010

By ALAN HENRY

Peter Warr at the opening race of the 2010 season in Bahrain, where he took part in the celebrations of the 60th anniversary of the F1 World Championship.

Photo: Bernard Asset

Right: The famous photograph of Warr greeting Ayrton Senna after the Brazilian's first grand prix win at Estoril in 1985.

Photo: Autocourse archive

PETER WARR

PETER WARR, who died in October at the age of 72, earned his place in recent F1 history as the keeper of the flame at the legendary Lotus team following the sudden death of its founder, Colin Chapman, in 1982, and he proved an adept and persuasive motor racing manager when he attracted the dynamic young Ayrton Senna to drive for the British squad at the start of the 1985 season.

Originally, Warr nurtured his own racing ambitions, eventually purchasing a Lotus 7 that had been specially built for Graham Hill to drive in the traditional Boxing Day Brands Hatch fixture in 1959. He raced it enthusiastically for a couple of seasons before switching to the single-seater Formula Junior category. He won the Eifelrennen at the Nürburgring at the wheel of a Lotus 20 and made two trips to Japan for races at the newly opened Suzuka circuit, winning the 1963 Japanese Grand Prix, then a sports car race, driving a Lotus 23B.

Warr retired from racing in 1964 and originally intended to follow Lotus when it moved to Hethel, Norfolk, in 1966. But when it came to the crunch, he decided not to go and left the team, in part because the job he really wanted as Lotus F1 manager had gone to his colleague, Andrew Ferguson. Then one day in 1969, Ferguson tipped off Warr that he was leaving the company, too. Chapman judged Warr to be the right man for the vacant post, so he was signed up just before the 1969 US Grand Prix at Watkins Glen, the race where Graham Hill crashed heavily and broke his legs in one of the works Lotus 49s while the other one sped to the maiden Formula One victory for Austrian driver Jochen Rindt.

Warr managed the team through the golden years of the Lotus 72, suffering the tragedy of Rindt's death at Monza in 1970 and then presiding over the team's rebirth in 1972, when Emerson Fittipaldi became the youngest ever world champion up to that point. This dominance continued into 1973, when Ronnie Peterson joined Fittipaldi in the Lotus squad, but over the next two years the team's fortunes began to wane, not helped in the spring of 1975 when Warr broke both legs in a road accident.

At the 1976 British GP, Warr was approached by the Austro-Canadian oil millionaire Walter Wolf, who had just acquired the assets of the bankrupt Williams team. Wolf wanted a clean-sheet approach for 1977 and offered Warr the job of masterminding the whole project. He quickly accepted the new challenge. Chapman bade him good fortune and suggested that he regard his detour to Wolf as temporary leave of absence.

Jody Scheckter took the new Wolf to second place in the 1977 world championship, a success that was as impressive as it was unexpected. But in the summer of 1981 came the call from Colin Chapman. It was time for Warr to return to Lotus, but just 16 months later he was faced with telling the team the tragic news that their leader had died from a sudden heart attack. Warr was thrust unwillingly into the Lotus driving seat, a task sometimes complicated by a sparky relationship with his boss's protégé, Nigel Mansell, who drove for the team until the end of 1984.

Although Lotus was fighting against the F1 tide during the 1980s, Warr made some inspired decisions to put a brake on that decline, most notably signing the brilliant Ayrton Senna for the 1985 season, and it seems somehow appropriate that Senna won the marque its last grand prix victory on the streets of Detroit in 1987. Warr left Lotus in 1989 and, after a brief period as secretary of the British Racing Drivers' Club, retired to France, where he lived until his death.

Photo: Autocourse archive

Photo: Autocourse archive

TREVOR TAYLOR

THE death of TREVOR TAYLOR, who succumbed to cancer in September, at the age of 73, severed one of the remaining major links to the epic 1960s era of Jimmy Clark, alongside whom the Yorkshireman drove for two grand prix seasons (1962 and 1963) in the Team Lotus line-up. A highly regarded and popular driver, Taylor admitted that he was in awe of Clark – "That fine man" was how he described him – and he never really managed to emerge from the twice world champion's shadow during his brief spell in the F1 limelight.

Taylor was the son of a garage owner from Wickersley, near Rotherham, and he emerged as a rising star to watch in the cut and thrust of 500cc F3 during the late 1950s, initially competing with a JAP-engined Staride before switching to an ex-Stuart Lewis-Evans Cooper-Norton. Ten victories in 1958 earned him the British F3 title and, after a frustrating year wrestling with his own F2 Cooper in 1959, he accepted an invitation to run his own newly purchased Lotus 18 as a second works car alongside Clark for the following season.

The two Lotus drivers shared the 1960 British Formula Junior title, and Taylor retained it solo in 1961 before joining Clark in the works Lotus F1 line-up as successor to Innes Ireland, whose services Colin Chapman had dispensed with only weeks after he'd won the team its first grand prix victory at Watkins Glen at the end of 1961.

Taylor's relationship with Lotus promised much, but delivered disappointingly little. The yellow-suited Yorkshireman took one of the type 24s to second place, behind Graham Hill's BRM V8, in the 1962 Dutch GP at Zandvoort, a year after he had trailed home last in the same race as a deputy for the injured Ireland, who had been recovering from a bad crash at Monaco. Then Taylor was lucky to survive a massive accident after colliding with the tempestuous Willy Mairesse's Ferrari 156 during the Belgian GP at Spa-Francorchamps, and he walked away from another huge shunt at Rouen, where he had slammed into the back of Maurice Trintignant's stalled car on the pit entry.

Chapman kept faith with Taylor into the 1963 season, but his second year was highlighted by a horrifying shunt at Enna, the high-speed Sicilian circuit, where he was tossed out of his type 25 and went rolling down the track for 50 yards. He escaped with bruising and grazes, but by now he had lost Chapman's confidence and was dropped in favour of Peter Arundell in 1964. Taylor joined Innes Ireland in the BRP-BRM squad run by Alfred Moss and Ken Gregory, but scored just a single championship point for a sixth at Watkins Glen before the team closed its doors.

After plumbing the depths at the wheel of the hopeless Shannon-Climax in the 1966 British GP at Brands Hatch, Taylor attempted to rebuild his career in sports cars, first with a Lotus 47 and later with a Lola T70, in which he won the 1969 Tourist Trophy. Driving the Surtees F5000 car in the newly instigated series for V8-engined single-seaters, he narrowly lost out in the title battle to works McLaren driver Peter Gethin. At the end of 1972, he finally retired and, despite a couple of unfortunate business reversals in later years, he never displayed any resentment that his racing career had fallen short of his own expectations.

IS THERE MORE TO LIFE THAN FORMULA ONE?
Probably not!
But, at Fellow Productions, recognised as one of the most experienced film production companies in F1 and MotoGP, we're now also increasingly in demand to extend our talents in other areas of production, such as commercials and high-end corporate films for a host of well-known worldwide brands. Formula One attracts many international sponsors keen to associate their brand with the excitement and glamour of the sport. Our skill in combining these elements into powerful films has helped us forge lasting client relationships. Whatever your message, we have the in-house experience and creativity to produce programming that truly engages an audience and enhances brand recognition.
For more information on how we can help you promote your brand or product please contact:
Mark Ratcliff
mark@fellowproductions.com
Tel: + 44 20 7449 2379
Or to receive a copy of our showreel please contact:
Ravinder Cheema
rav@fellowproductions.com
www.fellowproductions.com
Fellow PRODUCTIONS

TEAM-BY-TEAM

FORMULA 1 REVIEW

Team Reviews: MARK HUGHES

Car Specifications: ALAN HENRY

Car Illustrations: ADRIAN DEAN

Photo: Peter J Fox

1

JENSON BUTTON

2

LEWIS HAMILTON

VODAFONE McLAREN MERCEDES

ALTHOUGH it figured in the title fight for most of the season – and at the halfway stage its drivers were 1-2 and the team led the constructors' table – this wasn't a classic McLaren performance. The MP4-25 was hanging on as the third fastest car most of the time, its performance flattered by a great driver line-up, some good strategic calls and the relative unreliability of the Red Bull.

Jenson Button fitted right in to his new environment, and his easy-going persona ensured that there was none of the friction of the Hamilton/Alonso period. He took two very smart early-season victories and gave good direction to the engineering team, but usually was a vital couple of tenths slower than the swashbuckling Hamilton, who won three times.

The car was conceived around an innovative new aero feature that subsequently became all the rage – the F-duct. On the straights, this rear wing stalling device directed air away from the wing through pressure changes induced by the driver moving his leg over a hole within tubing that stretched from an inlet duct on the front of the car, through the cockpit and along the top of the engine cover to the wing. The result was a much more efficient trade-off between downforce in the corners and low drag down the straights. Since the McLaren was the only car configured around this device, it was generally more effective than the add-ons of rival cars. A yet more efficient version was evolved later in the season.

Another distinguishing feature of the car's design was its extreme length. Tim Goss led the design team and explained the thinking behind this: "The philosophy of the car was to get the absolute maximum out of the diffusers. The legalisation of those [through placement of appropriate bodywork slots] was actually quite a complex process to get the biggest, widest, longest diffuser. This car has a particularly long gearbox and long rear wheelbase, so despite the fact that the fuel tank was getting longer for the additional fuel capacity, we still stretched the gearbox, and it can be seen that the car is still a little bit bulbous around fuel tank area. That was to try and push the engine as far forward to get the gearbox as long as possible, to get the rear wishbone forward leg as far forward as possible because that, to some extent, dictates the start of the diffuser's inlet duct."

The previous season's legalisation of the double diffuser led to a 2010 generation of car that sought to take maximum advantage of the rule interpretation, and the McLaren was extreme in this. However, that big diffuser needed feeding, and that is where the car's Achilles' heel was inadvertently built in. Such was the diffuser's area that it was prone to stalling as the rear ride height increased beyond a critical point (as in slow-speed corners or heavy braking). Furthermore, the car's extreme length only exacerbated that tendency, in that the longer the car, the greater the rear ride height increases for a given amount of dive

McLAREN-MERCEDES MP4-25

SPONSORS	Mercedes-Benz • Vodafone • Exon Mobil • Boss • Santander • TAG Heuer • Diagio • Hilton • Kenwood • SAP • Olympus • Aigo Lenovo • Fedex • X trade Brokers • Aon • Akzo Nobel • Bridgestone • Akebono • Enkei • Faram • GS Yuasa • Kangaro TV • Koni NGK • Sonax • Sparco • Steinmetz • Targetti • Technogym • Yamazaki • Mazak • Sports Marketing Surveys
ENGINE	*Type:* Mercedes-Benz F0108X *No of cylinders:* V8 2.4-litre *Spark plugs:* NGK *Electronics:* McLaren Electronics ECU *Fuel:* Mobil unleaded *Oil:* Mobil 1
TRANSMISSION	*Gearbox:* McLaren Racing 7-speed longitudinal, semi-automatic 'e-shift' *Clutch:* AP Racing carbon-carbon multi-plate
CHASSIS	*Front and rear suspension:* Double wishbone/pushrod operating inboard mounted torsion-bar/damper units *Dampers:* Koni *Wheel diameter:* 13in front and rear *Wheels:* Enkei, magnesium forged *Tyres:* Bridgestone Potenza *Brake discs and pads:* Carbone Industrie *Brake callipers:* Akebono six-piston *Steering:* McLaren power assisted *Instruments:* McLaren Electronic Systems *Battery:* GS Yuasa *Radio systems:* Kenwood
DIMENSIONS:	*Wheelbase:* not given *Dimensions:* not given
	Formula weight: 620kg, including driver and camera

VODAFONE McLAREN MERCEDES: PERSONNEL

Team Principal: Martin Whitmarsh
Managing Director: Jonathan Neale
Engineering Director: Paddy Lowe
Design & Development Director: Neil Oatley
Chief Engineer MP4-25: Tim Goss
Team Manager: Dave Redding
Chief Mechanic: Pete Vale
Chief Aerodynamicist: Doug McKiernan
Head of Aerodynamics: John Iley
Principal Race Engineer: Phil Prew
Race engineer LH: Andy Latham
Race engineer JB: Dave Robson

Above: Engineering director, Paddy Lowe.
Photos: Peter J Fox

Above right: Jonathan Neale, the team's managing director.
Photo: Vodafone McLaren Mercedes

Right: Team principal, Martin Whitmarsh.

Top: Lewis Hamilton took a resounding win at Spa in the Belgian Grand Prix.
Photos: Peter J Fox

at the front, thus sometimes creating an inconsistent flow to the diffuser, which triggered its weak point all the more. The only way to break this vicious cycle was to run the car extremely stiffly, to keep it within a very narrow ride-height window. So in stark contrast to McLarens of recent years, it hated bumps and kerbs. This hurt it on some tracks more than others.

It was quick in Melbourne, China, Turkey, Montreal, Spa and Abu Dhabi, but struggled badly at Monaco, Silverstone and Hungary. Before the Ferrari came on strong, and taking advantage of various Red Bull mishaps, the team scored three 1-2s in the first half of the season. But as an average, the car qualified around 0.4 second slower than the Red Bull. It tended to race more competitively than it qualified, partly because it seemed to behave better on full tanks, partly because the team made some good strategic calls. In Melbourne, these were actually led by Button. In China, they came from the team.

"The pattern of the first half of our season was largely driven by F-duct sensitivity," said Goss, "in that at circuits like Canada that was particularly sensitive to it, it played into our hands. At around that time, we had closed the gap to the Red Bull, but then we fell back a little. We were a little slow off the mark with the blown diffuser – which we got on to as soon as we saw it on the Red Bull, but maybe not as hard as we could have. We were working on another aero feature that we thought was going to be a really big winner, but because we were concentrating on that and our tunnel resource was going into that, we didn't look as hard as we should have at the blown diffuser. A little bit later, we realised the value in it and dropped our other project to concentrate on the blown diffuser."

Not only did the blown diffuser debut later than most, but when it did appear – at Silverstone – it was problematical, and was removed for qualifying and the race. It finally debuted at Hockenheim with corrective work to control the temperatures and prevent the underfloor from deforming. It was made progressively more effective thereafter, a good step change occurring when Mercedes perfected the software to maintain good exhaust flow to the diffuser even when off-throttle.

Button gradually evolved away from Hamilton in some of his preferences, notably in his use of Brembo brakes from Silverstone onwards, rather than the Carbone Industry versions traditionally used. Jenson preferred the more progressive initial feel, even if the material did lack the ultimate in stopping power.

During Suzuka Friday practice, the F-duct was blown on to the rear wing's main profile rather than the flap – as pioneered by Force India – which increased the amount of stall. It wasn't used for the race there, but was fitted in two of the three subsequent events. The team was also experimenting from Korea with a modification to the way the brake bias changed rearward as the speed bled off, but Button felt that this may have been partially why he endured such a nightmare race there, one that effectively ended his title campaign. Hamilton hung on until the final round.

Third place in the drivers' and second in the constructors' must be considered a pretty decent result given the competitive limitations of the car.

Left: Jenson and Lewis celebrate their 1-2 success in the Canadian Grand Prix.
Photo: Peter J Fox

Far left: The Vodafone McLaren Mercedes team pose for a celebratory photo in Montreal.
Photo: Vodafone McLaren Mercedes

Below right: Lewis in action in the Singapore Grand PrixHamilton.
Photo: Peter J Fox

Above: Lewis Hamilton takes his pitstop in Malaysia.

Left: As the reigning world champion, Jenson Button fitted in well into his new environment at McLaren.
Photos: Peter J Fox

3

MICHAEL SCHUMACHER

4

NICO ROSBERG

MERCEDES GP PETRONAS F1 TEAM

THE perilous high-wire miracle that was Brawn's 2009 championship victory was revealed by Mercedes's 2010 season. In terms of resource and critical attention, that title was achieved by borrowing from the future, a future that duly came to pass with a comparatively mediocre performance from the team in 2010 as it morphed from Brawn into Mercedes. The struggle of returning seven-times world champion Michael Schumacher to recapture his former prowess overshadowed a more worrying underperformance from the Mercedes MGP 001.

Team principal Ross Brawn laid most of the blame at his own door, saying that he had failed to put together a strong enough engineering core team. But in mitigation, it would have been tough for anyone to have kept his eye fully on the ball when so many of them were in the air; at the time of the car's conception, Brawn was immersed in complex and long-running negotiations to secure the team's future, trying to win the 2009 title and having to cope with culling 40 per cent of the staff.

"We basically carved 40 per cent out of everything we had, and it was as crude as that," said Brawn of the enforced 2009 staff cuts that impacted so hard upon the 2010 car. "We had no other mechanism to go through the company and say, 'Two from here, five from there.' It happened very quickly, and the only fair way was to say to every department that they had to lose 40 per cent of their staff, and that takes a while to settle down. After you've done that, and this is not an excuse, but then starting a new car you don't feel very confident about taking on anything that's too ambitious, whereas the year before we did some fairly ambitious things."

The most fundamental limitation of the car's concept was a gearbox of insufficient length to maximise the double diffuser's inlet tract. The Red Bull, McLaren and Ferrari were all far more extreme in the way they treated this requirement. It also went against the prevailing fashion in eschewing a three-plane front wing in favour of a two-plane, and in the relative shortness of its wheelbase.

In its initial form, the car was a respectable performer and even started from the front row in Malaysia, albeit aided by the weather conditions. As the season progressed, however, so the car fell further off the pace. In part, this was down to unproductive development as the team wrestled with how to incorporate the blown diffuser and F-duct technology introduced on rival cars.

The car's razor-edged engine cover – designed to minimise blockage to the rear wing in yaw – precluded a conventional F-duct. Instead, a highly-intricate arrangement was devised whereby the foot controlled duct opened into a tubing route that ran below the floor, then up through the inside of hollow rear wing endplates. Eventually it was developed into a highly-efficient package – the car being fastest down

MERCEDES MGP 001

SPONSORS	Petronas • Aabar • Autonomy • Bridgestone • Deutsche Post • MIG Bank • Graham • Henri Lloyd • Monster • Ray-Ban
ENGINE	*Type:* Mercedes-Benz FO108X *No of Cylinders:* V8 *Spark plugs:* NGK *Electronics:* McLaren Electronic Systems FIA standard ECU & FIA homologated electronic & electrical system *Fuel:* Petronas *Oil:* Petronas
TRANSMISSION	*Gearbox:* 7-speed unit with carbon-composite maincase *Clutch:* Carbon plate
CHASSIS	*Front and rear suspension:* Wishbone and pushrod activated torsion springs and rockers *Dampers:* Sachs *Wheel diameter:* 360mm front and rear *Wheels:* BBS, forged magnesium *Tyres:* Bridgestone Potenza *Brake discs and pads:* Brembo *Brake callipers:* Brembo *Steering:* Power assisted rack and pinion *Radiators:* Marston *Fuel tank:* ATL *Instruments:* Carbon-fibre construction
DIMENSIONS	*Length:* 4800mm *Width:* 1800mm *Height:* 950mm *Formula weight:* 620kg

MERCEDES GP PETRONAS F1 TEAM: PERSONNEL

Team Principal: Ross Brawn
Chief Executive Officer: Nick Fry
Chief Operating Officer: Rob Thomas
Vice President, Mercedes-Benz Motorsport: Norbert Haug
M.D; Mercedes-Benz High Performance Engines: Thomas Fuhr
Head of Aerodynamics: Loic Bigois
Head of Vehicle Engineering & Dynamics: Craig Wilson
Chief Designer: John Owen
Chief Engineer: Russell Cooley
Sporting Director: Ron Meadows
Chief Race Engineer: Simon Cole
Senior Race Engineer, Michael Schumacher: Andrew Shovlin
Senior Race Engineer, Nico Rosberg: Jock Clear
Chief Mechanic: Matthew Deane

Above: Calling the shots – Norbert Haug, Mercedes vice president of motorsport.

Above left: Ross Brawn. He and his team were unable to conjure up the magic of their 2009 season as Brawn.

Left: The three-pointed star. Mercedes Benz was back as a stand-alone manufacturer for the first time since 1955.

Top: Michael Schumacher was tempted out of retirement to try to add to his magnificent record of seven world championships.
Photos: Peter J Fox

Above: Michael Schumacher failed to sparkle in a car that struggled to meet expectations.
Photo: Peter J Fox

Top right: Nico Rosberg prepared himself well during his first season with the team.
Photo: Paul-Henri Cahier

Above right: CEO Nick Fry enjoyed a calmer year after the ups and downs of the Honda and Brawn era.
Photo: Jad Sherif/WRi2

Opposite, top: Nico Rosberg came of age in 2010, handling his position in the team with great tact.

Opposite: 'The Silver Arrow' is prepared for the season's opening race in Bahrain.
Photos: Peter J Fox

the long straight of South Korea – but it took a time to iron out various leakages and pressure changes. "There were pros and cons of doing it the way we did," accepted Brawn. "We did wonder whether to take a step back, get back on to a conventional engine cover and introduce it that way. But we decided to persevere with what we had, and I'm not sure it was the right decision. We probably set ourselves a bigger task than we might have done. We thought it was going to be more straightforward than it was, and there are probably a couple of things we would have done later on in the year with the floor that we couldn't do because the floor obviously carries the channels for the F-duct. It's one of those things where conceptually you get a bit tied up, and if we were doing it again for next year, we would do it very differently."

From Barcelona, the car featured a slightly longer wheelbase, achieved through altering the angle of the front wishbones. This was to achieve the desired weight distribution, moving it a little rearwards to take some strain off the weaker front Bridgestones used in 2010.

The incorporation of a blown floor was even more problematic than that of the F-duct. Introduced at Valencia, it suffered serious heat related problems, was redesigned and even briefly discarded before being re-introduced. But even when working properly, it did not seem to deliver as much performance as those on other cars. "We are only now starting to understand the nuances of exhaust energised diffusers," admitted Brawn in Japan. "We definitely haven't taken as much advantage from it as others have. This was another area in which we were constrained by the layout of the transmission. We toyed with idea of whether to have another go at it, but decided in the end, with the size of the team and the resources we had, we needed to deploy our efforts in other areas."

The car's characteristics were that it was pretty good on slow- and medium-speed corners, with strong braking and traction, but lost out quite significantly in high-speed aero dominated corners, where it suffered a serious lack of front downforce. Nico Rosberg was better able to maximise the car's low- and medium-speed strengths than Michael Schumacher. In the high-speed, car-limited, sections, there was little between them. "Michael's deficit was generally in slow-speed technique, not high speed, where bravery and car control are the factors, and where they were very evenly matched," said Brawn, who admitted to being slightly mystified about the former champion's lack of progress through the year. "I'm hoping that with the new car and new tyres, and a winter to reflect on it, and a bit of testing, we will have two fully competitive drivers next year."

PETRONAS
SYNTIUM
SYNTIUM

PETRONAS
PETRONAS
3

5

SEBASTIAN VETTEL

6

MARK WEBBER

RED BULL RACING

IN just its fifth year of existence, Red Bull added its name to the illustrious list of world champion F1 constructors. It did so with a devastatingly fast car that demonstrated a clear aerodynamic superiority over everything else. But given such a technical advantage, the team made somewhat heavy weather of its campaign. This was down to a mix of early-season unreliability and a driver dynamic between Mark Webber and Sebastian Vettel that proved difficult to manage.

In conceiving the RB6, technical director Adrian Newey sought to take full advantage of the twin-diffuser concept, a feature that had been added to the 2009 RB5, but had not been intrinsic to its configuration. Accordingly, a new, much longer, even narrower gearbox casing maximised the length of the diffuser slot for a more powerful airflow. Consideration was given to ditching the 2009 car's unique pull-rod rear suspension, on account of the low mounted rockers forming a partial exit blockage to the diffuser, but in the end Newey decided to retain the feature. It brought significant benefits to the upper-body airflow, and he mitigated against the blockage by creating space elsewhere, using a step-up mechanism to move the gearbox up out of the way. In effect, it allowed him to have his aerodynamic cake and eat it, something of which his design hero, Colin Chapman, would have been proud.

Despite continuing strong feeling within the team that the Renault engine was lacking in horsepower, the unit was retained. "McLaren blocked us from having the Mercedes," admitted Newey, "and we looked at the Cosworth, which I think was a good engine, but their funding was relatively weak, and as such their engine was probably underdeveloped. We couldn't bankroll an engine development programme, and so we stayed with Renault. That sounds as if it was by default, but Renault as a partner treats us extremely well, and I'm very happy with them and have never felt as if we were being treated as a number-two team to the works team. We've had parity, we can have open and frank discussions in terms of what we'd like for the chassis side out of the engine, but there is no doubt that they froze the engine much earlier in 2006 [than others]; they didn't keep working on it like some others and haven't done since the freeze came in. The result is all our analysis suggests that we are at least four per cent behind a Mercedes, which, at most circuits, is getting on for half a second a lap." Given that the RB6's average qualifying advantage over the McLaren-Mercedes was around 0.4 second, that would imply its aerodynamic superiority was in the order of almost a second. Needless to say, McLaren disagrees strongly with Newey's analysis.

In the final pre-season Barcelona test, the car appeared with another feature that would serve only to enhance that aero superiority: an exhaust-blown diffuser. Using a new, low mounted exhaust layout to

©

RED BULL RB6

SPONSORS	Total • Rauch • Pepe Jeans • FXDD • Casio • Singha Beer • LogwIn • Red Bull mobile • Hangar Seven
INNOVATION PARTNERS	Platform Computing • Simens • Ansys • Hexagon Metrology • Fir-Tex • DHG • OZ Racing • Agie Chamilies
TEAM SUPPLIERS	Renault • Bridgestone • Puma • Sabelt • Nutilus
SUPPLIERS	P&O Ferries • VW Commercial Vehicles
ENGINE	*Type:* Renault R27-2010 *No of cylinders:* V8 *Spark plugs:* Champion *Electronics:* McLaren Electronic Systems
	Fuel: Total *Oil:* Total
TRANSMISSION	*Gearbox:* 7-speed longitudinally mounted, with hydraulic system for shift and clutch operation *Clutch:* AP Racing
CHASSIS	*Front suspension:* Aluminium uprights, carbon wishbones, pushrod activated inboard springs, anti-roll bar
	Rear suspension: Aluminium uprights, carbon wishbones, pull-rod activated inboard springs, anti-roll bar *Dampers:* Multimatic
	Wheel diameter: 13in, front and rear *Wheels:* OZ *Tyres:* Bridgestone Potenza *Brake pads, discs and callipers:* Brembo
	Steering: Red Bull *Radiators:* Marston/Red Bull *Fuel tank:* Red Bull/ATL
DIMENSIONS	*Length:* As regulated by overhang limits *Height:* 950mm *Width:* 1800mm *Wheelbase:* 3000mm
	Formula weight: 620kg

route the gases through a bodywork slot and into the diffuser's central section gave a very significant boost in downforce and re-introduced a concept first tried in 1983 by Renault, but which fell out of favour in the early 1990s. Stick-on dummy exhaust exits that mimicked the original conventional exhausts fooled no one, and from the moment of that test, almost every other team was hard at work on its own similar system. It did mean that Red Bull went into the season with an even bigger head start.

The early fruits of that advantage were not what they might have been, though. The team took just one victory – albeit a resounding 1-2 in Malaysia – from the first four races, despite starting each event from pole. Vettel was heading for a straightforward victory in the opening round in Bahrain when a spark plug failed, slowing him to a fourth-place finish. In Australia, he was controlling the race again when a wheel attachment failure intervened. In the changeable conditions of China, the race was lost to an early pit stop for wet tyres for both cars that proved unnecessary and had to be corrected with a further stop shortly afterwards.

It was only when the season reached Europe that the RB6 began to show its full capabilities. With an aggressive upgrade centred on a lower drop-away to the rear upper bodywork, but which comprised changes to every body surface other than the wings, it was a massive 0.8 second clear of the opposition

RED BULL RACING: PERSONNEL

Team Owner: Dietrich Mateschitz
Team Principal: Christian Horner
Director of Engineering: Adrian Newey
Chief Designer: Rob Marshall
Team Manager: Jonathan Wheatley
Chief Engineer Vehicle Dynamics: Mark Ellis
Chief Engineer Renault Engines: Fabrice Lom
Head of Aerodynamics: Peter Prodromou
Race Engineer, Vettel: Guillaume Rocquelin
Race Engineer, Webber: Ciaron Pilbeam

Above: Jonathan Wheatley.

Above left: Head of dynamics Peter Prodromou.

Above centre left: Adrian Newey.

Above centre right: Rob Marshall.

Left: Team principal Christian Horner.
Photos: Red Bull Racing

Top: Sebastian Vettel and Mark Webber took nine victories to win the constructors' championship for Red Bull Racing.
Photo: Peter J Fox

Above: Mark Webber took an emphatic victory in Hungary – one of four wins collected in 2010 by the Australian.

Top right: Sebastian Vettel and the Red Bull team celebrate his victory in Suzuka.
Photos: Peter J Fox

Right: Fabrice Lom, chief engineer responsible for Renault engines.
Photo: Red Bull Racing

Below: Ultimate joy for champion Vettel and Dietrich Mateschitz in Abu Dhabi.
Photo: Peter J Fox

Far right: Red Bull's stables at Milton Keynes.
Photo: Red Bull Racing

around Barcelona's long, fast sweeps. Mark Webber – who'd delighted Newey in qualifying by taking Turn Nine flat in sixth, accelerating all the way through, coming out 12mph faster than the best non-Red Bull – duly made his seasonal breakthrough to victory. In devastating form, he was set for the win even before Vettel suffered a brake disc failure late in the race.

With this and a similarly convincing victory at Monaco a week later, Webber went a long way to making amends for a scrappy start to the season, and in doing so laid down a very real claim to the world championship relatively late in his career. With the car in this form, he enhanced his already formidable qualifying speed with a mastery of the technique required to maximise the advantages of the blown diffuser. Creating the earliest possible opportunity in the corner to get on full throttle and thereby increase downforce was the key to this endeavour, and he was particularly adept at it. Later in the season, Renault – along with the other engine manufacturers – perfected software that maintained exhaust flow to the diffuser even off-throttle, thereby effectively neutralising the small advantage Webber enjoyed over Vettel in this department.

In the wake of his double defeat at Webber's hands, Vettel complained of difficult handling, and his chassis was duly replaced. An almost invisible crack was located and repaired, after which that chassis was used by Webber to win both the British and Hungarian Grands Prix. "There was a problem found which was upsetting the feeling Sebastian had for the car," said Newey. "It was confusing his senses slightly. But it was easily repaired."

With his new chassis, Vettel went into the Turkish Grand Prix weekend with his small edge in speed over Webber apparently restored, but this was prevented from being translated in qualifying by a broken rear roll bar mount. This gifted Webber his third straight pole, and with Vettel alongside him, the circumstances that ensured their controversial tangling in the race began to lock into place. As well as losing a likely 1-2 result, this incident created real turmoil in the team, which exposed a fault line of conflict between the marketing aims of the parent company providing the money and the straight racing choices made by the team.

That wasn't all Red Bull was up against either: politically, it found itself on the receiving end of a joint offensive from McLaren, Ferrari and Mercedes as they lobbied Charlie Whiting on various aspects of the RB6 through the season in an attempt to limit its performance advantage over them. Various minor modifications were made to the car at the FIA technical delegate's insistence, none of which seemed to materially affect its speed advantage. At Silverstone, a new front wing was introduced that caused further internal ructions when Vettel's damaged example was replaced on the eve of qualifying by the only other one – that previously on Webber's car. The changes made to the car concurrent with that wing's introduction appeared to allow it to run with the wing extremely close to the ground at speed. This caused not a little discontent from rivals, and led to more stringent wing and floor flexibility tests being introduced at Spa and Monza respectively. Again, it appeared to have little or no effect on the Red Bull's pace – nor on its apparent ability to run the front of the car very low, to aerodynamic advantage.

In all, the season was a graphic demonstration of Newey's continuing genius, exploited by a tough, efficient, experience honed little race team – but not without inflicting some internal battle scars.

Red Bull
MUMM
MUMM

FELIPE MASSA

FERNANDO ALONSO

SCUDERIA FERRARI MARLBORO

THE Scuderia bounced resoundingly back into championship contention after its underwhelming 2009 performance. While Fernando Alonso's leadership of the team seemed to lend it greater surefootedness, it was the conception of the car, specifically around a double diffuser, that gave it a basic level of competitiveness far in excess of that of the compromised 2009 car. However, in the car's initial form, it lacked the innovations of F-duct and blown diffuser (introduced by McLaren and Red Bull respectively), and much of the first part of Ferrari's season was limited as those devices were developed.

Alonso's opening race victory – inherited only after Sebastian Vettel's Red Bull encountered problems – wasn't added to until the car was running in blown-diffuser form in the latter half of the season. This feature was introduced at Valencia and was effective immediately, in contrast to the difficult adaptation by several other teams, but it wasn't until the German Grand Prix three races later that the competitive upsurge was rewarded with a victory. But from the moment of that controversial 'team orders' 1-2 at Hockenheim, Alonso was a factor everywhere, and he rounded off the team's season with a relentless sequence of victories and podiums that left the rival Red Bull and McLaren late-season campaigns looking decidedly brittle. For the first time under the team's new generation, it looked to have much the same swashbuckling confidence as the Brawn/Todt/Schumacher era.

In concept, the F10 was a long car, although not quite as extreme in this respect as the McLaren, allowing a long, slim gearbox to enhance the entry duct to the double diffuser. The capacity of the diffuser was further increased by a unique feature – the engine was tilted upwards to the rear by 3.5 degrees. This brought with it a penalty in that it raised the car's centre of gravity, and a careful trade-off had to be made, as technical director Aldo Costa explained: "This involved a pretty deep analysis to establish the threshold at which there was a net advantage. We had a much more extreme configuration in the tunnel, and what we ended up with was a compromise."

Not only did the narrow-bottomed gearbox casing create more flow capacity in the diffuser, but it also allowed more development potential. This left the team chasing three development paths early in the season: F-duct, blown floor and regular aero/diffuser evolution. The latter two, of course, were intrinsically related, so the regular aero development had to be held in abeyance while the blown floor programme caught up. This defined the competitive shape of Ferrari's season, in that while the Red Bull and McLaren were immediately on steep development paths, the Ferrari remained rather static early in the season. It received its F-duct for Barcelona, but subsequently this was found to be inefficient and was removed after Turkey; a revised version proved more effective.

The blown floor was a longer-lead item. "In general,

FERRARI F10

TITLE SPONSOR	Philip Morris
MAJOR SPONSORS	Fiat • Shell • Etihad • Bridgestone • AMD • Acer • Mubadala
ENGINE	*Type:* Ferrari 056 *No of cylinders (vee angle):* V8 (90-deg) *Electronics:* Magneti Marelli *Fuel:* Shell V-power *Oil:* Shell Helix Ultra
TRANSMISSION	*Gearbox:* Ferrari 7-speed, longitudinal, semi-automatic, sequentially controlled with quick-shift mechanism
CHASSIS	*Front and rear suspension:* Double carbon-fibre wishbones with pushrod activation of inboard torsion-bar springs
	Wheel diameter: 13in, front and rear *Wheels:* BBS *Tyres:* Bridgestone Potenza *Brakes:* Brembo ventilated carbon-fibre discs
DIMENSIONS	As regulations
	Formula weight: 620kg, including driver and camera

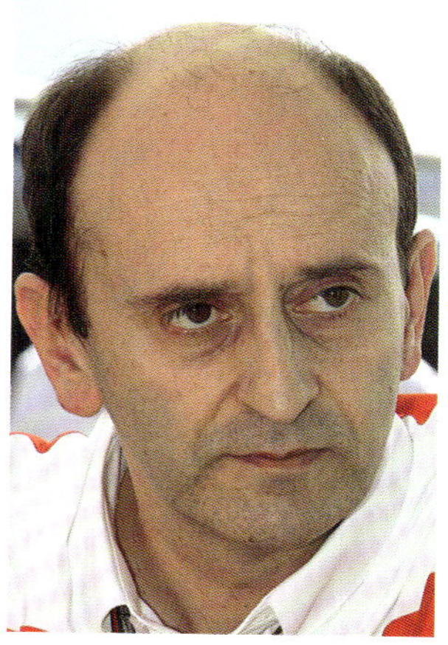

Above left: A family affair! Stefano Domenicali and his wife Silvia on the Monza podium are captured for posterity by father-in-law Ercole Colombo, the illustrious Italian F1 photographer (white shirt).
Photo: Bernard Asset

Top: Technical director Aldo Costa *(left)* and engine guru Luca Mamorini.
Photos: Jean-François Galeron/WRi2

Above right: Engineer Rob Smedley and Felipe Massa in discussion.

Right: Sporting director Chris Dyer.

Below: The magic of Ferrari always captivates the fans.
Photos: Peter J Fox

SCUDERIA FERRARI MARLBORO: PERSONNEL

General Director: Stefano Domenicali
Technical Director: Aldo Costa
Assistant Technical Director: Pat Fry
Sporting Director: Chris Dyer
Chief Designer: Nicolas Tombazis
Race Engineer, Alonso: Andrea Stella
Race Engineer, Massa: Rob Smedley
Race Engine Manager: Martino Binotto

the exhaust-blown diffuser was difficult," continued Costa, "an intense programme, not only as an aerodynamic concept, but it was also more difficult for the car layout, more intrusive, more demanding in terms of temperature generation, wishbone protection, floor protection, bodywork protection and longer-lead-time components. An exhaust is a long-lead component because you have the running of the engine dyno to verify and develop it."

During this period, as the factory was working furiously behind the scenes on the parallel developments, very little that was new appeared on the car, and after beginning the season within a couple of tenths of the fastest, by Spain it was around a second off the Red Bull, with almost the same deficit at Turkey. A very competitive race two weeks later in Montreal, despite no significant modifications, emphasised that while the car may have been increasingly lacking in the aero department, it was very good at tracks that demanded strong braking and traction. Alonso had already demonstrated as much during Monaco practice, before disastrously crashing out on Saturday morning, damaging the car so badly that he couldn't take part in qualifying.

The Valencia introduction of the blown floor saw the car qualify within 0.5 second of the Red Bull and only denied a strong podium finish by the inopportune timing of the safety car. At Silverstone, it was thwarted again by circumstances and officialdom, and at that stage Alonso was 49 points adrift. So it was somewhat startling to hear him on the radio saying, "We will win this championship." At the time, it seemed nothing more than a brave, defiant motivational message rather than a realistic prophecy. But after taking his third victory in four races at Korea, to vault into the lead of the championship with just two rounds to go, it was difficult not to be very impressed. Silverstone saw the introduction of a three-plane front wing in place of the original two-plane version, which worked better in maintaining the consistency not only of the front downforce, but also in the underfloor flow feeding the diffuser. A low-downforce/drag version of the two-piece wing was used for Monza and Spa, but elsewhere the three-piece item was preferred.

From Hockenheim onwards, the team – along with Red Bull – came under scrutiny for how the car appeared to be able to run its front wing much lower to the ground than demanded by the static minimum regulation height. But, like the Red Bull, it passed all the subsequent stringent flexibility tests.

An enlarged diffuser was introduced for Spa, the gearbox casing modifications necessary for its fitment having been on the car since Valencia. This change required the car to retake its rear crash test.

Realistically, the car was not as good as the Red Bull, but it was sufficiently close that the combination of Alonso's skills and Felipe Massa's underperformance made it very easy for Ferrari to operate with the mission of winning Alonso the title, with Massa in support. This was tough for Massa and his race engineer Rob Smedley, and the way the team order was sprung upon them was one of the few instances that demonstrated the relative inexperience of the team management.

The team needed a leader, and that's exactly what it got in Alonso, whose style was in stark contrast to the more relaxed approach of his predecessor, Kimi Räikkönen. Costa spoke for the whole team when he said, "The arrival of Fernando was very, very positive. He came with his big experience, a two-time champion with experience of big teams. Immediately he was positive, and it took him very little time to settle in the team, like he was here for ten years. Having him here was like black and white, like a switch. As soon as we started working with him, there was no issue at all. He was the most positive bloke of the team, always pushing, always optimistic, a real asset, in the car and outside it."

There is a sense that the 2010 success is just the beginning of a long, golden partnership between Alonso and Ferrari.

Above: An emotional Fernando Alonso takes the plaudits on the podium after his win in Korea.
Photo: Shell Motorsport

Left: Felipe Massa was cast into a supportive role throughout the 2010 season.
Photo: Peter J Fox

Far left: Alonso survived the terrible conditions to win in Korea and keep his title bid afloat.

Below: The Ferrari team celebrates a 1-3 finish at Monza.
Photos: Photo: Shell Motorsport

9

RUBENS BARRICHELLO

10

NICO HÜLKENBERG

AT&T WILLIAMS

AVERAGING around 0.9 second off the Red Bull made the Williams FW32 a lower Q3 car, and this was the competitive baseline from which the team fought over sixth place in the constructors' championship. In terms of competitiveness, it was locked in a tussle with the Renault and Force India, beginning slightly behind both of them, overhauling Force India at around Valencia time and actually emerging quickest of the group from Silverstone until Hungary, after which the Renault got F-duct parity and squeezed back ahead. These changes in form reflected the development race between the teams.

Aside from the changes everyone had to make adapting to the no-refuelling regulations, there was the additional challenge for the Grove-based team in configuring its car around a new engine, having reverted to Cosworth power after three years of Toyota.

"The biggest challenge to that was in anticipating the fuel consumption and therefore the size of tank required," said technical director Sam Michael. "We did that through looking at the data we had from 2006 when we last ran a Cosworth and then looking at the specific fuel consumption they were getting on their dyno for the 2010 version of the engine. A lot of effort went into that, and we got it spot on because the amount of fuel we had for the highest-capacity track was within 0.5kg of the tank capacity."

The new engine also impacted heavily upon the car's mechanical layout, as the clutch moved from the engine to the gearbox end, requiring new actuators and hydraulics. Williams was alone among the Cosworth teams in opting to do its own gearbox hydraulics and, in contrast to those who opted for the customer package, they were totally reliable.

In concept, the car was quite short in wheelbase – because of a fairly short gearbox – although competitively long in chassis length. "We put a lot of priority into the length," explained Michael. "We decided we'd rather make it longer to accommodate the big tank than wider. If you make it wider, you push the radiator out and make the sidepod undercut too small, which loses you downforce. So we didn't want to do anything to hurt the undercut." The shortness of the gearbox probably did compromise the diffuser performance, however.

A Barcelona aero upgrade didn't quite work as expected, and for the next four events the team was rather on the back foot, scoring just two points during this time. It didn't help that rival teams were beginning to get their F-ducts working while the Williams still didn't feature one, as it was proving difficult to fine-tune. "From Montreal, we changed our aero philosophy very significantly," said Michael. "We began to develop the aero in a very different direction to what we'd done for the last couple of years."

Rubens Barrichello was instrumental in this change concerning the targets that were being chased in CFD and tunnel data. "Sometimes something is better in

©

WILLIAMS FW32

SPONSORS	Philips • RBS • AT&T • Randstad • Accenture • Bridgestone • Hell • McGregor • Ridge • Thomson Reuters • Allianz • GAC • MAN PPG • RAYS • Sparco
ENGINE	*Type:* Cosworth 2.4L *No of cylinders (vee angle):* V8 (90-deg) *Fuel management and ignition systems:* Cosworth. *Engine material:* Block and pistons in aluminium, crankshaft in steel billet, connecting rods in titanium
TRANSMISSION	*Gearbox:* Williams F1 7-speed, seamless sequential semi-automatic shift, plus reverse gear, in an aluminium maincase *Gear selection:* Electro-hydraulic actuation *Clutch:* Carbon, multi-plate
CHASSIS	*Front suspension:* Carbon-fibre double wishbone arrangement, with composite toe-link and pushrod activated springs and anti-roll bar *Rear suspension:* Double wishbone and pushrod activated springs and anti-roll bar *Dampers:* Williams F1 *Wheels:* RAYS, forged magnesium *Tyres:* Bridgestone Potenza *Brakes:* 6-piston callipers all round, carbon discs and pads *Steering:* Williams D1 power assisted rack and pinion *Chassis electronics:* McLaren MES FIA standard electronic control unit *Cooling:* Aluminium oil, water and gearbox radiators
DIMENSIONS	*Length:* not given *Width:* 1800mm *Height:* not given *Wheelbase:* not given *Formula weight:* 620kg, including driver and camera

AT&T WILLIAMS: PERSONNEL

Team Principal: Frank Williams

Director of Engineering: Patrick Head

Chairman: Adam Parr

Chief Executive Officer: Alex Burns

Technical Director: Sam Michael

Non-Executive Director: Toto Wolff

General Counsel: Mark Biddle

Chief Designer: Ed Wood

Chief Aerodynamicist: Jon Tomlinson

Race Team Manager: Dickie Stanford

Race Engineer, Barrichello: Tony Ross

Race Engineer, Hülkenberg: Tom McCullough

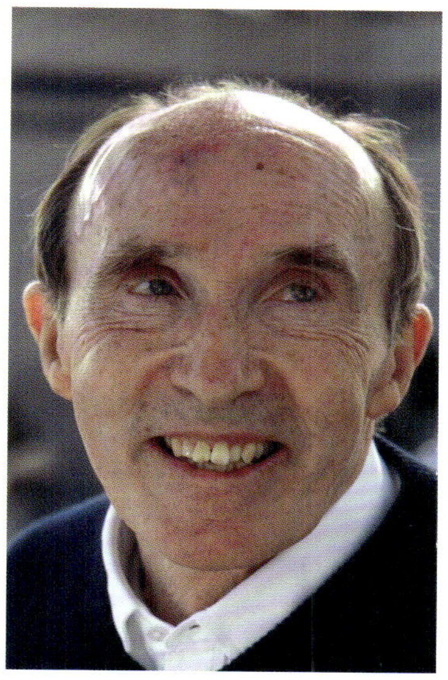

Above right:
Sir Frank Williams.
Photo: Jean-François Galeron/WRi2

Above far right:
Patrick Head.
Photo: Peter J Fox

Right: Adam Parr.
Photo: Jean-François Galeron/WRi2

Far right: Sam Michael.
Photo: Jean-François Galeron/WRi2

Top: Rubens Barrichello at Monaco.
Photo: Paul-Henri Cahier

theory," said Rubens, "but if you cannot be comfortable with it as a driver, it's not really an improvement."

The team was full of praise for the Brazilian veteran's contribution, feeling they had much better development direction from him than from other recent drivers. "In an era where there's no testing, he's been exceptional in what he's brought to the team," said Michael. "He's not an engineer, but is very good at telling you very quickly and efficiently what's working and what's not." He received similar praise for his engine feedback skills from Cosworth.

Another way in which the disruption of engine supply hurt the car's competitiveness was the fact that it prevented the team beginning the year with a blown diffuser, something of a frustration for Michael. "We were on to that long before the Red Bull ever appeared with it," he said. "We had it in the tunnel last October and it looked very good. We'd even developed it so that it blew directly into the central spat of the diffuser just like Red Bull, rather than around it like some other teams. But we couldn't get it on the car for the start of the season because at that point there wasn't the capacity to do two different exhaust layouts, and we weren't confident that we wouldn't just roast the car and have no back-up if we opted for the low exhaust from the start. So we said let's just go with a top-exit exhaust for the start of the year. But as soon as we saw Red Bull had made it work, we began to develop it. The exhaust programme is completely integrated with the bodywork and aero programmes, so it gets quite complicated and it took a time to do."

The system debuted in Valencia and was trouble-free immediately; with further tweaks, it gave a significant performance boost from Silverstone onwards. The F-duct was also debuted at Valencia and in its operation was rather different to everyone else's. To trigger it, the driver had to remove his leg from the hole in the duct's tubing. "We saw from CFD that the positive pressure inside the cockpit would easily be enough to stall the rear wing," explained Michael. "So the driver has his left leg over the hole, sealing the duct, then when he goes down the straight, he moves his leg off it and the air flows down the hole, through the chassis to the engine cover spine to the slot on the rear wing, which stalls. It's quite simple; we don't need to take any feed ducts from outside." There was some trouble adapting the system for the longer-legged Nico Hülkenberg, but this was sorted by the season's second half.

From Spa onwards, Cosworth was able to supply the engine software needed to maintain exhaust flow to the diffuser off-throttle, meaning the downforce boost was there right from the braking phase. Other teams had similar systems operating earlier into the season. "There was a bigger performance gain from that than from the initial fitment of the blown diffuser," said Michael. "It worked very well indeed immediately. On Rubens' first lap out of the pits in Spa, he said, 'Yep, I'm keeping this.'"

The car tended to show well early in the weekend when the track was green and become progressively less balanced as it rubbered in. In qualifying for the penultimate race, in Brazil, a dry line only formed in the last few minutes of qualifying, creating the ideal circumstances for the car – and rookie Nico Hülkenberg responded with a superb pole position, the team's first since Nürburgring 2005. He'd been the only driver able to generate the tyre temperatures necessary. But in the more normal situation of race day, it was back to earth with an eighth place, although those four points ensured the team leapfrogged Force India for sixth in the constructors'.

Barrichello's fourth place at Valencia was the best race result of the team's season, something that underlines there is plenty of scope for improvement at Williams. But it will be interesting to see whether the new development philosophy will have brought benefits to the conception of the 2011 car.

Above: Sir Jackie Stewart congratulates Patrick Head on Hülkenberg's pole position in Brazil.
Photo: Bernard Asset

Left: The rookie Hülkenberg and the vastly experienced Barrichello made a good blend for the Williams team.
Photo: Jean-François Galeron/WRi2

Top right: Despite his promising first season, Nico Hülkenberg's place in the Williams cockpit remained in doubt for 2011.

Top left: Celebration time for the team after Hülkenberg's surprise pole position.
Photos: Peter J Fox

11

ROBERT KUBICA

12

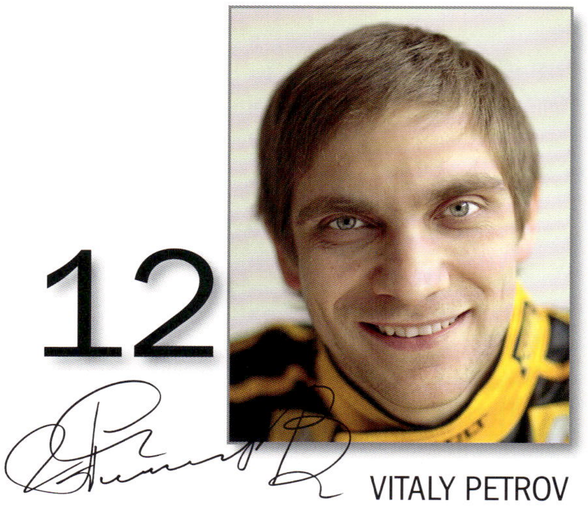

VITALY PETROV

RENAULT F1 TEAM

THERE was much that was promising about Renault's 2010 campaign, a season in which the team was under new ownership, retaining the parent company's name, but in reality leased by investment firm Genii Capital. The low-key Eric Boullier had replaced the disgraced Flavio Briatore as team principal, while Robert Kubica had taken over from the departing Fernando Alonso, but the technical core of the team remained much as before.

The R30 it conceived was a driveable, well-balanced car that allowed Kubica to star on several occasions, but which ultimately was an average of around 0.6 second slower than the identically powered Red Bull RB6, putting it on a similar performance level to the Mercedes. Given the extreme uncertainty surrounding the team at the end of the 2009 season, fifth place in the constructors' championship was a better performance than might have been expected.

Visually, the car was fairly standard looking, but the aerodynamic detailing around the front wing endplates reflected a CFD department that had been massively upgraded since the previous season. Against the fashion, the car continued its predecessor's wide, low nose theme, but to a less extreme degree. The stiffening rods between engine and gearbox that have distinguished Renaults since 2002 remained – and may well have played a part in what Kubica felt was the car's best asset: its driveability. "I always felt I could correct anything it did, and that gives you a lot of confidence to attack," he said.

As in previous years, the car was closer to the pace by the end of the season than at the beginning, a reflection of an effective development path. In fact, the facilities available for developing the car were rather better than those used in conceiving it, as technical director James Allison explained: "In November, we shut the tunnel down for four weeks and put a new rolling road in it. That month cost us around 0.2 second of performance in lost off-season development, but was more than repaid by the subsequent development rate."

The upgrade essentially consisted of replacing the canvas rolling road with a steel one. "It allowed us to get the right shape of squish on the model's tyres and to steer them to appropriate angles," said Allison. "In all, it gave us a much better, more realistic simulation with what was happening on track. It also speeds up and slows down much quicker than before, vastly increasing the throughput: extra valuable now that the resource restriction limits our access to the tunnel."

The obvious areas of development, once everyone's new cars had been launched, were F-duct and blown diffuser. Renault took longer than most in putting these features on its car, but when it did they were immediately very effective and problem-free. Other than that, most of the season's development centred on front wing endplate design – and floor. The

RENAULT R30

SPONSORS	Total • Bridgestone • TW Steel • Lada • HP • Trina Solar • EFG International • Snoras
ENGINE	*Type:* RS27-2010, 18,000rpm mandatory rev limit *No of cylinders (vee angle):* V8 (90-deg)
	Electronics: Magneti Marelli, McLaren Electronic Systems ECU as stipulated by FIA regulations *Fuel:* Total *Oil:* Total
TRANSMISSION	*Gearbox:* 7-speed semi-automatic, titanium, with reverse gear, 'Quickshift' system to maximise speed of gearshifts *Clutch:* AP Racing
CHASSIS	*Front suspension:* Carbon-fibre double wishbone with pushrod and rocker operated inboard torsion-bar/damper units
	Rear suspension: Carbon-fibre double wishbone with pushrod operated torsion bars and transverse mounted damper units
	Wheels: OZ, machined magnesium *Tyres:* Bridgestone Potenza *Brake pads and discs:* Hitco *Brake callipers:* AP Racing
	Fuel tank: ATL *Steering:* Renault F1 hydro-mechanical servo system (power assisted) *Instruments:* Renault F1 Team
DIMENSIONS	*Length:* 5050mm *Width:* 1800mm *Height:* 950mm *Front track:* 1450mm *Rear track:* 1400mm
	Formula weight: 620kg, with driver, cameras and ballast

RENAULT F1 TEAM: PERSONNEL

Chairman: Gerard Lopez
Team Principal: Eric Boullier
Managing Director: Bob Bell
Technical Director: James Allison
Chief Operating Officer: Patrick Louis
Chief Designer: Tim Densham
Deputy Technical Director: Naoki Tokunaga
Sporting Director: Steve Nielsen
Chief Race Engineer: Alan Permane
Head of Engine Track Operations: Remi Taffin
Head of Aerodynamics: Dirk de Beer
Chief Mechanic: Gavin Hudson
Race Engineer, Kubica: Simon Rennie
Race Engineer, Petrov: Mark Slade

Above right: Team principal Eric Boullier.
Photo: Peter J Fox

Above far right: James Allison, the team's technical director.
Photo: Jean-Francois Galeron/WRi2

Right: Renault's mechanics celebrate Kubica's second place in Melbourne.
Photo: Bernard Asset

TW STEEL
RENAULT
TOTAL

very wide diffuser had a lot of development potential, which was reflected in a total of seven different floor configurations through the year. "The rules are quite strict in sidepod area," explained Allison. "You can't put winglets and vanes there now, and to create the double-deck diffuser you have various slots, openings and holes that allow you to legalise what goes on, and by the time you've done all that, it really constrains the back end of the car quite a lot on the bodywork. So it's not very easy to just keep re-inventing things. If you come forward of that area, the gains you get from re-profiling a sidepod are very small. The gains are therefore in the front and the rear, the front wing and diffuser."

It wasn't until Valencia that the blown diffuser appeared on the car, and not until Spa did it receive an F-duct. Allison: "There was an earlier version of an F-duct that would have debuted at Silverstone. It looked quite good in CFD, but in the tunnel we couldn't make it work with the consistency I wanted it to have. Because I'd seen a lot of other teams struggle trying to make theirs work, it was plain it wasn't an easy thing to get right. So we canned it and chose a different direction." The version that debuted at Spa – and which catapulted the R30 to among the very fastest straight-line speeds – was reckoned to be worth 0.5 second per lap around the Belgian track. It blew directly on to the rear wing mainplane rather than the flap.

The blown floor initially didn't find favour with Kubica, who felt the driving style it imposed lost the car some of its driveability. "It impacted on our set-up and was quite a change in the way the car felt, a change that initially wasn't at all popular. In Valencia we ran it and it was okay, but with corners that didn't really reveal some of the uglier sides of what it does. The following weekend [at Silverstone] it wasn't quite so helpful, and we resolved to settle the matter in Budapest where we committed to doing a back-to-back, which completely dominated Friday because that's all we could do. It was not an easy thing to do, but really helpful because both drivers were able to get an immediate sensation of where it was good and bad. We could also definitively see that we were better with it than without. The drivers could remind themselves what the old car felt like, which was far from a bed of roses. They realised it was more that it was different than worse."

The car's driveability played a big part in Kubica putting the car on the front row in Monaco, and the second row at both Spa and Suzuka. Away from the drivers' tracks, it wasn't quite so competitive.

In 2011, with a car conceived with the benefit of the upgraded technical facilities, we will discover if this reconstituted team has the potential to ever again get close to those glory days of 2005–06.

Above: Technicians at work in the back of the garage in Malaysia.
Photo: Bernard Asset

Above right: Kubica celebrates his podium in Monaco.
Photo: Renault F1 Team

Right: Alan Permane, Eric Boullier, Robert Kubica and Simon Rennie in discussion.
Photo: Bernard Asset

Left: Fifth place in Hungary was the season's highlight for Vitaly Petrov.
Photos: Peter J Fox

Below: At work on Kubica's R30 during the Turkish GP.
Photo: Renault F1 Team

14

ADRIAN SUTIL

15

VITANTONIO LIUZZI

FORCE INDIA F1 TEAM

FORCE India continued to punch slightly above its weight in that, with a much smaller staff, it fought hard with Williams for sixth place in the constructors' championship. It did this despite quite a big reshuffle in senior technical personnel. In March, technical director James Key left, headed for Sauber. Mark Smith was promoted into the position, but before the year was out, it was announced that he too would be leaving. Joining Smith in moving to Lotus at the end of the season were designer Lewis Butler and aerodynamicist Marianne Hinson.

The die of the team's 2010 season had already been cast before these moves, with the design of the VJM03, a neat car that found its natural level in the upper midfield at the beginning of the year, sliding back to the lower midfield as the bigger teams around it developed their cars more. Interestingly, in terms of lap time, it was as close to the front of the field at the end of the year as at the beginning, at around a second off Red Bull, but by then Williams and Sauber had squeezed into the gap between to push the Force India out of Q3.

Adrian Sutil was a regular Q3 qualifier in the early season, getting in for the first four races straight, and it was only as Renault stretched its development legs that things became more marginal. He scored solid points results in the first half-season, backed up by a good fifth at Spa and Tonio Liuzzi's sixth in Korea.

Again the team used the Mercedes engine/McLaren gearbox package, the latter component defining the car as long. This enabled Simon Phillips's aero team to maximise the diffuser inlet in a similar way to the McLaren, using the long, narrow shape to accelerate the volume of airflow. Up front, a two-piece front wing was favoured and the car was, like its predecessor, invariably fast on the straights, but ultimately perhaps a little light on high-speed downforce.

"It was less extreme in this than last year's car," countered chief race engineer Dominic Harlow. "We had a better spread across a variety of tracks, and weren't only quick at Spa and Monza, although there was still a tendency towards showing better on higher-efficiency circuits. But equally at lower-speed places we were not really disadvantaged until later in the year when people started to really make their double diffusers work very well, and you saw some people with the top-end levels of downforce getting quite significantly higher: the Hungary, Singapore-type tracks."

This change in emphasis was a conscious decision made by the design team, project led by Akio Haga. "We made some changes to the way we developed our aero and quantified improvements," continued Harlow, "and that's what has flattened our performance across the tracks."

The two key technical add-ons of F-duct and blown diffuser were tackled immediately they were spotted on the McLaren and Red Bull respectively. The F-duct debuted at Turkey. "We opted to blow the main plane rather than the flap," said Harlow, "and it made our system quite powerful. Even early on, we looked to be

FORCE INDIA VJM03

SPONSORS	Kingfisher • Whyte and Mackay • Reebok • Medion Mobile • Airbus • Royal Challenge • Signature • Double Mint • Bridgestone
ENGINE	*Type:* Mercedes Benz F0108X *No of cylinders:* V8 2.4-litre *Spark plugs:* NGK *Oil:* Mobil 1
TRANSMISSION	*Gearbox:* McLaren Racing 7-speed, semi-automatic, 'e-shift' *Clutch:* AP Racing carbon
CHASSIS	*Front suspension:* Aluminium uprights with carbon-fibre composite wishbones, track rod and pushrod; inboard chassis mounted torsion springs, dampers and anti-roll bar assembly. *Rear suspension:* Aluminium uprights with carbon-fibre composite wishbones, track rod and pushrod; inboard gearbox mounted torsion springs, dampers and anti-roll bar assembly *Dampers:* Penske *Wheels:* BBS, forged *Tyres:* Bridgestone Potenza *Brake system:* AP Racing *Brake material:* Carbone Industrie
DIMENSIONS	*Length:* 4900mm *Height:* 950mm *Wheelbase:* 3500mm *Front track:* 1480mm *Rear track:* 1420mm *Formula weight:* 620kg, with driver and camera

Above: Adrian Sutil scored a creditable 47 points for the team to take 11th overall in the drivers' rankings.

Left: Reserve driver Paul di Resta – hoping for a full-time drive in F1 in 2011.

Photos: Peter J Fox

Above: Vijay Mallya.

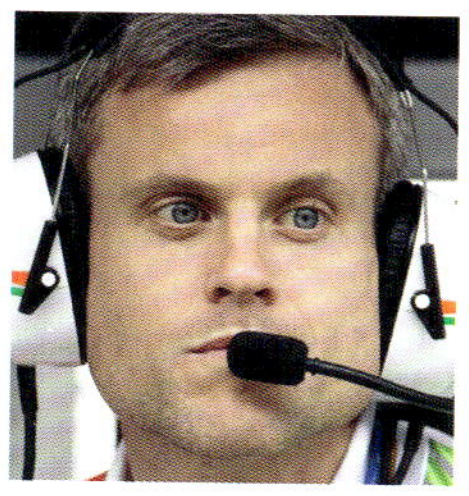

Left: Chief race engineer Dominic Harlow.

Below left: Team manager Andy Stevenson.

Photos: Peter J Fox

FORCE INDIA F1 TEAM: PERSONNEL

Chairman and Team Principal: Dr Vijay Mallya

Co-owner: Michiel Mol

Deputy Team Principal: Bob Fernley

Chief Operating Officer: Otmar Szafnauer

Team Manager: Andy Stevenson

Technical Director: Mark Smith

Engineering Director: Andy Green

Chief Race Engineer: Dominic Harlow

Race Engineer, Sutil: Brad Joyce

Race Engineer, Liuzzi: Gianpiero Lambiase

gaining quite a lot of top speed from it. But like most teams, we had some problems getting it working initially, and we improved and fine-tuned it from there."

Liuzzi struggled with the operation of the system far more than Sutil, which contributed to a very difficult season for the Italian. Had Liuzzi been able to score points with the same sort of frequency as his team-mate, it's likely there would have been a further place in the constructors' championship for the taking.

Incorporation of the blown diffuser, which was tried for the first time in Hungary practice and made its race debut at Spa, went relatively smoothly – generally a vindication of not trying to rush the project – although perhaps it wasn't as powerful a feature as on some cars, as Harlow explained: "We actually got quite a lot of help from McLaren and Mercedes in terms of what we needed to be able to run it, and in that sense it's quite an integrated project. It was a useful step, but I think we started from lower down the learning curve with it than with our F-duct, for example. I think we were a long way from getting what you can get from it, as represented by Red Bull, say."

Hand in hand with these developments came constant evolution of the front wing and floor, with a lot of intricate CFD-led detail around the endplates and front brake ducts that was particularly effective. A total of seven different floor designs were used through the season.

Force India's 2010 was perhaps lacking the dramatic sparkle of the 2009 highlights – there were no podiums or front-row starts – but it showed a team that was continuing to make respectable progress against better funded opposition. "The fact that we had to respond to two great whacking technical innovations that were not part of the original car has perhaps hurt us relative to the bigger teams," surmised Harlow, "because you need a lot of resource to do that sort of thing. Renault pulled away from us, Williams came from behind and were generally quicker in the second half. But overall, I think we've done quite a good job."

SCUDERIA TORO ROSSO

16

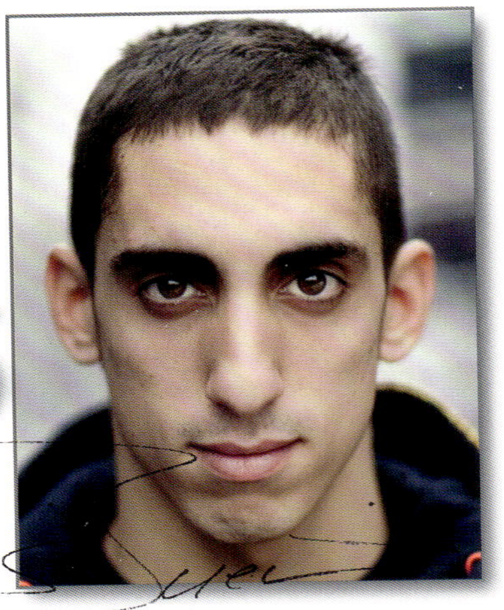

SÉBASTIEN BUEMI

17

JAIME ALGUERSUARI

THE regulations demanded that Toro Rosso went it alone for the first time in 2010, cut loose from the luxury of having its cars manufactured and delivered by Red Bull. So it wasn't too surprising that its season was less competitive than in 2009. That said, the Ferrari-powered STR5 took as its starting point 2009's Red Bull derived car, so there was still a certain legacy from that lineage. It retained, for example, the pull-rod rear suspension introduced on the 2009 car. With a staff of just 255, technical director Giorgio Ascanelli led the Faenza-based team back into the status of fully fledged constructor for the first time since its Minardi days, against not a few challenges, and emerged at the end of the season last of the 'established' teams, but comfortably clear of the three new outfits.

"We were ninth in the constructors', which, for our circumstances, I think was us doing our job," commented Ascanelli. "If we'd been tenth, we should have been shot. If we'd been eighth, it would have been extraordinary."

In conceiving the car, Ascanelli changed only what was really necessary from 2009's design. However, that still left a large vacuum of unknowns in what the best layout would be for a new big-tanked, no-refuelling car. "You have to decide at a very early stage where you sit the driver, how much fuel you need and where to put it, and what the configuration of the cooling is," he said. "There was no engineering data behind these decisions. Just, let's say, educated guesswork!"

Inevitably, some guesses were wrong, others less so: "We went for long and thin rather than short and wide, giving you a lot of space between the chassis bulkhead and the gearbox, and letting you have wishbones that are shaped for the double diffuser. That was okay. But we were suffering because our gearbox was too short, which meant there was not enough diffuser inlet, which limited us. It was the wrong choice of volumes in the end, but not a disaster."

Obstacles followed in the manufacture and wind-tunnel testing, all of them overcome with the make-do ingenuity of Ascanelli and his determined team. This was in the midst of establishing and expanding departments: "We took on 30 for the wind tunnel, went up from 17 to 30 in the drawing office, and the structural department was invented; we didn't have one! Overall, it was an extra 55 people. And … some of them have already left! I'm sure it's not easy working with me!" Ascanelli laughed as he put into vivid perspective life at the small end of the F1 scale.

The Bicester wind tunnel was used for the initial studies of the car, and again there were some basic problems to be overcome first, as Ascanelli recounted: "Well, there was no handbook! The car was ready before the tunnel, and the logistics of doing the car in Italy and having the tunnel in England is not

©

TORO ROSSO STR5

SPONSORS	Red Bull • Money Service Group • Hangar 7 • Bridgestone • Volkswagen • Advanti • USAG • Hexagon 8 Siemens • Dalco Magneti Marelli • Red Bull Mobile
ENGINE	*Type:* Ferrari Type 056 *No of cylinders (vee angle):* V8 (90-deg) *Spark plugs:* Champion *Electronics:* Magneti Marelli, McLaren Electronic Systems ECU as required by FIA rules *Fuel:* Shell *Oil:* Shell
TRANSMISSION	*Gearbox:* 7-speed longitudinally mounted with hydraulic system for power shift and clutch operation *Clutch:* Sachs triple-plate pull type
CHASSIS	*Front suspension:* Upper and lower carbon wishbones, torsion-bar springs with anti-roll bars, pushrod activated *Rear suspension:* Upper and lower carbon wishbones, torsion-bar springs with anti-roll bars, pull-rod activated *Dampers:* Sachs *Wheel diameter:* 13in, front and rear *Wheels:* OZ *Tyres:* Bridgestone Potenza *Brake discs, pads and callipers:* Brembo *Steering:* STR *Radiators:* Marston *Fuel tank:* ATL *Instruments:* MES
DIMENSIONS	*Not disclosed*
	Formula weight: 620kg, including driver and camera

SCUDERIA TORO ROSSO: PERSONNEL

Owner: Dietrich Mateschitz

Team Principal: Franz Tost

Technical Director: Giorgio Ascanelli

Chief Designer: Ben Butler

Head of Aero: Nicolo Petrucci

Chief Engineer: Laurent Mekies

Race Engineer, Buemi: Riccardo Adami

Race Engineer, Alguersuari: Andrea Landi

Team Manager: Gianfranco Fantuzzi

Above: Team principal Franz Tost.

Above right: The vastly experienced technical director, Giorgio Ascanelli.

Right: Team manager Gianfranco Fantuzzi.

Top: End-of-term photo at Abu Dhabi.

Photos: Toro Rosso/Red Bull

ideal. Also at this stage, we didn't know how to use the CFD!

"With the tunnel, first of all the rolling road had problems, then the chillers weren't working and there was a problem with repeatability of measurement. After ten days of hearing all this, I catch a plane over there. I arrive, say, 'Listen, I'm an old man. Do me a favour. Just hang the model there, and switch off the wind and the rolling road.' And guess what? The signal was drifting!"

What eventually emerged was a perfectly serviceable car with which Sébastien Buemi and Jaime Alguersuari were able to continue their F1 apprenticeships. The team understood quicker than many of the bigger outfits what the requirements were of the latest control tyres, and there were points in five of the first nine races. "When Williams messed up their update at Barcelona, and Sauber had a tricky time, too, we had a chance to take advantage. We were competitive with them at that point. But unfortunately this coincided with Seb having a bit of a dip in his own performance. I think he began the year believing Jaime wouldn't be anywhere near him, and when he was, it took a time for Seb to get his head around this."

There were three significant aero upgrades on the car through the season – a front wing package for Turkey, a diffuser change for Spa and a blown diffuser from Monza. There was also an F-duct rear wing at Monza, but it wasn't raced. "The F-duct was a difficult exercise," said Ascanelli. "It worked with the CFD, it worked in the tunnel; it's just a nightmare in terms of the technology. The accuracy of the parts, leakages, unwanted flexibility, which are actually changing the shape of the orifices… Unfortunately, I think the best race for the F-duct would have been Spa, but we were not in time because of these problems."

The learning curve continues into 2011, and you wouldn't bet against the team springing the odd surprise, even if the glory days of Monza 2008 seem long ago.

18

JARNO TRULLI

19

HEIKKI KOVALAINEN

LOTUS RACING

ARISING from the power struggle between the FIA and FOTA in 2009, the Tony Fernandes backed, Mike Gascoyne directed outfit brought the historic Team Lotus name back to the F1 grid for the first time since 1994. It was the most convincing of the three 'low-cost' new teams and took tenth place in the championship.

In the midst of the FIA/FOTA war, the governing body had invited new team entries for the 2010 world championship on the basis of a £40-million cost cap. That cap was never implemented, but Lotus was one of the three teams to commit regardless. It was a perilous plan in its initial stages, as Gascoyne explained: "When peace broke out between the FIA and FOTA, we didn't know if we would now get an entry, but we were still being encouraged to continue. Tony was telling me to do as little as possible, because obviously he didn't want to spend a fortune if we didn't get an entry.

So we did a ten-week plan from Silverstone, just to keep ourselves on target should we get the green light. But even then that was still around £1 million-worth of work. Then BMW announced its pull-out and we thought 'Great, we're safe,' but then it was announced that everyone would have to re-apply, and that Sauber was now in the frame."

It all panned out in the end, aided by Toyota's pull-out, which created two more spaces on the grid. This was fortuitous for Team Lotus in more ways than one: the closure of the Japanese giant's Cologne-based

Above: Tony Fernandes brought the famous Lotus name back into Formula One.

Right: Mike Gascoyne, who was in charge of starting the team from scratch.

Far right: Kovalainen speeds under the trees at Monte Carlo.

Photos: Peter J Fox

Bottom right: The Lotus name celebrated its 500th grand prix at Valencia.

Photo: Lukas Gorys

LOTUS T127

SPONSORS	1Malaysia • Tune Group • Naza • AirAsia • Maxis • CNN • Proton • Bridgestone • Hackett • PACT (Prince Andrew Charitable Trust)
SUPPLIERS/PARTNERS	Cosworth • CD Adapco • eBECS • VolPunlimited • 3CX • Rurol • LG • DuPont Refinish • Dell
ENGINE	*Type:* Cosworth GA *No of cylinders (vee angle):* V8 (90-deg)
	Electronics: McLaren Electronic Systems ECU (as required by FIA rules) and Lotus *Fuel:* BP *Lubricants:* BP
TRANSMISSION	Gearbox: Xtrac 7-speed longitudinal semi-automatic *Clutch:* AP Racing
CHASSIS	*Front and rear suspension:* Double wishbone and pushrod operated inboard springs and rockers *Dampers:* Penske
	Wheel diameter: 13in front and rear *Wheels:* BBS, forged magnesium *Tyres:* Bridgestone Potenza *Brake pads and discs:* Hitco
	Brake callipers: AP Racing *Steering:* Lotus *Radiators:* Lotus *Fuel tank:* ATL and Lotus *Instruments:* Lotus
DIMENSIONS	*Length:* About 5000mm *Width:* 1800mm *Height:* 950mm *Wheelbase:* 3250mm
	Formula weight: 620kg

F1 programme left a lot of experienced racing personnel on the market, many of whom had worked with Gascoyne when he had been Toyota's chassis technical director. "All the race team is ex-Toyota, and practically all the aero team, too.

A lot of contractors were companies we'd worked with at Toyota, and through my own Cologne-based company, MGI, we were ready to ramp up at short notice. When we got the go-ahead, we quickly ramped up to around 25 people on the design side. Jean-Claude Migeot at Aerolab had started an aero programme when we got an entry."

Meanwhile, the ex-TOM's factory in Hingham, Norfolk had been acquired as a base for the team. "It was September 14th when four of us went to this Marie Celeste factory. We had as our target a fire-up day of January 5th, and we were just 24 hours late."

The circumstances of the start-up defined the Lotus T127's design as conservative, with box-like sidepods and a short, wide configuration. "We were conservative with the cooling and had to design maximum-size brake ducts because we had no data, and obviously with no refuelling full tanks, brake wear was going to be significantly heavier. The fuel tank, again we had no data, because they hadn't run the Cosworth engine at 18,000rpm before. So we played safe there, too. The cell was quite wide, which compromised the radiators, which meant we couldn't cut things in more, which didn't help aerodynamically."

"Also, we were designing some of the earliest things you finalise, like side-impact tubes, nose box, so you can pass the crash tests, and don't forget we weren't going to get a chassis until mid-January. The thought of not passing the tests: that's it, you're dead. There was no second go at it, no spare capacity, so things like the radiator inlets were very generic. It would be crash tested a month before we did any wind-tunnel testing."

LOTUS RACING: PERSONNEL

Team Principal: Tony Fernandes
Deputy Team Principal: Kamarudin Meranun
Deputy Team Principal: S.M. Nasarudin
Chief Executive Officer: Riad Asmat
Chief Technical Officer: Mike Gascoyne
Chief Operating Officer: Keith Saunt
Deputy Technical Director/Sporting Director: Dieter Gass
Chief Designer: Lewis Butler
Head of Aerodynamics: Marianne Hinson
Head of Vehicle Dynamics: Elliot Dason-Barber
Chief Engineer: Jody Egginton
Race Engineer, Trulli: Gianluca Pisanello
Race Engineer, Kovalainen: Juan Pablo Ramirez
Team Manager: Graham Watson
Chief Mechanic: Phil Spencer

BRUNO SENNA

KARUN CHANDHOK

SAKON YAMAMOTO

CHRISTIAN KLIEN

20/21

HRT F110

SPONSORS	Region of Murcia • Embratel • Banco Cruzeiro do Sol • Jaypee • Ermis • Enzo Hotel • Cosworth • Bridgestone • Molta • Telewire PANDA • Black Button • Presezzi • OMP • Upsyuth • Phyto Garda • RuRoc • Jim Rickey • IT-Connect • Prolong
ENGINE	*Type:* Cosworth CA2010 *No of cylinders (vee angle):* V8 (90-deg) *Electronics:* Cosworth Electronics *Fuel:* Castrol *Oil:* Castrol
TRANSMISSION	Gearbox: X-Trac 7-speed longitudinal with quick-shift activation *Clutch:* Sachs
CHASSIS	*Front and rear suspension:* Carbon-fibre double wishbone with pushrod and rocker operated inboard damper units *Dampers:* Sachs. *Wheel diameter:* 13in, front and rear *Wheels:* OZ *Tyres:* Bridgestone Potenza *Brake pads, discs and callipers:* Brembo *Radiators:* Dallara *Fuel tank:* Dallara *Instruments:* McLaren
DIMENSIONS	*Width:* 1800mm *Height:* 1000mm *Wheelbase:* 3219mm *Formula weight:* 620kg, including driver and camera

HRT F1 TEAM

IT was a protracted and painful start-up for the Hispania Racing Team. Just getting to the end of the season had to be considered a result under financial circumstances that were forever on the edge. Originally, it was the project of Adrian Campos, but the one-time Minardi driver failed to attract the necessary investment once he'd secured the entry, and after a tortuous process Spanish businessman José Ramón Carabante took over the project to protect his original investment. He brought in former Midland F1 boss Colin Kolles as team principal.

The car – with standard Cosworth/Xtrac engine/transmission package – was commissioned to Dallara mid-way through 2009, but repeated late payments meant that even the design and build was a stop/start process. So compromised was the project by the financially induced difficulties that the Italian chassis manufacturer requested that its name not be carried on the car. Kolles inherited this set of difficulties and set about the seemingly impossible task of readying a team of two cars for the season's opening race, having missed all the pre-season tests.

The cars were still being completed as the Bahrain Grand Prix meeting got under way, by a crew that comprised German mechanics from Kolles's sports car and DTM teams, and a Spanish contingent from the Campos Meta F3 team. One car was completed in time for Bruno Senna to do three laps at the end of FP1, but the second wouldn't be driven by Karun Chandhok until qualifying! It was impressive in a desperate sort of way.

Kolles had hired former Honda technical director Geoff Willis as technical consultant three weeks before the beginning of the season, making it plain that there was zero development budget. "Essentially, we had a part-completed Dallara project," recalled Willis, "which we had to complete very quickly. We had a car build/manufacturing fortnight at the Dallara factory, and that was the first time our group of people worked together."

The car itself – the F110 – was quite generic in concept, but very dated in detail layout. "The tub was competitively stiff and light," said Willis, "but the level of detail refinement was years out of date. I've no issue with the car's level of performance. The way it came together, you couldn't reasonably expect anything else, but there had been a huge underestimation of how refined and professional F1 had become. Even the teams at the back of the F1 grid are at a level of refinement in packaging, quality, design, technology that was undreamed of ten years ago. If you look at a current F1 car, every single bit of it has been packaged incredibly tightly and cleverly, and the details are intricate. This is how we get the reliability; everything has been thought about: cooling, vibration, packaging; details that you almost forget now F1 has reached that level of refinement over the years. The difference between a GP2 car and an F1 car is absolutely night and day, so far apart. Maybe they thought this will be a super-duper GP2 car that needed to be 30 per cent better. Forget it; it needed to be ten times better."

Above, from left: Team owner Jose Ramon Carabante; team principal Dr Colin Kolles; reliability engineer Jacky Eeckalaert; and technical director Geoff Willis.

Below, clockwise from top left: Boris Bernes, Xavi Pujola, Richard Connell and Toni Cuquerella

Photos: Hispania Racing

Understandably, things were chaotic in the opening two races, but slowly the team began to gel into a slick racing-savvy operation that attacked its task of maximising the car's limited potential every weekend. Chandhok took the finish in the second race, and in Malaysia for race three both cars made it to the flag. In terms of performance, it qualified within one second of the Lotus in China, but with zero development it fell further back as the season progressed. Take the troublesome X-trac hydraulics out of the picture, and reliability was actually very solid.

"Its level of aero performance was probably between 130 and 150 points down on a Red Bull," avowed Willis. "It's had no aero refinement work, always had a fundamental understeer characteristic; we were never able to run it with enough weight forward, so couldn't match the weight distribution to the tyre characteristics. It couldn't be balanced aerodynamically and it had some slightly strange characteristics that have caused a few problems for the drivers. It needed an aero fix to cure that. You see the top teams improving their aero by four to five points a week, week-in, week-out, so the number of weeks you don't develop is the number of weeks you go backwards by."

Accepting the serious performance limitation, the team set about, in an analytical and professional way, finding the ultimate strategy for each track based not upon the conventional performance parameters, but on minimising time lost to blue flags. "You might think, why stop early?" said Willis. "Well, maybe as we're being lapped, we let the first three through very quickly because they aren't fighting each other. Then as soon as a gaggle comes, we pit then. There's maybe 12 blue flags we haven't suffered from. That adds up to a lot of time saved. We're quite well organised from a race engineering perspective. It's quite slick; we've not made many strategic mistakes and are quite aware of how some other bigger teams could really be doing that aspect better."

The financial squeeze was very much behind a regular shuffling of drivers from Silverstone onwards. Senna missed a race, replaced by Sakon Yamamoto, before it was Chandhok's turn to be stood down. He didn't reappear, and Yamamoto retained the seat – although in Singapore apparently he suffered 'food poisoning' and was replaced by Christian Klien. It would be unfair to judge any of the drivers in such uncompetitive circumstances.

For 2011, there is the promise of a transmission collaboration with Williams, but it would seem there are many hurdles to overcome before that becomes a reality. Then again, it's a team that's become quite used to clearing hurdles.

HRT F1 TEAM: PERSONNEL

Team Owner: Jose Ramon Carabante
Team Principal: Dr Colin Kolles
Director Business Affairs: Dr Manfred Ravetto
Technical Director: Geoff Willis
Reliability Engineer: Jacky Eeckalaert
Chief of Operations: Boris Bernes
Chief of Racing and Testing: Toni Cuquerella
Race Engineers Richard Connell, Xavi Pujolar

NICK HEIDFELD

22

PEDRO DE LA ROSA

KAMUI KOBAYASHI

23

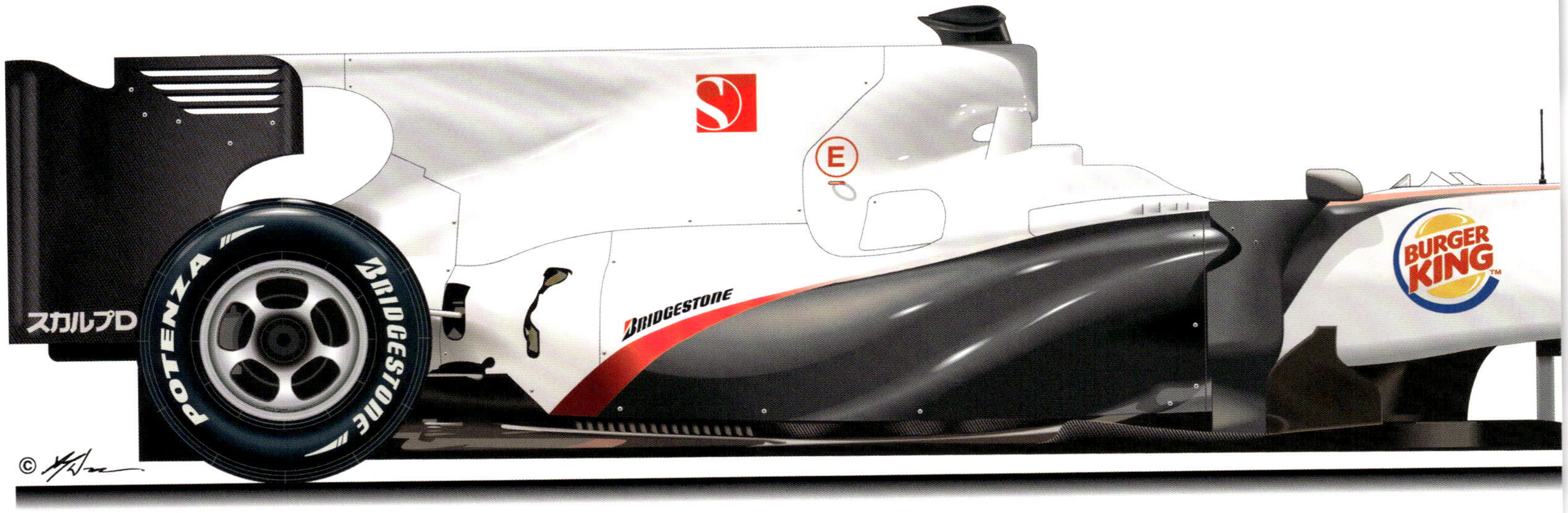

BMW SAUBER C29

SPONSORS	Certina • Bridgestone • Emil Frey • Mad-Croc • Ansys • Dalco • OZ • Skalp-D • Thormann • Walter Meier • ZF Sachs
ENGINE	*Type:* Ferrari 056 *No of cylinders (vee angle):* V8 (90-deg) *Electronics:* Magneti Marelli *Fuel:* Shell *Oil:* Shell
TRANSMISSION	*Gearbox: Ferrari longitudinal, semi-automatic, electronically controlled quick-shift mechanism Clutch: Carbon fibre*
CHASSIS	*Front and rear suspension:* Upper and lower wishones, pushrod activation of inboard mounted spring/damper units *Wheel diameter:* 13in, front and rear *Wheels:* OZ *Tyres:* Bridgestone Potenza *Brake callipers:* Brembo *Brake pads and discs:* Brembo, Carbone Industrie *Steering wheel:* BMW Sauber *Chassis electronics:* McLaren Electronic Systems
DIMENSIONS	*Length:* 4940mm *Width:* 1800mm *Height:* 1000mm *Front track:* 1495mm *Rear track:* 1410mm *Formula weight: 620kg, including driver and camera*

BMW SAUBER F1 TEAM

AFTER looking like it might not be on the grid at all, then an unpromising start with a car that was initially almost two seconds off the pace, Sauber turned its season around, and by the end of the year was challenging Williams and Force India hard for sixth place in the constructors' championship. By that time, the C29 had halved its deficit to the front to be nip-and-tuck as quick as the Williams, despite not having a blown diffuser.

When the planned purchase by the Qadbak group fell through, only the intervention of Peter Sauber in taking back ownership of the team following BMW's withdrawal kept it in play. That came late in the day, but the uncertainty did not affect the design and manufacture of the car, which used a Ferrari engine/gearbox package, rekindling a partnership last seen in 2005.

Long-time Sauber technical director Willi Rampf stayed on long enough to see the car's build through to completion, before moving on to semi-retirement. In his place, three weeks into the season, came former Force India technical director James Key. By the time he arrived, it was already very clear that the promising times seen in pre-season testing had been the product of a lighter fuel load than the opposition. New team drivers Pedro de la Rosa and Kamui Kobayashi were reporting very poor mechanical grip, and the speed-trap figures seemed to indicate a seriously high level of drag. There were also reliability issues.

For Key, who arrived in time for the Chinese Grand Prix, that was the bad news. The good news was that the team's facilities, built up during the BMW years, were fantastic: "On the aero side, the tunnel, the CFD, it's absolutely top class. You have the facilities to do more in a given time period than what I was used to at Force India. But it means you have to make sure the shape of the team is right to make best use of the resources. That's a bit tricky when you have more facilities than you can use in some cases. When you get that balance right, the manufacturing facilities mean things can happen so much quicker than what I've been used to. That was certainly a major part of how we were able to recover quite well from a difficult start."

Concurrent with changing the structure of the team and putting more emphasis on performance-related groups, Key took a long hard look at the car. Coming from a team that had a very aero-efficient machine, he didn't like the lift/drag numbers he was seeing, even though the team had been one of the earliest adaptors of the F-duct. "The numbers were about ten per cent higher than I'd expect of an aero-efficient car," he revealed. "But it was more than just that. Both drivers were complaining about mechanical grip and instability into slow corners, and it was clear the car was being set up too stiffly, that we'd got ourselves a bit hemmed in there. So before we even looked into bread-and-butter development, we had to prioritise how we set about sorting a number of specific problems on the car. From Barcelona and for the next few races, we used Fridays to experiment with set-up directions."

It was clear that the car's ultimate high-speed downforce capacity was quite respectable and, in concert with the F-duct at a time when few others had it, this gave pretty good performance in Spain, Kobayashi getting the car through to Q3 for the first time in the dry (he'd managed it in the wet conditions of Malaysia). "Yes, the team had done a great job with the F-duct. They had one on by China, which was an outstanding effort. It was a really good system, too, though initially a bit inconsistent," continued Key, "so we committed to getting a redesign on for Barcelona, which was a far more robust design for the same aero concept. That's where the Q3 came from."

Softening the car and deriving a new set of parameters around that brought driveability improvements, and thereafter the target was a mid-season upgrade that removed drag from the car and added some lower-speed downforce. "That ended up coming in three steps, Valencia, Silverstone and Hockenheim, because it's very difficult fundamentally changing aero characteristics because a lot of it is development legacy, the way it's built up over the previous months, and we had to unstitch a lot of that. There were mechanical updates, too, working on the suspension to get the consistency of balance through a corner. The instability was partly mechanical, partly aero. But the mechanical changes made a major difference in the slow corners, and that's where the most lap time is to be found."

De la Rosa's car suffered a disproportionate number of engine failures, for no apparent single reason. The failures stopped happening as suddenly as they'd started, but Pedro was already into his ninth engine by Monza. "That was all a bit strange," said a puzzled Key. "It was only one car that tended to get it, and we looked at it intensively, got Ferrari to check the installation, but nothing was particularly different. I think it was just bad luck. As a precaution, we changed the procedure on how we chilled the fuel on Saturday morning, changed it closer to what Ferrari were doing, just to be safe."

Although a blown diffuser was looked at in CFD and the tunnel, it never appeared on the car. "It took us a little while to realise just how potentially powerful it was," admitted Key. "But if we'd committed to it by the time, mid-season, we realised, we had the mid-season break, a load of refinement work to do to control the hot gases… It was a major project, and the earliest we could have got it on would have been Japan. So it was going to be a lot of aero time for a diffuser that was going to last four races. Also the cost: looking at how else we could use that budget, given that we were actually following a fruitful direction on general aero work, I felt it was a safer bet not doing it. It was a risk, but it didn't bite us too hard."

Given that a good blown diffuser was estimated at being worth upwards of 0.5 second per lap, the fact that Kobayashi could still occasionally get into Q3 underlines the fact that a very respectable design lay hidden beneath the C29's difficult gestation. Kamui's exciting racecraft brought in a late haul of points for the team, too. The late replacement of de la Rosa by Nick Heidfeld brought confirmation that the development direction being pursued was a fruitful one, although there was little noticeable difference in performance between the pair.

With a solid technical foundation established and new major Telmex sponsorship, things are looking much more promising for the Hinwil team than 12 months ago.

Above, centre left: Technical director James Key.

Above, near left: Monisha Kaltenborn.
Photos: Sauber F1 Team

Top left: Kamui Kobayashi was an ebullient presence with his feisty driving.
Photo: Peter J Fox

Below: Peter Sauber, who in 2010 celebrated 40 years in motor sport.
Photo: Sauber F1 Team

BMW SAUBER F1 TEAM: PERSONNEL

Team Principal: Peter Sauber
Managing Director: Monisha Kaltenborn
Technical Director: James Key
Chief Designer: Christoph Zimmerman
Head of Aerodynamics: Seamus Mullarkey
Team Manager: Beat Zehnder
Chief Race Engineer: Giampaolo Dall'ara
Race Engineer, Heidfeld/de la Rosa: Paul Russell
Race Engineer, Kobayashi: Francesco Nenci
Chief Mechanic: Urs Kuratle
Marketing Director: Alex Sauber

24

TIMO GLOCK

25

LUCAS DI GRASSI

VIRGIN RACING

THE team that subsequently became Virgin Racing was born of the FIA's attempts at generating new team blood by the proposed 'cost cap formula', which never happened. Those initial proposals offered cost-capped teams aerodynamic and engine advantages that piqued the interest of Manor Motorsport's John Booth and his business partner, Graham Lowden. They ran a Sheffield-based Formula 3 team using customer cars and had no facility to build an F1 car, but when it was suggested by key people within the governing body that it might be worth talking to Nick Wirth about that, a serious plan began to take shape.

Wirth's company, Wirth Research, had enjoyed success in sports car racing with an Acura designed entirely on CFD, without the use of a wind tunnel, and built in its Bicester factory. Wirth was interested in doing an F1 car in the same way, but had no desire to become an F1 team owner again, after his abortive Simtek operation of the 1990s. So there was common ground between the two entities. "We were introduced to Nick Wirth back in March '09," recalled Booth, "when the budget cap concept was introduced. There was going to be £30 million TV money, and that was going to be the cost of the season, and it all sounded a great idea. The week after the meeting, we were all pumped up and going for it, and started the application process. It was still a massive surprise when the announcement was made on June 12 that we had an entry: kind of, 'What shall we do now?' I think at that stage, Nick had a few sketches on the back of a fag packet..."

With a spirit of adventure, the unlikely bedfellows ploughed on, but their project almost came to grief at Silverstone in 2009 when the FOTA teams announced they were splitting from the FIA as from 2010. "We were signing with new sponsors," explained Booth, "and they've got the radio on in the afternoon, and the world blows up with walk-outs and splits! It was a massive setback for us." Part of the compromise that prevented the split was that there was no cost cap, nor any technical advantages for new teams. "We had to think about whether we could continue," said Booth.

The team had nothing like the £90–100 million required to design, build and race a two-car F1 team in the conventional manner. "It would have been impossible to ramp up the operation to utilise that amount of money," pointed out Booth. "That's even assuming it was out there, which it probably wasn't. We took the decision to continue, but within the financial framework we'd decided on for the original regulations. We could only do that because of Nick's CFD capability." The absence of a wind tunnel in the plans was the only thing that made the project financially feasible.

Richard Branson transferred his Virgin backing from the Brawn team of 2009 to this new project. It was a mutually good deal. Branson got a Virgin branded team through buying a small stake, but giving no gen-

VIRGIN RACING VR-01

SPONSORS	Antler • Ascends • Biotec • Bombril • Bridgestone • Carbon Green • Clear • CSC • Full Tilt Poker • FxPro • Kappa • LG MaRussia • Nexa Autocolour • Sorocred • St Tropez • UST Global • Virgin • Windreich
ENGINE	*Type:* Cosworth CA2010 *No of cylinders (vee angle):* V8 (90-deg) *Spark plugs:* Champion *Electronics:* FIA standard ECU and FIA homologated electronic and electrical systems *Oil:* BP
TRANSMISSION	*Gearbox:* Virgin Racing precision aluminium construction, longitudinal, 7-speed plus reverse with X-Trac internals *Clutch:* AP Racing
CHASSIS	*Front and rear suspension:* Double wishbone with pushrod operated rockers connected to roll torsion bars, dampers and anti-roll bar *Dampers:* Penske *Wheel diameter:* 13in, front and rear *Wheels:* BBS *Tyres:* Bridgestone Potenza. *Brake discs and pads:* Hitco *Brake callipers:* AP Racing *Steering:* VR hydraulic power assisted *Radiators:* VR *Instruments:* McLaren Electronic Systems
DIMENSIONS	*Length:* approx 5500mm *Width:* 1800mm *Height:* 950mm *Wheelbase:* about 3200mm *Formula weight:* 620kg, including driver and camera

Above: Nick Wirth designed the Virgin Racing VR-01 entirely by computer, without the aid of a wind tunnel.
Photo: Jea-François Galeron/WRi2

Top: Team principal John Booth, who brought his Manor Motorsport team into F1 on the back of investment from the Virgin Group.
Photo: Peter Nygaard/Grand Prix Photo

Above left: Brazilian Lucas di Grassi, who managed a season's best finish of 14th for the team.

Below: Team leader Timo Glock maintained his enthusiasm through a frustrating year.
Photos: Peter J Fox

uine sponsorship; the team got the Virgin brand to get them through the doors of other commercial entities.

Wirth and his team set about creating a car around the standard Cosworth engine/X-trac transmission project. Coincidentally, Wirth Research was also commissioned to create the hydraulic system to operate the X-trac gearbox that would be used not only by Virgin, but also the other new teams, Lotus and HRT. Ironically, the unreliability of this placed a major limitation on the car's initial development through curtailed testing.

The car, the VR-01, was a conventional design, albeit conservative around the sidepod area. It lacked the raw downforce of cars from the established teams, but generally was competitive on pace with the similarly conservative Lotus at around 104–105 per cent of a front running pace. However, it was realised even before the season began that it did not have enough fuel capacity to complete a race distance at some tracks. There were some extenuating circumstances – when the car was conceived, the fuel density limit was higher and there had been a mistaken assumption that topping up on the grid would be allowed. Whatever, a major redesign was necessary, with a new tub 13.5cm longer in the wheelbase. This was introduced for Timo Glock in Barcelona, while Lucas di Grassi was given his at Turkey, just in time before the high fuel requirements of Montreal.

Initially, the long car – nicknamed 'the limo' by the team – was slower than the short one, but some aerodynamic reconfiguring corrected this. The only full aero upgrade went on the car for Silverstone, comprising new front and rear wings and a new floor. This had been intended as the Barcelona package, delayed through the need to design and manufacture the longer-wheelbase car. Post-Silverstone, there were detail refinements only.

The team finished 12th and last in the constructors' championship, behind HRT, whose car was significantly slower, but who squeaked ahead on account of scoring more 14th-place finishes. Glock was always the team's cutting edge, invariably faster than rookie di Grassi, and was denied a possible South Korea finish that might have lifted the team above HRT only through being crashed into by Sébastien Buemi's Toro Rosso.

At the season's last race, in Abu Dhabi, it was announced that Russian supercar manufacturer Marussia had taken a stake in the team and would become a major sponsor from 2011. This will enable it to repay the venture capital that helped launch it; as a result, its footing looks secure into the future.

VIRGIN RACING: PERSONNEL

Team Principal: John Booth
CEO: Graeme Lowdon
Team Manager: Dave O'Neill
Technical Director: Nick Wirth
Head of Aerodynamics: Wirth Research
Chief Designer: Wirth Research
Chief Mechanic: Richard Wrenn
Head of Performance and Race Car Engineering: Mark Herd
Race Engineer, Glock: Dave Greenwood
Race Engineer, di Grassi: Mark Hutcheson

CHASSIS LOGBOOK 2010

COMPILED BY DAVID HAYHOE

McLAREN MP4-25

Photo: Vodafone McLaren Mercedes

ROUND 1 BAHRAIN GP

	McLAREN-MERCEDES	
1	Jenson Button	MP4-25/03
2	Lewis Hamilton	MP4-25/02
	MERCEDES	
3	Michael Schumacher	MGP W01/03
4	Nico Rosberg	MGP W01/02
	RED BULL-RENAULT	
5	Sebastian Vettel	RB6/3
6	Mark Webber	RB6/2
	FERRARI	
7	Felipe Massa	F10/281
8	Fernando Alonso	F10/283
	WILLIAMS-COSWORTH	
9	Rubens Barrichello	FW32/01
10	Nico Hülkenberg	FW32/03
	RENAULT	
11	Robert Kubica	R30/03
12	Vitaly Petrov	R30/02
	FORCE INDIA-MERCEDES	
14	Adrian Sutil	VJM03/03
15	Vitantonio Liuzzi	VJM03/01
	TORO ROSSO-FERRARI	
16	Sébastien Buemi	STR5/01
17	Jaime Alguersuari	STR5/03
	LOTUS-COSWORTH	
18	Jarno Trulli	T127/03
19	Heikki Kovalainen	T127/01
	HRT-COSWORTH	
20	Karun Chandhok	F110/01
21	Bruno Senna	F110/02
	BMW SAUBER-FERRARI	
22	Pedro de la Rosa	C29/03
23	Kamui Kobayashi	C29/02
	VIRGIN-COSWORTH	
24	Timo Glock	VR-01/02
25	Lucas Di Grassi	VR-01/01

ROUND 2 AUSTRALIAN GP

	McLAREN-MERCEDES	
1	Jenson Button	MP4-25/03
2	Lewis Hamilton	MP4-25/02
	MERCEDES	
3	Michael Schumacher	MGP W01/03
4	Nico Rosberg	MGP W01/02
	RED BULL-RENAULT	
5	Sebastian Vettel	RB6/3
6	Mark Webber	RB6/4
	FERRARI	
7	Felipe Massa	F10/281
8	Fernando Alonso	F10/283
	WILLIAMS-COSWORTH	
9	Rubens Barrichello	FW32/01
10	Nico Hülkenberg	FW32/03
	RENAULT	
11	Robert Kubica	R30/03
12	Vitaly Petrov	R30/02
	FORCE INDIA-MERCEDES	
14	Adrian Sutil	VJM03/03
14	Paul Di Resta	VJM03/03
15	Vitantonio Liuzzi	VJM03/01
	TORO ROSSO-FERRARI	
16	Sébastien Buemi	STR5/01
17	Jaime Alguersuari	STR5/03
	LOTUS-COSWORTH	
18	Jarno Trulli	T127/03
19	Heikki Kovalainen	T127/01
	HRT-COSWORTH	
20	Karun Chandhok	F110/01
21	Bruno Senna	F110/02
	BMW SAUBER-FERRARI	
22	Pedro de la Rosa	C29/03
23	Kamui Kobayashi	C29/02
	VIRGIN-COSWORTH	
24	Timo Glock	VR-01/02
25	Lucas Di Grassi	VR-01/01

ROUND 3 MALAYSIAN GP

	McLAREN-MERCEDES	
1	Jenson Button	MP4-25/03
2	Lewis Hamilton	MP4-25/01
	MERCEDES	
3	Michael Schumacher	MGP W01/03
4	Nico Rosberg	MGP W01/02
	RED BULL-RENAULT	
5	Sebastian Vettel	RB6/3
6	Mark Webber	RB6/4
	FERRARI	
7	Felipe Massa	F10/281
8	Fernando Alonso	F10/283
	WILLIAMS-COSWORTH	
9	Rubens Barrichello	FW32/01
10	Nico Hülkenberg	FW32/03
	RENAULT	
11	Robert Kubica	R30/03
12	Vitaly Petrov	R30/02
	FORCE INDIA-MERCEDES	
14	Adrian Sutil	VJM03/03
15	Vitantonio Liuzzi	VJM03/01
15	Paul Di Resta	VJM03/01
	TORO ROSSO-FERRARI	
16	Sébastien Buemi	STR5/01
17	Jaime Alguersuari	STR5/03
	LOTUS-COSWORTH	
18	Jarno Trulli	T127/03
19	Heikki Kovalainen	T127/01
19	Fairuz Fauzy	T127/01
	HRT-COSWORTH	
20	Karun Chandhok	F110/01
21	Bruno Senna	F110/02
	BMW SAUBER-FERRARI	
22	Pedro de la Rosa	C29/03
23	Kamui Kobayashi	C29/01
	VIRGIN-COSWORTH	
24	Timo Glock	VR-01/02
25	Lucas Di Grassi	VR-01/01

ROUND 4 CHINESE GP

	McLAREN-MERCEDES	
1	Jenson Button	MP4-25/02
2	Lewis Hamilton	MP4-25/01
	MERCEDES	
3	Michael Schumacher	MGP W01/03
4	Nico Rosberg	MGP W01/02
	RED BULL-RENAULT	
5	Sebastian Vettel	RB6/3
6	Mark Webber	RB6/4
	FERRARI	
7	Felipe Massa	F10/281
8	Fernando Alonso	F10/283
	WILLIAMS-COSWORTH	
9	Rubens Barrichello	FW32/01
10	Nico Hülkenberg	FW32/03
	RENAULT	
11	Robert Kubica	R30/03
12	Vitaly Petrov	R30/02
	FORCE INDIA-MERCEDES	
14	Adrian Sutil	VJM03/03
15	Vitantonio Liuzzi	VJM03/01
15	Paul Di Resta	VJM03/01
	TORO ROSSO-FERRARI	
16	Sébastien Buemi	STR5/01
17	Jaime Alguersuari	STR5/03
	LOTUS-COSWORTH	
18	Jarno Trulli	T127/03
19	Heikki Kovalainen	T127/01
	HRT-COSWORTH	
20	Karun Chandhok	F110/01
21	Bruno Senna	F110/02
	BMW SAUBER-FERRARI	
22	Pedro de la Rosa	C29/04
23	Kamui Kobayashi	C29/01
	VIRGIN-COSWORTH	
24	Timo Glock	VR-01/02
25	Lucas Di Grassi	VR-01/01

ROUND 5 SPANISH GP

	McLAREN-MERCEDES	
1	Jenson Button	MP4-25/03
2	Lewis Hamilton	MP4-25/04
	MERCEDES	
3	Michael Schumacher	MGP W01/01
4	Nico Rosberg	MGP W01/02
	RED BULL-RENAULT	
5	Sebastian Vettel	RB6/3
6	Mark Webber	RB6/4
	FERRARI	
7	Felipe Massa	F10/284
8	Fernando Alonso	F10/283
	WILLIAMS-COSWORTH	
9	Rubens Barrichello	FW32/04
10	Nico Hülkenberg	FW32/03
	RENAULT	
11	Robert Kubica	R30/03
12	Vitaly Petrov	R30/04
	FORCE INDIA-MERCEDES	
14	Adrian Sutil	VJM03/03
14	Paul Di Resta	VJM03/03
15	Vitantonio Liuzzi	VJM03/04
	TORO ROSSO-FERRARI	
16	Sébastien Buemi	STR5/02
17	Jaime Alguersuari	STR5/03
	LOTUS-COSWORTH	
18	Jarno Trulli	T127/03
19	Heikki Kovalainen	T127/01
	HRT-COSWORTH	
20	Karun Chandhok	F110/01
20	Christian Klien	F110/01
21	Bruno Senna	F110/02
	BMW SAUBER-FERRARI	
22	Pedro de la Rosa	C29/03
23	Kamui Kobayashi	C29/01
	VIRGIN-COSWORTH	
24	Timo Glock	VR-01/03
25	Lucas Di Grassi	VR-01/01

ROUND 7 TURKISH GP

	McLAREN-MERCEDES	
1	Jenson Button	MP4-25/03
2	Lewis Hamilton	MP4-25/01
	MERCEDES	
3	Michael Schumacher	MGP W01/01
4	Nico Rosberg	MGP W01/02
	RED BULL-RENAULT	
5	Sebastian Vettel	RB6/2
6	Mark Webber	RB6/4
	FERRARI	
7	Felipe Massa	F10/284
8	Fernando Alonso	F10/282
	WILLIAMS-COSWORTH	
9	Rubens Barrichello	FW32/04
10	Nico Hülkenberg	FW32/03
	RENAULT	
11	Robert Kubica	R30/03
12	Vitaly Petrov	R30/04
	FORCE INDIA-MERCEDES	
14	Adrian Sutil	VJM03/03
15	Vitantonio Liuzzi	VJM03/04
	TORO ROSSO-FERRARI	
16	Sébastien Buemi	STR5/02
17	Jaime Alguersuari	STR5/03
	LOTUS-COSWORTH	
18	Jarno Trulli	T127/03
19	Heikki Kovalainen	T127/01
	HRT-COSWORTH	
20	Karun Chandhok	F110/01
21	Bruno Senna	F110/02
21	Sakon Yamamoto	F110/02
	BMW SAUBER-FERRARI	
22	Pedro de la Rosa	C29/03
23	Kamui Kobayashi	C29/01
	VIRGIN-COSWORTH	
24	Timo Glock	VR-01/03
25	Lucas Di Grassi	VR-01/02

ROUND 8 CANADIAN GP

	McLAREN-MERCEDES	
1	Jenson Button	MP4-25/03
2	Lewis Hamilton	MP4-25/04
	MERCEDES	
3	Michael Schumacher	MGP W01/01
4	Nico Rosberg	MGP W01/02
	RED BULL-RENAULT	
5	Sebastian Vettel	RB6/2
6	Mark Webber	RB6/4
	FERRARI	
7	Felipe Massa	F10/284
8	Fernando Alonso	F10/282
	WILLIAMS-COSWORTH	
9	Rubens Barrichello	FW32/04
10	Nico Hülkenberg	FW32/03
	RENAULT	
11	Robert Kubica	R30/03
12	Vitaly Petrov	R30/04
	FORCE INDIA-MERCEDES	
14	Adrian Sutil	VJM03/03
15	Vitantonio Liuzzi	VJM03/01
	TORO ROSSO-FERRARI	
16	Sébastien Buemi	STR5/02
17	Jaime Alguersuari	STR5/03
	LOTUS-COSWORTH	
18	Jarno Trulli	T127/03
19	Heikki Kovalainen	T127/01
	HRT-COSWORTH	
20	Karun Chandhok	F110/01
21	Bruno Senna	F110/02
	BMW SAUBER-FERRARI	
22	Pedro de la Rosa	C29/03
23	Kamui Kobayashi	C29/01
	VIRGIN-COSWORTH	
24	Timo Glock	VR-01/03
25	Lucas Di Grassi	VR-01/02

ROUND 9 EUROPEAN GP

	McLAREN-MERCEDES	
1	Jenson Button	MP4-25/03
2	Lewis Hamilton	MP4-25/04
	MERCEDES	
3	Michael Schumacher	MGP W01/01
4	Nico Rosberg	MGP W01/02
	RED BULL-RENAULT	
5	Sebastian Vettel	RB6/2
6	Mark Webber	RB6/4
	FERRARI	
7	Felipe Massa	F10/284
8	Fernando Alonso	F10/285
	WILLIAMS-COSWORTH	
9	Rubens Barrichello	FW32/04
10	Nico Hülkenberg	FW32/03
	RENAULT	
11	Robert Kubica	R30/03
12	Vitaly Petrov	R30/04
	FORCE INDIA-MERCEDES	
14	Adrian Sutil	VJM03/03
14	Paul Di Resta	VJM03/03
15	Vitantonio Liuzzi	VJM03/01
	TORO ROSSO-FERRARI	
16	Sébastien Buemi	STR5/02
17	Jaime Alguersuari	STR5/03
	LOTUS-COSWORTH	
18	Jarno Trulli	T127/04
19	Heikki Kovalainen	T127/01
	HRT-COSWORTH	
20	Karun Chandhok	F110/03
20	Christian Klien	F110/03
21	Bruno Senna	F110/02
	BMW SAUBER-FERRARI	
22	Pedro de la Rosa	C29/04
23	Kamui Kobayashi	C29/02
	VIRGIN-COSWORTH	
24	Timo Glock	VR-01/03
25	Lucas Di Grassi	VR-01/02

ROUND 6 MONACO GP

	McLAREN-MERCEDES	
1	Jenson Button	MP4-25/03
2	Lewis Hamilton	MP4-25/01
	MERCEDES	
3	Michael Schumacher	MGP W01/01
4	Nico Rosberg	MGP W01/02
	RED BULL-RENAULT	
5	Sebastian Vettel	RB6/3
6	Mark Webber	RB6/4
	FERRARI	
7	Felipe Massa	F10/284
8	Fernando Alonso	F10/282 (283 Thu/Sat)
	WILLIAMS-COSWORTH	
9	Rubens Barrichello	FW32/04
10	Nico Hülkenberg	FW32/03
	RENAULT	
11	Robert Kubica	R30/03
12	Vitaly Petrov	R30/04
	FORCE INDIA-MERCEDES	
14	Adrian Sutil	VJM03/03
15	Vitantonio Liuzzi	VJM03/04
	TORO ROSSO-FERRARI	
16	Sébastien Buemi	STR5/02
17	Jaime Alguersuari	STR5/03
	LOTUS-COSWORTH	
18	Jarno Trulli	T127/03
19	Heikki Kovalainen	T127/01
	HRT-COSWORTH	
20	Karun Chandhok	F110/01
21	Bruno Senna	F110/02
	BMW SAUBER-FERRARI	
22	Pedro de la Rosa	C29/03
23	Kamui Kobayashi	C29/01
	VIRGIN-COSWORTH	
24	Timo Glock	VR-01/03
25	Lucas Di Grassi	VR-01/01

RENAULT R30

Photo: Renault F1 Team

CHASSIS LOGBOOK 2010

ROUND 10 BRITISH GP

	McLAREN-MERCEDES	
1	Jenson Button	MP4-25/03
2	Lewis Hamilton	MP4-25/04
	MERCEDES	
3	Michael Schumacher	MGP W01/01
4	Nico Rosberg	MGP W01/02
	RED BULL-RENAULT	
5	Sebastian Vettel	RB6/2
6	Mark Webber	RB6/3
	FERRARI	
7	Felipe Massa	F10/284
8	Fernando Alonso	F10/285
	WILLIAMS-COSWORTH	
9	Rubens Barrichello	FW32/04
10	Nico Hülkenberg	FW32/01
	RENAULT	
11	Robert Kubica	R30/03
12	Vitaly Petrov	R30/04
	FORCE INDIA-MERCEDES	
14	Adrian Sutil	VJM03/03
15	Vitantonio Liuzzi	VJM03/01
15	Paul Di Resta	VJM03/01
	TORO ROSSO-FERRARI	
16	Sébastien Buemi	STR5/02
17	Jaime Alguersuari	STR5/03
	LOTUS-COSWORTH	
18	Jarno Trulli	T127/04
18	Fairuz Fauzy	T127/04
19	Heikki Kovalainen	T127/01
	HRT-COSWORTH	
20	Karun Chandhok	F110/03
21	Sakon Yamamoto	F110/02
	BMW SAUBER-FERRARI	
22	Pedro de la Rosa	C29/04
23	Kamui Kobayashi	C29/02
	VIRGIN-COSWORTH	
24	Timo Glock	VR-01/03
25	Lucas Di Grassi	VR-01/02

ROUND 11 GERMAN GP

	McLAREN-MERCEDES	
1	Jenson Button	MP4-25/03
2	Lewis Hamilton	MP4-25/04
	MERCEDES	
3	Michael Schumacher	MGP W01/02
4	Nico Rosberg	MGP W01/04
	RED BULL-RENAULT	
5	Sebastian Vettel	RB6/2
6	Mark Webber	RB6/3
	FERRARI	
7	Felipe Massa	F10/284
8	Fernando Alonso	F10/285
	WILLIAMS-COSWORTH	
9	Rubens Barrichello	FW32/04
10	Nico Hülkenberg	FW32/01
	RENAULT	
11	Robert Kubica	R30/03
12	Vitaly Petrov	R30/04
	FORCE INDIA-MERCEDES	
14	Adrian Sutil	VJM03/03
15	Vitantonio Liuzzi	VJM03/01
	TORO ROSSO-FERRARI	
16	Sébastien Buemi	STR5/02
17	Jaime Alguersuari	STR5/03
	LOTUS-COSWORTH	
18	Jarno Trulli	T127/04
19	Heikki Kovalainen	T127/01
19	Fairuz Fauzy	T127/01
	HRT-COSWORTH	
20	Sakon Yamamoto	F110/03
21	Bruno Senna	F110/02
	BMW SAUBER-FERRARI	
22	Pedro de la Rosa	C29/04
23	Kamui Kobayashi	C29/02
	VIRGIN-COSWORTH	
24	Timo Glock	VR-01/03
25	Lucas Di Grassi	VR-01/02

ROUND 12 HUNGARIAN GP

	McLAREN-MERCEDES	
1	Jenson Button	MP4-25/03
2	Lewis Hamilton	MP4-25/02
	MERCEDES	
3	Michael Schumacher	MGP W01/02
4	Nico Rosberg	MGP W01/04
	RED BULL-RENAULT	
5	Sebastian Vettel	RB6/2
6	Mark Webber	RB6/3
	FERRARI	
7	Felipe Massa	F10/284
8	Fernando Alonso	F10/285
	WILLIAMS-COSWORTH	
9	Rubens Barrichello	FW32/04
10	Nico Hülkenberg	FW32/01
	RENAULT	
11	Robert Kubica	R30/03
12	Vitaly Petrov	R30/04
	FORCE INDIA-MERCEDES	
14	Adrian Sutil	VJM03/03
15	Vitantonio Liuzzi	VJM03/01
15	Paul Di Resta	VJM03/01
	TORO ROSSO-FERRARI	
16	Sébastien Buemi	STR5/02
17	Jaime Alguersuari	STR5/03
	LOTUS-COSWORTH	
18	Jarno Trulli	T127/04
19	Heikki Kovalainen	T127/01
	HRT-COSWORTH	
20	Sakon Yamamoto	F110/03
21	Bruno Senna	F110/02
	BMW SAUBER-FERRARI	
22	Pedro de la Rosa	C29/04
23	Kamui Kobayashi	C29/02
	VIRGIN-COSWORTH	
24	Timo Glock	VR-01/01 (03-Fri)
25	Lucas Di Grassi	VR-01/02

ROUND 13 BELGIAN GP

	McLAREN-MERCEDES	
1	Jenson Button	MP4-25/03
2	Lewis Hamilton	MP4-25/04
	MERCEDES	
3	Michael Schumacher	MGP W01/02
4	Nico Rosberg	MGP W01/04
	RED BULL-RENAULT	
5	Sebastian Vettel	RB6/5
6	Mark Webber	RB6/3
	FERRARI	
7	Felipe Massa	F10/284
8	Fernando Alonso	F10/285
	WILLIAMS-COSWORTH	
9	Rubens Barrichello	FW32/04
10	Nico Hülkenberg	FW32/01
	RENAULT	
11	Robert Kubica	R30/03
12	Vitaly Petrov	R30/04
	FORCE INDIA-MERCEDES	
14	Adrian Sutil	VJM03/03
15	Vitantonio Liuzzi	VJM03/01
	TORO ROSSO-FERRARI	
16	Sébastien Buemi	STR5/02
17	Jaime Alguersuari	STR5/03
	LOTUS-COSWORTH	
18	Jarno Trulli	T127/04
19	Heikki Kovalainen	T127/01
	HRT-COSWORTH	
20	Sakon Yamamoto	F110/03
21	Bruno Senna	F110/02
	BMW SAUBER-FERRARI	
22	Pedro de la Rosa	C29/03
23	Kamui Kobayashi	C29/01
	VIRGIN-COSWORTH	
24	Timo Glock	VR-01/01
25	Lucas Di Grassi	VR-01/02

LOTUS T127

Photo: Lotus Racing

RED BULL RB6

Photo: Red Bull Racing

ROUND 16 JAPANESE GP

	McLAREN-MERCEDES	
1	Jenson Button	MP4-25/01
2	Lewis Hamilton	MP4-25/02
	MERCEDES	
3	Michael Schumacher	MGP W01/05
4	Nico Rosberg	MGP W01/04
	RED BULL-RENAULT	
5	Sebastian Vettel	RB6/5
6	Mark Webber	RB6/6
	FERRARI	
7	Felipe Massa	F10/286
8	Fernando Alonso	F10/285
	WILLIAMS-COSWORTH	
9	Rubens Barrichello	FW32/04
10	Nico Hülkenberg	FW32/01
	RENAULT	
11	Robert Kubica	R30/05
12	Vitaly Petrov	R30/04
	FORCE INDIA-MERCEDES	
14	Adrian Sutil	VJM03/03
15	Vitantonio Liuzzi	VJM03/01
	TORO ROSSO-FERRARI	
16	Sébastien Buemi	STR5/02
17	Jaime Alguersuari	STR5/01
	LOTUS-COSWORTH	
18	Jarno Trulli	T127/04
19	Heikki Kovalainen	T127/01
	HRT-COSWORTH	
20	Sakon Yamamoto	F110/03
21	Bruno Senna	F110/02
	BMW SAUBER-FERRARI	
22	Nick Heidfeld	C29/03
23	Kamui Kobayashi	C29/04
	VIRGIN-COSWORTH	
24	Timo Glock	VR-01/01
25	Lucas di Grassi	VR-01/04
25	Jérôme d'Ambrosio	VR-01/04

ROUND 17 KOREAN GP

	McLAREN-MERCEDES	
1	Jenson Button	MP4-25/01
2	Lewis Hamilton	MP4-25/02
	MERCEDES	
3	Michael Schumacher	MGP W01/05
4	Nico Rosberg	MGP W01/04
	RED BULL-RENAULT	
5	Sebastian Vettel	RB6/5
6	Mark Webber	RB6/3
	FERRARI	
7	Felipe Massa	F10/284
8	Fernando Alonso	F10/285
	WILLIAMS-COSWORTH	
9	Rubens Barrichello	FW32/04
10	Nico Hülkenberg	FW32/01
	RENAULT	
11	Robert Kubica	R30/05
12	Vitaly Petrov	R30/04
	FORCE INDIA-MERCEDES	
14	Adrian Sutil	VJM03/03
15	Vitantonio Liuzzi	VJM03/04
	TORO ROSSO-FERRARI	
16	Sébastien Buemi	STR5/02
17	Jaime Alguersuari	STR5/01
	LOTUS-COSWORTH	
18	Jarno Trulli	T127/04
19	Heikki Kovalainen	T127/03
	HRT-COSWORTH	
20	Sakon Yamamoto	F110/03
21	Bruno Senna	F110/02
	BMW SAUBER-FERRARI	
22	Nick Heidfeld	C29/03
23	Kamui Kobayashi	C29/04
	VIRGIN-COSWORTH	
24	Timo Glock	VR-01/01
25	Lucas di Grassi	VR-01/02
25	Jérôme d'Ambrosio	VR-01/02

ROUND 14 ITALIAN GP

	McLAREN-MERCEDES	
1	Jenson Button	MP4-25/03
2	Lewis Hamilton	MP4-25/04
	MERCEDES	
3	Michael Schumacher	MGP W01/02
4	Nico Rosberg	MGP W01/04
	RED BULL-RENAULT	
5	Sebastian Vettel	RB6/5
6	Mark Webber	RB6/3
	FERRARI	
7	Felipe Massa	F10/284
8	Fernando Alonso	F10/285
	WILLIAMS-COSWORTH	
9	Rubens Barrichello	FW32/04
10	Nico Hülkenberg	FW32/01
	RENAULT	
11	Robert Kubica	R30/02
12	Vitaly Petrov	R30/04
	FORCE INDIA-MERCEDES	
14	Adrian Sutil	VJM03/03
14	Paul Di Resta	VJM03/03
15	Vitantonio Liuzzi	VJM03/01
	TORO ROSSO-FERRARI	
16	Sébastien Buemi	STR5/02
17	Jaime Alguersuari	STR5/03
	LOTUS-COSWORTH	
18	Jarno Trulli	T127/04
19	Heikki Kovalainen	T127/01
	HRT-COSWORTH	
20	Sakon Yamamoto	F110/03
21	Bruno Senna	F110/02
	BMW SAUBER-FERRARI	
22	Pedro de la Rosa	C29/03
23	Kamui Kobayashi	C29/01
	VIRGIN-COSWORTH	
24	Timo Glock	VR-01/01
25	Lucas Di Grassi	VR-01/04

ROUND 15 SINGAPORE GP

	McLAREN-MERCEDES	
1	Jenson Button	MP4-25/01
2	Lewis Hamilton	MP4-25/02
	MERCEDES	
3	Michael Schumacher	MGP W01/05
4	Nico Rosberg	MGP W01/04
	RED BULL-RENAULT	
5	Sebastian Vettel	RB6/5
6	Mark Webber	RB6/6
	FERRARI	
7	Felipe Massa	F10/286
8	Fernando Alonso	F10/285
	WILLIAMS-COSWORTH	
9	Rubens Barrichello	FW32/04
10	Nico Hülkenberg	FW32/01
	RENAULT	
11	Robert Kubica	R30/05
12	Vitaly Petrov	R30/04
	FORCE INDIA-MERCEDES	
14	Adrian Sutil	VJM03/03
15	Vitantonio Liuzzi	VJM03/01
	TORO ROSSO-FERRARI	
16	Sébastien Buemi	STR5/02
17	Jaime Alguersuari	STR5/03
	LOTUS-COSWORTH	
18	Jarno Trulli	T127/04
18	Fairuz Fauzy	T127/04
19	Heikki Kovalainen	T127/01
	HRT-COSWORTH	
20	Christian Klien	F110/03
21	Bruno Senna	F110/02
	BMW SAUBER-FERRARI	
22	Nick Heidfeld	C29/03
23	Kamui Kobayashi	C29/04
	VIRGIN-COSWORTH	
24	Timo Glock	VR-01/01
25	Lucas di Grassi	VR-01/04
25	Jérôme d'Ambrosio	VR-01/04

ROUND 18 BRAZILIAN GP

	McLAREN-MERCEDES	
1	Jenson Button	MP4-25/01
2	Lewis Hamilton	MP4-25/04
	MERCEDES	
3	Michael Schumacher	MGP W01/05
4	Nico Rosberg	MGP W01/01
	RED BULL-RENAULT	
5	Sebastian Vettel	RB6/5
6	Mark Webber	RB6/6
	FERRARI	
7	Felipe Massa	F10/284
8	Fernando Alonso	F10/285
	WILLIAMS-COSWORTH	
9	Rubens Barrichello	FW32/04
10	Nico Hülkenberg	FW32/01
	RENAULT	
11	Robert Kubica	R30/05
12	Vitaly Petrov	R30/02
	FORCE INDIA-MERCEDES	
14	Adrian Sutil	VJM03/03
15	Vitantonio Liuzzi	VJM03/04
	TORO ROSSO-FERRARI	
16	Sébastien Buemi	STR5/03
17	Jaime Alguersuari	STR5/01
	LOTUS-COSWORTH	
18	Jarno Trulli	T127/02
19	Heikki Kovalainen	T127/03
	HRT-COSWORTH	
20	Christian Klien	F110/03
21	Bruno Senna	F110/02
	BMW SAUBER-FERRARI	
22	Nick Heidfeld	C29/03
23	Kamui Kobayashi	C29/04
	VIRGIN-COSWORTH	
24	Timo Glock	VR-01/01
25	Lucas di Grassi	VR-01/02
25	Jérôme d'Ambrosio	VR-01/02

ROUND 19 ABU DHABI GP

	McLAREN-MERCEDES	
1	Jenson Button	MP4-25/01
2	Lewis Hamilton	MP4-25/04
	MERCEDES	
3	Michael Schumacher	MGP W01/05
4	Nico Rosberg	MGP W01/01
	RED BULL-RENAULT	
5	Sebastian Vettel	RB6/5
6	Mark Webber	RB6/6
	FERRARI	
7	Felipe Massa	F10/284
8	Fernando Alonso	F10/285
	WILLIAMS-COSWORTH	
9	Rubens Barrichello	FW32/04
10	Nico Hülkenberg	FW32/01
	RENAULT	
11	Robert Kubica	R30/05
12	Vitaly Petrov	R30/02
	FORCE INDIA-MERCEDES	
14	Adrian Sutil	VJM03/03
15	Vitantonio Liuzzi	VJM03/02
	TORO ROSSO-FERRARI	
16	Sébastien Buemi	STR5/03
17	Jaime Alguersuari	STR5/01
	LOTUS-COSWORTH	
18	Jarno Trulli	T127/02
19	Heikki Kovalainen	T127/03
19	Fairuz Fauzy	T127/03
	HRT-COSWORTH	
20	Christian Klien	F110/03
21	Bruno Senna	F110/02
	BMW SAUBER-FERRARI	
22	Nick Heidfeld	C29/03
23	Kamui Kobayashi	C29/04
	VIRGIN-COSWORTH	
24	Timo Glock	VR-01/01
25	Lucas di Grassi	VR-01/02

FIA FORMULA 1 WORLD CHAMPIONSHIP

GRANDS PRIX 2010

By SIMON ARRON and ALAN HENRY

Photo: Peter J Fox

Passionate about winning

FIA FORMULA 1 WORLD CHAMPIONSHIP · ROUND 1

BAHRAIN GRAND PRIX

SAKHIR CIRCUIT

Above: Sebastian Vettel threw down the gauntlet to his rivals by planting his Red Bull on pole position, but a sparking-plug problem hobbled his efforts in the race.

Main photo: An exultant Fernando Alonso opened his Ferrari career with a fortuitous victory, casting a significant straw into the F1 wind.
Photos: Peter J. Fox

SAKHIR QUALIFYING

"LOOK, I've just received a text from my mum. She has finally seen my car on TV." The most engaging stories in Bahrain weren't always the most obvious…

Karun Chandhok's momentary amusement reflected a step back in time, to when endless all-nighters were part of every Formula One mechanic's job description. During the build-up to the season's opening grand prix, the paddock air was ripe with the sound of carbon fibre being filed to fit – and, sometimes, a blasphemous symphony when it didn't.

It was hardly surprising that Chandhok's car had not been ready. The Hispania Racing Team had come into being only a couple of weeks before the campaign's dawn, when it had taken over the cash-strapped Campos Grand Prix project. And during a prolonged period of financial uncertainty, chassis supplier Dallara had halted development until it knew there would be a team to race its car…

After a last-minute rush, which included putting together most of a race crew from scratch, HRT transformed one carbon husk so that Bruno Senna could complete a few laps on Friday afternoon; car two was ready the following morning, except that hydraulic failure stranded it in the garage and obliged Chandhok to take his F1 bow during official qualifying. Not exactly ideal preparation, but those seven gentle laps felt like a victory of sorts. That's when Mrs Chandhok picked up her mobile.

Things were no more routine at the front, where Sebastian Vettel missed chunks of the Friday session after braking problems obliged him to have the system changed. The Red Bull RB6 ran sweetly on Saturday, though, and Vettel was fastest in all three qualifying sectors: in 2009, the team's forte had been quick, flowing corners. Now it could handle the slower, less challenging stuff, too – and quite a lot of it, as a new, half-mile loop had increased Bahrain's corner count to 23. Couched in PR terms, this was "a brand-new track layout that extends the existing 5.412km circuit to a thrilling 6.299km"; that'll be several more second- and third-gear corners, then.

"I have to admit I was not very happy yesterday," Vettel said. "I knew there was potential in the car, but I was just not putting it together, and my brake problems prevented me doing a lot of running. Things were better this morning, but at the end of qualifying the circuit became a bit more difficult with the conditions changing all the time. Finally, and I think I am speaking on behalf of all drivers, we should give some great respect to Felipe…"

Doubtless the sentiment was heartfelt, but it was also a cute bit of gamesmanship – a little nudge to remind Ferrari's star signing, Fernando Alonso, that he'd just been outqualified, and comfortably so, by team-mate Felipe Massa. For the Brazilian, this was a seamless resumption: he was competing in a grand prix for the first time since suffering serious head injuries the previous summer in Budapest, where flying debris had struck his crash helmet.

Massa was touched by Vettel's kind words. "It is fantastic to hear that," he said in response. "We are here to compete and race each other, but there is great respect between drivers, and that counts for more than anything else. I have been through difficult times, but now I'm here and 100 per cent ready to fight again."

Alonso, 0.366 seconds adrift of his team-mate, started third – and looked distinctly less happy than he claimed to be. A mistake in sector three ("I did my worst lap of the weekend at the worst possible time") dropped Mark Webber to sixth, behind Lewis Hamilton and Nico Rosberg, while defending champion Jenson Button began his new life with McLaren from eighth place.

Just ahead, Michael Schumacher was relegated to ordinary mortal status on his return from a three-year sabbatical. There were lots of new things to get used to, but he didn't have much testing time in which to do it. "I am satisfied with seventh," he said, "and appreciate everybody's efforts to support me as I get back into the swing of things."

It was also a neat parallel: that's where he had qualified his Jordan on his Formula One debut at Spa, 19 years earlier.

WE were, apparently, on the cusp of the most exciting season in Formula One history – a popular assumption based on Michael Schumacher's emergence from retirement, McLaren's title-rich Jenson Button/Lewis Hamilton alliance, Fernando Alonso's partnership with Ferrari, the first all-Mercedes grand prix car since 1955 (even though technically it was a Tyrrell, if you traced the bloodline far enough) and the unquestionable speed of Red Bull. If ever a race was poised to trip over its own hype, the 2010 Bahrain Grand Prix was a prime candidate.

There was, though, a distinct feelgood factor at the Sakhir International Circuit, most of it generated by the presence of all but two of the sport's living world champions – part of a celebration to honour the 60th anniversary of the F1 title's inauguration. Kimi Räikkönen and Nelson Piquet were indisposed, but the rest showed up and many participated enthusiastically in two pre-race parades. There was a little poetic licence (Nigel Mansell in the 1950 Thinwall Special), but John Surtees (Ferrari 1512), Emerson Fittipaldi (Lotus 72), Jackie Stewart (wearing a set of 1969 overalls that still fitted every bit as well as his Matra MS80) and Mario Andretti (Lotus 79) provided a strong emotional core. It was a rich seam of motorsport heritage in a land that has almost none.

"I'm not sure I'm feeling the big occasion," said Jody Scheckter, "but a lot of people seem to appreciate it. We're coming to a track and going through the motions as though we're going to take part in a race, but we're not. I suppose it's a bit like foreplay without the sex. You're looking forward to it, but you're not going to get it. Mind you, that has happened a few times before…" None of this prevented him from getting stuck in and sliding his Ferrari 312 T4 around as though it were still 1979. The grand prix had a tough act to follow.

Sebastian Vettel made a clean start to lead into Turn One, where Fernando Alonso plumped for the outside line and thereby claimed the inside at the following left-hand kink to usurp team-mate Felipe Massa. Just behind, Mark Webber's car hesitated momentarily when its engine breathed in excess oil and spewed dense white smoke across the circuit. Robert Kubica backed off in the belief that there might be something worth avoiding – and Adrian Sutil, ever a magnet for trouble during the opening moments of a race, ran into him, causing both to spin. "I don't think Sutil lifted," said Kubica. "He just hit me and the incident completely cooked my rear tyres." Sutil's view – "I don't really know what happened" – was more revealing than it might sound. Michael Schumacher and Jenson Button both overtook the momentarily faltering Webber, but the Australian swiftly repassed the defending champion.

Vettel was more than two seconds clear by the lap's end, with Alonso leading the pursuit. Massa was third, from Nico Rosberg, Lewis Hamilton, Schumacher, Webber, Button, Tonio Liuzzi, Rubens Barrichello, Vitaly Petrov, Kamui Kobayashi, Nico

Above: Back to school. The class of 2010 poses for an official photograph before the new term kicks off.
Photo: Peter J. Fox

Inset top right: Jody Scheckter poses with a Mercedes W196, as used by Fangio in 1954/5.

Inset top left: Friends reunited. Mario Andretti, Jackie Stewart and Emerson Fittipaldi.
Photos: Jean-François Galeron/WRi2

Above left: John Surtees in the Ferrari 1512 that he used during 1965.
Photo: Paul-Henri Cahier

Left: Bernie Ecclestone and Nigel Mansell.
Photo: Jean-François Galeron/WRi2

Far left: The Ferrari F1 garage is ablaze with light during the darkness of a desert evening at the Sakhir circuit.
Photo: Andrew Hone

Above: Alonso's debut outing with Ferrari served to put the rest of the F1 paddock on red alert.

Right: Tyre degradation was the major worry for all the teams, forcing them into largely similar conservative strategies.

Far right: McLaren's brilliantly simple F-duct would push its rivals into hasty redesigns for the subsequent races.

Facing page, top: Another Schumi? Entrepreneur Willi Weber chats intently with his new protégé, Nico Hülkenberg.

Facing page, centre: Michael was back with Mercedes, which had groomed him 20 years earlier in endurance racing.

Photos: Peter J. Fox

Facing page, bottom: Nico Rosberg started his season as he meant to go on in the Mercedes team, eclipsing 'new boy' Michael Schumacher.

Photo: Andrew Hone

Hülkenberg, Pedro de la Rosa, Jaime Alguersuari, Heikki Kovalainen, Sébastien Buemi, Timo Glock, Lucas di Grassi, Jarno Trulli, Kubica, Sutil, and the HRTs of Bruno Senna and Karun Chandhok, who both started from the pits.

The HRTs might only just have been built, but one was soon back in component form: Chandhok crashed at Turn 13 on the second lap after losing control over a bump. With so little preparation time, and never having driven the car on a full fuel load, he knew neither that it was there nor the likely consequences of hitting it.

Hülkenberg dropped to the tail of the field on lap three, after spinning at Turn Six and bouncing over a kerb. He made a precautionary pit stop, but the car was still driveable – if slightly less linear than before. Di Grassi's F1 debut ended at the same point when his gearbox lost hydraulic assistance.

There were no such concerns, though, for Vettel. He edged away from Alonso during the build-up to their one scheduled stop – the leaders switched from super-soft Bridgestones to mediums on laps 17 and 16 respectively – and subsequently remained more than three seconds clear. Alonso began to reduce the deficit ten laps later, but when it was down to about a second, Vettel responded with a couple of personal bests. "I had plenty in reserve and felt totally in control," he said.

At least he did until lap 33.

"All of a sudden, I heard a strange noise," he said, "and the car lost power." He experimented with different engine maps and began to zigzag gently down the main straight, to see whether he could induce a vibration that might cure the unwanted malaise. None of this was the result of radio instructions from the team – it was just another fragment in a growing body of evidence that the German has oodles of spare mental capacity when he's driving. He didn't have much motive power, however, and on lap 34 Alonso breezed into the lead. Vettel's Renault lost about ten per cent of its straight-line performance, so Massa and Hamilton (who had passed Rosberg as a result of their tyre stops) soon capitalised, too, but the Red Bull driver refused to give up. He found that some performance came back if he leaned off the fuel mixture, and a sequence of stunning times through the labyrinthine sector two, where power was less of an issue, helped keep him beyond others' reach. He remained vulnerable on the main straight of course – where he was having to use sixth gear rather than

seventh – but was lapping swiftly enough for it not to matter. People tend not to remember fourth places, but this was a particularly fine example of the genre, and his post-race reaction was as mature as his performance. "Obviously, I'm disappointed," he said, "because I know I should have won. There is a really nice trophy in Bahrain, too, so it's a shame not to take that home, but there's no champagne on the podium, so at least I didn't miss that…"

The problem was traced later to a faulty spark plug.

Ferrari had changed both drivers' engines before the start – a precautionary measure, and the originals were scheduled to be refitted during future free practice sessions – and Alonso had a wholly trouble-free afternoon. "I couldn't match Sebastian's pace on the softer tyre," he said, "but I was controlling my situation, looking after my rubber, and thought maybe I'd have a chance to attack towards the end." No such endeavour was required, however. "All victories require a little bit of luck," he continued, "and this one was lucky."

Vettel wasn't alone with his engine problems. Massa's V8 began running hot during the second half of the race, so he countered by switching to a richer mixture and easing off to ensure he had enough Shell to make it to the end. This was a minor blip, though, during an otherwise impressive comeback drive.

However, post-race talk focused less on the racers and more on the racing – or rather its absence. The new teams might have been easy prey for such as Kubica and Sutil as they attempted to claw their way back up the field, but they were three seconds or more off the pace around a long lap such as this.

"The new rules present a different challenge," said Hamilton, "but they definitely didn't make racing more exciting in terms of being able to overtake. After the start, I was close to Nico during the first part of the lap, but it was impossible to follow him as soon as we got to the fast sectors. There just wasn't enough grip to be able to stay with him, but I think we'll have an interesting season as everybody learns how to use the tyres."

Alonso was less optimistic. "Qualifying and the start will perhaps be the two key moments this year," he said. "Unfortunately, with no refuelling strategies, it will be very difficult to see any overtaking. After the first corner, positions will more or less be settled."

Interestingly, before the season Red Bull had pushed for two pit stops to be a mandatory minimum, to diversify the strategic permutations. This had been rejected by the majority, however, not least because rivals felt Red Bull was simply trying to protect itself against excessive tyre wear, something that didn't appear to be a factor in Bahrain.

Behind Vettel, Rosberg took fifth, ahead of Schumacher, who had been undone only by a subdued qualifying performance. In terms of race pace, there was precious little between the two Mercs. "I can live with that," Schumacher said, "and have every confidence that we'll improve the car. There's a long way to go, but we'll get there."

Button followed Schumacher across the line, after vaulting Webber in the wake of the tyre stops, but echoed his rivals' frustration about the sense

Above: Old faces, new places. Heikki Kovalainen's Lotus heads Russian debutant Vitaly Petrov's Renault, and the Virgins of Glock and di Grassi.
Photo: Peter J. Fox

Above right: The gorgeous Maserati 250F, which competed in an an era when refuelling was an integral part of grand prix racing.
Photo: Paul-Henri Cahier

Right: Lewis Hamilton opened his new season with a decent enough third place for McLaren.
Photo: Peter J. Fox

of stalemate. "I probably took things a little bit too easily at the start," he said. "After that, I paced myself until the final 20 laps, when I caught Michael, but I couldn't stay close enough through the middle sector to set up a passing opportunity."

Webber added, "The new rules mean we have to look after our tyres, so you can't get too close to the car ahead or take any risks. And compared with what we're used to, it feels like you're driving a boat, with all that fuel weight. It's not going to help the racing."

In the event's immediate slipstream, there were all manner of demands for a swift regulatory shake-up, a knee-jerk response that ignored one small detail: races in Bahrain have tended to be a bit like this ever since F1 first pitched up in 2004.

The new, extended scoring system enabled Liuzzi and Barrichello to celebrate points finishes at the start of the campaign, while Kubica and Sutil recovered to finish 11th and 12th, ahead of Alguersuari ("I feel I'm in much better shape than last year, when I had very little time to train and most of my races were just taxi drives."), Hülkenberg and Kovalainen – two laps down, but best of the new teams' representatives. Lotus had set out to put bulletproofing before speed and was rewarded with a double finish, although Trulli (17th) didn't actually take the chequered flag after losing his clutch and all hydraulic assistance during the race's final moments. Buemi was similarly immobile, his engine having cut suddenly when an electrical malady struck three laps from home.

Neither Sauber finished, hydraulic problems accounting for both Kobayashi and de la Rosa, and F1's first Russian lasted only 13 laps: Petrov's offside pushrod began chafing against the chassis (he and team-mate Kubica had opted for different front ride heights), which eventually caused a suspension mounting bolt to fracture. Senna dropped out after a water pipe separated from his radiator and cooked his Cosworth, while Glock stopped –like team-mate di Grassi – with a gearbox problem, although in this instance the cause was mechanical rather than hydraulic. The Virgin – the only contemporary F1 car crafted purely on computers, without the use of a wind tunnel – was a match for Lotus in terms of speed, though, and Glock engaged in a spirited battle with Kovalainen during the race's early stages.

Close racing was possible, it seemed, between cars that didn't generate a huge amount of downforce. Funny, that…

Simon Arron

EDITOR'S VIEW
REFUELLING PROS AND CONS

REFUELLING had been banned for 2010 in the expectation that it would improve the racing by removing an irritatingly variable factor from the F1 equation. In fact, on the basis of what we saw in a distinctly processional season-opener in Bahrain, the decision to scrap this strategic element made the racing even more predictable and processional than it had been before.

Formula One has had an on-off love affair with in-race refuelling stops since long before the official FIA world championship was inaugurated in 1950. As if to prove that there is nothing new under the sun, when the great Tazio Nuvolari made a refuelling stop on his way toward his epic victory for Alfa Romeo over the massed hordes of Mercedes and Auto Union in the 1935 German Grand Prix, problems with the refuelling equipment cost him two minutes and he was forced to watch his hard-earned lead evaporate. Okay, granted he got the lead back again, but the variable introduced by a refuelling stop was every bit as nerve-wracking a strategic factor then as it would be 70 years later.

In more recent years, a fair few competitors have briskly accelerated back into the race, confident that they had enough fuel to get to the chequered flag, only to be told over their radio link from the pit wall that their sophisticated refuelling rig had not delivered the intended allocation of five-star, making another unscheduled stop a matter of some urgency, with a consequent negative effect on track position.

Yet for all its apparent risks, refuelling remained a staple diet of the F1 business through to the end of the 2.5-litre F1 in 1960. Once the 1.5-litre era began in 1961, the theoretical benefits of refuelling were so marginal and disruptive – the drivers would have to climb from their cars to make it a practical proposition – that it just wasn't worth the candle.

True, Dan Gurney might not have lost what had looked to be a certain victory in the 1964 Belgian GP at Spa-Francorchamps if the Brabham team had had extra churns of fuel available when the American pitted a couple of laps from the finish, but generally it was something to be avoided.

It was not until 1982 that refuelling made a reappearance, when Gordon Murray, chief designer for Bernie Ecclestone's Brabham F1 team, decided to equip one of the squad's BT50s for in-race refuelling in an attempt to mitigate the effects of the very heavy fuel load required by the powerful BMW four-cylinder turbocharged engine in a non-stop race.

"It's perhaps a bit difficult to believe, but it started as a joke being bandied around the design office," recalled Murray. "It was a case of, 'Why don't we start light and make a pit stop?' The sums were fairly easy to do, working out whether the idea was worthwhile, because we knew how long a fresh set of tyres would be effective and, indeed, how much time you lost by keeping going on a worn set." The first such pit stop was scheduled for Piquet's BT50 in the 1982 British GP at Brands Hatch, but the Brabham rolled to a halt with electrical problems before it could prove whether this tactical move made sense or not.

In the event, most teams climbed aboard the refuelling bandwagon for 1983, but the FIA banned the procedure – concerned about the dangers of the high-pressure refuelling systems – at the end of that season. Eleven years later, it would return as a seemingly indispensable element of the F1 format until banned again for 2010.

The initial evidence was that getting rid of refuelling for the second time in just over a generation was of debatable benefit to the strategic fabric of the sport. One argument was that if a car had to stop for tyres, why not refuel as well? A counter-argument was that if a stop for tyres was necessary, why complicate it further with the potential hazards of a procedure that had seen Jos Verstappen's car almost incinerate the pits at Hockenheim in 1994? Ignited colours of Benetton indeed.

Alan Henry

FIA F1 WORLD CHAMPIONSHIP · ROUND 1

GULF AIR BAHRAIN GRAND PRIX

SAKHIR 12–14 MARCH 2010

RACE DISTANCE: 49 laps, 191.634 miles/308.405km

RACE WEATHER: Sunny (track 41–47°C, air 33–34°C)

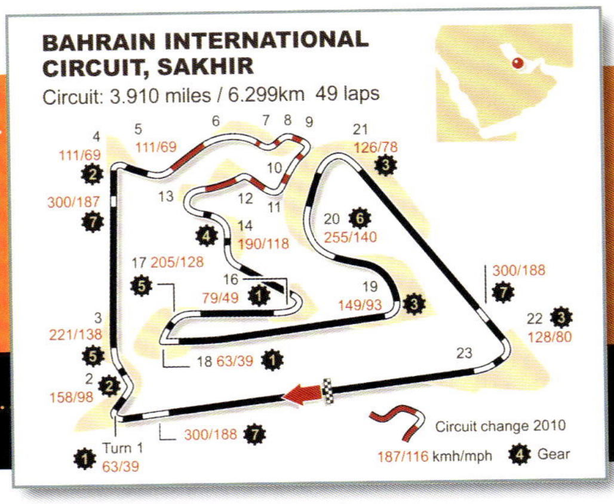

Pos.	Driver	Nat.	No.	Entrant	Car/Engine	Tyres	Laps	Time/Retirement	Speed (mph/km/h)	Gap to leader	Fastest race lap	
1	**Fernando Alonso**	E	8	Scuderia Ferrari Marlboro	Ferrari F10-056 V8	B	49	1h 39m 20.396s	115.744/186.272		1m 58.287s	45
2	**Felipe Massa**	BR	7	Scuderia Ferrari Marlboro	Ferrari F10-056 V8	B	49	1h 39m 36.495s	115.432/185.770	+ 16.099s	1m 59.732s	38
3	**Lewis Hamilton**	GB	2	Vodafone McLaren Mercedes	McLaren MP4-25-Mercedes FO108X V8	B	49	1h 39m 43.578s	115.295/185.550	+ 23.182s	1m 59.560s	42
4	**Sebastian Vettel**	D	5	Red Bull Racing	Red Bull RB6-Renault RS27 V8	B	49	1h 39m 59.195s	114.995/185.067	+ 38.799s	2m 00.218s	32
5	**Nico Rosberg**	D	4	Mercedes GP Petronas F1 Team	Mercedes MGP W01-Mercedes FO108X V8	B	49	1h 40m 00.609s	114.969/185.024	+ 40.213s	2m 00.236s	45
6	**Michael Schumacher**	GB	3	Mercedes GP Petronas F1 Team	Mercedes MGP W01-Mercedes FO108X V8	B	49	1h 40m 04.559s	114.389/184.902	+ 44.163s	2m 00.204s	45
7	**Jenson Button**	GB	1	Vodafone McLaren Mercedes	McLaren MP4-25-Mercedes FO108X V8	B	49	1h 40m 05.676s	114.872/184.868	+ 45.280s	1m 59.970s	45
8	**Mark Webber**	AUS	6	Red Bull Racing	Red Bull RB6-Renault RS27 V8	B	49	1h 40m 06.756s	114.851/184.834	+ 46.360s	1m 59.487s	45
9	**Vitantonio Liuzzi**	I	15	Force India F1 Team	Force India VJM03-Mercedes FO108X V8	B	49	1h 40m 13.404s	114.724/184.630	+ 53.008s	1m 59.906s	39
10	**Rubens Barrichello**	BR	9	AT&T Williams	Williams FW32-Cosworth CA2010 V8	B	49	1h 40m 22.885s	114.543/184.339	+ 1m 02.489s	1m 59.833s	47
11	Robert Kubica	PL	11	Renault F1 Team	Renault R30-RS27 V8	B	49	1h 40m 29.489s	114.417/184.137	+ 1m 09.093s	2m 00.474s	33
12	Adrian Sutil	D	14	Force India F1 Team	Force India VJM03-Mercedes FO108X V8	B	49	1h 40m 43.354s	114.155/183.715	+ 1m 22.958s	1m 59.393s	49
13	Jaime Alguersuari	E	17	Scuderia Toro Rosso	Toro Rosso STR5-Ferrari 056 V8	B	49	1h 40m 53.052s	113.973/183.421	+ 1m 32.656s	1m 59.964s	28
14	Nico Hülkenberg	D	10	AT&T Williams	Williams FW32-Cosworth CA2010 V8	B	48			+ 1 lap	2m 01.401s	34
15	Heikki Kovalainen	FIN	19	Lotus Racing	Lotus T127-Cosworth CA2010 V8	B	47			+ 2 laps	2m 02.701s	47
16	Sébastien Buemi	CH	16	Scuderia Toro Rosso	Toro Rosso STR5-Ferrari 056 V8	B	46	*electrics*		+ 3 laps	2m 00.080s	41
17	Jarno Trulli	I	18	Lotus Racing	Lotus T127-Cosworth CA2010 V8	B	46			+ 3 laps	2m 02.930s	34
	Pedro de la Rosa	E	22	BMW Sauber F1 Team	BMW Sauber C29-Ferrari 056 V8	B	28	*hydraulics*			2m 01.650s	27
	Bruno Senna	BR	21	HRT F1 Team	HRT F110-Cosworth CA2010 V8	B	17	*radiator/engine overheating*			2m 09.127s	14
	Timo Glock	D	24	Virgin Racing	Virgin VR-01-Cosworth CA2010 V8	B	16	*gearbox*			2m 07.062s	11
	Vitaly Petrov	RUS	12	Renault F1 Team	Renault R30-RS27 V8	B	13	*front suspension*			2m 04.307s	7
	Kamui Kobayashi	J	23	BMW Sauber F1 Team	BMW Sauber C29-Ferrari 056 V8	B	11	*hydraulics*			2m 05.044s	4
	Lucas di Grassi	BR	25	Virgin Racing	Virgin VR-01-Cosworth CA2010 V8	B	2	*hydraulics*			2m 09.361s	2
	Karun Chandhok	IND	20	HRT F1 Team	HRT F110-Cosworth CA2010 V8	B	1	*accident*			no time	

Fastest race lap: Fernando Alonso on lap 45, 1m 58.287s, 119.121mph/191.706km/h.

Lap record: Michael Schumacher (Ferrari F2004 V10), 1m 30.252s, 134.263mph/216.074km/h (2004) (3.366-mile/5.417km circuit).

Grid order	1	2	3	4	5	6	7	8	9	10	11	12	13	14	15	16	17	18	19	20	21	22	23	24	25	26	27	28	29	30	31	32	33	34	35	36	37	38
5 VETTEL	5	5	5	5	5	5	5	5	5	5	5	5	5	5	5	5	5	5	5	5	5	5	5	5	5	5	5	5	5	5	5	5	5	8	8	8	8	8
7 MASSA	8	8	8	8	8	8	8	8	8	8	8	8	8	8	8	8	7	8	8	8	8	8	8	8	8	8	8	8	8	8	8	8	8	5	7	7	7	7
8 ALONSO	7	7	7	7	7	7	7	7	7	7	7	7	7	7	7	7	8	7	7	7	7	7	7	7	7	7	7	7	7	7	7	7	7	7	5	5	5	2
2 HAMILTON	4	4	4	4	4	4	4	4	4	4	4	4	4	4	4	4	15	15	15	2	2	2	2	2	2	2	2	2	2	2	2	2	2	2	2	2	2	5
4 ROSBERG	2	2	2	2	2	2	2	2	2	2	2	2	2	2	2	6	9	9	2	15	4	4	4	4	4	4	4	4	4	4	4	4	4	4	4	4	4	4
6 WEBBER	3	3	3	3	3	3	3	3	3	3	3	3	3	3	6	1	2	2	4	4	3	3	3	3	3	3	3	3	3	3	3	3	3	3	3	3	3	3
3 SCHUMACHER	6	6	6	6	6	6	6	6	6	6	6	6	6	6	3	15	4	4	9	3	1	1	1	1	1	1	1	1	1	1	1	1	1	1	1	1	1	1
1 BUTTON	1	1	1	1	1	1	1	1	1	1	1	1	1	1	1	9	3	3	3	1	6	6	6	6	6	6	6	6	6	6	6	6	6	6	6	6	6	6
11 KUBICA	15	15	15	15	15	15	15	15	15	15	15	15	15	15	15	2	1	1	1	6	16	15	15	15	15	15	15	15	15	15	15	15	15	15	15	15	15	15
14 SUTIL	9	9	9	9	9	9	9	9	9	9	9	9	9	9	9	3	6	6	6	16	15	16	9	9	9	9	9	9	9	9	9	9	9	9	9	9	9	9
9 BARRICHELLO	12	12	12	12	12	12	12	12	12	12	12	12	12	22	16	16	16	16	16	9	9	9	16	16	11	11	11	11	11	11	11	11	11	11	11	11	11	11
15 LIUZZI	23	23	23	23	23	23	23	23	23	22	22	22	22	16	14	22	22	22	22	22	22	22	22	11	22	22	22	22	14	14	14	14	14	14	14	14	14	14
10 HULKENBERG	10	10	22	22	22	22	22	22	22	23	23	17	16	14	22	11	11	11	11	11	11	11	11	22	17	17	14	14	17	17	17	17	17	17	17	17	17	17
22 DE LA ROSA	22	22	17	17	17	17	17	17	17	17	17	16	17	11	11	17	17	17	17	17	17	17	17	17	16	14	17	17	16	16	16	16	16	16	16	16	16	16
16 BUEMI	17	17	16	16	16	16	16	16	16	16	16	14	14	17	17	14	14	14	14	14	14	14	14	14	14	16	16	16	10	10	10	10	10	10	10	10	10	10
23 KOBAYASHI	19	16	11	11	11	11	11	11	11	11	11	11	11	19	19	19	10	10	10	10	10	10	10	10	10	10	10	10	19	19	18	18	18	18	18	18	18	18
12 PETROV	16	19	19	19	14	14	14	14	14	14	14	19	24	10	10	10	19	19	19	19	19	19	19	19	19	19	19	19	18	18	19	19	19	19	19	19	19	19
17 ALGUERSUARI	24	11	24	14	19	19	19	19	19	19	19	24	19	24	18	18	18	18	18	18	18	18	18	18	18	18	18	18										
24 GLOCK	25	24	14	24	24	24	24	24	24	24	24	18	10	18	24	24	21																					
18 TRULLI	18	25	18	18	18	18	18	18	18	18	18	10	18	21	21	21																						
19 KOVALAINEN	11	14	10	21	21	10	10	10	10	10	21	21																										
25 DI GRASSI	14	18	21	21	10	10	21	21	21	21	21																											
21 SENNA	21	21																																				
20 CHANDHOK	20																																					

TIME SHEETS

PRACTICE 1 (FRIDAY)
Weather: Sunny
Temperatures: track 37–42°C, air 29–31°C

Pos.	Driver	Laps	Time
1	Adrian Sutil	18	1m 56.583s
2	Fernando Alonso	18	1m 56.766s
3	Robert Kubica	19	1m 57.041s
4	Felipe Massa	19	1m 57.055s
5	Jenson Button	19	1m 57.068s
6	Lewis Hamilton	19	1m 57.163s
7	Vitantonio Liuzzi	19	1m 57.194s
8	Nico Rosberg	15	1m 57.199s
9	Mark Webber	17	1m 57.255s
10	Michael Schumacher	16	1m 57.662s
11	Jaime Alguersuari	18	1m 57.722s
12	Nico Hülkenberg	20	1m 57.894s
13	Sebastian Vettel	17	1m 57.943s
14	Sébastien Buemi	13	1m 58.399s
15	Rubens Barrichello	11	1m 58.782s
16	Vitaly Petrov	13	1m 58.880s
17	Pedro de la Rosa	18	2m 00.250s
18	Kamui Kobayashi	11	2m 01.388s
19	Timo Glock	8	2m 03.680s
20	Heikki Kovalainen	21	2m 03.848s
21	Jarno Trulli	15	2m 03.970s
22	Lucas di Grassi	2	no time
23	Bruno Senna	3	no time

PRACTICE 2 (FRIDAY)
Weather: Sunny
Temperatures: track 44–47°C, air 33°C

Pos.	Driver	Laps	Time
1	Nico Rosberg	23	1m 55.409s
2	Lewis Hamilton	22	1m 55.854s
3	Michael Schumacher	23	1m 55.903s
4	Jenson Button	28	1m 56.076s
5	Sebastian Vettel	18	1m 56.459s
6	Nico Hülkenberg	26	1m 56.501s
7	Felipe Massa	30	1m 56.555s
8	Vitaly Petrov	26	1m 56.750s
9	Fernando Alonso	25	1m 57.140s
10	Pedro de la Rosa	24	1m 57.255s
11	Kamui Kobayashi	27	1m 57.352s
12	Adrian Sutil	29	1m 57.361s
13	Rubens Barrichello	21	1m 57.452s
14	Vitantonio Liuzzi	29	1m 57.833s
15	Robert Kubica	29	1m 58.155s
16	Jaime Alguersuari	31	1m 59.799s
17	Mark Webber	12	2m 00.444s
18	Heikki Kovalainen	23	2m 00.873s
19	Jarno Trulli	14	2m 00.990s
20	Timo Glock	3	2m 02.037s
21	Lucas di Grassi	21	2m 02.188s
22	Bruno Senna	17	2m 06.968s
23	Sébastien Buemi	1	no time

PRACTICE 3 (SATURDAY)
Weather: Sunny
Temperatures: track 43–45°C, air 32°C

Pos.	Driver	Laps	Time
1	Fernando Alonso	14	1m 54.099s
2	Nico Rosberg	13	1m 54.368s
3	Mark Webber	15	1m 54.500s
4	Michael Schumacher	13	1m 54.533s
5	Sebastian Vettel	16	1m 54.646s
6	Felipe Massa	14	1m 54.739s
7	Jenson Button	14	1m 55.000s
8	Robert Kubica	15	1m 55.331s
9	Vitantonio Liuzzi	11	1m 55.432s
10	Nico Hülkenberg	13	1m 55.461s
11	Adrian Sutil	13	1m 55.521s
12	Lewis Hamilton	8	1m 55.860s
13	Pedro de la Rosa	14	1m 56.063s
14	Rubens Barrichello	15	1m 56.259s
15	Sébastien Buemi	17	1m 56.295s
16	Jaime Alguersuari	16	1m 56.504s
17	Kamui Kobayashi	14	1m 56.530s
18	Vitaly Petrov	16	1m 56.811s
19	Timo Glock	10	1m 59.173s
20	Heikki Kovalainen	15	1m 59.789s
21	Jarno Trulli	5	2m 01.259s
22	Bruno Senna	11	2m 04.001s
23	Lucas di Grassi	2	no time

QUALIFYING (SATURDAY)
Weather: Sunny Temperatures: track 45–48°C, air 34°C

Pos.	Driver	First	Second	Third	Qualifying Tyre
1	Sebastian Vettel	1m 55.029s	1m 53.883s	1m 54.101s	Super-Soft
2	Felipe Massa	1m 55.313s	1m 54.331s	1m 54.242s	Super-Soft
3	Fernando Alonso	1m 54.612s	1m 54.172s	1m 54.608s	Super-Soft
4	Lewis Hamilton	1m 55.341s	1m 54.707s	1m 55.217s	Super-Soft
5	Nico Rosberg	1m 55.463s	1m 54.682s	1m 55.241s	Super-Soft
6	Mark Webber	1m 55.298s	1m 54.318s	1m 55.284s	Super-Soft
7	Michael Schumacher	1m 55.593s	1m 55.105s	1m 55.524s	Super-Soft
8	Jenson Button	1m 55.715s	1m 55.168s	1m 55.672s	Super-Soft
9	Robert Kubica	1m 55.511s	1m 54.963s	1m 55.885s	Super-Soft
10	Adrian Sutil	1m 55.213s	1m 54.996s	1m 56.309s	Medium
11	Rubens Barrichello	1m 55.969s	1m 55.330s		
12	Vitantonio Liuzzi	1m 55.628s	1m 55.653s		
13	Nico Hülkenberg	1m 56.375s	1m 55.857s		
14	Pedro de la Rosa	1m 56.428s	1m 56.237s		
15	Sébastien Buemi	1m 56.189s	1m 56.265s		
16	Kamui Kobayashi	1m 56.541s	1m 56.270s		
17	Vitaly Petrov	1m 56.167s	1m 56.619s		
18	Jaime Alguersuari	1m 57.071s			
19	Timo Glock	1m 59.728s			
20	Jarno Trulli	1m 59.852s			
21	Heikki Kovalainen	2m 00.313s			
22	Lucas di Grassi	2m 00.587s			
23	Bruno Senna	2m 03.240s			
24	Karun Chandhok	2m 04.904s			

FOR THE RECORD

1st GRAND PRIX (drivers): Chandhok, di Grassi, Hülkenberg, Petrov, Senna
1st GRAND PRIX (teams): HRT, Virgin
250th START: Michael Schumacher
80th 1-2 FINISH: Ferrari
10th FRONT ROW: Sebastian Vettel

DID YOU KNOW

This was the first grand prix for Lotus since Australia on 13th November, 1994.

This was the first race since 1993 in which refuelling was banned, and the first since the Pacific Grand Prix 1995 in which 24 cars were entered.

This was the first time since 1968 (Clark & Hill at Lotus) that two British world champions drove for the same team.

Fernando Alonso became the 37th driver to win a grand prix in a Ferrari.

POINTS

DRIVERS

1	Fernando Alonso	25
2	Felipe Massa	18
3	Lewis Hamilton	15
4	Sebastian Vettel	12
5	Nico Rosberg	10
6	Michael Schumacher	8
7	Jenson Button	6
8	Mark Webber	4
9	Vitantonio Liuzzi	3
10	Rubens Barrichello	1

CONSTRUCTORS

1	Ferrari	43
2	McLaren	21
3	Mercedes	18
4	Red Bull	16
5	Force India	2
6	Williams	1

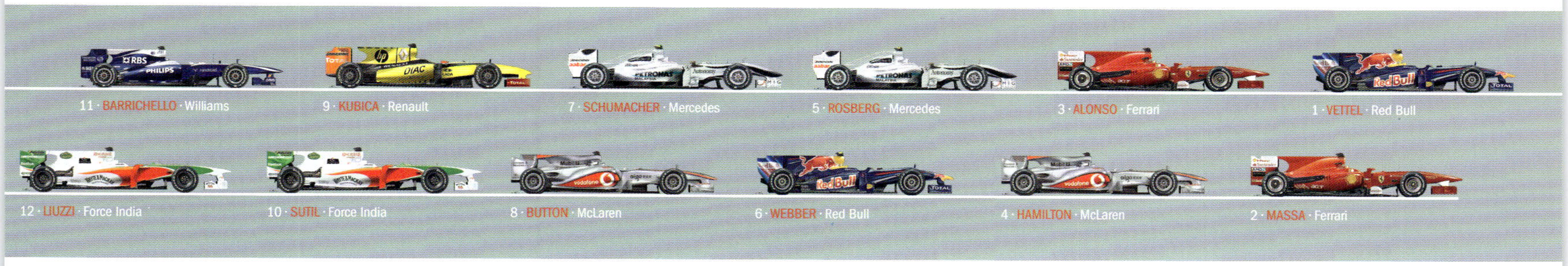

39	40	41	42	43	44	45	46	47	48	49	
8	8	8	8	8	8	8	8	8	8	8	1
7	7	7	7	7	7	7	7	7	7	7	2
2	2	2	2	2	2	2	2	2	2	2	3
5	5	5	5	5	5	5	5	5	5	5	
4	4	4	4	4	4	4	4	4	4	4	
3	3	3	3	3	3	3	3	3	3	3	6
1	1	1	1	1	1	1	1	1	1	1	7
6	6	6	6	6	6	6	6	6	6	6	8
15	15	15	15	15	15	15	15	15	15	15	
9	9	9	9	9	9	9	9	9	9	9	10
11	11	11	11	11	11	11	11	11	11	11	
14	14	14	14	14	14	14	14	14	14	14	
17	17	17	17	17	17	17	17	17	17	17	
16	16	16	16	16	16	16	16	*10*	*10*		
10	*10*	*10*	*10*	*10*	*10*	*10*	*10*	*19*			
18	*18*	*19*	*19*	*19*	*19*	*19*	*19*				
19	*19*	*18*	*18*	*18*	*18*	*18*	*18*				

21 Pit stop
14 One lap or more behind

RACE TYRE STRATEGIES

	Driver	Race Stint 1	Race Stint 2	Race Stint 3
1	Alonso	Super-Soft: 1-16	Medium: 17-49	
2	Massa	Super-Soft: 1-17	Medium: 18-49	
3	Hamilton	Super-Soft: 1-15	Medium: 16-49	
4	Vettel	Super-Soft: 1-17	Medium: 18-49	
5	Rosberg	Super-Soft: 1-16	Medium: 17-49	
6	Schumacher	Super-Soft: 1-15	Super-Soft: 16-49	
7	Button	Super-Soft: 1-16	Medium: 17-49	
8	Webber	Super-Soft: 1-16	Medium: 17-49	
9	Liuzzi	Medium: 1-20	Super-Soft: 21-49	
10	Barrichello	Medium: 1-19	Super-Soft: 20-49	
11	Kubica	Super-Soft: 1-12	Medium: 13-49	
12	Sutil	Medium: 1-15	Super-Soft: 16-49	
13	Alguersuari	Medium: 1-13	Super-Soft: 14-26	Medium: 27-49
14	Hülkenberg	Super-Soft: 1-3	Medium: 4-25	Super-Soft: 26-48
15	Kovalainen	Medium: 1-30	Super-Soft: 31-47	
16	Buemi	Medium: 1-25	Super-Soft: 26-46 (dnf)	
17	Trulli	Medium: 1-24	Super-Soft: 25-46	
	de la Rosa	Super-Soft: 1-14	Medium: 15-28 (dnf)	
	Senna	Super-Soft: 1-11	Super-Soft: 12-17 (dnf)	
	Glock	Medium: 1-16 (dnf)		
	Petrov	Medium: 1-13 (dnf)		
	Kobayashi	Medium: 1-11 (dnf)		
	di Grassi	Medium: 1-2 (dnf)		
	Chandhok	Super-Soft: 0 (dnf)		

The tyre regulations stipulate that the two dry tyre specifications must be used during the race.
The Super-Soft compound Bridgestone Potenza tyre is marked with a green stripe on the sidewall.

Photos: Peter J. Fox

FIA FORMULA 1 WORLD CHAMPIONSHIP · ROUND 2

AUSTRALIAN GRAND PRIX

MELBOURNE CIRCUIT

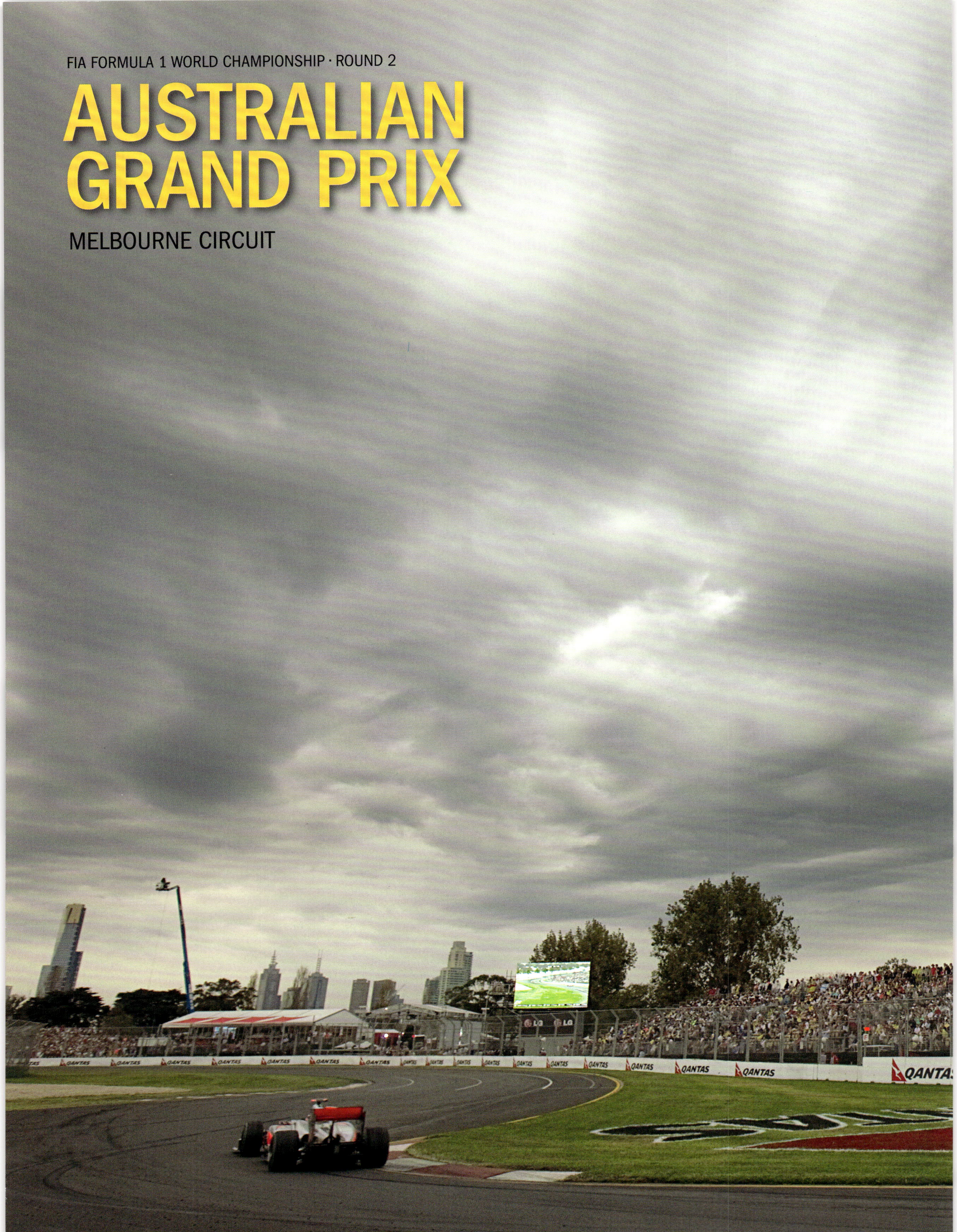

Main photo: Jenson Button heads for his first victory at the wheel of a McLaren beneath ominous skies over Albert Park.

Inset left: Jenson relishes a moment that vindicated his decision to switch teams after winning the 2009 title .

Photos: Peter J Fox

MELBOURNE QUALIFYING

FOR the first time since Australia hosted a world championship grand prix, in 1985, a homespun driver qualified on the front row. The local media, though, was focusing mainly on the bloke who lined up 11th, or Lewis Hamilton as he is popularly known. "GP ACE HOON SHAME" was the most prominent headline. It spoke volumes for the world's contemporary obsession with fluff and scandal. Hamilton's perceived misdemeanour was the kind of thing that used to be expected of Formula One drivers, and accepted as such. When leaving the circuit on Friday evening, he'd jinked out of the traffic queue as the lights turned green, passed a couple of cars ahead and executed a perfectly controlled power slide on to the broad main boulevard. Bruno Senna, one of those he'd overtaken, had been impressed by Hamilton's poise, but the Victorian State Police had a different perspective, and he was charged eventually with "deliberately losing control of a motor vehicle". Which, of course, is precisely what he hadn't done. In line with modern protocol, a trite public apology followed.

The subsequently overlooked Mark Webber sprang to Hamilton's defence and passed a couple of comments that juxtaposed the words "Australia" and "nanny state", at which point he started to get it in the neck, too. You had to dig quite a long way into the papers to establish that a motor race was taking place somewhere in Melbourne.

Conditions were overcast on Saturday, which encouraged everybody to complete banker laps at the start of the three qualifying sectors, but the rain held off and the result was the same at the end of each: Sebastian Vettel fastest, although he shaded Webber by just 0.116 seconds at the end of Q3, when both Red Bulls looked a touch ragged. "That's what happens when you are looking for time that probably wasn't there," said Webber. It was a mark of the Red Bulls' superiority that they were the only cars to breeze through Q2 without having to resort to the soft Bridgestone.

Fernando Alonso was an in-touch third for Ferrari, ahead of Jenson Button. "We lacked grip this morning," said the world champion, "but the car felt better in qualifying, except for Q3, when the balance went away. I had a bit of understeer, but it only cost me a tenth or two, so at best we're still half a second or so away from the pace-setters."

And Hamilton's 11th place? McLaren team principal Martin Whitmarsh described his charge as "distracted" in the wake of off-track events, but the driver himself thought otherwise. "Things haven't been easy today," he said, "but I've had great support. It's not as though I walked in here this morning and had everybody turn their backs on me. We work together through thick and thin. I put my hands up; I made a mistake and they supported me through it. I got in the car feeling quite good, to be honest. Q1 felt great, but in Q2 I struggled with the rear tyres for some reason."

Webber had been exposed to pressures of a very different kind. Did he feel as though he was bearing the hopes of a nation on his shoulders? "Not really," he said, "because I know tomorrow's papers will be wrapping fish and chips on Monday. They're very fickle, and most people down here obviously think this is the only race of the season. I have a much, much bigger thing in mind."

Above: Keeping the fans happy. Lewis Hamilton signs autographs for his supporters.
Photo: Paul-Henri Cahier

Left: No stopping him: Sebastian Vettel bagged yet another pole for Red Bull.

Right: Nico Rosberg eclipsed Schumacher again, finishing five places ahead of the former world champion.
Photos: Peter J Fox

Far right: Waiting on a friend? Back to journalism for Peter Windsor after his failed bid to get the USF1 team on to the 2010 grid.
Photo: Lukas Gorys

LEWIS HAMILTON
vodafone
AUSTRALIAN GRAND PRIX

PETRONAS
SYNTIUM

THE start might have been several hours away, but hospitality was already flowing freely. The clink of crystal flutes was momentarily drowned out, however, by the passing sound of history – the final race in the Tasman Cup Revival Series for Formula 5000 cars, a staple of the early 1970s. The corporate minority weren't the only ones for whom this was a champagne moment: second place was enough to secure the title for Kiwi Ken Smith, at the tender age of 68. It was an uplifting motif at the dawn of a positive day for the sport as a whole.

It took just a fortnight to stifle the mistaken assumption that grand prix racing had been condemned to a season of processional predictability. When Melbourne staged its first twilight race, in 2009, drivers had complained about the difficulty of picking out the correct racing line amid the setting sun's shadows. There were no such problems this time, not least because there was no sun: there were mild concerns, however, that it might be pitch dark by the time the race finished.

With the clouds came also rain, little more than mild drizzle, but enough to persuade the whole field to start on intermediates. For the second time in as many races, Sebastian Vettel made a clean start from pole, while Felipe Massa timed his getaway to perfection to beat Mark Webber to the Turn One apex and annex second. Just behind, though, there was mild pandemonium. Fernando Alonso attempted to claim space already occupied by Jenson Button, bounced off the McLaren and spun into Michael Schumacher, the Ferrari's gearbox inflicting significant damage to the Merc's floor and sidepod. Usually one of the most alert of all drivers, the Spaniard was partially caught out by the borderline uselessness of the outboard mirrors *du jour*. They might have sent out positive messages in the wind tunnel, but they weren't much help if you wanted to know what was going on in the immediate neighbourhood.

Consequently, Button dropped a couple of places, while Alonso slipped to last and Schumacher pitted at the lap's end, by which time the safety car had already been dispatched. The trigger had been a spectacular collision on the approach to Turn Six, where Kamui Kobayashi had lost a) his front wing and b) control. He speared right into the retaining wall and bounced back into the midfield pack, collecting Sébastien Buemi and the equally innocent Nico

Above: The boys at McLaren work on their strategies.
Photo: Jad Sherif/WRi2

Above right: Fernando Alonso blotted his copybook with a first-corner spin involving Button's McLaren.
Photo: Studio Colombo/WRi2

Left: Film star and qualified commercial pilot John Travolta was a guest of honour of race sponsor Qantas.
Photo: Peter J. Fox

Hülkenberg. Kobayashi had suffered two front wing failures in practice – the first after he had clipped a marker cone, the second because the team had not replaced a stay that had been damaged in the initial incident – and this one was put down to contact with another car shortly after the start, although Kobayashi couldn't pinpoint whom he'd hit.

All three were out on the spot and the race did not resume until the end of lap 4, with Vettel leading Massa, Webber, Robert Kubica (up from ninth), Nico Rosberg, Button, Hamilton (who had taken to the grass to avoid the first-corner nonsense), Adrian Sutil, Rubens Barrichello, Vitaly Petrov, Pedro de la Rosa, Tonio Liuzzi, Jaime Alguersuari, Heikki Kovalainen, Bruno Senna, Karun Chandhok, Timo Glock, Alonso, Lucas di Grassi and Schumacher. Both Virgins started from the pits – after having fresh fuel collectors fitted in the wake of persistent pick-up problems on Saturday – and Jarno Trulli was pushed straight into retirement from the grid after last-minute hydraulic problems. Senna joined him on the sidelines, for the same reason, almost as soon as the race restarted.

The rain-hit opening stages were manna for Hamilton's improvisational nous. He passed Button on lap six, but a few dry patches were beginning to

appear and the defending champion dived straight into the pits for a set of super-softs. Button is almost second to nobody when it comes to managing dry tyres on a damp track, but if his instincts were correct, he would have to make a single set of Bridgestones last almost 90 minutes. Then again, he's quite good at that, too. "My rear tyres were going away so quickly," he said, "that I knew there had to be enough grip to use slicks. The pit lane was absolutely saturated when I came in, though, and I thought I might have made a catastrophic decision."

His pessimism didn't improve when he slid off the road almost as soon as he'd left the pits, but it didn't take long for him to start setting the race's fastest sector times to date, at which point the pit lane became conspicuously busy. Many of the leading runners came in at the end of lap eight, but Vettel stayed out for one extra lap – and Webber for two. "When you're in front," said Red Bull sporting director Christian Horner, "you have to react to others around you. Jenson had run wide on his slicks and it looked as though he might have changed too soon. Sebastian had a comfortable cushion, so for us it was a matter of monitoring the track conditions and playing it safe."

Safe for Vettel meant keeping the lead, but while Webber's extra lap prevented him from being stacked behind his team-mate in the pits, it cost him a couple of positions. He also struggled to engage second as he rejoined – and then slid off at Turn One, which dropped him to sixth, behind Button, Kubica, Rosberg and Massa. The Pole had actually left the pits just ahead of Button, but he was easy prey on cold tyres, and the McLaren swept ahead at Turn Three.

Vettel had less than half a second in hand after his stop, but subsequently was able to increase that at will. He was 4.5 seconds clear of Button, and wholly in control, until lap 26, when he noticed a few sparks from the front left wheel. The team ordered him to pit, for a precautionary change, but he didn't get that far. "A big vibration was building up," he said, "and as soon as I touched the brakes for Turn 13, I had some sort of failure and went straight into the gravel." Initially, he suspected a brake problem, but it transpired that the wheel nut had worked loose – one of the locating pins had become fractionally misaligned – and damaged the wheel mounting.

That gifted Button the lead, from Kubica and Hamilton. Webber and Hamilton had both passed Massa on lap 16, but then tripped over each other and allowed the Ferrari back ahead – or two Ferraris in Webber's case, as the recovering Alonso had slipped through, too. Hamilton finally nailed the Brazilian six laps later, but the two cars touched on the main straight. That cost the McLaren a bit of wing and a ten-point frontal balance shift that deprived the Englishman of grip, but he was still able to usurp Rosberg on lap 26 (by which stage, Alonso and Webber had swapped places again, after the Spaniard had stumbled while trying to pass his own team-mate).

Schumacher, running well down, had struggled for many laps to pass Alguersuari, and on lap 29 he pitted for a second set of super-softs, which triggered a sequence of ultra-quick sector times. Webber, Rosberg and Hamilton were duly summoned in for fresh rubber.

In the Australian's case, Red Bull felt it a gamble worth taking: Webber's race had already been compromised and if the cars at the front trashed their tyres, a podium might be salvageable. McLaren made the call on Hamilton's behalf – a decision both parties would regret. "Lewis was losing time behind Kubica at that point," said team principal Martin Whitmarsh, "and we could see his left rear

tyre graining. Schumacher and Webber had changed tyres and were going very quickly. At the time, we felt it was the right call, but as the race wore on he – and we – could see it wasn't. With hindsight, if he'd stayed out, he could have finished second, but it was a team decision and I'm accountable." Part of the afternoon's main entertainment on Radio McLaren was an irate rant from 'Disgruntled of Stevenage'. Especially when he learned that those ahead weren't planning to stop again. "I was very surprised when Lewis pitted," said Kubica. "At first, I thought it must be a drive-through. He was much quicker than me and not too far behind Jenson. If he had managed to overtake me at that stage of the race, he would most probably have gone for it."

Mercedes brought Rosberg in because Hamilton seemed to have overtaken him a bit too easily. The team suspected that Nico might become a sitting duck for others, but in fact he'd lost out only because of the McLaren's superior top-end speed – a by-product of the team's aero regulator (by now frantically being copied almost everywhere) that stalled the rear wing along the straights to reduce drag.

Button, though, had no need to gamble. His pace and consistency on worn tyres were sensational. He was driving as quickly as required: no more, no less. From laps 31 to 44, he delivered a string of mid-1m 30s and then dipped into the 1m 29s as the fuel load lightened. On successive laps, his pace rarely shifted by more than a couple of tenths, give or take the occasional need to pass slower cars. "He wouldn't have wanted to push the tyres too hard right at the end," said Whitmarsh, "particularly the rears, but he had looked after them beautifully."

And besides, he'd already pulled out enough of a gap to eliminate any need to push.

Behind, Kubica did a similarly stellar job in a slightly less effective car to take second. "My guys did a fantastic job to get me ahead of Felipe at the stop," he said, "but there was no way I could fight with Jenson because he was too quick on the straights and already had heat in his tyres."

Massa benefited from Hamilton's stop to take third – his best result in Australia – while Alonso recovered almost imperceptibly from his early delay and inherited fourth as a result of the misguided two-stopping frenzy that broke out around half-distance. Hamilton and Webber used their fresh rubber to close down the two Ferraris, but there was no way through. Their four-car procession fell apart on lap 56, when Hamilton tried, but failed to get inside Alonso at Turn 13 and Webber harpooned the McLaren. Hamilton spun and lost a position to Rosberg as he scrabbled through the gravel, while Webber had to pit for a new nose and slipped to ninth, behind Liuzzi and Barrichello. "I apologised to Lewis afterwards," Webber said. "I simply got a bit too close and lost downforce." The stewards summoned him for a chat and issued a reprimand.

Schumacher claimed the final point – after taking an age to pass Alguersuari for a second time – and de la Rosa, Kovalainen and Chandhok (HRT's first finisher) were the only other drivers classified.

Sutil retired when his engine lapsed on to four cylinders soon after the restart, and Petrov spun into the Turn Three gravel within a couple of laps of switching to slicks. Neither Virgin completed the distance: a hydraulic leak stopped di Grassi, while Glock pulled in with 17 laps to go. Before the weekend, it had become apparent that the team's fuel tank would not be large enough to guarantee a full race distance at certain tracks, a detail it would be permitted to change later, but when Glock retired the team was keen that everybody should know he had not run dry: rather, some shims had fallen from the rear suspension (so that's all right, then).

There had been few such dramas at the front. "I had a big worry on about lap 15," Button said, "when the rear tyres started going away and I had a lot of graining. I thought, 'That's it, they're just going to swallow me up.' I took out a lot of front wing, closed the diff and just hoped for the best really. Towards the end, I could start pushing, got the balance back and the car felt very good. I was in a very happy place for the last 20 laps."

By then, he also had time to watch the trackside TV monitors and take in some of the chaos in his slipstream. "It seemed to be a much more exciting race than Bahrain," he said, "so hopefully we'll have a few more like it. Today was obviously unusual, and I don't know where we stand in terms of overall pace, but that's not always what racing is about."

Simon Arron

EDITOR'S VIEW
BUTTON CARVES A PLACE AT McLAREN

IT was the moment of vindication for Jenson Button. Some F1 insiders had not believed that it would come so quickly, others were confident that he would get the hang of working inside McLaren rather more promptly. Either way, winning the Australian GP after an outstandingly astute decision to make an early switch to slick rubber provided Button with a copybook psychological edge at an early stage in his relationship with the Woking superteam.

Jenson's decision to move to McLaren had signalled that he had surrounded himself with like-minded advisors who could see the logic behind his thinking. It was all very mature and reasoned. The first point was that McLaren had a matchless reputation, forged over three decades, for offering parity of equipment to its drivers. The second was that a team of McLaren's proven status would probably only come knocking once in an F1 driver's career. So the moment the approach had been made, in Jenson's mind it was almost inconceivable that he should turn it down. From the outset, it was clear that he was not worried about any pressure from the sitting tenant.

The first real sign of Jenson's steely self-belief about the 2010 season came on 7th January, when a group of British journalists was invited to participate in a telephone media conference as the snow lay on the ground deep and crisp and even. The newly crowned world champion radiated his customary affable assurance: confident, but not cocky; competitive, but not aggressive.

That same morning, former Ferrari ace Eddie Irvine, a man who knows all about challenging team-mates after his stint at Maranello alongside Michael Schumacher, was interviewed by ESPN and offered the view that Jenson must have been mad to switch from Brawn to McLaren. Drawing on his own experience with the great German star, which from the outset had seen him cast in a deferential role, he concluded that the pressure Button would face slotting in alongside young Lewis would be more than he could handle.

In Irvine's view, Hamilton would take him apart. He would be "murdered" by Lewis. It was a typically extreme opinion from the man who had come close to winning the 1999 world championship, still as controversial and outspoken as ever. But he would be proved incorrect. Button showed in Australia that he was not only clever, but also imperturbable under pressure.

They were qualities that would stand him in good stead as the season unfolded. Button's success had been a long time coming, but it was all the sweeter for the wait. Throughout 2009, he had seemed to grow comfortably into his own skin. Strolling through the paddock alone, he radiated the assurance of somebody very much at ease with himself and at peace with the world. He was pleasantly indulgent with the media, handling them with skill and forbearance. The boy had very definitely grown into the man.

Jenson's transition to McLaren was as seamless as it was effective. If Lewis didn't like the idea of a fellow Brit trying to rain on his personal parade, he hid it very well. You could see his point: "Hell, I was the man who effectively drove Fernando Alonso out of the McLaren team. I can handle anything." But Jenson would turn out to be a tougher nut than the Spaniard who, with the benefit of hindsight, significantly compromised his F1 career when he fell out with Ron Dennis and Martin Whitmarsh.

At the launch of the 2010 McLaren-Mercedes, Jenson seemed to take command. Slightly taller than Lewis, he seemed to be dictating the way in which they pulled the cover off to reveal the first MP4-25. Of course, the new kid on the block inevitably gets the most attention – initially, anyway – and Jenson seemed to be revelling in it without going over the top.

Alan Henry

Above: Robert Kubica stormed to a superb second place for Renault in Melbourne, signalling his competitive quality at the front of the field.

Right: John and Jenson Button get an early opportunity to celebrate victory with the McLaren team.

Photos: Jad Sherif/WRi2

FIA F1 WORLD CHAMPIONSHIP · ROUND 2

QANTAS AUSTRALIAN GRAND PRIX

MELBOURNE 26–28 MARCH 2010

RACE DISTANCE: 58 laps, 191.118 miles/307.574km

RACE WEATHER: Drizzle/cloudy (track 24–25°C, air 21–26°C)

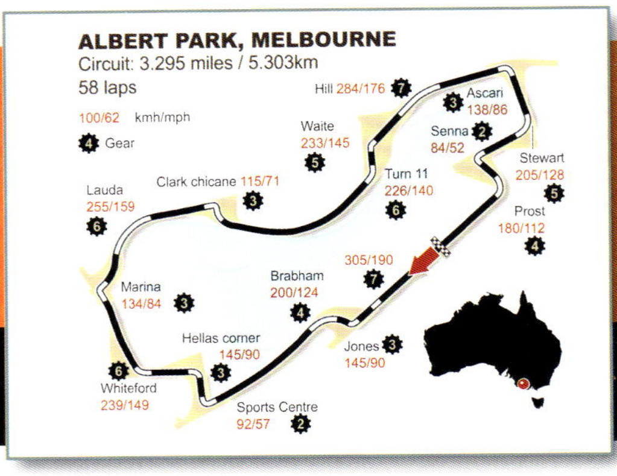

Pos.	Driver	Nat.	No.	Entrant	Car/Engine	Tyres	Laps	Time/Retirement	Speed (mph/km/h)	Gap to leader	Fastest race lap	
1	**Jenson Button**	GB	1	Vodafone McLaren Mercedes	McLaren MP4-25-Mercedes FO108X V8	B	58	1h 33m 36.531s	122.500/197.144		1m 29.291s	52
2	**Robert Kubica**	PL	11	Renault F1 Team	Renault R30-RS27 V8	B	58	1h 33m 48.565s	122.237/196.722	+ 12.034s	1m 29.570s	52
3	**Felipe Massa**	BR	7	Scuderia Ferrari Marlboro	Ferrari F10-056 V8	B	58	1h 33m 51.019s	122.184/196.636	+ 14.488s	1m 29.537s	52
4	**Fernando Alonso**	E	8	Scuderia Ferrari Marlboro	Ferrari F10-056 V8	B	58	1h 33m 52.835s	122.145/196.573	+ 16.304s	1m 29.707s	47
5	**Nico Rosberg**	D	4	Mercedes GP Petronas F1 Team	Mercedes MGP W01-Mercedes FO108X V8	B	58	1h 33m 53.214s	122.137/196.560	+ 16.683s	1m 28.489s	53
6	**Lewis Hamilton**	GB	2	Vodafone McLaren Mercedes	McLaren MP4-25-Mercedes FO108X V8	B	58	1h 34m 06.429s	121.851/196.100	+ 29.898s	1m 28.506s	47
7	**Vitantonio Liuzzi**	I	15	Force India F1 Team	Force India VJM03-Mercedes FO108X V8	B	58	1h 34m 36.378s	121.208/195.065	+ 59.847s	1m 29.685s	55
8	**Rubens Barrichello**	BR	9	AT&T Williams	Williams FW32-Cosworth CA2010 V8	B	58	1h 34m 37.067s	121.193/195.041	+ 1m 00.536s	1m 29.210s	58
9	**Mark Webber**	AUS	6	Red Bull Racing	Red Bull RB6-Renault RS27 V8	B	58	1h 34m 43.850s	121.049/194.809	+ 1m 07.319s	1m 28.358s	47
10	**Michael Schumacher**	GB	3	Mercedes GP Petronas F1 Team	Mercedes MGP W01-Mercedes FO108X V8	B	58	1h 34m 45.922s	121.005/194.738	+ 1m 09.391s	1m 29.185s	58
11	Jaime Alguersuari	E	17	Scuderia Toro Rosso	Toro Rosso STR5-Ferrari 056 V8	B	58	1h 34m 47.832s	120.964/194.672	+ 1m 11.301s	1m 29.713s	49
12	Pedro de la Rosa	E	22	BMW Sauber F1 Team	BMW Sauber C29-Ferrari 056 V8	B	58	1h 34m 50.615s	120.905/194.577	+ 1m 14.084s	1m 30.587s	54
13	Heikki Kovalainen	FIN	19	Lotus Racing	Lotus T127-Cosworth CA2010 V8	B	56			+ 2 laps	1m 33.638s	52
14	Karun Chandhok	IND	20	HRT F1 Team	HRT F110-Cosworth CA2010 V8	B	53			+ 5 laps	1m 35.045s	48
	Timo Glock	D	24	Virgin Racing	Virgin VR-01-Cosworth CA2010 V8	B	41	*rear suspension*			1m 34.230s	37
	Lucas di Grassi	BR	25	Virgin Racing	Virgin VR-01-Cosworth CA2010 V8	B	26	*hydraulics*			1m 36.607s	17
	Sebastian Vettel	D	5	Red Bull Racing	Red Bull RB6-Renault RS27 V8	B	25	*front wheel/spin*			1m 31.556s	22
	Adrian Sutil	D	14	Force India F1 Team	Force India VJM03-Mercedes FO108X V8	B	9	*engine*			1m 43.223s	6
	Vitaly Petrov	RUS	12	Renault F1 Team	Renault R30-RS27 V8	B	9	*spin*			1m 43.132s	6
	Bruno Senna	BR	21	HRT F1 Team	HRT F110-Cosworth CA2010 V8	B	4	*hydraulics*			2m 27.276s	4
	Sébastien Buemi	CH	16	Scuderia Toro Rosso	Toro Rosso STR5-Ferrari 056 V8	B	0	*accident*			no time	
	Nico Hülkenberg	D	10	AT&T Williams	Williams FW32-Cosworth CA2010 V8	B	0	*accident*			no time	
	Kamui Kobayashi	J	23	BMW Sauber F1 Team	BMW Sauber C29-Ferrari 056 V8	B	0	*accident*			no time	
NS	Jarno Trulli	I	18	Lotus Racing	Lotus T127-Cosworth CA2010 V8	B		*hydraulics*			no time	

Fastest race lap: Mark Webber on lap 47, 1m 28.358s, 134.255mph/216.061km/h.

Lap record: Michael Schumacher (Ferrari F2004 V10), 1m 24.125s, 141.010mph/226.933km/h (2004).

23 · SENNA · HRT | 21 · GLOCK · Virgin, started from pit lane | 19 · KOVALAINEN · Lotus | 17 · ALGUERSUARI · Toro Rosso | 15 · HÜLKENBERG · Williams | 13 · LIUZZI · Force India

24 · CHANDHOK · HRT | 22 · DI GRASSI · Virgin, started from pit lane | 20 · TRULLI · Lotus, non-starter from pit lane | 18 · PETROV · Renault | 16 · KOBAYASHI · BMW Sauber | 14 · DE LA ROSA · BMW Sauber

Grid order	1	2	3	4	5	6	7	8	9	10	11	12	13	14	15	16	17	18	19	20	21	22
5 VETTEL	5	5	5	5	5	5	5	5	6	6	5	5	5	5	5	5	5	5	5	5	5	5
6 WEBBER	7	7	7	7	7	6	6	6	14	5	1	1	1	1	1	1	1	1	1	1	1	1
8 ALONSO	6	6	6	6	6	7	7	15	5	1	11	11	11	11	11	11	11	11	11	11	11	11
1 BUTTON	11	11	11	11	11	11	11	17	1	11	4	4	4	4	4	4	4	4	4	4	4	4
7 MASSA	4	4	4	4	4	4	4	14	11	4	7	7	7	7	7	7	7	7	7	7	7	2
4 ROSBERG	1	1	1	1	1	2	2	11	4	7	6	6	6	6	6	2	2	2	2	2	2	7
3 SCHUMACHER	2	2	2	2	2	14	9	4	7	9	2	2	2	2	2	8	8	8	8	8	8	6
9 BARRICHELLO	14	14	14	14	14	9	12	24	9	2	9	9	9	8	8	6	6	6	6	6	6	8
11 KUBICA	9	9	9	9	9	12	14	7	15	22	22	22	8	9	9	9	9	9	9	9	9	9
14 SUTIL	12	12	12	12	12	22	22	9	17	8	8	8	22	22	22	22	22	22	22	22	15	15
2 HAMILTON	22	22	22	22	22	15	15	2	2	15	15	15	15	15	15	15	15	15	15	15	22	22
16 BUEMI	15	15	15	15	15	17	17	1	22	17	17	17	17	17	17	17	17	17	17	17	17	17
15 LIUZZI	17	17	17	17	17	8	8	22	8	3	3	3	3	3	3	3	3	3	3	3	3	3
22 DE LA ROSA	21	21	21	19	19	19	3	12	12	19	19	19	19	19	19	19	19	19	19	19	19	19
10 HULKENBERG	19	19	19	21	8	3	19	8	3	24	24	24	24	24	24	24	24	24	24	24	24	24
23 KOBAYASHI	20	20	20	20	24	24	24	25	25	20	20	20	20	20	20	20	20	20	20	25	25	25
17 ALGUERSUARI	24	24	24	24	3	25	25	3	24	25	25	25	25	25	25	25	25	25	25	20	20	20
12 PETROV	8	8	8	8	25	20	20	19	19													
19 KOVALAINEN	25	25	25	25	20	1	1	20	20													
18 TRULLI	3	3	3	3																		
21 SENNA																						
20 CHANDHOK																						
24 GLOCK																						
25 DI GRASSI																						

Grid order	23	24	25	26	27	28	29	30	31	32	33	34	35	36	37	38	39	40	41	42	43	44	45
5 VETTEL	5	5	5	1	1	1	1	1	1	1	1	1	1	1	1	1	1	1	1	1	1	1	1
6 WEBBER	1	1	1	11	11	11	11	11	11	11	11	11	11	11	11	11	11	11	11	11	11	11	11
8 ALONSO	11	11	11	2	2	2	2	2	2	2	2	7	7	7	7	7	7	7	7	7	7	7	7
1 BUTTON	4	4	4	4	4	4	4	4	4	4	7	8	8	8	8	8	8	8	8	8	8	8	8
7 MASSA	2	2	2	7	7	6	6	6	6	7	8	2	2	2	2	2	2	2	2	2	2	2	2
4 ROSBERG	7	7	7	6	6	7	7	7	7	8	4	6	6	6	6	6	6	6	6	6	6	6	6
3 SCHUMACHER	6	6	6	8	8	8	8	8	8	6	6	4	4	4	4	4	4	4	4	4	4	4	4
9 BARRICHELLO	8	8	8	9	9	9	9	9	15	15	15	15	15	15	15	15	15	15	15	15	15	15	15
11 KUBICA	9	9	9	15	15	15	15	15	22	22	22	22	22	22	22	22	22	22	22	22	22	22	22
14 SUTIL	15	15	15	22	22	22	22	22	9	9	9	9	9	9	9	9	9	9	9	9	9	9	9
2 HAMILTON	22	22	22	3	3	3	3	17	17	17	17	17	17	17	17	17	17	17	17	17	17	17	17
16 BUEMI	3	3	3	17	17	17	17	3	3	3	3	3	3	3	3	3	3	3	3	3	3	3	3
15 LIUZZI	17	17	17	19	19	19	19	19	19	19	19	19	19	19	19	19	19	19	19	19	19	19	19
22 DE LA ROSA	19	19	19	24	24	24	24	24	24	24	24	24	24	24	24	24	24	24	24	20	20	20	20
10 HULKENBERG	24	24	24	20	20	20	20	20	20	20	20	20	20	20	20	20	20	20	20				
23 KOBAYASHI	25	25	20	25																			
17 ALGUERSUARI	20	20	25																				
12 PETROV																							
19 KOVALAINEN																							
18 TRULLI																							
21 SENNA																							
20 CHANDHOK																							
24 GLOCK																							
25 DI GRASSI																							

21 Pit stop   *14 One lap or more behind*

TIME SHEETS

PRACTICE 1 (FRIDAY)

Weather: Sunny/cloudy

Temperatures: track 33–43°C, air 24–27°C

Pos.	Driver	Laps	Time
1	Robert Kubica	22	1m 26.927s
2	Nico Rosberg	18	1m 27.126s
3	Jenson Button	22	1m 27.482s
4	Felipe Massa	18	1m 27.511s
5	Sebastian Vettel	23	1m 27.686s
6	Fernando Alonso	21	1m 27.747s
7	Lewis Hamilton	22	1m 27.793s
8	Sébastien Buemi	21	1m 28.014s
9	Vitaly Petrov	25	1m 28.114s
10	Vitantonio Liuzzi	18	1m 28.192s
11	Paul di Resta	25	1m 28.537s
12	Michael Schumacher	19	1m 28.550s
13	Jaime Alguersuari	21	1m 28.572s
14	Mark Webber	22	1m 28.683s
15	Pedro de la Rosa	13	1m 29.465s
16	Rubens Barrichello	18	1m 29.712s
17	Nico Hülkenberg	26	1m 30.249s
18	Kamui Kobayashi	5	1m 31.588s
19	Jarno Trulli	13	1m 31.652s
20	Heikki Kovalainen	26	1m 31.654s
21	Lucas di Grassi	25	1m 32.831s
22	Bruno Senna	24	1m 33.401s
23	Karun Chandhok	19	1m 34.251s
24	Timo Glock	8	1m 34.925s

PRACTICE 2 (FRIDAY)

Weather: Cloudy/drizzle

Temperatures: track 24–26°C, air 20–21°C

Pos.	Driver	Laps	Time
1	Lewis Hamilton	13	1m 25.801s
2	Jenson Button	16	1m 26.076s
3	Mark Webber	22	1m 26.248s
4	Michael Schumacher	16	1m 26.511s
5	Vitaly Petrov	26	1m 26.732s
6	Sébastien Buemi	29	1m 26.832s
7	Adrian Sutil	22	1m 26.834s
8	Vitantonio Liuzzi	17	1m 26.835s
9	Rubens Barrichello	25	1m 26.904s
10	Nico Rosberg	22	1m 26.956s
11	Robert Kubica	28	1m 27.108s
12	Pedro de la Rosa	25	1m 27.108s
13	Kamui Kobayashi	23	1m 27.455s
14	Nico Hülkenberg	25	1m 27.545s
15	Fernando Alonso	20	1m 29.025s
16	Sebastian Vettel	19	1m 29.134s
17	Felipe Massa	21	1m 29.591s
18	Heikki Kovalainen	15	1m 29.860s
19	Jaime Alguersuari	43	1m 30.510s
20	Jarno Trulli	17	1m 30.695s
21	Timo Glock	9	1m 32.117s
22	Lucas di Grassi	2	no time
23	Karun Chandhok	1	no time

PRACTICE 3 (SATURDAY)

Weather: Cloudy

Temperatures: track 23°C, air 20–21°C

Pos.	Driver	Laps	Time
1	Mark Webber	16	1m 24.719s
2	Fernando Alonso	19	1m 24.929s
3	Michael Schumacher	17	1m 24.963s
4	Sebastian Vettel	19	1m 25.122s
5	Nico Rosberg	16	1m 25.366s
6	Jenson Button	20	1m 25.399s
7	Lewis Hamilton	14	1m 25.505s
8	Adrian Sutil	18	1m 25.525s
9	Felipe Massa	20	1m 25.549s
10	Vitantonio Liuzzi	19	1m 25.782s
11	Rubens Barrichello	17	1m 25.852s
12	Sébastien Buemi	21	1m 26.104s
13	Robert Kubica	21	1m 26.184s
14	Kamui Kobayashi	21	1m 26.275s
15	Jaime Alguersuari	17	1m 26.368s
16	Vitaly Petrov	19	1m 26.661s
17	Nico Hülkenberg	19	1m 26.804s
18	Pedro de la Rosa	18	1m 26.818s
19	Heikki Kovalainen	19	1m 29.539s
20	Jarno Trulli	16	1m 29.800s
21	Lucas di Grassi	18	1m 30.800s
22	Timo Glock	12	1m 31.114s
23	Karun Chandhok	11	1m 34.334s
24	Bruno Senna	8	1m 36.649s

QUALIFYING (SATURDAY)

Weather: Cloudy Temperatures: track 23°C, air 20–21°C

Pos.	Driver	First	Second	Third	Qualifying Tyre
1	Sebastian Vettel	1m 24.774s	1m 24.096s	1m 23.919s	Soft
2	Mark Webber	1m 25.286s	1m 24.276s	1m 24.035s	Soft
3	Fernando Alonso	1m 25.082s	1m 24.335s	1m 24.111s	Soft
4	Jenson Button	1m 24.897s	1m 24.531s	1m 24.675s	Soft
5	Felipe Massa	1m 25.548s	1m 25.010s	1m 24.837s	Soft
6	Nico Rosberg	1m 24.788s	1m 24.788s	1m 24.884s	Soft
7	Michael Schumacher	1m 25.351s	1m 24.871s	1m 24.927s	Soft
8	Rubens Barrichello	1m 25.702s	1m 25.085s	1m 25.217s	Soft
9	Robert Kubica	1m 25.588s	1m 25.122s	1m 25.372s	Soft
10	Adrian Sutil	1m 25.504s	1m 25.046s	1m 26.036s	Soft
11	Lewis Hamilton	1m 25.046s	1m 25.184s		
12	Sébastien Buemi	1m 26.061s	1m 25.638s		
13	Vitantonio Liuzzi	1m 26.170s	1m 25.743s		
14	Pedro de la Rosa	1m 26.089s	1m 25.747s		
15	Nico Hülkenberg	1m 25.866s	1m 25.748s		
16	Kamui Kobayashi	1m 26.251s	1m 25.777s		
17	Jaime Alguersuari	1m 26.095s	1m 26.089s		
18	Vitaly Petrov	1m 26.471s			
19	Heikki Kovalainen	1m 28.797s			
20	Jarno Trulli	1m 29.111s			
21	Timo Glock	1m 29.592s			
22	Lucas di Grassi	1m 30.185s			
23	Bruno Senna	1m 30.526s			
24	Karun Chandhok	1m 30.613s			

FOR THE RECORD

1st ALL FRONT ROW: Red Bull

30th PODIUM: Felipe Massa

10th PODIUM: Robert Kubica

DID YOU KNOW

Jenson Button became the 19th driver to win a grand prix in a McLaren.

Michael Schumacher reached the total of 14,000 F1 laps raced.

POINTS

DRIVERS

1	Fernando Alonso	37
2	Felipe Massa	33
3	Jenson Button	31
4	Lewis Hamilton	23
5	Nico Rosberg	20
6	Robert Kubica	18
7	Sebastian Vettel	12
8	Michael Schumacher	9
9	Vitantonio Liuzzi	8
10	Mark Webber	6
11	Rubens Barrichello	5

CONSTRUCTORS

1	Ferrari	70
2	McLaren	54
3	Mercedes	29
4	Renault	18
5	Red Bull	18
6	Force India	8
7	Williams	5

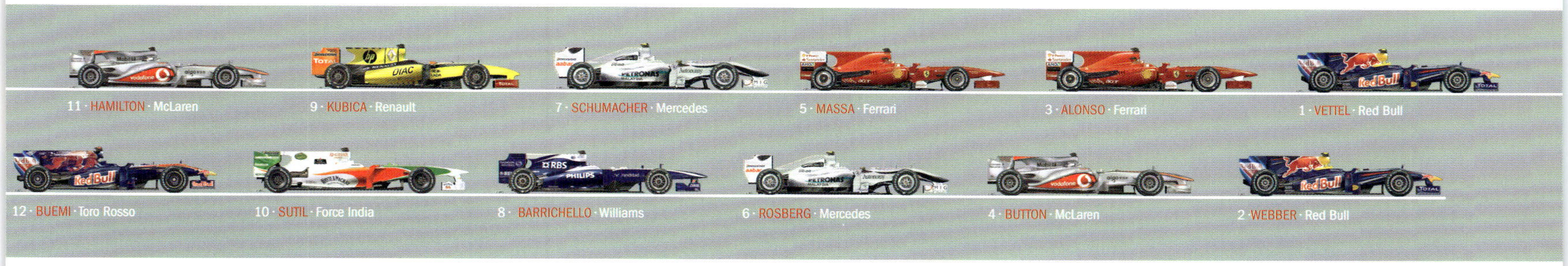

46	47	48	49	50	51	52	53	54	55	56	57	58	·
1	1	1	1	1	1	1	1	1	1	1	1	1	1
11	11	11	11	11	11	11	11	11	11	11	11	11	2
7	7	7	7	7	7	7	7	7	7	7	7	7	3
8	8	8	8	8	8	8	8	8	8	8	8	8	
2	2	2	2	2	2	2	2	2	2	4	4	4	
6	6	6	6	6	6	6	6	6	6	2	2	2	6
4	4	4	4	4	4	4	4	4	4	15	15	15	7
15	15	15	15	15	15	15	15	15	15	6	9	9	8
22	22	22	22	22	9	9	9	9	9	9	6	6	9
9	9	9	9	9	22	22	22	22	22	22	3	3	10
17	17	17	17	17	17	17	3	3	3	3	17	17	
3	3	3	3	3	3	3	17	17	17	17	22	22	
19	19	19	19	19	19	19	19	19	19	19			
20	20	20	20	20	20	20	20						

Safety car deployed on laps shown

RACE TYRE STRATEGIES

	Driver	Race Stint 1	Race Stint 2	Race Stint 3	Race Stint 4
1	Button	Inters: 1-6	Soft: 7-58		
2	Kubica	Inters: 1-8	Soft: 9-58		
3	Massa	Inters: 1-8	Soft: 9-58		
4	Alonso	Inters: 1-8	Soft: 9-58		
5	Rosberg	Inters: 1-8	Soft: 9-33	Soft: 34-58	
6	Hamilton	Inters: 1-8	Soft: 9-34	Soft: 35-58	
7	Liuzzi	Inters: 1-9	Soft: 10-58		
8	Barrichello	Inters: 1-8	Soft: 9-31	Hard: 32-58	
9	Webber	Inters: 1-10	Soft: 11-32	Soft: 33-56	Soft: 57-58
10	Schumacher	Inters: 1-3	Inters: 4-8	Soft: 9-29	Soft: 30-58
11	Alguersuari	Inters: 1-9	Soft: 10-27	Soft: 28-58	
12	de la Rosa	Inters: 1-8	Soft: 9-58		
13	Kovalainen	Inters: 1-8	Soft: 9-19		
14	Chandhok	Inters: 1-8	Hard: 9-46	Soft: 47-53	
	Glock	Inters: 1-9	Soft: 10-41 (dnf)		
	di Grassi	Inters: 1-10	Soft: 11-25	Soft: 26 (dnf)	
	Vettel	Inters: 1-9	Soft: 10-25 (dnf)		
	Sutil	Inters: 1-9 (dnf)			
	Petrov	Inters: 1-9 (dnf)			
	Senna	Inters: 1-4 (dnf)			
	Buemi	Inters: 0 (dnf)			
	Hülkenberg	Inters: 0 (dnf)			
	Kobayashi	Inters: 0 (dnf)			
dns	Trulli				

The tyre regulations stipulate that the two dry tyre specifications must be used during the race. The Soft compound Bridgestone Potenza tyre is marked with a green stripe on the sidewall.

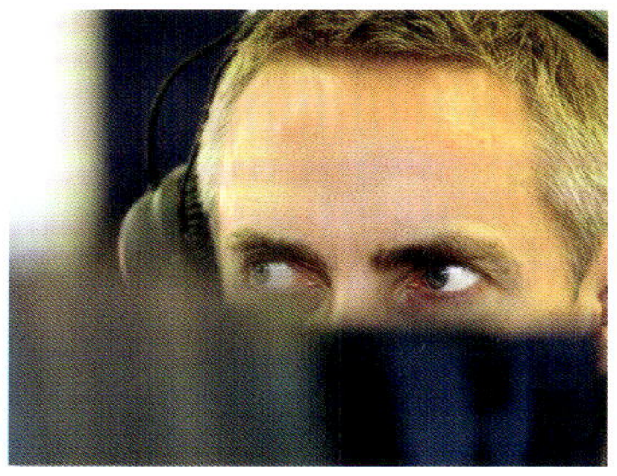

Photos: Peter J. Fox

RedBull

FIA FORMULA 1 WORLD CHAMPIONSHIP · ROUND 3

MALAYSIAN GRAND PRIX

SEPANG CIRCUIT

Mumm's the word! Sebastian Vettel celebrates victory at Sepang in time-honoured style.
Photo: Peter J Fox

SEPANG QUALIFYING

FOR all their highly trained strategists and cutting-edge predictive software, Formula One teams are sometimes best served by opening their eyes to the world immediately around them. And this was a case in point.

It shouldn't have mattered that the meteorological radars insisted conditions would improve: it began raining shortly before the start of qualifying and the Malaysian climate is more fickle than most. Things were just as likely to deteriorate as they were to improve, and completion of an early banker lap was the only common-sense strategy. That way, you were in the clear whatever happened. But still McLaren and Ferrari held back their drivers, as did Red Bull with Mark Webber. And then the rain resumed.

Better than most in delicate conditions, Webber and Jenson Button managed times that were good enough to progress into Q2, but Button wasn't convinced and speared into the gravel as he endeavoured to improve. He was eligible, but unable, to continue. Both Lewis Hamilton and Fernando Alonso spun before heading to the pits to swap intermediates for full wets, but that was as futile as their teams' tactics had been flawed.

"Do I feel frustrated?" said McLaren team principal Martin Whitmarsh. "Of course I do. We have learned lessons. The primary one is that in Q1 we are not just racing Ferrari and the other big boys. We need to get through to Q2 and cover the slower cars in those changeable conditions. But if I played you the weather radar and showed you what it showed us, you'd see why we did what we did."

Unlike Lotus (Heikki Kovalainen) and Virgin (Timo Glock), McLaren and Ferrari had to sit out Q2 (when, predictably, everybody did a banker lap at the start). Conditions improved in the middle of the session, but by the start of Q3 it was raining again – so much so that the red flag was soon brandished and proceedings were interrupted for 17 minutes while the monsoon abated.

There appeared to be only one logical tyre choice – full wets – when the session resumed, but the rain had eased and Webber's race engineer, Ciaran Pilbeam, suggested that a three-lap run on inter-mediates might be the way to go, assuming the Australian could keep the car on the track during the first part of the exercise. Webber concurred, and he was the only driver not to plump for wets. His first flying lap (1m 54.643s) was necessarily cautious, and three seconds off the pace. The second (1m 50.451s) put him on provisional pole, and the last (1m 49.327s) left him 1.346 seconds clear of Nico Rosberg, with Sebastian Vettel, Adrian Sutil, Nico Hülkenberg and Robert Kubica completing the top six.

"Full credit to Ciaran," said Webber. "The intermediate would have been totally the wrong tyre if it had lashed down with rain, but totally the right tyre if it held off for that little bit longer. It had already started to spit, but it was definitely the right tyre to be on in some parts of the track. In others, though, it was quite a high risk. I wasn't aware I was the only guy on inters, but in the end we made the right decision together. It was a tough hour for everyone, though, and I wouldn't throw egg at anybody, or any team."

Too late, Mark.

ALL that enterprise, all that lateral thinking, all gone to waste. Mark Webber might have played his cards right on Saturday, with a canny tyre choice that no rival dared emulate, but the Malaysian Grand Prix was only a few seconds old when he realised that he wasn't going to convert pole position to victory. From the outside, it looked like a schoolboy error, but in reality it was just another illustration of the relative uselessness of outboard mirrors.

Webber got away cleanly enough, but from third on the grid Sebastian Vettel made a corker of a start, towing past Nico Rosberg and then tucking in behind his team-mate for a second helping of slipstream. When they reached Turn One, Webber left a gaping hole to his right and Vettel exploited it to perfection. All of a sudden, the Australian's heart felt heavier than his fuel load.

"I didn't really know where Nico was," he said, "and Sebastian wasn't mega close when I last saw him, so things looked reasonable. You can't see much in these mirrors, though, and the track is so bloody wide that you wonder where the hell everyone is. I really thought Seb was on the outside, so I stayed pretty much in the middle to cover him and braked as late as I dared."

The cars ran wheel to wheel through the first two corners, but both drivers had been reminded pre-race to behave themselves for the team's sake – Red Bull didn't want to throw away its third winning position in as many grands prix – and Webber ceded as Vettel edged ahead. "The start was crucial," the German said. "I had good initial momentum off the line and got a good tow from Mark, so was able to gain, gain, gain."

Webber admitted he'd been caught napping. "The first time I saw Seb was when we were on the brakes," he said, "I couldn't hear him when we were at full throttle and I knew he wasn't beside me. He came in late, for sure, but it was fair. I thought, 'Oh God, I'm going to be here for the whole race unless he makes a mistake,' but we know how good he is..."

Behind, Rosberg held third from Robert Kubica, Adrian Sutil, Michael Schumacher, Nico Hülkenberg, Tonio Liuzzi, Vitaly Petrov, Kamui Kobayashi, Jaime Alguersuari, Sébastien Buemi, Lewis Hamilton (seven places gained during the opening lap), Felipe Massa, Jenson Button, Fernando Alonso, Jarno Trulli, Timo Glock, Lucas di Grassi, Bruno Senna, Heikki Kovalainen, Rubens Barrichello (Williams felt he might have lined up on the front row had Schumacher not delayed him during Q3, but it wouldn't have helped because his engine all but stalled on the line) and Karun Chandhok. Pedro de la Rosa didn't get as far as the start, a problem with his Sauber's pneumatic valve system forcing him to park en route to the grid.

It took Barrichello just a lap to usurp all the newcomers, but Hamilton's progress was more obviously spectacular. With the top four positions effectively settled by the time the field came out of the first corner, most of the interest was provided by those who had failed to respond correctly to the rain the previous afternoon. Hamilton passed the Toro Rossos on laps two and three, Kobayashi on lap four and Petrov on lap five, but was caught unawares when the Russian retaliated under braking for Turn One. The Englishman returned the favour at the end of the following lap and then zigzagged along the pit straight while Petrov tried to remain glued to the McLaren's rear wing.

Hamilton's conduct provoked outrage among some observers and prompted the stewards to issue a black-and-white 'conduct warning' flag, but Petrov didn't complain. Had the two cars been

Above: New Lotus team principal Tony Fernandes plays host to some of his sponsors and investors on the starting grid.
Photo: Paul-Henri Cahier

Top left: The Red Bull mechanics make a theatrical point.
Photo: Jean-François Galeron/WRi2

Above left: The eyes have it. Bruno Senna looks uncannily like his late uncle, Ayrton.
Photo: Paul-Henri Cahier

Left: An inspired choice. Mark Webber gambled on intermediate tyres in Q3 and was rewarded with pole position.
Photo: Jad Sherif/WRi2

adjacent at the time, you'd have shredded Hamilton's superlicence before he'd reached the braking zone, but, having recently discovered Petrov's robust streak, he was simply trying to break the tow. The ancient art of motor racing is all too easily forgotten sometimes.

Given the previous day's climatic peculiarities, McLaren decided to cover its options by starting Hamilton on hard tyres and Button on softs. "We thought there would be some rain, as there has every afternoon since we arrived," said team principal Martin Whitmarsh, "and we didn't think we'd get anywhere by copying what the 20 cars ahead were doing. Lewis wanted to run a long first stint on primes [hards]. Had there been some rain two-thirds of the way through, we might have looked like geniuses, but as it was his pace through the middle part of the race got him a solid points finish. As soon as Jenson became stuck in traffic, he had the ability to make an early stop and run to the end on the harder tyre. He couldn't have adopted the same tactic in reverse."

The split strategies set up a fascinating internal battle. Button initially made the slower progress of the two, not helped when Alonso overtook him on the second lap. He repassed the Ferrari on lap nine, but then pitted straight away for fresh tyres, Now running in clean air, he began lapping at the same pace as the Red Bulls, and it appeared that he and Hamilton would inevitably be quite close once the latter made his stop.

Leader Vettel switched from soft to hard Bridgestones on lap 23, one before Webber (who lost a couple of seconds when the front left wheel briefly jammed), while Rosberg and Kubica came in on laps 22 and 21 respectively. Hamilton didn't peel in until lap 30, by which stage others' stops had put him second on the road. "The two sides of the garage asked whether the drivers were free to race," Whitmarsh said, "and the answer was 'yes'. Both were told to push like hell, and we could see what was going to happen…"

The two McLarens were almost level as Hamilton rejoined, but his fresh, soft tyres gave him extra bite into Turn One and the issue was settled. Once clear of his team-mate, Hamilton swiftly caught Sutil – driving with increasing maturity, the German had run behind Kubica from the start – but a two-way Mercedes power struggle neutralised that particular battle, and Hamilton had to settle for sixth.

Button's worn rubber soon gave him additional problems, because both Ferraris had run long first stints on the prime and were in good shape after switching to softs on laps 26 (Massa) and 36 (Alonso). Massa caught Button on lap 34, but the Englishman defended robustly and continued to set a pace that belied his tyres' tattered state. Eventually, though, he ceded on lap 44, by which time Alonso was looming.

This had been a remarkable drive by the Spaniard. His clutch had begun misbehaving on the formation lap, but his subsequent pace offered absolutely no clues about his consequent – and constant – struggle to select gears. In the circumstances, his speed and consistency were sensational. Eventually, he passed Button by going deep into Turn One on lap 46, but

the world champion held a tighter, neater line and retaliated immediately. The same thing happened on lap 55, but this time Alonso's engine emitted a cloud of terminal white smoke moments after he had been repelled. Button deserved better than eighth place; Alonso simply deserved better.

Life was much quieter at the front of the field and, for the first time in the season, Vettel had a trouble-free race, although he didn't feel it had been wholly easy. "After the battle with Mark at the start, it was just a question of getting away from our competitors," he said. "I could see Mark and I were running at more or less the same pace. I think he was a little bit quicker at the beginning, but I was trying to save my tyres. The second stint felt very long in the extreme heat, and I was actually hoping for a bit of rain, just to cool me down."

He didn't get that, but he did receive a post-race summons from the stewards. They wanted him to explain why he'd passed Trulli's Lotus under yellow flags a couple of laps from home. The Italian was barely moving, however (he finished five laps in arrears), because he'd had chronic, deteriorating handling problems ever since Glock had hit him on lap three, an incident that led to the Virgin driver's retirement. The stewards judged that Vettel had slowed significantly when passing the Lotus and, in a welcome outbreak of common sense, decided to take no action.

The extended scoring system enabled Alguersuari and Hülkenberg to collect their maiden Formula One points. The two swapped places on lap 31, when the Spaniard pulled off the race's best move, taking a wide approach to Turn Four, slicing down the inside and then sweeping ahead around the outside of Turn Five. After the promise of Saturday, it was a disappointing result for Hülkenberg. It didn't help that he had been forced to make his tyre stop earlier than scheduled, on lap 13, because a faulty switch had left him unable to alter fuel mixtures and he'd been forced to come in to have a replacement steering wheel fitted.

Buemi finished 11th, having struggled with

Above: Defining moment of the race as Vettel gets the jump on pole-man Webber, the young German taking a lead he would never relinquish.
Photo: Paul-Henri Cahier

Facing page, top: Trying to keep cool: Rosberg clears his mind for the upcoming challenge.
Photo: Peter J Fox

Facing page, centre: Lewis Hamilton was embroiled in a lively little battle with Renault rookie Vitaly Petrov.
Photo: Lukas Gorys

Facing page, bottom: Adrian Sutil showed masterly discipline to complement his speed, ending up a fine fifth for Force India.
Photo: Jean-François Galeron/WRi2

Above: Lucas di Grassi did a smooth, competent job and brought his Virgin-Cosworth to the finish.
Photo: Paul-Henri Cahier

Right: The moving finger. Sebastian's crew poses for a victory photo.
Photos: Peter J Fox

Far right: A late-race engine failure was a bruisingly disappointing note on which Fernando Alonso ended his race in Malaysia.
Photos: Peter J Fox

understeer for much of the race after damaging his front wing in an opening-lap scuffle with Kobayashi. The team didn't replace it until he pitted for a second time, on lap 34. Williams called Barrichello in for an early tyre stop, as a tactical punt, on lap seven, but later had to bring him back in for fresh rubber; he ended up 12th, ahead of the parked Alonso, di Grassi, Chandhok, Senna (HRT's first double finish) and the dawdling Trulli. Kovalainen was still running, but unclassified, after a lengthy stop to resolve a hydraulic malfunction that was causing his Lotus to run too hot. He had lost a little time before that, when he pitted to replace a punctured left rear following a clash with di Grassi.

After his spirited early cameo, Petrov pulled in with a gearbox problem, while Liuzzi lost his throttle and Schumacher hung around in sixth only until lap ten, when his left rear wheel fell off after the nut somehow worked loose. Sauber, meanwhile, underlined that it could not be accused of giving its drivers unequal equipment: Kobayashi stopped on lap nine when his engine's pneumatic valve system followed de la Rosa's into hibernation.

In stark contrast, there was no stopping Vettel in the race's immediate aftermath. Smiling broadly, he gave a series of long and slightly rambling answers during the post-race press conference. "I'm sorry," he said, trying to compose himself. "I think I drank too much champagne on the podium. I'm not really used to this stuff and feel a bit tipsy…"

Simon Arron

EDITOR'S VIEW
ALONSO SHOWS HIS METTLE

FERNANDO Alonso has a cerebral personality beneath the skin – and it belies the rather light-hearted touch implied by his frequently pleasant outward demeanour. The qualities that marked him out as a talented freshman during his spell as a Renault test driver have coalesced over the years into a shrewd, hard-nosed and politically adept operator capable of maximising almost any situation presented to him.

In his new role as a Ferrari driver, these qualities have become an enhanced benefit in the potentially volatile hothouse environment at Maranello. The Spaniard had long been targeted by the Prancing Horse and, just as Niki Lauda, Jody Scheckter, Alain Prost, Nigel Mansell and Michael Schumacher had done before, he quickly discerned just how the Ferrari machine could be deployed to his personal advantage. Yet, as he displayed to brilliant effect at Sepang, he also has the temperament to play the long game if he can see benefit for the future.

Having won the opening race of the year in Bahrain and followed that up with a first-corner collision in Melbourne, Alonso was looking to Sepang as a race where he could consolidate his challenge for the world championship. In the end, even though he failed to score a point in Malaysia, the sheer quality of Fernando's drive, battling against technical problems, was enough to raise Maranello spirits. It generated a mood of thinly suppressed optimism for the balance of the season, although, to many on the touchlines, that might have seemed excessive, given the apparent strength of the McLaren and Red Bull opposition.

It was a classic demonstration of just how a world-class driver can salvage some crumbs of comfort from what starts as a deeply unpromising day. Having made an incorrect strategic call during rain-spoiled qualifying, Alonso and Felipe Massa were left trailing in 19th and 21st positions on the grid. Come the race, the Spaniard battled gearbox problems for much of the distance, then suffered an engine failure in the closing stages.

Almost from the start, things went wrong for Alonso. On the formation lap, his gearbox began to malfunction and he had no operative clutch from that point onwards. "I had first to shift down a gear, then press the throttle hard so that it would engage the specific gear for a corner.

"So it was probably the hardest race of my whole life in terms of driving, because I had to improvise for every corner. But even so, we looked on course to get a few points, which turned out not to be possible because of the engine failure towards the end."

With a sense of wry irony, he added, "But if the gearbox and the engine are going to break, it's better that it happens when you are ninth than when you are leading and you lose 25 points!"

You could say that the 2010 Malaysian Grand Prix turned out to be something of a fruitless affair for Fernando Alonso, but for Maranello the race delivered confirmation of the strength in depth offered by the Spanish driver. If there had been any reservations, surely his performance must have expunged them, even though there were still a few setbacks to come as Fernando meshed with the Prancing Horse.

In Malaysia, Alonso sent a signal that his alliance with Ferrari might well become one of the most outstanding in the team's substantial record book. He displayed performance and perspective in pretty much equal measure.

Alan Henry

FIA F1 WORLD CHAMPIONSHIP · ROUND 3

PETRONAS MALAYSIAN GRAND PRIX

KUALA LUMPUR 2–4 APRIL 2010

RACE DISTANCE: 56 laps, 192.879 miles/310.408km

RACE WEATHER: Sunny/cloudy (track 38–44°C, air 32–34°C)

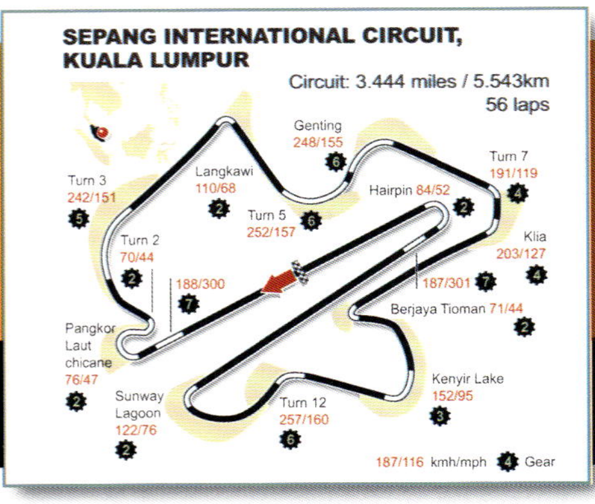

Pos.	Driver	Nat.	No.	Entrant	Car/Engine	Tyres	Laps	Time/Retirement	Speed (mph/km/h)	Gap to leader	Fastest race lap	
1	**Sebastian Vettel**	D	5	Red Bull Racing	Red Bull RB6-Renault RS27 V8	B	56	1h 33m 48.412s	123.367/198.540		1m 37.813s	53
2	**Mark Webber**	AUS	6	Red Bull Racing	Red Bull RB6-Renault RS27 V8	B	56	1h 33m 53.261s	123.261/198.369	+ 4.849s	1m 37.054s	53
3	**Nico Rosberg**	D	4	Mercedes GP Petronas F1 Team	Mercedes MGP W01-Mercedes FO108X V8	B	56	1h 34m 01.916s	123.072/198.065	+ 13.504s	1m 38.129s	53
4	**Robert Kubica**	PL	11	Renault F1 Team	Renault R30-RS27 V8	B	56	1h 34m 07.001s	122.961/197.887	+ 18.589s	1m 38.074s	55
5	**Adrian Sutil**	D	14	Force India F1 Team	Force India VJM03-Mercedes FO108X V8	B	56	1h 34m 09.471s	122.907/197.800	+ 21.059s	1m 38.160s	55
6	**Lewis Hamilton**	GB	2	Vodafone McLaren Mercedes	McLaren MP4-25-Mercedes FO108X V8	B	56	1h 34m 11.883s	122.855/197.716	+ 23.471s	1m 37.745s	32
7	**Felipe Massa**	BR	7	Scuderia Ferrari Marlboro	Ferrari F10-056 V8	B	56	1h 34m 15.480s	122.777/197.590	+ 27.068s	1m 37.784s	48
8	**Jenson Button**	GB	1	Vodafone McLaren Mercedes	McLaren MP4-25-Mercedes FO108X V8	B	56	1h 34m 26.330s	122.542/197.212	+ 37.918s	1m 38.501s	49
9	**Jaime Alguersuari**	E	17	Scuderia Toro Rosso	Toro Rosso STR5-Ferrari 056 V8	B	56	1h 34m 59.014s	121.839/196.081	+ 1m 10.602s	1m 39.489s	44
10	**Nico Hülkenberg**	D	10	AT&T Williams	Williams FW32-Cosworth CA2010 V8	B	56	1h 35m 01.811s	121.779/195.984	+ 1m 13.399s	1m 39.124s	51
11	Sébastien Buemi	CH	16	Scuderia Toro Rosso	Toro Rosso STR5-Ferrari 056 V8	B	56	1h 35m 07.350s	121.661/195.794	+ 1m 18.938s	1m 37.610s	54
12	Rubens Barrichello	BR	9	AT&T Williams	Williams FW32-Cosworth CA2010 V8	B	55			+ 1 lap	1m 39.428s	46
13	Fernando Alonso	E	8	Scuderia Ferrari Marlboro	Ferrari F10-056 V8	B	54	*engine*		+ 2 laps	1m 37.231s	41
14	Lucas di Grassi	BR	25	Virgin Racing	Virgin VR-01-Cosworth CA2010 V8	B	53			+ 3 laps	1m 43.224s	28
15	Karun Chandhok	IND	20	HRT F1 Team	HRT F110-Cosworth CA2010 V8	B	53			+ 3 laps	1m 44.790s	40
16	Bruno Senna	BR	21	HRT F1 Team	HRT F110-Cosworth CA2010 V8	B	52			+ 4 laps	1m 45.334s	39
17	Jarno Trulli	I	18	Lotus Racing	Lotus T127-Cosworth CA2010 V8	B	51			+ 5 laps	1m 43.753s	31
	Heikki Kovalainen	FIN	19	Lotus Racing	Lotus T127-Cosworth CA2010 V8	B	46				1m 42.701s	44
	Vitaly Petrov	RUS	12	Renault F1 Team	Renault R30-RS27 V8	B	32	*gearbox*			1m 40.693s	32
	Vitantonio Liuzzi	I	15	Force India F1 Team	Force India VJM03-Mercedes FO108X V8	B	12	*throttle*			1m 42.594s	9
	Michael Schumacher	GB	3	Mercedes GP Petronas F1 Team	Mercedes MGP W01-Mercedes FO108X V8	B	9	*rear wheel nut*			1m 42.084s	9
	Kamui Kobayashi	J	23	BMW Sauber F1 Team	BMW Sauber C29-Ferrari 056 V8	B	8	*engine*			1m 43.340s	6
	Timo Glock	D	24	Virgin Racing	Virgin VR-01-Cosworth CA2010 V8	B	2	*accident*			1m 46.388s	2
NS	Pedro de la Rosa	E	22	BMW Sauber F1 Team	BMW Sauber C29-Ferrari 056 V8	B		*engine*			no time	

Fastest race lap: Mark Webber on lap 53, 1m 37.054s, 127.757mph/205.605km/h.

Lap record: Juan Pablo Montoya (Williams FW26-BMW V10), 1m 34.223s, 131.596mph/211.782km/h (2004).

Grid order	1	2	3	4	5	6	7	8	9	10	11	12	13	14	15	16	17	18	19	20	21	22
6 WEBBER	5	5	5	5	5	5	5	5	5	5	5	5	5	5	5	5	5	5	5	5	5	5
4 ROSBERG	6	6	6	6	6	6	6	6	6	6	6	6	6	6	6	6	6	6	6	6	6	6
5 VETTEL	4	4	4	4	4	4	4	4	4	4	4	4	4	4	4	4	4	4	4	4	4	4
14 SUTIL	11	11	11	11	11	11	11	11	11	11	11	11	11	11	11	11	11	11	11	11	11	2
10 HULKENBERG	14	14	14	14	14	14	14	14	14	14	14	14	14	14	14	14	14	14	14	14	2	11
11 KUBICA	3	3	3	3	3	3	3	3	3	10	10	10	2	2	2	2	2	2	2	2	7	7
9 BARRICHELLO	10	10	10	10	10	10	10	10	10	15	15	2	10	17	17	17	17	17	7	7	8	8
3 SCHUMACHER	15	15	15	15	15	15	15	15	15	2	2	12	17	7	7	7	7	7	8	8	14	14
23 KOBAYASHI	12	12	12	12	2	12	2	2	2	12	12	17	16	8	8	8	8	8	17	1	1	1
15 LIUZZI	23	23	23	2	12	2	12	12	12	17	17	16	12	16	1	1	1	1	1	10	10	10
12 PETROV	17	17	2	23	23	23	23	23	17	16	16	7	7	1	10	10	10	10	10	12	12	17
22 DE LA ROSA	16	2	17	17	17	17	17	17	16	7	7	8	8	10	12	12	12	12	12	17	17	16
16 BUEMI	2	16	16	16	16	16	16	16	7	8	8	1	1	12	16	16	16	16	16	16	16	12
17 ALGUERSUARI	7	7	7	7	7	7	7	7	8	1	1	9	9	9	9	9	9	9	9	9	9	9
19 KOVALAINEN	1	8	8	8	8	8	8	8	1	9	9	25	25	25	25	25	25	25	25	25	25	25
24 GLOCK	8	1	1	1	1	1	1	1	9	25	25	18	18	18	18	18	18	18	18	18	18	18
1 BUTTON	18	9	9	9	9	9	9	25	25	19	18	20	20	20	20	21	20	20	20	20	20	20
18 TRULLI	24	18	25	25	25	25	25	19	19	18	20	21	21	21	21	20	21	21	21	21	21	21
8 ALONSO	25	24	19	19	19	19	19	9	18	20	21	19	19	19	19	19	19	19	19	19	19	19
2 HAMILTON	21	25	20	20	20	18	18	18	20	21	19	15										
7 MASSA	19	19	21	21	18	20	20	20	21													
20 CHANDHOK	9	20	18	18	21	21	21	21														
21 SENNA	20	21																				
25 DI GRASSI																						

Grid order	23	24	25	26	27	28	29	30	31	32	33	34	35	36	37	38	39	40	41	42	43	44	45
6 WEBBER	6	6	5	5	5	5	5	5	5	5	5	5	5	5	5	5	5	5	5	5	5	5	5
4 ROSBERG	5	5	2	2	2	2	2	6	6	6	6	6	6	6	6	6	6	6	6	6	6	6	6
5 VETTEL	2	2	6	6	6	6	6	2	4	4	4	4	4	4	4	4	4	4	4	4	4	4	4
14 SUTIL	4	4	4	4	4	4	4	4	11	11	11	11	11	11	11	11	11	11	11	11	11	11	11
10 HULKENBERG	11	11	11	11	11	11	11	11	8	8	8	8	8	14	14	14	14	14	14	14	14	14	14
11 KUBICA	7	7	7	8	8	8	8	8	14	14	14	14	14	2	2	2	2	2	2	2	2	2	2
9 BARRICHELLO	8	8	8	7	14	14	14	14	2	2	2	2	2	8	1	1	1	1	1	1	1	7	7
3 SCHUMACHER	14	14	14	14	1	1	1	1	1	1	1	1	1	1	7	7	7	7	7	7	7	1	1
23 KOBAYASHI	1	1	1	1	7	7	7	7	7	7	7	7	7	7	8	8	8	8	8	8	8	8	8
15 LIUZZI	10	10	10	10	10	10	10	10	17	17	17	17	17	17	17	17	17	17	17	17	17	17	17
12 PETROV	17	17	17	17	17	17	17	17	10	10	10	10	10	10	10	10	10	10	10	10	10	10	10
22 DE LA ROSA	16	16	16	16	16	16	16	16	16	16	16	16	9	9	9	9	9	9	9	9	16	16	16
16 BUEMI	12	12	12	12	12	12	12	12	12	12	9	9	16	16	16	16	16	16	16	16	9	9	9
17 ALGUERSUARI	9	9	9	9	9	9	9	9	9	9	25	25	25	25	25	25	25	25	25	25	25	25	25
19 KOVALAINEN	25	25	25	25	25	25	25	25	25	25	18	18	18	18	18	18	18	18	18	20	20	20	20
24 GLOCK	18	18	18	18	18	18	18	18	18	18	20	20	20	20	20	20	20	20	20	18	18	18	21
1 BUTTON	20	20	20	20	20	20	20	20	20	20	21	21	21	21	21	21	21	21	21	21	21	21	18
18 TRULLI	21	21	21	21	21	21	21	21	21	21	19	19	19	19	19	19	19	19	19	19	19	19	19
8 ALONSO	19	19	19	19	19	19	19	19	19	19													
2 HAMILTON																							
7 MASSA																							
20 CHANDHOK																							
21 SENNA																							
25 DI GRASSI																							

TIME SHEETS

PRACTICE 1 (FRIDAY)
Weather: Sunny
Temperatures: track 33-39°C, air 28-33°C

Pos.	Driver	Laps	Time
1	Lewis Hamilton	19	1m 34.921s
2	Nico Rosberg	19	1m 35.106s
3	Jenson Button	25	1m 35.207s
4	Michael Schumacher	14	1m 35.225s
5	Robert Kubica	22	1m 35.402s
6	Mark Webber	22	1m 35.479s
7	Adrian Sutil	20	1m 35.955s
8	Fernando Alonso	20	1m 35.959s
9	Sebastian Vettel	19	1m 36.043s
10	Sébastien Buemi	20	1m 36.100s
11	Felipe Massa	22	1m 36.451s
12	Kamui Kobayashi	28	1m 36.503s
13	Jaime Alguersuari	18	1m 36.645s
14	Vitaly Petrov	9	1m 36.712s
15	Paul di Resta	25	1m 36.891s
16	Pedro de la Rosa	24	1m 36.899s
17	Nico Hülkenberg	27	1m 37.802s
18	Rubens Barrichello	18	1m 38.278s
19	Jarno Trulli	21	1m 39.460s
20	Timo Glock	17	1m 39.755s
21	Lucas di Grassi	25	1m 40.159s
22	Fairuz Fauzy	19	1m 40.721s
23	Bruno Senna	27	1m 41.832s
24	Karun Chandhok	24	1m 41.966s

PRACTICE 2 (FRIDAY)
Weather: Sunny/partly cloudy
Temperatures: track 41-47°C, air 33-34°C

Pos.	Driver	Laps	Time
1	Lewis Hamilton	27	1m 34.175s
2	Sebastian Vettel	28	1m 34.441s
3	Nico Rosberg	30	1m 34.443s
4	Jenson Button	24	1m 34.538s
5	Michael Schumacher	30	1m 34.674s
6	Robert Kubica	34	1m 35.148s
7	Fernando Alonso	34	1m 35.581s
8	Sébastien Buemi	39	1m 35.660s
9	Vitaly Petrov	20	1m 35.872s
10	Adrian Sutil	32	1m 35.957s
11	Kamui Kobayashi	38	1m 36.018s
12	Vitantonio Liuzzi	34	1m 36.221s
13	Pedro de la Rosa	33	1m 36.325s
14	Jaime Alguersuari	39	1m 36.325s
15	Felipe Massa	30	1m 36.602s
16	Rubens Barrichello	26	1m 36.813s
17	Nico Hülkenberg	19	1m 37.415s
18	Jarno Trulli	34	1m 38.454s
19	Heikki Kovalainen	32	1m 38.530s
20	Mark Webber	13	1m 38.786s
21	Timo Glock	23	1m 39.061s
22	Lucas di Grassi	29	1m 39.158s
23	Karun Chandhok	27	1m 41.084s
24	Bruno Senna	32	1m 41.481s

PRACTICE 3 (SATURDAY)
Weather: Sunny/ cloudy
Temperatures: track 41-43°C, air 32-34°C

Pos.	Driver	Laps	Time
1	Mark Webber	17	1m 33.542s
2	Lewis Hamilton	14	1m 33.559s
3	Sebastian Vettel	17	1m 33.587s
4	Fernando Alonso	19	1m 33.751s
5	Michael Schumacher	15	1m 33.992s
6	Nico Rosberg	13	1m 34.090s
7	Jenson Button	16	1m 34.113s
8	Felipe Massa	15	1m 34.174s
9	Rubens Barrichello	13	1m 34.540s
10	Robert Kubica	17	1m 34.549s
11	Adrian Sutil	11	1m 34.623s
12	Sébastien Buemi	19	1m 34.673s
13	Nico Hülkenberg	13	1m 34.882s
14	Vitantonio Liuzzi	16	1m 34.957s
15	Jaime Alguersuari	16	1m 35.026s
16	Vitaly Petrov	17	1m 35.076s
17	Pedro de la Rosa	18	1m 35.477s
18	Kamui Kobayashi	19	1m 36.404s
19	Timo Glock	15	1m 37.299s
20	Jarno Trulli	16	1m 37.369s
21	Heikki Kovalainen	18	1m 38.161s
22	Lucas di Grassi	13	1m 38.783s
23	Bruno Senna	19	1m 39.868s
24	Karun Chandhok	16	1m 39.895s

QUALIFYING (SATURDAY)
Weather: Drizzle/rain/cloudy Temperatures: track 30-35°C, air 28-30°C

Pos.	Driver	First	Second	Third	Qualifying Tyre
1	Mark Webber	1m 51.886s	1m 48.210s	1m 49.327s	Soft
2	Nico Rosberg	1m 52.560s	1m 47.417s	1m 50.673s	Soft
3	Sebastian Vettel	1m 47.632s	1m 46.828s	1m 50.789s	Soft
4	Adrian Sutil	1m 49.479s	1m 47.085s	1m 50.914s	Soft
5	Nico Hülkenberg	1m 49.664s	1m 47.346s	1m 51.001s	Soft
6	Robert Kubica	1m 46.283s	1m 46.951s	1m 51.051s	Soft
7	Rubens Barrichello	1m 50.301s	1m 48.371s	1m 51.511s	Soft
8	Michael Schumacher	1m 52.239s	1m 48.400s	1m 51.717s	Soft
9	Kamui Kobayashi	1m 48.467s	1m 47.792s	1m 51.767s	Soft
10	Vitantonio Liuzzi	1m 49.922s	1m 48.238s	1m 52.254s	Soft
11	Vitaly Petrov	1m 47.952s	1m 48.760s		
12	Pedro de la Rosa	1m 47.153s	1m 48.771s		
13	Sébastien Buemi	1m 48.945s	1m 49.207s		
14	Jaime Alguersuari	1m 48.655s	1m 49.464s		
15	Heikki Kovalainen	1m 52.875s	1m 52.270s		
16	Timo Glock	1m 52.398s	1m 52.520s		
17	Jenson Button	1m 52.211s	no time		
18	Jarno Trulli	1m 52.884s			
19	Fernando Alonso	1m 53.044s			
20	Lewis Hamilton	1m 53.050s			
21	Felipe Massa	1m 53.283s			
22	Karun Chandhok	1m 56.299s			
23	Bruno Senna	1m 57.269s			
24	Lucas di Grassi	1m 59.977s			

FOR THE RECORD

1st FRONT ROW: Nico Rosberg
1st POINTS: Jaime Alguersuari, Nico Hülkenberg
10th PODIUM: Sebastian Vettel
20th PODIUM POSITION: Red Bull

DID YOU KNOW

The last time that three different constructors won the first three races of a season was 1990 (McLaren/ Ferrari/Williams).

Photos: Peter J. Fox

POINTS

DRIVERS

1	Felipe Massa	39
2	Fernando Alonso	37
3	Sebastian Vettel	37
4	Jenson Button	35
5	Nico Rosberg	35
6	Lewis Hamilton	31
7	Robert Kubica	30
8	Mark Webber	24
9	Adrian Sutil	10
10	Michael Schumacher	9
11	Vitantonio Liuzzi	8
12	Rubens Barrichello	5
13	Jaime Alguersuari	2
14	Nico Hülkenberg	1

CONSTRUCTORS

1	Ferrari	76
2	McLaren	66
3	Red Bull	61
4	Mercedes	44
5	Renault	30
6	Force India	18
7	Williams	6
8	Toro Rosso	2

11 · PETROV · Renault
9 · KOBAYASHI · BMW Sauber
7 · BARRICHELLO · Williams
5 · HÜLKENBERG · Williams
3 · VETTEL · Red Bull
1 · WEBBER · Red Bull
12 · DE LA ROSA · BMW Sauber
10 · LIUZZI · Force India
8 · SCHUMACHER · Mercedes
6 · KUBICA · Renault
4 · SUTIL · Force India
2 · ROSBERG · Mercedes

46	47	48	49	50	51	52	53	54	55	56	
5	5	5	5	5	5	5	5	5	5	5	1
6	6	6	6	6	6	6	6	6	6	6	2
4	4	4	4	4	4	4	4	4	4	4	3
11	11	11	11	11	11	11	11	11	11	11	
14	14	14	14	14	14	14	14	14	14	14	
2	2	2	2	2	2	2	2	2	2	2	6
7	7	7	7	7	7	7	7	7	7	7	7
1	1	1	1	1	1	1	1	1	1	1	8
8	8	8	8	8	8	8	8	8	17	17	9
17	17	17	17	17	17	17	17	17	10	10	10
10	10	10	10	10	10	10	10	10	16	16	
16	16	16	16	16	16	16	16	16	9		
9	9	9	9	9	9	9	9	9			
25	25	25	25	25	25	25	25				
20	20	20	20	20	20	20	20				
21	21	21	21	21	21	21					
18	18	18	18	18	18						
19											

21 Pit stop
14 One lap or more behind

RACE TYRE STRATEGIES

	Driver	Race Stint 1	Race Stint 2	Race Stint 3
1	Vettel	Soft: 1-23	Hard: 24-56	
2	Webber	Soft: 1-24	Hard: 25-56	
3	Rosberg	Soft: 1-22	Hard: 23-56	
4	Kubica	Soft: 1-21	Hard: 22-56	
5	Sutil	Soft: 1-20	Hard: 21-56	
6	Hamilton	Hard: 1-30	Soft: 31-56	
7	Massa	Hard: 1-26	Soft: 27-56	
8	Button	Soft: 1-9	Hard: 10-56	
9	Alguersuari	Hard: 1-19	Soft: 20-56	
10	Hülkenberg	Soft: 1-13	Hard: 14-56	
11	Buemi	Soft: 1-14	Soft: 15-34	Hard: 35-56
12	Barrichello	Soft: 1-7	Hard: 8-44	Hard: 45-55
13	Alonso	Hard: 1-36	Soft: 37-54 (dnf)	
14	di Grassi	Soft: 1-26	Hard: 27-53	
15	Chandhok	Soft: 1-15	Hard: 16-53	
16	Senna	Soft: 1-16	Hard: 17-52	
17	Trulli	Soft: 1-15	Hard: 16-51	
nc	Kovalainen	Soft: 1-11	Hard: 12-17	Hard: 18-46
	Petrov	Soft: 1-13	Hard: 14-32 (dnf)	
	Liuzzi	Soft: 1-12	Hard: 13 (dnf)	
	Schumacher	Soft: 1-9 (dnf)		
	Kobayashi	Soft: 1-8 (dnf)		
	Glock	Soft: 1 (dnf)		
	de la Rosa	dns		

The tyre regulations stipulate that the two dry tyre specifications must be used during the race. The Soft compound Bridgestone Potenza tyre is marked with a green stripe on the sidewall.

FIA FORMULA 1 WORLD CHAMPIONSHIP · ROUND 4

CHINESE GRAND PRIX

SHANGHAI CIRCUIT

Jenson Button overcame unpredictable weather and safety car interruptions to score his second victory in four starts for the McLaren team.
Photo: Peter J Fox

SHANGHAI QUALIFYING

RELENTLESS, ruthless – call him what you will, but you can't fault Sebastian Vettel's effectiveness. He wasn't particularly happy with his Red Bull RB6 during Saturday morning's third and final free practice session, when he trailed team-mate Mark Webber and Lewis Hamilton, so he pored over the telemetry data, poached a few elements of Webber's set-up and then used them to gain the upper hand.

Given that he did it while simultaneously tailoring his driving to the car's revised mannerisms, it was all the more impressive. "My guys missed lunch to sort the car," he said, "so I have to thank them for that. They just managed to get everything ready for qualifying, but the balance felt different, so I had to adapt. I drifted a bit wide through the first sequence of corners on my opening run in Q3, but I managed to put everything together on the second."

And then some. Second to fifth places were separated by just 0.173 seconds, but Vettel's improvisational 1m 34.558s lap put him 0.248 seconds clear of the rest. Astute management of Bridgestone's soft-compound tyre was critical, and Vettel bided his time, relatively speaking, nursing his rubber through the first part of the lap – where the endless scrabble through Turns One and Two takes a significant toll on the front left – and retaining useful extra bite where rivals had none.

Vettel was certain, too, that even greater delicacy would be required in the race. "I think it will definitely rain," he said, "but it's a question of when. The forecast looks quite bad, but we seem to be competitive at every type of circuit. Wet or dry, I think we'll be in good shape."

The vanquished Webber sought no excuses. "I was pretty happy with my lap," he said, "but Seb put in a really good one right at the end. The stopwatch doesn't lie."

Third for Ferrari, Fernando Alonso felt much the same way. "The Red Bulls seem unbeatable," he said. "Today was an accurate reflection of our potential, in qualifying at least, so I'm happy with the way things went." And if it should rain? "Hard to know," he said, "because when that happened during winter testing, teams were never running the same set-ups. We went pretty well in the wet in Australia, though…"

Jenson Button and Hamilton were fifth and sixth for McLaren. The defending champion was slightly off the pace in the first two phases of qualifying, but redressed the balance at the end. "The car felt much better in Q3," he said, "but it was a little bit too late by then. It felt quite different, balance-wise, and I had to play around with the differential and front wing in order to feel comfortable."

Hamilton was perplexed not to be able to challenge for pole. "I don't really know where I lost the time," he said, "The car felt great in Q1 and Q2, but in Q3 it started moving around a lot more, and it seemed as though the front end was bottoming out."

Both ended up behind Nico Rosberg, who capitalised on Mercedes GP's revised rear wing configuration to annex fourth – "quite a nice surprise", apparently – although team-mate Michael Schumacher was unable to balance the car to his liking, and ninth place reflected as much. More significantly, he was seven-tenths adrift of his compatriot – proof that old dogs and new tricks are not always mutually incompatible.

Right: Lewis Hamilton ran Button a close second at the chequered flag, after switching to a four-stop tyre strategy in a successful bid to vault up the field.
Photo: Jean-François Galeron/WRi2

Below: Vettel had pole, but the race-day weather would compromise his race.
Photo: Peter J Fox

"HOW long would it take to get home on the Trans-Siberian Railway?" The question was posed only half in jest. With almost all European air travel suspended, courtesy of a volcanic cloud drifting across from Iceland, potential escape routes from Shanghai dominated paddock conversation during the build-up to the Chinese Grand Prix. Just before the start, however, all eyes were on a different type of cloud, edging ominously towards the circuit.

The track was dry when Fernando Alonso made one of the most explosive starts in recent Formula One history. Explosive, but illegal. He burst through from third on the grid to usurp the Red Bulls of Mark Webber and Sebastian Vettel, who had started hesitantly from pole, but on lap four the Spaniard was ordered to serve a drive-through by way of retribution. By that stage, the race was already in the throes of significant pandemonium.

As the field headed down to Turn Six on the opening lap, Tonio Liuzzi lost control of his Force India. The Italian claimed the cold conditions had made it difficult to warm his brakes on the formation lap, but that particular truth was the same for

everybody. "As soon as I braked," he said, "the rear end locked completely." He spun around, reversing into the innocent Sébastien Buemi; Kamui Kobayashi – equally blameless – was caught up in the aftermath. All three were out on the spot, the safety car was dispatched and, simultaneously, it began to rain. Rubens Barrichello, Adrian Sutil and Jaime Alguersuari pitted immediately for intermediates, and most of the field followed suit one lap later, although Lewis Hamilton did so very late. "I wasn't sure whether or not the team was instructing me to come in," he said. "It was a bit of a miscommunication." By the time he'd made up his mind, he was already committed to Turn 16, and had to turn sharp right and enter the pits by driving straight through a gravel trap.

The flurry of stops compromised both Red Bull drivers. Webber, first in, ran straight into the team's front jack and damaged it, tweaking his front wing in the process and delaying Vettel, who was stacked up behind.

Nico Rosberg opted to stay out on dries and now led four like-minded colleagues: Jenson Button, Robert Kubica, Vitaly Petrov and Pedro de la Rosa, although the Spaniard's run towards the front didn't last long, because he pulled off with a dead engine after eight laps.

The race resumed on lap three, with Alonso running sixth from Heikki Kovalainen (the only other driver not to pit), Sutil, Barrichello, Alguersuari, Webber, Felipe Massa, Michael Schumacher, Hamilton, Vettel, Jarno Trulli, Nico Hülkenberg, Bruno Senna and Karun Chandhok, who had been obliged to start from the pits after having some hydraulic componentry changed under *parc fermé* conditions. The race had begun disastrously for Virgin: like many of the company's aeroplanes, its two F1 cars were grounded. Timo Glock had taken a punt on going to the grid on wets, but he had been pushed back to the garage when his Cosworth's pneumatic valve system lost air pressure. Lucas di Grassi's car was already there, with clutch trouble, but the Brazilian finally joined in on lap seven. It wasn't long, though, before the problem recurred.

The rain had more or less stopped when the race restarted, so all those on wets were soon in for dries – and Alonso had to pit twice, once to serve his drive-through. "Staying on dries was definitely the right thing to do," Button said, "although it didn't always feel like it because grip levels were changing by the lap."

He tracked Rosberg until lap 19, when the German ran wide at Turn 11, largely because it had started to rain again. During the next two laps, the whole field came in for intermediates, and Button resumed at the front, ahead of Rosberg and the Renaults. By now, Hamilton had fought back from 16th, after his corrective tyre stop on lap five, to seventh – and he'd done most of that the hard way. One of the highlights was a brief, but lively battle with Schumacher. This illustrated that there was absolutely nothing wrong with the German's track craft, but his positional awareness was rather offset by the fact he was bog slow.

When Button first took the lead, he had been almost 50 seconds ahead of his team-mate, but that advantage was reduced to just 3.2 seconds when the safety car reappeared on lap 21, this time because the track was littered with carbon debris after Alguersuari had shattered his front wing against the back of Senna's HRT, which had been rendered invisible in a shroud of spray.

The leaders bunched up significantly as the safety car's lights went out at the end of lap 25, and Hamilton immediately gained a place by edging Webber wide (completely off the track, in fact). Then he picked

off Schumacher, again, before dealing with Petrov and Kubica on laps 27 and 29 respectively. Rosberg proved a more stubborn adversary, but the conditions soon required fresh intermediates, and Hamilton was one of the first to make the change, on lap 37, one before the German. Fresh tyres were worth an extra three seconds or so per lap, and Hamilton's prompt call enabled him to move up to second.

Button came in for tyres on lap 38 and began to edge away as Hamilton radioed in to complain that his front left was shot. On lap 51, however, with five to go, the leader ran wide at the hairpin and Hamilton closed in once more. "I really struggled to put any heat into the tyres after that," Button said, "and it began raining quite hard once again during the final few laps, which made things very tricky." He didn't put a foot wrong, though: just like his Australian victory, it had been a masterclass in astute race management.

Hamilton would not have been a threat at all without the second safety car, but its intervention led to a frisson of tension on the McLaren pit wall, "There were some discussions about whether we should tell the drivers to ease up," team principal Martin Whitmarsh said, "but I felt we couldn't do it. They ran different strategies, and Lewis had to be given the opportunity to compete. Things sometimes go horribly wrong when you take such decisions, but they are both very sensible. Would it have been more comfortable if we'd told them to cruise at the end? Yes it would, and I'd have fewer grey hairs, but it was right to let them race, for the sake of the show."

And some show it had been, even if the locals – who, after seven seasons, have yet to embrace the concept of Formula One – didn't necessarily appreciate as much.

Hamilton faced another challenge after the race, when he and Vettel were hauled to race control to explain why they had driven side by side through the pits after their tyre stops on lap five. Both were judged to have driven dangerously and were given "the penalty of a reprimand" (ie. no penalty at all). The Englishman described his four-stop race as "quite eventful" – an understatement of the highest calibre.

Rosberg was satisfied with his second consecutive podium finish. "We made a good tyre call early on," he said. "I took advice from my team, and decided to give it a go and stay out. On the track, you are sayng, 'Please stop raining, please stop raining,' and it is just so on the edge. If it rains a little bit more, it is the wrong call; if it rains a little bit less, it is fine. It was nice to lead the race for quite a long time, but I think I got a little bit more tyre degradation than Jenson, and as soon as it started raining again, I struggled a little bit more and made a mistake. In general, though, I'm happy."

The second safety car annulled the worst effects of Alonso's drive-through and enabled him to shuffle his way back towards where he was supposed to be. He

Left: Rosberg drove well to achieve another strong podium finish, although the Mercedes driver had to give best to Hamilton in the closing stages.
Photo: Jean-François Galeron/WRi2

Below left: Contrasting, and sometimes confusing, images of China.
Photos: Peter J Fox

Below: No ceremony as Alonso barges his Ferrari ahead of team-mate Massa on the entry to the pit lane.
Photo: Andrew Hone

was up to fifth just before the final stops, during the course of which he vaulted Kubica. The Pole stopped on lap 37, one before Alonso, which should have given him an advantage, but new tyres provide no protection against lapped traffic, and the resultant delay allowed the Spaniard to annex fourth. Like Hamilton's, his had been a strong recovery, but his best move came on lap 19, when he passed team-mate Massa at the left-hander in the pit entry road as they came in together for intermediates. It was a wondrous piece of improvisation, the kind of move that separates champions from the rest (although Massa might not have thought so) – and Ferrari's mechanics were no less impressive as they juggled assorted tyres to make sure they had the correct Bridgestones ready for the car they were least expecting.

Vettel took sixth, his front wing slightly tweaked after an earlier brush with Sutil, and Petrov passed Webber for seventh when the Australian's final set of tyres wilted, largely because they were three laps older than the Russian's. Massa was an undistinguished ninth, from Schumacher, who spent much of the afternoon being bullied aside by younger rivals. "I did not manage my tyre strategy very well," he said. "It was one of those races you do not want to remember, but that has been true of the whole weekend, really." He spent almost as much time being overtaken as Hamilton and Alonso did overtaking.

Sutil, 11th, insisted that his first-lap tyre stop had been "the correct decision at the time, because it was raining quite a bit", although the final result hardly reflected as much. Barrichello, Alguersuari, Kovalainen, Hülkenberg, Senna and Chandhok completed the finishers, while Trulli dropped out with hydraulic gremlins. The Italian stopped on lap 17 and spent more than 11 minutes in the pits while the problem was rectified by the team, but the cure was only temporary.

The conclusion of one race heralded the start of another – that to get home. Four days would be regarded as a competitive time.

Simon Arron

JOHNNIE
WALKER
爱国者

EDITOR'S VIEW
THE PAINFUL TRUTH

THERE is almost always a moment early in every season when one reaches the (oft-premature) conclusion that a particular team is exerting such a decisive performance edge that it's no longer worth speculating on how the balance of the year will unfold. Done and dusted, the end of the story.

It wasn't like that after China, though. Look beyond the fact that all four pole positions so far in the season had fallen to the superb Red Bull RB6, even if this had only been parlayed into that single race victory at Sepang. Jenson Button's second win in four races not only demonstrated the obvious good sense shown by the world champion in making his switch to McLaren, but also the operational even-handedness displayed by McLaren towards him and Lewis Hamilton. It was obvious that the team was making good its promise to dispel any trace of partiality in the treatment of the two men.

Viewing F1 as a whole, the vista seemed promising going into the fourth race of the season, the final round of the initial 'global tour'. Yet there were unmistakable signs that the sport's new 'cut-price' era was turning out to be even more difficult than might have been expected initially. Going into Shanghai, there was no obvious sign of a performance breakthrough of any sort from either Virgin Racing or HRT, and while the re-emergent Lotus squad was clearly a cut above the other newcomers, there was no real indication of it becoming a serious challenger for a position at the back of the mainstream bunch.

Taking the longer view, there were also clear signals about the sport's commercial reality as the cars were fettled in the giant Shanghai pit complex. Two teams considered to be among the most likely future F1 contenders – Prodrive and Lola – confirmed that they would not be making formal applications for places on the World Championship Grand Prix grids in 2011.

Instead, Prodrive would concentrate on fielding Aston Martins in all appropriate sports car racing categories, as well as re-involving itself in the World Rally Championship in a long-term involvement with BMW's MINI brand. David Richards, the Prodrive founder, had thought long and hard about the possibility of entering F1, but eventually decided to stick with what he knew and what he believed to be the most commercially realistic route to pursue.

Prodrive and Lola made no secret that they were not totally convinced about the viability of the present F1 business model and how it applied to newcomers set on making a debut in the sport. At the time, some critics considered this stance to be sour grapes, but within another three months, their decisions were given further credibility when Bernie Ecclestone, no less, said that he would be surprised if all the new teams who had thrown their hats into the ring for 2010 actually survived the year.

It might have been a painful truth for the long-term outlook, but the message had more than a touch of commercial realism about it.

Alan Henry

Above: Karun Chandhok receives service from the HRT mechanics.

Left: Mark Webber takes a look at the McLaren after qualifying.

Photos: Jean-François Galeron/WRi2

FIA F1 WORLD CHAMPIONSHIP · ROUND 4

CHINESE GRAND PRIX

SHANGHAI 16–18 APRIL 2010

RACE DISTANCE: 56 laps, 189.559 miles/305.066km

RACE WEATHER: Drizzle/rain (track 22–25°C, air 19–21°C)

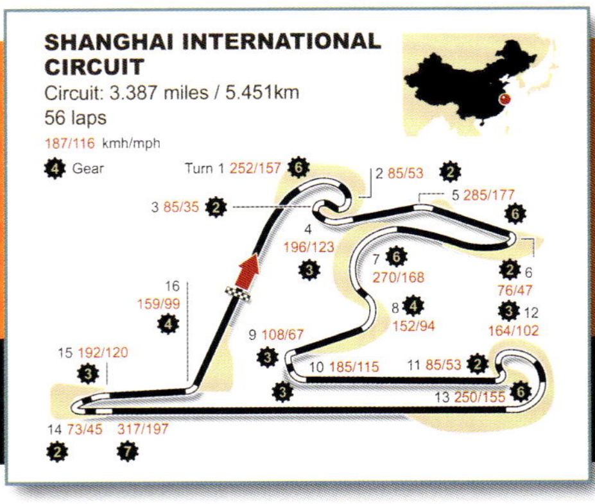

Pos.	Driver	Nat.	No.	Entrant	Car/Engine	Tyres	Laps	Time/Retirement	Speed (mph/km/h)	Gap to leader	Fastest race lap	
1	**Jenson Button**	GB	1	Vodafone McLaren Mercedes	McLaren MP4-25-Mercedes FO108X V8	B	56	1h 46m 42.163s	106.591/171.541		1m 42.886s	14
2	**Lewis Hamilton**	GB	2	Vodafone McLaren Mercedes	McLaren MP4-25-Mercedes FO108X V8	B	56	1h 46m 43.693s	106.565/171.500	+ 1.530s	1m 42.061s	13
3	**Nico Rosberg**	D	4	Mercedes GP Petronas F1 Team	Mercedes MGP W01-Mercedes FO108X V8	B	56	1h 46m 51.647s	106.433/171.287	+ 9.484s	1m 43.245s	14
4	**Fernando Alonso**	E	8	Scuderia Ferrari Marlboro	Ferrari F10-056 V8	B	56	1h 46m 54.032s	106.394/171.224	+ 11.869s	1m 44.134s	14
5	**Robert Kubica**	PL	11	Renault F1 Team	Renault R30-RS27 V8	B	56	1h 47m 04.376s	106.222/170.948	+ 22.213s	1m 43.630s	14
6	**Sebastian Vettel**	D	5	Red Bull Racing	Red Bull RB6-Renault RS27 V8	B	56	1h 47m 15.473s	106.039/170.653	+ 33.310s	1m 42.358s	14
7	**Vitaly Petrov**	RUS	12	Renault F1 Team	Renault R30-RS27 V8	B	56	1h 47m 29.763s	105.804/170.275	+ 47.600s	1m 43.801s	14
8	**Mark Webber**	AUS	6	Red Bull Racing	Red Bull RB6-Renault RS27 V8	B	56	1h 47m 34.335s	105.729/170.155	+ 52.172s	1m 42.609s	14
9	**Felipe Massa**	BR	7	Scuderia Ferrari Marlboro	Ferrari F10-056 V8	B	56	1h 47m 39.959s	105.637/170.006	+ 57.796s	1m 44.594s	14
10	**Michael Schumacher**	GB	3	Mercedes GP Petronas F1 Team	Mercedes MGP W01-Mercedes FO108X V8	B	56	1h 47m 43.912s	105.572/169.902	+ 1m 01.749s	1m 44.298s	14
11	Adrian Sutil	D	14	Force India F1 Team	Force India VJM03-Mercedes FO108X V8	B	56	1h 47m 45.037s	105.554/169.873	+ 1m 02.874s	1m 44.364s	14
12	Rubens Barrichello	BR	9	AT&T Williams	Williams FW32-Cosworth CA2010 V8	B	56	1h 47m 45.828s	105.541/169.852	+ 1m 03.665s	1m 45.559s	17
13	Jaime Alguersuari	E	17	Scuderia Toro Rosso	Toro Rosso STR5-Ferrari 056 V8	B	56	1h 47m 53.579s	105.415/169.649	+ 1m 11.416s	1m 43.755s	14
14	Heikki Kovalainen	FIN	19	Lotus Racing	Lotus T127-Cosworth CA2010 V8	B	55			+ 1 lap	1m 47.141s	14
15	Nico Hülkenberg	D	10	AT&T Williams	Williams FW32-Cosworth CA2010 V8	B	55			+ 1 lap	1m 44.549s	13
16	Bruno Senna	BR	21	HRT F1 Team	HRT F110-Cosworth CA2010 V8	B	54			+ 2 laps	1m 48.216s	16
17	Karun Chandhok	IND	20	HRT F1 Team	HRT F110-Cosworth CA2010 V8	B	52			+ 4 laps	1m 48.788s	15
	Jarno Trulli	I	18	Lotus Racing	Lotus T127-Cosworth CA2010 V8	B	26	*hydraulics*			1m 49.675s	14
	Lucas di Grassi	BR	25	Virgin Racing	Virgin VR-01-Cosworth CA2010 V8	B	8	*clutch*			1m 53.185s	7
	Pedro de la Rosa	E	22	BMW Sauber F1 Team	BMW Sauber C29-Ferrari 056 V8	B	7	*engine*			1m 47.739s	6
	Sébastien Buemi	CH	16	Scuderia Toro Rosso	Toro Rosso STR5-Ferrari 056 V8	B	0	*accident*			no time	
	Kamui Kobayashi	J	23	BMW Sauber F1 Team	BMW Sauber C29-Ferrari 056 V8	B	0	*accident*			no time	
	Vitantonio Liuzzi	I	15	Force India F1 Team	Force India VJM03-Mercedes FO108X V8	B	0	*accident*			no time	
NS	Timo Glock	D	24	Virgin Racing	Virgin VR-01-Cosworth CA2010 V8	B		*engine – valve system*			no time	

Fastest race lap: Lewis Hamilton on lap 13, 1m 42.061s, 119.473mph/192.273km/h.

Lap record: Michael Schumacher (Ferrari F2004 V10), 1m 32.238s, 132.196mph/212.749km/h (2004).

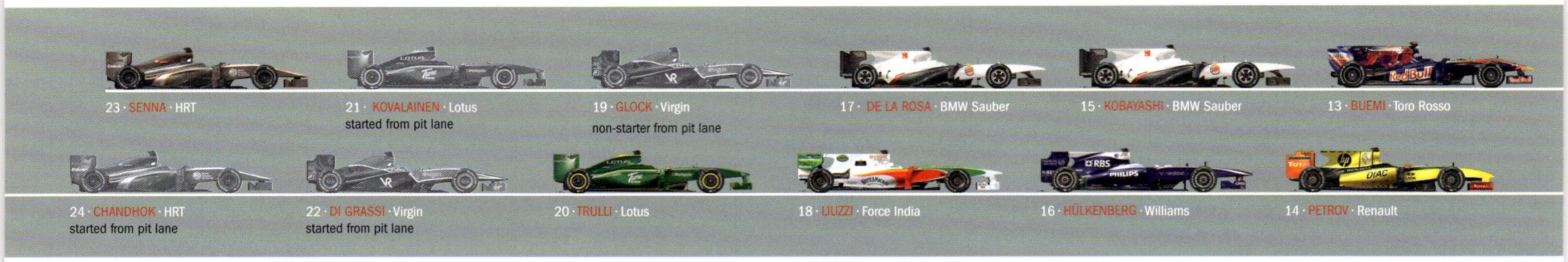

Grid order	1	2	3	4	5	6	7	8	9	10	11	12	13	14	15	16	17	18	19	20	21	22
5 VETTEL	8	8	4	4	4	4	4	4	4	4	4	4	4	4	4	4	4	4	1	1	1	1
6 WEBBER	6	6	1	1	1	1	1	1	1	1	1	1	1	1	1	1	1	1	4	4	4	4
8 ALONSO	5	4	11	11	11	11	11	11	11	11	1	11	11	11	11	11	11	11	11	11	11	11
4 ROSBERG	4	1	12	8	22	22	22	12	12	12	12	12	12	12	12	12	12	12	12	12	12	12
1 BUTTON	1	5	22	14	14	12	12	17	17	17	17	3	3	3	3	2	2	2	2	2	3	3
2 HAMILTON	2	11	8	22	12	17	17	19	3	3	3	2	2	2	2	3	5	5	5	5	6	6
7 MASSA	7	12	19	12	6	14	19	3	19	14	2	5	5	5	5	5	3	3	3	3	2	2
11 KUBICA	3	7	14	9	8	19	3	14	14	19	14	6	6	6	6	6	6	6	6	6	5	5
3 SCHUMACHER	11	22	9	17	17	6	14	5	5	5	5	14	14	14	14	14	14	17	17	14	14	14
14 SUTIL	12	19	17	6	7	7	6	6	2	2	6	17	17	17	17	17	17	14	14	8	8	8
9 BARRICHELLO	22	2	6	7	19	3	5	2	6	6	19	19	9	7	7	7	7	7	8	9	9	9
17 ALGUERSUARI	9	3	7	2	9	8	2	9	9	9	9	9	7	9	9	9	9	8	7	7	7	7
16 BUEMI	18	14	3	19	2	18	9	7	7	7	7	7	8	8	8	8	8	9	9	17	19	19
12 PETROV	19	9	2	5	5	9	18	18	8	8	8	8	19	19	19	19	19	19	19	19	10	10
23 KOBAYASHI	14	17	5	3	18	5	7	8	18	18	10	10	10	10	10	10	10	10	10	10	17	17
10 HULKENBERG	21	18	18	10	10	2	21	21	21	10	18	18	18	18	18	18	21	21	21	21	21	21
22 DE LA ROSA	10	21	10	18	3	21	8	10	10	21	21	21	21	21	21	21	18	20	20	20	20	20
15 LIUZZI	17	10	21	21	21	20	10	20	20	20	20	20	20	20	20	20	20	18	18	18	18	18
24 GLOCK	20	20	20	20	20	10	20	25														
18 TRULLI	25	25	25	25	25	25	25															
19 KOVALAINEN																						
25 DI GRASSI																						
21 SENNA																						
20 CHANDHOK																						

Grid order	23	24	25	26	27	28	29	30	31	32	33	34	35	36	37	38	39	40	41	42	43	44	45
5 VETTEL	1	1	1	1	1	1	1	1	1	1	1	1	1	1	1	1	1	1	1	1	1	1	1
6 WEBBER	4	4	4	4	4	4	4	4	4	4	4	4	4	4	4	4	2	2	2	2	2	2	2
8 ALONSO	11	1	11	11	11	11	2	2	2	2	2	2	2	2	2	8	4	4	4	4	4	4	4
4 ROSBERG	12	12	12	12	2	2	11	11	11	11	11	11	11	11	8	2	8	8	8	8	8	8	8
1 BUTTON	3	3	3	2	12	12	12	12	12	12	8	8	8	8	11	12	11	11	11	11	11	11	11
2 HAMILTON	6	6	2	14	14	14	8	8	8	8	5	5	5	5	5	11	5	5	5	5	5	5	5
7 MASSA	2	2	5	3	8	8	14	5	5	5	12	12	12	12	12	5	6	6	6	6	6	6	6
11 KUBICA	5	5	14	8	5	5	5	14	14	14	14	14	14	14	14	14	3	3	3	3	3	3	3
3 SCHUMACHER	14	14	8	5	3	3	3	3	3	3	3	3	3	7	7	7	17	17	17	17	17	17	12
14 SUTIL	8	8	9	9	9	9	9	7	7	7	7	7	7	3	9	6	12	12	12	12	12	12	7
9 BARRICHELLO	9	9	6	7	7	7	7	9	6	6	6	6	9	9	6	3	7	7	7	7	7	7	17
17 ALGUERSUARI	7	7	7	6	6	6	6	6	9	9	9	9	6	6	3	17	9	9	9	9	9	14	14
16 BUEMI	19	19	19	17	17	17	17	17	17	17	17	17	17	17	17	9	14	14	14	14	14	9	9
12 PETROV	17	17	17	19	19	19	19	19	19	19	19	19	19	19	19	19	19	19	19	19	19	19	19
23 KOBAYASHI	10	10	10	21	10	10	10	10	10	10	10	10	10	10	10	10	10	10	10	10	10	10	10
10 HULKENBERG	21	21	21	10	21	21	21	21	21	21	21	21	21	21	21	21	21	21	21	21	21	21	21
22 DE LA ROSA	20	20	20	20	20	20	20	20	20	20	20	20	20	20	20	20	20	20	20	20	20	20	20
15 LIUZZI	18	18	18	18																			
24 GLOCK																							
18 TRULLI																							
19 KOVALAINEN																							
25 DI GRASSI																							
21 SENNA																							
20 CHANDHOK																							

Safety car deployed on laps shown

TIME SHEETS

PRACTICE 1 (FRIDAY)

Weather: Sunny

Temperatures: track 19-26°C, air 12-15°C

Pos.	Driver	Laps	Time
1	Jenson Button	15	1m 36.677s
2	Nico Rosberg	17	1m 36.748s
3	Lewis Hamilton	19	1m 36.775s
4	Michael Schumacher	14	1m 37.509s
5	Sebastian Vettel	20	1m 37.601s
6	Robert Kubica	17	1m 37.716s
7	Vitaly Petrov	25	1m 37.745s
8	Mark Webber	17	1m 37.980s
9	Adrian Sutil	13	1m 38.008s
10	Felipe Massa	19	1m 38.098s
11	Jaime Alguersuari	19	1m 38.161s
12	Kamui Kobayashi	21	1m 38.375s
13	Pedro de la Rosa	19	1m 38.421s
14	Nico Hülkenberg	20	1m 38.569s
15	Paul di Resta	26	1m 38.618s
16	Rubens Barrichello	17	1m 38.678s
17	Sébastien Buemi	5	1m 39.939s
18	Jarno Trulli	22	1m 41.531s
19	Heikki Kovalainen	23	1m 41.779s
20	Timo Glock	19	1m 41.830s
21	Lucas di Grassi	27	1m 42.181s
22	Bruno Senna	23	1m 43.875s
23	Karun Chandhok	20	1m 43.949s
24	Fernando Alonso	6	no time

PRACTICE 2 (FRIDAY)

Weather: Sunny

Temperatures: track 24-27°C, air 15-16°C

Pos.	Driver	Laps	Time
1	Lewis Hamilton	26	1m 35.217s
2	Nico Rosberg	22	1m 35.465s
3	Jenson Button	26	1m 35.593s
4	Michael Schumacher	28	1m 35.602s
5	Sebastian Vettel	30	1m 35.791s
6	Mark Webber	29	1m 35.995s
7	Adrian Sutil	31	1m 36.254s
8	Jaime Alguersuari	43	1m 36.377s
9	Robert Kubica	29	1m 36.389s
10	Fernando Alonso	33	1m 36.604s
11	Felipe Massa	36	1m 36.944s
12	Vitaly Petrov	27	1m 36.986s
13	Pedro de la Rosa	32	1m 37.421s
14	Kamui Kobayashi	33	1m 37.431s
15	Rubens Barrichello	30	1m 37.657s
16	Vitantonio Liuzzi	31	1m 37.804s
17	Nico Hülkenberg	29	1m 37.867s
18	Jarno Trulli	35	1m 39.624s
19	Heikki Kovalainen	30	1m 39.947s
20	Timo Glock	27	1m 40.233s
21	Karun Chandhok	32	1m 41.008s
22	Lucas di Grassi	28	1m 41.107s
23	Bruno Senna	32	1m 41.345s

PRACTICE 3 (SATURDAY)

Weather: Sunny

Temperatures: track 27-32°C, air 18-19°C

Pos.	Driver	Laps	Time
1	Mark Webber	16	1m 35.323s
2	Lewis Hamilton	12	1m 35.564s
3	Sebastian Vettel	14	1m 35.691s
4	Jenson Button	14	1m 35.747s
5	Fernando Alonso	13	1m 35.857s
6	Nico Rosberg	12	1m 35.913s
7	Michael Schumacher	10	1m 36.262s
8	Robert Kubica	16	1m 36.343s
9	Felipe Massa	11	1m 36.416s
10	Kamui Kobayashi	16	1m 36.634s
11	Jaime Alguersuari	17	1m 36.879s
12	Vitantonio Liuzzi	16	1m 37.031s
13	Sébastien Buemi	18	1m 37.192s
14	Adrian Sutil	18	1m 37.240s
15	Vitaly Petrov	13	1m 37.339s
16	Rubens Barrichello	13	1m 37.585s
17	Pedro de la Rosa	19	1m 37.664s
18	Nico Hülkenberg	14	1m 37.784s
19	Timo Glock	15	1m 39.579s
20	Heikki Kovalainen	17	1m 39.616s
21	Lucas di Grassi	13	1m 39.749s
22	Jarno Trulli	16	1m 39.776s
23	Bruno Senna	19	1m 40.316s
24	Karun Chandhok	18	1m 41.141s

FOR THE RECORD

1st POINTS: Vitaly Petrov

DID YOU KNOW

The last time English drivers finished 1st and 2nd was Monaco 1969 (Graham Hill and Piers Courage), while the last time British drivers were 1st and 2nd was Austria 1999 (Irvine and Coulthard).

The last time that drivers of the same nationality were 1st and 2nd was Japan 2004 (Michael and Ralf Schumacher).

The last time that the same engine make powered the top three was Luxembourg 1997 (Villeneuve, Alesi and Frentzen with Renault power).

Photos: Peter J. Fox

QUALIFYING (SATURDAY)

Weather: Sunny Temperatures: track 31-32°C, air 21°C

Pos.	Driver	First	Second	Third	Qualifying Tyre
1	Sebastian Vettel	1m 36.317s	1m 35.280s	1m 34.558s	Soft
2	Mark Webber	1m 35.978s	1m 35.100s	1m 34.806s	Soft
3	Fernando Alonso	1m 35.987s	1m 35.235s	1m 34.913s	Soft
4	Nico Rosberg	1m 35.952s	1m 35.134s	1m 34.923s	Soft
5	Jenson Button	1m 36.122s	1m 35.443s	1m 34.979s	Soft
6	Lewis Hamilton	1m 35.641s	1m 34.928s	1m 35.034s	Soft
7	Felipe Massa	1m 36.076s	1m 35.290s	1m 35.180s	Soft
8	Robert Kubica	1m 36.348s	1m 35.550s	1m 35.364s	Soft
9	Michael Schumacher	1m 36.484s	1m 35.715s	1m 35.646s	Soft
10	Adrian Sutil	1m 36.671s	1m 35.665s	1m 35.963s	Soft
11	Rubens Barrichello	1m 36.664s	1m 35.748s		
12	Jaime Alguersuari	1m 36.618s	1m 36.047s		
13	Sébastien Buemi	1m 36.793s	1m 36.149s		
14	Vitaly Petrov	1m 37.031s	1m 36.311s		
15	Kamui Kobayashi	1m 37.044s	1m 36.422s		
16	Nico Hülkenberg	1m 37.049s	1m 36.647s		
17	Pedro de la Rosa	1m 37.050s	1m 37.020s		
18	Vitantonio Liuzzi	1m 37.161s			
19	Timo Glock	1m 39.278s			
20	Jarno Trulli	1m 39.399s			
21	Heikki Kovalainen	1m 39.520s			
22	Lucas di Grassi	1m 39.783s			
23	Bruno Senna	1m 40.469s			
24	Karun Chandhok	1m 40.578s			

POINTS

DRIVERS

1	Jenson Button	60
2	Nico Rosberg	50
3	Fernando Alonso	49
4	Lewis Hamilton	49
5	Sebastian Vettel	45
6	Felipe Massa	41
7	Robert Kubica	40
8	Mark Webber	28
9	Adrian Sutil	10
10	Michael Schumacher	10
11	Vitantonio Liuzzi	8
12	Vitaly Petrov	6
13	Rubens Barrichello	5
14	Jaime Alguersuari	2
15	Nico Hülkenberg	1

CONSTRUCTORS

1	McLaren	109
2	Ferrari	90
3	Red Bull	73
4	Mercedes	60
5	Renault	46
6	Force India	18
7	Williams	6
8	Toro Rosso	2

46	47	48	49	50	51	52	53	54	55	56	·
1	1	1	1	1	1	1	1	1	1	1	1
2	2	2	2	2	2	2	2	2	2	2	2
4	4	4	4	4	4	4	4	4	4	4	3
8	8	8	8	8	8	8	8	8	8	8	4
11	11	11	11	11	11	11	11	11	11	11	5
5	5	5	5	5	5	5	5	5	5	5	6
6	6	6	6	6	6	6	6	12	12	12	7
3	3	3	3	3	12	12	12	6	6	6	8
12	12	12	12	12	3	3	3	3	7	7	9
7	7	7	7	7	7	7	7	7	3	3	10
14	14	14	14	14	14	14	15	14	14	14	
9	9	9	9	9	9	9	9	9	9	9	
17	17	17	17	17	17	17	17	17	17	17	
19	19	19	19	19	19	19	19	19	19		
10	10	10	10	10	10	10	10	10	10		
21	21	21	21	21	21	21	21	21			
20	20	20	20	20	20	20					

21 Pit stop   *14 One lap or more behind*

RACE TYRE STRATEGIES

	Driver	Race Stint 1	Race Stint 2	Race Stint 3	Race Stint 4	Race Stint 5	Race Stint 6	Race Stint 7
1	Button	Soft: 1-20	Inters: 21-38	Inters: 39-56				
2	Hamilton	Soft: 1-2	Inters: 3-5	Hard: 6-20	Inters: 21-37	Inters: 38-56		
3	Rosberg	Soft: 1-20	Inters: 21-38	Inters: 39-56				
4	Alonso	Soft: 1-2	Inters: 3-5	Inters: 6-20	Soft: 21-37	Inters: 38-56		
5	Kubica	Soft: 1-20	Inters: 21-37	Inters: 38-56				
6	Vettel	Soft: 1-2	Inters: 3-5	Hard: 6-20	Inters: 21-37	Inters: 38-56		
7	Petrov	Soft: 1-20	Inters: 21-38	Inters: 39-56				
8	Webber	Soft: 1-2	Inters: 3-6	Hard: 7-19	Inters: 20-35	Inters: 36-56		
9	Massa	Soft: 1-2	Inters: 3-6	Soft: 7-19	Inters: 20-38	Inters: 39-56		
10	Schumacher	Soft: 1-2	Inters: 3-4	Soft: 5-19	Inters: 20-36	Inters: 37-56		
11	Sutil	Soft: 1	Inters: 2-6	Soft: 7-19	Inters: 20-38	Inters: 39-56		
12	Barrichello	Soft: 1	Inters: 2-5	Hard: 6-18	Inters: 19-37	Inters: 38-56		
13	Alguersuari	Soft: 1	Inters: 2-11	Soft: 12-19	Inters: 20	Inters: 21-34	Inters: 35-46	Inters: 47-56
14	Kovalainen	Soft: 1-19	Inters: 20-36	Inters: 37-55				
15	Hülkenberg	Soft: 1-2	Inters: 3-5	Hard: 6-19	Inters: 20-23	Hard: 24-25	Inters: 26-38	Inters: 39-55
16	Senna	Soft: 1-2	Inters: 3-12	Hard: 13-18	Inters: 19-41	Inters: 42-54		
17	Chandhok	Soft: 1-2	Inters: 3-11	Hard: 12-18	Inters: 19-41	Inters: 42-52		
	Trulli	Soft: 1-2	Inters: 3-12	Soft: 13-17	Inters: 18-21	Inters: 22-26 (dnf)		
	di Grassi	Inters: 1-8 (dnf)						
	de la Rosa	Soft: 1-7 (dnf)						
	Buemi	Soft: 0 (dnf)						
	Kobayashi	Soft: 0 (dnf)						
	Liuzzi	Soft: 0 (dnf)						
dns	Glock							

The tyre regulations stipulate that the two dry tyre specifications must be used during the race.
The Soft compound Bridgestone Potenza tyre is marked with a green stripe on the sidewall.

TOTAL

Having gained pole position, Mark Webber dominated proceedings for Red Bull at Catalunya.
Photo: Peter J Fox

FIA FORMULA 1 WORLD CHAMPIONSHIP · ROUND 5

SPANISH GRAND PRIX

CATALUNYA CIRCUIT

CATALUNYA QUALIFYING

"IT'S not often that you'll get to drive a car like this at a circuit like this, so go and enjoy it." Such was the final instruction from Red Bull Racing's sporting director, Christian Horner – and Mark Webber duly complied.

Cars with Adrian Newey's signature have traditionally worked well at an aerodynamically-dependent circuit such as Barcelona, and this time the Red Bull RB6 was in a league all of its own. The fall-out from Iceland's volcanic cloud might have compromised the teams' return from China, but it hadn't stifled the development race.

Almost everybody had significant modifications scheduled for Spain, but Red Bull hadn't so much brought an upgrade as a whole new car. Very little beyond the front wing had been carried forward from China, although the finishing touches were applied quite late. "I think the guys have slept for about five hours during the past two nights," Webber said after taking the third pole of his F1 career, 0.106 seconds quicker than team-mate Sebastian Vettel, but light years clear of the rest. "I'd like to dedicate today's result to them. I put together two good, solid laps and was marginally quicker than Seb after the first run. It's nice to be in that position: trying to build upon an existing advantage rather than playing catch-up."

Vettel admitted that his team-mate had been "unbeatable", despite their customary closeness. "It was only a tenth," he said, "but that was too much for me today."

Despite the raft of new parts, Red Bull had yet to introduce an F-duct, a detail that, potentially, exposed them to Lewis Hamilton's McLaren (third, but 0.834 seconds shy of Webber) on the long run to Turn One. "What can I tell you?" Hamilton said. "The Red Bulls are ridiculously fast through the quick corners. They already had more downforce efficiency than other teams and they've taken another step on top of that this weekend. Although I knew they'd be quick, I didn't expect them to be quite so far ahead. They probably aren't as strong as us down the straights, though, so we'll see how the start goes."

Fernando Alonso qualified fourth, ahead of championship leader Jenson Button, but Ferrari was fined $20,000 for releasing its Spanish talisman from the pits "in an unsafe manner" – he had been dispatched into the path of Nico Rosberg, although they didn't quite collide. Rosberg had other concerns, too, because the second Mercedes was finally being driven in the manner prescribed, dancing over kerbs and attacking the circuit with appropriate aggression. The car's wheelbase had been extended and, for the first time since he returned, Michael Schumacher was starting to look his trademark self.

He lined up sixth, two places ahead of Rosberg. "It was wholly unreasonable for people to expect Michael to come in and perform after three years away," said Mercedes team principal Ross Brawn. "He had to get used to new cars, new tyres and new regulations, but didn't have much chance to test. What we have seen today is a logical continuation of the progress we saw after the first three races.

"I believe his poor race in China was simply a blip. Nico had some understeer problems, but from now on I expect to see him and Michael trading places from race to race, It's our job to make sure they do so from nearer the front of the grid."

Robert Kubica separated the Mercs – but the mechanics were the day's star performers at Renault. Vitaly Petrov crashed the second car heavily during Saturday morning's final free practice and his crew did a stellar job to get it fixed, although the need for a fresh gearbox dictated a five-slot grid penalty.

Mark Webber had a different set of numbers on his mind: victory at the Catalunya circuit would make him the tenth driver to win the Spanish Grand Prix from pole position in as many years.

THIS, in many ways, was an acid test. Bahrain might have been a stinker, but since then Formula One had been bathed in the rich glow of entertainment. This, though, was Barcelona, scene of a thrilling wheel-to-wheel duel between Nigel Mansell and Ayrton Senna in 1991, but a circuit at which not much else had happened since. True to form, the 2010 Spanish Grand Prix lasted 1h 35m 44.101s, but was effectively settled within the first few seconds. It did, though, have its moments.

Mark Webber made a bright start from pole position, but team-mate Sebastian Vettel tucked into his slipstream, while Lewis Hamilton and Fernando Alonso capitalised on the superior straight-line performance their F-ducts allowed to join in for a few seconds. "It was quite tight into Turn One," Webber said, "and I knew we had some pretty quick cars behind us. That was a very important part of the race: I had to make sure I was still in the lead when I exited the corner."

He was, and Vettel clung on to second, with Hamilton and Alonso just slowing each other enough to dilute any challenge. Jenson Button settled into fifth, ahead of Michael Schumacher, Felipe Massa, Adrian Sutil, Jaime Alguersuari (a brilliant start from 15th), Robert Kubica, Nico Rosberg, Rubens Barrichello, Nico Hülkenberg, Tonio Liuzzi, Jarno Trulli, Kamui Kobayashi (who lost time at the first turn when Kubica nudged him through the gravel), Timo Glock (running the only revised Virgin with an expanded fuel tank), Karun Chandhok (who'd been given a five-place penalty for a gearbox change), Vitaly Petrov and Lucas di Grassi. Both Virgin drivers had been given five-place grid penalties for late nomination of gear ratios, not that it made much difference in the scheme of things.

Sébastien Buemi and Pedro de la Rosa headed for the pits after running into each other during the opening scramble. The Spaniard suffered a punctured left rear, and flailing rubber did enough damage to render the car more or less unusable, but he struggled on for 18 laps before parking up.

Bruno Senna made a spectacular start to vault from 24th to 17th by Turn Three. The downside? He failed to negotiate Turn Four. "The car just got away from me," he said, after extricating himself from the tyre wall. He would get plenty of extra mileage later, after arriving at Barcelona Airport to find the European travel industry in a state of some chaos following another waft of volcanic ash and enforced flight

Above: Understandably, Fernando Alonso was the centre of attention at his home race.
Photo: Paul-Henri Cahier

Above left, from top: Mark Webber with his race enginer Ciaran Pilbeam; Rob Smedley with Felipe Massa; and Robert Kubica with his Renault team engineers.

Left: After a slow start to the season, Rubens Barrichello secured some welcome points for Williams.
Photos: Peter J Fox

Above: Michael Schumacher battles to hold off Jenson Button on his way to a fine fourth place.
Photo: Peter J Fox

Top right: Jarno Trulli and Lotus were the best 'class B' finishers.
Photo: Jad Sherif/WRi2

Above right: Close call for Vettel as his Red Bull runs wide with brake problems. He avoided contact with the scenery and ended up third.
Photo: Studio Colombo/WRi2

cancellations. At that point, Senna and HRT team-mate Chandhok simply turned around and headed to Monte Carlo by road.

Poor Heikki Kovalainen didn't even have the opportunity to become embroiled in any first-lap nonsense: his Lotus's gearbox failed on the grid.

Once through the first corner, Webber was never headed again, although it would be a while before he enjoyed the luxury of respite. Vettel remained within touching distance until he made his mandatory tyre stop, on lap 16, but a jammed front right wheel nut cost the German a couple of seconds. He was still fractionally ahead of Hamilton when the Englishman rejoined after his own stop, one lap later (the same time as Webber's), but Vettel was on the outside line at Turn One and ran wide as the cars entered the corner together, which left Hamilton just enough space to reverse the order.

Once he'd annexed second, Hamilton was able to run at a similar pace to Webber, but the Australian was driving with unerring consistency. "I was just looking after car, engine and tyres," he said, although his devastating speed during the early part of his second stint implied haste rather than nurture. Not that he was alone: Hamilton, Vettel and Alonso were similarly relentless, and quite closely matched, but passing opportunities were predictably scarce, so Webber was home and dry.

To add a little context to the team's achievement, sporting director Christian Horner underlined the extent of the work that had been carried out since China. "One week ago," he said, "the floor of Mark's car was still part of a roll of carbon fibre. That's testimony to how hard the guys are working and how quickly they are transforming designs into actual components."

Webber gave praise, too. "Today's victory marks the culmination of a fantastic effort by the whole team," he said. "It started with everybody being out of position in the wake of Shanghai, but they all came to the factory to work during the recent bank holiday, and their eyes are almost popping out of their heads

as a result of the hours they've put in at the track this weekend. It's just boom, boom, boom. Everybody is tuned to the same channel, pushing hard."

In his immediate slipstream, the order shuffled twice during the closing laps. On lap 54, Vettel slid wide when his front right brake disc failed, gifting a position to Alonso. The German pitted for a precautionary check and was sent back out with instructions to nurse the car to the finish. "We could see some carbon shrapnel," said Horner, "so we suspect there was some form of delamination." During the final few laps, he barely dared touch the brakes at all, and the team was sufficiently concerned to suggest he should retire, but Vettel persuaded them that it was worth staying out. Despite not using the left-hand pedal, he was still able to lap within a couple of seconds of the pace – testimony to both the car and his own delicate touch.

His perseverance earned him an unexpected podium finish, too, because Hamilton retired on the penultimate lap when his left front wheel failed, the consequence of a stone becoming trapped and wearing away the metal. "He had a tyre deflation," said team principal Martin Whitmarsh, "but it doesn't appear to have been a tyre problem. His Bridgestones were in pretty good nick."

It was an unjust conclusion to a fine, measured drive. "I was just coaxing the car to the finish when I suddenly felt the steering go," he said. "I didn't sense anything odd before the accident; the car felt great, which is why it was such a surprise. I'm absolutely gutted that it happened so close to the finish, but that's motor racing."

His misfortune generated a sizeable cheer from the crowd, not least because Alonso inherited second. "It was nice to gain a couple of places towards the end," the Spaniard said, "but we have to be honest. Second is a fantastic result, but our performance was only so-so."

The rest were a long way short of even that. Button tracked Alonso during the opening stint, but a dragging clutch made him slow away from his tyre stop, on lap 16, and he dropped behind Schumacher. For all that the German felt more comfortable in the revised Mercedes, it wasn't particularly quick. "I am not too happy," he said, "because my only option today was to defend. I had no chance of making up positions unless the cars ahead had problems, but that's not how you want to go racing."

For the final 50 laps, Button was condemned to watching the Mercedes slither around, partly as a result of Schumacher's defensive technique, partly because it simply wasn't very good. "As everyone knows," Button said, "it's almost impossible to overtake around here, and Michael was moving about a bit to make sure I couldn't. It was frustrating because my car was quick, but that doesn't make any difference if you can't overtake. In the effort, I damaged my tyres quite a bit: I flat-spotted a front and hurt the rears under traction."

He also had to contend with an inoperative dashboard readout, which packed up early in the race. "The team was telling me over the radio to do

things on the steering wheel," he said, "but I couldn't tell whether or not I was doing the right things."

Felipe Massa was sixth and finished the race with a tweaked front wing, after he'd clipped Chandhok's HRT while lapping it, but it didn't make the car any worse than it already was. "The main difficulty was a lack of grip," he said, "especially in the third sector. The broken left front endplate didn't affect the handling much, and replacing it would have cost me at least three places, so it was right to stay out."

Sutil came home in seventh place after a solid, but uncharacteristically quiet afternoon, a performance that went largely unnoticed, because he was one of the few in midfield not be involved in a spat of some kind. Kubica took eighth for Renault, ahead of Barrichello and Alguersuari, the Spaniard not losing out too badly as the result of a collision with Chandhok on lap 28. The Indian subsequently retired with damaged front suspension, but Alguersuari escaped with a drive-through penalty (something team-mate Buemi also incurred, for rejoining unsafely after a tyre stop on lap 22). Hydraulic problems later caused the Swiss to drop out.

Petrov, Kobayashi and Rosberg (who complained that Kubica had pushed him wide on to the grass during the opening lap, although a jammed wheel nut in the pits cost him rather more time) were classified next, ahead of the stationary Hamilton, while Liuzzi, Hülkenberg (with downforce compromised by a damaged floor after he ran wide), Class B winner Trulli, Glock and di Grassi completed the finishers.

There would be a minor delay before the podium ceremony could take place, because the critical component – Webber – was momentarily absent. The Australian had vaulted from *parc fermé*, scrambled over the pit wall and run across the circuit before lobbing his crash helmet into the baying, appreciative mob in the main grandstand.

It was a spontaneous, extravagant gesture – and just the kind of post-race tonic from which the sport benefits. "Like my mechanics," he said, "fans don't always get the best deal."

Simon Arron

Left: Jaime Alguersuari grabbed the final point on offer with tenth place in his home race.
Photo: Peter J Fox

Below: Pirelli's motor sport activities manager, Mario Isola
Photo: Jad Sherif/WRi2

EDITOR'S VIEW
TALKING TYRES

THE talk was all about tyres in the run-up to the first round of the European leg of the F1 world championship. Not just about the comparative performance potential of the so-called 'prime' and 'option' at the Circuit de Catalunya, but in the wider context of just which manufacturer would step in at the start of 2011 to fill the void left by Bridgestone's planned departure from the sport.

It was a measure of the complexity of contemporary F1 politics that the final decision over the likely identity of the new supplier came in the wake of a FOTA meeting, after which Williams technical director Sam Michael commented to the effect that the choice was "between Avon and Michelin". It turned out to be Pirelli, a subtle signal from Jean Todt that it was the FIA who ultimately makes such weighty decisions, not an alliance of the competing teams.

Only two months later (August, 2010), Nick Heidfeld would begin testing Pirelli tyres at Mugello, using a Toyota TF109, in preparation for the Italian firm's big commitment in 2011.

Ever since Bridgestone had indicated its decision to withdraw, the F1 community had been suffused with speculation as to the possible identity of the Japanese tyre company's successor. There were those who felt that Bridgestone might even be persuaded to stay in. Others judged that this might provide a great opportunity for Michelin to return to the fray, but although some sympathetic noises emanated from the company, the wounds caused by events at the 2005 US GP at Indianapolis – where circumstances had conspired to cause all the Michelin runners to withdraw from the race due to technical problems with the rubber – still ran too deep.

In the end, it was Pirelli who signed up for the privilege of becoming F1's latest sole tyre supplier. Its racing pedigree was flawless. It had been in on the ground floor of the official world championship in 1950, providing the tyres on which Giuseppe Farina's Alfa Romeo 158 had won that year's British GP at Silverstone, and it had scored a total of 42 wins between then and 1991, albeit with a break from participation between 1958 and 1985.

Higher up the success rankings comes Dunlop with 83 wins between 1958 and 1970, and Michelin with 93 wins between 1978 and 2005. None comes close, however, to Goodyear's matchless record of 368 wins between 1965 and 1998, much of that period spent as the sport's sole supplier, not because the rules dictated it to be so, but because nobody stepped forward to offer a challenge.

"We much prefer a fight, to be honest," said Goodyear's legendary director of international racing, Leo Mehl, more than 30 years ago, "because the benefits in this business are pretty well split 50-50 between the advertising benefit and the technical feedback. But you run the danger of losing both benefits to some extent if you don't have the stimulus of competition. If you have a monopoly, for example, there is the ever-present danger that technical development may slow down slightly."

Such basic rules apply in much the same manner to this very day. Of course, while the F1 purists believe that a tyre war between major suppliers is all part of the sport's underlying fabric, the need to restrict tyre performance is obviously a prime factor to be borne in mind to prevent lap speeds from spiralling out of control.

"You can spend millions of pounds developing a new aerodynamic device and pick up a couple of tenths of a second a lap," mused one technical director. "In an unfettered tyre war, you can have a situation where you can, theoretically at least, slap on a fresh set of tyres which instantly picks you up over a second a lap, raising potential safety issues. That's why the tyre regulations have to be managed so carefully."

Alan Henry

Left: Webber scored his first win of the season to get his championship challenge into gear.
Photo: Paul-Henri Cahier

FIA F1 WORLD CHAMPIONSHIP · ROUND 4

GRAN PREMIO DE ESPAÑA

TELEFÓNICA

CATALUNYA 7–9 MAY 2010

RACE DISTANCE: 66 laps, 190.826 miles/307.104km

RACE WEATHER: Sunny/partly coudy (track 28–31°C, air 21–23°C)

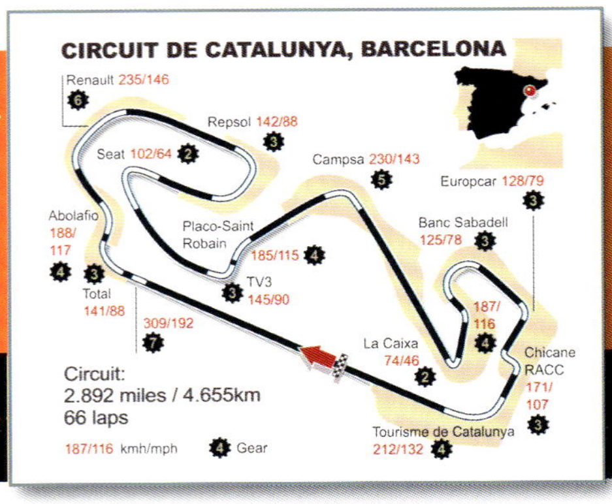

Pos.	Driver	Nat.	No.	Entrant	Car/Engine	Tyres	Laps	Time/Retirement	Speed (mph/km/h)	Gap to leader	Fastest race lap	
1	**Mark Webber**	AUS	6	Red Bull Racing	Red Bull RB6-Renault RS27 V8	B	66	1h 35m 44.101s	119.596/192.471		1m 24.828s	62
2	**Fernando Alonso**	E	8	Scuderia Ferrari Marlboro	Ferrari F10-056 V8	B	66	1h 36m 08.166s	119.097/191.668	+ 24.065s	1m 24.846s	57
3	**Sebastian Vettel**	D	5	Red Bull Racing	Red Bull RB6-Renault RS27 V8	B	66	1h 36m 35.439s	118.536/190.766	+ 51.338s	1m 25.176s	56
4	**Michael Schumacher**	GB	3	Mercedes GP Petronas F1 Team	Mercedes MGP W01-Mercedes FO108X V8	B	66	1h 36m 46.296s	118.315/190.409	+ 1m 02.195s	1m 25.529s	64
5	**Jenson Button**	GB	1	Vodafone McLaren Mercedes	McLaren MP4-25-Mercedes FO108X V8	B	66	1h 36m 47.829s	118.284/190.359	+ 1m 03.728s	1m 25.166s	64
6	**Felipe Massa**	BR	7	Scuderia Ferrari Marlboro	Ferrari F10-056 V8	B	66	1h 36m 49.868s	118.242/190.292	+ 1m 05.767s	1m 25.497s	64
7	**Adrian Sutil**	D	14	Force India F1 Team	Force India VJM03-Mercedes FO108X V8	B	66	1h 36m 57.042s	118.096/190.057	+ 1m 12.941s	1m 25.845s	65
8	**Robert Kubica**	PL	11	Renault F1 Team	Renault R30-RS27 V8	B	66	1h 36m 57.778s	118.081/190.033	+ 1m 13.677s	1m 25.466s	66
9	**Rubens Barrichello**	BR	9	AT&T Williams	Williams FW32-Cosworth CA2010 V8	B	65			+ 1 lap	1m 25.728s	59
10	**Jaime Alguersuari**	E	17	Scuderia Toro Rosso	Toro Rosso STR5-Ferrari 056 V8	B	65			+ 1 lap	1m 25.655s	63
11	Vitaly Petrov	RUS	12	Renault F1 Team	Renault R30-RS27 V8	B	65			+ 1 lap	1m 25.470s	63
12	Kamui Kobayashi	J	23	BMW Sauber F1 Team	BMW Sauber C29-Ferrari 056 V8	B	65			+ 1 lap	1m 26.083s	62
13	Nico Rosberg	D	4	Mercedes GP Petronas F1 Team	Mercedes MGP W01-Mercedes FO108X V8	B	65			+ 1 lap	1m 25.455s	50
14	Lewis Hamilton	GB	2	Vodafone McLaren Mercedes	McLaren MP4-25-Mercedes FO108X V8	B	64	*front wheel*		+ 2 laps	1m 24.357s	59
15	Vitantonio Liuzzi	I	15	Force India F1 Team	Force India VJM03-Mercedes FO108X V8	B	64	*engine*		+ 2 laps	1m 25.924s	63
16	Nico Hülkenberg	D	10	AT&T Williams	Williams FW32-Cosworth CA2010 V8	B	64			+ 2 laps	1m 26.863s	63
17	Jarno Trulli	I	18	Lotus Racing	Lotus T127-Cosworth CA2010 V8	B	63			+ 3 laps	1m 29.564s	56
18	Timo Glock	D	24	Virgin Racing	Virgin VR-01-Cosworth CA2010 V8	B	63			+ 3 laps	1m 29.776s	60
19	Lucas di Grassi	BR	25	Virgin Racing	Virgin VR-01-Cosworth CA2010 V8	B	62			+ 4 laps	1m 29.904s	47
	Sébastien Buemi	CH	16	Scuderia Toro Rosso	Toro Rosso STR5-Ferrari 056 V8	B	42	*hydraulics*			1m 26.724s	41
	Karun Chandhok	IND	20	HRT F1 Team	HRT F110-Cosworth CA2010 V8	B	27	*accident damage*			1m 32.041s	26
	Pedro de la Rosa	E	22	BMW Sauber F1 Team	BMW Sauber C29-Ferrari 056 V8	B	18	*accident damage*			1m 30.411s	9
	Bruno Senna	BR	21	HRT F1 Team	HRT F110-Cosworth CA2010 V8	B	0	*accident*			no time	
NS	Heikki Kovalainen	FIN	19	Lotus Racing	Lotus T127-Cosworth CA2010 V8	B		*gearbox software*				

Fastest race lap: Lewis Hamilton on lap 59, 1m 24.357s, 123.439mph/198.655km/h.

Lap record: Giancarlo Fisichella (Renault R25 V10), 1m 15.641s, 136.835mph/220.213km/h (2005) (2.875-mile/4.627km circuit).

Lap record *(current configuration)*: Kimi Räikkönen (Ferrari F2008 V8), 1m 21.670s, 127.500mph/205.191km/h (2008)

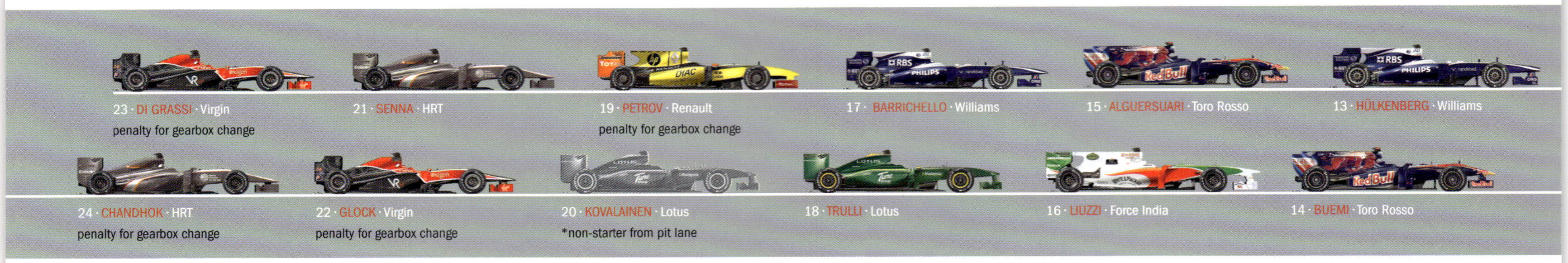

23 · DI GRASSI · Virgin
penalty for gearbox change

21 · SENNA · HRT

19 · PETROV · Renault
penalty for gearbox change

17 · BARRICHELLO · Williams

15 · ALGUERSUARI · Toro Rosso

13 · HÜLKENBERG · Williams

24 · CHANDHOK · HRT
penalty for gearbox change

22 · GLOCK · Virgin
penalty for gearbox change

20 · KOVALAINEN · Lotus
*non-starter from pit lane

18 · TRULLI · Lotus

16 · LIUZZI · Force India

14 · BUEMI · Toro Rosso

	Grid order	1	2	3	4	5	6	7	8	9	10	11	12	13	14	15	16	17	18	19	20	21	22	23	24	25	26	27	28	29	30	31	32	33	34	35	36	37	38	39	40	41	42	43	44	45	46	47	48	49	50	51	52
6	WEBBER	6	6	6	6	6	6	6	6	6	6	6	6	6	6	6	6	6	6	6	6	6	6	6	6	6	6	6	6	6	6	6	6	6	6	6	6	6	6	6	6	6	6	6	6	6	6	6	6	6	6	6	6
5	VETTEL	5	5	5	5	5	5	5	5	5	5	5	5	5	5	5	5	2	2	2	2	2	2	2	2	2	2	2	2	2	2	2	2	2	2	2	2	2	2	2	2	2	2	2	2	2	2	2	2	2	2	2	2
2	HAMILTON	2	2	2	2	2	2	2	2	2	2	2	2	2	2	2	2	5	5	5	5	5	5	5	5	5	5	5	5	5	5	5	5	5	5	5	5	5	5	5	5	5	5	5	5	5	5	5	5	5	5	5	5
8	ALONSO	8	8	8	8	8	8	8	8	8	8	8	8	8	8	8	8	14	8	8	8	8	8	8	8	8	8	8	8	8	8	8	8	8	8	8	8	8	8	8	8	8	8	8	8	8	8	8	8	8	8	8	8
1	BUTTON	1	1	1	1	1	1	1	1	1	1	1	1	1	1	1	1	8	3	3	3	3	3	3	3	3	3	3	3	3	3	3	3	3	3	3	3	3	3	3	3	3	3	3	3	3	3	3	3	3	3	3	3
3	SCHUMACHER	3	3	3	3	3	3	3	3	3	3	3	3	3	3	14	14	3	1	1	1	1	1	1	1	1	1	1	1	1	1	1	1	1	1	1	1	1	1	1	1	1	1	1	1	1	1	1	1	1	1	1	1
11	KUBICA	7	7	7	7	7	7	7	7	7	7	7	7	7	7	17	17	1	7	7	7	7	7	7	7	7	7	7	7	7	7	7	7	7	7	7	7	7	7	7	7	7	7	7	7	7	7	7	7	7	7	7	7
4	ROSBERG	14	14	14	14	14	14	14	14	14	14	14	14	14	14	11	11	7	14	14	14	14	14	14	14	14	14	14	14	14	14	14	14	14	14	14	14	14	14	14	14	14	14	14	14	14	14	14	14	14	14	14	14
7	MASSA	17	17	17	17	17	17	17	17	17	17	17	17	17	17	10	3	11	11	11	11	11	11	11	11	11	11	11	11	11	11	11	11	11	11	11	11	11	11	11	11	11	11	11	11	11	11	11	11	11	11	11	11
23	KOBAYASHI	11	11	11	11	11	11	11	11	11	11	11	11	11	11	9	10	9	9	9	9	9	9	9	9	9	9	9	9	9	9	9	9	9	9	9	9	9	9	9	9	9	9	9	9	9	9	9	9	9	9	9	9
14	SUTIL	4	4	4	4	4	4	4	4	4	4	4	4	4	9	3	7	10	10	10	10	10	10	17	17	17	17	17	17	17	17	17	17	17	17	17	17	17	17	17	17	17	17	17	17	17	17	17	17	17	17	17	17
22	DE LA ROSA	9	9	9	9	9	9	9	9	9	9	9	9	9	10	7	23	17	17	17	17	17	17	10	10	10	10	10	10	10	10	10	12	12	12	12	12	12	12	12	12	12	12	12	12	12	12	12	12	12	12	12	12
10	HULKENBERG	10	10	10	10	10	10	10	10	10	10	10	10	10	4	23	9	12	12	12	12	12	12	12	12	12	12	12	12	12	12	12	23	23	23	23	23	23	23	23	23	23	23	23	23	23	23	23	23	23	23	23	23
16	BUEMI	15	15	15	15	15	15	15	15	15	15	15	23	23	23	12	12	23	23	23	23	23	23	23	23	23	23	23	23	23	23	23	10	15	15	15	15	15	15	15	15	15	15	15	15	15	15	15	15	15	15	15	15
17	ALGUERSUARI	18	18	23	23	23	23	23	23	23	23	23	12	12	12	15	15	15	15	15	15	15	15	15	15	15	15	15	15	15	15	15	15	4	4	4	10	10	10	10	10	10	10	10	10	10	10	10	10	4	4	4	4
15	LIUZZI	23	23	12	12	12	12	12	12	12	12	12	15	15	15	16	16	16	16	16	16	16	4	4	4	4	4	4	4	4	4	4	4	10	10	10	4	4	4	4	4	4	4	4	4	4	4	4	4	10	10	10	10
9	BARRICHELLO	24	24	18	18	18	18	18	18	18	18	18	18	16	16	4	4	4	4	4	4	4	16	16	16	16	16	16	16	16	16	16	16	16	16	16	16	16	16	16	16	16	16	18	18	18	18	18	18	18	18	18	18
18	TRULLI	20	12	24	24	24	24	24	24	24	24	24	16	18	18	18	18	18	18	18	18	18	18	18	18	18	18	18	18	18	18	18	18	18	18	18	18	18	18	18	18	18	18	24	24	24	24	24	24	24	24	24	24
12	PETROV	12	20	20	20	20	20	20	16	16	16	16	24	24	24	24	24	24	24	24	24	24	20	20	20	20	20	24	24	24	24	24	24	24	24	24	24	24	24	24	24	24	24	25	25	25	25	25	25	25	25	25	25
19	KOVALAINEN	25	25	25	25	25	25	16	20	20	20	20	20	20	20	20	20	20	20	20	20	20	24	24	24	24	24	20	25	25	25	25	25	25	25	25	25	25	25	25	25	25	25										
21	SENNA	16	16	16	16	16	16	25	25	25	25	25	25	25	25	25	25	25	25	25	25	25	25	25	25	25	25	25																									
24	GLOCK	22	22	22	22	22	22	22	22	22	22	22	22	22	22	22	22	22	22																																		
25	DI GRASSI																																																				
20	CHANDHOK																																																				

TIME SHEETS

PRACTICE 1 (FRIDAY)
Weather: Sunny
Temperatures: track 18–23°C, air 15–17°C

Pos.	Driver	Laps	Time
1	Lewis Hamilton	21	1m 21.134s
2	Jenson Button	14	1m 21.672s
3	Michael Schumacher	12	1m 21.716s
4	Mark Webber	27	1m 22.011s
5	Sebastian Vettel	22	1m 22.026s
6	Nico Rosberg	19	1m 22.070s
7	Robert Kubica	22	1m 22.202s
8	Fernando Alonso	19	1m 22.258s
9	Vitaly Petrov	23	1m 22.397s
10	Kamui Kobayashi	26	1m 22.492s
11	Sébastien Buemi	24	1m 22.588s
12	Felipe Massa	22	1m 22.975s
13	Paul di Resta	21	1m 23.030s
14	Jaime Alguersuari	31	1m 23.110s
15	Vitantonio Liuzzi	19	1m 23.284s
16	Rubens Barrichello	22	1m 23.312s
17	Nico Hülkenberg	20	1m 23.471s
18	Heikki Kovalainen	17	1m 25.329s
19	Jarno Trulli	20	1m 26.244s
20	Timo Glock	23	1m 26.340s
21	Lucas di Grassi	24	1m 26.694s
22	Christian Klein	26	1m 27.250s
23	Bruno Senna	27	1m 27.752s
24	Pedro de la Rosa	3	no time

PRACTICE 2 (FRIDAY)
Weather: Cloudy/sunny
Temperatures: track 23–26°C, air 17–18°C

Pos.	Driver	Laps	Time
1	Sebastian Vettel	24	1m 19.965s
2	Mark Webber	35	1m 20.175s
3	Michael Schumacher	28	1m 20.757s
4	Fernando Alonso	30	1m 20.819s
5	Lewis Hamilton	23	1m 21.191s
6	Robert Kubica	36	1m 21.202s
7	Nico Rosberg	27	1m 21.271s
8	Felipe Massa	25	1m 21.302s
9	Jenson Button	26	1m 21.364s
10	Adrian Sutil	32	1m 21.518s
11	Pedro de la Rosa	37	1m 21.672s
12	Vitantonio Liuzzi	32	1m 21.904s
13	Kamui Kobayashi	29	1m 21.931s
14	Sébastien Buemi	37	1m 22.184s
15	Rubens Barrichello	33	1m 22.192s
16	Vitaly Petrov	35	1m 22.435s
17	Jaime Alguersuari	34	1m 22.449s
18	Nico Hülkenberg	7	1m 23.765s
19	Jarno Trulli	26	1m 24.209s
20	Heikki Kovalainen	22	1m 24.894s
21	Lucas di Grassi	30	1m 25.066s
22	Karun Chandhok	23	1m 25.972s
23	Bruno Senna	25	1m 26.152s
24	Timo Glock	21	1m 26.596s

PRACTICE 3 (SATURDAY)
Weather: Sunny
Temperatures: track 25–26°C, air 20°C

Pos.	Driver	Laps	Time
1	Sebastian Vettel	15	1m 20.528s
2	Mark Webber	11	1m 21.232s
3	Lewis Hamilton	14	1m 21.348s
4	Jenson Button	16	1m 21.376s
5	Michael Schumacher	14	1m 21.583s
6	Felipe Massa	16	1m 21.749s
7	Nico Rosberg	14	1m 22.013s
8	Fernando Alonso	15	1m 22.091s
9	Robert Kubica	20	1m 22.242s
10	Adrian Sutil	12	1m 22.377s
11	Sébastien Buemi	18	1m 22.400s
12	Kamui Kobayashi	11	1m 22.412s
13	Pedro de la Rosa	20	1m 22.527s
14	Nico Hülkenberg	16	1m 22.634s
15	Jaime Alguersuari	20	1m 22.926s
16	Rubens Barrichello	16	1m 22.953s
17	Vitantonio Liuzzi	12	1m 23.597s
18	Vitaly Petrov	5	1m 23.896s
19	Jarno Trulli	14	1m 24.610s
20	Heikki Kovalainen	11	1m 24.745s
21	Timo Glock	15	1m 25.722s
22	Lucas di Grassi	14	1m 25.855s
23	Karun Chandhok	18	1m 26.611s
24	Bruno Senna	6	1m 30.246s

QUALIFYING (SATURDAY)
Weather: Sunny Temperatures:track 34°C, air 22°C

Pos.	Driver	First	Second	Third	Qualifying Tyre
1	Mark Webber	1m 21.412s	1m 20.655s	1m 19.955s	Soft
2	Sebastian Vettel	1m 21.680s	1m 20.772s	1m 20.101s	Soft
3	Lewis Hamilton	1m 21.723s	1m 21.415s	1m 20.829s	Soft
4	Fernando Alonso	1m 21.957s	1m 21.549s	1m 20.937s	Soft
5	Jenson Button	1m 21.915s	1m 21.168s	1m 20.991s	Soft
6	Michael Schumacher	1m 22.528s	1m 21.557s	1m 21.294s	Soft
7	Robert Kubica	1m 22.488s	1m 21.599s	1m 21.353s	Soft
8	Nico Rosberg	1m 22.419s	1m 21.867s	1m 21.408s	Soft
9	Felipe Massa	1m 22.564s	1m 21.841s	1m 21.585s	Soft
10	Kamui Kobayashi	1m 22.577s	1m 21.725s	1m 21.984s	Soft
11	Adrian Sutil	1m 22.628s	1m 21.985s		
12	Pedro de la Rosa	1m 22.211s	1m 22.026s		
13	Nico Hülkenberg	1m 22.857s	1m 22.131s		
14	Vitaly Petrov	1m 22.976s	1m 22.139s		
15	Sébastien Buemi	1m 22.699s	1m 22.191s		
16	Jaime Alguersuari	1m 22.593s	1m 22.207s		
17	Vitantonio Liuzzi	1m 23.084s	1m 22.854s		
18	Rubens Barrichello	1m 23.125s			
19	Jarno Trulli	1m 24.674s			
20	Heikki Kovalainen	1m 24.748s			
21	Timo Glock	1m 25.475s			
22	Lucas di Grassi	1m 25.556s			
23	Karun Chandhok	1m 26.750s			
24	Bruno Senna	1m 27.122s			

FOR THE RECORD

10th FRONT ROW: Mark Webber
10th POLE POSITION: Red Bull

DID YOU KNOW

This was the 40th F1 Spanish Grand Prix, the 20th at Circuit de Catalunya and the 10th race in succession at Catalunya that the pole driver went on to win the race.

Photos: Peter J. Fox

POINTS

DRIVERS

1	Jenson Button	70
2	Fernando Alonso	67
3	Sebastian Vettel	60
4	Mark Webber	53
5	Nico Rosberg	50
6	Lewis Hamilton	49
7	Felipe Massa	49
8	Robert Kubica	44
9	Michael Schumacher	22
10	Adrian Sutil	16
11	Vitantonio Liuzzi	8
12	Rubens Barrichello	7
13	Vitaly Petrov	6
14	Jaime Alguersuari	3
15	Nico Hülkenberg	1

CONSTRUCTORS

1	McLaren	119
2	Ferrari	116
3	Red Bull	113
4	Mercedes	72
5	Renault	50
6	Force India	24
7	Williams	8
8	Toro Rosso	3

53	54	55	56	57	58	59	60	61	62	63	64	65	66	
6	6	6	6	6	6	6	6	6	6	6	6	6	6	1
2	2	2	2	2	2	2	2	2	2	2	2	8	8	2
5	5	8	8	8	8	8	8	8	8	8	8	5	5	3
8	8	5	5	5	5	5	5	5	5	5	5	3	3	4
3	3	3	3	3	3	3	3	3	3	3	3	1	1	5
1	1	1	1	1	1	1	1	1	1	1	1	7	7	6
7	7	7	7	7	7	7	7	7	7	7	7	14	14	7
14	14	14	14	14	14	14	14	14	14	14	14	11	11	8
11	11	11	11	11	11	11	11	11	11	11	11	9		9
9	9	9	9	9	9	9	9	9	9	9	9	17		10
17	17	17	17	17	17	17	17	17	17	17	17	12		
12	12	12	12	12	12	12	12	12	12	12	12	23		
23	23	23	23	23	23	23	23	23	23	23	23	4		
15	15	15	15	15	15	15	15	15	15	15	15			
4	4	4	4	4	4	4	4	4	4	4	4			
10	10	10	10	10	10	10	10	10	10	10	10			
18	18	18	18	18	18	18	18	18	18	18				
24	24	24	24	24	24	24	24	24	24	24				
25	25	25	25	25	25	25	25	25	25					

21 Pit stop *14 One lap or more behind*

RACE TYRE STRATEGIES

	Driver	Race Stint 1	Race Stint 2	Race Stint 3	Race Stint 4
1	Webber	Soft: 1-17	Hard: 18-66		
2	Alonso	Soft: 1-16	Hard: 17-66		
3	Vettel	Soft: 1-16	Hard: 17-54	Soft: 55-66	
4	Schumacher	Soft: 1-14	Hard: 15-66		
5	Button	Soft: 1-16	Hard: 17-66		
6	Massa	Soft: 1-14	Hard: 15-66		
7	Sutil	Soft: 1-17	Hard: 18-66		
8	Kubica	Soft: 1-16	Hard: 17-66		
9	Barrichello	Soft: 1-15	Hard: 16-65		
10	Alguersuari	Soft: 1-16	Hard: 17-34	Hard: 35-65	
11	Petrov	Soft: 1-13	Hard: 14-66		
12	Kobayashi	Soft: 1-16	Hard: 17-65		
13	Rosberg	Soft: 1-14	Hard: 15-35	Soft: 36-65	
14	Hamilton	Soft: 1-17	Hard: 18-64 (dnf)		
15	Liuzzi	Soft: 1-12	Hard: 13-64 (dnf)		
16	Hülkenberg	Soft: 1-16	Hard: 17-32	Soft: 33-64	
17	Trulli	Soft: 1-22	Hard: 23-63		
18	Glock	Soft: 1-21	Hard: 22-63		
19	di Grassi	Hard: 1-19	Soft: 20-62		
	Buemi	Soft: 1	Hard: 2-22	Hard: 23-29	Hard: 30-42 (dnf)
	Chandhok	Soft: 1-27	Hard: 28 (dnf)		
	de la Rosa	Soft: 1	Hard: 2-18 (dnf)		
	Senna	Soft: 1 (dnf)			
dns	Kovalainen				

The tyre regulations stipulate that the two dry tyre specifications must be used during the race. The Soft compound Bridgestone Potenza tyre is marked with a green stripe on the sidewall.

While Mark Webber celebrates his win in the Red Bull roof-top pool, Adrian Newey is about to be joined by Sebastian Vettel.
Photo: Peter J Fox

FIA FORMULA 1 WORLD CHAMPIONSHIP · ROUND 6

MONACO GRAND PRIX

MONTE CARLO CIRCUIT

Red Bull
Red Bull

MONTE CARLO QUALIFYING

YOU have to wonder, sometimes. Formula One drivers are happy to tackle Spa in the rain, or brake from 200mph at Monza in a car with precious little downforce, yet at Monaco they were fretting about the potentially obstructive consequences of having 24 cars on the track during the first part of qualifying. It's not so many years since 30 would have been allowed out for a full 60 minutes.

Fortunately, the notion of splitting qualifying into two groups was never more than idle banter. Predictably, the best drivers found time and space to set a decent lap, as they always have and always will. There was a lone exception, though: fastest in both free practice sessions on Thursday, Fernando Alonso didn't take part in qualifying at all after creaming into the wall at Massenet on Saturday morning. "It was my mistake," he said, "but I was also a bit unlucky. I hit the barriers at 90kph (56mph), and normally that would not be enough to write off a chassis." The Spaniard would have to start from the pits in his rebuilt car.

The Red Bull RB6's appetite for quick corners was a known quantity, but here was proof that now it could be trusted in a slower environment, too. For the second time in as many weekends, Mark Webber annexed pole, and the key was a single, four-lap run on Bridgestone's super-soft during Q3. Both his final two laps were good enough for pole: the second, a searing 1m 13.892s, would be the only time all weekend that a driver dipped below 1m 14s. "It's a nice feeling to get pole at Monaco," said Webber. "I brushed the barriers pretty hard at one point, but after that everything stayed together. I know it's going to be a long race, and track conditions change a lot here during a grand prix, but I'm optimistic that I can have a nice, clean afternoon."

Robert Kubica flattered the Renault R30 wonderfully once more to secure a spot on the front row, a laudable feat in a car that, by general consensus, was probably only fifth in the performance stakes at this stage of the campaign, behind Red Bull, Ferrari, McLaren and Mercedes. But Monaco allows drivers to make more of a difference.

Kubica completed a brace of two-lap runs in Q3, but fell 0.294 seconds short of the flying Webber. "It's a bit of a disappointment not to get pole after being so close," he said, "but the Red Bull was 1.5 seconds quicker than us in Barclelona, so there's no reason why we should have been in front of it here. You have to be realistic. Five months ago, remember, we were unsure whether the team would even be competing this year, yet here we are on the front row."

Sebastian Vettel wasted one of his Q3 laps when he locked up his rear tyres and slid across the chicane, but he beat Felipe Massa's surviving Ferrari to third. Lewis Hamilton and Jenson Button, winners for the past two seasons, were fifth and eighth for McLaren, split by the Mercedes MGP W01s of Nico Rosberg and Michael Schumacher, but Button wasn't best pleased with Massa, whom he accused of blocking tactics. "I don't know what Felipe was thinking," he said, "but I guess he wasn't looking in his mirrors."

Webber was looking rather further back as he attempted to become only the second Australian to win the Monaco GP, after Jack Brabham in 1959. "It will probably sink in a bit later," Webber said, "but it was Jack that first fired my dad's imagination and got him interested in racing, so I probably wouldn't be sitting here without him."

HISTORY will record only that Mark Webber controlled every centimetre of the 2010 Monaco Grand Prix – the principality's 68th – and that the top five positions did not alter beyond the first corner, but such prosaic statistics do not reflect the day's true effervescence. Yes, Webber was in a class of his own, but he was also a paragon of calm amid chaos.

The Australian made a couple of mistakes, but they weren't the sort that mattered. He broke the pit-lane speed limit during the pre-race installation laps, which earned him a 2,200-euro fine, and then made a less than flying start, the only aspect of the afternoon that was not, in his words, "absolutely faultless". At any other circuit, his average getaway might have been costly, but the run from the front of the grid to Ste Dévote is short. Even so, Robert Kubica felt Webber might be vulnerable. "Normally, I would have covered the inside to defend my position," the Pole said, "but Mark was slow pulling away and I thought I might have a chance to overtake. I got on the power a bit too early, though…" As his wheels began spinning, Sebastian Vettel pounced to make it a Red Bull one-two, with Kubica dropping to third, ahead of Felipe Massa, Lewis Hamilton, Rubens Barrichello, Michael Schumacher, Nico Rosberg, Tonio Liuzzi, Adrian Sutil, the slow-starting Jenson Button, Sébastien Buemi, Vitaly Petrov, Pedro de la Rosa, Kamui Kobayashi, Jaime Alguersuari, Heikki Kovalainen (who won a superior bottle of wine from one journalist, for becoming the first team-mate ever to outqualify Jarno Trulli in Monaco), Timo Glock, Trulli, Lucas di Grassi, Bruno Senna, Karun Chandhok and pit-lane starter Fernando Alonso, who made his mandatory tyre stop at the end of the opening lap, largely because the safety car had already been pressed into service.

The cause was Nico Hülkenberg, who failed to get away from 11th at the start of the formation lap when a faulty clutch paddle stranded him on the grid. Thus the German lined up at the back – and clipped one of the HRTs on the run through Ste Dévote. Minor damage morphed into major drama when his front wing failed in the tunnel and Hülkenberg slewed left into the wall, scattering debris far and wide.

Senna joined Alonso in pitting during the safety car interruption, on lap two, while Button stopped for rather different reasons. He had driven to the grid with his left-hand sidepod's cooling cover still in

Above: Felipe Massa threads the eye of an Armco needle as his Ferrari roars towards Tabac during qualifying.
Photo: Paul-Henri Cahier

Far left: Privileged spectators enjoy a close-up view of Vettel's Red Bull as it speeds up the hill towards Casino Square.

Left: Alonso fans proclaim their loyalty to the Ferrari driver, although on this particular weekend he would deliver them little but disappointment.
Photos: Peter J Fox

place, which caused his McLaren's Mercedes V8 to overheat. The team thought the engine might be all right once racing speeds contributed a little cooling air, but the safety car put paid to that and Button pulled off when a small fire broke out. "It was human error," he said, "and that's all there is to it. It was just one of those days."

Webber had been concerned that the Renault R30's ability to warm its tyres efficiently might have given Kubica a chance in the probable event of a restart, which finally came at the end of lap six, but Vettel was there as a buffer and the Australian's pace on cold tyres was sensational. He immediately pulled 1.4 seconds clear of his team-mate, a clue to the dominance that would follow.

Webber was almost nine seconds in front when Vettel made his mandatory tyre stop on lap 22, one before the leader, and carried on extending his advantage once they were both on the medium Bridgestone. By lap 30, he was 11.4 seconds to the good, but not for long. Williams might have thought its day had started badly, but things were about to get significantly worse.

Having run a strong sixth from the start, Barrichello slipped to tenth following the tyre stops and felt his FW32's behaviour had subsequently deteriorated, without obvious cause. On the 31st lap, he lost control on the run to Massenet and hit the barriers very hard, causing the safety car to be dispatched once more, this time until the end of lap 33. Initially, Williams suspected that Barrichello had suffered some form of suspension failure, but post-race investigations revealed that he had run over a loose drain cover, which had flipped up and broken his right rear wheel. One moment he was heading for what appeared to be a certain points finish, the next he was a passenger.

Webber immediately scarpered again when racing recommenced, this time pulling 1.1 seconds clear of Vettel within the lap, but no sooner had he built another useful lead than it was taken away. On lap 44, a loose drain cover – not the one Barrichello had hit, although it was nearby – was spotted close to Massenet, and the race was neutralised for two laps while the problem was fixed.

"I would certainly prefer not to have had the safety cars," Webber said, "because it's nice to build up a buffer and frustrating to have it taken away. It's never ideal to have your rhythm broken like that when you are leading, but I was totally open to it happening at some stage."

Nor would it be the last such interference. This time, the Australian dropped Vettel by almost two

Above: Webber delivered a classic Monaco victory, balancing blistering pace with just the right proportion of restraint and control.

Above left: Jenson Button's McLaren overheated into retirement almost before the race had started, due to some rare finger trouble on the part of his crew.
Photos: Peter J Fox

Left: Adrian Sutil scored more valuable points for Force India with another measured performance.
Photo: Jad Sherif/WRi2

seconds at the restart, although the German finally began to lap close to – or at – Webber's pace during this phase of the race. The contest, though, had long appeared settled.

Approaching Rascasse for the 74th time, Webber came up behind Trulli and Chandhok, who were squabbling over 14th, almost three laps down. The Italian thought he saw a gap to the inside, but hit the HRT before riding up and over it. Chandhok ducked, then contemplated restarting. It was only when he looked in his mirrors, to see whether both rear wheels were still attached, that he realised a Lotus was still perched on top of him.

"Jarno apologised straight away," Chandhok said. "He obviously had a bit of brain fade; even if I hadn't been there, I don't think he would have had enough steering lock to make the corner, given the line he took."

Webber lost a couple of seconds avoiding the fracas, but it could have ruined his whole weekend. "I saw Jarno making a lunge and wondered what the hell was going to happen," he said. "I just hoped I'd have an option to go down the inside… and that we'd finish under the safety car, if it came out, so that I didn't have to worry about doing one lap after yet another restart."

It did, so he didn't.

Vettel, Kubica and Massa had stayed fairly close throughout, swapping places only temporarily during the pit cycle, while the McLaren MP4-25's long wheelbase made it an unsuitable tool for Monaco, and Hamilton dropped away slightly prior to the safety car's fourth and final intervention.

The battle for sixth boiled down to a straight contest between strategic nous and ruthless opportunism – the latter won, but only temporarily. Alonso benefited from that canny first-lap stop – effectively free of charge, given the early safety car – and his ability to pass the slowest traffic relatively easily. By the time the tyre stops were over, he had been shuffled up to sixth. Toward the race's end, his Bridgestone mediums still had ample tread to spare, despite their long afternoon's toil.

As Webber ambled towards the chequered flag, the safety car pulled into the pits to allow cars to take the flag without any preceding clutter that might spoil the photographs. And as it did so, Schumacher elbowed Alonso aside to annex sixth. In previous seasons, drivers had not been permitted to resume racing after a restart until they had crossed the finishing line. This had been changed for 2010, however, to permit overtaking once they had passed the safety car line (by the pit entry), although article 40.13 of the regulations read: "If the safety car is still deployed at the beginning of the last lap, or is deployed during the last lap, it will enter the pit lane at the end of the lap and cars will take the chequered flag as normal, without overtaking."

This meant that there could be no further overtaking if the last lap began behind the safety car, but that's not actually what it said. Green flags were waved all the way along the pit straight, beyond the final corner, which implied the race was back on, In an official statement, Mercedes said, "We were fully aware of article 40.13, but believed that the combination of green lights and flags, plus the race control messages 'Safety car in this lap' and 'Track clear', indicated that the race was not finishing under the safety car and that drivers were free to race."

Above: Monaco served as another showcase for Robert Kubica's talents, the Pole bringing his Renault home in third.
Photo: Peter J Fox

Right: Happy man! Christian Horner holds aloft the constructors' trophy after another fine win for Red Bull.
Photo: Jad Sherif/WRi2

Far right: Heikki Kovalainen, in the Lotus, managed to hold off charging Fernando Alonso for two laps.
Photo: Peter Nygaard/GP Photo

Schumacher handled the moment brilliantly, but stewards deemed the offence worthy of a drive-through penalty. Since that was not servable, however, they converted it to a 20-second penalty. Forcing him to hand the place back to Alonso would have been appropriate, but with the race finishing as it did, the German was relegated to 12th. 'Stupid' is too kind a word: for possibly the first time in his career, virtually the whole paddock's sympathies were with Schumacher.

Thus his team-mate, Rosberg, inherited seventh, from Sutil, Liuzzi, Buemi and Alguersuari. No other cars were running at the end, although Petrov (who had lost a lap early on with a punctured right rear, then pitted shortly before the end with a gearbox problem), Chandhok and Trulli were classified. None of the new teams actually managed to get a car across the line. A failed steering joint accounted for Kovalainen, hydraulic problems floored Senna, and the Virgins succumbed to a loose right rear wheel (di Grassi) and suspension failure (Glock). Both Saubers were casualties, too: Kobayashi's gearbox broke and de la Rosa suffered hydraulic meltdown, the Spaniard receiving his first clue when his power steering suddenly became very heavy. A couple of weeks would pass before the habitually calm Peter Sauber described the C29 as "a really bad car, an unpleasant parting gift from BMW".

Webber had a slightly cheerier outlook on life. Victory gave him the championship lead for the first time in his Formula One career – he was level with Vettel on points, but ahead two to one on a countback of race victories – and he reflected on how life had changed since his previous victory in Monaco, in a round of the FIA F3000 Championship nine years beforehand. Back then, financial hardship had dictated that he share a hotel room with partner Ann, father Alan and other friends. "I think it was an old brothel," he said, "and dad was snoring all night, so I got no rest. I slept much better last night, and this has been the greatest day of my life. I'm predicting some very bad headaches tomorrow, but the team deserves them…"

Simon Arron

EDITOR'S VIEW
NEW TEAMS UNDER FIRE

A SINGLE week separated the Spanish and Monaco grands prix, scarcely enough time for the participants to draw breath, you might have thought, let alone for a streak of paranoia to emerge over just how demanding the process of qualifying might be on a track crowded out by the six competitors from the three new Formula One teams.

The concerns over the speed differentials between the fastest and slowest cars gave rise to scaremongering predictions that qualifying and the race at Monaco might be disastrous. Some drivers even suggested that the qualifying format should be adjusted to ensure that a reduced number of cars were on the track at any one time. Understandably, the FIA declined to make any such amendment to the schedule, pointing out that at no point so far in the season had any of the newcomers failed to qualify within the notional 107 per cent of the fastest car on the grid. As Lotus boss Tony Fernandes pointed out, "Every-body has to start somewhere."

In that respect, Monaco in 2010 was a very real indication that the three new teams were doing no better nor worse than might have been expected of them. After the first few races of the season, the newcomers had attracted much criticism from many quarters, to the effect that they were out of place in motor sport's most senior category and might be better off plying their trade in GP2 or a similar supporting category.

History teaches us the need for acute perspective when judging these issues and trying to arrive at an equitable conclusion. True, the Lotus, Virgin and HRT teams might have looked threadbare alongside McLaren and Red Bull, but think back to Monaco in 1968, when the third- and fourth-place Cooper-BRMS of Lucien Bianchi and Ludovico Scarfiotti finished four laps behind Graham Hill's Lotus 49B. Even by the modestly competitive standards of the day, this was a big gap, but nobody called for the drivers to be fired or the teams to be drummed out of the sport. The 2010 race was a reminder of just how far the sport had travelled, even in terms of the also-rans.

Of course, the return of Lotus to the streets of Monte Carlo for the first time since 1994 also contributed to the weekend's nostalgia quotient, many being quick to recall that this was the track where Stirling Moss had scored the marque's first GP victory in 1960, at the wheel of Rob Walker's Lotus 18.

Things were more relaxed and less structured in those days, so when US millionaire Lance Reventlow asked Moss if he would take a turn in one of his uncompetitive, but beautifully built, front-engined Scarabs during practice for the race, Stirl was quick to oblige. The Scarab was NBG, of course, being a couple of seasons late and many thousands of dollars short. And even the costs involved in those days were enough to frighten off Reventlow, whose mother owned Woolworths, let's not forget.

It was the equivalent of Mark Webber being asked to have a whirl in an HRT, but those were different times. Come to think of it, Mercedes tech chief Rudi Uhlenhaut was also invited to try out the Moss Maserati 250F during practice at Monaco in 1955. No mean driver himself, he didn't look too shabby by any manner or means.

Memo to Red Bull engineering boss, Adrian Newey: this year the Goodwood Festival of Speed in an RB5, next year the Monaco GP in an RB7. Just joking, Adrian. I think.

Alan Henry

GRAND PRIX DE MONACO

MONTE-CARLO 13–16 MAY 2010

RACE DISTANCE: 78 laps, 161.880 miles/260.520km

RACE WEATHER: Partly cloudy/sunny (track 29–39°C, air 21–22°C)

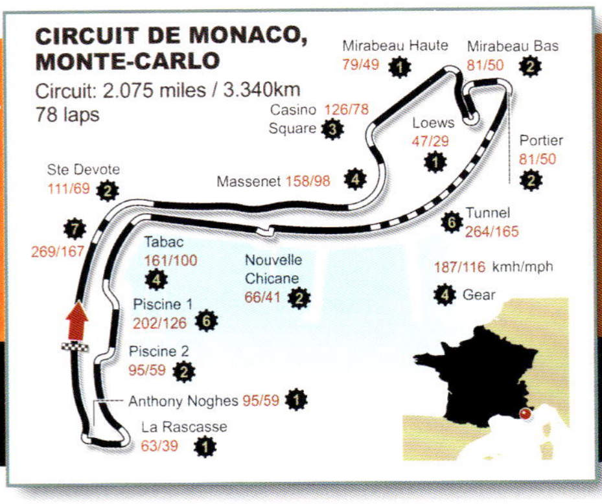

Pos.	Driver	Nat.	No.	Entrant	Car/Engine	Tyres	Laps	Time/Retirement	Speed (mph/km/h)	Gap to leader	Fastest race lap	
1	**Mark Webber**	AUS	6	Red Bull Racing	Red Bull RB6-Renault RS27 V8	B	78	1h 50m 13.355s	88.119/141.814		1m 15.318s	63
2	**Sebastian Vettel**	D	5	Red Bull Racing	Red Bull RB6-Renault RS27 V8	B	78	1h 50m 13.803s	88.114/141.805	+ 0.448s	1m 15.192s	71
3	**Robert Kubica**	PL	11	Renault F1 Team	Renault R30-RS27 V8	B	78	1h 50m 15.030s	88.097/141.778	+ 1.675s	1m 15.353s	72
4	**Felipe Massa**	BR	7	Scuderia Ferrari Marlboro	Ferrari F10-056 V8	B	78	1h 50m 16.021s	88.084/141.757	+ 2.666s	1m 15.503s	68
5	**Lewis Hamilton**	GB	2	Vodafone McLaren Mercedes	McLaren MP4-25-Mercedes FO108X V8	B	78	1h 50m 17.718s	88.061/141.721	+ 4.363s	1m 16.219s	68
6	**Fernando Alonso**	E	8	Scuderia Ferrari Marlboro	Ferrari F10-056 V8	B	78	1h 50m 19.696s	88.035/141.679	+ 6.341s	1m 15.905s	73
7	**Nico Rosberg**	D	4	Mercedes GP Petronas F1 Team	Mercedes MGP W01-Mercedes FO108X V8	B	78	1h 50m 20.006s	88.031/141.672	+ 6.651s	1m 15.959s	65
8	**Adrian Sutil**	D	14	Force India F1 Team	Force India VJM03-Mercedes FO108X V8	B	78	1h 50m 20.325s	88.027/141.665	+ 6.970s	1m 15.963s	72
9	**Vitantonio Liuzzi**	I	15	Force India F1 Team	Force India VJM03-Mercedes FO108X V8	B	78	1h 50m 20.660s	88.022/141.658	+ 7.305s	1m 16.142s	72
10	**Sébastien Buemi**	CH	16	Scuderia Toro Rosso	Toro Rosso STR5-Ferrari 056 V8	B	78	1h 50m 21.554s	88.010/141.639	+ 8.199s	1m 16.493s	68
11	Jaime Alguersuari	E	17	Scuderia Toro Rosso	Toro Rosso STR5-Ferrari 056 V8	B	78	1h 50m 22.490s	87.998/141.619	+ 9.135s	1m 16.381s	73
12	Michael Schumacher	GB	3	Mercedes GP Petronas F1 Team	Mercedes MGP W01-Mercedes FO108X V8	B	78	1h 50m 39.067s *	87.778/141.265	+ 25.712s	1m 15.580s	71
13	Vitaly Petrov	RUS	12	Renault F1 Team	Renault R30-RS27 V8	B	73	*rear suspension*		+ 5 laps	1m 16.405s	60
14	Karun Chandhok	IND	20	HRT F1 Team	HRT F110-Cosworth CA2010 V8	B	70	*accident*		+ 8 laps	1m 19.553s	69
15	Jarno Trulli	I	18	Lotus Racing	Lotus T127-Cosworth CA2010 V8	B	70	*accident*		+ 8 laps	1m 19.340s	69
	Heikki Kovalainen	FIN	19	Lotus Racing	Lotus T127-Cosworth CA2010 V8	B	58	*steering*			1m 18.401s	57
	Bruno Senna	BR	21	HRT F1 Team	HRT F110-Cosworth CA2010 V8	B	58	*hydraulics*			1m 20.130s	58
	Rubens Barrichello	BR	9	AT&T Williams	Williams FW32-Cosworth CA2010 V8	B	30	*rear suspension/spin*			1m 19.074s	22
	Kamui Kobayashi	J	23	BMW Sauber F1 Team	BMW Sauber C29-Ferrari 056 V8	B	26	*gearbox*			1m 18.775s	24
	Lucas di Grassi	BR	25	Virgin Racing	Virgin VR-01-Cosworth CA2010 V8	B	25	*rear wheel*			1m 22.255s	19
	Timo Glock	D	24	Virgin Racing	Virgin VR-01-Cosworth CA2010 V8	B	22	*rear suspension*			1m 20.775s	11
	Pedro de la Rosa	E	22	BMW Sauber F1 Team	BMW Sauber C29-Ferrari 056 V8	B	21	*hydraulics*			1m 19.270s	21
	Jenson Button	GB	1	Vodafone McLaren Mercedes	McLaren MP4-25-Mercedes FO108X V8	B	2	*sidepod cover/engine fire*			2m 14.285s	2
	Nico Hülkenberg	D	10	AT&T Williams	Williams FW32-Cosworth CA2010 V8	B	0	*front wing/accident*			no time	

* Michael Schumacher finished 6th, but was given a 20-second penalty for illegally overtaking on the final lap.

Fastest race lap: Sebastian Vettel on lap 71, 1m 15.192s, 99.364mph/159.910km/h.

Lap record: Michael Schumacher (Ferrari F2004 V10), 1m 14.439s, 100.369mph/161.528km/h (2004).

Grid order	1	2	3	4	5	6	7	8	9	10	11	12	13	14	15	16	17	18	19	20	21	22	23	24	25	26	27	28	29	30	31	32	33	34	35	36	37	38	39	40	41	42	43	44	45	46	47	48	49	50	51	52	53	54	55	56	57	58	59	60
6 WEBBER	6	6	6	6	6	6	6	6	6	6	6	6	6	6	6	6	6	6	6	6	6	6	6	6	6	6	6	6	6	6	6	6	6	6	6	6	6	6	6	6	6	6	6	6	6	6	6	6	6	6	6	6	6	6	6	6	6	6	6	6
11 KUBICA	5	5	5	5	5	5	5	5	5	5	5	5	5	5	5	5	5	5	5	5	5	4	4	4	4	4	4	5	5	5	5	5	5	5	5	5	5	5	5	5	5	5	5	5	5	5	5	5	5	5	5	5	5	5	5	5	5	5	5	5
5 VETTEL	11	11	11	11	11	11	11	11	11	11	11	11	11	11	11	11	11	11	11	11	4	5	5	5	5	5	5	11	11	11	11	11	11	11	11	11	11	11	11	11	11	11	11	11	11	11	11	11	11	11	11	11	11	11	11	11	11	11	11	11
7 MASSA	7	7	7	7	7	7	7	7	7	7	7	7	7	7	7	7	7	7	4	4	14	11	11	11	11	11	11	7	7	7	7	7	7	7	7	7	7	7	7	7	7	7	7	7	7	7	7	7	7	7	7	7	7	7	7	7	7	7	7	7
2 HAMILTON	2	2	2	2	2	2	2	2	2	2	2	2	2	2	2	2	9	9	14	14	11	23	23	23	23	7	7	2	2	2	2	2	2	2	2	2	2	2	2	2	2	2	2	2	2	2	2	2	2	2	2	2	2	2	2	2	2	2	2	2
4 ROSBERG	9	9	9	9	9	9	9	9	9	9	9	9	9	9	9	9	3	3	16	12	22	7	7	7	7	23	2	4	8	8	8	8	8	8	8	8	8	8	8	8	8	8	8	8	8	8	8	8	8	8	8	8	8	8	8	8	8	8	8	8
3 SCHUMACHER	3	3	3	3	3	3	3	3	3	3	3	3	3	3	3	3	4	4	12	22	23	2	2	2	2	2	8	8	3	3	3	3	3	3	3	3	3	3	3	3	3	3	3	3	3	3	3	3	3	3	3	3	3	3	3	3	3	3	3	3
1 BUTTON	4	4	4	4	4	4	4	4	4	4	4	4	4	4	4	4	15	15	7	23	7	8	8	8	8	8	3	3	4	4	4	4	4	4	4	4	4	4	4	4	4	4	4	4	4	4	4	4	4	4	4	4	4	4	4	4	4	4	4	4
9 BARRICHELLO	15	15	15	15	15	15	15	15	15	15	15	15	15	15	15	15	14	14	22	7	2	3	3	3	3	3	14	14	14	14	14	14	14	14	14	14	14	14	14	14	14	14	14	14	14	14	14	14	14	14	14	14	14	14	14	14	14	14	14	14
15 LIUZZI	14	14	14	14	14	14	14	14	14	14	14	14	14	14	14	14	16	16	23	17	8	14	14	14	14	14	9	9	9	9	15	15	15	15	15	15	15	15	15	15	15	15	15	15	15	15	15	15	15	15	15	15	15	15	15	15	15	15	15	15
10 HULKENBERG	1	1	16	16	16	16	16	16	16	16	16	16	16	16	16	16	12	12	17	2	3	9	9	9	9	9	15	15	15	15	16	16	16	16	16	16	16	16	16	16	16	16	16	16	16	16	16	16	16	16	16	16	16	16	16	16	16	16	16	16
14 SUTIL	16	16	12	12	12	12	12	12	12	12	12	12	12	12	12	12	22	22	2	8	9	15	15	15	15	15	16	16	16	16	17	17	17	17	17	17	17	17	17	17	17	17	17	17	17	17	17	17	17	17	17	17	17	17	17	17	17	17	17	17
16 BUEMI	12	12	22	22	22	22	22	22	22	22	22	22	22	22	22	22	23	23	8	3	15	16	16	16	16	16	12	12	12	17	*12*	*12*	*12*	*12*	*12*	*12*	*12*	*12*	*12*	*12*	*12*	*12*	*12*	*12*	*12*	*12*	*12*	*12*	*12*	*12*	*12*	*12*	*12*	*12*	*12*	*12*	*12*	*12*	*12*	*12*
12 PETROV	22	22	23	23	23	23	23	23	23	23	23	23	23	23	23	23	17	17	3	9	12	12	12	12	12	12	19	17	17	*12*	*19*	*19*	*19*	*19*	*19*	*19*	*19*	*19*	*19*	*19*	*19*	*19*	*19*	*19*	*19*	*19*	*19*	*19*	*19*	*19*	*19*	*19*	*19*	*19*	*19*	*19*	*19*	*19*	*20*	*20*
22 DE LA ROSA	23	23	17	17	17	17	17	17	17	17	17	17	17	17	17	17	2	2	9	16	16	19	19	19	19	19	17	*19*	*19*	*19*	*21*	*21*	*21*	*21*	*21*	*21*	*21*	*21*	*21*	*21*	*21*	*21*	*21*	*21*	*21*	*21*	*21*	*21*	*21*	*21*	*21*	*21*	*21*	*21*	*21*	*21*	*21*	*21*	*18*	*18*
23 KOBAYASHI	17	17	19	19	19	19	19	19	19	19	19	19	19	19	19	8	8	8	15	15	19	17	17	17	17	17	*21*	*21*	*21*	*21*	*20*	*20*	*20*	*20*	*20*	*20*	*20*	*20*	*20*	*20*	*20*	*20*	*20*	*20*	*20*	*20*	*20*	*20*	*20*	*20*	*20*	*20*	*20*	*20*	*20*	*20*	*20*	*20*		
17 ALGUERSUARI	19	19	24	24	24	24	24	24	24	24	24	24	24	8	8	19	19	19	19	19	17	24	18	18	18	*21*	*20*	*20*	*20*	*20*	*18*	*18*	*18*	*18*	*18*	*18*	*18*	*18*	*18*	*18*	*18*	*18*	*18*	*18*	*18*	*18*	*18*	*18*	*18*	*18*	*18*	*18*	*18*	*18*	*18*	*18*	*18*	*18*		
19 KOVALAINEN	24	24	18	18	18	18	18	18	18	18	8	8	8	24	24	24	24	24	24	24	24	18	25	25	*21*	*20*	*18*	*18*	*18*	*18*																														
18 TRULLI	18	18	25	25	25	25	25	25	25	8	18	18	18	18	18	18	18	18	18	18	18	25	21	*21*	*25*	*18*																																		
24 GLOCK	25	25	20	20	20	8	8	8	8	25	25	25	25	25	25	25	25	25	25	25	*25*	21	*20*	*20*	*20*																																			
25 DI GRASSI	21	20	8	8	8	20	20	20	20	20	20	20	20	20	20	20	20	20	*21*	*21*	*21*	*20*																																						
21 SENNA	20	8	21	21	21	21	21	21	21	21	21	21	21	21	21	21	21	21	*20*	*20*	*20*																																							
20 CHANDHOK	8	21																																																										
8 ALONSO																																																												

21 Pit stop   *14 One lap or more behind*

TIME SHEETS

PRACTICE 1 (THURSDAY)

Weather: Sunny

Temperatures: (track 28–32°C, air 21°C)

Pos.	Driver	Laps	Time
1	Fernando Alonso	32	1m 15.927s
2	Sebastian Vettel	27	1m 16.000s
3	Robert Kubica	28	1m 16.016s
4	Mark Webber	25	1m 16.382s
5	Felipe Massa	30	1m 16.517s
6	Michael Schumacher	21	1m 16.589s
7	Lewis Hamilton	32	1m 16.647s
8	Jenson Button	30	1m 16.692s
9	Adrian Sutil	23	1m 16.805s
10	Sébastien Buemi	31	1m 16.857s
11	Nico Rosberg	15	1m 17.149s
12	Rubens Barrichello	28	1m 17.331s
13	Vitantonio Liuzzi	27	1m 17.704s
14	Vitaly Petrov	39	1m 17.718s
15	Jaime Alguersuari	37	1m 17.991s
16	Nico Hülkenberg	39	1m 18.397s
17	Pedro de la Rosa	38	1m 18.434s
18	Kamui Kobayashi	32	1m 18.547s
19	Timo Glock	24	1m 19.527s
20	Heikki Kovalainen	32	1m 19.606s
21	Jarno Trulli	31	1m 19.902s
22	Lucas di Grassi	18	1m 20.566s
23	Bruno Senna	28	1m 21.688s
24	Karun Chandhok	6	1m 21.853s

PRACTICE 2 (THURSDAY)

Weather: Sunny/partly cloudy/drizzle

Temperatures: (track 27–41°C, air 19–22°C)

Pos.	Driver	Laps	Time
1	Fernando Alonso	36	1m 14.904s
2	Nico Rosberg	40	1m 15.013s
3	Sebastian Vettel	48	1m 15.099s
4	Felipe Massa	45	1m 15.120s
5	Michael Schumacher	38	1m 15.143s
6	Robert Kubica	39	1m 15.192s
7	Lewis Hamilton	32	1m 15.249s
8	Adrian Sutil	42	1m 15.460s
9	Jenson Button	38	1m 15.619s
10	Mark Webber	28	1m 15.620s
11	Vitaly Petrov	44	1m 15.746s
12	Sébastien Buemi	46	1m 16.276s
13	Nico Hülkenberg	48	1m 16.348s
14	Rubens Barrichello	38	1m 16.522s
15	Vitantonio Liuzzi	42	1m 16.528s
16	Pedro de la Rosa	36	1m 16.599s
17	Kamui Kobayashi	46	1m 16.818s
18	Jaime Alguersuari	28	1m 17.023s
19	Heikki Kovalainen	48	1m 18.184s
20	Lucas di Grassi	38	1m 18.478s
21	Jarno Trulli	13	1m 18.667s
22	Timo Glock	42	1m 18.721s
23	Karun Chandhok	36	1m 20.313s
24	Bruno Senna	11	1m 22.148s

PRACTICE 3 (SATURDAY)

Weather: Sunny

Temperatures: (track 25–29°C, air 21°C)

Pos.	Driver	Laps	Time
1	Robert Kubica	26	1m 14.806s
2	Felipe Massa	22	1m 14.852s
3	Mark Webber	25	1m 14.945s
4	Lewis Hamilton	25	1m 15.038s
5	Sebastian Vettel	26	1m 15.046s
6	Michael Schumacher	22	1m 15.236s
7	Nico Rosberg	20	1m 15.252s
8	Sébastien Buemi	22	1m 15.537s
9	Adrian Sutil	14	1m 15.659s
10	Jenson Button	22	1m 15.682s
11	Vitantonio Liuzzi	19	1m 15.691s
12	Jaime Alguersuari	27	1m 15.769s
13	Nico Hülkenberg	24	1m 16.164s
14	Rubens Barrichello	21	1m 16.232s
15	Vitaly Petrov	27	1m 16.240s
16	Fernando Alonso	6	1m 16.266s
17	Kamui Kobayashi	26	1m 16.644s
18	Pedro de la Rosa	23	1m 16.696s
19	Heikki Kovalainen	18	1m 17.782s
20	Jarno Trulli	26	1m 17.865s
21	Lucas di Grassi	25	1m 18.063s
22	Bruno Senna	25	1m 19.720s
23	Karun Chandhok	21	1m 19.781s
24	Timo Glock	3	no time

QUALIFYING (SATURDAY)

Weather: Sunny Temperatures: (track 31–34°C, air 21°C)

Pos.	Driver	First	Second	Third	Qualifying Tyre
1	Mark Webber	1m 15.035s	1m 14.462s	1m 13.826s	Super-Soft
2	Robert Kubica	1m 15.045s	1m 14.549s	1m 14.120s	Super-Soft
3	Sebastian Vettel	1m 15.110s	1m 14.568s	1m 14.227s	Super-Soft
4	Felipe Massa	1m 14.757s	1m 14.405s	1m 14.283s	Super-Soft
5	Lewis Hamilton	1m 15.676s	1m 14.527s	1m 14.432s	Super-Soft
6	Nico Rosberg	1m 15.188s	1m 14.375s	1m 14.544s	Super-Soft
7	Michael Schumacher	1m 15.649s	1m 14.691s	1m 14.590s	Super-Soft
8	Jenson Button	1m 15.623s	1m 15.150s	1m 14.637s	Super-Soft
9	Rubens Barrichello	1m 15.590s	1m 15.083s	1m 14.901s	Super-Soft
10	Vitantonio Liuzzi	1m 15.397s	1m 15.061s	1m 15.170s	Super-Soft
11	Nico Hülkenberg	1m 16.030s	1m 15.317s		
12	Adrian Sutil	1m 15.445s	1m 15.318s		
13	Sébastien Buemi	1m 15.961s	1m 15.413s		
14	Vitaly Petrov	1m 15.482s	1m 15.576s		
15	Pedro de la Rosa	1m 15.908s	1m 15.692s		
16	Kamui Kobayashi	1m 16.175s	1m 15.992s		
17	Jaime Alguersuari	1m 16.021s	1m 16.176s		
18	Heikki Kovalainen	1m 17.094s			
19	Jarno Trulli	1m 17.134s			
20	Timo Glock	1m 17.377s			
21	Lucas di Grassi	1m 17.864s			
22	Bruno Senna	1m 18.509s			
23	Karun Chandhok	1m 19.559s			
24	Fernando Alonso	no time			

FOR THE RECORD

50th START: **Vitantonio Liuzzi**

300th FRONT ROW POSITION: **Renault engine**

20th FRONT ROW POSITION: **Red Bull**

DID YOU KNOW

Pole and victory a week apart has only been achieved nine times before Mark Webber this weekend: Clark 1963, Brabham 1966, Hunt 1976, Piquet 1984, Senna 1988, Mansell 1992, Hill 1996, Hamilton 2007 and Button 2009.

Monaco 2010 saw the first top three all powered by Renault since Luxembourg 1997.

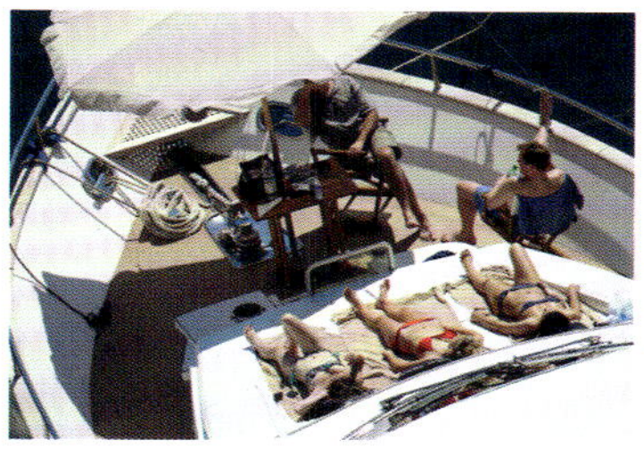

Photos: Peter J. Fox

POINTS

DRIVERS

1	Mark Webber	78
2	Sebastian Vettel	78
3	Fernando Alonso	75
4	Jenson Button	70
5	Felipe Massa	61
6	Robert Kubica	59
7	Lewis Hamilton	59
8	Nico Rosberg	56
9	Michael Schumacher	22
10	Adrian Sutil	20
11	Vitantonio Liuzzi	10
12	Rubens Barrichello	7
13	Vitaly Petrov	6
14	Jaime Alguersuari	3
15	Sébastien Buemi	1
16	Nico Hülkenberg	1

CONSTRUCTORS

1	Red Bull	156
2	Ferrari	136
3	McLaren	129
4	Mercedes	78
5	Renault	65
6	Force India	30
7	Williams	8
8	Toro Rosso	4

2	63	64	65	66	67	68	69	70	71	72	73	74	75	76	77	78	·
6	6	6	6	6	6	6	6	6	6	6	6	6	6	6	6	6	1
5	5	5	5	5	5	5	5	5	5	5	5	5	5	5	5	5	2
1	11	11	11	11	11	11	11	11	11	11	11	11	11	11	11	11	3
7	7	7	7	7	7	7	7	7	7	7	7	7	7	7	7	7	
2	2	2	2	2	2	2	2	2	2	2	2	2	2	2	2	2	
8	8	8	8	8	8	8	8	8	8	8	8	8	8	8	8	3	6
3	3	3	3	3	3	3	3	3	3	3	3	3	3	3	3	8	7
4	4	4	4	4	4	4	4	4	4	4	4	4	4	4	4	4	8
4	14	14	14	14	14	14	14	14	14	14	14	14	14	14	14	14	9
5	15	15	15	15	15	15	15	15	15	15	15	15	15	15	15	15	10
6	16	16	16	16	16	16	16	16	16	16	16	16	16	16	16	16	
7	17	17	17	17	17	17	17	17	17	17	17	17	17	17	17	17	
2	12	12	12	12	12	12	12	12	12	12	12						
0	20	20	20	20	20	20	20	20									
8	18	18	18	18	18	18	18	18									

Safety car deployed on laps shown

RACE TYRE STRATEGIES

	Driver	Race Stint 1	Race Stint 2	Race Stint 3
1	Webber	Super-Soft: 1-23	Medium: 24-78	
2	Vettel	Super-Soft: 1-22	Medium: 23-78	
3	Kubica	Super-Soft: 1-21	Medium: 22-78	
4	Massa	Super-Soft: 1-19	Medium: 20-78	
5	Hamilton	Super-Soft: 1-17	Medium: 18-78	
6	Alonso	Super-Soft: 1	Medium: 2-78	
7	Rosberg	Super-Soft: 1-28	Medium: 29-78	
8	Sutil	Super-Soft: 1-22	Medium: 23-78	
9	Liuzzi	Super-Soft: 1-19	Medium: 20-78	
10	Buemi	Super-Soft: 1-20	Medium: 21-78	
11	Alguersuari	Super-Soft: 1-21	Medium: 22-78	
12	Schumacher	Super-Soft: 1-19	Medium: 20-78	
13	Petrov	Super-Soft: 1-21	Medium: 22-30	Medium: 31-73
14	Chandhok	Super-Soft: 1-19	Medium: 20-70	
15	Trulli	Super-Soft: 1-26	Medium: 27-70	
	Kovalainen	Super-Soft: 1-28	Medium: 29-58 (dnf)	
	Senna	Super-Soft: 1-2	Medium: 3-58	
	Barrichello	Super-Soft: 1-19	Medium: 20-30 (dnf)	
	Kobayashi	Medium: 1-23 (dnf)		
	di Grassi	Super-Soft: 1-25	Medium: 26 (dnf)	
	Glock	Super-Soft: 1-22 (dnf)		
	de la Rosa	Super-Soft: 1-21 (dnf)		
	Button	Super-Soft: 1-2 (dnf)		
	Hülkenberg	Super-Soft: 0 (dnf)		

The tyre regulations stipulate that the two dry tyre specifications must be used during the race.
The Super-Soft compound Bridgestone Potenza tyre is marked with a green stripe on the sidewall.

FIA FORMULA 1 WORLD CHAMPIONSHIP · ROUND 7

TURKISH GRAND PRIX

ISTANBUL PARK CIRCUIT

Main photo: Lewis Hamilton can hardly believe his luck as he speeds past the hapless Red Bull pair to take an unlikely win for McLaren.
Photo: Studio Colombo/WRi2

Inset left: Vettel certainly was in no doubt about who was to blame for the all-Red Bull collision. And it wasn't him…
Photo: Peter J Fox

ISTANBUL QUALIFYING

"SLIGHTLY on the back foot," he called it, but then Mark Webber has never been one for hyperbole. The Australian suffered a blown engine during Friday afternoon's free practice session, but he had already completed 50 laps by then and, in any case, the Renault V8 was approaching the end of its anticipated life cycle.

The hydraulic problems that kept him in the pits during the first part of the Saturday morning session were more of an irritant, but none of this stifled his qualifying vim. Turn Eight apart, Istanbul Park has few obviously Red Bull-friendly corners, where peculiarly high levels of downforce matter, but the RB6 was almost 9mph faster than anything else through this ultra-quick left-hander. The McLarens worked much better here than they had two weekends earlier, when Monaco's tight confines had stifled the team's long chassis, but Lewis Hamilton still ended up 0.138 seconds shy of Webber's 1m 26.299s benchmark. "We are losing about 0.4 seconds to the Red Bulls through Turn Eight," the Englishman said.

Both might have been vanquished had Sebastian Vettel's run of technical misfortune not continued. Slightly off the pace in Monaco, the German had been given a fresh chassis for the weekend; the official explanation was that a small crack had been found in the original. Vettel likes to nickname his cars – the previous one had been 'Luscious Liz', this was 'Randy Mandy' – but he was probably calling it something else altogether when the brakes began locking during his final two laps. "It was very strange," said Vettel, who had been quickest on Saturday morning, and in both Q1 and Q2. "The car locked up going into Turn 12 on my first run, but that wasn't really a problem. Then it happened again two corners later and I thought, 'Okay, maybe I braked a little late,' but then I got confirmation that something was wrong when it happened again at the start of my second run. To be honest, I feel quite lucky that I'm still third."

Red Bull tried its own version of McLaren's cockpit operated aero vent on Friday, but discarded it ahead of qualifying. "It worked okay," Webber said, "but we came in to the weekend with our eyes wide open. It's a tricky project to get right, and fair play to McLaren, who got the jump on everybody else. We're not in a position to take risks. We never put stuff on the car if there's a chance it might make it slower, and we're not going to start now."

This was his third consecutive pole position, his fourth of the campaign and Red Bull's seventh in as many races. "I've known worse pressure," Webber added. "Last year, we clearly had a quick car, but it was a little bit snookered at some venues. This time, we've been to lots of different tracks and it works well at all of them."

Jenson Button lined up fourth, ahead of the two Mercedes-Benzes – Michael Schumacher outqualifying Nico Rosberg for only the second time – but it was a hugely disappointing session for Ferrari, ahead of its 800th world championship grand prix. The car had been respectably competitive on Friday, during long runs in race trim, but single-lap pace was a different matter. Felipe Massa – winner of the first three F1 races in Turkey – made it through to the final part of qualifying after a Q2 lap that was reckoned to be as fast as the car would go, but he started only eighth, four places ahead of Fernando Alonso. "Nothing strange happened today," the Spaniard said. "I deserve to be 12th on the evidence of what we have seen. I wasn't fast enough and don't think I could have got much more from the car. My fastest three laps were all pretty much the same, and when nine drivers are covered by just half a second…"

Right: Mark Webber was under extreme pressure from Lewis Hamilton in the early stages of the race.

Below: Vettel's sunny demeanour on the grid would change after the race.
Photos: Peter J Fox

Bottom left: Another milestone for the most famous team of them all.
Photo: Paul-Henri Cahier

Bottom: Hamilton's success at Istanbul Park served as a poignant tribute to the late Bruce McLaren close to the 40th anniversary of the team founder's death.
Photo: Jean-François Galeron WRi2

IF anything, it was a surprise it hadn't happened previously. Sebastian Vettel doesn't take prisoners; Mark Webber isn't renowned for concession. It was their collective attitude that gifted the 2010 Turkish Grand Prix to McLaren, but the underlying reasons were manifold.

The afternoon began conventionally enough, with Webber leading away from pole and Vettel outdragging Lewis Hamilton to cement a Red Bull one-two at Turn One, although Hamilton managed to recapture second within two corners. Momentarily delayed by his team-mate's slightly faltering start, Jenson Button was beaten away by Michael Schumacher, although he redressed that with a classy, brassy move before the lap was out, on the approach to the hairpin. This set the scene for the opening phase of the race, with the leading four cars pulling comfortably clear of the rest, more or less as one. Nico Rosberg sat sixth, behind his Mercedes team-mate, and Robert Kubica headed the pursuit, from Felipe Massa, Vitaly Petrov, Kamui Kobayashi, Adrian Sutil, Fernando Alonso, Pedro de la Rosa, Jaime Alguersuari, Tonio Liuzzi, Jarno Trulli, Heikki Kovalainen, Bruno Senna, Rubens Barrichello (who lost several places off the line when his anti-stall system kicked in unexpectedly), Timo Glock, Karun Chandhok and Lucas di Grassi. Nico Hülkenberg and Sébastien Buemi brushed wheels and headed for the pits at the end of the opening lap, with front and rear punctures respectively. "I made a good start," said Buemi, "but then de la Rosa was slow exiting Turn Two. I tried to go around him on the outside, but went a bit wide and Hülkenberg got past. I attempted to retake him at Turn Seven, on the outside, but I think he might have lost the front end of his car because he clipped my right rear."

At the front, the leaders consistently lapped within a tenth of each other – four evenly matched drivers in two identically competitive chassis. There was no overtaking – although Hamilton had a swift look to Webber's inside at Turn 12 on lap 12 – but none was required. The spectacle was compelling.

The rhythm was broken on lap 14, when Vettel was first to switch from soft to hard Bridgestones; next time around, Webber and Hamilton followed suit. The leader's stop wasn't great – 0.8 seconds slower than Vettel's or, in the Australian's words, "It felt as though they were putting fuel in" – but Hamilton's was 1.5 seconds more leisurely still, because his right rear wheel didn't relocate cleanly. Button stayed out until lap 17, but a couple of fastest laps weren't enough to alter his position in the pecking order. Webber continued to lead, but McLaren's fumble had dropped Hamilton behind Vettel.

And so the pursuit continued, as before, with four cars tied as one.

Before the start, Red Bull had been acutely aware of the McLaren threat and had opted to start the race without brimming either car's fuel tank. By running slightly lighter, it had hoped to break the opposition at the start and then control the pace toward the race's end. McLaren, though, had plumped for a similar strategy. Up on the pit counter, the economy alarms were starting to chime.

Above: Fernando Alonso prepares for a race that would only yield a disappointing eighth place.

Top: Timo Glock and Lucas di Grassi leave the pit lane; the Virgins were reliable to the finish.

Photos: Peter J Fox

On laps 36 – when he was 0.813 seconds clear of his team-mate – and 37, Webber posted times of 1m 30.511s and 1m 30.334s, but then he heeded an instruction to lean off his fuel mixture. On the following two laps, he managed a 1m 30.406s and a 1m 30.626s, but the effort to maintain equilibrium was starting to hurt his rear tyres, rather than his fuel consumption.

Running in traffic – and others' slipstream – Vettel had saved about 1.5kg of fuel, compared with Webber, and was able to continue with a slightly richer mixture. The difference in performance between their respective engine maps was minuscule, but significant: it equated to 0.18 seconds per lap, or about 1.5 metres down the long drag between Turns Nine and Turn 12.

On lap 40, Vettel got a particularly good exit from Nine and started to draw alongside his team-mate. Webber remained in the centre of the road, keeping Vettel on the dusty side of the track, and never deviated from his line. The German edged right as they approached the corner, but he did so before he was completely ahead. Irresistible force duly encountered immovable object: Vettel skated into the run-off area, his right rear suspension in tatters, while Webber escaped with a tweaked nose and, two laps later, a swift reparatory visit to the pits. Next time he passed the accident spot, Vettel was standing there, gesticulating, waving a finger at his temple – the international sign for 'idiot'.

Red Bull driver development manager Helmut Marko took Vettel's side: "Mark should have moved," he said, a few days before being barred from speaking to the press. Sporting director Christian Horner was less partial: he blamed both. "Mark didn't leave Sebastian enough space," he said, "but at the same time, Sebastian pulled across too soon. They have a duty to drive for the team, and what happened today cost us a race win and 28 championship points."

From where he'd been sitting, Webber saw only the other Red Bull going faster than he thought should have been feasible, but then he didn't have access to all the facts. He felt the team should have told Vettel to ease off, but that wasn't a realistic option with the McLarens so close. Up on the pit wall, indeed, quite the opposite was being contemplated: Webber's side of the garage was instructed to tell their man that he should be prepared to let Vettel go, but the competitive juices extend far beyond the cockpit and that message didn't percolate.

"If you look at the pictures," said Vettel, "I think it's clear that I had the inside line. I was focused on my braking point, but he touched my right rear wheel and I went off."

Webber's view? "Seb was obviously a bit quicker," he said, "but I wasn't about to make things easy. We're fighting for race wins, and the world championship. When he came down the inside, I just tried to keep him on the dirty side of the track, so that he'd struggle to brake for Turn 12. That way, I was hoping to get back ahead when we exited the corner. He cut across and hit me before we got there, though."

Analysing for BBC Radio 5 Live, former F1 racer Anthony Davidson took Webber's side. "The accident," he said, "was 100 per cent Vettel's fault."

Hamilton appreciated the moment, and not just because it gifted him the lead. "It was great to watch," he said. "It was like an action movie in 3D. Mark held his line, and I don't think there was necessarily a

Left: Although Vettel's race ended after the collision, Webber was able to pick up the pieces and recover to take third at the chequered flag.
Photos: Lukas Gorys

Below left: Kamui Kobayashi gave Sauber its first point of the season with a solid tenth place.

Below far left: An overheated Heikki Kovalainen takes on liquid.
Photos: Peter J Fox

Below: Nico Hülkenberg uses all the track, and a bit more besides, as he presses on hard at the wheel of the Williams FW32.
Photo: Paul-Henri Cahier

reason for Sebastian to move to the right. I had the best view in the house."

By now, McLaren had started to issue fuel conservation instructions of its own – a reflection of that searing early pace – and the following conversation took place.

McLaren: "Lewis, we need you to save fuel. Both cars are doing the same."

Hamilton: "Jenson's closing in on me, you guys."

McLaren: "Understood, Lewis."

Hamilton: "If I back off, is he going to pass me?"

McLaren: "No, Lewis, no…"

At this stage, a brief shower added an extra complication – dry tyres on a greasy track perfectly suit Button's delicate touch – and on lap 48 the reigning champion was suddenly on his team-mate's tail. Hamilton claimed he'd backed off a touch too much as a result of the fuel saving directive, and the duo ran side by side into Turn 12, with Button edging ahead through the subsequent right and left that lead on to the pit straight. Hamilton retained the inside line, though, and surged back ahead as they entered Turn One, forcing his team-mate slightly wide. It was hard, but entirely fair, although it stepped up the urgency of the messages about fuel economy. Thereafter, they settled down and ran to the flag in a more orderly fashion, and their post-race hug was every bit as genuine as the animosity simmering in a nearby garage. "The McLaren drivers proved it was possible for team-mates to fight closely," said Horner.

"We knew we had good race pace and would be able to stay with the Red Bulls," Hamilton said. "They were so fast through Turn Eight, though, that it was difficult to get close enough to set up a pass."

Ultimately, of course, that wouldn't be necessary. Hamilton dedicated his success to his father, Anthony, who had celebrated his 50th birthday on the previous Monday; it was also an appropriate result at the start of a week that marked the 40th anniversary of team founder Bruce McLaren's passing.

Webber trailed in third – with a clear championship lead over Button – and the order immediately behind remained fairly static from the start.

Schumacher took fourth, after leading team-mate Rosberg all afternoon, and Kubica was sixth, ahead of the out-of-sorts Ferraris, led by Massa. Alonso used gentle force to wrest eighth from Petrov with four laps to go, and their brush left the Russian with a punctured front right, which necessitated a pit stop that dropped him to 15th. Had he held the position, it would not have been Petrov's best result, but it had certainly been the most convincing performance of his fledgling F1 career. He came away with the consolation of fastest lap, courtesy of the fresh Bridgestones on which he finished the race. Sutil completed two of the afternoon's few passing manoeuvres, when he overtook Kobayashi on lap two and then again on lap 50. They completed the scorers; the Japanese driver's point was Sauber's first of the campaign. "The car worked best on the harder tyre," he said, "and that's why I only did a ten-lap stint on the softs. Towards the end, I could see the canvas through my front right, so I started to be very careful, especially through Turn Eight." The pit lane might have been a better option, but that's not how racing drivers think.

Kobayashi led team-mate de la Rosa across the line, with Alguersuari, Liuzzi, Barrichello, Petrov, Buemi, Hülkenberg, Glock and di Grassi completing the finishers. Chandhok was classified 20th, despite stopping six laps from the end with fuel pressure problems – the same malaise that had stopped team-mate Senna six laps beforehand.

The two Lotuses dropped out one lap apart, with hydraulic problems, but, like everybody from Schumacher backwards, they had been taking part in a different race.

Simon Arron

EDITOR'S VIEW
RED FACES AT RED BULL

EVENTS during the Turkish Grand Prix served as a stark reminder that all front-running F1 competitors totter precariously on a narrow line that separates superb wheel-to-wheel jousting from abject 'egg-on-face' humiliation. They also illustrated that keeping the lid on the bubbling cauldron of intra-team tension can be a thankless and exhausting task, even for the most disciplined and non-partisan of F1 operators.

In that respect, you would have to say that Red Bull proved it was a newcomer to this game, having grown to competitive maturity in a relatively short space of time. With that in mind, the sort of supremely embarrassing incident that left Webber and Vettel seething with indignation and mortification was a rite of passage the team was always likely to confront. From the pit wall, the McLaren management must have watched with a degree of wry amusement, having learned how this game works during the years of Lauda/Prost, Prost/Senna and Häkkinen/Coulthard over a period of more than two decades.

McLaren always worked hard behind the scenes to ensure that its arguments, for the most part, were kept very much in-house. After the controversy between Ayrton Senna and Alain Prost over who should have led into the first corner of the 1989 San Marino GP at Imola – a spat that ultimately led Prost to leave the team at the end of the year – team principal Ron Dennis sat both men down and allowed them to unburden their feelings. But he was sufficiently astute to do this away from the paddock's gaze, at a team test session on the remote Pembrey circuit in Wales, a week or so after the race that had generated so much trouble.

Of course, you could say that in those days Dennis had it easy. He alone was the man who commented about McLaren's position on any issue. That self-contained and polished approach continues to this day. At Istanbul Park, there was only the slightest of ripples on the Woking team's pond after Jenson Button had cheekily elbowed his way through to the lead, only to be repassed by Lewis. There was a touch of tension, but it was fleeting.

Obviously, the drivers could be relied upon to let rip in a situation like this, and such spontaneity, while obviously manna from heaven for the media, simply adds liberal helpings of unleaded to the flames of controversy. McLaren, happy to count to ten before offering any comment in situations like this, always manages to keep its jangled nerves under control, allowing the moment to pass as quickly as possible rather than lingering as a potential flashpoint for continued aggravation.

In the end, though, it seemed so obvious that Vettel had been the cause of the accident that it was almost laughable that there had been any sort of debate at all.

Alan Henry

Left: Jenson goes racing with Lewis, before the pair were urged to settle down to maintain a 1-2 finish.
Photo: Lukas Gorys

Below: "You're still my best pal, but don't race me when I'm in the lead!" Hamilton and Button share thoughts after their success.
Photo: Peter J Fox

Below: From the sublime to the ridiculous. Having basked in the glory at Monaco, two weeks later Christian Horner has to field a barrage of questions from the press in the aftermath of the race.
Photo: Peter J Fox

FIA F1 WORLD CHAMPIONSHIP · ROUND 7

TURKISH GRAND PRIX

ISTANBUL 28–30 MAY 2010

RACE DISTANCE: 58 laps, 192.250 miles/309.396km

RACE WEATHER: Sunny/cloudy/spitting/sunny (track 37–50°C, air 28–29°C)

Pos.	Driver	Nat.	No.	Entrant	Car/Engine	Tyres	Laps	Time/Retirement	Speed (mph/km/h)	Gap to leader	Fastest race lap	
1	**Lewis Hamilton**	GB	2	Vodafone McLaren Mercedes	McLaren MP4-25-Mercedes FO108X V8	B	58	1h 28m 47.620s	129.908/209.066		1m 30.075s	54
2	**Jenson Button**	GB	1	Vodafone McLaren Mercedes	McLaren MP4-25-Mercedes FO108X V8	B	58	1h 28m 50.265s	129.843/208.962	+ 2.645s	1m 29.895s	42
3	**Mark Webber**	AUS	6	Red Bull Racing	Red Bull RB6-Renault RS27 V8	B	58	1h 29m 11.905s	129.318/208.117	+ 24.285s	1m 29.195s	54
4	**Michael Schumacher**	GB	3	Mercedes GP Petronas F1 Team	Mercedes MGP W01-Mercedes FO108X V8	B	58	1h 29m 18.730s	129.153/207.852	+ 31.110s	1m 29.810s	53
5	**Nico Rosberg**	D	4	Mercedes GP Petronas F1 Team	Mercedes MGP W01-Mercedes FO108X V8	B	58	1h 29m 19.886s	129.125/207.807	+ 32.266s	1m 29.977s	52
6	**Robert Kubica**	PL	11	Renault F1 Team	Renault R30-RS27 V8	B	58	1h 29m 20.444s	129.112/207.786	+ 32.824s	1m 29.580s	57
7	**Felipe Massa**	BR	7	Scuderia Ferrari Marlboro	Ferrari F10-056 V8	B	58	1h 29m 24.255s	129.020/207.638	+ 36.635s	1m 29.996s	58
8	**Fernando Alonso**	E	8	Scuderia Ferrari Marlboro	Ferrari F10-056 V8	B	58	1h 29m 34.164s	128.782/207.255	+ 46.544s	1m 30.011s	56
9	**Adrian Sutil**	D	14	Force India F1 Team	Force India VJM03-Mercedes FO108X V8	B	58	1h 29m 36.649s	128.723/207.159	+ 49.029s	1m 29.959s	55
10	**Kamui Kobayashi**	J	23	BMW Sauber F1 Team	BMW Sauber C29-Ferrari 056 V8	B	58	1h 29m 53.270s	128.326/206.521	+ 1m 05.650s	1m 30.891s	42
11	Pedro de la Rosa	E	22	BMW Sauber F1 Team	BMW Sauber C29-Ferrari 056 V8	B	58	1h 29m 53.564s	128.319/206.510	+ 1m 05.944s	1m 30.421s	50
12	Jaime Alguersuari	E	17	Scuderia Toro Rosso	Toro Rosso STR5-Ferrari 056 V8	B	58	1h 29m 55.420s	128.275/206.439	+ 1m 07.800s	1m 29.535s	50
13	Vitantonio Liuzzi	I	15	Force India F1 Team	Force India VJM03-Mercedes FO108X V8	B	57			+ 1 lap	1m 31.421s	53
14	Rubens Barrichello	BR	9	AT&T Williams	Williams FW32-Cosworth CA2010 V8	B	57			+ 1 lap	1m 30.933s	53
15	Vitaly Petrov	RUS	12	Renault F1 Team	Renault R30-RS27 V8	B	57			+ 1 lap	1m 29.165s	57
16	Sébastien Buemi	CH	16	Scuderia Toro Rosso	Toro Rosso STR5-Ferrari 056 V8	B	57			+ 1 lap	1m 29.588s	57
17	Nico Hülkenberg	D	10	AT&T Williams	Williams FW32-Cosworth CA2010 V8	B	57			+ 1 lap	1m 30.620s	51
18	Timo Glock	D	24	Virgin Racing	Virgin VR-01-Cosworth CA2010 V8	B	55			+ 3 laps	1m 32.265s	48
19	Lucas di Grassi	BR	25	Virgin Racing	Virgin VR-01-Cosworth CA2010 V8	B	55			+ 3 laps	1m 33.257s	55
20	Karun Chandhok	IND	20	HRT F1 Team	HRT F110-Cosworth CA2010 V8	B	52	*fuel pump*		+ 6 laps	1m 34.585s	37
	Bruno Senna	BR	21	HRT F1 Team	HRT F110-Cosworth CA2010 V8	B	46	*fuel pressure*			1m 34.247s	35
	Sebastian Vettel	D	5	Red Bull Racing	Red Bull RB6-Renault RS27 V8	B	39	*accident*			1m 30.181s	37
	Heikki Kovalainen	FIN	19	Lotus Racing	Lotus T127-Cosworth CA2010 V8	B	33	*hydraulics*			1m 34.363s	26
	Jarno Trulli	I	18	Lotus Racing	Lotus T127-Cosworth CA2010 V8	B	32	*hydraulics*			1m 34.463s	26

Fastest race lap: Vitaly Petrov on lap 57, 1m 29.165s, 133.918mph/215.519km/h.

Lap record: Juan Pablo Montoya (McLaren MP4-20-Mercedes Benz V10), 1m 24.770s, 140.861mph/226.693km/h (2005).

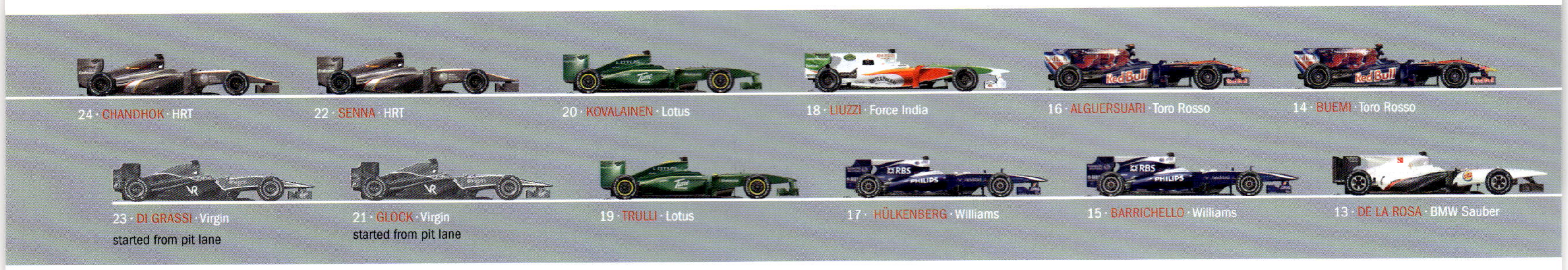

Grid order		1	2	3	4	5	6	7	8	9	10	11	12	13	14	15	16	17	18	19	20	21	22	23
6	WEBBER	6	6	6	6	6	6	6	6	6	6	6	6	6	6	6	1	1	6	6	6	6	6	6
2	HAMILTON	2	2	2	2	2	2	2	2	2	2	2	2	2	2	2	6	6	5	5	5	5	5	5
5	VETTEL	5	5	5	5	5	5	5	5	5	5	5	5	5	5	1	5	5	2	2	2	2	2	2
1	BUTTON	1	1	1	1	1	1	1	1	1	1	1	1	1	1	4	2	2	1	1	1	1	1	1
3	SCHUMACHER	3	3	3	3	3	3	3	3	3	3	3	3	3	3	5	3	3	3	3	3	3	3	3
4	ROSBERG	4	4	4	4	4	4	4	4	4	4	4	4	4	4	3	4	4	4	4	4	4	4	4
11	KUBICA	11	11	11	11	11	11	11	11	11	11	11	11	11	17	11	11	11	11	11	11	11	11	11
7	MASSA	7	7	7	7	7	7	7	7	7	7	7	7	7	11	7	7	7	7	7	7	7	7	7
12	PETROV	12	12	12	12	12	12	12	12	12	12	12	12	17	7	12	12	12	12	12	12	12	12	12
23	KOBAYASHI	23	14	14	14	14	14	14	14	14	14	14	14	15	12	8	8	8	8	8	8	8	8	8
14	SUTIL	14	23	23	23	23	23	23	23	23	23	8	22	12	8	23	23	23	23	23	23	23	23	23
8	ALONSO	8	8	8	8	8	8	8	8	8	8	22	17	8	23	14	14	14	14	14	14	14	14	14
22	DE LA ROSA	22	22	22	22	22	22	22	22	22	22	17	15	23	14	22	22	22	22	22	22	22	22	22
16	BUEMI	17	17	17	17	17	17	17	17	17	17	15	8	14	22	17	17	17	17	17	17	17	17	17
9	BARRICHELLO	10	15	15	15	15	15	15	15	15	15	23	23	22	15	15	15	15	15	15	15	15	15	15
17	ALGUERSUARI	15	18	9	9	9	9	9	9	9	9	18	18	19	19	19	19	10	10	10	10	10	10	10
10	HULKENBERG	18	9	18	18	18	18	18	18	18	18	19	19	18	18	10	10	19	19	9	9	9	9	9
15	LIUZZI	19	19	19	19	19	19	19	19	19	19	10	10	9	10	18	18	9	9	19	19	19	19	19
18	TRULLI	21	21	21	21	21	21	21	21	10	10	9	9	10	9	9	9	18	18	18	18	18	18	18
19	KOVALAINEN	9	24	24	24	24	24	24	10	21	21	21	21	21	21	21	21	21	21	24	24	24	24	24
24	GLOCK	24	20	20	20	10	10	10	24	24	24	24	24	24	24	24	24	24	24	21	21	16	16	24
21	SENNA	20	25	25	25	20	20	25	25	25	25	25	25	25	25	25	25	25	16	16	16	25	25	25
25	DI GRASSI	25	10	10	10	25	25	20	20	20	20	20	20	20	20	16	16	16	25	25	25	21	21	21
20	CHANDHOK	16	16	16	16	16	16	16	16	16	16	16	16	16	16	20	20	20	20	20	20	20	20	20

Grid order		24	25	26	27	28	29	30	31	32	33	34	35	36	37	38	39	40	41	42	43	44	45
6	WEBBER	6	6	6	6	6	6	6	6	6	6	6	6	6	6	6	6	2	2	2	2	2	2
2	HAMILTON	5	5	5	5	5	5	5	5	5	5	5	5	5	5	5	5	1	1	1	1	1	1
5	VETTEL	2	2	2	2	2	2	2	2	2	2	2	2	2	2	2	2	6	6	6	6	6	6
1	BUTTON	1	1	1	1	1	1	1	1	1	1	1	1	1	1	1	1	3	3	3	3	3	3
3	SCHUMACHER	3	3	3	3	3	3	3	3	3	3	3	3	3	3	3	3	4	4	4	4	4	4
4	ROSBERG	4	4	4	4	4	4	4	4	4	4	4	4	4	4	4	4	11	11	11	11	11	11
11	KUBICA	11	11	11	11	11	11	11	11	11	11	11	11	11	11	11	11	7	7	7	7	7	7
7	MASSA	7	7	7	7	7	7	7	7	7	7	7	7	7	7	7	7	12	12	12	12	12	12
12	PETROV	12	12	12	12	12	12	12	12	12	12	12	12	12	12	12	12	8	8	8	8	8	8
23	KOBAYASHI	8	8	8	8	8	8	8	8	8	8	8	8	8	8	8	8	23	23	23	23	23	23
14	SUTIL	23	23	23	23	23	23	23	23	23	23	23	23	23	23	23	23	14	14	14	14	14	14
8	ALONSO	14	14	14	14	14	14	14	14	14	14	14	14	14	14	14	14	22	22	22	22	22	22
22	DE LA ROSA	22	22	22	22	22	22	22	22	22	22	22	22	22	22	22	22	17	17	17	17	17	17
16	BUEMI	17	17	17	17	17	17	17	17	17	17	17	17	17	17	17	17	15	15	15	15	15	15
9	BARRICHELLO	15	15	15	15	15	15	15	15	15	15	15	15	15	15	15	15	9	9	9	9	9	9
17	ALGUERSUARI	10	10	10	10	10	9	9	9	9	9	9	9	9	9	9	9	16	16	16	16	16	10
10	HULKENBERG	9	9	9	9	9	10	10	10	10	10	10	10	10	10	16	16	10	10	10	10	10	16
15	LIUZZI	19	19	19	19	19	19	19	16	16	16	16	16	16	16	10	10	24	24	24	24	24	24
18	TRULLI	18	18	18	18	18	18	16	19	19	19	24	24	24	24	24	24	21	21	21	21	21	20
19	KOVALAINEN	16	16	16	16	16	16	18	18	18	24	21	21	21	21	21	21	20	20	20	20	20	21
24	GLOCK	24	24	24	24	24	24	24	24	24	21	20	20	20	20	20	20	25	25	25	25	25	25
21	SENNA	25	25	25	25	25	21	21	21	21	25	25	25	25	25	25	25						
25	DI GRASSI	21	21	21	21	21	25	25	25	25	20												
20	CHANDHOK	20	20	20	20	20	20	20	20	20													

TIME SHEETS

PRACTICE 1 (FRIDAY)

Weather: Sunny

Temperatures: track 35-43°C, air 26-27°C

Pos.	Driver	Laps	Time
1	Lewis Hamilton	20	1m 28.653s
2	Jenson Button	21	1m 29.615s
3	Michael Schumacher	24	1m 29.750s
4	Nico Rosberg	25	1m 29.855s
5	Sebastian Vettel	30	1m 29.867s
6	Robert Kubica	23	1m 30.061s
7	Vitaly Petrov	24	1m 30.065s
8	Mark Webber	26	1m 30.097s
9	Fernando Alonso	20	1m 30.294s
10	Adrian Sutil	17	1m 30.501s
11	Kamui Kobayashi	20	1m 30.615s
12	Vitantonio Liuzzi	21	1m 30.853s
13	Felipe Massa	22	1m 30.867s
14	Sébastien Buemi	24	1m 31.011s
15	Pedro de la Rosa	18	1m 31.238s
16	Nico Hülkenberg	23	1m 31.355s
17	Rubens Barrichello	19	1m 31.464s
18	Jaime Alguersuari	27	1m 31.735s
19	Heikki Kovalainen	24	1m 32.161s
20	Jarno Trulli	23	1m 32.990s
21	Karun Chandhok	13	1m 34.876s
22	Lucas di Grassi	21	1m 35.137s
23	Timo Glock	15	1m 35.583s
24	Sakon Yamamoto	26	1m 36.137s

PRACTICE 2 (FRIDAY)

Weather: Sunny

Temperatures: track 44-47°C, air 29-30°C

Pos.	Driver	Laps	Time
1	Jenson Button	30	1m 28.280s
2	Mark Webber	24	1m 28.378s
3	Sebastian Vettel	27	1m 28.590s
4	Lewis Hamilton	32	1m 28.672s
5	Fernando Alonso	30	1m 28.725s
6	Nico Rosberg	22	1m 28.914s
7	Michael Schumacher	22	1m 28.974s
8	Robert Kubica	34	1m 29.225s
9	Vitaly Petrov	36	1m 29.501s
10	Felipe Massa	26	1m 29.620s
11	Adrian Sutil	16	1m 29.629s
12	Nico Hülkenberg	17	1m 29.987s
13	Kamui Kobayashi	34	1m 30.053s
14	Pedro de la Rosa	34	1m 30.176s
15	Sébastien Buemi	32	1m 30.386s
16	Vitantonio Liuzzi	28	1m 30.627s
17	Rubens Barrichello	32	1m 30.766s
18	Jaime Alguersuari	37	1m 30.933s
19	Heikki Kovalainen	37	1m 31.610s
20	Lucas di Grassi	28	1m 33.013s
21	Jarno Trulli	11	1m 33.081s
22	Timo Glock	29	1m 33.312s
23	Bruno Senna	35	1m 33.420s
24	Karun Chandhok	25	1m 33.740s

PRACTICE 3 (SATURDAY)

Weather: Cloudy/partly cloudy

Temperatures: track 29-34° C, air 24-25°C

Pos.	Driver	Laps	Time
1	Sebastian Vettel	18	1m 27.086s
2	Nico Rosberg	16	1m 27.359s
3	Lewis Hamilton	14	1m 27.396s
4	Mark Webber	15	1m 27.553s
5	Robert Kubica	20	1m 27.784s
6	Fernando Alonso	18	1m 27.861s
7	Michael Schumacher	16	1m 27.879s
8	Jenson Button	17	1m 27.963s
9	Felipe Massa	20	1m 27.969s
10	Vitaly Petrov	18	1m 28.344s
11	Sébastien Buemi	22	1m 28.610s
12	Pedro de la Rosa	21	1m 28.652s
13	Jaime Alguersuari	21	1m 28.734s
14	Kamui Kobayashi	20	1m 29.036s
15	Nico Hülkenberg	18	1m 29.044s
16	Vitantonio Liuzzi	15	1m 29.211s
17	Rubens Barrichello	14	1m 29.305s
18	Jarno Trulli	19	1m 30.618s
19	Heikki Kovalainen	22	1m 30.884s
20	Timo Glock	21	1m 31.341s
21	Lucas di Grassi	16	1m 32.180s
22	Bruno Senna	22	1m 32.230s
23	Karun Chandhok	19	1m 32.762s
24	Adrian Sutil	1	no time

QUALIFYING (SATURDAY)

Weather: Sunny/Cloudy Temperatures: track 40-43°C, air 28°C

Pos.	Driver	First	Second	Third	Qualifying Tyre
1	Mark Webber	1m 27.500s	1m 26.818s	1m 26.295s	Soft
2	Lewis Hamilton	1m 27.667s	1m 27.013s	1m 26.433s	Soft
3	Sebastian Vettel	1m 27.067s	1m 26.729s	1m 26.760s	Soft
4	Jenson Button	1m 27.555s	1m 27.277s	1m 26.781s	Soft
5	Michael Schumacher	1m 27.756s	1m 27.438s	1m 26.857s	Soft
6	Nico Rosberg	1m 27.649s	1m 27.141s	1m 26.952s	Soft
7	Robert Kubica	1m 27.766s	1m 27.426s	1m 27.039s	Soft
8	Felipe Massa	1m 27.993s	1m 27.200s	1m 27.082s	Soft
9	Vitaly Petrov	1m 27.620s	1m 27.387s	1m 27.430s	Soft
10	Kamui Kobayashi	1m 28.158s	1m 27.434s	1m 28.122s	Soft
11	Adrian Sutil	1m 27.951s	1m 27.525s		
12	Fernando Alonso	1m 27.857s	1m 27.612s		
13	Pedro de la Rosa	1m 28.147s	1m 27.879s		
14	Sébastien Buemi	1m 28.534s	1m 28.273s		
15	Rubens Barrichello	1m 28.336s	1m 28.392s		
16	Jaime Alguersuari	1m 28.460s	1m 28.540s		
17	Nico Hülkenberg	1m 28.227s	1m 28.841s		
18	Vitantonio Liuzzi	1m 28.958s			
19	Jarno Trulli	1m 30.237s			
20	Heikki Kovalainen	1m 30.519s			
21	Timo Glock	1m 30.744s			
22	Bruno Senna	1m 31.266s			
23	Lucas di Grassi	1m 31.989s			
24	Karun Chandhok	1m 32.060s			

FOR THE RECORD

800th F1 WORLD CHAMPIONSHIP RACE: Ferrari (inc 1952 Indy 500)

50th START: Sebastian Vettel

30th PODIUM: Lewis Hamilton

30th FASTEST LAP: Renault

1st FASTEST LAP: Vitoly Petrov

DID YOU KNOW

This was the first time since 1998 that a constructor achieved pole in the first seven races of a season; that year, McLaren claimed pole in the first nine races.

POINTS

DRIVERS

1	Mark Webber	93
2	Jenson Button	88
3	Lewis Hamilton	84
4	Fernando Alonso	79
5	Sebastian Vettel	78
6	Robert Kubica	67
7	Felipe Massa	67
8	Nico Rosberg	66
9	Michael Schumacher	34
10	Adrian Sutil	22
11	Vitantonio Liuzzi	10
12	Rubens Barrichello	7
13	Vitaly Petrov	6
14	Jaime Alguersuari	3
15	Sébastien Buemi	1
16	Kamui Kobayashi	1
17	Nico Hülkenberg	1

CONSTRUCTORS

1	McLaren	172
2	Red Bull	171
3	Ferrari	146
4	Mercedes	100
5	Renault	73
6	Force India	32
7	Williams	8
8	Toro Rosso	4
9	BMW Sauber	1

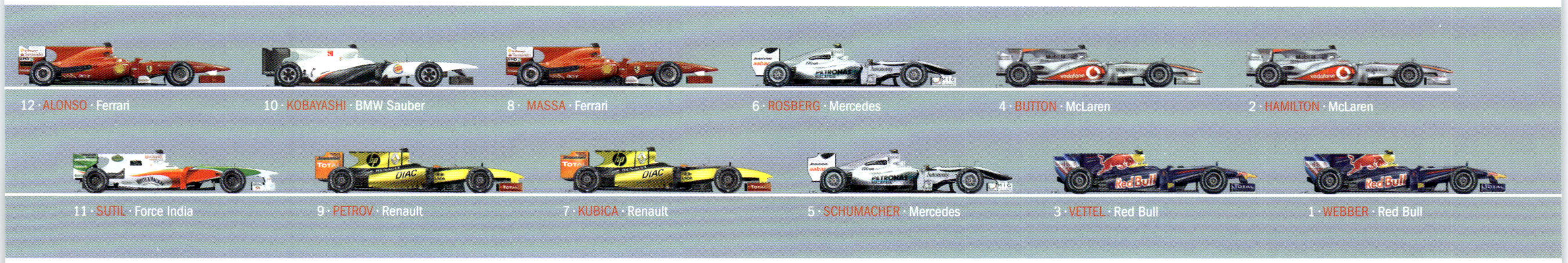

46	47	48	49	50	51	52	53	54	55	56	57	58	·
2	2	1	2	2	2	2	2	2	2	2	2	2	1
1	1	2	1	1	1	1	1	1	1	1	1	1	2
6	6	6	6	6	6	6	6	6	6	6	6	6	3
3	3	3	3	3	3	3	3	3	3	3	3	3	
4	4	4	4	4	4	4	4	4	4	4	4	4	
11	11	11	11	11	11	11	11	11	11	11	11	11	6
7	7	7	7	7	7	7	7	7	7	7	7	7	7
12	12	12	12	12	12	12	12	8	8	8	8	8	8
8	8	8	8	8	8	8	8	14	14	14	14	14	9
23	23	23	23	14	14	14	14	23	23	23	23	23	10
14	14	14	14	23	23	23	23	22	22	22	22	22	
22	22	22	22	22	22	22	22	17	17	17	17	17	
17	17	17	17	17	17	17	17	15	15	15	15		
15	15	15	15	15	15	15	15	9	9	9	9		
9	9	9	9	9	9	9	9	12	12	12	12		
10	10	16	16	16	16	16	16	16	16	16	16		
16	16	10	10	10	10	10	10	10	10	10	10		
24	24	24	24	24	24	24	24	24	24				
20	20	20	20	20	20	25	25	25	25				
25	25	25	25	25	25	20							
21													

21 Pit stop

14 One lap or more behind

RACE TYRE STRATEGIES

	Driver	Race Stint 1	Race Stint 2	Race Stint 3
1	Hamilton	Soft: 1-15	Hard: 16-58	
2	Button	Soft: 1-17	Hard: 18-58	
3	Webber	Soft: 1-15	Hard: 16-42	Hard: 43-58
4	Schumacher	Soft: 1-14	Hard: 15-58	
5	Rosberg	Soft: 1-15	Hard: 16-58	
6	Kubica	Soft: 1-13	Hard: 14-58	
7	Massa	Soft: 1-13	Hard: 14-58	
8	Alonso	Soft: 1-11	Hard: 12-58	
9	Sutil	Soft: 1-12	Hard: 13-58	
10	Kobayashi	Soft: 1-10	Hard: 11-58	
11	de la Rosa	Soft: 1-12	Hard: 13-58	
12	Alguersuari	Hard: 1-14	Soft: 15-41	Soft: 42-58
13	Liuzzi	Soft: 1-13	Hard: 14-57	
14	Barrichello	Soft: 1-10	Hard: 11-57	
15	Petrov	Soft: 1-12	Hard: 13-54	Soft: 55-57
16	Buemi	Hard: 1	Soft: 2-44	Soft: 45-57
17	Hülkenberg	Hard: 1	Soft: 2-37	Hard: 38-57
18	Glock	Hard: 1-32	Soft: 33-54	
19	di Grassi	Soft: 1-33	Hard: 34-54	
20	Chandhok	Hard: 1-21	Soft: 22-52	
	Senna	Soft: 1-20	Hard: 21-46 (dnf)	
	Vettel	Soft: 1-14	Hard: 15-39 (dnf)	
	Kovalainen	Soft: 1-33 (dnf)		
	Trulli	Hard: 1-32 (dnf)		

The tyre regulations stipulate that the two dry tyre specifications must be used during the race. The Soft compound Bridgestone Potenza tyre is marked with a green stripe on the sidewall.

Photos: Peter J. Fox

Left: A second win in as many races really fired up Lewis Hamilton's world championship challenge in Montreal.

Main photo: Hamilton had the edge on Sebastian Vettel's Red Bull, and the German driver eventually had to give best to Button and Alonso, finishing the day fourth.

Photos: Peter J Fox

FIA FORMULA 1 WORLD CHAMPIONSHIP · ROUND 8

CANADIAN GRAND PRIX

MONTREAL CIRCUIT

2

MONTREAL QUALIFYING

MARGINS, margins… Lewis Hamilton covets the Circuit Gilles Villeneuve, and always will. He recorded his first Formula One pole position at the track, in 2007, and followed it with his maiden victory one day later. Like Monaco, it's a claustrophobic circuit that permits drivers to make a difference. You just need to flirt a little more outrageously with the walls, but on Saturday morning Hamilton overstepped the mark at Turn Four.

It was little more than a gentle kiss and there was no visible damage, but the McLaren mechanics knuckled down to replace the right-hand suspension, front and rear, prior to qualifying. "I don't think I've ever seen them work so hard," Hamilton said. "It was like watching an orchestra."

He rewarded their endeavours with stellar 1m 15.105s lap that maintained his 100 per cent pole position strike rate at the venue and simultaneously ended Red Bull's seasonal monopoly. At a circuit where increments are usually measured in thousandths, he was fully 0.258 seconds clear of the field. He didn't make it back to the pits, however, because his car began to run low on fuel during his cooling-off lap and the team instructed him to switch off.

McLaren team principal Martin Whitmarsh denied that this had been a bit of brinkmanship – running the car as light as possible to embellish its driver's pole prospects – and insisted that it was simply the result of an error. As Hamilton hadn't completed his 'in' lap within the prescribed maximum time laid down by the stewards – an obligation to minimise speed differentials – the team was reprimanded and fined $10,000, but pole was safe.

"If he had returned to the pits," said Whitmarsh, "there would not have been enough fuel to provide the sample the regulations demand. We thought that was the dominant requirement."

Margins, margins…

Hamilton's performance advantage was partly down to his decision to qualify on the super-soft Bridgestone, while the second- and third-placed Red Bull drivers opted for the more durable medium. Mark Webber just had the edge on teammate Sebastian Vettel, but only until an unscheduled gearbox change earned him a five-place grid penalty and knocked him back to seventh.

"We expected McLaren to be strong, and Lewis did a very quick lap," said Webber, "but obviously he's on a different compound, and I'm delighted that we're so quick on rubber that will be more stable for us."

Hamilton denied that McLaren had taken an unnecessary tyre gamble, but his pace earlier in the session suggested that he could still have challenged for pole if he had plumped for the medium.

Vettel blamed traffic for his failure to go faster. "I didn't manage a clear lap until the very end of the session," he said, "but I'm happy with my situation. From what we saw yesterday, it is difficult to make the softer tyre last for more than a few laps."

Hamilton, though, was unconcerned. "We just have to take each day as it comes," he said. "We have had a few problems making the softer tyres last, but we don't know what track conditions will be like tomorrow and we'll just do our best to look after them as well as we can."

Fernando Alonso was an in-touch fourth for Ferrari, ahead of Jenson Button, and Tonio Liuzzi was a career-best sixth for Force India. The Italian was using a replacement chassis – he'd suffered handling problems in Turkey, which were traced to an incorrectly bonded floor – and relishing every second. All three would move up a place because of Webber's transmission woes.

Mercedes showed encouraging form during Friday's free practice, but both drivers struggled in low-fuel trim once again, and Michael Schumacher was knocked out in Q2, the only Mercedes powered driver to suffer such a fate.

AND so, to strategy. Would the McLarens' super-soft tyres melt within a matter of laps, or did the team's perceived madness conceal method? And how much would the safety car – deployed 20 times during the previous 11 Canadian Grands Prix – influence the outcome? The answers were "Yes", "Yes" and "Not at all" – and the upshot was one of the season's most absorbing contests. It was almost as though this was a different sport from the one that had attracted so much flak in the slipstream of Bahrain.

The cool, damp conditions of the first two days finally yielded to sunshine on race morning, but intermittent showers had cleaned the circuit throughout the build-up and precious little rubber had been laid down. And with so many slow corners leading on to long straights – "traction events", in the teams' argot – the Circuit Gilles Villeneuve is hard on rubber at the best of times.

Lewis Hamilton made a good start from pole position – something of a personal tradition in Canada – to lead away, while Sebastian Vettel maintained second, but only after a ferocious chop, legal but borderline, to repel Fernando Alonso. Jenson Button held fourth without resorting to violence, but there was plenty just behind. "I was trying to stay out of trouble," said Tonio Liuzzi. "I could see Felipe coming across, but I was more or less on the grass already and didn't have anywhere to go."

The fruits of the Italian's best F1 grid position were swiftly frittered as he and Massa touched going into the first left-hander. Once initial contact had been made, Massa barged the Force India twice more at Turn Two before Liuzzi finally spun around. Both headed immediately to the pits for repairs, as did Pedro de la Rosa, who spun to the left on the approach to the first corner after a punt from Vitaly Petrov. The Russian had jumped the start, for which he was eventually given a drive-through penalty, and he received the same punishment for causing a collision, too, although notice of that would not be served until lap 22.

The momentary pandemonium allowed Mark Webber to recapture two of the five positions his gearbox penalty had cost him and he ran fifth, ahead of Robert Kubica, Adrian Sutil, Michael Schumacher, Nico Hülkenberg, Jaime Alguersuari, Sébastien Buemi, Heikki Kovalainen, Nico Rosberg (who'd had to back off to avoid the shenanigans at Turn Two), Rubens Barrichello (whose anti-stall system briefly kicked in, again, on the grid), Jarno Trulli, Bruno Senna, Lucas di Grassi, Petrov, Karun Chandhok, Timo Glock and the pit-bound trio. Officially, Kamui Kobayashi completed the first lap, but only because he crawled through the timing beam on the pit straight. The Japanese driver had been fighting with Rosberg on the approach to the final chicane, but was edged wide over the kerbs and vaulted from there into the retaining wall on the opposite side of the circuit, crumpling his Sauber too badly to continue.

Above: Tonio Liuzzi's good qualifying position was ruined when he tangled with Felipe Massa's Ferrari at the first corner, but the Italian recovered well to score points for ninth place.
Photo: Jean-François Galeron/WRi2

Left, above and below: Shades or no shades for Nico Hülkenberg and Patrick Head.

Far left: Brakes take a greater hammering at the Circuit Gilles Villeneuve than probably any other circuit on the calendar.
Photos: Peter J Fox

Right: Fernando Alonso became tangled up in traffic, and as a result was jumped for second place by Jenson Button's McLaren.
Photo: Peter J Fox

Below: After dropping down the grid with a penalty, Mark Webber eventually had to settle for fifth.
Photo: Paul-Henri Cahier

Hamilton was one second clear within the first two laps, but then Vettel closed in as the softer Bridgestones began to wilt, a condition that enabled Webber to pass Button on lap four. One lap later, the tyre stops began, with Rosberg and Trulli peeling in. Button was next, and on lap seven Hamilton and Alonso came in, too. The McLaren wheel change wasn't particularly slick, though, and delayed Hamilton just enough to allow Alonso to draw alongside as they headed for the exit. The Spaniard had the inside line for Turn One and made the move stick.

Suddenly the Red Bulls were first and second, as many had predicted they would be, but so abrasive were the conditions that even the harder tyres were, in the words of Red Bull sporting director Christian Horner, "turning to cheese". Webber came in on lap 13, Vettel on 14. That momentarily promoted the yet-to-stop Buemi into the lead: the Swiss was due to pit imminently, but first he had a cameo part to play. Alonso and Hamilton caught him on lap 15, coming into the hairpin, and the Spaniard briefly contemplated a passing attempt, which cost

sufficient momentum to make him easy prey on the following straight. Hamilton was back ahead, with Button third after vaulting Vettel and Webber during the tyre stops.

Clearly, this was going to be a two-stop race, and Hamilton pitted again on lap 26. Alonso's tyres were still in reasonable nick and this was a potential opportunity for him to gain ground on a clear track, but then he lost a couple of seconds while lapping the inattentive Trulli and the balance of power remained unaffected. Alonso pitted on lap 28 and rejoined half a second in arrears. Catching that Lotus had been a significant turning point.

Now Hamilton needed to make a set of mediums last for 44 laps, but finally the track had started to rubber in, so tyre abuse diminished and the pit lane became more tranquil. Hamilton would not be headed again. "It was difficult to know how much to save your tyres and how much to push," he said. "It has been the most challenging race of the year so far. Fernando had great pace, and it was always a case of trying to get through the traffic without allowing him to pass. I just knuckled down and tried to do the best job I could."

Red Bull had opted to split its strategies after the first stop: Vettel was sent out for a short second stint on super-softs, while Webber continued on mediums. "We wanted to cover both options," said Horner. "The safety car is rarely too far away in Montreal, except on a day like today, but if it had appeared, then one or other of our drivers might have benefited. Ultimately, though, there was nothing in the strategies."

Having spent the middle part of the race nursing his tyres, and defending against Vettel, Button gradually began to increase his pace and put pressure on Alonso. "You do everything you can to nurse the tyres," he said. "You play around with the diff and remove a bit of front wing, but during the first few laps even that wasn't enough. Pitting early on the soft actually helped me, because it moved me closer to the battle at the front, and once I was on the harder tyre everything began to work very well. You still had to be careful, though, because it would have been easy to grain the tyres."

His pursuit of Alonso yielded dividends on lap 56 when, for the third time that afternoon, traffic intervened to the Spaniard's detriment. This time, Chandhok's HRT was the obstacle. "I thought he was letting me through," Alonso said, "but he was just taking a different line to mine." The Ferrari driver was momentarily obliged to back off, and that gave Button enough of an edge to draft past between Turns Seven and Eight. Once ahead, he immediately began to close on Hamilton, but the leader had performance left in the tank, and underlined as much by setting his fastest time of the day with just eight laps to go. Game over.

For Alonso, there were mixed feelings. "I think we were 50 seconds behind the McLarens in Turkey," he said, "so to be fighting for victory here is a sign that we are moving in the right direction. We are back in the fight, but this is a race we could have won. Sometimes traffic helps you, sometimes it hurts you. Today, I lost out."

Vettel dropped off the leaders' pace in the second half of the race, so as not to aggravate a transmission

oil leak, but he took fourth – just – from the closing Webber. "Given that we weren't expected to do all that well this weekend," said Horner, "it has been a useful bit of damage limitation."

Despite his unproductive opening lap, Rosberg managed to salvage sixth for Mercedes. "I was able to pull off some good overtaking moves," he said, "and our race pace was strong. It was really difficult to manage the tyres. I tried to drive smoothly to control the graining, but every time I looked in my mirrors it was getting worse. Thankfully, the primes held after my second stop."

Kubica took seventh – and was allowed to keep it, despite an incident at the end of lap 26. The Pole had just been passed by Sutil, but when the German braked for the chicane, at the lap's end, Kubica sliced past and cut across his rival's bows so as not to compromise his entry to the pit lane. It was the instinctive response of a committed racer, the kind of thing that saves a few tenths, but the stewards saw it differently and reprimanded the Renault driver for dangerous behaviour.

The two cars had touched when trading places shortly beforehand and Sutil suffered a deflated right rear when he reached Turn One. A full lap at reduced pace cost him several positions, although eventually he clawed his way back to tenth by passing Schumacher on the final lap.

Buemi's pre-planned three-strop strategy minimised the need for tyre preservation and enabled him to take eighth, ahead of Liuzzi, one of the afternoon's star performers. Following his early brush with Massa, he switched immediately to the harder tyre and launched a spirited recovery drive that incorporated some of the race's liveliest moments, not least on the final lap, when he usurped Schumacher (which involved the Geman brushing wheels for the umpteenth time during the day – he collected a puncture shortly after forcing Kubica on to the grass on lap 13). "It was okay racing with Michael," Liuzzi said, "because he does things very cleanly." The stewards investigated the incident, but eventually concurred, although it was something of a minority view.

The bottom line? The Italian finally looked like the racing driver he has always promised to be. "I qualified near the front because we were genuinely quicker than some of the top teams," he said, "not because of peculiar circumstances. It was definitely one of my better race weekends, even if what happened on lap one was a low point in my career."

Sutil followed Liuzzi past Schumacher moments later, but it was hardly a surprise that the Mercedes driver was struggling: he had been running the same set of super-softs for 37 laps.

Alguersuari, Hülkenberg, Barrichello and Massa were next, the last describing his afternoon as "horrible". The only other finishers were Class B winner Kovalainen, who was 15th, from Petrov, Chandhok and di Grassi. Glock dropped out when his power steering failed, while brake problems, a blown engine and loss of second gear accounted for Trulli, de la Rosa and Senna respectively.

After the initial skirmish with Liuzzi, for which he blamed the Italian, obviously, Massa spent most of the race struggling to carve through traffic. On lap 63, he was running behind Schumacher, and his attempted pass prompted the German to edge him on to the grass approaching the chicane. Massa broke the speed limit when subsequently he pitted for repairs, but there wasn't time to serve a drive-through, so 20 seconds were added to his race time.

"Towards the end," said Schumacher, "I was trying as hard as I could to defend myself, but it was only possible to a certain degree. Today, our weapons were not very sharp."

The same could not be said of the robustness of his defensive technique.

Simon Arron

Left: Jenson Button heads Fernando Alonso on his way to second place.
Photo: Peter J Fox

Right: Valentino Rossi discusses handling with his Ferrari engineers at a test in Catalunya in February 2010. The MotoGP star has signed for Ducati for 2011–12.
Photo: Studio Colombo/WRi2

Bottom: More trophies for McLaren's Woking display.
Photo: Peter J Fox

EDITOR'S VIEW
FERRARI HINTS AT SEAT FOR ROSSI

FERRARI president Luca di Montezemolo originally took over the management of Maranello's F1 team in 1973 and was one of the crucial catalysts responsible for reviving the team's fortunes after one of the most depressing performance slumps in its history. Anybody who was present at the 1973 British Grand Prix could hardly have failed to notice the arthritic pace displayed by Jacky Ickx in the Ferrari 312B3, which spent much of the race battling with Howden Ganley's Iso Marlboro. That was a Williams by any other name – and one racing at a time well before Sir Frank's team had scaled the peaks as a credible winning force.

Stick with me, please; there really is a relevant point here. On the Wednesday before the 2010 Canadian GP, Montezemolo reiterated his belief that the three new teams on the F1 grid were "a joke" and that the sport would be better served by the top teams being permitted to field a third car.

"Giving this car to a good young driver or [to] Valentino Rossi would be better than a team being four seconds [a lap] behind," he said. Or indeed than a works Ferrari almost being lapped by the winning McLaren, as was the case all those years ago at the home of British motor racing. It was an interesting point, unquestionably, but there is always a great danger attached to any display of frenzied expectancy in the F1 business. And when a pivotal figure such as di Montezemolo begins to voice controversial opinions, inevitably one ends up looking for a hidden agenda.

Ferrari has always been something of a weather vane by which the prevailing wind in the F1 paddock can be checked. While it might be unfair to suggest that di Montezemolo is the kind of guy who sets his watch by the last clock he passed, the notion that Rossi might seriously contemplate a switch from his current comfort zone on two wheels might have been little more than grandstanding on the part of the Ferrari supremo.

At first glance, the prospect of somebody at last picking up the torch previously carried by John Surtees, as the only man to win world championships on two wheels and four, unquestionably exudes a tantalising magic. In practical terms, however, the gamble and sheer uncertainty involved – for both parties – would be too much for it ever to have a realistic hope of coming to fruition.

Was Ferrari just seeking to further strengthen its status and influence within the turbulent waters of F1 politics? At a time when the teams were all trying to strike a better deal with Bernie Ecclestone for a bigger share of the commercial rights from the start of 2013, any window dressing that could add to the allure of the Prancing Horse would surely be too good to pass up. Whether it was a third car and/or Valentino Rossi, Montezemolo's speculation would help burnish Ferrari's already indispensable position at the cutting edge of the F1 action.

The fact that it would almost certainly be neither was a detail swept away on the swirling vortex of F1's speculative storm. Luca knew it, the rest of the paddock knew it, but what the hell, it made good copy in the media centre for a couple of days.

Alan Henry

FIA F1 WORLD CHAMPIONSHIP · ROUND 8

GRAND PRIX DU CANADA

MONTRÉAL 11-13 JUNE 2010

RACE DISTANCE: 70 laps, 189.686 miles/305.270km

RACE WEATHER: Sunny (track 35-39°C, air 27-28°C)

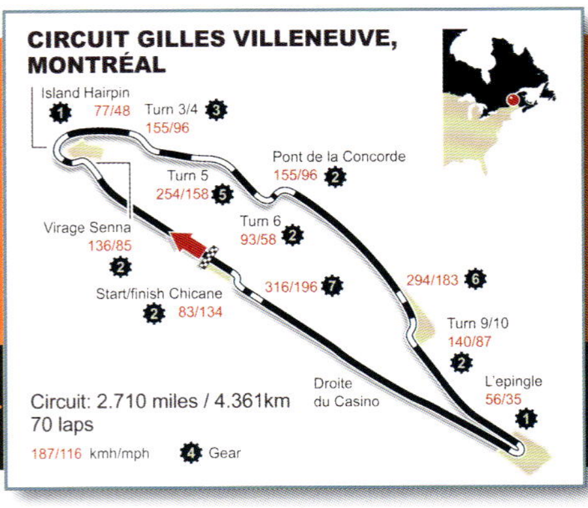

Pos.	Driver	Nat.	No.	Entrant	Car/Engine	Tyres	Laps	Time/Retirement	Speed (mph/km/h)	Gap to leader	Fastest race lap	
1	**Lewis Hamilton**	GB	2	Vodafone McLaren Mercedes	McLaren MP4-25-Mercedes FO108X V8	B	70	1h 33m 53.456s	121.216/195.079		1m 17.806s	62
2	**Jenson Button**	GB	1	Vodafone McLaren Mercedes	McLaren MP4-25-Mercedes FO108X V8	B	70	1h 33m 55.710s	121.168/195.001	+ 2.254s	1m 18.144s	66
3	**Fernando Alonso**	E	8	Scuderia Ferrari Marlboro	Ferrari F10-056 V8	B	70	1h 34m 02.670s	121.018/194.760	+ 9.214s	1m 18.207s	44
4	**Sebastian Vettel**	D	5	Red Bull Racing	Red Bull RB6-Renault RS27 V8	B	70	1h 34m 31.273s	120.408/193.778	+ 37.817s	1m 18.417s	62
5	**Mark Webber**	AUS	6	Red Bull Racing	Red Bull RB6-Renault RS27 V8	B	70	1h 34m 32.747s	120.377/193.728	+ 39.291s	1m 18.148s	62
6	**Nico Rosberg**	D	4	Mercedes GP Petronas F1 Team	Mercedes MGP W01-Mercedes FO108X V8	B	70	1h 34m 49.540s	120.022/193.156	+ 56.084s	1m 17.832s	68
7	**Robert Kubica**	PL	11	Renault F1 Team	Renault R30-RS27 V8	B	70	1h 34m 50.756s	119.996/193.115	+ 57.300s	1m 16.972s	67
8	**Sébastien Buemi**	CH	16	Scuderia Toro Rosso	Toro Rosso STR5-Ferrari 056 V8	B	69			+ 1 lap	1m 19.784s	39
9	**Vitantonio Liuzzi**	I	15	Force India F1 Team	Force India VJM03-Mercedes FO108X V8	B	69			+ 1 lap	1m 19.349s	66
10	**Adrian Sutil**	D	14	Force India F1 Team	Force India VJM03-Mercedes FO108X V8	B	69			+ 1 lap	1m 19.530s	68
11	Michael Schumacher	GB	3	Mercedes GP Petronas F1 Team	Mercedes MGP W01-Mercedes FO108X V8	B	69			+ 1 lap	1m 19.577s	44
12	Jaime Alguersuari	E	17	Scuderia Toro Rosso	Toro Rosso STR5-Ferrari 056 V8	B	69			+ 1 lap	1m 19.842s	69
13	Nico Hülkenberg	D	10	AT&T Williams	Williams FW32-Cosworth CA2010 V8	B	69			+ 1 lap	1m 18.912s	64
14	Rubens Barrichello	BR	9	AT&T Williams	Williams FW32-Cosworth CA2010 V8	B	69			+ 1 lap	1m 19.175s	65
15	Felipe Massa	BR	7	Scuderia Ferrari Marlboro	Ferrari F10-056 V8	B	69*			+ 1 lap	1m 18.325s	45
16	Heikki Kovalainen	FIN	19	Lotus Racing	Lotus T127-Cosworth CA2010 V8	B	68			+ 2 laps	1m 20.654s	65
17	Vitaly Petrov	RUS	12	Renault F1 Team	Renault R30-RS27 V8	B	68			+ 2 laps	1m 19.453s	58
18	Karun Chandhok	IND	20	HRT F1 Team	HRT F110-Cosworth CA2010 V8	B	66			+ 4 laps	1m 21.884s	47
19	Lucas di Grassi	BR	25	Virgin Racing	Virgin VR-01-Cosworth CA2010 V8	B	65			+ 5 laps	1m 21.937s	49
	Timo Glock	D	24	Virgin Racing	Virgin VR-01-Cosworth CA2010 V8	B	50	*accident/steering*			1m 21.669s	43
	Jarno Trulli	I	18	Lotus Racing	Lotus T127-Cosworth CA2010 V8	B	42	*brakes/vibration*			1m 20.791s	38
	Pedro de la Rosa	E	22	BMW Sauber F1 Team	BMW Sauber C29-Ferrari 056 V8	B	30	*engine*			1m 20.574s	21
	Bruno Senna	BR	21	HRT F1 Team	HRT F110-Cosworth CA2010 V8	B	13	*gearbox*			1m 24.524s	5
	Kamui Kobayashi	J	23	BMW Sauber F1 Team	BMW Sauber C29-Ferrari 056 V8	B	1	*accident*			no time	

*Massa received 20-sec penalty for speeding in the pit lane. It did not affect his placing.

Fastest race lap: Robert Kubica on lap 67, 1m 16.972s, 126.738mph/203.965km/h.

Lap record: Rubens Barrichello (Ferrari F2004 V10), 1m 13.622s, 132.505mph/213.246km/h (2004).

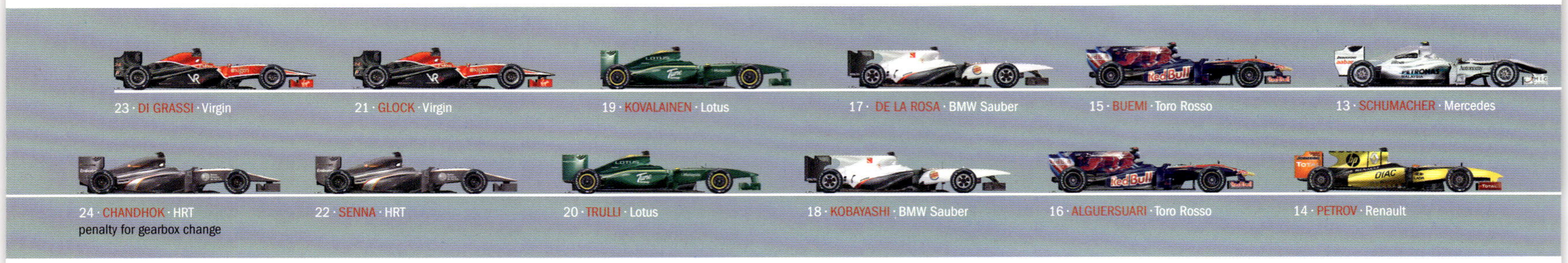

Grid order	1	2	3	4	5	6	7	8	9	10	11	12	13	14	15	16	17	18	19	20	21	22	23	24	25	26	27
2 HAMILTON	2	2	2	2	2	2	5	5	5	5	5	5	5	16	2	2	2	2	2	2	2	2	2	2	2	8	8
5 VETTEL	5	5	5	5	5	5	6	6	6	6	6	6	16	8	8	8	8	8	8	8	8	8	8	8	8	1	6
8 ALONSO	8	8	8	8	8	8	11	11	3	3	3	16	8	2	1	1	1	1	1	1	1	1	1	1	1	5	2
1 BUTTON	1	1	1	1	6	6	3	3	16	16	16	8	2	1	5	5	5	5	5	5	5	5	5	5	5	6	1
15 LIUZZI	6	6	6	6	1	11	16	16	8	8	8	2	1	5	6	6	6	6	6	6	6	6	6	6	6	2	5
7 MASSA	11	11	11	11	11	3	19	8	2	2	2	1	6	6	11	11	11	11	11	11	11	11	11	11	11	14	16
6 WEBBER	14	14	14	14	3	16	8	19	19	1	1	3	3	11	14	14	14	14	14	14	14	14	14	14	14	16	11
11 KUBICA	3	3	3	3	14	17	2	2	1	19	11	11	11	14	16	16	16	16	16	16	16	16	16	16	16	4	4
14 SUTIL	10	10	10	10	10	19	1	1	11	11	14	14	14	19	4	4	4	4	4	4	4	4	4	4	4	11	3
4 ROSBERG	17	17	17	17	16	9	25	14	14	14	19	19	19	10	19	10	10	10	10	10	10	10	10	17	3	3	10
9 BARRICHELLO	16	16	16	16	17	1	14	25	25	25	25	10	10	4	10	17	17	17	17	17	17	17	17	3	17	10	17
10 HULKENBERG	19	19	19	19	19	25	12	12	12	10	10	4	4	3	17	3	3	3	3	3	3	3	3	10	10	17	14
3 SCHUMACHER	4	4	4	9	9	14	24	24	24	4	4	17	17	17	3	22	22	15	15	15	15	15	15	15	15	15	15
12 PETROV	9	9	9	4	25	12	17	10	10	12	17	25	25	22	22	15	15	19	7	7	7	7	19	22	22	22	22
16 BUEMI	18	18	18	18	12	21	10	17	17	17	12	12	22	15	15	19	19	7	19	19	19	19	22	19	19	9	9
17 ALGUERSUARI	21	25	25	25	21	24	9	4	4	9	24	22	24	24	7	7	7	22	22	22	22	22	9	9	9	19	19
22 DE LA ROSA	25	21	21	21	24	10	21	9	9	24	22	24	15	12	12	12	12	18	18	18	9	9	18	18	18	7	7
23 KOBAYASHI	12	12	12	12	20	20	4	21	21	22	21	21	12	7	18	18	18	9	9	9	18	18	7	7	7	18	18
19 KOVALAINEN	20	20	24	24	4	4	20	20	22	21	18	15	18	18	20	25	25	25	25	25	25	25	25	25	25	25	25
18 TRULLI	24	24	20	20	18	22	22	22	20	20	20	18	7	25	25	20	9	20	24	24	24	24	24	24	12	12	12
24 GLOCK	23	22	22	22	22	18	18	18	18	18	15	20	20	20	9	9	20	24	12	12	12	12	12	12	24	24	24
21 SENNA	22	15	15	15	15	15	15	15	15	15	7	7	21	9	24	24	24	12	20	20	20	20	20	20	20	20	20
25 DI GRASSI	15	7	7	7	7	7	7	7	7	7	9	9	9														
20 CHANDHOK	7																										

Grid order	28	29	30	31	32	33	34	35	36	37	38	39	40	41	42	43	44	45	46	47	48	49	50	51	52	53	54
2 HAMILTON	6	6	6	6	6	6	6	6	6	6	6	6	6	6	6	6	6	6	6	6	6	6	2	2	2	2	2
5 VETTEL	2	2	2	2	2	2	2	2	2	2	2	2	2	2	2	2	2	2	2	2	2	2	8	8	8	8	8
8 ALONSO	8	8	8	8	8	8	8	8	8	8	8	8	8	8	8	8	8	8	8	8	8	8	1	1	1	1	1
1 BUTTON	1	1	1	1	1	1	1	1	1	1	1	1	1	1	1	1	1	1	1	1	1	1	5	5	5	5	5
15 LIUZZI	5	5	5	5	5	5	5	5	5	5	5	5	5	5	5	5	5	5	5	5	5	5	6	6	6	6	6
7 MASSA	16	16	16	16	16	16	16	11	11	11	11	11	11	11	11	11	11	11	11	11	11	11	11	11	11	11	11
6 WEBBER	11	11	11	11	11	11	11	4	4	4	4	4	4	4	4	4	4	4	4	4	4	4	4	4	4	4	4
11 KUBICA	4	4	4	4	4	4	4	16	16	16	16	16	16	16	16	16	16	16	16	16	16	16	3	3	3	3	3
14 SUTIL	3	3	3	3	3	17	17	17	17	17	17	17	17	17	3	3	3	3	3	3	3	3	16	16	16	16	16
4 ROSBERG	10	17	17	17	17	3	3	3	3	3	3	3	3	3	10	10	10	10	10	10	10	10	10	10	10	10	10
9 BARRICHELLO	17	10	10	10	10	10	10	10	10	10	10	10	10	10	14	14	14	14	14	14	14	14	14	14	14	7	7
10 HULKENBERG	15	14	14	14	14	14	14	14	14	14	14	14	14	14	17	17	17	17	17	17	17	7	7	7	7	14	14
3 SCHUMACHER	14	15	15	15	15	15	15	15	15	15	15	15	15	15	15	15	15	15	15	15	7	17	17	17	17	17	17
12 PETROV	22	22	7	7	7	7	7	7	7	7	7	7	7	7	7	7	7	7	7	7	7	15	15	15	15	15	15
16 BUEMI	9	9	22	19	9	9	9	9	9	9	9	9	9	9	9	9	9	9	9	9	9	9	9	9	9	9	9
17 ALGUERSUARI	7	7	19	9	19	19	19	19	19	19	19	19	19	19	19	19	19	19	19	19	19	19	19	12	12	12	12
22 DE LA ROSA	19	19	9	18	18	18	18	18	18	18	18	18	12	12	12	12	12	12	12	12	12	12	19	19	19	19	19
23 KOBAYASHI	18	18	18	25	25	12	12	12	12	12	12	12	20	20	20	20	20	24	24	24	25	25	25	25	25	25	25
19 KOVALAINEN	25	25	25	12	12	25	25	25	25	25	25	25	18	24	24	24	24	25	25	25	20	20	20	20	20	20	20
18 TRULLI	12	12	12	24	20	20	20	20	20	20	20	20	24	25	25	25	25	20	20	20	24	24	24				
24 GLOCK	24	24	24	20	24	24	24	24	24	24	24	24	25	18	18												
21 SENNA	20	20	20																								
25 DI GRASSI																											
20 CHANDHOK																											

TIME SHEETS

PRACTICE 1 (FRIDAY)
Weather: Cloudy/sunny
Temperatures: track 19-24°C, air 17-19°C

Pos.	Driver	Laps	Time
1	Jenson Button	23	1m 18.127s
2	Michael Schumacher	19	1m 18.285s
3	Lewis Hamilton	19	1m 18.352s
4	Nico Rosberg	23	1m 18.356s
5	Sebastian Vettel	27	1m 18.549s
6	Robert Kubica	19	1m 18.662s
7	Fernando Alonso	21	1m 18.726s
8	Vitantonio Liuzzi	25	1m 19.097s
9	Nico Hülkenberg	31	1m 19.282s
10	Rubens Barrichello	19	1m 19.313s
11	Adrian Sutil	12	1m 19.373s
12	Felipe Massa	21	1m 19.511s
13	Vitaly Petrov	24	1m 19.549s
14	Mark Webber	26	1m 19.609s
15	Kamui Kobayashi	33	1m 20.186s
16	Sébastien Buemi	27	1m 20.320s
17	Pedro de la Rosa	21	1m 20.584s
18	Jaime Alguersuari	28	1m 20.823s
19	Heikki Kovalainen	24	1m 21.869s
20	Karun Chandhok	27	1m 21.977s
21	Jarno Trulli	12	1m 22.543s
22	Bruno Senna	28	1m 22.701s
23	Timo Glock	20	1m 22.713s
24	Lucas di Grassi	4	no time

PRACTICE 2 (FRIDAY)
Weather: Cloudy/partly cloudy
Temperatures: track 24-26°C, air 20-21°C

Pos.	Driver	Laps	Time
1	Sebastian Vettel	32	1m 16.877s
2	Fernando Alonso	35	1m 16.963s
3	Nico Rosberg	34	1m 17.151s
4	Mark Webber	33	1m 17.273s
5	Felipe Massa	33	1m 17.401s
6	Adrian Sutil	28	1m 17.415s
7	Lewis Hamilton	29	1m 17.522s
8	Robert Kubica	36	1m 17.529s
9	Michael Schumacher	34	1m 17.688s
10	Vitantonio Liuzzi	35	1m 17.903s
11	Jenson Button	33	1m 17.961s
12	Rubens Barrichello	27	1m 18.385s
13	Nico Hülkenberg	41	1m 18.447s
14	Vitaly Petrov	40	1m 18.582s
15	Pedro de la Rosa	34	1m 18.658s
16	Kamui Kobayashi	38	1m 19.142s
17	Sébastien Buemi	32	1m 19.168s
18	Jaime Alguersuari	41	1m 19.274s
19	Heikki Kovalainen	35	1m 19.969s
20	Karun Chandhok	29	1m 20.879s
21	Bruno Senna	31	1m 21.097s
22	Jarno Trulli	11	1m 21.346s
23	Timo Glock	25	1m 21.488s
24	Lucas di Grassi	30	1m 21.577s

PRACTICE 3 (SATURDAY)
Weather: Sunny/cloudy
Temperatures: track 20-21°C, air 18-20°C

Pos.	Driver	Laps	Time
1	Lewis Hamilton	15	1m 16.058s
2	Mark Webber	16	1m 16.340s
3	Fernando Alonso	19	1m 16.495s
4	Michael Schumacher	15	1m 16.536s
5	Sebastian Vettel	16	1m 16.582s
6	Robert Kubica	18	1m 16.653s
7	Adrian Sutil	15	1m 16.673s
8	Jenson Button	16	1m 16.699s
9	Vitantonio Liuzzi	15	1m 16.814s
10	Vitaly Petrov	18	1m 16.982s
11	Nico Hülkenberg	16	1m 17.121s
12	Felipe Massa	16	1m 17.231s
13	Jaime Alguersuari	22	1m 17.331s
14	Kamui Kobayashi	20	1m 17.548s
15	Pedro de la Rosa	16	1m 17.609s
16	Sébastien Buemi	21	1m 17.633s
17	Rubens Barrichello	18	1m 17.789s
18	Nico Rosberg	4	1m 17.979s
19	Jarno Trulli	15	1m 19.013s
20	Heikki Kovalainen	16	1m 19.447s
21	Timo Glock	22	1m 19.536s
22	Lucas di Grassi	20	1m 19.844s
23	Bruno Senna	18	1m 20.325s
24	Karun Chandhok	1	no time

QUALIFYING (SATURDAY)
Weather: Partly cloudy/cloudy Temperatures: track 26-28°C, air 22°C

Pos.	Driver	First	Second	Third	Qualifying Tyre
1	Lewis Hamilton	1m 15.889s	1m 15.528s	1m 15.105s	Super-Soft
2	Mark Webber	1m 16.423s	1m 15.692s	1m 15.373s	Medium
3	Sebastian Vettel	1m 16.129s	1m 15.556s	1m 15.420s	Medium
4	Fernando Alonso	1m 16.171s	1m 15.597s	1m 15.435s	Super-Soft
5	Jenson Button	1m 16.371s	1m 15.742s	1m 15.520s	Super-Soft
6	Vitantonio Liuzzi	1m 17.086s	1m 16.171s	1m 15.648s	Super-Soft
7	Felipe Massa	1m 16.673s	1m 16.314s	1m 15.688s	Super-Soft
8	Robert Kubica	1m 16.370s	1m 15.682s	1m 15.715s	Medium
9	Adrian Sutil	1m 16.495s	1m 16.295s	1m 15.881s	Super-Soft
10	Nico Rosberg	1m 16.350s	1m 16.001s	1m 16.071s	Super-Soft
11	Rubens Barrichello	1m 16.880s	1m 16.434s		
12	Nico Hülkenberg	1m 16.770s	1m 16.438s		
13	Michael Schumacher	1m 16.598s	1m 16.492s		
14	Vitaly Petrov	1m 16.569s	1m 16.844s		
15	Sébastien Buemi	1m 17.356s	1m 16.928s		
16	Jaime Alguersuari	1m 17.027s	1m 17.029s		
17	Pedro de la Rosa	1m 17.611s	1m 17.384s		
18	Kamui Kobayashi	1m 18.019s			
19	Heikki Kovalainen	1m 18.237s			
20	Jarno Trulli	1m 18.698s			
21	Timo Glock	1m 18.941s			
22	Bruno Senna	1m 19.484s			
23	Lucas di Grassi	1m 19.675s			
24	Karun Chandhok	1m 27.757s			

FOR THE RECORD

1st LAP LED: Sébastien Buemi
1st FASTEST LAP: Robert Kubica

DID YOU KNOW

Rubens Barrichello became the first driver to complete 15,000 F1 race laps.

POINTS

DRIVERS

1	Lewis Hamilton	109
2	Jenson Button	106
3	Mark Webber	103
4	Fernando Alonso	94
5	Sebastian Vettel	90
6	Nico Rosberg	74
7	Robert Kubica	73
8	Felipe Massa	67
9	Michael Schumacher	34
10	Adrian Sutil	23
11	Vitantonio Liuzzi	12
12	Rubens Barrichello	7
13	Vitaly Petrov	6
14	Sébastien Buemi	5
15	Jaime Alguersuari	3
16	Kamui Kobayashi	1
17	Nico Hülkenberg	1

CONSTRUCTORS

1	McLaren	215
2	Red Bull	193
3	Ferrari	161
4	Mercedes	108
5	Renault	79
6	Force India	35
7	Toro Rosso	8
8	Williams	8
9	BMW Sauber	1

5	56	57	58	59	60	61	62	63	64	65	66	67	68	69	70	
2	2	2	2	2	2	2	2	2	2	2	2	2	2	2	2	1
8	1	1	1	1	1	1	1	1	1	1	1	1	1	1	1	2
1	8	8	8	8	8	8	8	8	8	8	8	8	8	8	8	3
5	5	5	5	5	5	5	5	5	5	5	5	5	5	5	5	4
6	6	6	6	6	6	6	6	6	6	6	6	6	6	6	6	5
1	11	11	11	4	4	4	4	4	4	4	4	4	4	4	4	6
4	4	4	4	11	11	11	11	11	11	11	11	11	11	11	11	7
3	3	3	3	3	16	16	16	16	16	16	16	16	16	16		8
6	16	16	16	16	3	3	3	3	3	3	3	3	3	15		9
0	10	10	7	7	7	7	7	15	15	15	15	15	15	14		10
7	7	7	15	15	15	15	15	14	14	14	14	14	14	3		
4	14	14	14	14	14	14	14	17	17	17	17	17	17	17		
5	15	15	17	17	17	17	17	10	10	10	10	10	10	10		
7	17	17	10	10	10	10	10	9	9	9	9	9	9	9		
9	9	9	9	9	9	9	9	7	7	7	7	7	7	7		
2	19	19	19	19	19	19	19	19	19	19	19	19	19			
9	12	12	12	12	12	12	12	12	12	12	12	12	12			
5	25	20	20	20	20	20	20	20	20	20	20					
0	20	25	25	25	25	25	25	25	25	25						

21 Pit stop   *14 One lap or more behind*

RACE TYRE STRATEGIES

	Driver	Race Stint 1	Race Stint 2	Race Stint 3	Race Stint 4	Race Stint 5
1	Hamilton	S-Soft: 1-7	Med: 8-26	Med: 27-70		
2	Button	S-Soft: 1-6	Med: 7-27	Med: 28-70		
3	Alonso	S-Soft: 1-7	Med: 8-28	Med: 29-70		
4	Vettel	Med: 1-14	S-Soft: 15-27	Med: 28-70		
5	Webber	Med: 1-13	Med: 14-50	S-Soft: 51-70		
6	Rosberg	S-Soft: 1-5	Med: 6-27	Med: 28-70		
7	Kubica	Med: 1-9	Med: 10-26	Med: 27-59	S-Soft: 60-70	
8	Buemi	Med: 1-15	Med: 16-35	Med: 36-50	S-Soft: 51-69	
9	Liuzzi	S-Soft: 1	Med: 2-24	Med: 25-69		
10	Sutil	S-Soft: 1-6	Med: 7-27	Med: 28-69		
11	Schumacher	Med: 1-12	Med: 13-14	Med: 15-33	S-Soft: 34-69	
12	Alguersuari	S-Soft: 1-7	Med: 8-25	Med: 26-42	Med: 43-69	
13	Hülkenberg	Med: 1-6	Med: 7-24	Med: 25-29	Med: 30-58	S-Soft: 59-69
14	Barrichello	S-Soft: 1-7	Med: 8-11	Med: 12-30	Med: 31-69	
15	Massa	S-Soft: 1	Med: 2-23	Med: 24-41	Med: 42-63	S-Soft: 64-69
16	Kovalainen	Med: 1-16	Med: 17-32	Med: 33-51	S-Soft: 52-68	
17	Petrov	Med: 1-13	Med: 14-18	Med: 19-24	Med: 25-56	S-Soft: 57-68
18	Chandhok	Med: 1-19	Med: 20-45	S-Soft: 46-66		
19	di Grassi	Med: 1-14	Med: 15-28	Med: 29-40	S-Soft: 41-65	
	Glock	Med: 1-15	Med: 16-24	Med: 25-32	S-Soft: 33-48	S-Soft: 49-50 (dnf)
	Trulli	S-Soft: 1-5	Med: 6-30	Med: 31-40	Med: 41-42 (dnf)	
	de la Rosa	Med: 1	Med: 2-18	Med: 19-30 (dnf)		
	Senna	Med: 1-13 (dnf)				
	Kobayashi	S-Soft: 1 (dnf)				

The tyre regulations stipulate that the two dry tyre specifications must be used during the race.
The Super-Soft compound Bridgestone Potenza tyre is marked with a green stripe on the sidewall.

Photos: Peter J. Fox

star
movistar
movistar
movistar
movistar
movistar
movistar
movistar

FIA FORMULA 1 WORLD CHAMPIONSHIP · ROUND 9

GRAND PRIX OF EUROPE

VALENCIA CIRCUIT

Vettel takes the chequered flag to win the European GP.
Photo: Peter J Fox

VALENCIA QUALIFYING

FROM the moment Sebastian Vettel felt the car dart sideways, he knew he'd left himself only a single shot at pole position, but he is impervious to pressure. He might have mucked up his first Q3 run around Valencia's portside roads, but the second was a precision masterclass, and the German's 1m 37.587s lap put him just beyond the reach of Red Bull team-mate Mark Webber. It was the team's eighth pole position of the campaign.

Despite the statistics, however, Vettel admitted to a slight feeling of surprise. "In theory, this kind of circuit shouldn't really be our strongest," he said, "but the car feels very good. I had a huge moment in the first sector on my initial Q3 run, so knew I'd have to throw everything at the second. It worked, though. With our new F-duct and a few other bits and pieces added to the car, the mechanics only slept for an hour or two last night. This is the best way to say thanks."

Webber, all of 0.075 seconds adrift – yet another illustration of the competitive glue that bonds the Red Bull duo – also paid tribute. "I'm not going to roll out a list of excuses," he said. "I just wasn't quick enough. If you were to pick a circuit on which to race the opposition, you probably wouldn't choose this one, but this is a sensational result for Red Bull. I know we keep going on about what a good job the team is doing, but you just have to look at the mechanics' eyes to see how hard they've been working. Seb and I just do a bit of driving."

Red Bull was racing for the first time with its F-duct – trialled during practice in Turkey, but then discarded pending further development – but it was by no means alone in bringing significant embellishments to Valencia. Ferrari, Mercedes and Renault all introduced lowered exhaust systems, an old idea reprised by Red Bull at the season's dawn. The benefits? Exhaust gases accelerate the flow of air over the car's diffuser, but complex surface treatments, typically a zirconia-based ceramic coating, are required to minimise the risk of potentially deleterious side-effects, such as spontaneous combustion.

Despite their upgrades, all three teams were beaten to third place by Lewis Hamilton's McLaren, even though the championship leader had wasted his second Q3 lap by locking his rear wheels at Turn 12. "We were quite a long way off in free practice this morning," he said, "and with all our main rivals having made changes, I thought we might struggle. After my mistake at the end, I doubted I'd be able to hang on to third, so all in all I'm delighted."

Team-mate Jenson Button was a disappointed seventh, behind Fernando Alonso, Felipe Massa and Robert Kubica. "Things were looking good until the last corner of my final lap in Q3," he said. "I was pretty happy with the car, but then got a bit of oversteer through the quick right-hander before the final corner and that set the car up poorly for what followed. I locked up, ran wide and lost two-tenths. That's massive; I could have been fourth on the grid."

There was greater encouragement, though, for Williams, which put both cars into Q3 on merit: Nico Hülkenberg and Rubens Barrichello posted identical times, but the German got there first.

The potential pitfalls of the mid-season development race were illustrated by Mercedes' plight, with Nico Rosberg and Michael Schumacher both knocked out during the second phase of qualifying. "We are not making the tyres work well at the moment," said team principal Ross Brawn. "We are pushing very hard to develop the car, and in pushing so hard, you sometimes trip up."

Right: Lewis Hamilton managed to serve a drive-through penalty and still take second place for McLaren.

Below left: Jaime Alguersuari watches proceedings.

Below: Star in the ascendent. Paul di Resta had another outing for Force India during Friday free practice, impressing again with his composure.

Photos: Peter J Fox

MARK Webber was flat in seventh when it happened – 306km/h (190.14mph) according to the Red Bull telemetry. Normally, he wouldn't have needed to worry about slowing just yet for Turn 12, but this time Heikki Kovalainen's Lotus lay ahead, having been shuffled in front of the Red Bull through circumstance. When the Finn hit the left-hand pedal, he did so precisely 80 metres earlier than Webber's customary braking point. Small wonder that the Australian was taken by surprise. The 2010 Grand Prix of Europe's enduring image was not the calm methodology of Sebastian Vettel's victory – only the second of a campaign that should already have yielded several more – but the violent flight that precipitated his team-mate's first retirement of the year.

Now in its third season as a grand prix host, the Valencia street circuit felt more structured and mature than hitherto, a track that was steadily finding its feet. It was an inescapable truth that it had yet to provide any evidence of suitability for actual racing, but this would be a far more vibrant contest than the two that had gone before.

Vettel started well enough from pole position, but Webber, alongside, might not have lost as many places had he completed the first lap on foot. Lewis Hamilton, Fernando Alonso and Felipe Massa picked him off almost straight away; Jenson Button and Robert Kubica dispatched him in a simultaneous pincer movement on the approach to Turn Eight. Then Rubens Barrichello joined in, elbowing Webber wide and creating space for Nico Hülkenberg to usurp the Australian and knock him back from second to ninth within less than half a lap.

Hamilton had a look to Vettel's inside at Turn Two, an ultra-tight right-hander, and they brushed gently, the Englishman incurring mild front wing damage that was more aesthetic than detrimental. Even so, he was 1.6 seconds adrift by the end of the lap.

Behind Webber, Sébastien Buemi ran tenth, ahead of Michael Schumacher, Adrian Sutil, Tonio Liuzzi, Nico Rosberg, Vitaly Petrov, Jaime Alguersuari, Pedro de la Rosa, Kamui Kobayashi, Kovalainen, Lucas di Grassi, Timo Glock, Karun Chandhok and Bruno Senna, with Jarno Trulli heading for the pits to replace a front wing that had been knocked during the initial scramble. He wasn't sure whom he'd hit nor, indeed, who had hit him from behind, an impact that triggered gearbox problems that required another, much lengthier pit stop on lap three. In the meantime, de la Rosa passed Alguersuari, so come what may, there had already been one more proper passing manoeuvre than 2009's corresponding fixture had yielded.

While Vettel continued to pull away comfortably at the front, Red Bull tried to fathom a way of minimising the damage inflicted by Webber's poor start. With overtaking a scarce commodity, it opted to call him in for his mandatory tyre change on lap seven: if they could send him out in a bit of clean air, he could at least make better use of his car's true potential and, perhaps, benefit later. It was a slow stop, though – the team had to replace a faulty front left wheel nut – and he slipped to 19th, behind Kovalainen.

The Finn was perfectly entitled to defend when the two cars approached Turn 12 for the ninth time, and Webber respected as much. As previously mentioned, however, he did not anticipate that Kovalainen would hit the brakes quite so soon. Usually, blue flags require a Lotus driver to step aside for an approaching Red Bull, because such situations occur only during lappery, but this was a race for position: it was a misunderstanding borne of unfamiliarity. The impact sent Kovalainen sharp left into the wall, a sizeable impact, but not one that many noticed because all eyes were on Webber, who was launched almost vertically before his car somersaulted back to the asphalt and ploughed, right way up, into the tyre wall, whereupon he calmly unclipped his belts and sauntered away without a scratch.

"Heikki seemed to be going to the left," Webber said, "and I prepared to move to his inside. He then edged back to the right, though, and I realised he was defending. Fair enough, he's entitled to do that, so I thought I'd try around his outside, but then he braked..."

Webber might have been doing 190mph when he hit the Lotus, but all of a sudden the world slowed down. "It felt as though I had plenty of time to think," he said. "I knew I was a long way from the ground, but had no idea quite how far I'd gone. I wondered if this might hurt and was scrolling the track through my mind, trying to remember whether there were any bridges or anything to hit at that point, because that would have been pretty serious. The car righted itself pretty quickly, though, and I had quite a soft landing. If something like that is going to happen, it was probably the best place on the track for it. I was definitely lucky."

The safety car was deployed, and the incident conditioned almost every other aspect of the race.

Vettel and Hamilton had passed the pit entrance before the safety car was scrambled, and Alonso was so close to the final corner that it was too late to change course. Massa could have come in, but Ferrari appeared to be dozing, so Kubica led the rush. Renault had already intended to bring Petrov in on that lap, for a scheduled change, so the mechanics had to scramble to fetch Kubica's tyres, which dropped him behind both Button and Barrichello.

Right: Felipe Massa waves to the crowd as he walks back following his accident.
Photo: Peter Nygaard/GP Photo

Far right: Kobayashi elbowed his Sauber through to seventh place on the final lap, after another demonstration of audacity and exuberance.
Photos: Peter J Fox

Below: Adrian Sutil rides the high kerbing with confidence on his way to a promising sixth place.
Photo: Jean-François Galeron/WRi2

Below right: Nicolas Todt.

Bottom right: Jenson Button.
Photos: Peter J Fox

As some of those who had missed the pit entrance reached the exit, meanwhile, the safety car emerged. Vettel was well clear, but Hamilton was adjacent and hesitated briefly before deciding he was ahead and, therefore, entitled to accelerate clear. "I was coming around Turn One and saw the safety car pretty much alongside," he said, "but I thought I'd already passed it and so continued." The Ferraris, though, had no option but to line up behind, which meant a calamitous loss of time, especially for Massa, who would be stacked up behind his team-mate when they finally reached the pits.

In ordinary circumstances, the safety car driver is entitled to wave through any following cars until the race leader is lined up just behind, but in this instance the priority was to keep the track as clear as possible, so as not to impede the medical car (which wasn't required, although that much wasn't yet obvious).

Alonso was outraged by Hamilton's conduct: he felt the Englishman had blatantly and unlawfully passed the safety car and, as the afternoon wore on, became increasingly obsessed with wanting to know how the FIA planned to hang, draw and quarter his foe. It wasn't that simple a call to make, however, because TV replays were inconclusive, and it took stewards 14 laps to calculate that he really had committed the offence of which Alonso was so convinced. He was duly handed a drive-through penalty, but the race's changing complexion rendered that irrelevant.

Most teams brought both drivers in for immediate tyre changes at the time of Webber's accident, but Sauber didn't. Kobayashi stayed out and moved up to third on the road, behind Vettel and Hamilton, with Button, Barrichello, Kubica, Buemi, Sutil, Hülkenberg, Alonso, de la Rosa, Petrov, Rosberg, Liuzzi, di Grassi, Glock, Massa, Alguersuari, Chandhok, Senna, Schumacher and the distant Trulli completing the order. McLaren changed Hamilton's front wing when he came in – "If we hadn't," said team principal Martin Whitmarsh, "we were concerned that his front tyres might suffer as the race wore on." – but the pit sequence was disastrous for Schumacher, who had been running just ahead of Kobayashi prior to the race's neutralisation. He didn't come in until lap 11, though, and then was held at the pit exit until everybody else had passed. "In our view," said Mercedes team principal Ross Brawn, "the regulations are clear. The exit light should not turn red until the line of cars has formed fully behind the safety car. We would like the FIA to look into this, because there was no line formed and Hamilton was more than 18 seconds ahead of Kobayashi when Michael came in."

The team had intended to send him back out somewhere within that 18-second window, but potential opportunity morphed into frustration as the exit light remained resolutely red.

Vettel locked his front right at the last corner, just as the race resumed at the end of lap 14, but the ensuing flat spot was only mild and didn't bother him unduly. He continued to lead comfortably, with Hamilton a second or so adrift. Kobayashi was doing a decent job in the Sauber, but was more than 15 seconds in arrears when Hamilton served his drive-through on lap 27 – and that was just enough for the Englishman to keep second place as Vettel inherited a suddenly comfortable lead he was able to maintain to the finish.

"When I first saw the safety car boards, I had just come on to the main straight," the German said, "and

I thought that might be tough for us because some of the cars closest behind might effectively get a free pit stop, but in fact they were in the same situation as me."

With tyre wear no real concern on either compound, Kobayashi stayed out on his original medium Bridgestones until lap 53, which finally freed Button, but that would be the trigger for an engaging little cameo. Kobayashi's stop dropped him to ninth, but with low fuel and fresh super-soft rubber, he was able to pick off Alonso and Buemi during the final two laps, to follow Barrichello, Kubica and Sutil across the line. Sutil pulled off the afternoon's best move, on lap 39, momentarily locking wheels with Buemi on the run to Turn 12 before squeezing ahead around the outside.

Kobayashi's late progress did little to suppress Alonso's foul mood, and later he claimed that the race had been "manipulated", although in truth the bit to which he referred – Hamilton's penalty – had been monitored meticulously.

Hülkenberg's promising weekend reaped no reward. Beaten away by Barrichello at the start, he lost time stacked behind his team-mate in the pits and retired, with a potential points finish in sight, when an overheating exhaust ignited the back of his Williams and frayed the bodywork. This, in turn, cut into his right rear tyre and obliged him to pull off, whereupon he gave the Turn 12 tyre wall a hearty kick (which wasn't quite as hard as Webber had hit it).

De la Rosa should have claimed the final point, from Petrov, Rosberg, Liuzzi, Massa, Alguersuari, Schumacher, Liuzzi, di Grassi, Glock, Chandhok, Senna and Trulli, but "should have" and "did" are not one and the same.

Glock was docked 20 seconds for ignoring blue flags on lap 37, when he continued to race Senna as Kobayashi and Button came up to lap them. The two backmarkers actually touched in the incident, which obliged both to make second pit stops – Senna for a fresh front wing and Glock to replace a punctured rear tyre. Normally, the offence would have been punishable by a drive-through, but as the ruling was made after the race, he was given a time penalty that dropped him behind Chandhok.

There was, however, more significant post-race shuffling slightly farther north in the classification. Button, Barrichello, Kubica, Sutil, Buemi, de la Rosa, Petrov, Liuzzi and – peculiarly – the retired Hülkenberg had five seconds added to their race times, for lapping at speeds that were perceived to be too quick when heading for the pits after the safety car boards had been shown.

The main consequences? Alonso gained a position at Buemi's expense and de la Rosa slipped out of the top ten, to be replaced by Rosberg. It was hard to know, though, quite what Kubica, Button or Barrichello in particular could have done, given that they were almost at the end of a lap that had legitimately been completed at racing speed. "There was no time to lift off or hit the brakes," said Button, "so to be honest, I can't really see why I was called to the stewards."

At the time, he and Kubica had been negotiating the 180mph kink just before the pit entry. To comply with the stewards' wishes would have meant backing off abruptly and, in all probability, crashing.

Absurd is too kind a word.

Simon Arron

Left: Rubens Barrichello followed his 2009 victory for Brawn at Valencia by storming to fourth place in his Williams-Cosworth.
Photo: Jad Sherif/WRi2

Below left: A victor's wave from a delighted Vettel.
Photo: Peter Nygaard/Grand Prix Photo

Bottom left: Mark Webber counts himself lucky to escape unscathed from that massive accident.
Photo: Lukas Gorys

Below: The rugged Australian walks away shaken, but not stirred.
Photo: Peter Nygaard/Grand Prix Photo

EDITOR'S VIEW
WEBBER SURVIVES DUE TO F1 SAFETY REGIME

IT was as if two generations of F1 engineering safety had been compressed into about 20 seconds, the amount of time that passed between Mark Webber's Red Bull striking the rear of Heikki Kovalainen's Lotus T127 and the moment when the last piece of debris tumbled to a halt on the track at Valencia. In that short space of time, everything the sport had learned in terms of structural impact resistance, cockpit security, fuel retention and circuit safety was strained almost to breaking point – and passed the test with flying colours.

There was still a handful of old timers working in the F1 paddock who could remember what it used to be like. Forty years earlier, almost to the weekend, Piers Courage had perished in the blazing wreckage of Frank Williams's de Tomaso 505 during the Dutch GP at Zandvoort. There was no possibility of his surviving the inferno, even though the impact was significantly less than that suffered by Webber's wayward machine, which successfully retained every drop of its fuel load within its single safety cell.

Instead of contemplating the stark possibility of the first fatal accident in F1 since Ayrton Senna's tragic crash in the 1994 San Marino GP at Imola, the commentators were left to dwell on the thankfully trivial issue of just where the fault lay for this spectacular high-speed collision. Some felt that it was cut and dried, barely meriting anything more than cursory discussion. Webber had transgressed the first law of the M25 – if the white van that's been tailgating your Mondeo for the past 10 miles finally runs into you, then it's down to him, squire. So it was Webber's fault.

The alternative view was that Kovalainen had chosen to race a car that was significantly quicker than his own, which, while entirely legitimate and his own affair, seemed an abject waste of effort, given than Webber would have breezed past him shortly afterwards. On the other hand, some observers considered that Heikki may have weaved unnecessarily, catching Webber momentarily off guard. Either way, what in previous generations might have been a massive disaster was triggered in a split second.

There were also those who thought it slightly surprising that the stewards failed to point a finger of blame. Perhaps they were too busy trying to reach a conclusion as to whether or not Lewis Hamilton had gained an unfair advantage in the queue behind the safety car after it had been deployed in the wake of Webber's accident – an issue that consumed Fernando Alonso's conversation over the radio waves for pretty much the balance of the race. Given that Mark had survived such a terrible accident with little more than a mild increase in his pulse rate, there would have been nothing to be gained by giving him a ticket for a traffic violation to round off his day.

It might have been a worthwhile moment to reflect that it was entirely appropriate that McLaren had gained an excellent result by finishing second and third in the European GP, given that the team had bequeathed possibly the biggest technical legacy that helped Webber survive his accident. In 1981, John Barnard and Ron Dennis introduced the first F1 carbon-fibre composite monocoque, which utterly changed the sport's technical landscape. Contributions to further enhance safety followed from other engineers, the FIA and the circuit designers, but if there was a seminal moment when motor racing safety emerged from the dark ages, that was probably it. Twenty-nine years later, it helped save Mark Webber's life.

Alan Henry

FIA F1 WORLD CHAMPIONSHIP · ROUND 9

TELEFÓNICA GRAND PRIX OF EUROPE

VALENCIA 25–27 JUNE 2010

RACE DISTANCE: 57 laps, 191.931 miles/308.883km

RACE WEATHER: Sunny (track 43–45°C, air 27–28°C)

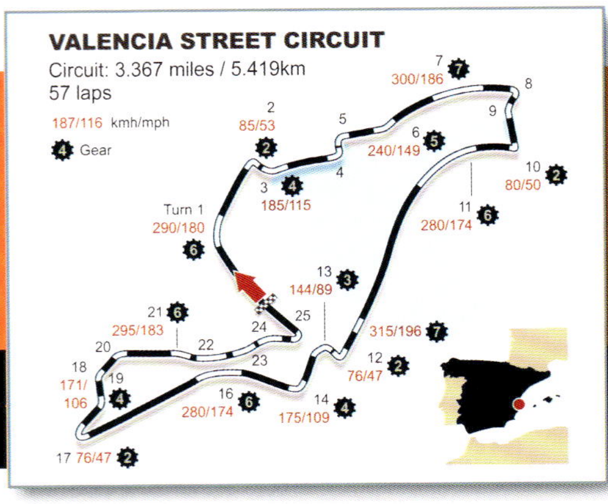

Pos.	Driver	Nat.	No.	Entrant	Car/Engine	Tyres	Laps	Time/Retirement	Speed (mph/km/h)	Gap to leader	Fastest race lap	
1	**Sebastian Vettel**	D	5	Red Bull Racing	Red Bull RB6-Renault RS27 V8	B	57	1h 40m 29.571s	114.593/184.420		1m 39.141s	52
2	**Lewis Hamilton**	GB	2	Vodafone McLaren Mercedes	McLaren MP4-25-Mercedes FO108X V8	B	57	1h 40m 34.613s	114.498/184.266	+ 5.042s	1m 39.156s	56
3	**Jenson Button**	GB	1	Vodafone McLaren Mercedes	McLaren MP4-25-Mercedes FO108X V8	B	57	1h 40m 42.229s *	114.353/184.034	+ 12.658s	1m 38.766s	54
4	**Rubens Barrichello**	BR	9	AT&T Williams	Williams FW32-Cosworth CA2010 V8	B	57	1h 40m 55.198s *	114.109/183.640	+ 25.627s	1m 39.489s	56
5	**Robert Kubica**	PL	11	Renault F1 Team	Renault R30-RS27 V8	B	57	1h 40m 56.693s *	114.081/183.595	+ 27.122s	1m 39.542s	55
6	**Adrian Sutil**	D	14	Force India F1 Team	Force India VJM03-Mercedes FO108X V8	B	57	1h 40m 59.739s *	114.023/183.502	+ 30.168s	1m 39.803s	52
7	**Kamui Kobayashi**	J	23	BMW Sauber F1 Team	BMW Sauber C29-Ferrari 056 V8	B	57	1h 41m 00.536s	114.008/183.478	+ 30.965s	1m 39.517s	57
8	**Fernando Alonso**	E	8	Scuderia Ferrari Marlboro	Ferrari F10-056 V8	B	57	1h 41m 02.380s	113.973/183.422	+ 32.809s	1m 39.889s	50
9	**Sébastien Buemi**	CH	16	Scuderia Toro Rosso	Toro Rosso STR5-Ferrari 056 V8	B	57	1h 41m 05.870s *	113.908/183.317	+ 36.299s	1m 40.084s	53
10	**Nico Rosberg**	D	4	Mercedes GP Petronas F1 Team	Mercedes MGP W01-Mercedes FO108X V8	B	57	1h 41m 13.953s	113.756/183.073	+ 44.382s	1m 39.878s	57
11	Felipe Massa	BR	7	Scuderia Ferrari Marlboro	Ferrari F10-056 V8	B	57	1h 41m 16.192s	113.714/183.005	+ 46.621s	1m 40.208s	52
12	Pedro de la Rosa	E	22	BMW Sauber F1 Team	BMW Sauber C29-Ferrari 056 V8	B	57	1h 41m 16.985s *	113.699/182.981	+ 47.414s	1m 40.430s	56
13	Jaime Alguersuari	E	17	Scuderia Toro Rosso	Toro Rosso STR5-Ferrari 056 V8	B	57	1h 41m 17.810s	113.684/182.957	+ 48.239s	1m 40.327s	55
14	Vitaly Petrov	RUS	12	Renault F1 Team	Renault R30-RS27 V8	B	57	1h 41m 17.858s *	113.683/182.955	+ 48.287s	1m 40.100s	57
15	Michael Schumacher	GB	3	Mercedes GP Petronas F1 Team	Mercedes MGP W01-Mercedes FO108X V8	B	57	1h 41m 18.397s	113.673/182.939	+ 48.826s	1m 38.968s	53
16	Vitantonio Liuzzi	I	15	Force India F1 Team	Force India VJM03-Mercedes FO108X V8	B	57	1h 41m 20.461s *	113.634/182.877	+ 50.890s	1m 40.305s	52
17	Lucas di Grassi	BR	25	Virgin Racing	Virgin VR-01-Cosworth CA2010 V8	B	56			+ 1 lap	1m 42.414s	45
18	Karun Chandhok	IND	20	HRT F1 Team	HRT F110-Cosworth CA2010 V8	B	55			+ 2 laps	1m 43.820s	51
19	Timo Glock	D	24	Virgin Racing	Virgin VR-01-Cosworth CA2010 V8	B	55	**		+ 2 laps	1m 42.319s	48
20	Bruno Senna	BR	21	HRT F1 Team	HRT F110-Cosworth CA2010 V8	B	55			+ 2 laps	1m 42.927s	55
21	Jarno Trulli	I	18	Lotus Racing	Lotus T127-Cosworth CA2010 V8	B	53			+ 4 laps	1m 41.770s	53
	Nico Hülkenberg	D	10	AT&T Williams	Williams FW32-Cosworth CA2010 V8	B	49	*exhaust* *			1m 40.790s	46
	Heikki Kovalainen	FIN	19	Lotus Racing	Lotus T127-Cosworth CA2010 V8	B	8	*accident*			1m 46.130s	8
	Mark Webber	AUS	6	Red Bull Racing	Red Bull RB6-Renault RS27 V8	B	8	*accident*			1m 44.064s	5

* Includes 5-sec post-race penalty for speeding while safety car was deployed. ** Includes 20-sec post-race penalty for ignoring blue flags.

Fastest race lap: Jenson Button on lap 54, 1m 38.766s, 122.734mph/197.521km/h.

Lap record: Timo Glock (Toyota TF109 V8), 1m 38.683s, 122.837mph/197.687km/h (2009).

Grid order	1	2	3	4	5	6	7	8	9	10	11	12	13	14	15	16	17	18	19	20	21	22	23
5 VETTEL	5	5	5	5	5	5	5	5	5	5	5	5	5	5	5	5	5	5	5	5	5	5	5
6 WEBBER	2	2	2	2	2	2	2	2	2	2	2	2	2	2	2	2	2	2	2	2	2	2	2
2 HAMILTON	8	8	8	8	8	8	8	8	8	3	3	23	23	23	23	23	23	23	23	23	23	23	23
8 ALONSO	7	7	7	7	7	7	7	7	7	23	23	1	1	1	1	1	1	1	1	1	1	1	1
7 MASSA	11	11	11	11	11	11	11	11	3	1	1	9	9	9	9	9	9	9	9	9	9	9	9
11 KUBICA	1	1	1	1	1	1	1	1	17	9	9	11	11	11	11	11	11	11	11	11	11	11	11
1 BUTTON	9	9	9	9	9	9	9	9	1	11	11	16	16	16	16	16	16	16	16	16	16	16	16
10 HULKENBERG	10	10	10	10	10	10	10	10	23	16	16	14	14	14	14	14	14	14	14	14	14	14	14
9 BARRICHELLO	6	6	6	6	6	6	16	16	9	8	14	10	10	10	8	8	8	8	8	8	8	8	8
12 PETROV	16	16	16	16	16	16	3	3	11	14	10	8	8	8	10	10	10	10	10	10	10	10	10
16 BUEMI	3	3	3	3	3	3	14	14	16	10	8	22	22	22	22	22	22	22	22	22	22	22	22
4 ROSBERG	14	14	14	14	14	14	15	15	14	22	22	12	12	12	12	12	12	12	12	12	12	12	12
14 SUTIL	15	15	15	15	15	15	4	12	10	12	12	4	4	4	4	4	4	4	4	4	4	4	4
15 LIUZZI	4	4	4	4	4	4	12	22	22	4	4	15	15	15	15	15	15	15	15	15	15	15	15
3 SCHUMACHER	12	12	12	12	12	12	22	17	12	7	15	25	25	25	7	7	7	7	7	7	7	7	7
22 DE LA ROSA	17	22	22	22	22	22	17	23	15	15	25	24	24	24	25	17	17	17	17	17	17	17	17
17 ALGUERSUARI	22	17	17	17	17	17	23	4	4	17	24	7	7	7	17	3	3	3	3	3	3	3	3
23 KOBAYASHI	23	23	23	23	23	23	6	19	25	25	7	17	17	17	24	25	25	25	25	25	25	25	25
18 TRULLI	19	19	19	19	19	19	19	6	24	24	17	3	20	20	3	24	24	24	24	24	24	24	24
19 KOVALAINEN	25	25	25	25	25	25	25	25	21	21	21	20	21	21	20	20	20	20	20	20	20	20	20
25 DI GRASSI	24	24	24	24	24	24	24	24	20	20	20	21	3	3	21	21	21	21	21	21	21	21	21
24 GLOCK	20	20	20	20	20	20	20	20	18	18	18	18	18	18	18	18	18	18	18	18	18	18	18
20 CHANDHOK	21	21	21	21	21	21	21	21															
21 SENNA	18	18	18	18	18	18	18	18															

Grid order	24	25	26	27	28	29	30	31	32	33	34	35	36	37	38	39	40	41	42	43	44	45
5 VETTEL	5	5	5	5	5	5	5	5	5	5	5	5	5	5	5	5	5	5	5	5	5	5
6 WEBBER	2	2	2	2	2	2	2	2	2	2	2	2	2	2	2	2	2	2	2	2	2	2
2 HAMILTON	23	23	23	23	23	23	23	23	23	23	23	23	23	23	23	23	23	23	23	23	23	23
8 ALONSO	1	1	1	1	1	1	1	1	1	1	1	1	1	1	1	1	1	1	1	1	1	1
7 MASSA	9	9	9	9	9	9	9	9	9	9	9	9	9	9	9	9	9	9	9	9	9	9
11 KUBICA	11	11	11	11	11	11	11	11	11	11	11	11	11	11	11	11	11	11	11	11	11	11
1 BUTTON	16	16	16	16	16	16	16	16	16	16	16	16	16	16	16	14	14	14	14	14	14	14
10 HULKENBERG	14	14	14	14	14	14	14	14	14	14	14	14	14	14	14	16	16	16	16	16	16	16
9 BARRICHELLO	8	8	8	8	8	8	8	8	8	8	8	8	8	8	8	8	8	8	8	8	8	8
12 PETROV	10	10	10	10	10	10	10	10	10	10	10	10	10	10	10	10	10	10	10	10	10	10
16 BUEMI	22	22	22	22	22	22	22	22	22	22	22	22	22	22	22	22	22	22	22	22	22	22
4 ROSBERG	12	12	12	12	12	12	12	12	12	12	12	12	12	12	12	12	12	12	12	12	12	12
14 SUTIL	4	4	4	4	4	4	4	4	4	4	4	4	4	4	4	4	4	4	4	4	4	4
15 LIUZZI	15	15	15	15	15	15	15	15	15	15	15	15	15	15	15	15	15	15	15	15	15	15
3 SCHUMACHER	7	7	7	7	7	7	7	7	7	7	7	7	7	7	7	7	7	7	7	7	7	7
22 DE LA ROSA	17	17	17	17	17	17	17	17	17	17	17	17	17	17	17	17	17	17	17	17	17	17
17 ALGUERSUARI	3	3	3	3	3	3	3	3	3	3	3	3	3	3	3	3	3	3	3	3	3	3
23 KOBAYASHI	25	25	25	25	25	25	25	25	25	25	25	25	25	25	25	25	25	25	25	25	25	25
18 TRULLI	20	20	20	20	20	20	20	20	20	20	20	20	20	20	20	20	20	20	20	20	20	20
19 KOVALAINEN	21	21	21	21	21	21	21	21	21	21	21	21	21	24	24	24	24	24	24	24	24	24
25 DI GRASSI	24	24	24	24	24	24	24	24	24	24	24	24	24	21	21	21	21	21	21	21	21	21
24 GLOCK	18	18	18	18	18	18	18	18	18	18	18	18	18	18	18	18	18	18	18	18	18	18
20 CHANDHOK																						
21 SENNA																						

21 Pit stop   *14 One lap or more behind*   Safety car deployed on laps shown

TIME SHEETS

PRACTICE 1 (FRIDAY)
Weather: Sunny
Temperatures: track 32-37°C, air 25-26°C

Pos.	Driver	Laps	Time
1	Nico Rosberg	16	1m 41.175s
2	Lewis Hamilton	19	1m 41.339s
3	Jenson Button	21	1m 41.383s
4	Robert Kubica	20	1m 41.715s
5	Felipe Massa	21	1m 42.182s
6	Sebastian Vettel	24	1m 42.216s
7	Mark Webber	17	1m 42.275s
8	Michael Schumacher	18	1m 42.312s
9	Fernando Alonso	22	1m 42.421s
10	Rubens Barrichello	21	1m 42.463s
11	Nico Hülkenberg	23	1m 42.707s
12	Vitaly Petrov	17	1m 42.962s
13	Sébastien Buemi	23	1m 43.310s
14	Vitantonio Liuzzi	19	1m 43.380s
15	Pedro de la Rosa	21	1m 43.397s
16	Paul di Resta	18	1m 43.437s
17	Kamui Kobayashi	21	1m 43.729s
18	Jaime Alguersuari	21	1m 44.183s
19	Heikki Kovalainen	21	1m 44.491s
20	Timo Glock	23	1m 45.653s
21	Bruno Senna	17	1m 47.123s
22	Jarno Trulli	18	1m 47.285s
23	Christian Klien	14	1m 47.343s
24	Lucas di Grassi	24	1m 47.356s

PRACTICE 2 (FRIDAY)
Weather: Sunny
Temperatures: track 44-46°C, air 29-30°C

Pos.	Driver	Laps	Time
1	Fernando Alonso	33	1m 39.283s
2	Sebastian Vettel	27	1m 39.339s
3	Mark Webber	29	1m 39.427s
4	Nico Rosberg	22	1m 39.650s
5	Lewis Hamilton	24	1m 39.749s
6	Robert Kubica	28	1m 39.880s
7	Felipe Massa	22	1m 39.947s
8	Adrian Sutil	30	1m 40.020s
9	Jenson Button	27	1m 40.029s
10	Rubens Barrichello	33	1m 40.174s
11	Michael Schumacher	24	1m 40.287s
12	Vitantonio Liuzzi	33	1m 40.387s
13	Vitaly Petrov	29	1m 40.618s
14	Kamui Kobayashi	34	1m 40.906s
15	Pedro de la Rosa	30	1m 40.945s
16	Sébastien Buemi	35	1m 41.115s
17	Nico Hülkenberg	30	1m 41.371s
18	Jaime Alguersuari	36	1m 41.457s
19	Heikki Kovalainen	31	1m 42.467s
20	Jarno Trulli	30	1m 42.993s
21	Timo Glock	14	1m 43.811s
22	Lucas di Grassi	27	1m 43.854s
23	Bruno Senna	24	1m 44.095s
24	Karun Chandhok	21	1m 44.566s

PRACTICE 3 (SATURDAY)
Weather: Sunny
Temperatures: track 30-40°C, air 25-26°C

Pos.	Driver	Laps	Time
1	Sebastian Vettel	14	1m 38.052s
2	Robert Kubica	17	1m 38.154s
3	Mark Webber	13	1m 38.313s
4	Adrian Sutil	17	1m 38.500s
5	Fernando Alonso	18	1m 38.513s
6	Rubens Barrichello	15	1m 38.623s
7	Vitantonio Liuzzi	17	1m 38.676s
8	Felipe Massa	16	1m 38.686s
9	Jenson Button	16	1m 38.769s
10	Lewis Hamilton	15	1m 38.816s
11	Nico Rosberg	15	1m 38.822s
12	Sébastien Buemi	16	1m 39.050s
13	Nico Hülkenberg	15	1m 39.105s
14	Vitaly Petrov	16	1m 39.113s
15	Michael Schumacher	14	1m 39.222s
16	Jaime Alguersuari	18	1m 39.392s
17	Kamui Kobayashi	16	1m 39.527s
18	Pedro de la Rosa	16	1m 39.699s
19	Heikki Kovalainen	19	1m 41.303s
20	Jarno Trulli	20	1m 41.428s
21	Timo Glock	17	1m 41.955s
22	Lucas di Grassi	18	1m 42.354s
23	Bruno Senna	18	1m 42.611s
24	Karun Chandhok	19	1m 42.622s

QUALIFYING (SATURDAY)
Weather: Sunny Temperatures: track 44-45°C, air 27°C

Pos.	Driver	First	Second	Third	Qualifying Tyre
1	Sebastian Vettel	1m 38.324s	1m 38.015s	1m 37.587s	Super-Soft
2	Mark Webber	1m 38.549s	1m 38.041s	1m 37.662s	Super-Soft
3	Lewis Hamilton	1m 38.697s	1m 38.158s	1m 37.969s	Super-Soft
4	Fernando Alonso	1m 38.472s	1m 38.179s	1m 38.075s	Super-Soft
5	Felipe Massa	1m 38.657s	1m 38.046s	1m 38.127s	Super-Soft
6	Robert Kubica	1m 38.132s	1m 38.062s	1m 38.137s	Super-Soft
7	Jenson Button	1m 38.360s	1m 38.399s	1m 38.210s	Super-Soft
8	Nico Hülkenberg	1m 38.843s	1m 38.523s	1m 38.428s	Super-Soft
9	Rubens Barrichello	1m 38.449s	1m 38.326s	1m 38.428s	Super-Soft
10	Vitaly Petrov	1m 39.004s	1m 38.552s	1m 38.523s	Super-Soft
11	Sébastien Buemi	1m 39.096s	1m 38.586s		
12	Nico Rosberg	1m 38.752s	1m 38.627s		
13	Adrian Sutil	1m 39.021s	1m 38.851s		
14	Vitantonio Liuzzi	1m 38.969s	1m 38.884s		
15	Michael Schumacher	1m 38.994s	1m 39.234s		
16	Pedro de la Rosa	1m 39.003s	1m 39.264s		
17	Jaime Alguersuari	1m 39.128s	1m 39.458s		
18	Kamui Kobayashi	1m 39.343s			
19	Jarno Trulli	1m 40.658s			
20	Heikki Kovalainen	1m 40.882s			
21	Lucas di Grassi	1m 42.086s			
22	Timo Glock	1m 42.140s			
23	Karun Chandhok	1m 42.600s			
24	Bruno Senna	1m 42.851s			

FOR THE RECORD

10th WIN: Red Bull
500th GRAND PRIX: Lotus

DID YOU KNOW

This was the 20th Grand Prix of Europe (12 held in Germany, 5 in Spain and 3 in Britain).

On only two previous occasions have 21 cars been classified in a grand prix: Britain in 1952 and Turkey in 2007.

POINTS

DRIVERS

1	Lewis Hamilton	127
2	Jenson Button	121
3	Sebastian Vettel	115
4	Mark Webber	103
5	Fernando Alonso	98
6	Robert Kubica	83
7	Nico Rosberg	75
8	Felipe Massa	67
9	Michael Schumacher	34
10	Adrian Sutil	31
11	Rubens Barrichello	19
12	Vitantonio Liuzzi	12
13	Kamui Kobayashi	7
14	Sébastien Buemi	7
15	Vitaly Petrov	6
16	Jaime Alguersuari	3
17	Nico Hülkenberg	1

CONSTRUCTORS

1	McLaren	248
2	Red Bull	218
3	Ferrari	165
4	Mercedes	109
5	Renault	89
6	Force India	43
7	Williams	20
8	Toro Rosso	10
9	BMW Sauber	7

46	47	48	49	50	51	52	53	54	55	56	57	
5	5	5	5	5	5	5	5	5	5	5	5	1
2	2	2	2	2	2	2	2	2	2	2	2	2
23	23	23	23	23	23	23	1	1	1	1	1	3
1	1	1	1	1	1	1	9	9	9	9	9	4
9	9	9	9	9	9	9	11	11	11	11	11	5
11	11	11	11	11	11	11	14	14	14	14	14	6
14	14	14	14	14	14	14	23	16	16	16	23	7
16	16	16	16	16	16	16	16	8	8	23	16	8
8	8	8	8	8	8	8	8	23	23	8	8	9
10	10	10	10	22	22	22	22	22	22	22	22	10
22	22	22	22	12	12	12	12	12	12	12	12	
12	12	12	12	4	4	4	4	4	4	4	4	
4	4	4	4	15	15	15	15	15	15	15	15	
15	15	15	15	7	7	7	7	7	7	7	7	
7	7	7	7	17	17	17	17	17	17	17	17	
17	17	17	17	3	3	3	3	3	3	3	3	
3	3	3	3	25	25	25	25	25	25	25		
25	25	25	25	20	20	20	20	20	24			
20	20	20	20	24	24	24	24	24	20			
24	24	24	24	21	21	21	21	21	21			
21	21	21	21	18	18	18	18					
18	18	18	18									

RACE TYRE STRATEGIES

	Driver	Race Stint 1	Race Stint 2	Race Stint 3	Race Stint 4
1	Vettel	S-Soft: 1-10	Med: 11-57		
2	Hamilton	S-Soft: 1-10	Med: 11-57		
3	Button	S-Soft: 1-9	Med: 10-57		
4	Barrichello	Med: 1-9	S-Soft: 10-57		
5	Kubica	Med: 1-9	Med: 10-57		
6	Sutil	S-Soft: 1-9	Med: 10-57		
7	Kobayashi	Med: 1-53	S-Soft: 54-57		
8	Alonso	S-Soft: 1-10	Med: 11-57		
9	Buemi	S-Soft: 1-9	Med: 10-57		
10	Rosberg	S-Soft: 1-8	Med: 9-57		
11	Massa	S-Soft: 1-10	Med: 11-57		
12	de la Rosa	S-Soft: 1-9	Med: 10-57		
13	Alguersuari	S-Soft: 1-10	Med: 11-57		
14	Petrov	S-Soft: 1-9	Med: 10-57		
15	Schumacher	Med 1-11	S-Soft: 12-13	Med: 14-36	S-Soft: 37-57
16	Liuzzi	S-Soft: 1-9	Med: 10-57		
17	di Grassi	Med 1-42	S-Soft: 43-56		
18	Chandhok	S-Soft: 1-9	Med: 10-55		
19	Glock	Med 1-24	S-Soft: 25-36	S-Soft: 37-55	
20	Senna	Med: 1-11	S-Soft: 12-37	Med: 38-55	
21	Trulli	Med: 1	S-Soft: 2-3	Med: 4-53	
	Hülkenberg	S-Soft: 1-9	Med: 10-49 (dnf)		
	Kovalainen	Med: 1-8 (dnf)			
	Webber	S-Soft: 1-8 (dnf)			

The tyre regulations stipulate that the two dry tyre specifications must be used during the race.
The Super-Soft compound Bridgestone Potenza tyre is marked with a green stripe on the sidewall.

Photo: Peter J. Fox

Mark Webber drove a flawless race to add victory in the British Grand Prix to his burgeoning CV.
Photo: Peter J Fox

FIA FORMULA 1 WORLD CHAMPIONSHIP · ROUND 10

BRITISH GRAND PRIX

SILVERSTONE CIRCUIT

SILVERSTONE QUALIFYING

MARK Webber's face looked almost as thunderous as Red Bull's performance. The Australian is normally one of the sport's most fluent and engaging speakers, but in the immediate aftermath of qualifying at Silverstone – a circuit he adores – his answers were curt, his discontent manifest. And it had nothing to do with the sliver by which he trailed team-mate Sebastian Vettel.

The German had endured a trying start to his weekend. Brake problems had plagued him on Friday, and his front wing – a new design, freshly introduced – had sheared from its mountings on Saturday morning. The team had only two available, one per chassis, and Webber wasn't best pleased when technical director Adrian Newey pinched his and fitted it to Vettel's car. The German used it to good effect to beat Webber by 0.143 seconds – and the new front wing was said to be worth about two-tenths.

"The car feels unbelievable around here," Vettel said. "It's not often that you get to drive a car like this at a track like this. The cornering speeds are unbelievable and I think we'll be quick in race trim, too. The forecast for tomorrow is sunny; England is becoming more tropical, probably the place you should all go to invest."

Webber's demeanour was the polar opposite. "I think the team will be very happy," was his terse summary of the session. He'd be starting from the dirtier side of the track, too, which would mean having to defend against the dependably aggressive Fernando Alonso at the start. Later, Webber added, "I wear my heart on my sleeve; it's just the way I am."

Red Bull sporting director Christian Horner insisted the wing decision had been difficult, but logical, based on championship positions and performance in the final free practice session, when Vettel had been fractionally faster. In addition, it was the result of finger trouble on the team's part rather than anything Vettel had done. "It's not a matter of having a number-one driver," he said. "If the situation arose again, we would use the same criteria, but we only had one wing and I couldn't cut it in half."

Alonso lost some time during his final lap, when he happened upon Michael Schumacher's trundling Mercedes, but acknowledged that it had made little difference. "It cost me a bit," the Spaniard said, "but it didn't explain the missing seven-tenths."

Lewis Hamilton's fourth place was a reward for some splendid teamwork on McLaren's part. It introduced its exhaust-blown diffuser for the first time on Friday, but the system overheated parts of the bodywork and created a handling imbalance. "We were carrying out running repairs throughout the day," said team principal Martin Whitmarsh, "but we learned some useful things."

That evening, test driver Gary Paffett was dispatched to the team's Woking factory, where he spent almost six hours conducting back-to-back tests on the team's simulator. As a result, McLaren decided to ditch its new floor – which, in any case, had originally been scheduled to make its first appearance in Germany – and refit the previous version, although some new parts, including a revised front wing, were retained (on both cars in this instance).

Despite the team having to start with a clean sheet of paper on Saturday, the initial results were encouraging. Both chassis felt well balanced, but Jenson Button's car lost rear grip when it mattered. "The car felt fine this morning and we didn't alter it at all before qualifying," he said, "so I have no idea what happened." He started 14th, ten places behind his team-mate, who described his Q3 lap as "the best I've ever driven. Sometimes you realise that there is absolutely nothing more you could have got from the car."

Nico Rosberg, Robert Kubica, Felipe Massa and Rubens Barrichello completed the top eight, the latter benefiting from a new exhaust-blown diffuser that had been retained for the race.

Further back, Tonio Liuzzi picked up a five-place grid penalty for impeding Nico Hülkenberg during Q2, and HRT implemented the season's first driver change. It dropped Bruno Senna to accommodate Sakon Yamamoto, a decision that owed plenty to finance, but nothing at all to performance.

Generally, drivers approved of Silverstone's revised layout. The circuit had been extended since 2009, with Bridge Corner bypassed and a new infield section added, while down at Club Corner there was the emerging skeleton of a new pit and paddock complex, the first visible fruits of the investment justified by the circuit's new long-term British GP deal, awarded after Donington Park's rival bid collapsed.

In the past, Bernie Ecclestone had often accused Silverstone of looking like a building site – and worse – and now it really did, albeit for the best possible reasons.

Above: Fernando Alonso casts a shrewd eye over the Red Bull RB6 after qualifying.

Top left: Home-town support for Jenson Button.

Above left: An animated Sebastian Vettel during practice.

Left: Jenson Button and Lewis Hamilton are interviewed by legendary Murray Walker.

Main photo: Silverstone was blessed with fine weather.
Photos: Peter J Fox

Inset, opposite: Mark Webber simmers with indignation at the post-qualifying media conference, after Red Bull's only new-spec front wing had been given to Vettel.
Photo: Peter Nygaard/GP Photo

RED Bull RB6 chassis three is the car Sebastian Vettel discarded after crushing defeats in Barcelona and Monaco, but there didn't seem to be too much wrong with it as the field raced toward Copse on the opening lap.

Mark Webber had little option but to use Vettel's cast-off, following his 190mph somersault in Valencia, and the dirtier side of the circuit hadn't, after all, been too bad a starting point. Red Bull later identified a software malfunction that had caused Vettel to falter as he tried to convert pole position into the lead but, given the events of the past 24 hours, it was blatantly obvious that Webber wasn't about to concede as the two cars approached the right-hander side by side. Vettel attempted a defensive chop, but it was never really on: his team-mate was already there. One year earlier, Silverstone had been the scene of a celebratory wake as it prepared to stage the British Grand Prix for what appeared to be the final time. Now, it was the theatre for uncompromising motorsport at its best.

Webber had no reason to budge. He'd beaten Vettel away and simply claimed the track to which he was entitled as they breezed through Copse. An older head than Vettel's might have accepted defeat in the short term and tucked in behind, but the German persisted with the outside line and, with Webber sticking resolutely to the conventional racing route, duly ran wide over the kerbs – not that Webber left him much choice. In his determination, Vettel had also left a gap to the inside, and the closely following Lewis Hamilton, seldom shy, poked his nose in. The subsequent contact was fleeting and gentle – such that neither driver noticed it – but the consequences became apparent when Vettel reached Becketts and his right rear Bridgestone deflated at the best part of 190mph. As everybody else filtered right, he bounced away to the left and did a remarkably good job of keeping the car pointing more or less straight.

Fernando Alonso had been slow away from third, beaten by both Robert Kubica and Nico Rosberg, and at Becketts Felipe Massa slipped ahead, too. The Brazilian's right rear clipped his team-mate's front wing, however, and he joined Vettel in dawdling to the pits, his savaged Bridgestone in tatters.

Thus Webber led from Hamilton, Kubica, Rosberg, Alonso, Rubens Barrichello, Michael Schumacher, Jenson Button (a fabulous start from 14th), Kamui Kobayashi, Adrian Sutil, Pedro de la Rosa (who lost a couple of places when he was forced wide at Copse), Vitaly Petrov, Nico Hülkenberg, Sébastien Buemi, Jaime Alguersuari (one of only three drivers, along with the Force India duo, on the harder tyre), Jarno Trulli, Heikki Kovalainen, Timo Glock, Tonio Liuzzi, Luca di Grassi, Karun Chandhok, Sakon Yamamoto and the two stragglers.

Hamilton harassed Webber for the first two laps, but the Australian soon began to edge away. "It was a good battle with Lewis," he said, "and I really enjoyed the first part of the race. We might not have been wheel to wheel, but I was just watching the pit boards, his and mine, to monitor the gap. It's interesting that they sometimes said different things, but only by a tenth or so. We were pushing each other as hard as we could, but it's fair to say I had the better car."

And then some.

Hamilton came in for his mandatory tyre stop on lap 16, switching from soft to hard Bridgestones, and Webber did likewise one lap later. Subsequently, he continued to extend his advantage and was six seconds clear by lap 28, when the safety car was deployed to allow marshals to sweep fragments of

shredded Sauber from the pit straight. Sutil had triggered the interruption two laps beforehand by attempting to pass de la Rosa via the novel means of driving through, rather than around, him. The rear end of the Sauber was badly damaged and the team retired the Spaniard soon afterwards as a precaution. The Force India carried on as though nothing had happened, and the team's post-race press release made mention of Sutil passing de la Rosa and the Sauber's "rear wing falling apart", but didn't actually cite the cause.

Webber was swiftly back into his stride when the race resumed at the end of lap 30. "There's always a bit of a concern when the safety car comes out," he said, "but I'd had a good gap before and there was a reason for that." He duly pulled away again – he was 1.3 seconds ahead within a lap, 2.5 seconds within three – and was able to engage cruise mode before the end to secure his third victory of the season. As he took the flag, the team came on the radio to offer the customary post-race congratulations. "Yeah," replied Webber, "not bad for a number-two driver." A wonderful one-liner, although later he admitted that it probably created more problems than it solved.

"Silverstone has always been a very special circuit for me," he said. "I have won here in Formula Ford, F3000, sports cars and now F1. At the start of the year, [partner] Ann told me, 'If you don't do anything else this year, at least make sure you bloody well win Monaco and Silverstone.'"

Mission accomplished.

Opening lap and safety car interlude apart, it was a quiet afternoon at the front of the field, and Hamilton was content with second, particularly so, in light of the manner in which McLaren had been obliged to reconfigure its cars on Friday night. "I don't think this is a miracle result," he said. "It's just a reflection of all the hard work the team has put in. On pure pace, I cannot challenge the Ferraris and Red Bulls, but it was down to the start. I managed to creep my way forwards and that was a real blessing."

Rosberg and Kubica swapped places in the wake of their tyre stops, on laps 15 and 13 respectively, but both remained ahead of Alonso. At least, they did until lap 17, when the Spaniard pulled off a spectacular pass at Vale, moving up to fourth at Kubica's expense. Spectacular, but highly illegal – all

Above: Nico Rosberg and girlfriend Vivian look pleased with life after the German took third.
Photo: Lukas Gorys

Top: Silverstone's Richard Phillips breathed a sigh of relief that the revised Silverstone circuit configuration was so well received by the F1 fraternity.
Photo: Jean-François Galeron/WRi2

Left: Fernando Alonso and Robert Kubica at close quarters. The Ferrari driver would be handed a drive-through penalty for straying beyond the track limits while passing the Renault.
Photo: Studio Colombo/WRi2

Above left: Sebastien Vettel is hung out to dry on the opening lap of the race. Team-mate Mark Webber is about to take full advantage.
Photo: Peter Nygaard/GP Photo

four wheels of the Ferrari were off the circuit and he was almost as close to the A43 as he was to the racing line. One of the season's more predictable radio communications followed, as officials informed Ferrari that Alonso would have to hand the position back, but two things occurred while this conversation was going on. Firstly, Alonso passed Alguersuari, who had yet to stop, to complicate the concession of one position. Secondly, Kubica retired with left-hand driveshaft failure and was no longer available for a place swap. Thus Alonso was handed a drive-through instead, just as the safety car came out to deal with the aforementioned Sauber debris. As the whole field had bunched up by the time Alonso served his penalty, he dropped 12 places rather than the one originally intended – and that was no less outrageous than his original manoeuvre, which had been little more than impudent opportunism.

s"There's no point arguing," Alonso said. "The stewards are always right."

This left Rosberg with a clear run to third, ahead of Button, one of the afternoon's star turns. Having gained six places on the opening lap, he vaulted Barrichello and Schumacher during the tyre stops but his early brio did cause unforeseen complications. "Because he was so far back on the grid, we assumed he wouldn't be running at his natural pace and gambled on a lighter fuel load," said team principal Martin Whitmarsh. "He made a great start, though, and was immediately running rather faster than we'd anticipated." Consequently, he was obliged to turn down his revs long before the race's end, which compromised his pursuit of third place.

"Jenson was close," Rosberg said, "but it was a bit easier to keep him behind than it had been with Alonso at the start, because the McLaren seemed to struggle a bit more through high-speed corners. If Fernando had stayed there, my race might have been a bit more difficult."

Barrichello underlined Williams's improving form with a strong run to fifth, ahead of Kobayashi, who was every bit as brisk and consistent as he had been during the second part of the race in Valencia. "I was pretty confident before the start," Kobayashi said, "because I can really feel how the car is getting better and better. I had no chance to overtake anybody this time, but I still enjoyed the race. It wasn't especially hard – I didn't even break sweat."

The safety car was manna for Vettel, who ran non-stop after his early puncture. The German had worked his way ahead of the newcomers by the time of the race's neutralisation, but he was still only 17th, almost a lap behind Webber and 45 seconds behind Alguersuari's tenth-placed Toro Rosso (although the Spaniard still hadn't pitted). The interruption brought him more or less back on terms with everybody, though, and he progressed swiftly after the restart, carving his way up to eighth and exerting huge pressure on Sutil during the closing stages. This involved occasional use of the grass, but finally he elbowed his compatriot aside in the new section of the circuit to annex seventh. Hit by Sutil when they swapped places at Brooklands shortly after the restart, Schumacher tried to follow Vettel through, but the door was shut firmly and the elder statesman had to settle for ninth, ahead of Hülkenberg, Liuzzi, Buemi and Petrov, whose hopes of a possible points finish were dashed when a puncture forced an unscheduled second stop on lap 40. At the time, he had been running just behind Hülkenberg.

Just after half-distance, Alonso got on the radio to instruct Ferrari to cease all communications. "The race was lost," he said, "and there was no point them telling me about gaps; I could see where the other cars were. After my penalty, it was more or less like a test session. There wasn't much to do other than enjoy driving." A late stop for fresh rubber did enable him to secure fastest lap, whatever that was worth.

The Spaniard finished in front of Massa, who made an unscheduled stop after losing control at Woodcote and spinning into the pit entry. "I don't know what to do," he said, "because bad luck seems to be following me around." True to a point, but there was also a bit of bad driving involved.

Lotus was the best of the new teams, Trulli taking 15th from Kovalainen, Glock, Chandhok and Yamamoto, but di Grassi dropped out early with hydraulic pump failure. Fading brakes pitched Alguersuari out of 11th place and into the Luffield gravel shortly before the end.

Given the events of the previous day, justice could hardly have felt more poetic for Webber. Afterwards, he revealed that quite a few of his rivals had teased him gently as they lapped the circuit on a flat-bed truck during the pre-race parade.

"Some of the other guys asked whether I'd like to swap front wings with them," he said, "although Seb wasn't one of them."

Simon Arron

Left: Rubens Barrichello impressed again for Williams with a good run to fifth place. Here he is tailed by Kobayashi and Sutil.
Photo: Peter J Fox

Below: Mark Webber delights with another brilliant win after a frustrating time in practice and qualifying.
Photo: Peter Nygaard/GP Photo

EDITOR'S VIEW
WEBBER STAMPS HIS AUTHORITY

THE run-up to the British Grand Prix is always a period rich in controversy, diversity and intensive gossip. At least in 2010 the British Racing Drivers' Club, long-time owner of Silverstone, was spared its customary role at the epicentre of all this chat and discussion. Silverstone's future as the home and host of the BGP had finally been sealed on a long-term basis, and had been marked with a dramatically modernised track layout and the skeleton of a state-of-the-art pit complex growing on the exit of Club corner. This was intended to be used for the first time at the 2011 event.

The revised circuit had been designed and conceived originally with the MotoGP competitors in mind, and during the period when many still expected that the British GP would definitely be switching to Donington Park. But as the prospects for the circuit near Derby steadily dwindled during the last couple of months of 2009, and Silverstone eventually regained its F1 date, the BRDC began toying with the idea of using the so-called 'Arena' circuit for the 2010 British GP.

"The new sections of the circuit were initially brought in to comply with MotoGP safety regulations, but the 'Arena' complex was always designed with both two- and four-wheeled racing in mind," said Silverstone managing director Richard Phillips. "We have been very careful, working closely with drivers and riders, to make sure we are improving and enhancing what Silverstone already has to offer – from a driver's, rider's and spectator's point of view."

The great thing about the circuit changes was the fact that they had successfully retained the Silverstone 'flavour' while enhancing the track's reputation as one of the best places on the world championship calendar where fans could witness F1 cars straining at the leash on just about every section of the lap. That, and just enough spicy edge between Red Bull team-mates Sebastian Vettel and Mark Webber, delivered the sort of fiercely charged, high-octane confrontation that the sophisticated British race fans always relish. And in the context of the 2010 season to date, that meant the intense scrutiny continued to fall on the Red Bull RB6 teamsters.

Although during the countdown to the race, McLaren was pinning its hopes for a strong performance on its new diffuser package – and 1994 winner Damon Hill tipped Button to come out on top as the McLaren intra-team rivalry seemed set to boil over – Webber expressed a certain scepticism about what he clearly thought were McLaren's carefully crafted efforts to create an image of an easy relationship between their two men. Mark reckoned that it was all a case of 'smoke and mirrors', and that it was not possible to have a "warm, fuzzy, beautiful relationship when a team-mate is also a competitor."

Certainly, Webber demonstrated that he was no push-over when it came to the Silverstone race. He managed successfully to keep in check his simmering discontent over his team's decision to give the second new-spec nosecone to Vettel during qualifying, and responded in the best way possible by producing a stunning GP victory in front of what one might realistically describe as his adoptive home crowd.

Watching Webber mastering his Red Bull through the swoops and sweeps of Silverstone inevitably put one in mind of Alan Jones back in 1979, at the wheel of the seminal Williams FW07. The two men exuded that formidable, hewn-from-the-solid demeanour that, once roused into action, will not easily be stilled, be it by team-mate or rival – or both.

Alan Henry

FIA F1 WORLD CHAMPIONSHIP · ROUND 10

SANTANDER BRITISH GRAND PRIX

SILVERSTONE 9–11 JULY 2010

RACE DISTANCE: 52 laps, 190.281 miles/306.227km

RACE WEATHER: Sunny (track 33–36°C, air 24°C)

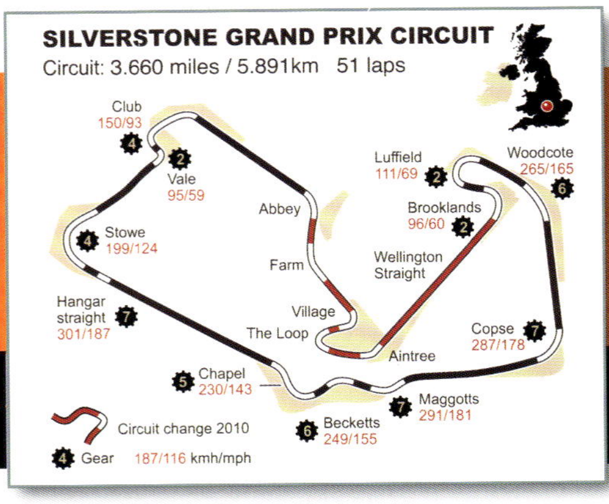

Pos.	Driver	Nat.	No.	Entrant	Car/Engine	Tyres	Laps	Time/Retirement	Speed (mph/km/h)	Gap to leader	Fastest race lap	
1	**Mark Webber**	AUS	6	Red Bull Racing	Red Bull RB6-Renault RS27 V8	B	52	1h 24m 38.200s	134.892/217.088		1m 32.364s	45
2	**Lewis Hamilton**	GB	2	Vodafone McLaren Mercedes	McLaren MP4-25-Mercedes FO108X V8	B	52	1h 24m 39.560s	134.856/217.030	+ 1.360s	1m 32.758s	43
3	**Nico Rosberg**	D	4	Mercedes GP Petronas F1 Team	Mercedes MGP W01-Mercedes FO108X V8	B	52	1h 24m 59.507s	134.329/216.181	+ 21.307s	1m 32.952s	50
4	**Jenson Button**	GB	1	Vodafone McLaren Mercedes	McLaren MP4-25-Mercedes FO108X V8	B	52	1h 25m 00.186s	134.311/216.152	+ 21.986s	1m 33.003s	52
5	**Rubens Barrichello**	BR	9	AT&T Williams	Williams FW32-Cosworth CA2010 V8	B	52	1h 25m 09.656s	134.061/215.751	+ 31.456s	1m 33.615s	50
6	**Kamui Kobayashi**	J	23	BMW Sauber F1 Team	BMW Sauber C29-Ferrari 056 V8	B	52	1h 25m 10.371s	134.043/215.721	+ 32.171s	1m 33.558s	52
7	**Sebastian Vettel**	D	5	Red Bull Racing	Red Bull RB6-Renault RS27 V8	B	52	1h 25m 14.934s	133.924/215.529	+ 36.734s	1m 31.967s	52
8	**Adrian Sutil**	D	14	Force India F1 Team	Force India VJM03-Mercedes FO108X V8	B	52	1h 25m 19.132s	133.814/215.352	+ 40.932s	1m 34.337s	42
9	**Michael Schumacher**	GB	3	Mercedes GP Petronas F1 Team	Mercedes MGP W01-Mercedes FO108X V8	B	52	1h 25m 19.799s	133.796/215.324	+ 41.599s	1m 34.171s	47
10	**Nico Hülkenberg**	D	10	AT&T Williams	Williams FW32-Cosworth CA2010 V8	B	52	1h 25m 20.212s	133.785/215.306	+ 42.012s	1m 33.989s	48
11	Vitantonio Liuzzi	I	15	Force India F1 Team	Force India VJM03-Mercedes FO108X V8	B	52	1h 25m 20.659s	133.774/215.288	+ 42.459s	1m 34.018s	51
12	Sébastien Buemi	CH	16	Scuderia Toro Rosso	Toro Rosso STR5-Ferrari 056 V8	B	52	1h 25m 25.827s	133.639/215.071	+ 47.627s	1m 32.980s	52
13	Vitaly Petrov	RUS	12	Renault F1 Team	Renault R30-RS27 V8	B	52	1h 25m 37.574s	133.333/214.579	+ 59.374s	1m 32.484s	52
14	Fernando Alonso	E	8	Scuderia Ferrari Marlboro	Ferrari F10-056 V8	B	52	1h 25m 40.585s	133.255/214.453	+ 1m 02.385s	1m 30.874s	52
15	Felipe Massa	BR	7	Scuderia Ferrari Marlboro	Ferrari F10-056 V8	B	52	1h 25m 45.689s	133.123/214.240	+ 1m 07.489s	1m 31.646s	52
16	Jarno Trulli	I	18	Lotus Racing	Lotus T127-Cosworth CA2010 V8	B	51			+ 1 lap	1m 36.519s	44
17	Heikki Kovalainen	FIN	19	Lotus Racing	Lotus T127-Cosworth CA2010 V8	B	51			+ 1 lap	1m 36.251s	48
18	Timo Glock	D	24	Virgin Racing	Virgin VR-01-Cosworth CA2010 V8	B	50			+ 2 laps	1m 36.415s	49
19	Karun Chandhok	IND	20	HRT F1 Team	HRT F110-Cosworth CA2010 V8	B	50			+ 2 laps	1m 38.798s	40
20	Sakon Yamamoto	J	21	HRT F1 Team	HRT F110-Cosworth CA2010 V8	B	50			+ 2 laps	1m 38.309s	50
	Jaime Alguersuari	E	17	Scuderia Toro Rosso	Toro Rosso STR5-Ferrari 056 V8	B	44	*brakes*			1m 33.748s	43
	Pedro de la Rosa	E	22	BMW Sauber F1 Team	BMW Sauber C29-Ferrari 056 V8	B	29	*accident/rear wing*			1m 35.883s	23
	Robert Kubica	PL	11	Renault F1 Team	Renault R30-RS27 V8	B	19	*driveshaft*			1m 36.846s	12
	Lucas di Grassi	BR	25	Virgin Racing	Virgin VR-01-Cosworth CA2010 V8	B	9	*hydraulics*			1m 40.641s	7

Fastest race lap: Fernando Alonso on lap 52, 1m 30.874s, 145.012mph/233.373km/h.

Lap record: Nigel Mansell (Williams FW11B-Honda V6 turbo), 1m 09.832s, 153.059mph/246.324km/h (1987) (2.969-mile/4.778km circuit)

Lap record (previous configuration): Michael Schumacher (Ferrari F2004 V10), 1m 18.739s, 146.053mph/235.049km/h (2004) (3.194-mile/ 5.141km circuit).

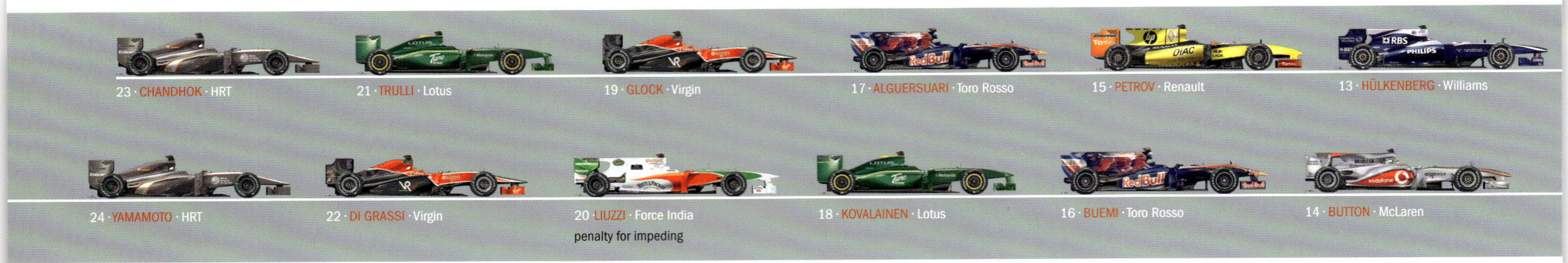

Grid order	1	2	3	4	5	6	7	8	9	10	11	12	13	14	15	16	17	18	19	20	21
5 VETTEL	6	6	6	6	6	6	6	6	6	6	6	6	6	6	6	6	6	6	6	6	6
6 WEBBER	2	2	2	2	2	2	2	2	2	2	2	2	2	2	2	2	2	2	2	2	2
8 ALONSO	11	11	11	11	11	11	11	11	11	11	11	11	4	4	4	1	1	1	1	1	1
2 HAMILTON	4	4	4	4	4	4	4	4	4	4	4	4	11	1	1	10	10	10	10	10	10
4 ROSBERG	8	8	8	8	8	8	8	8	8	8	8	1	1	14	14	17	17	4	4	4	4
11 KUBICA	9	9	9	9	9	9	9	9	9	9	9	8	14	12	10	4	4	17	8	8	8
7 MASSA	3	3	3	3	3	3	3	3	3	3	1	9	12	10	16	11	8	8	17	17	17
9 BARRICHELLO	1	1	1	1	1	1	1	1	1	1	23	14	10	16	12	8	11	11	9	9	9
22 DE LA ROSA	23	23	23	23	23	23	23	23	23	23	14	22	22	17	17	16	9	9	23	23	23
3 SCHUMACHER	14	14	14	14	14	14	14	14	14	14	3	23	16	11	11	9	23	23	3	3	3
14 SUTIL	22	22	22	22	22	22	22	22	22	22	22	12	17	8	8	23	3	3	22	22	22
23 KOBAYASHI	12	12	12	12	12	12	12	12	12	12	12	10	8	9	9	3	22	22	14	14	14
10 HULKENBERG	10	10	10	10	10	10	10	10	10	10	10	16	9	23	23	22	14	14	12	12	12
1 BUTTON	16	16	16	16	16	16	16	16	16	16	16	17	23	3	3	14	12	12	15	15	15
12 PETROV	17	17	17	17	17	17	17	17	17	17	17	3	3	22	22	12	15	15	16	16	16
16 BUEMI	18	18	18	18	18	18	18	18	18	15	15	15	15	15	15	15	16	16	7	7	7
17 ALGUERSUARI	19	19	19	19	19	15	15	15	15	18	18	18	18	18	18	18	18	7	18	18	18
19 KOVALAINEN	24	15	15	15	15	19	19	19	19	19	19	19	19	19	7	19	7	18	19	19	19
24 GLOCK	15	24	24	24	24	24	24	24	24	24	24	24	7	7	19	7	19	19	11	24	24
15 LIUZZI	25	25	25	25	25	25	25	25	7	7	7	7	24	24	24	24	24	24	24	5	5
18 TRULLI	20	20	20	20	20	20	20	20	20	20	20	20	20	20	20	5	5	5	5	20	20
25 DI GRASSI	21	21	21	21	21	21	21	7	21	21	21	21	21	5	5	20	20	20	20	21	21
20 CHANDHOK	7	7	7	7	7	7	7	21	25	5	5	5	5	21	21	21	21	21	21		
21 YAMAMOTO	5	5	5	5	5	5	5	5	5												

Grid order	22	23	24	25	26	27	28	29	30	31	32	33	34	35	36	37	38	39	40	41	42
5 VETTEL	6	6	6	6	6	6	6	6	6	6	6	6	6	6	6	6	6	6	6	6	6
6 WEBBER	2	2	2	2	2	2	2	2	2	2	2	2	2	2	2	2	2	2	2	2	2
8 ALONSO	10	10	10	10	10	4	4	4	4	4	4	4	4	4	4	4	4	4	4	4	4
2 HAMILTON	4	4	4	4	4	8	8	8	1	1	1	1	1	1	1	1	1	1	1	1	1
4 ROSBERG	8	8	8	8	8	1	1	1	9	9	9	9	9	9	9	9	9	9	9	9	9
11 KUBICA	1	1	1	1	1	10	9	9	23	23	23	23	23	23	23	23	23	23	23	23	23
7 MASSA	17	17	17	17	17	17	23	23	3	3	14	14	14	14	14	14	14	14	14	14	14
9 BARRICHELLO	9	9	9	9	9	9	3	3	14	14	3	3	3	3	3	3	3	3	5	5	5
22 DE LA ROSA	23	23	23	23	23	23	17	14	10	10	10	10	10	10	10	10	5	5	3	3	3
3 SCHUMACHER	3	3	3	3	3	3	14	10	12	12	12	12	12	12	12	5	10	10	10	10	10
14 SUTIL	22	22	22	22	14	14	10	12	17	17	17	17	5	5	5	12	12	12	17	17	17
23 KOBAYASHI	14	14	14	14	12	12	12	17	8	16	7	5	17	17	17	17	17	17	15	15	15
10 HULKENBERG	12	12	12	12	22	15	16	16	16	7	5	7	7	7	7	7	7	15	8	8	8
1 BUTTON	15	15	15	15	15	16	7	7	7	5	15	15	15	15	15	15	15	8	12	16	16
12 PETROV	16	16	16	16	16	7	15	5	5	15	16	16	8	8	8	8	8	16	16	12	12
16 BUEMI	7	7	7	7	7	22	22	22	15	8	8	8	16	16	16	16	16	7	7	7	7
17 ALGUERSUARI	18	18	18	5	5	5	5	15	18	18	18	18	18	18	18	18	18	18	18	18	18
19 KOVALAINEN	24	24	5	18	18	18	18	18	24	24	24	24	24	24	24	24	24	24	24	24	24
24 GLOCK	19	5	24	24	24	24	24	24	19	19	19	19	19	19	19	19	19	19	19	19	19
15 LIUZZI	5	19	19	19	19	19	19	19	20	20	20	20	20	20	20	20	20	20	20	20	20
18 TRULLI	20	20	20	20	20	20	20	20	21	21	21	21	21	21	21	21	21	21	21	21	21
25 DI GRASSI	21	21	21	21	21	21	21	21													
20 CHANDHOK																					
21 YAMAMOTO																					

TIME SHEETS

PRACTICE 1 (FRIDAY)

Weather: Sunny

Temperatures: track 27–34°C, air 22–26°C

Pos.	Driver	Laps	Time
1	Sebastian Vettel	22	1m 32.280s
2	Lewis Hamilton	16	1m 32.614s
3	Robert Kubica	21	1m 32.725s
4	Mark Webber	23	1m 32.747s
5	Adrian Sutil	18	1m 32.968s
6	Nico Rosberg	21	1m 33.318s
7	Nico Hülkenberg	19	1m 33.377s
8	Jenson Button	20	1m 33.519s
9	Michael Schumacher	18	1m 33.955s
10	Rubens Barrichello	17	1m 34.016s
11	Sébastien Buemi	21	1m 34.132s
12	Vitaly Petrov	22	1m 34.365s
13	Fernando Alonso	20	1m 34.490s
14	Paul di Resta	22	1m 34.580s
15	Kamui Kobayashi	16	1m 34.710s
16	Pedro de la Rosa	17	1m 34.901s
17	Felipe Massa	21	1m 35.037s
18	Jaime Alguersuari	27	1m 35.318s
19	Heikki Kovalainen	16	1m 36.747s
20	Timo Glock	11	1m 37.330s
21	Lucas di Grassi	15	1m 37.518s
22	Karun Chandhok	21	1m 38.735s
23	Fairuz Fauzy	11	1m 39.510s
24	Sakon Yamamoto	27	1m 39.673s

PRACTICE 2 (FRIDAY)

Weather: Sunny

Temperatures: track 39–41°C, air 29–30°C

Pos.	Driver	Laps	Time
1	Mark Webber	15	1m 31.234s
2	Fernando Alonso	26	1m 31.626s
3	Sebastian Vettel	25	1m 31.875s
4	Felipe Massa	25	1m 32.099s
5	Nico Rosberg	29	1m 32.166s
6	Michael Schumacher	28	1m 32.660s
7	Vitaly Petrov	28	1m 32.745s
8	Lewis Hamilton	22	1m 32.757s
9	Adrian Sutil	27	1m 32.787s
10	Rubens Barrichello	33	1m 32.967s
11	Robert Kubica	30	1m 33.019s
12	Nico Hülkenberg	29	1m 33.164s
13	Jenson Button	24	1m 33.200s
14	Kamui Kobayashi	23	1m 33.402s
15	Vitantonio Liuzzi	27	1m 33.728s
16	Sébastien Buemi	36	1m 33.836s
17	Pedro de la Rosa	29	1m 34.051s
18	Jaime Alguersuari	36	1m 34.643s
19	Heikki Kovalainen	25	1m 35.465s
20	Lucas di Grassi	24	1m 36.237s
21	Timo Glock	21	1m 36.553s
22	Karun Chandhok	27	1m 37.019s
23	Sakon Yamamoto	32	1m 38.303s
24	Jarno Trulli	3	1m 42.901s

PRACTICE 3 (SATURDAY)

Weather: Sunny/partly cloudy

Temperatures: track 29–31°C, air 24–26°C

Pos.	Driver	Laps	Time
1	Sebastian Vettel	14	1m 30.958s
2	Mark Webber	15	1m 30.992s
3	Fernando Alonso	10	1m 31.101s
4	Nico Rosberg	15	1m 31.188s
5	Felipe Massa	16	1m 31.240s
6	Robert Kubica	18	1m 31.519s
7	Lewis Hamilton	16	1m 31.549s
8	Michael Schumacher	14	1m 31.555s
9	Pedro de la Rosa	18	1m 31.559s
10	Rubens Barrichello	16	1m 31.581s
11	Vitaly Petrov	17	1m 31.698s
12	Jenson Button	16	1m 31.703s
13	Nico Hülkenberg	17	1m 31.867s
14	Kamui Kobayashi	16	1m 31.947s
15	Adrian Sutil	13	1m 31.994s
16	Sébastien Buemi	18	1m 32.235s
17	Jaime Alguersuari	20	1m 32.331s
18	Vitantonio Liuzzi	18	1m 32.723s
19	Heikki Kovalainen	20	1m 34.339s
20	Lucas di Grassi	17	1m 35.479s
21	Jarno Trulli	11	1m 36.098s
22	Karun Chandhok	16	1m 36.286s
23	Timo Glock	6	1m 36.640s
24	Sakon Yamamoto	18	1m 37.178s

QUALIFYING (SATURDAY)

Weather: Sunny Temperatures: track 34–36°C, air 27–28°C

Pos.	Driver	First	Second	Third	Qualifying Tyre
1	Sebastian Vettel	1m 30.841s	1m 30.480s	1m 29.615s	Soft
2	Mark Webber	1m 30.858s	1m 30.114s	1m 29.758s	Soft
3	Fernando Alonso	1m 30.997s	1m 30.700s	1m 30.426s	Soft
4	Lewis Hamilton	1m 31.297s	1m 31.118s	1m 30.556s	Soft
5	Nico Rosberg	1m 31.626s	1m 31.085s	1m 30.625s	Soft
6	Robert Kubica	1m 31.680s	1m 31.344s	1m 31.040s	Soft
7	Felipe Massa	1m 31.313s	1m 31.010s	1m 31.172s	Soft
8	Rubens Barrichello	1m 31.424s	1m 31.126s	1m 31.175s	Soft
9	Pedro de la Rosa	1m 31.533s	1m 31.327s	1m 31.274s	Soft
10	Michael Schumacher	1m 32.058s	1m 31.022s	1m 31.430s	Soft
11	Adrian Sutil	1m 31.109s	1m 31.399s		
12	Kamui Kobayashi	1m 31.851s	1m 31.421s		
13	Nico Hülkenberg	1m 32.144s	1m 31.635s		
14	Jenson Button	1m 31.435s	1m 31.699s		
15	Vitantonio Liuzzi	1m 32.226s	1m 31.708s		
16	Vitaly Petrov	1m 31.638s	1m 31.796s		
17	Sébastien Buemi	1m 31.901s	1m 32.012s		
18	Jaime Alguersuari	1m 32.430s			
19	Heikki Kovalainen	1m 34.405s			
20	Timo Glock	1m 34.775s			
21	Jarno Trulli	1m 34.864s			
22	Lucas di Grassi	1m 35.212s			
23	Karun Chandhok	1m 36.576s			
24	Sakon Yamamoto	1m 36.968s			

FOR THE RECORD

10th POLE POSITION: **Sebastian Vettel**

20th PODIUM: **Mercedes Benz**

POINTS

DRIVERS

1	Lewis Hamilton	145
2	Jenson Button	133
3	Mark Webber	128
4	Sebastian Vettel	121
5	Fernando Alonso	98
6	Nico Rosberg	90
7	Robert Kubica	83
8	Felipe Massa	67
9	Michael Schumacher	36
10	Adrian Sutil	35
11	Rubens Barrichello	29
12	Kamui Kobayashi	15
13	Vitantonio Liuzzi	12
14	Sébastien Buemi	7
15	Vitaly Petrov	6
16	Jaime Alguersuari	3
17	Nico Hülkenberg	2

CONSTRUCTORS

1	McLaren	278
2	Red Bull	249
3	Ferrari	165
4	Mercedes	126
5	Renault	89
6	Force India	47
7	Williams	31
8	BMW Sauber	15
9	Toro Rosso	10

43	44	45	46	47	48	49	50	51	52	-
6	6	6	6	6	6	6	6	6	6	1
2	2	2	2	2	2	2	2	2	2	2
4	4	4	4	4	4	4	4	4	4	3
1	1	1	1	1	1	1	1	1	1	
9	9	9	9	9	9	9	9	9	9	
23	23	23	23	23	23	23	23	23	23	6
14	14	14	14	14	14	14	14	5	5	7
5	5	5	5	5	5	5	5	14	14	8
3	3	3	3	3	3	3	3	3	3	9
10	10	10	10	10	10	10	10	10	10	10
17	17	15	15	15	15	15	15	15	15	
15	15	8	8	8	8	8	16	16	16	
8	8	16	16	16	16	16	12	12	12	
16	16	12	12	12	12	12	8	8	8	
12	12	7	7	7	7	7	7	7	7	
7	7	*18*	*18*	*18*	*18*	*18*	*18*	*18*		
18	*18*	*24*	*19*	*19*	*19*	*19*	*19*	*19*		
24	*24*	*19*	*24*	*24*	*24*	*24*	*24*			
19	*19*	*20*	*20*	*20*	*20*	*20*	*20*			
20	*20*	*21*	*21*	*21*	*21*	*21*	*21*			
21	*21*									

21 Pit stop *14 One lap or more behind*

Safety car deployed on laps shown

RACE TYRE STRATEGIES

	Driver	Race Stint 1	Race Stint 2	Race Stint 3	Race Stint 4
1	Webber	Soft: 1-17	Hard: 18-52		
2	Hamilton	Soft: 1-16	Hard: 17-52		
3	Rosberg	Soft: 1-15	Hard: 16-52		
4	Button	Soft: 1-21	Hard: 22-52		
5	Barrichello	Soft: 1-12	Hard: 13-52		
6	Kobayashi	Soft: 1-12	Hard: 13-52		
7	Vettel	Soft: 1	Hard: 2-52		
8	Sutil	Soft: 1-15	Hard: 16-52		
9	Schumacher	Soft: 1-11	Hard: 12-52		
10	Hülkenberg	Soft: 1-27	Hard: 28-52		
11	Liuzzi	Hard: 1-28	Soft: 29-52		
12	Buemi	Soft: 1-16	Hard: 17-52		
13	Petrov	Soft: 1-15	Hard: 16-40	Hard: 41-52	
14	Alonso	Soft: 1-12	Hard: 13-30	Hard: 31-49	Soft: 50-52
15	Massa	Soft: 1	Hard: 2-39	Hard: 40-52	
16	Trulli	Soft: 1-25	Hard: 26-51		
17	Kovalainen	Soft: 1-22	Hard: 23-51		
18	Glock	Soft: 1-24	Hard: 25-50		
19	Chandhok	Soft: 1-22	Hard: 23-50		
20	Yamamoto	Soft: 1-10	Hard: 11-53		
	Alguersuari	Hard: 1-28	Soft: 29-44 (dnf)		
	de la Rosa	Soft: 1-13	Hard: 14-26	Hard: 27-29 (dnf)	
	Kubica	Soft: 1-10 (dnf)			
	di Grassi	Hard: 1-9 (dnf)			

The tyre regulations stipulate that the two dry tyre specifications must be used during the race. The Soft compound Bridgestone Potenza tyre is marked with a green stripe on the sidewall.

Photos: Peter J. Fox

Bird's eye view of the Hockenheim stadium section, with the pack strung out under an ominously grey sky.
Photo: Peter J Fox

FIA FORMULA 1 WORLD CHAMPIONSHIP · ROUND 11

GERMAN GRAND PRIX

HOCKENHEIM CIRCUIT

Panasonic
ntander

HOCKENHEIM QUALIFYING

THE scaled-down klaxon and firecracker sonata told its own tale. Ten years ago, Hockenheim would have gone berserk when Michael Schumacher achieved little more than a successful exit from his pit garage, but these were subdued times (and not just because Schumacher was a lacklustre 11th). There was little sign of the dense thicket of humanity that used to cluster around the circuit entrance throughout a grand prix weekend, but finally – in the middle of Saturday afternoon – Sebastian Vettel breathed some life into the audience.

Two thousandths of a second were all it took.

The session began disruptively – Tonio Liuzzi prompted a red flag after losing control at the final turn and spinning across the road into the pit wall, to his Force India's significant detriment – and ended thrillingly. Fernando Alonso appeared to be on course to take Ferrari's first pole position of 2010, but then Vettel conjured a 1m 13.791s lap to defeat him by the aforementioned 0.002 seconds: it was his third consecutive pole and Red Bull's tenth of the campaign. That stirred the crowd, but first they faced a brief, edgy wait. Custom might dictate that, in dry weather, circuit conditions peak in the final moments of qualifying, and Alonso – fastest after the first Q3 runs – was last to venture out. His final effort, though, was not quite enough.

"I wanted to make sure I had a clear track on my out lap," Vettel said, "to prepare my tyres properly without interference from other cars. I knew I only had one shot at pole. The lap could perhaps have been a little bit better, It is very easy to overdrive, and take the edge off the tyres, but in the end it was okay, even if the margin was almost nothing. There are no prizes for today, though, other than being able to go to sleep with a nice feeling inside."

Alonso declared himself happy with such a slender deficit. "We have often been half a second slower than Red Bull in Q3," he said, "so I'm encouraged to be so close. We didn't expect to be quite so competitive at Silverstone two weeks ago, because high-speed corners don't really suit us, so we knew we'd be in good shape when we came to circuits like this." Felipe Massa backed him up with a strong run to third, ahead of Mark Webber and the two McLarens, Jenson Button pipping Lewis Hamilton as the team committed to race with an exhaust-blown diffuser for the first time.

McLaren's weekend got off to an unproductive start, Hamilton damaging all four corners of his chassis when he crashed coming out of Turn Three after only eight laps of practice on Friday morning. "I hit the rev limiter," he said, "but the wheels spun when I changed gear and the car began to oversteer. I put a wheel on the grass while I was trying to sort it all out, and after that I was a passenger." That left Button to do the lion's share of the evaluation work, but cool, showery conditions reduced the day's relevance.

"Lewis's accident didn't set us back too much," said McLaren team principal Martin Whitmarsh, "The variable weather made it difficult to reach too many firm conclusions about the new floor, but it seems to work as it is supposed to. It opens up interesting development opportunities and, so far, I'd say we have released less than half its potential."

The unseasonal conditions also minimised fears about possible tyre induced chaos, with Bridgestone having brought along an ambitious cocktail of hard and super-soft compounds, the latter of which might have wilted if Hockenheim had been its traditional furnace. "The super-soft is strong enough to do a reasonable stint," said Vettel, "and it won't really matter how many laps you do on the hard tyre because the wear rate is negligible. We could probably use it next weekend in Hungary, too."

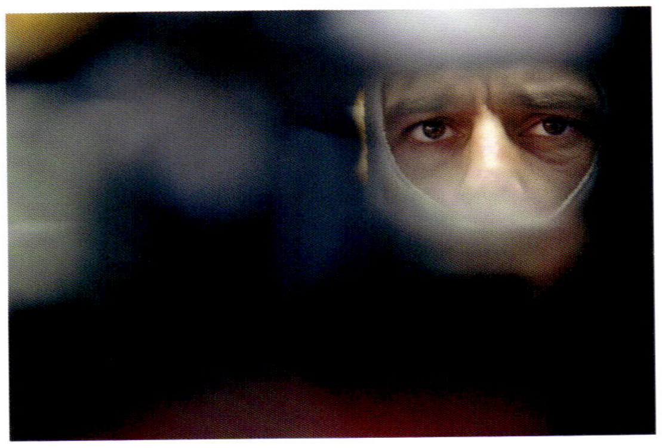

IT wasn't so much what Ferrari did that caused offence – it was the manner of execution and the team's gauche attempts to blur the truth. The 2010 German Grand Prix began explosively and continued in a similar vein, but for entirely different reasons. Fernando Alonso came away with his second win of the campaign, but such trifles were hardly mentioned.

Alonso's afternoon began brightly enough, the Spaniard drawing alongside Sebastian Vettel when the pole winning Red Bull's engine bogged down as its driver released the clutch, The German's brief loss of momentum forced him to defend aggressively by veering to the right, but Alonso is immune to intimidation and squeezed through the minuscule gap he'd been left. This fleeting duel compromised their approaches to Turn One, however, and allowed Felipe Massa to sweep around the outside to vault from third to first in a single hit. Lewis Hamilton breezed past Mark Webber to annex fourth, while Jenson Button slipped to sixth and both Williams drivers wasted decent qualifying performances by frittering three positions apiece before they'd reached Turn Two.

There was a rich seam of chaos at the heart of midfield. Jaime Alguersuari rammed Toro Rosso team-mate Sébastien Buemi at the hairpin, and did so with sufficient force to precipitate the Swiss driver's retirement once they had both trundled back to the pits. Both Force Indias came in, too, after Tonio Liuzzi snagged team-mate Adrian Sutil shortly after the start. The Italian required a new front wing and, in the splendid muddle that ensued, the two drivers' tyres became jumbled: Sutil was dispatched with three hard Bridgestones plus a super-soft that should have been on Liuzzi's car, and vice versa. Both were soon back in for the error to be rectified, and the team was reprimanded for a breach of the tyre regulations, although the offence was comedic rather than wilful.

As the second lap began, Massa led from Alonso, Vettel, Hamilton, Webber, Button, Robert Kubica, Michael Schumacher, Nico Rosberg, Kamui Kobayashi, Rubens Barrichello, Vitaly Petrov, Nico Hülkenberg, Pedro de la Rosa, Jarno Trulli, Heikki Kovalainen, Lucas di Grassi, Bruno Senna (back with HRT, after missing Silverstone), Sakon Yamamoto (still with HRT, this time at Karun Chandhok's expense) and Timo Glock, with the surviving Force India/Toro Rosso cast bringing up the rear. Trulli wasn't destined to last long, though: he coasted to the pits on lap two, without any gears, and all attempts at repair failed. He managed one more slow lap before finally parking up.

Massa's lead created scope for pleasing symmetry,

Above: Alonso and Vettel momentarily distract each other as the pack jostles into the first right-hander on the opening lap, allowing Massa to surge around the outside into the lead.
Photo: Studio Colombo/WRi2

Top left: Michael Schumacher was back at his home grand prix, but not as the all-conquering hero he had hoped to be.
Photo: Peter Nygaard/GP Photo

Centre left: Jenson Button and his engineer deep in contemplation on chassis set-up.

Above left: Mark Webber was not a contender for victory at Hockenheim: the Australian qualified fourth and finished sixth.
Photos: Peter J Fox

Left: Nico Hülkenberg takes up his position on the grid.
Photo: Paul-Henri Cahier

because it was the first anniversary of the Hungarian GP qualifying accident that had left the Brazilian with serious head injuries, but sentiment and motorsport are rarely complementary.

The leader was 1.5 seconds clear of Alonso by lap 13, when the Spaniard made his mandatory tyre stop to swap from super-softs to hards, and still 0.7 seconds to the good after he shadowed the move one lap later. Button led the field at this stage, as the only one of the original top six yet to stop, and a lengthy 22-lap stint enabled the McLaren driver to vault Webber. Once he'd pitted though, the Ferraris resumed control, with Vettel tagging along behind.

Alonso contemplated a move at the hairpin, on lap 21, but there was no way through and stalemate ensued until the race was well into its second half, when Massa's race engineer, Rob Smedley, came on the radio to tell the Brazilian, "Alonso is faster than you. Can you confirm you understand?" Clearly Felipe did, for on lap 49 he backed off at the hairpin exit. He didn't exactly wave Alonso through, but it was so obvious a gesture that he might as well have done. That triggered another radio transmission. "Good lad," said Smedley. "Just stick with it now. Sorry."

Alonso subsequently crossed the line with more than four seconds in hand and gave his team-mate a hug in *parc fermé*, but Smedley had already offered verbal consolation. "That was very, very magnanimous," he said to Massa. "You won't know what this means, but I'll explain it to you later."

Given the ban on team orders, Ferrari denied any such tactics. "We felt Fernando was quicker at that stage of the race," said sporting director Stefano Domenicali, "and simply passed the information on to Felipe. After that, it is up to the drivers to decide what is best for the team."

Why, though, had Domenicali not been the one on the radio, giving instructions, coded or otherwise? The tone of Smedley's comments told the world all it needed to know, yet he shouldn't have been put in that position, given that it was as much of a sacrifice for him as it was for Massa. Back in the day, former sporting director Jean Todt was the one who gave the commands. Ironically, of course, it was Todt-led Ferrari's clumsy execution of team orders that caused the practice to be banned, after Rubens Barrichello backed off to let Michael Schumacher through at the final corner of the 2002 Austrian GP. Now, eight years on, the Todt-led FIA's World Motor Sport Council would be investigating Ferrari's conduct.

Massa insisted, without great conviction, that it had been his decision alone to let Alonso pass, and claimed, too, that he had been struggling slightly on the harder tyre, a flimsy excuse that was not supported by his lap times. The Spaniard, meanwhile, reacted angrily when someone suggested victory had been handed to him in an inappropriate manner.

"I don't think that's true," he said. "The championship is over 19 races, not one. Sometimes we win, sometimes we lose, but the important thing today is that we won, and I think we deserved it. We've had a competitive car for the past two races, but didn't score any points. Winning is always special, but there's no point getting too excited. There's still a long way to go and we need to stay focused, because in a few days we will be back on track."

In the wake of all this froth and denial, both drivers were summoned to meet the stewards, along with Smedley and Ferrari team manager Massimo Rivola. Subsequently, the team was found guilty of breaching Article 39.1 of the 2010 sporting regulations ("team orders that interfere with a race result are prohibited") and Article 151c of the 2010 international sporting code ("any act prejudicial to the interests of competition or the interests of motorsport generally"). Ferrari was fined $100,000 – the maximum on-the-spot punishment that could be imposed – and a later WMSC tribunal, in September, declined to sanction further penalties. The FIA was sure that Ferrari had given illegal team orders, but the rule banning them, difficult to police in ordinary circumstances, was to be reviewed.

In truth, the practice had never gone away: consider how Heikki Kovalainen moved aside for McLaren team-mate Lewis Hamilton at Hockenheim in 2008, to support the Englishman's title bid. Hamilton thanked the Finn publicly, yet nothing was said. It was the same when Massa eased up at Interlagos in 2007, to help Kimi Räikkönen win the world championship, and when Räikkönen reciprocated in an effort to assist Massa's ultimately unsuccessful title tilt one year later.

The difference between these incidents and Austria 2002 is that Ferrari had no reason to do what it did back then: it won 15 of that season's 17 races and had no meaningful opposition. This time, it was simply doing what was best to abet the title chances of one driver who had more points than the other, and who had consistently been the team's quicker performer. As a result, the intensity of the five-way title fight remained undiminished, so Ferrari's actions were hardly prejudicial to the interests of the sport. However, the situation could have been more subtly – and more honestly – managed.

The overbearing scent of post-race scandal superseded the previously dominant debate – about the legality or otherwise of the allegedly flexible front wings used by Red Bull and Ferrari, both of which passed scrutineering – and rather masked the fact that, despite what you might have deduced from the

Above: "Alonso is faster than you…" Massa takes up station behind the Spaniard after allowing him past on lap 50.
Photo: Paul-Henri Cahier

Top left: Nico Rosberg sees the funny side of things in conversation with Hamilton and Button.
Photo: Peter J. Fox

Above left: Felipe Massa was understandably very crestfallen when he appeared at the post-race media conference.
Photo: Paul-Henri Cahier

colossal ink spillage that followed, this had been a fairly quiet Sunday.

Vettel and Hamilton were third and fourth all afternoon, and the German, best of the home drivers, was all but ignored during the post-race press conference (amused though he was by the verbal jousting between journalists and the two Ferrari drivers). "Can I go?" he asked at one point, making as if to leave before Alonso dragged him back. Somebody then asked him about team orders. "Don't you have another question," he said. "Yeah, maybe they should have crashed. I don't know, I haven't seen the incident because I was too far back. I don't know what you're all talking about, but I can guess."

Button and Webber remained similarly static after trading places during the pit stops. At one point, the Englishman's consistent pace on super-softs looked as though it might carry him ahead of Hamilton, too, but in the end he was left to give chase. "I think Lewis and I got the maximum from the car today," he said, "but it isn't quite quick enough at the moment." Despite that, they continued to run first and second in the championship.

Kubica was just as seventh at the end as he had been at the beginning, although the two Mercedes drivers did trade places, Rosberg moving ahead in the wake of a lengthy 24-lap opening stint. In his first home race since 2006, Schumacher trailed home ninth, one lap in arrears and scarcely on the radar.

Petrov claimed the final point – "a pleasant surprise", as he put it, because he hadn't realised he was running in the top ten – ahead of Kobayashi, Barrichello and Hülkenberg. A disappointing end to the weekend, that, for Williams, after both cars made it through to Q3. Ultimately, poor starts from the grubbier side of the grid were their downfall, although technical director Sam Michael conceded that keeping Hülkenberg out for 34 laps on super-softs had probably been "a bit too long". The team had nothing to lose at that stage, though, with the car running outside the points, and was hoping it might capitalise in the event of a safety car interruption. With so much procession and so little actual racing, however, that was never particularly likely.

The finishers were completed by de la Rosa, Alguersuari, Liuzzi, Sutil (who had to make an unscheduled stop after ploughing through the Sachskurve gravel trap on his 34th lap), Glock and Senna. De la Rosa started on hard tyres and stayed out for 51 laps, but his hopes of making places on the super-softs were swiftly dashed: he was following Barrichello when the pair came up to lap Kovalainen's Lotus on lap 58. The Finn saw the Williams behind him when he tried to move aside at Turn Two, but not the Sauber: the impact forced Kovalainen to retire – he had been the best of the newcomers at the time, after suspension failure had caused di Grassi to spin out a few laps earlier – and obliged de la Rosa to pit for a new nose. Yamamoto departed, unnoticed, after 16 laps, when electrical trouble caused his engine to cut.

On days such as this, people often question F1's credibility. What did it say, for instance, to those who had placed a wager on a Massa victory? Betting, though, is not motor racing's *raison d'être*. Those who gamble seriously on the equestrian equivalent do so after studying facts, bloodlines and relevant data – it's not the same thing as sticking a tenner on the Grand National because you quite like a horse's name. Given the championship situation, no student of recent history would have placed a bet on Massa, because team orders have been around since the Renault brothers were sitting on their grandma's lap.

Always have, always will.

Simon Arron

Left: Vettel uses all of the road, and then some, en route to third place for Red Bull.
Photo: Jad Sherif/WRi2

Below: Lewis Hamilton drove with his customary zest and determination, but could not improve on fourth place at the chequered flag.

Below right: Getting by with a little help from his friends, Alonso took top spot on the rostrum for the first time since the Bahrain GP.
Photos: Peter J. Fox

EDITOR'S VIEW
FERRARI SLAMMED FOR TEAM ORDERS

INEVITABLY, delving into history in a bid to justify contemporary decisions is fraught with potential risks, as Luca di Montezemolo was reminded in the aftermath of Ferrari's controversial and humiliating instruction to Felipe Massa to concede the lead to Fernando Alonso at Hockenheim. His efforts to justify the decision on the grounds that Ferrari always puts team effort before individual achievement was fair enough, but it only told part of the story.

The complete truth of the matter is that Ferrari has an established standing order that its drivers hold position when they get to the front of the field. Thus, according to that well-practised Maranello tradition, Alonso should have followed Massa all the way to the chequered flag from the moment he completed the opening lap in second position.

Many years ago, it was confirmed to the writer by Piero Ferrari, son of the late *Commendatore*, that team instructions in such circumstances have always been for the two cars to hold station in the order they assume first and second places.

It was the adherence to this convention that ensured Jody Scheckter was not challenged by team-mate Gilles Villeneuve in the closing stages of the 1979 Italian GP at Monza, victory in which secured the world title for the South African. It was also a major bone of contention at Imola three years later, when Didier Pironi overtook Villeneuve against team orders to win the San Marino GP.

Granted, the era of Jean Todt and Michael Schumacher brought with it an apparent recalibration of Ferrari's strategic priorities, the German driver imposing his dominance on the team's operations, whether through contractual priority or simply the force of his character and driving ability. But whenever there was any sort of intra-team rift, the cracks were always papered over by falling back on the old mantra that the team's interests were the priority.

Niki Lauda, a man well versed in the political machinations at Maranello, certainly did not mince his words when asked to comment on the strategic decision at Hockenheim. Speaking to the *Daily Mail*, Lauda said he couldn't understand why the team had taken the decision at this stage of the season and why Massa hadn't been given the opportunity to secure victory himself.

"This was the most stupid thing I have ever seen from Ferrari," he said. "Why did they do it? They did not need to because the championship is alive for another eight races.

"Why could Massa not have a chance to win, a year since he had the accident that could have cost his life?"

The Austrian also hit out at Alonso for the manner in which he had dealt with the press in the immediate aftermath of the race, when he denied that team orders had been issued.

"I've never heard a driver talk such bull****," he said. "He has no character."

Of course, the ultimate irony is that Ferrari's on-track strategy directly contradicted its statements. If team interests were the priority, it would not have interfered with Massa's race. By favouring Alonso, Ferrari proved that the Spaniard's interest in winning the drivers' world championship was the most crucial imperative.

Alan Henry

FIA F1 WORLD CHAMPIONSHIP · ROUND 11

GROSSER PREIS SANTANDER VON DEUTSCHLAND

HOCKENHEIM 23–25 JULY 2010

RACE DISTANCE: 67 laps, 190.424 miles/306.458km

RACE WEATHER: Sunny/cloudy (track 27–30°C, air 22–24°C)

HOCKENHEIM-RING, HOCKENHEIM

Circuit: 2.842 miles / 4.574km

67 laps

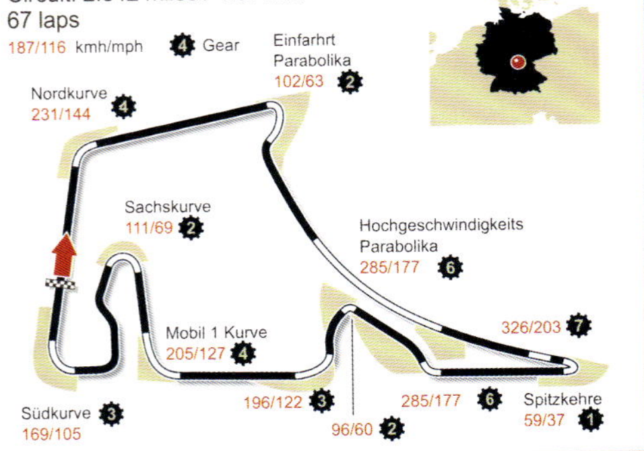

Pos.	Driver	Nat.	No.	Entrant	Car/Engine	Tyres	Laps	Time/Retirement	Speed (mph/km/h)	Gap to leader	Fastest race lap	
1	**Fernando Alonso**	E	8	Scuderia Ferrari Marlboro	Ferrari F10-056 V8	B	67	1h 27m 38.864s	130.356/209.788		1m 15.880s	66
2	**Felipe Massa**	BR	7	Scuderia Ferrari Marlboro	Ferrari F10-056 V8	B	67	1h 27m 43.060s	130.252/209.621	+ 4.196s	1m 16.097s	66
3	**Sebastian Vettel**	D	5	Red Bull Racing	Red Bull RB6-Renault RS27 V8	B	67	1h 27m 43.985s	130.229/209.584	+ 5.121s	1m 15.824s	67
4	**Lewis Hamilton**	GB	2	Vodafone McLaren Mercedes	McLaren MP4-25-Mercedes FO108X V8	B	67	1h 28m 05.760s	129.693/208.720	+ 26.896s	1m 16.503s	65
5	**Jenson Button**	GB	1	Vodafone McLaren Mercedes	McLaren MP4-25-Mercedes FO108X V8	B	67	1h 28m 08.346s	129.629/208.618	+ 29.482s	1m 16.451s	65
6	**Mark Webber**	AUS	6	Red Bull Racing	Red Bull RB6-Renault RS27 V8	B	67	1h 28m 22.470s	129.284/208.063	+ 43.606s	1m 16.678s	57
7	**Robert Kubica**	PL	11	Renault F1 Team	Renault R30-RS27 V8	B	66			+ 1 lap	1m 17.166s	62
8	**Nico Rosberg**	D	4	Mercedes GP Petronas F1 Team	Mercedes MGP W01-Mercedes FO108X V8	B	66			+ 1 lap	1m 16.609s	66
9	**Michael Schumacher**	GB	3	Mercedes GP Petronas F1 Team	Mercedes MGP W01-Mercedes FO108X V8	B	66			+ 1 lap	1m 17.088s	66
10	**Vitaly Petrov**	RUS	12	Renault F1 Team	Renault R30-RS27 V8	B	66			+ 1 lap	1m 17.198s	62
11	Kamui Kobayashi	J	23	BMW Sauber F1 Team	BMW Sauber C29-Ferrari 056 V8	B	66			+ 1 lap	1m 17.100s	63
12	Rubens Barrichello	BR	9	AT&T Williams	Williams FW32-Cosworth CA2010 V8	B	66			+ 1 lap	1m 17.029s	63
13	Nico Hülkenberg	D	10	AT&T Williams	Williams FW32-Cosworth CA2010 V8	B	66			+ 1 lap	1m 16.836s	61
14	Pedro de la Rosa	E	22	BMW Sauber F1 Team	BMW Sauber C29-Ferrari 056 V8	B	66			+ 1 lap	1m 16.527s	61
15	Jaime Alguersuari	E	17	Scuderia Toro Rosso	Toro Rosso STR5-Ferrari 056 V8	B	66			+ 1 lap	1m 16.971s	66
16	Vitantonio Liuzzi	I	15	Force India F1 Team	Force India VJM03-Mercedes FO108X V8	B	65			+ 2 laps	1m 16.596s	64
17	Adrian Sutil	D	14	Force India F1 Team	Force India VJM03-Mercedes FO108X V8	B	65			+ 2 laps	1m 16.687s	65
18	Timo Glock	D	24	Virgin Racing	Virgin VR-01-Cosworth CA2010 V8	B	64			+ 3 laps	1m 18.211s	62
19	Bruno Senna	BR	21	HRT F1 Team	HRT F110-Cosworth CA2010 V8	B	63			+ 4 laps	1m 20.861s	57
	Heikki Kovalainen	FIN	19	Lotus Racing	Lotus T127-Cosworth CA2010 V8	B	56	*accident*			1m 20.664s	51
	Lucas di Grassi	BR	25	Virgin Racing	Virgin VR-01-Cosworth CA2010 V8	B	50	*spin*			1m 20.703s	49
	Sakon Yamamoto	J	20	HRT F1 Team	HRT F110-Cosworth CA2010 V8	B	19	*gearbox*			1m 23.541s	16
	Jarno Trulli	I	18	Lotus Racing	Lotus T127-Cosworth CA2010 V8	B	3	*gearbox*			2m 14.452s	2
	Sébastien Buemi	CH	16	Scuderia Toro Rosso	Toro Rosso STR5-Ferrari 056 V8	B	1	*accident/rear wing*			no time	

Fastest race lap: Sebastian Vettel on lap 67, 1m 15.824s, 134.941mph/217.166km/h.

Lap record: Riccardo Patrese (Williams FW14B V10), 1m 41.591s, 150.060mph/241.498km/h (1992) (4.235-mile/6.815km circuit)

Lap record (current configuration): Kimi Räikkönen (McLaren MP4-19B-Mercedes Benz V10), 1m 13.780s, 138.679mph/223.182km/h (2004).

Grid order		1	2	3	4	5	6	7	8	9	10	11	12	13	14	15	16	17	18	19	20	21	22	23	24	25	26
5	VETTEL	7	7	7	7	7	7	7	7	7	7	7	7	7	7	1	1	1	1	1	1	1	1	7	7	7	7
8	ALONSO	8	8	8	8	8	8	8	8	8	8	8	8	8	2	7	7	7	7	7	7	7	7	8	8	8	8
7	MASSA	5	5	5	5	5	5	5	5	5	5	5	5	2	1	8	8	8	8	8	8	8	8	5	5	5	5
6	WEBBER	2	2	2	2	2	2	2	2	2	2	2	2	6	8	5	5	5	5	5	5	5	5	2	2	2	2
1	BUTTON	6	6	6	6	6	6	6	6	6	6	6	6	1	5	11	11	2	2	2	2	2	2	1	1	1	1
2	HAMILTON	1	1	1	1	1	1	1	1	1	1	1	1	5	11	2	2	4	4	4	4	6	6	6	6	6	6
11	KUBICA	11	11	11	11	11	11	11	11	11	11	11	11	11	4	4	4	6	6	6	6	4	4	4	4	10	10
9	BARRICHELLO	3	3	3	3	3	3	3	3	3	3	3	3	3	6	6	6	11	12	12	12	12	12	12	10	22	22
4	ROSBERG	4	4	4	4	4	4	4	4	4	4	4	4	4	3	12	12	12	10	10	10	10	10	10	22	11	11
10	HULKENBERG	23	23	23	23	23	23	23	23	23	23	23	23	23	23	23	10	10	22	22	22	22	22	22	11	4	4
3	SCHUMACHER	9	9	9	9	9	9	9	9	9	9	9	9	9	12	10	22	22	11	11	11	11	11	11	3	3	3
23	KOBAYASHI	12	12	12	12	12	12	12	12	12	12	12	12	12	10	22	3	3	3	3	3	3	3	3	12	12	12
12	PETROV	10	10	10	10	10	10	10	10	10	10	10	10	10	9	3	23	23	23	23	23	23	23	23	23	23	23
22	DE LA ROSA	22	22	22	22	22	22	22	22	22	22	22	22	22	22	9	9	9	9	9	9	9	9	9	9	9	9
17	ALGUERSUARI	18	19	19	19	19	19	19	19	19	19	19	19	19	19	19	19	19	19	19	19	19	17	17	17	17	14
16	BUEMI	19	25	25	25	25	25	25	25	25	25	25	25	25	25	25	25	25	25	17	17	17	19	19	14	14	17
18	TRULLI	25	21	21	21	21	21	21	21	21	21	21	21	21	21	21	21	17	17	25	14	14	14	14	19	25	25
19	KOVALAINEN	21	20	20	24	24	24	24	24	24	24	24	24	24	24	17	17	21	14	14	25	25	25	25	25	15	15
14	SUTIL	14	24	24	20	20	20	20	20	20	20	20	17	17	17	24	24	14	21	21	21	24	24	24	24	24	24
21	SENNA	20	14	14	14	17	17	17	17	17	17	17	20	20	14	14	14	24	24	24	24	21	15	15	15	19	19
15	LIUZZI	24	17	17	17	15	14	14	14	14	14	14	14	14	20	20	20	20	15	15	15	15	21	21	21	21	21
20	YAMAMOTO	15	15	15	15	14	15	15	15	15	15	15	15	15	15	15	15	15	20	20							
24	GLOCK	16	18	18																							
25	DI GRASSI	17																									

Grid order		27	28	29	30	31	32	33	34	35	36	37	38	39	40	41	42	43	44	45	46	47	48	49	50	51	52
5	VETTEL	7	7	7	7	7	7	7	7	7	7	7	7	7	7	7	7	7	7	7	7	7	7	8	8	8	8
8	ALONSO	8	8	8	8	8	8	8	8	8	8	8	8	8	8	8	8	8	8	8	8	8	8	7	7	7	7
7	MASSA	5	5	5	5	5	5	5	5	5	5	5	5	5	5	5	5	5	5	5	5	5	5	5	5	5	5
6	WEBBER	2	2	2	2	2	2	2	2	2	2	2	2	2	2	2	2	2	2	2	2	2	2	2	2	2	2
1	BUTTON	1	1	1	1	1	1	1	1	1	1	1	1	1	1	1	1	1	1	1	1	1	1	1	1	1	1
2	HAMILTON	6	6	6	6	6	6	6	6	6	6	6	6	6	6	6	6	6	6	6	6	6	6	6	6	6	6
11	KUBICA	10	10	10	10	10	10	10	22	22	22	22	22	22	22	22	22	22	22	22	22	22	22	22	22	11	11
9	BARRICHELLO	22	22	22	22	22	22	22	11	11	11	11	11	11	11	11	11	11	11	11	11	11	11	11	11	22	4
4	ROSBERG	11	11	11	11	11	11	11	4	4	4	4	4	4	4	4	4	4	4	4	4	4	4	4	4	4	3
10	HULKENBERG	4	4	4	4	4	4	4	10	3	3	3	3	3	3	3	3	3	3	3	3	3	3	3	3	3	12
3	SCHUMACHER	3	3	3	3	3	3	3	3	12	12	12	12	12	12	12	12	12	12	12	12	12	12	12	12	12	23
23	KOBAYASHI	12	12	12	12	12	12	12	12	23	23	23	23	23	23	23	23	23	23	23	23	23	23	23	23	23	9
12	PETROV	23	23	23	23	23	23	23	23	9	9	9	9	9	9	9	9	9	9	9	9	9	9	9	9	9	10
22	DE LA ROSA	9	9	9	9	9	9	9	9	10	10	10	10	10	10	10	10	10	10	10	10	10	10	10	10	10	22
17	ALGUERSUARI	14	14	14	14	14	14	14	17	17	17	17	17	17	17	17	17	17	17	17	17	17	17	17	17	17	17
16	BUEMI	17	17	17	17	17	17	17	14	15	15	15	15	15	15	15	15	15	15	15	15	15	15	15	15	15	15
18	TRULLI	25	15	15	15	15	15	15	15	14	14	14	14	14	14	14	14	14	14	14	14	14	14	14	14	14	14
19	KOVALAINEN	15	25	25	25	25	25	25	25	25	25	25	25	25	25	25	25	25	25	25	25	25	25	25	24	24	24
14	SUTIL	24	24	24	24	24	24	24	24	24	24	24	24	24	24	24	24	24	24	24	24	24	24	24	19	19	19
21	SENNA	19	19	19	19	19	19	19	19	19	19	19	19	19	19	19	19	19	19	19	19	19	19	19	21	21	21
15	LIUZZI	21	21	21	21	21	21	21	21	21	21	21	21	21	21	21	21	21	21	21	21	21	21	21	25		
20	YAMAMOTO																										
24	GLOCK																										
25	DI GRASSI																										

TIME SHEETS

PRACTICE 1 (FRIDAY)

Weather: Rain/cloudy

Temperatures: track 20-21°C, air 19-20°C

Pos.	Driver	Laps	Time
1	Adrian Sutil	20	1m 25.701s
2	Felipe Massa	27	1m 26.850s
3	Jenson Button	16	1m 26.936s
4	Rubens Barrichello	21	1m 26.947s
5	Vitaly Petrov	21	1m 26.948s
6	Nico Rosberg	20	1m 27.448s
7	Sébastien Buemi	31	1m 28.114s
8	Nico Hülkenberg	24	1m 28.193s
9	Vitantonio Liuzzi	19	1m 28.300s
10	Pedro de la Rosa	23	1m 28.486s
11	Sebastian Vettel	21	1m 28.735s
12	Timo Glock	21	1m 28.735s
13	Robert Kubica	20	1m 28.903s
14	Mark Webber	13	1m 29.048s
15	Jarno Trulli	17	1m 29.280s
16	Jaime Alguersuari	34	1m 29.366s
17	Lewis Hamilton	8	1m 29.429s
18	Lucas di Grassi	19	1m 29.500s
19	Fernando Alonso	15	1m 29.684s
20	Kamui Kobayashi	17	1m 29.690s
21	Fairuz Fauzy	27	1m 30.938s
22	Bruno Senna	23	1m 31.720s
23	Michael Schumacher	13	1m 32.450s
24	Sakon Yamamoto	26	1m 32.791s

PRACTICE 2 (FRIDAY)

Weather: Cloudy/drizzle/cloudy

Temperatures: track 21-23°C, air 21°C

Pos.	Driver	Laps	Time
1	Fernando Alonso	35	1m 16.265s
2	Sebastian Vettel	26	1m 16.294s
3	Felipe Massa	37	1m 16.438s
4	Mark Webber	40	1m 16.585s
5	Nico Rosberg	32	1m 16.827s
6	Michael Schumacher	20	1m 16.971s
7	Lewis Hamilton	10	1m 17.004s
8	Robert Kubica	37	1m 17.009s
9	Rubens Barrichello	37	1m 17.056s
10	Nico Hülkenberg	44	1m 17.204s
11	Kamui Kobayashi	44	1m 17.336s
12	Vitaly Petrov	35	1m 17.547s
13	Pedro de la Rosa	39	1m 17.573s
14	Adrian Sutil	38	1m 17.701s
15	Jenson Button	36	1m 17.739s
16	Vitantonio Liuzzi	33	1m 17.871s
17	Sébastien Buemi	45	1m 18.147s
18	Jaime Alguersuari	48	1m 19.327s
19	Timo Glock	30	1m 19.553s
20	Jarno Trulli	34	1m 20.008s
21	Lucas di Grassi	31	1m 20.106s
22	Heikki Kovalainen	37	1m 20.377s
23	Bruno Senna	37	1m 21.988s
24	Sakon Yamamoto	37	1m 23.066s

PRACTICE 3 (SATURDAY)

Weather: Drizzle/cloudy

Temperatures: track 20-22°C, air 19-20°C

Pos.	Driver	Laps	Time
1	Sebastian Vettel	18	1m 15.103s
2	Fernando Alonso	21	1m 15.387s
3	Mark Webber	16	1m 15.708s
4	Felipe Massa	20	1m 15.854s
5	Nico Rosberg	20	1m 16.046s
6	Lewis Hamilton	13	1m 16.207s
7	Michael Schumacher	16	1m 16.473s
8	Rubens Barrichello	23	1m 16.481s
9	Robert Kubica	20	1m 16.646s
10	Nico Hülkenberg	17	1m 16.743s
11	Kamui Kobayashi	19	1m 16.882s
12	Sébastien Buemi	21	1m 16.990s
13	Jenson Button	15	1m 17.037s
14	Vitaly Petrov	20	1m 17.148s
15	Pedro de la Rosa	19	1m 17.220s
16	Jaime Alguersuari	21	1m 17.341s
17	Vitantonio Liuzzi	22	1m 17.538s
18	Heikki Kovalainen	11	1m 19.193s
19	Jarno Trulli	10	1m 19.607s
20	Bruno Senna	9	1m 20.533s
21	Sakon Yamamoto	14	1m 21.538s
22	Lucas di Grassi	10	1m 23.444s
23	Timo Glock	7	1m 23.873s
24	Adrian Sutil	2	no time

QUALIFYING (SATURDAY)

Weather: Cloudy/sunny/cloud Temperatures: track 23-26°C, air 20-22°C

Pos.	Driver	First	Second	Third	Qualifying Tyre
1	Sebastian Vettel	1m 15.152s	1m 14.249s	1m 13.791s	Super-Soft
2	Fernando Alonso	1m 14.808s	1m 14.081s	1m 13.793s	Super-Soft
3	Felipe Massa	1m 15.216s	1m 14.478s	1m 14.290s	Super-Soft
4	Mark Webber	1m 15.334s	1m 14.340s	1m 14.347s	Super-Soft
5	Jenson Button	1m 15.823s	1m 14.716s	1m 14.427s	Super-Soft
6	Lewis Hamilton	1m 15.505s	1m 14.488s	1m 14.566s	Super-Soft
7	Robert Kubica	1m 15.736s	1m 14.835s	1m 15.079s	Super-Soft
8	Rubens Barrichello	1m 16.398s	1m 14.698s	1m 15.109s	Super-Soft
9	Nico Rosberg	1m 16.178s	1m 15.018s	1m 15.179s	Super-Soft
10	Nico Hülkenberg	1m 16.387s	1m 14.943s	1m 15.339s	Super-Soft
11	Michael Schumacher	1m 16.084s	1m 15.026s		
12	Kamui Kobayashi	1m 15.951s	1m 15.084s		
13	Vitaly Petrov	1m 16.521s	1m 15.307s		
14	Adrian Sutil	1m 16.220s	1m 15.467s		
15	Pedro de la Rosa	1m 16.450s	1m 15.550s		
16	Jaime Alguersuari	1m 16.664s	1m 15.588s		
17	Sébastien Buemi	1m 16.029s	1m 15.974s		
18	Jarno Trulli	1m 17.583s			
19	Heikki Kovalainen	1m 18.300s			
20	Timo Glock	1m 18.343s			
21	Bruno Senna	1m 18.592s			
22	Vitantonio Liuzzi	1m 18.952s			
23	Sakon Yamamoto	1m 19.844s			
24	Lucas di Grassi	no time			

FOR THE RECORD

150th START: **Fernando Alonso**

10th FASTEST LAP: **Red Bull**

DID YOU KNOW

2010 was the 40th anniversary of the first German Grand Prix at Hockenheim.

This was Ferrari's 20th victory at the German Grand Prix

POINTS

DRIVERS

1	Lewis Hamilton	157
2	Jenson Button	143
3	Mark Webber	136
4	Sebastian Vettel	136
5	Fernando Alonso	123
6	Nico Rosberg	94
7	Robert Kubica	89
8	Felipe Massa	85
9	Michael Schumacher	38
10	Adrian Sutil	35
11	Rubens Barrichello	29
12	Kamui Kobayashi	15
13	Vitantonio Liuzzi	12
14	Vitaly Petrov	7
15	Sébastien Buemi	7
16	Jaime Alguersuari	3
17	Nico Hülkenberg	2

CONSTRUCTORS

1	McLaren	300
2	Red Bull	272
3	Ferrari	208
4	Mercedes	132
5	Renault	96
6	Force India	47
7	Williams	31
8	BMW Sauber	15
9	Toro Rosso	10

53	54	55	56	57	58	59	60	61	62	63	64	65	66	67
8	8	8	8	8	8	8	8	8	8	8	8	8	8	8
7	7	7	7	7	7	7	7	7	7	7	7	7	7	7
5	5	5	5	5	5	5	5	5	5	5	5	5	5	5
2	2	2	2	2	2	2	2	2	2	2	2	2	2	2
1	1	1	1	1	1	1	1	1	1	1	1	1	1	1
6	6	6	6	6	6	6	6	6	6	6	6	6	6	6
11	11	11	11	11	11	11	11	11	11	11	11	11	11	
4	4	4	4	4	4	4	4	4	4	4	4	4	4	
3	3	3	3	3	3	3	3	3	3	3	3	3	3	
12	12	12	12	12	12	12	12	12	12	12	12	12	12	
23	23	23	23	23	23	23	23	23	23	23	23	23	23	
9	9	9	9	9	9	9	9	9	9	9	9	9	9	
22	22	22	22	22	10	10	10	10	10	10	10	10	10	
10	10	10	10	10	22	11	11	11	11	11	11	11	11	
17	17	17	17	17	17	17	17	17	17	17	17	17	17	
15	15	15	15	15	15	15	15	15	15	15	15	15		
14	14	14	14	14	14	14	14	14	14	14	14	14		
19	19	19	24	24	24	24	24	24	24	24	24			
24	24	24	21	21	21	21	21	21	21	21				
21	21	21	19											

21 Pit stop *14 One lap or more behind*

RACE TYRE STRATEGIES

	Driver	Race Stint 1	Race Stint 2	Race Stint 3	Race Stint 4
1	Alonso	Super-Soft: 1-13	Hard: 14-67		
2	Massa	Super-Soft: 1-14	Hard: 15-67		
3	Vettel	Super-Soft: 1-12	Hard: 13-67		
4	Hamilton	Super-Soft: 1-14	Hard: 15-67		
5	Button	Super-Soft: 1-22	Hard: 23-67		
6	Webber	Super-Soft: 1-13	Hard: 14-67		
7	Kubica	Super-Soft: 1-17	Hard: 18-66		
8	Rosberg	Super-Soft: 1-24	Hard: 25-66		
9	Schumacher	Super-Soft: 1-14	Hard: 15-66		
10	Petrov	Super-Soft: 1-23	Hard: 24-66		
11	Kobayashi	Super-Soft; 1-15	Hard: 16-66		
12	Barrichello	Super-Soft: 1-14	Hard: 15-66		
13	Hülkenberg	Super-Soft: 1-34	Hard: 35-66		
14	de la Rosa	Hard: 1-51	Super-Soft: 52-58	Hard: 59-66	
15	Alguersuari	Hard: 1	Super-Soft: 2-25	Super-Soft: 26-66	
16	Liuzzi	Hard: 1	Super-Soft: 2-5	Hard: 6-62	Super-Soft: 63-65
17	Sutil	Super-Soft: 1	Hard: 2-4	Hard: 5-34	Super-Soft: 35-65
18	Glock	Hard: 1-52	Super-Soft: 53-64		
19	Senna	Super-Soft: 1-21	Hard: 22-39	Hard: 40-63	
	Kovalainen	Super-Soft: 1-24	Hard: 25-56 (dnf)		
	di Grassi	Hard: 1-50 (dnf)			
	Yamamoto	Super-Soft 1-17	Hard: 18-19 (dnf)		
	Trulli	Hard: 1-2	Super-Soft: 3 (dnf)		
	Buemi	Hard: 1 (dnf)			

The tyre regulations stipulate that the two dry tyre specifications must be used during the race.
The Super-Soft compound Bridgestone Potenza tyre is marked with a green stripe on the sidewall.

Photos: Peter J. Fox

FIA FORMULA 1 WORLD CHAMPIONSHIP · ROUND 12

HUNGARIAN GRAND PRIX

HUNGARORING CIRCUIT

Left: Mark Webber is elated after securing his fourth win of the season in the Red Bull RB6.
Photo: Peter J Fox

Main photo: They're off! The starting lights go out at the Hungaroring, and the two Red Bulls are about to lead the sprint to the first corner.
Photo: Peter J Fox

HUNGARORING QUALIFYING

"WE have to be realistic," said Fernando Alonso. "Sometimes we are able to match Red Bull's race pace, but that's when they qualify a couple of tenths ahead of us, not 1.2 seconds..."

At the Hungaroring, a circuit with a proliferation of corners and no major straights worth the name, the Red Bull RB6 was in a class all its own. Sebastian Vettel and Mark Webber had traded fastest laps throughout the first day and a half, but in Q3 – when such things mattered most – the German managed a magical 1m 18.772s that put him 0.411s clear of his team-mate. And Webber was first to pay tribute. "I didn't get a clean run today," he said, "but that was a great lap from Seb."

And then some.

"I don't think there's any big secret," said Vettel, who annexed his seventh pole of the campaign in Red Bull's 100th grand prix. "I played around a little with the front wing, the differential and tyre pressures – sometimes fine-tuning the tyres can find you three tenths. We knew we were in good shape yesterday, but didn't know quite how good. If you look back just a few days to Germany, Ferrari was quickest in the race. I don't think any of the cars has changed a great deal since then, but it's very clear that this circuit suits us. It isn't an easy track – the bumps are quite harsh and that makes the car very nervous, but I felt confident. Everything just works, basically."

Alonso was best of the rest, ahead of team-mate Felipe Massa – who visited medical staff early in the weekend, to thank them for the efficient way they dealt with the serious head injury he'd suffered here in 2009 (when suspension debris from Rubens Barrichello's Brawn struck him on the crash helmet during qualifying). If he harboured any reservations, they didn't show in his car's body language – and he was particularly good to watch through Turn Five, a fast, uphill right-hander, where he looked more aggressive than most as he embraced the exit kerb "To be honest," Massa said, "I don't remember anything about the accident, even though I've watched it many times. Now, when you're sitting in the car and you close your visor, you don't think about such things."

Barrichello, eighth for Williams, offered an interesting insight into his compatriot's mindset. "I don't think Felipe will fear anything," he said. "Three or four months ago we were back in Brazil, playing poker. He told me he had a surprise for me and put the helmet from the accident on the table. He had fun with it, but it completely destroyed my night and I started losing money..."

Lewis Hamilton was fifth for McLaren – a car that team principal Martin Whitmarsh described as "the fastest with fixed wings". Rivals remained convinced that Red Bull and Ferrari were using front wings that flexed illegally when their cars were on the move, although intense technical scrutiny had yet to reveal anything amiss.

Hamilton's team-mate Jenson Button was only 11th – having been unable to find a favourable balance on Bridgestone's super-soft tyre in Q2 – but his problems were small beer compared with those of Michael Schumacher. "My set-up is targeted more towards the race than qualifying," said the German, after qualifying 14th. "It worked OK this morning, but became less effective as track temperatures rose."

On a day of surprisingly large numbers, the eight places and, in Q2, 0.819s that separated him from team-mate Nico Rosberg were among the most eye-catching.

Right: Sebastian Vettel momentarily drops too far back behind team-mate Webber, who is tucked in tight behind the Mercedes safety car. That fleeting few seconds of inattention cost him any chance of a victory.
Photo: GP Photo/Peter Nygaard

Below: Sébastien Buemi deep in consultation with the Toro Rosso technical crew.

Below left: Tyre matters. Discarded stencils to denote left- or right-hand tyres and individual markings show the attention to detail required.
Photos: Peter J Fox

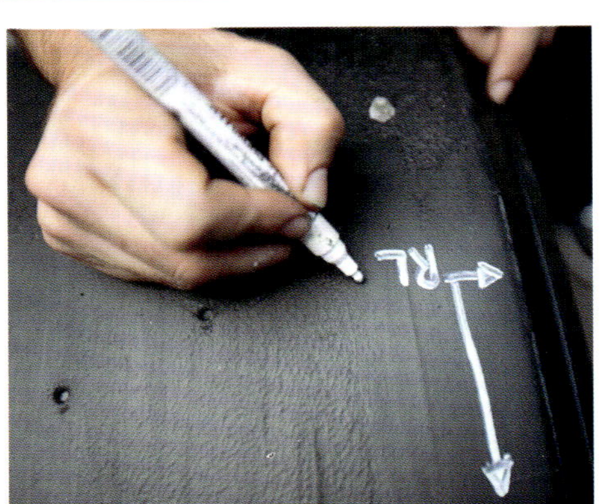

IT was but a moment's inattention, wholly insignificant in the scheme of things, but the consequences were disproportionately dramatic. Sebastian Vettel should have won the Hungarian Grand Prix very comfortably, and his defeat stemmed not from a misjudged apex or a fumbled tyre stop, but because he had failed to spot that the safety car's lights had just been extinguished – a new and peculiar twist in the canon of motor racing excuses. Red Bull team-mate Mark Webber wasn't complaining, though.

The Australian hadn't been in a particularly positive frame of mind at the start, as Vettel streaked away from pole and Fernando Alonso thrust his Ferrari through from third on the grid to beat Webber into Turn One. "When Fernando came past me," he said, "I thought, 'Here we go, it's Budapest again.'"

The Hungaroring is traditionally very dirty off the racing line, and Webber knew better than most that he was likely to be a sitting duck. Back in 2003, he'd qualified his Jaguar an improbable third at the same venue, taken second at the start and then, armed only with a middling car, delayed most of the field until the first round of pit stops. Alonso was the main beneficiary that day, scorching away to cement his maiden F1 success.

Vettel's margin of superiority might have been substantial during qualifying, but it was nothing compared with what followed. With a Ferrari behind him, rather than Webber, he pulled 1.349 seconds clear during the opening lap and almost doubled that advantage within two. Felipe Massa ran fourth, ahead of Vitaly Petrov, Lewis Hamilton, Nico Rosberg, Robert Kubica, Rubens Barrichello, Nico Hülkenberg, Pedro de la Rosa, Adrian Sutil, Michael Schumacher (who lost time by running wide at Turn One), Tonio Liuzzi, Jenson Button, Kamui Kobayashi (who described his start as "good", a masterclass in understatement given that he'd lined up at the back), Jarno Trulli, Jaime Alguersuari, Sébastien Buemi, Lucas di Grassi, Heikki Kovalainen, Timo Glock, Bruno Senna and Sakon Yamamoto. Alguersuari would be the race's first casualty, with a blown engine on lap two. He didn't see any warning alarms on his dash, but a dense plume of trailing smoke provided a more obvious clue.

With Webber trapped – Alonso's Ferrari was faster down the pit straight and gave him ample protection on the approach to Turn One, the only feasible passing spot – Vettel continued to pull away and stalemate beckoned.

Button and Liuzzi made the race's first scheduled stops, on lap 14; soon after rejoining, the Italian lost a significant section of his front wing, which had been scuffed during the opening lap and finally shook itself apart. A large chunk of debris landed in the middle of Turn 11, not a major issue, but it was more easily retrievable if the race was neutralised behind the safety car.

Vettel's radio had been faulty from the start and he was struggling to hear engineer Guillaume Rocquelin, but as he came out of the final corner, he spotted a trackside 'SC' board just in time and swerved right, across a stout kerb, to squeeze into the pit lane at the last possible moment. Tactically, it was the logical thing to do, and almost everybody else peeled in, too. Webber stayed out, though, assuming the race lead.

The pit lane was chaotic rather than merely busy. Renault gave Kubica the signal to depart just as the incoming Sutil was aiming for the adjacent Force India pit: the subsequent impact put the German out on the spot, while Kubica rejoined after repairs, but was handed a stop-go penalty for causing a collision. In the end, that simply became a 'stop' penalty: having examined the unusual loads to which Kubica's front suspension had been subjected, the team opted to withdraw the car on safety grounds.

Life was no more straightforward at Mercedes, where the lollipop man gave Rosberg the signal to go as soon as he saw the right rear wheel crew moving away from the car. The nut had flown from the air-gun, however, and one of the team was scurrying into the garage to locate a replacement. Rosberg wobbled only a few metres before the wheel worked loose, scythed through the middle of the Sauber pit and eventually bowled over Williams mechanic Nigel Hope, who was not seriously hurt and soon returned to duty.

Mercedes and Renault were later fined $50,000 apiece for "unsafe conduct".

At the front, Webber's plan was to stay out for as long as possible in a bid to build a big enough lead to be able to make his tyre change and rejoin in front of Alonso. He was about to be handed an unexpected bonus, however. When the race restarted at the end of lap 17, Vettel wasn't paying full attention. "I didn't see the safety car lights go out," he said, "and with my radio not working, I hadn't heard any message. I really thought we had one more slow lap to do."

Right: A close call in the pit lane: Nico Rosberg's Mercedes sheds its right rear wheel as he accelerates back into the race. Meanwhile, Sutil's Force India and Kubica's Renault become embroiled in their own private tangle.
Photo: Peter J Fox

Below: Nico Hülkenberg had his best race of the season to date for the Williams team.

Bottom: Pedro de la Rosa scored some useful points for Sauber.
Photos: Jean-François Galeron/WRi2

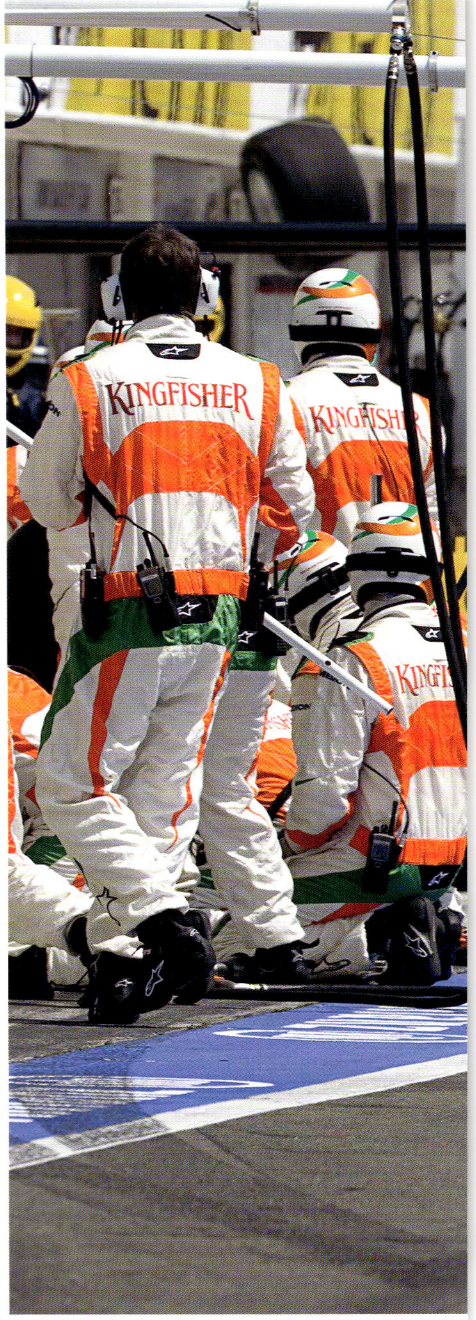

The rules dictate that drivers must remain within ten lengths of each other before a restart, to prevent teams from using one car tactically to benefit the other, but with Webber alert and Vettel napping, the gap between the Red Bulls was significantly more. The German was handed a drive-through penalty, served on lap 31, and thereafter was condemned to spend the afternoon where Webber had started it, behind Alonso.

There was still ample life in Webber's original set of super-soft Bridgestones and his pace during the next phase of the race was sensational – several series of ultra-quick laps, with an occasional pause to allow his tyres a little respite.

"It was a brilliant performance," said Red Bull sporting director Christian Horner. "Mark did a run of what were effectively qualifying laps."

Before the race, teams expected the super-soft to be raceable for 30 laps or so, but Webber stayed out for 43. "The front left was pretty much finished by then," he said. "I needed to build a lead of about 20 seconds to stay ahead of the Ferrari. I was aiming for a bit more, though, to reduce the pressure on the guys during the stop."

In the space of 26 laps, he'd stretched his lead to 23.7 seconds, and his fourth victory of the year was secure.

"By the time I switched to the mediums," he said, "the others had already done 20-odd laps on theirs and the race was pretty much in the bag. I know Seb had some difficulties before the restart, so today was a bit of a gift for me, but I've not had many of those, so I'll take it."

It was a fitting way to celebrate a double landmark: his 150th F1 start and Red Bull's 100th. And it was also enough to put him back in the championship lead, not least because Hamilton retired. The Englishman had moved up to fourth after passing Massa during the tyre stops, but gearbox failure stopped him six laps beyond the restart.

As he had done earlier with Webber, Alonso absorbed Vettel's persistent pressure to take second, but acknowledged that he had been a touch fortunate. "After all this year's bad luck," he said, "I think we remain in credit. If we receive five or six more presents like this, it still won't be enough."

Vettel, heart pounding away stoutly on his sleeve, took a while to comprehend why he had been given a drive-through – and he wasn't particularly impressed when the truth percolated. "I'm obviously disappointed," he said. "Last week at Hockenheim, one team [hello, Ferrari, that means you] clearly breached a rule, but received a penalty that didn't affect the result. Today, I made a small mistake and it cost me a race I should have won."

He had just cause to be irritated, too. At the time of his perceived offence, there were bigger gaps between cars further back in the field (21 seconds from Liuzzi to Kovalainen, for instance), but he was the only driver punished.

Massa completed a largely anonymous afternoon in fourth place, but there were some intriguing cameos in his slipstream. Petrov and Hülkenberg scored the best results of their fledgling F1 careers: circumstance helped, but their consistent speed was the main contributory factor. The Russian had run slightly wide on lap two, allowing Hamilton to reclaim a place he'd lost at the start, but otherwise drove faultlessly. "It feels wonderful," he said, "because everything ran almost perfectly today. I made a good start, and managed to pass Rosberg and Hamilton into the first corner. After that, I didn't block Lewis too much, because I had a problem with my tyre warm-up and was having to fight the car. I decided to let him through rather than risk a mistake that might cost me more positions."

Having followed team-mate Barrichello at the start, Hülkenberg benefited from the safety car's intervention because the Brazilian had started the race on medium tyres and felt the interruption had come too soon to risk switching to super-softs. Eventually he stayed out until lap 55, whereupon his stop dropped him from fifth to 11th, behind ancient nemesis Schumacher,

Barrichello had been quicker than the German all weekend, and that was amplified by a fresh set of super-softs against Schumacher's part-worn mediums. Catching was one thing, though, and passing quite another. He was given an opportunity with four laps to go, however, when Schumacher made a mistake at the last corner and lost momentum coming on to the pit straight. As Barrichello drew to his rival's right, he found himself squeezed ever more

EDITOR'S VIEW
SAME OLD SCHUMACHER

SIX years of partnering Michael Schumacher at Ferrari had certainly given Rubens Barrichello a shrewd and deep understanding of the German driver's psyche, to the point where he knew he would be wasting his breath if he were to remonstrate with the 41-year-old after he had lunged his Mercedes toward the Brazilian's Williams at 190mph on the pit straight at Hungaroring.

Schumacher's three-year absence in (temporary) retirement from F1 had clearly dulled some memories of the starkly uncompromising nature of his unique brand of 'professional foul'. Suddenly, we seemed to be on fast rewind to Michael's halcyon days at Ferrari, when he invented the controversial 'one move' technique, which sometimes saw him steering hard right or left straight off the starting grid.

It is a bad habit that has been picked up by several of the younger generation of drivers, notably Sebastian Vettel, who had very nearly pushed Fernando Alonso's Ferrari into the pit wall as he accelerated away from the grid at Hockenheim the weekend before the Hungarian race.

Rubens did not mince his words, balancing his annoyance with a resigned and measured tone of delivery. He thought it was the most dangerous move he'd seen at any time during his career.

"I like a fair fight," he told German TV straight after the race, "but that wasn't fair here. If Michael wants to go to heaven, in the event that he is going to heaven, then I don't really care. But I don't want to go before him." Strong, some would say extreme, words, and more than enough to revive old enmities and open barely healed sores.

Asked directly whether he would be seeking out Schumacher, Barrichello was adamant that it would not change his long established behavioural pattern. "No, I don't want to, because it won't resolve [anything]," he said. "You know Michael: you talk to him and he always thinks he's right. I just think I'm a fair guy and justice was done today in a way. He's been out of F1 for three years, and we can see he hasn't changed; he's still the same guy.

"I was lucky that the wall finished at that point, because I was millimetres from it. You wouldn't expect someone with so much experience to do that; you would expect someone with ten races to do that kind of thing. But for him, who has been through so many things... He's carrying something from the past that was not necessary today."

On the Monday after the race, having been hit with a $100,000 fine by the stewards, the Mercedes driver said he agreed with the stewards' decision and apologised to Barrichello if the Brazilian felt his driving was dangerous.

"Yesterday, right after the race, I was still in the heat of the action, but after I watched the incident with Rubens again, I must say that the stewards were right with their assessment: the move against him was too hard," Schumacher wrote on his website.

"I wanted to make it hard for him to pass me. I clearly showed him that I didn't want to let him pass, but... I wasn't seeking to endanger him with my move. If he feels I was, then I'm sorry, this wasn't my intention."

Whether Schumacher's belated magnanimity was a case of 'too little, too late' was something for Barrichello to ponder, but there could be little doubt that the multiple champion knew exactly what he was doing. A cynic might be forgiven for concluding that Schumacher only apologised after he saw the way the wind was blowing the day after the race. And possibly after Mercedes had whispered forcefully into his ear.

Alan Henry

Above: Vitaly Petrov delivered an accomplished drive to fourth place for Renault, his best F1 result so far.
Photo: Jean-François Galeron/WRi2

Left: The Williams of Rubens Barrichello is forced into the pit lane exit after a ruthless attempt by Michael Schumacher to prevent the Brazilian from overtaking.
Photo: Sutton Photgraphic

tightly against the pit wall. "Michael had been driving quite dirtily for a few laps," he said, "and there was no way I was going to back off."

Schumacher's vain defence included a brutal 190mph chop that obliged Barrichello to use the pit lane exit road – a good job that the wall ended where it did, and that no other car was coming out – and the Brazilian eventually managed to find his way back to the racing line after flirting with the dirt. It was admirable commitment for the sake of a solitary championship point, but he was fuming about Schumacher's conduct. "It was one of the worst bits of driving I've experienced," he said, "but there's no point talking to Michael about it because he'll think he was right."

The stewards didn't and handed Schumacher a ten-position grid penalty for Belgium, although that wasn't as great a deterrent as it might have been. Schumacher mumbled various excuses about not having known where Rubens was, and having given him space to the other side, but he did eventually issue an apology of sorts by sending Barrichello a text message.

"Michael," said the Brazilian, "knew exactly where I was."

Between the Williams duo, the two Sauber drivers gave a good account of themselves, although de la Rosa, seventh, was as steady as team-mate Kobayashi had been spectacular. The theory runs that overtaking borders on the impossible at the Hungaroring, but apparently that theory was unknown in Japan.

Button had a frustrating afternoon and spent almost all of it studying the Sauber C29's rear-wing profile. He'd made a good start from 11th, but then lost several places when he was bundled wide at the first corner, a situation from which he never really recovered. McLaren team principal Martin Whitmarsh described his performance as "patient and determined", but "mediocre" was probably a more honest assessment. It simply wasn't his weekend at the circuit where he had scored his first win in 2006.

Buemi finished 12th, behind Schumacher, and the order was completed by Liuzzi, Kovalainen, Trulli, Glock, Senna, di Grassi and Yamamoto. The evenly matched Lotus drivers had a good day, beating the other new teams and enjoying a close fight with each other. Trulli had originally dropped behind Kovalainen as a result of not pitting during the safety car period, but they were absolutely together by the race's end, their duel interrupted only when they had to step aside to allow Webber to lap them for a third time.

As at Hockenheim, one week before, the race took place to a backdrop of rumours about the allegedly flexible front wings Red Bull and Ferrari were supposed to be using – and a more stringent series of tests that might be implemented during the summer recess.

The topic cropped up yet again after the race, but Webber just smiled. "Yeah," he quipped. "I think the wing is worth at least one second per lap, if not two. It's like our adjustable front ride height control. It's like everything else that constantly comes up. Our guys have broken their balls to design a car within the spirit of the regulations, and every time the FIA tests it, we pass."

Simon Arron

FIA F1 WORLD CHAMPIONSHIP · ROUND 12

ENI MAGYAR NAGYDÍJ

BUDAPEST 30 JULY–1 AUGUST 2010

RACE DISTANCE: 70 laps, 190.531 miles/306.630km

RACE WEATHER: Sunny (track 38–41°C, air 29°C)

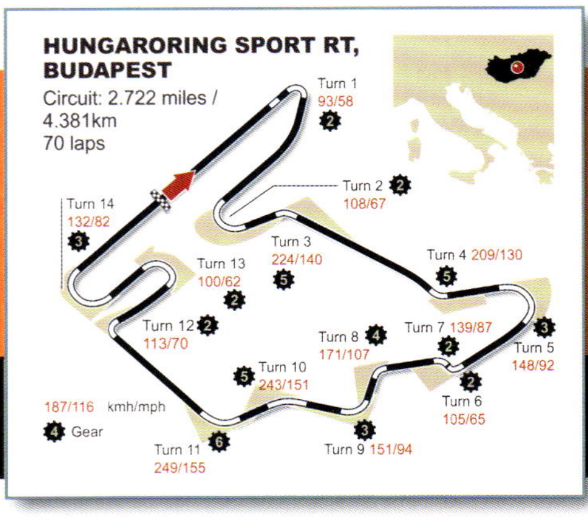

Pos.	Driver	Nat.	No.	Entrant	Car/Engine	Tyres	Laps	Time/Retirement	Speed (mph/km/h)	Gap to leader	Fastest race lap	
1	**Mark Webber**	AUS	6	Red Bull Racing	Red Bull RB6-Renault RS27 V8	B	70	1h 41m 05.571s	113.083/181.989		1m 22.651s	46
2	**Fernando Alonso**	E	8	Scuderia Ferrari Marlboro	Ferrari F10-056 V8	B	70	1h 41m 23.392s	112.751/181.455	+ 17.821s	1m 23.195s	67
3	**Sebastian Vettel**	D	5	Red Bull Racing	Red Bull RB6-Renault RS27 V8	B	70	1h 41m 24.823s	112.725/181.413	+ 19.252s	1m 22.362s	70
4	**Felipe Massa**	BR	7	Scuderia Ferrari Marlboro	Ferrari F10-056 V8	B	70	1h 41m 33.045s	112.573/181.168	+ 27.474s	1m 23.329s	69
5	**Vitaly Petrov**	RUS	12	Renault F1 Team	Renault R30-RS27 V8	B	70	1h 42m 18.763s	111.734/179.819	+ 1m 13.192s	1m 23.799s	61
6	**Nico Hülkenberg**	D	10	AT&T Williams	Williams FW32-Cosworth CA2010 V8	B	70	1h 42m 22.294s	111.670/179.715	+ 1m 16.723s	1m 24.204s	66
7	**Pedro de la Rosa**	E	22	BMW Sauber F1 Team	BMW Sauber C29-Ferrari 056 V8	B	69			+ 1 lap	1m 24.342s	65
8	**Jenson Button**	GB	1	Vodafone McLaren Mercedes	McLaren MP4-25-Mercedes FO108X V8	B	69			+ 1 lap	1m 24.205s	61
9	**Kamui Kobayashi**	J	23	BMW Sauber F1 Team	BMW Sauber C29-Ferrari 056 V8	B	69			+ 1 lap	1m 24.282s	68
10	**Rubens Barrichello**	BR	9	AT&T Williams	Williams FW32-Cosworth CA2010 V8	B	69			+ 1 lap	1m 22.811s	68
11	Michael Schumacher	GB	3	Mercedes GP Petronas F1 Team	Mercedes MGP W01-Mercedes FO108X V8	B	69			+ 1 lap	1m 25.372s	64
12	Sébastien Buemi	CH	16	Scuderia Toro Rosso	Toro Rosso STR5-Ferrari 056 V8	B	69			+ 1 lap	1m 25.449s	58
13	Vitantonio Liuzzi	I	15	Force India F1 Team	Force India VJM03-Mercedes FO108X V8	B	69			+ 1 lap	1m 25.358s	58
14	Heikki Kovalainen	FIN	19	Lotus Racing	Lotus T127-Cosworth CA2010 V8	B	67			+ 3 laps	1m 27.457s	64
15	Jarno Trulli	I	18	Lotus Racing	Lotus T127-Cosworth CA2010 V8	B	67			+ 3 laps	1m 27.429s	58
16	Timo Glock	D	24	Virgin Racing	Virgin VR-01-Cosworth CA2010 V8	B	67			+ 3 laps	1m 27.674s	59
17	Bruno Senna	BR	21	HRT F1 Team	HRT F110-Cosworth CA2010 V8	B	67			+ 3 laps	1m 28.093s	61
18	Lucas di Grassi	BR	25	Virgin Racing	Virgin VR-01-Cosworth CA2010 V8	B	66			+ 4 laps	1m 27.287s	62
19	Sakon Yamamoto	J	20	HRT F1 Team	HRT F110-Cosworth CA2010 V8	B	66			+ 4 laps	1m 29.278s	59
	Lewis Hamilton	GB	2	Vodafone McLaren Mercedes	McLaren MP4-25-Mercedes FO108X V8	B	23	*gearbox*			1m 26.258s	22
	Robert Kubica	PL	11	Renault F1 Team	Renault R30-RS27 V8	B	23	*accident/front suspension*			1m 26.825s	21
	Nico Rosberg	D	4	Mercedes GP Petronas F1 Team	Mercedes MGP W01-Mercedes FO108X V8	B	15	*wheel nut loose/wheel lost*			1m 27.954s	13
	Adrian Sutil	D	14	Force India F1 Team	Force India VJM03-Mercedes FO108X V8	B	15	*accident*			1m 28.177s	12
	Jaime Alguersuari	E	17	Scuderia Toro Rosso	Toro Rosso STR5-Ferrari 056 V8	B	1	*engine*			no time	

Fastest race lap: Sebastian Vettel on lap 70, 1m 22.362s, 118.987mph/191.491km/h.

Lap record: Michael Schumacher (Ferrari F2004 V10), 1m 19.071s, 123.939mph/199.461km/h (2004).

Grid order	1	2	3	4	5	6	7	8	9	10	11	12	13	14	15	16	17	18	19	20	21	22	23	24	25	26	27
5 VETTEL	5	5	5	5	5	5	5	5	5	5	5	5	5	5	5	6	6	6	6	6	6	6	6	6	6	6	6
6 WEBBER	8	8	8	8	8	8	8	8	8	8	8	8	8	8	6	5	5	5	5	5	5	5	5	5	5	5	5
8 ALONSO	6	6	6	6	6	6	6	6	6	6	6	6	6	6	8	8	8	8	8	8	8	8	8	8	8	8	8
7 MASSA	7	7	7	7	7	7	7	7	7	7	7	7	7	7	7	2	2	2	2	2	2	2	2	7	7	7	7
2 HAMILTON	12	2	2	2	2	2	2	2	2	2	2	2	2	2	2	7	7	7	7	7	7	7	7	9	9	9	9
4 ROSBERG	2	12	12	12	12	12	12	12	12	12	12	12	12	12	12	23	9	9	9	9	9	9	9	12	12	12	12
12 PETROV	4	4	4	4	4	4	4	4	4	4	4	4	4	4	4	9	12	12	12	12	12	12	12	10	10	10	10
11 KUBICA	11	11	11	11	11	11	11	11	11	11	11	11	11	11	11	12	10	10	10	10	10	10	10	22	22	22	22
22 DE LA ROSA	9	9	9	9	9	9	9	9	9	9	9	9	9	9	9	10	22	22	22	22	22	22	22	1	1	1	1
10 HÜLKENBERG	10	10	10	10	10	10	10	10	10	10	10	10	10	10	10	22	1	1	1	1	1	1	1	23	23	23	23
1 BUTTON	22	22	22	22	22	22	22	22	22	22	22	22	22	22	22	1	3	23	23	23	23	23	23	3	3	3	3
9 BARRICHELLO	14	14	14	14	14	14	14	14	14	14	14	14	14	14	14	3	23	3	3	3	3	3	3	16	16	16	16
14 SUTIL	3	3	3	3	3	3	3	3	3	3	3	3	3	3	3	16	16	16	16	16	16	16	16	15	15	15	15
3 SCHUMACHER	15	15	15	1	1	1	1	1	1	1	1	1	1	23	23	18	18	15	15	15	15	15	15	19	19	19	19
16 BUEMI	1	1	1	23	23	23	23	23	23	23	23	23	23	1	16	15	15	18	18	18	19	19	19	18	18	18	18
15 LIUZZI	23	23	23	15	15	15	15	15	15	15	15	15	15	16	1	19	19	19	19	19	18	18	18	24	24	24	24
17 ALGUERSUARI	18	18	18	16	16	16	16	16	16	16	16	16	16	15	18	24	24	24	24	24	24	24	24	21	21	21	21
24 GLOCK	17	16	16	18	18	18	18	18	18	18	18	18	18	18	25	21	21	21	21	21	21	21	21	20	20	20	20
19 KOVALAINEN	16	25	25	25	25	25	25	25	25	25	25	25	25	25	19	25	11	11	11	11	11	11	20	25	25	25	25
18 TRULLI	25	19	19	19	19	19	19	19	19	19	19	19	19	19	15	20	20	20	20	20	20	20	25				
25 DI GRASSI	19	24	24	24	24	24	24	24	24	24	24	24	24	24	24	11	25	25	25	25	25	25	11				
21 SENNA	24	21	21	21	21	21	21	21	21	21	21	21	21	21	21												
23 KOBAYASHI	21	20	20	20	20	20	20	20	20	20	20	20	20	20	20												
20 YAMAMOTO	20																										

Grid order	28	29	30	31	32	33	34	35	36	37	38	39	40	41	42	43	44	45	46	47	48	49	50	51	52	53	54
5 VETTEL	6	6	6	6	6	6	6	6	6	6	6	6	6	6	6	6	6	6	6	6	6	6	6	6	6	6	6
6 WEBBER	5	5	5	5	8	8	8	8	8	8	8	8	8	8	8	8	8	8	8	8	8	8	8	8	8	8	8
8 ALONSO	8	8	8	8	5	5	5	5	5	5	5	5	5	5	5	5	5	5	5	5	5	5	5	5	5	5	5
7 MASSA	7	7	7	7	7	7	7	7	7	7	7	7	7	7	7	7	7	7	7	7	7	7	7	7	7	7	7
2 HAMILTON	9	9	9	9	9	9	9	9	9	9	9	9	9	9	9	9	9	9	9	9	9	9	9	9	9	9	9
4 ROSBERG	12	12	12	12	12	12	12	12	12	12	12	12	12	12	12	12	12	12	12	12	12	12	12	12	12	12	12
12 PETROV	10	10	10	10	10	10	10	10	10	10	10	10	10	10	10	10	10	10	10	10	10	10	10	10	10	10	10
11 KUBICA	22	22	22	22	22	22	22	22	22	22	22	22	22	22	22	22	22	22	22	22	22	22	22	22	22	22	22
22 DE LA ROSA	1	1	1	1	1	1	1	1	1	1	1	1	1	1	1	1	1	1	1	1	1	1	1	1	1	1	1
10 HÜLKENBERG	23	23	23	23	23	23	23	23	23	23	23	23	23	23	23	23	23	23	23	23	23	23	23	23	23	23	23
1 BUTTON	3	3	3	3	3	3	3	3	3	3	3	3	3	3	3	3	3	3	3	3	3	3	3	3	3	3	3
9 BARRICHELLO	16	16	16	16	16	16	16	16	16	16	16	16	16	16	16	16	16	16	16	16	16	16	16	16	16	16	16
14 SUTIL	15	15	15	15	15	15	15	15	15	15	15	15	15	15	15	15	15	15	15	15	15	15	15	15	15	15	15
3 SCHUMACHER	19	19	19	19	19	19	19	19	19	19	19	19	19	19	19	19	19	19	19	19	19	19	19	19	19	19	19
16 BUEMI	18	18	18	18	18	18	18	18	18	18	18	18	18	18	18	18	18	18	18	18	18	18	18	18	18	18	18
15 LIUZZI	24	24	24	24	24	24	24	24	24	24	24	24	24	24	24	24	24	24	24	24	24	24	24	24	24	24	24
17 ALGUERSUARI	21	21	21	21	21	21	21	21	21	21	21	21	21	21	21	21	21	21	21	21	21	21	21	21	21	21	21
24 GLOCK	20	25	25	25	25	25	25	25	25	25	25	25	25	25	25	25	25	25	25	25	25	25	25	25	25	25	25
19 KOVALAINEN	25	20	20	20	20	20	20	20	20	20	20	20	20	20	20	20	20	20	20	20	20	20	20	20	20	20	20
18 TRULLI																											
25 DI GRASSI																											
21 SENNA																											
23 KOBAYASHI																											
20 YAMAMOTO																											

21 Pit stop   *14 One lap or more behind*

TIME SHEETS

PRACTICE 1 (FRIDAY)

Weather: Sunny

Temperatures: track 26-35°C, air 21-26°C

Pos.	Driver	Laps	Time
1	Sebastian Vettel	29	1m 20.976s
2	Mark Webber	27	1m 21.106s
3	Robert Kubica	21	1m 22.072s
4	Jenson Button	17	1m 22.444s
5	Rubens Barrichello	25	1m 22.601s
6	Pedro de la Rosa	24	1m 22.764s
7	Fernando Alonso	25	1m 22.772s
8	Nico Rosberg	25	1m 22.777s
9	Michael Schumacher	26	1m 22.792s
10	Nico Hülkenberg	25	1m 22.966s
11	Adrian Sutil	19	1m 23.003 s
12	Felipe Massa	26	1m 23.007s
13	Vitaly Petrov	24	1m 23.249s
14	Kamui Kobayashi	23	1m 23.327s
15	Paul di Resta	19	1m 23.520s
16	Sébastien Buemi	22	1m 23.780s
17	Jaime Alguersuari	28	1m 23.868s
18	Lewis Hamilton	15	1m 24.075s
19	Jarno Trulli	22	1m 25.032s
20	Heikki Kovalainen	23	1m 25.210s
21	Timo Glock	21	1m 25.990s
22	Lucas di Grassi	17	1m 26.686s
23	Bruno Senna	34	1m 26.990s
24	Sakon Yamamoto	24	1m 28.157s

PRACTICE 2 (FRIDAY)

Weather: Cloudy/sunny

Temperatures: track 28-34°C, air 24-25°C

Pos.	Driver	Laps	Time
1	Sebastian Vettel	33	1m 20.087s
2	Fernando Alonso	34	1m 20.584s
3	Mark Webber	36	1m 20.597s
4	Felipe Massa	33	1m 20.986s
5	Vitaly Petrov	33	1m 21.195s
6	Lewis Hamilton	30	1m 21.308s
7	Robert Kubica	37	1m 21.375s
8	Nico Hülkenberg	41	1m 21.623s
9	Jenson Button	33	1m 21.730s
10	Michael Schumacher	31	1m 21.773s
11	Pedro de la Rosa	38	1m 21.809s
12	Rubens Barrichello	36	1m 21.844s
13	Nico Rosberg	28	1m 22.039s
14	Kamui Kobayashi	37	1m 22.212s
15	Jaime Alguersuari	43	1m 22.469s
16	Adrian Sutil	22	1m 22.507s
17	Sébastien Buemi	38	1m 22.602s
18	Vitantonio Liuzzi	36	1m 23.138s
19	Jarno Trulli	37	1m 24.553s
20	Timo Glock	35	1m 25.376s
21	Lucas di Grassi	32	1m 25.669s
22	Bruno Senna	33	1m 26.745s
23	Sakon Yamamoto	32	1m 26.798s
24	Heikki Kovalainen	5	1m 27.705s

PRACTICE 3 (SATURDAY)

Weather: Sunny

Temperatures: track 28-32°C, air 24-25°C

Pos.	Driver	Laps	Time
1	Mark Webber	17	1m 19.574s
2	Sebastian Vettel	15	1m 20.058s
3	Fernando Alonso	19	1m 20.724s
4	Robert Kubica	19	1m 21.066s
5	Felipe Massa	16	1m 21.264s
6	Lewis Hamilton	17	1m 21.376s
7	Vitaly Petrov	15	1m 21.399s
8	Nico Rosberg	18	1m 21.422s
9	Jenson Button	18	1m 21.473s
10	Nico Hülkenberg	18	1m 21.513s
11	Rubens Barrichello	19	1m 21.705s
12	Michael Schumacher	15	1m 21.939s
13	Pedro de la Rosa	21	1m 22.151s
14	Kamui Kobayashi	20	1m 22.337s
15	Jaime Alguersuari	19	1m 22.427s
16	Sébastien Buemi	22	1m 22.508s
17	Adrian Sutil	14	1m 22.918s
18	Vitantonio Liuzzi	8	1m 23.708s
19	Lucas di Grassi	19	1m 24.547s
20	Jarno Trulli	22	1m 24.576s
21	Heikki Kovalainen	22	1m 24.623s
22	Timo Glock	17	1m 24.805s
23	Bruno Senna	21	1m 26.479s
24	Sakon Yamamoto	21	1m 27.176s

QUALIFYING (SATURDAY)

Weather: Sunny Temperatures: track 32-37°C, air 26°C

Pos.	Driver	First	Second	Third	Qualifying Tyre
1	Sebastian Vettel	1m 20.417s	1m 19.573s	1m 18.773s	Super-Soft
2	Mark Webber	1m 21.132s	1m 19.531s	1m 19.184s	Super-Soft
3	Fernando Alonso	1m 21.278s	1m 20.237s	1m 19.987s	Super-Soft
4	Felipe Massa	1m 21.299s	1m 20.857s	1m 20.331s	Super-Soft
5	Lewis Hamilton	1m 21.455s	1m 20.877s	1m 20.499s	Super-Soft
6	Nico Rosberg	1m 21.212s	1m 20.811s	1m 21.082s	Super-Soft
7	Vitaly Petrov	1m 21.558s	1m 20.797s	1m 21.229s	Super-Soft
8	Robert Kubica	1m 21.159s	1m 20.867s	1m 21.328s	Super-Soft
9	Pedro de la Rosa	1m 21.891s	1m 21.273s	1m 21.411s	Super-Soft
10	Nico Hülkenberg	1m 21.598s	1m 21.275s	1m 21.710s	Super-Soft
11	Jenson Button	1m 21.422s	1m 21.292s		
12	Rubens Barrichello	1m 21.478s	1m 21.331s		
13	Adrian Sutil	1m 22.080s	1m 21.517s		
14	Michael Schumacher	1m 21.840s	1m 21.630s		
15	Sébastien Buemi	1m 21.982s	1m 21.897s		
16	Vitantonio Liuzzi	1m 21.789s	1m 21.927s		
17	Jaime Alguersuari	1m 21.978s	1m 21.998s		
18	Kamui Kobayashi	1m 22.222s			
19	Timo Glock	1m 24.050s			
20	Heikki Kovalainen	1m 24.120s			
21	Jarno Trulli	1m 24.199s			
22	Lucas di Grassi	1m 25.118s			
23	Bruno Senna	1m 26.391s			
24	Sakon Yamamoto	1m 26.453s			

FOR THE RECORD

150th START: **Mark Webber**

100th GRAND PRIX: **Red Bull**

30th PODIUM POSITION: **Red Bull**

DID YOU KNOW

This was the 25th Hungarian Grand Prix (McLaren 9 wins, Williams 7, Ferrari 5, Benetton 1, Honda 1, Red Bull 1, Renault 1).

POINTS

DRIVERS

1	Mark Webber	161
2	Lewis Hamilton	157
3	Sebastian Vettel	151
4	Jenson Button	147
5	Fernando Alonso	141
6	Felipe Massa	97
7	Nico Rosberg	94
8	Robert Kubica	89
9	Michael Schumacher	38
10	Adrian Sutil	35
11	Rubens Barrichello	30
12	Vitaly Petrov	17
13	Kamui Kobayashi	17
14	Vitantonio Liuzzi	12
15	Nico Hülkenberg	10
16	Sébastien Buemi	7
17	Pedro de la Rosa	6
18	Jaime Alguersuari	3

CONSTRUCTORS

1	Red Bull	312
2	McLaren	304
3	Ferrari	238
4	Mercedes	132
5	Renault	106
6	Force India	47
7	Williams	40
8	BMW Sauber	23
9	Toro Rosso	10

5	56	57	58	59	60	61	62	63	64	65	66	67	68	69	70	
6	6	6	6	6	6	6	6	6	6	6	6	6	6	6	6	1
8	8	8	8	8	8	8	8	8	8	8	8	8	8	8	8	2
5	5	5	5	5	5	5	5	5	5	5	5	5	5	5	5	3
7	7	7	7	7	7	7	7	7	7	7	7	7	7	7	7	
2	12	12	12	12	12	12	12	12	12	12	12	12	12	12	12	
9	10	10	10	10	10	10	10	10	10	10	10	10	10	10	10	6
0	22	22	22	22	22	22	22	22	22	22	22	22	22	22		7
2	1	1	1	1	1	1	1	1	1	1	1	1	1	1		8
1	23	23	23	23	23	23	23	23	23	23	23	23	23	23		9
3	3	3	3	3	3	3	3	3	3	9	9	9	9	9		10
3	9	9	9	9	9	9	9	9	9	3	3	3	3	3		
6	16	16	16	16	16	16	16	16	16	16	16	16	16	16		
5	15	15	15	15	15	15	15	15	15	15	15	15	15	15		
9	19	19	19	19	19	19	19	19	19	19	19	19				
8	18	18	18	18	18	18	18	18	18	18	18	18				
4	24	24	24	24	24	24	24	24	24	24	24	24				
1	21	21	21	21	21	21	21	21	21	21	21	21				
5	25	25	25	25	25	25	25	25	25	25	25					
0	20	20	20	20	20	20	20	20	20	20	20					

Safety car deployed on laps shown

RACE TYRE STRATEGIES

	Driver	Race Stint 1	Race Stint 2	Race Stint 3
1	Webber	Super-Soft: 1-43	Medium: 44-70	
2	Alonso	Super-Soft: 1-15	Medium: 16-70	
3	Vettel	Super-Soft: 1-15	Medium: 16-31	Medium: 32-70
4	Massa	Super-Soft: 1-15	Medium: 16-70	
5	Petrov	Super-Soft: 1-15	Medium: 16-70	
6	Hülkenberg	Super-Soft: 1-15	Medium: 16-70	
7	de la Rosa	Super-Soft: 1-15	Medium: 16-69	
8	Button	Super-Soft: 1-14	Medium: 15-69	
9	Kobayashi	Super-Soft: 1-16	Medium: 17-69	
10	Barrichello	Medium: 1-55	Super-Soft: 56-69	
11	Schumacher	Super-Soft: 1-15	Medium: 16-69	
12	Buemi	Medium: 1-15	Super-Soft: 16-69	
13	Liuzzi	Medium: 1-14	Super-Soft: 15-69	
14	Kovalainen	Super-Soft: 1-15	Medium: 16-66	
15	Trulli	Super-Soft: 1-20	Medium: 21-66	
16	Glock	Super-Soft: 1-15	Medium: 16-66	
17	Senna	Super-Soft: 1-15	Medium: 16-66	
18	di Grassi	Super-Soft: 1-15	Medium: 16	Medium: 17-66
19	Yamamoto	Medium: 1-14	Super-Soft: 15-66	
	Hamilton	Super-Soft: 1-15	Medium: 16-23 (dnf)	
	Kubica	Super-Soft: 1-15	Medium: 16-22	Medium: 23 (dnf)
	Rosberg	Super-Soft: 1-15 (dnf)		
	Sutil	Super-Soft: (dnf)		
	Alguersuari	Medium: 1 (dnf)		

The tyre regulations stipulate that the two dry tyre specifications must be used during the race.
The Super-Soft compound Bridgestone Potenza tyre is marked with a green stripe on the sidewall.

Photos: Peter J. Fox

vodafone
vodafone

FIA FORMULA 1 WORLD CHAMPIONSHIP · ROUND 13

Inset left: Lewis Hamilton kisses his winner's trophy.
Photo: Peter Nygaard/WRi2

Main photo: Hamilton mastered the tricky conditions with typical aplomb to take his third win of the season.
Photo: Andrew Hone

BELGIAN GRAND PRIX

SPA-FRANCORCHAMPS CIRCUIT

SPA-FRANCORCHAMPS QUALIFYING

USUALLY, you'd expect to see a Virgin poke its nose out first, or perhaps an HRT. The start of qualifying is an opportunity for so-called minnows to gain a few minutes of uninterrupted TV exposure, but this time the sharks were basking at the end of the pit lane.

The Ardennes weather is capricious at the best of times, and right now there was a palpable hint of moisture in the air. Everybody rushed out in a bid to set a time while most of the circuit was still dry, and the opening few minutes looked more like a scene from a 1970s Formula Ford race as drivers summoned every ounce of brutal obstinacy in a bid to create a bit of clear track space. It was motorsport at its most compellingly selfish, although none of it mattered because the rain began in earnest before anybody completed a timed lap. Besides, the red flag was soon fluttering after Vitaly Petrov crashed at Liège (curiously, its correct name is seldom used, but it's the downhill left-hander beyond Rivage).

The conditions might have been unsettled, but ultimately the same could not be said of the qualifying order, with Mark Webber heading a familiar-looking top six. The Australian set his decisive 1m 45.778s lap on his first run in Q3. "We knew that would be a pretty important moment," he said. "The weather is always unpredictable here, but I think today has been unusual even by Spa's standards. I was pretty happy with the lap, and then it began to rain again, so I knew it was going to be difficult to improve."

Nobody told Lewis Hamilton as much. The Englishman was first on the road at the start of Q3 and found it tricky to assess the conditions. "It was hard to tell whether some dark patches on the circuit were due to rain, or whether the asphalt was a slightly different colour," he said. "I was a bit too wary on my first run, because I didn't realise quite how dry some corners were."

He made amends on his second. Having picked through a localised shower that affected only La Source, the first corner, he hurled caution to the wind to close to within one-tenth of Webber.

Renault introduced its F-duct later than most, but it worked spectacularly well straight out of the box, and Robert Kubica took third, despite not getting a second lap in Q3 after fuel pick-up problems caused his engine to cut. By the time he'd coasted in, there wasn't sufficient time to go out again. "I'm happy with the result, though," he said, "because it underlines the positive steps we have taken with the car. I'm not sure we're in a position to challenge for victory just yet, but you never know."

Sebastian Vettel, Jenson Button and Felipe Massa completed the top six and, of the usual front-runners, only Fernando Alonso (tenth) was mildly displaced after running horribly wide while trying to conjure a decent lap toward the session's end.

It was a tough day for Mercedes: Michael Schumacher knew before the start that he faced a ten-position penalty for his thuggery in Budapest, while team-mate Nico Rosberg was docked five places for an unscheduled gearbox change. They weren't the only ones to be hit: Sébastien Buemi was penalised three positions for impeding Rosberg, Timo Glock five for doing likewise to Sakon Yamamoto (if such a thing were possible) and Pedro de la Rosa ten for an engine change that took him one over the maximum allocation of eight.

The outlook was brighter at Williams, where both Rubens Barrichello and Nico Hülkenberg made it through to Q3 – and the Brazilian celebrated his landmark 300th grand prix. Belgium was due to be the 833rd F1 world championship race, and Barrichello had competed in 36.014 per cent of them – a quirky statistic, and astonishing with it. Predictably, his trademark enthusiasm remained undimmed.

"Earlier in my career," he said, "I always used to think breaks between races were too short. Things are different now, although I don't really know why. We have just been away for three weeks, and after the first of those I was itching to drive again. My wife is terrified; she thinks I'll race forever."

How had he spent the summer recess? Watching video highlights of his early career and transferring them to DVD...

IT looked momentarily like an easy victory cast asunder. The temptation to pit at the end of the previous lap had been strong, but at that stage there was still more moisture in the air than there was on the track. Spa has an awkwardly long lap, though, capable of accommodating contrasting climates simultaneously – and now the race-long leader was skittering through the gravel trap at Rivage. Life, though, is seldom straightforward in Lewis Hamilton's world.

Hamilton grabbed the early initiative when Mark Webber bogged down on pole position – the Australian had been slow away on the formation lap, too, so he adjusted a few clutch settings, but found that they increased his car's reluctance to move. He swiftly dropped to sixth, behind Robert Kubica, Jenson Button (who made a splendid start), Sebastian Vettel and Felipe Massa, but the race was only about 90 seconds old when a familiar neighbour – the rain – dropped in. The whole field was on slicks (the Mercedes drivers, Rubens Barrichello and Timo Glock on hards, the rest on softs) and Hamilton – first to discover that there was virtually no grip on the approach to the chicane – led a mass assault on the escape road. Almost alone among the top half of the field, Webber and Adrian Sutil managed to follow the prescribed route – Sutil losing a place in the process, as Nico Hülkenberg took a route-one approach that went unpunished by the stewards – but the only casualty of the mess was Barrichello, who slammed into the side of Fernando Alonso while the Spaniard was trying to thread through the turn without vaulting the kerbs. The Brazilian's 300th grand prix thus lasted less than a lap. "Hopefully," he said, "my 301st will be better." Despite the ferocity of the impact, Alonso was able to continue after pitting for repairs, and in the process he switched to intermediates. The Spaniard wasn't the only one so inclined: Pedro de la Rosa, Heikki Kovalainen, Timo Glock and Sébastien Buemi dived in for wets, too.

Button – his front wing mildly scuffed after a brush on lap one – lost places to Vettel and Massa while everybody was scrambling over the kerbs, but immediately reclaimed them in one neat move at La Source (although the Brazilian relinquished his position voluntarily, in the wake of what had just happened). He picked up another, too, on the run to Les Combes, after Kubica all but lost control at Raidillon. Vettel was almost caught out as well, putting a wheel on the grass as he moved left to avoid the Pole. Despite having to wrestle to retain control, he managed to find a spare hand to shake a fist at Kubica. The frantic pace was quickly suppressed by the safety car's intervention, to allow Barrichello's car to be removed, but there was still time for Webber to breeze past Massa before Les Combes: straight-line speed might not have been Red Bull's forte, but it had trimmed the RB6's wings to enhance top-end performance and still had enough aerodynamic strength in reserve to be quick through the sweeps of sector two.

With the race neutralised, Hamilton led from Button, Kubica, Vettel, Webber, Massa, Hülkenberg, Sutil, Tonio Liuzzi, Nico Rosberg, Vitaly Petrov (up to 11th from the back within two laps, after avoiding all the early chaos), Kamui Kobayashi (who pitted at the lap's end, to make a tactical tyre switch, from soft to hard), Michael Schumacher, Jaime Alguersuari (who came in on lap two for intermediates), Jarno Trulli, Lucas di Grassi, Sakon Yamamoto, Bruno Senna (another to pit for intermediates), de la Rosa. Alonso, Kovalainen, Glock (who made his second stop, this time to revert to dry rubber) and Buemi.

Glock had the correct idea: de la Rosa, Kovalainen and Senna all returned to switch to dries at the end of lap three, just as the race restarted, while Alguersuari and Alonso followed suit next time around. Senna might as well not have bothered rejoining: his suspension fractured on lap five, causing him to spin at Stavelot. In the absence of any convenient skips, he returned the HRT to its pit.

Vettel wrested third from Kubica within moments of the restart, while Hamilton was able to ease away at the front. Button's frontal damage might have been slight, but it was enough to take the edge off his performance. "I had to dial maximum angle into the wing," he said. "That made the rear end twitchy without actually giving me any more front grip."

Ultimately, the tattered wing would be the least of his

Above: Alonso and Massa lead the queue towards the pit lane exit before the rain intensified.

Photo: Paul-Henri Cahier

Right: Jarno Trulli hurls his Lotus at Eau Rouge as he battles to make up time.

Photo: Andrew Hone

Above: A rare error cost Renault's Robert Kubica second place.
Photo: Peter J Fox

Top right: Mark Webber kept his championship prospects wide open with a strong drive to second place.
Photo: Paul-Henri Cahier

Above right: Rubens Barrichello didn't have much to celebrate after his 300th grand prix start.
Photo: Peter J Fox

Right: Once again, Adrian Sutil impressed in the adverse conditions to take a strong fifth place.
Photo: Andrew Hone

problems. By lap 16, with Hamilton almost ten seconds to the good, it began drizzling again, not sufficiently hard to warrant a tyre change, but enough to make the circuit awkwardly greasy. On the approach to the chicane, Vettel lost control – Red Bull felt he'd been caught out because Button braked early, although the Englishman denied he'd done anything of the kind – and slithered to the left before looping back around and ramming Button amidships. The German later claimed his car had been thrown off balance when he hit a bump under braking.

Button retired on the spot, while Vettel carried on after pitting for a replacement front wing, although he would also be handed a drive-through penalty for causing an avoidable collision. "I wouldn't have expected a move like that from a junior formula driver," said McLaren team principal Martin Whitmarsh.

Not long after serving his penalty, Vettel was hit by Liuzzi as they negotiated the chicane: the Italian pitted immediately for a new front wing, but Vettel carried on until his left rear tyre deflated, and he had to complete half a lap at a crawl before coming in for a replacement.

Kubica and Webber moved up to second and third upon Button's demise, but the leaders were engaged in a tactical waiting game. Heavy rain was forecast and they wanted to synchronise their tyre stops with its arrival. The cocktail of long stints and heavy fuel had taken their toll on the soft rear Bridgestones, however, and they weren't going to last as long as the dry conditions. Webber was first of the top three to pit, on lap 22, while Kubica and Hamilton followed suit on laps 23 and 24 respectively.

It would be another 12 laps before the predicted deluge finally arrived, which is where we came in…

Hamilton sailed past the pit entry at the end of his 34th lap, as did Kubica, Webber and Massa. Fifth-placed Sutil was first to commit to wets, and most of those behind did likewise. "I was thinking about coming in," Sutil said, "and then the team instructed me on the radio. We had the same idea more or less simultaneously, but it was quite tricky because some areas at the top of the circuit were still dry, and it would have been very easy to destroy a set of intermediates within a lap."

Ultimately, the timing of the tyre stops made little difference: laps 34 and 35 were equally suitable, although Hamilton first had his brush with calamity at Rivage, where he just kissed the tyre wall with his front wing before teetering back on to the track. As he had been 11 seconds clear at the end of the previous lap, he was able to recover without losing his lead,

and the top four all came in for tyres at the lap's end, Hamilton resuming in the lead.

The stops were a touch more dramatic for Kubica. "I had to adjust a number of settings on the steering wheel, to allow for the switch to wets," he said. "I couldn't do it on the circuit, because it was too wet, so I did it in the pits. Unfortunately, I became distracted." He locked his brakes, overshot his marker and clipped a couple of mechanics with his front wing: it took a couple of seconds for Renault to untangle the mess, and that was enough to gift second place to Webber. Most drivers opted to switch to intermediates at this point, although Vettel – a distant 17th in the wake of his penalty and other misfortunes – went for full wets.

The lone renegade amid this glut of tyre changes was Hülkenberg, although in his case it was a poorly calculated gamble. The German's bright early showing had been negated by an electronic problem that meant he had a choice between full throttle and almost none at all. He stalled when he made his tyre stop, on lap 16, and lost several places as a consequence. Staying on dries was a punt to make amends, but the cocktail of slicks, a wet track and no driveability prompted a litany of errors, although he remained out for three laps before conceding to the inevitable.

Hamilton continued to lead comfortably until lap 38, when the safety car appeared for the second time to allow marshals to shift Alonso's car, the Spaniard having crashed on the way into Rivage as the rain intensified. The interruption was brief – de la Rosa, Buemi and Liuzzi all switched to full wets, while Vettel came in for a fresh set – and the race resumed at the end of lap 40, "I was kind of hoping it might stay out a little longer," Hamilton said, but he completed the final three laps without mishap and edged away to secure victory in a race that he had controlled perfectly for all but a few seconds. That was enough to restore his championship lead, but only by three points from the ultra-consistent Webber – one of the few not to have put a foot wrong all afternoon – and Kubica. "Given the conditions," Webber said, "I think you'd have got long odds on the top three qualifiers finishing on the podium, although the order

is, obviously, slightly the wrong way around for me. In the end, I'm happy with second, though; you have to take as much as you can from races like this if you are in the running for the championship."

Massa's fourth place was the culmination of one of his best races of the season – he'd outperformed Alonso all weekend – and Sutil took fifth after a similarly worthy drive. For all his occasional appetite for misadventure, the German maintained his custom of driving flawlessly in difficult conditions. He also pointed out that he'd spent most of the weekend driving one-handed through Eau Rouge and Blanchimont, to get the best from his F-duct.

There had been a sharp intake of breath on the Mercedes pit wall on lap 11, when Petrov had passed Rosberg going into Les Combes, and the closely following Schumacher had attempted to capitalise on his team-mate's consequent loss of momentum. Schumacher went around the outside at the complex's second right-hander and his rear wheel just clipped Rosberg's left front, but neither car sustained any damage. Rosberg lost two positions, to Kobayashi and Alonso, when stacked behind his team-mate during the rain-enforced tyre stop, but that was also the Mercedes drivers' only stop. A long first stint on hard tyres paid off and enabled them to pass Petrov.

With Alonso having removed himself from the equation, Rosberg dealt with both Kobayashi and Schumacher at the final restart, slipstreaming up to sixth at Les Combes. "The car ahead [Sutil] was slow through Eau Rouge," Schumacher said, "and that allowed Nico to get a run on me."

They finished sixth and seventh, ahead of Kobayashi (another solid performance in the wake of the team's disastrous Saturday), Petrov and Alguersuari, although the Toro Rosso driver was later given a 20-second time penalty when the stewards ruled that he had gained an unfair advantage by cutting the chicane right at the end in his efforts to keep Liuzzi behind. The Italian thus moved up to tenth, while Alguersuari dropped to 13th, behind de la Rosa and Buemi. The final point might have been de la Rosa's, but he dropped two places by running wide through the gravel at Stavelot on the penultimate lap. "I can't really complain about finishing 12th after an engine change forced me to start last," he said, "but I should have scored a point. I was on full wets, though, and there wasn't enough rain to prevent me destroying them. They went off quite quickly and I made a mistake while trying to put pressure on Petrov."

Hülkenberg, Vettel, Kovalainen, di Grassi, Glock, Trulli and Yamamoto completed the finishers. Trulli had been best placed of the new teams' drivers, but he spun at Pouhon on lap 39 and handed the initiative to di Grassi, who then lost out to Kovalainen at the final restart.

Such, though, were minor details. "I think somebody was looking after me today," Hamilton said.

True to a point, but this was more a matter of meritocracy than luck.

Simon Arron

Left: Vettel made a serious mistake by slamming into Jenson Button's McLaren early in the race.
Photo: Studio Colombo/WRi2

Below: Belgian hero Jacky Ickx, who so nearly won the world championship 40 years earlier.
Photo: Peter Nygaard/GP Photo

Below left: One day, you might be in F1. Jos Verstappen and his young racer son, Max, in the pit lane.
Photo: Frits Van Eldik/WRi2

Below: Alonso put in a strong performance for Ferrari, but a small slip pitched him into the barriers.
Photo: Perer J Fox

EDITOR'S VIEW
VETTEL AND THE LEARNING CURVE

DWELLING on Sebastian Vettel's driving error, which resulted in the unfortunate elimination of Jenson Button from the Belgian Grand Prix, dominated a disproportionate amount of people's time in the aftermath of this tricky and challenging race. It was absolutely beyond dispute that Vettel had made a significant mistake, which had caused his Red Bull to T-bone Button's McLaren in a cloud of steam and flying debris, but this was a race that reminded us the dividing line between 'hero' and 'zero' can be unpredictably narrow – witness Lewis Hamilton's tippy-toes excursion across a gravel trap to within spitting distance of an unyielding barrier. Had he not rescued the situation through a combination of driving genius and great good fortune, the McLaren record book would have looked barren indeed at the end of this particular contest.

As it was, Hamilton drove with deft control after a demonstration of his now mature and rounded talent, which was every bit as prominent as Vettel's uptight and seemingly over-anxious handling of an unpredictable unfolding situation. Yet if one trawls through the F1 history books, the record of bright young stars tripping over their own brimming optimism during their second or third year in the sport's most senior category is plain for all to see.

Go back ten years and consider Jenson Button's second and third world championship seasons, driving for the frustratingly uncompetitive Benetton-Renault squad. He seemed distracted, inconsistent and all at sea. Only when he switched to the BAR-Honda outfit for 2003 – his fourth season in F1 – did he start to make the consistent progress that led to his first GP win in Hungary 2006, and his relentless march thereafter to become one of the most polished and consistent of the sport's proven front-runners. So dwelling too long on Vettel's occasional setbacks in no way should have blinded experienced observers to his fast maturing talent, even though Mark Webber frequently matched his performance in terms of sheer pace. Examine the CVs of the leading drivers, and they will be seeking to hide skeletons in their cupboards, embarrassing memories of days when they got it all badly wrong. In that respect, Vettel probably has fewer than most.

You had to take your hat off to Fernando Alonso at Spa, even though the Ferrari team leader's race ended with broken suspension following a spin over a greasy kerb into a barrier. The twice world champion deserved full marks for driving flat out up to that point, mentally shrugging aside any possible damage deep in his Ferrari's chassis after being mauled at high speed by Rubens Barrichello's Williams at the end of the opening lap. Proof, perhaps, that a certain lack of imagination is required to spice the reservoir of natural talent with which the really great drivers are blessed.

Alan Henry

FIA F1 WORLD CHAMPIONSHIP · ROUND 13

BELGIAN GRAND PRIX

SPA-FRANCORCHAMPS 27–29 AUGUST 2010

RACE DISTANCE: 44 laps, 191.415 miles/308.052km

RACE WEATHER: Cloudy/sunny/rain (track 17–20°C, air 15–17°C)

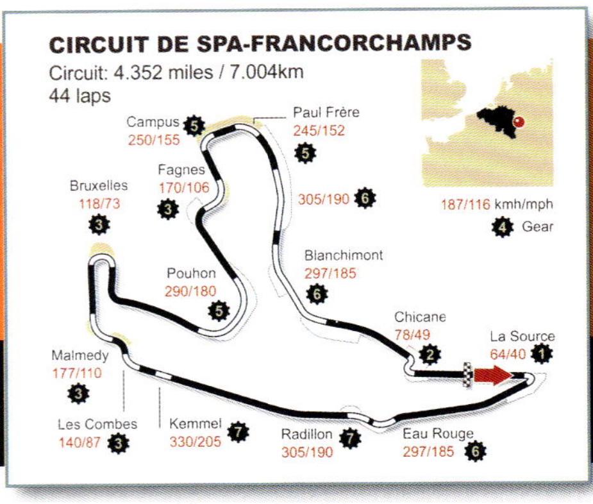

Pos.	Driver	Nat.	No.	Entrant	Car/Engine	Tyres	Laps	Time/Retirement	Speed (mph/km/h)	Gap to leader	Fastest race lap	
1	**Lewis Hamilton**	GB	2	Vodafone McLaren Mercedes	McLaren MP4-25-Mercedes FO108X V8	B	44	1h 29m 04.268s	128.940/207.509		1m 49.069s	32
2	**Mark Webber**	AUS	6	Red Bull Racing	Red Bull RB6-Renault RS27 V8	B	44	1h 29m 05.839s	128.902/207.448	+ 1.571s	1m 49.395s	32
3	**Robert Kubica**	PL	11	Renault F1 Team	Renault R30-RS27 V8	B	44	1h 29m 07.761s	128.856/207.374	+ 3.493s	1m 49.807s	29
4	**Felipe Massa**	BR	7	Scuderia Ferrari Marlboro	Ferrari F10-056 V8	B	44	1h 29m 12.532s	128.741/207.189	+ 8.264s	1m 50.111s	26
5	**Adrian Sutil**	D	14	Force India F1 Team	Force India VJM03-Mercedes FO108X V8	B	44	1h 29m 13.362s	128.721/207.157	+ 9.094s	1m 50.477s	25
6	**Nico Rosberg**	D	4	Mercedes GP Petronas F1 Team	Mercedes MGP W01-Mercedes FO108X V8	B	44	1h 29m 16.627s	128.642/207.030	+ 12.359s	1m 51.688s	31
7	**Michael Schumacher**	GB	3	Mercedes GP Petronas F1 Team	Mercedes MGP W01-Mercedes FO108X V8	B	44	1h 29m 19.816s	128.566/206.907	+ 15.548s	1m 51.914s	32
8	**Kamui Kobayashi**	J	23	BMW Sauber F1 Team	BMW Sauber C29-Ferrari 056 V8	B	44	1h 29m 20.946s	128.539/206.864	+ 16.678s	1m 51.749s	29
9	**Vitaly Petrov**	RUS	12	Renault F1 Team	Renault R30-RS27 V8	B	44	1h 29m 28.119s	128.367/206.587	+ 23.851s	1m 51.175s	32
10	**Vitantonio Liuzzi**	I	15	Force India F1 Team	Force India VJM03-Mercedes FO108X V8	B	44	1h 29m 39.099s	128.105/206.165	+ 34.831s	1m 52.267s	31
11	Pedro de la Rosa	E	22	BMW Sauber F1 Team	BMW Sauber C29-Ferrari 056 V8	B	44	1h 29m 40.287s	128.077/206.120	+ 36.019s	1m 52.537s	31
12	Sébastien Buemi	CH	16	Scuderia Toro Rosso	Toro Rosso STR5-Ferrari 056 V8	B	44	1h 29m 44.163s	127.985/205.972	+ 39.895s	1m 52.966s	30
13	Jaime Alguersuari	E	17	Scuderia Toro Rosso	Toro Rosso STR5-Ferrari 056 V8	B	44	1h 29m 53.725s *	127.758/205.606	+ 49.457s	1m 51.576s	31
14	Nico Hülkenberg	D	10	AT&T Williams	Williams FW32-Cosworth CA2010 V8	B	43			+ 1 lap	1m 51.864s	28
15	Sebastian Vettel	D	5	Red Bull Racing	Red Bull RB6-Renault RS27 V8	B	43			+ 1 lap	1m 50.868s	22
16	Heikki Kovalainen	FIN	19	Lotus Racing	Lotus T127-Cosworth CA2010 V8	B	43			+ 1 lap	1m 55.797s	23
17	Lucas Di Grassi	BR	25	Virgin Racing	Virgin VR-01-Cosworth CA2010 V8	B	43			+ 1 lap	1m 55.705s	25
18	Timo Glock	D	24	Virgin Racing	Virgin VR-01-Cosworth CA2010 V8	B	43			+ 1 lap	1m 55.268s	31
19	Jarno Trulli	I	18	Lotus Racing	Lotus T127-Cosworth CA2010 V8	B	43			+ 1 lap	1m 55.103s	24
20	Sakon Yamamoto	J	20	HRT F1 Team	HRT F110-Cosworth CA2010 V8	B	42			+ 2 laps	1m 55.484s	31
	Fernando Alonso	E	8	Scuderia Ferrari Marlboro	Ferrari F10-056 V8	B	37	*accident*			1m 51.374s	29
	Jenson Button	GB	1	Vodafone McLaren Mercedes	McLaren MP4-25-Mercedes FO108X V8	B	15	*accident*			1m 52.879s	6
	Bruno Senna	BR	21	HRT F1 Team	HRT F110-Cosworth CA2010 V8	B	5	*rear suspension*			2m 20.201s	5
	Rubens Barrichello	BR	9	AT&T Williams	Williams FW32-Cosworth CA2010 V8	B	0	*accident*			no time	

* includes 20-sec penalty for leaving the track and gaining an advantage

Fastest race lap: Lewis Hamilton on lap 32, 1m 49.069s, 143.648mph/ 231.178km/h.

Lap record: Kimi Räikkönen (McLaren MP4-19-Mercedes Benz V8), 1m 45.108s, 148.465mph/238.931km/h (2004) (4.335-mile/6.976km circuit)

Lap record (current configuration): Sebastian Vettel (Red Bull RB5-Renault V8), 1m 47.263s, 146.066mph/235.070km/h (2009).

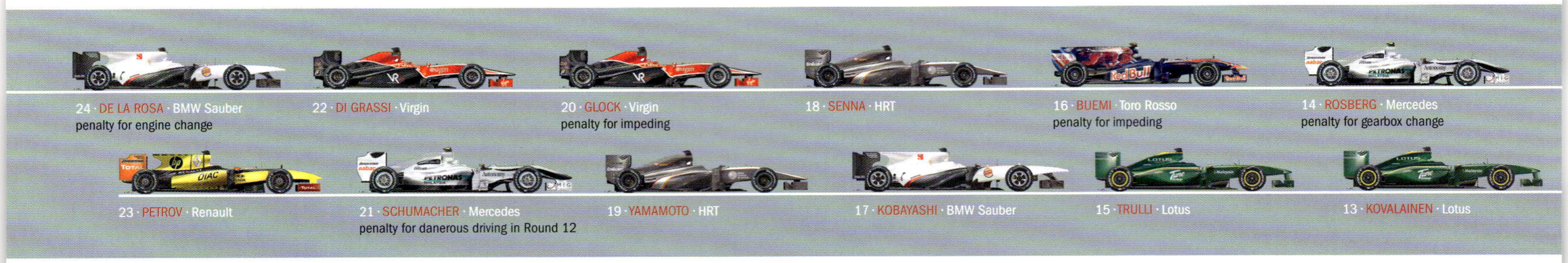

24 · DE LA ROSA · BMW Sauber
penalty for engine change

22 · DI GRASSI · Virgin

20 · GLOCK · Virgin
penalty for impeding

18 · SENNA · HRT

16 · BUEMI · Toro Rosso
penalty for impeding

14 · ROSBERG · Mercedes
penalty for gearbox change

23 · PETROV · Renault

21 · SCHUMACHER · Mercedes
penalty for danerous driving in Round 12

19 · YAMAMOTO · HRT

17 · KOBAYASHI · BMW Sauber

15 · TRULLI · Lotus

13 · KOVALAINEN · Lotus

Grid order	1	2	3	4	5	6	7	8	9	10	11	12	13	14	15	16	17	18	19	20	21	22	23	24	25	26	27	28	29	30	31	32	33	34	35	36
6 WEBBER	2	2	2	2	2	2	2	2	2	2	2	2	2	2	2	2	2	2	2	2	2	2	2	2	2	2	2	2	2	2	2	2	2	2	2	2
2 HAMILTON	11	1	1	1	1	1	1	1	1	1	1	1	1	1	1	11	11	11	11	11	11	11	11	11	11	11	11	11	11	11	11	11	11	11	11	6
11 KUBICA	5	11	11	5	5	5	5	5	5	5	5	5	5	5	5	6	6	6	6	6	6	7	7	6	6	6	6	6	6	6	6	6	6	6	6	11
5 VETTEL	7	5	5	11	11	11	11	11	11	11	11	11	11	11	11	7	7	7	7	7	7	6	6	7	7	7	7	7	7	7	7	7	7	7	7	7
1 BUTTON	1	6	6	6	6	6	6	6	6	6	6	6	6	6	6	14	14	14	14	14	14	3	3	3	14	14	14	14	14	14	14	14	14	14	14	14
7 MASSA	6	7	7	7	7	7	7	7	7	7	7	7	7	7	7	5	3	3	3	3	3	4	4	14	3	3	3	3	3	3	3	3	3	3	3	3
9 BARRICHELLO	10	10	10	14	14	14	14	14	14	14	14	14	14	14	14	10	4	4	4	4	4	23	14	4	4	4	4	4	4	4	4	4	4	23	23	23
14 SUTIL	14	14	14	10	10	10	10	10	10	10	10	10	10	10	10	3	23	23	23	23	23	14	23	23	23	23	23	23	23	23	23	23	23	8	8	8
10 HULKENBERG	4	15	15	15	15	15	15	15	15	4	12	12	12	12	12	4	8	8	8	8	8	8	8	8	8	8	8	8	8	8	8	8	8	4	4	4
8 ALONSO	17	4	4	4	4	4	4	4	4	12	3	3	3	3	3	12	12	12	12	12	12	12	12	12	12	12	12	12	12	12	12	12	12	12	12	12
17 ALGUERSUARI	15	12	12	12	12	12	12	12	12	3	4	4	4	4	4	23	15	15	15	15	15	15	15	15	5	17	17	17	17	17	17	17	17	17	17	17
15 LIUZZI	23	23	3	3	3	3	3	3	3	23	23	23	23	23	23	8	5	5	5	22	22	22	22	22	17	22	22	22	22	22	22	22	22	10	22	22
19 KOVALAINEN	20	3	18	18	18	23	23	23	23	15	15	15	15	15	8	15	22	22	22	5	17	17	17	5	22	10	10	10	10	10	10	10	10	22	10	10
4 ROSBERG	3	17	25	25	23	18	18	18	8	8	8	8	8	8	15	22	17	17	17	17	5	5	5	17	15	15	15	15	15	15	15	15	15	15	15	15
18 TRULLI	12	18	20	23	25	25	25	22	22	22	22	22	22	22	22	17	10	10	10	10	10	10	10	10	10	16	16	16	16	16	16	16	16	16	16	16
16 BUEMI	18	25	17	20	20	22	22	8	18	17	17	17	17	17	17	16	16	16	16	16	16	16	16	16	16	18	18	18	18	18	18	18	18	5	5	18
23 KOBAYASHI	25	20	8	24	24	20	8	25	25	18	18	16	16	16	16	18	18	18	18	18	18	18	18	18	18	25	25	25	25	25	25	25	5	18	18	5
21 SENNA	22	21	23	17	22	24	20	17	17	25	16	18	18	18	18	25	25	25	25	25	25	25	25	25	25	24	24	24	24	24	24	5	25	24	25	25
20 YAMAMOTO	19	22	22	8	16	8	24	20	16	16	25	25	25	25	25	24	24	24	24	24	24	24	24	24	24	5	19	19	19	5	5	24	24	25	24	24
24 GLOCK	21	8	24	22	8	16	16	16	20	24	24	24	24	24	24	19	19	19	19	19	19	19	19	19	19	19	5	5	5	19	19	19	19	19	19	19
3 SCHUMACHER	24	19	19	16	17	17	17	24	24	20	20	20	19	19	19	20	20	20	20	20	20	20	20	20	20	20	20	20	20	20	20	20	20	20	20	20
25 DI GRASSI	8	24	21	19	19	19	19	19	19	19	19	19	20	20	20																					
12 PETROV	16	16	16	21	21																															
22 DE LA ROSA																																				

21 Pit stop

14 One lap or more behind

TIME SHEETS

PRACTICE 1 (FRIDAY)

Weather: Rain/drizzle/partly cloudy
Temperatures: track 18-19°C, air 18°C

Pos.	Driver	Laps	Time
1	Fernando Alonso	17	2m 00.797s
2	Lewis Hamilton	7	2m 01.567s
3	Robert Kubica	14	2m 02.081s
4	Sebastian Vettel	11	2m 02.450s
5	Adrian Sutil	14	2m 02.646s
6	Jenson Button	6	2m 02.913s
7	Mark Webber	11	2m 02.926s
8	Kamui Kobayashi	17	2m 03.401s
9	Rubens Barrichello	7	2m 03.424s
10	Michael Schumacher	9	2m 03.489s
11	Felipe Massa	17	2m 03.601s
12	Nico Hülkenberg	17	2m 03.649s
13	Nico Rosberg	6	2m 03.654s
14	Pedro de la Rosa	17	2m 03.851s
15	Vitantonio Liuzzi	12	2m 04.145s
16	Jaime Alguersuari	16	2m 04.250s
17	Vitaly Petrov	15	2m 04.690s
18	Sébastien Buemi	6	2m 05.680s
19	Timo Glock	18	2m 05.697s
20	Lucas Di Grassi	14	2m 06.695s
21	Jarno Trulli	15	2m 07.189s
22	Bruno Senna	13	2m 07.737s
23	Heikki Kovalainen	15	2m 07.955s
24	Sakon Yamamoto	18	2m 10.507s

PRACTICE 2 (FRIDAY)

Weather: Partly cloudy/sunny
Temperatures: track 21-25°C, air 19-20°C

Pos.	Driver	Laps	Time
1	Fernando Alonso	25	1m 49.032s
2	Adrian Sutil	17	1m 49.157s
3	Lewis Hamilton	14	1m 49.248s
4	Robert Kubica	20	1m 49.282s
5	Felipe Massa	23	1m 49.588s
6	Sebastian Vettel	19	1m 49.689s
7	Jenson Button	20	1m 49.755s
8	Pedro de la Rosa	27	1m 50.081s
9	Rubens Barrichello	22	1m 50.128s
10	Kamui Kobayashi	24	1m 50.200s
11	Vitaly Petrov	24	1m 50.251s
12	Michael Schumacher	23	1m 50.341s
13	Nico Rosberg	21	1m 50.382s
14	Jaime Alguersuari	25	1m 50.682s
15	Nico Hülkenberg	20	1m 50.831s
16	Vitantonio Liuzzi	17	1m 51.520s
17	Sébastien Buemi	25	1m 51.523s
18	Mark Webber	19	1m 51.636s
19	Heikki Kovalainen	15	1m 53.480s
20	Jarno Trulli	21	1m 53.639s
21	Lucas Di Grassi	17	1m 54.325s
22	Bruno Senna	24	1m 55.751s
23	Sakon Yamamoto	21	1m 56.039s
24	Timo Glock	3	2m 03.179s

PRACTICE 3 (SATURDAY)

Weather: Cloudy/sunny/drizzle/rain
Temperatures: track 17-25°C, air 15-18°C

Pos.	Driver	Laps	Time
1	Mark Webber	10	1m 46.106s
2	Lewis Hamilton	17	1m 46.223s
3	Sebastian Vettel	12	1m 46.396s
4	Jenson Button	17	1m 46.397s
5	Robert Kubica	17	1m 46.492s
6	Fernando Alonso	11	1m 46.627s
7	Felipe Massa	10	1m 46.962s
8	Adrian Sutil	15	1m 47.064s
9	Nico Hülkenberg	16	1m 47.160s
10	Kamui Kobayashi	17	1m 47.296s
11	Pedro de la Rosa	15	1m 47.388s
12	Vitaly Petrov	15	1m 47.406s
13	Rubens Barrichello	14	1m 47.512s
14	Michael Schumacher	16	1m 47.695s
15	Nico Rosberg	9	1m 47.837s
16	Sébastien Buemi	20	1m 47.905s
17	Jaime Alguersuari	18	1m 47.981s
18	Vitantonio Liuzzi	8	1m 48.692s
19	Jarno Trulli	14	1m 50.600s
20	Bruno Senna	9	1m 51.133s
21	Heikki Kovalainen	14	1m 51.384s
22	Lucas Di Grassi	13	1m 51.517s
23	Timo Glock	10	1m 51.669s
24	Sakon Yamamoto	13	1m 52.001s

QUALIFYING (SATURDAY)

Weather: Sunny/rain Temperatures: track 17-25°C, air 15-18°C

Pos.	Driver	First	Second	Third	Qualifying Tyre
1	Mark Webber	1m 57.352s	1m 47.253s	1m 45.778s	Soft
2	Lewis Hamilton	1m 56.706s	1m 46.211s	1m 45.863s	Soft
3	Robert Kubica	1m 56.041s	1m 47.320s	1m 46.100s	Soft
4	Sebastian Vettel	1m 58.487s	1m 47.245s	1m 46.127s	Soft
5	Jenson Button	1m 57.981s	1m 46.790s	1m 46.206s	Soft
6	Felipe Massa	1m 58.323s	1m 47.322s	1m 46.314s	Soft
7	Rubens Barrichello	1m 55.757s	1m 47.797s	1m 46.602s	Hard
8	Adrian Sutil	1m 58.730s	1m 47.292s	1m 46.659s	Soft
9	Nico Hülkenberg	1m 55.442s	1m 47.821s	1m 47.053s	Soft
10	Fernando Alonso	1m 57.023s	1m 47.544s	1m 47.441s	Soft
11	Michael Schumacher	1m 56.313s	1m 47.874s		
12	Nico Rosberg	1m 54.826s	1m 47.885s		
13	Jaime Alguersuari	1m 58.944s	1m 48.267s		
14	Vitantonio Liuzzi	2m 01.102s	1m 48.680s		
15	Sébastien Buemi	2m 00.386s	1m 49.209s		
16	Heikki Kovalainen	2m 01.343s	1m 50.980s		
17	Timo Glock	2m 01.316s	1m 52.049s		
18	Jarno Trulli	2m 01.491s			
19	Kamui Kobayashi	2m 02.284s			
20	Bruno Senna	2m 03.612s			
21	Sakon Yamamoto	2m 03.941s			
22	Pedro de la Rosa	2m 05.294s			
23	Lucas Di Grassi	2m 18.754s			
24	Vitaly Petrov	no time			

FOR THE RECORD

30TH FRONT ROW POSITION: Red Bull

Photos: Peter J. Fox

DRIVERS

1	Lewis Hamilton	182
2	Mark Webber	179
3	Sebastian Vettel	151
4	Jenson Button	147
5	Fernando Alonso	141
6	Felipe Massa	109
7	Robert Kubica	104
8	Nico Rosberg	102
9	Adrian Sutil	45
10	Michael Schumacher	44
11	Rubens Barrichello	30
12	Kamui Kobayashi	21
13	Vitaly Petrov	19
14	Vitantonio Liuzzi	13
15	Nico Hülkenberg	10
16	Sébastien Buemi	7
17	Pedro de la Rosa	6
18	Jaime Alguersuari	3

CONSTRUCTORS

1	Red Bull	330
2	McLaren	329
3	Ferrari	250
4	Mercedes	146
5	Renault	123
6	Force India	58
7	Williams	40
8	BMW Sauber	27
9	Toro Rosso	10

37	38	39	40	41	42	43	44	
2	2	2	2	2	2	2	2	1
6	6	6	6	6	6	6	6	2
11	11	11	11	11	11	11	11	3
7	7	7	7	7	7	7	7	
14	14	14	14	14	14	14	14	
3	3	3	3	4	4	4	4	6
23	23	23	23	3	3	3	3	7
8	4	4	4	23	23	23	23	8
4	12	12	12	12	12	12	12	9
12	17	17	17	22	17	17	17	10
17	22	22	22	17	15	15	15	
22	15	15	15	15	22	22	22	
15	16	16	16	16	16	16	16	
16	10	10	10	10	10	10		
10	18	18	5	5	5	5		
18	5	5	19	19	19	19		
5	25	25	25	25	25	25		
25	19	19	24	24	24	24		
19	24	24	18	18	18	18		
24	20	20	20	20	20			
20								

Safety car deployed on laps shown

RACE TYRE STRATEGIES

	Driver	Race Stint 1	Race Stint 2	Race Stint 3	Race Stint 4	Race Stint 5	Race Stint 6
1	Hamilton	Soft: 1-24	Hard: 25-35	Inters: 36-44			
2	Webber	Soft: 1-23	Hard: 24-34	Inters: 35-44			
3	Kubica	Soft: 1-23	Hard: 24-35	Inters: 36-44			
4	Massa	Soft: 1-23	Hard: 24-35	Inters: 36-44			
5	Sutil	Soft: 1-21	Hard: 22-34	Inters: 35-44			
6	Rosberg	Hard: 1-34	Inters: 35-44				
7	Schumacher	Hard: 1-34	Inters: 35-44				
8	Kobayashi	Soft: 1-2	Hard: 3-34	Inters: 35-44			
9	Petrov	Soft: 1-16	Hard: 17-34	Inters: 35-44			
10	Liuzzi	Soft: 1-10	Hard: 11-34	Inters: 35-44			
11	de la Rosa	Soft: 1	Inters: 2-3	Soft: 4-34	Inters: 35-38	Wet: 39-44	
12	Buemi	Soft: 1	Inters: 2-3	Soft: 4-33	Inters: 34-37	Wet: 38-44	
13	Alguersuari	Soft: 1-2	Inters: 3-4	Soft: 5-34	Inters: 35-44		
14	Hülkenberg	Soft: 1-16	Hard: 17-37	Wet: 38-43			
15	Vettel	Soft: 1-16	Hard: 17-20	Hard: 21-26	Soft: 27-33	Wet: 34-36	Wet: 37-43
16	Kovalainen	Soft: 1	Inters: 2-3	Soft: 4-33	Inters: 34-43		
17	di Grassi	Soft: 1-33	Inters: 34-43				
18	Glock	Hard: 1	Wet: 2	Soft: 3-32	Wet: 33-43		
19	Trulli	Soft: 1-33	Inters: 34-43				
20	Yamamoto	Soft: 1-13	Soft: 14-32	Wet: 33-42			
	Alonso	Soft: 1	Inters: 2-4	Hard: 5-34	Inters: 35-37 (dnf)		
	Button	Soft: 1-15 (dnf)					
	Senna	Soft: 1-2	Inters: 3	Hard: 4-5 (dnf)			
	Barrichello	Hard: 0 (dnf)					

The tyre regulations stipulate that the two dry tyre specifications must be used during the race.
The Super-Soft compound Bridgestone Potenza tyre is marked with a green stripe on the sidewall.

FIA FORMULA 1 WORLD CHAMPIONSHIP · ROUND 14

ITALIAN GRAND PRIX

MONZA CIRCUIT

Nothing like it! Alonso's Ferrari surrounded by Maranello personnel on the evocative Monza grid, waiting to start another memorable afternoon for the Prancing Horse.

Photo: Peter J Fox

F
ETIHAD
FIAT
V-Power
MAKE ROADS SAFE

MONZA QUALIFYING

FERNANDO Alonso called it "a nice surprise", but most would label it perfect timing. Ferrari had not been on pole position since Brazil 2008 – 31 races beforehand – and there could have been no finer location at which to terminate the drought. The *tifosi* responded with customary aplomb, albeit at mildly reduced volume, because quite a few grandstands were only half full. Even Monza isn't immune to recession.

Alonso lapped in 1m 21.952s on his first run in Q3, but failed to improve on his second and had to wait to see whether that time would suffice. "We have held pole position provisionally a few times this year," he said, "but on each occasion, somebody has gone faster right at the end of the session, and I knew Jenson [Button] had still to complete his lap." The McLaren driver finished 0.122 seconds adrift, however.

"I set out to do a solid banker lap at the start of Q3," Alonso added, "and then pushed a little harder on the second run. With the low-downforce configuration we use here, though, it is very easy to make mistakes and I was unable to improve. A calmer approach turned out to be the best one."

Even before he secured his first pole position as a Ferrari driver, the weekend had been quite lively. "When I arrived on Thursday," he said, "I was in a Fiat 500 painted a very Ferrari shade of red. I could see people running behind us and that made it feel a very special occasion."

Button profited from his decision to stick with McLaren's F-duct, which team-mate Lewis Hamilton discarded after trying it in Friday morning's free practice. Hamilton was running a less steeply raked rear wing, so there wasn't much for the F-duct to stall down the long straights, and he felt sure his preternatural car control would be enough to tame the car's twitchier tendencies. He was almost 10mph quicker than his team-mate through the speed trap, but Button's superior balance gave him an edge around the lap as a whole, and he finished three places ahead. "We weren't sure which approach to take when we came here," Button said, "but I'm sure I've made the right decision. I feel very comfortable with the car as it is: I can brake later and carry more speed into the corners. So far it has worked well, and I'm sure I'll be in good shape for the race."

Felipe Massa took third for Ferrari, and fourth represented a good recovery for Mark Webber. It wasn't so much that this was expected to be the least Red Bull-friendly venue of the season (a point underlined by Sebastian Vettel's sixth place), more that the Australian's running time had been limited by a faulty sensor on Friday afternoon and an airbox fire on Saturday morning. "I'd have settled for fourth at the start of the session," he said.

Nico Hülkenberg's eighth place for Williams wasn't the best grid position of his fledgling F1 career, but it was a product of consistent speed rather than peculiar circumstance and, consequently, his most convincing qualifying performance to date, He outpaced team-mate Rubens Barrichello from the start – and at Monza, that's as good a barometer as any.

Above: Jenson Button fended off Alonso brilliantly in the first phase of the race, the McLaren driver narrowly being leapfrogged when Fernando stayed out one more lap before making his tyre stop. Note the flat spot on Jenson's right front Bridgestone.
Photo: Paul-Henri Cahier

Left: Different attention spans from designer fans.
Photo: Peter J Fox

FROM Jenson Button's perspective, it was hard to tell how close Fernando Alonso's Ferrari might be – the McLaren's mirrors were shaking too much and the Englishman was aware only of a vibrating red dot. But then the Italian Grand Prix was a passing blur for everybody, little more than 75 minutes of racing that altered the world championship's complexion yet again. Alonso had the quicker car, Button the seamless artistry, and a finely balanced duel finally tipped in the Spaniard's favour after the race's tactical evolution was dictated by a driver running more than 20 seconds behind the leaders.

Button made the brighter start from the so-called slower side of the grid and earned himself a predictably brutal defensive chop from the pole-sitter, but the Spaniard swerved too late towards a non-existent gap and Button was able to claim the line into the first corner. Alonso's appetite for a scrap cost him significant momentum and Ferrari team-mate Felipe Massa immediately drew alongside, the two cars touching lightly and allowing Button to ease far enough ahead to immunise himself against slipstreamed retaliation.

The two Ferraris remained side by side most of the way to the second chicane, with Lewis Hamilton on their tail. Alonso had the inside and duly claimed the corner, with Massa tucked in, correctly, just behind. "I was following the normal line," the Brazilian said, "when I felt a thump."

That was because Hamilton – the campaign's most consistently impressive performer to this point – had blotted his copybook with a gross misjudgement. There was never enough space to attempt a pass and he simply drove into the Ferrari's left rear wheel, at which point the McLaren's right front briefly buckled through 45 degrees. Such details didn't discourage Hamilton, who continued until the mangled McLaren failed to respond to his steering inputs at the first Lesmo, where he skated irretrievably into the gravel and prompted a lusty cheer from the grandstands (which appeared to contain most of Spain).

"When Lewis watches the replay in slow motion, he'll probably realise it was the wrong thing to do," said McLaren team principal Martin Whitmarsh, "but he's an aggressive racing driver who has to make split-second decisions and I wouldn't want his approach to change, because that's what makes him who he is."

Button was 0.621 seconds clear by the end of the opening lap, with Alonso and Massa spearheading the pursuit. Nico Rosberg ran fourth, from namesake Hülkenberg, Sebastian Vettel, Michael Schumacher and Mark Webber, who had been mugged at the first chicane and then ran fractionally wide at the second, dropping from fourth to ninth faster than you could say "flexible front wing". Sébastien Buemi completed the top ten, ahead of Rubens Barrichello, Pedro de la Rosa, Jaime Alguersuari, Tonio Liuzzi, Vitaly Petrov, Jarno Trulli, Timo Glock, Lucas di Grassi, Heikki Kovalainen, Sakon Yamamoto, Bruno Senna and Adrian Sutil. The last had run wide at the first chicane and then did so again at Parabolica. When he escaped from the gravel, the German pitted immediately to take a tactical punt on a set of hard Bridgestones.

Kamui Kobayashi failed to complete the lap. He had experienced a loss of gears during the installation laps and had returned to the pits, from where he started after the team had fitted a fresh ECU. He immediately sensed that the gearbox had suffered internal damage, however, and pulled off at the second Lesmo.

The gap at the front remained stable for a while, although it wasn't large enough to deter Alonso from taking an occasional peek down the inside at Turn One. "Mentally," Button explained, "it was very tough, because I never knew quite how far behind Fernando was. It's hard to judge when the mirrors vibrate so much."

The Spaniard continually sought a faster exit from Parabolica, which might have enabled him to get a run on the McLaren as they drafted along the pit straight, but the opportunity never arose. "Jenson simply wasn't making any mistakes," Alonso said. "He was driving superbly." That much was true of both, and it was a delight to watch: Button was swift and consistent, Alonso a constant bundle of energy as he tried to coax more speed from the Ferrari and

corrected frequent, fleeting slides as he teetered through Parabolica.

The tyre stops would be decisive, but it was difficult to gauge the best time to come in. The first three – Massa was still there, within touch – were well clear of the rest after 15 laps, but not far enough that they could make a tyre stop and rejoin ahead of the pack (which didn't contain too many shrinking violets, with Rosberg still leading Kubica, Hülkenberg and Vettel, although Webber was now eighth after repassing Schumacher at the start of lap six).

There was a degree of scepticism when the Red Bulls swapped places on lap 20, but this had nothing to do with team tactics. Vettel suddenly lost straight-line performance and the team feared his engine was on the way out, although the problem soon cleared. Initially, it was thought that Vettel's airbox might have ingested a visor tear-off, but the telemetry revealed that brake pressure had momentarily been applied on the straight, the front calipers having bound on following an impact with a kerb.

The midfield runners began making scheduled stops from lap 16 – Alguersuari and de la Rosa were the first to come in – and there was an unfortunate incident when Yamamoto followed suit on lap 22. HRT gave him the signal to go while a radio engineer was still hunched over the cockpit. He was duly sent flying, although no serious injuries were caused. The cash-strapped team was later fined $20,000 for unsafe release.

Kubica was first of the faster runners to switch from softs to hards, on lap 33, and on his out lap he set the quickest sector-three time of the race. His first flying lap, a 1m 25.768s, was a personal best and within a couple of tenths of the leaders' pace. It looked as though the moment to change was ripe and the rest of the leading group reacted swiftly. Rosberg and Webber came in on lap 35, Button on 36 and Alonso on 37 – the latter pair both receiving radio instructions to "push like hell", a superfluous, patronising habit common to most teams.

Button spent 22.955 seconds in the pits, Alonso 22.194. The Spaniard's in-lap was quicker, too – 1m 28.594s to 1m 29.169s – and that was enough to give him a half-length lead as he rejoined.

On cold tyres, the Spaniard chucked his Ferrari mildly sideways in his bid to repel Button at the first chicane. The Englishman looked for space to the inside and outside, but emerged from the corner just behind and the race was effectively lost. Massa set a string of fastest laps while the two leaders were changing tyres, a detail that might have brought him into contention had he not subsequently overshot his pit bay during his own stop.

"I can't complain about our strategy," Whitmarsh said. "As the cars behind us cascaded in and switched to the hard tyre, we could see it was quicker and at that point you want to get on to the faster tyre as swiftly as possible. It would have been nice if Ferrari had come in at the same time as us, but it would have been a foolish thing for them to do. The bottom line is that Fernando was faster and our stop was a few tenths slower."

The race's closing stages passed off without major drama and Alonso completed his third win of the campaign in his first race as a Ferrari driver at Monza. He has had worse days.

"It is an important result in championship terms," he said, "especially considering what happened to Hamilton and Webber. Our title chances do not, though, hinge on what happens to the others. We need to find some consistency; sometimes we are

Left: Luca di Montezemolo was beside himself with delight at Ferrari's first Monza win since Schumacher in 2006.
Photo: Peter J Fox

Far left: Nico Hülkenberg drove an impressive race to bag seventh place for the Williams squad.
Photo: Paul-Henri Cahier

Below: After victory in Belgium, Lewis Hamilton came back to earth with a bump at Monza.
Photo: Peter J Fox

not performing at 100 per cent, and that's where we need to concentrate our efforts."

Button and Massa completed the podium, while Vettel had moved up to fourth courtesy of the day's best bit of improvisation: he stayed out on his Bridgestone softs until the end of the 52nd and penultimate lap. "Initially," said Red Bull sporting director Christian Horner, "we were planning to ditch the soft tyres after about 15 laps, but Seb still seemed to be running well."

Vettel was fourth on the road from lap 36, once the others had stopped, and – shades of Webber in Budapest – needed to put about 23 seconds between himself and Rosberg if he wanted to stay there. He was 22.2 seconds clear by lap 51, at which point the Mercedes driver lost a couple of seconds in traffic and Vettel's damage limitation was complete. "I'd forgotten what it was like to have grip," he said, after a single lap on hard Bridgestones, but Horner paid tribute to the discarded originals. "They lasted pretty well," he said. "Seb could have driven home on them."

Rosberg took fifth from Webber, who had a frustrating time following Hülkenberg during the second half of the race, The Australian had emerged just behind Kubica (whose tyre change had been rather slower than his subsequent pace) after the tyre stops, but passed the Pole on lap 37 and then encountered a stubborn defensive methodology from Williams's raw recruit, who bypassed the second part of the first chicane on three occasions. "He seemed to go through it every other lap," Webber said.

The stewards had earlier handed Alguersuari a drive-through for doing the same thing, but took no action against Hülkenberg, and Webber had to wait until lap 50 before he managed to slip ahead on the approach to the second chicane.

"I did cut the first corner," Hülkenberg said, "but I was trying hard and struggling a bit with my brake pedal. I didn't get a penalty, so I think it was okay, even though it was on the limit." Webber thought it "beyond" rather than "on", and so did almost everybody else. The German's fighting spirit, however, had been beyond reproach.

Kubica took eighth, from Schumacher, with Barrichello completing the top ten. The Brazilian suffered slight nose damage when he was forced wide in the initial jam at the opening corner, and that dropped him behind Buemi, which rather conditioned his afternoon. The Swiss stayed out until lap 33, at which point Barrichello made use of some clean air and moved ahead after his own stop four laps later.

Behind the Toro Rosso, Liuzzi and Petrov completed the unlapped runners, ahead of de la Rosa, Alguersuari and Sutil. The last had been hoping for a safety car, after his early stop, but it would have profited him little because eventually he had to pit again after damaging his car's nose. He had been following de la Rosa at the time and wasn't sure whether he'd clipped the Spaniard or a kerb, but either way the result was the same.

Glock, Kovalainen and Yamamoto completed the finishers, although di Grassi was classified, despite pitting just before the end with broken suspension. Trulli and Senna were the only casualties beyond the first lap, with failed gearbox and hydraulics respectively, but such details were scarcely noticed as the annual track invasion began.

"I can only compare the crowd reaction with my 2006 victory in Spain," Alonso said. "It's a very special feeling, and it's hard finding the words to describe it."

Simon Arron

EDITOR'S VIEW
ALONSO ESTABLISHES HIS TRUE STATUS

IT was a particularly busy time off-track in the run-up to the Italian Grand Prix, with Ferrari breathing a very audible and understandable sigh of relief after the FIA World Motor Sport Council had decided to apply no further sanction in the aftermath of the imposition of team orders that had eased Fernando Alonso's path to victory at Hockenheim several weeks earlier.

Unquestionably, the governing body had faced a dilemma. It could only act on the basis of hard and incontrovertible evidence, rather than speculation and hearsay. In fact, FIA president Jean Todt seemed convinced that team orders had been applied, but the decision not to impose further punishment stemmed from the fact that there had been ambiguities in the way the rules had been applied on previous occasions.

Yet not penalising Ferrari beyond the $100,000 fine that had already been levied on the team by the stewards of the meeting in Germany was seen by some as a poor compromise. Red Bull Racing team principal Christian Horner even went so far as to muse that, in effect, a tariff had been placed on team orders,

"And if you want to pay up $100,000 for the privilege [of infringing the rule], then it perhaps sends a message that you can," he said.

Similarly, Lewis Hamilton had very firm thoughts about how this ruling would impact on the balance of the world championship. "Some people like to win the championship in a different way, as we have seen in the past," said the 2008 title holder very pointedly. "I think Jenson and myself would be proud to go neck and neck to the end, and if we end up losing the championship to somebody like Fernando because he has the whole team behind him, I don't think I would feel too bad about it. I would feel I had worked my hardest and done my best."

Everybody felt they knew precisely what Hamilton was talking about, namely his somewhat strained relationship that had developed with Alonso during their 2007 season at McLaren. Yet the trouble with taking the stance Lewis adopted – no matter how understandable – is that there is always a set of circumstances lurking that conspires to nip your backside at the most inopportune moment.

On this occasion, it was Hamilton's exuberance on the opening lap of the race, which saw him sucked into a wheel-to-wheel confrontation with Felipe Massa's Ferrari at the second chicane. Ferrari's inclination to impose team orders on its drivers had nothing to do with Lewis's regrettable slip, which cost him a possible 25 points at a stroke. It was an extremely unfortunate episode, but at least with McLaren you know exactly where you are, their drivers being permitted to hurl themselves into unfettered action with friend and foe alike.

Not surprisingly, Ferrari was elated to have registered its first Italian Grand Prix win since Michael Schumacher's victorious swansong four years earlier. With the assistance and collaboration of Ross Brawn and Jean Todt, Michael had turned Maranello into his private fiefdom. Now Fernando Alonso had done the same in front of the adoring *tifosi*, his Monza victory in one of the famous scarlet machines amounting to a symbolic rite of passage, which cemented the Spaniard's heroic status in the minds of the Italian fans.

Felipe Massa, trailing home in a worthy third place, had been consigned to number-two status more comprehensively and decisively than was possible by the imposition of team orders. It was always going to turn out like that for the increasingly bewildered and dispirited Brazilian.

Alan Henry

Above: Felipe Massa took third place, but inevitably was overshadowed by the winner.

Left: Alonso could hardly have done a better job for his adoring fans.

Top left: The *tifosi* flood the track as Alonso, Domenicalli and Massa soak up the applause.
Photos: Peter J Fox

FIA F1 WORLD CHAMPIONSHIP · ROUND 14

GRAN PREMIO SANTANDER D'ITALIA

MONZA 10–12 SEPTEMBER 2010

RACE DISTANCE: 53 laps, 190.587 miles/306.720km

RACE WEATHER: Sunny (track 33–36°C, air 25°C)

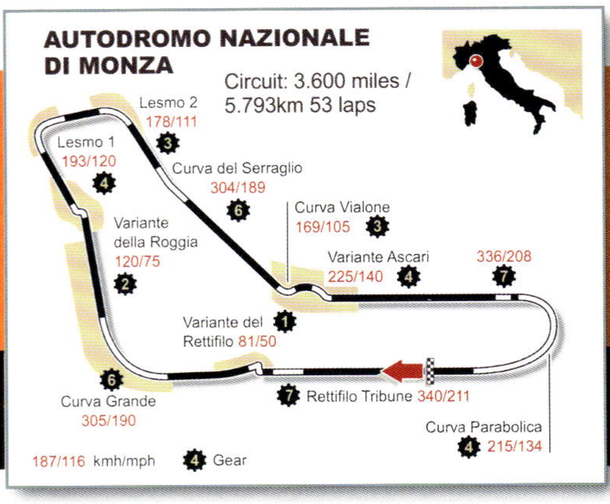

Pos.	Driver	Nat.	No.	Entrant	Car/Engine	Tyres	Laps	Time/Retirement	Speed (mph/km/h)	Gap to leader	Fastest race lap	
1	**Fernando Alonso**	E	8	Scuderia Ferrari Marlboro	Ferrari F10-056 V8	B	53	1h 16m 24.572s	149.657/240.849		1m 24.139s	52
2	**Jenson Button**	GB	1	Vodafone McLaren Mercedes	McLaren MP4-25-Mercedes FO108X V8	B	53	1h 16m 27.510s	149.561/240.695	+ 2.938s	1m 24.598s	46
3	**Felipe Massa**	BR	7	Scuderia Ferrari Marlboro	Ferrari F10-056 V8	B	53	1h 16m 28.795s	149.519/240.627	+ 4.223s	1m 24.575s	51
4	**Sebastian Vettel**	D	5	Red Bull Racing	Red Bull RB6-Renault RS27 V8	B	53	1h 16m 52.768s	148.742/239.377	+ 28.196s	1m 24.493s	50
5	**Nico Rosberg**	D	4	Mercedes GP Petronas F1 Team	Mercedes MGP W01-Mercedes FO108X V8	B	53	1h 16m 54.514s	148.685/239.286	+ 29.942s	1m 24.491s	52
6	**Mark Webber**	AUS	6	Red Bull Racing	Red Bull RB6-Renault RS27 V8	B	53	1h 16m 55.848s	148.643/239.217	+ 31.276s	1m 24.278s	52
7	**Nico Hülkenberg**	D	10	AT&T Williams	Williams FW32-Cosworth CA2010 V8	B	53	1h 16m 57.384s	148.593/239.137	+ 32.812s	1m 24.576s	52
8	**Robert Kubica**	PL	11	Renault F1 Team	Renault R30-RS27 V8	B	53	1h 16m 58.600s	148.554/239.075	+ 34.028s	1m 24.560s	48
9	**Michael Schumacher**	GB	3	Mercedes GP Petronas F1 Team	Mercedes MGP W01-Mercedes FO108X V8	B	53	1h 17m 09.520s	148.204/238.511	+ 44.948s	1m 24.947s	49
10	**Rubens Barrichello**	BR	9	AT&T Williams	Williams FW32-Cosworth CA2010 V8	B	53	1h 17m 28.785s	147.589/237.522	+ 1m 04.213s	1m 25.239s	48
11	Sébastien Buemi	CH	16	Scuderia Toro Rosso	Toro Rosso STR5-Ferrari 056 V8	B	53	1h 17m 29.628s	147.563/237.479	+ 1m 05.056s	1m 25.224s	51
12	Vitantonio Liuzzi	I	15	Force India F1 Team	Force India VJM03-Mercedes FO108X V8	B	53	1h 17m 30.678s	147.530/237.426	+ 1m 06.106s	1m 25.102s	51
13	Vitaly Petrov	RUS	12	Renault F1 Team	Renault R30-RS27 V8	B	53	1h 17m 43.491s	147.124/236.773	+ 1m 18.919s	1m 24.644s	53
14	Pedro de la Rosa	E	22	BMW Sauber F1 Team	BMW Sauber C29-Ferrari 056 V8	B	52			+ 1 lap	1m 26.325s	47
15	Jaime Alguersuari	E	17	Scuderia Toro Rosso	Toro Rosso STR5-Ferrari 056 V8	B	52			+ 1 lap	1m 25.472s	51
16	Adrian Sutil	D	14	Force India F1 Team	Force India VJM03-Mercedes FO108X V8	B	52			+ 1 lap	1m 24.937s	51
17	Timo Glock	D	24	Virgin Racing	Virgin VR-01-Cosworth CA2010 V8	B	51			+ 2 laps	1m 27.765s	50
18	Heikki Kovalainen	FIN	19	Lotus Racing	Lotus T127-Cosworth CA2010 V8	B	51			+ 2 laps	1m 27.822s	50
19	Sakon Yamamoto	J	20	HRT F1 Team	HRT F110-Cosworth CA2010 V8	B	51			+ 2 laps	1m 28.875s	45
20	Lucas Di Grassi	BR	25	Virgin Racing	Virgin VR-01-Cosworth CA2010 V8	B	50	*suspension*		+ 3 laps	1m 28.171s	46
	Jarno Trulli	I	18	Lotus Racing	Lotus T127-Cosworth CA2010 V8	B	46	*gearbox*			1m 29.017s	30
	Bruno Senna	BR	21	HRT F1 Team	HRT F110-Cosworth CA2010 V8	B	11	*hydraulics*			1m 30.880s	10
	Lewis Hamilton	GB	2	Vodafone McLaren Mercedes	McLaren MP4-25-Mercedes FO108X V8	B	0	*accident*			no time	
	Kamui Kobayashi	J	23	BMW Sauber F1 Team	BMW Sauber C29-Ferrari 056 V8	B	0	*gearbox*			no time	

Fastest race lap: Fernando Alonso on lap 52, 1m 24.139s, 154.014mph/ 247.861km/h.

Lap record: Rubens Barrichello (Ferrari F2004 V10), 1m 21.046s, 159.892mph/257.320km/h (2004).

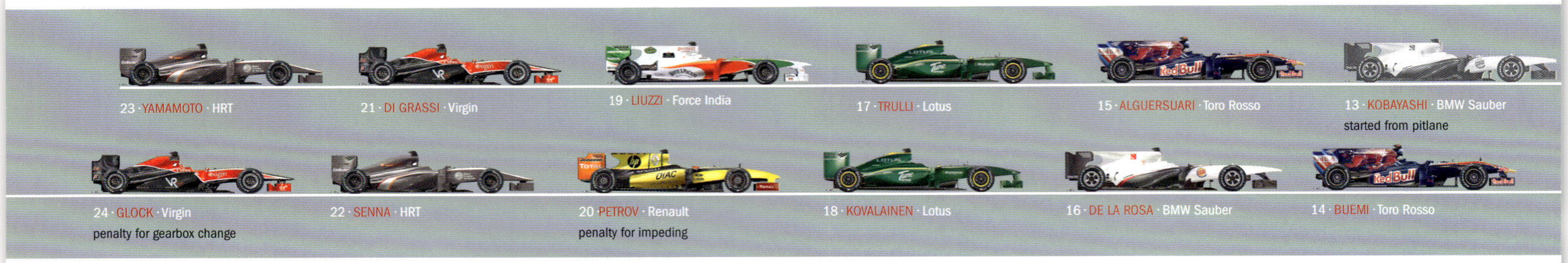

Grid order	1	2	3	4	5	6	7	8	9	10	11	12	13	14	15	16	17	18	19	20	21	22	23	24	25	26	27	28	29	30	31	32	33	34	35	36	37	38	39	40	41	42
8 ALONSO	1	1	1	1	1	1	1	1	1	1	1	1	1	1	1	1	1	1	1	1	1	1	1	1	1	1	1	1	1	1	1	1	1	1	1	8	7	7	8	8	8	8
1 BUTTON	8	8	8	8	8	8	8	8	8	8	8	8	8	8	8	8	8	8	8	8	8	8	8	8	8	8	8	8	8	8	8	8	8	8	8	7	8	8	1	1	1	1
7 MASSA	7	7	7	7	7	7	7	7	7	7	7	7	7	7	7	7	7	7	7	7	7	7	7	7	7	7	7	7	7	7	7	7	7	7	7	1	1	1	7	7	7	7
6 WEBBER	4	4	4	4	4	4	4	4	4	4	4	4	4	4	4	4	4	4	4	4	4	4	4	4	4	4	4	4	4	4	4	4	4	4	10	5	5	5	5	5	5	5
2 HAMILTON	11	11	11	11	11	11	11	11	11	11	11	11	11	11	11	11	11	11	11	11	11	11	11	11	11	11	11	11	11	11	11	11	10	10	4	10	4	4	4	4	4	4
5 VETTEL	10	10	10	10	10	10	10	10	10	10	10	10	10	10	10	10	10	10	10	10	10	10	10	10	10	10	10	10	10	10	10	10	6	6	5	3	10	10	10	10	10	10
4 ROSBERG	5	5	5	5	5	5	5	5	5	5	5	5	5	5	5	5	5	5	5	6	6	6	6	6	6	6	6	6	6	6	6	6	11	5	6	4	6	6	6	6	6	6
10 HULKENBERG	3	3	3	3	3	6	6	6	6	6	6	6	6	6	6	6	6	6	6	5	5	5	5	5	5	5	5	5	5	5	5	5	5	3	3	11	11	11	11	11	11	11
11 KUBICA	6	6	6	6	6	3	3	3	3	3	3	3	3	3	3	3	3	3	3	3	3	3	3	3	3	3	3	3	3	3	3	3	3	11	11	6	9	3	3	3	3	3
9 BARRICHELLO	16	16	16	16	16	16	16	16	16	16	16	16	16	16	16	16	16	16	16	16	16	16	16	16	16	16	16	16	16	16	16	16	9	9	9	9	3	12	12	12	12	12
14 SUTIL	9	9	9	9	9	9	9	9	9	9	9	9	9	9	9	9	9	9	9	9	9	9	9	9	9	9	9	9	9	9	9	9	16	12	12	12	12	9	9	9	9	9
3 SCHUMACHER	22	22	22	22	22	22	22	22	22	15	15	15	15	15	15	15	15	15	15	15	15	15	15	15	15	15	15	15	15	15	15	12	12	16	16	16	16	16	16	16	16	16
23 KOBAYASHI	17	17	15	15	15	15	15	15	15	22	22	22	22	22	22	22	22	12	12	12	12	12	12	12	12	12	12	12	12	12	12	15	15	15	15	15	15	15	15	15	15	15
16 BUEMI	15	15	17	17	17	17	17	17	17	17	17	17	17	17	17	12	12	22	22	22	22	22	22	22	22	22	22	22	22	22	22	22	22	22	22	22	22	22	22	22	22	22
17 ALGUERSUARI	12	12	12	12	12	12	12	12	12	12	12	12	12	12	12	17	18	18	17	17	14	14	14	14	14	14	14	14	14	14	14	14	14	14	14	14	*17*	17	17	17	17	*17*
22 DE LA ROSA	18	18	18	18	18	18	18	18	18	18	18	18	18	18	18	18	17	17	18	14	17	18	18	18	*18*	*17*	*17*	*17*	*17*	*17*	*17*	*17*	*17*	*17*	*17*	*17*	*14*	*14*	*14*	*14*	*14*	*14*
18 TRULLI	24	24	24	24	24	24	24	24	24	24	24	24	24	24	24	14	14	14	14	18	18	24	17	17	*17*	*18*	*18*	*18*	*18*	*18*	*18*	*18*	*18*	*18*	*18*	*24*	*24*	*24*	*24*	*24*	*24*	*24*
19 KOVALAINEN	25	25	25	25	19	19	19	19	19	19	19	19	19	19	19	24	24	24	24	24	24	19	24	*24*	*25*	*24*	*24*	*24*	*24*	*24*	*24*	*24*	*24*	*24*	*24*	*19*	*19*	*19*	*19*	*19*	*19*	*19*
15 LIUZZI	19	19	19	19	25	25	25	25	25	25	25	25	14	14	14	19	19	19	19	19	19	17	*19*	*25*	*24*	*19*	*19*	*19*	*19*	*19*	*19*	*19*	*19*	*19*	*19*	*18*	*18*	*18*	*18*	*25*	*25*	*25*
12 PETROV	20	20	20	20	20	20	20	20	20	20	14	14	25	25	25	25	25	25	25	25	*25*	*25*	*25*	*19*	*19*	*25*	*25*	*25*	*25*	*25*	*25*	*25*	*25*	*25*	*25*	*25*	*25*	*25*	*25*	*18*	*18*	*18*
25 DI GRASSI	21	21	21	21	21	21	21	21	21	21	20	20	20	20	20	20	20	20	20	*20*	*20*	*20*	*20*	*20*	*20*	*20*	*20*	*20*	*20*	*20*	*20*	*20*	*20*	*20*	*20*	*20*	*20*	*20*	*20*	*20*	*20*	*20*
21 SENNA	14	14	14	14	14	14	14	14	14	14	21																															
20 YAMAMOTO																																										
24 GLOCK																																										

21 Pit stop   *14 One lap or more behind*

TIME SHEETS

PRACTICE 1 (FRIDAY)

Weather: Sunny
Temperatures: track 25-31°C, air 18°-22°C

Pos.	Driver	Laps	Time
1	Jenson Button	28	1m 23.693s
2	Sebastian Vettel	27	1m 23.790s
3	Lewis Hamilton	25	1m 23.967s
4	Robert Kubica	25	1m 24.120s
5	Nico Rosberg	30	1m 24.129s
6	Mark Webber	26	1m 24.446s
7	Vitantonio Liuzzi	19	1m 24.512s
8	Fernando Alonso	24	1m 24.543s
9	Felipe Massa	22	1m 24.648s
10	Michael Schumacher	26	1m 24.756s
11	Nico Hülkenberg	28	1m 24.841s
12	Paul Di Resta	23	1m 24.923s
13	Vitaly Petrov	25	1m 25.292s
14	Sébastien Buemi	29	1m 25.318s
15	Pedro de la Rosa	20	1m 25.320s
16	Kamui Kobayashi	24	1m 25.334s
17	Jaime Alguersuari	19	1m 25.897s
18	Timo Glock	19	1m 26.772s
19	Jarno Trulli	12	1m 26.898s
20	Lucas Di Grassi	17	1m 26.956s
21	Heikki Kovalainen	14	1m 27.374s
22	Bruno Senna	8	1m 28.256s
23	Rubens Barrichello	4	1m 28.516s
24	Sakon Yamamoto	17	1m 29.870s

PRACTICE 2 (FRIDAY)

Weather: Sunny
Temperatures: track 35-37°C, air 24-26°C

Pos.	Driver	Laps	Time
1	Sebastian Vettel	27	1m 22.839s
2	Fernando Alonso	32	1m 22.915s
3	Felipe Massa	20	1m 23.061s
4	Lewis Hamilton	22	1m 23.154s
5	Jenson Button	38	1m 23.210s
6	Mark Webber	23	1m 23.415s
7	Rubens Barrichello	31	1m 23.708s
8	Robert Kubica	32	1m 23.709s
9	Nico Hülkenberg	30	1m 23.852s
10	Nico Rosberg	29	1m 23.857s
11	Adrian Sutil	35	1m 24.181s
12	Vitantonio Liuzzi	36	1m 24.380s
13	Vitaly Petrov	21	1m 24.407s
14	Michael Schumacher	29	1m 24.448s
15	Sébastien Buemi	35	1m 24.517s
16	Pedro de la Rosa	32	1m 24.547s
17	Kamui Kobayashi	31	1m 24.785s
18	Jaime Alguersuari	24	1m 25.106s
19	Jarno Trulli	38	1m 26.204s
20	Heikki Kovalainen	41	1m 26.306s
21	Lucas Di Grassi	31	1m 26.631s
22	Timo Glock	25	1m 26.676s
23	Sakon Yamamoto	5	1m 29.498s
24	Bruno Senna	3	no time

PRACTICE 3 (SATURDAY)

Weather: Sunny
Temperatures: track 31-33°C, air 23°C

Pos.	Driver	Laps	Time
1	Lewis Hamilton	19	1m 22.498s
2	Sebastian Vettel	21	1m 22.545s
3	Fernando Alonso	15	1m 22.644s
4	Felipe Massa	16	1m 22.648s
5	Jenson Button	19	1m 22.724s
6	Nico Rosberg	17	1m 22.946s
7	Mark Webber	9	1m 23.082s
8	Nico Hülkenberg	18	1m 23.129s
9	Robert Kubica	20	1m 23.209s
10	Adrian Sutil	19	1m 23.303s
11	Rubens Barrichello	19	1m 23.450s
12	Sébastien Buemi	20	1m 23.673s
13	Michael Schumacher	21	1m 23.896s
14	Kamui Kobayashi	24	1m 23.908s
15	Jaime Alguersuari	17	1m 23.909s
16	Vitaly Petrov	19	1m 23.967s
17	Pedro de la Rosa	19	1m 24.191s
18	Vitantonio Liuzzi	15	1m 24.439s
19	Jarno Trulli	14	1m 25.788s
20	Heikki Kovalainen	16	1m 25.925s
21	Timo Glock	18	1m 26.434s
22	Lucas Di Grassi	19	1m 26.682s
23	Bruno Senna	18	1m 27.471s
24	Sakon Yamamoto	14	1m 28.730s

QUALIFYING (SATURDAY)

Weather: Sunny Temperatures: track 37-38°C, air 27°C

Pos.	Driver	First	Second	Third	Qualifying Tyre
1	Fernando Alonso	1m 22.646s	1m 22.297s	1m 21.962s	Soft
2	Jenson Button	1m 23.085s	1m 22.354s	1m 22.084s	Soft
3	Felipe Massa	1m 22.421s	1m 22.610s	1m 22.293s	Soft
4	Mark Webber	1m 23.431s	1m 22.706s	1m 22.433s	Soft
5	Lewis Hamilton	1m 22.830s	1m 22.394s	1m 22.623s	Soft
6	Sebastian Vettel	1m 23.235s	1m 22.701s	1m 22.675s	Soft
7	Nico Rosberg	1m 23.529s	1m 23.055s	1m 23.027s	Soft
8	Nico Hülkenberg	1m 23.516s	1m 22.989s	1m 23.037s	Soft
9	Robert Kubica	1m 23.234s	1m 22.880s	1m 23.039s	Soft
10	Rubens Barrichello	1m 23.695s	1m 23.142s	1m 23.328s	Soft
11	Adrian Sutil	1m 23.493s	1m 23.199s		
12	Michael Schumacher	1m 23.840s	1m 23.388s		
13	Kamui Kobayashi	1m 24.273s	1m 23.659s		
14	Sébastien Buemi	1m 23.744s	1m 23.681s		
15	Vitaly Petrov	1m 24.086s	1m 23.819s		
16	Jaime Alguersuari	1m 24.083s	1m 23.919s		
17	Pedro de la Rosa	1m 24.442s	1m 24.044s		
18	Jarno Trulli	1m 25.540s			
19	Heikki Kovalainen	1m 25.742s			
20	Vitantonio Liuzzi	1m 25.774s			
21	Timo Glock	1m 25.934s			
22	Lucas Di Grassi	1m 25.974s			
23	Bruno Senna	1m 26.847s			
24	Sakon Yamamoto	1m 27.020s			

FOR THE RECORD

30th PODIUM: Jenson Button

DID YOU KNOW

This was the 60th Formula One grand prix at Monza (present every year of the world championship apart from 1980).

POINTS

DRIVERS

1	Mark Webber	187
2	Lewis Hamilton	182
3	Fernando Alonso	166
4	Jenson Button	165
5	Sebastian Vettel	163
6	Felipe Massa	124
7	Robert Kubica	112
8	Nico Rosberg	108
9	Michael Schumacher	46
10	Adrian Sutil	45
11	Rubens Barrichello	31
12	Kamui Kobayashi	21
13	Vitaly Petrov	19
14	Nico Hülkenberg	16
15	Vitantonio Liuzzi	13
16	Sébastien Buemi	7
17	Pedro de la Rosa	6
18	Jaime Alguersuari	3

CONSTRUCTORS

1	Red Bull	350
2	McLaren	347
3	Ferrari	290
4	Mercedes	158
5	Renault	127
6	Force India	58
7	Williams	47
8	BMW Sauber	27
9	Toro Rosso	10

43	44	45	46	47	48	49	50	51	52	53	-
8	8	8	8	8	8	8	8	8	8	8	1
1	1	1	1	1	1	1	1	1	1	1	2
7	7	7	7	7	7	7	7	7	7	7	3
5	5	5	5	5	5	5	5	5	5	5	
4	4	4	4	4	4	4	4	4	4	4	
10	10	10	10	10	10	10	6	6	6	6	6
6	6	6	6	6	6	6	10	10	10	10	7
11	11	11	11	11	11	11	11	11	11	11	8
3	3	3	3	3	3	3	3	3	3	3	9
12	12	12	12	12	12	12	9	9	9	9	10
9	9	9	9	9	9	9	16	16	16	16	
16	16	16	16	16	16	16	15	15	15	15	
15	15	15	15	15	15	15	12	12	12	12	
22	22	22	22	22	22	22	22	22	22		
17	17	17	17	17	17	17	17	17	17		
14	14	14	14	14	14	14	14	14	14		
24	24	24	24	24	24	24	24	24			
19	19	19	19	19	19	19	19	19			
25	25	25	25	25	25	25	20	20			
18	18	18	18	20	20	20	25				
20	20	20	20								

RACE TYRE STRATEGIES

	Driver	Race Stint 1	Race Stint 2	Race Stint 3
1	Alonso	Soft: 1-37	Hard: 38-53	
2	Button	Soft: 1-36	Hard: 37-53	
3	Massa	Soft: 1-38	Hard: 39-53	
4	Vettel	Soft: 1-52	Hard: 53	
5	Rosberg	Soft: 1-35	Hard: 36-53	
6	Webber	Soft: 1-35	Hard: 36-53	
7	Hülkenberg	Soft: 1-36	Hard: 37-53	
8	Kubica	Soft: 1-33	Hard: 34-53	
9	Schumacher	Soft: 1-36	Hard: 37-53	
10	Barrichello	Soft: 1-37	Hard: 38-53	
11	Buemi	Soft: 1-33	Hard: 34-53	
12	Liuzzi	Soft: 1-31	Hard: 32-53	
13	Petrov	Hard: 1-49	Soft: 50-53	
14	de la Rosa	Soft: 1-17	Hard: 18-52	
15	Alguersuari	Hard: 1-16	Soft: 17-21	Soft: 22-52
16	Sutil	Soft: 1-2	Hard: 3-36	Soft: 37-52
17	Glock	Soft: 1-24	Hard: 25-51	
18	Kovalainen	Soft: 1-23	Hard: 24-51	
19	Yamamoto	Soft: 1-22	Hard: 23-51	
20	di Grassi	Soft: 1-25	Hard:26-50	
	Trulli	Soft: 1-25	Hard: 26-46 (dnf)	
	Senna	Soft: 1-11 (dnf)		
	Hamilton	Soft: 0 (dnf)		
	Kobayashi	Hard: 0 (dnf)		

The tyre regulations stipulate that the two dry tyre specifications must be used during the race. The Soft compound Bridgestone Potenza tyre is marked with a green stripe on the sidewall.

Photos: Peter J. Fox

FIA FORMULA 1 WORLD CHAMPIONSHIP · ROUND 15

SINGAPORE GRAND PRIX

MARINA BAY CIRCUIT

Fernando Alonso's Ferrari is almost like an impressionist painting as it streaks along the shoreline.
Photo: Peter J Fox

MARINA BAY QUALIFYING

THE forecast suggested more rain and another Red Bull pole position, but neither materialised. The serial pace-setter might have been quickest throughout free practice, but – five years to the day since he had clinched his first Formula One world title – Fernando Alonso had a fractional edge when it mattered.

After conducting tests on Friday, Ferrari opted to dispense with its F-duct because the advantages were felt to be negligible on a circuit with few significant straights. Qualifying began badly for the team, though, when an electronic problem stranded Felipe Massa before the Brazilian had completed a timed lap. "We have some experimental parts this weekend," Alonso said, "but after Felipe's problem, we reset my engine to minimise any risk of a repeat. In any case, today's conditions weren't easy because we've had very little running in completely dry conditions. At the start of qualifying, I still wasn't 100 per cent confident in the car. I was happy with both Q3 runs, though: my lap times were similar, although I had no idea whether that would be good enough for first, second, fourth or wherever. To be on pole is good news, and I was a bit surprised to see the Red Bulls behind, but if it rains tomorrow anything could happen."

The team made a mistake in Q2 – programming the wrong engine map into Alonso's car – but pressed the correct buttons before Q3, and the Spaniard responded with a 1m 45.390s, enough to put him just 0.067 seconds clear of Sebastian Vettel.

The German described qualifying as "messy". On his first Q3 run, he got a little too close to Michael Schumacher's Mercedes and had to follow it for a significant chunk of the lap. "I misjudged the gap," he said. "I was about three seconds behind Michael when I crossed the line, which I thought would be enough to allow me a clear run, but I caught him within about five corners."

That left Vettel a single shot at the top spot and he almost wasted that, too, gently brushing the wall at Turn 13, but the time loss was minimal. "The car was definitely good enough for pole," Vettel said, "but I just didn't get it together."

At least, in his case, the problem was temporary. Teammate Mark Webber had struggled all weekend to put clean laps together and never looked like challenging for pole. "I've had real trouble getting into a rhythm," he said, "and there are a few places where I know I lost time on most of my laps."

He lined up behind the McLarens of Lewis Hamilton and Jenson Button as the title chasing quintet locked out the top five places.

"I can't complain," Hamilton said. "I lost time on my first run, because I got a bit too close to Jenson, and then simply didn't do a very good job on my second. I'm on the clean side of the grid, though, and we've been making good starts of late. I'm expecting an extremely tricky race, especially if it rains at some stage, because we've seen how long it takes for the track to dry. I think the Red Bulls are beatable, though; Fernando has proved that."

With Massa starting at the back anyway, Ferrari opted to give him his ninth engine of the season (one over the allocated eight) and a fresh gearbox. Technically, that was worth a grid penalty of 15 places, although in the circumstances it made absolutely no difference. Nico Hülkenberg slipped from 12th to 17th, however, as a result of his Williams's transmission being changed.

Nick Heidfeld started 14th on his return to Sauber, which had dropped Pedro de la Rosa, while Christian Klien prepared for his first F1 start since Monza 2006 after replacing Sakon Yamamoto at HRT. Officially the Japanese driver had suffered a bout of food poisoning, although his cheery demeanour around the paddock suggested that the problem had more to do with sponsorship than anything he might have eaten.

Above: Former F1 drivers Stefan Johansson, Danny Sullivan and Eddie Cheever chew over old times.
Photo: Jean-François Galeron/WRi2

Above centre: Nick Heidfeld was behind the wheel of a Sauber once again.

Top: Alonso finds time for a brief interview just before the start.
Photos: Peter J Fox

Right: Christian Klien took over behind the wheel of the HRT.
Photo: Lukas Gorys

Above right: Vettel crosses the Anderson Bridge on his way to second place.
Photo: Peter J Fox

HE'D shadowed the Ferrari from the start and now, as Fernando Alonso peeled in to make his mandatory tyre stop, Sebastian Vettel tracked him once more. On the surface, it appeared a curious decision, as though Red Bull was unwilling to attempt strategic improvisation, but circumstance left the team little choice. If Vettel were to beat the Spaniard, he'd have to pass him on the circuit. Alonso had been flawless all weekend, however, and remained so to score his second victory against the Singaporean nightscape.

Both drivers had made good starts from the front row and Alonso issued his customary defensive chop on the run to Turn One – as good a deterrent as any – to lead from Vettel, Lewis Hamilton, Jenson Button, Mark Webber, Nico Rosberg, Robert Kubica, Rubens Barrichello, Michael Schumacher, Vitaly Petrov, Kamui Kobayashi, Sébastien Buemi, Nico Hülkenberg, Adrian Sutil, Tonio Liuzzi, Heikki Kovalainen, Jarno Trulli, Timo Glock, Christian Klien, Lucas di Grassi, Jaime Alguersuari (who had started from the pit lane after his Toro Rosso had developed a coolant leak) and Bruno Senna. Felipe Massa headed straight to the pits for a tactical tyre change (as he was at the back anyway, he wanted to gain time in clear air in the hope that a safety car might profit him later – a plan that had worked for Alonso in Monaco), while Nick Heidfeld stopped for a fresh nose, having spent a significant proportion of the opening lap bumping into Liuzzi.

That had brisk consequences, because the Italian's rear suspension had taken a significant hit, and a toe-link fractured on lap two, causing him to wobble to a halt with his car in a precarious position. The safety car was duly dispatched, albeit far too soon to be of any assistance to Massa.

Red Bull contemplated a strategic punt – was it worthwhile calling Vettel in? – but eventually it summoned Webber instead. Initially, the Australian queried the decision – he would be required to nurse a set of medium Bridgestones for the best part of two hours – but he heeded the instruction and, with most of the second half of the field adopting the same tactic, dropped only to 11th, behind Rosberg, Kubica, Barrichello, Schumacher, Kobayashi and Glock, the last three of whom he picked off fairly swiftly after the race resumed at the end of lap five. "When I came out," said Webber, "it was clear that I was in a reasonable position. I saw Kamui brushing walls and jumping kerbs, so thought I'd better get past as soon as possible, Things were going to be interesting if he carried on driving like that for the next two hours."

Webber needed to remain within 25 seconds of the two McLarens to have a chance of taking third place when eventually they came in for fresh rubber, and although subsequently he was unable to pass the tenacious Barrichello, the Williams was swift enough to keep Webber on target. It helped that Hamilton and Button had been forced to proceed with a degree of caution, to keep their rear super-softs in shape.

Webber wasn't the only one keeping an eye on the McLarens. Alonso had a slight edge on the softer rubber in the opening stages of the race, so Vettel preferred to keep a watching brief, but their pace remained relentless. Neither, though, could afford to make a mandatory tyre stop until Hamilton had done likewise, for they would have rejoined behind him and lost time when they could least afford it, with their fresh tyres' potential at its most effective.

Eventually, Hamilton came in on lap 28, rejoining about six seconds behind Webber, and he left a big enough gap on the track to accommodate the two leaders. While they were running hard at the front, their teams had been focusing on the car in third.

"Our main hope," said Red Bull sporting director Christian Horner, "was that we'd be able to pit one lap before Ferrari and benefit from an extra lap of new-tyre pace. As soon as we saw Alonso coming in, though, we knew we'd have to pass him on the track. Should we have stayed out for an extra couple of laps, to try a different tactic? No, because the benefit of the new tyres was such that Seb would have dropped further behind."

Alonso was 1.8 seconds clear when the leaders pitted on lap 29, and the pressure was further relieved when Vettel faltered as he left the pits. "Our best option was to come in and put pressure on Ferrari in the pits," the German said, "because everyone knows our stops are very strong. Unfortunately, I had a bit of a wobble with the getaway procedure and Ferrari made a clean stop, so that was that."

Button stopped at the same time, rejoining behind Webber and Hamilton, but another potential twist lay just around the corner. Remember what Webber had said about Kobayashi's technique earlier in the race?

The Japanese driver was still on his original set of super-softs, which were fairly well shredded by lap 31, and simply misjudged Turn 18, the second-gear left-hander that passes beneath a grandstand. The car came to rest nose-first against the wall and Senna, next on the scene, had no chance to react. The HRT slammed into the stricken Sauber, triggering another short safety car interlude. The stewards investigated the Brazilian's conduct at the scene of waved yellow flags, but took no punitive action after establishing that he'd done all he could to avoid a collision: he had been defeated by time and space.

When the race restarted, at the end of lap 35, Vettel and Webber were separated by the lapped Virgins of di Grassi and Glock, the latter having driven a splendid cameo earlier in the race. After electing not to pit during the first safety car period, he wound up in the top half of the field and – Webber apart – managed to hold off a gaggle of faster cars for quite some time. His technique had been a treat to witness, although it involved nothing more complicated than putting his car in the right place at the right time – the ancient art of racecraft.

The same situation applied now, Glock responding immediately to the blue flags and moving aside to give quicker traffic a clear passage, but di Grassi was less attentive. He impeded Webber quite badly at the exit of Turn Five – and Hamilton is never one to let an opportunity pass. The McLaren driver dived to Webber's right and drew alongside on the approach to the left-hander at Turn Seven, but the Australian was within his rights to stake a claim for the inside line. He was still there when Hamilton turned in. The McLaren's left rear wheel connected with the Red Bull's right front: Hamilton was out on the spot with suspension damage, but Webber was able to continue, albeit with the affected wheel now significantly out of balance. "I couldn't see Mark," said Hamilton, "and thought I was ahead." He had been, but insufficiently so: for the second consecutive race, he went away without scoring (no bonus points being awarded for throwing your steering wheel a significant distance, something for which he appeared to possess a natural aptitude).

"Lewis had to have a go," said Webber, "because he saw it was very difficult for me to clear the Virgins. When we have backmarkers in the queue at a restart, it's not easy for the guy in front. Lewis had a pretty good run on me, but it was a key point in the race and neither of us wanted to give an inch. He was a little bit ahead, but it was incredibly tight. We didn't hit that hard, but it could have been enough to put us both out of the race."

Applying common sense, which seemed to be an ever more prominent feature of Jean Todt's presidential code, the FIA stewards – guided by 1985 Indy 500 winner Danny Sullivan – decreed it a racing incident and took no further action. They were of like mind soon afterwards when Schumacher and Heidfeld, who had collided gently at Turn Five on lap 31, did so again six laps and two corners later, this time with greater force. Heidfeld was barged into the tyre wall, where he remained, while his assailant returned to the pits for repairs.

With Webber hamstrung by a cocktail of old tyres and fresh vibration, the first two were able to pull well clear (although the Australian was still quick enough to contain the following Button).

The pit stops had altered the performance equation at the front. Vettel was, potentially, slightly faster on the medium Bridgestones, but Alonso's relentless consistency under pressure meant the balance of power remained unchanged. "It was difficult at the end," Alonso said, "because there was a group of cars ahead and I had to manage the gap to them without running the risk of overtaking under yellow flags, or anything like that." As he had all evening, he controlled the situation to perfection.

The yellow flags appeared on lap 58, after Kovalainen had spun on his own oil and then driven on, spewing lubricant and belching increasingly vigorous flames. The Finn was looking for somewhere sensible to stop, but considered the pit lane a bad

Left: Fernando Alonso looks supremely relaxed and content with his latest trophy.
Photo: Peter J Fox

Far left: Lucas di Grassi unwittingly triggered the collision between Mark Webber and Lewis Hamilton. Team-mate Timo Glock, following here, drove an engaging little cameo.
Photo: Paul-Henri Cahier

Below: Jenson gives his version of the race to the massed ranks of TV and radio reporters.
Photo: Peter J Fox

idea, so parked on the main straight instead. He then hopped over the pit counter, borrowed an extinguisher from the Williams garage and returned to deal with the blaze, although the Lotus continued to smoulder gently as Alonso took the flag to score the 25th victory of his F1 career. "I was pushing Fernando as hard as I could," said Vettel, "and hoped he might clip one of the walls or something, but he drove very well."

Webber duly took a distant third, from Button, with Rosberg and Barrichello completing the top six ahead of Kubica, who had had a busier night than most. A right rear puncture had forced the Pole to make an unscheduled stop on lap 45, dropping him from sixth to 12th, but he had capitalised on a fresh set of mediums to recover five of the lost positions with an engaging series of passes, the best of which involved sweeping past Sutil around the outside of Turn Seven.

Sutil and Hülkenberg were next to cross the line, but long after the race – at 1.30 the following morning in the Williams driver's case – both were handed drive-through penalties for taking short cuts on the opening lap. The stewards might have been a tad slow to react to the Sutil incident, at Turn Seven, but only investigated Hülkenberg in the wake of a successful protest from Force India, who felt the German had passed Liuzzi illegally.

As drive-throughs are not technically servable on Mondays, both drivers were given 20-second time penalties, which dropped them to ninth and tenth, behind Massa. Predictably, the Ferrari driver had spent the whole race in traffic and, given that his tyres had done all but the opening lap, he was understandably powerless to repel Kubica in the final stages.

Petrov was next, happy with his pace, but less so with Hülkenberg, who had bundled him wide at Turn Seven as early as lap seven, costing the Russian three places and dropping both behind Sutil. Alguersuari, Schumacher, Buemi and di Grassi completed the survivors, although Kovalainen's frazzled Lotus was classified 16th. Hydraulic problems accounted for Glock, Klien and Trulli, the last of whom had run at the back after sustaining a puncture on lap six.

Nobody was able to explain quite how Webber had avoided a similar fate. After the race, the Australian's right front tyre was found to be loose on its wheel, a consequence of his brush with Hamilton 25 laps before, yet somehow it hadn't deflated. "There was quite a gap between rubber and rim," said Horner. "I have never seen anything like it." Had the circuit featured a genuinely quick left-hander, the tyre would not have survived. A slice of championship luck?

Perhaps, but Alonso was beginning to display championship form.

Simon Arron

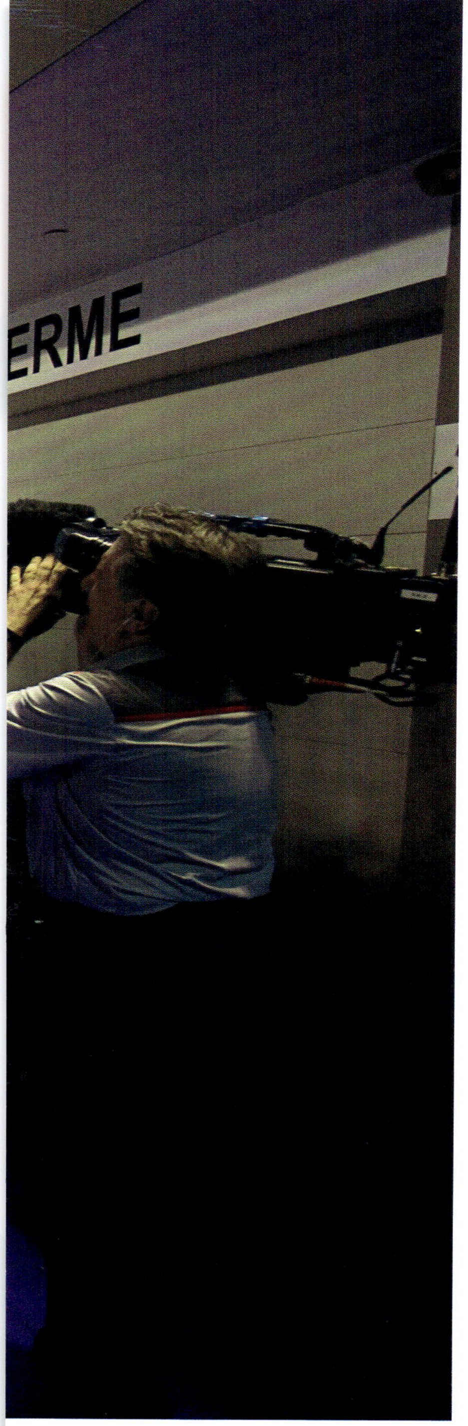

EDITOR'S VIEW
VETTEL DEMONSTRATES TRUE RACECRAFT

Left: Fernando Alonso's second win in as many races catapulted him back into the heart of the world championship battle.
Photo: Peter J Fox

Below left: Heikki Kovalainen wisely refrained from steering his blazing Lotus into the pit lane.
Photo: Jad Sherif/WRi2

Bottom: Sebastian Vettel reflects on his hard earned second place.
Photo: Paul-Henri Cahier

THERE are occasions in the F1 business when winning isn't everything and a driver can bask in the satisfaction of a job particularly well done, even if his efforts don't quite earn him the top spot on the podium. Sebastian Vettel's drive to second place in the third running of the Singapore GP at the Marina Bay circuit was, in my view, one such red-letter day.

A seemingly perfect qualifying run had been spoiled when the young German driver brushed the wall and, as a direct consequence, had to settle for second place on the starting grid. Of course, handing Fernando Alonso an inch in the tussle for pole position is to guarantee that the Spaniard takes a mile: it ensured that the battle for the lead of the 61-lap race was as gripping as it was unpredictable. Here was the best driver of the current generation dishing out a master class to possibly the best member of the next.

Watching the relentless nature of Vettel's chase put me in mind of the 1972 South African GP, when Graham Hill kept his Brabham ahead of new boy Niki Lauda's March in an admittedly modest contest for sixth place. Graham, by then past his best, but still the most experienced driver on the grid by a country mile, climbed from the cockpit at race's end and – after a theatrical pause – said deadpan, "I reckon I should send him a bill for that driving lesson!"

For Vettel, the first element of his driving lesson came on the run from the starting grid to the first corner. Obviously, this was the point where the race could be won or lost – and notice I said 'could' rather than 'would'. Alonso protected his line with meticulous precision and, ten seconds into the battle, Vettel found himself with a mountain to climb.

Yet neither driver seemed to fumble any catch or curved ball that was flung at them. Alonso's skill in traffic was simply breathtaking. It might seem an obvious point, but I'm always in awe of the manner in which truly great drivers hijack situations to their own advantage. Thus it was with Alonso. Not only did he shimmy through gaps with effortless ease, but also he controlled the pace so that he and the pursuing Red Bull never bunched up too tightly against backmarkers, thereby neutralising any real possibility of a do-or-die overtaking manoeuvre from Vettel.

Looking at the contest from the other side, it would have been all too easy for Vettel to have become flustered and over-driven his way into a potentially terminal incident. But instead he was the perfect pursuer, sometimes dropping back subtly to cool his brakes before discreetly ramping up the pressure once again. Very clever drivers like Vettel know what's likely to work and what isn't under such torrid circumstances, and the only way past the Ferrari would have been to worry Alonso into an error. Some chance!

The day will surely come, not soon, but inevitably, when Alonso loses his lustre and the top brass at Maranello start thinking about who will take over from the man from Oviedo as the Prancing Horse's flag carrier. On the basis of what we saw during 2010 in general, and at Singapore in particular, the guy they call 'Schumi with a smile' surely will be set for pole position.

Alan Henry

FIA F1 WORLD CHAMPIONSHIP · ROUND 15

SINGTEL SINGAPORE GRAND PRIX

SINGAPORE 24–26 SEPTEMBER 2010

RACE DISTANCE: 61 laps, 192.200 miles/309.316km

RACE WEATHER: Dark (track 31–32°C, air 29°C)

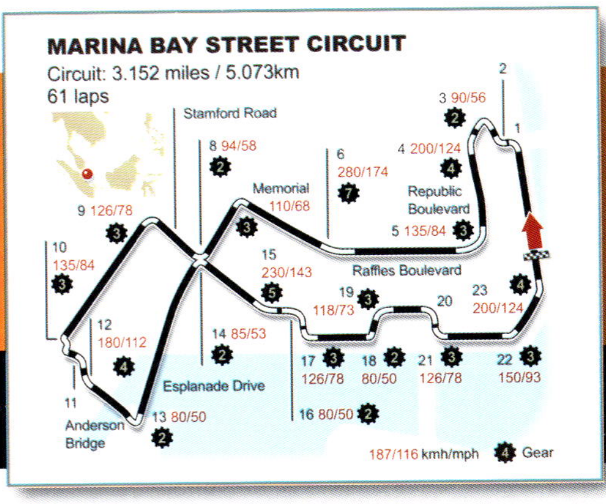

Pos.	Driver	Nat.	No.	Entrant	Car/Engine	Tyres	Laps	Time/Retirement	Speed (mph/km/h)	Gap to leader	Fastest race lap	
1	**Fernando Alonso**	E	8	Scuderia Ferrari Marlboro	Ferrari F10-056 V8	B	61	1h 57m 53.579s	97.817/157.422		1m 47.976s	58
2	**Sebastian Vettel**	D	5	Red Bull Racing	Red Bull RB6-Renault RS27 V8	B	61	1h 57m 53.872s	97.813/157.415	+ 0.293s	1m 48.141s	59
3	**Mark Webber**	AUS	6	Red Bull Racing	Red Bull RB6-Renault RS27 V8	B	61	1h 58m 22.720s	97.416/156.776	+ 29.141s	1m 49.706s	54
4	**Jenson Button**	GB	1	Vodafone McLaren Mercedes	McLaren MP4-25-Mercedes FO108X V8	B	61	1h 58m 23.963s	97.399/156.748	+ 30.384s	1m 49.711s	61
5	**Nico Rosberg**	D	4	Mercedes GP Petronas F1 Team	Mercedes MGP W01-Mercedes FO108X V8	B	61	1h 58m 42.973s	97.139/156.330	+ 49.394s	1m 50.125s	55
6	**Rubens Barrichello**	BR	9	AT&T Williams	Williams FW32-Cosworth CA2010 V8	B	61	1h 58m 49.680s	97.048/156.183	+ 56.101s	1m 50.334s	52
7	**Robert Kubica**	PL	11	Renault F1 Team	Renault R30-RS27 V8	B	61	1h 59m 20.138s	96.635/155.519	+ 1m 26.559s	1m 49.255s	56
8	**Felipe Massa**	BR	7	Scuderia Ferrari Marlboro	Ferrari F10-056 V8	B	61	1h 59m 46.876s	96.275/154.940	+ 1m 53.297s	1m 52.079s	45
9	**Adrian Sutil**	D	14	Force India F1 Team	Force India VJM03-Mercedes FO108X V8	B	61	2h 00m 05.995s *	96.020/154.529	+ 2m 12.416s	1m 52.473s	45
10	**Nico Hülkenberg**	D	10	AT&T Williams	Williams FW32-Cosworth CA2010 V8	B	61	2h 00m 06.370s *	96.015/154.521	+ 2m 12.791s	1m 52.213s	45
11	Vitaly Petrov	RUS	12	Renault F1 Team	Renault R30-RS27 V8	B	60			+ 1 lap	1m 51.903s	46
12	Jaime Alguersuari	E	17	Scuderia Toro Rosso	Toro Rosso STR5-Ferrari 056 V8	B	60			+ 1 lap	1m 52.333s	43
13	Michael Schumacher	GB	3	Mercedes GP Petronas F1 Team	Mercedes MGP W01-Mercedes FO108X V8	B	60			+ 1 lap	1m 49.680s	54
14	Sébastien Buemi	CH	16	Scuderia Toro Rosso	Toro Rosso STR5-Ferrari 056 V8	B	60			+ 1 lap	1m 49.710s	59
15	Lucas Di Grassi	BR	25	Virgin Racing	Virgin VR-01-Cosworth CA2010 V8	B	59			+ 2 laps	1m 52.513s	55
16	Heikki Kovalainen	FIN	19	Lotus Racing	Lotus T127-Cosworth CA2010 V8	B	58	*accident/ fuel pressure valve/fire*		+ 3 laps	1m 53.051s	53
	Timo Glock	D	24	Virgin Racing	Virgin VR-01-Cosworth CA2010 V8	B	49	*hydraulics*			1m 53.559s	38
	Nick Heidfeld	D	22	BMW Sauber F1 Team	BMW Sauber C29-Ferrari 056 V8	B	36	*accident*			1m 52.475s	29
	Lewis Hamilton	GB	2	Vodafone McLaren Mercedes	McLaren MP4-25-Mercedes FO108X V8	B	35	*accident*			1m 50.750s	31
	Christian Klien	A	20	HRT F1 Team	HRT F110-Cosworth CA2010 V8	B	31	*hydraulics*			1m 57.766s	23
	Kamui Kobayashi	J	23	BMW Sauber F1 Team	BMW Sauber C29-Ferrari 056 V8	B	30	*accident*			1m 53.957s	22
	Bruno Senna	BR	21	HRT F1 Team	HRT F110-Cosworth CA2010 V8	B	29	*accident damage*			1m 57.962s	19
	Jarno Trulli	I	18	Lotus Racing	Lotus T127-Cosworth CA2010 V8	B	27	*hydraulics*			1m 56.386s	20
	Vitantonio Liuzzi	I	15	Force India F1 Team	Force India VJM03-Mercedes FO108X V8	B	1	*accident/rear suspension*			no time	

* includes 20-sec penalty for leaving the track and gaining an advantage.

Fastest race lap: Fernando Alonso on lap 58, 1m 47.976s, 105.097mph/169.137km/h.

Lap record: Kimi Räikkönen (Ferrari F2008 V8), 1m 45.599s, 107.336mph/172.740km/h (2008) (3.148-mile/5.067km circuit).

Grid order	1	2	3	4	5	6	7	8	9	10	11	12	13	14	15	16	17	18	19	20	21	22	23	24
8 ALONSO	8	8	8	8	8	8	8	8	8	8	8	8	8	8	8	8	8	8	8	8	8	8	8	8
5 VETTEL	5	5	5	5	5	5	5	5	5	5	5	5	5	5	5	5	5	5	5	5	5	5	5	5
2 HAMILTON	2	2	2	2	2	2	2	2	2	2	2	2	2	2	2	2	2	2	2	2	2	2	2	2
1 BUTTON	1	1	1	1	1	1	1	1	1	1	1	1	1	1	1	1	1	1	1	1	1	1	1	1
6 WEBBER	6	6	4	4	4	4	4	4	4	4	4	4	4	4	4	4	4	4	4	4	4	4	4	4
9 BARRICHELLO	4	4	11	11	11	11	11	11	11	11	11	11	11	11	11	11	11	11	11	11	11	11	11	11
4 ROSBERG	11	11	9	9	9	9	9	9	9	9	9	9	9	9	9	9	9	9	9	9	9	9	9	9
11 KUBICA	9	9	3	3	3	3	3	3	3	3	6	6	6	6	6	6	6	6	6	6	6	6	6	6
3 SCHUMACHER	3	3	6	23	23	23	6	6	6	6	3	3	3	3	3	3	3	3	3	3	3	3	3	3
23 KOBAYASHI	12	12	23	24	24	6	23	23	23	23	23	23	23	23	23	23	23	23	23	23	23	23	23	23
17 ALGUERSUARI	23	23	24	6	6	24	24	24	24	24	24	24	24	24	14	14	14	14	14	14	14	14	14	14
12 PETROV	16	16	12	12	12	12	14	14	14	14	14	14	14	14	24	10	10	10	10	10	10	10	10	10
16 BUEMI	10	10	16	10	10	10	10	10	10	10	10	10	10	10	10	7	7	7	7	7	7	7	7	7
22 HEIDFELD	14	14	10	14	14	14	7	7	7	7	7	7	7	7	7	12	12	12	12	12	12	12	12	12
14 SUTIL	15	19	14	7	7	7	12	12	12	12	12	12	12	12	12	16	16	16	16	16	16	16	16	16
15 LIUZZI	19	24	19	16	16	16	16	16	16	16	16	16	16	16	16	17	17	17	17	17	17	17	17	17
10 HULKENBERG	18	18	18	19	19	17	17	17	17	17	17	17	17	17	17	24	24	24	24	24	24	24	24	24
24 GLOCK	24	20	17	18	18	19	19	19	19	19	19	19	19	19	19	19	19	22	22	22	22	22	22	22
19 KOVALAINEN	20	17	20	17	17	25	25	25	25	25	25	25	25	22	22	22	22	19	19	19	19	19	19	19
25 DI GRASSI	25	25	25	25	25	20	20	20	22	22	22	22	22	25	25	25	25	25	25	25	25	25	25	25
18 TRULLI	17	21	21	20	20	21	21	22	20	20	20	20	20	20	20	20	20	20	20	20	*20*	*20*	*20*	*20*
20 KLIEN	21	7	7	21	21	22	22	21	21	21	21	21	21	21	21	21	21	21	21	*21*	*21*	*21*	*21*	*21*
21 SENNA	7	22	22	22	22	18	18	*18*	*18*	*18*	*18*	*18*	*18*	*18*	*18*	*18*	*18*	*18*	*18*	*18*	*18*	*18*	*18*	*18*
7 MASSA	22																							

Grid order	25	26	27	28	29	30	31	32	33	34	35	36	37	38	39	40	41	42	43	44	45	46	47
8 ALONSO	8	8	8	8	8	8	8	8	8	8	8	8	8	8	8	8	8	8	8	8	8	8	8
5 VETTEL	5	5	5	5	5	5	5	5	5	5	5	5	5	5	5	5	5	5	5	5	5	5	5
2 HAMILTON	2	2	2	1	4	11	11	6	6	6	6	6	6	6	6	6	6	6	6	6	6	6	6
1 BUTTON	1	1	1	2	11	4	9	11	2	2	2	1	1	1	1	1	1	1	1	1	1	1	1
6 WEBBER	4	4	4	4	1	9	6	9	1	1	1	4	4	4	4	4	4	4	4	4	4	4	4
9 BARRICHELLO	11	11	11	11	9	6	2	2	4	4	4	11	11	11	11	11	11	11	11	11	9	9	9
4 ROSBERG	9	9	9	9	6	2	1	1	11	11	11	9	9	9	9	9	9	9	9	9	11	14	14
11 KUBICA	6	6	6	6	2	1	4	4	9	9	9	14	14	14	14	14	14	14	14	14	14	10	10
3 SCHUMACHER	3	3	3	3	3	23	14	14	14	14	14	10	10	10	10	10	10	10	10	10	10	7	7
23 KOBAYASHI	23	23	23	23	23	14	10	10	10	10	10	7	7	7	7	7	7	7	7	7	7	12	12
17 ALGUERSUARI	14	14	14	14	14	10	7	7	7	7	7	12	12	12	12	12	12	12	12	12	12	16	16
12 PETROV	10	10	10	10	10	7	12	12	12	12	12	17	17	17	17	17	16	16	16	16	16	17	11
16 BUEMI	7	7	7	7	7	12	16	17	17	17	17	22	16	16	16	16	17	17	17	17	17	11	17
22 HEIDFELD	12	12	12	12	12	16	17	16	22	22	22	3	19	19	19	19	19	19	19	19	19	19	19
14 SUTIL	16	16	16	16	16	3	22	22	3	3	3	16	3	3	3	3	3	3	3	3	3	3	3
15 LIUZZI	17	17	17	17	17	17	3	3	16	16	16	19	*24*	*24*	*24*	*24*	*24*	*24*	*24*	*24*	*24*	*24*	*24*
10 HULKENBERG	24	24	24	22	22	22	24	19	19	19	19	*24*	*25*	*25*	*25*	*25*	*25*	*25*	*25*	*25*	*25*	*25*	*25*
24 GLOCK	22	22	22	24	24	24	19	*25*	*25*	*25*	*24*	*25*											
19 KOVALAINEN	19	19	*19*	*19*	19	19	*25*	*24*	*24*	*24*	*25*												
25 DI GRASSI	*25*	*25*	*25*	*25*	25	25	*20*																
18 TRULLI	*20*	*20*	*20*	*20*	*20*	*20*																	
20 KLIEN	*21*	*21*	*21*	*21*	*21*																		
21 SENNA	*18*	*18*	*18*																				
7 MASSA																							

21 Pit stop

14 One lap or more behind

TIME SHEETS

PRACTICE 1 (FRIDAY)
Weather: Sunny/dusk/dark
Temperatures: track 29°C, air 28-29°C

Pos.	Driver	Laps	Time
1	Mark Webber	10	1m 54.589s
2	Michael Schumacher	24	1m 54.708s
3	Adrian Sutil	15	1m 54.827s
4	Sebastian Vettel	12	1m 55.137s
5	Jaime Alguersuari	20	1m 55.160s
6	Jenson Button	12	1m 55.333s
7	Vitantonio Liuzzi	15	1m 55.510s
8	Sébastien Buemi	15	1m 55.523s
9	Robert Kubica	11	1m 55.672s
10	Vitaly Petrov	20	1m 55.914s
11	Fernando Alonso	12	1m 56.090s
12	Kamui Kobayashi	22	1m 56.339s
13	Nick Heidfeld	18	1m 56.458s
14	Nico Rosberg	8	1m 56.598s
15	Heikki Kovalainen	12	1m 56.603s
16	Rubens Barrichello	17	1m 56.615s
17	Nico Hülkenberg	14	1m 56.840s
18	Lewis Hamilton	9	1m 56.884s
19	Felipe Massa	22	1m 57.760s
20	Timo Glock	19	1m 59.034s
21	Jérôme D'Ambrosio	16	1m 59.275s
22	Bruno Senna	23	1m 59.783s
23	Christian Klien	17	2m 03.424s
24	Fairuz Fauzy	11	2m 05.694s

PRACTICE 2 (FRIDAY)
Weather: Dark
Temperatures: track 29°C, air 28°C

Pos.	Driver	Laps	Time
1	Sebastian Vettel	29	1m 46.660s
2	Mark Webber	27	1m 47.287s
3	Jenson Button	28	1m 47.690s
4	Fernando Alonso	20	1m 47.718s
5	Lewis Hamilton	28	1m 47.818s
6	Rubens Barrichello	31	1m 48.302s
7	Felipe Massa	28	1m 48.341s
8	Nico Rosberg	26	1m 48.679s
9	Robert Kubica	15	1m 48.855s
10	Michael Schumacher	31	1m 48.889s
11	Nico Hülkenberg	32	1m 49.153s
12	Kamui Kobayashi	30	1m 49.438s
13	Nick Heidfeld	26	1m 49.558s
14	Vitaly Petrov	30	1m 49.608s
15	Vitantonio Liuzzi	28	1m 49.896s
16	Adrian Sutil	11	1m 49.984s
17	Jaime Alguersuari	31	1m 50.191s
18	Sébastien Buemi	35	1m 50.896s
19	Heikki Kovalainen	30	1m 51.878s
20	Timo Glock	22	1m 52.150s
21	Lucas Di Grassi	25	1m 53.431s
22	Jarno Trulli	27	1m 53.526s
23	Bruno Senna	27	1m 54.725s
24	Christian Klien	25	1m 55.542s

PRACTICE 3 (SATURDAY)
Weather: Dusk/dark
Temperatures: track 29° C, air 28°C

Pos.	Driver	Laps	Time
1	Sebastian Vettel	15	1m 48.028s
2	Fernando Alonso	16	1m 48.650s
3	Lewis Hamilton	12	1m 49.000s
4	Felipe Massa	18	1m 49.023s
5	Nico Rosberg	17	1m 49.056s
6	Mark Webber	13	1m 49.212s
7	Nico Hülkenberg	17	1m 49.304s
8	Robert Kubica	16	1m 49.520s
9	Adrian Sutil	15	1m 49.916s
10	Sébastien Buemi	16	1m 49.949s
11	Vitaly Petrov	15	1m 50.040s
12	Rubens Barrichello	16	1m 50.053s
13	Jenson Button	12	1m 50.060s
14	Jaime Alguersuari	16	1m 50.067s
15	Michael Schumacher	14	1m 50.067s
16	Vitantonio Liuzzi	16	1m 50.868s
17	Nick Heidfeld	15	1m 51.016s
18	Kamui Kobayashi	17	1m 51.027s
19	Timo Glock	14	1m 52.340s
20	Heikki Kovalainen	15	1m 53.146s
21	Lucas Di Grassi	15	1m 53.297s
22	Jarno Trulli	17	1m 53.681s
23	Christian Klien	16	1m 54.826s
24	Bruno Senna	16	1m 55.367s

QUALIFYING (SATURDAY)
Weather: Dark Temperatures: track 29°C, air 28°C

Pos.	Driver	First	Second	Third	Qualifying Tyre
1	Fernando Alonso	1m 46.541s	1m 45.809s	1m 45.390s	Super-Soft
2	Sebastian Vettel	1m 46.960s	1m 45.561s	1m 45.457s	Super-Soft
3	Lewis Hamilton	1m 48.296s	1m 46.042s	1m 45.571s	Super-Soft
4	Jenson Button	1m 48.032s	1m 46.490s	1m 45.944s	Super-Soft
5	Mark Webber	1m 47.088s	1m 45.908s	1m 45.977s	Super-Soft
6	Rubens Barrichello	1m 48.183s	1m 47.019s	1m 46.236s	Super-Soft
7	Nico Rosberg	1m 48.554s	1m 46.783s	1m 46.443s	Super-Soft
8	Robert Kubica	1m 47.657s	1m 46.949s	1m 46.593s	Super-Soft
9	Michael Schumacher	1m 48.425s	1m 47.160s	1m 46.702s	Super-Soft
10	Kamui Kobayashi	1m 48.908s	1m 47.599s	1m 47.884s	Super-Soft
11	Jaime Alguersuari	1m 48.127s	1m 47.666s		
12	Nico Hülkenberg	1m 47.984s	1m 47.674s		
13	Vitaly Petrov	1m 48.906s	1m 48.165s		
14	Sébastien Buemi	1m 49.063s	1m 48.502s		
15	Nick Heidfeld	1m 48.696s	1m 48.557s		
16	Adrian Sutil	1m 48.496s	1m 48.899s		
17	Vitantonio Liuzzi	1m 48.988s	1m 48.961s		
18	Timo Glock	1m 50.721s			
19	Heikki Kovalainen	1m 50.915s			
20	Lucas Di Grassi	1m 51.107s			
21	Jarno Trulli	1m 51.641s			
22	Christian Klien	1m 52.946s			
23	Bruno Senna	1m 54.174s			
24	Felipe Massa	no time			

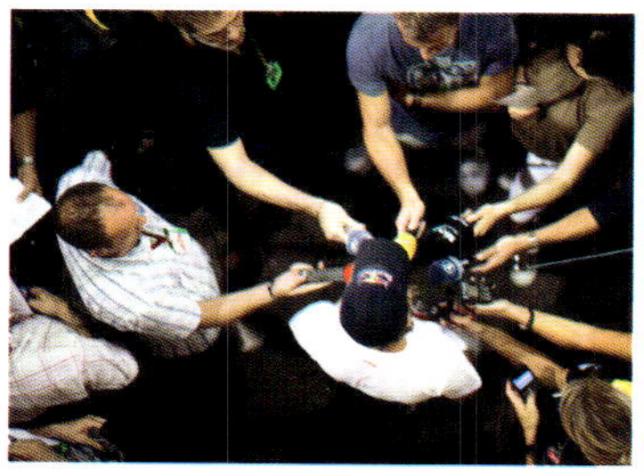

FOR THE RECORD

60th PODIUM: Fernando Alonso
50th START: Timo Glock
50th GRAND PRIX: Force India
50oth POINT: Jenson Button
20th POLE POSITION: Fernando Alonso

DID YOU KNOW

This was Rubens Barrichello's 300th start, including the 1998 Belgian GP, where he retired at the first start. Some sources exclude that race, thus making Japan his 300th race.

POINTS

DRIVERS

1	Mark Webber	202
2	Fernando Alonso	191
3	Lewis Hamilton	182
4	Sebastian Vettel	181
5	Jenson Button	177
6	Felipe Massa	128
7	Nico Rosberg	122
8	Robert Kubica	114
9	Adrian Sutil	47
10	Michael Schumacher	46
11	Rubens Barrichello	39
12	Kamui Kobayashi	21
13	Vitaly Petrov	19
14	Nico Hülkenberg	17
15	Vitantonio Liuzzi	13
16	Sébastien Buemi	7
17	Pedro de la Rosa	6
18	Jaime Alguersuari	3

CONSTRUCTORS

1	Red Bull	383
2	McLaren	359
3	Ferrari	319
4	Mercedes	168
5	Renault	133
6	Force India	60
7	Williams	56
8	BMW Sauber	27
9	Toro Rosso	10

48	49	50	51	52	53	54	55	56	57	58	59	60	61	
8	8	8	8	8	8	8	8	8	8	8	8	8	8	1
5	5	5	5	5	5	5	5	5	5	5	5	5	5	2
6	6	6	6	6	6	6	6	6	6	6	6	6	6	3
1	1	1	1	1	1	1	1	1	1	1	1	1	1	
4	4	4	4	4	4	4	4	4	4	4	4	4	4	
9	9	9	9	9	9	9	9	9	9	9	9	9	9	6
14	14	14	14	14	14	14	11	11	11	11	11	11	11	7
10	10	10	10	10	10	11	14	14	14	14	14	14	14	8
7	7	7	7	7	11	10	10	10	10	10	10	10	10	9
12	12	12	12	11	7	7	7	7	7	7	7	7	7	10
16	16	16	11	12	12	12	12	12	12	12	12	12		
11	11	11	16	17	17	17	17	17	17	17	17	17		
17	17	17	17	16	19	19	19	19	3	3	3	3		
19	19	19	19	19	3	3	3	3	19	16	16	16		
3	3	3	3	3	16	16	16	16	16	19	25			
24	25	25	25	25	25	25	25	25	25	25				
25	24													

Safety car deployed on laps shown

RACE TYRE STRATEGIES

	Driver	Race Stint 1	Race Stint 2	Race Stint 3	Race Stint 4
1	Alonso	Super-Soft: 1-29	Medium: 30-61		
2	Vettel	Super-Soft: 1-29	Medium: 30-61		
3	Webber	Super-Soft: 1-3	Medium: 4-61		
4	Button	Super-Soft: 1-29	Medium: 30-61		
5	Rosberg	Super-Soft: 1-30	Medium: 31-61		
6	Barrichello	Super-Soft: 1-32	Medium: 33-61		
7	Kubica	Super-Soft: 1-32	Medium: 33-45	Medium: 46-61	
8	Massa	Super-Soft: 1	Medium: 2-61		
9	Sutil	Super-Soft: 1-32	Medium: 33-61		
10	Hülkenberg	Super-Soft: 1-3	Medium: 4-61		
11	Petrov	Super-Soft: 1-3	Medium: 4-60		
12	Alguersuari	Super-Soft: 1-3	Medium: 4-60		
13	Schumacher	Super-Soft: 1-30	Medium: 31-37	Super-Soft: 38-60	
14	Buemi	Super-Soft: 1-3	Medium:4-32	Medium: 33-52	Super-Soft: 53-60
15	di Grassi	Super-Soft: 1-3	Medium: 4-41	Medium: 42-59	
16	Kovalainen	Super-Soft: 1-3	Medium: 4-34	Medium: 35-58	
	Glock	Medium: 1-31	Super-Soft: 31-49 (dnf)		
	Heidfeld	Medium: 1	Super-Soft: 2-2	Medium: 3-36 (dnf)	
	Hamilton	Super-Soft: 1-28	Medium: 29-35 (dnf)		
	Klien	Super-Soft: 1-3	Medium: 4-31 (dnf)		
	Kobayashi	Super-Soft: 1-30 (dnf)			
	Senna	Super-Soft: 1-3	Medium: 4-29 (dnf)		
	Trulli	Super-Soft: 1-3	Medium: 4-6	Medium: 7-25	Super-Soft: 26-27 (dnf)
	Liuzzi	Medium: 1 (dnf)			

The tyre regulations stipulate that the two dry tyre specifications must be used during the race.
The Super-Soft compound Bridgestone Potenza tyre is marked with a green stripe on the sidewall.

Photos: Peter J. Fox

Red Bull

FIA FORMULA 1 WORLD CHAMPIONSHIP · ROUND 16

JAPANESE GRAND PRIX

SUZUKA CIRCUIT

Sebastian Vettel reprised his 2009 success with a storming and dominant victory for Red Bull at Suzuka.
Photo: Peter J Fox

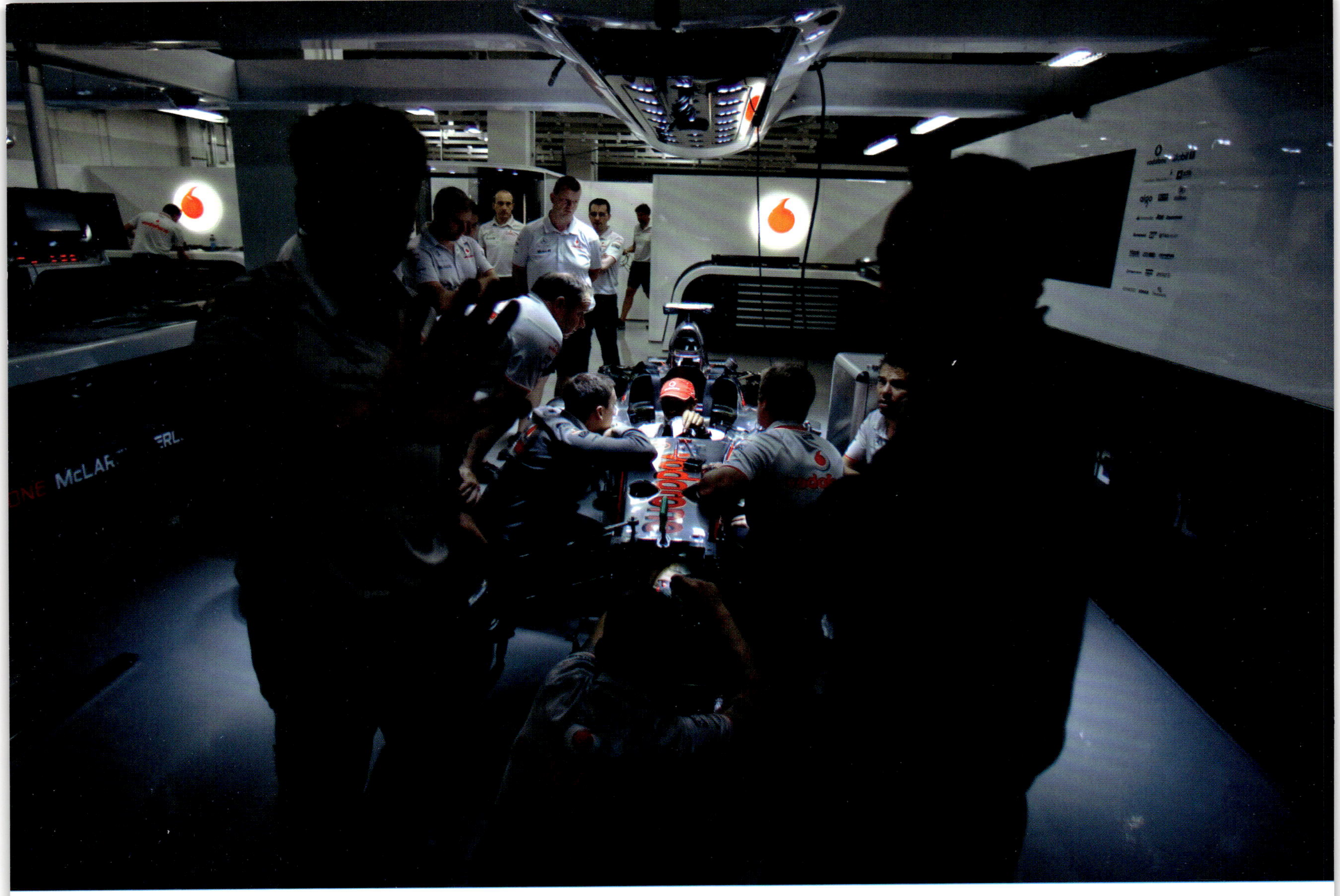

SYNTIUM

Above: Black as night – the Mercedes safety car resembles a submarine in the pit lane.
Photo: Paul-Henri Cahier

Left: Vettel runs for cover.
Photo: Lukas Gorys

Top: Stick or twist? Glock and di Grassi trade cards rather than practice times.

Top left: Keep out! The McLaren crew and Lewis Hamilton need all the time they can get after his mishaps in practice.

Far left: Give us a push! The Mercedes crew attends to Michael Schumacher.
Photos: Peter J Fox

Left: Lewis checks out the handling on his spare chassis.
Photo: Peter Nygaard/Grand Prix Photo

SUZUKA QUALIFYING

IN the Virgin garage, drivers Timo Glock and Lucas di Grassi amused themselves by playing cards. Outside, mechanics from various teams were preoccupied with creating small boats from assorted bits of waste. It wasn't what the Japanese Grand Prix promoter had in mind when Suzuka was redeveloped, but in the right circumstances the pit lane doubled as a marvellous river.

A conventional qualifying session had been in doubt since the morning, when only seven of the 24 drivers had bothered with anything more than an installation lap during final free practice. Incessant since daybreak, the rain showed no sign of relenting and the track was totally undriveable by 2pm, when qualifying should have started. The safety car was dispatched for half-hourly track inspections, but with no sign of the weather breaking – and darkness fast approaching – the session's cancellation was inevitable, and it was rescheduled for 10am on Sunday. But then rain induced chaos has been a frequent feature ever since Japan hosted its maiden Formula One grand prix in 1976.

"The decision to cancel was absolutely right," said Sebastian Vettel, who had been quickest in Friday's two practice sessions, "because there was too much standing water." Bridgestone's wet-weather F1 tyres were capable of dispersing 61 litres of water per second, but even they couldn't have coped.

The following morning's outlook was much brighter, and Vettel maintained his breezy form, nicking pole position from Red Bull team-mate Mark Webber by less than a tenth.

"We came here with quite a bit of confidence," the German said, "because this track is kind of made for our car, especially the first sector. We like it when there aren't too many straights. After all yesterday's confusion, I'm pleased the sun came out. We've had a good start to the day, but the most important bit is yet to come."

Lewis Hamilton's weekend began badly, when he crashed at Degner after relatively few laps on Friday morning, damaging a new-spec rear wing. That left Jenson Button to evaluate a package of new parts on his own, but Hamilton looked the more convincing on Sunday morning as they qualified sixth and third respectively (Button was the only driver in the top ten to opt for the harder, prime tyre), although Hamilton then had to take a five-position grid penalty in the wake of an unscheduled gearbox change. The team hadn't noticed a damaged driveshaft, a direct consequence of his Singaporean clash with Webber a fortnight beforehand.

Not for the first time at a circuit where narrow margins for error allow the driver to make a difference, Robert Kubica flattered his Renault and inherited Hamilton's third place, ahead of Fernando Alonso.

"One of the R30's best characteristics is that it's an easy car to control," the Pole said. "It's fairly straightforward to take it to the limit and, if you stray beyond, it's not hard to get it back. When I was driving for BMW, I remember following Fernando's Renault and thinking, 'Damn, he's much better than me on used tyres because he looks much more in control.' The first time I drove a Renault, I immediately realised why."

It was a disappointing morning for more than 2,000 fans in the bespoke Kamui Kobayashi grandstand at The Esses – the local hero lined up only 14th, three places behind his team-mate, Nick Heidfeld, after making a mistake at the chicane.

It wasn't the first time Suzuka qualifying had taken place on race morning – it happened in 2004, when the threat of an approaching typhoon had persuaded organisers to cancel the second phase of the weekend: now, as then, it gave Sunday a fresh sense of purpose and proved that grands prix could ordinarily be accommodated within two days rather than three.

"I think I prefer the usual timetable," quipped Red Bull sporting director Christian Horner. "If nothing else, it gives me more than three hours to savour pole position…"

Above: Wham! The unlucky Tonio Liuzzi's Force India is smashed from the track by Massa's Ferrari.
Photo: Peter Nygaard/Grand Prix Photo

Above right: Sebastian Vettel is congratulated on his latest success by an admiring Adrian Newey.
Photo: Peter J Fox

Right: Mercedes team-mates Schumacher and Rosberg go wheel to wheel.
Photo: Peter Nygaard/Grand Prix Photo

FOR a moment, all logic was suspended. The sight of two Red Bulls tearing towards Turn One was a microcosm of the season as a whole, but why on earth was that yellow thing darting between them? There were many unexpected elements to the 2010 Japanese Grand Prix, but the final result – a second consecutive Suzuka victory for Sebastian Vettel – wasn't among them.

Vettel got away from the line better than team-mate Mark Webber, but neither was a match for Robert Kubica, who managed to split them before Turn One. "I could see Robert," said Vettel, "and clearly he had a bit of momentum, but fortunately the straight wasn't long enough for him to challenge me."

Kubica's wasn't the only Renault to make an immediate impact. In the midfield maelstrom, Vitaly Petrov carved to the left and drove straight into the innocent Nico Hülkenberg, whose Williams suffered irreparable front suspension damage. The Russian's car ricocheted into the sleepers on the left and he climbed out to collect a five-position grid penalty in Korea, an inevitable by-product of the collision creation process. It was poor timing for Petrov: Renault had made it clear it wanted to keep him in 2011, if only he could smooth out the untidier edges of his racecraft. If only…

The carbon shrapnel was still settling when Felipe Massa veered to the right on the approach to Turn One. Still moist after the previous day's deluge, the grass offered no purchase and, bereft of steering, Massa tracked a straight course that continued until he met something solid – in this instance, Tonio Liuzzi's Force India, which was deflected into the left-hand tyre wall at high speed. "I made a good start," the Italian said, "and was minding my own business when I suddenly noticed this out-of-control red rocket." The stewards categorised this one as a normal racing incident and took no further action.

"I think I was really cursed today," Massa said. "This morning I failed to get into Q3 because of traffic, and in the race I didn't even get through the first two corners. Nico Rosberg, who was in front of me on the grid, got away poorly and I tried to move to the left, but Adrian Sutil was already there. Then I switched to the right, but in so doing, I found myself on the grass and at that point the car took off on its own."

It was the continuation of a violent theme that had begun, bizarrely, during the pre-race installation laps, when Lucas di Grassi crashed heavily at 130R. "There is no evidence that anything broke," said Virgin sporting director John Booth, "but plenty to suggest Lucas hit a kerb."

The safety car was deployed while the pit straight and Turn One were cleared of debris, and Vettel led from Kubica, Webber, Fernando Alonso, Jenson Button, the fast-starting Lewis Hamilton. Rubens Barrichello, Michael Schumacher, Nick Heidfeld, Sutil, Jaime Alguersuari, Kamui Kobayashi, Sébastien Buemi, Heikki Kovalainen and Sakon Yamamoto. Rosberg, Jarno Trulli and Bruno Senna all came in

immediately to switch from soft to hard Bridgestones, while Timo Glock went from hards to softs for one lap, then pitted again next time around to reverse the process.

For as long as Kubica remained where he was, Vettel had every chance of making a decent break, but that buffer vanished before the restart. The Pole had been aware of an odd vibration from the start and the cause became apparent on lap three, when his right rear wheel fell off. As his car now needed rescuing, too, the race remained neutralised until the end of lap six. It was originally thought that a wheel-gun miscalibration had been the cause of Kubica's problem, but later it transpired that a morsel of debris had become wedged between the retaining pin and the nut, which consequently had not been secured properly.

The following Webber had spotted the unfolding drama and was passing radio messages to race director Charlie Whiting, asking whether he could overtake under the safety car because he didn't fancy negotiating a stray wheel. The problem was safely resolved before he received an answer, however.

The Red Bulls edged away from Alonso when the race finally resumed, but not by much, with Button and Hamilton (suffering an ear infection, to add to the weekend's growing catalogue of woes) next up.

With Alonso so close, Red Bull was keeping a wary eye on the Ferrari pit. "We felt there would be a significant performance gain during the first lap on fresh prime tyres," said the team's sporting director, Christian Horner, "so we wanted to bring Sebastian in on the same lap as Alonso, and Mark no more than one lap later, to cover ourselves."

As Ferrari prepared to switch tyres on lap 24, Red Bull did likewise: Vettel came in first and Webber followed next time around, the crew's efforts being just enough to keep both ahead of Alonso. Hamilton had pitted on lap 22 and still lay fifth, so Button – still on his original primes – was artificially shuffled to the front.

The Englishman had selected to qualify and start on the harder tyre because he preferred the balance it gave him. He was also concerned that the soft Bridgestones might be particularly fragile on a clean, rain washed circuit. In Sunday's heat, however, the track rubbered in quite quickly and tyre wear was less exaggerated than had been anticipated.

By this stage of the race, it was evident that a switch to fresh rubber – of either compound – would be advantageous, but McLaren left Button out for an eternity. "We had a bit of a rest behind Jenson," said Vettel, "because we couldn't just drive through him." Webber added, "Although he wasn't really in the race for the lead, Jenson potentially had a part to play in backing us up towards Fernando, and I had to get the balance right. I didn't want to get so close to Seb that I killed my tyres."

McLaren team principal Martin Whitmarsh denied Button was being used as a defensive pawn – to enable Hamilton to catch the leading group, as he was now doing. "Some teams might race like

Above: Heikki Kovalainen's 12th place might not seem much, but it helped ensure that Lotus would take a sizeable share of the constructors' kitty for 2011.

Right: Kobayashi brings a breath of fresh air into F1.
Photos: Peter J Fox

that," he said, "but we don't." Not too many people believed him, because there was no other plausible reason to delay the leader's tyre change. It was either rubbish strategy or else an astute ploy that any hard-nosed racing team would use. And given the race's evolution, Button was destined to rejoin in fifth place, come what may.

He finally pitted on lap 38 and rejoined 8.5 seconds behind his team-mate, although they swapped places again on lap 44, largely because Hamilton had lost third gear and would be reduced to a virtual cruise for the final 15 laps, using only fourth to seventh in a bid to nurse his transmission. With the rest so far back, however, his fifth place was secure.

There were no such foibles at the front, Vettel taking the flag less than one second clear as Webber kept a watchful eye on the scarlet menace that had been hounding him all afternoon. "This one is down to the team," Vettel said. "Most of the guys didn't sleep from Thursday until Saturday, because they were working so hard on the car, so it was probably a good thing qualifying was delayed; they got some well-earned rest. It's almost as though this circuit was designed for our chassis: the high-speed corners are always a pleasure, and the lighter the fuel load became, the more fun it was to drive. I love this circuit."

It showed.

Behind the leading group, Rosberg's early tyre stop helped promote him to what was effectively sixth – just ahead of team-mate Schumacher – after the latter had pitted on lap 23. Then the pair engaged in a lively duel that ended six laps from the end, when Rosberg lost his left rear wheel at Turn Seven. "It clearly wasn't finger trouble," said team principal Ross Brawn, "because the wheel had been on the car for 46 laps. Quite a few teams reported loose wheels at the end of the race, although ours was obviously the most extreme example. The physical loads have changed this year, with cars running much longer stints on heavier fuel loads, and the problem was probably due to a particular circuit characteristic."

Thus Schumacher took sixth, ahead of Kobayashi, who provided a significant chunk of the afternoon's entertainment.

Sauber imitated Button's strategy by starting the local hero on a set of primes and switching him to softs on lap 38. The Japanese driver had a lively start to the race, dispatching several rivals with a series of (mostly) neat moves at the hairpin, but by the end of his unnecessarily long first stint, his pace was fading. During his stop, he surrendered positions to Alguersuari and Sutil, both of whom he had previously passed, and thus was obliged to do it all over again. But being Kobayashi, he did. The Red Bulls might have hogged the limelight, but this was the day's brightest cameo, although the car was quite tatty by the end (largely because he and Alguersuari banged wheels when Kobayashi passed the Spaniard for the second time, on lap 44).

Heidfeld made it a good day for Sauber by taking eighth, while Barrichello and Buemi completed the top ten. Alguersuari had been running ahead of Heidfeld, but had to pit for a fresh nose after his brush with Kobayashi, which dropped him to 11th.

Lotus obtained its best result of the campaign, with Kovalainen and Trulli evenly matched in 12th and 13th, while Glock, Senna and Yamamoto all made it to the finish. The stationary Rosberg was classified and, officially, Sutil was the only driver to retire after the early restart. The Force India driver spun on his own oil – at 130R, of all places – but didn't hit anything and beat a smoky retreat to the pits.

"We needed to perform," said Kovalainen, "and could not have done any more. We were only lapped once; our pace was amazing."

These things are relative.

Simon Arron

EDITOR'S VIEW
KOBAYASHI: THE RISING SON OF JAPAN

SUZUKA remains one of the greatest F1 circuits on the planet, and the Japanese passion for F1 has in no way been dented by the absence of Honda and Toyota from the starting grids, even on their home turf. All of this serves to prove, of course, that in the mind of the viewing public, the overriding priority is the person driving the car, not the identity of the machine itself.

Kamui Kobayashi, who ironically came to prominence driving for Toyota in the closing races of the 2009 season, has now emerged as easily the most convincing Japanese driver on the regular F1 beat since Honda insisted that Satoru Nakajima – father of future Williams driver Kazuki – was foisted on Team Lotus alongside Ayrton Senna in 1987 as a condition of being supplied with Honda 1.5-litre turbo V6 engines. Satoru was a nice bloke who didn't make any waves, but he had all the qualities that Ayrton wanted in a team-mate during his Lotus phase. He was amenable, obliging and rather slow.

Later we had the amusing Ukyo Katayama as a member of the Tyrrell team. He was better than Nakajima, although his greatest claim to fame was reducing McLaren team-mates Senna and Gerhard Berger to sobs and quivering gales of laughter when he misunderstood a question at a press conference and proceeded to trot out a lengthy joke, the punch line of which was "so elephant say to snake, 'You got no ears, you no snake, you Niki Lauda.'" It guaranteed Katayama heroic status within the F1 paddock, if not out on the circuit.

Subsequently, Takuma Sato looked a convincing runner at the wheel of Honda-powered Jordans and BARs, bagging a third place in the 2004 US Grand Prix at Indianapolis, only for his star to fade; he shuffled out of the F1 exit door via a brief spell with the precarious Super Aguri team. Earlier, his storming drive to fifth place for Jordan in the 2002 Japanese GP had reminded many observers of a one-armed paper hanger at the top of a ladder in a gale. One just held one's breath and hoped that it would not end in tears. Impressively, it didn't.

Having mastered Interlagos and Abu Dhabi with impressive aplomb at the tail end of 2009, Kobayashi again proved highly competent and assured at Suzuka this time around, qualifying his Sauber 14th and then storming to a decent seventh, a few seconds behind Michael Schumacher's Mercedes. Kobayashi is one of those supremely energetic drivers who takes every opportunity that is thrown his way and seldom appears to be marking time or taking it easy.

You might logically argue that he only bagged a useful helping of points in front of his home crowd because both the Renaults dropped out, Felipe Massa stupidly ran Tonio Liuzzi off the track at the first corner and Nico Hulkenberg had his Williams driven off the road by Vitaly Petrov. I just hope that Kobayashi gets into a top car at some stage in the future or, better still, that Sauber manages to give him just that.

Alan Henry

FIA F1 WORLD CHAMPIONSHIP · ROUND 16

JAPANESE GRAND PRIX

SUZUKA 8–10 OCTOBER 2010

RACE DISTANCE: 53 laps, 191.054 miles/307.471km

RACE WEATHER: Sunny (track 31–34°C, air 25–26°C)

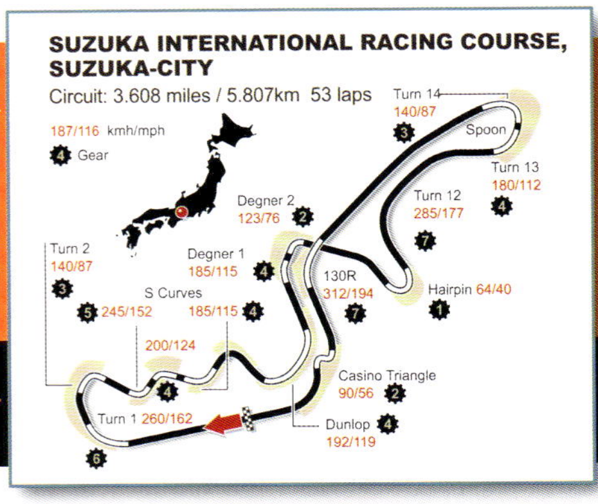

Pos.	Driver	Nat.	No.	Entrant	Car/Engine	Tyres	Laps	Time/Retirement	Speed (mph/km/h)	Gap to leader	Fastest race lap	
1	**Sebastian Vettel**	D	5	Red Bull Racing	Red Bull RB6-Renault RS27 V8	B	53	1h 30m 27.323s	126.727/203.948		1m 33.653s	51
2	**Mark Webber**	AUS	6	Red Bull Racing	Red Bull RB6-Renault RS27 V8	B	53	1h 30m 28.228s	126.706/203.914	+ 0.905s	1m 33.474s	53
3	**Fernando Alonso**	E	8	Scuderia Ferrari Marlboro	Ferrari F10-056 V8	B	53	1h 30m 30.044s	126.664/203.846	+ 2.721s	1m 33.823s	53
4	**Jenson Button**	GB	1	Vodafone McLaren Mercedes	McLaren MP4-25-Mercedes FO108X V8	B	53	1h 30m 40.845s	126.412/203.441	+ 13.522s	1m 33.529s	53
5	**Lewis Hamilton**	GB	2	Vodafone McLaren Mercedes	McLaren MP4-25-Mercedes FO108X V8	B	53	1h 31m 06.918s	125.810/202.471	+ 39.595s	1m 35.182s	35
6	**Michael Schumacher**	GB	3	Mercedes GP Petronas F1 Team	Mercedes MGP W01-Mercedes FO108X V8	B	53	1h 31m 27.256s	125.344/201.721	+ 59.933s	1m 34.853s	52
7	**Kamui Kobayashi**	J	23	BMW Sauber F1 Team	BMW Sauber C29-Ferrari 056 V8	B	53	1h 31m 31.361s	125.250/201.570	+ 1m 04.038s	1m 34.486s	50
8	**Nick Heidfeld**	DE	22	BMW Sauber F1 Team	BMW Sauber C29-Ferrari 056 V8	B	53	1h 31m 36.971s	125.122/201.364	+ 1m 09.648s	1m 35.521s	52
9	**Rubens Barrichello**	BR	9	AT&T Williams	Williams FW32-Cosworth CA2010 V8	B	53	1h 31m 38.169s	125.094/201.320	+ 1m 10.846s	1m 35.597s	53
10	**Sébastien Buemi**	CH	16	Scuderia Toro Rosso	Toro Rosso STR5-Ferrari 056 V8	B	53	1h 31m 40.129s	125.050/201.249	+ 1m 12.806s	1m 35.116s	52
11	Jaime Alguersuari	E	17	Scuderia Toro Rosso	Toro Rosso STR5-Ferrari 056 V8	B	52			+ 1 lap	1m 34.365s	49
12	Heikki Kovalainen	FIN	19	Lotus Racing	Lotus T127-Cosworth CA2010 V8	B	52			+ 1 lap	1m 37.620s	51
13	Jarno Trulli	I	18	Lotus Racing	Lotus T127-Cosworth CA2010 V8	B	51			+ 2 laps	1m 39.710s	28
14	Timo Glock	D	24	Virgin Racing	Virgin VR-01-Cosworth CA2010 V8	B	51			+ 2 laps	1m 39.813s	51
15	Bruno Senna	BR	21	HRT F1 Team	HRT F110-Cosworth CA2010 V8	B	51			+ 2 laps	1m 40.329s	49
16	Sakon Yamamoto	J	20	HRT F1 Team	HRT F110-Cosworth CA2010 V8	B	50			+ 3 laps	1m 39.806s	33
17	Nico Rosberg	D	4	Mercedes GP Petronas F1 Team	Mercedes MGP W01-Mercedes FO108X V8	B	47	*rear wheel lost/accident*		+ 6 laps	1m 36.108s	44
	Adrian Sutil	D	14	Force India F1 Team	Force India VJM03-Mercedes FO108X V8	B	44	*oil leak*			1m 36.319s	43
	Robert Kubica	PL	11	Renault F1 Team	Renault R30-RS27 V8	B	2	*rear wheel lost*			2m 41.378s	2
	Nico Hülkenberg	D	10	AT&T Williams	Williams FW32-Cosworth CA2010 V8	B	0	*accident*			no time	
	Felipe Massa	BR	7	Scuderia Ferrari Marlboro	Ferrari F10-056 V8	B	0	*accident*			no time	
	Vitaly Petrov	RUS	12	Renault F1 Team	Renault R30-RS27 V8	B	0	*accident*			no time	
	Vitantonio Liuzzi	I	15	Force India F1 Team	Force India VJM03-Mercedes FO108X V8	B	0	*accident*			no time	
NS	Lucas Di Grassi	BR	25	Virgin Racing	Virgin VR-01-Cosworth CA2010 V8	B		*accident on formation lap*			no time	

Fastest race lap: Mark Webber on lap 53, 1m 33.474s, 138.968mph/223.647km/h.

Lap record: Kimi Räikkönen (McLaren MP4-20-Mercedes Benz V10), 1m 31.540s, 141.904mph/228.372km/h (2005).

Grid order	1	2	3	4	5	6	7	8	9	10	11	12	13	14	15	16	17	18	19	20	21
5 VETTEL	5	5	5	5	5	5	5	5	5	5	5	5	5	5	5	5	5	5	5	5	5
6 WEBBER	11	11	6	6	6	6	6	6	6	6	6	6	6	6	6	6	6	6	6	6	6
11 KUBICA	6	6	8	8	8	8	8	8	8	8	8	8	8	8	8	8	8	8	8	8	8
8 ALONSO	8	8	1	1	1	1	1	1	1	1	1	1	1	1	1	1	1	1	1	1	1
1 BUTTON	1	1	2	2	2	2	2	2	2	2	2	2	2	2	2	2	2	2	2	2	2
4 ROSBERG	2	2	9	9	9	9	3	3	3	3	3	3	3	3	3	3	3	3	3	3	3
9 BARRICHELLO	9	9	3	3	3	3	9	9	9	9	9	9	9	9	9	9	9	9	9	9	23
2 HAMILTON	3	3	22	22	22	22	22	22	22	22	22	22	22	22	22	22	22	22	23	23	16
10 HULKENBERG	4	22	14	14	14	14	14	14	14	14	14	14	14	14	14	14	14	23	17	17	17
3 SCHUMACHER	22	14	17	17	17	17	17	17	17	17	17	17	23	23	23	23	23	17	16	16	4
22 HEIDFELD	14	17	23	23	23	23	23	23	23	23	23	23	17	17	17	17	17	14	4	4	22
7 MASSA	17	23	16	16	16	16	16	16	16	16	16	16	16	16	16	16	16	16	22	22	9
12 PETROV	18	16	4	4	4	4	4	4	4	4	4	4	4	4	4	4	4	4	14	14	14
23 KOBAYASHI	23	4	19	19	19	19	19	19	19	19	19	19	19	19	19	19	19	19	19	19	19
14 SUTIL	16	19	20	20	20	20	20	20	20	20	20	20	20	20	18	18	18	18	18	18	18
17 ALGUERSUARI	19	20	18	18	18	18	18	18	18	18	18	18	18	18	20	20	20	20	20	20	20
15 LIUZZI	24	18	21	21	21	21	24	24	24	24	24	24	24	24	24	24	24	24	24	24	24
16 BUEMI	21	21	24	24	24	24	21	21	21	21	21	21	21	21	21	21	21	21	21	21	21
18 TRULLI	20	24																			
19 KOVALAINEN																					
25 DI GRASSI																					
24 GLOCK																					
21 SENNA																					
20 YAMAMOTO																					

Grid order	22	23	24	25	26	27	28	29	30	31	32	33	34	35	36	37	38	39	40	41	42
5 VETTEL	5	5	5	6	1	1	1	1	1	1	1	1	1	1	1	1	1	5	5	5	5
6 WEBBER	6	6	6	1	5	5	5	5	5	5	5	5	5	5	5	5	5	6	6	6	6
11 KUBICA	8	8	8	5	6	6	6	6	6	6	6	6	6	6	6	6	6	8	8	8	8
8 ALONSO	1	1	1	8	8	8	8	8	8	8	8	8	8	8	8	8	8	2	2	2	2
1 BUTTON	2	3	23	2	2	2	2	2	2	2	2	2	2	2	2	2	2	1	1	1	1
4 ROSBERG	3	23	2	23	23	23	23	23	23	23	23	23	23	23	23	23	23	4	4	4	4
9 BARRICHELLO	23	2	16	16	16	16	16	4	4	4	4	4	4	4	4	4	4	3	3	3	3
2 HAMILTON	16	16	4	4	4	4	4	3	3	3	3	3	3	3	3	3	3	22	22	22	22
10 HULKENBERG	4	4	3	3	3	3	3	22	22	22	22	22	22	22	22	22	22	9	9	9	9
3 SCHUMACHER	22	22	22	22	22	22	22	9	9	9	9	9	9	9	9	9	9	14	14	14	14
22 HEIDFELD	9	9	9	9	9	9	9	14	14	14	14	14	14	14	14	14	14	17	17	17	17
7 MASSA	14	14	14	14	14	14	14	17	17	17	17	17	17	17	17	17	17	23	23	23	23
12 PETROV	17	17	17	17	17	17	17	16	16	16	16	16	16	16	16	16	16	16	16	16	16
23 KOBAYASHI	19	19	19	19	19	19	19	19	19	19	19	19	19	19	*19*	*19*	*19*	*19*	*19*	*19*	*19*
14 SUTIL	18	18	18	18	18	18	18	18	18	18	*18*	*18*	*18*	*18*	*18*	*18*	*18*	*18*	*18*	*18*	*18*
17 ALGUERSUARI	*20*	*20*	*20*	*20*	*20*	*20*	*20*	*20*	*20*	*24*	*24*	*24*	*24*	*24*	*24*	*24*	*24*	*24*	*24*	*24*	*24*
15 LIUZZI	*24*	*24*	*24*	*24*	*24*	*24*	*24*	*24*	*24*	*21*	*21*	*21*	*21*	*21*	*21*	*21*	*21*	*21*	*21*	*21*	*21*
16 BUEMI	*21*	*21*	*21*	*21*	*21*	*21*	*21*	*21*	*21*	*20*	*20*	*20*	*20*	*20*	*20*	*20*	*20*	*20*	*20*	*20*	*20*
18 TRULLI																					
19 KOVALAINEN																					
25 DI GRASSI																					
24 GLOCK																					
21 SENNA																					
20 YAMAMOTO																					

21 Pit stop *14 One lap or more behind* Safety car deployed on laps shown

TIME SHEETS

PRACTICE 1 (FRIDAY)

Weather: Cloudy/sunny
Temperatures: track 27–31°C, air 24–26°C

Pos.	Driver	Laps	Time
1	Sebastian Vettel	23	1m 32.585s
2	Mark Webber	23	1m 32.633s
3	Robert Kubica	23	1m 33.129s
4	Adrian Sutil	13	1m 33.639s
5	Lewis Hamilton	9	1m 33.643s
6	Rubens Barrichello	21	1m 33.677s
7	Nico Hülkenberg	24	1m 33.707s
8	Michael Schumacher	20	1m 33.739s
9	Nick Heidfeld	23	1m 33.791s
10	Nico Rosberg	9	1m 33.831s
11	Felipe Massa	25	1m 33.929s
12	Jenson Button	19	1m 34.042s
13	Fernando Alonso	23	1m 34.169s
14	Kamui Kobayashi	19	1m 34.271s
15	Vitaly Petrov	24	1m 34.373s
16	Vitantonio Liuzzi	21	1m 34.379s
17	Sébastien Buemi	26	1m 34.991s
18	Jaime Alguersuari	22	1m 35.684s
19	Heikki Kovalainen	25	1m 36.949s
20	Timo Glock	17	1m 37.329s
21	Jarno Trulli	23	1m 37.388s
22	Jérôme D'Ambrosio	23	1m 37.778s
23	Bruno Senna	28	1m 38.814s
24	Sakon Yamamoto	26	1m 39.443s

PRACTICE 2 (FRIDAY)

Weather: Sunny/cloudy
Temperatures: track 28–32°C, air 24–26°C

Pos.	Driver	Laps	Time
1	Sebastian Vettel	32	1m 31.465s
2	Mark Webber	29	1m 31.860s
3	Robert Kubica	32	1m 32.200s
4	Fernando Alonso	34	1m 32.362s
5	Felipe Massa	35	1m 32.519s
6	Jenson Button	28	1m 32.533s
7	Vitaly Petrov	32	1m 32.703s
8	Michael Schumacher	27	1m 32.831s
9	Adrian Sutil	26	1m 32.842s
10	Nico Hülkenberg	26	1m 32.851s
11	Nico Rosberg	26	1m 32.880s
12	Kamui Kobayashi	31	1m 33.471s
13	Lewis Hamilton	8	1m 33.481s
14	Rubens Barrichello	16	1m 33.564s
15	Nick Heidfeld	33	1m 33.697s
16	Sébastien Buemi	32	1m 34.005s
17	Jaime Alguersuari	37	1m 34.055s
18	Vitantonio Liuzzi	33	1m 34.310s
19	Heikki Kovalainen	37	1m 36.095s
20	Jarno Trulli	33	1m 36.333s
21	Lucas Di Grassi	28	1m 36.630s
22	Timo Glock	28	1m 36.834s
23	Bruno Senna	33	1m 37.352s
24	Sakon Yamamoto	34	1m 37.831s

PRACTICE 3 (SATURDAY)

Weather: Drizzle/rain
Temperatures: track 21°C, air 20°C

Pos.	Driver	Laps	Time
1	Jaime Alguersuari	9	1m 55.902s
2	Timo Glock	6	2m 07.497s
3	Lucas Di Grassi	1	no time
4	Sakon Yamamoto	1	no time
5	Bruno Senna	1	no time
6	Sébastien Buemi	4	no time
7	Nick Heidfeld	1	no time
8	Felipe Massa	1	no time
9	Nico Hülkenberg	2	no time
10	Rubens Barrichello	1	no time
11	Kamui Kobayashi	1	no time
12	Heikki Kovalainen	1	no time
13	Nico Rosberg	1	no time
14	Vitantonio Liuzzi	1	no time
15	Mark Webber	1	no time
16	Michael Schumacher	1	no time
17	Fernando Alonso	1	no time
18	Vitaly Petrov	1	no time
19	Jenson Button	3	no time
20	Jarno Trulli	1	no time
21	Sebastian Vettel	1	no time
22	Adrian Sutil	1	no time
23	Robert Kubica	2	no time
24	Lewis Hamilton	3	no time

QUALIFYING (SUNDAY)

Weather: Sunny Temperatures: track 30–33°C, air 26°C

Pos.	Driver	First	Second	Third	Qualifying Tyre
1	Sebastian Vettel	1m 32.035s	1m 31.184s	1m 30.785s	Soft
2	Mark Webber	1m 32.476s	1m 31.241s	1m 30.853s	Soft
3	Lewis Hamilton	1m 32.809s	1m 31.523s	1m 31.169s	Soft
4	Robert Kubica	1m 32.808s	1m 32.042s	1m 31.231s	Soft
5	Fernando Alonso	1m 32.555s	1m 31.819s	1m 31.352s	Soft
6	Jenson Button	1m 32.636s	1m 31.763s	1m 31.378s	Hard
7	Nico Rosberg	1m 32.238s	1m 31.886s	1m 31.494s	Soft
8	Rubens Barrichello	1m 32.361s	1m 31.874s	1m 31.535s	Soft
9	Nico Hülkenberg	1m 32.211s	1m 31.926s	1m 31.559s	Soft
10	Michael Schumacher	1m 32.513s	1m 32.073s	1m 31.846s	Soft
11	Nick Heidfeld	1m 33.011s	1m 32.187s		
12	Felipe Massa	1m 32.721s	1m 32.321s		
13	Vitaly Petrov	1m 32.849s	1m 32.422s		
14	Kamui Kobayashi	1m 32.783s	1m 32.427s		
15	Adrian Sutil	1m 33.186s	1m 32.659s		
16	Jaime Alguersuari	1m 33.471s	1m 33.071s		
17	Vitantonio Liuzzi	1m 33.216s	1m 33.154s		
18	Sébastien Buemi	1m 33.568s			
19	Jarno Trulli	1m 35.346s			
20	Heikki Kovalainen	1m 35.464s			
21	Lucas Di Grassi	1m 36.265s			
22	Timo Glock	1m 36.332s			
23	Bruno Senna	1m 37.270s			
24	Sakon Yamamoto	1m 37.365s			

FOR THE RECORD

20th FRONT ROW: Sebastian Vettel

POINTS

DRIVERS

1	Mark Webber	220
2	Fernando Alonso	206
3	Sebastian Vettel	206
4	Lewis Hamilton	192
5	Jenson Button	189
6	Felipe Massa	128
7	Nico Rosberg	122
8	Robert Kubica	114
9	Michael Schumacher	54
10	Adrian Sutil	47
11	Rubens Barrichello	41
12	Kamui Kobayashi	27
13	Vitaly Petrov	19
14	Nico Hülkenberg	17
15	Vitantonio Liuzzi	13
16	Sébastien Buemi	8
17	Pedro de la Rosa	6
18	Nick Heidfeld	4
19	Jaime Alguersuari	3

CONSTRUCTORS

1	Red Bull	426
2	McLaren	381
3	Ferrari	334
4	Mercedes	176
5	Renault	133
6	Force India	60
7	Williams	58
8	BMW Sauber	37
9	Toro Rosso	11

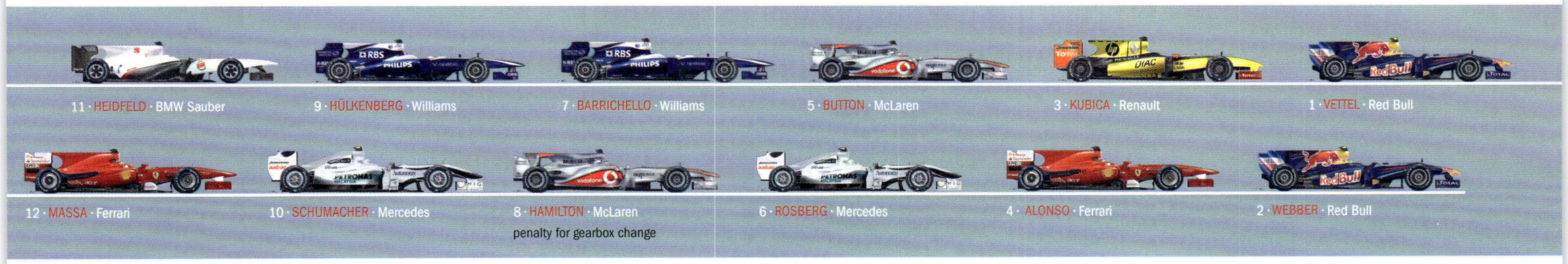

43	44	45	46	47	48	49	50	51	52	53	-
5	5	5	5	5	5	5	5	5	5	5	1
6	6	6	6	6	6	6	6	6	6	6	2
8	8	8	8	8	8	8	8	8	8	8	3
2	1	1	1	1	1	1	1	1	1	1	
1	2	2	2	2	2	2	2	2	2	2	
4	4	4	4	4	3	3	3	3	3	3	6
3	3	3	3	3	22	23	23	23	23	23	7
22	22	22	22	22	23	22	22	22	22	22	8
9	9	9	9	9	9	9	9	9	9	9	9
14	23	23	23	23	16	16	16	16	16	16	10
17	16	16	16	16	17	17	17	17	17		
23	14	17	17	17	19	19	19	19	19		
16	17	19	19	19	18	18	18	18			
19	19	18	18	18	24	24	24	24			
18	18	24	24	24	21	21	21	21			
24	24	21	21	21	20	20	20				
21	21	20	20	20							
20	20										

RACE TYRE STRATEGIES

	Driver	Race Stint 1	Race Stint 2	Race Stint 3
1	Vettel	Soft: 1-24	Hard: 25-53	
2	Webber	Soft: 1-25	Hard: 26-53	
3	Alonso	Soft: 1-24	Hard: 25-53	
4	Button	Hard: 1-38	Soft: 39-53	
5	Hamilton	Soft: 1-22	Hard: 23-53	
6	Schumacher	Soft: 1-23	Hard: 23-53	
7	Kobayashi	Hard: 1-38	Soft: 39-53	
8	Heidfeld	Soft: 1-18	Hard: 19-53	
9	Barrichello	Soft: 1-20	Hard: 21-53	
10	Buemi	Hard: 1-28	Soft: 29-53	
11	Alguersuari	Soft: 1-21	Hard: 22-44	Soft: 45-52
12	Kovalainen	Soft: 1-35	Hard: 36-52	
13	Trulli	Soft: 1	Hard: 2-51	
14	Glock	Hard: 1	Soft: 2	Hard: 3-51
15	Senna	Soft: 1	Hard: 2-51	
16	Yamamoto	Soft: 1-31	Hard: 32-50	
17	Rosberg	Soft: 1	Hard: 2-47	
	Sutil	Soft: 1-18	Hard: 19-44 (dnf)	
	Kubica	Soft: 1-2 (dnf)		
	Hülkenberg	Soft: 1 (dnf)		
	Massa	Hard: 1 (dnf)		
	Petrov	Soft: 1 (dnf)		
	Liuzzi	Hard: 1 (dnf)		

The tyre regulations stipulate that the two dry tyre specifications must be used during the race. The Soft compound Bridgestone Potenza tyre is marked with a green stripe on the sidewall.

Photos: Peter J. Fox

FIA FORMULA 1 WORLD CHAMPIONSHIP · ROUND 17

KOREAN GRAND PRIX

YEONGAM CIRCUIT

Serious expressions from Alonso, Hamilton and Massa as the podium ceremony protocol for the inaugural Korean Grand Prix took place in dank, dark conditions
Photo: Bernard Asset

YEONGAM QUALIFYING

HIRE cars cost $1,000 per week, everybody would have to stay in brothels and the circuit was located in a quagmire, so best take your Wellingtons...

The Korean Grand Prix was a rich seam of wild rumours long before the race was finally confirmed – and most turned out to be wildly inaccurate. It would have been an exaggeration to describe the venue as "finished" – it had been certificated only nine days before any car turned a wheel, rather than the usual 90 (or 60 in the case of a street circuit, which is what the Korea International Circuit will become when the neighbouring city is eventually built), but the most important bit was complete and required only some cosmetic fine-tuning (the subtle alteration of a few barrier angles and kerb profiles) between Friday's free practice sessions and Saturday qualifying. Its three distinctly themed sectors – echoes of Monza, Silverstone and Monaco respectively – were a hit with the drivers, and challenging diversity rendered it an instant classic. "If I could find anything to criticise," said championship leader Mark Webber, "I'd be clutching at straws."

The Australian was rather less enthralled about the starting line-up after qualifying second to Red Bull team-mate Sebastian Vettel. The peripheral construction work (grandstands were still being erected on Thursday) left the whole site dirty and, off the racing line, that was particularly true of the track. The clean side of a circuit usually offers extra purchase that's worth about eight metres at the start of a race, but here it was reckoned to be nearer 20.

"I have felt more comfortable as the weekend has gone on," Vettel said. "Even so, it is quite hard to understand the best approach at certain corners, because there are some awkward cambers and it would be very easy to make a mistake."

His pace concealed the limited track time he'd had during free practice – he had picked up a puncture on Friday and had always intended to sit out much of Saturday morning, to restrict wear on a Renault V8 that was approaching its last scheduled race.

He and Webber adopted slightly different strategies in Q3, the German opting for a one-lap final run while Webber (who took his eighth and final new engine of the season before qualifying) was fuelled slightly more heavily for two, because his car felt less balanced on its first flying lap with soft tyres. The gap between them was the customary micron, with Fernando Alonso just 0.181 seconds off pole in third.

The Ferrari wouldn't be an obvious threat to the Red Bulls on the long run between Turns Two and Three – it was fractionally slower through the speed trap – but Nico Rosberg's Mercedes (fifth, behind Lewis Hamilton) just might. The Anglo-German team might have ceased development long since, to focus on its 2011 car, but its F-duct was working very well (Rosberg was quickest of all on the straight), and a stable chassis package gave the team a better understanding of where to find extra fractions of lap time. "There's probably a lesson in that, somewhere," said team principal Ross Brawn.

Rosberg escaped without penalty after impeding Alonso during Q2: the stewards ruled that the German had done his best to keep out of the way. Team-mate Michael Schumacher was reprimanded for blocking Williams driver Rubens Barrichello, but retained ninth place because the Brazilian was in the first – and slower – phase of a two-lap run.

While Hamilton was an in-touch fourth, McLaren team-mate Jenson Button struggled to generate tyre heat, and his dwindling prospects of a successful title defence looked ever bleaker when he qualified only seventh. "We were quick in practice," Hamilton said, "but I don't know where the Red Bulls found that extra half-second."

Above: The Mercedes SLS safety car was deployed for a large portion of the race. Here, Vettel and Webber's Red Bulls hold station behind it at the head of the pack.

Top left: Concerned race director Charlie Whiting oversees work on the new track.

Above centre left: The stands were still under construction as the meeting began.

Above left: Red Bull's test driver, Daniel Ricciardo, who looks a great prospect for a bright F1 future.

Left: Tour de Korea? Alonso puts in some energetic legwork to familiarise himself with the circuit.

Photos: Peter J Fox

THERE are times when television directors need to summon up every ounce of editing discretion to conjure crowd scenes that make half-empty racetracks appear busy, but that was never an issue at the Korea International Circuit. Outside, the venue's main three-lane highway was barely visible beneath a tapestry of abandoned cars as 80,000 people flocked to embrace the nation's first world championship grand prix. But would it actually happen?

In the wake of so many rumours and counter-rumours about the circuit's likely readiness ahead of the appointed date, it was ironic that the weather threatened to undo the constructional graft. Persistent morning drizzle never really abated, and by mid-afternoon it was absolutely tipping down. Timo Glock and Felipe Massa both spun during their reconnaissance laps, while Bruno Senna ran horribly wide at Turn Three (but with large parts of the infrastructure unfinished, there was nothing much for him to hit).

The start was put back by ten minutes while conditions were assessed, and eventually the field was unleashed behind the safety car. The adverse weather was a bonus for Mark Webber, who knew he might struggle to hang on to second if the race had started conventionally on a dry track, but the spray was a serious handicap for almost everybody bar Sebastian Vettel, who led the field in grid order (Senna, last anyway, made a quick pit stop at the end of the first lap before rejoining). Fernando Alonso described the conditions as "The worst I've ever experienced" and Jenson Button came on the radio to tell McLaren, "I can't even see my front tyres. I'm driving completely blind and just waiting to hit somebody." Race control got the message and on lap three the red flag was shown, the field returning to the grid in the order they'd left it.

There was another potential problem looming, because the combination of a 3pm start and Korea's relatively early sunsets (when, indeed, it has some sun) meant that the light might not hold for a full race distance – and 49 minutes elapsed before lap four finally began, again behind the safety car.

The drivers' radio reactions were entertainingly diverse as the procession continued. Lewis Hamilton couldn't wait to get going. On lap eight, he was fizzing about the improved conditions, and two laps later added, "They really should start the race." At this point, Webber was asked what he thought about the conditions and replied, "I can't really see much difference." By lap 16, Hamilton was claiming that conditions were almost ripe for intermediates; shortly beforehand, an FIA official had emerged from race control and conducted a scientific experiment: he stuck out an open palm to see whether it was still raining.

Finally, at the end of lap 17, the safety car withdrew and Vettel led the field away, with Webber holding second from Alonso and Nico Rosberg passing Hamilton under braking for Turn Three: cannily, Mercedes had softened both its cars during the long break and the decision bore immediate fruit.

Massa held fifth from Button, Michael Schumacher, Robert Kubica, Nico Hülkenberg, Adrian Sutil, Rubens Barrichello, Kamui Kobayashi, Nick Heidfeld, Jaime Alguersuari, Tonio Liuzzi, Sébastien Buemi, Timo Glock, Vitaly Petrov (who served a five-place grid penalty following his start-line conduct in Japan), Heikki Kovalainen, Salon Yamamoto, Senna, Jarno Trulli (who had spun at the first turn, forcing Senna wide) and di Grassi, who pitted for intermediates as the race resumed.

Within two laps, the safety car appeared once again, this time because Webber had taken a bit too

much kerb coming out of Turn 12 before spinning across the track, hitting the wall on one side and then slewing back into his rivals' path. Alonso missed him, but Rosberg couldn't. The circuit was littered with cranes, but they were part of the architectural programme and couldn't be used to shift stranded cars. "The accident was totally my fault," said Webber, watching his championship lead heading towards evaporation after only his second non-finish of the campaign.

The race resumed at the end of lap 23, with Vettel taking a bold line over the potentially treacherous kerbs at the final corner to open a significant gap over Alonso – he was 2.1 seconds clear by the lap's end. There was more carnage during the lap, when Trulli tried to bulldoze Senna aside at Turn Six. The Lotus lost its nose and the Italian headed back to the pits for repairs, although he retired a couple of laps later when his hydraulics failed – scarcely a first, and a problem that had first become apparent during the longest safety car period, when his power steering had become a tad heavy.

Di Grassi disappeared at the same point after spinning into the tyre wall at Turn 14, a hint that it was still perhaps a touch too early for intermediates. "I went off trying to avoid a collision with Yamamoto," he said, although in reality he'd simply crashed while trying to pass him.

There was rather greater disruption on lap 31, when Buemi made an ill-judged attempt to wrest 12th from Glock at Turn Three. No, a Virgin shouldn't have been that far up, but the German had driven with his customary splendour in mixed conditions and had gained positions as the balance of the cluttered midfield either made mistakes or, in the case of both Saubers, made premature stops to switch to inters.

Two laps earlier, Buemi had crudely elbowed Kovalainen wide at Turn Ten, and now he simply hit Glock squarely in the midriff, earning himself a five-position grid penalty in Brazil. Glock restarted, but went only as far as the pits, and the race was neutralised to allow Buemi's dog-eared Toro Rosso to be retrieved. At this rate, safety car driver Bernd Mayländer was going to be a classified finisher.

Mayländer emerged just too late for either Vettel or Alonso to peel in for a timely tyre change in the improving conditions. Hamilton made it, though, followed by Massa, Schumacher, Kubica and everybody else who hadn't previously switched. The two leaders came in next time around, and Alonso locked up as he stopped parking slightly askew and delaying the crew members working on his front right

wheel. That cost him a bit of time and second place, as Hamilton nipped ahead, but Massa – leading the rest of the pack – drove at a suitably leisurely pace on his out lap, to ensure his team-mate could rejoin without further positional loss.

The pit glitch was but a temporary setback for Alonso. As Vettel made yet another awesome restart at the end of lap 34, again flirting with the slippery Turn 18 kerbs (he pulled 1.5 seconds clear, this time), Hamilton immediately ran wide at Turn One and dropped back to third. "I was really struggling with my brakes," he said, "and simply locked the fronts."

The gap between the front two now stabilised and the race finally appeared to have settled down. "I think Sebastian was quicker on full wets," Alonso said, "but I was able to keep pace with him a little more easily on intermediates."

He was 1.2 seconds adrift at the start of the 44th lap, when Vettel began to complain about the fading light. The German radioed in about the particularly poor visibility at Turn One, although it didn't help that he had chosen a medium visor tint. McLaren asked Hamilton what he thought about the conditions. "They're fine," came the predictable response.

One lap later, Vettel's comments became manna for conspiracy theorists. The Red Bull suddenly faltered on the pit straight and Alonso swept by into Turn One. Had the race-long leader been dropping hints about an early stoppage because he'd seen some worrying temperature messages on his dash?

Not at all, according to sporting director Christian Horner. "We had absolutely no idea until Seb came on the radio shouting, 'engine problem'," he said. After 1,600 kilometres, 400 short of its theoretical life cycle, his Renault V8 had suffered a con-rod failure, a cruel blow after a weekend when he had done absolutely everything right. "It's just one of those things," Vettel said, his mood remarkably sanguine. "That's life."

What should have been his championship lead passed instead to Alonso, who reeled off the final ten laps without incident. "I think it's one of the trickiest victories of my career," he said. "Prior to the race, we had no experience of driving here on wet tyres. Then

Above: The murky conditions ensured the safety car stayed in place for a large part of the race.

Above left: Alonso leads Hamilton, Rosberg, Massa and Button.

Right: The novel attraction of F1 kept the crowds glued to their seats, even in the rain.

Left: The track needed a huge amount of work to make it raceworthy

Photos: Peter J Fox

EDITOR'S VIEW
END-OF-SEASON JITTERS AT RED BULL

Above: Mark Webber's wrecked Red Bull RB6 presents a forlorn sight at the edge of the circuit.
Photo: Peter J Fox

Top: Sebastian Vettel reports to his crew on the pit wall following his retirement from the lead.
Photo: Dieter Mathis/WRi2

ONE has to hope that the comments attributed to Gerhard Berger, to the effect that Mark Webber intentionally had attempted to take out another driver as he crashed out of the Korean Grand Prix, were somehow misquoted or misinterpreted. If not, then the popular Austrian driver was surely guilty, at the very least, of a huge misjudgement for airing such contentious and controversial views.

Apparently, Berger had suggested that, after bouncing off the wall, as Webber spun back across the circuit it had been his intention deliberately to take out one of his championship rivals, Lewis Hamilton or Fernando Alonso, rather than spearing into the hapless Nico Rosberg's Mercedes. Whatever the thinking behind Gerhard's observations, Red Bull team principal Christian Horner stepped up to the plate with a rigorous defence of his driver, which must have been reassuring for the Australian, who sometimes has felt that the RBR top brass has not always supported his cause.

"As with every incident in F1, opinions will always be made without all the facts," Horner told the *Daily Telegraph Sport*. "Just to be absolutely clear, Mark's intention was *not* to take out another driver after his crash in the Korean Grand Prix, and it is ridiculous to suggest otherwise.

"After Mark's impact with the wall, it was clear on the TV and from the data that his car was badly damaged. However, the natural and immediate instinct of any competitive driver is not to give up and to keep going.

"In the atrocious conditions, Mark made the snap decision to continue, as every driver would in that situation. It's absurd to suggest that Mark would ever deliberately take out another driver. Mark accepted immediate blame for this incident, which in itself deserves credit."

Even so, Horner's sympathetic, and entirely logical, remarks did not entirely mollify Webber as the F1 caravan continued its late-season global tour towards Interlagos and the penultimate race of the schedule. On his arrival in São Paulo, Mark said that he believed that his championship challenge had been an inconvenience to the Red Bull squad, which really preferred Sebastian Vettel to be the driver with his name up in lights.

"I don't think I was maybe meant to be in the hunt," said Webber with an insouciant grin, "so it has been maybe quite inconvenient, but I've enjoyed every minute of it."

Horner was thrust into the spotlight again in a bid to smooth the Australian driver's ruffled feathers. "The team would be greatly hurt to see Mark has said that, *if* he has said that," he remarked. "I can only think it's been taken out of context because he has a great deal of support within the team."

It all seemed like a touch of end-of-season nerves.

Alan Henry

we switched to intermediates, again with no previous reference points, and finally we finished the race in very dark conditions on a slippery track with tyres that were virtually slicks."

Dark? By the time he reached the podium, it was nightfall.

Hamilton and Massa completed the top three, and despite being 21 points adrift, the Englishman insisted the title was still winnable. "Generally, our qualifying pace isn't good enough," he said, "but we have some positive new things coming. It's not impossible."

The task looked exactly that for Button, who had struggled all weekend to generate adequate tyre and brake temperatures. A premature switch to intermediates left him nursing frayed tyres towards the end, and eventually he spun at Turn 17. Keeping the car out of the wall at that moment was probably his weekend's zenith and he trailed in 12th.

Schumacher took fourth, equalling his best result of the campaign, although this was his most impressive performance. The softened suspension tweak helped, of course, but one mid-race move on Button was ripe with Schumacher trademarks – firm and aggressive, with no hint of recent clumsiness. "I think the gathering darkness was Michael's biggest concern," said Mercedes team principal Ross Brawn. "He was becoming distracted by the lights on his steering wheel and didn't know how to adjust the brightness, so we had to explain it to him over the radio."

Kubica ordinarily excels in such conditions, but Renault had only one specification of F-duct rear wing available – unlike the wide choice at others' disposal – and the Pole was obliged to live with whatever balance that generated. He nursed his intermediates well, though, and was able to move up to fifth in the later stages, forcing Barrichello into a mistake (which dropped the Brazilian to seventh, behind the faultless Liuzzi) and profiting from a slow puncture that obliged Hülkenberg to make a late pit stop, dropping him from sixth to tenth.

Kobayashi and Heidfeld occupied the slots between the Williams team-mates. Having struggled initially on their intermediates, both spent the middle part of the race trying to swat aside the effervescent Sutil, who would move ahead, make a mistake, drop back and try again. Eventually, on lap 47, the German took a wild swipe at Kobayashi on the approach to Turn Five – and the Force India driver retired with buckled suspension. He was still given a five-place grid penalty for Interlagos, though.

Alguersuari, the aforementioned Button, Kovalainen, Senna and Yamamoto completed the finishers, while Petrov dropped out at the end of lap 40, when he misjudged Turn 18 and smote the pit lane entry barriers with significant force.

The greater impact, though, was made by Korea. For all its mildly incomplete air, this had been a tremendous first event at a circuit with authentic character.

Simon Arron

Above: Cats with the cream? Alonso and Massa reflect on a great day for the Scuderia.
Photo: Jean-Francois Galeron/WRi2

Below: Rare sight in 2010 as Schumacher's Mercedes outbrakes a struggling Button's McLaren.
Photo: Studio Colombo/WRi2

FIA F1 WORLD CHAMPIONSHIP · ROUND 17

KOREAN GRAND PRIX

YEONGAM 22–24 OCTOBER 2010

RACE DISTANCE: 55 laps, 191.774 miles/308.630km

RACE WEATHER: Drizzle/rain/cloudy (track 19–21°C, air 19–20°C)

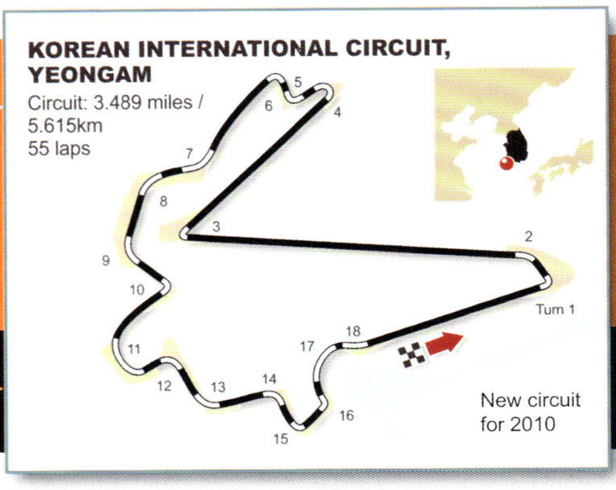

Pos.	Driver	Nat.	No.	Entrant	Car/Engine	Tyres	Laps	Time/Retirement	Speed (mph/km/h)	Gap to leader	Fastest race lap	
1	**Fernando Alonso**	E	8	Scuderia Ferrari Marlboro	Ferrari F10-056 V8	B	55	2h 48m 20.810s	68.349/109.997		1m 50.257s	42
2	**Lewis Hamilton**	GB	2	Vodafone McLaren Mercedes	McLaren MP4-25-Mercedes FO108X V8	B	55	2h 48m 35.809s	68.248/109.834	+ 14.999s	1m 50.430s	42
3	**Felipe Massa**	BR	7	Scuderia Ferrari Marlboro	Ferrari F10-056 V8	B	55	2h 48m 51.678s	68.141/109.662	+ 30.868s	1m 50.502s	44
4	**Michael Schumacher**	GB	3	Mercedes GP Petronas F1 Team	Mercedes MGP W01-Mercedes FO108X V8	B	55	2h 49m 00.498s	68.082/109.567	+ 39.688s	1m 51.835s	43
5	**Robert Kubica**	PL	11	Renault F1 Team	Renault R30-RS27 V8	B	55	2h 49m 08.544s	68.028/109.480	+ 47.734s	1m 51.604s	45
6	**Vitantonio Liuzzi**	I	15	Force India F1 Team	Force India VJM03-Mercedes FO108X V8	B	55	2h 49m 14.381s	67.989/109.417	+ 53.571s	1m 51.371s	45
7	**Rubens Barrichello**	BR	9	AT&T Williams	Williams FW32-Cosworth CA2010 V8	B	55	2h 49m 30.067s	67.884/109.248	+ 1m 09.257s	1m 51.564s	45
8	**Kamui Kobayashi**	J	23	BMW Sauber F1 Team	BMW Sauber C29-Ferrari 056 V8	B	55	2h 49m 38.699s	67.826/109.156	+ 1m 17.889s	1m 53.086s	42
9	**Nick Heidfeld**	D	22	BMW Sauber F1 Team	BMW Sauber C29-Ferrari 056 V8	B	55	2h 49m 40.917s	67.811/109.132	+ 1m 20.107s	1m 53.263s	42
10	**Nico Hülkenberg**	D	10	AT&T Williams	Williams FW32-Cosworth CA2010 V8	B	55	2h 49m 41.661s	67.807/109.124	+ 1m 20.851s	1m 51.982s	43
11	Jaime Alguersuari	E	17	Scuderia Toro Rosso	Toro Rosso STR5-Ferrari 056 V8	B	55	2h 49m 44.956s	67.785/109.089	+ 1m 24.146s	1m 51.962s	43
12	Jenson Button	GB	1	Vodafone McLaren Mercedes	McLaren MP4-25-Mercedes FO108X V8	B	55	2h 49m 50.749s	67.746/109.027	+ 1m 29.939s	1m 52.193s	42
13	Heikki Kovalainen	FIN	19	Lotus Racing	Lotus T127-Cosworth CA2010 V8	B	54			+ 1 lap	1m 55.018s	43
14	Bruno Senna	BR	21	HRT F1 Team	HRT F110-Cosworth CA2010 V8	B	53			+ 2 laps	1m 59.290s	30
15	Sakon Yamamoto	J	20	HRT F1 Team	HRT F110-Cosworth CA2010 V8	B	53			+ 2 laps	1m 58.313s	36
	Adrian Sutil	D	14	Force India F1 Team	Force India VJM03-Mercedes FO108X V8	B	46	*accident*			1m 52.601s	40
	Sebastian Vettel	D	5	Red Bull Racing	Red Bull RB6-Renault RS27 V8	B	45	*engine*			1m 50.375s	44
	Vitaly Petrov	RUS	12	Renault F1 Team	Renault R30-RS27 V8	B	39	*accident*			1m 53.031s	39
	Timo Glock	D	24	Virgin Racing	Virgin VR-01-Cosworth CA2010 V8	B	31	*accident*			1m 58.102s	29
	Sébastien Buemi	CH	16	Scuderia Toro Rosso	Toro Rosso STR5-Ferrari 056 V8	B	30	*accident*			1m 56.768s	27
	Lucas Di Grassi	BR	25	Virgin Racing	Virgin VR-01-Cosworth CA2010 V8	B	25	*spin*			2m 02.635s	25
	Jarno Trulli	I	18	Lotus Racing	Lotus T127-Cosworth CA2010 V8	B	25	*hydraulics*			2m 05.161s	20
	Mark Webber	AUS	6	Red Bull Racing	Red Bull RB6-Renault RS27 V8	B	18	*accident*			2m 00.025s	18
	Nico Rosberg	D	4	Mercedes GP Petronas F1 Team	Mercedes MGP W01-Mercedes FO108X V8	B	18	*accident*			2m 00.652s	18

Race stopped after 3 laps due to heavy rain and restarted for remaining 52 laps. Official race times above include period of inactivity.

Fastest race lap: Fernando Alonso on lap 42, 1m 50.257s, 113.919mph/183.335km/h.

Lap record: no previous race.

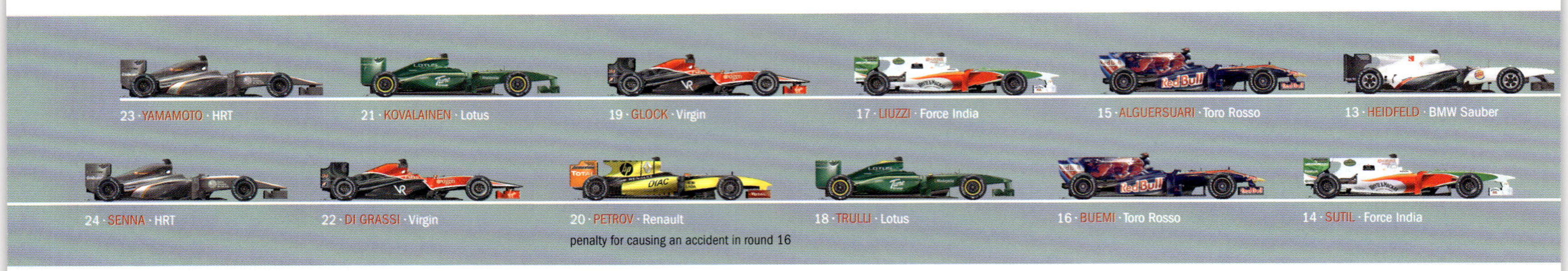

23 · YAMAMOTO · HRT
21 · KOVALAINEN · Lotus
19 · GLOCK · Virgin
17 · LIUZZI · Force India
15 · ALGUERSUARI · Toro Rosso
13 · HEIDFELD · BMW Sauber
24 · SENNA · HRT
22 · DI GRASSI · Virgin
20 · PETROV · Renault
penalty for causing an accident in round 16
18 · TRULLI · Lotus
16 · BUEMI · Toro Rosso
14 · SUTIL · Force India

	Grid order	1	2	3	4	5	6	7	8	9	10	11	12	13	14	15	16	17	18	19	20	21	22
5	VETTEL	5	5	5	5	5	5	5	5	5	5	5	5	5	5	5	5	5	5	5	5	5	5
6	WEBBER	6	6	6	6	6	6	6	6	6	6	6	6	6	6	6	6	6	6	8	8	8	8
8	ALONSO	8	8	8	8	8	8	8	8	8	8	8	8	8	8	8	8	8	8	2	2	2	2
2	HAMILTON	2	2	2	2	2	2	2	2	2	2	2	2	2	2	2	2	2	4	7	7	7	7
4	ROSBERG	4	4	4	4	4	4	4	4	4	4	4	4	4	4	4	4	4	2	1	1	1	1
7	MASSA	7	7	7	7	7	7	7	7	7	7	7	7	7	7	7	7	7	7	3	3	3	3
1	BUTTON	1	1	1	1	1	1	1	1	1	1	1	1	1	1	1	1	1	1	11	11	11	11
11	KUBICA	11	11	11	11	11	11	11	11	11	11	11	11	11	11	11	11	11	3	10	10	10	10
3	SCHUMACHER	3	3	3	3	3	3	3	3	3	3	3	3	3	3	3	3	3	11	9	9	9	9
9	BARRICHELLO	9	9	9	9	9	9	9	9	9	9	9	9	9	9	9	9	9	10	14	14	14	14
10	HULKENBERG	10	10	10	10	10	10	10	10	10	10	10	10	10	10	10	10	10	14	15	15	15	15
23	KOBAYASHI	23	23	23	23	23	23	23	23	23	23	23	23	23	23	23	23	23	9	17	17	17	17
22	HEIDFELD	22	22	22	22	22	22	22	22	22	22	22	22	22	22	22	22	22	23	22	24	24	24
14	SUTIL	14	14	14	14	14	14	14	14	14	14	14	14	14	14	14	14	14	22	24	19	19	19
17	ALGUERSUARI	17	17	17	17	17	17	17	17	17	17	17	17	17	17	17	17	17	17	23	12	20	20
16	BUEMI	16	16	16	16	16	16	16	16	16	16	16	16	16	16	16	16	16	15	12	20	22	22
15	LIUZZI	15	15	15	15	15	15	15	15	15	15	15	15	15	15	15	15	15	16	16	22	23	23
18	TRULLI	18	18	18	18	18	18	18	18	18	18	18	18	18	18	18	18	18	24	19	18	18	12
24	GLOCK	24	24	24	24	24	24	24	24	24	24	24	24	24	24	24	24	24	12	20	23	12	25
12	PETROV	12	12	12	12	12	12	12	12	12	12	12	12	12	12	12	12	12	19	21	25	25	16
19	KOVALAINEN	19	19	19	19	19	19	19	19	19	19	19	19	19	19	19	19	19	20	18	16	16	21
25	DI GRASSI	25	25	25	20	20	20	20	20	20	20	20	20	20	20	20	20	20	21	25	21	21	18
20	YAMAMOTO	20	20	20	21	21	21	21	21	21	21	21	21	21	21	21	21	21	18				
21	SENNA	21	21	21	25	25	25	25	25	25	25	25	25	25	25	25	25	25	25				

	Grid order	23	24	25	26	27	28	29	30	31	32	33	34	35	36	37	38	39	40	41	42	43	44
5	VETTEL	5	5	5	5	5	5	5	5	5	5	5	5	5	5	5	5	5	5	5	5	5	5
6	WEBBER	8	8	8	8	8	8	8	8	8	8	2	2	8	8	8	8	8	8	8	8	8	8
8	ALONSO	2	2	2	2	2	2	2	2	2	2	8	8	2	2	2	2	2	2	2	2	2	2
2	HAMILTON	7	7	7	7	7	7	7	7	7	7	7	7	7	7	7	7	7	7	7	7	7	7
4	ROSBERG	1	1	1	1	3	3	3	3	3	3	3	3	3	3	3	3	3	3	3	3	3	3
7	MASSA	3	3	3	3	1	10	10	11	11	9	9	9	9	9	9	9	9	9	9	9	9	9
1	BUTTON	11	11	11	10	10	11	11	9	9	12	12	12	12	12	12	12	12	10	10	10	10	10
11	KUBICA	10	10	10	11	11	9	9	10	17	10	10	10	10	10	10	10	10	11	11	11	11	11
3	SCHUMACHER	9	9	9	9	9	1	17	17	15	11	11	11	11	11	11	11	11	15	15	15	15	15
9	BARRICHELLO	14	14	14	14	14	15	15	15	12	23	23	23	23	15	15	15	15	23	23	23	23	23
10	HULKENBERG	15	15	15	15	15	17	24	12	10	15	15	15	15	23	23	23	23	22	22	22	22	22
23	KOBAYASHI	17	17	17	17	17	14	12	24	23	1	1	1	1	22	14	22	22	17	17	14	14	14
22	HEIDFELD	24	24	24	24	24	24	16	16	1	22	22	22	22	14	22	14	17	14	14	17	17	17
14	SUTIL	19	19	19	19	19	19	23	23	22	14	14	14	14	17	17	17	14	1	1	1	1	1
17	ALGUERSUARI	20	20	20	12	12	12	1	1	14	17	17	17	17	1	1	1	1	19	19	19	19	19
16	BUEMI	22	23	12	16	16	16	22	22	24	21	21	21	19	19	19	19	21	21	21	21	21	*21*
15	LIUZZI	23	12	16	23	23	23	19	19	19	19	19	19	21	21	21	21	19	20	20	*20*	*20*	*20*
18	TRULLI	12	16	23	22	22	22	14	14	21	20	20	20	20	20	20	20	20					
24	GLOCK	25	22	22	21	21	21	21	21	*20*													
12	PETROV	16	25	25	20	20	20	20	*20*														
19	KOVALAINEN	21	21	21																			
25	DI GRASSI	18	18	*18*																			
20	YAMAMOTO																						
21	SENNA																						

Safety car deployed on laps shown

TIME SHEETS

PRACTICE 1 (FRIDAY)

Weather: Sunny
Temperatures: track 23-30°C, air 18-21°C

Pos.	Driver	Laps	Time
1	Lewis Hamilton	15	1m 40.887s
2	Robert Kubica	18	1m 40.968s
3	Nico Rosberg	21	1m 41.152s
4	Sebastian Vettel	18	1m 41.371s
5	Jenson Button	16	1m 41.940s
6	Michael Schumacher	25	1m 42.022s
7	Mark Webber	23	1m 42.202s
8	Nick Heidfeld	18	1m 42.293s
9	Nico Hülkenberg	21	1m 42.678s
10	Rubens Barrichello	23	1m 42.883s
11	Vitaly Petrov	22	1m 42.896s
12	Felipe Massa	25	1m 43.054s
13	Kamui Kobayashi	20	1m 43.309s
14	Adrian Sutil	18	1m 43.602s
15	Fernando Alonso	21	1m 43.928s
16	Sébastien Buemi	23	1m 43.940s
17	Vitantonio Liuzzi	21	1m 44.887s
18	Jaime Alguersuari	26	1m 45.141s
19	Timo Glock	20	1m 45.588s
20	Jérôme d'Ambrosio	17	1m 46.613s
21	Heikki Kovalainen	22	1m 47.115s
22	Sakon Yamamoto	29	1m 50.347s
23	Bruno Senna	15	1m 50.821s
24	Jarno Trulli	11	1m 51.701s

PRACTICE 2 (FRIDAY)

Weather: Sunny/cloudy
Temperatures: track 28-32°C, air 21-22°C

Pos.	Driver	Laps	Time
1	Mark Webber	23	1m 37.942s
2	Fernando Alonso	30	1m 38.132s
3	Lewis Hamilton	29	1m 38.279s
4	Robert Kubica	29	1m 38.718s
5	Jenson Button	19	1m 38.726s
6	Felipe Massa	32	1m 38.820s
7	Sebastian Vettel	22	1m 39.204s
8	Vitaly Petrov	28	1m 39.267s
9	Nico Rosberg	29	1m 39.268s
10	Kamui Kobayashi	26	1m 39.564s
11	Nick Heidfeld	25	1m 39.588s
12	Michael Schumacher	26	1m 39.598s
13	Rubens Barrichello	35	1m 39.812s
14	Vitantonio Liuzzi	27	1m 39.881s
15	Adrian Sutil	22	1m 39.971s
16	Nico Hülkenberg	30	1m 40.478s
17	Jaime Alguersuari	29	1m 40.578s
18	Sébastien Buemi	32	1m 40.896s
19	Heikki Kovalainen	29	1m 42.773s
20	Jarno Trulli	19	1m 42.801s
21	Timo Glock	26	1m 43.115s
22	Lucas Di Grassi	29	1m 44.039s
23	Sakon Yamamoto	19	1m 45.166s
24	Bruno Senna	3	1m 46.649s

PRACTICE 3 (SATURDAY)

Weather: Cloudy
Temperatures: track 22-24°C, air 19-21°C

Pos.	Driver	Laps	Time
1	Robert Kubica	15	1m 37.354s
2	Lewis Hamilton	16	1m 37.402s
3	Fernando Alonso	15	1m 37.426s
4	Mark Webber	13	1m 37.441s
5	Nico Rosberg	12	1m 37.629s
6	Felipe Massa	16	1m 37.955s
7	Jenson Button	15	1m 38.419s
8	Nico Hülkenberg	17	1m 38.501s
9	Michael Schumacher	12	1m 38.630s
10	Adrian Sutil	18	1m 38.632s
11	Vitaly Petrov	14	1m 38.668s
12	Rubens Barrichello	16	1m 38.733s
13	Sébastien Buemi	21	1m 39.058s
14	Kamui Kobayashi	16	1m 39.145s
15	Jaime Alguersuari	21	1m 39.159s
16	Sebastian Vettel	9	1m 39.780s
17	Nick Heidfeld	17	1m 40.289s
18	Vitantonio Liuzzi	15	1m 41.591s
19	Jarno Trulli	15	1m 41.623s
20	Timo Glock	17	1m 41.853s
21	Heikki Kovalainen	19	1m 42.095s
22	Lucas Di Grassi	19	1m 43.111s
23	Bruno Senna	19	1m 43.417s
24	Sakon Yamamoto	20	1m 43.880s

QUALIFYING (SATURDAY)

Weather: Cloudy Temperatures: track 24-26°C, air 22°C

Pos.	Driver	First	Second	Third	Qualifying Tyre
1	Sebastian Vettel	1m 37.123s	1m 36.074s	1m 35.585s	Soft
2	Mark Webber	1m 37.373s	1m 36.039s	1m 35.659s	Soft
3	Fernando Alonso	1m 37.144s	1m 36.287s	1m 35.766s	Soft
4	Lewis Hamilton	1m 37.113s	1m 36.197s	1m 36.062s	Soft
5	Nico Rosberg	1m 37.708s	1m 36.791s	1m 36.535s	Soft
6	Felipe Massa	1m 37.515s	1m 36.169s	1m 36.571s	Soft
7	Jenson Button	1m 38.123s	1m 37.064s	1m 36.731s	Soft
8	Robert Kubica	1m 37.703s	1m 37.179s	1m 36.824s	Soft
9	Michael Schumacher	1m 37.980s	1m 37.077s	1m 36.950s	Soft
10	Rubens Barrichello	1m 38.257s	1m 37.511s	1m 36.998s	Soft
11	Nico Hülkenberg	1m 38.115s	1m 37.620s		
12	Kamui Kobayashi	1m 38.429s	1m 37.643s		
13	Nick Heidfeld	1m 38.171s	1m 37.715s		
14	Adrian Sutil	1m 38.572s	1m 37.783s		
15	Vitaly Petrov	1m 38.174s	1m 37.799s		
16	Jaime Alguersuari	1m 38.583s	1m 37.853s		
17	Sébastien Buemi	1m 38.621s	1m 38.594s		
18	Vitantonio Liuzzi	1m 38.955s			
19	Jarno Trulli	1m 40.521s			
20	Timo Glock	1m 40.748s			
21	Heikki Kovalainen	1m 41.768s			
22	Lucas Di Grassi	1m 42.325s			
23	Sakon Yamamoto	1m 42.444s			
24	Bruno Senna	1m 43.283s			

FOR THE RECORD

1ST GRAND PRIX: South Korea

DID YOU KNOW

This is the 68th venue, and South Korea is the 29th country to host an F1 World Championship grand prix.

POINTS

DRIVERS

1	Fernando Alonso	231
2	Mark Webber	220
3	Lewis Hamilton	210
4	Sebastian Vettel	206
5	Jenson Button	189
6	Felipe Massa	143
7	Robert Kubica	124
8	Nico Rosberg	122
9	Michael Schumacher	66
10	Rubens Barrichello	47
11	Adrian Sutil	47
12	Kamui Kobayashi	31
13	Vitantonio Liuzzi	21
14	Vitaly Petrov	19
15	Nico Hülkenberg	18
16	Sébastien Buemi	8
17	Pedro de la Rosa	6
18	Nick Heidfeld	6
19	Jaime Alguersuari	3

CONSTRUCTORS

1	Red Bull	426
2	McLaren	399
3	Ferrari	374
4	Mercedes	188
5	Renault	143
6	Force India	68
7	Williams	65
8	BMW Sauber	43
9	Toro Rosso	11

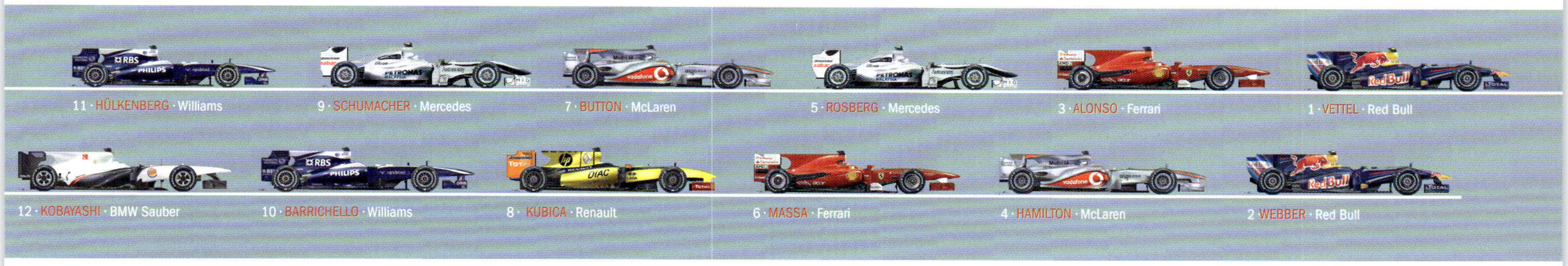

45	46	47	48	49	50	51	52	53	54	55	
5	8	8	8	8	8	8	8	8	8	8	1
8	2	2	2	2	2	2	2	2	2	2	2
2	7	7	7	7	7	7	7	7	7	7	3
7	3	3	3	3	3	3	3	3	3	3	
3	9	9	9	9	9	9	11	11	11	11	
9	10	10	10	10	10	11	15	15	15	15	6
10	11	11	11	11	11	15	9	9	9	9	7
11	15	15	15	15	15	10	23	23	23	23	8
15	23	23	23	23	23	23	22	22	22	22	9
23	14	22	22	22	22	22	17	17	17	10	10
22	22	17	17	17	17	17	10	10	10	17	
14	17	1	1	1	1	1	1	1	1	1	
17	1	19	*19*	*19*	*19*	*19*	*19*	*19*	*19*		
1	19	*21*	*21*	*21*	*21*	*21*	*21*	*21*			
19	*21*	*20*	*20*	*20*	*20*	*20*	*20*	*20*			
21	*20*										
20											

21 Pit stop *14 One lap or more behind*

RACE TYRE STRATEGIES

	Driver	Race Stint 1	Race Stint 2	Race Stint 3	Race Stint 4
1	Alonso	Wet: 1-32	Inters: 33-55		
2	Hamilton	Wet: 1-31	Inters: 32-55		
3	Massa	Wet: 1-31	Inters: 32-55		
4	Schumacher	Wet: 1-31	Inters: 32-55		
5	Kubica	Wet: 1-31	Inters: 32-55		
6	Liuzzi	Wet: 1-31	Inters: 32-55		
7	Barrichello	Wet: 1-31	Inters: 32-55		
8	Kobayashi	Wet: 1-19	Inters: 20-55		
9	Heidfeld	Wet: 1-19	Inters: 20-55		
10	Hülkenberg	Wet: 1-30	Inters: 31-51	Inters: 52-55	
11	Alguersuari	Wet: 1-31	Inters: 32-55		
12	Button	Wet: 1-28	Inters: 29-55		
13	Kovalainen	Wet: 1-31	Inters: 32-38	Inters: 39-54	
14	Senna	Wet: 1	Wet: 2-19	Inters: 20-53	
15	Yamamoto	Wet: 1-26	Inters: 27-53		
	Sutil	Wet: 1-28	Inters: 28-46 (dnf)		
	Vettel	Wet: 1-32	Inters: 33-45 (dnf)		
	Petrov	Wet: 1-20	Inters: 21-39 (dnf)		
	Glock	Wet: 1-31 (dnf)			
	Buemi	Wet: 1-19	Inters: 20-30 (dnf)		
	di Grassi	Wet: 1-4	Wet: 5-13	Wet: 14-17	Inters: 18-25 (dnf)
	Trulli	Wet: 1-21	Inters: 22-24	Inters: 25 (dnf)	
	Webber	Wet: 1-18 (dnf)			
	Rosberg	Wet: 1-18 (dnf)			

The tyre regulations stipulate that the two dry tyre specifications must be used during the race. However the race was run under wet conditions using full wet and intermediate compound tyres.

Photos: Peter J. Fox

FIA FORMULA 1 WORLD CHAMPIONSHIP · ROUND 18

BRAZILIAN GRAND PRIX

INTERLAGOS CIRCUIT

Stretching his legs: Sebastian Vettel crests the rise by the Interlagos pits, already decisively ahead of team-mate Mark Webber after a couple of laps of the Brazilian GP.

Photo: Peter J Fox

INTERLAGOS QUALIFYING

THE 23-year-old pronounced himself happy with car and tyres, then parked up. He had been respectably quick to that point but, with the track becoming faster as the session progressed, his earlier lap time gradually merged with the anonymity of lower midfield, a statistic that might forever be erased from the memory.

"A lot of young drivers would become flustered when they're only 15th fastest or whatever," said Williams engineering director Patrick Head, "but Nico Hülkenberg is not like that. The car was exactly as he wanted it, so there didn't seem much point playing around. His attitude is very mature."

Even so, nobody suspected what lay around the corner.

Saturday morning at Interlagos had been very wet and the circuit was still sodden when qualifying began. The faintest hint of a dry line began to appear halfway through Q3, and with five minutes to go Lewis Hamilton came in to the pits for slicks. His out-lap looked horribly treacherous, but sector times soon began to plummet and this was clearly the way to go.

Hülkenberg had been planning to switch to a fresh set of intermediates, until engineer Tom McCullough pointed out that team-mate Rubens Barrichello had plumped for slicks, so the youngster followed suit and the results were startling. The Williams had excelled all season on 'green' tracks, circuits washed clean by rain, but had tended to slip down the hierarchy as the surface rubbered in. This, though, was a snapshot in time, a key moment of the weekend when conditions were ideal for the FW32 – and Hülkenberg didn't waste the opportunity. Each of his final two laps was good enough for pole, and the best of them was more than a second clear of the Red Bulls of Sebastian Vettel and Mark Webber. "At first, I thought I'd missed out by only a tenth," said Vettel, "but then I had a closer look at the numbers..."

At the circuit where it had scored its most recent F1 victory, in 2004, Williams had annexed its first pole since the 2005 Grand Prix of Europe – and a first for Cosworth since France 1999. Barrichello was sixth, after failing to get his tyres up to a suitable temperature – partly, he felt, because he had been slowed by the slightly cautious Lewis Hamilton, just ahead – and the Williams duo had four title contenders between them, with championship leader Fernando Alonso tagging along behind Vettel, Webber and Hamilton. Outsider Jenson Button struggled again with his brakes, as he had in Korea, and started only in 11th spot.

"I can't believe I've done it," Hülkenberg said. "I tried to squeeze as much out of the car as I could, but conditions were tricky because parts of the circuit were still very wet. I just did my best to avoid the damp patches. This is a very emotional moment and I can't really find the words to describe it. I'm still shaking.

"Tomorrow, my best option would be to make a good start and drive away from these guys, but in the dry I accept that's probably not going to happen. I don't want to get in the way of the title fight, but at the same time I have to look after my own interests."

With rumours rife that his place in the team might be in jeopardy (Williams had constantly been linked with sponsor-rich Venezuelan Pastor Maldonado, Hülkenberg's successor as GP2 champion), the German could not have picked a finer moment to astonish the F1 paddock. "He has just given us all a bit of a driving lesson," said Webber.

The Australian was facing pressure of a different kind, however, following remarks he had made to the effect that Red Bull didn't provide him with the same level of emotional support that Vettel enjoyed. Webber insisted, though, that he remained in a positive frame of mind. "Korea apart," he said, "I'm very happy with the way I've been driving, and that wouldn't have been possible if I wasn't happy with my situation. I'm really pleased with the way things have gone today, because in such difficult conditions it would have been just as easy to qualify 17th as third."

Above: A crucial moment at the start as Vettel gets the jump on pole-man Nico Hülkenberg's Williams in the scramble for the tricky, downhill, left-hand first corner.
Photo: Paul-Henri Cahier

Left: The centre of attention. Nico Hülkenberg poses with the Red Bull pair of Vettel and Webber for the traditional pole-position photo.
Photo: Peter J Fox

A NEOPHYTE on pole, four world title contenders in his wake, and a first corner that encourages aggression and compromises defence. Few races are blessed with such a potentially explosive cocktail, but the 2010 Brazilian Grand Prix was effectively settled by the time the first apex had been hit. Nico Hülkenberg earned the rare distinction of leading a Formula One world championship grand prix during his rookie season – even if the lap chart didn't record as much – but his moment in the spotlight was fleeting.

The pre-race headlines were dominated not by the four drivers actively pursuing the title, but by the man who was about to surrender it: on Saturday evening, one of McLaren's chauffeur-driven cars – a bulletproof Mercedes B-class containing Jenson Button, his father John, manager Richard Goddard and physio Mike Collier was waiting at a set of traffic lights, only a couple of minutes from the circuit, when an armed gang approached. "We could see some guys on the pavement," said Button, "and they looked a bit suspicious, but I didn't think anything of it. Richard then noticed that one of them had a baton, and I spotted another fiddling with his trousers. That's when I realised he had a gun. As soon as I said that, our driver looked across at them and they charged towards us."

Their chauffeur, local man Daniel Toni, floored the throttle, bounced off several cars in the queue ahead and carved an escape route. "As we looked back," said Button, "we could see that two of the gang had handguns and one appeared to be holding an automatic weapon."

That same evening, three Sauber engineers had their belongings stolen after being held up at gunpoint. Interlagos is a wonderful racetrack with an atmosphere to match, but it is too often tarnished by the musk of menace. "You hear about these things happening," Button said, "but until you're involved, you've no idea how scary it is." For him, the race would be the easy bit.

The same applied to Sebastian Vettel, albeit for different reasons. Hülkenberg made a fine start from pole, but Vettel's was better. "Nico didn't leave me a great deal of room down the inside," he said, "but there was just enough. I was praying there wouldn't be any debris on that part of the circuit, because I was nowhere near the conventional line."

Hülkenberg's tenure of second was almost as brief. "I had a good run through Turns One and Two, and then lined Nico up," said Mark Webber. "I was waiting for him to brake into Turn Four and thought, 'Hmm, that's going to be a bit deep; I don't know if you're going to hit the apex.' Thankfully, he didn't and that opened up my race a bit."

Lewis Hamilton and Fernando Alonso crossed the line almost as one at the lap's end, the Spaniard edging ahead on the approach to Turn One. Hamilton stuck to the inside, though, and didn't give his rival space to make the corner, but this positional reversal was brief. Alonso sliced ahead again at Turn Four and set about hassling Hülkenberg.

Robert Kubica slotted into sixth, ahead of Rubens Barrichello, Felipe Massa, Button, Michael Schumacher, Nico Rosberg, Nick Heidfeld, Kamui Kobayashi, Jaime Alguersuari, Sébastien Buemi, Tonio Liuzzi, Heikki Kovalainen, Timo Glock, Jarno Trulli, Lucas di Grassi, Adrian Sutil, Vitaly Petrov (who dropped almost to the back after jinking to avoid

Above: Mark Webber takes a few moments to ponder how a potentially crucial day might unfold.
Photo: Studio Colombo/WRi2

Top: After escaping an unpleasant armed robbery attempt, Jenson Button seeks sanctuary in the cockpit of his McLaren.
Photo: Studio Colombo/WRi2

Above right: Robert Kubica and Nico Hülkenberg look to use more than a touch of kerb as they tackle the tight infield section of the circuit.
Photo: Studio Colombo/WRi2

Alguersuari and becoming snagged on the kerb at Turn Two) and Bruno Senna. It was Christian Klien's turn to drive the HRT this weekend – no explanation was offered, nor any sought – but faltering fuel pressure caused him to miss the start and he didn't join in until the leaders were on their fourth lap.

Vettel was 1.6 seconds clear of Webber after one lap, 2.5 seconds within five and then the gap stabilised. Alonso felt he might be able to match the Red Bulls' pace in race trim, but first he had to shift Hülkenberg. That took until lap seven, by which stage the opposition was more than ten seconds up the road. Then Hamilton began shadowing the Williams, but he remained wedged behind until the German made his mandatory tyre stop on lap 14.

By now, the Red Bulls were engaged in a brisk stalemate. Vettel pitted on lap 25, to swap from super-soft to medium Bridgestones, and Webber did the same next time around. The margin between them fluctuated occasionally, usually through the unpredictable whims of lapped traffic, but their relentless rhythm remained unaltered until lap 51, when the safety car appeared. The cause was Liuzzi – or, rather, his rear suspension, which fractured and pitched him hard into the Turn Two tyre wall. The Italian escaped with a sore foot, but the car was badly crumpled and the race remained neutralised until the end of lap 55.

Alonso and Hamilton remained third and fourth on the road, ahead of the effervescent Button, Rosberg and Schumacher. Having lost a place to Schumacher on the third lap, when the German got a better exit from Turn Three, Button made his mandatory tyre stop on lap ten: such was his pace in clean air that he was easily able to clear both Mercs after their stops (Rosberg moved ahead of Schumacher after staying out for six laps longer). There was a chance Button would pass Hamilton, too, when the latter pitted on lap 20, but conveniently he put in a slower lap shortly beforehand so as not to compromise his team-mate's already slender title chances. To keep his own hopes alive, Button had needed to finish at least second and hope the rest were nowhere.

With the safety car in situ, Hamilton and Button

peeled in for fresh mediums and super-softs respectively. Rosberg came in for super-softs, but the team fitted the wrong compound due to a miscommunication: with the race neutralised, however, he was able to return and have the problem rectified without further loss of position (although the first stop had dropped him behind Schumacher).

"Had the other front-runners' older tyres started to degrade in the final laps," said McLaren team principal Martin Whitmarsh, "our drivers would have been well placed to capitalise. In the event, there was very little such degradation, so we derived no demonstrable benefit. There was no disadvantage either, though, so it was worth trying."

Schumacher didn't bother waiting to find out that much: almost as soon as the race resumed, he waved Rosberg through, in the misguided assumption that new tyres would be significantly quicker.

Vettel had two layers of protection at the restart – Hülkenberg and Kubica, both now lapped – while five cars separated Webber from Alonso. "I had been running quite a conservative engine setting," the Spaniard said, "because during the first part of the race, I was controlling the gap to Hamilton. After the safety car, I turned up the revs in an effort to put pressure on Mark, but by the time I got through the traffic he was about five seconds up the road."

That didn't soften his approach, though: he duly brought the gap down, but Webber had the situation under control, despite a few engine worries. His Renault V8 had started overheating on lap 35, due to a dip in water pressure, and he was obliged to turn down the wick. "It was looking a bit marginal," he said, "but we got it to the line." He finished the afternoon 4.2 seconds behind Vettel – and eight points behind Alonso, a margin that could have been just one had Red Bull taken an alternative stance in the title race.

With Hamilton finishing fourth and Button fifth, the sport was poised for its first four-way title showdown, although nothing less than victory – and a bit of good fortune – would suffice for Hamilton in Abu Dhabi.

For Button, Brazil had been very similar to 2009: a fine drive to fifth from an indifferent grid position. Last time, though, it had been enough to clinch the world title rather than ensure he couldn't.

For all the persistent uncertainties in the title contest, one key issue was resolved: Red Bull's fourth 1-2 of the campaign meant that the team was guaranteed the world championship for constructors at only its sixth attempt. "I first visited the team's factory in 2005," Vettel said. "I was a small boy; I had just obtained my driving licence and I went all the way from Germany to Milton Keynes. Someone showed me around and I was fascinated: stars in my eyes, looking up to F1. To be part of the team that has clinched a first championship is incredible. I really don't know how to put it into words."

Webber did: "Today is all about the team," he said. "I feel really stoked for them."

Rosberg and Schumacher took sixth and seventh, ahead of Hülkenberg, who had been plagued by a vibration, but still managed to ward off Kubica from lap 15, when they emerged together from their simultaneous tyre stops, to the end. "I expected to finish somewhere between fifth and tenth," he

Above: The Red Bull team poses for a celebratory photo after clinching the constructors' championship.
Photos: Peter J Fox

Right: Vettel's finger says it all.

Above right: Adrian Newey – making notes, making history.
Photo: Paul-Henri Cahier

said, "so I'll settle for eighth." The final point fell to Kobayashi, who ran a long 48-lap first stint on medium tyres, but didn't have quite enough straight-line speed to make much progress on fresh super-softs towards the end. He did pass both Toro Rossos, though. Alguersuari crossed the line 11th, but Buemi slipped to 13th after ceding a place to Sutil at Turn One, with ten laps to go. This was actually one of the race's best moves, the German using his trademark aggression to throw the Force India sideways as he passed around the outside – a lot of effort for 12th place, but worth the investment.

Barrichello might have challenged for points, but a jammed right rear wheel nut slowed his first stop, and he then made a second after a clash with Alguersuari punctured his front left tyre. He wasn't the only local favourite to suffer in the pits: Massa rejoined with a loose front right wheel after his first scheduled stop, on lap 12, and had to come straight back in because the nut had cross-threaded. From last place, he recovered to 13th, but then chucked away a couple of positions by running wide at Turn One during a comedic attempt to usurp Buemi. Actually, wide doesn't do it justice: he was most of the way to Rio.

Heidfeld had been running 14th, but picked up a drive-through penalty for ignoring blue flags: he accepted that the penalty was "wholly justified", but hadn't realised Rosberg was trying to lap him. That probably said more about Mercedes than Heidfeld's momentary inattention. He slipped to 17th, behind Petrov, with Kovalainen, Trulli, Glock, Senna and Klien concluding a remarkably complete set of finishers. Di Grassi was still running, too, albeit nine laps down and unclassified, after spending six-and-a-half minutes in the pits for rear suspension repairs.

Afterwards, Vettel was pressed long and hard on the subject of team tactics. If the order were the same in Abu Dhabi seven days hence, with him leading Webber, Alonso third and his own title hopes beyond salvation, would he step aside to help the team. He didn't answer directly, but dropped hints that he might. "I think the situation is pretty clear," he said.

Simon Arron

EDITOR'S VIEW
RED BULL BUILDS SUCCESS ON SOLID FOOTING

MARK Webber might have got the tabloid media buzzing in the paddock at Interlagos with some strategically placed observations about his treatment in the corridors of power at Red Bull Racing, but in reality his relationship with Sebastian Vettel had been remarkably tranquil, given the intensity of their battle for the 2010 world championship.

If you want to think aggravation, then think back to 1988 and 1989, when Ayrton Senna and Alain Prost lived in a state of thinly controlled, armed neutrality – at best – during their time together in the McLaren-Honda line-up. Or Nigel Mansell versus Nelson Piquet at Williams just before that. Or Alan Jones versus Carlos Reutemann in the early 1980s. Make no mistake, Vettel against Webber might look like a vicious catfight, but at least they seem able to bear to be in each other's company. And that's more than you can say about the aforementioned pairings.

Objectively, it's hard imagine how Vettel and Webber could have done a better job in the São Paulo suburbs. They ran 1-2 from the start, and the only slight technical problem was a touch of unexpected overheating from Mark's Renault V8, which obliged him to ease back slightly in the closing stages to make sure he kept on top of Fernando Alonso's third-place Ferrari.

Yet for Red Bull Racing, the real joy was in winning the constructors' championship little more than five years after the drinks company had bought the moribund Jaguar team – which previously had thrived as Stewart Grand Prix – for a reputed one-dollar fee in exchange for assuming its debts. It was a shrewd move indeed, providing a rock-solid foundation on which Christian Horner and subsequently Adrian Newey built a lean fighting machine. For Renault, it was a ninth constructors' championship success since its first with Williams in 1992.

"I think we have been fortunate in a way, in that the rules are still to some extent in their infancy," said Newey. "We are the second year into a very big set of regulation changes and with some fairly significant winter changes this year, and that helps to differentiate.

"If you can come up with fresh ideas, new ideas that steal a march, then that happens. If you get to a position where we got to at the end of 2008, where we were many years into very stable regulations, then it becomes very difficult to find new avenues."

The only thing one can be pretty sure of is that, on the evidence of the past couple of decades, Newey will find a way of maximising the potential of any regulations that are placed in front of him.

Alan Henry

FIA F1 WORLD CHAMPIONSHIP · ROUND 18

GRANDE PRÊMIO PETROBRAS DO BRASIL

SÃO PAULO 5–7 NOVEMBER 2010

RACE DISTANCE: 71 laps, 190.083 miles/305.909km

RACE WEATHER: Sunny (track 39–42°C, air 24°C)

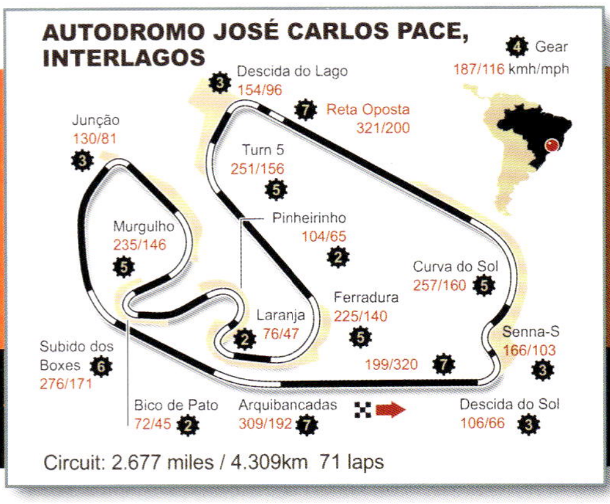

Pos.	Driver	Nat.	No.	Entrant	Car/Engine	Tyres	Laps	Time/Retirement	Speed (mph/km/h)	Gap to leader	Fastest race lap	
1	**Sebastian Vettel**	D	5	Red Bull Racing	Red Bull RB6-Renault RS27 V8	B	71	1h 33m 11.803s	122.375/196.944		1m 14.283s	70
2	**Mark Webber**	AUS	6	Red Bull Racing	Red Bull RB6-Renault RS27 V8	B	71	1h 33m 16.046s	122.282/196.794	+ 4.243s	1m 14.047s	69
3	**Fernando Alonso**	E	8	Scuderia Ferrari Marlboro	Ferrari F10-056 V8	B	71	1h 33m 18.610s	122.226/196.704	+ 6.807s	1m 13.855s	67
4	**Lewis Hamilton**	GB	2	Vodafone McLaren Mercedes	McLaren MP4-25-Mercedes FO108X V8	B	71	1h 33m 26.437s	122.055/196.429	+ 14.634s	1m 13.851s	66
5	**Jenson Button**	GB	1	Vodafone McLaren Mercedes	McLaren MP4-25-Mercedes FO108X V8	B	71	1h 33m 27.396s	122.035/196.396	+ 15.593s	1m 13.932s	71
6	**Nico Rosberg**	D	4	Mercedes GP Petronas F1 Team	Mercedes MGP W01-Mercedes FO108X V8	B	71	1h 33m 47.123s	121.607/195.707	+ 35.320s	1m 14.184s	65
7	**Michael Schumacher**	GB	3	Mercedes GP Petronas F1 Team	Mercedes MGP W01-Mercedes FO108X V8	B	71	1h 33m 55.259s	121.431/195.425	+ 43.456s	1m 15.219s	71
8	**Nico Hülkenberg**	D	10	AT&T Williams	Williams FW32-Cosworth CA2010 V8	B	70			+ 1 lap	1m 14.985s	70
9	**Robert Kubica**	PL	11	Renault F1 Team	Renault R30-RS27 V8	B	70			+ 1 lap	1m 15.161s	61
10	**Kamui Kobayashi**	J	23	BMW Sauber F1 Team	BMW Sauber C29-Ferrari 056 V8	B	70			+ 1 lap	1m 14.748s	65
11	Jaime Alguersuari	E	17	Scuderia Toro Rosso	Toro Rosso STR5-Ferrari 056 V8	B	70			+ 1 lap	1m 15.695s	68
12	Adrian Sutil	D	14	Force India F1 Team	Force India VJM03-Mercedes FO108X V8	B	70			+ 1 lap	1m 14.997s	64
13	Sébastien Buemi	CH	16	Scuderia Toro Rosso	Toro Rosso STR5-Ferrari 056 V8	B	70			+ 1 lap	1m 15.935s	69
14	Rubens Barrichello	BR	9	AT&T Williams	Williams FW32-Cosworth CA2010 V8	B	70			+ 1 lap	1m 15.227s	69
15	Felipe Massa	BR	7	Scuderia Ferrari Marlboro	Ferrari F10-056 V8	B	70			+ 1 lap	1m 15.330s	69
16	Vitaly Petrov	RUS	12	Renault F1 Team	Renault R30-RS27 V8	B	70			+ 1 lap	1m 15.485s	70
17	Nick Heidfeld	D	22	BMW Sauber F1 Team	BMW Sauber C29-Ferrari 056 V8	B	70			+ 1 lap	1m 15.068s	68
18	Heikki Kovalainen	FIN	19	Lotus Racing	Lotus T127-Cosworth CA2010 V8	B	69			+ 2 laps	1m 17.161s	69
19	Jarno Trulli	I	18	Lotus Racing	Lotus T127-Cosworth CA2010 V8	B	69			+ 2 laps	1m 17.316s	69
20	Timo Glock	D	24	Virgin Racing	Virgin VR-01-Cosworth CA2010 V8	B	69			+ 2 laps	1m 17.695s	66
21	Bruno Senna	BR	21	HRT F1 Team	HRT F110-Cosworth CA2010 V8	B	69			+ 2 laps	1m 17.731s	66
22	Christian Klien	A	20	HRT F1 Team	HRT F110-Cosworth CA2010 V8	B	65			+ 6 laps	1m 17.690s	63
	Lucas di Grassi	BR	25	Virgin Racing	Virgin VR-01-Cosworth CA2010 V8	B	62				1m 16.767s	60
	Vitantonio Liuzzi	I	15	Force India F1 Team	Force India VJM03-Mercedes FO108X V8	B	49	*accident*			1m 16.940s	37

Fastest race lap: Lewis Hamilton on lap 66, 1m 13.851s, 130.519mph/210.049km/h.

Lap record: Juan Pablo Montoya (Williams FW26-BMW V10), 1m 11.473s, 134.862mph/217.038km/h (2004)

24 · SENNA · HRT
penalty for gearbox change

22 · SUTIL · Force India
penalty for causing an accident in round 17

20 · KOVALAINEN · Lotus

18 · TRULLI · Lotus

16 · LIUZZI · Force India

14 · ALGUERSUARI · Toro Rosso

23 · KLIEN · HRT
started from pitlane

21 · DI GRASSI · Virgin

19 · BUEMI · Toro Rosso
penalty for causing an accident in round 17

17 · GLOCK · Virgin

15 · HEIDFELD · BMW Sauber

13 · ROSBERG · Mercedes

Grid order	1	2	3	4	5	6	7	8	9	10	11	12	13	14	15	16	17	18	19	20	21	22	23	24	25	26	27	28
10 HULKENBERG	5	5	5	5	5	5	5	5	5	5	5	5	5	5	5	5	5	5	5	5	5	5	5	5	6	6	5	5
5 VETTEL	6	6	6	6	6	6	6	6	6	6	6	6	6	6	6	6	6	6	6	6	6	6	6	6	5	5	6	6
6 WEBBER	10	10	10	10	10	10	8	8	8	8	8	8	8	8	8	8	8	8	8	8	8	8	8	8	8	8	8	8
2 HAMILTON	8	8	8	8	8	8	10	10	10	10	10	10	10	2	2	2	2	2	2	2	4	4	4	4	4	4	2	2
8 ALONSO	2	2	2	2	2	2	2	2	2	2	2	2	2	3	3	3	3	3	3	4	23	23	23	23	23	2	23	23
9 BARRICHELLO	11	11	11	11	11	11	11	11	11	11	11	11	11	10	4	4	4	4	4	3	2	2	2	2	2	23	1	1
11 KUBICA	9	9	9	9	9	9	9	9	9	9	9	9	3	4	16	16	16	23	23	23	1	1	1	1	1	1	4	4
3 SCHUMACHER	7	7	7	7	7	7	7	7	7	7	7	3	4	11	23	23	23	16	1	1	14	14	14	14	14	14	14	14
7 MASSA	1	1	3	3	3	3	3	3	3	3	3	4	22	17	17	14	14	14	14	14	3	3	3	3	3	3	3	3
12 PETROV	3	3	1	1	1	1	1	1	1	1	4	22	9	16	15	12	1	1	10	10	10	10	10	10	10	10	10	10
1 BUTTON	4	4	4	4	4	4	4	4	4	4	22	7	17	22	14	15	12	12	11	11	11	11	11	11	11	11	11	11
23 KOBAYASHI	22	22	22	22	22	22	22	22	22	22	17	17	16	23	12	1	10	10	22	22	22	22	22	22	22	22	22	22
4 ROSBERG	23	17	17	17	17	17	17	17	17	17	1	16	23	15	1	10	11	11	12	17	17	17	17	17	17	17	17	17
17 ALGUERSUARI	17	16	16	16	16	16	16	16	16	16	16	23	15	14	10	11	22	22	17	9	9	9	9	9	9	9	9	9
22 HEIDFELD	16	23	23	23	23	23	23	23	23	23	23	15	14	12	11	22	17	17	9	16	16	16	16	16	16	16	16	16
15 LIUZZI	15	15	15	15	15	15	15	15	15	15	15	14	12	1	22	17	9	9	16	15	15	15	15	15	15	15	15	15
24 GLOCK	19	19	19	19	14	14	14	14	14	14	14	12	1	9	9	9	15	15	15	12	12	7	7	7	7	7	7	7
18 TRULLI	24	24	24	14	19	12	12	12	12	12	12	1	19	19	19	19	18	18	18	7	7	12	12	12	12	12	12	12
16 BUEMI	18	18	14	24	12	19	19	19	19	19	19	19	7	24	24	18	19	7	7	18	25	25	25	25	25	25	19	19
19 KOVALAINEN	25	14	12	12	24	24	24	24	24	24	24	24	24	18	18	24	7	25	25	25	21	21	21	19	19	19	25	18
25 DI GRASSI	14	12	18	18	18	18	18	18	18	18	18	18	18	25	25	25	25	21	21	21	19	19	19	18	18	18	18	24
14 SUTIL	12	25	25	25	25	25	25	25	25	25	25	25	25	21	21	21	21	19	19	19	18	18	18	21	24	24	24	25
20 KLIEN	21	21	21	21	21	21	21	21	21	21	21	21	21	7	7	7	24	24	24	24	24	24	24	24	21	21	21	21
21 SENNA	20	20	20	20	20	20	20	20	20	20	20	20	20	20	20	20	20	20	20	20	20	20	20	20	20	20	20	20

Grid order	29	30	31	32	33	34	35	36	37	38	39	40	41	42	43	44	45	46	47	48	49	50	51	52	53	54	55
10 HULKENBERG	5	5	5	5	5	5	5	5	5	5	5	5	5	5	5	5	5	5	5	5	5	5	5	5	5	5	5
5 VETTEL	6	6	6	6	6	6	6	6	6	6	6	6	6	6	6	6	6	6	6	6	6	6	6	6	6	6	6
6 WEBBER	8	8	8	8	8	8	8	8	8	8	8	8	8	8	8	8	8	8	8	8	8	8	8	8	8	8	8
2 HAMILTON	2	2	2	2	2	2	2	2	2	2	2	2	2	2	2	2	2	2	2	2	2	2	2	2	2	2	2
8 ALONSO	23	1	1	1	1	1	1	1	1	1	1	1	1	1	1	1	1	1	1	1	1	1	1	1	1	1	1
9 BARRICHELLO	1	23	23	23	23	23	23	23	23	23	4	4	4	4	4	4	4	4	4	4	4	4	4	3	3	3	3
11 KUBICA	4	4	4	4	4	4	4	4	4	4	23	23	23	23	23	23	23	23	23	23	14	3	3	4	4	4	4
3 SCHUMACHER	14	14	14	14	14	14	14	14	14	14	14	14	14	14	14	14	14	14	14	14	3	14	10	10	10	10	10
7 MASSA	3	3	3	3	3	3	3	3	3	3	3	3	3	3	3	3	3	3	3	3	10	10	11	11	11	11	11
12 PETROV	10	10	10	10	10	10	10	10	10	10	10	10	10	10	10	10	10	10	10	10	11	11	17	17	17	17	17
1 BUTTON	11	11	11	11	11	11	11	11	11	11	11	11	11	11	11	11	11	11	11	11	22	17	16	16	16	16	23
23 KOBAYASHI	22	22	22	22	22	22	22	22	22	22	22	22	22	22	22	22	22	22	22	22	17	16	23	23	23	23	16
4 ROSBERG	17	17	17	17	17	17	17	17	17	17	17	17	17	17	17	17	17	17	17	17	16	22	14	14	14	14	14
17 ALGUERSUARI	9	9	9	9	9	16	16	16	16	16	16	16	16	16	16	16	16	16	16	16	7	23	22	22	22	22	22
22 HEIDFELD	16	16	16	16	16	7	7	7	7	7	7	7	7	7	7	7	7	7	7	7	23	7	7	7	7	7	7
15 LIUZZI	15	15	7	7	7	15	15	15	15	15	15	15	15	15	15	15	15	15	15	15	15	12	12	12	12	12	12
24 GLOCK	7	7	15	15	15	12	12	12	12	12	12	12	12	12	12	12	12	12	12	12	12	9	9	9	9	9	9
18 TRULLI	12	12	12	12	12	9	9	9	9	9	9	9	9	9	9	9	9	9	9	9	9	19	19	19	19	19	19
16 BUEMI	19	19	19	19	19	19	19	19	19	19	19	19	19	19	19	19	19	19	19	19	19	18	18	18	18	18	18
19 KOVALAINEN	18	18	18	18	18	18	18	18	18	18	18	18	18	18	18	18	18	18	18	18	18	24	24	24	24	24	24
25 DI GRASSI	24	24	24	24	24	24	24	24	24	24	24	24	24	24	24	24	24	24	24	24	24	21	21	21	21	21	21
14 SUTIL	21	21	21	21	21	21	21	21	21	21	21	21	21	21	21	21	21	21	21	21	21	20	20	20	20	20	20
20 KLIEN	25	25	25	25	25	25	25	25	25	25	25	20	20	20	20	20	20	20	20	20	20	25	25	25	25	25	25
21 SENNA	20	20	20	20	20	20	20	20	20	20	20	20	25	25	25	25	25	25	25	25	25						

TIME SHEETS

PRACTICE 1 (FRIDAY)
Weather: Sunny
Temperatures: track 33–39°C, air 26–28°C

Pos.	Driver	Laps	Time
1	Sebastian Vettel	23	1m 12.328s
2	Mark Webber	28	1m 12.810s
3	Lewis Hamilton	24	1m 12.845s
4	Jenson Button	24	1m 13.267s
5	Robert Kubica	24	1m 13.370s
6	Nico Rosberg	26	1m 13.516s
7	Rubens Barrichello	26	1m 13.546s
8	Michael Schumacher	25	1m 13.643s
9	Adrian Sutil	26	1m 13.918s
10	Nick Heidfeld	23	1m 14.000s
11	Kamui Kobayashi	23	1m 14.004s
12	Nico Hülkenberg	29	1m 14.155s
13	Fernando Alonso	20	1m 14.246s
14	Felipe Massa	26	1m 14.267s
15	Vitaly Petrov	23	1m 14.370s
16	Vitantonio Liuzzi	26	1m 14.487s
17	Jaime Alguersuari	30	1m 14.618s
18	Sébastien Buemi	29	1m 14.734s
19	Jarno Trulli	25	1m 15.603s
20	Timo Glock	20	1m 15.860s
21	Heikki Kovalainen	26	1m 16.057s
22	Jérôme d'Ambrosio	28	1m 16.707s
23	Christian Klien	18	1m 16.839s
24	Bruno Senna	30	1m 17.360s

PRACTICE 2 (FRIDAY)
Weather: Partly cloudy
Temperatures: track 39–41°C, air 30–31°C

Pos.	Driver	Laps	Time
1	Sebastian Vettel	28	1m 11.968s
2	Mark Webber	34	1m 12.072s
3	Fernando Alonso	36	1m 12.328s
4	Lewis Hamilton	33	1m 12.656s
5	Felipe Massa	19	1m 12.677s
6	Robert Kubica	37	1m 12.882s
7	Jenson Button	33	1m 13.206s
8	Nick Heidfeld	40	1m 13.222s
9	Nico Rosberg	34	1m 13.333s
10	Michael Schumacher	36	1m 13.346s
11	Rubens Barrichello	37	1m 13.520s
12	Kamui Kobayashi	41	1m 13.610s
13	Nico Hülkenberg	39	1m 13.725s
14	Adrian Sutil	32	1m 13.741s
15	Vitaly Petrov	26	1m 13.818s
16	Vitantonio Liuzzi	37	1m 14.045s
17	Sébastien Buemi	33	1m 14.304s
18	Jaime Alguersuari	37	1m 14.578s
19	Jarno Trulli	47	1m 14.984s
20	Heikki Kovalainen	43	1m 15.101s
21	Lucas di Grassi	35	1m 15.433s
22	Bruno Senna	42	1m 16.070s
23	Christian Klien	38	1m 16.082s
24	Timo Glock	35	1m 16.150s

PRACTICE 3 (SATURDAY)
Weather: Rain/cloudy
Temperatures: track 22°C, air 21°C

Pos.	Driver	Laps	Time
1	Sebastian Vettel	28	1m 11.968s
2	Mark Webber	34	1m 12.072s
3	Fernando Alonso	36	1m 12.328s
4	Lewis Hamilton	33	1m 12.656s
5	Felipe Massa	19	1m 12.677s
6	Robert Kubica	37	1m 12.882s
7	Jenson Button	33	1m 13.206s
8	Nick Heidfeld	40	1m 13.222s
9	Nico Rosberg	34	1m 13.333s
10	Michael Schumacher	36	1m 13.346s
11	Rubens Barrichello	37	1m 13.520s
12	Kamui Kobayashi	41	1m 13.610s
13	Nico Hülkenberg	39	1m 13.725s
14	Adrian Sutil	32	1m 13.741s
15	Vitaly Petrov	26	1m 13.818s
16	Vitantonio Liuzzi	37	1m 14.045s
17	Sébastien Buemi	33	1m 14.304s
18	Jaime Alguersuari	37	1m 14.578s
19	Jarno Trulli	47	1m 14.984s
20	Heikki Kovalainen	43	1m 15.101s
21	Lucas di Grassi	35	1m 15.433s
22	Bruno Senna	42	1m 16.070s
23	Christian Klien	38	1m 16.082s
24	Timo Glock	35	1m 16.150s

QUALIFYING (SATURDAY)
Weather: Cloudy Temperatures: track 20–22°C, air 19–20°C

Pos.	Driver	First	Second	Third	Qualifying Tyre
1	Nico Hülkenberg	1m 20.050s	1m 19.144s	1m 14.470s	Super-Soft
2	Sebastian Vettel	1m 19.160s	1m 18.691s	1m 15.519s	Super-Soft
3	Mark Webber	1m 19.025s	1m 18.516s	1m 15.637	Super-Soft
4	Lewis Hamilton	1m 19.931s	1m 18.921s	1m 15.747s	Super-Soft
5	Fernando Alonso	1m 18.987s	1m 19.010s	1m 15.989s	Super-Soft
6	Rubens Barrichello	1m 19.799s	1m 18.925s	1m 16.203s	Super-Soft
7	Robert Kubica	1m 19.249s	1m 18.877s	1m 16.552s	Inter
8	Michael Schumacher	1m 19.879s	1m 18.923s	1m 16.925s	Super-Soft
9	Felipe Massa	1m 19.778s	1m 19.200s	1m 17.101s	Super-Soft
10	Vitaly Petrov	1m 20.189s	1m 19.153s	1m 17.656s	Inter
11	Jenson Button	1m 19.905s	1m 19.288s		
12	Kamui Kobayashi	1m 19.741s	1m 19.385s		
13	Nico Rosberg	1m 20.153s	1m 19.486s		
14	Jaime Alguersuari	1m 20.158s	1m 19.581s		
15	Sébastien Buemi	1m 20.096s	1m 19.847s		
16	Nick Heidfeld	1m 20.174s	1m 19.899s		
17	Vitantonio Liuzzi	1m 20.592s	1m 20.357s		
18	Adrian Sutil	1m 20.830s			
19	Timo Glock	1m 22.130s			
20	Jarno Trulli	1m 22.250s			
21	Heikki Kovalainen	1m 22.378s			
22	Lucas di Grassi	1m 22.810s			
23	Christian Klien	1m 23.083s			
24	Bruno Senna	1m 23.796s			

FOR THE RECORD

1st WORLD CONSTRUCTORS' CHAMPIONSHIP:
Red Bull
FIRST POLE POSITION: Nico Hülkenberg
20th PODIUM: Mark Webber

DID YOU KNOW

This was the first pole for a Cosworth-powered car since France 1999 (Barrichello in a Stewart), and Williams's first since the European Grand Prix of 2005.

This was only the second time that 22 cars had been classified in a grand prix, the first being the 1952 British Grand Prix.

POINTS

DRIVERS

1	Fernando Alonso	246
2	Mark Webber	238
3	Sebastian Vettel	231
4	Lewis Hamilton	222
5	Jenson Button	199
6	Felipe Massa	143
7	Nico Rosberg	130
8	Robert Kubica	126
9	Michael Schumacher	72
10	Rubens Barrichello	47
11	Adrian Sutil	47
12	Kamui Kobayashi	32
13	Nico Hülkenberg	22
14	Vitantonio Liuzzi	21
15	Vitaly Petrov	19
16	Sébastien Buemi	8
17	Pedro de la Rosa	6
18	Nick Heidfeld	6
19	Jaime Alguersuari	3

CONSTRUCTORS

1	Red Bull	469
2	McLaren	421
3	Ferrari	389
4	Mercedes	202
5	Renault	145
6	Williams	69
7	Force India	68
8	BMW Sauber	44
9	Toro Rosso	11

56	57	58	59	60	61	62	63	64	65	66	67	68	69	70	71	
5	5	5	5	5	5	5	5	5	5	5	5	5	5	5	5	1
6	6	6	6	6	6	6	6	6	6	6	6	6	6	6	6	2
8	8	8	8	8	8	8	8	8	8	8	8	8	8	8	8	3
2	2	2	2	2	2	2	2	2	2	2	2	2	2	2	2	
1	1	1	1	1	1	1	1	1	1	1	1	1	1	1	1	
4	4	4	4	4	4	4	4	4	4	4	4	4	4	4	4	6
3	3	3	3	3	3	3	3	3	3	3	3	3	3	3	3	7
10	10	10	10	10	10	10	10	10	10	10	10	10	10	10		8
11	11	11	11	11	11	11	11	11	11	11	11	11	11	11		9
17	17	17	17	17	17	17	17	23	23	23	23	23	23	23		10
23	23	23	23	23	23	23	23	17	17	17	17	17	17	17		
16	16	16	16	16	14	14	14	14	14	14	14	14	14	14		
14	7	7	14	14	16	16	16	16	16	16	16	16	16	16		
7	14	14	22	22	22	22	22	7	7	7	7	9	9	9		
22	22	22	7	7	7	7	7	12	12	12	12	12	7	7		
12	12	12	12	12	12	12	12	9	9	9	9	7	12	12		
9	9	9	9	9	9	9	9	22	22	22	22	22	22	22		
19	19	19	19	19	19	19	19	19	19	19	19	19	19			
18	18	18	18	18	18	18	18	18	18	18	18	18	18			
24	24	24	24	24	24	24	24	24	24	24	24	24	24			
21	21	21	21	21	21	21	21	21	21	21	21	21	21			
20	20	20	20	20	20	20	20	20	20							
25	25	25	25	25	25	25										

21 Pit stop
Safety car deployed
14 One lap or more behind

RACE TYRE STRATEGIES

	Driver	Race Stint 1	Race Stint 2	Race Stint 3	Race Stint 4
1	Vettel	Super-Soft: 1-25	Medium: 26-71		
2	Webber	Super-Soft: 1-26	Medium: 27-71		
3	Alonso	Super-Soft: 1-24	Medium: 25-71		
4	Hamilton	Super-Soft: 1-20	Medium: 21-51	Medium: 52-71	
5	Button	Super-Soft: 1-11	Medium: 12-52	Super-Soft: 53-71	
6	Rosberg	Super-Soft: 1-26	Medium: 27-51	Medium: 52-54	Super-Soft: 55-71
7	Schumacher	Super-Soft: 1-20	Medium: 21-71		
8	Hülkenberg	Super-Soft: 1-14	Medium: 15-70		
9	Kubica	Super-Soft: 1-14	Medium: 15-70		
10	Kobayashi	Medium: 1-48	Super-Soft: 49-70		
11	Alguersuari	Super-Soft: 1-15	Medium: 16-70		
12	Sutil	Medium: 1-50	Super-Soft: 51-70		
13	Buemi	Super-Soft: 1-18	Medium: 19-70		
14	Barrichello	Super-Soft: 1-13	Medium: 14-34	Super-Soft: 35-50	Super-Soft: 51-70
15	Massa	Super-Soft: 1-12	Medium: 13	Medium: 14-50	Super-Soft: 51-70
16	Petrov	Super-Soft: 1-19	Medium: 20-50	Super-Soft: 51-70	
17	Heidfeld	Super-Soft: 1-14	Medium: 15-50	Super-Soft: 51-64	Super-Soft: 65-70
18	Kovalainen	Super-Soft: 1-17	Medium: 20-69		
19	Trulli	Super-Soft: 1-20	Medium: 21-69		
20	Glock	Super-Soft: 1-16	Medium: 17-69		
21	Senna	Super-Soft: 1-24	Medium: 25-69		
22	Klien	Super-Soft: 1-11	Medium: 12-45	Medium: 46-65	
	di Grassi	Super-Soft: 1-28	Medium: 29-40	Medium: 41-57	Super-Soft: 58-62 (nc)
	Liuzzi	Super-Soft: 1-16	Medium: 17-49 (dnf)		

The tyre regulations stipulate that the two dry tyre specifications must be used during the race.
The Super-Soft compound Bridgestone Potenza tyre is marked with a green stripe on the sidewall.

FIA FORMULA 1 WORLD CHAMPIONSHIP · ROUND 19

ABU DHABI GRAND PRIX

YAS MARINA CIRCUIT

A magical tableau to mark the end of a dramatic season that could not have been scripted.
Photo: Paul-Henri Cahier

ETIHAD AIRWAYS
ABU DHABI
GRAND PRIX
YAS MARINA CIRCUIT 2010
ETIHAD
FIA

YAS MARINA QUALIFYING

CUSTOMARILY the gap was about seven-hundredths, but on a day when he most needed to shift the marginal balance of power in his favour, Mark Webber fell more than half a second short.

"We were struggling to generate tyre temperature on our first flying lap," the Australian said, "and on a long circuit such as this, there isn't time to do two two-lap runs. Maybe a one and a two would have been better..."

In the end, he and Red Bull team-mate Sebastian Vettel did a single Q3 run each, the German completing three laps and Webber four. "It's not easy trying to prepare your tyres properly when you have a few laps of fuel on board," Webber said, "and I just didn't judge it quite right today."

Vettel did, though, and a 1m 39.394s gave him his tenth pole of the campaign and a 0.531-second margin over his team-mate, who qualified fifth behind the McLarens of Lewis Hamilton and Jenson Button, with Fernando Alonso's Ferrari sandwiched in the middle.

"It was a very tricky session," Vettel said, "because conditions change a lot here between the afternoon and the evening, as the temperature drops. It was hard to know which tyre would work best. I opted to do only one run in Q3, although with hindsight, it would probably have been a little bit quicker if we had done two. I was concerned, though, that the options might not quite be up to temperature on the first lap." All three of his laps were quick – he did a 1m 39.448s and a 1m 39.457s either side of his best – but only the second of them was good enough to pip Hamilton to pole.

The McLaren driver survived a brush with Felipe Massa in Q2, the two cars coming close at Turn Eight and the Englishman knocking over a camera bollard as he took evasive action, but he escaped with a mildly scuffed front wing.

Alonso was caught in a knot of cars trying to start a final lap at the end of the session and just made it across the line before the chequered flag fell. The margin was tighter still for Massa, just behind, but the Brazilian backed off before radioing in to check whether he was clear to continue, rather than doing things the other way around. He had actually started his lap before the flag fell, but his hesitation cost him four-tenths and left him sixth. With a little more common sense, he could have been even closer to his team-mate, to play a more useful protective role in the title contest.

How did points leader Alonso plan to manage his race?

"First of all we need to see how the start goes," he said. "Normally after the first 10 or 20 metres, you know how well you've started the race. If it's good, you can think about attacking; if you feel something has gone wrong, you try to defend. I will react accordingly, but we won't win the championship at the first corner. All we can do there is lose it, so we will see what happens."

Nico Rosberg looked as though he might play an unexpected role in the pole battle, having been searingly quick on medium tyres in Q2, but Mercedes had used up all its fresh sets by Q3 and its car was not as effective on the supersofts. In any case, Rosberg wanted to start on the latter because an early safety car period would allow him to switch to the harder tyre, a tactic that wouldn't work at all in reverse.

Within 24 hours, this would have particular significance...

Above: The start was absolutely crucial for Sebastian Vettel, who just managed to keep his Red Bull ahead of Lewis Hamilton's McLaren. The young German was able to dictate the pace of the race from then onwards.

Left: The quartet of championship challengers pose for a friendly photo before the dramatic finale.

Photos: Peter J Fox

OUTSIDE, Norbert Vettel – father of the new world champion – was physically assaulting German TV anchor Kai Ebel, in a good-natured attempt to rip off an expensive and decidedly ostentatious pair of trousers. Upstairs, Mark Webber was lying quietly in his room, surrounded by his immediate family and chatting pragmatically about what might have been. Nearby, McLaren team principal Martin Whitmarsh was graciously accepting defeat in a contest that had, in recent weeks, looked increasingly difficult to win. And Ferrari was frantically selecting reverse gear, asking the world not to think too badly of a bizarre race strategy that left Fernando Alonso helpless to defend his points lead.

By the standards of the season as a whole, the 2010 finale was relatively straightforward – a race short on incident, yet ripe with confusing data that shuffled the odds in a manner unforeseen. Advantage Sebastian Vettel.

The German didn't take many risks during the afternoon's course, largely because he didn't need to, but after making a bright start from pole, he made a bold pitch for the racing line at Turn One, despite the likelihood of Lewis Hamilton sticking his nose in. The German left a partial gap that ordinarily might have been tempting, but while Hamilton had less to lose than the other title contenders, he also needed to win. He duly slotted in behind, with Jenson Button beating Fernando Alonso off the line to take third, while Mark Webber and Felipe Massa maintained grid order in fifth and sixth.

Yas Marina would offer more proper racing opportunities if the original circuit plan – a long straight run to the hairpin – had been followed, but the health-and-safety police had felt that the high approach speeds would have been unsuitable, given the proximity of the adjacent grandstands, so a fiddly chicane was inserted just beforehand. Mercedes team-mates Nico Rosberg and Michael Schumacher arrived here side by side, but the senior statesman was on the dirtier outside line and looped into a spin as soon as he tried turning right. The car came to rest broadside, and Schumacher had just started to edge forwards when Tonio Liuzzi arrived. Boxed in and wholly blameless, the Italian smashed into the Mercedes and rose up over its cockpit, his detached front left wheel coming worryingly close to striking Schumacher's helmet. The two drivers were laughing and joking as they strolled back to the pits together, but it had been a close call – and striking testimony to the integrity of modern cockpit design.

The safety car was dispatched immediately and drivers were diverted around the chicane for the next couple of laps, via the bit of racetrack that isn't, while Rosberg, Vitaly Petrov, Jaime Alguersuari, Bruno Senna, Lucas di Grassi and Christian Klien all peeled in immediately to switch from super-softs to the Bridgestone medium, which was tough enough to do several Abu Dhabi GPs without risk of degradation.

Just before the restart at the end of lap five, Hamilton slithered wide over the kerbs when the leader slowed, in preparation for launch, and the two cars were several lengths apart as they crossed the line, the German pulling 1.2 seconds clear within the lap. Button, Alonso, Webber and Massa headed the pursuit, from Rubens Barrichello, Kamui Kobayashi, Robert Kubica, Adrian Sutil, Nick Heidfeld, Sébastien Buemi, Nico Hülkenberg, Rosberg (who lost no time at all among the back-markers), Heikki Kovalainen, Jarno Trulli, Petrov, Alguersuari, Timo Glock, di Grassi, Senna and Klien.

On lap eight, Webber ran a touch too wide coming out of Turn 19 and gave the barrier a glancing blow with his right rear. No damage was done, but it was

Above: The view from the grand-stands was splendid, even if there was little overtaking on offer.

Top right: Jaime Alguersuari profited from the introduction of the safety car, but drove very well thereafter, to keep Felipe Massa in check.
Photos: Peter J Fox

Centre right: Lewis Hamilton gave it his best shot, but his McLaren wasn't quite quick enough.
Photo: Simon Arron

symptomatic of a wider malaise. The Australian had discussed the merits of a safety car pit stop with his crew during the opening lap, but the notion had been discarded. His rear tyres were already in poor shape, though, and the team could see as much from the telemetry. On lap 11, he came in to change. "He was towards the back of the leading group and wasn't going to win the world title from there," said Red Bull sporting director Christian Horner, "so there was nothing to lose."

Webber rejoined 16th, behind Alguersuari, but managed to pass him within two laps – and Ferrari now faced a strategic dilemma. It needed to cover Webber, in case his strategy paid dividends, yet Vettel was the greater title threat. "They were aiming at two tongs," said Webber, "but only had one hammer."

That wasn't quite the case, for on lap 13 Ferrari summoned Massa in the hope that he might rejoin ahead of Webber – already lapping very quickly on the mediums – and give Alonso an extra layer of protection. The Brazilian came out behind Alguersuari, however, and would remain jammed there for the balance of the race. "The Toro Rosso was pulling 316kph [196mph] on the straights without a tow," Massa said, "but even in his slipstream, I was only getting 312."

That ploy having failed, Ferrari called in Alonso on lap 15 – to the incredulity of most rival teams. It was obvious that such a move at this stage of the race would drop him behind Rosberg and Petrov, neither of whom would be stopping again and both of whom were much faster than the Ferrari at the end of the longest straight, the lone mildly viable passing spot. If Vettel were to win, Alonso needed to finish fourth, and Ferrari had just created a couple of extra impediments. Furthermore, Kubica was flying along on a set of mediums and clearly was planning a long first stint, so it would be difficult to clear him, too.

There was, however, some misleading data. Immediately after the restart, Vettel had lapped consistently in the 1m 45s, but on lap 11 he dipped into the 1m 46s and his times began to drift as

Hamilton edged closer. The leader's tyres were graining – a clue that an early switch to mediums might be advisable; Bridgestone's pre-race forecast had suggested the super-softs would be good for only 12–15 laps – but the problem soon stabilised and Vettel dipped back into the 1m 45s just as Alonso was entering the pit lane.

The Spaniard rejoined 12th, just ahead of Webber, but behind Petrov – and the Renault's straight-line advantage soon became apparent. On lap 22 – by now well aware that its title hopes had been seriously compromised – Ferrari came on the radio and underlined the desperate urgency for progress. Next time around, the Spaniard tried to dive past Petrov at Turn Eight, but he was much too far back and slithered hopelessly wide. There being absolutely no consequences for carelessness at many parts of the track, however, he was able to continue without further loss of place. That, though, wouldn't help.

"With hindsight," said Ferrari sporting director Stefano Domenicali, "it is obvious that we made a mistake, but at the time we thought we were doing the right thing. We wanted to pit before the tyres deteriorated and, although we realised that we'd come out behind some of the cars that had already stopped, we didn't imagine it would be so difficult to pass them."

Both Alonso and Webber would remain hemmed in behind Petrov to the end.

Barring technical misfortune, the Spaniard's lone hope was that Hamilton could now work his way past Vettel. The McLaren driver came in for tyres on lap 25, but crucially rejoined just behind Kubica, the last place in the world he needed to be. Vettel peeled in next time around and the Red Bull crew did a fantastic job in the face of extreme pressure, getting its man back out just ahead of the Pole. The gap between the top two had previously been stable at about 1.8 seconds, but by the time Kubica finally pitted, on lap 46, it had grown to 12.8 seconds. "I am sure the team brought me in for the right reasons," Hamilton said, "but unfortunately I came out behind a Renault and there was no way past, because I was on the rev limiter before the end of the main straight."

Horner described the tension on the Red Bull pit counter as "unbearable" during the closing stages. "At one point," he said, "I think I forgot to breathe."

Vettel asked the team to give him clear pit-board messages, because his left-hand radio channel was cutting out intermittently, but it was working well enough for him to hear most of what race engineer Guillaume Roquelin ('Rocky') was saying. "For the final ten ten laps," he said, "I was wondering what was going on. Rocky was trying to give me advice every lap, to help me carry the car home. I was thinking, 'Why is he nervous? We must be in a bloody good position.' I hadn't really been looking at the screens, because I didn't want any distractions, although I knew one of the Ferraris was stuck behind a Renault. As I crossed the line, he came on the radio very silently and said, 'It is looking good, but we have to wait until all the cars finish.' I didn't know what he meant, but then he started screaming that we'd won

Above: Follow my leader. Jaime Alguersuari's Toro Rosso leads Felipe Massa's Ferrari and Nick Heidfeld's Sauber as the trio scrap for the last few points on offer.

Opposite: The McLaren boys toast the new world champion on the podium.
Photos: Paul-Henri Cahier

Top right: That's my boy! Vettel is hugged by father Norbert.

Centre right: A Joyous day for Austria, as Hemut Marko embraces Red Bull team boss Dieter Mateschitz.
Photos: Peter J Fox

the world championship."

Hamilton duly took second, ahead of Button, who led for a while after the front two stopped and nursed his super-softs until lap 39 before pitting. The clincher for Vettel was the sight of Rosberg crossing the line in fourth, having moved stealthily and swiftly through the field as others made less profitable pit stops than his own. Kubica took fifth after another stellar performance, particularly as a clutch problem had cost him a couple of positions at the start, but then he was one of the few who had managed to pass any cars of similar calibre. The worthy Petrov had been spirited to sixth by the end, with the two erstwhile title contenders just behind.

After the flag, Alonso drew alongside the Russian and started making assorted obscene gestures, an act of utter gracelessness. Two years beforehand, team-mate Massa had lost the world title at the season's final corner and handled defeat with tears and dignity, the way it should be done. Alonso is a wonderful tenacious competitor, but his post-race actions lost him a lot of respect and earned him a derogatory retaliatory hand signal from Petrov, whose perspective was wholly fair. "If I were in his position, I'd be angry, too," Petrov said, "but he should be angry with himself or his team. I just drove a normal race and did nothing wrong; it is just very difficult to overtake here."

Alguersuari and Massa completed the top ten, ahead of Heidfeld (who, unlike Alonso, had ended up gaining three positions as the result of a lap-15 stop) and Barrichello, whose early vim had been compromised by a later stop that dropped him back into traffic. There would be more positive news on the following afternoon, however, when Williams confirmed that it was extending the Brazilian's contract into 2011 – his 19th consecutive F1 season. Sutil, Kobayashi (another to lose out during the stops), Buemi, Hülkenberg (who would be dropped by Williams 24 hours later – one of the season's shorter-sighted decisions), Kovalainen, di Grassi, Senna and Klien completed the finishers after a race in which the tension matched the hype, although the action fell somewhat short. Trulli pitted to replace a broken front wing on lap 28, then stopped just before the end when his rear wing flew off, although he was still classified 21st. Glock was the only other retirement after the opening lap, gearbox failure forcing him to stop when he was running behind Kovalainen.

Vettel is usually one of the most garrulous members of the paddock cast, but he struggled to speak through his tears during the cooling-off lap. His trademark composure was restored by the time he reached the press conference, however.

"I guess I am pretty empty at this stage." he said. "I don't know what to say, but doubtless I'll find a reason to talk forever… It is unbelievable. For some reason, it doesn't feel like this is happening. I guess it will sink in when I finally go to sleep, but I think it might be daylight before that happens."

In a campaign of relentless twists and turns, it was appropriate that he should assume the championship lead for the first and only time as he crossed the finishing line in Abu Dhabi. His judgement could hardly have been more perfect.

Simon Arron

EDITOR'S VIEW
ALONSO: NEARLY, BUT NOT QUITE

Below: Alonso was sanguine about his failure to take the title.

Bottom: Ferrari pitted to ensure they had Webber's Red Bull covered. but they miscalculated their ability to deal with the opposition ahead.

Photos: Peter J Fox

SEBASTIAN Vettel will have raised more than a few smiles by pointing out that James Hunt only led the 1976 world championship at the final race of the season, the young German proving that he's either very widely read or extremely well briefed. My money's on the latter, to be honest, but either way it was a nice touch of historical perspective on the part of the youngest ever title holder, who was not even born until 12 years after James's memorable achievement really began to put the sport into top gear in terms of global media interest.

Vettel's implicit point that "it's not over until it's over" may be the most overworked epithet in the F1 business, but it's no less true for all that. The grand prix community arrived back in the United Arab Emirates, just a couple of hundred miles from where Alonso had opened his score by winning in Bahrain at the start of the year, confidently expecting that the Spaniard would breeze his way to a third title crown.

Alonso believed he would get the job done too, having suggested as early as Silverstone that he would overturn a 47-point championship deficit to win the title. And as he punched home wins in Monza, Singapore and Korea, it began to seem as though the lad from Oviedo was going to pull it off, well against the odds.

Yet circumstances caught up with him when a strategic blunder resulted in his being hemmed in by the inspired Vitaly Petrov at Yas Marina, the Russian Renault driver having put on hold his seemingly magnetic attraction for trackside barriers. Suddenly Alonso's own goals from earlier in the campaign – the jump-start in China and the practice crash at Monaco – began to assume a significance that could not be brushed aside. Alonso's fans may be right that he is one of the complete drivers currently racing in F1, but he is far from infallible. And that was proved very clearly at Abu Dhabi.

Of course, having hyped up the whole of Italy to believe that the day of glory was at hand, Ferrari president Luca di Montezemolo was at the receiving end of a resignation call, on the basis that it was a disgrace that Ferrari had thrown away the world championship through tactical incompetence. I'm delighted to say that di Montezemolo stood his ground, more or less saying that he wasn't going to be lectured in that manner by some daft politician who'd never done anything worthwhile. So that was alright then. Love his style!

Alan Henry

Passionate about engineering

FIA F1 WORLD CHAMPIONSHIP · ROUND 19

ETIHAD AIRWAYS ABU DHABI GRAND PRIX

YAS MARINA 12–14 NOVEMBER 2010

RACE DISTANCE: 55 laps, 189.739 miles/305.355km

RACE WEATHER: Sunny/dusk/dark (track 30–32°C, air 28°C)

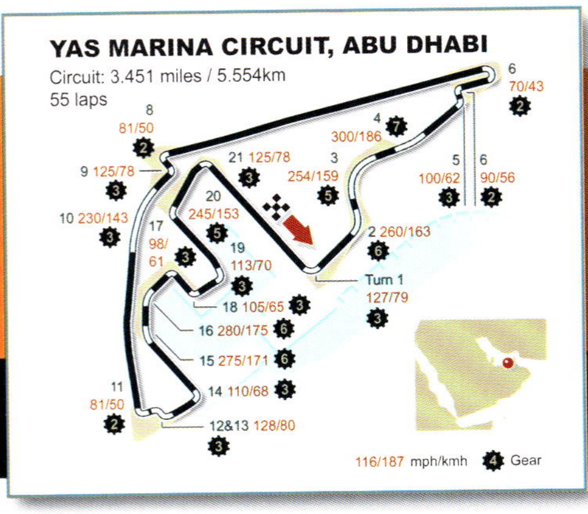

Pos.	Driver	Nat.	No.	Entrant	Car/Engine	Tyres	Laps	Time/Retirement	Speed (mph/km/h)	Gap to leader	Fastest race lap	
1	**Sebastian Vettel**	D	5	Red Bull Racing	Red Bull RB6-Renault RS27 V8	B	55	1h 39m 36.837s	114.284/183.923		1m 41.739s	50
2	**Lewis Hamilton**	GB	2	Vodafone McLaren Mercedes	McLaren MP4-25-Mercedes FO108X V8	B	55	1h 39m 46.999s	114.090/183.610	+ 10.162s	1m 41.274s	47
3	**Jenson Button**	GB	1	Vodafone McLaren Mercedes	McLaren MP4-25-Mercedes FO108X V8	B	55	1h 39m 47.884s	114.073/183.583	+ 11.047s	1m 41.636s	48
4	**Nico Rosberg**	D	4	Mercedes GP Petronas F1 Team	Mercedes MGP W01-Mercedes FO108X V8	B	55	1h 40m 07.584s	113.699/182.981	+ 30.747s	1m 41.711s	52
5	**Robert Kubica**	PL	11	Renault F1 Team	Renault R30-RS27 V8	B	55	1h 40m 15.863s	113.543/182.729	+ 39.026s	1m 41.753s	51
6	**Vitaly Petrov**	RUS	12	Renault F1 Team	Renault R30-RS27 V8	B	55	1h 40m 20.357s	113.458/182.593	+ 43.520s	1m 42.311s	52
7	**Fernando Alonso**	E	8	Scuderia Ferrari Marlboro	Ferrari F10-056 V8	B	55	1h 40m 20.634s	113.453/182.585	+ 43.797s	1m 42.227s	52
8	**Mark Webber**	AUS	6	Red Bull Racing	Red Bull RB6-Renault RS27 V8	B	55	1h 40m 21.080s	113.444/182.571	+ 44.243s	1m 42.196s	52
9	**Jaime Alguersuari**	E	17	Scuderia Toro Rosso	Toro Rosso STR5-Ferrari 056 V8	B	55	1h 40m 27.038s	113.333/182.391	+ 50.201s	1m 42.727s	49
10	**Felipe Massa**	BR	7	Scuderia Ferrari Marlboro	Ferrari F10-056 V8	B	55	1h 40m 27.705s	113.319/182.370	+ 50.868s	1m 42.725s	52
11	Nick Heidfeld	D	22	BMW Sauber F1 Team	BMW Sauber C29-Ferrari 056 V8	B	55	1h 40m 28.388s	113.307/182.350	+ 51.551s	1m 42.673s	52
12	Rubens Barrichello	BR	9	AT&T Williams	Williams FW32-Cosworth CA2010 V8	B	55	1h 40m 34.523s	113.191/182.164	+ 57.686s	1m 42.669s	50
13	Adrian Sutil	D	14	Force India F1 Team	Force India VJM03-Mercedes FO108X V8	B	55	1h 40m 35.162s	113.180/182.145	+ 58.325s	1m 42.695s	52
14	Kamui Kobayashi	J	23	BMW Sauber F1 Team	BMW Sauber C29-Ferrari 056 V8	B	55	1h 40m 36.395s	113.157/182.108	+ 59.558s	1m 42.733s	53
15	Sébastien Buemi	CH	16	Scuderia Toro Rosso	Toro Rosso STR5-Ferrari 056 V8	B	55	1h 40m 40.015s	113.089/181.999	+ 1m 03.178s	1m 42.573s	50
16	Nico Hülkenberg	D	10	AT&T Williams	Williams FW32-Cosworth CA2010 V8	B	55	1h 40m 41.600s	113.059/181.951	+ 1m 04.763s	1m 42.397s	51
17	Heikki Kovalainen	FIN	19	Lotus Racing	Lotus T127-Cosworth CA2010 V8	B	54			+ 1 lap	1m 45.378s	52
18	Lucas Di Grassi	BR	25	Virgin Racing	Virgin VR-01-Cosworth CA2010 V8	B	53			+ 2 laps	1m 46.126s	50
19	Bruno Senna	BR	21	HRT F1 Team	HRT F110-Cosworth CA2010 V8	B	53			+ 2 laps	1m 46.255s	52
20	Christian Klien	A	20	HRT F1 Team	HRT F110-Cosworth CA2010 V8	B	53			+ 2 laps	1m 46.646s	44
21	Jarno Trulli	I	18	Lotus Racing	Lotus T127-Cosworth CA2010 V8	B	51	*rear wing*		+ 4 laps	1m 45.979s	42
	Timo Glock	D	24	Virgin Racing	Virgin VR-01-Cosworth CA2010 V8	B	43	*gearbox*			1m 46.837s	39
	Michael Schumacher	GB	3	Mercedes GP Petronas F1 Team	Mercedes MGP W01-Mercedes FO108X V8	B	0	*accident*			no time	
	Vitantonio Liuzzi	I	15	Force India F1 Team	Force India VJM03-Mercedes FO108X V8	B	0	*accident*			no time	

Fastest race lap: Lewis Hamilton on lap 47, 1m 41.274s, 122.677mph/197.428km/h.

Lap record: Sebastian Vettel (Red Bull RB5-Renault V8), 1m 40.279s, 123.894mph/199.387km/h (2009).

Grid order	1	2	3	4	5	6	7	8	9	10	11	12	13	14	15	16	17	18	19	20	21	22
5 VETTEL	5	5	5	5	5	5	5	5	5	5	5	5	5	5	5	5	5	5	5	5	5	5
2 HAMILTON	2	2	2	2	2	2	2	2	2	2	2	2	2	2	2	2	2	2	2	2	2	2
8 ALONSO	1	1	1	1	1	1	1	1	1	1	1	1	1	1	1	1	1	1	1	1	1	1
1 BUTTON	8	8	8	8	8	8	8	8	8	8	8	8	8	8	8	9	9	23	23	23	23	23
6 WEBBER	6	6	6	6	6	6	6	6	6	6	7	7	7	9	9	23	23	11	11	11	11	11
7 MASSA	7	7	7	7	7	7	7	7	7	7	6	9	9	23	23	11	11	9	14	14	14	14
9 BARRICHELLO	9	9	9	9	9	9	9	9	9	9	9	23	23	11	11	14	14	14	16	16	16	16
3 SCHUMACHER	4	23	23	23	23	23	23	23	23	23	23	11	11	14	14	16	16	16	4	4	4	4
4 ROSBERG	23	14	14	14	14	11	11	11	11	11	11	14	14	22	22	4	4	4	10	10	10	10
12 PETROV	14	11	11	11	11	14	14	14	14	14	14	22	22	16	16	10	10	10	12	12	12	12
11 KUBICA	12	22	22	22	22	22	22	22	22	22	22	16	16	4	4	12	12	12	8	8	8	8
23 KOBAYASHI	11	16	16	16	16	16	16	16	16	16	16	4	4	10	10	8	8	8	6	6	6	6
14 SUTIL	22	10	10	10	10	10	10	10	4	4	4	10	10	12	12	6	6	6	17	17	17	17
22 HEIDFELD	16	19	19	19	19	4	4	4	10	10	10	12	12	6	6	17	17	17	7	7	7	7
10 HULKENBERG	10	18	18	18	18	19	19	12	12	12	12	17	17	17	17	7	7	7	22	22	22	22
15 LIUZZI	19	24	24	24	4	18	12	19	17	17	17	6	6	7	7	22	22	22	9	9	9	9
17 ALGUERSUARI	17	4	4	4	24	12	18	17	19	19	19	19	19	19	19	19	19	19	19	19	19	19
16 BUEMI	18	12	12	12	12	17	17	18	18	18	18	18	18	18	18	18	18	18	18	18	18	18
18 TRULLI	24	17	17	17	17	24	24	24	24	24	24	24	24	24	24	24	24	24	24	24	24	24
19 KOVALAINEN	21	25	25	25	25	25	25	25	25	25	25	25	25	25	25	25	25	25	25	25	25	25
24 GLOCK	25	21	21	21	21	21	21	21	21	21	21	21	21	21	21	21	21	21	21	21	21	21
25 DI GRASSI	20	20	20	20	20	20	20	20	20	20	20	20	20	20	20	20	20	20	20	20	20	20
21 SENNA																						
20 KLIEN																						

Grid order	23	24	25	26	27	28	29	30	31	32	33	34	35	36	37	38	39	40	41	42	43	44
5 VETTEL	5	5	1	1	1	1	1	1	1	1	1	1	1	1	1	1	1	5	5	5	5	5
2 HAMILTON	2	1	5	5	5	5	5	5	5	5	5	5	5	5	5	5	5	11	11	11	11	11
8 ALONSO	1	23	11	11	11	11	11	11	11	11	11	11	11	11	11	11	11	2	2	2	2	2
1 BUTTON	23	11	23	2	2	2	2	2	2	2	2	2	2	2	2	2	2	1	1	1	1	1
6 WEBBER	11	2	2	23	23	23	23	23	23	23	14	14	14	14	14	14	14	14	14	14	14	14
7 MASSA	14	14	14	14	14	14	14	14	14	14	23	16	16	16	4	4	4	4	4	4	4	4
9 BARRICHELLO	16	16	16	16	16	16	16	16	16	16	16	4	4	4	16	12	12	12	12	12	12	12
3 SCHUMACHER	4	4	4	4	4	4	4	4	4	4	4	10	10	12	12	8	8	8	8	8	8	8
4 ROSBERG	10	10	10	10	10	10	10	10	10	10	10	12	12	8	8	6	6	6	6	6	6	6
12 PETROV	12	12	12	12	12	12	12	12	12	12	12	8	8	10	6	17	17	17	17	17	17	17
11 KUBICA	8	8	8	8	8	8	8	8	8	8	8	6	6	6	17	7	7	7	7	7	7	7
23 KOBAYASHI	6	6	6	6	6	6	6	6	6	6	6	17	17	17	7	22	22	22	22	22	22	22
14 SUTIL	17	17	17	17	17	17	17	17	17	17	17	7	7	7	22	9	9	9	9	9	9	9
22 HEIDFELD	7	7	7	7	7	7	7	7	7	7	7	22	22	22	9	23	23	23	23	23	23	23
10 HULKENBERG	22	22	22	22	22	22	22	22	22	22	22	9	9	9	23	16	16	16	16	16	16	16
15 LIUZZI	9	9	9	9	9	9	9	9	9	9	9	23	23	23	10	10	10	10	10	10	10	10
17 ALGUERSUARI	19	19	19	19	19	19	19	19	19	19	19	19	19	19	19	19	19	19	19	19	19	19
16 BUEMI	18	18	18	18	18	24	24	24	24	24	24	24	24	24	24	24	24	24	24	24	24	25
18 TRULLI	24	24	24	24	24	18	25	25	25	25	25	25	25	25	25	25	25	25	25	25	25	21
19 KOVALAINEN	25	25	25	25	25	25	21	21	21	21	21	21	21	21	21	21	21	21	21	21	21	20
24 GLOCK	21	21	21	21	21	21	20	20	20	20	20	20	20	20	20	20	20	20	20	20	20	18
25 DI GRASSI	20	20	20	20	20	20	18	18	18	18	18	18	18	18	18	18	18	18	18	18	18	
21 SENNA																						
20 KLIEN																						

Safety car deployed on laps shown

TIME SHEETS

PRACTICE 1 (FRIDAY)

Weather: Sunny

Temperatures: track 35–38°C, air 29°C

Pos.	Driver	Laps	Time
1	Sebastian Vettel	18	1m 42.760s
2	Lewis Hamilton	16	1m 43.369s
3	Jenson Button	19	1m 43.785s
4	Mark Webber	19	1m 43.840s
5	Robert Kubica	19	1m 44.080s
6	Fernando Alonso	17	1m 44.121s
7	Michael Schumacher	19	1m 44.199s
8	Kamui Kobayashi	18	1m 44.604s
9	Nico Rosberg	19	1m 44.718s
10	Nick Heidfeld	19	1m 44.737s
11	Felipe Massa	18	1m 45.160s
12	Vitaly Petrov	21	1m 45.445s
13	Rubens Barrichello	15	1m 45.474s
14	Adrian Sutil	20	1m 45.552s
15	Vitantonio Liuzzi	14	1m 45.585s
16	Jaime Alguersuari	20	1m 46.003s
17	Nico Hülkenberg	19	1m 46.644s
18	Sébastien Buemi	22	1m 47.105s
19	Timo Glock	19	1m 48.450s
20	Jarno Trulli	17	1m 48.472s
21	Lucas Di Grassi	13	1m 49.375s
22	Bruno Senna	18	1m 49.590s
23	Christian Klien	17	1m 50.274s
24	Fairuz Fauzy	18	1m 51.705s

PRACTICE 2 (FRIDAY)

Weather: Sunny/dusk

Temperatures: track 28–30°C, air 27–29°C

Pos.	Driver	Laps	Time
1	Lewis Hamilton	25	1m 40.888s
2	Sebastian Vettel	28	1m 41.145s
3	Fernando Alonso	29	1m 41.314s
4	Mark Webber	29	1m 41.315s
5	Robert Kubica	31	1m 41.576s
6	Felipe Massa	21	1m 41.583s
7	Vitaly Petrov	31	1m 42.096s
8	Jenson Button	28	1m 42.132s
9	Vitantonio Liuzzi	31	1m 42.203s
10	Nico Rosberg	29	1m 42.222s
11	Michael Schumacher	29	1m 42.246s
12	Nico Hülkenberg	32	1m 42.449s
13	Adrian Sutil	21	1m 42.535s
14	Kamui Kobayashi	26	1m 42.768s
15	Rubens Barrichello	37	1m 42.914s
16	Nick Heidfeld	34	1m 42.950s
17	Jaime Alguersuari	17	1m 43.128s
18	Sébastien Buemi	33	1m 43.584s
19	Heikki Kovalainen	36	1m 45.180s
20	Timo Glock	31	1m 45.259s
21	Jarno Trulli	35	1m 45.612s
22	Lucas Di Grassi	29	1m 46.053s
23	Christian Klien	32	1m 47.210s
24	Bruno Senna	28	1m 47.434s

PRACTICE 3 (SATURDAY)

Weather: Sunny

Temperatures: track 40–41°C, air 29°C

Pos.	Driver	Laps	Time
1	Sebastian Vettel	18	1m 40.696s
2	Mark Webber	15	1m 40.829s
3	Lewis Hamilton	13	1m 41.280s
4	Fernando Alonso	14	1m 41.490s
5	Jenson Button	17	1m 41.578s
6	Vitaly Petrov	17	1m 41.689s
7	Michael Schumacher	18	1m 41.690s
8	Nico Rosberg	17	1m 41.729s
9	Robert Kubica	18	1m 41.877s
10	Nick Heidfeld	20	1m 41.893s
11	Nico Hülkenberg	18	1m 41.934s
12	Felipe Massa	14	1m 41.978s
13	Rubens Barrichello	15	1m 42.316s
14	Kamui Kobayashi	16	1m 42.566s
15	Adrian Sutil	18	1m 42.587s
16	Vitantonio Liuzzi	14	1m 42.858s
17	Jaime Alguersuari	20	1m 42.993s
18	Sébastien Buemi	18	1m 43.344s
19	Heikki Kovalainen	15	1m 44.876s
20	Jarno Trulli	23	1m 45.048s
21	Timo Glock	20	1m 45.050s
22	Bruno Senna	16	1m 45.490s
23	Lucas Di Grassi	22	1m 45.629s
24	Christian Klien	17	1m 46.464s

QUALIFYING (SATURDAY)

Weather: Sunny/dusk/dark Temperatures: track 28–30°C, air 27–28°C

Pos.	Driver	First	Second	Third	Qualifying Tyre
1	Sebastian Vettel	1m 40.318s	1m 39.874s	1m 39.394s	Super-Soft
2	Lewis Hamilton	1m 40.335s	1m 40.119s	1m 39.425s	Super-Soft
3	Fernando Alonso	1m 40.170s	1m 40.311s	1m 39.792s	Super-Soft
4	Jenson Button	1m 40.870s	1m 40.014s	1m 39.823s	Super-Soft
5	Mark Webber	1m 40.690s	1m 40.074s	1m 39.925s	Super-Soft
6	Felipe Massa	1m 40.942s	1m 40.323s	1m 40.202s	Super-Soft
7	Rubens Barrichello	1m 40.904s	1m 40.476s	1m 40.203s	Super-Soft
8	Michael Schumacher	1m 41.222s	1m 40.452s	1m 40.516s	Super-Soft
9	Nico Rosberg	1m 40.231s	1m 40.060s	1m 40.589s	Super-Soft
10	Vitaly Petrov	1m 41.018s	1m 40.658s	1m 40.901s	Super-Soft
11	Robert Kubica	1m 41.336s	1m 40.780s		
12	Kamui Kobayashi	1m 41.045s	1m 40.783s		
13	Adrian Sutil	1m 41.473s	1m 40.914s		
14	Nick Heidfeld	1m 41.409s	1m 41.113s		
15	Nico Hülkenberg	1m 41.015s	1m 41.418s		
16	Vitantonio Liuzzi	1m 41.681s	1m 41.642s		
17	Jaime Alguersuari	1m 41.707s	1m 41.738s		
18	Sébastien Buemi	1m 41.824s			
19	Jarno Trulli	1m 43.516s			
20	Heikki Kovalainen	1m 43.712s			
21	Timo Glock	1m 44.095s			
22	Lucas Di Grassi	1m 44.510s			
23	Bruno Senna	1m 45.085s			
24	Christian Klien	1m 45.296s			

FOR THE RECORD

1st WORLD DRIVERS' CHAMPIONSHIP: Sebastian Vettel

10th WIN: Sebastian Vettel

20th POLE POSITION: Red Bull

DID YOU KNOW

Sebastian Vettel became the youngest ever F1 world champion at the age of 23 years, 4 months and 11 days.

The Mercedes Formula 1 safety car celebrated its 250th grand prix at Abu Dhabi. The first time it appeared was at the 1996 French Grand Prix (C 36 AMG). In 2010, it was an SLS AMG 6.3L V8.

POINTS

DRIVERS

1	Sebastian Vettel	256
2	Fernando Alonso	252
3	Mark Webber	242
4	Lewis Hamilton	240
5	Jenson Button	214
6	Felipe Massa	144
7	Nico Rosberg	142
8	Robert Kubica	136
9	Michael Schumacher	72
10	Rubens Barrichello	47
11	Adrian Sutil	47
12	Kamui Kobayashi	32
13	Vitaly Petrov	27
14	Nico Hülkenberg	22
15	Vitantonio Liuzzi	21
16	Sébastien Buemi	8
17	Pedro de la Rosa	6
18	Nick Heidfeld	6
19	Jaime Alguersuari	5

CONSTRUCTORS

1	Red Bull	498
2	McLaren	454
3	Ferrari	396
4	Mercedes	214
5	Renault	163
6	Williams	69
7	Force India	68
8	BMW Sauber	44
9	Toro Rosso	13

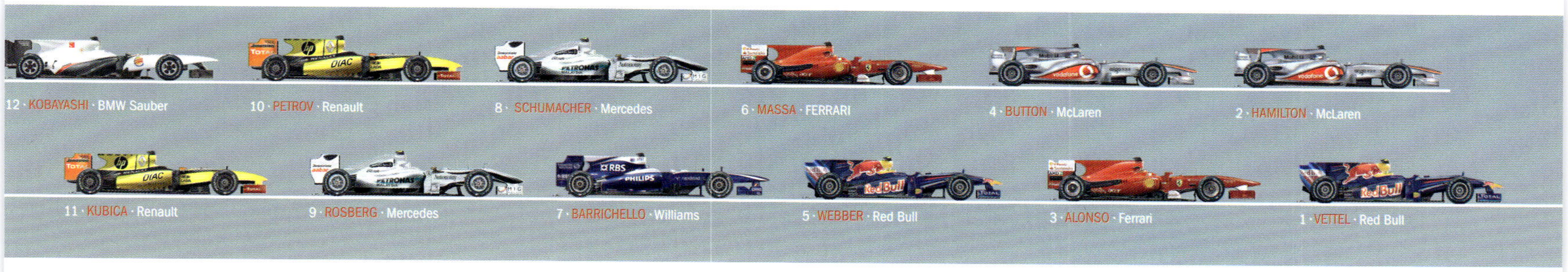

45	46	47	48	49	50	51	52	53	54	55	
5	5	5	5	5	5	5	5	5	5	5	1
11	2	2	2	2	2	2	2	2	2	2	2
2	11	1	1	1	1	1	1	1	1	1	3
1	1	14	4	4	4	4	4	4	4	4	
14	14	4	11	11	11	11	11	11	11	11	
4	4	11	12	12	12	12	12	12	12	12	6
12	12	12	8	8	8	8	8	8	8	8	7
8	8	8	6	6	6	6	6	6	6	6	8
6	6	6	17	17	17	17	17	17	17	17	
17	17	17	7	7	7	7	7	7	7	7	10
7	7	7	22	22	22	22	22	22	22	22	
22	22	22	9	9	9	9	9	9	9	9	
9	9	9	14	14	14	14	14	14	14	14	
23	23	23	23	23	23	23	23	23	23	23	
16	16	16	16	16	16	16	16	16	16	16	
10	10	10	10	10	10	10	10	10	10	10	
19	19	19	19	19	19	19	19	19	19		
25	25	25	25	25	25	25	25	25			
21	21	21	21	21	21	21	21	21			
20	20	20	20	20	20	20	20	20			
18	18	18	18	18	18	18					

21 Pit stop

14 One lap or more behind

RACE TYRE STRATEGIES

	Driver	Race Stint 1	Race Stint 2
1	Vettel	Super-Soft: 1-24	Medium: 25-55
2	Hamilton	Super-Soft: 1-23	Medium: 24-55
3	Button	Super-Soft: 1-39	Medium: 40-55
4	Rosberg	Super-Soft: 1	Medium: 2-55
5	Kubica	Medium: 1-46	Super-Soft: 47-55
6	Petrov	Super-Soft: 1	Medium: 2-55
7	Alonso	Super-Soft: 1-15	Medium: 16-55
8	Webber	Super-Soft: 1-11	Medium: 12-55
9	Alguersuari	Super-Soft: 1	Medium: 2-55
10	Massa	Super-Soft: 1-13	Medium: 14-55
11	Heidfeld	Super-Soft: 1-15	Medium: 16-55
12	Barrichello	Super-Soft: 1-18	Medium: 19-55
13	Sutil	Medium: 1-14	Super-Soft: 48-55
14	Kobayashi	Super-Soft: 1-33	Medium: 34-55
15	Buemi	Medium: 1-37	Super-Soft: 38-55
16	Hülkenberg	Medium: 1-36	Super-Soft: 37-55
17	Kovalainen	Medium: 1-41	Super-Soft: 42-54
18	di Grassi	Super-Soft: 1	Medium: 2-53
19	Senna	Super-Soft: 1	Medium: 2-53
20	Klien	Super-Soft: 1	Medium: 2-53
21	Trulli	Medium: 1-28	Super-Soft: 29-51
	Glock	Medium: 1-40	Super-Soft: 41-43 (dnf)
	Schumacher	Super-Soft: 1 (dnf)	
	Liuzzi	Medium: 1 (dnf)	

The tyre regulations stipulate that the two dry tyre specifications must be used during the race.
The Super-Soft compound Bridgestone Potenza tyre is marked with a green stripe on the sidewall.

Photos: Peter J. Fox

STATISTICS

DRIVERS' POINTS TABLE

Compiled by DAVID HAYHOE

Place	Driver	Nationality	Date of birth	Car	Bahrain	Australia	Malaysia	China	Spain	Monaco	Turkey	Canada	Europe	Britain	Germany	Hungary	Belgium	Italy	Singapore	Japan	Korea	Brazil	Abu Dhabi	Points
1	**Sebastian VETTEL**	D	3/7/87	Red Bull-Renault	4p	Rp	1	6p	3	2f	R	4	1p	7p	3pf	3pf	15	4	2	1p	Rp	1	1p	**256**
2	**Fernando ALONSO**	E	29/7/81	Ferrari	1f	4	13*	4	2	6	8	3	8	14f	1	2	R	1pf	1pf	3	1f	3	7	**252**
3	**Mark WEBBER**	AUS	27/8/76	Red Bull-Renault	8	9f	2pf	8	1p	1p	3p	5	R	1	6	1	2p	6	3	2f	R	2	8	**242**
4	**Lewis HAMILTON**	GB	7/1/85	McLaren-Mercedes	3	6	6	2f	14*f	5	1	1p	2	2	4	R	1f	R	R	5	2	4f	2f	**240**
5	**Jenson BUTTON**	GB	19/1/80	McLaren-Mercedes	7	1	8	1	5	R	2	2	3f	4	5	8	R	2	4	4	12	5	3	**214**
6	**Felipe MASSA**	BR	25/4/81	Ferrari	2	3	7	9	6	4	7	15	11	15	2	4	4	3	8	R	3	15	10	**144**
7	**Nico ROSBERG**	D	27/6/85	Mercedes	5	5	3	3	13	7	5	6	10	3	8	R	6	5	5	17*	R	6	4	**142**
8	**Robert KUBICA**	PL	7/12/84	Renault	11	2	4	5	8	3	6	7f	5	R	7	R	3	8	7	R	5	9	5	**136**
9	**Michael SCHUMACHER**	D	3/1/69	Mercedes	6	10	R	10	4	12	4	11	15	9	9	11	7	9	13	6	4	7	R	**72**
10	**Rubens BARRICHELLO**	BR	23/5/72	Williams-Cosworth	10	8	12	12	9	R	14	14	4	5	12	10	R	10	6	R	7	14	12	**47**
11	**Adrian SUTIL**	D	11/1/83	Force India-Mercedes	12	R	5	11	7	8	9	10	6	8	17	R	5	16	9	R	R	12	13	**47**
12	**Kamui KOBAYASHI**	J	13/9/86	BMW Sauber-Ferrari	R	R	R	R	12	R	10	R	7	6	11	9	8	R	R	7	8	10	14	**32**
13	**Vitaly PETROV**	RUS	8/9/84	Renault	R	R	R	7	11	13*	15f	17	14	13	10	5	9	13	11	R	R	16	6	**27**
14	**Nico HÜLKENBERG**	D	19/8/87	Williams-Cosworth	14	R	10	15	16	R	17	13	R	10	13	6	14	7	10	R	10	8p	16	**22**
15	**Vitantonio LIUZZI**	I	6/8/80	Force India-Mercedes	9	7	R	R	15*	9	13	9	16	11	16	13	10	12	R	R	6	R	R	**21**
16	**Sébastien BUEMI**	CH	31/10/88	Toro Rosso-Ferrari	16*	R	11	R	R	10	16	8	9	12	R	12	12	11	14	10	R	13	15	**8**
17	**Pedro de la ROSA**	E	24/2/71	BMW Sauber-Ferrari	R	12	NS	R	R	R	11	R	12	R	14	7	11	14	-	-	-	-	-	**6**
18	**Nick HEIDFELD**	D	10/5/77	BMW Sauber-Ferrari	-	-	-	-	-	-	-	-	-	-	-	-	-	-	R	8	9	17	11	**6**
19	**Jaime ALGUERSUARI**	E	23/3/90	Toro Rosso-Ferrari	13	11	9	13	10	11	12	12	13	R	15	R	13	15	12	11	11	11	9	**5**
20	**Heikki KOVALAINEN**	FIN	19/10/81	Lotus-Cosworth	15	13	NC	14	NS	R	R	16	R	17	R	14	16	18	16*	12	13	18	17	-
21	**Jarno TRULLI**	I	13/7/74	Lotus-Cosworth	17	NS	17	R	17	15*	R	R	21	16	R	15	19	R	R	13	R	19	21*	-
22	**Karun CHANDHOK**	IND	19/1/84	HRT-Cosworth	R	14	15	17	R	14*	20*	18	18	19	-	-	-	-	-	-	-	-	-	-
23	**Bruno SENNA**	BR	15/10/83	HRT-Cosworth	R	R	16	16	R	R	R	R	20	-	19	17	R	R	R	15	14	21	19	-
24	**Lucas di GRASSI**	BR	11/8/84	Virgin-Cosworth	R	R	14	R	19	R	19	19	17	R	R	18	17	20*	15	NS	R	NC	18	-
25	**Timo GLOCK**	D	18/3/82	Virgin-Cosworth	R	R	R	NS	18	R	18	R	19	18	18	16	18	17	R	14	R	20	R	-
26	**Sakon YAMAMOTO**	J	9/7/82	HRT-Cosworth	-	-	-	-	-	-	AP	-	-	20	R	19	20	19	-	16	15	-	-	-
27	**Christian KLIEN**	A	7/2/83	HRT-Cosworth	-	-	-	-	AP	-	-	-	AP	-	-	-	-	-	R	-	-	22	20	-
	Jérôme d'AMBROSIO	B	27/12/85	Virgin-Cosworth	-	-	-	-	-	-	-	-	-	-	-	-	-	-	AP	AP	AP	AP	-	-
	Paul di RESTA	GB	16/4/86	Force India-Mercedes	-	AP	AP	AP	AP	-	-	-	AP	AP	-	AP	-	AP	-	-	-	-	-	-
	Fairuz FAUZY	MAL	24/10/82	Lotus-Cosworth	-	-	AP	-	-	-	-	-	-	AP	AP	-	-	-	AP	-	-	-	AP	-

KEY: AP - Also practiced NC - Non-classified NS - Non-starter R - Retired * Placed but retired f - fastest lap p - pole position

POINTS AND PERCENTAGES

Compiled by DAVID HAYHOE

GRID POSITIONS: 2010

Pos	Driver	Starts	Best	Worst	Average
1	Sebastian Vettel	19	1	6	1.95
2	Mark Webber	19	1	7	2.79
3	Lewis Hamilton	19	1	20	5.16
4	Fernando Alonso	19	1	24	5.79
5	Jenson Button	19	2	17	6.84
6	Robert Kubica	19	2	11	6.95
7	Nico Rosberg	19	2	14	7.37
8	Felipe Massa	19	2	24	7.74
9	Rubens Barrichello	19	6	17	9.42
10	Michael Schumacher	19	5	21	9.95
11	Nico Hülkenberg	19	1	17	11.21
12	Adrian Sutil	19	4	22	12.16
13	Nick Heidfeld	5	11	15	13.40
14	Kamui Kobayashi	19	9	23	13.95
15	Vitaly Petrov	19	7	23	14.16
16	Pedro de la Rosa	13	9	24	14.62
17	Sébastien Buemi	19	11	19	14.79
18	Vitantonio Liuzzi	19	5	21	15.05
19	Jaime Alguersuari	19	11	18	15.26
20	Jarno Trulli	18	15	21	18.78
21	Heikki Kovalainen	18	13	21	18.83
22	Timo Glock	18	16	24	20.22
23	Lucas di Grassi	18	20	24	22.06
24	Bruno Senna	18	18	24	22.39
25	Sakon Yamamoto	7	19	24	22.71
26	Christian Klien	3	22	24	23.00
27	Karun Chandhok	10	21	24	23.20

RETIREMENTS: 2010

Number of cars to have retired

Grand Prix	Starters	At 1/4 distance	At 1/2 distance	At 3/4 distance	At full distance	Percentage of finishers
Bahrain	24	3	6	7	8	66.7
Australia	23	6	8	9	9	60.9
Malaysia	23	4	4	5	6	73.9
China	23	5	6	6	6	73.9
Spain	23	1	3	4	6	73.9
Monaco	24	2	7	8	12	50.0
Turkey	24	0	0	3	5	79.2
Canada	24	2	3	5	5	79.2
Europe	24	2	2	2	3	87.5
Britain	24	1	2	3	4	83.3
Germany	24	3	3	4	5	79.2
Hungary	24	3	5	5	5	79.2
Belgium	24	2	3	3	4	83.3
Italy	24	3	3	3	5	79.2
Singapore	24	1	4	7	9	62.5
Japan	23	5	5	5	7	69.6
Korea	24	0	4	7	9	62.5
Brazil	24	0	0	1	1	95.8
Abu Dhabi	24	2	2	2	4	83.3

LAP LEADERS: 2010

Grand Prix	Vettel	Webber	Button	Alonso	Hamilton	Massa	Rosberg	Buemi	Total
Bahrain	33	-	-	16	-	-	-		49
Australia	23	2	33	-	-	-	-	-	58
Malaysia	54	2	-	-	-	-	-	-	56
China	-	-	38	2	-	-	16	-	56
Spain	-	66	-	-	-	-	-	-	66
Monaco	-	78	-	-	-	-	-	-	78
Turkey	-	37	3	-	18	-	-	-	58
Canada	7	22	-	2	38	-	-	1	70
Europe	57	-	-	-	-	-	-	-	57
Britain	-	52	-	-	-	-	-	-	52
Germany	-	-	8	19	-	40	-	-	67
Hungary	15	55	-	-	-	-	-	-	70
Belgium	-	-	-	-	44	-	-	-	44
Italy	-	-	35	16	-	2	-	-	53
Singapore	-	-	-	61	-	-	-	-	61
Japan	39	1	13	-	-	-	-	-	53
Korea	45	-	-	10	-	-	-	-	55
Brazil	69	2	-	-	-	-	-	-	71
Abu Dhabi	40	-	15	-	-	-	-	-	55
Total	382	317	145	126	100	42	16	1	1129
(Per cent)	*33.8*	*28.1*	*12.8*	*11.2*	*8.9*	*3.7*	*1.4*	*0.1*	*100.0*

CAREER PERFORMANCES: 2010

Driver	Nationality	Races	Championships	Wins	2nd places	3rd places	4th places	5th places	6th places	7th places	8th places	9th places	10th places	Pole positions	Fastest laps	Points
Jaime Alguersuari	E	**27**	-	-	-	-	-	-	-	-	-	2	1	-	-	**5**
Fernando Alonso	E	**158**	2	26	21	16	16	9	6	7	6	1	6	20	18	**829**
Rubens Barrichello	BR	**304**	-	11	29	28	20	18	13	14	7	10	20	14	17	**654**
Sébastien Buemi	CH	**36**	-	-	-	-	-	-	-	2	3	1	2	-	-	**14**
Jenson Button	GB	**189**	1	9	8	14	15	22	7	10	13	5	8	7	3	**541**
Karun Chandhok	IND	**10**	-	-	-	-	-	-	-	-	-	-	-	-	-	**-**
Pedro de la Rosa	E	**85**	-	-	1	-	-	4	4	2	5	1	2	-	1	**35**
Lucas di Grassi	BR	**18**	-	-	-	-	-	-	-	-	-	-	-	-	-	**-**
Timo Glock	D	**54**	-	-	2	1	3	-	2	5	1	4	3	-	1	**51**
Lewis Hamilton	GB	**71**	1	14	13	9	4	6	3	3	-	2	1	18	8	**496**
Nick Heidfeld	D	**172**	-	-	8	4	10	9	16	12	10	13	13	1	2	**225**
Nico Hülkenberg	D	**19**	-	-	-	-	-	-	1	1	1	-	4	1	-	**22**
Christian Klien	A	**49**	-	-	-	-	-	1	1	1	5	5	2	-	-	**14**
Kamui Kobayashi	J	**21**	-	-	-	-	-	-	2	2	2	2	2	-	-	**35**
Heikki Kovalainen	FIN	**70**	-	1	2	1	4	7	3	5	6	3	3	1	2	**105**
Robert Kubica	PL	**76**	-	1	5	6	7	9	4	7	6	5	1	1	1	**273**
Vitantonio Liuzzi	I	**63**	-	-	-	-	-	-	2	1	2	5	4	-	-	**26**
Felipe Massa	BR	**133**	-	11	11	11	9	8	9	7	6	13	8	15	12	**464**
Vitaly Petrov	RUS	**19**	-	-	-	-	-	1	1	1	-	1	1	-	1	**27**
Nico Rosberg	D	**89**	-	-	1	4	4	9	8	6	7	6	6	-	2	**217.5**
Michael Schumacher	D	**268**	7	91	43	20	14	10	9	8	4	4	4	68	76	**1441**
Bruno Senna	BR	**18**	-	-	-	-	-	-	-	-	-	-	-	-	-	**-**
Adrian Sutil	D	**71**	-	-	-	-	1	2	1	1	3	3	2	-	1	**53**
Jarno Trulli	I	**234**	-	1	4	6	16	14	14	15	13	14	9	4	1	**246.5**
Sebastian Vettel	D	**62**	1	10	4	5	8	3	3	1	4	1	-	15	6	**381**
Mark Webber	AUS	**157**	-	6	8	6	3	6	12	13	10	12	8	6	6	**411.5**
Sakon Yamamoto	J	**21**	-	-	-	-	-	-	-	-	-	-	-	-	-	-

Note: As is now common practice, drivers retiring on the formation lap are not counted as having started.
Where races have been subject to a restart, those retiring during an initial race are included as having started.

ALL TIME RECORDS

STARTS

Rubens Barrichello	304
Michael Schumacher	268
Riccardo Patrese	256
David Coulthard	246
Jarno Trulli	234
Giancarlo Fisichella	229
Gerhard Berger	210
Andrea de Cesaris	208
Nelson Piquet	204
Jean Alesi	201
Alain Prost	199
Michele Alboreto	194

WINS

Michael Schumacher	91
Alain Prost	51
Ayrton Senna	41
Nigel Mansell	31
Jackie Stewart	27
Fernando Alonso	26
Jim Clark	25
Niki Lauda	25
Juan Manuel Fangio	24
Nelson Piquet	23
Damon Hill	22
Mika Häkkinen	20

FASTEST LAPS

Michael Schumacher	76
Alain Prost	41
Kimi Räikkönen	35
Nigel Mansell	30
Jim Clark	28
Mika Häkkinen	25
Niki Lauda	24
Juan Manuel Fangio	23
Nelson Piquet	23
Gerhard Berger	21
Damon Hill	19
Stirling Moss	19
Ayrton Senna	19

YOUNGEST STARTERS

Jaime Alguersuari	19y 04m 03d
Mike Thackwell	19y 05m 29d
Ricardo Rodriguez	19y 06m 27d
Fernando Alonso	19y 07m 03d
Esteban Tuero	19y 10m 14d
Chris Amon	19y 10m 20d
Sebastian Vettel	19y 11m 14d
Eddie Cheever	20y 01m 22d
Jenson Button	20y 01m 22d
Tarso Marques	20y 02m 12d
Sébastien Buemi	20y 04m 29d
Peter Collins	20y 06m 12d

YOUNGEST WINNERS

Sebastian Vettel	21y 02m 11d
Fernando Alonso	22y 00m 26d
Bruce McLaren	22y 03m 12d
Lewis Hamilton	22y 05m 03d
Kimi Räikkönen	23y 05m 06d
Robert Kubica	23y 06m 01d
Jacky Ickx	23y 06m 06d
Michael Schumacher	23y 07m 27d
Emerson Fittipaldi	23y 09m 22d
Mike Hawthorn	24y 02m 25d
Jody Scheckter	24y 04m 11d
Elio de Angelis	24y 04m 20d

POLE POSITIONS

Michael Schumacher	68
Ayrton Senna	65
Jim Clark	33
Alain Prost	33
Nigel Mansell	32
Juan Manuel Fangio	29
Mika Häkkinen	26
Niki Lauda	24
Nelson Piquet	24
Fernando Alonso	20
Damon Hill	20

YOUNGEST ON POLE

Sebastian Vettel	21y 02m 11d
Fernando Alonso	21y 07m 23d
Rubens Barrichello	22y 03m 05d
Lewis Hamilton	22y 05m 03d
Andrea de Cesaris	22y 10m 04d
Nico Hülkenberg	23y 02m 19d
Robert Kubica	23y 03m 30d
Jacky Ickx	23y 07m 03d
Kimi Räikkönen	23y 08m 12d
David Coulthard	24y 00m 13d
Jenson Button	24y 03m 06d
Eugenio Castellotti	24y 07m 26d

WORLD CHAMPIONSHIPS

Michael Schumacher	7
Juan Manuel Fangio	5
Alain Prost	4
Jack Brabham	3
Niki Lauda	3
Nelson Piquet	3
Ayrton Senna	3
Jackie Stewart	3
Fernando Alonso	2
Alberto Ascari	2
Jim Clark	2
Emerson Fittipaldi	2
Mika Häkkinen	2
Graham Hill	2

YOUNGEST CHAMPIONS

Sebastian Vettel	23y 04m 11d
Lewis Hamilton	23y 09m 26d
Fernando Alonso	24y 01m 27d
Emerson Fittipaldi	25y 08m 29d
Michael Schumacher	25y 10m 10d
Niki Lauda	26y 06m 16d
Jacques Villeneuve	26y 06m 17d
Jim Clark	27y 06m 04d
Kimi Räikkönen	28y 00m 04d
Jochen Rindt	28y 05m 16d
Ayrton Senna	28y 07m 09d
James Hunt	29y 01m 25d

PODIUMS

Michael Schumacher	154
Alain Prost	106
Ayrton Senna	80
Rubens Barrichello	68
Fernando Alonso	63
David Coulthard	62
Kimi Räikkönen	62
Nelson Piquet	60
Nigel Mansell	59
Niki Lauda	54
Mika Häkkinen	51
Gerhard Berger	48

Pastor Maldonado scored six feature-race wins to underpin his successful 2010 GP2 title assault.
Photo: GP2 Media Services

GP2 REVIEW by CRAIG LLEWELLYN

PASTOR THE MASTER

AFTER three years of unfulfilled promise – and more than the odd rash moment – 2010 was seen as something of a make-or-break season for Pastor Maldonado's bid to return Venezuela to Formula One, but, like Giorgio Pantano before him, the GP2 Series veteran finally made his mark in a positive way.

The mercurial Maracay native had never previously bettered fifth overall in any set of GP2 standings, but having been snapped up by the rebranded Rapax team, formerly the Piquet Sports outfit that had run him in 2008, he emerged as a dominant force. Having been expected to produce more with multiple champion ART Grand Prix in 2009, only to be overshadowed by rookie Nico Hülkenberg, Maldonado knew that he had to come good this time around, but still made a slow start to the campaign.

Although not quite as slow as Hülkenberg's scoreless opening round a year earlier, the Venezuelan started with sixth place in the Barcelona feature, having qualified only ninth, and followed that up with the bottom step of the podium in Sunday's sprint, behind Rapax team-mate Luiz Razia and rookie winner Fabio Leimer. Monaco, a happy hunting ground in anything he had raced there previously, saw Maldonado settle for second behind Sergio Perez, having failed to make the front row after crashing in a qualifying shoot-out, and finish well outside the points after being penalised for a jump start in the sprint.

It was in Turkey that the Venezuelan's season finally kicked into a higher gear, starting with a feature-race victory that owed much to a legal lightning start and early pace that had pole-man Davide Valsecchi settling for second within a handful of laps. Picking up a couple of places to earn the final point on Sunday ensured that Maldonado left Istanbul Park in sole possession of the championship lead, having shared it with Dani Clos after Barcelona and dropped behind Perez in Monaco. He never looked back.

Although still unable to qualify on pole, he overcame the loss of a couple of places early on in Valencia to benefit from others' misfortune, pouncing on an error from ART replacement Jules Bianchi to claim the lead, and victory, before again making up places in the sprint to bag a 15-point weekend haul that would stand as the best of the season. With pole-man Perez suffering misfortune in both races and failing to add to his post-Turkey tally, and Clos only scoring on Saturday, Maldonado opened out a handy 15-point lead over the Spaniard as the series headed into an unscheduled mid-season break.

There had been a stand-alone race planned for the Portimao circuit, which had staged the 2009 finale, but 'contractual problems' resulted in it being canned, providing a four-week hiatus while the F1 circus visited Canada for the teams to recoup. When the action resumed, however, so did Maldonado.

Once more edged out of pole position at Silverstone, the Rapax driver made amends at the first turn, passing Bianchi and disappearing ten seconds up the road to claim victory number three. Adding another fourth place on Sunday stretched his lead over Clos to 19 points, and over Perez to 26.

The run continued in Germany, Hungary and Belgium, where Maldonado converted starts of second, fourth and second into feature-race victories, but his apparent charge to the championship was slowed slightly by a sudden inability to add to his total on Sunday morning. A collision with series returnee Romain Grosjean while disputing the minor points accounted for the Venezuelan at Hockenheim, while tagging Sam Bird and damaging his front wing resulted in a black flag in Hungary. Then further damage halted his participation in race two at Spa, although the broken wheel was picked up in a typical opening-lap skirmish in the Ardennes.

Clos and Perez did their level best to keep the veteran honest, with the Racing Engineering driver claiming his first GP2 win in the Istanbul sprint, and Barwa Addax's Mexican adding similar successes at Silverstone, Hockenheim and Spa, but there were too many low or non-scores in between that prevented either from keeping the points gap manageable.

Clos was Maldonado's main opposition through the first five rounds, a consistent scoring run only broken by back-to-back retirements in the Monaco and Valencia sprints, but a pointless weekend in Hungary was followed by a back-breaking start-line shunt at Spa, and despite not missing a round, the Spaniard didn't add to his tally until the Abu Dhabi finale.

Given eight weeks between Monza and the final double-header, a healed Clos qualified on the front row at Yas Marina, only for a penalty to dump him back to 12th. Undaunted, he claimed two fourth-place finishes to round out the year, only narrowly missing out on the top three overall.

Perez was able to take advantage of the Spaniard's mid-season misfortune, even though he went home empty-handed from Turkey and with only the two-point pole bonus to his credit from Valencia. Four straight podium finishes between Silverstone and Budapest vaulted him past Clos, but his hold on second overall remained shaky even as the field headed to Monza for the penultimate round.

Ironically, the race billed as the championship showdown – despite the season finishing in Abu Dhabi in November – was something of an anti-climax, with none of the top three heading to Italy leaving with an addition to their points tally.

Maldonado arrived at the royal park with 27 points in hand over Perez, but the two remaining contenders only qualified eighth and seventh respectively, after Maldonado's spin had stymied more than one of his rivals, and their position proved perilous in the opening laps. Maldonado was ahead of Perez when

he catapulted himself over the back of Grosjean at a restart, but the Mexican failed to capitalise when he succumbed to a soft accident with Michael Herck.

Neither man scored on Sunday either, although Maldonado didn't really need to, as Perez required victory and the fastest-lap bonus to ensure that battle progressed. As it happened, they were eliminated in the same incident, with Perez's lap-two off at the Parabolica triggering a chain reaction that also accounted for the Venezuelan. Clos, meanwhile, was unable to mount a new assault on second overall, having been caught up in a first-lap accident on Saturday and paying for his lowly grid start with 12th in the sprint.

Perez finally secured second overall with victory in the Abu Dhabi feature race and another non-score on Sunday, while Maldonado failed to score in either race in the UAE, leaving the final margin between them at 16 points.

The leaders' Monza mishaps opened the way for ART to finally claim its first victories of a season that had promised much, but all too often had proved frustrating.

F3 Euroseries champion Bianchi opened a few eyes with pole position in Barcelona – although a number of newcomers shone in the session, including team-mate Bird – but both were first-lap victims: Bianchi was caught out by an over-ambitious Christian Vietoris, and Bird by his own failings at the start. The Briton, however, was able to give a good indication of his pace by defying the Circuit de Catalunya's reputation as an overtaking-free zone and recovering from last to ninth at the flag.

Bianchi claimed another pole in Britain, but had to settle for second behind Maldonado, adding to other early podiums in Monaco and Valencia, before he, too, suffered back injuries after a race-one crash in Hungary, going pointless for a couple of rounds.

Bird, meanwhile, could lay claim to being perhaps the unluckiest driver in the field, as several promising positions went begging through no fault of his own. The Briton, who had secured the desired ART seat after a strong Asia Series showing, claimed his maiden podium in Istanbul's feature race, and repeated the feat in Valencia, but his run tailed off after fourth at Silverstone was followed by an engine problem on Sunday, and more bad luck as his motor cut when starting from pole in Hungary.

At Monza, however, ART was back, with Bianchi claiming a third pole of the year, only for Bird to jump him at the start and disappear. The Frenchman was comfortable in second and, despite starting from row four on Sunday, the pair proved that their form was no fluke by coming through to third and fourth at the flag – and into the top five overall. Bird added another podium in Abu Dhabi for good measure, finishing the

Above: Sergio Perez won the most glamorous GP2 Series round of all in Monaco, en route to second overall in the standings and an F1 seat with Sauber.

Left: Euro Formula 3 champion Jules Bianchi could not deliver ART Grand Prix the championship and had to be content with third in the series, behind Maldonado and Perez.

Photos: GP2 Media Services

year just four points off a team-mate later appointed as Ferrari test driver for 2011.

Between them, the top five scorers garnered 13 of the season's 20 wins, with the remainder scattered through the field.

Arden's Charles Pic lived up to a reputation forged in World Series by Renault by claiming the opening round in Spain, before Leimer took an unexpected sprint-race win for Tiago Monteiro's Ocean Racing Technology team after making the most of pole on the partially reversed grid system.

Jerome d'Ambrosio endured a strange up-and-down season, winning the sprint race in Monaco from pole, but later being dropped by DAMS for the Hockenheim double-header as the team attempted to sort its underperformance through the middle of the year. The Belgian returned in Hungary and scored more regularly thereafter, before being picked up by Virgin Racing to run in Friday practice at four of the final F1 rounds.

F3 graduate Marcus Ericsson claimed a brief moment in the spotlight by winning race two for Super Nova in Valencia, but scored on just two other occasions, while Giacomo Ricci put DPR back on top on Sunday in Hungary. The Italian had started the season with an opening-race podium, but existed on a race-to-race basis and vanished immediately after his biggest success. Racing Engineering's Christian Vietoris finally triumphed in race two at Monza after enduring a season almost as trying as Bird's – including missing the finale with appendicitis – while iSport's Davide Valsecchi salvaged a disappointing campaign with victory in the Abu Dhabi sprint.

The Italian was among those who should perhaps have done better, along with iSport team-mate Oliver Turvey, having largely dominated the preceding Asia Series. Valsecchi was nearly unbeatable in the 'winter championship', but, like Kamui Kobayashi before him, found the switch back to more modern machinery tougher than he imagined.

The Italian took pole in Turkey, continuing an affinity with the Istanbul Park circuit, despite his monster qualifying smash there in 2008, but his podium finish behind Maldonado was one of only two in 2010. Turvey, meanwhile, fared a little better, scoring regularly in the second half of the season, and making the podium in the Monza and Abu Dhabi feature races, to finish sixth overall.

Dropping behind Turvey in the standings, Giedo van der Garde put in some of the more aggressive performances of the year, and was rewarded with second in the Monaco, Valencia and Spa sprints, but, like Bianchi, he was unable to cap his season with a maiden-series success.

Former race winner Alvaro Parente made a belated return to the series, and claimed second and third places on his first weekend back at Spa, while Grosjean – who had appeared a title contender before his F1 call-up in 2009 – twice made the podium, in Belgium and Abu Dhabi, after making sporadic appearances with DAMS, initially replacing d'Ambrosio, then the injured Ho-Pin Tung.

Back injuries were a theme of the year, with Josef Kral coming off worst of all in an aerial accident reminiscent of Mark Webber's in Valencia. Thankfully, the young Czech was able to return in Abu Dhabi – and duly opened his points account.

With Razia making a strong start to the year, including a brace of sprint-race podiums in Barcelona and Istanbul, and a return to the top three at Yas Marina, Rapax held off Barwa Addax at the head of the teams' championship, with ART's strong finish earning it third overall.

While Maldonado and Perez will likely be gone – the Mexican having already been snapped up by Sauber for F1 in 2011, and the champion linked to both Williams and HRT – before the end of the season, GP2 will introduce its third iteration of Dallara-Renault and a revised field for its seventh year.

The new car, the GP2/11, is designed to both look and behave like its bigger F1 cousin, having adopted the latest set of aero rules operating in the top flight, with wider front and narrower rear wings. While outright performance is not the goal, the series' technical chiefs expect the new machine to be slightly faster than its predecessor, something the teams will discover when it debuts in the Asia Series.

In an effort to make the off-season competition more relevant, it will now use the same car as the main championship, having previously employed the original-specification Dallara, and feature *all* the same teams.

Thus Racing Engineering will embark on its first Asia Series, as will GP2 newcomers Carlin and Team AirAsia. Trevor Carlin's eponymous squad has been knocking on the door for some time and is added to the roster at the expense of Durango, which dropped out before the 2010 campaign got under way. AirAsia, however, is an intriguing addition, stemming from Lotus Racing boss Tony Fernandes's desire to expand his team's influence down the ladder. The British-based operation takes the place of DPR, which bows out after six seasons, but could go head to head with an ART team bolstered by the technical support of Proton owned Group Lotus.

Left: Sam Bird leads Jules Bianchi at Monza. The ART duo made the top five in the GP2 Series standings.

Right: iSport's Oliver Turvey improved as the year went on, climbing to sixth place in the final points.

Below right: Dani Clos claimed a maiden GP2 Series victory in Turkey. It should have been a 1-2 for Racing Engineering as rookie Christian Vietoris gave chase, until mechanical problems struck.

Below: Davide Valsecchi dominated the GP2 Asia Series, but did not return to the top of the main series podium until the action returned to Abu Dhabi.

Photos: GP2 Media Services

GP3 REVIEW by CRAIG LLEWELLYN

THREE: A MAGIC NUMBER?

THE all-new GP3 Series slotted seamlessly on to the Formula One bill alongside older brother GP2 and provided a champion already with links to the top flight, but whether the single-seater ladder needed another option for those with grand prix aspirations remained questionable.

Mexico's Esteban Gutierrez strolled to the inaugural title with F3 and GP2 front-runner ART Grand Prix, taking five wins, three pole positions and six fastest laps from the 16 races. Such was his cushion over nearest rival Robert Wickens that he could afford three non-scores in his final four outings. He wrapped up the crown with a maximum 13-point haul from the feature race at Monza, before failing to trouble the scorers as he attempted to bow out in style in the finale.

The brainchild of GP2 organiser Bruno Michel, GP3 was fast-tracked on to the F1 support bill with ten teams drawn from various backgrounds, including GP2, F3, Renault World Series and, in the case of Status Grand Prix, the top of the A1GP tree. Each squad was contracted to run three of the bespoke Renault-powered Dallaras at each round – a feat achieved everywhere but Hungary – and drew its talent from each of the obvious feeder series, although some drivers were clearly on board as much for their backing as for their ability.

Having failed to set the world alight in the F3 Euroseries, former FBMW Europe champion Gutierrez quickly stamped his authority on the new category and, having allowed lesser lights – including highly-rated ART team-mate Alexander Rossi – to steal a march on him at the Barcelona opener, rattled off four wins in the following four rounds to establish a points lead he would never lose.

Four of the Mexican's five wins came in the Saturday afternoon feature races, with only Hockenheim seeing him top the podium in Sunday's sprint outing. However, he also appeared on the podium in both races at the Circuit de Catalunya, in Silverstone's sprint and in the Hungaroring feature, making it all the more surprising when he failed to score at all.

Already on Sauber's books as test driver, Telmex backed Gutierrez has been retained for 2011, but his next move must surely be to GP2, although it remains to be seen whether that will be with ART or Telmex backed Barwa Addax.

Wickens ended the season as Gutierrez's nearest rival and, indeed, was the next most successful in terms of race wins, claiming three successes in the second half of the season. The Canadian struggled for reliability early on, however, posting four non-scores in the first four rounds and having to come from fourth on the leaderboard to eventually secure runner-up honours.

Having finally broken through in race one at Hockenheim, Wickens showed the sort of form that had made him a star in A1GP, and benefited from the close ties with Status Grand Prix, which had run him in the now-defunct nation-vs-nation series to produced a 53-point tally for the Swiss driver, putting him almost equi-distant between Wickens and Rossi, but fully 35 behind the new champion.

Three other drivers won races in the inaugural season. Rio Haryanto's Sunday success in Turkey helped him to fifth overall and, as the best placed of the four drivers to represent Manor Motorsport during the year, a test in the Virgin Racing F1 car. Wickens's team-mate, Daniel Morad, won the sprint race at Silverstone, opening the Status account, but struggled with poor fortune elsewhere, while Adrien Tambay belied his late entrance to the series by winning on his fourth start, at Spa.

Among those who went home empty-handed, Roberto Merhi – combining F3 and GP3 in a busy year – and Britons Dean Smith and James Jakes probably deserved better. Adrian Quaife-Hobbs, Felipe Guimaraes and Josef Newgarden appeared at the front from time to time, but had just a brace of podiums between them, while former F3 and A1GP front-runner Renger van der Zande was strangely muted, appearing just once in the top three while leading the RSC Mücke Motorsport attack. The Dutchman's team-mate, Nigel Melker, opened the year with back-to-back poles, but they were his only scores, while Newgarden, Muller and visiting F3 Euroseries regular Daniel Juncadella also topped qualifying.

In all, 27 drivers scored at least a point during the season, and eventual British F3 champion Jean-Eric Vergne, who turned out in rounds one and three, hinted that he could have been a force before he opted to concentrate on other commitments, landing an F1 test with Toro Rosso at the end of the season.

The general inexperience of the field often resulted in accidents and penalties, but on the whole the racing was entertaining, the upshot of an underpowered car that allowed those behind to remain in touch with the man they were chasing. Not only did the car lack grunt in its output, but it also struggled aurally. However, it was the copious amounts of grip produced by its GP2-style ground-effect technology that helped cast doubt over GP3's value to the single-seater ladder.

With the similarly grip-over-power afflicted F3 already long-established – and F2, AutoGP and WSbR all cluttering the space behind GP2 – GP3's arrival had a direct affect on numbers, in the F3 Euroseries in particular. The cost of a season is similar, although less than competing in F2, but its first year was a solid one, once early gremlins had been eradicated. With both Mark Webber and Ralf Schumacher lending their names to teams – tying up with Arden and Mücke respectively – it has the backing to go far.

win again at Spa and Monza. The Belgian success also highlighted a different aspect of his racecraft as, having moved to the front in a typically time-consuming Ardennes downpour, the Canadian backed up the field as the safety car withdrew, running the clock down to avoid having to complete another, potentially ruinous, lap.

Although Rossi won the second outing in Barcelona, it was Norwegian Pal Varhaug who had the honour of taking the first ever victory in GP3. The Jenzer Motorsport driver faded thereafter, however, failing to add to the ten points he accrued in Spain and finishing a distant 13th overall.

Rossi was more successful, adding another sprint race win in Hungary, but the American would still only finish fourth in the standings after Varhaug's Jenzer team-mate, Nico Muller, put together a stronger run-in, including a feature-race victory in Hungary to go with his earlier sprint success in Valencia. Two further podium finishes in the final couple of double-headers

Above: Robert Wickens survived a brush with the wall to take a clever victory behind the pace car at Spa in the feature race.

Top left: Esteban Gutierrez won five times en route to claiming the inaugural GP3 series title with ART Grand Prix.

Left: The young Mexican looks to have a strong future having already been a part of Sauber's F1 squad for a year

Photos: GP3 Media

ALESHIN PROVES HIS POINT

WORLD SERIES BY RENAULT REVIEW by OLLIE BARSTOW

Russia's Mikhail Aleshin celebrated victory in the World Series by Renault opener at Motorland Aragon; he would celebrate again when he took the title in the final round in Spain.

Inset above: Catching and passing rival Daniel Ricciardo at Barcelona was key to Aleshin claiming the crown.
Photos: World Series by Renault

Below: Esteban Guerrieri *(left)* appeared unstoppable at Silverstone – as elsewhere in 2010 – but a race-one exclusion for a rogue piece of tape denied him a double win and, ultimately, a shot at the title. He made his displeasure known as he celebrated victory on the race-two podium.
Photo: World Series by Renault

AS far as title deciders go, the final act of the 2010 Formula Renault 3.5 Series could not have offered a more tantalising script. The scenario: two drivers going head to head in a 22-lap sprint to the title. The protagonists: Mikhail Aleshin, a seasoned contender with a point to prove, and Daniel Ricciardo, a young up-and-comer tipped for superstardom. The plot: whichever driver finishes ahead of the other takes the spoils. The twist: the balancing act of treacherous weather conditions.

Appropriately enough, the race, held around the Circuit de Catalunya, was befitting of its billing, culminating in the title being decided just corners from the chequered flag.

As the drivers tip-toed around the opening bends, feeling their way on the slippery surface, initially it was advantage Ricciardo, while Aleshin trailed in fourth. The pair would emerge nose-to-tail in the former's favour, however, following the pit stops, Aleshin unlucky not to leapfrog his rival when he misjudged his entry into the box.

Just to throw another curve ball into proceedings, Aleshin made things particularly difficult for himself when he ran on at La Caixa with fewer than ten laps remaining, losing four seconds to his rival. Nonetheless, he put his head down, rose to the occasion and swiftly made up the margin to set up an enthralling head-to-head with just two laps remaining.

With momentum on his side, Aleshin stalked Ricciardo, who was struggling for grip in his Tech 1 car, and when the Australian wobbled on the exit of Campsa, the Russian pounced, found the traction and completed the decisive move of the season.

A determined Ricciardo did attempt to respond on the final lap, but instead spun out of the penultimate bend, Aleshin subsequently crossing the line as the new champion just as his defeated rival – the favourite pre-season – clumsily turned himself around.

It was the exciting culmination of a tale that had been played out over several months, because while Aleshin and Ricciardo would head into the cliff hanger of a final race exactly as they had started their 2010 story – on level pegging – it remained a season of twists and turns for the championship's key players.

Indeed, Aleshin and Ricciardo approached the 2010 FR3.5 campaign from very different angles, the former attempting his fourth season in this category after a moderately successful, but brief, foray to Formula 2 in 2009, while the latter was continuing his rapid rise up the motorsport ladder following his dominant British Formula 3 title win.

To put it into context: when Ricciardo was just starting out competing in the Formula BMW Asia series back in 2006, Aleshin was embarking on his first season of Formula Renault 3.5 racing.

With Red Bull engineering his carefully plotted career path, he was placed at former champion Tech 1 Racing alongside another of the Austrian drinks company's favoured sons, Brendon Hartley.

Aleshin, meanwhile, returned to Carlin Motorsport, the team with whom he'd spent three seasons between 2006 and 2008 – ironically also under Red Bull's guidance – with only one win to show for it. His team-mate would be American Jake Rosenzweig.

As one of the most respected rungs on the motorsport ladder for the next 'Sebastian Vettel' and 'Robert Kubica', the 2010 grid was brimming with precocious young talent.

At Draco, winner in 2009 with Bertrand Baguette, Nathanael Berthon was one of several rookies making their debut, together with former Formula Renault 2.0 Eurocup rival and champion Albert Costa, who stuck with Epsilon Euskadi. Other notables included Esteban Guerrieri with ISR; Stefano Coletti and Greg Mansell, son of Nigel, at Comtec; Italian F3 champion Daniele Zampieri at Pons; FR3.5 race winner Jon Lancaster at Fortec; as well as British F3 runner-up Walter Grubmuller and sports car ace Jan Charouz at 2008 winner P1 Motorsport.

The winter also brought a few team changes, too, with ISR joining the series, while KMP split from SG Formula to enter its own outfit under the Russian flag, and Mofaz was rebranded Junior Team Lotus in a nod to the newly formed F1 team.

The regulations would receive their own tweaks for the new season as well, with a qualifying session for each race to replace the reverse-grid format, while the first race of a weekend would see the cars set up in low-aero configuration in an effort to prompt more overtaking.

Having played host to the season finale in 2009, Motorland Aragon was granted the opportunity to raise the curtain for 2010, and while Ricciardo caused the first cut with pole position for the opener, it was fellow front-row sitter Aleshin who drew the blood when he out-dragged his rival to lead into the opening bend, a move that – unbeknown to them at the time –ultimately would decide the title just metres into the season.

Indeed, Aleshin went on to victory – only his second in 51 FR3.5 starts – while Ricciardo had to make do with third after an attempt to pass instead dropped him behind Zampieri.

Nonetheless, Ricciardo seized the initiative in race two with another podium place, while Aleshin finished outside the points in 11th position, leaving the Australian in charge heading to the second round at Spa-Francorchamps.

It was Ricciardo's turn to hit problems in Belgium as he limped to a 13th-place finish in the opening race, while Aleshin steadied some nerves with a second win in three races after fending off both Hartley and a fever that had dogged him throughout the weekend. It was an important psychological boost for Aleshin, who also won the opening round of the 2007 season, only to fail to live up to early expectations.

A fourth- and fifth-place finish for the pair in favour of Aleshin, during the weather disrupted race two, kept things fairly even in the standings heading to the blue-riband fifth round, held around the streets of Monaco. The jewel in the FR3.5 crown, victory here can be considered a minor title win in itself, but the race was of particular importance to Ricciardo, who was racing under the noses – and scrutiny – of the Red Bull bosses.

Ricciardo rose to the challenge, though, first securing a crucial third pole of the season before cruising to a stylish maiden FR3.5 victory. If his Red Bull mentors expected nothing less than a win, certainly they were given perfection with it.

The win, though faultless, earned Ricciardo minor rewards in the standings, as Aleshin followed him home in second, the latter staying ahead by seven points with already a third of the season completed.

Not that the title battle had been reduced to a strict head-to-head, with Sten Pentus and Guerrieri each registering victories of their own during the opening events.

Guerrieri's start to the season had been far from plain sailing, the Argentine – a mainstay of the European racing scene since 2003 – securing a rolling contract with ISR for 2010. Two retirements during the Aragon opener signalled a dismal beginning for Guerrieri, as did an accident during qualifying at Spa-Francorchamps that ruled him out of the first race.

He struck back with a dominant victory in the

Right: Despite an interrupted season, Argentina's Esteban Guerrieri showed his class with six race wins; he was a title contender until the final round in Barcelona.

Bottom: Reigning British F3 champion Daniel Ricciardo claimed four race wins on his way to a close second in the standings.

Below: Albert Costa bounced back from pre-season injury to end the campaign fifth overall.

Photos: World Series by Renault

sodden second race after capitalising on ten drivers – including the top three of Rosenzweig, Zampieri and Ricciardo – being given penalties for changing their tyres after the deadline. However, it wasn't enough for potential sponsors to cough up, Guerrieri being forced to withdraw from the following Monaco round.

Such an injustice would be the first of several misdemeanours that would afflict Guerrieri, who showed exactly what he was capable of during round four at Brno, when he took a crushing double victory. It was a dominant event for the Czech-based ISR team, Filip Salaquarda – son of team owner Igor Salaquarda – starting both races from pole, although it was team-mate Guerrieri who would prevail when it mattered.

With indifferent races for Aleshin and Ricciardo – who could only manage a single ninth and fifth respectively between them – Guerrieri suddenly found himself launched into a title fight that had seemed very unlikely two weeks earlier when he was standing on the sidelines.

Moving on to France for the fifth round of the season at Magny-Cours, Aleshin regained his momentum with a hard-fought win after overhauling the in-form Guerrieri for a third victory of the season.

Sixth in the first race, Ricciardo regained some of his composure with a confident run to second place in race two. It could have been a win, Ricciardo leading comfortably in the damp conditions, only to be handed a drive-through penalty for having changed his tyres after the allotted deadline.

It prompted an entertaining charge by Ricciardo as he fought his way back to the front, even capitalising on a late shower that forced several drivers – including Aleshin – off the circuit to move into second place. However, he would run out of laps to hunt down Berthon, who became another new winner with a fine maiden victory on home soil for Draco. Berthon would prove one of the year's finds, the Frenchman outpacing his more experienced team-mate, Julian Leal, to challenge for the podium frequently.

Following his trip across the gravel trap, Aleshin recovered to fourth to keep the series lead pegged at ten points over Ricciardo, while Guerrieri was seven points further back.

A trip to Hungary for the sixth round at the Hungaroring awaited the trio next, although only Aleshin and Ricciardo would reach the start line after Guerrieri's ISR team was forced to withdraw from the event when it found cracks in its chassis. With no chance to conduct repairs, ISR opted for the safe option by pulling both Guerrieri and Salaquarda out.

Guerrieri's rivals duly took advantage, Ricciardo dominating the opening race around the tight and twisty Budapest circuit to win from lights to flag, while Aleshin continued to keep him honest with a run to second position.

Race two shook things up somewhat for the protagonists, as fairly average qualifying efforts – Aleshin fifth, Ricciardo seventh – enabled Pentus to snatch the headlines with a second victory of the season from pole position. Aleshin finished third, with Ricciardo in sixth ensuring the former would head into the summer break with a 12-point advantage.

Returning to action two months later at Hockenheim, Ricciardo signalled his intentions to

claw back ground on Aleshin with a victory in the opening race, but a drive-through penalty for speeding in the pit lane cost him the chance to build on that in the second encounter. Indeed, with Aleshin only managing a modest fifth and fourth himself, it was a missed opportunity for Ricciardo.

Now separated by eight points in Aleshin's favour, with just two rounds and four races remaining, Ricciardo was given another chance to put pressure on his rival after the former – the master of consistency up to that point – endured an unusually out-of-character performance at Silverstone, the Russian managing just a sixth and 11th-place finish on Carlin's home ground.

In Ricciardo's defence, his first retirement of the season in race one was not of his own doing, the Australian retiring spectacularly when Lancaster's attempts to defend his line off the grid instead tipped Ricciardo into series of brutal barrel rolls down the home straight. While Ricciardo was unhurt, the same couldn't be said for his burgeoning title hopes.

As average as his performance had been at Silverstone, Aleshin remarkably caught another break in the same race when Guerrieri was disqualified from victory in bizarre circumstances.

A win and second place at Hockenheim had put Guerrieri into outside title contention once again, a status he would go on to strengthen with a win from pole position at Silverstone. However, word would filter through that he had been excluded when it was discovered that tape had been used to secure a piece of the bodywork on his car following a smash in qualifying. Although not performance enhancing, it flouted the regulations and forced officials to take the win – and 15 points – away from him.

The error may have been spotted had team manager Salaquarda not been barred from the pit lane as a punishment for an earlier altercation with Zampieri, one that also prevented the Italian from starting the first race. For Guerrieri, it was merely the latest blow in a season of setbacks, although this in particular would prove especially detrimental once the season was over…

Later it would transpire that the protest had come from the Tech 1 team, who duly benefited when Jean-Eric Vergne was upped to a belated first place. The Frenchman – Ricciardo's recently crowned successor as British Formula 3 champion in 2010 – was competing in only his third FR3.5 race after being promoted by Red Bull to replace Hartley, the Kiwi's failure to win during the first half of the season being met with a firm boot from the company's young-driver programme and therefore his Tech 1 drive.

Guerrieri struck back with victory in race two, appropriately overtaking Ricciardo on the final lap to take yet another win – his fifth of the season. Ricciardo could also be pleased with his fight back following the acrobatics of the opening encounter, not least because it kept him within three points of Aleshin with just two races remaining.

And so attentions turned to the showdown, Ricciardo closer to Aleshin than he had been since losing the series lead at Spa. Things were about to get closer, though, when Ricciardo stormed to victory from pole position in race one, but while Aleshin had no answer to his rival's pace, his second-place finish kept things perfectly even with just one race to go.

The scene was set for an exciting 'winner takes all' battle, the spoils finally going to Aleshin, the 23-year-old keeping his cool in the rain to catch and pass Ricciardo late on, bringing a thrilling conclusion to a thrilling season.

Up ahead, Guerrieri was completing a sixth win of the season to end it 15 points adrift of the series lead. A sobering thought for both Aleshin and Ricciardo was that had Guerrieri kept his win at Silverstone, or started in Hungary or Monaco, then most likely he would have been crowned champion.

Elsewhere, Pentus's two race wins earned him an excellent fourth in the standings for Fortec, ahead of top rookie competitor Costa. The Spaniard failed to win a race for Epsilon Euskadi, but his three podiums and fifth overall signals him as a star in waiting.

Coletti was another prolific podium winner in 2010 without actually completing a race win, although the Monegasque driver could be pleased with his confident progression from Formula 3 in sixth overall, ahead of Berthon and, remarkably, Vergne, the rising star's four podiums in just six races lifting him to eighth in the standings. Appropriately enough, it placed him just ahead of the man he replaced, Hartley, who retained tenth and was instrumental in Tech 1 winning the teams' title for the second time. He finished just adrift of Zampieri, whose score sheet included two podiums, but also three exclusions.

Outside the top ten, Salaquarda claimed a podium on home soil at Brno on the way to 11th overall, ahead of Nelson Panciatici, who had a solid rookie season as the top representative for Junior Team Lotus. Pre-season title contender Lancaster was a disappointing 13th after a fraught year in the second Fortec car, ahead of Anton Nebylitskiy and Mansell.

Turning attentions to 2011, the FR3.5 continues to go from strength to strength as a prominent breeding ground. A 13th team will join in the form of Italian outfit BVM Target, while the series will be brought further into line with Formula One with the adoption of its points system.

As for Aleshin, Ricciardo and Guerrieri, justice should ensure that their stories continue onwards and upwards in 2011 – if for no other reason than to reward them for keeping us on the edge of our seats all year.

STONEMAN ROLLS TO VICTORY

FORMULA 2 REVIEW by OLLIE BARSTOW

FOLLOWING a successful return to the motorsport fraternity in 2009, the FIA Formula 2 Championship continued into 2010 looking to build on the solid foundation it had established during its comeback year.

Revived after an absence of 25 years under the stewardship of former F1 driver Jonathan Palmer, F2 2009 proved the esteemed moniker still had a place in the motorsport hierarchy with the decision to supply the package directly to drivers – rather than teams – doing a fine job of maintaining a level playing field by rewarding driver skill over team ability.

With Williams F1 supplying the chassis, as well as the opportunity to test its F1 challenger as a prize for winning championship, the re-imagined series attracted a strong calibre of racer in 2009 title winner Andy Soucek, as well as vice-champions Robert Wickens and Mikhail Aleshin.

However, having attempted to provide a reputable alternative to the likes of GP2, Formula Renault 3.5 and Formula 3, F2 received another significant rival in the form of GP3 2010, which offered a similar package with the emphasis of competitive racing on a budget.

Its arrival had a direct effect on F2 in 2010, luring away the likes of Wickens, Mirko Bortolotti and Tobias Hegewald – all front-runners in 2009 – as well as intercepting a number of drivers graduating from F3 or Formula Renault.

As a consequence, grid numbers were down in 2010, although the series retained its reputation as a competitive breeding ground for those who did submit an entry.

Among those returning for a second crack at the title were Kazim Vasiliauskas, Philipp Eng, Nicola de Marco and Jolyon Palmer – son of series organiser Jonathan Palmer – while notable debutants included Dean Stoneman from Formula Renault UK, Sergey Afanasiev from the cancelled International Formula Master series and Will Bratt from the also defunct Formula 3000 Euroseries.

With a nine-round calendar once again dictated by its supporting role to the World Touring Car Championship, Formula 2 did at least get the opportunity to steal the spotlight for its opener with a stand-alone event held at Silverstone.

A total of 22 drivers would raise the curtain on the 2010 season, with – appropriately enough – early honours going to Palmer, who became the first British driver to win an F2 race since 1983. It is also worth noting that the man he succeeded for this role was none other than his father, Jonathan.

Following it up with a run to second position in the second race, behind Eng, Palmer – who had scored just once during 2009 with a run to sixth at Imola – came away from the opening round with the initial lead in the standings.

A trip to Morocco and the high-speed street circuit in Marrakech provided a unique challenge for the field ahead of race two, with nearly every driver experiencing some kind of drama at the walled venue.

Indeed, Palmer's retirement from second position in race one – and unspectacular fifth from race two – duly handed Eng the lead in the standings, the Austrian firming his status as a title favourite with a 1-2 finish. His results were matched by Stoneman, who kept the British flag flying with a maiden victory during the opening race to also move ahead of Palmer in the standings.

A trip to the equally high-speed, but significantly less-confined Monza would see Palmer produce a career defining weekend, in which he scored double victory from double pole position.

It was an almost perfect performance, although Palmer benefited from a stroke of luck in the first race when early leader Johan Jokinen was handed a drive-through penalty for an infringement on the grid. Nonetheless, he displayed his mettle by keeping a charging Stoneman behind him, the British duo crossing swords for the first time properly in what would become a two-way exchange for the crown.

Palmer went on to further his cause with a dominant performance in race two, enabling him to leap back to the head of the standings at the expense of Stoneman – who held firm in second – and Eng, whose fine start to the season was brought to a sudden halt by two failures to score in Italy. Bratt and

Above and left: Dean Stoneman pressed his championship challenge to perfection.

Below: That's my boy! Jonathan Palmer applauds as his son Jolyon takes the plaudids after his win at Silverstone.

Photos: LAT Photographic

Afanasiev kept a watching brief in fourth and fifth, although evidence suggested that with a third of the season already completed, the championship battle would go one of three ways.

In fact, the following event at Zolder would all but reduce the trio to a mere duo, after Eng suffered another disastrous event, finishing outside the points in both races, whereas Palmer and Stoneman resumed their battle up front.

This time, it was Stoneman who would take the honours with a commanding race-one victory, although Palmer kept him honest with a run to second from fifth on the grid, before reducing the margin again by beating his countryman to second in race two. Victory, meanwhile, went the way of local favourite Benjamin Bailly, the 20-year-old scoring his first international race win from pole position.

With Stoneman breathing down his neck in the standings, Palmer upped the pressure at Portimao with a well-timed fourth win of the season, the youngster resisting the attentions of the in-form Bailly and also Jack Clarke, who in turn broke his F2 podium duck on his 25th start. Even better for Palmer, Stoneman failed to score after he was robustly elbowed off the track during a dispute for tarmac with Eng, the 'Silver Lining' backed driver only able to recover to 11th.

Nonetheless, Stoneman responded in supreme fashion during race two with a third victory of the season, although with Palmer is second position, it was he who held an advantage of 26 points as the drivers entered the latter half of the season.

A return to Brands Hatch would see the next phase of the title battle played out on home turf, both drivers eager to claim bragging rights in front of the British fans. Appropriately enough, it was here where the championship pendulum would begin to swing back in favour of Stoneman, who cruised to victory in race one while Palmer lumbered to an eighth-place finish – a result that lost him 21 points in the process.

A pivotal moment in the championship battle occurred during race two, when Stoneman and Palmer collided while disputing third, the former's attempt to pass at Paddock Hill Bend resulting in Palmer crashing out. Although Stoneman's eventual podium would see him inherit the series lead, a post-race penalty would drop him down to 12th and therefore ensure that Palmer retained a five-point advantage. Erstwhile title contender Eng claimed his third win of the season to end a run of poor form, while Tom Gladdis, Jack Clarke and Will Bratt would also enjoy home podium success at Brands Hatch.

With the end of the season approaching and tempers flaring after their Brands Hatch collision, Palmer and Stoneman continued their battle at Brno, the latter snatching the lead after the first race with a run to second, before Palmer took it back by winning race two.

A visit to Oschersleben formed the basis of the penultimate round, the German event proving the pivotal moment of the season as Stoneman delivered a dominant performance that would not only help him secure the championship lead, but also put him almost out of reach with just one round remaining.

Indeed, after stamping his authority on proceedings with a 15-second win in the treacherous weather conditions of race one, Stoneman followed it up with victory in the second race to complete a perfect 50 points haul at a crucial moment. By contrast, Palmer could only manage a third in race one, before a poor qualifying position – coupled with Oschersleben's minimal overtaking opportunities – consigned him to a lowly 12th in race two. That meant Palmer – having begun the weekend with a four-point lead – would leave Germany 31 points behind.

It also meant that Stoneman merely needed to keep an eye on the top ten at the Valencia finale to confirm the inevitable. Indeed, while his runs to ninth and third were hardly a vintage way to seal a title, they were more than enough to keep Palmer at bay and claim the first international crown of his burgeoning career.

A disappointing end to the season would see Palmer finish an unrepresentative 42 points adrift in the final standings, although the fact that he commanded an almost three-figure advantage over third was indicative of his and Stoneman's dominance over the year. Indeed, the final event in Spain was the first – and only – of the year that wouldn't see either driver on the top step of the podium, the honours going instead to de Marco, who was also a winner at Brno, and Vasiliauskas, who literally bounced back from a race-one overturn to claim the final win of the season.

In the overall standings, Afanasiev capitalised on a consistent score sheet of finishing each of the final seven races inside the top five to confirm third position, just ahead of Lithuanian Vasiliauskas, who posted six podiums, but four DNFs on the way to fourth place.

A pre-season favourite, Bratt ended his maiden F2 campaign with fifth position after claiming four podiums, his strong finishing record enabling him to edge out race winners Eng – who never recovered from a mid-season lull – Bailly and de Marco in sixth, seventh and eighth respectively.

With season two completed, attentions now turn to 2011, with series organisers already announcing a raft of changes that will see its support slot with the WTCC dropped in favour of an F1 inspired calendar, while the budget for the package will be reduced to £225,000. Intended to bulk up a grid that, while entertaining, lacked the big names – and sponsors – that made the inaugural season such a success, F2 2010 still offered proof that there is most certainly a place for its unique concept on the motorsport ladder.

FORMULA 3 REVIEW by CRAIG LLEWELLYN

MORTARA PAINTS NEW PICTURE

Right: Edoardo Mortara stepped back to F3 and claimed the 2010 Euroseries title for Signature.

Far right: Mortara claimed five straight feature race wins, including here at Norisring, to secure the F3 Euroseries crown.
Photos: F3 Euroseries

Below: Signature team mate Marco Wittmann showed the inate strength of Signature – and the Volkswagen engine – in taking second place overall behind Mortara.
Photo: Jakob Ebrey/LAT Photgraphic

STEPPING back in an attempt to go forward can often be a tricky and dangerous move, but Edoardo Mortara accomplished the move with ease as he brought to an end the ART era in F3's Euroseries.

In the other major F3 competition, meanwhile, Frenchman Jean-Eric Vergne exhibited a similar level of dominance as he wrapped up the British title in his first year in the category.

After enduring a trying season in GP2 in 2009, Italian Mortara was helped in his brave decision by Volkswagen's desire to have a proven front-runner leading its assault on the Euroseries. Having already reverted to F3 and triumphed in Macau at the end of last season, 'Edo' was persuaded to stay with the Signature team, knowing that a good season could help rebuild a battered reputation.

He had little to fear from F3, having finished as runner-up to Nico Hülkenberg in 2008 with the then fledgling Signature-VW combination, and started the year as he meant to go on, winning the opening skirmish at Paul Ricard and finishing second in the sprint race that followed. Then Hockenheim brought a brace of podium finishes, before Mortara embarked on a run of five straight weekends when he claimed victory in the higher-scoring feature race.

The wins at Valencia, Norisring, Nürburgring and Zandvoort were all accomplished from pole, which provided valuable bonus points, while that at Brands Hatch combined with a season ending success back at Hockenheim to sandwich his worst weekend of the year, at Oschersleben.

The five-meeting run of feature-race success effectively broke the back of the opposition, led by Signature team-mate Marco Wittmann, with Mortara's first non-score – the result of a collision with the German – not coming until Zandvoort in August. Admittedly, he followed that up by not adding to his tally in the three sprint races that followed, courtesy of two more early collisions and a disqualification, but the damage was already done, with the title, ironically, wrapped up at Oschersleben.

Wittmann, in his second season in the Euroseries, confirmed Signature and VW's emergence as the combination to beat by claiming second overall, ahead of the two ART drivers expected to lead the championship charge.

Although he closed to within a point of Mortara after round two, where he took his only win of the year, a pointless trip to Valencia severely dented Wittmann's ambitions, although consistent scoring thereafter – including seven podiums – kept him out of the clutches of pre-season favourite Valtteri Bottas.

Buoyed by a deal to become Williams's F1 test driver, the Finn was tipped to lead ART Grand Prix to a sixth straight championship title, but he never really recovered from two poor opening rounds, which yielded only nine points. Although subsequently he took wins in the Norisring sprint and Oschersleben feature, there was too much ground for Bottas to make up, and even a second successive non-championship Masters victory at Zandvoort couldn't soften the blow.

Bottas had to overcome new ART team-mate Alexander Sims to wind up third overall, the Briton having opened the season with victory in the Paul Ricard sprint race after switching from Mücke Motorsport over the winter. Only three further podiums went Sims's way, however, blighting his challenge.

The remaining race wins were spread between Roberto Merhi, Daniel Juncadella, Jim Pla, Kevin Magnussen and Antonio Felix da Costa, who equalled Christian Klien's record of three successes en route to claiming the rookie-of-the-year title. Along with Laurens Vanthoor, each could lay claim to a front running role in 2011, although again the Euroseries looks set to face competition for numbers from GP3.

The British series followed a familiar theme as Carlin and Red Bull combined to put a rookie into the champion's seat for the third year in succession.

Having taken Jaime Alguersuari and Daniel Ricciardo to the crown in 2008 and 2009 respectively, the renowned talent spotters plucked Vergne from a successful season in Formula Renault and gave him the tools – including the potent VW engine used by Mortara – to get the job done.

Like Mortara, Vergne started strongly, winning

two of the three opening weekend races on a new-look British schedule that called for a short sprint, with semi-reversed grid – and from mid-season, pit-stops – between rounds of 30 and 40 minutes respectively. With the longer races' grids determined by qualifying, the Frenchman's immediate speed – also demonstrated in World Series by Renault testing over the winter – stood him in good stead.

Although he had to settle for a single podium in round two at Silverstone, Vergne was back on top of the sprint-race podium on home soil at Magny-Cours and, from there, it was unusual to see the Carlin driver outside the top three as he recorded ten victories in the rounds leading up to the Brands Hatch finale. He backed them up with five seconds and a third, only the reverse-grid sprints at Hockenheim, Rockingham and Snetterton spoiling the run.

By the time the series visited Norfolk, however, it mattered little, for Vergne's run had already secured the crown. With his mind perhaps on other things – having already won for the first time in the World Series by Renault – the Frenchman ended his season on a low note, recording his only DNF after a trip into the gravel during the final race at Brands, but his winning margin was still an impressive 99 points.

Second overall was disputed throughout the season by the two leading British contenders, before James Calado came out ahead of Oli Webb. The success ensured that Carlin claimed another 1-2 in the championship standings, as its man added another five race wins to the tally.

Although the first two came on Vergne's off-days at Silverstone, Racing Steps Foundation backed Calado twice beat the Frenchman in a straight fight – at Thruxton and Snetterton – before rounding out the year with victory in the finale at Brands Hatch.

A long way ahead of his fellow Briton through the opening five triple-headers, Webb faltered at Spa, and the gap between them narrowed to a single point next time out at Thruxton. Then two poor results at Silverstone saw the tables turned on the Fortec driver, as Calado eased ahead, and the gap kept increasing to the end, despite Webb taking race-one victory at Brands Hatch.

Such were Webb's results towards the end of the season that fourth-placed Adriano Buzaid finished just 12 points adrift in the final standings. The Brazilian, racing with Carlin, started slowly, but came on strong as the year progressed, returning to the top step at Silverstone and Snetterton amid a run of seven straight podiums, as he opened out a gap to those behind him in the points race.

The remaining wins went the way of Hitech's Gabriel Dias, who took three sprint races; reigning National Class champion Daniel McKenzie, who triumphed twice in reverse-grid affairs for Fortec; FBMW graduate Felipe Nasr (Räikkönen Robertson Racing); and the unheralded Rupert Svendsen-Cook, who claimed the first ever sprint for Carlin at Oulton Park. Of these, Nasr wound up best placed in the standings, claiming fifth overall, with Dias, Svendsen-Cook and McKenzie in sixth, seventh and ninth respectively. Hitech's William Buller and RRR's Carlos Huertas completed the top ten.

The National Class was, for the most part, a two-horse race between T-Sport's Menasheh Idafar and FFord champion James Cole, which ultimately went the way of the former on account of his 18 wins to Cole's 11. Idafar ended the season with seven straight successes, including a stunning third place overall in the wet Brands Hatch finale. For the record, Juan Carlos Sistos picked up the one win not claimed by the T-Sport duo, triumphing for Motul Team West-Tec at Silverstone in August.

Having given Finland its first Masters title in 2009, Bottas returned to Zandvoort to repeat the feat in 2010. At the time of his success, he still hadn't broken through to the top step in the Euroseries, but the victory, from pole, in the first of the year's stand-alone 'classics' at least helped propel him to two wins later in the year.

Second again in qualifying, Bottas nonetheless overcame ART team-mate Sims in a race that started behind the safety car due to rain, but was made to wait as Merhi – one of the few to change to wets on the grid – moved from fourth to lead briefly. Once in front, though, the slick shod Bottas made the most of drying conditions to give ART a seventh consecutive Masters crown. Sims and Wittmann completed the podium, with Vergne claiming a creditable fourth for the British series, ahead of Mortara.

With only the Sud-Am title still to be decided as *AUTOCOURSE* went to press, a host of new names were crowned as champions of the respective national series.

Yuji Kunimoto succeeded GP2 graduate Marcus Ericsson as All-Japan F3 champion after a dominant campaign that saw him open with ten straight wins. Strangely, he failed to top the podium after that, but still emerged with a 58-point advantage as Petronas Team TOM's continued its stranglehold on the series.

Team-mate Rafael Suzuki claimed the next three races to take the team's run to 13 wins, before Hideki Yamauchi (Hanashima Racing) and Koki Saga (Denso Team Le Beausset) rounded out the year with a victory apiece. Second overall, however, went to the winless Yuhi Sekiguchi (ThreeBond Racing) on the basis of 11 podium appearances in 16 races. The National Class was a far closer affair, with HFDP Racing's Takashi Kobayashi edging to a three-point win over TOM'S Spirit's Naoya Gamou.

The battle for the three places warranting a Ferrari F1 test ensured that F3 Italia went to the wire, before eventually being settled in favour of Cesar Ramos. The Brazilian interloper claimed victory in the very last race at Monza to ensure that he came out on top of a three-way scrap with Monegasque Stephane Richelmi and Italian Andrea Caldarelli, with Daniel Mancinelli keeping a watching brief should he be able to slip into one of the top three spots.

Richelmi actually claimed more wins than anyone, taking four to the three each of Caldarelli, Ramos and Sergio Campana, but the Brazilian underpinned his title with five podiums in the first six races, allowing the BVM-Target driver to withstand the better results of his rivals later on. With the title on the line, Ramos came good again in the finale to top a table containing 42 names, among them rookie champion Gaby Chaves, who finished tenth overall for Eurointernational.

Already an F3 veteran at 21, Tom Dillmann finally claimed a title when he beat off the challenge of Daniel Abt and Kevin Magnussen for the ATS Formel 3 Cup in Germany. The Frenchman, driving for HS Technik Motorsport, took six wins during the year and claimed the crown by chasing closest rival Abt across the line at the Oschersleben finale. Abt, the son of touring car expert Christian, had the weight of multiple champion van Amersfoort Racing behind him and won twice, but ultimately came up eight points short of the title.

Bizarrely, Abt also finished second in the rookie championship, behind Magnussen, who finished third overall in the main competition. The Dane, son of ex-F1 and sports car ace Jan Magnussen, won three times, with the remaining victories going to Step Dusseldorp, Felix Rosenqvist, Jimmy Eriksson, Willi Steindl and Nico Monien.

Britain's Ben Barker came out on top of perhaps the closest title race of them all, requiring the bonus point for fastest lap in the season finale at Sandown to claim the Australian Championship. The FFord graduate, in only his second season of single-seater racing, went into the final triple-header with an eight-point advantage after winning six of the previous nine races, but was fortunate that race two at Sandown was axed after an accident and that his rebuilt Team BRM Dallara was 0.05 second faster than team-mate, and main rival, Mitch Evans's when it mattered. Tom Tweedie finished third overall, 12 points back, but retained his National Class title.

World Series by Renault refugee Marco Barba put his experience to good use in claiming the second Euro F3 Open crown for the Cedars team after a second long battle with Motul Team West-Tec's Callum Macleod and RP Motorsport's Davide Fumanello, while Phillipe Chuard secured the Austrian Formel 3 Cup for his eponymous team. The only repeat winner in 2010 was Jani Tammi (Oakra F3 Motorsport), who triumphed in the Nordic F3 Masters a year on from claiming the NEZ Cup.

Meanwhile, F3 Sud-Americana Petrobras was set to go down to the final round at Interlagos, with Bruno Andrade looking to give Cesario Formula yet another title triumph. He was leading sole rival Yann Cuhna (Bassan Motorsport) by 29 points with one double-header to run.

Far left: Carlin and Red Bull combined to put a rookie Jean Eric Vergne into the champion's seat for the third year in succession.

Right: Oli Brown took took the fight to Carlin.
Photos: LAT Photographic

Above: Valtteri Bottas became the first driver to win the F3 Masters at Zandvoort twice, but still couldn't crack the Euroseries.
Photo: F3 Euroseries

Left: Yuji Kunimoto romped home as the Japanese F3 champion after a dominant campaign that saw him open with ten straight wins.
Photo: LAT Photographic

Below: Ben Barker maintained Britain's recent run of success 'down under' by claiming the 2010 Australian F3 title for Team BRM.

SPORTS & GT REVIEW by GARY WATKINS

CHANGING TIMES

Bulletproof Audi reliability paid dividends for Mike Rockenfeller, Timo Bernhard and Romain Dumas, who took victory with the LMP1 R15 in the Le Mans 24 Hours.
Photo: Drew Gibson/LAT Photographic

TDI
TDI
MAHLE
BOSCH

AUDI started the new decade at the Le Mans 24 Hours as it had begun the last: with a 1-2-3 victory. The result may have been the same, but that's where the similarities between the 2000 and 2010 events ended. The German manufacturer dominated at the start of the new century, but ten years on it got lucky. Its revised 'R15-plus' wasn't a match on speed for arch-rival Peugeot's well-proven 908, yet Audi ended up with a clean sweep of the podium positions after the French cars hit trouble.

Le Mans 2010 was decided on reliability. Audi won because it didn't have technical issues; of its three crews, Timo Bernhard, Mike Rockenfeller and Romain Dumas came out on top because their R15 TDI turbo-diesel had the cleanest run through the 24 hours. It was as simple as that.

The Peugeot 908 HDi had a bigger advantage in terms of lap time over the Audi than in 2009. There had been moments during that year when the best of the German cars appeared as though they would keep the 'Pugs' honest. This time, Audi seemed out of it almost from the get-go.

Peugeot topped the leaderboard for two-thirds of the race, and the 908 turbo-diesel driven by Franck Montagny, Stephane Sarrazin and Nicolas Minassian was nearly two laps to the good when the famous Le Mans clock ticked towards 7am on Sunday. Then smoke started billowing from the right-hand exhaust and Montagny was left head in hands at the side of the track.

The retirement of the leading Peugeot didn't mean the end of the manufacturer's challenge for a second straight victory at La Sarthe, even though the other three 908s had all run into problems earlier. The car Briton Anthony Davidson shared with Alex Wurz and Marc Gené had been delayed in the seventh hour with alternator failure. Yet such was the performance advantage of the 908 that this car was on the way to making up all three of the laps lost before it, too, went bang in the 21st hour.

The one remaining, semi-works 908, run by the French ORECA team, had lost four laps to driveshaft failure, but was still in the hunt for a podium when the engine problem struck in the 22nd hour. The other Peugeot, which Sébastien Bourdais had put on pole, was an early casualty, a wishbone mounting plate having pulled out of the monocoque during the second hour.

Peugeot's problems were centred on a new-specification con-rod, which failed on the three cars still running in the latter stages. The component had come through on-track race simulations and dyno testing without problems, but the pace of the 2010 Le Mans 24 Hours caught out the Peugeot Sport squad. So fast was the race that Audi broke the all-time distance record set by the Porsche 917 of Helmut Marko and Gijs van Lennep in 1971 on a much faster iteration of the Circuit de la Sarthe.

That wasn't the only bit of history made at Le Mans in 2010. Bernhard joined the elite band of drivers who have won the big three sports car classics, while Rockenfeller became the first man in more than 20 years to win 24-hour classics at Le Mans and Daytona in the same season.

Their Audi produced a near-faultless run: its only delay came when it needed a replacement wing

mirror, the result of a pit-lane encounter with an errant cameraman.

The second-placed R15, driven by Marcel Fassler, Benoît Treluyer and André Lotterer, lost contact with the Bernard/Dumas/Rockenfeller car in the ninth hour when Treluyer damaged the nose running over kerbs. Meanwhile, the Audi regarded as most likely to take the fight to the Peugeots, driven by the 2008 winning crew of Allan McNish, Tom Kristensen and Rinaldo Capello, dropped out of contention in the fifth hour.

Through no fault of his own, Kristensen collided with the GT2-class BMW M3 driven by Le Mans debutant Andy Priaulx. The loss of three laps to repairs left no way back for the Audi, which finished third and last of the R15s.

The promise of a level playing field between the diesels and petrol LMP1 prototypes proved empty. Rule tweaks designed to close the gap were overcome by the turbo-diesels' development, and then some.

ORECA's bid for victory with Peugeot may have come to nought, but its own Courage-based design powered by an AIM-badged Judd V10 came through to fourth as the first petrol-powered car in the hands of Andy Meyrick, Soheil Ayari and Didier André. Fifth place went to the best of the LMP2 prototypes, the British Strakka team's HPD ARX-01c.

The car that had started life as an Acura dominated the class in the hands of Danny Watts, Jonny Kane and team boss Nick Leventis. The expected challenge from the works backed HPD, run by Le Mans debutant Highcroft Racing, only briefly materialised.

The GT1 class withered and died at Le Mans in 2010. Race organiser the Automobile Club de l'Ouest announced on the Thursday before the race that these cars wouldn't be invited back in 2011. Victory in a class that once attracted mega-buck attacks from Chrysler, Chevrolet and Aston Martin went to a privately run car produced by a manufacturer that no longer exists. The Saleen S7R, entered by the French Larbre team, had a relatively trouble-free run in the hands of Julien Canal, Gabriele Gardel and Roland Berville to claim GT1 honours.

Porsche took victory in the ultra-competitive GT2 division, although its ageing 911 GT3-RSR wasn't the

Above: Top of the LMP2 class was the Nick Leventis/Danny Watts/Jonny Kane HPD ARX-01c of Strakka Racing, which finished fifth.
Photo: Drew Gibson/LAT Photographic

Above left: A kaleidoscope of lights for the Tom Kristensen/Rinaldo Capello/Allan McNish Audi Sport Team Joest car at Le Mans.
Photo: Jeff Bloxham/LAT Photographic

Top: Sarthe GT honours went to the Marc Lieb/Richard Lietz/Wolf Henzler Felbermayr-Proton Porsche 911 GT3-RSR.
Photo: Alastair Staley/LAT Photographic

fastest car. The Felbermayr-Proton entry, driven by Marc Lieb, Richard Lietz and Wolf Henzler, benefited from problems encountered by the Risi Competizione Ferrari and factory Chevrolet squads.

The GT2 division produced the best racing in the series that ran to Le Mans rules on both sides of the Atlantic. The American Le Mans Series may have lacked cars in the LMP1 and P2 classes, but the strength in depth in GT2 went some way toward making up for this shortfall. Ferrari, Porsche, Chevrolet and BMW went head to head, with Flying Lizards Porsche drivers Jörg Bergmeister and Patrick Long coming out on top in the drivers' standings, and BMW in the manufacturers' rankings.

Porsche also won in Europe, Lieb and Lietz doing the business with the Felbermayr-Proton squad. Their win in the season opening Paul Ricard Eight Hours unexpectedly gave them double points when the winning Audi passed the 1500km mark, giving them a massive head-start in the points. Their big rival, the AF Corse Ferrari 430 GT driven by Gianmaria Bruni and Jaime Melo, failed to score, which left no way back in a five-round championship.

Highcroft may have failed to achieve success at Le Mans, but it sealed a second straight ALMS crown. The prototype classes, P1 and P2, were combined in America because of the lack of entries, but David Brabham and Simon Pagenaud took three overall victories in their P2-spec HPD to seal the title.

The LMP1 drivers' title in Europe went to Sarrazin, whose points tally, garnered at the wheel of an ORECA Peugeot in four of the races and a works car at the Spa 1,000km, was more than enough to give him the crown. The P2 crown went to the British RML team, whose drivers Tommy Erdos and Mike Newton took a second title in four years.

A new initiative for 2010 was the introduction of the Intercontinental Le Mans Cup by the ACO. A mini-series of three end-of-season events was organised in preparation for a seven-race calendar, including the Le Mans 24 Hours, in 2012. The idea was to take the premier rounds of the series running to Le Mans rules in Europe and North America, and add a couple of Asian races.

Peugeot's victories at the final round of the LMS and ALMS, at Silverstone and Road Atlanta, put it well ahead in the manufacturers' points – there was no drivers' classification – before the finale at Zhuhai in China in November.

The ILMC quickly came to be regarded as the true successor to the world sports car series of 1953–92. That's something the new-for-2010 FIA GT1 World Championship wasn't, and the man behind the series made no bones about it.

Stephane Ratel had abandoned the endurance format of the FIA GT Championship in favour of a TV-friendly arrangement of two one-hour races. Full factory teams were banned, while the performance of the six car types that participated in the series was balanced by a committee headed by FIA technical consultant and former Lotus designer Peter Wright.

Inevitably, this so-called Balance of Performance, a more overt form of what had gone before in FIA GTs, was controversial, and the committee clearly didn't get it right for the series opener in Abu Dhabi. By a couple of races into the championship, however, the cries of foul had turned into nothing more than paddock grumblings.

Controversial or not, the BoP ensured some excellent racing in the new series. After five weekends of the championship, each of the six makes involved had tasted victory.

The Maserati MC12, one of three old-style GT1 cars 'grandfathered' in to compete against a new generation of machinery, once again had the edge. It wasn't always the most competitive car, but it was consistently competitive. That, combined with the famed reliability of the Vitaphone Racing squad, ensured that Michael Bartels and Andrea Bertolini were well ahead in the points as the championship headed off to the final two events in South America.

Class also told in Grand American's Rolex sponsored series. Chip Ganassi Racing duo Scott Pruett and Memo Rojas dominated, winning nine of the 12 events in their BMW-engined Riley to notch up a second title together in three years.

Ganassi again failed to win the season opening Daytona 24 Hours, victory going to the Riley-Porsche run by Brumos Racing under the Action Express banner. The participation of the likes of Rockenfeller once again proved the international appeal of the historic race, even if the schism in sports car racing ensured that it stood aloof from the global aspirations of the FIA and the ACO.

Above: Spa-Francorchamps in Belgium, with the Peugeot 908 of Montagny, Sarrazin and Minassian in control.
Photo: Jeff Bloxham/LAT Photographic

Left: The RML Lola HPD coupe of Tommy Erdos, Mike Newton and Andy Wallace at Paul Ricard.
Photo: Drew Gibson/LAT Photographic

Right: Highcroft Racing's Simon Pagenaud, Marino Franchitti and David Brabham celebrate overall victory in the ALMS round at Monterey, California.
Photo: Dan R Boyd/LAT Photographic

Far right: The Chip Ganassi BMW Riley of Scott Pruett and Memo Rojas was dominant in the GrandAm series.
Photo: LAT Photographic

PEUGEOT
TOTAL
2
P1
MICHELIN
PEUGEOT HDi FAP

RACEWAY
GUNA SECA
1ST PLACE
MONTEREY
LE MANS
presented by
TEQUILA
PATRÓN
TEQUILA
PATRÓN

SUNTRUST
10
BMW Power
TELMEX
01
DINAN

On his way to the BTCC title, Jason Plato, in his Chevrolet leads the pack up the hill towards Druids at Brands Hatch.
Photo: Malcolm Griffiths/LAT Photographic

TOURING CAR REVIEW by MATT SALISBURY

FOUR-ACT DRAMA

Above: The vastly experienced Yvan Muller, 2010 WTCC champion for Chevrolet.
Photo: Kevin Wood/LAT Photographic

Top right: Gordon Shedden works his BTCC Honda Civic through the chicane at Knockhill
Photo: Jakob Ebrey/LAT Photographic

Above right: Tom Onslow-Cole and Tom Chilton embrace at Donington.
Photo: Malcolm Griffiths/LAT Photographic

Right: Matt Neal took five wins in his Honda Racing Civic and, with team-mate Shedden, bagged the manufacturers' title.
Photo: Jakob Ebrey/LAT Photographic

ACTION, drama and controversy. If that's what you were looking for in 2010, then the world of touring cars was the place to be. As *AUTOCOURSE* closed for press, the World Touring Car Championship still had one round to run on the streets of Macau, but after controversy in the penultimate event of the season, Yvan Muller had already secured his second championship crown. The British Touring Car Championship was decided in favour of Jason Plato, following a dramatic four-way fight for honours, while in the German series, three drivers went to Shanghai for the final DTM race still in contention for the title. Down under, it's anyone's guess as to who will emerge on top of a titanic battle for the V8 Supercar Championship.

Ahead of the WTCC season finale, it appeared that the fight for the title once again would go to the wire, with Muller holding a lead of 37 points over multiple champion Andy Priaulx following the preceding round at Okayama. However, that event had seen BMW Team RBM switch to a non-homologated sequential gearbox, which ultimately would end Priaulx's hopes of overhauling the Frenchman.

Despite stewards at the event allowing the change to take place, an appeal by Chevrolet led to the FIA Court of Appeal excluding both Priaulx and team-mate Augusto Farfus from the results, which in turn handed Muller an unassailable lead in the standings going into the final round. The ruling also left Chevrolet within touching distance of the manufacturers' title.

"This time, I can go to Macau with a more relaxed spirit, but we have to keep in mind that anything can happen," Muller said. "We need to stay completely focused and work well on the Cruze, which has been excellent on all types of circuits this year."

The fact that the title was decided in the courtroom was a somewhat disappointing end to what had been another hard-fought battle for championship honours, with Muller proving to be the man to beat from the opening round. Having joined Chevrolet following the departure of SEAT's factory team, the Frenchman took victory first time out in Brazil and was a model of consistency through the season as he gained a further two victories and finished on the podium an impressive 13 times. Priaulx, meanwhile, had emerged as Muller's closest rival after a season that saw him win six times, making him the most successful driver in series history in terms of wins. However, the decision to exclude him from the Okayama results meant instead that he headed to Macau fighting only for the runner-up slot.

Going into the season finale, that position was held by Gabriele Tarquini, the man who had lifted the 2009 championship to become the oldest winner of an FIA world title. Now running under the SR-Sport banner after SEAT's departure, the Italian won five times at the wheel of his SEAT Leon TDi, although his own hopes of taking a second title were ended in Japan when he crashed out while leading the second race.

The diesel-powered Leon remained a potent force throughout the year, with former F1 racer Tiago Monteiro also winning twice in the car to leave SEAT equal with BMW in terms of race wins. Colin Turkington clinched BMW's seventh win of the year in Japan, albeit following Farfus's exclusion from the results, with his maiden victory being the highlight of an impressive campaign from the reigning BTCC champion, who took part in selected events during the year. The other three victories of 2010 went to Chevrolet, with Rob Huff winning on two occasions and Alain Menu securing victory once. Huff had looked a championship contender early in the season, but a zero score in Portugal would severely dent his hopes.

Looking to the future, plenty of questions remain unanswered about how the grid will shape up for 2011. Although BMW has developed a 1.6-litre

turbocharged engine to meet new regulations coming into play, the manufacturer has yet to confirm whether it will field a factory team in the series. However, there will be a new name on the grid on a full-time basis after Volvo confirmed it will be represented by the Polestar Racing team ahead of a possible full works entry for 2012. Ford could also be represented after it revealed it is working on developing an S2000 version of its new Focus ST for use by customer teams.

One key change for 2011 will be a new qualifying format, where the grid for race two is decided by the results of the opening phase of the two-part qualifying session, a move made by series bosses to stop the practice of drivers slowing towards the end of race one to benefit from the reverse-grid rules that previously had been employed. The calendar also sees a few amendments, with a proposed race in Argentina being cancelled and the British event moving from Brands Hatch to a re-opened Donington Park. Suzuka takes over from Okayama as venue for the Japanese race, while China will also host an event at a circuit yet to be announced.

Having finished second in three of the previous four seasons, Jason Plato returned to the top of the pile in the British Touring Car Championship as he clinched the title for the second time. In doing so, he also joined Andy Rouse at the head of the all-time winners list after seven victories took his career total to 60.

Again, Plato raced for the RML team, although now with factory backing from Chevrolet and armed with a new car in the Cruze. The team's experience of running the car in the WTCC meant Plato was on the pace from the outset, and victories at Rockingham and Oulton Park meant he reached the halfway stage of the season second to long-time rival Matt Neal in the standings.

However, a double win at Snetterton after the summer break saw Plato take a lead he would keep through to the season's end, with further wins at Knockhill and a double on Finals Day at Brands Hatch giving him the championship crown.

"It means a lot to win the title, but it's more the style in which we won: we did it properly," he said. "I have so much respect for Ray Mallock and RML, and I'm as pleased for them as I am for myself. This is the best touring car team in the world, and I want to win for them again next year."

Plato certainly didn't have it all his own way, with Honda Racing pair Neal and Gordon Shedden, and Team Aon's Tom Onslow-Cole all in contention for the title going into the final round. Neal and Gordon Shedden won five times apiece over the course of the season, but despite missing out on the drivers' title, their results were enough to give Honda the Manufacturers'/Constructors' Championship and the HiQ Teams title. Onslow-Cole, meanwhile, was one of the star performers in his Ford Focus ST, which featured an LPG-powered turbo engine that was one of the talking points of the year.

The straight-line speed of the car would be a bone of contention for rival teams, and series bosses moved to reign in the performance of the car at Silverstone – where it promptly won all three races. Despite winning four times during the course of the season, failure to score in any of the three races on Finals Day not only cost Onslow-Cole the chance to

fight for the overall title, but also saw him lose the lead of the Independents' championship to team-mate Tom Chilton.

Chilton won three times in total during the season, including twice at Silverstone, where Onslow-Cole appeared to be asked to move over, and edged out Steven Kane for the Indy title. Kane took his maiden victory in the opening rounds of the year at Thruxton where Fabrizio Giovanardi also won twice for Triple Eight. However, it would be the only time the Italian appeared all season due to sponsorship issues. Other winners during 2010 were Mat Jackson, who took his only win of a tough campaign on the Brands Hatch GP circuit, and Andrew Jordan, who won at Croft and in the final race of the year on the shorter Brands Hatch Indy layout.

As ever, there were notable performers elsewhere, including Paul O'Neill in the older BTC-spec Honda Integra run by Team sunshine.co.uk with Tech-Speed. Despite his ageing car, O'Neill headed the Independents' championship early in the year and could have topped the overall standings had it not been for a retirement in round nine at Brands Hatch. Three overall podium finishes almost saw him win the BTCC Fans' Favourite award for a second straight season, although he just missed out on the honour to newcomer Shaun Hollamby, who secured plenty of supporters after electing to run a Volkswagen Golf with his small AmD Milltek Racing team.

Another rookie, Alex MacDowall, impressed with a number of strong qualifying performances as Plato's team-mate at Chevrolet, while the season finale saw Ben Collins make his BTCC debut in a third Airwaves BMW. Although he would fail to score, the addition to the grid of the man formally known as 'The Stig', from hit TV show *Top Gear*, secured plenty of headlines.

During 2010, BTCC fans saw a glimpse of the future as three teams – including Jordan's Pirtek Racing outfit – elected to run the Next Generation Touring Car engine, which will form the basis of the championship moving forwards. A full-blown NGTC car, designed to bring down the costs involved in competing in the series, also completed a demonstration run during the final round of the year in the hands of James Thompson, and two new teams have already confirmed plans to run NGTC cars in 2011. While others are expected to do the same, teams will also have the option of following Jordan's lead by fitting the NGTC engine to an S2000 car, with Honda among those set to go down that route.

Over in Germany, the fight to be 2010 DTM champion came down to three drivers with one race left to run at the time *AUTOCOURSE* closed for press.

After back-to-back titles in 2008 and 2009, Timo Scheider saw his chances of a third straight title come to an end as the fight for the championship became an all Mercedes affair going into the season finale on the streets of Shanghai.

Gary Paffett was the early championship leader after taking victory in the opening round of the year at Hockenheim, but it was the man who finished second to him in the first race of the campaign who would then start to cement his place at the top of the standings, as Bruno Spengler reeled off five straight podium finishes, including victories at Lausitz and the Nürburgring.

That left the Canadian with a 17-point lead over Paffett and Paul di Resta going to Zandvoort, but when Paffett headed a 1-2 finish ahead of his fellow Brit in Holland, and Spengler could only manage seventh, the tide started to turn. Di Resta duly took three successive wins at Brands Hatch, Oschersleben and Hockenheim to overhaul Spengler, who failed to finish for the first time in 2010 in the final race on German soil.

However, when di Resta could only manage ninth at Adria after an incident on the opening lap, Spengler clinched a third place that meant he held a three-point lead heading to China. Second place in the same race for Paffett, his first trip to the podium after his Zandvoort win, ensured he also retained a chance of winning the title in Shanghai, although he was nine points behind Spengler with only ten available.

With the top three in the championship sharing seven victories, only three other drivers had taken to the top step of the podium prior to the final round. Jamie Green clinched victory at the Norisring, while Mattias Ekstrom and Scheider earned the only two victories for Audi as they struggled to match Mercedes for results during the year.

Away from the racetrack, the big story within the DTM surrounded speculation that BMW was planning to join the series, with confirmation coming in October that it would do battle with Audi and Mercedes from 2012, when new regulations are brought in, with a car based on the M3. Those new regulations will also come ahead of a planned new series being run in America for the latest generation DTM cars in 2013.

The changes will all come after the 2011 season, which again will be decided over 11 races, one of which will be held in Austria at the redeveloped Red Bull Ring. The DTM will also hold a Race of Champions-style knock-out event at the Olympic Stadium in Munich, although that event won't count for championship points.

The 2009 V8 Supercar Championship went the way of Team Vodafone driver Jamie Whincup, who wrapped up a second straight title after *AUTOCOURSE 2009–2010* went to press.

Despite the switch from Ford to Holden over the winter, Whincup remained in contention for a third straight title after another impressive season, which included victory in the opening four races of the year. In all, Whincup had nine victories heading into the final rounds, but found himself 50 points behind Ford rival James Courtney, a winner on four occasions

Left: Paul di Resta in the Mercedes C-Klasse at Hockenheim. The Brit was in the hunt with Bruno Spengler and Gary Paffett for top honours in the DTM.

Right: DTM race winner Bruno Spengler receives a champagne shower from Gary Paffett on the podium at the Nürburgring.
Photos: LAT Photographic

Below: A rumble of thunder. The massed field of V8 Supercars at the start of the L&H 500 at Phillip Island.
Photo: Mark Horsburgh/LAT

himself. However, with 600 points still available, any one of six drivers still held a mathematical chance of taking the championship. Among those six was Whincup's team-mate, Craig Lowndes, who clinched victory in the two big endurance events at Phillip Island and Bathurst alongside V8 legend Mark Skaife.

Aside from the endurance races, one of the biggest draws of the season proved to be the annual visit to Surfers Paradise, with the event running to a new format for 2010. Each team brought in an international driver to take part in the race weekend alongside its regulars, with Le Mans winner David Brabham, IndyCar champion Helio Castroneves and F1 title winner Jacques Villeneuve among those who lined up on the grid.

From 2011, the V8 Supercar Championship has been handed international status by the FIA in a move that will allow the series to compete at up to six international venues and in 12 Australasian events each year for the next five years. In 2011, Abu Dhabi and Hamilton will host the two events outside Australia, with 12 championship meetings on home soil as well as a race supporting the Australian GP.

"This is tremendous news for the sport, and we thank the FIA for their endorsement and recognition of V8 Supercars as a major international player, particularly in the Asia Pacific region," V8 Supercars CEO Martin Whitaker said. "After an enormous amount of hard work by CAMS, and with the support of the FIA Touring Car Commission, this gives V8 Supercars flexibility in exploring further expansion of the sport."

IZOD
TARGET

CHASING AN AUDIENCE

UNITED STATES RACING REVIEW by GORDON KIRBY

Main photo: After a number of years in the doldrums, the Indy Racing League is reshaping itself and hoping for a vibrant future.
Photo: Phillip Abbott/LAT Photographic

Inset: Even NASCAR has felt the pinch in the recession-hit USA.
Photo: Nigel Kinrade/LAT Photographic

Above: The remarkable Jimmy Johnson emerged as the NASCAR Sprint Cup champion for the fifth consecutive occasion.
Photo: Nigel Kinrade/LAT Photographic

Top right: Denny Hamlin just missed out in the title battle with Johnson.

Above right: Kevin Harvick was another formidable presence in 2010.
Photos: LAT South USA

Right: Racing at close quarters is the enduring appeal of NASCAR.
Photo: Brian Czobat/LAT Photographic

TIME and again in 2010 at races of all types, in conversations with decidedly untrendy, feet-on-the-ground folk, the word 'relevance' regularly came up. In most cases – at NASCAR and IndyCar races – the word was used to describe what's desperately lacking in these traditional forms of American motor racing. In other cases – exclusively, I have to say, at ALMS races – the word described the strongest suit of what has emerged, despite the absence of Audi and Penske, as the USA's most international and technologically driven racing series. But there's no question that for me personally, 'relevance' was the word of the year.

Sadly, NASCAR and IndyCar have become increasingly irrelevant in recent years as both forms of racing struggle with dwindling crowds and declining TV ratings. NASCAR remains the big dog of American racing, way ahead of any other series, but over the past few years American stock car racing has witnessed a big drop in ticket sales and TV ratings, and in 2010 the trend reached alarming levels. NASCAR's TV ratings have fallen by 15–20 per cent over each of the past two years, although they remain more than ten times larger than IndyCar, which was lucky to attract a national TV audience of more than 300,000 people for most of its 2010 races.

The shrinking pool of viewers has begun to have a serious impact on sponsorship revenues, and everyone in NASCAR is worried about the future of what only a few years ago was the gold standard of American racing. No fewer than 100,000 seats were unoccupied at July's Brickyard 400 NASCAR race at Indianapolis, and every NASCAR track, including Charlotte in the heart of North Carolina's stock car country and the legendary half-mile Bristol bullring in the mountains of Tennessee, has struggled with slow ticket sales. Bristol had enjoyed an unbroken 30-year run of sell-outs until 2010, when some 30,000 seats remained vacant for the track's two Sprint Cup races.

Conventional wisdom held that while NASCAR's blue-collar fan base – many of whom have lost their jobs in the economic downturn of the past two years – could no longer afford hotels, travel and US$100 tickets, they would continue to watch on TV. But that theory has been blown apart, as the all-important TV ratings have suffered a similar decline. One result is that more and more cars appear with different sponsors keyed to individual races, and top drivers and their cars often wear unfamiliar logos and paint jobs at many events. Good for business perhaps, but bad for the clear identities that were part of NASCAR's strength for many years.

NASCAR's top-level Sprint Cup Championship saw defending champion Jimmie Johnson locked in a fierce battle with Denny Hamlin for a fifth straight title crown. Hamlin led into the final race at Homestead-Miami, but a spin early in the race thwarted his ambitions, and Johnson came home in second place, which was enough to clinch the championship.

In recent years, Johnson has established himself as the lead driver in Rick Hendrick's four-car Chevrolet team beside four-times champion Jeff Gordon, NASCAR's most popular driver Dale Earnhardt Jr and veteran Mark Martin. Johnson, 35, is a cool customer who works well with crew chief Chad Knaus; more often than not, they are able to tune and adapt their car to best suit the changing track conditions that occur over the course of 400- and 500-mile oval races.

NASCAR and oval racing in general are much more difficult than many uninformed observers believe, and the most successful drivers are those who make the correct changes to their cars through the many pit stops required to get to the end of a typical NASCAR race. This is where Johnson and Knaus are so much better than any other team, but Johnson is also a tremendous driver who's capable of hanging on to a loose or oversteering car as well as making impressive

passes in crowded quarters.

Johnson is a California native who maintains a townhouse in New York City and speaks softly without a trace of Carolina twang. His personality and image are not at all those of the classic Southern stock car driver, and he trails far behind team-mate Dale Earnhardt Jr in NASCAR's most popular driver ratings. But he is certainly the class of today's field and has entirely rewritten the record books by becoming the first driver in NASCAR's history to win four championships in a row. A fifth successive title in 2010 elevated him into a unique category and put him on a path to becoming one of NASCAR's greatest drivers of all-time, in company with seven-times champions Richard Petty and Dale Earnhardt.

Johnson's strongest challengers in 2010 were Denny Hamlin and Kevin Harvick. Hamlin, 30, started racing Cup cars in 2005 and drives for Joe Gibbs's three-car Toyota team. He scored his seventh win of the year at Martinsville at the end of October and closed to within six points of Johnson. Although not as consistent as Johnson, Hamlin was unbeatable on occasion and is also a tough cookie who can trade paint with the best of them.

Kevin Harvick is the lead driver for Richard Childress's three-car team of Chevrolets. He replaced the late Dale Earnhardt following his death at Daytona in February 2001, and he enjoyed his most competitive season in 2010. A two-time second-division champion, Harvick led the Sprint Cup championship for most of the year.

Consolodating his reputation was Kyle Busch, NASCAR's *enfant terrible* and one of Hamlin's Joe Gibbs team-mates. Without doubt, Busch is one of NASCAR's most talented and outspoken drivers, and he has attracted a legion of fans as well as an equally large number of detractors. In some races, Kyle is unbeatable, but he lacks Jimmie Johnson's consistency. Four-times champion Jeff Gordon considers young Busch to be the most naturally talented driver to race in NASCAR in many years, so it will be interesting to see if Kyle can mature into a champion.

Gordon ran strongly all season. At 39, he has been racing Cup cars for 19 years, and although he's still a front-runner, he had yet to win a race in 2010 at press time. He won the last of his four championships in 2001.

Other top contenders in 2010 included two-times champion Tony Stewart, who has raced his own Chevrolets in recent years, plus Roush-Fenway Ford drivers Carl Edwards and Greg Biffle. Fast and tough-minded, Stewart is one of NASCAR's most popular drivers. He, too, is unbeatable on occasion, but nothing like as consistent as Johnson. The same can be said of Edwards and Biffle. Edwards, it has to be said, was disppointing in 2010.

Juan Pablo Montoya also had a disappointing year, his fourth in NASCAR with Earnhardt-Ganassi Racing. He was unable to win a race all year and failed to make the season-ending 'Chase for the Cup' featuring the year's top 12 drivers. He was overshadowed by his team-mate, Jamie McMurrary, who won the season opening Daytona 500 and also took the Brickyard

Above: The Nevada desert makes a dramatic backdrop as the NASCAR field provides an alternative attraction to gambling.
Photo: Lesley Ann Miller/LAT Photographic

Above right: Dario Franchitti took a memorable second Indy 500 win. The Speedway holds a special place in the Scotsman's heart, as his hero is the 1965 winner, Jim Clark.
Photo: Walt Kuhn/LAT Photographic

400 at Indianapolis in July. Still, Montoya is enjoying life in NASCAR and has no regrets about turning his back on Formula One.

"Absolutely, it was the right move, 120 per cent," Montoya declared. "I have zero regrets about it and I really enjoy what I'm doing. Like everything, some years are better than others and some weeks are better than others, especially in NASCAR. I think in open-wheel racing when you have a good car, you have a good car all the time. But in NASCAR, you have a good car one week and the next week you don't even know what hit you. But that's what makes it interesting."

Despite its problems, NASCAR continues to draw full fields of 43 cars with three or four non-qualifiers at most races. There's no question that NASCAR's field is the deepest and strongest of any form of worldwide motorsport, with all but the last few drivers and cars capable of winning most races

Montoya pointed out that if you're in a top F1 team, you're unlikely to ever qualify outside the top ten, but in NASCAR you're sometimes 20th or even 30th on the grid. "Sometimes you are in peoples' way," he said, shaking his head. "It's incredible because when you're off on set-up, it's painful. For a driver, it's really, really hard."

FRANCHITTI REIGNS SUPREME

The IndyCar championship was won in 2010 for the second year in a row by Dario Franchitti, who also won the Indianapolis 500 for a second time. Franchitti has raced Indy cars since 1997, battling for the CART championship with Montoya in 1999. He tried NASCAR in 2008 with Earnhardt-Ganassi Racing after winning his first IndyCar title and Indy 500 with Andretti-Green Racing in 2007, but his move to stock cars came at exactly the wrong time as the economy tanked and Chip Ganassi was unable to find the sponsorship to properly support the experiment. Two-thirds of the way through the year, Dario found himself without a ride and Ganassi proposed a return to Indy cars, which the Scotsman enthusiastically accepted.

The move proved exactly the right thing, as Franchitti has emerged with Ganassi's team as the fastest, smartest and most consistent IndyCar driver. At Indianapolis, he took command of the race on the opening lap and scored an excellent victory, but for most of the year he trailed Penske driver Will Power in the championship. Dario came on strong at the end of the season, however, and overhauled Power in the final race.

"I was in a similar situation in 2007," Franchitti

said. "I lost a pretty massive lead in the championship through one thing and another, so I think I know what Will was going through. But it's the situation you're presented with, and you just do the best you can. We definitely managed to find some pace in the last part of the season. It was a typical season with the ebb and flow. One guy is strong and then the other guy is strong. It just goes that way, so you've just got to try and be as consistent as possible and do the job.

"Obviously it's fun when you're up front and winning, but it's been like a breath of fresh air. It's been fantastic for me. I've really enjoyed it. When I did NASCAR in '08, it showed me what I was missing. I just love driving in the IndyCar series. I love being part of the team. It's what I love doing, and I think you should always follow your heart."

Franchitti and Ganassi team-mate Scott Dixon, IndyCar champion in 2008, have formed an excellent partnership over the last two years. "You learn from your team-mates," Franchitti said. "I've learned so much from all my team-mates and none more so than Scott. There are times when I wonder, 'How the hell does he do that?' He pushes you, and I've learned a tremendous amount from him on certain types of tracks, and that works the other way, too.

"When you work together, you absolutely get better results, but it's a tough thing to do. All these secrets are hard won, and you're giving them to someone else who's going to go out and try and beat you, and in a lot of cases does just that. But you've got to understand that if you give it out to your team-mate, you'll receive it back."

Regular winners for many years, Franchitti and Dixon are great racers. Without doubt, Franchitti is one of the world's best drivers, a fair and true racer, and Dixon is darn near as good, scoring three wins in 2010 and taking third in the championship. They're also civilised, soft-spoken gentlemen, and Franchitti stands out from today's crowd of drivers by enjoying a rare passion for the sport's history. His hero is Jim Clark, and he enjoyed a sublime day at Indianapolis in September when he drove Clark's superbly restored 1965 Indy 500 winning Lotus 38. "It was," Dario quietly declared, "one of the highlights my career."

Championship rival Power enjoyed his first full season with Roger Penske's three-car team. Power is a quiet, reserved Australian, who joined Penske in 2009 as a part-time driver, but broke his back in a nasty accident at Infineon Raceway in August 2009. Power arrived in the United States in 2006 with a solid reputation earned in Australia and three seasons racing in Europe. He ran in the Champ Car World Series in 2006 and 2007 for Derrick Walker's Team Australia operation. In 2007, he was a Champ Car title contender, winning two races, taking four poles and finishing fourth in points. In 2008, he joined the unified IRL series with KV Racing, before moving to Team Penske. In 2010, Power rebounded in style from his back injuries, winning five races and taking eight poles, only to crash in the season finale and lose the championship to Franchitti.

Power's team-mates, Helio Castroneves and Ryan Briscoe, operated in his shadow for most of the year. It was Castroneves's tenth year with Team Penske and 13th in Indy cars. Helio remains quick and competitive in most races, and is always a threat at Indianapolis. He won three races in 2010 and finished fourth in the championship. Briscoe is fast and sometimes smooth, but still prone to small, but costly mistakes. He won one race and finished fifth in points as the Ganassi and Penske teams dominated IndyCar racing.

The only other drivers to win races in 2010 were Tony Kanaan and Ryan Hunter-Reay, each of whom managed to take just one race. But such is the parlous state of IndyCar that Kanaan and Hunter-Reay lost their sponsors and rides at the end of the season, and were searching for work as we closed for

Dario Franchitti's return to open-wheel racing from NASCAR proved a wise decision, the Scot using all his experience to win the Indy Racing League title.
Photo: Michael Levitt/LAT Photographic

Above: Team Penske's Will Power was perhaps the quickest driver in the Indy Racing League, winning five races and taking the pole eight times.
Photo: Phillip Abbot/LAT Photographic

Top right: The big one. Dario Franchitti receives the plaudits after winning his second Indy 500.
Photo: Dan Streck/LAT Photographic

Above right: As his mechanics try in vain to repair his car, Will Power ponders his championship slipping away at the dramatic Homestead finale.
Photo: Michael Levitt/LAT Photographic

Right: Marco Andretti, Will Power and Helio Castroneves run three-abreast at Chicagoland.
Photo: Phillip Abbott/LAT Photographic

press. Poor crowds and dismal TV ratings have made it extremely difficult to sell sponsorship, and it's sad to report that there was a record number of empty seats for the 2010 Indianapolis 500.

Randy Bernard was hired in March 2010 to take over the reins of IndyCar. The former boss of America's Professional Bull Riders Association, Bernard replaced Tony George, who was removed from power in the summer of 2009. George had founded the IRL series in 1996, ultimately scoring a pyrrhic victory over CART's former team owners when Champ Car was absorbed by the IRL at the beginning of 2008.

But by then, Indy car racing was a mere shadow of its once great self. Over a decade-and-a-half, George spent between US$400 million and $800 million to win his battle with CART and Champ Car, but in June 2009, his mother and three sisters decided that enough was enough. They voted him out of power, ultimately choosing Bernard to replace him. "I'm focused on how are we going to make IndyCar bigger," Bernard said. "How are we going to expand our audience? [Series sponsor] Izod have done a great job of sponsorship activation, but it's very important for me now to take that a step further. I want to make sure it's about building our image in the pop culture, and among our youth and mainstream America.

"We need to better leverage and activate our endemic sponsors, like Honda and Firestone, to do like Izod have done and reach those 15 to 20 million fans we lost in the mid-nineties. We know those fans are still out there. It's true that a bunch of them hate us. They despise us. But I like to call them 'the influencers'. I think we have to reach them and convince them with passion about why they need to come back."

After months of debate and proposals from five different car builders – Dallara, Lola, Swift, BAT and Delta Wing – IndyCar decided in July to continue with a new Dallara-Honda combination for 2012–15; Dallara has committed to build its Indy cars at a new facility in Indiana, across the road from the Indianapolis Motor Speedway. The Italian chassis builder will receive tax breaks from the city and state goverments worth US$5 million.

IndyCar hopes to bring variety to the table by encouraging other car builders or engine builders to design their own unique aerodynamic platforms – front and rear wings, sidepods and engine cover. Top team owner Roger Penske announced that his team would not build an 'aero kit', but Lotus has committed to produce a package, and Randy Bernard hopes to encourage one or two more to follow suit.

The 2012 Dallara's price has been pegged at US$385,000, a 45-per-cent reduction over the current car. Dallara's aero kit is priced at US$36,000, and kits produced by other manufacturers may cost no more than US$70,000. Dallara will offer a US$150,000 discount on the first 28 cars bought by teams located in the state of Indiana. The first new Dallara rolling chassis is scheduled to be ready in October 2011, with deliveries to teams starting in December.

Bernard admits that it will take a year or two to attract new engine manufacturers and aero kit builders. "I think we have to be realistic and not set our expectations too high," he said. "Our goal is to be looking at the long term. We know that engine and chassis manufacturers were under deadlines right now to get moving. So we think it's going to be pretty darn hard to see other engine manufacturers by 2012. We're optimistic, but our goal is to have some interest from other engine manufacturers and aero manufacturers in 2013 for sure."

THE DELTA WING

Many people, including most IndyCar team owners, were very disappointed that the radical Delta Wing design was rejected by IndyCar. The Delta Wing was funded by Chip Ganassi and designed by former Lola engineer Ben Bowlby, who has worked as Ganassi's chief of R&D since 2003. Bowlby's car weighs only 800lb and is an extremely low-drag design intended for the new generation of 1.6-litre 'Global Racing Engines'. In theory, the car is capable of lapping the Indianapolis Motor Speedway at over 230mph with only 300bhp.

The Delta Wing has no wings. Instead, it's fitted with a vertical stabliser and has an extreme rear weight bias, with 72 per cent of its weight on the rear wheels. The tiny, 10-inch front tyres are hidden within the nose, and the aim is not only to substantially reduce drag, but also to make the car much more raceable and capable of running in close quarters than the modern breed of single-seater.

Brian Lisles is general manager of Newman/Haas Racing and was one of the engineers Bowlby consulted when designing the Delta Wing. Along with most IndyCar engineers and team owners, Lisles was a strong supporter of the Delta Wing.

"The reason a lot of the team owners looked very hard at and were supportive of the Delta Wing was because the Delta Wing had the possibility of generating sufficient additional media coverage and interest, so that we had a chance of increasing our audience," Lisles said. "Three months of getting those weird, strange cars on TV and in the press could have been enough to kick-start the series, or at least move it along a little bit. The seven- to thirteen-year-old kids were really excited by the Delta Wing, and if you get them excited, dad will take them to the race to see it. That's how you build a new audience, which we desperately need."

But the revolutionary concept proved difficult for some people to get their minds around. Many fans hoped the Delta Wing would help rejuvenate Indy car racing, but the concept was rejected in favour of a renewed Dallara-Honda combination.

Nevertheless, there's lots of conversation about the Delta Wing concept going on with engine manufacturers and sanctioning bodies around the world. "The genie is out of the bottle," designer Bowlby remarked. "This concept is going to come to life and go racing somewhere around the world. I believe we will bring it to life ourselves, sooner rather than later. We hope to build and test a prototype in 2011, and race it in 2012."

RELEVANCY IN THE ALMS

Duncan Dayton's Honda-based Highcroft HPD ARX-01c won the team's second American Le Mans Series championship in a row in 2010, with David Brabham, Simon Pagenaud and Marino Franchitti driving. The Highcroft team won three races, and its trio of drivers completed the year without damaging a single piece of bodywork or putting any marks on their car, a superb achievement. The Highcroft team's championship rivals included Greg Pickett's Cytosports Porsche RS Spyder, Rob Dyson's Lola-Mazda coupe and Paul Drayson's Lola-Judd. Brit Johnny Cocker scored Drayson's first ALMS win at

Above: Still going strong. Scott Pruett enjoyed a record breaking year, sharing Chip Ganassi's Grand-Am Riley with Memo Rojas.
Photo: LAT Photographic

Above right: Paul Drayson and Johnny Cocker took a memorable win at Elkhart Lake.
Photo: Dan R. Boyd/LAT Photographic

Top: The Highcroft HPD ARX-01c took the ALMS title in the capable hands of David Brabham, Simon Pagenaud and Marino Franchitti.
Photo: Lesley Ann Miller/LAT Photographic

Elkhart Lake in August.

The loss in recent years of factory or factory backed P1 and P2 teams from Audi, Porsche and Acura has left the ALMS with a thin field of prototypes, and the series is looking for the right way forward. Rob Dyson is a long-time supporter of American sports car racing. His Lola-Mazda ran in 2010 on isobutanol, a biofuel developed by BP/Castrol.

"What I like about the ALMS is the variety of different automobiles, and the variety of different types of engines and powerplants you can bring," Dyson remarked. "There's a little more science and hot rodding you can do in the ALMS. That's what makes it so much fun. We've made a lot of changes in our cars, and fortunately the rules allow us to do all the things we do. We run against a couple of normally aspirated V8s, and I think the variety is interesting. I believe the ALMS has the fan base because the cars are so interesting. The fans come to see different cars and engines race. That's what it's all about."

While NASCAR and IndyCar lost crowds and TV ratings, particularly among the youth market, the ALMS enjoyed an increase in crowds in 2010, including a big increase in the all-important 18–35 age group. The 2010 Petit Le Mans ALMS season-closer at Road Atlanta drew a record crowd of 124,000 spectators over three days, 11,000 more than the previous Petit Le Mans record.

The GT2 championship was a feature of the 2010 ALMS, with teams from Porsche, Ferrari, Corvette and BMW fighting for the championship. The GT2 drivers' championship was taken by Joerg Bergmeister and Patrick Long aboard the Flying Lizard Porsche 911 RSR, while Bobby Rahal's BMW squad took the GT2 team championship in its first year in the ALMS.

Two-times champion team owner Duncan Dayton is an unabashed fan of the ALMS series. "There's great competition in the ALMS down through all four classes," he said. "If you want to see a really exciting motor race, as opposed to some of the processions that we see in other series, you've got to come watch an ALMS race. I have to say that the racing has been spectacular in the ALMS in every year that we've been involved. Look at the last-lap passes and battles we saw at Long Beach and Elkhart Lake, and at Laguna Seca, where a six-hour race wasn't decided until the last 20 minutes. To have that incredible competition among a bunch of different car and engine combinations is fantastic."

Dayton believes deeply in the ALMS's commitment to encouraging new technology. "I think the ALMS is the only relevant form of motor sports in America today," he said. "Clearly the presence of the manufacturers and their interest in the series demonstrates that it's the only venue where they can showcase and develop their technology, and bring it to the marketplace very quickly.

"I think you will continue to see the manufacturers invest their R&D dollars heavily in the ALMS because it is applicable and relevant to what they are doing on a day-to-day basis. A lot of other manufacturers have hybrids in the pipeline, and the ACO is going to allow them in the coming years at Le Mans. I think encouraging hybrid technology is going to bring a lot of excitement to Le Mans and the ALMS series, and will energise a lot of other manufacturers to get back into racing."

GANASSI'S FOURTH GRAND-AM TITLE

Chip Ganassi also runs a team in the Grand-Am sports car series, which is backed by NASCAR and godfathered by Jimmy France, younger brother of the late Bill France Jr. Veteran Scott Pruett leads Ganassi's Grand-Am team, co-driving with Mexican Memo Rojas. In 2010, the duo took the team's fourth championship in the past six years, winning nine of 11 races, a Grand-Am record. They drove a BMW-powered Riley after running Lexus engines the previous five years.

"We've had a record breaking year, and it's been a lot of fun," Pruett grinned. "I'm having a great time, and Memo is going real good. He's really stepped up his game over the last couple of years and did a terrific job this year. Can you believe it? I'm still going at it at 52, and still one of the guys to beat. I have no complaints and I'm thankful. The great part is I'm still having such a fun time. I'm really loving the driving, and I think that helps you stay motivated to work out every day, and to be sharp and do what you've got to do."

Pruett says Ganassi's multiple teams provide a key to their success in IndyCar and Grand-Am. "We're fortunate because we can pull resources from Chip's NASCAR and IndyCar teams at whatever level we need. We're able to up our game to get more performance out of the car and all the components, and when we have an engine in the BMW with better driveability and a little bit more torque, it was the last little bit that we needed to put it over the top.

"We're doing the same thing next year. Everybody couldn't have been more pleased with the success we've had this year. I mean, how could you not be? For me, I'll go do it another year. Again, I've just been blessed to be doing what I do at this level, and having the performance and kind of record breaking seasons we've had. I would have never thought it was possible. This will be my eighth year with Chip and his organisation. We've won four championships, and if we didn't win the championship, we finished second. So it's a great home for me."

Runner-up in the Grand-Am championship was Wayne Taylor's Dallara-Ford, driven by Max Angelelli and Ricky Taylor, followed by defending champions Alex Gurney and Jon Fogarty in Bob Stallings's Gainsco Riley-Chevrolet.

America's other notable champions in 2010 were Frenchman J.K. Vernay, who won the Indy Lights championship, and Derek Daly's 18-year-old son, Conor, who dominated the Star-Mazda championship. Vernay beat Canadian James Hinchcliffe to the Indy Lights title and hopes to graduate to Indy cars in 2011, while young Daly has his sights set on racing in Europe in the 2011 GP3 series.

Below left: New Indy Lights champion J.K. Vernay kisses the Firehawk Cup.
Photo: Lesley Ann Miller/LAT Photographic

Below: Chris Dyson, Guy Smith and Andy Meyrick shared the Lola-Mazda in the ALMS LMP2 class.
Photo: Dan R. Boyd/LAT Photographic

Bottom: Canadian James Hinchcliffe, a perennial contender in the support classes, just lost out to Vernay in a close-fought Indy LIghts title battle.
Photo: Dan Streck/LAT Photographic

KARTING REVIEW by RUSSELL ATKINS

A GOOD YEAR FOR THE BRITS

Above: British leading lights Harry Crawley (40) and James Singleton (24) shine through the spray in the Euro Max Challenge at Wackersdorf in Germany.

Inset: Singleton and Crawley enjoy the perks of their success.

Photos: Bas Kaligis

Top right: Ash Hand was a prolific winner in Formula Kart Stars (FKS), with eight victories from 12 finals deservedly earning him the Junior Max crown.

Above right: Tom Harvey celebrates one of the most extraordinary triumphs of the season in FKS at Genk in Belgium.

Right: George Russell reprised his outstanding MSA Cadet class success from 2009 with double British Mini Max title glory in 2010.

Photos: Chris Walker/www.kartpix.net

IT was very much a year for the Brits in karting, 2010. Invariably a strong breeding ground for future talent – prior to this season, the two most recent F1 world champions, lest we forget, had climbed the British karting ladder – the sport saw no fewer than nine drivers toasting major victories on the international stage, with many others able to point to similar success stories.

That being the case, it seems only right that we should begin this review in Britain, with the Formula Kart Stars Championship (FKS), the same series that once set Lewis Hamilton on the fast track towards the big time. In the MSA British Cadet class, a three-way tussle for glory ultimately was settled in the Ellough Park finale between Welsh hotshot Tom Harvey, Fusion Motorsport team-mate Nathan Aston and the pair's Eclipse Motorsport rival, Connor Jupp. Along the way, Harvey had triumphed at Rowrah, Whilton Mill – a superb double, earning the 12-year-old the moniker 'Whilton Wizard' – and in a nail-biting thriller at Genk in Belgium, where any one of 17 drivers could have won going into the last lap. Cumbrian speed demon Aston, for his part, had ascended the top step of the podium on home turf at Rowrah and in Genk, while Jupp had prevailed at Glan Y Gors and Three Sisters.

When it all came down to Ellough, though, an off-colour weekend for Harvey, who had tyre woes, reduced it to a two-horse race, and while Jupp did all he possibly could with a sublime double victory, it was not quite enough to overcome Aston, who finished third in both finals, ending the campaign dead level on points and deservedly clinching the coveted crown on countback.

Stepping up to Mini Max level, George Russell repeated his dominant form from 2009 in Cadets to make it two championship successes in swift succession, ascending the highest step of the rostrum five times and only missing out on a top-three finish on two occasions as he stamped his authority on proceedings and firmly marked himself out as one to watch. Adam Glear ran the Strawberry Racing ace the closest – triumphing at Rowrah and Glan Y Gors – with Bobby Thompson winding up third.

In the more powerful Junior Max category, it was all about one driver – Ash Hand. Seamlessly ruling the roost, the Nuneaton-based star claimed a staggering eight victories – comprising unchallenged doubles at Rowrah, Whilton Mill, Genk and Three Sisters – to break all records in a magnificent campaign. Victory in 15 of his 24 heat races revealed even more of an incredible story.

Reigning Mini Max champion Jack Barlow ended proceedings as runner-up, with Josh Parker and Declan Jones tied on points for third, while rookie

Luke Whitworth stunned by registering a podium finish in the very last round at Ellough on his return to competition following an eight-week lay-off with a badly broken arm. Remarkable enough in itself, but given the Rotherham teenager had only begun karting at the end of the previous year, his achievement in a national championship was quite extraordinary. Keep tabs on him in 2011.

In KF3, finally, it was an impressive whitewash for Ben Barnicoat, the Mick Barrett Racing charger demonstrating the benefit of a year's experience at that level as he saw off the challenges of class newcomers Charlie Robertson and Matthew Graham in a small, but no less eagerly contested field.

In British championship Super 1, the duels for glory were every bit as tense. In the Cadet class, Harvey

gained his revenge for his FKS near-miss with a superb title triumph, going on a mid-season rout of four consecutive victories that cemented his success. With the Bonvilston speed demon sweeping to an impressive ten rostrum finishes from 12 starts, the destiny of the laurels was never really in any doubt; fellow front-runners Jupp and Lando Norris claimed second and third, while FKS champion Aston wound up sixth.

In KF3, this time Barnicoat had to give best to Jake Dennis, as the Racing Steps backed star went one spot higher than he had managed the season before. Barnicoat won as many races as Dennis, but ultimately ended up paying the price for finishing outside the top ten in the Shenington curtain-raiser. Jake Dalton was the only other driver who was really ever in the same ballpark as the pair.

It was European front-runner Jacob Nørtoft who comfortably claimed the KF2 crown, the Dane being beaten just once in the eight opening outings. Alex Walker sealed the runner-up honours, with KF3 graduate Callum Bowyer doing a praiseworthy job indeed to snatch third place overall, belying the fact that, at only 16, he was giving away years in both age and experience to many of his adversaries.

In Super KF, meanwhile, something of a dampener was put on proceedings when the class was canned

Top: FKS champion Nathan Aston celebrates victory in his own inimitable manner in the MSA Cadet Class.

Above: Luke Whitworth, one of the indisputable 'finds' of 2010, belied a complete lack of prior racing experience.

Top right: Girls do love a winner, as Super 1 Series front-runner Callum Bowyer discovers.

Above right: Matt Parry made up for his near miss in 2009 with the Super 1 Junior Max laurels in 2010.

Photos: Chris Walker/www.kartpix.net

due to insufficient numbers before the campaign had reached its conclusion, leaving ultra-successful karting veteran Mark Litchfield as champion from Jonathan Walker and Elliot Burton.

Moving over to the Rotax classes, Russell made it cause for a double celebration in Mini Max, although not by much, as the 12-year-old saw off Harry Webb's challenge by a scant three points, with the impressively consistent Jack Aitken only another four points further in arrears in third.

In Junior Max, Matt Parry atoned for having narrowly failed to lift the laurels 12 months earlier by pipping Jack Marshall to the top spot, with Sean Babington finishing third. Barlow ended up as the best placed first-year driver in fourth. Mention should also be made of plucky Junior Max rookie Harry Crawley, who was Parry's principal challenger early on before his bid was cruelly crushed by a rib injury at the worst possible time. The young Dartford star's brilliant victory over the eventual champion, following an enthralling wheel-to-wheel duel at Whilton Mill, was one of the highlights of the season, while FKS king Hand put a run of torrid ill-fortune in Super 1 behind him to thoroughly dominate the final meeting at Three Sisters to show what might have been.

In Senior Max, Tom Fawcett prevailed at the end of a three-way scrap for the laurels with Jake Ball and John Stewart, and in the Rotax Max 177 'heavyweight' class, six-times race winner Lucas Orrock got the verdict over runner-up and prolific podium finisher David Griffiths by six points, with Stephen Cobb rounding out the top three.

Before leaving the national scene, we must also pay tribute to the heroes of Kartmasters, the blue-riband meeting on the British karting calendar. Jupp finally got to lay claim to a title he could call his own in 2010 by edging season-long rival Harvey to the Comer Cadet trophy by a mere 0.06 second. Mini Max glory went the way of the man of the season, Russell, with Babington overcoming defending 'GP' champion Hand for the Junior Max crown.

In KF3, FKS champion Barnicoat was not to be denied – although Daniel Vaughan pushed him all the way to the chequered flag – while 2009 British and European champion Jordan Chamberlain demonstrated his class to emerge victorious in KF2, with Litchfield a close second. Tom Grice completed the podium in third, and Bowyer once again punched above his weight in fourth.

There was a star turn in Senior Rotax from Jack Hawksworth, the Bradford ace who was more accustomed to competing at the sharp end in the KZ1 gearbox class on European shores, but who returned to the UK to race a direct-drive kart for the first time in over a year. In a performance that earned him the coveted Driver of the Day accolade out of some 228 entrants, the 19-year-old belied a lack of prior testing to see off rivals of the calibre of seven-times Kartmasters winner Michael Simpson to triumph brilliantly and add another prestigious trophy to his overflowing cabinet.

Hawksworth is a former Junior Rotax European Champion and Junior Rotax world championship runner-up in the hotly contested Rotax Max Euro Challenge. In 2010, that series again delivered some real seat-of-the-pants action – and once more, the Brits excelled.

The series kicked off with the Winter Cup at Malaga in Spain, where British front-runner James Singleton stunned the paddock by storming to pole position on his international Junior Rotax debut, outpacing both the reigning European and world champions along the way. He turned heads by ending up on the podium in the final, too, just pipped to second place by countryman Jack Barlow as Ukyo Sasahara stole the top spot.

The main championship subsequently took in

Left: Jack Hawksworth celebrates sweeping all before him to claim the coveted Kartmasters GP trophy and Driver of the Day award; the 19-year-old was a regular front-runner on the international scene, too.

Photo: Chris Walker/www.kartpix.net

Below: Jordan King shows them who's boss in the WSK Master Series at Castelletto in Italy.

Photo: Gregory Heirman/FotoFormulaK

rounds at Wackersdorf in Germany, Bruck in Austria and Genk. Notable performances came from Tristan Viidas in Junior Rotax at Salbris and Harry Crawley at Wackersdorf, the latter battling back from troubled heats to storm through the spray in torrential conditions and triumph in the Junior Rotax final. The 13-year-old simply drove away from the pursuing pack to lead home Singleton in a British 1-2 in as dominant a performance as was witnessed all season.

Barlow brilliantly headed a Strawberry Racing 1-2, ahead of Joel Affolter in Juniors at Bruck, with Ed Brand giving the British contingent even more reason to cheer by defeating Joey Van Splunteren in Senior Max. In the Genk finale, victories for the on-form Jack Aitken in Junior Rotax, Sean Babington in a one-off Senior Rotax appearance, Christophe Adams in Max Masters and Simas Juodvirsis in DD2 meant that the successful dozen who would go on to compete in the prestigious Rotax International Open at Zuera in Spain comprised Affolter, Aitken and Barlow (Junior Rotax); Van Splunteren, Brand and Mats Van Den Brand (Senior Max); Adams, Matias Laine and Florent Lambert (Max Masters); and Andreas Jensen, Patrick Pearce and Maik Barten (DD2) – a third of them British drivers.

Right: Red Bull backed Alex Albon notches up another triumph on the European stage, with countryman Callan O'Keeffe *(left)* and Max Verstappen joining him on the rostrum following the KF3 World Cup at Braga in Portugal.

Below: An overjoyed Jake Dennis takes the win for Under-18 World Championship glory.

Bottom right: Flanked by Jordan Chamberlain *(left)* and Nicolaj Møller-Madsen, precocious McLaren-Mercedes protégé Nyck de Vries proves that good things come in small packages in the CIK-FIA World Championship outing at Zuera in Spain.

Photos: Chris Walker/www.kartpix.net

Staying in Europe, the WSK International Series split into the WSK Euro Series, WSK World Series and WSK Master Series in 2010. The Euro Series attracted the greatest numbers and took place over five rounds at La Conca, Lonato, Zuera, Genk and Sarno. Among the 38 Super KF class competitors, it was Armand Convers who got the better of McLaren backed Nyck de Vries for the honours. KZ1 laurels went the way of 2009 World Cup winner Jonathan Thonon from Bas Lammers; Energy Corse's Paolo de Conto utterly dominated KZ2, tallying almost twice the points total of his nearest adversary, female racer Beitske Visser; Ignazio d'Agosto strolled to KF2 class success; and in KF3, it was the Max Verstappen show, with Alex Albon a lonely second.

In the World Series held at Portimao in Portugal, Millville in America and Sharm El Sheikh in Egypt, Convers and de Vries replicated their Euro Series duel in Super KF – with the same outcome in the Frenchman's favour after de Vries was excluded in Egypt, although the precociously talented Dutchman took away the consolation prize of two grand final victories to none for his arch-rival. Jonathan Thonon waltzed away with KZ2 class glory; Sébastien Bailly overcame d'Agosto in the Sharm El Sheikh finale to clinch the KF2 title, with Chris Lock also leapfrogging the luckless Italian, who endured an Egyptian nightmare; and in KF3, Verstappen comfortably made it a brace of WSK trophies.

The Master Series was held at Siena, Val Vibrata and Castelletto – all in Italy – and saw Visser gain her revenge with the KZ2 title. In KF2, Antonio Giovinazzi was unbeatable, but special mention should go to Jordan King, who was the architect of a stupendous triumph at Castelletto that earned the Hugo Boss brand ambassador the runner-up spot in the standings following a fraught six-way tussle; compatriot Lock wound up third. Nicklas Nielsen narrowly overcame Visoui – 'bridesmaid' for a second time – in KF3 to pinch the crown from under his Romanian rival's nose.

Of perhaps greatest significance on the international stage, though, are the CIK-FIA races, bearing the official endorsement of the sport's governing body – and a happy stomping-ground indeed for British competitors in 2010. In the showcase meeting, de Vries tasted victory champagne by overhauling long-time race leader Jordan Chamberlain to seal world championship glory at Zuera, while in the KF3 World Cup at Braga, it was Red Bull supported Albon who showed the rest how to do it, with countryman Callan O'Keeffe in third sandwiching runner-up Verstappen.

The KZ1 World Cup at Braga in Portugal yielded a runaway victory for Bas Lammers from Intrepid team-mate Jérémy Iglesias. McLaren-Mercedes Young Driver Programme member Oliver Rowland, meanwhile, produced an even more dominant showing to clinch the Super KF/KF1 World Cup laurels at Suzuka, leaving his pursuers quite literally trailing in his wheel tracks as he won the pre-final by nigh-on 20 seconds and the grand final by almost 15 – given that de Vries was one of those giving chase, no mean feat at all.

The European KZ1 and KZ2 Championship was held at Sarno in Italy and Varennes in France, with Lammers and Iglesias reprising their World Cup efforts to give Intrepid a commanding 1-2 – dividing the four race wins neatly between themselves – and Jack Hawksworth doing a fine job against the odds to place sixth. Again, de Conto dominated KZ2.

The European KF2 Championship was claimed by Nicolaj Møller-Madsen from Bailly, while there was a supreme triumph for the highly rated Albon in the European KF3 Championship at the same meeting, the 14-year-old taking the chequered flag almost five seconds clear of Pierre Gasly. Harrison Scott and Jake Dennis were practically as one in third and fourth, very nearly making it an all-British podium lock-out.

In the European Superkart Championship, Gavin Bennett secured a hat trick of titles by adding to his successes in 2007 and 2009, dominating the last four races at Assen in the Netherlands and Le Mans in France; the only track the Brit didn't win at, somewhat ironically, was his home circuit of Silverstone.

In the inaugural Under-18 World Championship, Dennis ensured that the theme of British success was well preserved, mounting the highest step of the rostrum at Wackersdorf as he saw off Finland's Matias Köykkä for the trophy, with Adam Stirling third following a brilliant victory at Alcañiz in Spain.

In the glamorous Monaco Kart Cup, finally, while Charles Leclerc soaked up the plaudits for KF3 class victory, it was Albon who stole the headlines once more by scything his way up the order from 28th, following a pre-final disaster, to an excellent fourth – with overtaking being just about as easy as it is in the Principality's grand prix. In KZ1, meanwhile, Norman Nato pipped de Conto to the top spot by barely a quarter of a second, with Rowland a solid fifth, while Hawksworth had masterfully worked his way through the pack from 22nd to seventh when, with barely a handful of laps remaining, the former Margutti Trophy winner's daring charge unfortunately ended in the barriers. No matter, though – he had already well and truly made his mark.

FORMULA KART STARS
THE ROAD TO FORMULA 1
THROUGH RACING AND EDUCATION

BERNIE ECCLESTONE

I have a feeling that in the future the Formula 1 World Champions may well come from within the ranks of FKS and this is the reason that Formula One Mangement supports FKS

LEWIS HAMILTON

I wouldn't be in Formula One if I hadn't come through this series

FORMULA KART STARS 2010 BRITISH KART CHAMPIONS

I have won two major UK championships, Formula Kart Stars and Kartmasters and 2nd in Super 1. It has been a privilege to race in Formula Kart Stars because it was the first big championship I have won in my junior karting career. I would like to thank everyone for all of the help and support that they have given me throughout the season. This will be the first step on the ladder to be the youngest Formula 1 World Champion ever!

Ben Barnicoat

It's been a brilliant season and to come away as Formula Kart Stars MSA British Cadet champion is just fantastic. I've learnt so much this year about all the aspects that make a winner and I am much more competitive because of that. Gathering experience is essential and hopefully I can continue to learn and win next year.

Nathan Aston

I have enjoyed a fantastic year in Formula Kart Stars in 2010, and winning the title in a championship that carries the support of two of the sport's true greats – Lewis Hamilton and Bernie Ecclestone – makes me tremendously proud, and definitely ranks as my finest achievement to-date. Competing in FKS has enabled me to develop all the skills required for a successful motorsport career, and I would also like to say a special 'thank you' to Mark Collings of CRG

Ash Hand

Again, what another incredible year for me, winning Formula Kart Stars for the second year running. Last year I was MSA British Cadet Champion and this year Mini Max at 12 years old. 2010 has been a hat trick of championships for me, being crowned FKS and Super 1 champion. I also won Kartmasters Grand Prix for the third year running in three different classes. I would like to thank everyone that has helped me achieve these results.

George Russell

GINETTA
JUNIOR CHAMPIONSHIP 2011

'The next step for FKS drivers'

Want to be part of the UK's highest profile Junior racing series?

Contact Stewart Linn on:
0113 385 4165
GINETTA.COM

VITAL MOTORSPORT

Vital Motorsport Trackside and Mail order specialists are proud to support and work closely with the Formula Kart Stars Championship

Formula Kart Stars
Snowball Farm
Westbury
Brackley
Northamptonshire
NN13 5JP
United Kingdom

www.formulakartstars.com
debbie.sellers@formulakartstars.com
Tel: +44 (0)7973 553179

MAJOR RESULTS

OTHER CHAMPIONSHIP RACING SERIES WORLDWIDE

Compiled by DAVID HAYHOE and JOÃO PAULO CUHNA - www.forix.com

GP2 Series

All cars are Dallara GP2-08-Renault.

GP2 SERIES, Circuit de Catalunya, Montmeló, Barcelona, Spain, 8/9 May. Round 1. 37 and 25 laps of the 2.892-mile/4.655-km circuit.
Race 1 (106.944 miles/172.109 km).
1 Charles Pic, F, 57m 54.177s, 110.816 mph/178.342 km/h; **2** Giacomo Ricci, I, 57m 55.666s; **3** Daniel Clos, E, 57m 58.386s; **4** Sergio Pérez, MEX, 57m 59.288s; **5** Oliver Turvey, GB, 58m 12.516s; **6** Pastor Maldonado, YV, 58m 24.388s; **7** Luiz Razia, BR, 58m 24.745s; **8** Fabio Leimer, CH, 58m 28.498s; **9** Sam Bird, GB, 58m 30.138s; **10** Davide Valsecchi, I, 58m 38.241s; **11** Marcus Ericsson, S, 58m 44.529s; **12** Josef Kral, CZ, 58m 45.859s; **13** Ho-Pin Tung, CN, 58m 47.627s; **14** Alberto Valério, BR, 58m 54.014s; **15** Rodolfo Gonzalez, YV, 59m 00.357s; **16** Adrian Zaugg, ZA, 59m 00.571s; **17** Michael Herck, RO, 59m 00.866s; **18** Max Chilton, GB, 59m 05.749s; **19** Vlado Arabadjiev, BG, 59m 10.469s; **20** Giedo van der Garde, NL, 59m 11.350s; **21** Jérôme D'Ambrosio, B, 12 laps (DNF-wheel loose); **22** Jules Bianchi, F, 0 (DNF-accident); **23** Christian Vietoris, D, 0 (DNF-accident); **24** Johnny Cecotto Jr., YV, 0 (DNF-accident).
Fastest race lap: Bird, 1m 31.754s, 113.487 mph/182.640 km/h.
Pole position: Bianchi, 1m 27.727s, 118.697 mph/191.024 km/h.

Race 2 (72.234 miles/116.249 km).
1 Fabio Leimer, CH, 38m 31.849s, 112.482 mph/181.022 km/h; **2** Luiz Razia, BR, 38m 32.604s; **3** Pastor Maldonado, YV, 38m 36.699s; **4** Sam Bird, GB, 38m 46.123s; **5** Oliver Turvey, GB, 38m 58.634s; **6** Daniel Clos, E, 38m 59.282s; **7** Charles Pic, F, 39m 00.308s; **8** Giacomo Ricci, I, 39m 00.926s; **9** Giedo van der Garde, NL, 39m 01.738s; **10** Ho-Pin Tung, CN, 39m 03.172s; **11** Davide Valsecchi, I, 39m 11.077s; **12** Jules Bianchi, F, 39m 11.413s; **13** Jérôme D'Ambrosio, B, 39m 11.510s; **14** Rodolfo Gonzalez, YV, 39m 23.232s; **15** Adrian Zaugg, ZA, 39m 23.820s; **16** Max Chilton, GB, 39m 24.322s; **17** Johnny Cecotto Jr., YV, 39m 25.338s; **18** Christian Vietoris, D, 39m 25.978s; **19** Josef Kral, CZ, 39m 26.621s; **20** Vlado Arabadjiev, BG, 39m 28.237s; **21** Michael Herck, RO, 39m 38.310s; **22** Marcus Ericsson, S, 2 laps (DNF-hydraulics); **23** Alberto Valério, BR, 0 (DNF-spin).
Did not start: Sergio Pérez, MEX (engine).
Fastest race lap: Leimer, 1m 31.229s, 114.140 mph/183.691 km/h.
Pole position: Leimer.
Championship points: Drivers: 1 Pic, 10; **2** Leimer, 8; **3** Ricci, 8; **4** Razia, 7; **5** Clos, 7; **6** Maldonado, 7.
Teams: 1 Rapax, 14; **2** Arden International, 10; **3** Ocean Racing Technology, 8.

GP2 SERIES, Monte-Carlo Street Circuit, Monaco, 14/15 May. Round 2. 42 and 30 laps of the 2.075-mile/3.340-km circuit.
Race 1 (87.166 miles/140.280 km).
1 Sergio Pérez, MEX, 1h 00m 32.223s, 86.392 mph/139.035 km/h; **2** Pastor Maldonado, YV, 1h 00m 32.840s; **3** Daniel Clos, E, 1h 00m 42.911s; **4** Jules Bianchi, F, 1h 00m 44.340s; **5** Alberto Valério, BR, 1h 00m 46.340s; **6** Giedo van der Garde, NL, 1h 00m 49.560s; **7** Luiz Razia, BR, 1h 01m 08.190s; **8** Jérôme D'Ambrosio, B, 1h 01m 09.626s; **9** Johnny Cecotto Jr., YV, 1h 01m 18.758s; **10** Rodolfo Gonzalez, YV, 1h 01m 25.278s; **11** Charles Pic, F, 1h 01m 26.200s; **12** Marcus Ericsson, S, 1h 01m 27.136s; **13** Josef Kral, CZ, 1h 01m 29.794s; **14** Christian Vietoris, D, 1h 01m 30.859s; **15** Oliver Turvey, GB, 1h 01m 32.165s; **16** Michael Herck, RO, 1h 01m 35.231s; **17** Giacomo Ricci, I, 1h 01m 35.642s; **18** Sam Bird, GB, 1h 01m 56.383s; **19** Davide Valsecchi, I, 21 laps (DNF-accident); **20** Vlado Arabadjiev, BG, 19 (DNF-accident); **21** Ho-Pin Tung, CN, 13 (DNF-accident); **22** Fabio Leimer, CH, 0 (DNF-accident); **23** Adrian Zaugg, ZA, 0 (DNF-stalled); **24** Max Chilton, GB, 0 (DNF-stalled).
Fastest race lap: Pérez, 1m 21.823s, 91.311 mph/146.951 km/h.
Pole position: Clos, 1m 37.572s, 76.572 mph/123.232 km/h.

Race 2 (62.261 miles/100.200 km).
1 Jérôme D'Ambrosio, B, 43m 43.804s, 85.425 mph/137.479 km/h; **2** Giedo van der Garde, NL, 43m 44.155s; **3** Jules Bianchi, F, 43m 44.882s; **4** Johnny Cecotto Jr., YV, 43m 46.723s; **5** Luiz Razia, BR, 43m 50.376s; **6** Sergio Pérez, MEX, 43m 51.061s; **7** Charles Pic, F, 43m 51.707s; **8** Josef Kral, CZ, 43m 52.641s; **9** Marcus Ericsson, S, 43m 53.235s; **10** Sam Bird, GB, 43m 53.850s; **11** Pastor Maldonado, YV, 43m 54.269s; **12** Adrian Zaugg, ZA, 43m 55.043s; **13** Vlado Arabadjiev, BG, 43m 56.395s; **14** Max Chilton, GB, 44m 09.050s; **15** Oliver Turvey, GB, 44m 09.265s; **16** Davide Valsecchi, I, 44m 09.507s; **17** Fabio Leimer, CH, 44m 09.867s; **18** Michael Herck, RO, 22 laps (DNF-engine); **19** Ho-Pin Tung, CN, **20** (DNF-gearbox); **20** Giacomo Ricci, I, 17 (DNF-engine); **21** Alberto Valério, BR, 14 (DNF-accident); **22** Rodolfo Gonzalez, YV, 14 (DNF-accident); **23** Daniel Clos, E, 8 (DNF-accident); Did not start: Christian Vietoris, D (sensor).
Fastest race lap: Bird, 1m 22.052s, 91.056 mph/146.541 km/h.
Pole position: D'Ambrosio.

Championship points: Drivers: 1 Pérez, 17; **2** Maldonado, 15; **3** Clos, 15; **4** Razia, 11; **5** Bianchi, 11; **6** Pic, 10.
Teams: 1 Rapax, 26; **2** Barwa Addax Team, 25; **3** ART Grand Prix, 16.

GP2 SERIES, Istanbul Speed Park, Tuzla, Turkey, 29/30 May. Round 3. 32 and 23 laps of the 3.317-mile/5.338-km circuit.
Race 1 (106.011 miles/170.608 km).
1 Pastor Maldonado, YV, 52m 33.219s, 121.031 mph/194.781 km/h; **2** Davide Valsecchi, I, 52m 52.750s; **3** Sam Bird, GB, 52m 56.546s; **4** Giedo van der Garde, NL, 52m 59.348s; **5** Luiz Razia, BR, 52m 59.965s; **6** Michael Herck, RO, 53m 03.663s; **7** Christian Vietoris, D, 53m 09.938s; **8** Daniel Clos, E, 53m 14.688s; **9** Max Chilton, GB, 53m 21.801s; **10** Jérôme D'Ambrosio, B, 53m 23.067s; **11** Ho-Pin Tung, CN, 53m 23.534s; **12** Johnny Cecotto Jr., YV, 53m 29.215s; **13** Fabio Leimer, CH, 53m 40.020s; **14** Oliver Turvey, GB, 53m 41.611s; **15** Josef Kral, CZ, 53m 55.683s; **16** Rodolfo Gonzalez, YV, 53m 57.008s; **17** Alberto Valério, BR, 29 laps (DNF-brakes); **18** Vlado Arabadjiev, BG, 27 (DNF-brakes); **19** Adrian Zaugg, ZA, 27 (DNF-engine); **20** Giacomo Ricci, I, 25 (DNF-accident); **21** Marcus Ericsson, S, 11 (DNF-engine); **22** Charles Pic, F, 1 (DNF-accident); **23** Jules Bianchi, F, 1 (DNF-accident).
Disqualified: Sergio Pérez, MEX, finished 4th in 52m 59.172s (car underweight).
Fastest race lap: Maldonado, 1m 37.010s, 123.087 mph/198.090 km/h.
Pole position: Valsecchi, 1m 34.860s, 125.877 mph/202.580 km/h.

Race 2 (76.159 miles/122.566 km).
1 Daniel Clos, E, 37m 25.211s, 122.114 mph/196.523 km/h; **2** Luiz Razia, BR, 37m 34.081s; **3** Giedo van der Garde, NL, 37m 38.207s; **4** Davide Valsecchi, I, 37m 38.690s; **5** Michael Herck, RO, 37m 39.714s; **6** Pastor Maldonado, YV, 37m 44.329s; **7** Sergio Pérez, MEX, 37m 45.291s; **8** Jérôme D'Ambrosio, B, 37m 45.699s; **9** Ho-Pin Tung, CN, 37m 49.079s; **10** Sam Bird, GB, 37m 54.771s; **11** Max Chilton, GB, 37m 56.877s; **12** Johnny Cecotto Jr., YV, 38m 01.370s; **13** Jules Bianchi, F, 38m 05.760s; **14** Josef Kral, CZ, 38m 05.836s; **15** Fabio Leimer, CH, 38m 13.655s; **16** Rodolfo Gonzalez, YV, 38m 13.893s; **17** Giacomo Ricci, I, 38m 14.272s; **18** Oliver Turvey, GB, 22 laps; **19** Alberto Valério, BR, 21; **20** Adrian Zaugg, ZA, 17 (DNF-engine); **21** Christian Vietoris, D, 9 (DNF-engine); **22** Marcus Ericsson, S, 5 (DNF-accident); **23** Vlado Arabadjiev, BG, 3 (DNF-accident);
Did not start: Charles Pic, F (illness).
Fastest race lap: Turvey, 1m 36.770s, 123.393 mph/198.582 km/h.
Pole position: Clos.
Championship points: Drivers: 1 Maldonado, 27; **2** Clos, 23; **3** Razia, 20; **4** Pérez, 17; **5** van der Garde, 17; **6** Valsecchi, 13.
Teams: 1 Rapax, 47; **2** Barwa Addax Team, 34; **3** Racing Engineering, 25.

GP2 SERIES, Valencia Street Circuit, Spain, 26/27 June. Round 4. 30 and 22 laps of the 3.367-mile/5.419-km circuit.
Race 1 (101.016 miles/162.570 km).
1 Pastor Maldonado, YV, 56m 55.681s, 106.467 mph/171.342 km/h; **2** Jules Bianchi, F, 57m 03.977s; **3** Sam Bird, GB, 57m 11.775s; **4** Giedo van der Garde, NL, 57m 12.469s; **5** Daniel Clos, E, 57m 34.655s; **6** Charles Pic, F, 57m 38.096s; **7** Marcus Ericsson, S, 57m 38.595s; **8** Michael Herck, RO, 57m 39.403s; **9** Alberto Valério, BR, 57m 44.189s; **10** Davide Valsecchi, I, 57m 46.092s; **11** Sergio Pérez, MEX, 57m 46.989s; **12** Christian Vietoris, D, 57m 51.019s; **13** Vlado Arabadjiev, BG, 29 laps (DNF-engine); **14** Adrian Zaugg, ZA, 29; **15** Fabio Leimer, CH, 25 (DNF-battery); **16** Giacomo Ricci, I, 0 (DNF-accident); **17** Johnny Cecotto Jr., YV, 0 (DNF-accident); **18** Luiz Razia, BR, 0 (DNF-accident); **19** Oliver Turvey, GB, 0 (DNF-accident); **20** Josef Kral, CZ, 0 (DNF-accident); **21** Jérôme D'Ambrosio, B, 0 (DNF-accident); **22** Ho-Pin Tung, CN, 0 (DNF-accident); **23** Rodolfo Gonzalez, YV, 0 (DNF-accident); **24** Max Chilton, GB, 0 (DNF-accident).
Fastest race lap: Maldonado, 1m 47.528s, 112.733 mph/181.426 km/h.
Pole position: Pérez, 1m 45.337s, 115.077 mph/185.199 km/h.

Race 2 (74.079 miles/119.218 km).
1 Marcus Ericsson, S, 45m 33.442s, 97.563 mph/157.012 km/h; **2** Giedo van der Garde, NL, 45m 34.325s; **3** Michael Herck, RO, 45m 38.562s; **4** Pastor Maldonado, YV, 45m 38.734s; **5** Charles Pic, F, 45m 42.675s; **6** Davide Valsecchi, I, 45m 51.220s; **7** Daniel Clos, E, 45m 51.757s; **8** Jérôme D'Ambrosio, B, 45m 52.352s; **9** Vlado Arabadjiev, BG, 45m 54.760s; **10** Sam Bird, GB, 45m 57.273s; **11** Max Chilton, GB, 45m 59.439s; **12** Oliver Turvey, GB, 46m 03.829s; **13** Ho-Pin Tung, CN, 46m 06.155s; **14** Johnny Cecotto Jr., YV, 46m 06.836s; **15** Adrian Zaugg, ZA, 21 laps; **16** Sergio Pérez, MEX, 21; **17** Luiz Razia, BR, 15 (DNF-accident); **18** Rodolfo Gonzalez, YV, 1 (DNF-accident); **19** Josef Kral, CZ, 1 (DNF-accident); **20** Jules Bianchi, F, 0 (DNF-accident); **21** Alberto Valério, BR, 0 (DNF-accident); **22** Christian Vietoris, D, 0 (DNF-accident); **23** Fabio Leimer, CH, 0 (DNF-accident); **24** Giacomo Ricci, I, 0 (DNF-accident).
Fastest race lap: Pérez, 1m 47.514s, 112.747 mph/181.449 km/h.
Pole position: Herck.

Championship points: Drivers: 1 Maldonado, 42; **2** Clos, 27; **3** van der Garde, 27; **4** Razia, 20; **5** Pérez, 19; **6** Bianchi, 19.
Teams: 1 Rapax, 62; **2** Barwa Addax Team, 46; **3** ART Grand Prix, 36.

GP2 SERIES, Silverstone Grand Prix Circuit, Towcester, Northamptonshire, Great Britain, 10/11 July. Round 5. 29 and 21 laps of the 3.660-mile/5.891-km circuit.
Race 1 (106.089 miles/170.734 km).
1 Pastor Maldonado, YV, 50m 21.479s, 126.402 mph/203.424 km/h; **2** Jules Bianchi, F, 50m 31.604s; **3** Daniel Clos, E, 50m 41.028s; **4** Sam Bird, GB, 50m 42.458s; **5** Sergio Pérez, MEX, 50m 53.518s; **6** Christian Vietoris, D, 50m 57.218s; **7** Davide Valsecchi, I, 50m 59.181s; **8** Oliver Turvey, GB, 51m 00.232s; **9** Giedo van der Garde, NL, 51m 00.566s; **10** Charles Pic, F, 51m 01.324s; **11** Jérôme D'Ambrosio, B, 51m 01.580s; **12** Marcus Ericsson, S, 51m 15.428s; **13** Giacomo Ricci, I, 51m 16.385s; **14** Alberto Valério, BR, 51m 23.611s; **15** Adrian Zaugg, ZA, 51m 33.452s; **16** Rodolfo Gonzalez, YV, 51m 34.304s; **17** Fabio Leimer, CH, 51m 35.693s; **18** Johnny Cecotto Jr., YV, 51m 37.592s; **19** Max Chilton, GB, 51m 39.284s; **20** Luca Filippi, I, 51m 55.131s; **21** Vlado Arabadjiev, BG, 51m 55.722s; **22** Michael Herck, RO, 28 laps; **23** Luiz Razia, BR, 18 (DNF-alternator); **24** Ho-Pin Tung, CN, 12 (DNF-gearbox).
Fastest race lap: Maldonado, 1m 41.663s, 129.622 mph/208.606 km/h.
Pole position: Bianchi, 1m 39.189s, 132.855 mph/213.809 km/h.

Race 2 (76.805 miles/123.606 km).
1 Sergio Pérez, MEX, 35m 54.531s, 128.333 mph/206.532 km/h; **2** Oliver Turvey, GB, 36m 09.917s; **3** Daniel Clos, E, 36m 10.528s; **4** Pastor Maldonado, YV, 36m 10.957s; **5** Jules Bianchi, F, 36m 12.131s; **6** Davide Valsecchi, I, 36m 16.298s; **7** Giedo van der Garde, NL, 36m 17.283s; **8** Charles Pic, F, 36m 18.738s; **9** Luca Filippi, I, 36m 19.014s; **10** Christian Vietoris, D, 36m 19.588s; **11** Jérôme D'Ambrosio, B, 36m 20.384s; **12** Giacomo Ricci, I, 36m 20.508s; **13** Fabio Leimer, CH, 36m 24.723s; **14** Michael Herck, RO, 36m 25.038s; **15** Ho-Pin Tung, CN, 36m 25.434s; **16** Luiz Razia, BR, 36m 40.259s; **17** Vlado Arabadjiev, BG, 36m 43.244s; **18** Marcus Ericsson, S, 36m 44.487s; **19** Max Chilton, GB, 36m 44.745s; **20** Rodolfo Gonzalez, YV, 36m 49.987s; **21** Adrian Zaugg, ZA, 37m 13.844s; **22** Alberto Valério, BR, 20 laps; **23** Johnny Cecotto Jr., YV, 19.
Did not start: Sam Bird, GB (engine).
Fastest race lap: Pérez, 1m 41.610s, 129.689 mph/208.715 km/h.
Pole position: Turvey.
Championship points: Drivers: 1 Maldonado, 56; **2** Clos, 37; **3** Bianchi, 31; **4** Pérez, 30; **5** van der Garde, 27; **6** Bird, 22.
Teams: 1 Rapax, 76; **2** Barwa Addax Team, 57; **3** ART Grand Prix, 53.

GP2 SERIES, Hockenheimring Grand Prix Circuit, Heidelberg, Germany, 24/25 July. Round 6. 38 and 27 laps of the 2.842-mile/4.574-km circuit.
Race 1 (108.002 miles/173.812 km).
1 Pastor Maldonado, YV, 54m 07.807s, 119.713 mph/192.660 km/h; **2** Sergio Pérez, MEX, 54m 11.673s; **3** Charles Pic, F, 54m 20.230s; **4** Daniel Clos, E, 54m 20.707s; **5** Jules Bianchi, F, 54m 30.982s; **6** Marcus Ericsson, S, 54m 34.206s; **7** Adrian Zaugg, ZA, 54m 46.401s; **8** Oliver Turvey, GB, 54m 50.639s; **9** Michael Herck, RO, 54m 53.100s; **10** Luca Filippi, I, 54m 53.194s; **11** Alberto Valério, BR, 54m 55.085s; **12** Giedo van der Garde, NL, 54m 56.590s; **13** Johnny Cecotto Jr., YV, 54m 59.915s; **14** Sam Bird, GB, 55m 00.792s; **15** Vlado Arabadjiev, BG, 55m 10.652s; **16** Giacomo Ricci, I, 37 laps (DNF-spin); **17** Davide Valsecchi, I, 37; **18** Rodolfo Gonzalez, YV, 37; **19** Max Chilton, GB, 36; **20** Romain Grosjean, F, 35; **21** Fabio Leimer, CH, 34 (DNF-accident); **22** Ho-Pin Tung, CN, 9 (DNF-accident); **23** Luiz Razia, BR, 4 (DNF-accident); **24** Christian Vietoris, D, 0 (DNF-accident).
Fastest race lap: Bianchi, 1m 23.527s, 122.496 mph/197.138 km/h.
Pole position: Pic, 1m 41.638s, 100.668 mph/162.010 km/h.

Race 2 (76.738 miles/123.498 km).
1 Sergio Pérez, MEX, 38m 02.071s, 121.055 mph/194.819 km/h; **2** Oliver Turvey, GB, 38m 08.409s; **3** Adrian Zaugg, ZA, 38m 10.182s; **4** Jules Bianchi, F, 38m 15.646s; **5** Sam Bird, GB, 38m 17.019s; **6** Daniel Clos, E, 38m 19.167s; **7** Luca Filippi, I, 38m 19.457s; **8** Michael Herck, RO, 38m 23.358s; **9** Giedo van der Garde, NL, 38m 24.563s; **10** Christian Vietoris, D, 38m 25.777s; **11** Giacomo Ricci, I, 38m 26.606s; **12** Alberto Valério, BR, 38m 30.052s; **13** Luiz Razia, BR, 38m 30.305s; **14** Ho-Pin Tung, CN, 38m 31.268s; **15** Vlado Arabadjiev, BG, 38m 34.603s; **16** Max Chilton, GB, 38m 40.009s; **17** Charles Pic, F, 38m 42.332s; **18** Davide Valsecchi, I, 38m 43.545s; **19** Romain Grosjean, F, 24 laps (DND-accident); **20** Pastor Maldonado, YV, 24 (DNF-accident); **21** Rodolfo Gonzalez, YV, 23 (DNF-accident); **22** Johnny Cecotto Jr., YV, 14 (DNF-accident); **23** Marcus Ericsson, S, 2 (DNF-accident); **24** Fabio Leimer, CH, 1 (DNF-accident).
Fastest race lap: Pérez, 1m 23.110s, 123.110 mph/198.127 km/h.
Pole position: Turvey.

Championship points: Drivers: 1 Maldonado, 66; **2** Pérez, 45; **3** Clos, 43; **4** Bianchi, 39; **5** van der Garde, 27; **6** Bird, 24.
Teams: 1 Rapax, 86; **2** Barwa Addax Team, 72; **3** ART Grand Prix, 63.

GP2 SERIES, Hungaroring, Mogyorod, Budapest, Hungary, 31 July/1 August. Round 7. 37 and 28 laps of the 2.722-mile/4.381-km circuit.
Race 1 (100.698 miles/162.057 km).
1 Pastor Maldonado, YV, 1h 18m 45.734s, 76.710 mph/123.452 km/h; **2** Christian Vietoris, D, 1h 18m 51.599s; **3** Sergio Pérez, MEX, 1h 18m 52.245s; **4** Oliver Turvey, GB, 1h 18m 52.843s; **5** Giedo van der Garde, NL, 1h 18m 55.959s; **6** Jérôme D'Ambrosio, B, 1h 18m 57.778s; **7** Michael Herck, RO, 1h 18m 58.221s; **8** Giacomo Ricci, I, 1h 18m 58.675s; **9** Davide Valsecchi, I, 1h 18m 59.272s; **10** Luiz Razia, BR, 1h 19m 00.115s; **11** Charles Pic, F, 1h 19m 04.374s; **12** Marcus Ericsson, S, 1h 19m 07.439s; **13** Sam Bird, GB, 1h 19m 11.078s; **14** Luca Filippi, I, 1h 19m 13.794s; **15** Adrian Zaugg, ZA, 1h 19m 15.450s; **16** Daniel Clos, E, 1h 19m 16.232s; **17** Max Chilton, GB, 1h 19m 17.888s; **18** Vlado Arabadjiev, BG, 36 laps; **19** Alberto Valério, BR, 24 (DNF-accciddent); **20** Fabio Leimer, CH, 14 (DNF-engine); **21** Johnny Cecotto Jr., YV, 9 (DNF-accident); **22** Jules Bianchi, F, 0 (DNF-accident); **23** Ho-Pin Tung, CN, 0 (DNF-accident); **24** Rodolfo Gonzalez, YV, 0 (DNF-accident).
Fastest race lap: Maldonado, 1m 30.767s, 107.968 mph/173.759 km/h.
Pole position: Bird, 1m 27.864s, 111.536 mph/179.500 km/h.

Race 2 (76.198 miles/122.628 km).
1 Giacomo Ricci, I, 42m 56.588s, 106.462 mph/171.335 km/h; **2** Christian Vietoris, D, 43m 03.685s; **3** Davide Valsecchi, I, 43m 13.300s; **4** Giedo van der Garde, NL, 43m 16.296s; **5** Oliver Turvey, GB, 43m 17.243s; **6** Luca Filippi, I, 43m 18.971s; **7** Daniel Clos, E, 43m 23.473s; **8** Adrian Zaugg, ZA, 43m 26.666s; **9** Charles Pic, F, 43m 27.915s; **10** Marcus Ericsson, S, 43m 35.982s; **11** Fabio Leimer, CH, 43m 37.198s; **12** Alberto Valério, BR, 43m 39.598s; **13** Johnny Cecotto Jr., YV, 43m 46.257s; **14** Vlado Arabadjiev, BG, 43m 54.488s; **15** Rodolfo Gonzalez, YV, 44m 07.417s; **16** Max Chilton, GB, 44m 08.461s; **17** Jérôme D'Ambrosio, B, 12 laps (DNF-hydraulics); **18** Sam Bird, GB, 9 (DNF-hydraulics); **19** Michael Herck, RO, 9 (DNF-gearbox); **20** Luiz Razia, BR, 2 (DNF-accident); **21** Sergio Pérez, MEX, 2 (DNF-accident).
Disqualified: Pastor Maldonado, YV, 6 laps (failed to obey instruction to pit with loose bodywork)
Did not start: Jules Bianchi, F (injured); Ho-Pin Tung, CN (injured).
Fastest race lap: Herck, 1m 30.764s, 107.972 mph/173.764 km/h.
Pole position: Ricci.
Championship points: Drivers: 1 Maldonado, 77; **2** Pérez, 51; **3** Clos, 43; **4** Bianchi, 39; **5** van der Garde, 34; **6** Bird, 26.
Teams: 1 Rapax, 97; **2** Barwa Addax Team, 85; **3** ART Grand Prix, 65.

GP2 SERIES, Circuit de Spa-Francorchamps, Stavelot, Belgium, 28/29 August. Round 8. 25 and 18 laps of the 4.352-mile/7.004-km circuit.
Race 1 (108.725 miles/174.976 km).
1 Pastor Maldonado, YV, 52m 27.763s, 124.345 mph/200.114 km/h; **2** Álvaro Parente, P, 52m 28.006s; **3** Romain Grosjean, F, 52m 32.529s; **4** Charles Pic, F, 52m 41.578s; **5** Luca Filippi, I, 52m 43.848s; **6** Oliver Turvey, GB, 52m 48.880s; **7** Sergio Pérez, MEX, 52m 49.476s; **8** Rodolfo Gonzalez, YV, 52m 55.138s; **9** Giedo van der Garde, NL, 52m 58.597s; **10** Johnny Cecotto Jr., YV, 53m 00.105s; **11** Christian Vietoris, D, 53m 00.535s; **12** Fabio Leimer, CH, 53m 01.405s; **13** Marcus Ericsson, S, 53m 02.695s; **14** Jules Bianchi, F, 53m 08.060s; **15** Adrian Zaugg, ZA, 53m 09.153s; **16** Luiz Razia, BR, 53m 13.316s; **17** Max Chilton, GB, 24 laps; **18** Davide Valsecchi, I, 24; **19** Vlado Arabadjiev, BG, 22 (DNF-spin); **20** Jérôme D'Ambrosio, B, 20 (DNF-engine); **21** Michael Herck, RO, 18 (DNF-accident damage); **22** Fabrizio Crestani, I, 2 (DNF-accident); **23** Sam Bird, GB, 0 (DNF-accident); **24** Daniel Clos, E, 0 (DNF-accident).
Fastest race lap: Valsecchi, 1m 58.285s, 132.455 mph/213.166 km/h.
Pole position: D'Ambrosio, 2m 15.942s, 115.251 mph/185.479 km/h.

Race 2 (78.260 miles/125.948 km).
1 Sergio Pérez, MEX, 41m 51.924s, 112.160 mph/180.504 km/h; **2** Giedo van der Garde, NL, 41m 54.498s; **3** Álvaro Parente, P, 41m 55.507s; **4** Rodolfo Gonzalez, YV, 41m 56.750s; **5** Oliver Turvey, GB, 41m 58.984s; **6** Romain Grosjean, F, 41m 59.961s; **7** Marcus Ericsson, S, 42m 00.664s; **8** Davide Valsecchi, I, 42m 01.396s; **9** Adrian Zaugg, ZA, 42m 02.206s; **10** Luiz Razia, BR, 42m 02.511s; **11** Max Chilton, GB, 42m 03.554s; **12** Sam Bird, GB, 42m 04.095s; **13** Michael Herck, RO, 42m 04.477s; **14** Fabrizio Crestani, I, 42m 05.193s; **15** Charles Pic, F, 11 laps (DNF-accident); **16** Vlado Arabadjiev, BG, 9 (DNF-electrics); **17** Jérôme D'Ambrosio, B, 8 (DNF-electronics); **18** Christian Vietoris, D, 6 (DNF-accident); **19** Johnny Cecotto Jr., YV, 5 (DNF-accident); **20** Jules Bianchi, F, 4 (DNF-accident); **21** Luca Filippi, I, 2 (DNF-accident damage); **22** Fabio Leimer, CH, 1 (DNF-accident); **23** Pastor Maldonado, YV, 0 (DNF-accident damage).
Did not start: Daniel Clos, E (injured).

Fastest race lap: Pérez, 1m 57.014s, 133.894 mph/215.481 km/h.
Pole position: Gonzalez.
Championship points: Drivers: 1 Maldonado, 87; **2** Pérez, 60; **3** Clos, 43; **4** van der Garde, 39; **5** Bianchi, 39; **6** Turvey, 30.
Teams: 1 Rapax, 107; **2** Barwa Addax Team, 99; **3** ART Grand Prix, 65.

GP2 SERIES, Autodromo Nazionale di Monza, Milan, Italy, 11/12 September. Round 9. 30 and 21 laps of the 3.600-mile/5.793-km circuit.
Race 1 (107.796 miles/173.481 km).
1 Sam Bird, GB, 49m 27.229s, 130.783 mph/210.476 km/h; **2** Jules Bianchi, F, 49m 35.814s; **3** Oliver Turvey, GB, 49m 44.397s; **4** Christian Vietoris, D, 49m 45.478s; **5** Jérôme D'Ambrosio, B, 49m 46.590s; **6** Adrian Zaugg, ZA, 49m 48.418s; **7** Edoardo Piscopo, I, 49m 51.847s; **8** Max Chilton, GB, 49m 55.891s; **9** Davide Valsecchi, I, 50m 14.062s; **10** Fabrizio Crestani, I, 50m 15.002s; **11** Charles Pic, F, 50m 17.723s; **12** Álvaro Parente, P, 50m 27.159s; **13** Romain Grosjean, F, 29 laps; **14** Fabio Leimer, CH, 23 (DNF-hydraulics); **15** Pastor Maldonado, YV, 7 (DNF-accident damage); **16** Sergio Pérez, MEX, 5 (DNF-accident); **17** Michael Herck, RO, 5 (DNF-accident); **18** Marcus Ericsson, S, 3 (DNF-accident); **19** Luiz Razia, BR, 3 (DNF-accident); **20** Brendon Hartley, NZ, 2 (DNF-accident); **21** Daniel Clos, E, 0 (DNF-accident); **22** Luca Filippi, I, 0 (DNF-accident); **23** Giedo van der Garde, NL, 0 (DNF-accident).
Did not start: Rodolfo Gonzalez, YV (accident).
Fastest race lap: Bird, 1m 32.438s, 140.186 mph/225.608 km/h.
Pole position: Bianchi, 1m 30.269s, 143.555 mph/231.029 km/h.

Race 2 (75.400 miles/121.344 km).
1 Christian Vietoris, D, 32m 28.733s, 139.289 mph/224.165 km/h; **2** Jérôme D'Ambrosio, B, 32m 29.781s; **3** Sam Bird, GB, 32m 29.917s; **4** Jules Bianchi, F, 32m 35.522s; **5** Max Chilton, GB, 32m 38.218s; **6** Oliver Turvey, GB, 32m 38.650s; **7** Adrian Zaugg, ZA, 32m 42.163s; **8** Charles Pic, F, 32m 44.360s; **9** Álvaro Parente, P, 32m 47.654s; **10** Luiz Razia, BR, 32m 50.301s; **11** Marcus Ericsson, S, 32m 54.479s; **12** Daniel Clos, E, 32m 56.844s; **13** Sergio Pérez, MEX, 32m 57.466s; **14** Luca Filippi, I, 33m 00.235s; **15** Fabrizio Crestani, I, 33m 01.778s; **16** Davide Valsecchi, I, 33m 41.494s; **17** Romain Grosjean, F, 18 laps (DNF-accident damage); **18** Brendon Hartley, NZ, 9 (DNF-exhaust); **19** Giedo van der Garde, NL, 5 (DNF-accident); **20** Michael Herck, RO, 2 (DNF-engine); **21** Edoardo Piscopo, I, 2 (DNF-accident); **22** Rodolfo Gonzalez, YV, 1 (DNF-accident); **23** Pastor Maldonado, YV, 0 (DNF-accident).
Did not start: Fabio Leimer, CH (hydraulics).
Fastest race lap: Bird, 1m 31.954s, 140.924 mph/226.796 km/h.
Pole position: Chilton.
Championship points: Drivers: 1 Maldonado, 87; **2** Pérez, 60; **3** Bianchi, 52; **4** Clos, 43; **5** Bird, 42; **6** van der Garde, 39.
Teams: 1 Rapax, 107; **2** Barwa Addax Team, 99; **3** ART Grand Prix, 94.

GP2 SERIES, Yas Marina Circuit, Abu Dhabi, United Arab Emirates, 13/14 November. Round 10. 31 and 22 laps of the 3.451-mile/5.554-km circuit.
Race 1 (106.913 miles/172.059 km).
1 Sergio Pérez, MEX, 59m 53.752s, 107.098 mph/172.358 km/h; **2** Oliver Turvey, GB, 1h 00m 14.817s; **3** Sam Bird, GB, 1h 00m 23.447s; **4** Daniel Clos, E, 1h 00m 24.194s; **5** Davide Valsecchi, I, 1h 00m 30.366s; **6** Romain Grosjean, F, 1h 00m 31.927s; **7** Luiz Razia, BR, 1h 00m 32.948s; **8** Josef Kral, CZ, 1h 00m 33.476s; **9** Brendon Hartley, NZ, 1h 00m 34.431s; **10** Rodolfo Gonzalez, YV, 1h 00m 43.456s; **11** Marcus Ericsson, S, 1h 00m 49.112s; **12** Max Chilton, GB, 1h 00m 51.677s; **13** Fabrizio Crestani, I, 1h 00m 52.086s; **14** Jérôme D'Ambrosio, B, 1h 00m 52.588s; **15** James Jakes, GB, 1h 00m 54.979s; **16** Michael Herck, RO, 1h 00m 55.930s; **17** Pastor Maldonado, YV, 1h 01m 07.861s; **18** Jules Bianchi, F, 1h 01m 23.398s; **19** Federico Leo, I, 1h 01m 30.057s; **20** Charles Pic, F, 30 laps; **21** Ho-Pin Tung, CN, 11 (DNF); **22** Fabio Leimer, CH, 7 (DNF); **23** Adrian Zaugg, ZA, 0 (DNF); **24** Giedo van der Garde, NL, 0 (DNF).
Fastest race lap: Pérez, 1m 50.749s, 112.181 mph/180.537 km/h.
Pole position: Turvey, 1m 48.559s, 114.444 mph/184.180 km/h.

Race 2 (75.853 miles/122.073 km).
1 Davide Valsecchi, I, 40m 59.120s, 111.043 mph/178.707 km/h; **2** Luiz Razia, BR, 41m 00.045s; **3** Romain Grosjean, F, 41m 04.227s; **4** Daniel Clos, E, 41m 04.717s; **5** Josef Kral, CZ, 41m 16.973s; **6** Brendon Hartley, NZ, 41m 21.044s; **7** Jérôme D'Ambrosio, B, 41m 23.785s; **8** Pastor Maldonado, YV, 41m 24.291s; **9** Michael Herck, RO, 41m 24.792s; **10** Charles Pic, F, 41m 31.045s; **11** Max Chilton, GB, 41m 34.601s; **12** Ho-Pin Tung, CN, 41m 35.774s; **13** Fabrizio Crestani, I, 41m 36.948s; **14** Fabio Leimer, CH, 41m 37.521s; **15** Rodolfo Gonzalez, YV, 41m 38.084s; **16** Oliver Turvey, GB, 41m 45.636s; **17** Jules Bianchi, F, 41m 46.687s; **18** James Jakes, GB, 41m 50.898s; **19** Giedo van der Garde, NL, 42m 15.500s; **20** Marcus Ericsson, S, 18 laps (DNF); **21** Federico Leo, I, 10 (DNF); **22** Sam Bird, GB, 4 (DNF); **23** Sergio Pérez, MEX, 4 (DNF); **24** Adrian Zaugg, ZA, 0 (DNS).
Fastest race lap: van der Garde, 1m 50.110s, 112.832 mph/181.585 km/h.
Pole position: Kral.

Final championship points
Drivers: 1 Pastor Maldonado, YV, 87; **2** Sergio Pérez, MEX, 71; **3** Jules Bianchi, F, 52; **4** Daniel Clos, E, 51; **5** Sam Bird, GB, 48; **6** Oliver Turvey, GB, 47; **7** Giedo van der Garde, NL, 39; **8** Davide Valsecchi, I, 31; **9** Christian Vietoris, D, 29; **10** Charles Pic, F, 28; **11** Luiz Razia, BR, 28; **12** Jérôme D'Ambrosio, B, 21; **13** Giacomo Ricci, I, 16; **14** Romain Grosjean, F, 14; **15** Álvaro Parente, P, 13; **16** Michael Herck, RO, 12; **17** Marcus Ericsson, S, 11; **18** Adrian Zaugg, ZA, 9; **19** Fabio Leimer, CH, 8; **20** Luca Filippi, I, 5; **21** Rodolfo Gonzalez, YV, 4; **22** Alberto Valério, BR, 4; **23** Johnny Cecotto Jr., YV, 3; **24** Josef Kral, CZ, 3; **25** Max Chilton, GB, 3; **26** Edoardo Piscopo, I, 2; **27** Brendon Hartley, NZ, 1.
Teams: 1 Rapax, 115; **2** Barwa Addax Team, 110; **3** ART Grand Prix, 100; **4** Racing Engineering, 80; **5** iSport International, 78; **6** DAMS, 35; **7** Arden International, 32; **8** DPR, 28; **9** Super Nova Racing, 19; **10** Scuderia Coloni, 18; **11** Trident Racing, 14; **12** Ocean Racing Technology, 11.

GP2 Asia Series

All cars are Dallara-Renault.

2009–2010

GP2 ASIA SERIES, Yas Marina Circuit, Abu Dhabi, UAE, 31 October/1 November. Round 1. 33 and 22 laps of the 3.451-mile/5.554-km circuit.
Race 1 (113.815 miles/183.167 km).
1 Davide Valsecchi, I, 1h 07m 49.810s, 100.676 mph/162.022 km/h; **2** Luca Filippi, I, 1h 07m 54.691s; **3** James Jakes, GB, 1h 07m 55.984s; **4** Alexander Rossi, USA, 1h 07m 56.992s; **5** Josef Kral, CZ, 1h 07m 58.030s; **6** Christian Vietoris, D, 1h 08m 03.110s; **7** Johnny Cecotto Jr., YV, 1h 08m 05.270s; **8** Oliver Turvey, GB, 1h 08m 06.033s; **9** Edoardo Piscopo, I, 1h 08m 06.525s; **10** Roldán Rodríguez, E, 1h 08m 06.689s; **11** Marcus Ericsson, S, 1h 08m 11.496s; **12** Will Bratt, GB, 1h 08m 12.349s; **13** Michael Herck, RO, 1h 08m 12.691s; **14** Rodolfo Gonzalez, YV, 1h 08m 13.213s; **15** Daniel Zampieri, I, 1h 08m 13.596s; **16** Max Chilton, GB, 1h 08m 14.941s; **17** Fabio Leimer, CH, 1h 08m 19.829s; **18** Sam Bird, GB, 31 laps; **19** Charles Pic, F, 28 (DNF); **20** Vlado Arabadjiev, BG, 25 (DNF); **21** Plamen Kralev, BG, 24 (DNF); **22** Luiz Razia, BR, 12 (DNF); **23** Giacomo Ricci, I, 8 (DNF); **24** Diego Nunes, BR, 0 (DNF).
Fastest race lap: Valsecchi, 1m 53.341s, 109.615 mph/176.409 km/h.
Pole position: Valsecchi, 1m 51.964s, 110.963 mph/178.578 km/h.

Race 2 (75.853 miles/122.073 km).
1 Christian Vietoris, D, 43m 18.814s, 105.074 mph/169.101 km/h; **2** Davide Valsecchi, I, 43m 21.261s; **3** Josef Kral, CZ, 43m 22.009s; **4** Oliver Turvey, GB, 43m 25.430s; **5** Alexander Rossi, USA, 43m 26.234s; **6** Johnny Cecotto Jr., YV, 43m 26.525s; **7** Edoardo Piscopo, I, 43m 27.051s; **8** Luca Filippi, I, 43m 28.950s; **9** Michael Herck, RO, 43m 29.544s; **10** James Jakes, GB, 43m 30.457s; **11** Luiz Razia, BR, 43m 30.695s; **12** Marcus Ericsson, S, 43m 31.129s; **13** Diego Nunes, BR, 43m 31.707s; **14** Roldán Rodríguez, E, 43m 32.117s; **15** Charles Pic, F, 43m 32.591s; **16** Rodolfo Gonzalez, YV, 43m 33.245s; **17** Max Chilton, GB, 43m 38.299s; **18** Sam Bird, GB, 43m 40.235s; **19** Vlado Arabadjiev, BG, 17 laps (DNF); **20** Fabio Leimer, CH, 14 (DNF); **21** Will Bratt, GB, 14 (DNF); **22** Daniel Zampieri, I, 5 (DNF); **23** Giacomo Ricci, I, 1 (DNF); **24** Plamen Kralev, BG, 0 (DNF).
Fastest race lap: Bird, 1m 52.070s, 110.858 mph/178.409 km/h.
Pole position: Turvey.
Championship points: Drivers: 1 Valsecchi, 19; **2** Vietoris, 9; **3** Filippi, 8; **4** Kral, 8; **5** Rossi, 7; **6** Jakes, 6.
Teams: 1 iSport International, 23; **2** Super Nova Racing, 14; **3** DAMS, 9.

GP2 ASIA SERIES, Yas Marina Circuit, Abu Dhabi, UAE, 5/6 February. Round 2. 33 and 21 laps of the 3.451-mile/5.554-km circuit.
Race 1 (113.815 miles/183.167 km).
1 Oliver Turvey, GB, 1h 04m 55.310s, 105.186 mph/169.280 km/h; **2** Davide Valsecchi, I, 1h 04m 55.928s; **3** Jules Bianchi, F, 1h 04m 57.899s; **4** Javier Villa, E, 1h 05m 02.682s; **5** Giacomo Ricci, I, 1h 05m 05.869s; **6** Alexander Rossi, USA, 1h 05m 09.028s; **7** Michael Herck, RO, 1h 05m 15.110s; **8** Max Chilton, GB, 1h 05m 19.705s; **9** Josef Kral, CZ, 1h 05m 22.767s; **10** Charles Pic, F, 1h 05m 29.036s; **11** Will Bratt, GB, 1h 05m 29.610s; **12** Sergio Pérez, MEX, 1h 05m 46.595s; **13** Vlado Arabadjiev, BG, 1h 06m 00.700s; **14** Luca Filippi, I, 32 laps; **15** Alberto Valério, BR, 32; **16** Plamen Kralev, BG, 32; **17** Marcus Ericsson, S, 30; **18** Fabio Leimer, CH, 27 (DNF); **19** Giedo van der Garde, NL, 25 (DNF); **20** Daniel Zampieri, I, 23 (DNF); **21** Daniel Clos, E, 9 (DNF); **22** Christian Vietoris, D, 7 (DNF); **23** Sam Bird, GB, 4 (DNF); **24** Edoardo Piscopo, I, 0 (DNF).
Fastest race lap: Arabadjiev, 1m 51.872s, 111.054 mph/178.725 km/h.
Pole position: Pic, 1m 52.497s, 110.438 mph/177.732 km/h.

Race 2 (72.402 miles/116.519 km).
1 Davide Valsecchi, I, 41m 00.566s, 105.929 mph/170.476 km/h; **2** Michael Herck, RO, 41m 02.535s; **3** Giacomo Ricci, I, 41m 04.793s; **4** Sergio Pérez, MEX, 41m 12.184s; **5** Oliver Turvey, GB, 41m 12.801s; **6** Max Chilton, GB, 41m 20.185s; **7** Jules Bianchi, F, 41m 20.584s; **8** Charles Pic, F, 41m 21.252s; **9** Alexander Rossi, USA, 41m 26.946s; **10** Vlado Arabadjiev, BG, 41m 27.604s; **11** Javier Villa, E, 41m 27.966s; **12** Marcus Ericsson, S, 41m 28.873s; **13** Daniel Clos, E, 41m 30.140s; **14** Christian Vietoris, D, 41m 31.559s; **15** Daniel Zampieri, I, 41m 32.257s; **16** Edoardo Piscopo, I, 41m 32.779s; **17** Luca Filippi, I, 41m 35.420s; **18** Alberto Valério, BR, 41m 40.215s; **19** Giedo van der Garde, NL, 42m 04.263s; **20** Plamen Kralev, BG, 42m 07.785s; **21** Will Bratt, GB, 18 laps; **22** Fabio Leimer, CH, 16 (DNF); **23** Josef Kral, CZ, 0 (DNF); **24** Sam Bird, GB, 0 (DNF).
Fastest race lap: Valsecchi, 1m 52.061s, 110.867 mph/178.424 km/h.
Pole position: Chilton.
Championship points: Drivers: 1 Valsecchi, 35; **2** Turvey, 16; **3** Rossi, 10; **4** Vietoris, 9; **5** Filippi, 8; **6** Kral, 8.
Teams: 1 iSport International, 51; **2** DPR, 15; **3** Super Nova Racing, 14.

GP2 ASIA SERIES, Bahrain International Circuit, Sakhir, Bahrain, 26/27 February. Round 3. 34 and 23 laps of the 3.363-mile/5.412-km circuit.
Race 1 (114.184 miles/183.762 km).
1 Davide Valsecchi, I, 1h 02m 05.146s, 110.348 mph/177.588 km/h; **2** Luca Filippi, I, 1h 02m 07.938s; **3** Javier Villa, E, 1h 02m 11.213s; **4** Giacomo Ricci, I, 1h 02m 11.384s; **5** Charles Pic, F, 1h 02m 18.172s; **6** Álvaro Parente, P, 1h 02m 22.923s; **7** Sergio Pérez, MEX, 1h 02m 29.094s; **8** Adrian Zaugg, ZA, 1h 02m 30.625s; **9** Oliver Turvey, GB, 1h 02m 34.399s; **10** Jules Bianchi, F, 1h 02m 38.384s; **11** Daniel Zampieri, I, 1h 02m 39.655s; **12** Yelmer Buurman, NL, 1h 02m 44.659s; **13** Sam Bird, GB, 1h 02m 45.561s; **14** Christian Vietoris, D, 1h 02m 46.896s; **15** Edoardo Piscopo, I, 1h 02m 50.925s; **16** Will Bratt, GB, 1h 02m 51.949s; **17** Vlado Arabadjiev, BG, 1h 02m 53.723s; **18** Max Chilton, GB, 1h 03m 10.232s; **19** Jake Rosenzweig, USA, 1h 03m 11.357s; **20** Fabio Leimer, CH, 1h 03m 28.531s; **21** Josef Kral, CZ, 1h 03m 58.195s; **22** Plamen Kralev, BG, 33 laps; **23** Michael Herck, RO, 32; **24** Alexander Rossi, USA, 26 (DNF).
Fastest race lap: Villa, 1m 47.035s, 113.105 mph/182.026 km/h.
Pole position: Bianchi, 1m 43.474s, 116.998 mph/188.290 km/h.

Race 2 (77.193 miles/124.230 km).
1 Charles Pic, F, 41m 11.960s, 112.418 mph/180.920 km/h; **2** Giacomo Ricci, I, 41m 15.546s; **3** Javier Villa, E, 41m 21.331s; **4** Sam Bird, GB, 41m 34.348s; **5** Edoardo Piscopo, I, 41m 35.153s; **6** Oliver Turvey, GB, 41m 37.070s; **7** Vlado Arabadjiev, BG, 41m 37.826s; **8** Daniel Zampieri, I, 41m 40.910s; **9** Christian Vietoris, D, 41m 44.459s; **10** Yelmer Buurman, NL, 41m 45.036s; **11** Josef Kral, CZ, 41m 45.449s; **12** Max Chilton, GB, 41m 48.397s; **13** Michael Herck, RO, 41m 48.654s; **14** Jake Rosenzweig, USA, 41m 59.749s; **15** Fabio Leimer, CH, 42m 01.249s; **16** Plamen Kralev, BG, 42m 39.798s; **17** Sergio Pérez, MEX, 42m 41.613s; **18** Luca Filippi, I, 42m 48.792s; **19** Adrian Zaugg, ZA, 22 laps; **20** Davide Valsecchi, I, 22; **21** Jules Bianchi, F, 19; **22** Will Bratt, GB, 2 (DNF); **23** Alexander Rossi, USA, 2 (DNF); **24** Álvaro Parente, P, 0 (DNF).
Fastest race lap: Bianchi, 1m 46.499s, 113.675 mph/182.942 km/h.
Pole position: Zaugg.
Championship points: Drivers: 1 Valsecchi, 45; **2** Ricci, 19; **3** Turvey, 17; **4** Filippi, 16; **5** Villa, 16; **6** Pic, 12.
Teams: 1 iSport International, 62; **2** Arden International, 28; **3** DPR, 26.

GP2 ASIA SERIES, Bahrain International Circuit, Sakhir, Bahrain, 13/14 March. Round 4. 29 and 20 laps of the 3.914-mile/6.299-km circuit.
Race 1 (113.354 miles/182.425 km).
1 Luca Filippi, I, 1h 06m 15.383s, 102.650 mph/165.199 km/h; **2** Davide Valsecchi, I, 1h 06m 17.441s; **3** Charles Pic, F, 1h 06m 19.373s; **4** Álvaro Parente, P, 1h 06m 22.246s; **5** Giacomo Ricci, I, 1h 06m 23.468s; **6** Sam Bird, GB, 1h 06m 30.228s; **7** Javier Villa, E, 1h 06m 30.688s; **8** Edoardo Piscopo, I, 1h 06m 30.886s; **9** Oliver Turvey, GB, 1h 06m 31.067s; **10** Jules Bianchi, F, 1h 06m 33.881s; **11** Alexander Rossi, USA, 1h 06m 37.411s; **12** Vlado Arabadjiev, BG, 1h 06m 37.643s; **13** Yelmer Buurman, NL, 1h 06m 41.520s; **14** Daniel Clos, E, 1h 06m 42.132s; **15** Will Bratt, GB, 1h 06m 43.414s; **16** Josef Kral, CZ, 1h 06m 45.591s; **17** Jake Rosenzweig, USA, 1h 06m 47.182s; **18** Michael Herck, RO, 1h 07m 03.480s; **19** Max Chilton, GB, 28 laps; **20** Christian Vietoris, D, 21 (DNF); **21** Plamen Kralev, BG, 20 (DNF); **22** Rodolfo Gonzalez, YV, 15 (DNF); **23** Luiz Razia, BR, 1 (DNF); **24** Fabio Leimer, CH, 0 (DNF).
Fastest race lap: Filippi, 2m 09.823s, 108.535 mph/174.671 km/h.
Pole position: Filippi, 2m 07.087s, 110.872 mph/178.432 km/h.

Race 2 (78.127 miles/125.734 km).
1 Giacomo Ricci, I, 43m 47.744s, 107.034 mph/172.255 km/h; **2** Sam Bird, GB, 43m 53.113s; **3** Álvaro Parente, P, 43m 57.329s; **4** Davide Valsecchi, I, 44m 03.439s; **5** Alexander Rossi, USA, 44m 04.303s; **6** Javier Villa, E, 44m 11.024s; **7** Yelmer Buurman, NL, 44m 13.147s; **8** Luca Filippi, I, 44m 13.693s; **9** Vlado Arabadjiev, BG, 44m 16.821s; **10** Josef Kral, CZ, 44m 18.524s; **11** Oliver Turvey, GB, 44m 19.940s; **12** Daniel Clos, E, 44m 22.779s; **13** Luiz Razia, BR, 44m 26.372s; **14** Christian Vietoris, D, 44m 33.311s; **15** Max Chilton, GB, 44m 35.117s; **16** Will Bratt, GB, 44m 39.565s; **17** Jake Rosenzweig, USA, 44m 40.801s; **18** Plamen Kralev, BG, 44m 59.994s; **19** Charles Pic, F, 45m 31.858s; **20** Jules Bianchi, F, 17 laps (DNF); **21** Rodolfo Gonzalez, YV, 16 (DNF); **22** Michael Herck, RO, 16 (DNF).
Did not start: Edoardo Piscopo, I (rear wheel lost); Fabio Leimer, CH (engine).
Fastest race lap: Bianchi, 2m 09.787s, 108.566 mph/174.720 km/h.
Pole position: Piscopo.

Final championship points.
Drivers: 1 Davide Valsecchi, I, 56; **2** Luca Filippi, I, 29; **3** Giacomo Ricci, I, 29; **4** Javier Villa, E, 19; **5** Charles Pic, F, 18; **6** Oliver Turvey, GB, 17; **7** Sam Bird, GB, 12; **8** Álvaro Parente, P, 12; **9** Alexander Rossi, USA, 12; **10** Christian Vietoris, D, 9; **11** Josef Kral, CZ, 8; **12** Jules Bianchi, F, 8; **13** Michael Herck, RO, 7; **14** James Jakes, GB, 6; **15** Sergio Pérez, MEX, 5; **16** Edoardo Piscopo, I, 3; **17** Johnny Cecotto Jr., YV, 3; **18** Max Chilton, GB, 2; **19** Adrian Zaugg, ZA, 1.
Teams: 1 iSport International, 73; **2** Arden International, 37; **3** DPR, 36; **4** Malaysia Qi-Meritus.Com, 34; **5** ART Grand Prix, 20; **6** Super Nova Racing, 14; **7** DAMS, 12; **8** Scuderia Coloni, 12; **9** Ocean Racing Technology, 9; **10** Barwa Addax Team, 5; **11** Trident Racing, 4.

FIA Formula 2 Championship

All cars are Williams-Audi turbo.

FIA FORMULA TWO CHAMPIONSHIP, Silverstone Grand Prix Circuit, Towcester, Northamptonshire, Great Britain, 18 April. Round 1. 2 x 23 laps of the 3.194-mile/5.141-km circuit.
Race 1 (73.473 miles/118.243 km).
1 Jolyon Palmer, GB, 38m 16.660s, 115.168 mph/185.345 km/h; **2** Dean Stoneman, GB, 38m 19.671s; **3** Sergei Afanasiev, RUS, 38m 23.744s; **4** Philipp Eng, A, 38m 26.592s; **5** Kazim Vasiliauskas, LT, 38m 28.241s; **6** Will Bratt, GB, 38m 29.043s; **7** Mihai Marinescu, RO, 38m 40.485s; **8** Armaan Ebrahim, IND, 38m 43.541s; **9** Nicola de Marco, I, 38m 48.503s; **10** Benjamin Lariche, F, 38m 50.902s.
Fastest race lap: Palmer, 1m 38.985s, 116.180 mph/186.973 km/h.
Pole position: Palmer, 1m 36.380s, 119.320 mph/192.027 km/h.

Race 2 (73.473 miles/118.243 km).
1 Philipp Eng, A, 38m 07.958s, 115.606 mph/186.050 km/h; **2** Jolyon Palmer, GB, 38m 08.765s; **3** Johan Jokinen, DK, 38m 24.188s; **4** Jack Clarke, GB, 38m 28.529s; **5** Will Bratt, GB, 38m 29.376s; **6** Sergei Afanasiev, RUS, 38m 36.025s; **7** Kazim Vasiliauskas, LT, 38m 41.401s; **8** Mihai Marinescu, RO, 38m 43.289s; **9** Armaan Ebrahim, IND, 38m 52.984s; **10** Nicola de Marco, I, 38m 54.807s.
Fastest race lap: Eng, 1m 38.733s, 116.476 mph/187.451 km/h.
Pole position: Eng, 1m 36.992s, 118.567 mph/190.815 km/h.

FIA FORMULA TWO CHAMPIONSHIP, Circuit de Marrakech, Morocco, 1/2 May. Round 2. 19 and 17 laps of the 2.824-mile/4.545-km circuit.
Race 1 (53.659 miles/86.355 km).
1 Dean Stoneman, GB, 42m 59.528s, 74.886 mph/120.517 km/h; **2** Philipp Eng, A, 43m 00.805s; **3** Kelvin Snoeks, NL, 43m 01.348s; **4** Ivan Samarin, RUS, 43m 02.013s; **5** Ricardo Teixeira, ANG, 43m 03.028s; **6** Armaan Ebrahim, IND, 43m 03.309s; **7** Paul Rees, GB, 43m 04.261s; **8** Sergei Afanasiev, RUS, 43m 04.979s; **9** Benjamin Lariche, F, 43m 06.236s; **10** Kazim Vasiliauskas, LT, 43m 06.910s.
Fastest race lap: Stoneman, 1m 31.817s, 110.729 mph/178.202 km/h.
Pole position: Stoneman, 1m 32.559s, 109.842 mph/176.773 km/h.

Race 2 (48.010 miles/77.265 km).
1 Philipp Eng, A, 35m 42.174s, 80.682 mph/129.846 km/h; **2** Dean Stoneman, GB, 35m 44.129s; **3** Will Bratt, GB, 35m 47.320s; **4** Kazim Vasiliauskas, LT, 35m 50.708s; **5** Jolyon Palmer, GB, 35m 58.161s; **6** Armaan Ebrahim, IND, 35m 59.025s; **7** Sergei Afanasiev, RUS, 36m 02.549s; **8** Paul Rees, GB, 36m 03.959s; **9** Kelvin Snoeks, NL, 36m 07.164s; **10** Benjamin Lariche, F, 36m 11.027s.
Fastest race lap: Stoneman, 1m 31.312s, 111.342 mph/179.187 km/h.
Pole position: Eng, 1m 30.186s, 112.732 mph/181.425 km/h.

FIA FORMULA TWO CHAMPIONSHIP, Autodromo Nazionale di Monza, Milan, Italy, 22/23 May. Round 3. 21 and 18 laps of the 3.600-mile/5.793-km circuit.
Race 1 (75.400 miles/121.344 km).
1 Jolyon Palmer, GB, 38m 49.352s, 116.529 mph/187.536 km/h; **2** Dean Stoneman, GB, 38m 50.164s; **3** Kazim Vasiliauskas, LT, 38m 54.362s; **4** Will Bratt, GB, 38m 55.102s; **5** Mihai Marinescu, RO, 39m 01.023s; **6** Benjamin Bailly, B, 39m 02.209s; **7** Johan Jokinen, DK, 39m 06.060s; **8** Benjamin Lariche, F, 39m 11.962s; **9** Paul Rees, GB, 39m 13.385s; **10** Plamen Kralev, BG, 39m 15.548s.
Fastest race lap: Jokinen, 1m 41.416s, 127.776 mph/205.636 km/h.
Pole position: Palmer, 1m 41.722s, 127.392 mph/205.017 km/h.

Race 2 (64.601 miles/103.965 km).
1 Jolyon Palmer, GB, 30m 51.520s, 125.606 mph/202.144 km/h; **2** Sergei Afanasiev, RUS, 30m 55.437s; **3** Will Bratt, GB, 30m 55.933s; **4** Dean Stoneman, GB, 31m 02.551s; **5** Armaan Ebrahim, IND, 31m 04.955s; **6** Benjamin Bailly, B, 31m 06.011s; **7** Paul Rees, GB, 31m 06.975s; **8** Ivan Samarin, RUS, 31m 12.424s; **9** Benjamin Lariche, F, 31m 13.833s; **10** Parthiva Sureshwaren, IND, 31m 14.268s.
Fastest race lap: Marinescu, 1m 41.439s, 127.747 mph/205.589 km/h.
Pole position: Palmer, 1m 39.935s, 129.670 mph/208.683 km/h.

FIA FORMULA TWO CHAMPIONSHIP, Circuit Zolder, Heusden-Zolder, Belgium, 19/20 June. Round 4. 25 and 22 laps of the 2.485-mile/4.000-km circuit.
Race 1 (62.137 miles/100.000 km).
1 Dean Stoneman, GB, 38m 01.434s, 98.049 mph/157.795 km/h; **2** Jolyon Palmer, GB, 38m 08.958s; **3** Kazim Vasiliauskas, LT, 38m 10.524s; **4** Sergei Afanasiev, RUS, 38m 11.285s; **5** Armaan Ebrahim, IND, 38m 14.580s; **6** Benjamin Bailly, B, 38m 16.798s; **7** Ivan Samarin, RUS, 38m 21.591s; **8** Mihai Marinescu, RO, 38m 22.771s; **9** Ricardo Teixeira, ANG, 38m 32.506s; **10** Nicola de Marco, I, 38m 33.649s.
Fastest race lap: Stoneman, 1m 24.324s, 106.111 mph/170.769 km/h.
Pole position: Stoneman, 1m 23.200s, 107.545 mph/173.076 km/h.

Race 2 (54.681 miles/88.000 km).
1 Benjamin Bailly, B, 31m 10.817s, 105.221 mph/169.337 km/h; **2** Jolyon Palmer, GB, 31m 14.636s; **3** Dean Stoneman, GB, 31m 15.693s; **4** Jack Clarke, GB, 31m 17.386s; **5** Will Bratt, GB, 31m 17.990s; **6** Mihai Marinescu, RO, 31m 23.157s; **7** Kazim Vasiliauskas, LT, 31m 25.542s; **8** Ivan Samarin, RUS, 31m 33.880s; **9** Benjamin Lariche, F, 31m 42.871s; **10** Kelvin Snoeks, NL, 31m 44.422s.
Fastest race lap: Afanasiev, 1m 24.038s, 106.472 mph/171.351 km/h.
Pole position: Bailly, 1m 22.353s, 108.651 mph/174.857 km/h.

FIA FORMULA TWO CHAMPIONSHIP, Autódromo Internacional do Algarve, Portimão, Portugal, 3/4 July. Round 5. 22 and 19 laps of the 2.891-mile/4.653-km circuit.
Race 1 (63.607 miles/102.366 km).
1 Jolyon Palmer, GB, 37m 35.402s, 101.527 mph/163.393 km/h; **2** Benjamin Bailly, B, 37m 38.028s; **3**

Jack Clarke, GB, 37m 39.729s; **4** Kazim Vasiliauskas, LT, 37m 41.163s; **5** Nicola de Marco, I, 37m 42.165s; **6** Ricardo Teixeira, ANG, 37m 46.186s; **7** Armaan Ebrahim, IND, 37m 46.699s; **8** Benjamin Lariche, F, 37m 49.700s; **9** Sergei Afanasiev, RUS, 37m 50.991s; **10** Natalia Kowalska, PL, 37m 58.024s.
Fastest race lap: Palmer, 1m 37.707s, 106.527 mph/171.439 km/h.
Pole position: Palmer, 1m 35.700s, 108.761 mph/175.034 km/h.

Race 2 (54.934 miles/88.407 km).
1 Dean Stoneman, GB, 31m 37.784s, 104.206 mph/167.703 km/h; **2** Jolyon Palmer, GB, 31m 41.882s; **3** Benjamin Bailly, B, 31m 42.748s; **4** Mihai Marinescu, RO, 31m 52.832s; **5** Will Bratt, GB, 31m 57.216s; **6** Philipp Eng, A, 31m 57.703s; **7** Nicola de Marco, I, 32m 02.367s; **8** Ivan Samarin, RUS, 32m 04.570s; **9** Natalia Kowalska, PL, 32m 04.913s; **10** Benjamin Lariche, F, 32m 06.239s.
Fastest race lap: Stoneman, 1m 39.223s, 104.899 mph/168.819 km/h.
Pole position: Palmer, 1m 35.193s, 109.340 mph/175.966 km/h.

FIA FORMULA TWO CHAMPIONSHIP, Brands Hatch GP Circuit, West Kingsdown, Dartford, Kent, Great Britain,
17/18 July. Round 6. 28 and 24 laps of the 2.301-mile/3.703-km circuit.
Race 1 (64.408 miles/103.654 km).
1 Dean Stoneman, GB, 36m 38.208s, 105.480 mph/169.753 km/h; **2** Jack Clarke, GB, 36m 46.389s; **3** Ivan Samarin, RUS, 36m 49.344s; **4** Will Bratt, GB, 36m 49.515s; **5** Tom Gladdis, GB, 36m 50.095s; **6** Sergei Afanasiev, RUS, 36m 51.615s; **7** Nicola de Marco, I, 36m 53.096s; **8** Jolyon Palmer, GB, 36m 54.018s; **9** Armaan Ebrahim, IND, 36m 54.407s; **10** Philipp Eng, A, 36m 55.860s.
Fastest race lap: Stoneman, 1m 17.582s, 106.769 mph/171.828 km/h.
Pole position: Stoneman, 1m 15.758s, 109.339 mph/175.965 km/h.

Race 2 (55.204 miles/88.842 km).
1 Philipp Eng, A, 31m 32.628s, 105.004 mph/168.987 km/h; **2** Tom Gladdis, GB, 31m 33.173s; **3** Will Bratt, GB, 31m 40.895s; **4** Nicola de Marco, I, 31m 44.669s; **5** Sergei Afanasiev, RUS, 31m 45.471s; **6** Mihai Marinescu, RO, 31m 46.361s; **7** Armaan Ebrahim, IND, 31m 47.356s; **8** Jack Clarke, GB, 31m 48.610s; **9** Ivan Samarin, RUS, 31m 53.782s; **10** Benjamin Lariche, F, 31m 54.222s.
Fastest race lap: Stoneman, 1m 17.937s, 106.282 mph/171.045 km/h.
Pole position: Kazim Vasiliauskas, LT, 1m 16.061s, 108.904 mph/175.264 km/h.

FIA FORMULA TWO CHAMPIONSHIP, Automotodrom Brno Masaryk Circuit, Brno, Czech Republic, 31 July/1 August. Round 7. 20 and 17 laps of the 3.357-mile/5.403-km circuit.
Race 1 (67.145 miles/108.060 km).
1 Nicola de Marco, I, 36m 20.232s, 110.870 mph/178.428 km/h; **2** Dean Stoneman, GB, 36m 23.322s; **3** Sergei Afanasiev, RUS, 36m 26.025s; **4** Benjamin Bailly, B, 36m 28.187s; **5** Jolyon Palmer, GB, 36m 34.208s; **6** Philipp Eng, A, 36m 38.457s; **7** Kelvin Snoeks, NL, 36m 43.109s; **8** Will Bratt, GB, 36m 43.669s; **9** Ricardo Teixeira, ANG, 36m 48.163s; **10** Benjamin Lariche, F, 36m 48.900s.
Fastest race lap: de Marco, 1m 48.246s, 111.654 mph/179.690 km/h.
Pole position: Stoneman, 1m 45.597s, 114.455 mph/184.198 km/h.

Race 2 (57.074 miles/91.851 km).
1 Jolyon Palmer, GB, 31m 04.799s, 110.180 mph/177.318 km/h; **2** Dean Stoneman, GB, 31m 06.993s; **3** Kazim Vasiliauskas, LT, 31m 16.057s; **4** Sergei Afanasiev, RUS, 31m 17.604s; **5** Benjamin Bailly, B, 31m 18.955s; **6** Nicola de Marco, I, 31m 24.612s; **7** Benjamin Lariche, F, 31m 25.752s; **8** Kelvin Snoeks, NL, 31m 26.316s; **9** Jack Clarke, GB, 31m 29.067s; **10** Will Bratt, GB, 31m 31.091s.
Fastest race lap: Palmer, 1m 48.913s, 110.970 mph/178.590 km/h.
Pole position: Stoneman, 1m 45.683s, 114.362 mph/184.048 km/h.

FIA FORMULA TWO CHAMPIONSHIP, Motorsport Arena Oschersleben, Germany, 4/5 September. Round 8. 24 and 23 laps of the 2.297-mile/3.696-km circuit.
Race 1 (55.118 miles/88.704 km).
1 Dean Stoneman, GB, 40m 11.982s, 82.266 mph/132.395 km/h; **2** Kazim Vasiliauskas, LT, 40m 27.775s; **3** Jolyon Palmer, GB, 40m 28.448s; **4** Sergei Afanasiev, RUS, 40m 38.940s; **5** Benjamin Bailly, B, 40m 49.195s; **6** Will Bratt, GB, 40m 55.975s; **7** Philipp Eng, A, 41m 02.758s; **8** Kelvin Snoeks, NL, 41m 10.977s; **9** Nicola de Marco, I, 41m 30.015s; **10** Ricardo Teixeira, ANG, 41m 33.039s.
Fastest race lap: de Marco, 1m 39.164s, 83.374 mph/134.177 km/h.
Pole position: Afanasiev, 1m 20.376s, 102.863 mph/165.541 km/h.

Race 2 (52.822 miles/85.008 km).
1 Dean Stoneman, GB, 31m 40.254s, 100.069 mph/161.046 km/h; **2** Kazim Vasiliauskas, LT, 31m 42.220s; **3** Sergei Afanasiev, RUS, 31m 47.143s; **4** Kelvin Snoeks, NL, 31m 53.290s; **5** Benjamin Bailly, B, 31m 56.499s; **6** Mihai Marinescu, RO, 31m 57.330s; **7** Will Bratt, GB, 31m 57.943s; **8** Ivan Samarin, RUS, 32m 04.871s; **9** Philipp Eng, A, 32m 05.155s; **10** Armaan Ebrahim, IND, 32m 05.711s.
Fastest race lap: Vasiliauskas, 1m 21.578s, 101.347 mph/163.102 km/h.
Pole position: Stoneman, 1m 22.314s, 100.441 mph/161.644 km/h.

FIA FORMULA TWO CHAMPIONSHIP, Circuit de la Comunitat Valenciana Ricardo Tormo, Cheste, Valencia, Spain, 18/19 September. Round 9. 25 and 21 laps of the 2.489-mile/4.005-km circuit.
Race 1 (62.215 miles/100.125 km).
1 Nicola de Marco, I, 37m 59.082s, 98.273 mph/158.155 km/h; **2** Will Bratt, GB, 38m 00.292s; **3** Armaan Ebrahim, IND, 38m 16.897s; **4** Philipp Eng, A, 38m 18.224s; **5** Sergei Afanasiev, RUS, 38m 20.788s; **6** Benjamin Lariche, F, 38m 22.128s; **7** Jolyon Palmer, GB, 38m 22.749s; **8** Benjamin Bailly, B, 38m 23.099s; **9** Dean Stoneman, GB, 38m 24.492s; **10** Ivan Samarin, RUS, 38m 29.289s.
Fastest race lap: Bratt, 1m 29.255s, 100.374 mph/161.537 km/h.
Pole position: de Marco, 1m 26.348s, 103.753 mph/166.975 km/h.

Race 2 (52.260 miles/84.105 km).
1 Kazim Vasiliauskas, LT, 31m 37.175s, 99.167 mph/159.594 km/h; **2** Jack Clarke, GB, 31m 39.692s; **3** Dean Stoneman, GB, 31m 45.504s; **4** Ivan Samarin, RUS, 31m 58.260s; **5** Sergei Afanasiev, RUS, 32m 00.101s; **6** Mihai Marinescu, RO, 32m 01.244s; **7** Armaan Ebrahim, IND, 32m 01.571s; **8** Kelvin Snoeks, NL, 32m 02.228s; **9** Benjamin Bailly, B, 32m 05.055s; **10** Ramón Piñeiro, E, 32m 06.072s.
Fastest race lap: Vasiliauskas, 1m 28.748s, 100.947 mph/162.459 km/h.
Pole position: Vasiliauskas, 1m 25.923s, 104.266 mph/167.801 km/h.

Final championship points
1 Dean Stoneman, GB, 284; **2** Jolyon Palmer, GB, 242; **3** Sergei Afanasiev, RUS, 157; **4** Kazim Vasiliauskas, LT, 153; **5** Will Bratt, GB, 144; **6** Philipp Eng, A, 142; **7** Benjamin Bailly, B, 130; **8** Nicola de Marco, I, 98; **9** Jack Clarke, GB, 81; **10** Armaan Ebrahim, IND, 78; **11** Mihai Marinescu, RO, 68; **12** Ivan Samarin, RUS, 64; **13** Kelvin Snoeks, NL, 48; **14** Benjamin Lariche, F, 33; **15** Tom Gladdis, GB, 28; **16** Ricardo Teixeira, ANG, 23; **17** Johan Jokinen, DK, 21; **18** Paul Rees, GB, 18; **19** Natalia Kowalska, PL, 3; **20** Parthiva Sureshwaren, IND, 1; **21** Plamen Kralev, BG, 1; **22** Ramón Piñeiro, E, 1.

All-Japan Formula Nippon Championship

All cars are Swift FN09.

ALL-JAPAN FORMULA NIPPON CHAMPIONSHIP, Suzuka International Racing Course, Suzuka-shi, Mie Prefecture, Japan, 18 April. Round 1. 37 laps of the 3.608-mile/5.807-km circuit, 133.507 miles/214.859 km.
1 Takashi Kogure, J (-Honda), 1h 05m 05.402s, 123.067 mph/198.057 km/h; **2** João Paulo de Oliveira, BR (-Toyota), 1h 05m 06.664s; **3** André Lotterer, D (-Toyota), 1h 05m 08.544s; **4** Kohei Hirate, J (-Toyota), 1h 05m 33.682s; **5** Takuya Izawa, J (-Honda), 1h 05m 36.295s; **6** Loïc Duval, F (-Honda), 1h 05m 42.604s; **7** Naoki Yamamoto, J (-Honda), 1h 05m 43.602s; **8** Koudai Tsukakoshi, J (-Honda), 1h 05m 50.837s; **9** Yuji Ide, J (-Honda), 1h 06m 12.942s; **10** Hiroaki Ishiura, J (-Toyota), 1h 06m 25.406s.
Fastest race lap: Hirate, 1m 43.167s, 125.911 mph/202.635 km/h.
Pole position: Kogure, 1m 38.917s, 131.321 mph/211.341 km/h.

ALL-JAPAN FORMULA NIPPON CHAMPIONSHIP, Twin Ring Motegi, Motegi-machi, Haga-gun, Tochigi Prefecture, Japan, 23 May. Round 2. 52 laps of the 2.983-mile/4.801-km circuit, 155.127 miles/249.652 km.
1 João Paulo de Oliveira, BR (-Toyota), 1h 35m 31.811s, 97.431 mph/156.800 km/h; **2** Koudai Tsukakoshi, J (-Honda), 1h 36m 12.398s; **3** André Lotterer, D (-Toyota), 1h 36m 15.541s; **4** Loïc Duval, F (-Honda), 1h 36m 50.974s; **5** Naoki Yamamoto, J (-Honda), 1h 37m 10.730s; **6** Takashi Kogure, J (-Honda), 1h 37m 18.608s; **7** Kohei Hirate, J (-Toyota), 51 laps; **8** Kazuya Oshima, J (-Toyota), 51; **9** Yuji Ide, J (-Honda), 51; **10** Kei Cozzolino, I (-Toyota), 51.
Fastest race lap: de Oliveira, 1m 48.533s, 98.952 mph/159.247 km/h.
Pole position: de Oliveira, 1m 33.967s, 114.290 mph/183.933 km/h.

ALL-JAPAN FORMULA NIPPON CHAMPIONSHIP, Fuji International Speedway, Sunto-gun, Shizuoka Prefecture, Japan, 18 July. Round 3. 44 laps of the 2.835-mile/4.563-km circuit, 124.754 miles/200.772 km.
1 Kohei Hirate, J (-Toyota), 1h 06m 05.040s, 113.269 mph/182.288 km/h; **2** André Lotterer, D (-Toyota), 1h 06m 17.833s; **3** João Paulo de Oliveira, BR (-Toyota), 1h 06m 19.930s; **4** Kazuya Oshima, J (-Toyota), 1h 06m 24.363s; **5** Takashi Kogure, J (-Honda), 1h 06m 25.382s; **6** Hiroaki Ishiura, J (-Toyota), 1h 06m 30.363s; **7** Naoki Yamamoto, J (-Honda), 1h 06m 31.531s; **8** Kei Cozzolino, I (-Toyota), 1h 06m 37.967s; **9** Takuya Izawa, J (-Honda), 1h 06m 54.046s; **10** Yuji Ide, J (-Honda), 1h 06m 58.646s.
Fastest race lap: Hirate, 1m 29.142s, 114.504 mph/184.277 km/h.
Pole position: Loïc Duval, F (-Honda), 1m 25.999s, 118.689 mph/191.012 km/h.

ALL-JAPAN FORMULA NIPPON CHAMPIONSHIP, Twin Ring Motegi, Motegi-machi, Haga-gun, Tochigi Prefecture, Japan, 8 August. Round 4. 52 laps of the 2.983-mile/4.801-km circuit, 155.127 miles/249.652 km.
1 Loïc Duval, F (-Honda), 1h 27m 17.626s, 106.624 mph/171.594 km/h; **2** Takashi Kogure, J (-Honda), 1h 27m 18.659s; **3** Kohei Hirate, J (-Toyota), 1h 27m 26.104s; **4** Naoki Yamamoto, J (-Honda), 1h 27m 37.348s; **5** Kazuya Oshima, J (-Toyota), 1h 27m 43.134s; **6** João Paulo de Oliveira, BR (-Toyota), 1h 27m 43.785s; **7** Katsuyuki Hiranaka, J (-Toyota), 1h 28m 05.887s; **8** Hiroaki Ishiura, J (-Toyota), 1h 28m 10.153s; **9** Yuji Ide, J (-Honda), 1h 28m 37.852s; **10** Koudai Tsukakoshi, J (-Honda), 1h 28m 39.595s.
Fastest race lap: de Oliveira, 1m 38.240s, 109.319 mph/175.932 km/h.
Pole position: Kogure, 1m 35.347s, 112.636 mph/181.271 km/h.

ALL-JAPAN FORMULA NIPPON CHAMPIONSHIP, Sportsland-SUGO International Course, Shibata-gun, Miyagi Prefecture, Japan, 26 September. Round 5. 62 laps of the 2.302-mile/3.704-km circuit, 142.704 miles/229.660 km.
1 Kazuya Oshima, J (-Toyota), 1h 17m 52.542s, 109.948 mph/176.944 km/h; **2** Loïc Duval, F (-Honda), 1h 17m 55.889s; **3** André Lotterer, D (-Toyota), 1h 17m 56.080s; **4** Hiroaki Ishiura, J (-Toyota), 1h 18m 09.200s; **5** Takashi Kogure, J (-Honda), 1h 18m 18.511s; **6** Takuya Izawa, J (-Honda), 1h 18m 25.799s; **7** Kei Cozzolino, I (-Toyota), 1h 18m 25.931s; **8** Tsugio Matsuda, J (-Toyota), 1h 18m 48.499s; **9** Yuji Ide, J (-Honda), 1h 18m 51.730s; **10** Takuto Iguchi, J (-Toyota), 1h 18m 59.577s.
Fastest race lap: Lotterer, 1m 09.301s, 119.566 mph/192.423 km/h.
Pole position: Duval, 1m 05.843s, 125.846 mph/202.529 km/h.

ALL-JAPAN FORMULA NIPPON CHAMPIONSHIP, Autopolis International Racing Course, Kamit-suemura, Hita-gun, Oita Prefecture, Japan, 17 October. Round 6. 50 laps of the 2.904-mile/4.674-km circuit, 145.214 miles/233.700 km.
1 André Lotterer, D (-Toyota), 1h 26m 07.759s, 101.160 mph/162.802 km/h; **2** João Paulo de Oliveira, BR (-Toyota), 1h 26m 09.257s; **3** Hiroaki Ishiura, J (-Toyota), 1h 26m 22.057s; **4** Kei Cozzolino, I (-Toyota), 1h 26m 38.131s; **5** Naoki Yamamoto, J (-Honda), 1h 27m 02.842s; **6** Takuto Iguchi, J (-Toyota), 1h 27m 14.488s; **7** Katsuyuki Hiranaka, J (-Toyota), 1h 27m 23.177s; **8** Kohei Hirate, J (-Toyota), 1h 27m 23.441s; **9** Takashi Kogure, J (-Honda), 27 laps (DNF); **10** Tsugio Matsuda, J (-Toyota), 17 (DNF).
Fastest race lap: Cozzolino, 1m 34.340s, 110.827 mph/178.359 km/h.
Pole position: Kazuya Oshima, J (-Toyota), 1m 31.973s, 113.679 mph/182.949 km/h.

ALL-JAPAN FORMULA NIPPON CHAMPIONSHIP, Suzuka International Racing Course, Suzuka-shi, Mie Prefecture, Japan, 7 November. Round 7. 20 and 28 laps of the 3.608-mile/5.807-km circuit.
Race 7 (72.166 miles/116.140 km).
1 Loïc Duval, F (-Honda), 34m 31.275s, 125.429 mph/201.858 km/h; **2** Takashi Kogure, J (-Honda), 34m 32.652s; **3** André Lotterer, D (-Toyota), 34m 33.308s; **4** João Paulo de Oliveira, BR (-Toyota), 34m 35.282s; **5** Kazuya Oshima, J (-Toyota), 34m 47.288s; **6** Naoki Yamamoto, J (-Honda), 34m 50.598s; **7** Hiroaki Ishiura, J (-Toyota), 35m 03.818s; **8** Yuji Ide, J (-Honda), 35m 04.953s; **9** Kohei Hirate, J (-Toyota), 35m 06.187s; **10** Koudai Tsukakoshi, J (-Honda), 35m 08.331s.
Fastest race lap: Duval, 1m 42.622s, 126.580 mph/203.711 km/h.
Pole position: Duval, 1m 40.828s, 128.832 mph/207.335 km/h.

Race 8 (101.032 miles/162.596 km).
1 João Paulo de Oliveira, BR (-Toyota), 49m 31.945s, 122.383 mph/196.957 km/h; **2** André Lotterer, D (-Toyota), 49m 34.517s; **3** Takashi Kogure, J (-Honda), 49m 35.023s; **4** Loïc Duval, F (-Honda), 49m 53.683s; **5** Naoki Yamamoto, J (-Honda), 49m 53.778s; **6** Kohei Hirate, J (-Toyota), 49m 54.259s; **7** Kazuya Oshima, J (-Toyota), 49m 58.759s; **8** Yuji Ide, J (-Honda), 49m 59.400s; **9** Tsugio Matsuda, J (-Toyota), 50m 15.499s; **10** Hiroaki Ishiura, J (-Toyota), 50m 16.310s.
Fastest race lap: Kogure, 1m 43.216s, 125.852 mph/202.538 km/h.
Pole position: de Oliveira, 1m 40.379s, 129.408 mph/208.263 km/h.

Final championship points
Drivers: 1 João Paulo de Oliveira, BR, 47.5; **2** André Lotterer, D, 43; **3** Loïc Duval, F, 39.5; **4** Takashi Kogure, J, 38; **5** Kohei Hirate, J, 25.5; **6** Kazuya Oshima, J, 24; **7** Naoki Yamamoto, J, 20.5; **8** Hiroaki Ishiura, J, 16; **9** Koudai Tsukakoshi, J, 9; **10** Kei Cozzolino, I, 8; **11** Takuya Izawa, J, 7; **12** Katsuyuki Hiranaka, J, 4; **13** Takuto Iguchi, J, 3; **14** Yuji Ide, J, 1; **15** Tsugio Matsuda, J, 1.
Teams: 1 Team Impul, 68; **2** Petronas Team Tom's, 66; **3** Nakajima Racing, 56.5; **4** DoCoMo Team Dandelion Racing, 40.5; **5** Team LeMans, 24; **6** HFDP Racing, 9; **7** KCMG, 4; **8** Deliziefollie Cerumo/Inging, 3; **9** Motul Team Mugen, 1; **10** Kondo Racing, 1.

GP3 Series

GP3 SERIES, Circuit de Catalunya, Montmeló, Barcelona, Spain, 8/9 May. Round 1. 16 and 15 laps of the 2.892-mile/4.655-km circuit.
Race 1 (46.201 miles/74.354 km).
1 Pål Varhaug, N, 26m 58.573s, 102.760 mph/165.376 km/h; **2** Robert Wickens, CDN, 27m 00.136s; **3** Esteban Gutierrez, MEX, 27m 00.531s; **4** Dean Smith, GB, 27m 02.019s; **5** Jean-Eric Vergne, F, 27m 05.295s; **6** Simon Trummer, CH, 27m 07.307s; **7** Lucas Foresti, BR, 27m 12.177s; **8** Alexander Rossi, USA, 27m 12.781s; **9** James Jakes, GB, 27m 14.420s; **10** Miki Monràs, E, 27m 15.201s.
Fastest race lap: Adrian Quaife-Hobbs, GB, 1m 40.299s, 103.818 mph/167.080 km/h.
Pole position: Nigel Melker, NL, 1m 52.602s, 92.475 mph/148.825 km/h.

Race 2 (43.309 miles/69.699 km).
1 Alexander Rossi, USA, 27m 06.594s, 95.851 mph/154.258 km/h; **2** Lucas Foresti, BR, 27m 17.129s; **3** Esteban Gutierrez, MEX, 27m 17.599s; **4** Robert Wickens, CDN, 27m 18.293s; **5** Dean Smith, GB, 27m 20.748s; **6** Pedro Nunes, BR, 27m 23.676s; **7** James Jakes, GB, 27m 24.131s; **8** Simon Trummer, CH, 27m 24.940s; **9** Nico Müller, CH, 27m 25.531s; **10** Oliver Oakes, GB, 27m 31.500s.
Fastest race lap: Rossi, 1m 38.501s, 105.714 mph/170.130 km/h.
Pole position: Rossi.

GP3 SERIES, Istanbul Speed Park, Tuzla, Turkey, 29/30 May. Round 2. 2 x 15 laps of the 3.317-mile/5.338-km circuit.
Race 1 (49.624 miles/79.862 km).
1 Esteban Gutierrez, MEX, 26m 56.811s, 110.492 mph/177.821 km/h; **2** James Jakes, GB, 27m 07.324s; **3** Felipe Guimarães, BR, 27m 13.132s; **4** Alexander Rossi, USA, 27m 16.234s; **5** Daniel Morad, CDN, 27m 18.831s; **6** Nico Müller, CH, 27m 22.227s; **7** Miki Monràs, E, 27m 22.397s; **8** Rio Haryanto, RI, 27m 23.426s; **9** Doru Sechelariu, RO, 27m 24.853s; **10** Josef Newgarden, USA, 27m 26.764s.
Fastest race lap: Gutierrez, 1m 47.305s, 111.278 mph/179.085 km/h.
Pole position: Nigel Melker, NL, 1m 46.361s, 112.266 mph/180.675 km/h.

Race 2 (49.624 miles/79.862 km).
1 Rio Haryanto, RI, 27m 08.058s, 109.729 mph/176.592 km/h; **2** Miki Monràs, E, 27m 10.264s; **3** Alexander Rossi, USA, 27m 12.039s; **4** Nico Müller, CH, 27m 13.671s; **5** Daniel Morad, CDN, 27m 14.436s; **6** Felipe Guimarães, BR, 27m 16.528s; **7** Esteban Gutierrez, MEX, 27m 16.968s; **8** James Jakes, GB, 27m 18.497s; **9** Doru Sechelariu, RO, 27m 19.419s; **10** Dean Smith, GB, 27m 24.269s.
Fastest race lap: Robert Wickens, CDN, 1m 47.346s, 111.236 mph/179.017 km/h.
Pole position: Haryanto.

GP3 SERIES, Valencia Street Circuit, Spain, 26/27 June. Round 3. 2 x 14 laps of the 3.367-mile/5.419-km circuit.
Race 1 (47.141 miles/75.866 km).
1 Esteban Gutierrez, MEX, 28m 00.338s, 100.995 mph/162.537 km/h; **2** Robert Wickens, CDN, 28m 02.822s; **3** Roberto Merhi, E, 28m 09.037s; **4** Jean-Eric Vergne, F, 28m 11.972s; **5** Miki Monràs, E, 28m 12.368s; **6** Rio Haryanto, RI, 28m 21.170s; **7** Nico Müller, CH, 28m 21.753s; **8** James Jakes, GB, 28m 23.673s; **9** Tobias Hegewald, D, 28m 29.984s; **10** Stefano Coletti, MC, 28m 30.872s.
Fastest race lap: Gutierrez, 1m 58.748s, 102.081 mph/164.284 km/h.
Pole position: Gutierrez, 1m 58.653s, 102.163 mph/164.415 km/h.

Race 2 (47.141 miles/75.866 km).
1 Nico Müller, CH, 28m 01.567s, 100.922 mph/162.418 km/h; **2** Roberto Merhi, E, 28m 04.775s; **3** James Jakes, GB, 28m 08.208s; **4** Rio Haryanto, RI, 28m 16.990s; **5** Adrian Quaife-Hobbs, GB, 28m 18.621s; **6** Stefano Coletti, MC, 28m 19.739s; **7** Esteban Gutierrez, MEX, 28m 20.346s; **8** Pål Varhaug, N, 28m 26.564s; **9** Pablo Sánchez, MEX, 28m 27.716s; **10** Mirko Bortolotti, I, 28m 31.384s.
Fastest race lap: Merhi, 1m 58.845s, 101.998 mph/164.149 km/h.
Pole position: Jakes.

GP3 SERIES, Silverstone Grand Prix Circuit, Towcester, Northamptonshire, Great Britain, 10/11 July. Round 4. 2 x 14 laps of the 3.660-mile/5.891-km circuit.
Race 1 (51.182 miles/82.369 km).
1 Esteban Gutierrez, MEX, 26m 40.761s, 115.104 mph/185.242 km/h; **2** Rio Haryanto, RI, 26m 44.392s; **3** Nico Müller, CH, 26m 50.962s; **4** Tobias Hegewald, D, 26m 53.090s; **5** Alexander Rossi, USA, 26m 55.177s; **6** Dean Smith, GB, 26m 56.160s; **7** Daniel Morad, CDN, 26m 58.727s; **8** Mirko Bortolotti, I, 26m 59.370s; **9** Robert Wickens, CDN, 26m 59.947s; **10** Stefano Coletti, MC, 27m 02.201s.
Fastest race lap: Gutierrez, 1m 53.307s, 116.301 mph/187.169 km/h.
Pole position: Gutierrez, 1m 51.451s, 118.238 mph/190.286 km/h.

Race 2 (51.182 miles/82.369 km).
1 Daniel Morad, CDN, 26m 35.990s, 115.448 mph/185.795 km/h; **2** Alexander Rossi, USA, 26m 41.527s; **3** Esteban Gutierrez, MEX, 26m 41.616s; **4** Nico Müller, CH, 26m 42.106s; **5** Robert Wickens, CDN, 26m 42.859s; **6** Tobias Hegewald, D, 26m 43.704s; **7** Renger van der Zande, NL, 26m 46.862s; **8** Oliver Oakes, GB, 26m 52.483s; **9** Pål Varhaug, N, 26m 55.216s; **10** Josef Newgarden, USA, 26m 55.981s.
Fastest race lap: Morad, 1m 52.955s, 116.664 mph/187.752 km/h.
Pole position: Bortolotti.

GP3 SERIES, Hockenheimring Grand Prix Circuit, Heidelberg, Germany, 24/25 July. Round 5. 2 x 17 laps of the 2.842-mile/4.574-km circuit.
Race 1 (48.317 miles/77.758 km).
1 Robert Wickens, CDN, 29m 40.963s, 97.666 mph/157.178 km/h; **2** James Jakes, GB, 29m 43.358s; **3** Renger van der Zande, NL, 29m 44.542s; **4** Esteban Gutierrez, MEX, 29m 44.963s; **5** Stefano Coletti, MC, 29m 52.299s; **6** Mirko Bortolotti, I, 29m 52.866s; **7** Felipe Guimarães, BR, 29m 53.474s; **8** Daniel Juncadella, E, 30m 01.315s; **9** Dean Smith, GB, 30m 01.935s; **10** Doru Sechelariu, RO, 30m 02.312s.
Fastest race lap: Wickens, 1m 33.080s, 109.924 mph/176.905 km/h.
Pole position: Josef Newgarden, USA, 1m 47.176s, 95.466 mph/153.638 km/h.

Race 2 (48.317 miles/77.758 km).
1 Esteban Gutierrez, MEX, 32m 14.652s, 89.907 mph/144.692 km/h; **2** Daniel Juncadella, E, 32m 15.009s; **3** Stefano Coletti, MC, 32m 15.762s; **4** Mirko Bortolotti, I, 32m 16.336s; **5** Robert Wickens, CDN, 32m 21.056s; **6** Pedro Nunes, BR, 32m 22.548s; **7** Felipe Guimarães, BR, 32m 23.287s; **8** Alexander Rossi, USA, 32m 24.184s; **9** Daniel Morad, CDN, 32m 24.532s; **10** Michael Christensen, DK, 32m 27.576s.
Fastest race lap: Gutierrez, 1m 31.853s, 111.392 mph/179.269 km/h.
Pole position: Juncadella.

GP3 SERIES, Hungaroring, Mogyorod, Budapest, Hungary, 31 July/1 August. Round 6. 2 x 16 laps of the 2.722-mile/4.381-km circuit.
Race 1 (43.531 miles/70.056 km).
1 Nico Müller, CH, 26m 27.400s, 98.721 mph/158.877 km/h; **2** Esteban Gutierrez, MEX, 26m 28.850s; **3** Stefano Coletti, MC, 26m 41.916s; **4** Robert Wickens, CDN, 26m 42.256s; **5** Dean Smith,

GB, 26m 45.632s; **6** António Félix da Costa, P, 26m 51.946s; **7** Josef Newgarden, USA, 26m 52.246s; **8** Alexander Rossi, USA, 26m 53.399s; **9** Renger van der Zande, NL, 26m 55.473s; **10** Michael Christensen, DK, 26m 57.208s.
Fastest race lap: Gutierrez, 1m 38.280s, 99.715 mph/ 160.476 km/h.
Pole position: Müller, 1m 36.991s, 101.040 mph/ 162.608 km/h.

Race 2 (43.531 miles/70.056 km).
1 Alexander Rossi, USA, 26m 27.165s, 98.736 mph/ 158.900 km/h; **2** Robert Wickens, CDN, 26m 32.127s; **3** Dean Smith, GB, 26m 38.324s; **4** Stefano Coletti, MC, 26m 39.564s; **5** Esteban Gutierrez, MEX, 26m 40.422s; **6** Nico Müller, CH, 26m 42.686s; **7** Adrian Quaife-Hobbs, GB, 26m 45.908s; **8** Mirko Bortolotti, I, 26m 51.392s; **9** Adrien Tambay, F, 26m 56.993s; **10** Oliver Oakes, GB, 26m 57.552s.
Fastest race lap: Wickens, 1m 38.332s, 99.662 mph/ 160.391 km/h.
Pole position: Rossi.

GP3 SERIES, Circuit de Spa-Francorchamps, Stavelot, Belgium, 28/29 August. Round 7. 9 and 12 laps of the 4.352-mile/7.004-km circuit.
Race 1 (39.092 miles/62.912 km).
1 Robert Wickens, CDN, 30m 10.463s, 77.731 mph/ 125.096 km/h; **2** Roberto Merhi, E, 30m 10.982s; **3** Adrian Quaife-Hobbs, GB, 30m 14.557s; **4** Nico Müller, CH, 30m 14.678s; **5** Daniel Juncadella, E, 30m 15.420s; **6** Dean Smith, GB, 30m 16.141s; **7** Pedro Nunes, BR, 30m 16.511s; **8** Simon Trummer, CH, 30m 18.203s; **9** Miki Monràs, E, 30m 19.102s; **10** Michael Christensen, DK, 30m 20.745s.
Fastest race lap: Müller, 2m 13.498s, 117.361 mph/ 188.874 km/h.
Pole position: Wickens, 2m 19.944s, 111.955 mph/ 180.174 km/h.

Race 2 (52.148 miles/83.924 km).
1 Adrien Tambay, F, 30m 11.408s, 103.639 mph/ 166.790 km/h; **2** Alexander Rossi, USA, 30m 11.853s; **3** Miki Monràs, E, 30m 12.611s; **4** Dean Smith, GB, 30m 14.196s; **5** Adrian Quaife-Hobbs, GB, 30m 14.515s; **6** Nico Müller, CH, 30m 17.539s; **7** Esteban Gutierrez, MEX, 30m 23.568s; **8** Tobias Hegewald, D, 30m 25.245s; **9** Felipe Guimarães, BR, 30m 29.605s; **10** Oliver Oakes, GB, 30m 31.202s.
Fastest race lap: Müller, 2m 13.050s, 117.756 mph/ 189.510 km/h.
Pole position: Trummer.

GP3 SERIES, Autodromo Nazionale di Monza, Milan, Italy, 11/12 September. Round 8. 16 and 15 laps of the 3.600-mile/5.793-km circuit.
Race 1 (57.402 miles/92.379 km).
1 Esteban Gutierrez, MEX, 28m 26.731s, 121.077 mph/ 194.854 km/h; **2** Robert Wickens, CDN, 28m 27.726s; **3** Rio Haryanto, RI, 28m 28.835s; **4** Nico Müller, CH, 28m 29.387s; **5** Mirko Bortolotti, I, 28m 30.424s; **6** Roberto Merhi, E, 28m 31.270s; **7** Josef Newgarden, USA, 28m 31.617s; **8** Nigel Melker, NL, 28m 33.654s; **9** Daniel Morad, CDN, 28m 36.879s; **10** Tobias Hegewald, D, 28m 37.620s.
Fastest race lap: Gutierrez, 1m 45.131s, 123.261 mph/ 198.369 km/h.
Pole position: Gutierrez, 1m 43.425s, 125.294 mph/ 201.641 km/h.

Race 2 (53.802 miles/86.586 km).
1 Robert Wickens, CDN, 26m 20.507s, 122.547 mph/ 197.221 km/h; **2** Mirko Bortolotti, I, 26m 22.125s; **3** Nico Müller, CH, 26m 22.446s; **4** Roberto Merhi, E, 26m 23.547s; **5** Josef Newgarden, USA, 26m 24.937s; **6** Miki Monràs, E, 26m 30.111s; **7** Daniel Morad, CDN, 26m 33.202s; **8** Leonardo Cordeiro, BR, 26m 35.781s; **9** Oliver Oakes, GB, 26m 36.380s; **10** Michael Christensen, DK, 26m 38.205s.
Fastest race lap: Pål Varhaug, N, 1m 43.843s, s124.790 mph/200.830 km/h.
Pole position: Melker.

Final Championship points.
Drivers: **1** Esteban Gutierrez, MEX, 88; **2** Robert Wickens, CDN, 71; **3** Nico Müller, CH, 53; **4** Alexander Rossi, USA, 38; **5** Rio Haryanto, RI, 27; **6** Roberto Merhi, E, 26; **7** Dean Smith, GB, 24; **8** James Jakes, GB, 21; **9** Stefano Coletti, MC, 18; **10** Miki Monràs, E, 17; **11** Mirko Bortolotti, I, 16; **12** Daniel Morad, CDN, 15; **13** Pål Varhaug, N, 10; **14** Daniel Juncadella, E, 10; **15** Adrian Quaife-Hobbs, GB, 10; **16** Felipe Guimarães, BR, 9; **17** Jean-Eric Vergne, F, 9; **18** Josef Newgarden, USA, 8; **19** Lucas Foresti, BR, 7; **20** Adrien Tambay, F, 6; **21** Renger van der Zande, NL, 6; **22** Tobias Hegewald, D, 6; **23** Nigel Melker, NL, 5; **24** Pedro Nunes, BR, 4; **25** Simon Trummer, CH, 4; **26** António Félix da Costa, P, 3; **27** Leonardo Cordeiro, BR, 1.
Teams: **1** ART Grand Prix, 130; **2** Status Grand Prix, 86; **3** Jenzer Motorsport, 67; **4** Manor Racing, 64; **5** Carlin, 42; **6** Tech **1** Racing, 37; **7** Atech CRS GP, 26; **8** Addax Team, 25; **9** MW Arden, 18; **10** RSC Mucke Motorsport, 17.

British Formula 3 International Series

BRITISH FORMULA 3 INTERNATIONAL SERIES, Oulton Park Circuit, Tarporley, Cheshire, Great Britain, 3/5 April. 19, 13 and 26 laps of the 2.692-mile/ 4.332-km circuit.
Round 1 (51.148 miles/82.315 km).
1 Jean-Eric Vergne, F (Dallara F308-Volkswagen), 30m 21.288s, 101.100 mph/162.705 km/h; **2** Oliver Webb, GB (Dallara F308-Mercedes Benz), 30m 24.779s; **3** Adriano Buzaid, BR (Dallara F308-Volkswagen), 30m 27.085s; **4** Carlos Huertas, CO (Dallara F308-Mercedes Benz), 30m 30.986s; **5** Rupert Svendsen-Cook, GB (Dallara F308-Volkswagen), 30m 32.452s; **6** Daisuke Nakajima, J (Dallara F308-Mercedes Benz), 30m 33.860s; **7** Gabriel Dias, BR (Dallara F310-Volkswagen), 30m 37.029s; **8** Jazeman Jaafar, MAL (Dallara F308-Volkswagen), 30m 38.230s; **9** Daniel McKenzie, GB (Dallara F308-Mercedes Benz), 30m 39.059s; **10** William Buller, GB (Dallara F310-Volkswagen), 30m 41.393s.
Fastest race lap: Vergne, 1m 29.073s, 108.800 mph/ 175.097 km/h.
Pole position: Vergne, 1m 28.810s, 109.122 mph/ 175.616 km/h.

Round 2 (34.996 miles/56.321 km).
1 Rupert Svendsen-Cook, GB (Dallara F308-Volkswagen), 20m 08.175s, 104.277 mph/167.818 km/h; **2** Daisuke Nakajima, J (Dallara F308-Mercedes Benz), 20m 08.833s; **3** Carlos Huertas, CO (Dallara F308-Mercedes Benz), 20m 11.343s; **4** Adriano Buzaid, BR (Dallara F308-Volkswagen), 20m 11.793s; **5** Jean-Eric Vergne, F (Dallara F308-Volkswagen), 20m 12.675s; **6** Jazeman Jaafar, MAL (Dallara F308-Volkswagen), 20m 15.592s; **7** Daniel McKenzie, GB (Dallara F308-Mercedes Benz), 20m 16.091s; **8** Oliver Webb, GB (Dallara F308-Mercedes Benz), 20m 16.415s; **9** William Buller, GB (Dallara F310-Volkswagen), 20m 17.553s; **10** Alex Brundle, GB (Dallara F310-Volkswagen), 20m 19.035s.
Fastest race lap: Vergne, 1m 29.664s, 108.083 mph/ 173.943 km/h.
Pole position: Dias.

Round 3 (69.992 miles/112.641 km).
1 Jean-Eric Vergne, F (Dallara F308-Volkswagen), 39m 00.158s, 107.672 mph/173.282 km/h; **2** Oliver Webb, GB (Dallara F308-Mercedes Benz), 39m 01.535s; **3** Rupert Svendsen-Cook, GB (Dallara F308-Volkswagen), 39m 26.070s; **4** Gabriel Dias, BR (Dallara F310-Volkswagen), 39m 27.051s; **5** Adriano Buzaid, BR (Dallara F308-Volkswagen), 39m 27.702s; **6** James Calado, GB (Dallara F308-Volkswagen), 39m 28.289s; **7** Daisuke Nakajima, J (Dallara F308-Mercedes Benz), 39m 32.134s; **8** Jay Bridger, GB (Dallara F308-Mercedes Benz), 39m 40.499s; **9** Alex Brundle, GB (Dallara F310-Volkswagen), 39m 42.995s; **10** Daniel McKenzie, GB (Dallara F308-Mercedes Benz), 39m 43.182s.
Fastest race lap: Vergne, 1m 29.064s, 108.811 mph/ 175.115 km/h.
Pole position: Vergne, 1m 28.751s, 109.195 mph/ 175.732 km/h.

BRITISH FORMULA 3 INTERNATIONAL SERIES, Silverstone Grand Prix Circuit, Towcester, Northamptonshire, Great Britain, 1/2 May. 14, 10 and 20 laps of the 3.660-mile/5.891-km circuit.
Round 4 (51.247 miles/82.474 km).
1 James Calado, GB (Dallara F308-Volkswagen), 27m 01.234s, 113.795 mph/183.136 km/h; **2** Oliver Webb, GB (Dallara F308-Mercedes Benz), 27m 02.249s; **3** Daisuke Nakajima, J (Dallara F308-Mercedes Benz), 27m 03.377s; **4** Jean-Eric Vergne, F (Dallara F308-Volkswagen), 27m 04.542s; **5** Carlos Huertas, CO (Dallara F308-Mercedes Benz), 27m 07.414s; **6** Esteban Gutierrez, MEX (Dallara F308-Mercedes Benz), 27m 08.155s; **7** Jazeman Jaafar, MAL (Dallara F308-Volkswagen), 27m 09.847s; **8** Gabriel Dias, BR (Dallara F310-Volkswagen), 27m 10.682s; **9** Adriano Buzaid, BR (Dallara F308-Volkswagen), 27m 12.086s; **10** Rupert Svendsen-Cook, GB (Dallara F308-Volkswagen), 27m 17.945s.
Fastest race lap: Calado, 1m 54.731s, 114.858 mph/ 184.846 km/h.
Pole position: Calado, 1m 53.267s, 116.343 mph/ 187.235 km/h.

Round 5 (36.605 miles/58.910 km).
1 Alexander Sims, GB (Dallara F308-Mercedes Benz), 22m 05.371s, 99.427 mph/160.012 km/h; **2** Gabriel Dias, BR (Dallara F310-Volkswagen), 22m 13.659s; **3** Daisuke Nakajima, J (Dallara F308-Mercedes Benz), 22m 14.757s; **4** Esteban Gutierrez, MEX (Dallara F308-Mercedes Benz), 22m 14.812s; **5** Jean-Eric Vergne, F (Dallara F308-Volkswagen), 22m 18.050s; **6** Adriano Buzaid, BR (Dallara F308-Volkswagen), 22m 18.320s; **7** Jazeman Jaafar, MAL (Dallara F308-Volkswagen), 22m 27.877s; **8** Carlos Huertas, CO (Dallara F308-Mercedes Benz), 22m 28.680s; **9** James Calado, GB (Dallara F308-Volkswagen), 22m 32.200s; **10** Luiz Felipe Nasr, BR (Dallara F308-Mercedes Benz), 22m 33.245s.
Fastest race lap: Sims, 2m 10.176s, 101.230 mph/ 162.914 km/h.
Pole position: Dias.

Round 6 (73.210 miles/117.820 km).
1 James Calado, GB (Dallara F308-Volkswagen), 41m 03.787s, 106.971 mph/172.154 km/h; **2** Oliver Webb, GB (Dallara F308-Mercedes Benz), 41m 04.843s; **3** Luiz Felipe Nasr, BR (Dallara F308-Mercedes Benz), 41m 06.680s; **4** Alexander Sims, GB (Dallara F308-Mercedes Benz), 41m 07.730s; **5** Adriano Buzaid, BR (Dallara F308-Volkswagen), 41m 10.350s; **6** Jean-Eric Vergne, F (Dallara F308-Volkswagen), 41m 11.037s; **7** Jazeman Jaafar, MAL (Dallara F308-Volkswagen), 41m 12.682s; **8** Gabriel Dias, BR (Dallara F310-Volkswagen), 41m 13.454s; **9** Esteban Gutierrez, MEX (Dallara F308-Mercedes Benz), 41m 14.327s; **10** William Buller, GB (Dallara F310-Volkswagen), 41m 19.715s.
Fastest race lap: Webb, 1m 55.027s, 114.562 mph/ 184.370 km/h.
Pole position: Calado, 1m 53.198s, 116.413 mph/ 187.349 km/h.

BRITISH FORMULA 3 INTERNATIONAL SERIES, Circuit de Nevers, Magny-Cours, France, 22/23 May. 19, 7 and 25 laps of the 2.741-mile/4.411-km circuit.
Round 7 (52.076 miles/83.809 km).
1 Oliver Webb, GB (Dallara F308-Mercedes Benz), 30m 20.722s, 102.967 mph/165.710 km/h; **2** Gabriel Dias, BR (Dallara F310-Volkswagen), 30m 26.677s; **3** William Buller, GB (Dallara F310-Volkswagen), 30m 29.443s; **4** Jean-Eric Vergne, F (Dallara F308-Volkswagen), 30m 29.849s; **5** Carlos Huertas, CO (Dallara F308-Mercedes Benz), 30m 37.535s; **6** James Calado, GB (Dallara F308-Volkswagen), 30m 37.973s; **7** Jazeman Jaafar, MAL (Dallara F308-Volkswagen), 30m 44.906s; **8** Adriano Buzaid, BR (Dallara F308-Volkswagen), 30m 45.270s; **9** Daisuke Nakajima, J (Dallara F308-Mercedes Benz), 30m 47.004s; **10** Jay Bridger, GB (Dallara F308-Mercedes Benz), 30m 48.664s.
Fastest race lap: Webb, 1m 34.816s, 104.066 mph/ 167.478 km/h.
Pole position: Vergne, 1m 33.296s, 105.761 mph/ 170.206 km/h.

Round 8 (19.186 miles/30.877 km).
1 Jean-Eric Vergne, F (Dallara F308-Volkswagen), 11m 14.889s, 102.342 mph/164.704 km/h; **2** Oliver Webb, GB (Dallara F308-Mercedes Benz), 11m 19.126s; **3** William Buller, GB (Dallara F310-Volkswagen), 11m 21.347s; **4** Daisuke Nakajima, J (Dallara F308-Mercedes Benz), 11m 21.496s; **5** Hywel Lloyd, GB (Dallara F308-Mercedes Benz), 11m 21.866s; **6** Luiz Felipe Nasr, BR (Dallara F308-Mercedes Benz), 11m 22.041s; **7** Lucas Foresti, BR (Dallara F308-Volkswagen), 11m 22.491s; **8** Daniel McKenzie, GB (Dallara F308-Mercedes Benz), 11m 23.551s; **9** Jay Bridger, GB (Dallara F308-Mercedes Benz), 11m 24.053s; **10** Rupert Svendsen-Cook, GB (Dallara F308-Volkswagen), 11m 24.624s.
Gabriel Dias, finished 1st in 12m 14.189s, but given 1-min penalty for jumping the start.
Disqualified: Jazeman Jaafar, MAL (Dallara F308-Volkswagen), finished 3rd in 11m 19.958s (caused accident).
Fastest race lap: Vergne, 1m 35.378s, 103.452 mph/ 166.491 km/h.
Pole position: Jaafar.

Round 9 (68.522 miles/110.275 km).
1 Oliver Webb, GB (Dallara F308-Mercedes Benz), 40m 00.344s, 102.767 mph/165.388 km/h; **2** Jean-Eric Vergne, F (Dallara F308-Volkswagen), 40m 01.026s; **3** Gabriel Dias, BR (Dallara F310-Volkswagen), 40m 21.745s; **4** James Calado, GB (Dallara F308-Volkswagen), 40m 22.602s; **5** Daniel McKenzie, GB (Dallara F308-Mercedes Benz), 40m 28.875s; **6** Rupert Svendsen-Cook, GB (Dallara F308-Volkswagen), 40m 36.292s; **7** Luiz Felipe Nasr, BR (Dallara F308-Mercedes Benz), 40m 36.829s; **8** Hywel Lloyd, GB (Dallara F308-Mercedes Benz), 40m 44.390s; **9** Lucas Foresti, BR (Dallara F308-Volkswagen), 40m 46.581s; **10** Jazeman Jaafar, MAL (Dallara F308-Volkswagen), 40m 48.922s.
Fastest race lap: Webb, 1m 35.449s, 103.375 mph/ 166.367 km/h.
Pole position: Vergne, 1m 33.123s, 105.957 mph/ 170.522 km/h.

BRITISH FORMULA 3 INTERNATIONAL SERIES, Hockenheimring Grand Prix Circuit, Heidelberg, Germany, 29/30 May. 16, 13 and 25 laps of the 2.842-mile/4.574-km circuit.
Round 10 (45.474 miles/73.184 km).
1 Jean-Eric Vergne, F (Dallara F308-Volkswagen), 25m 28.768s, 107.084 mph/172.336 km/h; **2** Jazeman Jaafar, MAL (Dallara F308-Volkswagen), 25m 47.960s; **3** Daniel McKenzie, GB (Dallara F308-Mercedes Benz), 25m 50.060s; **4** James Calado, GB (Dallara F308-Volkswagen), 25m 50.860s; **5** Adriano Buzaid, BR (Dallara F308-Volkswagen), 25m 58.054s; **6** Jay Bridger, GB (Dallara F308-Mercedes Benz), 25m 59.320s; **7** Gabriel Dias, BR (Dallara F310-Volkswagen), 25m 59.829s; **8** Oliver Webb, GB (Dallara F308-Mercedes Benz), 26m 06.917s; **9** James Cole, GB (Dallara F307-Mugen Honda), 26m 08.426s; **10** William Buller, GB (Dallara F310-Volkswagen), 26m 10.201s.
Fastest race lap: Vergne, 1m 34.568s, 108.194 mph/ 174.122 km/h.
Pole position: Vergne, 1m 33.830s, 109.045 mph/ 175.491 km/h.

Round 11 (36.948 miles/59.462 km).
1 Gabriel Dias, BR (Dallara F310-Volkswagen), 20m 54.072s, 106.064 mph/170.694 km/h; **2** Oliver Webb, GB (Dallara F308-Mercedes Benz), 20m 55.237s; **3** Adriano Buzaid, BR (Dallara F308-Volkswagen), 20m 56.052s; **4** Jay Bridger, GB (Dallara F308-Mercedes Benz), 20m 57.721s; **5** Jean-Eric Vergne, F (Dallara F308-Volkswagen), 20m 58.246s; **6** James Calado, GB (Dallara F308-Volkswagen), 20m 59.751s; **7** William Buller, GB (Dallara F310-Volkswagen), 21m 00.732s; **8** Jazeman Jaafar, MAL (Dallara F308-Volkswagen), 21m 04.813s; **9** Rupert Svendsen-Cook, GB (Dallara F308-Volkswagen), 21m 11.751s; **10** Carlos Huertas, CO (Dallara F308-Mercedes Benz), 21m 18.132s.
Fastest race lap: Dias, 1m 34.695s, 108.049 mph/ 173.888 km/h.
Pole position: Webb.

Round 12 (71.054 miles/114.350 km).
1 Jean-Eric Vergne, F (Dallara F308-Volkswagen), 39m 58.368s, 106.653 mph/171.641 km/h; **2** William Buller, GB (Dallara F310-Volkswagen), 40m 19.966s; **3** Jazeman Jaafar, MAL (Dallara F308-Volkswagen), 40m 20.563s; **4** Adriano Buzaid, BR (Dallara F308-Volkswagen), 40m 21.517s; **5** Gabriel Dias, BR (Dallara F310-Volkswagen), 40m 22.735s; **6** James Calado, GB (Dallara F308-Volkswagen), 40m 23.218s; **7** Daisuke Nakajima, J (Dallara F308-Mercedes Benz), 40m 24.239s; **8** Rupert Svendsen-Cook, GB (Dallara F308-Volkswagen), 40m 38.107s; **9** Lucas Foresti, BR (Dallara F308-Volkswagen), 40m 45.213s; **10** Alex Brundle, GB (Dallara F310-Volkswagen), 40m 54.882s.
Fastest race lap: Vergne, 1m 35.185s, 107.493 mph/ 172.993 km/h.
Pole position: Vergne, 1m 33.779s, 109.104 mph/ 175.587 km/h.

BRITISH FORMULA 3 INTERNATIONAL SERIES, Rockingham Motor Speedway, Corby, Northamptonshire, Great Britain, 17/18 July. 24, 16 and 31 laps of the 1.940-mile/3.122-km circuit.
Round 13 (46.560 miles/74.931 km).
1 Jean-Eric Vergne, F (Dallara F308-Volkswagen), 29m 38.641s, 94.238 mph/151.661 km/h; **2** Carlos Huertas, CO (Dallara F308-Mercedes Benz), 29m 38.923s; **3** Oliver Webb, GB (Dallara F308-Mercedes Benz), 29m 43.241s; **4** James Calado, GB (Dallara F308-Volkswagen), 29m 43.882s; **5** William Buller, GB (Dallara F310-Volkswagen), 29m 59.236s; **6** Gabriel Dias, BR (Dallara F310-Volkswagen), 29m 59.838s; **7** Luiz Felipe Nasr, BR (Dallara F308-Mercedes Benz), 30m 00.369s; **8** Daniel McKenzie, GB (Dallara F308-Mercedes Benz), 30m 01.021s; **9** Adriano Buzaid, BR (Dallara F308-Volkswagen), 30m 01.757s; **10** Daisuke Nakajima, J (Dallara F308-Mercedes Benz), 30m 03.607s.
Fastest race lap: Vergne, 1m 12.991s, 95.683 mph/ 153.986 km/h.
Pole position: Webb, 1m 12.271s, 96.636 mph/ 155.521 km/h.

Round 14 (31.040 miles/49.954 km).
1 Daniel McKenzie, GB (Dallara F308-Mercedes Benz), 20m 06.462s, 92.621 mph/149.059 km/h; **2** Daisuke Nakajima, J (Dallara F308-Mercedes Benz), 20m 07.575s; **3** Adriano Buzaid, BR (Dallara F308-Volkswagen), 20m 15.250s; **4** Gabriel Dias, BR (Dallara F310-Volkswagen), 20m 24.692s; **5** William Buller, GB (Dallara F310-Volkswagen), 20m 26.147s; **6** James Calado, GB (Dallara F308-Volkswagen), 20m 26.736s; **7** Carlos Huertas, CO (Dallara F308-Mercedes Benz), 20m 27.127s; **8** Oliver Webb, GB (Dallara F308-Mercedes Benz), 20m 27.858s; **9** Jean-Eric Vergne, F (Dallara F308-Volkswagen), 20m 28.813s; **10** Lucas Foresti, BR (Dallara F308-Volkswagen), 20m 32.089s.
Fastest race lap: McKenzie, 1m 13.269s, 95.319 mph/ 153.402 km/h.
Pole position: Nakajima.

Round 15 (60.140 miles/96.786 km).
1 Luiz Felipe Nasr, BR (Dallara F308-Mercedes Benz), 40m 15.189s, 89.642 mph/144.265 km/h; **2** Jean-Eric Vergne, F (Dallara F308-Volkswagen), 40m 30.841s; **3** James Calado, GB (Dallara F308-Volkswagen), 40m 36.997s; **4** Adriano Buzaid, BR (Dallara F308-Volkswagen), 40m 40.201s; **5** William Buller, GB (Dallara F310-Volkswagen), 40m 42.554s; **6** Oliver Webb, GB (Dallara F308-Mercedes Benz), 40m 44.077s; **7** James Cole, GB (Dallara F307-Mugen Honda), 40m 50.564s; **8** Menasheh Idafar, GB (Dallara F307-Mugen Honda), 40m 51.220s; **9** Hywel Lloyd, GB (Dallara F308-Mercedes Benz), 40m 52.544s; **10** Jay Bridger, GB (Dallara F308-Mercedes Benz), 40m 57.524s.
Fastest race lap: Nasr, 1m 14.256s, 94.053 mph/ 151.363 km/h.
Pole position: Webb, 1m 12.147s, 96.802 mph/ 155.788 km/h.

BRITISH FORMULA 3 INTERNATIONAL SERIES, Circuit de Spa-Francorchamps, Stavelot, Belgium, 30/31 July. 13, 8 and 17 laps of the 4.352-mile/7.004-km circuit.
Round 16 (56.577 miles/91.052 km).
1 Jean-Eric Vergne, F (Dallara F308-Volkswagen), 29m 36.710s, 114.637 mph/184.491 km/h; **2** James Calado, GB (Dallara F308-Volkswagen), 29m 37.824s; **3** Rupert Svendsen-Cook, GB (Dallara F308-Volkswagen), 29m 49.194s; **4** Oliver Webb, GB (Dallara F308-Mercedes Benz), 29m 50.117s; **5** Adriano Buzaid, BR (Dallara F308-Volkswagen), 29m 50.944s; **6** Daniel McKenzie, GB (Dallara F308-Mercedes Benz), 29m 51.587s; **7** Luiz Felipe Nasr, BR (Dallara F308-Mercedes Benz), 29m 53.942s; **8** Lucas Foresti, BR (Dallara F308-Volkswagen), 29m 54.818s; **9** Hywel Lloyd, GB (Dallara F308-Mercedes Benz), 29m 56.742s; **10** Daniel Juncadella, E (Dallara F309-Mercedes Benz), 29m 57.964s.
Fastest race lap: Vergne, 2m 15.842s, 115.336 mph/ 185.615 km/h.
Pole position: Vergne, 2m 14.676s, 116.335 mph/ 187.222 km/h.

Round 17 (34.817 miles/56.032 km).
1 Jean-Eric Vergne, F (Dallara F308-Volkswagen), 18m 22.251s, 113.712 mph/183.002 km/h; **2** Luiz Felipe Nasr, BR (Dallara F308-Mercedes Benz), 18m 22.910s; **3** Daniel McKenzie, GB (Dallara F308-Mercedes Benz), 18m 30.550s; **4** James Calado, GB (Dallara F308-Volkswagen), 18m 35.379s; **5** Oliver Webb, GB (Dallara F308-Mercedes Benz), 18m 35.730s; **6** Carlos Muñoz, CO (Dallara F308-Mercedes Benz), 18m 36.258s; **7** Rupert Svendsen-Cook, GB (Dallara F308-Volkswagen), 18m 36.404s; **8** Hywel Lloyd, GB (Dallara F308-Mercedes Benz), 18m 37.500s; **9** Daisuke Nakajima, J (Dallara F308-Mercedes Benz), 18m 39.486s; **10** Alexander Sims, GB (Dallara F308-Mercedes Benz), 18m 50.023s.
Fastest race lap: Nasr, 2m 16.662s, 114.644 mph/ 184.501 km/h.
Pole position: Nasr.

Round 18 (73.985 miles/119.068 km).
1 Jean-Eric Vergne, F (Dallara F308-Volkswagen), 39m 05.769s, 113.543 mph/182.731 km/h; **2** James Calado, GB (Dallara F308-Volkswagen), 39m 09.548s; **3** Alexander Sims, GB (Dallara F308-Mercedes Benz), 39m 27.744s; **4** Gabriel Dias, BR (Dallara F310-Volkswagen), 39m 29.332s; **5** Luiz Felipe Nasr, BR (Dallara F308-Mercedes Benz), 39m 29.494s; **6** Daniel Juncadella, E (Dallara F309-Mercedes Benz), 39m 30.099s; **7** Rupert Svendsen-Cook, GB (Dallara F308-Volkswagen), 39m 30.859s; **8** Jazeman Jaafar, MAL (Dallara F308-Volkswagen), 39m 32.989s; **9** Adriano Buzaid, BR (Dallara F308-Volkswagen), 39m 33.074s; **10** Daniel McKenzie, GB (Dallara F308-Mercedes Benz), 39m 34.368s.
Fastest race lap: Vergne, 2m 16.987s, 114.372 mph/ 184.064 km/h.
Pole position: Webb, 2m 14.476s, 116.507 mph/ 187.501 km/h.

BRITISH FORMULA 3 INTERNATIONAL SERIES, Thruxton Circuit, Andover, Hampshire, Great Britain, 7/8 August. 27, 17 and 33 laps of the 2.356-mile/3.792-km circuit.
Round 19 (63.612 miles/102.374 km).
1 James Calado, GB (Dallara F308-Volkswagen), 30m 32.030s, 124.999 mph/201.167 km/h; **2** Jean-Eric Vergne, F (Dallara F308-Volkswagen), 30m 32.335s; **3** Rupert Svendsen-Cook, GB (Dallara F308-Volkswagen), 30m 46.417s; **4** Adriano Buzaid, BR (Dallara F308-Volkswagen), 30m 50.869s; **5** Oliver Webb, GB (Dallara F308-Mercedes Benz), 30m 56.486s; **6** Lucas Foresti, BR (Dallara F308-Volkswagen), 30m 57.088s; **7** Luiz Felipe Nasr, BR (Dallara F308-Mercedes Benz), 30m 57.306s; **8** Daniel McKenzie, GB (Dallara F308-Mercedes Benz), 30m 58.893s; **9** William Buller, GB (Dallara F310-Volkswagen), 31m 02.666s; **10** Carlos Huertas, CO (Dallara F308-Mercedes Benz), 31m 04.875s.
Fastest race lap: Calado, 1m 07.312s, 126.004 mph/ 202.784 km/h.
Pole position: Vergne, 1m 06.196s, 128.128 mph/ 206.202 km/h.

Round 20 (40.052 miles/64.457 km).
1 Jean-Eric Vergne, F (Dallara F308-Volkswagen), 19m 09.854s, 125.396 mph/201.805 km/h; **2** James Calado, GB (Dallara F308-Volkswagen), 19m 11.492s; **3** Oliver Webb, GB (Dallara F308-Mercedes Benz), 19m 13.069s; **4** Rupert Svendsen-Cook, GB (Dallara F308-Volkswagen), 19m 17.729s; **5** Daniel McKenzie, GB (Dallara F308-Mercedes Benz), 19m 18.842s; **6** Adriano Buzaid, BR (Dallara F308-Volkswagen), 19m 20.294s; **7** Jazeman Jaafar, MAL (Dallara F308-Volkswagen), 19m 26.118s; **8** Carlos Huertas, CO (Dallara F308-Mercedes Benz), 19m 26.530s; **9** Gabriel Dias, BR (Dallara F310-Volkswagen), 19m 29.754s; **10** Jay Bridger, GB (Dallara F308-Mercedes Benz), 19m 34.476s.
Fastest race lap: Vergne, 1m 06.752s, 127.061 mph/204.485 km/h.
Pole position: Nasr.

Round 21 (77.748 miles/125.123 km).
1 Jean-Eric Vergne, F (Dallara F308-Volkswagen), 40m 52.546s, 114.123 mph/183.663 km/h; **2** Oliver Webb, GB (Dallara F308-Mercedes Benz), 41m 00.442s; **3** James Calado, GB (Dallara F308-Volkswagen), 41m 02.240s; **4** Adriano Buzaid, BR (Dallara F308-Volkswagen), 41m 05.081s; **5** Rupert Svendsen-Cook, GB (Dallara F308-Volkswagen), 41m 09.030s; **6** Luiz Felipe Nasr, BR (Dallara F308-Mercedes Benz), 41m 11.955s; **7** Lucas Foresti, BR (Dallara F308-Volkswagen), 41m 13.585s; **8** Jay Bridger, GB (Dallara F308-Mercedes Benz), 41m 20.974s; **9** Daniel McKenzie, GB (Dallara F308-Mercedes Benz), 41m 22.080s; **10** Alex Brundle, GB (Dallara F310-Volkswagen), 41m 27.692s.
Fastest race lap: Vergne, 1m 07.264s, 126.094 mph/202.928 km/h.
Pole position: Vergne, 1m 06.148s, 128.221 mph/206.352 km/h.

BRITISH FORMULA 3 INTERNATIONAL SERIES, Silverstone Grand Prix Circuit, Towcester, Northamptonshire, Great Britain, 14/15 August. 16, 11 and 23 laps of the 3.195-mile/5.141-km circuit.
Round 22 (51.112 miles/82.257 km).
1 James Calado, GB (Dallara F308-Volkswagen), 30m 48.609s, 99.536 mph/160.187 km/h; **2** Jean-Eric Vergne, F (Dallara F308-Volkswagen), 30m 55.802s; **3** Lucas Foresti, BR (Dallara F308-Volkswagen), 31m 10.177s; **4** Adriano Buzaid, BR (Dallara F308-Volkswagen), 31m 11.359s; **5** Luiz Felipe Nasr, BR (Dallara F308-Mercedes Benz), 31m 12.134s; **6** Rupert Svendsen-Cook, GB (Dallara F308-Volkswagen), 31m 21.252s; **7** Carlos Huertas, CO (Dallara F308-Mercedes Benz), 31m 22.284s; **8** Daniel McKenzie, GB (Dallara F308-Mercedes Benz), 31m 23.137s; **9** Oliver Webb, GB (Dallara F308-Mercedes Benz), 31m 30.486s; **10** Daisuke Nakajima, J (Dallara F308-Mercedes Benz), 32m 00.482s.
Fastest race lap: Vergne, 1m 41.258s, 113.573 mph/182.778 km/h.
Pole position: Vergne, 1m 47.869s, 106.612 mph/171.576 km/h.

Round 23 (35.140 miles/56.552 km).
1 Adriano Buzaid, BR (Dallara F308-Volkswagen), 19m 08.094s, 110.184 mph/177.324 km/h; **2** Carlos Huertas, CO (Dallara F308-Mercedes Benz), 19m 10.784s; **3** Jean-Eric Vergne, F (Dallara F308-Volkswagen), 19m 11.547s; **4** Luiz Felipe Nasr, BR (Dallara F308-Mercedes Benz), 19m 12.635s; **5** James Calado, GB (Dallara F308-Volkswagen), 19m 14.299s; **6** Rupert Svendsen-Cook, GB (Dallara F308-Volkswagen), 19m 22.861s; **7** Oliver Webb, GB (Dallara F308-Mercedes Benz), 19m 23.366s; **8** Jazeman Jaafar, MAL (Dallara F308-Volkswagen), 19m 23.880s; **9** Hywel Lloyd, GB (Dallara F308-Mercedes Benz), 19m 25.606s; **10** Daniel McKenzie, GB (Dallara F308-Mercedes Benz), 19m 27.304s.
Fastest race lap: Huertas, 1m 41.621s, 113.167 mph/182.125 km/h.
Pole position: Huertas.

Round 24 (73.474 miles/118.244 km).
1 Jean-Eric Vergne, F (Dallara F308-Volkswagen), 41m 01.289s, 107.465 mph/172.949 km/h; **2** Adriano Buzaid, BR (Dallara F308-Volkswagen), 41m 02.501s; **3** Oliver Webb, GB (Dallara F308-Mercedes Benz), 41m 07.523s; **4** James Calado, GB (Dallara F308-Volkswagen), 41m 08.569s; **5** Lucas Foresti, BR (Dallara F308-Volkswagen), 41m 21.511s; **6** Rupert Svendsen-Cook, GB (Dallara F308-Volkswagen), 41m 26.061s; **7** Gabriel Dias, BR (Dallara F310-Volkswagen), 41m 27.184s; **8** Alex Brundle, GB (Dallara F310-Volkswagen), 41m 30.477s; **9** William Buller, GB (Dallara F310-Volkswagen), 41m 31.270s; **10** Daniel McKenzie, GB (Dallara F308-Mercedes Benz), 41m 31.967s.
Fastest race lap: Vergne, 1m 41.235s, 113.599 mph/182.819 km/h.
Pole position: Vergne, 1m 45.944s, 108.549 mph/174.693 km/h.

BRITISH FORMULA 3 INTERNATIONAL SERIES, Snetterton Circuit, Thetford, Norfolk, Great Britain, 29/30 August. 26, 18 and 38 laps of the 1.952-mile/3.141-km circuit.
Round 25 (50.752 miles/81.677 km).
1 Jean-Eric Vergne, F (Dallara F308-Volkswagen), 30m 04.032s, 101.277 mph/162.989 km/h; **2** Adriano Buzaid, BR (Dallara F308-Volkswagen), 30m 07.667s; **3** Luiz Felipe Nasr, BR (Dallara F308-Mercedes Benz), 30m 08.134s; **4** Oliver Webb, GB (Dallara F308-Mercedes Benz), 30m 17.734s; **5** Daisuke Nakajima, J (Dallara F308-Mercedes Benz), 30m 20.109s; **6** Gabriel Dias, BR (Dallara F310-Volkswagen), 30m 20.776s; **7** William Buller, GB (Dallara F310-Volkswagen), 30m 21.279s; **8** James Calado, GB (Dallara F308-Volkswagen), 30m 26.005s; **9** Daniel McKenzie, GB (Dallara F308-Mercedes Benz), 30m 35.776s; **10** Jazeman Jaafar, MAL (Dallara F308-Volkswagen), 30m 39.034s.
Fastest race lap: Buller, 1m 02.146s, 113.075 mph/181.977 km/h.
Pole position: Buzaid, 1m 00.994s, 115.211 mph/185.414 km/h.

Round 26 (35.136 miles/56.546 km).
1 Gabriel Dias, BR (Dallara F310-Volkswagen), 20m 40.081s, 102.001 mph/164.154 km/h; **2** Adriano Buzaid, BR (Dallara F308-Volkswagen), 20m 40.474s; **3** William Buller, GB (Dallara F310-Volkswagen), 20m 42.876s; **4** Daisuke Nakajima, J (Dallara F308-Mercedes Benz), 20m 44.995s; **5** Luiz Felipe Nasr, BR (Dallara F308-Mercedes Benz), 20m 47.384s; **6** Daniel McKenzie, GB (Dallara F308-Mercedes Benz), 20m 47.968s; **7** James Calado, GB (Dallara F308-Volkswagen), 20m 48.678s; **8** Jean-Eric Vergne, F (Dallara F308-Volkswagen), 20m 52.386s; **9** Jazeman Jaafar, MAL (Dallara F308-Volkswagen), 21m 00.850s; **10** Maxim Snegirev, RUS (Dallara F308-Mercedes Benz), 21m 08.370s.
Fastest race lap: Calado, 1m 04.400s, 109.118 mph/175.608 km/h.
Pole position: Dias.

Round 27 (74.176 miles/119.375 km).
1 Adriano Buzaid, BR (Dallara F308-Volkswagen), 39m 11.397s, 113.563 mph/182.763 km/h; **2** Jean-Eric Vergne, F (Dallara F308-Volkswagen), 39m 18.935s; **3** James Calado, GB (Dallara F308-Volkswagen), 39m 19.362s; **4** Daisuke Nakajima, J (Dallara F308-Mercedes Benz), 39m 25.679s; **5** Luiz Felipe Nasr, BR (Dallara F308-Mercedes Benz), 39m 26.711s; **6** Jazeman Jaafar, MAL (Dallara F308-Volkswagen), 39m 32.048s; **7** Carlos Huertas, CO (Dallara F308-Mercedes Benz), 39m 33.364s; **8** Gabriel Dias, BR (Dallara F310-Volkswagen), 39m 34.572s; **9** William Buller, GB (Dallara F310-Volkswagen), 39m 37.517s; **10** Rupert Svendsen-Cook, GB (Dallara F308-Volkswagen), 39m 53.319s.
Fastest race lap: Buzaid, 1m 01.200s, 114.823 mph/184.790 km/h.
Pole position: Buzaid, 1m 00.948s, 115.298 mph/185.554 km/h.

BRITISH FORMULA 3 INTERNATIONAL SERIES, Brands Hatch Grand Prix Circuit, West Kingsdown, Dartford, Kent, Great Britain, 25/26 September. 23, 15 and 26 laps of the 2.301-mile/3.703-km circuit.
Round 28 (52.921 miles/85.168 km).
1 Oliver Webb, GB (Dallara F308-Mercedes Benz), 30m 00.505s, 105.811 mph/170.287 km/h; **2** James Calado, GB (Dallara F308-Volkswagen), 30m 03.133s; **3** Adriano Buzaid, BR (Dallara F308-Volkswagen), 30m 10.891s; **4** Rupert Svendsen-Cook, GB (Dallara F308-Volkswagen), 30m 20.715s; **5** Carlos Huertas, CO (Dallara F308-Mercedes Benz), 30m 29.014s; **6** William Buller, GB (Dallara F310-Volkswagen), 30m 29.224s; **7** Daniel McKenzie, GB (Dallara F308-Mercedes Benz), 30m 29.556s; **8** Jean-Eric Vergne, F (Dallara F308-Volkswagen), 30m 30.734s; **9** Daisuke Nakajima, J (Dallara F308-Mercedes Benz), 30m 31.410s; **10** Luiz Felipe Nasr, BR (Dallara F308-Mercedes Benz), 30m 31.862s.
Fastest race lap: Webb, 1m 17.443s, 106.959 mph/172.134 km/h.
Pole position: Webb, 1m 17.670s, 106.646 mph/171.631 km/h.

Round 29 (34.514 miles/55.544 km).
1 Daniel McKenzie, GB (Dallara F308-Mercedes Benz), 19m 43.432s, 104.990 mph/168.965 km/h; **2** Carlos Huertas, CO (Dallara F308-Mercedes Benz), 19m 46.893s; **3** Adriano Buzaid, BR (Dallara F308-Volkswagen), 19m 48.567s; **4** Jean-Eric Vergne, F (Dallara F308-Volkswagen), 19m 49.155s; **5** James Calado, GB (Dallara F308-Volkswagen), 19m 49.955s; **6** Rupert Svendsen-Cook, GB (Dallara F308-Volkswagen), 19m 51.494s; **7** Oliver Webb, GB (Dallara F308-Mercedes Benz), 19m 53.457s; **8** Daisuke Nakajima, J (Dallara F308-Mercedes Benz), 19m 56.901s; **9** Luiz Felipe Nasr, BR (Dallara F308-Mercedes Benz), 19m 58.564s; **10** Alex Brundle, GB (Dallara F310-Volkswagen), 19m 59.006s.
Fastest race lap: Nasr, 1m 17.461s, 106.934 mph/172.094 km/h.
Pole position: McKenzie.

Round 30 (59.823 miles/96.276 km).
1 James Calado, GB (Dallara F308-Volkswagen), 40m 09.900s, 89.366 mph/143.821 km/h; **2** William Buller, GB (Dallara F310-Volkswagen), 40m 18.052s; **3** Menasheh Idafar, GB (Dallara F307-Mugen Honda), 40m 40.086s; **4** Adderly Fong, HK (Dallara F308-Mercedes Benz), 40m 41.521s; **5** Jay Bridger, GB (Dallara F308-Mercedes Benz), 40m 46.454s; **6** Daniel McKenzie, GB (Dallara F308-Mercedes Benz), 40m 46.778s; **7** Luiz Felipe Nasr, BR (Dallara F308-Mercedes Benz), 40m 48.311s; **8** Carlos Huertas, CO (Dallara F308-Mercedes Benz), 40m 51.920s; **9** Adriano Buzaid, BR (Dallara F308-Volkswagen), 40m 58.568s; **10** Oliver Webb, GB (Dallara F308-Mercedes Benz), 41m 03.357s.
Fastest race lap: Calado, 1m 21.515s, 101.616 mph/163.535 km/h.
Pole position: McKenzie, 1m 17.525s, 106.846 mph/171.952 km/h.

Final championship points
1 Jean-Eric Vergne, F, 392; **2** James Calado, GB, 293; **3** Oliver Webb, GB, 250; **4** Adriano Buzaid, BR, 238; **5** Luiz Felipe Nasr, BR, 136; **6** Gabriel Dias, BR, 135; **7** Rupert Svendsen-Cook, GB, 131; **8** William Buller, GB, 111; **9** Daniel McKenzie, GB, 109; **10** Carlos Huertas, CO, 104; **11** Daisuke Nakajima, J, 97; **12** Jazeman Jaafar, MAL, 85; **13** Lucas Foresti, BR, 45; **14** Jay Bridger, GB, 37; **15** Hywel Lloyd, GB, 23; **16** Adderly Fong, HK, 12; **17** Alex Brundle, GB, 11; **18** Maxim Snegirev, RUS, 1.
National class: **1** Menasheh Idafar, GB, 435; **2** James Cole, GB, 418; **3** Juan Carlos Sistos, MEX, 72; **4** Luiz Razia, BR, 23.

Formula 3 Euro Series

FORMULA 3 EURO SERIES, Circuit ASA Paul Ricard, Le Beausset, France, 10/11 April. 19 and 14 laps of the 3.630-mile/5.842-km circuit.
Round 1 (68.971 miles/110.998 km).
1 Edoardo Mortara, I (Dallara F308-Volkswagen), 36m 15.649s, 114.125 mph/183.666 km/h; **2** Marco Wittmann, D (Dallara F308-Volkswagen), 36m 16.437s; **3** Alexander Sims, GB (Dallara F308-Mercedes Benz), 36m 21.685s; **4** Daniel Juncadella, E (Dallara F308-Mercedes Benz), 36m 26.572s; **5** Roberto Merhi, E (Dallara F308-Mercedes Benz), 36m 36.800s; **6** Adrian Quaife-Hobbs, GB (Dallara F308-Volkswagen), 36m 42.995s; **7** Jim Pla, F (Dallara F308-Mercedes Benz), 36m 43.779s; **8** António Félix da Costa, P (Dallara F308-Volkswagen), 36m 48.561s; **9** Valtteri Bottas, FIN (Dallara F308-Mercedes Benz), 36m 54.436s; **10** Matias Laine, FIN (Dallara F308-Volkswagen), 37m 03.252s.
Fastest race lap: Wittmann, 1m 53.533s, 115.105 mph/185.243 km/h.
Pole position: Juncadella, 1m 52.624s, 116.034 mph/186.738 km/h.

Round 2 (50.821 miles/81.788 km).
1 Alexander Sims, GB (Dallara F308-Mercedes Benz), 26m 56.953s, 113.148 mph/182.094 km/h; **2** Edoardo Mortara, I (Dallara F308-Volkswagen), 27m 04.430s; **3** Marco Wittmann, D (Dallara F308-Volkswagen), 27m 05.510s; **4** Roberto Merhi, E (Dallara F308-Mercedes Benz), 27m 06.472s; **5** Laurens Vanthoor, B (Dallara F308-Volkswagen), 27m 07.291s; **6** Valtteri Bottas, FIN (Dallara F308-Mercedes Benz), 27m 08.568s; **7** Daniel Juncadella, E (Dallara F308-Mercedes Benz), 27m 11.454s; **8** António Félix da Costa, P (Dallara F308-Volkswagen), 27m 13.618s; **9** Adrian Quaife-Hobbs, GB (Dallara F308-Volkswagen), 27m 14.281s; **10** Nicolas Marroc, F (Dallara F308-Mercedes Benz), 27m 15.534s.
Fastest race lap: Juncadella, 1m 54.311s, 114.321 mph/183.982 km/h.
Pole position: da Costa.

FORMULA 3 EURO SERIES, Hockenheimring Grand Prix Circuit, Heidelberg, Germany, 24/25 April. 18 and 25 laps of the 2.842-mile/4.574-km circuit.
Round 3 (51.159 miles/82.332 km).
1 Marco Wittmann, D (Dallara F308-Volkswagen), 28m 16.473s, 108.561 mph/174.713 km/h; **2** Edoardo Mortara, I (Dallara F308-Volkswagen), 28m 22.884s; **3** Valtteri Bottas, FIN (Dallara F308-Mercedes Benz), 28m 27.960s; **4** Roberto Merhi, E (Dallara F308-Mercedes Benz), 28m 28.500s; **5** Adrian Quaife-Hobbs, GB (Dallara F308-Volkswagen), 28m 30.828s; **6** Esteban Gutierrez, MEX (Dallara F308-Mercedes Benz), 28m 32.844s; **7** António Félix da Costa, P (Dallara F308-Volkswagen), 28m 35.718s; **8** Daniel Juncadella, E (Dallara F308-Mercedes Benz), 28m 38.185s; **9** Matias Laine, FIN (Dallara F308-Volkswagen), 28m 42.656s; **10** Nicolas Marroc, F (Dallara F308-Mercedes Benz), 28m 42.851s.
Fastest race lap: Mortara, 1m 33.246s, 109.729 mph/176.591 km/h.
Pole position: Wittmann, 1m 33.021s, 109.994 mph/177.018 km/h.

Round 4 (71.054 miles/114.350 km).
1 Roberto Merhi, E (Dallara F308-Mercedes Benz), 39m 44.989s, 107.252 mph/172.605 km/h; **2** Daniel Juncadella, E (Dallara F308-Mercedes Benz), 39m 45.588s; **3** Edoardo Mortara, I (Dallara F308-Volkswagen), 39m 46.401s; **4** Marco Wittmann, D (Dallara F308-Volkswagen), 39m 47.093s; **5** Valtteri Bottas, FIN (Dallara F308-Mercedes Benz), 39m 49.235s; **6** Jim Pla, F (Dallara F308-Mercedes Benz), 40m 06.678s; **7** Adrian Quaife-Hobbs, GB (Dallara F308-Volkswagen), 40m 14.350s; **8** Alexander Sims, GB (Dallara F308-Mercedes Benz), 40m 14.762s; **9** António Félix da Costa, P (Dallara F308-Volkswagen), 40m 17.488s; **10** Matias Laine, FIN (Dallara F308-Volkswagen), 40m 30.980s.
Fastest race lap: Bottas, 1m 34.407s, 108.379 mph/174.419 km/h.
Pole position: Juncadella.

FORMULA 3 EURO SERIES, Circuit de la Comunitat Valenciana Ricardo Tormo, Cheste, Valencia, Spain, 22/23 May. 20 and 27 laps of the 2.489-mile/4.005-km circuit.
Round 5 (49.772 miles/80.100 km).
1 Edoardo Mortara, I (Dallara F308-Volkswagen), 30m 04.467s, 99.297 mph/159.803 km/h; **2** Valtteri Bottas, FIN (Dallara F308-Mercedes Benz), 30m 05.197s; **3** Alexander Sims, GB (Dallara F308-Mercedes Benz), 30m 09.098s; **4** Roberto Merhi, E (Dallara F308-Mercedes Benz), 30m 18.077s; **5** Laurens Vanthoor, B (Dallara F308-Volkswagen), 30m 20.371s; **6** António Félix da Costa, P (Dallara F308-Volkswagen), 30m 25.735s; **7** Kevin Magnussen, DK (Dallara F308-Volkswagen), 30m 28.187s; **8** Nicolas Marroc, F (Dallara F308-Mercedes Benz), 30m 29.627s; **9** Daniel Juncadella, E (Dallara F308-Mercedes Benz), 30m 30.041s; **10** Carlos Muñoz, CO (Dallara F308-Mercedes Benz), 30m 33.252s.
Fastest race lap: Juncadella, 1m 29.171s, 100.469 mph/161.689 km/h.
Pole position: Mortara, 1m 28.583s, 101.136 mph/162.763 km/h.

Round 6 (67.192 miles/108.135 km).
1 Kevin Magnussen, DK (Dallara F308-Volkswagen), 40m 52.638s, 98.625 mph/158.721 km/h; **2** Nicolas Marroc, F (Dallara F308-Mercedes Benz), 41m 02.759s; **3** Laurens Vanthoor, B (Dallara F308-Volkswagen), 41m 03.385s; **4** Valtteri Bottas, FIN (Dallara F308-Mercedes Benz), 41m 03.893s; **5** Alexander Sims, GB (Dallara F308-Mercedes Benz), 41m 06.550s; **6** Edoardo Mortara, I (Dallara F308-Volkswagen), 41m 07.081s; **7** Marco Wittmann, D (Dallara F308-Volkswagen), 41m 07.631s; **8** Jim Pla, F (Dallara F308-Mercedes Benz), 41m 08.500s; **9** Daniel Juncadella, E (Dallara F308-Mercedes Benz), 41m 09.267s; **10** Matias Laine, FIN (Dallara F308-Volkswagen), 41m 30.597s.
Fastest race lap: Magnussen, 1m 29.716s, 99.859 mph/160.707 km/h.
Pole position: Marroc.

FORMULA 3 EURO SERIES, Norisring, Nürnberg (Nuremberg), Germany, 3/4 July. 35 and 48 laps of the 1.429-mile/2.300-km circuit.
Round 7 (50.020 miles/80.500 km).
1 Edoardo Mortara, I (Dallara F308-Volkswagen), 30m 27.998s, 98.509 mph/158.534 km/h; **2** Marco Wittmann, D (Dallara F308-Volkswagen), 30m 29.066s; **3** Valtteri Bottas, FIN (Dallara F308-Mercedes Benz), 30m 29.664s; **4** Alexander Sims, GB (Dallara F308-Mercedes Benz), 30m 30.678s; **5** Roberto Merhi, E (Dallara F308-Mercedes Benz), 30m 31.661s; **6** Carlos Muñoz, CO (Dallara F308-Mercedes Benz), 30m 32.903s; **7** António Félix da Costa, P (Dallara F308-Volkswagen), 30m 33.454s; **8** Matias Laine, FIN (Dallara F308-Volkswagen), 30m 35.890s; **9** Laurens Vanthoor, B (Dallara F308-Volkswagen), 30m 38.728s; **10** Nicolas Marroc, F (Dallara F308-Mercedes Benz), 26 laps.
Fastest race lap: Mortara, 48.983s, 105.035 mph/169.038 km/h.
Pole position: Mortara, 48.963s, 105.078 mph/169.107 km/h.

Round 8 (68.599 miles/110.400 km).
1 Valtteri Bottas, FIN (Dallara F308-Mercedes Benz), 39m 42.130s, 103.671 mph/166.842 km/h; **2** Marco Wittmann, D (Dallara F308-Volkswagen), 39m 44.067s; **3** Edoardo Mortara, I (Dallara F308-Volkswagen), 39m 44.654s; **4** Alexander Sims, GB (Dallara F308-Mercedes Benz), 39m 50.021s; **5** Laurens Vanthoor, B (Dallara F308-Volkswagen), 39m 55.588s; **6** Daniel Juncadella, E (Dallara F308-Mercedes Benz), 40m 08.209s; **7** Matias Laine, FIN (Dallara F308-Volkswagen), 40m 14.545s; **8** Jim Pla, F (Dallara F308-Mercedes Benz), 40m 17.712s; **9** Carlos Muñoz, CO (Dallara F308-Mercedes Benz), 40m 17.908s; **10** Nicolas Marroc, F (Dallara F308-Mercedes Benz), 40m 18.876s.
Fastest race lap: Mortara, 48.941s, 105.126 mph/169.183 km/h.
Pole position: Laine.

FORMULA 3 EURO SERIES, Nürburgring, Nürburg/Eifel, Germany, 7/8 August. 22 and 20 laps of the 2.255-mile/3.629-km circuit.
Round 9 (49.609 miles/79.838 km).
1 Edoardo Mortara, I (Dallara F308-Volkswagen), 30m 57.701s, 96.136 mph/154.716 km/h; **2** Laurens Vanthoor, B (Dallara F308-Volkswagen), 30m 59.088s; **3** Roberto Merhi, E (Dallara F308-Mercedes Benz), 31m 02.130s; **4** Alexander Sims, GB (Dallara F308-Mercedes Benz), 31m 02.658s; **5** Marco Wittmann, D (Dallara F308-Volkswagen), 31m 03.482s; **6** Valtteri Bottas, FIN (Dallara F308-Mercedes Benz), 31m 09.119s; **7** António Félix da Costa, P (Dallara F308-Volkswagen), 31m 16.613s; **8** Jim Pla, F (Dallara F308-Mercedes Benz), 31m 17.417s; **9** Nicolas Marroc, F (Dallara F308-Mercedes Benz), 31m 19.313s; **10** Christopher Zanella, CH (Dallara F308-Volkswagen), 31m 28.117s.
Fastest race lap: Mortara, 1m 23.631s, 97.067 mph/156.215 km/h.
Pole position: Mortara, 1m 22.658s, 98.210 mph/158.054 km/h.

Round 10 (45.099 miles/72.580 km).
1 António Félix da Costa, P (Dallara F308-Volkswagen), 30m 35.113s, 88.472 mph/142.383 km/h; **2** Marco Wittmann, D (Dallara F308-Volkswagen), 30m 35.893s; **3** Alexander Sims, GB (Dallara F308-Mercedes Benz), 30m 44.458s; **4** Jim Pla, F (Dallara F308-Mercedes Benz), 30m 47.343s; **5** Roberto Merhi, E (Dallara F308-Mercedes Benz), 30m 49.006s; **6** Edoardo Mortara, I (Dallara F308-Volkswagen), 30m 49.858s; **7** Valtteri Bottas, FIN (Dallara F308-Mercedes Benz), 30m 50.409s; **8** Nicolas Marroc, F (Dallara F308-Mercedes Benz), 30m 53.445s; **9** Carlos Muñoz, CO (Dallara F308-Mercedes Benz), 30m 57.608s; **10** Daniel Juncadella, E (Dallara F308-Mercedes Benz), 31m 03.887s.
Fastest race lap: Juncadella, 1m 23.920s, 96.733 mph/155.677 km/h.
Pole position: Pla.

FORMULA 3 EURO SERIES, Circuit Park Zandvoort, Netherlands, 21/22 August. 19 and 26 laps of the 2.676-mile/4.307-km circuit.
Round 11 (50.849 miles/81.833 km).
1 Edoardo Mortara, I (Dallara F308-Volkswagen), 29m 38.034s, 102.954 mph/165.688 km/h; **2** Valtteri Bottas, FIN (Dallara F308-Mercedes Benz), 29m 39.029s; **3** Marco Wittmann, D (Dallara F308-Volkswagen), 29m 39.440s; **4** Alexander Sims, GB (Dallara F308-Mercedes Benz), 29m 54.508s; **5** Roberto Merhi, E (Dallara F308-Mercedes Benz), 29m 54.863s; **6** Carlos Muñoz, CO (Dallara F308-Mercedes Benz), 29m 56.067s; **7** Laurens Vanthoor, B (Dallara F308-Volkswagen), 29m 56.649s; **8** António Félix da Costa, P (Dallara F308-Volkswagen), 29m 57.359s; **9** Christopher Zanella, CH (Dallara F308-Volkswagen), 30m 01.852s; **10** Jim Pla, F (Dallara F308-Mercedes Benz), 30m 07.257s.
Fastest race lap: Mortara, 1m 32.153s, 104.549 mph/168.255 km/h.
Pole position: Mortara, 1m 31.281s, 105.548 mph/169.862 km/h.

Round 12 (69.582 miles/111.982 km).
1 António Félix da Costa, P (Dallara F308-Volkswagen), 40m 53.306s, 102.106 mph/164.323 km/h; **2** Laurens Vanthoor, B (Dallara F308-Volkswagen), 40m 53.571s; **3** Roberto Merhi, E (Dallara F308-Mercedes Benz), 40m 54.839s; **4** Carlos Muñoz, CO (Dallara F308-Mercedes Benz), 40m 56.207s; **5** Alexander Sims, GB (Dallara F308-Mercedes Benz), 41m 04.405s; **6** Marco Wittmann, D (Dallara F308-Volkswagen), 41m 04.653s; **7** Christopher Zanella, CH (Dallara F308-Volkswagen), 41m 24.851s; **8** Mika Mäki, FIN (Dallara F308-Volkswagen), 41m 25.512s; **9** Daniel Juncadella, E (Dallara F308-Mercedes Benz), 41m 25.985s; **10** Matias Laine, FIN (Dallara F308-Volkswagen), 41m 27.073s.
Fastest race lap: Mortara, 1m 32.750s, 103.876 mph/167.172 km/h.
Pole position: da Costa.

FORMULA 3 EURO SERIES, Brands Hatch Indy Circuit, West Kingsdown, Dartford, Kent, Great Britain, 4/5 September. 41 and 55 laps of the 1.199-mile/1.929-km circuit.
Round 13 (49.144 miles/79.089 km).
1 Edoardo Mortara, I (Dallara F308-Volkswagen), 28m 19.770s, 104.083 mph/167.505 km/h; **2** Laurens Vanthoor, B (Dallara F308-Volkswagen), 28m 23.531s; **3** Marco Wittmann, D (Dallara F308-Volkswagen), 28m 24.176s; **4** Valtteri Bottas, FIN (Dallara F308-Mercedes Benz), 28m 24.516s; **5** Alexander Sims, GB (Dallara F308-Mercedes Benz), 28m 25.493s; **6** Daniel Juncadella, E (Dallara F308-Mercedes Benz), 28m 27.139s; **7** Carlos Muñoz, CO (Dallara F308-Mercedes

Benz), 28m 36.209s; **8** António Félix da Costa, P (Dallara F308-Volkswagen), 28m 36.930s; **9** Mika Mäki, FIN (Dallara F308-Volkswagen), 28m 44.142s; **10** Matias Laine, FIN (Dallara F308-Volkswagen), 28m 45.532s.
Fastest race lap: Wittmann, 40.953s, 105.366 mph/169.570 km/h.
Pole position: Vanthoor, 40.696s, 106.031 mph/170.641 km/h.

Round 14 (65.924 miles/106.095 km).
1 António Félix da Costa, P (Dallara F308-Volkswagen), 39m 17.350s, 100.676 mph/162.022 km/h; **2** Carlos Muñoz, CO (Dallara F308-Mercedes Benz), 39m 19.988s; **3** Daniel Juncadella, E (Dallara F308-Mercedes Benz), 39m 20.707s; **4** Valtteri Bottas, FIN (Dallara F308-Mercedes Benz), 39m 21.862s; **5** Marco Wittmann, D (Dallara F308-Volkswagen), 39m 22.859s; **6** Matias Laine, FIN (Dallara F308-Volkswagen), 39m 27.630s; **7** Laurens Vanthoor, B (Dallara F308-Volkswagen), 39m 28.262s; **8** Alexander Sims, GB (Dallara F308-Mercedes Benz), 39m 29.449s; **9** Mika Mäki, FIN (Dallara F308-Volkswagen), 39m 48.054s; **10** Roberto Merhi, E (Dallara F308-Mercedes Benz), 39m 48.230s.
Fastest race lap: da Costa, 41.201s, 104.732 mph/168.549 km/h.
Pole position: da Costa.

FORMULA 3 EURO SERIES, Motorsport Arena Oschersleben, Germany, 18/19 September. 22 and 29 laps of the 2.297-mile/3.696-km circuit.
Round 15 (50.525 miles/81.312 km).
1 Valtteri Bottas, FIN (Dallara F308-Mercedes Benz), 30m 16.369s, 100.139 mph/161.158 km/h; **2** Alexander Sims, GB (Dallara F308-Mercedes Benz), 30m 38.510s; **3** António Félix da Costa, P (Dallara F308-Volkswagen), 30m 39.157s; **4** Daniel Juncadella, E (Dallara F308-Mercedes Benz), 30m 43.817s; **5** Roberto Merhi, E (Dallara F308-Mercedes Benz), 30m 46.506s; **6** Edoardo Mortara, I (Dallara F308-Volkswagen), 30m 56.984s; **7** Marco Wittmann, D (Dallara F308-Volkswagen), 30m 57.792s; **8** Carlos Muñoz, CO (Dallara F308-Mercedes Benz), 30m 58.907s; **9** Jim Pla, F (Dallara F308-Mercedes Benz), 30m 59.586s; **10** Nicolas Marroc, F (Dallara F308-Mercedes Benz), 31m 00.173s.
Fastest race lap: Bottas, 1m 20.623s, 102.548 mph/165.035 km/h.
Pole position: Bottas, 1m 20.412s, 102.817 mph/165.468 km/h.

Round 16 (66.601 miles/107.184 km).
1 Jim Pla, F (Dallara F308-Mercedes Benz), 40m 26.450s, 98.813 mph/159.023 km/h; **2** Marco Wittmann, D (Dallara F308-Volkswagen), 40m 28.601s; **3** Nicolas Marroc, F (Dallara F308-Mercedes Benz), 40m 30.301s; **4** Laurens Vanthoor, B (Dallara F308-Volkswagen), 40m 30.823s; **5** Renger van der Zande, NL (Dallara F308-Volkswagen), 40m 42.147s; **6** Daniel Juncadella, E (Dallara F308-Mercedes Benz), 40m 42.555s; **7** Tobias Hegewald, D (Dallara F308-Volkswagen), 40m 49.234s; **8** Alexander Sims, GB (Dallara F308-Mercedes Benz), 28 laps; **9** Roberto Merhi, E (Dallara F308-Mercedes Benz), 28; **10** Carlos Muñoz, CO (Dallara F308-Mercedes Benz), 27.
Fastest race lap: Bottas, 1m 21.651s, 101.257 mph/162.957 km/h.
Pole position: Muñoz.

FORMULA 3 EURO SERIES, Hockenheimring Grand Prix Circuit, Heidelberg, Germany, 16/17 October. 17 and 30 laps of the 2.321-mile/3.736-km circuit.
Round 17 (39.465 miles/63.512 km).
1 Edoardo Mortara, I (Dallara F309-Volkswagen), 31m 16.386s, 75.716 mph/121.853 km/h; **2** Valtteri Bottas, FIN (Dallara F308-Mercedes Benz), 31m 18.176s; **3** Marco Wittmann, D (Dallara F308-Volkswagen), 31m 24.347s; **4** Alexander Sims, GB (Dallara F308-Mercedes Benz), 31m 31.033s; **5** Roberto Merhi, E (Dallara F308-Mercedes Benz), 31m 34.571s; **6** Laurens Vanthoor, B (Dallara F308-Volkswagen), 31m 44.445s; **7** Christopher Zanella, CH (Dallara F308-Volkswagen), 31m 50.152s; **8** Daniel Juncadella, E (Dallara F309-Mercedes Benz), 31m 51.386s; **9** António Félix da Costa, P (Dallara F308-Volkswagen), 32m 04.330s; **10** Matias Laine, FIN (Dallara F308-Volkswagen), 32m 18.259s.
Fastest race lap: Bottas, 1m 42.841s, 81.263 mph/130.781 km/h.
Pole position: Mortara, 1m 18.604s, 106.320 mph/171.106 km/h.

Round 18 (69.643 miles/112.080 km).
1 Daniel Juncadella, E (Dallara F309-Mercedes Benz), 40m 15.720s, 103.785 mph/167.026 km/h; **2** Roberto Merhi, E (Dallara F308-Mercedes Benz), 40m 19.747s; **3** Valtteri Bottas, FIN (Dallara F308-Mercedes Benz), 40m 30.177s; **4** António Félix da Costa, P (Dallara F308-Volkswagen), 40m 38.138s; **5** Alexander Sims, GB (Dallara F308-Mercedes Benz), 40m 38.634s; **6** Carlos Muñoz, CO (Dallara F308-Mercedes Benz), 40m 45.041s; **7** Marco Wittmann, D (Dallara F308-Volkswagen), 40m 45.597s; **8** Nicolas Marroc, F (Dallara F308-Mercedes Benz), 40m 46.136s; **9** Matias Laine, FIN (Dallara F308-Volkswagen), 40m 49.556s; **10** Sandro Zeller, CH (Dallara F306-Mercedes Benz), 29 laps.
Fastest race lap: Juncadella, 1m 19.742s, 104.803 mph/168.664 km/h.
Pole position: Juncadella.

Final championship points
Drivers: **1** Edoardo Mortara, I, 101; **2** Marco Wittmann, D, 76; **3** Valtteri Bottas, FIN, 74; **4** Alexander Sims, GB, 63; **5** Roberto Merhi, E, 56; **6** Laurens Vanthoor, B, 42; **7** António Félix da Costa, P, 40; **8** Daniel Juncadella, E, 35; **9** Carlos Muñoz, CO, 18; **10** Jim Pla, F, 13; **11** Nicolas Marroc, F, 10; **12** Kevin Magnussen, DK, 8; **13** Adrian Quaife-Hobbs, GB, 7; **14** Matias Laine, FIN, 3; **15** Christopher Zanella, CH, 2; **16** Tobias Hegewald, D, 1.
Rookies: **1** António Félix da Costa, P, 40; **2** Daniel Juncadella, E, 35; **3** Carlos Muñoz, CO, 18; **4** Jim Pla, F, 13.
Teams: 1 Signature, 193; **2** ART Grand Prix, 148; **3** Mücke Motorsport, 74.
Nations: **1** Italy, 96; **2** Spain, 90; **3** Germany, 76; **4** Finland, 76.

ATS Formel-3-Cup

ATS FORMEL-3-CUP, Motorsport Arena Oschersleben, Germany, 10/11 April. 2 x 22 laps of the 2.297-mile/3.696-km circuit.
Round 1 (50.525 miles/81.312 km).
1 Kevin Magnussen, DK (Dallara F307-Volkswagen), 30m 18.166s, 100.040 mph/160.999 km/h; **2** Daniel Abt, D (Dallara F307-Volkswagen), 30m 18.971s; **3** Tom Dillmann, F (Dallara F307-Volkswagen), 30m 24.356s; **4** Stef Dusseldorp, NL (Dallara F307-Volkswagen), 30m 25.623s; **5** Markus Pommer, D (Dallara F307-Mercedes Benz), 30m 31.611s; **6** Gary Hauser, L (Dallara F307-Mercedes Benz), 30m 51.795s; **7** Willi Steindl, A (Dallara F307-Volkswagen), 30m 52.670s; **8** Jimmy Eriksson, S (Dallara F307-Volkswagen), 31m 02.264s; **9** Kevin Friesacher, A (Dallara F307-Volkswagen), 31m 04.257s; **10** Rene Binder, A (Dallara F307-Volkswagen), 31m 06.468s.
Fastest race lap: Abt, 1m 21.449s, 101.508 mph/163.361 km/h.
Pole position: Abt, 1m 20.477s, 102.734 mph/165.334 km/h.

Round 2 (50.525 miles/81.312 km).
1 Stef Dusseldorp, NL (Dallara F307-Volkswagen), 30m 15.698s, 100.176 mph/161.218 km/h; **2** Kevin Magnussen, DK (Dallara F307-Volkswagen), 30m 20.729s; **3** Daniel Abt, D (Dallara F307-Volkswagen), 30m 21.847s; **4** Jimmy Eriksson, S (Dallara F307-Volkswagen), 30m 31.349s; **5** Marco Sörensen, DK (Dallara F307-Mercedes Benz), 30m 35.878s; **6** Markus Pommer, D (Dallara F307-Mercedes Benz), 30m 37.103s; **7** Tom Dillmann, F (Dallara F307-Volkswagen), 30m 37.281s; **8** Luis Derani, BR (Dallara F307-Volkswagen), 30m 50.046s; **9** Willi Steindl, A (Dallara F307-Volkswagen), 30m 50.498s; **10** Alon Day, IL (Dallara F307-Volkswagen), 30m 51.053s.
Fastest race lap: Dillmann, 1m 21.101s, 101.943 mph/164.062 km/h.
Pole position: Dillmann, 1m 20.239s, 103.039 mph/165.825 km/h.

ATS FORMEL-3-CUP, Sachsenring, Oberlungwitz, Germany, 8/9 May. 2 x 25 laps of the 2.265-mile/3.645-km circuit.
Round 3 (56.622 miles/91.125 km).
1 Tom Dillmann, F (Dallara F307-Volkswagen), 31m 16.061s, 108.654 mph/174.861 km/h; **2** Felix Rosenqvist, S (Dallara F307-Volkswagen), 31m 21.016s; **3** Stef Dusseldorp, NL (Dallara F307-Volkswagen), 31m 22.015s; **4** Daniel Abt, D (Dallara F307-Volkswagen), 31m 24.816s; **5** Kevin Magnussen, DK (Dallara F307-Volkswagen), 31m 31.155s; **6** Gary Hauser, L (Dallara F307-Mercedes Benz), 31m 43.459s; **7** Willi Steindl, A (Dallara F307-Volkswagen), 31m 52.757s; **8** Nikolai Martsenko, RUS (Dallara F307-Opel), 31m 58.755s; **9** Luis Derani, BR (Dallara F307-Volkswagen), 31m 59.827s; **10** Markus Pommer, D (Dallara F307-Mercedes Benz), 32m 00.278s.
Fastest race lap: Dillmann, 1m 14.258s, 109.801 mph/176.708 km/h.
Pole position: Dillmann, 1m 13.348s, 111.164 mph/178.901 km/h.

Round 4 (56.622 miles/91.125 km).
1 Tom Dillmann, F (Dallara F307-Volkswagen), 31m 12.530s, 108.859 mph/175.191 km/h; **2** Daniel Abt, D (Dallara F307-Volkswagen), 31m 23.675s; **3** Kevin Magnussen, DK (Dallara F307-Volkswagen), 31m 24.825s; **4** Marco Sörensen, DK (Dallara F307-Mercedes Benz), 31m 27.433s; **5** Gary Hauser, L (Dallara F307-Mercedes Benz), 31m 37.523s; **6** Jimmy Eriksson, S (Dallara F307-Volkswagen), 31m 39.800s; **7** Willi Steindl, A (Dallara F307-Volkswagen), 31m 45.658s; **8** Markus Pommer, D (Dallara F307-Mercedes Benz), 31m 52.212s; **9** Luis Derani, BR (Dallara F307-Volkswagen), 31m 55.278s; **10** Alon Day, IL (Dallara F307-Volkswagen), 31m 58.251s.
Fastest race lap: Dusseldorp, 1m 14.201s, 109.886 mph/176.844 km/h.
Pole position: Dusseldorp, 1m 13.482s, 110.961 mph/178.574 km/h.

ATS FORMEL-3-CUP, Hockenheimring Grand Prix Circuit, Heidelberg, Germany, 29/30 May. 16 and 19 laps of the 2.842-mile/4.574-km circuit.
Round 5 (45.474 miles/73.184 km).
1 Nico Monien, D (Dallara F307-Mercedes Benz), 25m 59.288s, 104.989 mph/168.963 km/h; **2** Kevin Magnussen, DK (Dallara F307-Volkswagen), 26m 00.934s; **3** Tom Dillmann, F (Dallara F307-Volkswagen), 26m 02.229s; **4** Luis Derani, BR (Dallara F307-Volkswagen), 26m 14.870s; **5** Daniel Abt, D (Dallara F307-Volkswagen), 26m 15.334s; **6** Jimmy Eriksson, S (Dallara F307-Volkswagen), 26m 17.012s; **7** Marco Sörensen, DK (Dallara F307-Mercedes Benz), 26m 18.207s; **8** Markus Pommer, D (Dallara F307-Mercedes Benz), 26m 19.821s; **9** Nikolai Martsenko, RUS (Dallara F307-Opel), 26m 28.592s; **10** Alon Day, IL (Dallara F307-Volkswagen), 26m 32.715s.
Fastest race lap: Abt, 1m 36.095s, 106.475 mph/171.355 km/h.
Pole position: Abt, 1m 34.320s, 108.479 mph/174.580 km/h.

Round 6 (54.001 miles/86.906 km).
1 Tom Dillmann, F (Dallara F307-Volkswagen), 30m 33.574s, 106.024 mph/170.629 km/h; **2** Stef Dusseldorp, NL (Dallara F307-Volkswagen), 30m 35.024s; **3** Daniel Abt, D (Dallara F307-Volkswagen), 30m 41.807s; **4** Alon Day, IL (Dallara F307-Volkswagen), 30m 42.793s; **5** Kevin Magnussen, DK (Dallara F307-Volkswagen), 30m 45.590s; **6** Luis Derani, BR (Dallara F307-Volkswagen), 31m 02.308s; **7** Jimmy Eriksson, S (Dallara F307-Volkswagen), 31m 03.479s; **8** Felix Rosenqvist, S (Dallara F307-Volkswagen), 31m 07.955s; **9** Luis Jorge Sá Silva, ANG (Dallara F307-Volkswagen), 31m 20.209s; **10** Marco Sörensen, DK (Dallara F307-Mercedes Benz), 31m 21.617s.
Fastest race lap: Dillmann, 1m 35.654s, 106.966 mph/172.145 km/h.
Pole position: Dillmann, 1m 33.956s, 108.899 mph/175.257 km/h.

ATS FORMEL-3-CUP, Nationale Circuit Assen, Netherlands, 17/18 July. 2 x 20 laps of the 2.830-mile/4.555-km circuit.
Round 7 (56.607 miles/91.100 km).
1 Felix Rosenqvist, S (Dallara F307-Volkswagen), 31m 13.761s, 108.757 mph/175.028 km/h; **2** Daniel Abt, D (Dallara F307-Volkswagen), 31m 15.883s; **3** Stef Dusseldorp, NL (Dallara F307-Volkswagen), 31m 28.224s; **4** Alon Day, IL (Dallara F307-Volkswagen), 31m 33.100s; **5** Willi Steindl, A (Dallara F307-Volkswagen), 31m 33.302s; **6** Markus Pommer, D (Dallara F307-Mercedes Benz), 31m 33.785s; **7** Kevin Magnussen, DK (Dallara F307-Volkswagen), 31m 34.227s; **8** Tom Dillmann, F (Dallara F307-Volkswagen), 31m 36.538s; **9** Gary Hauser, L (Dallara F307-Mercedes Benz), 31m 41.993s; **10** Jimmy Eriksson, S (Dallara F307-Volkswagen), 31m 44.771s.
Fastest race lap: Dillmann, 1m 32.315s, 110.375 mph/177.631 km/h.
Pole position: Abt, 1m 30.352s, 112.773 mph/181.490 km/h.

Round 8 (56.607 miles/91.100 km).
1 Daniel Abt, D (Dallara F307-Volkswagen), 31m 16.893s, 108.576 mph/174.736 km/h; **2** Felix Rosenqvist, S (Dallara F307-Volkswagen), 31m 18.247s; **3** Stef Dusseldorp, NL (Dallara F307-Volkswagen), 31m 18.727s; **4** Tom Dillmann, F (Dallara F307-Volkswagen), 31m 22.370s; **5** Kevin Magnussen, DK (Dallara F307-Volkswagen), 31m 38.258s; **6** Willi Steindl, A (Dallara F307-Volkswagen), 31m 41.856s; **7** Markus Pommer, D (Dallara F307-Mercedes Benz), 31m 42.191s; **8** Sandro Zeller, CH (Dallara F307-Mercedes Benz), 31m 44.660s; **9** Gary Hauser, L (Dallara F307-Mercedes Benz), 31m 46.864s; **10** Luis Derani, BR (Dallara F307-Volkswagen), 31m 54.276s.
Fastest race lap: Abt, 1m 32.684s, 109.935 mph/176.924 km/h.
Pole position: Abt, 1m 30.829s, 112.181 mph/180.537 km/h.

ATS FORMEL-3-CUP, Nürburgring, Nürburg/Eifel, Germany, 24/25 July. 2 x 22 laps of the 2.248-mile/3.618-km circuit.
Round 9 (49.459 miles/79.596 km).
1 Tom Dillmann, F (Dallara F307-Volkswagen), 30m 17.385s, 97.971 mph/157.669 km/h; **2** Felix Rosenqvist, S (Dallara F307-Volkswagen), 30m 41.065s; **3** Willi Steindl, A (Dallara F307-Volkswagen), 30m 42.060s; **4** Rene Binder, A (Dallara F307-Volkswagen), 30m 53.982s; **5** Daniel Abt, D (Dallara F307-Volkswagen), 30m 56.224s; **6** Markus Pommer, D (Dallara F307-Mercedes Benz), 30m 56.892s; **7** Jimmy Eriksson, S (Dallara F307-Volkswagen), 31m 00.334s; **8** Alon Day, IL (Dallara F307-Volkswagen), 31m 03.506s; **9** Riccardo Brutschin, D (ARTTech F24-Opel), 31m 08.734s; **10** Nikolai Martsenko, RUS (Dallara F307-Opel), 31m 09.470s.
Fastest race lap: Dillmann, 1m 21.347s, 99.490 mph/160.114 km/h.
Pole position: Abt, 1m 20.948s, 99.981 mph/160.903 km/h.

Round 10 (49.459 miles/79.596 km).
1 Tom Dillmann, F (Dallara F307-Volkswagen), 30m 11.950s, 98.265 mph/158.142 km/h; **2** Felix Rosenqvist, S (Dallara F307-Volkswagen), 30m 17.545s; **3** Daniel Abt, D (Dallara F307-Volkswagen), 30m 18.542s; **4** Stef Dusseldorp, NL (Dallara F307-Volkswagen), 30m 19.573s; **5** Willi Steindl, A (Dallara F307-Volkswagen), 30m 30.390s; **6** Alon Day, IL (Dallara F307-Volkswagen), 30m 31.146s; **7** Kevin Magnussen, DK (Dallara F307-Volkswagen), 30m 36.645s; **8** Markus Pommer, D (Dallara F307-Mercedes Benz), 30m 37.448s; **9** Jimmy Eriksson, S (Dallara F307-Volkswagen), 30m 39.327s; **10** Rene Binder, A (Dallara F307-Volkswagen), 30m 50.254s.
Fastest race lap: Dillmann, 1m 21.378s, 99.452 mph/160.053 km/h.
Pole position: Dillmann, 1m 20.020s, 101.140 mph/162.769 km/h.

ATS FORMEL-3-CUP, Nationale Circuit Assen, Netherlands, 7/8 August. 20 and 18 laps of the 2.830-mile/4.555-km circuit.
Round 11 (56.607 miles/91.100 km).
1 Stef Dusseldorp, NL (Dallara F307-Volkswagen), 31m 17.709s, 108.528 mph/174.660 km/h; **2** Kevin Magnussen, DK (Dallara F307-Volkswagen), 31m 26.233s; **3** Jimmy Eriksson, S (Dallara F307-Volkswagen), 31m 44.263s; **4** Tom Dillmann, F (Dallara F307-Volkswagen), 31m 44.830s; **5** Luis Derani, BR (Dallara F307-Volkswagen), 31m 47.754s; **6** Felix Rosenqvist, S (Dallara F307-Volkswagen), 31m 48.544s; **7** Markus Pommer, D (Dallara F307-Mercedes Benz), 31m 49.251s; **8** Rene Binder, A (Dallara F307-Volkswagen), 31m 52.261s; **9** Bernd Herndlhofer, A (Dallara F307-Mercedes Benz), 31m 53.474s; **10** Daniel Abt, D (Dallara F307-Volkswagen), 31m 53.512s.
Fastest race lap: Dusseldorp, 1m 32.883s, 109.700 mph/176.545 km/h.
Pole position: Dusseldorp, 1m 32.023s, 110.725 mph/178.195 km/h.

Round 12 (50.946 miles/81.990 km).
1 Felix Rosenqvist, S (Dallara F307-Volkswagen), 31m 18.166s, 97.652 mph/157.155 km/h; **2** Markus Pommer, D (Dallara F307-Mercedes Benz), 31m 37.112s; **3** Rene Binder, A (Dallara F307-Volkswagen), 31m 40.233s; **4** Kevin Magnussen, DK (Dallara F307-Volkswagen), 31m 41.233s; **5** Tom Dillmann, F (Dallara F307-Volkswagen), 31m 52.988s; **6** Bernd Herndlhofer, A (Dallara F307-Mercedes Benz), 31m 53.427s; **7** Alon Day, IL (Dallara F307-Volkswagen), 32m 04.346s; **8** Willi Steindl, A (Dallara F307-Volkswagen), 32m 04.589s; **9** Jimmy Eriksson, S (Dallara F307-Volkswagen), 32m 29.278s; **10** Gary Hauser, L (Dallara F307-Mercedes Benz), 32m 30.172s.
Fastest race lap: Dillmann, 1m 33.178s, 109.352 mph/175.986 km/h.
Pole position: Rosenqvist, 1m 31.799s, 110.995 mph/178.629 km/h.

ATS FORMEL-3-CUP, EuroSpeedway Lausitz, Klettwitz, Dresden, Germany, 14/15 August. 2 x 23 laps of the 2.139-mile/3.442-km circuit.
Round 13 (49.191 miles/79.166 km).
1 Kevin Magnussen, DK (Dallara F307-Volkswagen), 31m 17.345s, 94.330 mph/151.809 km/h; **2** Jimmy Eriksson, S (Dallara F307-Volkswagen), 31m 20.934s; **3** Stef Dusseldorp, NL (Dallara F307-Volkswagen), 31m 21.189s; **4** Daniel Abt, D (Dallara F307-Volkswagen), 31m 24.644s; **5** Tom Dillmann, F (Dallara F307-Volkswagen), 31m 24.921s; **6** Willi Steindl, A (Dallara F307-Volkswagen), 31m 26.776s; **7** Luis Derani, BR (Dallara F307-Volkswagen), 31m 34.711s; **8** Felix Rosenqvist, S (Dallara F307-Volkswagen), 31m 35.883s; **9** Gary Hauser, L (Dallara F307-Mercedes Benz), 31m 48.002s; **10** Alon Day, IL (Dallara F307-Volkswagen), 31m 54.402s.
Fastest race lap: Dusseldorp, 1m 19.397s, 96.975 mph/156.066 km/h.
Pole position: Abt, 1m 15.475s, 102.014 mph/164.176 km/h.

Round 14 (49.191 miles/79.166 km).
1 Jimmy Eriksson, S (Dallara F307-Volkswagen), 30m 14.267s, 97.609 mph/157.087 km/h; **2** Felix Rosenqvist, S (Dallara F307-Volkswagen), 30m 14.661s; **3** Markus Pommer, D (Dallara F307-Mercedes Benz), 30m 16.714s; **4** Daniel Abt, D (Dallara F307-Volkswagen), 30m 21.609s; **5** Alon Day, IL (Dallara F307-Volkswagen), 30m 22.623s; **6** Stef Dusseldorp, NL (Dallara F307-Volkswagen), 30m 26.841s; **7** Gary Hauser, L (Dallara F307-Mercedes Benz), 30m 32.402s; **8** Tom Dillmann, F (Dallara F307-Volkswagen), 30m 34.117s; **9** Kevin Magnussen, DK (Dallara F307-Volkswagen), 30m 40.466s; **10** Riccardo Brutschin, D (ARTTech F24-Opel), 30m 56.619s.
Fastest race lap: Abt, 1m 17.497s, 99.353 mph/159.893 km/h.
Pole position: Dillmann, 1m 38.337s, 78.297 mph/126.008 km/h.

ATS FORMEL-3-CUP, Nürburgring, Nürburg/Eifel, Germany, 28/29 August. 13 and 16 laps of the 3.199-mile/5.148-km circuit.
Round 15 (41.585 miles/66.924 km).
1 Kevin Magnussen, DK (Dallara F307-Volkswagen), 28m 30.325s, 87.530 mph/140.866 km/h; **2** Daniel Abt, D (Dallara F307-Volkswagen), 28m 39.496s; **3** Marco Sörensen, DK (Dallara F307-Mercedes Benz), 28m 48.644s; **4** Stef Dusseldorp, NL (Dallara F307-Volkswagen), 28m 54.735s; **5** Felix Rosenqvist, S (Dallara F307-Volkswagen), 28m 55.829s; **6** Kevin Kleveros, S (Dallara F307-Volkswagen), 29m 21.765s; **7** Willi Steindl, A (Dallara F307-Volkswagen), 29m 24.913s; **8** Alon Day, IL (Dallara F307-Volkswagen), 29m 26.460s; **9** Tom Dillmann, F (Dallara F307-Volkswagen), 29m 29.884s; **10** Gary Hauser, L (Dallara F307-Mercedes Benz), 29m 41.393s.
Fastest race lap: Dillmann, 1m 54.268s, 100.778 mph/162.187 km/h.
Pole position: Sörensen, 2m 18.023s, 83.434 mph/134.273 km/h.

Round 16 (51.181 miles/82.368 km).
1 Tom Dillmann, F (Dallara F307-Volkswagen), 30m 31.391s, 100.608 mph/161.912 km/h; **2** Daniel Abt, D (Dallara F307-Volkswagen), 30m 33.810s; **3** Stef Dusseldorp, NL (Dallara F307-Volkswagen), 30m 36.644s; **4** Felix Rosenqvist, S (Dallara F307-Volkswagen), 30m 38.054s; **5** Kevin Magnussen, DK (Dallara F307-Volkswagen), 30m 38.762s; **6** Jimmy Eriksson, S (Dallara F307-Volkswagen), 30m 52.610s; **7** Alon Day, IL (Dallara F307-Volkswagen), 30m 54.043s; **8** Willi Steindl, A (Dallara F307-Volkswagen), 31m 00.793s; **9** Luis Derani, BR (Dallara F307-Volkswagen), 31m 10.292s; **10** Nikolai Martsenko, RUS (Dallara F307-Opel), 31m 11.043s.
Fastest race lap: Dillmann, 1m 53.436s, 101.518 mph/163.377 km/h.
Pole position: Dillmann, 1m 55.627s, 99.594 mph/160.281 km/h.

ATS FORMEL-3-CUP, Motorsport Arena Oschersleben, Germany, 2/3 October. 22 and 18 laps of the 2.297-mile/3.696-km circuit.
Round 17 (50.525 miles/81.312 km).
1 Daniel Abt, D (Dallara F307-Volkswagen), 30m 26.045s, 99.609 mph/160.304 km/h; **2** Tom Dillmann, F (Dallara F307-Volkswagen), 30m 27.643s; **3** Stef Dusseldorp, NL (Dallara F307-Volkswagen), 30m 29.885s; **4** Kevin Magnussen, DK (Dallara F307-Volkswagen), 30m 45.998s; **5** Klaus Bachler, A (Dallara F307-Volkswagen), 30m 50.851s; **6** Markus Pommer, D (Dallara F307-Mercedes Benz), 30m 54.560s; **7** Willi Steindl, A (Dallara F307-Volkswagen), 30m 55.286s; **8** Alon Day, IL (Dallara F307-Volkswagen), 30m 55.815s; **9** Luis Derani, BR (Dallara F307-Volkswagen), 30m 59.521s; **10** Bernd Herndlhofer, A (Dallara F307-Mercedes Benz), 30m 59.956s.
Fastest race lap: Abt, 1m 21.890s, 100.961 mph/162.481 km/h.
Pole position: Dusseldorp, 1m 20.676s, 102.480 mph/164.926 km/h.

Round 18 (41.339 miles/66.528 km).
1 Willi Steindl, A (Dallara F307-Volkswagen), 25m 18.982s, 97.973 mph/157.672 km/h; **2** Felix Rosenqvist, S (Dallara F307-Volkswagen), 25m 19.444s; **3** Kevin Magnussen, DK (Dallara F307-Volkswagen), 25m 21.416s; **4** Luis Derani, BR (Dallara F307-Volkswagen), 25m 22.413s; **5** Klaus Bachler, A (Dallara F307-Volkswagen), 25m 24.337s; **6** Nigel Melker, NL (Dallara F307-Mercedes Benz), 25m 24.945s; **7** Markus Pommer, D (Dallara F307-Mercedes Benz), 25m 29.614s; **8** Sandro Zeller, CH (Dallara F307-Mercedes Benz), 25m 41.479s; **9** Alon Day, IL (Dallara F307-Volkswagen), 25m 41.490s; **10** Nikolai Martsenko, RUS (Dallara F307-Opel), 25m 53.183s.
Fastest race lap: Dillmann, 1m 22.415s, 100.318 mph/161.446 km/h.
Pole position: Dillmann, 1m 20.452s, 102.766 mph/165.386 km/h.

Final championship points
Formel-3-Cup: **1** Tom Dillmann, F, 120; **2** Daniel Abt, D, 112; **3** Kevin Magnussen, DK, 96; **4** Stef Dusseldorp, NL, 88; **5** Felix Rosenqvist, S, 83; **6** Jimmy Eriksson, S, 43; **7** Willi Steindl, A, 43; **8** Markus Pommer, D, 40; **9** Alon Day, IL, 26; **10** Luis Derani, BR, 20; **11** Marco Sörensen, DK, 18; **12** Rene Binder, A, 12; **13** Gary

Hauser, L, 12; **14** Nico Monien, D, 10; **15** Klaus Bachler, A, 8; **16** Bernd Herndlhofer, A, 3; **17** Sandro Zeller, CH, 3; **18** Nikolai Martsenko, RUS, 1.
Formel-3-Trophy: **1** Riccardo Brutschin, D, 142; **2** Alexey Karachev, RUS, 121; **3** Aki Sandberg, FIN, 93.
Rookie Cup: **1** Kevin Magnussen, DK, 128; **2** Daniel Abt, D, 125; **3** Felix Rosenqvist, S, 106.

Italian Formula 3 Championship

ITALIAN FORMULA 3 CHAMPIONSHIP, Autodromo Internazionale di Misano, Misano Adriatico, Rimini, Italy, 24/25 April. Round 1. 13 and 20 laps of the 2.626-mile/4.226-km circuit.
Race 1 (34.137 miles/54.938 km).
1 Andrea Caldarelli, I (Dallara F310-FPT), 24m 56.430s, 82.123 mph/132.165 km/h; **2** Christopher Zanella, CH (Mygale M-10-FPT), 24m 57.216s; **3** César Ramos, BR (Dallara F310-FPT), 24m 57.754s; **4** Tom Dillmann, F (Dallara F310-FPT), 24m 58.633s; **5** Stéphane Richelmi, MC (Dallara F310-FPT), 24m 59.699s; **6** Kevin Giovesi, I (Dallara F310-FPT), 25m 00.464s; **7** Matt Lee, USA (Mygale M-10-FPT), 25m 00.920s; **8** Gabby Chaves, CO (Mygale M-10-FPT), 25m 01.709s; **9** Frédéric Vervisch, B (Dallara F310-FPT), 25m 02.814s; **10** Samuele Buttarelli, I (Dallara F310-FPT), 25m 03.583s.
Fastest race lap: Dillmann, 1m 50.180s, 85.798 mph/138.079 km/h.
Pole position: Zanella, 1m 54.361s, 82.661 mph/133.031 km/h.

Race 2 (52.518 miles/84.520 km).
1 Stéphane Richelmi, MC (Dallara F310-FPT), 31m 03.587s, 101.452 mph/163.272 km/h; **2** Tom Dillmann, F (Dallara F310-FPT), 31m 04.193s; **3** César Ramos, BR (Dallara F310-FPT), 31m 04.533s; **4** Andrea Caldarelli, I (Dallara F310-FPT), 31m 06.221s; **5** Christopher Zanella, CH (Mygale M-10-FPT), 31m 11.406s; **6** Daniel Mancinelli, I (Dallara F310-FPT), 31m 11.790s; **7** Frédéric Vervisch, B (Dallara F310-FPT), 31m 20.233s; **8** Jesse Krohn, FIN (Dallara F310-FPT), 31m 28.587s; **9** Kevin Giovesi, I (Dallara F310-FPT), 31m 32.312s; **10** Edoardo Liberati, I (Dallara F310-FPT), 31m 33.099s.
Fastest race lap: Mancinelli, 1m 31.766s, 103.015 mph/165.786 km/h.
Pole position: Richelmi.

ITALIAN FORMULA 3 CHAMPIONSHIP, Hockenheimring Grand Prix Circuit, Heidelberg, Germany, 12/13 June. Round 2. 19 and 18 laps of the 2.842-mile/4.574-km circuit.
Race 1 (54.001 miles/86.906 km).
1 Daniel Mancinelli, I (Dallara F310-FPT), 30m 53.377s, 104.891 mph/168.806 km/h; **2** Sergio Campana, I (Dallara F310-FPT), 31m 14.187s; **3** Jesse Krohn, FIN (Dallara F310-FPT), 31m 16.162s; **4** Stéphane Richelmi, MC (Dallara F310-FPT), 31m 16.860s; **5** Andrea Caldarelli, I (Dallara F310-FPT), 31m 17.342s; **6** Gabby Chaves, CO (Mygale M-10-FPT), 31m 24.779s; **7** Christopher Zanella, CH (Mygale M-10-FPT), 31m 25.102s; **8** Samuele Buttarelli, I (Dallara F310-FPT), 31m 25.427s; **9** Frédéric Vervisch, B (Dallara F310-FPT), 31m 26.018s; **10** Kevin Giovesi, I (Mygale M-10-FPT), 31m 26.345s.
Fastest race lap: Mancinelli, 1m 36.716s, 105.791 mph/170.255 km/h.
Pole position: Chaves, 1m 52.925s, 90.606 mph/145.817 km/h.

Race 2 (51.159 miles/82.332 km).
1 César Ramos, BR (Dallara F310-FPT), 29m 04.776s, 105.555 mph/169.875 km/h; **2** Daniel Mancinelli, I (Dallara F310-FPT), 29m 05.420s; **3** Samuele Buttarelli, I (Dallara F310-FPT), 29m 07.631s; **4** Matt Lee, USA (Mygale M-10-FPT), 29m 18.903s; **5** Christopher Zanella, CH (Mygale M-10-FPT), 29m 27.526s; **6** Jesse Krohn, FIN (Dallara F310-FPT), 29m 32.631s; **7** Momo Barri, I (Dallara F310-FPT), 29m 42.612s; **8** Kevin Giovesi, I (Mygale M-10-FPT), 29m 44.351s; **9** Alberto Cerqui, I (Dallara F310-FPT), 29m 48.332s; **10** Tyler Dueck, CDN (Dallara F308-FPT), 29m 49.309s.
Fastest race lap: Ramos, 1m 36.154s, 106.409 mph/171.250 km/h.
Pole position: Krohn.

ITALIAN FORMULA 3 CHAMPIONSHIP, Autodromo Enzo e Dino Ferrari, Imola, Italy, 4 July. Round 3. 2 x 18 laps of the 3.050-mile/4.909-km circuit.
Race 1 (54.906 miles/88.362 km).
1 Daniel Mancinelli, I (Dallara F310-FPT), 31m 09.384s, 105.735 mph/170.164 km/h; **2** César Ramos, BR (Dallara F310-FPT), 31m 09.986s; **3** Frédéric Vervisch, B (Dallara F310-FPT), 31m 17.034s; **4** Stéphane Richelmi, MC (Dallara F310-FPT), 31m 22.502s; **5** Jesse Krohn, FIN (Dallara F310-FPT), 31m 25.451s; **6** Sergio Campana, I (Dallara F310-FPT), 31m 28.152s; **7** Edoardo Liberati, I (Dallara F310-FPT), 31m 35.725s; **8** Andrea Caldarelli, I (Dallara F310-FPT), 31m 36.013s; **9** Matt Lee, USA (Mygale M-10-FPT), 31m 38.246s; **10** Christopher Zanella, CH (Mygale M-10-FPT), 31m 38.415s.
Fastest race lap: Ramos, 1m 42.891s, 106.725 mph/171.758 km/h.
Pole position: Mancinelli, 1m 41.994s, 107.664 mph/173.269 km/h.

Race 2 (54.906 miles/88.362 km).
1 Stéphane Richelmi, MC (Dallara F310-FPT), 31m 24.075s, 104.910 mph/168.837 km/h; **2** César Ramos, BR (Dallara F310-FPT), 31m 24.563s; **3** Jesse Krohn, FIN (Dallara F310-FPT), 31m 37.418s; **4** Andrea Caldarelli, I (Dallara F310-FPT), 31m 38.947s; **5** Daniel Mancinelli, I (Dallara F310-FPT), 31m 40.464s; **6** Edoardo Liberati, I (Dallara F310-FPT), 31m 43.127s; **7** Christopher Zanella, CH (Mygale M-10-FPT), 31m 43.407s; **8** Gianmarco Raimondo, CDN (Dallara F310-FPT), 31m 44.398s; **9** Samuele Buttarelli, I (Dallara F310-FPT), 31m 45.196s; **10** Kevin Giovesi, I (Mygale M-10-FPT), 31m 45.925s.
Fastest race lap: Ramos, 1m 43.411s, 106.189 mph/170.894 km/h.
Pole position: Liberati.

ITALIAN FORMULA 3 CHAMPIONSHIP, Autodromo Internazionale del Mugello, Scarperia, Firenze (Florence), Italy, 24/25 July. Round 4. 17 and 16 laps of the 3.259-mile/5.245-km circuit.
Race 1 (55.405 miles/89.165 km).
1 Andrea Caldarelli, I (Dallara F310-FPT), 30m 06.872s, 110.387 mph/177.651 km/h; **2** Daniel Mancinelli, I (Dallara F310-FPT), 30m 13.642s; **3** Samuele Buttarelli, I (Dallara F310-FPT), 30m 15.605s; **4** César Ramos, BR (Dallara F310-FPT), 30m 16.056s; **5** Stéphane Richelmi, MC (Dallara F310-FPT), 30m 22.842s; **6** Sergio Campana, I (Dallara F310-FPT), 30m 23.170s; **7** Gabby Chaves, CO (Mygale M-10-FPT), 30m 34.997s; **8** Jesse Krohn, FIN (Dallara F310-FPT), 30m 35.516s; **9** Christopher Zanella, CH (Mygale M-10-FPT), 30m 36.393s; **10** Momo Barri, I (Dallara F310-FPT), 30m 41.073s.
Fastest race lap: Caldarelli, 1m 44.851s, 111.899 mph/180.084 km/h.
Pole position: Caldarelli, 1m 43.721s, 113.118 mph/182.046 km/h.

Race 2 (52.145 miles/83.920 km).
1 Stéphane Richelmi, MC (Dallara F310-FPT), 31m 00.700s, 100.888 mph/162.364 km/h; **2** Sergio Campana, I (Dallara F310-FPT), 31m 01.301s; **3** Samuele Buttarelli, I (Dallara F310-FPT), 31m 01.729s; **4** César Ramos, BR (Dallara F310-FPT), 31m 02.425s; **5** Christopher Zanella, CH (Mygale M-10-FPT), 31m 22.091s; **6** Daniel Mancinelli, I (Dallara F310-FPT), 31m 23.116s; **7** Andrea Caldarelli, I (Dallara F310-FPT), 31m 27.196s; **8** Gabby Chaves, CO (Mygale M-10-FPT), 31m 39.448s; **9** Edoardo Liberati, I (Dallara F310-FPT), 31m 39.738s; **10** Jesse Krohn, FIN (Dallara F310-FPT), 31m 40.474s.
Fastest race lap: Buttarelli, 1m 45.973s, 110.714 mph/178.177 km/h.
Pole position: Liberati.

ITALIAN FORMULA 3 CHAMPIONSHIP, Autodromo Riccardo Paletti, Varano dei Melegari, Parma, Italy, 29 August. Round 5. 27 and 28 laps of the 1.476-mile/2.375-km circuit.
Race 1 (39.845 miles/64.125 km).
1 Stéphane Richelmi, MC (Dallara F310-FPT), 29m 29.143s, 81.080 mph/130.486 km/h; **2** César Ramos, BR (Dallara F310-FPT), 29m 30.316s; **3** Andrea Caldarelli, I (Dallara F310-FPT), 29m 31.118s; **4** Christopher Zanella, CH (Mygale M-10-FPT), 29m 32.463s; **5** Matt Lee, USA (Dallara F310-FPT), 29m 39.788s; **6** Sergio Campana, I (Dallara F310-FPT), 29m 41.885s; **7** Daniel Mancinelli, I (Dallara F310-FPT), 29m 44.339s; **8** Jesse Krohn, FIN (Dallara F310-FPT), 29m 44.913s; **9** Gabby Chaves, CO (Mygale M-10-FPT), 29m 46.331s; **10** Kevin Giovesi, I (Mygale M-10-FPT), 29m 48.298s.
Fastest race lap: Ramos, 1m 03.181s, 84.087 mph/135.325 km/h.
Pole position: Richelmi, 1m 02.482s, 85.028 mph/136.839 km/h.

Race 2 (41.321 miles/66.500 km).
1 Jesse Krohn, FIN (Dallara F310-FPT), 29m 57.339s, 82.764 mph/133.196 km/h; **2** Sergio Campana, I (Dallara F310-FPT), 30m 00.904s; **3** Daniel Mancinelli, I (Dallara F310-FPT), 30m 02.596s; **4** Christopher Zanella, CH (Mygale M-10-FPT), 30m 02.911s; **5** Andrea Caldarelli, I (Dallara F310-FPT), 30m 03.336s; **6** César Ramos, BR (Dallara F310-FPT), 30m 03.677s; **7** Matt Lee, USA (Dallara F310-FPT), 30m 06.457s; **8** Stéphane Richelmi, MC (Dallara F310-FPT), 30m 07.450s; **9** Kevin Giovesi, I (Mygale M-10-FPT), 30m 08.203s; **10** Gabby Chaves, CO (Mygale M-10-FPT), 30m 09.384s.
Fastest race lap: Ramos, 1m 03.299s, 83.930 mph/135.073 km/h.
Pole position: Krohn.

ITALIAN FORMULA 3 CHAMPIONSHIP, Autodromo di Vallelunga, Campagnano di Roma, Italy, 25/26 September. Round 6. 2 x 17 laps of the 2.538-mile/4.085-km circuit.
Race 1 (43.151 miles/69.445 km).
1 César Ramos, BR (Dallara F310-FPT), 29m 36.819s, 87.428 mph/140.702 km/h; **2** Daniel Mancinelli, I (Dallara F310-FPT), 29m 45.092s; **3** Stéphane Richelmi, MC (Dallara F310-FPT), 29m 45.397s; **4** Christopher Zanella, CH (Mygale M-10-FPT), 29m 56.521s; **5** Nicolas Marroc, F (Dallara F310-FPT), 29m 56.778s; **6** Francesco Castellacci, I (Dallara F308-FPT), 30m 00.484s; **7** Edoardo Liberati, I (Dallara F310-FPT), 30m 00.986s; **8** Jesse Krohn, FIN (Dallara F310-FPT), 30m 01.474s; **9** Momo Barri, I (Dallara F310-FPT), 30m 02.628s; **10** Andrea Roda, I (Dallara F310-FPT), 30m 07.630s.
Fastest race lap: Ramos, 1m 31.316s, 100.068 mph/161.045 km/h.
Pole position: Ramos, 1m 30.361s, 101.126 mph/162.747 km/h.

Race 2 (43.151 miles/69.445 km).
1 Sergio Campana, I (Dallara F310-FPT), 30m 34.608s, 84.674 mph/136.269 km/h; **2** Edoardo Liberati, I (Dallara F310-FPT), 30m 37.586s; **3** Samuele Buttarelli, I (Dallara F310-FPT), 30m 43.890s; **4** Gabby Chaves, CO (Mygale M-10-FPT), 30m 44.176s; **5** Andrea Caldarelli, I (Dallara F310-FPT), 30m 44.871s; **6** Stéphane Richelmi, MC (Dallara F310-FPT), 30m 45.651s; **7** César Ramos, BR (Dallara F310-FPT), 30m 46.218s; **8** Christopher Zanella, CH (Mygale M-10-FPT), 30m 46.552s; **9** Jesse Krohn, FIN (Dallara F310-FPT), 30m 50.023s; **10** Gianmarco Raimondo, CDN (Dallara F310-FPT), 30m 51.632s.
Fastest race lap: Ramos, 1m 31.218s, 100.176 mph/161.218 km/h.
Pole position: Buttarelli.

ITALIAN FORMULA 3 CHAMPIONSHIP, Autodromo Internazionale del Mugello, Scarperia, Firenze (Florence), Italy, 9/10 October. Round 7. 2 x 17 laps of the 3.259-mile/5.245-km circuit.
Race 1 (55.405 miles/89.165 km).
1 Andrea Caldarelli, I (Dallara F310-FPT), 29m 55.145s, 111.108 mph/178.812 km/h; **2** Stéphane Richelmi, MC (Dallara F310-FPT), 29m 57.730s; **3** Sergio Campana, I (Dallara F310-FPT), 30m 11.632s; **4** César Ramos, BR (Dallara F310-FPT), 30m 16.234s; **5** Gabby Chaves, CO (Mygale M-10-FPT), 30m 16.725s; **6** Christopher Zanella, CH (Mygale M-10-FPT), 30m 21.416s; **7** Jesse Krohn, FIN (Dallara F310-FPT), 30m 27.380s; **8** Nicolas Marroc, F (Dallara F310-FPT), 30m 28.271s; **9** Kevin Giovesi, I (Mygale M-10-FPT), 30m 30.571s; **10** Momo Barri, I (Dallara F310-FPT), 30m 36.205s.
Fastest race lap: Caldarelli, 1m 44.098s, 112.708 mph/181.386 km/h.
Pole position: Caldarelli, 1m 42.088s, 114.927 mph/184.958 km/h.

Race 2 (55.405 miles/89.165 km).
1 Sergio Campana, I (Dallara F310-FPT), 30m 00.773s, 110.761 mph/178.253 km/h; **2** Stéphane Richelmi, MC (Dallara F310-FPT), 30m 01.450s; **3** Nicolas Marroc, F (Dallara F310-FPT), 30m 08.098s; **4** César Ramos, BR (Dallara F310-FPT), 30m 08.464s; **5** Daniel Mancinelli, I (Dallara F310-FPT), 30m 09.104s; **6** Andrea Caldarelli, I (Dallara F310-FPT), 30m 09.529s; **7** Gabby Chaves, CO (Mygale M-10-FPT), 30m 13.445s; **8** Edoardo Liberati, I (Dallara F310-FPT), 30m 14.000s; **9** Samuele Buttarelli, I (Dallara F310-FPT), 30m 17.704s; **10** Gianmarco Raimondo, CDN (Dallara F310-FPT), 30m 23.664s.
Fastest race lap: Campana, 1m 44.385s, 112.398 mph/180.888 km/h.
Pole position: Marroc.

ITALIAN FORMULA 3 CHAMPIONSHIP, Autodromo Nazionale di Monza, Milan, Italy, 23/24 October. Round 8. 15 and 17 laps of the 3.600-mile/5.793-km circuit.
Race 1 (53.994 miles/86.895 km).
1 Sergio Campana, I (Dallara F310-FPT), 30m 56.063s, 104.726 mph/168.540 km/h; **2** Andrea Caldarelli, I (Dallara F310-FPT), 30m 56.385s; **3** Edoardo Liberati, I (Dallara F310-FPT), 30m 58.999s; **4** Daniel Mancinelli, I (Dallara F310-FPT), 31m 01.854s; **5** Christopher Zanella, CH (Mygale M-10-FPT), 31m 05.237s; **6** Gianmarco Raimondo, CDN (Dallara F310-FPT), 31m 05.405s; **7** Nicolas Marroc, F (Dallara F310-FPT), 31m 07.475s; **8** César Ramos, BR (Dallara F310-FPT), 31m 07.626s; **9** David Fumanelli, I (Dallara F310-FPT), 31m 08.788s; **10** Alberto Cerqui, I (Dallara F310-FPT), 31m 09.097s.
Fastest race lap: Caldarelli, 1m 47.909s, 120.087 mph/193.262 km/h.
Pole position: Ramos, 1m 46.066s, 122.174 mph/196.620 km/h.

Race 2 (61.193 miles/98.481 km).
1 César Ramos, BR (Dallara F310-FPT), 30m 56.339s, 118.672 mph/190.984 km/h; **2** Stéphane Richelmi, MC (Dallara F310-FPT), 30m 58.150s; **3** Daniel Mancinelli, I (Dallara F310-FPT), 31m 02.681s; **4** Andrea Caldarelli, I (Dallara F310-FPT), 31m 03.144s; **5** Nicolas Marroc, F (Dallara F310-FPT), 31m 05.405s; **6** Matt Lee, USA (Dallara F310-FPT), 31m 05.893s; **7** Gabby Chaves, CO (Mygale M-10-FPT), 31m 07.472s; **8** Gianmarco Raimondo, CDN (Dallara F310-FPT), 31m 09.261s; **9** Samuele Buttarelli, I (Dallara F310-FPT), 31m 09.737s; **10** Edoardo Liberati, I (Dallara F310-FPT), 31m 10.546s.
Fastest race lap: Liberati, 1m 47.855s, 120.148 mph/193.359 km/h.
Pole position: Marroc.

Final championship points
1 César Ramos, BR, 161; **2** Stéphane Richelmi, MC, 153; **3** Andrea Caldarelli, I, 148; **4** Daniel Mancinelli, I, 138; **5** Sergio Campana, I, 114; **6** Christopher Zanella, CH, 90; **7** Jesse Krohn, FIN, 66; **8** Samuele Buttarelli, I, 50; **9** Edoardo Liberati, I, 44; **10** Gabby Chaves, CO, 44; **11** Matt Lee, USA, 31; **12** Nicolas Marroc, F, 30; **13** Tom Dillmann, F, 22; **14** Frédéric Vervisch, B, 20; **15** Kevin Giovesi, I, 18; **16** Gianmarco Raimondo, CDN, 14; **17** Momo Barri, I, 8; **18** Francesco Castellacci, I, 6; **19** Alberto Cerqui, I, 3; **20** David Fumanelli, I, 2; **21** Andrea Roda, I, 1; **22** Tyler Dueck, CDN, 1.
Rookies: **1** Gabby Chaves, CO, 195; **2** Kevin Giovesi, I, 170; **3** Gianmarco Raimondo, CDN, 135.

All-Japan Formula 3 Championship

ALL-JAPAN FORMULA 3 CHAMPIONSHIP, Suzuka International Racing Course, Suzuka-shi, Mie Prefecture, Japan, 17/18 April. 12 and 17 laps of the 3.608-mile/5.807-km circuit.
Round 1 (43.300 miles/69.684 km).
1 Yuji Kunimoto, J (Dallara F308-Toyota), 23m 00.109s, 112.947 mph/181.770 km/h; **2** Kouki Saga, J (Dallara F308-Toyota), 23m 01.983s; **3** Alexandre Imperatori, CH (Dallara F308-Mugen Honda), 23m 10.716s; **4** Rafael Suzuki, BR (Dallara F308-Toyota), 23m 11.625s; **5** Yuhi Sekiguchi, J (Dallara F308-Nissan), 23m 20.288s; **6** Hiroki Yoshida, J (Dallara F308-Toyota), 23m 22.861s; **7** Takashi Kobayashi, J (Dallara F307-Toyota), 23m 24.671s; **8** Katsumasa Chiyo, J (Dallara F305-Toyota), 23m 28.380s; **9** Kazuki Miura, J (Dallara F307-Toyota), 23m 31.708s; **10** Kimiya Sato, J (Dallara F306-Toyota), 23m 36.134s.
Fastest race lap: Kunimoto, 1m 53.781s, 114.166 mph/183.732 km/h.
Pole position: Kunimoto, 1m 53.749s, 114.198 mph/183.784 km/h.

Round 2 (61.341 miles/98.719 km).
1 Yuji Kunimoto, J (Dallara F308-Toyota), 32m 38.752s, 112.739 mph/181.436 km/h; **2** Kouki Saga, J (Dallara F308-Toyota), 32m 46.201s; **3** Rafael Suzuki, BR (Dallara F308-Toyota), 32m 52.982s; **4** Yuhi Sekiguchi, J (Dallara F308-Nissan), 33m 02.517s; **5** Hiroki Yoshida, J (Dallara F308-Toyota), 33m 07.348s; **6** Takashi Kobayashi, J (Dallara F307-Toyota), 33m 15.558s; **7** Katsumasa Chiyo, J (Dallara F305-Toyota), 33m 22.483s; **8** Naoya Gamou, J (Dallara F306-Toyota), 33m 38.901s; **9** Yoshitaka Kuroda, J (Dallara F307-Toyota), 33m 40.190s; **10** Daiki Sasaki, J (Dallara F306-Toyota), 33m 43.804s.
Fastest race lap: Kunimoto, 1m 54.430s, 113.518 mph/182.690 km/h.
Pole position: Saga, 1m 52.778s, 115.181 mph/185.366 km/h.

ALL-JAPAN FORMULA 3 CHAMPIONSHIP, Twin Ring Motegi, Motegi-machi, Haga-gun, Tochigi Prefecture, Japan, 22/23 May. 14 and 20 laps of the 2.983-mile/4.801-km circuit.
Round 3 (41.765 miles/67.214 km).
1 Yuji Kunimoto, J (Dallara F308-Toyota), 25m 03.489s, 100.003 mph/160.939 km/h; **2** Yuhi Sekiguchi, J (Dallara F308-Nissan), 25m 04.871s; **3** Alexandre Imperatori, CH (Dallara F308-Mugen Honda), 25m 11.050s; **4** Kouki Saga, J (Dallara F308-Toyota), 25m 14.676s; **5** Rafael Suzuki, BR (Dallara F308-Toyota), 25m 15.145s; **6** Hiroki Yoshida, J (Dallara F308-Toyota), 25m 26.998s; **7** Katsumasa Chiyo, J (Dallara F305-Toyota), 25m 33.849s; **8** Takashi Kobayashi, J (Dallara F307-Toyota), 25m 35.223s; **9** Kazuki Miura, J (Dallara F307-Toyota), 25m 48.463s; **10** Gary Thompson, IRL (Dallara F306-Toyota), 25m 49.937s.
Fastest race lap: Kunimoto, 1m 46.683s, 100.668 mph/162.009 km/h.
Pole position: Kunimoto, 1m 45.851s, 101.459 mph/163.282 km/h.

Round 4 (59.664 miles/96.020 km).
1 Yuji Kunimoto, J (Dallara F308-Toyota), 35m 43.959s, 100.184 mph/161.231 km/h; **2** Alexandre Imperatori, CH (Dallara F308-Mugen Honda), 35m 48.120s; **3** Yuhi Sekiguchi, J (Dallara F308-Nissan), 35m 53.354s; **4** Rafael Suzuki, BR (Dallara F308-Toyota), 35m 54.018s; **5** Takashi Kobayashi, J (Dallara F307-Toyota), 36m 25.499s; **6** Naoya Gamou, J (Dallara F306-Toyota), 36m 27.963s; **7** Kouki Saga, J (Dallara F308-Toyota), 36m 29.428s; **8** Kimiya Sato, J (Dallara F306-Toyota), 36m 39.293s; **9** Gary Thompson, IRL (Dallara F306-Toyota), 36m 44.089s; **10** Katsumasa Chiyo, J (Dallara F305-Toyota), 36m 45.313s.
Fastest race lap: Kunimoto, 1m 46.460s, 100.879 mph/162.348 km/h.
Pole position: Kunimoto, 1m 45.701s, 101.603 mph/163.514 km/h.

ALL-JAPAN FORMULA 3 CHAMPIONSHIP, Fuji International Speedway, Sunto-gun, Shizuoka Prefecture, Japan, 12/13 June. 15 and 21 laps of the 2.835-mile/4.563-km circuit.
Round 5 (42.341 miles/68.141 km).
1 Yuji Kunimoto, J (Dallara F308-Toyota), 24m 10.783s, 105.065 mph/169.086 km/h; **2** Yuhi Sekiguchi, J (Dallara F308-Nissan), 24m 23.820s; **3** Rafael Suzuki, BR (Dallara F308-Toyota), 24m 27.532s; **4** Alexandre Imperatori, CH (Dallara F308-Mugen Honda), 24m 30.808s; **5** Kouki Saga, J (Dallara F308-Toyota), 24m 31.910s; **6** Takashi Kobayashi, J (Dallara F307-Toyota), 24m 41.721s; **7** Naoya Gamou, J (Dallara F306-Toyota), 24m 45.817s; **8** Katsuaki Kubota, J (Dallara F308-Toyota), 24m 51.146s; **9** Kimiya Sato, J (Dallara F306-Toyota), 24m 51.527s; **10** Gary Thompson, IRL (Dallara F306-Toyota), 25m 03.840s.
Fastest race lap: Kunimoto, 1m 36.228s, 106.072 mph/170.707 km/h.
Pole position: Kunimoto, 1m 34.887s, 107.572 mph/173.120 km/h.

Round 6 (59.353 miles/95.519 km).
1 Yuji Kunimoto, J (Dallara F308-Toyota), 38m 28.375s, 92.563 mph/148.966 km/h; **2** Rafael Suzuki, BR (Dallara F308-Toyota), 38m 31.624s; **3** Yuhi Sekiguchi, J (Dallara F308-Nissan), 38m 44.332s; **4** Alexandre Imperatori, CH (Dallara F308-Mugen Honda), 38m 46.232s; **5** Kouki Saga, J (Dallara F308-Toyota), 38m 48.098s; **6** Takashi Kobayashi, J (Dallara F307-Toyota), 38m 58.282s; **7** Naoya Gamou, J (Dallara F306-Toyota), 39m 12.038s; **8** Tsubasa Mekaru, J (Dallara F305/307-Toyota), 39m 13.839s; **9** Katsuaki Kubota, J (Dallara F308-Toyota), 39m 15.161s; **10** Gary Thompson, IRL (Dallara F306-Toyota), 39m 15.994s.
Fastest race lap: Kunimoto, 1m 35.546s, 106.830 mph/171.926 km/h.
Pole position: Kunimoto, 1m 34.841s, 107.624 mph/173.204 km/h.

ALL-JAPAN FORMULA 3 CHAMPIONSHIP, Fuji International Speedway, Sunto-gun, Shizuoka Prefecture, Japan, 17/18 July. 15 and 21 laps of the 2.835-mile/4.563-km circuit.
Round 7 (42.341 miles/68.141 km).
1 Yuji Kunimoto, J (Dallara F308-Toyota), 24m 21.721s, 104.279 mph/167.821 km/h; **2** Yuhi Sekiguchi, J (Dallara F308-Nissan), 24m 37.397s; **3** Rafael Suzuki, BR (Dallara F308-Toyota), 24m 38.348s; **4** Alexandre Imperatori, CH (Dallara F308-Mugen Honda), 24m 42.539s; **5** Kouki Saga, J (Dallara F308-Toyota), 24m 46.880s; **6** Kimiya Sato, J (Dallara F306-Toyota), 24m 56.472s; **7** Katsumasa Chiyo, J (Dallara F305-Toyota), 24m 59.661s; **8** Takashi Kobayashi, J (Dallara F307-Toyota), 25m 00.115s; **9** Gary Thompson, IRL (Dallara F306-Toyota), 25m 07.380s; **10** Naoya Gamou, J (Dallara F306-Toyota), 25m 08.906s.
Fastest race lap: Kunimoto, 1m 36.648s, 105.612 mph/169.965 km/h.
Pole position: Kunimoto, 1m 36.105s, 106.208 mph/170.926 km/h.

Round 8 (59.353 miles/95.519 km).
1 Yuji Kunimoto, J (Dallara F308-Toyota), 34m 14.648s, 103.993 mph/167.361 km/h; **2** Rafael Suzuki, BR (Dallara F308-Toyota), 34m 32.816s; **3** Alexandre Imperatori, CH (Dallara F308-Mugen Honda), 34m 39.813s; **4** Yuhi Sekiguchi, J (Dallara F308-Nissan), 34m 40.978s; **5** Kouki Saga, J (Dallara F308-Toyota), 34m 47.261s; **6** Naoya Gamou, J (Dallara F306-Toyota), 34m 49.673s; **7** Takashi Kobayashi, J (Dallara F307-Toyota), 35m 02.643s; **8** Kimiya Sato, J (Dallara F306-Toyota), 35m 04.510s; **9** Katsumasa Chiyo, J (Dallara F305-Toyota), 35m 09.696s; **10** Daiki Sasaki, J (Dallara F306-Toyota), 35m 10.081s.
Fastest race lap: Kunimoto, 1m 37.060s, 105.163 mph/169.244 km/h.
Pole position: Kunimoto, 1m 36.091s, 106.224 mph/170.950 km/h.

ALL-JAPAN FORMULA 3 CHAMPIONSHIP, Twin Ring Motegi, Motegi-machi, Haga-gun, Tochigi Prefecture, Japan, 7/8 August. 14 and 20 laps of the 2.983-mile/4.801-km circuit.
Round 9 (41.765 miles/67.214 km).
1 Yuji Kunimoto, J (Dallara F308-Toyota), 25m 20.670s,

98.873 mph/159.121 km/h; **2** Yuhi Sekiguchi, J (Dallara F308-Nissan), 25m 22.441s; **3** Hideki Yamauchi, J (Dallara F308-Toyota), 25m 23.956s; **4** Kouki Saga, J (Dallara F308-Toyota), 25m 29.731s; **5** Alexandre Imperatori, CH (Dallara F308-Mugen Honda), 25m 31.619s; **6** Rafael Suzuki, BR (Dallara F308-Toyota), 25m 32.385s; **7** Naoya Gamou, J (Dallara F306-Toyota), 25m 45.607s; **8** Takashi Kobayashi, J (Dallara F307-Toyota), 25m 47.484s; **9** Daiki Sasaki, J (Dallara F306-Toyota), 25m 53.482s; **10** Kimiya Sato, J (Dallara F306-Toyota), 25m 56.252s.
Fastest race lap: Sekiguchi, 1m 47.708s, 99.710 mph/160.467 km/h.
Pole position: Kunimoto, 1m 46.996s, 100.373 mph/161.535 km/h.

Round 10 (59.664 miles/96.020 km).
1 Yuji Kunimoto, J (Dallara F308-Toyota), 36m 24.131s, 98.341 mph/158.265 km/h; **2** Yuhi Sekiguchi, J (Dallara F308-Nissan), 36m 31.837s; **3** Hideki Yamauchi, J (Dallara F308-Toyota), 36m 32.854s; **4** Rafael Suzuki, BR (Dallara F308-Toyota), 36m 42.069s; **5** Alexandre Imperatori, CH (Dallara F308-Mugen Honda), 36m 42.962s; **6** Kouki Saga, J (Dallara F308-Toyota), 36m 57.864s; **7** Naoya Gamou, J (Dallara F306-Toyota), 37m 01.586s; **8** Gary Thompson, IRL (Dallara F306-Toyota), 37m 19.028s; **9** Katsumasa Chiyo, J (Dallara F305-Toyota), 37m 19.435s; **10** Daiki Sasaki, J (Dallara F306-Toyota), 37m 21.022s.
Fastest race lap: Kunimoto, 1m 48.100s, 99.348 mph/159.885 km/h.
Pole position: Kunimoto, 1m 47.198s, 100.184 mph/161.231 km/h.

ALL-JAPAN FORMULA 3 CHAMPIONSHIP, Okayama International Circuit (TI Circuit Aida), Aida Gun, Okayama Prefecture, Japan, 4/5 September. 18 and 25 laps of the 2.301-mile/3.703-km circuit.
Round 11 (41.417 miles/66.654 km).
1 Rafael Suzuki, BR (Dallara F308-Toyota), 26m 30.507s, 93.744 mph/150.867 km/h; **2** Yuji Kunimoto, J (Dallara F308-Toyota), 26m 35.321s; **3** Yuhi Sekiguchi, J (Dallara F308-Nissan), 26m 36.370s; **4** Kouki Saga, J (Dallara F308-Toyota), 26m 42.558s; **5** Alexandre Imperatori, CH (Dallara F308-Mugen Honda), 26m 56.545s; **6** Naoya Gamou, J (Dallara F306-Toyota), 26m 57.367s; **7** Takashi Kobayashi, J (Dallara F307-Toyota), 26m 58.193s; **8** Hideki Yamauchi, J (Dallara F308-Toyota), 26m 58.558s; **9** Kazuki Miura, J (Dallara F307-Toyota), 27m 01.990s; **10** Gary Thompson, IRL (Dallara F306-Toyota), 27m 06.322s.
Fastest race lap: Sekiguchi, 1m 27.667s, 94.487 mph/152.062 km/h.
Pole position: Yamauchi, 1m 26.117s, 96.187 mph/154.799 km/h.

Round 12 (57.523 miles/92.575 km).
1 Rafael Suzuki, BR (Dallara F308-Toyota), 36m 48.998s, 93.746 mph/150.869 km/h; **2** Yuhi Sekiguchi, J (Dallara F308-Nissan), 36m 51.550s; **3** Hideki Yamauchi, J (Dallara F308-Toyota), 36m 58.137s; **4** Yuji Kunimoto, J (Dallara F308-Toyota), 37m 03.661s; **5** Kouki Saga, J (Dallara F308-Toyota), 37m 05.419s; **6** Alexandre Imperatori, CH (Dallara F308-Mugen Honda), 37m 24.338s; **7** Naoya Gamou, J (Dallara F306-Toyota), 37m 25.118s; **8** Takashi Kobayashi, J (Dallara F307-Toyota), 37m 25.819s; **9** Katsumasa Chiyo, J (Dallara F305-Toyota), 37m 30.020s; **10** Kazuki Miura, J (Dallara F307-Toyota), 37m 32.052s.
Fastest race lap: Suzuki, 1m 27.615s, 94.543 mph/152.152 km/h.
Pole position: Suzuki, 1m 26.119s, 96.185 mph/154.795 km/h.

ALL-JAPAN FORMULA 3 CHAMPIONSHIP, Sportsland-SUGO International Course, Shibata-gun, Miyagi Prefecture, Japan, 25/26 September. 18 and 25 laps of the 2.302-mile/3.704-km circuit.
Round 13 (41.430 miles/66.676 km).
1 Rafael Suzuki, BR (Dallara F308-Toyota), 23m 06.081s, 107.605 mph/173.173 km/h; **2** Hideki Yamauchi, J (Dallara F308-Toyota), 23m 06.766s; **3** Yuji Kunimoto, J (Dallara F308-Toyota), 23m 07.427s; **4** Alexandre Imperatori, CH (Dallara F308-Mugen Honda), 23m 18.528s; **5** Naoya Gamou, J (Dallara F306-Toyota), 23m 27.205s; **6** Daiki Sasaki, J (Dallara F306-Toyota), 23m 31.599s; **7** Takashi Kobayashi, J (Dallara F307-Toyota), 23m 32.042s; **8** Kazuki Miura, J (Dallara F307-Toyota), 23m 35.123s; **9** Katsumasa Chiyo, J (Dallara F305-Toyota), 23m 35.553s; **10** Yoshitaka Kuroda, J (Dallara F307-Toyota), 23m 53.769s.
Fastest race lap: Sekiguchi, 1m 16.011s, 109.011 mph/175.437 km/h.
Pole position: Yamauchi, 1m 14.513s, 111.203 mph/178.964 km/h.

Round 14 (57.542 miles/92.605 km).
1 Hideki Yamauchi, J (Dallara F308-Toyota), 32m 05.853s, 107.563 mph/173.107 km/h; **2** Kouki Saga, J (Dallara F308-Toyota), 32m 08.108s; **3** Rafael Suzuki, BR (Dallara F308-Toyota), 32m 10.857s; **4** Yuji Kunimoto, J (Dallara F308-Toyota), 32m 11.954s; **5** Alexandre Imperatori, CH (Dallara F308-Mugen Honda), 32m 16.777s; **6** Naoya Gamou, J (Dallara F306-Toyota), 32m 33.988s; **7** Kimiya Sato, J (Dallara F306-Toyota), 32m 38.892s; **8** Gary Thompson, IRL (Dallara F306-Toyota), 32m 41.128s; **9** Katsumasa Chiyo, J (Dallara F305-Toyota), 32m 42.145s; **10** Takashi Kobayashi, J (Dallara F307-Toyota), 32m 43.147s.
Fastest race lap: Kunimoto, 1m 16.103s, 108.880 mph/175.225 km/h.
Pole position: Yamauchi, 1m 14.285s, 111.544 mph/179.513 km/h.

ALL-JAPAN FORMULA 3 CHAMPIONSHIP, Autopolis International Racing Course, Kamit-sue-mura, Hitagun, Oita Prefecture, Japan, 16/17 October. 14 and 20 laps of the 2.904-mile/4.674-km circuit.
Round 15 (40.660 miles/65.436 km).
1 Kouki Saga, J (Dallara F308-Toyota), 27m 48.994s, 87.703 mph/141.145 km/h; **2** Hideki Yamauchi, J (Dallara F308-Toyota), 27m 49.335s; **3** Yuhi Sekiguchi, J (Dallara F308-Nissan), 27m 51.652s; **4** Alexandre Imperatori, CH (Dallara F308-Mugen Honda), 27m 55.776s; **5** Yuji Kunimoto, J (Dallara F308-Toyota), 28m 00.054s; **6** Takashi Kobayashi, J (Dallara F307-Toyota), 28m 06.527s; **7** Yoshitaka Kuroda, J (Dallara F307-Toyota), 28m 17.738s; **8** Hiroki Yoshida, J (Dallara F306-Toyota), 28m 19.177s; **9** Katsumasa Chiyo, J (Dallara F305-Toyota), 28m 34.707s; **10** Daiki Sasaki, J (Dallara F306-Toyota), 28m 52.362s.
Fastest race lap: Saga, 1m 41.148s, 103.368 mph/166.354 km/h.
Pole position: Yamauchi, 1m 39.326s, 105.264 mph/169.406 km/h.

Round 16 (58.086 miles/93.480 km).
1 Kouki Saga, J (Dallara F308-Toyota), 34m 14.683s, 101.772 mph/163.786 km/h; **2** Yuhi Sekiguchi, J (Dallara F308-Nissan), 34m 16.418s; **3** Alexandre Imperatori, CH (Dallara F308-Mugen Honda), 34m 34.484s; **4** Naoya Gamou, J (Dallara F306-Toyota), 34m 46.510s; **5** Katsumasa Chiyo, J (Dallara F305-Toyota), 35m 00.325s; **6** Kazuki Miura, J (Dallara F307-Toyota), 35m 07.960s; **7** Gary Thompson, IRL (Dallara F306-Toyota), 35m 08.463s; **8** Hiroki Yoshida, J (Dallara F306-Toyota), 35m 15.563s; **9** Yoshitaka Kuroda, J (Dallara F307-Toyota), 18 laps; **10** Kimiya Sato, J (Dallara F306-Toyota), 17 (DNF).
Fastest race lap: Saga, 1m 41.603s, 102.905 mph/165.609 km/h.
Pole position: Yamauchi, 1m 39.013s, 105.597 mph/169.941 km/h.

Final championship points
Championship Class Drivers: 1 Yuji Kunimoto, J, 139; **2** Yuhi Sekiguchi, J, 81; **3** Rafael Suzuki, BR, 78; **4** Kouki Saga, J, 68; **5** Alexandre Imperatori, CH, 52; **6** Hideki Yamauchi, J, 45; **7** Hiroki Yoshida, J, 5; **8** Katsuaki Kubota, J, 4.
National Class Drivers: 1 Takashi Kobayashi, J, 124; **2** Naoya Gamou, J, 121; **3** Katsumasa Chiyo, J, 66; **4** Kimiya Sato, J, 43.
Championship Class Teams: 1 Petronas Team Tom's, 137; **2** ThreeBond Racing, 78; **3** Denso Team Le Beausset, 65; **4** Toda Racing, 52.
National Class Teams: 1 HFDP Racing, 114; **2** Tom's Spirit, 109; **3** Denso Team Le Beausset, 64.
4 Team Nova, 59.

Major Non-Championship Formula 3

2009

The following races were run after AUTOCOURSE 2009–2010 went to press.

FIA F3 WORLD CUP, MACAU GP, Circuito da Guia, Macau, 21/22 November. 10 and 15 laps of the 3.803-mile/6.120-km circuit.
Race 1 (38.028 miles/61.200 km).
1 Jean-Karl Vernay, F (Dallara F308-Volkswagen), 31m 52.192s, 71.593 mph/115.218 km/h; **2** Marcus Ericsson, S (Dallara F308-Toyota), 31m 52.463s; **3** Edoardo Mortara, I (Dallara F308-Volkswagen), 31m 53.286s; **4** Valtteri Bottas, FIN (Dallara F308-Mercedes Benz), 31m 53.779s; **5** Laurens Vanthoor, B (Dallara F308-Volkswagen), 31m 54.370s; **6** Daniel Ricciardo, AUS (Dallara F308-Volkswagen), 31m 56.790s; **7** Sam Bird, GB (Dallara F308-Mercedes Benz), 31m 58.285s; **8** Takuto Iguchi, J (Dallara F308-Toyota), 31m 58.857s; **9** Roberto Merhi, E (Dallara F308-Mercedes Benz), 32m 00.264s; **10** Mika Mäki, FIN (Dallara F308-Volkswagen), 32m 01.442s.
Fastest race lap: Vernay, 2m 10.906s, 104.579 mph/168.303 km/h.
Pole position: Ericsson, 2m 10.042s, 105.274 mph/169.422 km/h.

Race 2 (57.042 miles/91.800 km).
1 Edoardo Mortara, I (Dallara F308-Volkswagen), 53m 07.769s, 64.418 mph/103.671 km/h; **2** Jean-Karl Vernay, F (Dallara F308-Volkswagen), 53m 08.915s; **3** Sam Bird, GB (Dallara F308-Mercedes Benz), 53m 18.751s; **4** Marcus Ericsson, S (Dallara F308-Toyota), 53m 22.757s; **5** Valtteri Bottas, FIN (Dallara F308-Mercedes Benz), 53m 26.957s; **6** Takuto Iguchi, J (Dallara F308-Toyota), 53m 29.175s; **7** Renger van der Zande, NL (Dallara F308-Mercedes Benz), 53m 29.828s; **8** Mika Mäki, FIN (Dallara F308-Volkswagen), 53m 36.774s; **9** Yuji Kunimoto, J (Dallara F308-Toyota), 53m 41.117s; **10** Jules Bianchi, F (Dallara F308-Mercedes Benz), 53m 43.530s.
Fastest race lap: Mortara, 2m 10.732s, 104.718 mph/168.527 km/h.
Pole position: Vernay.

2010

ZANDVOORT MASTERS OF FORMULA 3, Circuit Park Zandvoort, Netherlands, 6 June. 25 laps of the 2.676-mile/4.307-km circuit, 66.906 miles/107.675 km.
1 Valtteri Bottas, FIN (Dallara F308-Mercedes Benz), 41m 38.851s, 96.389 mph/155.123 km/h; **2** Alexander Sims, GB (Dallara F308-Mercedes Benz), 41m 39.982s; **3** Marco Wittmann, D (Dallara F308-Volkswagen), 41m 49.905s; **4** Jean-Eric Vergne, F (Dallara F308-Volkswagen), 41m 51.544s; **5** Edoardo Mortara, I (Dallara F308-Volkswagen), 41m 57.414s; **6** Gabriel Dias, BR (Dallara F308-Volkswagen), 42m 46.568s; **7** Lucas Foresti, BR (Dallara F308-Volkswagen), 42m 50.017s; **8** Wayne Boyd, GB (Dallara F308-Mercedes Benz), 42m 52.935s; **9** Hywel Lloyd, GB (Dallara F308-Mercedes Benz), 42m 54.078s; **10** William Buller, GB (Dallara F308-Volkswagen), **24** laps.
Disqualified: Rio Haryanto, RI (Dallara F308-Mercedes Benz), completed **24** laps (for ignoring yellow flags and dangerous driving resulting in an accident).
Fastest race lap: Vergne, 1m 32.788s, 103.833 mph/167.103 km/h.
Pole position: Sims, 1m 30.956s, 105.924 mph/170.469 km/h.

Results of the Macau races will be given in AUTOCOURSE 2011–2012.

World Series by Renault Formula Renault 3.5

All cars are Dallara-Renault.

FORMULA RENAULT 3.5, MotorLand Aragón, Alcañiz, Aragon, Spain, 17/18 April. Round 1. 21 and 26 laps of the 3.321-mile/5.344-km circuit.
Race 1 (69.733 miles/112.224 km).
1 Mikhail Aleshin, RUS, 47m 25.281s, 88.229 mph/141.991 km/h; **2** Daniel Zampieri, I, 47m 33.045s; **3** Daniel Ricciardo, AUS, 47m 41.587s; **4** Jon Lancaster, GB, 47m 50.077s; **5** Nelson Panciatici, F, 47m 58.394s; **6** Brendon Hartley, NZ, 48m 00.278s; **7** Jake Rosenzweig, USA, 48m 04.900s; **8** Greg Mansell, GB, 48m 10.217s; **9** Daniil Move, RUS, **20** laps; **10** Walter Grubmüller, A, 19.
Fastest race lap: Zampieri, 2m 04.999s, 95.634 mph/153.908 km/h.
Pole position: Ricciardo, 2m 01.886s, 98.076 mph/157.839 km/h.

Race 2 (86.336 miles/138.944 km).
1 Sten Pentus, EST, 46m 37.629s, 111.097 mph/178.793 km/h; **2** Daniel Ricciardo, AUS, 46m 50.802s; **3** Nathanaël Berthon, F, 47m 00.231s; **4** Albert Costa, E, 47m 10.534s; **5** Federico Leo, I, 47m 11.039s; **6** Brendon Hartley, NZ, 47m 11.998s; **7** Daniil Move, RUS, 47m 12.709s; **8** Walter Grubmüller, A, 47m 20.533s; **9** Nelson Panciatici, F, 47m 25.328s; **10** Victor Garcia, E, 47m 26.233s.
Fastest race lap: Pentus, 1m 45.001s, 113.848 mph/183.221 km/h.
Pole position: Ricciardo, 1m 58.709s, 100.701 mph/162.063 km/h.

FORMULA RENAULT 3.5, Circuit de Spa-Francorchamps, Stavelot, Belgium, 1/2 May. Round 2. 22 and 17 laps of the 4.351-mile/7.003-km circuit.
Race 1 (95.732 miles/154.066 km).
1 Mikhail Aleshin, RUS, 46m 26.663s, 123.673 mph/199.032 km/h; **2** Sten Pentus, EST, 46m 32.768s; **3** Stefano Coletti, MC, 46m 45.558s; **4** Albert Costa, E, 46m 45.894s; **5** Greg Mansell, GB, 46m 47.161s; **6** Federico Leo, I, 46m 47.829s; **7** Walter Grubmüller, A, 46m 51.448s; **8** Jan Charouz, CZ, 46m 56.331s; **9** Jon Lancaster, GB, 46m 56.716s; **10** Anton Nebylitskiy, RUS, 46m 56.837s.
Fastest race lap: Hartley, 2m 05.547s, 124.776 mph/200.807 km/h.
Pole position: Aleshin, 2m 02.151s, 128.245 mph/206.390 km/h.

Race 2 (73.975 miles/119.051 km).
1 Esteban Guerrieri, RA, 45m 25.474s, 97.711 mph/157.251 km/h; **2** Daniel Zampieri, I, 45m 28.782s; **3** Stefano Coletti, MC, 45m 42.631s; **4** Mikhail Aleshin, RUS, 45m 43.789s; **5** Daniel Ricciardo, AUS, 45m 47.395s; **6** Brendon Hartley, NZ, 45m 49.643s; **7** Jon Lancaster, GB, 46m 01.290s; **8** Jake Rosenzweig, USA, 46m 04.169s; **9** Jan Charouz, CZ, 46m 16.233s; **10** Nathanaël Berthon, F, 46m 16.837s.
Fastest race lap: Guerrieri, 2m 27.796s, 105.992 mph/170.578 km/h.
Pole position: Rosenzweig, 2m 28.117s, 105.762 mph/170.208 km/h.

FORMULA RENAULT 3.5, Monte-Carlo Street Circuit, Monaco, 16 May. Round 3. 31 laps of the 2.075-mile/3.340-km circuit, 64.337 miles/103.540 km.
1 Daniel Ricciardo, AUS, 45m 40.072s, 84.527 mph/136.034 km/h; **2** Mikhail Aleshin, RUS, 45m 41.165s; **3** Albert Costa, E, 46m 01.175s; **4** Brendon Hartley, NZ, 46m 07.057s; **5** Stefano Coletti, MC, 46m 08.352s; **6** Sten Pentus, EST, 46m 11.301s; **7** Jon Lancaster, GB, 46m 12.113s; **8** Filip Salaquarda, CZ, 46m 32.687s; **9** Nelson Panciatici, F, 46m 33.592s; **10** Daniil Move, RUS, 46m 34.416s.
Fastest race lap: Hartley, 1m 26.906s, 85.970 mph/138.356 km/h.
Pole position: Ricciardo, 1m 26.230s, 86.644 mph/139.441 km/h.

FORMULA RENAULT 3.5, Automotodrom Brno Masaryk Circuit, Brno, Czech Republic, 5/6 June. Round 4. 26 and 24 laps of the 3.357-mile/5.403-km circuit.
Race 1 (87.289 miles/140.478 km).
1 Esteban Guerrieri, RA, 46m 47.517s, 111.928 mph/180.130 km/h; **2** Brendon Hartley, NZ, 46m 49.421s; **3** Anton Nebylitskiy, RUS, 46m 50.511s; **4** Ómar Leal, CO, 46m 51.932s; **5** Keisuke Kunimoto, J, 46m 58.552s; **6** Sten Pentus, EST, 46m 59.528s; **7** Jan Charouz, CZ, 47m 04.257s; **8** Nathanaël Berthon, F, 47m 05.335s; **9** Stefano Coletti, MC, 47m 14.233s; **10** Jon Lancaster, GB, 47m 21.739s.
Fastest race lap: Aleshin, 1m 45.642s, 114.406 mph/184.119 km/h.
Pole position: Salaquarda, 1m 42.685s, 117.701 mph/189.422 km/h.

Race 2 (80.574 miles/129.672 km).
1 Esteban Guerrieri, RA, 45m 59.313s, 105.123 mph/169.179 km/h; **2** Nathanaël Berthon, F, 46m 00.490s; **3** Filip Salaquarda, CZ, 46m 04.994s; **4** Walter Grubmüller, A, 46m 05.802s; **5** Daniel Ricciardo, AUS, 46m 06.519s; **6** Brendon Hartley, NZ, 46m 12.143s; **7** Jon Lancaster, GB, 46m 13.194s; **8** Nelson Panciatici, F, 46m 28.665s; **9** Mikhail Aleshin, RUS, 46m 28.954s; **10** Albert Costa, E, 46m 29.667s.
Fastest race lap: Ricciardo, 1m 44.591s, 115.556 mph/185.970 km/h.
Pole position: Salaquarda, 1m 41.013s, 119.649 mph/192.557 km/h.

FORMULA RENAULT 3.5, Circuit de Nevers, Magny-Cours, France, 19/20 June. Round 5. 25 and 30 laps of the 2.741-mile/4.411-km circuit.
Race 1 (68.522 miles/110.275 km).
1 Mikhail Aleshin, RUS, 47m 06.881s, 87.261 mph/140.433 km/h; **2** Esteban Guerrieri, RA, 47m 21.772s; **3** Stefano Coletti, MC, 47m 23.799s; **4** Nelson Panciatici, F, 47m 31.657s; **5** Daniel Zampieri, I, 47m 44.544s; **6** Daniel Ricciardo, AUS, 47m 49.778s; **7** Sten Pentus, EST, 47m 50.823s; **8** Albert Costa, E, 48m 11.070s; **9** Nathanaël Berthon, F, 48m 23.139s; **10** Jon Lancaster, GB, 48m 27.661s.
Fastest race lap: Pentus, 1m 50.663s, 89.163 mph/143.495 km/h.
Pole position: Guerrieri, 1m 27.619s, 112.613 mph/181.234 km/h.

Race 2 (82.226 miles/132.330 km).
1 Nathanaël Berthon, F, 46m 04.729s, 107.067 mph/172.309 km/h; **2** Daniel Ricciardo, AUS, 46m 04.979s; **3** Filip Salaquarda, CZ, 46m 17.966s; **4** Mikhail Aleshin, RUS, 46m 25.475s; **5** Albert Costa, E, 46m 27.148s; **6** Bruno Méndez, E, 47m 00.276s; **7** Stefano Coletti, MC, 47m 00.704s; **8** Sten Pentus, EST, 47m 02.371s; **9** Nelson Panciatici, F, 47m 11.888s; **10** Esteban Guerrieri, RA, 47m 20.164s *.
** finished 9th but given a 10-sec penalty for blocking.*
Fastest race lap: Ricciardo, 1m 28.854s, 111.048 mph/178.715 km/h.
Pole position: Ricciardo, 1m 26.390s, 114.216 mph/183.812 km/h.

FORMULA RENAULT 3.5, Hungaroring, Mogyorod, Budapest, Hungary, 3/4 July. Round 6. 28 and 24 laps of the 2.722-mile/4.381-km circuit.
Race 1 (76.222 miles/122.668 km).
1 Daniel Ricciardo, AUS, 47m 14.151s, 96.819 mph/155.815 km/h; **2** Mikhail Aleshin, RUS, 47m 27.909s; **3** Sten Pentus, EST, 47m 43.861s; **4** Brendon Hartley, NZ, 47m 45.305s; **5** Nelson Panciatici, F, 47m 52.996s; **6** Albert Costa, E, 47m 53.496s; **7** Jan Charouz, CZ, 47m 53.947s; **8** Jake Rosenzweig, USA, 48m 16.391s; **9** Keisuke Kunimoto, J, 48m 16.970s; **10** Anton Nebylitskiy, RUS, 48m 17.496s.
Fastest race lap: Ricciardo, 1m 36.613s, 101.435 mph/163.245 km/h.
Pole position: Ricciardo, 1m 33.168s, 105.186 mph/169.281 km/h.

Race 2 (65.333 miles/105.144 km).
1 Sten Pentus, EST, 39m 00.851s, 100.476 mph/161.701 km/h; **2** Albert Costa, E, 39m 07.143s; **3** Mikhail Aleshin, RUS, 39m 09.772s; **4** Daniel Zampieri, I, 39m 10.340s; **5** Greg Mansell, GB, 39m 12.084s; **6** Daniel Ricciardo, AUS, 39m 14.841s; **7** Anton Nebylitskiy, RUS, 39m 15.374s; **8** Jake Rosenzweig, USA, 39m 30.048s; **9** Brendon Hartley, NZ, 39m 30.390s; **10** Stefano Coletti, MC, 39m 35.994s.
Fastest race lap: Aleshin, 1m 35.251s, 102.886 mph/165.579 km/h.
Pole position: Pentus, 1m 32.957s, 105.425 mph/169.665 km/h.

FORMULA RENAULT 3.5, Hockenheimring Grand Prix Circuit, Heidelberg, Germany, 4/5 September. Round 7. 30 and 31 laps of the 2.842-mile/4.574-km circuit.
Race 1 (85.265 miles/137.220 km).
1 Daniel Ricciardo, AUS, 46m 47.111s, 109.348 mph/175.978 km/h; **2** Esteban Guerrieri, RA, 46m 50.028s; **3** Jon Lancaster, GB, 46m 59.626s; **4** Daniel Zampieri, I, 47m 02.227s; **5** Mikhail Aleshin, RUS, 47m 06.402s; **6** Greg Mansell, GB, 47m 06.607s; **7** Stefano Coletti, MC, 47m 07.565s; **8** Albert Costa, E, 47m 09.250s; **9** Nathanaël Berthon, F, 47m 11.651s; **10** Anton Nebylitskiy, RUS, 47m 12.239s.
Fastest race lap: Guerrieri, 1m 29.595s, 114.199 mph/183.787 km/h.
Pole position: Ricciardo, 1m 27.061s, 117.523 mph/189.136 km/h.

Race 2 (88.107 miles/141.794 km).
1 Esteban Guerrieri, RA, 46m 47.925s, 112.960 mph/181.792 km/h; **2** Stefano Coletti, MC, 46m 53.816s; **3** Nathanaël Berthon, F, 46m 59.037s; **4** Mikhail Aleshin, RUS, 47m 01.830s; **5** Jean-Eric Vergne, F, 47m 02.361s; **6** Sten Pentus, EST, 47m 12.912s; **7** Filip Salaquarda, CZ, 47m 13.666s; **8** Jon Lancaster, GB, 47m 17.052s; **9** Ómar Leal, CO, 47m 17.697s; **10** Federico Leo, I, 47m 23.875s.
Fastest race lap: Guerrieri, 1m 28.921s, 115.065 mph/185.180 km/h.
Pole position: Guerrieri, 1m 26.415s, 118.402 mph/190.550 km/h.

FORMULA RENAULT 3.5, Silverstone Grand Prix Circuit, Towcester, Northamptonshire, Great Britain, 18/19 September. Round 8. 2 x 25 laps of the 3.667-mile/5.901-km circuit.
Race 1 (91.668 miles/147.525 km).
1 Jean-Eric Vergne, F, 45m 57.394s, 119.679 mph/192.605 km/h; **2** Albert Costa, E, 46m 07.603s; **3** Stefano Coletti, MC, 46m 15.400s; **4** Nelson Panciatici, F, 46m 17.029s; **5** Filip Salaquarda, CZ, 46m 18.026s; **6** Mikhail Aleshin, RUS, 46m 21.437s; **7** Anton Nebylitskiy, RUS, 46m 21.992s; **8** Victor Garcia, E, 46m 22.432s; **9** Daniil Move, RUS, 46m 28.224s; **10** Greg Mansell, GB, 46m 28.641s.
Fastest race lap: Jon Lancaster, GB, 1m 48.638s, 121.505 mph/195.544 km/h.
Pole position: Lancaster, 1m 44.673s, 126.108 mph/202.952 km/h.

Race 2 (91.668 miles/147.525 km).
1 Esteban Guerrieri, RA, 46m 02.792s, 119.445 mph/192.229 km/h; **2** Daniel Ricciardo, AUS, 46m 03.367s; **3** Jean-Eric Vergne, F, 46m 10.381s; **4** Filip Salaquarda, CZ, 46m 16.149s; **5** Anton Nebylitskiy, RUS, 46m 16.844s; **6** Daniel Zampieri, I, 46m 17.957s; **7** Sten Pentus, EST, 46m 23.457s; **8** Albert Costa, E, 46m 26.296s; **9** Nelson Panciatici, F, 46m 27.474s; **10** Ómar Leal, CO, 46m 32.183s.
Fastest race lap: Lancaster, 1m 48.165s, 122.037 mph/196.399 km/h.
Pole position: Ricciardo, 1m 45.149s, 125.537 mph/202.033 km/h.

FORMULA RENAULT 3.5, Circuit de Catalunya, Montmeló, Barcelona, Spain, 9/10 October. Round 9. 28 and 22 laps of the 2.892-mile/4.655-km circuit.
Race 1 (80.990 miles/130.340 km).
1 Daniel Ricciardo, AUS, 45m 45.264s, 106.205 mph/

170.921 km/h; **2** Mikhail Aleshin, RUS, 46m 11.485s; **3** Jean-Eric Vergne, F, 46m 20.521s; **4** Esteban Guerrieri, RA, 46m 35.756s; **5** Albert Costa, E, 46m 48.532s; **6** Nathanaël Berthon, F, 46m 48.819s; **7** Federico Leo, I, 47m 00.748s; **8** Filip Salaquarda, CZ, 47m 02.012s; **9** Greg Mansell, GB, 47m 02.641s; **10** Stefano Coletti, MC, 47m 08.871s.
Fastest race lap: Ricciardo, 1m 36.689s, 107.695 mph/173.318 km/h.
Pole position: Ricciardo, 1m 34.217s, 110.520 mph/177.865 km/h.

Race 2 (63.635 miles/102.410 km).
1 Esteban Guerrieri, RA, 47m 08.118s, 81.002 mph/130.360 km/h; **2** Jean-Eric Vergne, F, 47m 32.302s; **3** Mikhail Aleshin, RUS, 47m 33.349s; **4** Daniel Ricciardo, AUS, 47m 42.089s; **5** Stefano Coletti, MC, 47m 55.410s; **6** Nelson Panciatici, F, 47m 57.987s; **7** Anton Nebylitskiy, RUS, 47m 58.793s; **8** Jan Charouz, CZ, 48m 02.900s; **9** Jon Lancaster, GB, 48m 03.808s; **10** Albert Costa, E, 48m 08.065s.
Fastest race lap: Guerrieri, 1m 59.282s, 87.296 mph/140.490 km/h.
Pole position: Guerrieri, 1m 56.515s, 89.369 mph/143.826 km/h.

Final championship points
Drivers: 1 Mikhail Aleshin, RUS, 138; **2** Daniel Ricciardo, AUS, 136; **3** Esteban Guerrieri, RA, 123; **4** Sten Pentus, EST, 78; **5** Albert Costa, E, 78; **6** Stefano Coletti, MC, 76; **7** Nathanaël Berthon, F, 60; **8** Jean-Eric Vergne, F, 53; **9** Daniel Zampieri, I, 51; **10** Brendon Hartley, NZ, 50; **11** Filip Salaquarda, CZ, 44; **12** Nelson Panciatici, F, 44; **13** Jon Lancaster, GB, 39; **14** Anton Nebylitskiy, RUS, 31; **15** Greg Mansell, GB, 23; **16** Walter Grubmüller, A, 16; **17** Federico Leo, I, 16; **18** Jan Charouz, CZ, 16; **19** Jake Rosenzweig, USA, 13; **20** Julián Leal, CO, 11; **21** Daniil Move, RUS, 9; **22** Keisuke Kunimoto, J, 8; **23** Bruno Méndez, E, 5; **24** Victor Garcia, E, 4.
Teams: 1 Tech **1** Racing, 239; **2** ISR, 167; **3** Carlin, 151.

FIA GT1 World Championship

FIA GT1 WORLD CHAMPIONSHIP, Yas Marina Circuit, Abu Dhabi, United Arab Emirates, 17 April. Round 1. 28 laps of the 3.451-mile/5.554-km circuit, 96.631 miles/155.512 km.
1 Romain Grosjean/Thomas Mutsch, F/D (Ford GT), 1h 01m 14.892s, 94.661 mph/152.342 km/h; **2** Andreas Zuber/Marc Hennerici, A/D (Chevrolet Corvette Z06), 1h 01m 37.953s; **3** Mike Hezemans/Andrea Piccini, NL/I (Chevrolet Corvette Z06), 1h 01m 41.377s; **4** Andrea Bertolini/Michael Bartels, I/D (Maserati MC 12 GT1), 1h 01m 48.967s; **5** Ricardo Zonta/Rafael Daniel, BR/BR (Lamborghini Murciélago R-SV), 1h 02m 04.388s; **6** Miguel Ramos/Enrique Bernoldi, P/BR (Maserati MC 12 GT1), 1h 02m 07.951s; **7** Matteo Bobbi/Bert Longin, I/B (Maserati MC 12 GT1), 1h 02m 15.457s; **8** Christopher Haase/Peter Kox, D/NL (Lamborghini Murciélago R-SV), 1h 02m 27.586s; **9** Alexandros Margaritis/Altfrid Heger, GR/D (Maserati MC 12 GT1), 1h 02m 39.365s; **10** Alex Müller/Xavier Maassen, D/NL (Chevrolet Corvette Z06), 1h 02m 41.146s.
Fastest race lap: Grosjean/Mutsch, 2m 07.376s, 97.537 mph/156.971 km/h.
Pole position: Grosjean/Mutsch.
(Zuber/Hennerici qualified for pole by winning the qualifying race but were docked 10 places for a 'balance of performance' irregularity)

FIA GT1 WORLD CHAMPIONSHIP, Silverstone Grand Prix Circuit, Towcester, Northamptonshire, Great Britain, 2 May. Round 2. 28 laps of the 3.660-mile/5.891-km circuit, 102.524 miles/164.996 km.
1 Jamie Campbell-Walter/Warren Hughes, GB/GB (Nissan GT-R), 1h 01m 46.717s, 99.572 mph/160.245 km/h; **2** Frédéric Makowiecki/Thomas Accary, F/F (Aston Martin DB9), 1h 01m 48.602s; **3** Frank Kechele/Jos Menten, D/NL (Lamborghini Murciélago R-SV), 1h 01m 57.001s; **4** Matteo Bobbi/Bert Longin, I/B (Maserati MC 12 GT1), 1h 01m 57.592s; **5** Stefan Mücke/Christoffer Nygaard, D/DK (Aston Martin DB9), 1h 01m 57.768s; **6** Alexandros Margaritis/Altfrid Heger, GR/D (Maserati MC 12 GT1), 1h 01m 58.504s; **7** Andrea Bertolini/Michael Bartels, I/D (Maserati MC 12 GT1), 1h 02m 06.027s; **8** Bas Leinders/Maxime Martin, B/B (Ford GT), 1h 02m 09.130s; **9** Seiji Ara/Max Nilsson, J/S (Nissan GT-R), 1h 02m 14.425s; **10** Markus Palttala/Renaud Kuppens, FIN/B (Ford GT), 1h 02m 15.507s.
Disqualified: Darren Turner/Tomas Enge, GB/CZ (Aston Martin DBR9), finished 1st in 1h 01m 21.561s (skid plank wear).
Fastest race lap: Makowiecki/Accary, 2m 00.549s, 109.314 mph/175.925 km/h.
Pole position: Makowiecki/Accary.

FIA GT1 WORLD CHAMPIONSHIP, Automotodrom Brno Masaryk Circuit, Brno, Czech Republic, 23 May. Round 3. 28 laps of the 3.357-mile/5.403-km circuit, 94.004 miles/151.284 km.
1 Romain Grosjean/Thomas Mutsch, F/D (Ford GT), 1h 00m 46.852s, 92.795 mph/149.340 km/h; **2** Darren Turner/Tomas Enge, GB/CZ (Aston Martin DB9), 1h 00m 47.569s; **3** Michael Krumm/Peter Dumbreck, D/GB (Nissan GT-R), 1h 00m 47.818s; **4** Clivio Piccione/Jonathan Hirschi, MC/CH (Aston Martin DB9), 1h 00m 48.405s; **5** Andrea Bertolini/Michael Bartels, I/D (Maserati MC 12 GT1), 1h 00m 48.618s; **6** Miguel Ramos/Enrique Bernoldi, P/BR (Maserati MC 12 GT1), 1h 00m 55.909s; **7** Nicky Pastorelli/Dominik Schwager, NL/D (Lamborghini Murciélago R-SV), 1h 01m 00.137s; **8** Marc Hennerici/Stefan Rosina, D/SK (Chevrolet Corvette Z06), 1h 01m 03.565s; **9** Frédéric Makowiecki/Stéphane Sarrazin, F/F (Aston Martin DB9), 1h 01m 07.726s; **10** Karl Wendlinger/Henri Moser, A/CH (Nissan GT-R), 1h 01m 09.514s.
Fastest race lap: Stefan Mücke/Christoffer Nygaard, D/DK (Aston Martin DB9), 1m 57.382s, 102.964 mph/165.705 km/h.
Pole position: Bertolini/Bartels.

FIA GT1 WORLD CHAMPIONSHIP, Circuit ASA Paul Ricard, Le Beausset, France, 4 July. Round 4. 28 laps of the 3.630-mile/5.842-km circuit, 101.641 miles/163.576 km.
1 Andrea Bertolini/Michael Bartels, I/D (Maserati MC **12** GT1), 1h 00m 30.245s, 100.794 mph/162.213 km/h; **2** Michael Krumm/Peter Dumbreck, D/GB (Nissan GT-R), 1h 00m 37.302s; **3** Alexandros Margaritis/Altfrid Heger, GR/D (Maserati MC 12 GT1), 1h 00m 54.878s; **4** Bas Leinders/Maxime Martin, B/B (Ford GT), 1h 00m 56.454s; **5** Marc Hennerici/Andrea Piccini, D/I (Chevrolet Corvette Z06), 1h 00m 59.915s; **6** Xavier Maassen/Mike Hezemans, NL/NL (Chevrolet Corvette Z06), 1h 01m 06.069s; **7** Romain Grosjean/Thomas Mutsch, F/D (Ford GT), 1h 01m 16.423s; **8** Jamie Campbell-Walter/Warren Hughes, GB/GB (Nissan GT-R), 1h 01m 24.609s; **9** Frédéric Makowiecki/Thomas Accary, F/F (Aston Martin DB9), 1h 01m 26.944s; **10** Ricardo Zonta/Rafael Daniel, BR/BR (Lamborghini Murciélago R-SV), 1h 01m 27.471s.
Fastest race lap: Stefan Mücke/Christoffer Nygaard, D/DK (Aston Martin DB9), 2m 05.972s, 103.738 mph/166.951 km/h.
Pole position: Bertolini/Bartels.

FIA GT1 WORLD CHAMPIONSHIP, Circuit de Spa-Francorchamps, Stavelot, Belgium, 31 July. Round 5. 24 laps of the 4.352-mile/7.004-km circuit, 104.373 miles/167.972 km.
1 Ricardo Zonta/Frank Kechele, BR/D (Lamborghini Murciélago R-SV), 1h 01m 02.392s, 102.594 mph/165.110 km/h; **2** Alex Müller/Altfrid Heger, D/D (Maserati MC 12 GT1), 1h 01m 05.645s; **3** Richard Westbrook/Thomas Mutsch, GB/D (Ford GT), 1h 01m 09.067s; **4** Miguel Ramos/Enrique Bernoldi, P/BR (Maserati MC 12 GT1), 1h 01m 09.466s; **5** Frédéric Makowiecki/Thomas Accary, F/F (Aston Martin DB9), 1h 01m 10.328s; **6** Darren Turner/Tomas Enge, GB/CZ (Aston Martin DB9), 1h 01m 10.666s; **7** Andrea Bertolini/Michael Bartels, I/D (Maserati MC 12 GT1), 1h 01m 12.133s; **8** Nico Verdonck/Bert Longin, B/B (Maserati MC 12 GT1), 1h 01m 12.983s; **9** Nicky Pastorelli/Dominik Schwager, NL/D (Lamborghini Murciélago R-SV), 1h 01m 13.176s; **10** Clivio Piccione/Jonathan Hirschi, MC/CH (Aston Martin DB9), 1h 01m 16.313s.
Fastest race lap: Oliver Gavin/Pertti Kuismanen, GB/FIN (Chevrolet Corvette Z06), 2m 20.965s, 111.144 mph/178.869 km/h.
Pole position: Xavier Maassen/Jos Menten, NL/NL (Chevrolet Corvette ZX06).

FIA GT1 WORLD CHAMPIONSHIP, Nürburgring, Nürburg/Eifel, Germany, 29 August. Round 6. 30 laps of the 3.192-mile/5.137-km circuit, 95.760 miles/154.110 km.
1 Darren Turner/Tomas Enge, GB/CZ (Aston Martin DB9), 1h 00m 59.709s, 94.197 mph/151.595 km/h; **2** Christopher Haase/Peter Kox, D/NL (Lamborghini Murciélago R-SV), 1h 01m 09.256s; **3** Marc Hennerici/Alexandros Margaritis, D/GR (Chevrolet Corvette Z06), 1h 01m 12.727s; **4** Clivio Piccione/Jonathan Hirschi, MC/CH (Aston Martin DB9), 1h 01m 13.891s; **5** Stefan Mücke/Christoffer Nygaard, D/DK (Aston Martin DB9), 1h 01m 14.818s; **6** Andrea Bertolini/Michael Bartels, I/D (Maserati MC 12 GT1), 1h 01m 16.201s; **7** Frédéric Makowiecki/Yann Clairay, F/F (Aston Martin DB9), 1h 01m 19.634s; **8** Jamie Campbell-Walter/Warren Hughes, GB/GB (Nissan GT-R), 1h 01m 24.543s; **9** Alessandro Pier Guidi/Bert Longin, I/B (Maserati MC 12 GT1), 1h 01m 24.807s; **10** Karl Wendlinger/Henri Moser, A/CH (Nissan GT-R), 1h 01m 40.143s.
Fastest race lap: Pier Guidi/Longin, 1m 58.370s, 97.078 mph/156.232 km/h.
Pole position: Turner/Enge.

FIA GT1 WORLD CHAMPIONSHIP, Autódromo Internacional do Algarve, Portimão, Portugal, 19 September. Round 7. 34 laps of the 2.891-mile/4.653-km circuit, 98.131 miles/157.927 km.
1 Andrea Bertolini/Michael Bartels, I/D (Maserati MC 12 GT1), 1h 00m 19.722s, 97.596 mph/157.066 km/h; **2** Richard Westbrook/Thomas Mutsch, GB/D (Ford GT), 1h 00m 21.124s; **3** Marc Hennerici/Alexandros Margaritis, D/GR (Chevrolet Corvette Z06), 1h 00m 35.204s; **4** Michael Krumm/Peter Dumbreck, D/GB (Nissan GT-R), 1h 00m 44.345s; **5** Bas Leinders/Maxime Martin, B/B (Ford GT), 1h 00m 51.667s; **6** Frédéric Makowiecki/Yann Clairay, F/F (Aston Martin DB9), 1h 00m 52.205s; **7** Christopher Haase/Peter Kox, D/NL (Lamborghini Murciélago R-SV), 1h 00m 52.572s; **8** Jos Menten/Frank Kechele, NL/D (Lamborghini Murciélago R-SV), 1h 00m 54.567s; **9** Alex Müller/Altfrid Heger, D/D (Maserati MC 12 GT1), 1h 01m 01.670s; **10** Darren Turner/Tomas Enge, GB/CZ (Aston Martin DB9), 1h 01m 03.217s.
Fastest race lap: Alessandro Pier Guidi/Nikolaus Mayr-Melnhof, I/A (Maserati MC 12 GT1), 1m 43.275s, 100.779 mph/162.189 km/h.
Pole position: Krumm/Dumbreck.

FIA GT1 WORLD CHAMPIONSHIP, Circuito de Navarra, Los Arcos, Spain, 24 October. Round 8. 37 laps of the 2.444-mile/3.933-km circuit, 90.423 miles/145.521 km.
1 Ricardo Zonta/Frank Kechele, BR/D (Lamborghini Murciélago R-SV), 1h 01m 30.476s, 88.205 mph/141.953 km/h; **2** Frédéric Makowiecki/Yann Clairay, F/F (Aston Martin DB9), 1h 01m 42.373s; **3** Jamie Campbell-Walter/Warren Hughes, GB/GB (Nissan GT-R), 1h 01m 42.828s; **4** Darren Turner/Tomas Enge, GB/CZ (Aston Martin DB9), 1h 01m 43.444s; **5** Bas Leinders/Maxime Martin, B/B (Ford GT), 1h 02m 06.502s; **6** Andrea Bertolini/Michael Bartels, I/D (Maserati MC 12 GT1), 1h 02m 10.787s; **7** Nicolas Armindo/Neel Jani, F/CH (Ford GT), 1h 02m 21.499s; **8** Marc Hennerici/Alexandros Margaritis, D/GR (Chevrolet Corvette Z06), 1h 02m 30.546s; **9** Nicky Pastorelli/Dominik Schwager, NL/D (Lamborghini Murciélago R-SV), 1h 02m 30.838s; **10** Markus Palttala/Matteo Bobbi, FIN/I (Ford GT), 1h 02m 43.743s.
Fastest race lap: Zonta/Kechele, 1m 37.027s, 90.674 mph/145.926 km/h.
Pole position: Zonta/Kechele.

Provisional championship points
Drivers: 1 Andrea Bertolini/Michael Bartels, I/D, 130; **2** Thomas Mutsch, D, 95; **3** Marc Hennerici. D 84; **4** Frank Kechele, D, 83; **5** Darren Turner/Tomas Enge, GB/CZ, 78; **6** Ricardo Zonta, BR, 75; **7** Frédéric Makowiecki, F, 72; **8** Alexandra Margaritis, GR, 69; **9** Romain Grosjean, CH, 62; **10** Michael Krumm/Peter Dumbreck, D/GB, 57.
Teams: 1 Vitaphone Racing Team, 160; **2** Reiter, 142; **3** Sumo Power GT, 114; **4** Hexis AMR, 110; **5** Young Driver AMR, 110; **6** Matech Competition, 101; **7** Triple H Team Hegersport, 80; **8** Marc VDS Racing Team, 46; **9** Mad-Croc Racing, 17; **10** All-Inkl.com Münnich Motorsport, 12; **11** Swiss Racing Team, 5.

Results of the Brazil and Argentina races will be given in AUTOCOURSE 2011–2012.

Le Mans Series

LE MANS SERIES, Circuit ASA Paul Ricard, Le Beausset, France, 11 April. Round 1. 266 laps of the 3.598-mile/5.791-km circuit, 957.164 miles/1540.406 km.
1 Rinaldo Capello/Allan McNish, I/GB (Audi R15), 8h 00m 36.415s, 119.494 mph/192.307 km/h (1st LMP1 class); **2** Adrián Fernández/Harold Primat/Stefan Mücke, MEX/CH/D (Lola B08/60-Aston Martin), 261 laps; **3** Andrea Belicchi/Jean-Christophe Boullion/Guy Smith, I/F/GB (Lola B10/60 Coupé-Rebellion), 261; **4** Olivier Panis/Nicolas Lapierre/Stéphane Sarrazin, F/F/F (Peugeot 908), 258; **5** Soheil Ayari/Didier André/Loïc Duval, F/F/F (Oreca 01-AIM), 258; **6** Pierre Ragues/Franck Mailleux/Vanina Ickx, F/F/B (Lola B08/60-Aston Martin), 256; **7** Nick Leventis/Danny Watts/Jonny Kane, GB/GB/GB (HPD ARX-01c), 250 (1st LMP2 class); **8** Richard Hein/Guillaume Moreau, MC/F (Pescarolo 01-Mazda), 250; **9** Tommy Erdos/Mike Newton/Andy Wallace, BR/GB/GB (Lola B08/80-HPD), 249; **10** Mathieu Lahaye/Jacques Nicolet, F/F (Pescarolo 01-Mazda), 249.
Fastest race lap: Capello/McNish, 1m 42.541s, 126.330 mph/203.309 km/h.
Pole position: Panis/Lapierre/Sarrazin, 1m 41.195s, 128.011 mph/206.014 km/h.

LE MANS SERIES, Circuit de Spa-Francorchamps, Stavelot, Belgium, 9 May. Round 2. 139 laps of the 4.352-mile/7.004-km circuit, 604.940 miles/973.556 km.
1 Pedro Lamy/Sébastien Bourdais/Simon Pagenaud, P/F/F (Peugeot 908), 6h 00m 39.012s, 100.641 mph/161.966 km/h (1st LMP1 class); **2** Franck Montagny/Stéphane Sarrazin/Nicolas Minassian, F/F/F (Peugeot 908), 6h 01m 47.320s; **3** Rinaldo Capello/Tom Kristensen/Allan McNish, I/DK/GB (Audi R15), 6h 02m 05.227s; **4** Marc Gené/Alexander Wurz/Anthony Davidson, E/A/GB (Peugeot 908), 138 laps; **5** Timo Bernhard/Romain Dumas/Mike Rockenfeller, D/F/D (Audi R15), 137; **6** Miguel Pais do Amaral/Olivier Pla, P/F (Ginetta-Zytek 09S-Zytek), 130 (1st LMP2 class); **7** Tommy Erdos/Mike Newton/Andy Wallace, BR/GB/GB (Lola B08/80-HPD), 130; **8** Richard Hein/Guillaume Moreau, MC/F (Pescarolo 01-Judd), 129; **9** Mathieu Lahaye/Jacques Nicolet, F/F (Pescarolo 01-Judd), 128; **10** Ferdinando Geri/Andrea Piccini/Giacomo Piccini, I/I/I (Lola B09/80-Judd), 128.
Fastest race lap: Montagny/Sarrazin/Minassian, 1m 59.797s, 130.783 mph/210.476 km/h.
Pole position: Lamy/Bourdais/Pagenaud, 1m 57.884s, 132.906 mph/213.891 km/h.

1000 KM DO ALGARVE, Autódromo Internacional do Algarve, Portimão, Portugal, 17 July. Round 3. 215 laps of the 2.892-mile/4.655-km circuit, 621.884 miles/1000.825 km.
1 Olivier Panis/Nicolas Lapierre/Stéphane Sarrazin, F/F/F (Peugeot 908), 5h 48m 30.820s, 107.063 mph/172.301 km/h; **2** Nicolas Prost/Neel Jani, F/CH (Lola B10/60 Coupé-Rebellion), 210 laps; **3** Pierre Ragues/Franck Mailleux/Vanina Ickx, F/F/B (Lola B08/60-Aston Martin), 209; **4** Tommy Erdos/Mike Newton/Ben Collins, BR/GB/GB (Lola B08/80-HPD), 201; **5** Karim Ojjeh/Tim Greaves/Thor-Christian Ebbesvik, SA/GB/N (Ginetta-Zytek 09S-Zytek), 193; **6** Jody Firth/Warren Hughes, GB/GB (Oreca FLM 09), 193; **7** Gianmaria Bruni/Jaime Melo Jr., I/BR (Ferrari 430 GT2), 192; **8** Andrea Barlesi/Alessandro Cicognani/Gary Chalandon, I/I/F (Oreca FLM 09), 191; **9** Giancarlo Fisichella/Toni Vilander/Jean Alesi, I/FIN/F (Ferrari 430 GT2), 191; **10** Marc Lieb/Richard Lietz, D/A (Porsche 997 GT3 RSR), 191.
Fastest race lap: Panis/Lapierre/Sarrazin, 1m 32.375s, 112.724 mph/181.412 km/h.
Pole position: Panis/Lapierre/Sarrazin, 1m 30.681s, 114.830 mph/184.801 km/h.

LE MANS SERIES, Hungaroring, Mogyorod, Budapest, Hungary, 22 August. Round 4. 206 laps of the 2.722-mile/4.381-km circuit, 560.779 miles/902.486 km.
1 Nick Leventis/Danny Watts/Jonny Kane, GB/GB/GB (HPD ARX-01c), 6h 01m 02.752s, 93.192 mph/149.978 km/h; **2** Miguel Pais do Amaral/Olivier Pla, P/F (Ginetta-Zytek 09S-Zytek), 205 laps; **3** Mathieu Lahaye/Jacques Nicolet, F/F (Pescarolo 01-Judd), 204; **4** Tommy Erdos/Mike Newton/Ben Collins, BR/GB/GB (Lola B08/80-HPD), 202; **5** Karim Ojjeh/Tim Greaves/Thor-Christian Ebbesvik, SA/GB/N (Ginetta-Zytek 09S-Zytek), 201; **6** Piergiuseppe Perazzini/Marco Cioci/Luca Pirri Ardizzone, I/I/I (Lola B09/80-Judd), 200; **7** Greg Mansell/Leo Mansell, GB/GB (Ginetta-Zytek 09S-Zytek), 199; **8** Nicolas Prost/Neel Jani, F/CH (Lola B10/60 Coupé-Rebellion), 193; **9** Richard Hein/Guillaume Moreau, MC/F (Pescarolo 01-Judd), 192; **10** Marc Lieb/Richard Lietz, D/A (Porsche 997 GT3 RSR), 192.
Fastest race lap: Olivier Panis/Nicolas Lapierre/Stéphane Sarrazin, F/F/F (Peugeot 908), 1m 34.934s, 103.229 mph/166.132 km/h.
Pole position: Leventis/Watts/Kane, 1m 32.431s, 106.025 mph/170.631 km/h.

AUTOSPORT 1000 KM OF SILVERSTONE, Silverstone Grand Prix Circuit, Towcester, Northamptonshire, Great Britain, 12 September. Round 5. 170 laps of the 3.660-mile/5.891-km circuit, 622.285 miles/1001.470 km.
1 Anthony Davidson/Nicolas Minassian, GB/F (Peugeot 908), 5h 11m 41.835s, 119.786 mph/192.777 km/h; **2** Nicolas Lapierre/Stéphane Sarrazin, F/F (Peugeot 908), 5h 12m 24.755s; **3** Timo Bernhard/Rinaldo Capello, D/I (Audi R15-Plus), 5h 13m 28.192s; **4** Juan Barazi/Sam Hancock/Stefan Mücke, DK/GB/D (Lola B09/60-Aston Martin), 167 laps; **5** Nicolas Prost/Neel Jani, F/CH (Lola B10/60 Coupé-Rebellion), 165; **6** Pierre Ragues/Franck Mailleux/Vanina Ickx, F/F/B (Lola B09/60-Aston Martin), 164; **7** Leo Mansell/Greg Mansell, GB/GB (Ginetta-Zytek 09S-Zytek), 161; **8** Nick Leventis/Danny Watts/Jonny Kane, GB/GB/GB (HPD ARX-01c), 160; **9** Miguel Pais do Amaral/Olivier Pla, P/F (Ginetta-Zytek 09S-Zytek), 160; **10** Richard Hein/Guillaume Moreau, MC/F (Pescarolo 01-Judd), 160.
Fastest race lap: Lapierre/Sarrazin, 1m 44.338s, 126.299 mph/203.258 km/h.
Pole position: Tom Kristensen/Allan McNish, DK/GB (Audi R15-Plus), 1m 43.475s, 127.352 mph/204.953 km/h.

Final championship points
LM P1 Drivers: 1 Stéphane Sarrazin, F, 78; **2** Nicolas Lapierre, F, 63; **3** Rinaldo Capello, I, 57; **4** Vanina Ickx/Franck Mailleux/Pierre Ragues, B/F/F, 55; **5** Neel Jani/Nicolas Prost, CH/F, 52; **6** Allan McNish, GB, 45; **7** Andrea Belicchi/Jean-Christophe Boullion, I/F, 44; **8** Olivier Panis, F, 39; **9** Stefan Mücke, D, 38; **10** Leo Mansell/Greg Mansell, GB/GB, 34.
LMP 2 Drivers: 1 Tommy Erdos/Mike Newton, BR/GB, 75; **2** Nick Leventis/Jonny Kane/Danny Watts, GB/GB/GB, 69; **3** Jacques Nicolet/Mathieu Lahaye, F/F, 53; **4** Guillaume Moreau/Richard Hein, F/MC, 52.
GT1 Drivers:1 Gabriele Gardel/Patrice Goueslard, CH/F, 97; **2** Fernando Rees, BR, 64; **3** Julien Canal, F, 33.
GT2 Drivers: 1 Marc Lieb/Richard Lietz, D/A, 87; **2** Giancarlo Fisichella/Toni Vilander, I/FIN, 66; **2** Jean Alesi, F, 66; **3** Christian Ried/Martin Ragginger, D/A, 55.
Formula Le Mans Drivers: 1 Gary Chalandon/Andrea Barlesi,F/I, 59; **2** Steve Zacchia, CH, 57; **3** Alessandro Cicognani, I, 46; **4** Luca Moro, I, 44.
LM P1 Manufacturers: 1 Peugeot, 112; **2** Lola B10/60 – Rebellion, 96; **3** Lola Aston Martin, 93; **4** Audi, 67; **5** Ginetta Zytek, 40; **6** Oreca AIM, 17; **7** Lola Coupé Judd, 7.
LM P2 Manufacturers: 1 Pescarolo – Judd, 105; **2** Ginetta Zytek, 90; **3** Lola HPD, 74,
LM GT1 Manufacturers: 1 Saleen, 121; **2** Ford – Matech, 33; **3** Corvette, 10.
LM GT2 Manufacturers: 1 Porsche, 159; **2** Ferrari, 156; **3** Spyker, 38.
LM P1 Teams: 1 Team Oreca Matmut (no. 4), 63; **2** Signature Plus (no. 008), 55; **3** Rebellion Racing (no. 12), 52.
LM P2 Teams: 1 RML (no. 25), 75; **2** Strakka Racing (no. 42), 69; **3** OAK Racing (no. 24), 53.
LM GT1 Teams: 1 Larbre Competition (no. 50), 97; **2** Atlas EFX-Team FS (no. 66); **3** Marc VDS Racing (no. 70), 18.
LM GT2 Teams: 1 Team Felbermayr Proton (no. 77), 87; **2** AF Corse (no. 95), 66; **3** AF Corse (no. 96), 59.
Formula Le Mans Teams: 1 DAMS (no. 43), 59; **2** Hope Polevision Racing (no. 47), 57; **3** Boutsen Energy Racing (no. 45), 41.

American Le Mans Series

58th MOBIL 1 TWELVE HOURS OF SEBRING, Sebring International Raceway, Florida, USA, 20 March. Round 1. 367 laps of the 3.700-mile/5.955-km circuit, 1357.900 miles/2185.328 km.
1 Marc Gené/Alexander Wurz/Anthony Davidson, E/A/GB (Peugeot 908), 12h 00m 54.362s, 113.016 mph/181.881 km/h (1st P1 class); **2** Pedro Lamy/Sébastien Bourdais/Nicolas Minassian, P/F/F (Peugeot 908), 12h 01m 08.179s; **3** Stefan Mücke/Harold Primat/Adrián Fernández, D/CH/MEX (Lola B09/60-Aston Martin), 364 laps; **4** Greg Pickett/Klaus Graf/Sascha Maassen, USA/D/D (Porsche RS Spyder Evo), 353 (1st P2 class); **5** David Brabham/Simon Pagenaud/Marino Franchitti, AUS/F/GB (HPD ARX-01c), 349; **6** Jaime Melo Jr./Gianmaria Bruni/Pierre Kaffer, BR/I/D (Ferrari 430 GT2), 331 (1st GT2 class); **7** Bill Auberlen/Tom Milner/Dirk Werner, USA/USA/D (BMW M3 E92), 330; **8** Dirk Müller/Joey Hand/Andy Priaulx, D/USA/GB (BMW M3 E92), 330; **9** Jörg Bergmeister/Patrick Long/Marc Lieb, D/USA/D (Porsche 997 GT3 RSR), 329; **10** Scott Tucker/Christophe Bouchut/Mark Wilkins, USA/F/CDN (Oreca FLM 09), 327 (1st PC class).
Fastest race lap: Bourdais, 1m 44.972s, 126.890 mph/204.211 km/h.
Pole position: Gené/Wurz/Davidson, 1m 45.214s, 126.599 mph/203.741 km/h.

TEQUILA PATRÓN ALMS AT LONG BEACH, Long Beach Street Circuit, California, USA, 17 April. Round 2. 67 laps of the 1.968-mile/3.167-km circuit, 131.856 miles/212.202 km.
1 David Brabham/Simon Pagenaud, AUS/F (HPD ARX-01c), 1h 40m 47.723s, 78.489 mph/126.316 km/h; **2** Adrián Fernández/Harold Primat, MEX/CH (Lola B09/60-Aston Martin), 1h 40m 48.076s; **3** Greg Pickett/Klaus Graf, USA/D (Porsche RS Spyder Evo), 1h 40m 57.195s; **4** Chris Dyson/Guy Smith, USA/GB (Lola B09/86-Mazda), 1h 40m 58.626s; **5** Gunnar Jeannette/Elton Julian, USA/USA (Oreca FLM 09), 66 laps; **6** Scott Tucker/Christophe Bouchut, USA/F (Oreca FLM 09), 65; **7** Tom Sutherland/J.R. Hildebrand, USA/USA (Oreca FLM 09), 65; **8** Jörg Bergmeister/Patrick Long, D/USA (Porsche 997 GT3 RSR), 65; **9** Tomy Drissi/Ken Davis, USA/USA (Lola B06/10-AER), 65; **10** Jan Magnussen/Johnny O'Connell, DK/USA (Chevrolet Corvette C6.R), 65.
Fastest race lap: Pagenaud, 1m 14.124s, 95.580 mph/153.821 km/h.
Pole position: Fernández/Primat, 1m 13.213s, 96.769 mph/155.735 km/h.

AMERICAN LE MANS SERIES, Mazda Raceway Laguna Seca, Monterey, California, USA, 22 May. Round 3. 237 laps of the 2.238-mile/3.602-km circuit, 530.406 miles/853.606 km.
1 David Brabham/Simon Pagenaud/Marino Franchitti, AUS/F/GB (HPD ARX-01c), 6h 00m 09.654s, 88.361 mph/142.204 km/h; **2** Greg Pickett/Klaus Graf/Sascha Maassen, USA/D/D (Porsche RS Spyder Evo), 230 laps; **3** Scott Tucker/Christophe Bouchut/Mark Wilkins, USA/F/CDN (Oreca FLM 09), 229; **4** Tom Sutherland/Tom Weickardt/Kyle Marcelli, USA/USA/CDN (Oreca FLM 09),

229; **5** Jörg Bergmeister/Patrick Long, D/USA (Porsche 997 GT3 RSR), 227; **6** Dirk Müller/Joey Hand, D/USA (BMW M3 E92), 227; **7** Olivier Beretta/Oliver Gavin, MC/GB (Chevrolet Corvette C6.R), 227; **8** Jaime Melo Jr./Gianmaria Bruni, BR/I (Ferrari 430 GT2), 225; **9** Scott Sharp/Johannes van Overbeek, USA/USA (Ferrari 430 GT2), 225; **10** Jan Magnussen/Johnny O'Connell, DK/USA (Chevrolet Corvette C6.R), 224.
Fastest race lap: Smith, 1m 14.262s, 108.491 mph/174.600 km/h.
Pole position: Chris Dyson/Guy Smith/Andrew Meyrick, USA/GB/GB (Lola B09/86-Mazda), 1m 12.338s, 111.377 mph/179.244 km/h.

LARRY H. MILLER DEALERSHIPS UTAH GRAND PRIX, Miller Motorsports Park, Tooele, Utah, USA, 11 July. Round 4. 91 laps of the 3.048-mile/4.905-km circuit, 277.368 miles/446.381 km.
1 David Brabham/Simon Pagenaud, AUS/F (HPD ARX-01c), 2h 45m 43.162s, 100.423 mph/161.615 km/h; **2** Jonathan Cocker/Emanuele Pirro, GB/I (Lola B09/60-Judd), 2h 46m 02.278s; **3** Greg Pickett/Klaus Graf, USA/D (Porsche RS Spyder Evo), 2h 47m 13.536s; **4** Jon Field/Clint Field, USA/USA (Lola B06/10-AER), 88 laps; **5** Scott Tucker/Christophe Bouchut, USA/F (Oreca FLM 09), 86; **6** Gunnar Jeannette/Christian Zugel, USA/USA (Oreca FLM 09), 85; **7** Alex Figge/Max Hyatt, USA/USA (Oreca FLM 09), 85; **8** Scott Tucker/Andy Wallace, USA/GB (Oreca FLM 09), 85; **9** Jaime Melo Jr./Gianmaria Bruni, BR/I (Ferrari 430 GT2), 85; **10** Bill Auberlen/Tom Milner, USA/USA (BMW M3 E92), 85.
Fastest race lap: Pirro, 1m 36.291s, 113.954 mph/183.392 km/h.
Pole position: Brabham/Pagenaud, 1m 34.350s, 116.298 mph/187.164 km/h.

AMERICAN LE MANS NORTHEAST GRAND PRIX, Lime Rock Park, Lakeville, Connecticut, USA, 24 July. Round 5. 171 laps of the 1.500-mile/2.414-km circuit, 256.500 miles/412.797 km.
1 Greg Pickett/Klaus Graf, USA/D (Porsche RS Spyder Evo), 2h 45m 04.386s, 93.231 mph/150.041 km/h; **2** David Brabham/Simon Pagenaud, AUS/F (HPD ARX-01c), 2h 45m 32.196s; **3** Gunnar Jeannette/Elton Julian, USA/USA (Oreca FLM 09), 162 laps (DNF-not running); **4** Tom Papadopoulos/Alex Figge, USA/USA (Oreca FLM 09), 162; **5** Jörg Bergmeister/Patrick Long, D/USA (Porsche 997 GT3 RSR), 161; **6** Bill Auberlen/Tom Milner, USA/USA (BMW M3 E92), 161; **7** Dirk Müller/Joey Hand, D/USA (BMW M3 E92), 161; **8** Mika Salo/Pierre Kaffer, FIN/D (Ferrari 430 GT2), 160; **9** Olivier Beretta/Oliver Gavin, MC/GB (Chevrolet Corvette C6.R), 159; **10** Scott Tucker/Andy Wallace, USA/GB (Oreca FLM 09), 158.
Fastest race lap: Brabham, 50.056s, 107.879 mph/173.614 km/h.
Pole position: Brabham/Pagenaud, 58.106s, 92.933 mph/149.562 km/h.

ACURA SPORTS CAR CHALLENGE, Mid-Ohio Sports Car Course, Lexington, Ohio, USA, 7 August. Round 6. 119 laps of the 2.258-mile/3.634-km circuit, 268.702 miles/432.434 km.
1 Chris Dyson/Guy Smith, USA/GB (Lola B09/86-Mazda), 2h 45m 17.657s, 97.535 mph/156.968 km/h; **2** David Brabham/Simon Pagenaud, AUS/F (HPD ARX-01c), 2h 45m 18.163s; **3** Scott Tucker/Christophe Bouchut, USA/F (Oreca FLM 09), 115 laps; **4** Bryan Willman/Tomy Drissi, USA/USA (Lola B06/10-AER), 114; **5** Ricardo Gonzalez/Luis Diaz, MEX/MEX (Oreca FLM 09), 114; **6** Gunnar Jeannette/Elton Julian, USA/USA (Oreca FLM 09), 113; **7** Brian Wong/Kyle Marcelli, USA/CDN (Oreca FLM 09), 113; **8** Scott Tucker/Andy Wallace, USA/GB (Oreca FLM 09), 113; **9** Jaime Melo Jr./Gianmaria Bruni, BR/I (Ferrari 430 GT2), 112; **10** Olivier Beretta/Oliver Gavin, MC/GB (Chevrolet Corvette C6.R), 112.
Fastest race lap: Pagenaud, 1m 12.463s, 112.178 mph/180.534 km/h.
Pole position: Paul Drayson/Jonathan Cocker, GB/GB (Lola B09/60-Judd), 1m 10.034s, 116.069 mph/186.795 km/h.

TIME WARNER CABLE ROAD RACE SHOWCASE, Road America, Elkhart Lake, Wisconsin, USA, 22 August. Round 7. 69 laps of the 4.048-mile/6.515-km circuit, 279.312 miles/449.509 km.
1 Paul Drayson/Jonathan Cocker, GB/GB (Lola B09/60-Judd), 2h 45m 15.756s, 101.406 mph/163.198 km/h; **2** Klaus Graf/Timo Bernhard, D/D (Porsche RS Spyder Evo), 2h 45m 16.807s; **3** David Brabham/Simon Pagenaud, AUS/F (HPD ARX-01c), 2h 45m 20.671s; **4** Chris Dyson/Guy Smith, USA/GB (Lola B09/86-Mazda), 2h 45m 21.818s; **5** Gunnar Jeannette/Elton Julian, USA/USA (Oreca FLM 09), 67 laps; **6** Ricardo Gonzalez/Luis Diaz, MEX/MEX (Oreca FLM 09), 67; **7** Dirk Müller/Joey Hand, D/USA (BMW M3 E92), 66; **8** Jörg Bergmeister/Patrick Long, D/USA (Porsche 997 GT3 RSR), 66; **9** Olivier Beretta/Oliver Gavin, MC/GB (Chevrolet Corvette C6.R), 66; **10** Jan Magnussen/Johnny O'Connell, DK/USA (Chevrolet Corvette C6.R), 66.
Fastest race lap: Cocker, 1m 52.420s, 129.628 mph/208.616 km/h.
Pole position: Drayson/Cocker, 1m 49.554s, 133.019 mph/214.073 km/h.

MOBIL 1 PRESENTS GRAND PRIX OF MOSPORT, Mosport International Raceway, Bowmanville, Ontario, Canada, 29 August. Round 8. 99 laps of the 2.459-mile/3.957-km circuit, 243.441 miles/391.780 km.
1 Klaus Graf/Romain Dumas, D/F (Porsche RS Spyder Evo), 2h 19m 01.795s, 105.059 mph/169.077 km/h; **2** David Brabham/Simon Pagenaud, AUS/F (HPD ARX-01c), 2h 19m 06.415s; **3** Tony Burgess/Johnny Mowlem, CDN/GB (Lola B06/10-AER), 98 laps; **4** Gunnar Jeannette/Elton Julian, USA/USA (Oreca FLM 09), 95; **5** Scott Tucker/Christophe Bouchut, USA/F (Oreca FLM 09), 95; **6** Paul Drayson/Jonathan Cocker, GB/GB (Lola B09/60-Judd), 95; **7** Chris Dyson/Guy Smith, USA/GB (Lola B09/86-Mazda), 94; **8** Christian Zugel/Frankie Montecalvo, USA/USA (Oreca FLM 09), 93; **9** Scott Tucker/Andy Wallace, USA/GB (Oreca FLM 09), 93; **10** Ricardo Gonzalez/Luis Diaz, MEX/MEX (Oreca FLM 09), 92.
Fastest race lap: Cocker, 1m 07.962s, 130.255 mph/209.625 km/h.
Pole position: Graf/Dumas, 1m 06.956s, 132.212 mph/212.774 km/h.

PETIT LE MANS, Road Atlanta Motorsports Center, Braselton, Georgia, USA, 2 October. Round 9. 394 laps of the 2.540-mile/4.088-km circuit, 1000.760 miles/1610.567 km.
1 Pedro Lamy/Franck Montagny/Stéphane Sarrazin, P/F/F (Peugeot 908), 9h 10m 43.451s, 109.030 mph/175.467 km/h; **2** Marc Gené/Alexander Wurz/Anthony Davidson, E/A/GB (Peugeot 908), 9h 11m 45.132s; **3** Rinaldo Capello/Tom Kristensen/Allan McNish, I/DK/GB (Audi R15-Plus), 392 laps; **4** David Brabham/Simon Pagenaud/Marino Franchitti, AUS/F/GB (HPD ARX-01c), 383; **5** Jon Field/Clint Field/Ben Devlin, USA/USA/GB (Lola B06/10-AER), 383; **6** Marcel Fässler/André Lotterer/Benoît Treluyer, CH/D/F (Audi R15-Plus), 377; **7** Klaus Graf/Sascha Maassen/Lucas Luhr, D/D/D (Porsche RS Spyder Evo), 372; **8** Paul Drayson/Jonathan Cocker/Emanuele Pirro, GB/GB/I (Lola B09/60-Judd), 369; **9** Jacques Nicolet/Frédéric Da Rocha/Patrice Lafargue, F/F/F (Pescarolo 01-Judd), 359; **10** Oliver Gavin/Jan Magnussen/Emmanuel Collard, GB/DK/F (Chevrolet Corvette C6.R), 355.
Fastest race lap: Montagny, 1m 07.948s, 134.573 mph/216.575 km/h.
Pole position: Gené/Wurz/Davidson, 1m 07.187s, 136.097 mph/219.028 km/h.

Final championship points
LMP Drivers: 1 Simon Pagenaud/David Brabham, F/AUS, 182; **2** Klaus Graf, D, 162; **3** Jonathan Cocker, GB, 110; **4** Chris Dyson, USA, 98; **5** Paul Drayson, GB, 94; **6** Guy Smith, GB, 92; **7** Marino Franchitti, GB, 81; **8** Greg Pickett, USA, 79; **9** Sascha Maassen, D, 77; **10** Clint Field, USA, 69.
LMPC Drivers: 1 Scott Tucker, USA, 183; **2** Gunnar Jeannette, USA, 169; **3** Elton Julian, USA, 153; **4** Christophe Bouchut, F, 147; **5** Kyle Marcelli, CDN, 101.
GT Drivers: 1 Patrick Long/Jörg Bergmeister, USA/D, 157; **2** Gianmaria Bruni, I, 140; **3** Bill Auberlen/Tom Milner, USA/USA, 125.
GTC Drivers: 1 Tim Pappas/Jeroen Bleekemolen, NL/NL, 146; **2** Shane Lewis, USA, 126; **3** Andy Lally, USA, 113.
LMP Chassis Manufacturers: 1 Honda Performance Development, 182; **2** Lola, 173; **3** Porsche, 162.
GT Automobile Manufacturers: 1 BMW, 158; **2** Porsche, 157; **3** Ferrari, 155.
LMP Engine Manufacturers: 1 Honda Performance Development, 182; **2** Porsche, 162; **3** AER, 112.

Asian Le Mans Series

ASIAN LE MANS SERIES, Okayama International Circuit (TI Circuit Aida), Aida Gun, Okayama Prefecture, Japan, 31 October/1 November. 126 and 128 laps of the 2.301-mile/3.703-km circuit.
Race 1 (289.918 miles/466.578 km).
1 Christophe Tinseau/Shinji Nakano, F/J (Pescarolo 01-Judd), 3h 00m 24.018s, 96.424 mph/155.180 km/h; **2** Nicolas Lapierre/Loïc Duval, F/F (Courage-Oreca LC70-AIM), 3h 00m 30.948s; **3** Stefan Mücke/Harold Primat, D/CH (Lola B09/60-Aston Martin), 124 laps; **4** Oliver Jarvis/Christian Bakkerud, GB/DK (Audi R10), 124; **5** Matteo Cressoni/Hideki Noda/Christijan Albers, I/J/NL (Audi R10), 122; **6** Paul Drayson/Jonathan Cocker, GB/GB (Lola B09/60-Judd), 121; **7** Jacques Nicolet/Richard Hein/Mathieu Lahaye, F/MC/F (Pescarolo 01-Mazda), 116; **8** Damien Toulemonde/Frédéric Da Rocha/José Ibanez, F/F/F (Courage LC75-AER), 116; **9** Shigekazu Wakisaka/Shogo Mitsuyama, J/J (Courage-Oreca LC70-YGK), 115; **10** Atsushi Yogo/Hiroyuki Iiri, J/J (Lamborghini Murcielago), 113.
Fastest race lap: Cocker, 1m 21.735s, 101.344 mph/163.097 km/h.
Pole position: Drayson/Cocker, 1m 19.143s, 104.663 mph/168.439 km/h.

Race 2 (294.520 miles/473.984 km).
1 Stefan Mücke/Harold Primat, D/CH (Lola B09/60-Aston Martin), 3h 01m 08.944s, 97.550 mph/156.992 km/h; **2** Christophe Tinseau/Shinji Nakano, F/J (Pescarolo 01-Judd), 3h 02m 09.121s; **3** Nicolas Lapierre/Loïc Duval, F/F (Courage-Oreca LC70-AIM), 3h 02m 17.423s; **4** Paul Drayson/Jonathan Cocker, GB/GB (Lola B09/60-Judd), 127 laps; **5** Oliver Jarvis/Christian Bakkerud, GB/DK (Audi R10), 127; **6** Matteo Cressoni/Hideki Noda/Christijan Albers, I/J/NL (Audi R10), 125; **7** Jacques Nicolet/Richard Hein/Mathieu Lahaye, F/MC/F (Pescarolo 01-Mazda), 118; **8** Akihiro Tsuzuki/Takeshi Tsuchiya, J/J (Aston Martin DBR9), 115; **9** Atsushi Yogo/Hiroyuki Iiri, J/J (Lamborghini Murcielago), 114; **10** Roland Berville/Stéphane Lemeret/Carlo van Dam, F/B/NL (Saleen S7R-Ford), 114.
Fastest race lap: Cocker, 1m 20.561s, 102.821 mph/165.474 km/h.
Pole position: Drayson/Cocker.

Final championship points
P1 Teams: 1 no.17 Sora Racing, 18; **2** no.007 Aston Martin Racing, 15; **3** no.10 Team ORECA Matmut AIM, 14; **4** no.15 Kolles, 10; **5** no.87 Drayson Racing, 9; **6** no.14 Kolles, 7; **7** no.11 Tokai University YGK Power, 2.
P2 Teams: 1 no.24 Oak Racing, 21; **2** no.28 Jose Ibanez, 16.
GT1 Teams: 1 no.69 JLOC, 18; **2** no.61 Hitotsuyama Team Nova, 15; **3** no.50 Larbre Competition, 14; **4** no.68 JLOC, 10.
GT2 Teams: 1 no.89 Hankook Team Farnbacher, 16; **2** no.92 Rahal Letterman Racing Team, 14; **3** no.88 Team Felbermayr-Proton, 13; **4** no.77 Team Felbermayr-Proton, 9; **5** no.71 Team Daishin, 9.

Super GT Series (Japan)

Cars are Nissan GT-R, Lexus SC430 and Honda HSV-010.

SUZUKA GT 300km, Suzuka International Racing Course, Ino-Cho, Suzuka-shi, Mie Prefecture, Japan, 21 March. Round 1. 52 laps of the 3.608-mile/5.807-km circuit, 187.632 miles/301.964 km.
1 João Paulo de Oliveira/Hironobu Yasuda, BR/J (Nissan), 1h 53m 23.333s, 99.285 mph/159.784 km/h; **2** Daisuke Ito/Björn Wirdheim, J/S (Lexus), 1h 53m 32.655s; **3** Takuya Izawa/Naoki Yamamoto, J/J (Honda), 1h 53m 38.730s; **4** Juichi Wakisaka/André Lotterer, J/D (Lexus), 1h 53m 41.287s; **5** André Couto/Kohei Hirate, P/J (Lexus), 1h 53m 42.659s; **6** Hiroaki Ishiura/Kazuya Oshima, J/J (Lexus), 1h 53m 43.696s; **7** Toshihiro Kaneishi/Koudai Tsukakoshi, J/J (Honda), 1h 54m 09.841s; **8** Satoshi Motoyama/Benoît Treluyer, J/F (Nissan), 1h 54m 55.666s; **9** Yuji Tachikawa/Richard Lyons, J/GB (Lexus), 51 laps; **10** Ryo Michigami/Yuki Nakayama, J/J (Honda), 51.
Fastest race lap: Kogure, 1m 55.555s, 112.413 mph/180.911 km/h.
Pole position: Takashi Kogure/Loïc Duval, J/F (Honda).

OKAYAMA GT300km, Okayama International Circuit (TI Circuit Aida), Aida Gun, Okayama Prefecture, Japan, 4 April. Round 2. 82 laps of the 2.301-mile/3.703-km circuit, 188.677 miles/303.646 km.
1 Takashi Kogure/Loïc Duval, J/F (Honda), 2h 02m 26.084s, 92.462 mph/148.803 km/h; **2** Yuji Tachikawa/Richard Lyons, J/GB (Lexus), 2h 02m 37.884s; **3** Juichi Wakisaka/André Lotterer, J/D (Lexus), 2h 02m 40.293s; **4** Tsugio Matsuda/Ronnie Quintarelli, J/I (Nissan), 2h 02m 40.796s; **5** Daisuke Ito/Björn Wirdheim, J/S (Lexus), 2h 03m 11.825s; **6** Ralph Firman/Yuji Ide, IRL/J (Honda), 2h 03m 14.750s; **7** Toshihiro Kaneishi/Koudai Tsukakoshi, J/J (Honda), 2h 03m 23.369s; **8** Takuya Izawa/Naoki Yamamoto, J/J (Honda), 2h 03m 37.757s; **9** Hiroaki Ishiura/Kazuya Oshima, J/J (Lexus), 81 laps; **10** André Couto/Kohei Hirate, P/J (Lexus), 81.
Fastest race lap: Duval, 1m 26.647s, 95.599 mph/153.851 km/h.
Pole position: Kogure/Duval.

FUJI GT 400km, Fuji International Speedway, Sunto-gun, Shizuoka Prefecture, Japan, 2 May. Round 3. 88 laps of the 2.835-mile/4.563-km circuit, 249.508 miles/401.544 km.
1 Hiroaki Ishiura/Kazuya Oshima, J/J (Lexus), 2h 25m 00.795s, 103.235 mph/166.140 km/h; **2** Juichi Wakisaka/André Lotterer, J/D (Lexus), 2h 25m 05.536s; **3** Daisuke Ito/Björn Wirdheim, J/S (Lexus), 2h 25m 23.670s; **4** Yuji Tachikawa/Richard Lyons, J/GB (Lexus), 2h 25m 42.694s; **5** Toshihiro Kaneishi/Koudai Tsukakoshi, J/J (Honda), 2h 25m 52.482s; **6** Tsugio Matsuda/Ronnie Quintarelli, J/I (Nissan), 2h 26m 12.735s; **7** Takashi Kogure/Loïc Duval, J/F (Honda), 2h 26m 18.492s; **8** João Paulo de Oliveira/Hironobu Yasuda, BR/J (Nissan), 87 laps; **9** Ryo Michigami/Yuki Nakayama, J/J (Honda), 87; **10** Takuya Izawa/Naoki Yamamoto, J/J (Honda), 87.
Fastest race lap: Oshima, 1m 35.612s, 106.755 mph/171.806 km/h.
Pole position: Ishiura/Oshima.

SUPER GT INTERNATIONAL SERIES MALAYSIA, Sepang International Circuit, Jalan Pekeliling, Kuala Lumpur, Malaysia, 20 June. Round 4. 54 laps of the 3.444-mile/5.542-km circuit, 185.957 miles/299.268 km.
1 Tsugio Matsuda/Ronnie Quintarelli, J/I (Nissan), 1h 50m 54.084s, 100.606 mph/161.910 km/h; **2** Satoshi Motoyama/Benoît Treluyer, J/F (Nissan), 1h 51m 07.417s; **3** Takashi Kogure/Loïc Duval, J/F (Honda), 1h 51m 10.757s; **4** Daisuke Ito/Björn Wirdheim, J/S (Lexus), 1h 51m 22.326s; **5** Takuya Izawa/Naoki Yamamoto, J/J (Honda), 1h 51m 24.893s; **6** Yuji Tachikawa/Richard Lyons, J/GB (Lexus), 1h 51m 48.158s; **7** Hiroaki Ishiura/Kazuya Oshima, J/J (Lexus), 1h 51m 49.423s; **8** Juichi Wakisaka/André Lotterer, J/D (Lexus), 1h 52m 01.625s; **9** João Paulo de Oliveira/Hironobu Yasuda, BR/J (Nissan), 1h 52m 14.423s; **10** André Couto/Kohei Hirate, P/J (Lexus), 1h 52m 18.427s.
Fastest race lap: Treluyer, 1m 59.495s, 103.745 mph/166.962 km/h.
Pole position: Matsuda/Quintarelli.

SUGO GT 300km, Sportsland-SUGO International Course, Shibata-gun, Miyagi Prefecture, Japan, 25 July. Round 5. 81 laps of the 2.302-mile/3.704-km circuit, 186.426 miles/300.024 km.
1 Toshihiro Kaneishi/Koudai Tsukakoshi, J/J (Honda), 1h 50m 27.577s, 101.263 mph/162.968 km/h; **2** Takashi Kogure/Loïc Duval, J/F (Honda), 1h 50m 27.602s; **3** Daisuke Ito/Björn Wirdheim, J/S (Lexus), 1h 50m 40.210s; **4** Tsugio Matsuda/Ronnie Quintarelli, J/I (Nissan), 1h 50m 44.043s; **5** João Paulo de Oliveira/Hironobu Yasuda, BR/J (Nissan), 1h 51m 05.414s; **6** Satoshi Motoyama/Benoît Treluyer, J/F (Nissan), 1h 51m 23.696s; **7** Juichi Wakisaka/André Lotterer, J/D (Lexus), 1h 51m 41.880s; **8** Takuya Izawa/Naoki Yamamoto, J/J (Honda), 1h 51m 42.051s; **9** Yuji Tachikawa/Richard Lyons, J/GB (Lexus), 80 laps; **10** André Couto/Kohei Hirate, P/J (Lexus), 79.
Fastest race lap: Treluyer, 1m 17.691s, 106.648 mph/171.633 km/h.
Pole position: Motoyama/ Treluyer.

39th INTERNATIONAL POKKA GT SUMMER SPECIAL, Suzuka International Racing Course, Suzuka-shi, Mie Prefecture, Japan, 22 August. Round 6. 121 laps of the 3.608-mile/5.807-km circuit, 436.605 miles/702.647 km.
1 Ralph Firman/Yuji Ide/Takashi Kobayashi, IRL/J/J (Honda), 4h 07m 10.085s, 105.985 mph/170.567 km/h; **2** Satoshi Motoyama/Benoît Treluyer, J/F (Nissan), 4h 07m 32.397s; **3** Takuya Izawa/Naoki Yamamoto, J/J (Honda), 4h 07m 35.825s; **4** Toshihiro Kaneishi/Koudai Tsukakoshi, J/J (Honda), 4h 09m 01.246s; **5** Hiroaki Ishiura/Kazuya Oshima, J/J (Lexus), 4h 09m 07.990s; **6** Yuji Tachikawa/Richard Lyons, J/GB (Lexus), 120 laps; **7** Ryo Michigami/Yuki Nakayama, J/J (Honda), 120; **8** André Couto/Kohei Hirate, P/J (Lexus), 120; **9** Takashi Kogure/Loïc Duval, J/F (Honda), 120; **10** Juichi Wakisaka/André Lotterer, J/D (Lexus), 120.
Fastest race lap: Treluyer, 1m 57.676s, 110.386 mph/177.650 km/h.
Pole position: Firman/ Ide/Kobayashi.

MOTEGI GT 250km, Twin Ring Motegi, Motegi-machi, Haga-gun, Tochigi Prefecture, Japan, 24 October. Round 7. 53 laps of the 2.983-mile/4.801-km circuit, 158.120 miles/254.469 km.
1 Juichi Wakisaka/André Lotterer, J/D (Lexus), 1h 37m 19.525s, 97.478 mph/156.877 km/h; **2** Takashi Kogure/Loïc Duval, J/F (Honda), 1h 37m 20.251s; **3** Toshihiro Kaneishi/Koudai Tsukakoshi, J/J (Honda), 1h 37m 35.252s; **4** Hiroaki Ishiura/Kazuya Oshima, J/J (Lexus), 1h 37m 35.631s; **5** Tsugio Matsuda/Ronnie Quintarelli, J/I (Nissan), 1h 37m 52.251s; **6** Takuya Izawa/Naoki Yamamoto, J/J (Honda), 1h 37m 52.887s; **7** Ralph Firman/Yuji Ide, IRL/J (Honda), 1h 37m 56.148s; **8** Satoshi Motoyama/Benoît Treluyer, J/F (Nissan), 1h 38m 04.121s; **9** Ryo Michigami/Yuki Nakayama, J/J (Honda), 1h 38m 10.766s; **10** João Paulo de Oliveira/Hironobu Yasuda, BR/J (Nissan), 1h 38m 25.102s.
Fastest race lap: Duval, 1m 46.770s, 100.591 mph/161.887 km/h.
Pole position: Kogure/Duval.

Final championship points
GT500: 1 Takashi Kogure/Loïc Duval, J/F, 67; **2** André Lotterer/Juichi Wakisaka, D/J, 62; **3** Koudai Tsukakoshi/Toshihiro Kaneishi, J/J, 53; **4** Björn Wirdheim/Daisuke Ito, S/J, 51; **5** Ronnie Quintarelli/Tsugio Matsuda, I/J, 47; **6** Hiroaki Ishiura/Kazuya Oshima, J/J, 45; **7** Benoît Treluyer/Satoshi Motoyama, F/J, 41; **8** Naoki Yamamoto/Takuya Izawa, J/J, 40; **9** Richard Lyons/Yuji Tachikawa, GB/J, 37; **10** João Paulo de Oliveira/Hironobu Yasuda, BR/J, 32.
GT300: 1 Masataka Yanagida/Kazuki Hoshino, J/J, 64; **2** Morio Nitta/Shinichi Takagi, J/J, 55; **3** Nobuteru Taniguchi/Ryo Orime, J/J, 52.

Other Sports Car races

GRAND AMERICAN ROLEX SPORTS CAR, Daytona International Speedway, Daytona Beach, Florida, USA, 30 January. 755 laps of the 3.560-mile/5.729-km circuit, 2687.800 miles/4325.595 km (Grand-Am round 1).
1 João Barbosa/Terry Borcheller/Ryan Dalziel/Mike Rockenfeller, P/USA/GB/D (Riley-Porsche), 24h 00m 47.762s, 111.930 mph/180.134 km/h; **2** Massimiliano Papis/Scott Pruett/Memo Rojas/Justin Wilson, I/USA/MEX/GB (Riley-BMW), 24h 01m 40.065s; **3** Christophe Bouchut/Ryan Hunter-Reay/Lucas Luhr/Scott Tucker/Richard Westbrook, F/USA/D/USA/GB (Riley-BMW), 751 laps; **4** Colin Braun/Nic Jönsson/Tracy Krohn/Ricardo Zonta, USA/S/USA/BR (Lola-Ford), 735; **5** Burt Frisselle/Oswaldo Negri Jr./John Pew/Mark Wilkins, USA/BR/USA/CDN (Riley-Ford), 726; **6** Max Angelelli/Pedro Lamy/Ricky Taylor/Wayne Taylor, I/P/USA/ZA (Dallara-Ford), 711; **7** A.J. Allmendinger/Brian Frisselle/Mark Patterson/Michael Valiante, USA/USA/USA/CDN (Riley-Ford), 707; **8** Jonathan Bomarito/Nick Ham/David Haskell/Sylvain Tremblay, USA/USA/USA/USA (Mazda RX-8), 707; **9** Jörg Bergmeister/Patrick Long/Seth Neiman/Johannes van Overbeek, D/USA/USA/USA (Porsche 911 GT3 Cup), 703; **10** Ted Ballou/Kelly Collins/Pat Flanagan/Wolf Henzler/Andy Lally, USA/USA/USA/D/USA (Porsche 911 GT3 Cup), 691.
Fastest race lap: Angelelli/Lamy/Taylor (Ricky)/Taylor (Wayne), 1m 41.101s, 126.764 mph/204.007 km/h.
Pole position: Angelelli/Lamy/Taylor (Ricky)/Taylor (Wayne), 1m 40.681s, 127.293 mph/204.858 km/h.

ADAC-ZÜRICH-24h-RENNEN, Nürburgring Nordschleife Circuit, Nürburg/Eifel, Germany, 14-15 May. 154 laps of the 15.769-mile/25.378-km circuit, 2428.450 miles/ 3908.212 km.
1 Jörg Muller/Augusto Farfus Jr./Uwe Alzen/Pedro Lamy, D/BR/D/P Bmw M3 E92), 24h 00m 18.168s, 101.188 mph/162.847 km/h; **2** Dominik Farnbacher/Allan Simonsen/Leh Keen/Marco Seefried, D/DK/USA/D (Ferrari 430 GTC), 154 Laps; **3** Dennis Rostek/Luca Ludwig/Marc Bronzel/Markus Winkelhock, D/D/D/D (Audi R8 LMS), 153; **4** Marko Hartung/Patrick Söderlund/Edward Sandström/Martin Öhlin, D/S/S/S (BMW Z4 GT3), 152; **5** Christer Jöns/Sean Paul Breslin/Johannes Stuck/Kenneth Heyer, D/IRL/D/D (Audi R8 LMS), 152; **6** Jürgen Alzen/Dominik Schwager/Thomas Jäger/Sascha Bert, D/D/D/D (Porsche GT3 Cup S), 151; **7** Dirk Werner/Dirk Müller/Andy Priaulx/Dirk Adorf, D/D/GB/D (BMW M3 E92), 150; **8** Michael Zehe/Marco Schlep/Alexander Roloff/Mark Bullitt, D/D/D/USA (Porsche GT3 Cup S), 150; **9** Stefan Aust/Rudi Adams/Jochen Übler/Markus Grossmann, D/D/D/D (BMW Z4 GT3), 149; **10** Matthias Weiland/Rodney Forbes/Kai Riemer/David Horn, D/AUS/D/D (Porsche 997 GT3 Cup), 148.
Fastest race lap: Marc Lieb/Timo Bernhard/Romain Dumas/Marcel Tiemann, D/D/F/D (Porsche GT3 R), 8m 28.587s, 111.621 mph/ 179.636 km/h.
Pole position: Mattias Ekström/Oliver Jarvis/Timo Scheider/Marco Werner, S/GB/D/D (Audi R8), 8m 24.753s, 112.469 mph/181.001 km.h.

SPA 24 HOURS, Circuit de Spa-Francorchamps, Stavelot, Belgium, 29 July-1 August. 541 laps of the 4.352-mile/7.004-km circuit, 2354.477 miles/3789.164 km.
1 Jorg Bergmeister/Romain Dumas/Martin Ragginger/Wolf Henzler, D/F/A/D (Porsche 911 GT3-RSR), 24h 00m 27.341s, 98.108 mph/ 157.889 km/h (1st GT2 class); **2** Patrick Pilet/Raymond Narac/Patrick Long/Richard Lietz, F/F/USA/A (Porsche 911 GT3-RSR), 24h 01m 44.163s; **3** Dirk Muller/Dirk Werner/Dirk Adorf, D/D/D (BMW M3), 540 laps (1st GTN class); **4** Uwe Alzen/Jorg Muller/Pedro Lamy, D/D/P (BMW M3), 534; **5** Michael Waltrip/Nicola Cadei/Robert Kauffmann/Marco Cioci, USA/I/USA/I (Ferrari 430 GT), 519; **6** Jurgen Haring/Dimitrios Konstantinou/Aranaud Peyroles/Gilles Vannelet, D/D/F/F (Porsche 911 GT3-R), 518 (1st GT3 class); **7** Paul Van Splunteren/Nick Hommerson/Louis Machiels/Phil Bastiaans, NL/NL/B/NL (Porsche 911 GT3-RSR), 515; **8** Maxime Martin/Bas Leinders/Marc Duez, B/B/B (Ford GT), 512; **9** Richard Dean/Mark Blundell/Zak Brown/Eddie Cheever, GB/GB/USA/USA (Audi R8 LMS), 503; **10** Stefan Johansson/Alain Li/Mark Patterson/Emil Assentato, S/PRC/USA/USA (Audi R8 LMS), 501.
Fastest race lap: Muller (Dirk), 2m 21.430s, mph/178.281 km/h.
Pole position: Gianmaria Bruni/ Bert Longin/Eric van de Poele/Toni Vilander, I/B/B/FIN (Ferrari 430 GT), 2m 22.403s, 110.022 mph/ 177.063 km/h.

78th 24 HEURES DU MANS, Circuit International Du Mans, Les Raineries, Le Mans, France, 12-13 June. 397 laps of the 8.469-mile/13.629-km circuit, 3362.061 miles/5410.713 km.
1 Mike Rockenfeller/Timo Bernhard/Romain Dumas, D/D/F

(Audi R15-Plus), 24h 01m 23.694s, 139.950 mph/225.228 km/h (1st LMP1 class); **2** André Lotterer/Marcel Fässler/Benoît Treluyer, D/CH/F (Audi R15-Plus), 396 laps; **3** Tom Kristensen/Rinaldo Capello/Allan McNish, DK/I/GB (Audi R15-Plus), 394; **4** Soheil Ayari/Didier André/Andrew Meyrick, F/F/GB (Oreca 01-AIM), 369; **5** Nick Leventis/Danny Watts/Jonny Kane, GB/GB/GB (HPD ARX-01c), 367; **6** Harold Primat/Stefan Mücke/Adrián Fernández, CH/D/MEX (Lola B09/60-Aston Martin), 365; **7** Mathieu Lahaye/Guillaume Moreau/Jan Charouz, F/F/CZ (Pescarolo 01-Judd), 361 (1st LMP2 class); **8** Mike Newton/Tommy Erdos/Andy Wallace, GB/BR/GB (Lola B08/80-HPD), 358; **9** Jacques Nicolet/Richard Hein/Jean-François Yvon, F/MC/F (Pescarolo 01-Judd), 341; **10** Karim Ojjeh/Tim Greaves/Gary Chalandon, SA/GB/F (Ginetta-Zytek 09S-Zytek), 341; **11** Marc Lieb/Richard Lietz/Wolf Henzler, D/A/D (Porsche 997 GT3 RSR), 338 (1st GT2 class); **12** Dominik Farnbacher/Allan Simonsen/Leh Keen, D/DK/USA (Ferrari 430 GT2), 336; **13** Roland Berville/Julien Canal/Gabriele Gardel, F/F/CH (Saleen S7R-Ford), 331 (1st GT1 class); **14** Marco Holzer/Richard Westbrook/Timo Scheider, D/GB/D (Porsche 997 GT3 RSR), 327; **15** Stéphane Grégoire/Jérôme Policand/David Hart, F/F/NL (Chevrolet Corvette C6.R), 327; **16** Giancarlo Fisichella/Jean Alesi/Toni Vilander, I/F/FIN (Ferrari 430 GT2), 323; **17** Raymond Narac/Patrick Pilet/Patrick Long, F/F/USA (Porsche 997 GT3 RSR), 321; **18** Pierre Bruneau/Marc Rostan/Ralph Meichtry, F/F/CH (Radical SR9-Judd), 321; **19** Jörg Müller/Augusto Farfus Jr./Uwe Alzen, D/BR/D (BMW M3 E92), 320; **20** Miguel Pais do Amaral/Olivier Pla/Warren Hughes, P/F/GB (Ginetta-Zytek 09S-Zytek), 318; **21** Paul van Splunteren/Niek Hommerson/Louis Machiels, NL/NL/B (Porsche 997 GT3 RSR), 317; **22** Christoffer Nygaard/Tomas Enge/Peter Kox, DK/CZ/NL (Aston Martin DBR9), 311; **23** Philippe Salini/Stephane Salini/Tristan Gommendy, F/F/F (WR LMP2008-Zytek), 308; **24** Horst Felbermayr Sr./Horst Felbermayr Jr./Miroslav Konopka, A/A/SK (Porsche 997 GT3 RSR), 304; **25** David Brabham/Marino Franchitti/Marco Werner, AUS/GB/D (HPD ARX-01c), 296; **26** Jean de Pourtales/Hideki Noda/Jonathan Kennard, F/J/GB (Lola B08/47-Judd), 291; **27** Tom Coronel/Peter Dumbreck/Jeroen Bleekemolen, NL/GB/NL (Spyker C8 Laviolette GT2-R-Audi), 280; **28** Olivier Panis/Nicolas Lapierre/Loïc Duval, F/F/F (Peugeot 908), 373 (DNF-engine); **29** Darren Turner/Juan Barazi/Sam Hancock, GB/DK/GB (Lola B09/60-Aston Martin), 368 (DNF-engine); **30** Alexander Wurz/Marc Gené/Anthony Davidson, A/E/GB (Peugeot 908), 360 (DNF-engine); **31** Christian Bakkerud/Oliver Jarvis/Christijan Albers, DK/GB/NL (Audi R10), 331 (DNF-gearbox); **32** Pierre Ragues/Vanina Ickx/Franck Mailleux, F/B/F (Lola B09/60-Aston Martin), 302 (DNF-accident damage); **33** Nicolas Minassian/Stéphane Sarrazin/Franck Montagny, F/F/F (Peugeot 908), 264 (DNF-engine); **34** Oliver Gavin/Olivier Beretta/Emmanuel Collard, GB/MC/F (Chevrolet Corvette C6.R), 255 (DNF-engine); **35** Paul Drayson/Jonathan Cocker/Emanuele Pirro, GB/GB/I (Lola B09/60-Judd), 254; **36** Julien Jousse/Xavier Maassen/Patrice Goueslard, F/NL/F (Chevrolet Corvette C6.R), 238 (DNF-transmission); **37** Jan Magnussen/Johnny O'Connell/Antonio Garcia, DK/USA/E (Chevrolet Corvette C6.R), 225 (DNF-engine); **38** Tracy Krohn/Nic Jönsson/Eric van de Poele, USA/S/B (Ferrari 430 GT2), 197 (DNF-engine); **39** Scott Tucker/Manuel Rodrigues/Christophe Bouchut, USA/F/F (Audi R10), 182 (DNF-accident damage); **40** Nicolas Prost/Neel Jani/Marco Andretti, F/CH/USA (Lola B10/60 Coupé-Rebellion), 175 (DNF-gearbox); **41** Thomas Mutsch/Romain Grosjean/Jonathan Hirschi, D/F/CH (Ford GT), 171 (DNF-engine); **42** Andrea Belicchi/Jean-Christophe Boullion/Guy Smith, I/F/GB (Lola B10/60 Coupé-Rebellion), 143 (DNF-accident); **43** Atsushi Yogo/Koji Yamanishi/Hiroyuki Iiri, J/J/J (Lamborghini Murciélago R-SV), 138 (DNF-gearbox); **44** Jaime Melo Jr./Gianmaria Bruni/Pierre Kaffer, BR/I/D (Ferrari 430 GT2), 116 (DNF-gearbox); **45** Robert Bell/Tim Sugden/Bryce Miller, GB/GB/USA (Aston Martin V8 Vantage), 71 (DNF-accident); **46** Seth Neiman/Darren Law/Jörg Bergmeister, USA/CDN/D (Porsche 997 GT3 RSR), 61 (DNF-engine); **47** Natacha Gachnang/Rahel Frey/Cyndie Allemann, CH/CH/CH (Ford GT), 59 (DNF-engine/fire); **48** Luca Pirri Ardizzone/Marco Cioci/Piergiuseppe Perazzini, I/I/I (Lola B09/80-Judd), 57 (DNF-suspension); **49** Andy Priaulx/Dirk Müller/Dirk Werner, GB/D/D (BMW M3 E92), 53 (DNF-fuel sensor); **50** Julien Schell/Frédéric Da Rocha/David Zollinger, F/F/F (Norma M200-Judd), 40 (DNF-transmission); **51** Sébastien Bourdais/Pedro Lamy/Simon Pagenaud, F/P/F (Peugeot 908), 38 (DNF-suspension); **52** Eric De Doncker/Bas Leinders/Markus Palttala, B/B/FIN (Ford GT), 26 (DNF-accident); **53** Nigel Mansell/Greg Mansell/Leo Mansell, GB/GB/GB (Ginetta-Zytek 09S-Zytek), 4 (DNF-accident); **54** Paul Gentilozzi/Ryan Dalziel/Marc Goossens, USA/GB/B (Jaguar XKR-S), 4 (DNF-misfire); **55** Michael Lewis/Bryan Willman/Tony Burgess, USA/USA/CDN (Lola B06/10-AER), 1 (DNF-gearbox).

Did not start: Mika Salo/ Matias Russo/ Luis Perez Companc, FIN/ RA/ RA (Ferrari 430 GT) (accident).

Fastest race lap: Panis/Lapierre/Duval, 3m 19.074s, 153.145 mph/246.463 km/h.

Pole position: Bourdais/Lamy/Pagenaud, 3m 19.711s, 152.657 mph/245.677 km/h.

V8 Supercar Championship

2009

The following races were run after AUTOCOURSE 2009–2010 went to press.

BIG POND 300, Barbagallo Raceway Wanneroo, Perth, Western Australia, Australia, 21/22 November. Round 13. 42 and 84 laps of the 1.501-mile/2.415-km circuit.

Race 1 (63.026 miles/101.430 km).

1 Jamie Whincup, AUS (Ford Falcon FG), 41m 33.5350s, 90.992 mph/146.437 km/h; **2** Todd Kelly, AUS (Holden Commodore VE), 41m 45.6079s; **3** Mark Winterbottom, AUS (Ford Falcon FG), 41m 46.2628s; **4** James Courtney, AUS (Ford Falcon FG), 41m 53.0689s; **5** Will Davison, AUS (Holden Commodore VE), 42m 00.8186s; **6** Craig Lowndes, AUS (Ford Falcon FG), 42m 07.0906s; **7** Rick Kelly, AUS (Holden Commodore VE), 42m 12.1149s; **8** Greg Murphy, NZ (Holden Commodore VE), 42m 14.6409s; **9** Russell Ingall, AUS (Holden Commodore VE), 42m 15.5895s; **10** Steven Johnson, AUS (Ford Falcon FG), 42m 21.5166s.

Fastest race lap: Kelly, 56.6498s, 95.361 mph/153.469 km/h.

Pole position: Lowndes, 57.1862s, 94.466 mph/152.029 km/h.

Race 2 (126.051 miles/202.860 km).

1 Craig Lowndes, AUS (Ford Falcon FG), 1h 27m 42.4547s, 86.230 mph/138.774 km/h; **2** Steven Johnson, AUS (Ford Falcon FG), 1h 27m 53.6154s; **3** Garth Tander, AUS (Holden Commodore VE), 1h 27m 56.2563s; **4** Jamie Whincup, AUS (Ford Falcon FG), 1h 27m 56.5016s; **5** Russell Ingall, AUS (Holden Commodore VE), 1h 28m 03.1085s; **6** Jason Bright, AUS (Ford Falcon BF), 1h 28m 06.7945s; **7** Jason Bargwanna, AUS (Holden Commodore VE), 1h 28m 07.6654s; **8** Steven Richards, NZ (Ford Falcon FG), 1h 28m 10.7172s; **9** Cameron McConville, AUS (Holden Commodore VE), 1h 28m 13.6528s; **10** James Courtney, AUS (Ford Falcon FG), 1h 28m 13.8336s.

Fastest race lap: Michael Caruso, AUS (Holden Commodore VE), 57.3380s, 94.216 mph/151.627 km/h.

Pole position: Whincup, 57.1146s, 94.585 mph/152.220 km/h.

SYDNEY TELESTRA 500, Sydney Olympic Park Street Race, New South Wales, Australia, 5/6 December. Round 14. 2 x 74 laps of the 2.113-mile/3.400-km circuit.

Race 1 (156.337 miles/251.600 km).

1 Garth Tander, AUS (Holden Commodore VE), 2h 05m 49.8020s, 74.546 mph/119.971 km/h; **2** Mark Winterbottom, AUS (Ford Falcon FG), 2h 05m 52.6368s; **3** Jason Bright, AUS (Ford Falcon BF), 2h 05m 57.8859s; **4** Lee Holdsworth, AUS (Holden Commodore VE), 2h 05m 58.3116s; **5** Jamie Whincup, AUS (Ford Falcon FG), 2h 06m 00.4782s; **6** Michael Caruso, AUS (Holden Commodore VE), 2h 06m 08.4705s; **7** Jason Bargwanna, AUS (Holden Commodore VE), 2h 06m 10.3059s; **8** Steven Richards, NZ (Ford Falcon FG), 2h 06m 10.6254s; **9** Rick Kelly, AUS (Holden Commodore VE), 2h 06m 11.0878s; **10** Shane van Gisbergen, NZ (Ford Falcon FG), 2h 06m 21.0511s.

Fastest race lap: Holdsworth, 1m 30.8818s, 83.686 mph/134.680 km/h.

Pole position: Tander, 1m 29.8489s, 84.648 mph/136.228 km/h.

Race 2 (156.337 miles/251.600 km).

1 James Courtney, AUS (Ford Falcon FG), 2h 08m 16.0105s, 73.130 mph/117.692 km/h; **2** Michael Caruso, AUS (Holden Commodore VE), 2h 08m 19.9192s; **3** Mark Winterbottom, AUS (Ford Falcon FG), 2h 08m 26.6970s; **4** Russell Ingall, AUS (Holden Commodore VE), 2h 08m 29.2888s; **5** Fabian Coulthard, NZ (Ford Falcon FG), 2h 08m 30.9702s; **6** Shane van Gisbergen, NZ (Ford Falcon FG), 2h 08m 36.7798s; **7** Greg Murphy, NZ (Holden Commodore VE), 2h 08m 41.9143s; **8** Will Davison, AUS (Holden Commodore VE), 2h 08m 48.8577s; **9** Alex Davison, AUS (Ford Falcon FG), 2h 08m 58.8421s; **10** Steven Johnson, AUS (Ford Falcon FG), 2h 09m 29.1305s.

Fastest race lap: Lowndes, 1m 30.9782s, 83.597 mph/134.537 km/h.

Pole position: Holdsworth, 1m 29.3047s, 85.164 mph/137.058 km/h.

Final championship points

Drivers: **1** Jamie Whincup, AUS, 3349; **2** Will Davison, AUS, 3044; **3** Garth Tander, AUS, 2916; **4** Craig Lowndes, AUS, 2592; **5** Mark Winterbottom, AUS, 2414; **6** Steven Johnson, AUS, 2255; **7** James Courtney, AUS, 2192; **8** Rick Kelly, AUS, 2162; **9** Russell Ingall, AUS, 2048; **10** Lee Holdsworth, AUS, 2006; **11** Michael Caruso, AUS, 1977; **12** Shane van Gisbergen, NZ, 1970; **13** Steven Richards, NZ, 1780; **14** Jason Richards, NZ, 1756; **15** Fabian Coulthard, NZ, 1665; **16** Alex Davison, AUS, 1648; **17** Paul Dumbrell, AUS, 1627; **18** Todd Kelly, AUS, 1624; **19** Jason Bright, AUS, 1607; **20** Cameron McConville, AUS, 1565.

Teams: 1 Holden Racing Team, 5650; **2** Triple Eight Race Engineering, 5573; **3** Dick Johnson Racing, 4357.

2010

YAS V8 400, Yas Marina Circuit, Abu Dhabi, UAE, 19/20 February. Round 1. 2 x 43 laps of the 2.920-mile/4.700-km circuit.

Race 1 (125.579 miles/202.100 km).

1 Jamie Whincup, AUS (Holden Commodore VE), 1h 28m 04.434s, 85.550 mph/137.679 km/h; **2** Craig Lowndes, AUS (Holden Commodore VE), 1h 28m 05.373s; **3** Mark Winterbottom, AUS (Ford Falcon FG), 1h 28m 06.386s; **4** James Courtney, AUS (Ford Falcon FG), 1h 28m 16.312s; **5** Lee Holdsworth, AUS (Holden Commodore VE), 1h 28m 17.455s; **6** Shane van Gisbergen, NZ (Ford Falcon FG), 1h 28m 26.665s; **7** Paul Dumbrell, AUS (Ford Falcon FG), 1h 28m 28.098s; **8** Jonathon Webb, AUS (Ford Falcon FG), 1h 28m 35.704s; **9** Alex Davison, AUS (Ford Falcon FG), 1h 28m 39.734s; **10** Rick Kelly, AUS (Holden Commodore VE), 1h 28m 42.024s.

Fastest race lap: van Gisbergen, 1m 59.114s, 88.265 mph/142.048 km/h.

Pole position: Whincup, 1m 58.114s, 89.012 mph/143.251 km/h.

Race 2 (125.579 miles/202.100 km).

1 Jamie Whincup, AUS (Holden Commodore VE), 1h 27m 28.373s, 86.138 mph/138.625 km/h; **2** Mark Winterbottom, AUS (Ford Falcon FG), 1h 27m 32.435s; **3** Shane van Gisbergen, NZ (Ford Falcon FG), 1h 27m 40.204s; **4** Rick Kelly, AUS (Holden Commodore VE), 1h 27m 45.729s; **5** Craig Lowndes, AUS (Holden Commodore VE), 1h 27m 46.626s; **6** James Courtney, AUS (Ford Falcon FG), 1h 27m 59.924s; **7** Lee Holdsworth, AUS (Holden Commodore VE), 1h 28m 03.837s; **8** Steven Johnson, AUS (Ford Falcon FG), 1h 28m 03.992s; **9** Russell Ingall, AUS (Holden Commodore VE), 1h 28m 07.763s; **10** Jason Bright, AUS (Holden Commodore VE), 1h 28m 10.466s.

Fastest race lap: van Gisbergen, 1m 58.737s, 88.545 mph/142.499 km/h.

Pole position: Winterbottom, 1m 58.037s, 89.070 mph/143.344 km/h.

DESERT 400, Bahrain International Circuit, Sakhir, Bahrain, 26/27 February. Round 2. 2 x 37 laps of the 3.363-mile/5.412-km circuit.

Race 1 (124.426 miles/200.244 km).

1 Jamie Whincup, AUS (Holden Commodore VE), 1h 21m 37.4276s, 91.462 mph/147.195 km/h; **2** Mark Winterbottom, AUS (Ford Falcon FG), 1h 21m 40.8428s; **3** Craig Lowndes, AUS (Holden Commodore VE), 1h 21m 49.2215s; **4** Garth Tander, AUS (Holden Commodore VE), 1h 21m 50.8473s; **5** Shane van Gisbergen, NZ (Ford Falcon FG), 1h 22m 03.5046s; **6** James Courtney, AUS (Ford Falcon FG), 1h 22m 04.8363s; **7** Russell Ingall, AUS (Holden Commodore VE), 1h 22m 15.8139s; **8** Will Davison, AUS (Holden Commodore VE), 1h 22m 17.0904s; **9** Rick Kelly, AUS (Holden Commodore VE), 1h 22m 20.5786s; **10** Michael Caruso, AUS (Holden Commodore VE), 1h 22m 21.4866s.

Fastest race lap: Whincup, 2m 07.5480s, 94.915 mph/152.751 km/h.

Pole position: Whincup, 2m 04.5189s, 97.224 mph/156.467 km/h.

Race 2 (124.426 miles/200.244 km).

1 Jamie Whincup, AUS (Holden Commodore VE), 1h 21m 06.4169s, 92.045 mph/148.133 km/h; **2** Mark Winterbottom, AUS (Ford Falcon FG), 1h 21m 11.2673s; **3** Shane van Gisbergen, NZ (Ford Falcon FG), 1h 21m 23.5424s; **4** Rick Kelly, AUS (Holden Commodore VE), 1h 21m 24.9421s; **5** Lee Holdsworth, AUS (Holden Commodore VE), 1h 21m 31.4192s; **6** Will Davison, AUS (Holden Commodore VE), 1h 21m 31.7058s; **7** James Courtney, AUS (Ford Falcon FG), 1h 21m 36.7812s; **8** Jason Richards, NZ (Holden Commodore VE), 1h 21m 40.9443s; **9** Michael Caruso, AUS (Holden Commodore VE), 1h 21m 41.1803s; **10** Paul Dumbrell, AUS (Ford Falcon FG), 1h 21m 41.7746s.

Fastest race lap: van Gisbergen, 2m 06.9097s, 95.393 mph/153.520 km/h.

Pole position: Whincup, 2m 05.3684s, 96.565 mph/155.407 km/h.

CLIPSAL 500, Adelaide Steet Circuit, South Australia, Australia, 13/14 March. Round 3. 2 x 78 laps of the 2.001-mile/3.220-km circuit.

Race 1 (156.064 miles/251.160 km).

1 Garth Tander, AUS (Holden Commodore VE), 1h 59m 06.5574s, 78.615 mph/126.519 km/h; **2** James Courtney, AUS (Ford Falcon FG), 1h 59m 10.5994s; **3** Lee Holdsworth, AUS (Holden Commodore VE), 1h 59m 12.9954s; **4** Jamie Whincup, AUS (Holden Commodore VE), 1h 59m 15.4375s; **5** Paul Dumbrell, AUS (Ford Falcon FG), 1h 59m 15.7080s; **6** Jason Bright, AUS (Holden Commodore VE), 1h 59m 21.3300s; **7** Fabian Coulthard, NZ (Holden Commodore VE), 1h 59m 22.0990s; **8** Michael Caruso, AUS (Holden Commodore VE), 1h 59m 22.5547s; **9** Will Davison, AUS (Holden Commodore VE), 1h 59m 23.1838s; **10** Russell Ingall, AUS (Holden Commodore VE), 1h 59m 30.4843s.

Fastest race lap: Courtney, 1m 22.3924s, 87.422 mph/140.692 km/h.

Pole position: Whincup, 1m 21.5887s, 88.283 mph/142.078 km/h.

Race 2 (156.064 miles/251.160 km).

1 Garth Tander, AUS (Holden Commodore VE), 1h 58m 01.9244s, 79.332 mph/127.673 km/h; **2** James Courtney, AUS (Ford Falcon FG), 1h 58m 02.9009s; **3** Mark Winterbottom, AUS (Ford Falcon FG), 1h 58m 04.0557s; **4** Shane van Gisbergen, NZ (Ford Falcon FG), 1h 58m 05.2895s; **5** Paul Dumbrell, AUS (Ford Falcon FG), 1h 58m 05.6827s; **6** Rick Kelly, AUS (Holden Commodore VE), 1h 58m 08.0552s; **7** Tony D'Alberto, AUS (Holden Commodore VE), 1h 58m 08.9525s; **8** Steven Johnson, AUS (Ford Falcon FG), 1h 58m 09.6524s; **9** Jason Richards, NZ (Holden Commodore VE), 1h 58m 10.1537s; **10** Michael Caruso, AUS (Holden Commodore VE), 1h 58m 11.9871s.

Fastest race lap: Courtney, 1m 21.9502s, 87.894 mph/141.451 km/h.

Pole position: Tander, 1m 20.9560s, 88.973 mph/143.188 km/h.

ITM 400 HAMILTON, Hamilton City Street Circuit, New Zealand, 17/18 April. Round 4. 2 x 59 laps of the 2.113-mile/3.400-km circuit.

Race 1 (124.647 miles/200.600 km).

1 Jamie Whincup, AUS (Holden Commodore VE), 1h 30m 34.7140s, 82.567 mph/132.879 km/h; **2** Garth Tander, AUS (Holden Commodore VE), 1h 30m 37.1357s; **3** James Courtney, AUS (Ford Falcon FG), 1h 30m 38.6537s; **4** Craig Lowndes, AUS (Holden Commodore VE), 1h 30m 40.3749s; **5** Michael Caruso, AUS (Holden Commodore VE), 1h 30m 44.9118s; **6** Steven Johnson, AUS (Ford Falcon FG), 1h 30m 47.1219s; **7** Mark Winterbottom, AUS (Ford Falcon FG), 1h 30m 49.5484s; **8** Rick Kelly, AUS (Holden Commodore VE), 1h 30m 50.7122s; **9** Paul Dumbrell, AUS (Ford Falcon FG), 1h 30m 51.3373s; **10** Lee Holdsworth, AUS (Holden Commodore VE), 1h 30m 51.5758s.

Fastest race lap: Whincup, 1m 23.2780s, 91.327 mph/146.977 km/h.

Pole position: Whincup, 1m 23.2690s, 91.337 mph/146.993 km/h.

Race 2 (124.647 miles/200.600 km).

1 Jamie Whincup, AUS (Holden Commodore VE), 1h 27m 53.1931s, 85.096 mph/136.949 km/h; **2** Garth Tander, AUS (Holden Commodore VE), 1h 27m 59.4247s; **3** Michael Caruso, AUS (Holden Commodore VE), 1h 28m 12.7851s; **4** Lee Holdsworth, AUS (Holden Commodore VE), 1h 28m 16.0745s; **5** Will Davison, AUS (Holden Commodore VE), 1h 28m 25.3073s; **6** Rick Kelly, AUS (Holden Commodore VE), 1h 28m 33.1928s; **7** Shane van Gisbergen, NZ (Ford Falcon FG), 1h 28m 40.5135s; **8** Todd Kelly, AUS (Holden Commodore VE), 1h 28m 41.2185s; **9** Jason Bargwanna, AUS (Holden Commodore VE), 1h 28m 42.9263s; **10** Jonathon Webb, AUS (Ford Falcon FG), 1h 28m 43.2192s.

Disqualified: Steven Johnson, AUS (Ford Falcon FG), finished 5th in 1h 28m 20.5671s (rear brake infringement).

Fastest race lap: Whincup, 1m 23.4397s, 91.150 mph/146.692 km/h.

Pole position: Tander, 1m 23.0349s, 91.595 mph/147.407 km/h.

CITY OF IPSWICH 300, Queensland Raceway, Ipswich, Queensland, Australia, 1/2 May. Round 5. 38 and 65 laps of the 1.942-mile/3.126-km circuit.

Race 1 (73.811 miles/118.788 km).

1 James Courtney, AUS (Ford Falcon FG), 46m 13.2975s, 95.814 mph/154.197 km/h; **2** Craig Lowndes, AUS (Holden Commodore VE), 46m 26.7392s; **3** Shane van Gisbergen, NZ (Ford Falcon FG), 46m 28.1442s; **4** Jamie Whincup, AUS (Holden Commodore VE), 46m 33.3587s; **5** Garth Tander, AUS (Holden Commodore VE), 46m 35.0518s; **6** Steven Johnson, AUS (Ford Falcon FG), 46m 35.5375s; **7** Lee Holdsworth, AUS (Holden Commodore VE), 46m 36.5549s; **8** Rick Kelly, AUS (Holden Commodore VE), 46m 39.7938s; **9** Mark Winterbottom, AUS (Ford Falcon FG), 46m 46.2188s; **10** Jonathon Webb, AUS (Ford Falcon FG), 46m 55.3722s.

Fastest race lap: Courtney, 1m 10.5896s, 99.060 mph/159.422 km/h.

Pole position: Tander, 1m 09.8526s, 100.105 mph/161.104 km/h.

Race 2 (126.256 miles/203.190 km).

1 James Courtney, AUS (Ford Falcon FG), 1h 26m 25.0810s, 87.659 mph/141.074 km/h; **2** Garth Tander, AUS (Holden Commodore VE), 1h 26m 36.5978s; **3** Shane van Gisbergen, NZ (Ford Falcon FG), 1h 26m 38.5506s; **4** Russell Ingall, AUS (Holden Commodore VE), 1h 26m 41.8045s; **5** Craig Lowndes, AUS (Holden Commodore VE), 1h 26m 42.0570s; **6** Michael Caruso, AUS (Holden Commodore VE), 1h 26m 45.2341s; **7** Rick Kelly, AUS (Holden Commodore VE), 1h 26m 46.1303s; **8** Steven Johnson, AUS (Ford Falcon FG), 1h 26m 46.8157s; **9** Steven Richards, NZ (Ford Falcon FG), 1h 26m 51.7842s; **10** Tony D'Alberto, AUS (Holden Commodore VE), 1h 26m 53.0316s.

Fastest race lap: Caruso, 1m 10.8600s, 98.682 mph/158.814 km/h.

Pole position: Whincup, 1m 09.7934s, 100.190 mph/161.241 km/h.

WINTON MOTOR RACEWAY, Winton Motor Raceway, Benalla, Victoria, Australia, 15/16 May. Round 6. 40 and 64 laps of the 1.864-mile/3.000-km circuit.

Race 1 (74.565 miles/120.000 km).

1 James Courtney, AUS (Ford Falcon FG), 57m 49.1567s, 77.376 mph/124.525 km/h; **2** Craig Lowndes, AUS (Holden Commodore VE), 57m 52.9595s; **3** Jamie Whincup, AUS (Holden Commodore VE), 58m 05.5998s; **4** Steven Johnson, AUS (Ford Falcon FG), 58m 06.7431s; **5** Shane van Gisbergen, NZ (Ford Falcon FG), 58m 09.4880s; **6** Todd Kelly, AUS (Holden Commodore VE), 58m 23.2202s; **7** Jason Bright, AUS (Holden Commodore VE), 58m 24.8963s; **8** Michael Caruso, AUS (Holden Commodore VE), 58m 27.2035s; **9** Tony D'Alberto, AUS (Holden Commodore VE), 58m 27.9046s; **10** Lee Holdsworth, AUS (Holden Commodore VE), 58m 28.6529s.

Fastest race lap: Slade, 1m 23.1445s, 80.712 mph/129.894 km/h.

Pole position: Courtney, 1m 21.8739s, 81.965 mph/131.910 km/h.

Race 2 (119.303 miles/192.000 km).

1 James Courtney, AUS (Ford Falcon FG), 1h 37m 31.2546s, 73.401 mph/118.128 km/h; **2** Craig Lowndes, AUS (Holden Commodore VE), 1h 37m 37.1058s; **3** Lee Holdsworth, AUS (Holden Commodore VE), 1h 37m 39.1169s; **4** Rick Kelly, AUS (Holden Commodore VE), 1h 37m 39.5454s; **5** Michael Caruso, AUS (Holden Commodore VE), 1h 37m 42.1799s; **6** Mark Winterbottom, AUS (Ford Falcon FG), 1h 37m 44.6509s; **7** Tim Slade, AUS (Ford Falcon FG), 1h 37m 46.3035s; **8** Garth Tander, AUS (Holden Commodore VE), 1h 37m 46.7690s; **9** Tony D'Alberto, AUS (Holden Commodore VE), 1h 37m 47.1032s; **10** Paul Dumbrell, AUS (Ford Falcon FG), 1h 37m 50.1453s.

Fastest race lap: Reindler, AUS (Holden Commodore VE), 1m 23.4879s, 80.380 mph/129.360 km/h.

Pole position: Kelly (Rick), 1m 21.8487s, 81.990 mph/131.950 km/h.

SKYCITY TRIPLE CROWN, Hidden Valley Raceway, Darwin, Northern Territory, Australia, 19/20 June. Round 7. 42 and 69 laps of the 1.783-mile/2.870-km circuit.

Race 1 (74.900 miles/120.540 km).

1 Mark Winterbottom, AUS (Ford Falcon FG), 51m 17.8454s, 87.606 mph/140.989 km/h; **2** Jamie Whincup, AUS (Holden Commodore VE), 51m 18.6329s; **3** Shane van Gisbergen, NZ (Ford Falcon FG), 51m 39.5262s; **4** Jason Richards, NZ (Holden Commodore VE), 51m 45.1517s; **5** James Courtney, AUS (Ford Falcon FG), 51m 48.0660s; **6** Tim Slade, AUS (Ford Falcon FG), 51m 48.5215s; **7** Craig Lowndes, AUS (Holden Commodore VE), 51m 49.7414s; **8** Paul Dumbrell, AUS (Ford Falcon FG), 51m 50.5396s; **9** Todd Kelly, AUS (Holden Commodore VE), 51m 52.8658s; **10** Garth Tander, AUS (Holden Commodore VE), 51m 53.6014s.

Fastest race lap: Whincup, 1m 11.0922s, 90.305 mph/145.332 km/h.

Pole position: Winterbottom, 1m 09.6854s, 92.128 mph/148.266 km/h.

Race 2 (123.050 miles/198.030 km).

1 Jamie Whincup, AUS (Holden Commodore VE), 1h 24m 35.0111s, 87.286 mph/140.474 km/h; **2** Mark Winterbottom, AUS (Ford Falcon FG), 1h 24m 39.0120s; **3** Shane van Gisbergen, NZ (Ford Falcon FG), 1h 24m 41.8694s; **4** James Courtney, AUS (Ford Falcon FG), 1h 24m 51.9046s; **5** Craig Lowndes, AUS (Holden Commodore VE), 1h 24m 57.8860s; **6** Tim Slade, AUS (Ford Falcon FG), 1h 25m 00.5727s; **7** Jason Richards, NZ (Holden Commodore VE), 1h 25m 03.2143s; **8** Todd Kelly, AUS (Holden Commodore VE), 1h 25m 09.1128s; **9** Rick Kelly, AUS (Holden Commodore VE), 1h 25m 09.8990s; **10** Steven Richards, NZ (Ford Falcon FG), 1h 25m 10.9152s.

Fastest race lap: Tander, 1m 09.9507s, 91.779 mph/ 147.704 km/h.
Pole position: Alex Davison, AUS (Ford Falcon FG), 1m 10.0614s, 91.634 mph/147.470 km/h.

SUCROGEN TOWNSVILLE 400, Townsville Street Circuit, Queensland, Australia, 10/11 July. Round 8. 72 and 71 laps of the 1.783-mile/2.870-km circuit.
Race 1 (128.400 miles/206.640 km).
1 Jamie Whincup, AUS (Holden Commodore VE), 1h 31m 16.3310s, 84.406 mph/135.839 km/h; **2** Garth Tander, AUS (Holden Commodore VE), 1h 31m 25.5609s; **3** Mark Winterbottom, AUS (Ford Falcon FG), 1h 31m 35.3148s; **4** Lee Holdsworth, AUS (Holden Commodore VE), 1h 31m 45.8190s; **5** James Courtney, AUS (Ford Falcon FG), 1h 31m 46.2099s; **6** Russell Ingall, AUS (Holden Commodore VE), 1h 32m 08.8904s; **7** Jason Richards, NZ (Holden Commodore VE), 1h 32m 12.5312s; **8** Shane van Gisbergen, NZ (Ford Falcon FG), 1h 32m 13.8508s; **9** Steven Richards, NZ (Ford Falcon FG), 1h 32m 16.8086s; **10** Paul Dumbrell, AUS (Ford Falcon FG), 1h 32m 17.4765s.
Fastest race lap: Tander, 1m 13.7640s, 87.034 mph/ 140.068 km/h.
Pole position: Whincup, 1m 13.3223s, 87.558 mph/ 140.912 km/h.

Race 2 (126.617 miles/203.770 km).
1 Mark Winterbottom, AUS (Ford Falcon FG), 1h 36m 49.3580s, 78.463 mph/126.274 km/h; **2** James Courtney, AUS (Ford Falcon FG), 1h 36m 50.5930s; **3** Garth Tander, AUS (Holden Commodore VE), 1h 36m 53.8343s; **4** Paul Dumbrell, AUS (Ford Falcon FG), 1h 36m 59.0363s; **5** Steven Richards, NZ (Ford Falcon FG), 1h 37m 02.5296s; **6** Will Davison, AUS (Holden Commodore VE), 1h 37m 02.6429s; **7** Shane van Gisbergen, NZ (Ford Falcon FG), 1h 37m 03.2945s; **8** Jason Richards, NZ (Holden Commodore VE), 1h 37m 03.7756s; **9** Jonathon Webb, AUS (Ford Falcon FG), 1h 37m 04.8484s; **10** Jason Bargwanna, AUS (Holden Commodore VE), 1h 37m 13.0597s.
Fastest race lap: Whincup, 1m 13.5250s, 87.317 mph/ 140.523 km/h.
Pole position: Whincup, 1m 12.7275s, 88.274 mph/ 142.064 km/h.

L&H 500, Phillip Island Grand Prix Circuit, Cowes, Victoria, Australia, 11/12 September. Round 9. 14, 14 and 113 laps of the 2.762-mile/4.445-km circuit.
Race 1 (38.668 miles/62.230 km).
1 Steve Owen, AUS (Holden Commodore VE), 25m 54.9169s, 89.525 mph/144.077 km/h; **2** Jason Bargwanna, AUS (Holden Commodore VE), 25m 56.0523s; **3** Shane van Gisbergen, NZ (Ford Falcon FG), 25m 57.2055s; **4** Garth Tander, AUS (Holden Commodore VE), 25m 58.1418s; **5** Jason Richards, NZ (Holden Commodore VE), 25m 58.4815s; **6** Todd Kelly, AUS (Holden Commodore VE), 25m 59.1027s; **7** Dean Canto, AUS (Ford Falcon FG), 26m 04.6334s; **8** Tony D'Alberto, AUS (Holden Commodore VE), 26m 11.8639s; **9** Jonathon Webb, AUS (Ford Falcon FG), 26m 11.9655s; **10** Greg Murphy, NZ (Holden Commodore VE), 26m 14.4916s.
Fastest race lap: Owen, 1m 34.1144s, 105.649 mph/ 170.027 km/h.
Pole position: Owen, 1m 32.3273s, 107.694 mph/ 173.318 km/h.

Race 2 (38.668 miles/62.230 km).
1 Rick Kelly, AUS (Holden Commodore VE), 24m 05.1814s, 96.323 mph/155.017 km/h; **2** Craig Lowndes, AUS (Holden Commodore VE), 24m 06.6593s; **3** James Courtney, AUS (Ford Falcon FG), 24m 08.8277s; **4** Steven Richards, NZ (Ford Falcon FG), 24m 09.3623s; **5** Mark Winterbottom, AUS (Ford Falcon FG), 24m 09.7075s; **6** Will Davison, AUS (Holden Commodore VE), 24m 10.1786s; **7** Marcus Marshall, AUS (Ford Falcon FG), 24m 10.6808s; **8** Tim Slade, AUS (Ford Falcon FG), 24m 11.4563s; **9** Fabian Coulthard, NZ (Holden Commodore VE), 24m 12.1006s; **10** Alex Davison, AUS (Ford Falcon FG), 24m 14.6130s.
Fastest race lap: Kelly (Rick), 1m 33.7775s, 106.029 mph/170.637 km/h.
Pole position: Kelly (Rick), 1m 32.4448s, 107.558 mph/ 173.097 km/h.

Race 3 (312.105 miles/502.285 km).
1 Craig Lowndes/Mark Skaife, AUS/AUS (Holden Commodore VE), 3h 11m 47.3551s, 97.640 mph/157.136 km/h; **2** Mark Winterbottom/Luke Youlden, AUS/AUS (Ford Falcon FG), 3h 11m 50.6421s; **3** Jason Richards/ Andrew Jones, NZ/AUS (Holden Commodore VE), 3h 11m 52.3708s; **4** Rick Kelly/Owen Kelly, AUS/AUS (Holden Commodore VE), 3h 11m 53.0488s; **5** Tim Slade/Jack Perkins, AUS/AUS (Ford Falcon FG), 3h 12m 07.0705s; **6** Jonathon Webb/David Russell, AUS/AUS (Ford Falcon FG), 3h 12m 15.8363s; **7** Paul Dumbrell/Dean Canto, AUS/AUS (Ford Falcon FG), 3h 12m 17.3036s; **8** Russell Ingall/Paul Morris, AUS/AUS (Holden Commodore VE), 3h 12m 17.4491s; **9** Garth Tander/Cameron McConville, AUS/AUS (Holden Commodore VE), 3h 12m 18.8532s; **10** Alex Davison/David Brabham, AUS/AUS (Ford Falcon FG), 3h 12m 23.0519s.
Fastest race lap: Lowndes/Skaife, 1m 34.8014s, 104.884 mph/168.794 km/h.
Pole position: Jamie Whincup, AUS (Holden Commodore VE).

SUPERCHEAP AUTO BATHURST 1000, Mount Panorama, Bathurst, New South Wales, Australia, 10 October. Round 10. 161 laps of the 3.861-mile/ 6.213-km circuit, 621.553 miles/1000.293 km.
1 Craig Lowndes/Mark Skaife, AUS/AUS (Holden Commodore VE), 6h 12m 51.4153s, 100.020 mph/160.966 km/h; **2** Jamie Whincup/Steve Owen, AUS/AUS (Holden Commodore VE), 6h 12m 51.5886s; **3** Garth Tander/ Cameron McConville, AUS/AUS (Holden Commodore VE), 6h 12m 52.6649s; **4** Jason Bright/Matthew Halliday, AUS/NZ (Holden Commodore VE), 6h 12m 53.7856s; **5** James Courtney/Warren Luff, AUS/AUS (Ford Falcon FG), 6h 12m 57.6154s; **6** Greg Murphy/Allan Simonsen, NZ/ DK (Holden Commodore VE), 6h 12m 58.4983s; **7** Lee Holdsworth/David Besnard, AUS/AUS (Holden Commodore VE), 6h 12m 58.9621s; **8** Russell Ingall/Paul Morris, AUS/AUS (Holden Commodore VE), 6h 13m 01.2865s; **9** Mark Winterbottom/Luke Youlden, AUS/AUS (Ford Falcon FG), 6h 13m 02.1909s; **10** Michael Caruso/Greg Ritter, AUS/AUS (Holden Commodore VE), 6h 13m 02.7375s.
Fastest race lap: Bright/Halliday, 2m 08.8215s, 107.886 mph/173.626 km/h.
Pole position: Winterbottom/Youlden, 2m 07.5377s, 108.972 mph/175.374 km/h.

ARMOR ALL GOLD COAST 600, Surfer's Paradise Steet Circuit, Queensland, Australia, 23/24 October. Round 11. 2 x 102 laps of the 1.839-mile/2.960-km circuit.
Race 1 (187.604 miles/301.920 km).
1 Garth Tander/Cameron McConville, AUS/AUS (Holden Commodore VE), 2h 20m 00.6981s, 80.395 mph/129.383 km/h; **2** Craig Lowndes/Andy Priaulx, AUS/ GB (Holden Commodore VE), 2h 20m 02.5530s; **3** Shane van Gisbergen/John McIntyre, NZ/AUS (Ford Falcon FG), 2h 20m 04.6282s; **4** Michael Caruso/Patrick Long, AUS/USA (Holden Commodore VE), 2h 20m 05.9298s; **5** Alex Davison/David Brabham, AUS/AUS (Ford Falcon FG), 2h 20m 25.7409s; **6** Jamie Whincup/Steve Owen, AUS/ AUS (Holden Commodore VE), 2h 20m 26.1390s; **7** Jason Bright/Alain Menu, AUS/CH (Holden Commodore VE), 2h 20m 26.6205s; **8** Jonathon Webb/Sébastien Bourdais, AUS/F (Ford Falcon FG), 2h 20m 27.4299s; **9** Karl Reindler/Fabrizio Giovanardi, AUS/I (Holden Commodore VE), 2h 20m 40.2605s; **10** James Courtney/Warren Luff, AUS/AUS (Ford Falcon FG), 2h 20m 40.4481s.
Fastest race lap: Lowndes/Priaulx, 1m 13.1879s, 90.470 mph/145.597 km/h.
Pole position: Tander/McConville, 1m 12.6841s, 91.097 mph/146.607 km/h.

Race 2 (187.604 miles/301.920 km).
1 Jamie Whincup/Steve Owen, AUS/AUS (Holden Commodore VE), 2h 29m 37.7468s, 75.227 mph/ 121.067 km/h; **2** Shane van Gisbergen/John McIntyre, NZ/AUS (Ford Falcon FG), 2h 29m 37.9521s; **3** Mark Winterbottom/Luke Youlden, AUS/AUS (Ford Falcon FG), 2h 29m 38.2327s; **4** James Courtney/Warren Luff, AUS/ AUS (Ford Falcon FG), 2h 29m 39.3828s; **5** Paul Dumbrell/Jacques Villeneuve, AUS/CDN (Ford Falcon FG), 2h 29m 55.6009s; **6** Rick Kelly/Owen Kelly, AUS/AUS (Holden Commodore VE), 2h 29m 59.8298s; **7** Will Davison/ Ryan Briscoe, AUS/AUS (Holden Commodore VE), 2h 30m 01.3036s; **8** Russell Ingall/Jack Perkins, AUS/AUS (Holden Commodore VE), 2h 30m 01.5675s; **9** Lee Holdsworth/Greg Ritter, AUS/AUS (Holden Commodore VE), 2h 30m 03.8231s; **10** Craig Lowndes/Andy Priaulx, AUS/GB (Holden Commodore VE), 2h 30m 08.5735s.
Fastest race lap: Courtney/Luff, 1m 13.1332s, 90.537 mph/145.706 km/h.
Pole position: Winterbottom/Youlden, 1m 12.0389s, 91.913 mph/147.920 km/h.

FALKEN TASMANIA CHALLENGE, Symmons Plains Raceway, Launceston, Tasmania, Australia, 13/14 November. Round 12. 50 and 84 laps of the 1.498-mile/ 2.411-km circuit.
Race 1 (74.906 miles/120.550 km).
1 Craig Lowndes, AUS (Holden Commodore VE), 44m 18.2888s, 101.442 mph/163.255 km/h; **2** Garth Tander, AUS (Holden Commodore VE), 44m 22.4467s; **3** Greg Murphy, NZ (Holden Commodore VE), 44m 26.2765s; **4** Paul Dumbrell, AUS (Ford Falcon FG), 44m 28.5598s; **5** Mark Winterbottom, AUS (Ford Falcon FG), 44m 29.9273s; **6** Jamie Whincup, AUS (Holden Commodore VE), 44m 30.7412s; **7** Russell Ingall, AUS (Holden Commodore VE), 44m 30.9234s; **8** Steven Richards, NZ (Ford Falcon FG), 44m 37.2765s; **9** Michael Caruso, AUS (Holden Commodore VE), 44m 38.1626s; **10** Lee Holdsworth, AUS (Holden Commodore VE), 44m 38.3734s.
Fastest race lap: Lowndes, 51.7334s, 104.250 mph/ 167.775 km/h.
Pole position: Tander, 51.9836s, 103.749 mph/ 166.968 km/h.

Race 2 (125.843 miles/202.524 km).
1 Mark Winterbottom, AUS (Ford Falcon FG), 1h 25m 58.9978s, 87.814 mph/141.323 km/h; **2** Paul Dumbrell, AUS (Ford Falcon FG), 1h 25m 59.7487s; **3** Jason Bright, AUS (Holden Commodore VE), 1h 26m 00.2869s; **4** Russell Ingall, AUS (Holden Commodore VE), 1h 26m 02.2258s; **5** Greg Murphy, NZ (Holden Commodore VE), 1h 26m 13.6502s; **6** Garth Tander, AUS (Holden Commodore VE), 1h 26m 14.5292s; **7** Todd Kelly, AUS (Holden Commodore VE), 1h 26m 19.9126s; **8** Fabian Coulthard, NZ (Holden Commodore VE), 1h 26m 21.0579s; **9** Steven Richards, NZ (Ford Falcon FG), 1h 26m 21.6164s; **10** Lee Holdsworth, AUS (Holden Commodore VE), 1h 26m 22.2802s.
Fastest race lap: Davison, 51.9669s, 103.782 mph/ 167.021 km/h.
Pole position: Winterbottom, 59.4007s, 90.794 mph/ 146.119 km/h.

Provisional championship points
Drivers: **1** James Courtney, AUS, 2662; **2** Jamie Whincup, AUS, 2612; **3** Mark Winterbottom, AUS, 2462; **4** Craig Lowndes, AUS, 2405; **5** Garth Tander, AUS, 2328; **6** Shane van Gisbergen, NZ, 2178; **7** Rick Kelly, AUS, 1946; **8** Lee Holdsworth, AUS, 1919; **9** Paul Dumbrell, AUS, 1848; **10** Michael Caruso, AUS, 1835; **11** Russell Ingall, AUS, 1676; **12** Steven Johnson, AUS, 1589; **13** Jason Richards, NZ, 1547; **14** Jonathon Webb, AUS, 1525; **15** Tim Slade, AUS, 1442; **16** Jason Bright, AUS, 1408; **17** Steven Richards, NZ, 1291; **18** Todd Kelly, AUS, 1273; **19** Greg Murphy, NZ, 1249; **20** Alex Davison, AUS, 1179.
Teams: **1** Team Vodafone, 5017; **2** Jim Beam Racing, 4261; **3** Fujitsu Racing/GRM, 3769.

Results of the Sandown and Sydney races will be given in AUTOCOURSE 2011–2012.

Non-Championship Australian V8 race

MANUFACTURERS CHALLENGE, Albert Park Circuit, Melbourne, Victoria, Australia, 26-28 March. 3 x 13 laps of the 3.295-mile/5.303-km circuit.
Race 1 (42.837 miles/ 68.939 km).
1 James Courtney, AUS (Ford Falcon FG), 25m 58.8986s, 98.924 mph/ 159.202 km/h; **2** Garth Tander, AUS (Holden Commodore VE), 25m 59.1581s; **3** Shane van Gisbergen, NZ (Ford Falcon FG), 25m 59.6025s; **4** Craig Lowndes, AUS (Holden Commodore VE), 26m 00.0777s; **5** Jamie Whincup, AUS (Holden Commodore VE), 26m 00.6228s; **6** Todd Kelly, AUS (Holden Commodore VE), 26m 11.4193s.
Fastest lap: Tander, 1m 58.2996s, 100.275 mph / 161.377 km/h.
Pole position: Tander, 1m 57.1666s, 101.244 mph/ 162.937 km/h.

Race 2 (42.837 miles/ 68.939 km).
1 Garth Tander, AUS (Holden Commodore VE), 25m 58.1135s, 100.275 mph/ 161.377 km/h; **2** Jamie Whincup, AUS (Holden Commodore VE), 25m 58.4906s; **3** James Courtney, AUS (Ford Falcon FG), 26m 02.4591s; **4** Shane van Gisbergen, NZ (Ford Falcon FG), 26m 04.1028s; **5** Mark Winterbottom, AUS (Ford Falcon FG), 26m 04.8568s; **6** Will Davison, AUS (Holden Commodore VE), 26m 08.6272s.
Fastest lap: Courtney, 1m 58.5781s, 100.039 mph/ 160.998 km/h.
Pole position: Courtney.

Race 3 (42.837 miles/ 68.939 km).
1 Garth Tander, AUS (Holden Commodore VE), 29m 11.2684s, 88.057 mph/ 141.715 km/h; **2** Shane van Gisbergen, NZ (Ford Falcon FG), 29m 14.1384s; **3** Will Davison, AUS (Holden Commodore VE), 29m 15.3758s; **4** Craig Lowndes, AUS (Holden Commodore VE), 29m 15.6634s; **5** Steven Johnson, AUS (Ford Falcon FG), 29m 17.9811s; **6** Paul Dumbrell, AUS (Holden Commodore VE), 29m 18.7240s.
Fastest lap: Tander, 1m 59.3602s, 99.384 mph/ 159.943 km/h.
Pole position: Tander.

Overall
1 Garth Tander, AUS (Holden Commodore VE); **2** Shane van Gisbergen, NZ (Ford Falcon FG); **3** Craig Lowndes, AUS (Holden Commodore VE); **4** Will Davison, AUS (Holden Commodore VE); **5** Steven Johnson, AUS (Ford Falcon FG); **6** Paul Dumbrell, AUS (Holden Commodore VE); **7** James Courtney, AUS (Ford Falcon FG); **8** Jamie Whincup, AUS (Ford Falcon FG); **9** Lee Holdsworth, AUS (Holden Commodore VE); **10** Jason Richards, NZ (Holden Commodore VE).

FIA World Touring Car Championship

2009

The following races were run after AUTOCOURSE 2009–2010 went to press.

RACE OF MACAU, Circuito da Guia, Macau, 22 November. 9 and 7 laps of the 3.803-mile/6.120-km circuit.
Round 23 (34.225 miles/55.080 km).
1 Robert Huff, GB (Chevrolet Cruze), 23m 02.627s, 89.113 mph/143.413 km/h; **2** Gabriele Tarquini, I (SEAT Leon TDI), 23m 10.579s; **3** Jordi Gené, E (SEAT Leon TDI), 23m 11.623s; **4** Alain Menu, CH (Chevrolet Cruze), 23m 12.955s; **5** Yvan Muller, F (SEAT Leon TDI), 23m 16.161s; **6** Tiago Monteiro, P (SEAT Leon TDI), 23m 18.144s; **7** Jörg Müller, D (BMW 320si), 23m 18.409s; **8** Augusto Farfus Jr., BR (BMW 320si), 23m 18.594s; **9** Alessandro Zanardi, I (BMW 320si), 23m 18.928s; **10** Sergio Hernández, E (BMW 320si), 23m 19.154s.
Fastest race lap: Monteiro, 2m 32.076s, 90.021 mph/ 144.874 km/h.
Pole position: Huff, 2m 32.141s, 89.982 mph/ 144.813 km/h.

Round 24 (26.620 miles/42.840 km).
1 Augusto Farfus Jr., BR (BMW 320si), 22m 20.166s, 71.506 mph/115.078 km/h; **2** Jörg Müller, D (BMW 320si), 22m 20.967s; **3** Yvan Muller, F (SEAT Leon TDI), 22m 21.367s; **4** Tiago Monteiro, P (SEAT Leon TDI), 22m 22.146s; **5** Gabriele Tarquini, I (SEAT Leon TDI), 22m 23.981s; **6** Jordi Gené, E (SEAT Leon TDI), 22m 25.184s; **7** Nicola Larini, I (Chevrolet Cruze), 22m 25.525s; **8** Robert Huff, GB (Chevrolet Cruze), 22m 26.061s; **9** Alessandro Zanardi, I (BMW 320si), 22m 26.333s; **10** Rickard Rydell, S (SEAT Leon TDI), 22m 26.878s.
Fastest race lap: Müller, 2m 32.671s, 89.670 mph/ 144.310 km/h.
Pole position: Farfus Jr.

Final championship points
Drivers: **1** Gabriele Tarquini, I, 127; **2** Yvan Muller, F, 123; **3** Augusto Farfus Jr., BR, 113; **4** Andy Priaulx, GB, 84; **5** Robert Huff, GB, 80; **6** Jörg Müller, D, 76; **7** Rickard Rydell, S, 64; **8** Jordi Gené, E, 48; **9** Tiago Monteiro, P, 44; **10** Alain Menu, CH, 41; **11** Sergio Hernández, E, 36; **12** Alessandro Zanardi, I, 31; **13** Nicola Larini, I, 27; **14** Tom Coronel, NL, 15; **15** Felix Porteiro, E, 10; **16** Franz Engstler, D, 7; **17** James Thompson, GB, 6; **18** Stefano D'Aste, I, 3; **19** Eric Cayrolle, F, 1.
Manufacturers: **1** SEAT, 314; **2** BMW, 311; **3** Chevrolet, 215; **4** Lada, 83.
Drivers (Yokohama Independents' Trophy): **1** Tom Coronel, NL, 233; **2** Felix Porteiro, E, 220; **3** Franz Engstler, D, 158; **4** Stefano D'Aste, I, 137; **5** Tom Boardman, GB, 99.
Teams (Yokohama Independents' Trophy): 1 SUNRED Engineering, 304; **2** Scuderia Proteam Motorsport, 239; **3** Liqui Moly Team Engstler, 212; **4** Wiechers-Sport, 150; **5** Colak Racing Team Ingra, 32.

2010

RACE OF BRAZIL, Autódromo Internacional de Curitiba, Brazil, 7 March. 16 and 14 laps of the 2.296-mile/3.695-km circuit.
Round 1 (36.735 miles/59.120 km).
1 Yvan Muller, F (Chevrolet Cruze), 26m 57.181s, 81.776 mph/131.606 km/h; **2** Robert Huff, GB (Chevrolet Cruze), 26m 58.234s; **3** Alain Menu, CH (Chevrolet Cruze), 27m 02.763s; **4** Gabriele Tarquini, I (SEAT Leon TDI), 27m 04.317s; **5** Andy Priaulx, GB (BMW 320si), 27m 08.806s; **6** Augusto Farfus Jr., BR (BMW 320si), 27m 09.279s; **7** Jordi Gené, E (SEAT Leon TDI), 27m 11.560s; **8** Tom Coronel, NL (SEAT Leon TDI), 27m 11.828s; **9** Fredy Barth, CH (SEAT Leon TDI), 27m 15.954s; **10** Norbert Michelisz, H (SEAT Leon TDI), 27m 17.540s.
Fastest race lap: Huff, 1m 33.904s, 88.020 mph/ 141.655 km/h.
Pole position: Muller (Yvan), 1m 23.725s, 98.721 mph/ 158.877 km/h.

Round 2 (32.144 miles/51.730 km).
1 Gabriele Tarquini, I (SEAT Leon TDI), 20m 13.311s, 95.372 mph/153.487 km/h; **2** Jordi Gené, E (SEAT Leon TDI), 20m 14.587s; **3** Alain Menu, CH (Chevrolet Cruze), 20m 18.718s; **4** Yvan Muller, F (Chevrolet Cruze), 20m 19.296s; **5** Robert Huff, GB (Chevrolet Cruze), 20m 21.606s; **6** Augusto Farfus Jr., BR (BMW 320si), 20m 21.907s; **7** Tiago Monteiro, P (SEAT Leon TDI), 20m 23.730s; **8** Michel Nykjær, DK (SEAT Leon TDI), 20m 25.119s; **9** Norbert Michelisz, H (SEAT Leon TDI), 20m 30.887s; **10** Sergio Hernández, E (BMW 320si), 20m 37.555s.
Fastest race lap: Tarquini, 1m 25.803s, 96.330 mph/ 155.029 km/h.
Pole position: Coronel.

RACE OF MOROCCO, Circuit de Marrakech, Morocco, 2 May. 2 x 13 laps of the 2.824-mile/4.545-km circuit.
Round 3 (36.714 miles/59.085 km).
1 Gabriele Tarquini, I (SEAT Leon TDI), 32m 12.815s, 68.381 mph/110.049 km/h; **2** Robert Huff, GB (Chevrolet Cruze), 32m 13.932s; **3** Tiago Monteiro, P (SEAT Leon TDI), 32m 14.607s; **4** Fredy Barth, CH (SEAT Leon TDI), 32m 15.251s; **5** Tom Coronel, NL (SEAT Leon TDI), 32m 16.328s; **6** Yvan Muller, F (Chevrolet Cruze), 32m 18.430s; **7** Norbert Michelisz, H (SEAT Leon TDI), 32m 20.715s; **8** Andy Priaulx, GB (BMW 320si), 32m 21.707s; **9** Alain Menu, CH (Chevrolet Cruze), 32m 22.928s; **10** Augusto Farfus Jr., BR (BMW 320si), 32m 24.774s.
Fastest race lap: Barth, 1m 46.925s, 95.084 mph/ 153.023 km/h.
Pole position: Tarquini, 1m 45.830s, 96.067 mph/ 154.606 km/h.

Round 4 (36.714 miles/59.085 km).
1 Andy Priaulx, GB (BMW 320si), 36m 15.763s, 60.746 mph/97.761 km/h; **2** Yvan Muller, F (Chevrolet Cruze), 36m 16.600s; **3** Tom Coronel, NL (SEAT Leon TDI), 36m 16.991s; **4** Tiago Monteiro, P (SEAT Leon TDI), 36m 17.227s; **5** Fredy Barth, CH (SEAT Leon TDI), 36m 17.712s; **6** Gabriele Tarquini, I (SEAT Leon TDI), 36m 18.158s; **7** Michel Nykjær, DK (SEAT Leon TDI), 36m 20.318s; **8** Jordi Gené, E (SEAT Leon TDI), 36m 21.128s; **9** Mehdi Bennani, MA (BMW 320si), 36m 21.679s; **10** Norbert Michelisz, H (SEAT Leon TDI), 36m 21.872s.
Fastest race lap: Gené, 1m 47.894s, 94.230 mph/ 151.648 km/h.
Pole position: Priaulx.

RACE OF ITALY, Autodromo Nazionale di Monza, Milan, Italy, 23 May. 2 x 9 laps of the 3.600-mile/5.793-km circuit.
Round 5 (32.204 miles/51.828 km).
1 Andy Priaulx, GB (BMW 320si), 18m 32.008s, 104.258 mph/167.787 km/h; **2** Augusto Farfus Jr., BR (BMW 320si), 18m 32.256s; **3** Robert Huff, GB (Chevrolet Cruze), 18m 33.661s; **4** Yvan Muller, F (Chevrolet Cruze), 18m 33.828s; **5** Tom Coronel, NL (SEAT Leon TDI), 18m 34.279s; **6** Fredy Barth, CH (SEAT Leon TDI), 18m 34.316s; **7** Gabriele Tarquini, I (SEAT Leon TDI), 18m 34.383s; **8** Michel Nykjær, DK (SEAT Leon TDI), 18m 34.734s; **9** Tiago Monteiro, P (SEAT Leon TDI), 18m 35.251s; **10** Harry Vaulkhard, GB (Chevrolet Lacetti), 18m 41.040s.
Mehdi Bennani, MA (BMW 320si), finished 10th in 18m 35.980s, but given a 30-sec penalty for cutting a chicane.
Fastest race lap: Tarquini, 2m 01.590s, 106.575 mph/ 171.517 km/h.
Pole position: Farfus Jr., 2m 00.672s, 107.386 mph/ 172.822 km/h.

Round 6 (32.204 miles/51.828 km).
1 Yvan Muller, F (Chevrolet Cruze), 18m 29.805s, 104.465 mph/168.120 km/h; **2** Tom Coronel, NL (SEAT Leon TDI), 18m 30.317s; **3** Robert Huff, GB (Chevrolet Cruze), 18m 30.627s; **4** Augusto Farfus Jr., BR (BMW 320si), 18m 30.806s; **5** Andy Priaulx, GB (BMW 320si), 18m 31.547s; **6** Jordi Gené, E (SEAT Leon TDI), 18m 33.300s; **7** Tiago Monteiro, P (SEAT Leon TDI), 18m 34.002s; **8** Norbert Michelisz, H (SEAT Leon TDI), 18m 34.385s; **9** Alain Menu, CH (Chevrolet Cruze), 18m 34.904s; **10** Leonel Pernía, RA (Chevrolet Cruze), 18m 39.723s.
Fastest race lap: Priaulx, 2m 01.860s, 106.339 mph/ 171.137 km/h.
Pole position: Nykjær.

RACE OF BELGIUM, Circuit Zolder, Heusden-Zolder, Belgium, 20 June. 2 x 13 laps of the 2.485-mile/4.000-km circuit.
Round 7 (32.311 miles/52.000 km).
1 Gabriele Tarquini, I (SEAT Leon TDI), 21m 54.209s, 88.510 mph/142.443 km/h; **2** Yvan Muller, F (Chevrolet Cruze), 21m 56.838s; **3** Alain Menu, CH (Chevrolet Cruze), 21m 57.265s; **4** Tiago Monteiro, P (SEAT Leon TDI), 21m 57.768s; **5** Robert Huff, GB (Chevrolet Cruze), 21m 58.075s; **6** Norbert Michelisz, H (SEAT Leon TDI), 21m 58.401s; **7** Andy Priaulx, GB (BMW 320si), 21m 59.036s; **8** Tom Coronel, NL (SEAT Leon TDI), 22m 03.504s; **9** Augusto Farfus Jr., BR (BMW 320si), 22m 03.662s; **10** Fredy Barth, CH (SEAT Leon TDI), 22m 03.864s.
Fastest race lap: Priaulx, 1m 40.138s, 89.354 mph/ 143.801 km/h.
Pole position: Tarquini, 1m 38.265s, 91.057 mph/ 146.542 km/h.

Round 8 (32.311 miles/52.000 km).
1 Andy Priaulx, GB (BMW 320si), 21m 52.091s, 88.652 mph/142.673 km/h; **2** Robert Huff, GB (Chevrolet Cruze), 21m 53.140s; **3** Tiago Monteiro, P (SEAT

Leon TDI), 21m 53.845s; **4** Alain Menu, CH (Chevrolet Cruze), 21m 54.389s; **5** Yvan Muller, F (Chevrolet Cruze), 21m 56.875s; **6** Gabriele Tarquini, I (SEAT Leon TDI), 21m 57.879s; **7** Norbert Michelisz, H (SEAT Leon TDI), 21m 58.374s; **8** Augusto Farfus Jr., BR (BMW 320si), 21m 58.754s; **9** Sergio Hernández, E (BMW 320si), 22m 05.582s; **10** Tom Coronel, NL (SEAT Leon TDI), 22m 06.901s.
Fastest race lap: Priaulx, 1m 40.181s, 89.315 mph/143.739 km/h.
Pole position: Priaulx.

RACE OF PORTUGAL, Autódromo Internacional do Algarve, Portimão, Portugal, 4 July. 2 x 11 laps of the 2.891-mile/4.653-km circuit.
Round 9 (31.804 miles/51.183 km).
1 Tiago Monteiro, P (SEAT Leon TDI), 21m 38.194s, 88.194 mph/141.934 km/h; **2** Yvan Muller, F (Chevrolet Cruze), 21m 39.226s; **3** Gabriele Tarquini, I (SEAT Leon TDI), 21m 39.781s; **4** Augusto Farfus Jr., BR (BMW 320si), 21m 40.020s; **5** Alain Menu, CH (Chevrolet Cruze), 21m 47.001s; **6** Tom Coronel, NL (SEAT Leon TDI), 21m 49.917s; **7** Norbert Michelisz, H (SEAT Leon TDI), 21m 50.756s; **8** Fredy Barth, CH (SEAT Leon TDI), 21m 58.367s; **9** Sergio Hernández, E (BMW 320si), 22m 01.307s; **10** Darryl O'Young, HK (Chevrolet Lacetti), 22m 01.439s.
Fastest race lap: Tarquini, 1m 56.984s, 88.973 mph/143.188 km/h.
Pole position: Monteiro, 1m 55.372s, 90.216 mph/145.189 km/h.

Round 10 (31.804 miles/51.183 km).
1 Gabriele Tarquini, I (SEAT Leon TDI), 21m 49.935s, 87.403 mph/140.662 km/h; **2** Yvan Muller, F (Chevrolet Cruze), 21m 51.671s; **3** Alain Menu, CH (Chevrolet Cruze), 21m 53.179s; **4** Andy Priaulx, GB (BMW 320si), 21m 53.505s; **5** Augusto Farfus Jr., BR (BMW 320si), 21m 54.029s; **6** Tom Coronel, NL (SEAT Leon TDI), 21m 56.136s; **7** Tiago Monteiro, P (SEAT Leon TDI), 21m 56.448s; **8** Fredy Barth, CH (SEAT Leon TDI), 22m 00.142s; **9** Darryl O'Young, HK (Chevrolet Lacetti), 22m 02.686s; **10** Colin Turkington, GB (BMW 320si), 22m 03.544s.
Fastest race lap: Jordi Gené, E (SEAT Leon TDI), 1m 57.902s, 88.280 mph/142.073 km/h.
Pole position: Barth.

RACE OF GREAT BRITAIN, Brands Hatch Grand Prix Circuit, West Kingsdown, Dartford, Kent, Great Britain, 18 July. 2 x 16 laps of the 2.301-mile/3.703-km circuit.
Round 11 (36.796 miles/59.218 km).
1 Yvan Muller, F (Chevrolet Cruze), 28m 05.204s, 78.605 mph/126.503 km/h; **2** Robert Huff, GB (Chevrolet Cruze), 28m 05.500s; **3** Colin Turkington, GB (BMW 320si), 28m 06.052s; **4** Gabriele Tarquini, I (SEAT Leon TDI), 28m 07.819s; **5** Tom Coronel, NL (SEAT Leon TDI), 28m 08.362s; **6** Augusto Farfus Jr., BR (BMW 320si), 28m 09.561s; **7** Andy Priaulx, GB (BMW 320si), 28m 10.374s; **8** Tiago Monteiro, P (SEAT Leon TDI), 28m 10.499s; **9** Norbert Michelisz, H (SEAT Leon TDI), 28m 10.709s; **10** Jordi Gené, E (SEAT Leon TDI), 28m 11.307s.
Fastest race lap: Priaulx, 1m 34.078s, 88.047 mph/141.699 km/h.
Pole position: Muller, 1m 32.481s, 89.568 mph/144.146 km/h.

Round 12 (36.796 miles/59.218 km).
1 Andy Priaulx, GB (BMW 320si), 27m 05.324s, 81.501 mph/131.164 km/h; **2** Colin Turkington, GB (BMW 320si), 27m 05.723s; **3** Gabriele Tarquini, I (SEAT Leon TDI), 27m 06.718s; **4** Tom Coronel, NL (SEAT Leon TDI), 27m 07.178s; **5** Yvan Muller, F (Chevrolet Cruze), 27m 08.361s; **6** Robert Huff, GB (Chevrolet Cruze), 27m 08.742s; **7** Norbert Michelisz, H (SEAT Leon TDI), 27m 10.225s; **8** Augusto Farfus Jr., BR (BMW 320si), 27m 10.853s; **9** Michel Nykjær, DK (SEAT Leon TDI), 27m 11.359s; **10** Jordi Gené, E (SEAT Leon TDI), 27m 11.805s.
Fastest race lap: Priaulx, 1m 34.791s, 87.385 mph/140.633 km/h.
Pole position: Priaulx.

RACE OF THE CZECH REPUBLIC, Automotodrom Brno Masaryk Circuit, Brno, Czech Republic, 1 August. 12 and 10 laps of the 3.357-mile/5.403-km circuit.
Round 13 (40.287 miles/64.836 km).
1 Robert Huff, GB (Chevrolet Cruze), 28m 46.901s, 83.985 mph/135.160 km/h; **2** Gabriele Tarquini, I (SEAT Leon TDI), 28m 47.697s; **3** Alain Menu, CH (Chevrolet Cruze), 28m 48.937s; **4** Augusto Farfus Jr., BR (BMW 320si), 28m 49.246s; **5** Andy Priaulx, GB (BMW 320si), 28m 59.775s; **6** Colin Turkington, GB (BMW 320si), 29m 00.103s; **7** Michel Nykjær, DK (SEAT Leon TDI), 29m 01.157s; **8** Kristian Poulsen, DK (BMW 320si), 29m 02.581s; **9** Tiago Monteiro, P (SEAT Leon TDI), 29m 03.425s; **10** Stefano D'Aste, I (BMW 320si), 29m 05.681s.
Fastest race lap: Farfus Jr., 2m 12.167s, 91.446 mph/147.168 km/h.
Pole position: Huff, 2m 10.860s, 92.359 mph/148.638 km/h.

Round 14 (33.573 miles/54.030 km).
1 Andy Priaulx, GB (BMW 320si), 22m 22.054s, 90.057 mph/144.933 km/h; **2** Colin Turkington, GB (BMW 320si), 22m 24.308s; **3** Alain Menu, CH (Chevrolet Cruze), 22m 25.407s; **4** Robert Huff, GB (Chevrolet Cruze), 22m 27.401s; **5** Augusto Farfus Jr., BR (BMW 320si), 22m 27.778s; **6** Tiago Monteiro, P (SEAT Leon TDI), 22m 29.555s; **7** Darryl O'Young, HK (Chevrolet Lacetti), 22m 32.266s; **8** Fredy Barth, CH (SEAT Leon TDI), 22m 33.752s; **9** Stefano D'Aste, I (BMW 320si), 22m 34.635s; **10** Tom Coronel, NL (SEAT Leon TDI), 22m 38.638s.
Fastest race lap: Tarquini, 2m 12.737s, 91.053 mph/146.536 km/h.
Pole position: O'Young.

RACE OF GERMANY, Motorsport Arena Oschersleben, Germany, 5 September. 2 x 14 laps of the 2.297-mile/3.696-km circuit.
Round 15 (32.152 miles/51.744 km).
1 Alain Menu, CH (Chevrolet Cruze), 22m 50.427s, 84.461 mph/135.927 km/h; **2** Augusto Farfus Jr., BR (BMW 320si), 22m 50.918s; **3** Yvan Muller, F (Chevrolet Cruze), 22m 55.165s; **4** Tiago Monteiro, P (SEAT Leon TDI), 22m 57.855s; **5** Andy Priaulx, GB (BMW 320si), 22m 58.272s; **6** Tom Coronel, NL (SEAT Leon TDI), 23m 27.262s *; **7** Michel Nykjær, DK (SEAT Leon TDI), 23m 33.490s *; **8** Norbert Michelisz, H (SEAT Leon TDI), 23m 36.614s *; **9** Kristian Poulsen, DK (BMW 320si), 23m 36.876s *; **10** Sergio Hernández, E (BMW 320si), 23m 38.324s *.
Fastest race lap: Menu, 1m 36.543s, 85.637 mph/137.820 km/h.
Pole position: Farfus Jr., 1m 38.070s, 84.304 mph/135.674 km/h.
** includes 30-sec penalty*

Round 16 (32.152 miles/51.744 km).
1 Andy Priaulx, GB (BMW 320si), 22m 51.499s, 84.395 mph/135.821 km/h; **2** Augusto Farfus Jr., BR (BMW 320si), 22m 54.228s; **3** Yvan Muller, F (Chevrolet Cruze), 23m 00.239s; **4** Michel Nykjær, DK (SEAT Leon TDI), 23m 01.803s; **5** Tom Coronel, NL (SEAT Leon TDI), 23m 02.481s; **6** Kristian Poulsen, DK (BMW 320si), 23m 03.488s; **7** Robert Huff, GB (Chevrolet Cruze), 23m 08.190s; **8** Alain Menu, CH (Chevrolet Cruze), 23m 08.742s; **9** Gabriele Tarquini, I (SEAT Leon TDI), 23m 09.418s; **10** Jordi Gené, E (SEAT Leon TDI), 23m 10.692s.
Fastest race lap: Tarquini, 1m 36.890s, 85.330 mph/137.326 km/h.
Pole position: Michelisz.

RACE OF SPAIN, Circuit de la Comunitat Valenciana Ricardo Tormo, Cheste, Valencia, Spain, 19 September. 2 x 13 laps of the 2.489-mile/4.005-km circuit.
Round 17 (32.352 miles/52.065 km).
1 Gabriele Tarquini, I (SEAT Leon TDI), 23m 11.124s, 83.720 mph/134.735 km/h; **2** Yvan Muller, F (Chevrolet Cruze), 23m 11.637s; **3** Robert Huff, GB (Chevrolet Cruze), 23m 17.442s; **4** Jordi Gené, E (SEAT Leon TDI), 23m 21.073s; **5** Andy Priaulx, GB (BMW 320si), 23m 21.668s; **6** Tiago Monteiro, P (SEAT Leon TDI), 23m 22.790s; **7** Fredy Barth, CH (SEAT Leon TDI), 23m 24.858s; **8** Alain Menu, CH (Chevrolet Cruze), 23m 25.645s; **9** Michel Nykjær, DK (SEAT Leon TDI), 23m 27.710s; **10** Tom Coronel, NL (SEAT Leon TDI), 23m 28.341s.
Fastest race lap: Tarquini, 1m 45.811s, 84.669 mph/136.261 km/h.
Pole position: Tarquini, 1m 44.111s, 86.051 mph/138.486 km/h.

Round 18 (32.352 miles/52.065 km).
1 Tiago Monteiro, P (SEAT Leon TDI), 23m 29.770s, 82.613 mph/132.953 km/h; **2** Yvan Muller, F (Chevrolet Cruze), 23m 30.489s; **3** Gabriele Tarquini, I (SEAT Leon TDI), 23m 33.225s; **4** Andy Priaulx, GB (BMW 320si), 23m 33.555s; **5** Jordi Gené, E (SEAT Leon TDI), 23m 33.953s; **6** Robert Huff, GB (Chevrolet Cruze), 23m 34.752s; **7** Michel Nykjær, DK (SEAT Leon TDI), 23m 37.018s; **8** Augusto Farfus Jr., BR (BMW 320si), 23m 37.595s; **9** Tom Coronel, NL (SEAT Leon TDI), 23m 38.794s; **10** Kristian Poulsen, DK (BMW 320si), 23m 39.895s.
Fastest race lap: Monteiro, 1m 46.719s, 83.948 mph/135.102 km/h.
Pole position: Menu.

Okayama International Circuit (TI Circuit Aida), Aida Gun, Okayama Prefecture, Japan, 31 October. 2 x 16 laps of the 2.301-mile/3.703-km circuit.
Round 19 (36.815 miles/59.248 km).
1 Robert Huff, GB (Chevrolet Cruze), 31m 46.668s, 69.510 mph/111.866 km/h; **2** Yvan Muller, F (Chevrolet Cruze), 31m 51.599s; **3** Norbert Michelisz, H (SEAT Leon TDI), 31m 56.410s; **4** Colin Turkington, GB (BMW 320si), 31m 57.978s; **5** Gabriele Tarquini, I (SEAT Leon TDI), 32m 00.544s; **6** Michel Nykjær, DK (SEAT Leon TDI), 32m 01.569s; **7** Alain Menu, CH (Chevrolet Cruze), 32m 16.690s; **8** Robert Dahlgren, S (Volvo C30), 32m 17.745s; **9** Yukinori Taniguchi, J (Chevrolet Lacetti), 32m 59.816s; **10** Darryl O'Young, HK (Chevrolet Lacetti), 33m 02.663s.
Disqualified: Andy Priaulx, GB (BMW 320si), finished 2nd in 31m 49.645s; Augusto Farfus Jr., BR (BMW 320si), finished 4th in 31m 55.264s (both used illegal gearbox).
Fastest race lap: Muller, 1m 51.813s, 74.082 mph/119.224 km/h.
Pole position: Priaulx, 1m 36.972s, 85.420 mph/137.470 km/h.

Round 20 (36.815 miles/59.248 km).
1 Colin Turkington, GB (BMW 320si), 33m 48.074s, 65.349 mph/105.170 km/h; **2** Yvan Muller, F (Chevrolet Cruze), 33m 48.798s; **3** Robert Huff, GB (Chevrolet Cruze), 33m 49.896s; **4** Alain Menu, CH (Chevrolet Cruze), 33m 50.900s; **5** Robert Dahlgren, S (Volvo C30), 33m 51.239s; **6** Michel Nykjær, DK (SEAT Leon TDI), 33m 52.248s; **7** Norbert Michelisz, H (SEAT Leon TDI), 33m 53.506s; **8** Tom Coronel, NL (SEAT Leon TDI), 33m 53.975s; **9** Darryl O'Young, HK (Chevrolet Lacetti), 33m 55.135s; **10** Franz Engstler, D (BMW 320si), 33m 55.687s.
Disqualified: Farfus Jr. finished 1st in 33m 47.799s, 65.358 mph/105.184 km/h (used illegal gearbox).
Fastest race lap: Nykjær, 1m 53.478s, 72.995 mph/117.474 km/h.
Pole position: Nykjær.

Provisional championship points
Drivers: **1** Yvan Muller, F, 301; **2** Gabriele Tarquini, I, 246; **3** Andy Priaulx, GB, 240; **4** Robert Huff, GB, 236; **5** Alain Menu, CH, 167; **6** Tiago Monteiro, P, 158; **7** Augusto Farfus Jr., BR, 149; **8** Tom Coronel, NL, 128; **9** Colin Turkington, GB, 97; **10** Norbert Michelisz, H, 69; **11** Michel Nykjær, DK, 66; **12** Jordi Gené, E, 61; **13** Fredy Barth, CH, 51; **14** Kristian Poulsen, DK, 16; **15** Darryl O'Young, HK, 15; **16** Sergio Hernández, E, 7; **17** Yukinori Taniguchi, J, 4; **18** Stefano D'Aste, I, 3; **19** Mehdi Bennani, MA, 2; **20** Franz Engstler, D, 2; **21** Harry Vaulkhard, GB, 1; **22** Leonel Pernía, RA, 1.
Manufacturers: **1** Chevrolet, 645; **2** SEAT, 571; **3** BMW, 544.
Drivers (Yokohama Independents' Trophy): **1** Sergio Hernández, E, 124; **2** Darryl O'Young, HK, 103; **3** Kristian Poulsen, DK, 97; **4** Franz Engstler, D, 95; **5** Stefano D'Aste, I, 88.
Teams (Yokohama Independents' Trophy): **1** Scuderia Proteam Motorsport, 206; **2** bamboo engineering, 181; **3** Liqui Moly Team Engstler, 127; **4** Poulsen Motorsport, 91; **5** Wiechers-Sport, 70.

Results of the Macau races will be given in AUTOCOURSE 2011–2012.

German Touring Car Championship (DTM)

GERMAN TOURING CAR CHAMPIONSHIP (DTM), Hockenheimring Grand Prix Circuit, Heidelberg, Germany, 25 April. Round 1. 39 laps of the 2.842-mile/4.574-km circuit, 110.844 miles/178.386 km.
1 Gary Paffett, GB (Mercedes C-Klasse 09), 1h 02m 31.580s, 106.365 mph/171.178 km/h; **2** Bruno Spengler, CDN (Mercedes C-Klasse 09), 1h 02m 32.147s; **3** Jamie Green, GB (Mercedes C-Klasse 08), 1h 02m 33.421s; **4** Paul Di Resta, GB (Mercedes C-Klasse 09), 1h 02m 33.831s; **5** Mike Rockenfeller, D (Audi A4 DTM 08), 1h 02m 34.781s; **6** Mattias Ekström, S (Audi A4 DTM 09), 1h 02m 35.000s; **7** Timo Scheider, D (Audi A4 DTM 09), 1h 02m 44.647s; **8** Miguel Molina, E (Audi A4 DTM 08), 1h 02m 45.083s; **9** Ralf Schumacher, D (Mercedes C-Klasse 09), 1h 02m 48.491s; **10** Alexandre Prémat, F (Audi A4 DTM 08), 1h 03m 00.089s.
Fastest race lap: Spengler, 1m 33.855s, 109.017 mph/175.445 km/h.
Pole position: Paffett, 1m 33.214s, 109.766 mph/176.652 km/h.

GERMAN TOURING CAR CHAMPIONSHIP (DTM), Circuit de la Comunitat Valenciana Ricardo Tormo, Cheste, Valencia, Spain, 23 May. Round 2. 45 laps of the 2.489-mile/4.005-km circuit, 111.987 miles/180.225 km.
1 Mattias Ekström, S (Audi A4 DTM 09), 1h 09m 56.290s, 96.073 mph/154.615 km/h; **2** Bruno Spengler, CDN (Mercedes C-Klasse 09), 1h 09m 59.837s; **3** Alexandre Prémat, F (Audi A4 DTM 08), 1h 10m 00.904s; **4** Timo Scheider, D (Audi A4 DTM 09), 1h 10m 01.564s; **5** Paul Di Resta, GB (Mercedes C-Klasse 09), 1h 10m 04.929s; **6** Mike Rockenfeller, D (Audi A4 DTM 08), 1h 10m 09.102s; **7** Gary Paffett, GB (Mercedes C-Klasse 09), 1h 10m 12.735s; **8** Miguel Molina, E (Audi A4 DTM 08), 1h 10m 13.406s; **9** Jamie Green, GB (Mercedes C-Klasse 08), 1h 10m 14.672s; **10** Susie Stoddart, GB (Mercedes C-Klasse 08), 1h 10m 27.331s.
Fastest race lap: Ekström, 1m 30.971s, 98.481 mph/158.490 km/h.
Pole position: Ekström, 1m 29.565s, 100.027 mph/160.978 km/h.

GERMAN TOURING CAR CHAMPIONSHIP (DTM), EuroSpeedway Lausitz, Klettwitz, Dresden, Germany, 6 June. Round 3. 52 laps of the 2.161-mile/3.478-km circuit, 112.379 miles/180.856 km.
1 Bruno Spengler, CDN (Mercedes C-Klasse 09), 1h 12m 32.740s, 92.945 mph/149.580 km/h; **2** Paul Di Resta, GB (Mercedes C-Klasse 09), 1h 12m 37.282s; **3** Jamie Green, GB (Mercedes C-Klasse 08), 1h 12m 38.063s; **4** Mike Rockenfeller, D (Audi A4 DTM 08), 1h 12m 41.090s; **5** Gary Paffett, GB (Mercedes C-Klasse 09), 1h 12m 45.098s; **6** Martin Tomczyk, D (Audi A4 DTM 09), 1h 12m 48.028s; **7** Susie Stoddart, GB (Mercedes C-Klasse 08), 1h 12m 49.845s; **8** Timo Scheider, D (Audi A4 DTM 09), 1h 12m 59.170s; **9** Ralf Schumacher, D (Mercedes C-Klasse 09), 1h 13m 07.273s; **10** Markus Winkelhock, D (Audi A4 DTM 08), 1h 13m 15.359s.
Fastest race lap: Rockenfeller, 1m 19.957s, 97.303 mph/156.594 km/h.
Pole position: Di Resta, 1m 18.772s, 98.767 mph/158.950 km/h.

GERMAN TOURING CAR CHAMPIONSHIP (DTM), Norisring, Nürnberg (Nuremberg), Germany, 4 July. Round 4. 82 laps of the 1.429-mile/2.300-km circuit, 117.191 miles/188.600 km.
1 Jamie Green, GB (Mercedes C-Klasse 08), 1h 08m 05.282s, 103.270 mph/166.197 km/h; **2** Mattias Ekström, S (Audi A4 DTM 09), 1h 08m 05.873s; **3** Bruno Spengler, CDN (Mercedes C-Klasse 09), 1h 08m 07.192s; **4** Oliver Jarvis, GB (Audi A4 DTM 09), 1h 08m 15.228s; **5** Timo Scheider, D (Audi A4 DTM 09), 1h 08m 17.597s; **6** Gary Paffett, GB (Mercedes C-Klasse 09), 1h 08m 19.803s; **7** Alexandre Prémat, F (Audi A4 DTM 08), 1h 08m 21.116s; **8** Martin Tomczyk, D (Audi A4 DTM 09), 1h 08m 21.382s; **9** Maro Engel, D (Mercedes C-Klasse 08), 1h 08m 27.436s; **10** Paul Di Resta, GB (Mercedes C-Klasse 09), 1h 08m 36.818s.
Fastest race lap: Ralf Schumacher, D (Mercedes C-Klasse 09), 48.616s, 105.828 mph/170.314 km/h.
Pole position: Schumacher, 48.721s, 105.600 mph/169.947 km/h.

GERMAN TOURING CAR CHAMPIONSHIP (DTM), Nürburgring, Nürburg/Eifel, Germany, 8 August. Round 5. 49 laps of the 2.255-mile/3.629-km circuit, 110.493 miles/177.821 km.
1 Bruno Spengler, CDN (Mercedes C-Klasse 09), 1h 10m 27.488s, 94.092 mph/151.427 km/h; **2** Paul Di Resta, GB (Mercedes C-Klasse 09), 1h 10m 30.331s; **3** Gary Paffett, GB (Mercedes C-Klasse 09), 1h 10m 36.074s; **4** Timo Scheider, D (Audi A4 DTM 09), 1h 10m 42.796s; **5** Jamie Green, GB (Mercedes C-Klasse 08), 1h 10m 49.078s; **6** Ralf Schumacher, D (Mercedes C-Klasse 09), 1h 10m 49.820s; **7** Mattias Ekström, S (Audi A4 DTM 09), 1h 10m 54.756s; **8** Maro Engel, D (Mercedes C-Klasse 08), 1h 10m 57.259s; **9** Mike Rockenfeller, D (Audi A4 DTM 08), 1h 11m 01.430s; **10** David Coulthard, GB (Mercedes C-Klasse 08), 1h 11m 07.048s.
Fastest race lap: Spengler, 1m 24.372s, 96.215 mph/154.843 km/h.
Pole position: Ekström, 1m 23.817s, 96.852 mph/155.868 km/h.

GERMAN TOURING CAR CHAMPIONSHIP (DTM), Circuit Park Zandvoort, Netherlands, 22 August. Round 6. 42 laps of the 2.676-mile/4.307-km circuit, 112.402 miles/180.894 km.
1 Gary Paffett, GB (Mercedes C-Klasse 09), 1h 07m 04.346s, 100.550 mph/161.820 km/h; **2** Paul Di Resta, GB (Mercedes C-Klasse 09), 1h 07m 04.742s; **3** Timo Scheider, D (Audi A4 DTM 09), 1h 07m 16.584s; **4** Mattias Ekström, S (Audi A4 DTM 09), 1h 07m 23.005s; **5** Miguel Molina, E (Audi A4 DTM 08), 1h 07m 23.656s; **6** Oliver Jarvis, GB (Audi A4 DTM 09), 1h 07m 24.914s; **7** Bruno Spengler, CDN (Mercedes C-Klasse 09), 1h 07m 25.232s; **8** Martin Tomczyk, D (Audi A4 DTM 09), 1h 07m 26.052s; **9** Ralf Schumacher, D (Mercedes C-Klasse 09), 1h 07m 26.459s; **10** Jamie Green, GB (Mercedes C-Klasse 08), 1h 07m 27.226s.
Fastest race lap: Scheider, 1m 32.967s, 103.633 mph/166.782 km/h.
Pole position: Scheider, 1m 31.590s, 105.191 mph/169.289 km/h.

GERMAN TOURING CAR CHAMPIONSHIP (DTM), Brands Hatch Indy Circuit, West Kingsdown, Dartford, Kent, Great Britain, 5 September. Round 7. 98 laps of the 1.199-mile/1.929-km circuit, 117.465 miles/189.042 km.
1 Paul Di Resta, GB (Mercedes C-Klasse 09), 1h 10m 05.552s, 100.552 mph/161.822 km/h; **2** Bruno Spengler, CDN (Mercedes C-Klasse 09), 1h 10m 12.995s; **3** Timo Scheider, D (Audi A4 DTM 09), 1h 10m 15.810s; **4** Miguel Molina, E (Audi A4 DTM 08), 1h 10m 16.271s; **5** Gary Paffett, GB (Mercedes C-Klasse 09), 1h 10m 18.332s; **6** Oliver Jarvis, GB (Audi A4 DTM 09), 1h 10m 29.382s; **7** Martin Tomczyk, D (Audi A4 DTM 09), 1h 10m 29.538s; **8** Alexandre Prémat, F (Audi A4 DTM 08), 1h 10m 31.241s; **9** Mike Rockenfeller, D (Audi A4 DTM 08), 1h 10m 31.745s; **10** Jamie Green, GB (Mercedes C-Klasse 08), 1h 10m 32.125s.
Fastest race lap: Molina, 41.896s, 102.994 mph/165.753 km/h.
Pole position: Di Resta, 41.278s, 104.536 mph/168.235 km/h.

GERMAN TOURING CAR CHAMPIONSHIP (DTM), Motorsport Arena Oschersleben, Germany, 19 September. Round 8. 50 laps of the 2.297-mile/3.696-km circuit, 114.829 miles/184.800 km.
1 Paul Di Resta, GB (Mercedes C-Klasse 09), 1h 11m 05.254s, 96.919 mph/155.977 km/h; **2** Bruno Spengler, CDN (Mercedes C-Klasse 09), 1h 11m 06.525s; **3** Mattias Ekström, S (Audi A4 DTM 09), 1h 11m 08.816s; **4** Gary Paffett, GB (Mercedes C-Klasse 09), 1h 11m 09.856s; **5** Mike Rockenfeller, D (Audi A4 DTM 08), 1h 11m 27.150s; **6** Alexandre Prémat, F (Audi A4 DTM 08), 1h 11m 31.255s; **7** Jamie Green, GB (Mercedes C-Klasse 08), 1h 11m 31.963s; **8** Martin Tomczyk, D (Audi A4 DTM 09), 1h 11m 35.505s; **9** Ralf Schumacher, D (Mercedes C-Klasse 09), 1h 11m 40.795s; **10** Susie Stoddart, GB (Mercedes C-Klasse 08), 1h 11m 56.340s.
Fastest race lap: Timo Scheider, D (Audi A4 DTM 09), 1m 22.991s, 99.622 mph/160.326 km/h.
Pole position: Di Resta, 1m 21.394s, 101.576 mph/163.472 km/h.

GERMAN TOURING CAR CHAMPIONSHIP (DTM), Hockenheimring Grand Prix Circuit, Heidelberg, Germany, 17 October. Round 9. 47 laps of the 2.321-mile/3.736-km circuit, 109.108 miles/175.592 km.
1 Paul Di Resta, GB (Mercedes C-Klasse 09), 1h 07m 27.578s, 97.043 mph/156.175 km/h; **2** Timo Scheider, D (Audi A4 DTM 09), 1h 07m 38.110s; **3** Mike Rockenfeller, D (Audi A4 DTM 08), 1h 07m 42.280s; **4** Gary Paffett, GB (Mercedes C-Klasse 09), 1h 07m 47.119s; **5** Martin Tomczyk, D (Audi A4 DTM 09), 1h 07m 47.584s; **6** Oliver Jarvis, GB (Audi A4 DTM 09), 1h 07m 47.915s; **7** Susie Stoddart, GB (Mercedes C-Klasse 08), 1h 07m 48.524s; **8** Jamie Green, GB (Mercedes C-Klasse 08), 1h 07m 48.854s; **9** Maro Engel, D (Mercedes C-Klasse 08), 46 laps; **10** Bruno Spengler, CDN (Mercedes C-Klasse 09), **23** (DNF-rear suspension).
Fastest race lap: Di Resta, 1m 20.120s, 104.308 mph/167.868 km/h.
Pole position: Scheider, 1m 37.399s, 85.804 mph/138.088 km/h.

GERMAN TOURING CAR CHAMPIONSHIP (DTM), Autodromo Adria International Raceway, Adria, Italy, 31 October. Round 10. 38 laps of the 1.679-mile/2.702-km circuit, 63.800 miles/102.676 km.
1 Timo Scheider, D (Audi A4 DTM 09), 1h 15m 01.965s, 51.018 mph/82.105 km/h; **2** Gary Paffett, GB (Mercedes C-Klasse 09), 1h 15m 10.877s; **3** Bruno Spengler, CDN (Mercedes C-Klasse 09), 1h 15m 11.703s; **4** Markus Winkelhock, D (Audi A4 DTM 08), 1h 15m 18.930s; **5** Oliver Jarvis, GB (Audi A4 DTM 09), 1h 15m 19.973s; **6** Martin Tomczyk, D (Audi A4 DTM 09), 1h 15m 24.492s; **7** Maro Engel, D (Mercedes C-Klasse 08), 1h 15m 36.389s; **8** Mattias Ekström, S (Audi A4 DTM 09), 1h 15m 43.211s; **9** Paul Di Resta, GB (Mercedes C-Klasse 09), 1h 15m 45.722s; **10** David Coulthard, GB (Mercedes C-Klasse 08), 1h 15m 48.998s.
Fastest race lap: Ekström, 1m 21.722s, 73.961 mph/119.028 km/h.
Pole position: Paffett, 1m 10.471s, 85.769 mph/138.031 km/h.

Provisional championship points
Drivers: **1** Bruno Spengler, CDN, 66; **2** Paul Di Resta, GB, 63; **3** Gary Paffett, GB, 57; **4** Timo Scheider, D, 47; **5** Mattias Ekström, S, 35; **6** Jamie Green, GB, 29; **7** Mike Rockenfeller, D, 22; **8** Oliver Jarvis, GB, 18; **9** Martin Tomczyk, D, 15; **10** Alexandre Prémat, F, 12; **11** Miguel Molina, E, 11; **12** Markus Winkelhock, D, 5; **13** Susie Stoddart, GB, 4; **14** Ralf Schumacher, D, 3; **15** Maro Engel, D, 3.
Teams: **1** Salzgitter / Mercedes-Benz Bank AMG, 123; **2** Laureus AMG Mercedes, 66; **3** Audi Sport Team Abt, 65; **4** Audi Sport Team Abt Sportsline, 50; **5** Audi Sport Team Phoenix, 34; **6** TV Spielfilm / Junge Sterne AMG Mercedes, 33; **7** Audi Sport Rookie Team Abt, 11; **8** Audi Sport Team Rosberg, 5; **9** GQ AMG Mercedes, 3.

Result of the Shanghai race will be given in AUTOCOURSE 2011–2012.

British Touring Car Championship

BRITISH TOURING CAR CHAMPIONSHIP, Thruxton Circuit, Andover, Hampshire, Great Britain, 4 April. 16, 16 and 18 laps of the 2.356-mile/3.792-km circuit.
Round 1 (37.696 miles/60.666 km).
1 Fabrizio Giovanardi, I (Vauxhall Vectra), 21m 35.259s, 104.771 mph/168.612 km/h; **2** Jason Plato, GB (Chevrolet Cruze), 21m 38.519s; **3** Mat Jackson, GB (BMW 320si E90), 21m 41.715s; **4** Paul O'Neill, GB (Honda Integra), 21m 42.124s; **5** Tom Boardman, GB (SEAT Leon), 21m 44.646s; **6** Philip Glew, GB (Vauxhall Vectra), 21m 44.998s; **7** Alex MacDowall, GB (Chevrolet Cruze), 21m 50.025s; **8** David Pinkney, GB (Vauxhall Vectra), 21m 59.970s; **9** John George, GB (Honda Integra), 22m 07.807s; **10** Andy Neate, GB (BMW 320si E90), 22m 11.755s.
Fastest race lap: Shedden, 1m 18.473s, 108.083 mph/173.942 km/h.
Pole position: Shedden, 1m 24.061s, 100.898 mph/162.379 km/h.

Round 2 (37.696 miles/60.666 km).
1 Fabrizio Giovanardi, I (Vauxhall Vectra), 21m 32.829s, 104.967 mph/168.929 km/h; **2** Matt Neal, GB (Honda Civic), 21m 35.258s; **3** Paul O'Neill, GB (Honda Integra), 21m 36.837s; **4** Jason Plato, GB (Chevrolet Cruze), 21m 37.875s; **5** Mat Jackson, GB (BMW 320si E90), 21m 38.973s; **6** Alex MacDowall, GB (Chevrolet Cruze), 21m 39.673s; **7** Philip Glew, GB (Vauxhall Vectra), 21m 39.957s; **8** Steven Kane, GB (BMW 320si E90), 21m 46.138s; **9** Rob Collard, GB (BMW 320si E90), 21m 47.731s; **10** David Pinkney, GB (Vauxhall Vectra), 21m 49.686s.
Fastest race lap: Plato, 1m 19.094s, 107.234 mph/172.577 km/h.
Pole position: Giovanardi.

Round 3 (42.408 miles/68.249 km).
1 Steven Kane, GB (BMW 320si E90), 25m 29.299s, 99.829 mph/160.659 km/h; **2** Mat Jackson, GB (BMW 320si E90), 25m 30.395s; **3** Jason Plato, GB (Chevrolet Cruze), 25m 30.842s; **4** Gordon Shedden, GB (Honda Civic), 25m 31.032s; **5** Fabrizio Giovanardi, I (Vauxhall Vectra), 25m 31.206s; **6** Paul O'Neill, GB (Honda Integra), 25m 37.680s; **7** Tom Onslow-Cole, GB (Ford Focus ST), 25m 38.335s; **8** Tom Chilton, GB (Ford Focus ST), 25m 38.942s; **9** Alex MacDowall, GB (Chevrolet Cruze), 25m 40.662s; **10** David Pinkney, GB (Vauxhall Vectra), 25m 41.302s.
Fastest race lap: Collard, 1m 18.562s, 107.960 mph/173.745 km/h.
Pole position: Collard.

BRITISH TOURING CAR CHAMPIONSHIP, Rockingham Motor Speedway, Corby, Northamptonshire, Great Britain, 25 April. 3 x 16 laps of the 1.940-mile/3.122-km circuit.
Round 4 (31.040 miles/49.954 km).
1 Matt Neal, GB (Honda Civic), 23m 38.434s, 78.779 mph/126.783 km/h; **2** Gordon Shedden, GB (Honda Civic), 23m 46.667s; **3** Jason Plato, GB (Chevrolet Cruze), 23m 47.352s; **4** Tom Boardman, GB (SEAT Leon), 23m 53.402s; **5** Steven Kane, GB (BMW 320si E90), 23m 55.278s; **6** Paul O'Neill, GB (Honda Integra), 23m 55.561s; **7** Andrew Jordan, GB (Vauxhall Vectra), 24m 12.525s; **8** Tom Onslow-Cole, GB (Ford Focus ST), 24m 12.942s; **9** Martin Johnson, GB (Vauxhall Astra Coupe), 24m 29.696s; **10** Rob Collard, GB (BMW 320si E90), 24m 34.643s.
Fastest race lap: Collard, 1m 25.732s, 81.463 mph/131.102 km/h.
Pole position: Chilton, 1m 23.363s, 83.778 mph/134.827 km/h.

Round 5 (31.040 miles/49.954 km).
1 Jason Plato, GB (Chevrolet Cruze), 23m 06.392s, 80.600 mph/129.714 km/h; **2** Rob Collard, GB (BMW 320si E90), 23m 06.882s; **3** Steven Kane, GB (BMW 320si E90), 23m 08.305s; **4** Mat Jackson, GB (BMW 320si E90), 23m 09.825s; **5** Andrew Jordan, GB (Vauxhall Vectra), 23m 21.755s; **6** Tom Chilton, GB (Ford Focus ST), 23m 24.517s; **7** Tom Onslow-Cole, GB (Ford Focus ST), 23m 27.526s; **8** Paul O'Neill, GB (Honda Integra), 23m 27.797s; **9** Matt Neal, GB (Honda Civic), 23m 30.222s; **10** James Nash, GB (Vauxhall Vectra), 23m 38.031s.
Fastest race lap: Plato, 1m 25.019s, 82.146 mph/132.201 km/h.
Pole position: Neal.

Round 6 (31.040 miles/49.954 km).
1 Matt Neal, GB (Honda Civic), 23m 09.696s, 80.408 mph/129.405 km/h; **2** Paul O'Neill, GB (Honda Integra), 23m 15.185s; **3** Steven Kane, GB (BMW 320si E90), 23m 17.513s; **4** Andrew Jordan, GB (Vauxhall Vectra), 23m 19.965s; **5** Jason Plato, GB (Chevrolet Cruze), 23m 20.491s; **6** Rob Collard, GB (BMW 320si E90), 23m 20.843s; **7** Tom Onslow-Cole, GB (Ford Focus ST), 23m 22.399s; **8** James Nash, GB (Vauxhall Vectra), 23m 23.313s; **9** Andy Neate, GB (BMW 320si E90), 23m 23.704s; **10** Tom Boardman, GB (SEAT Leon), 23m 25.876s.
Fastest race lap: Neal, 1m 25.066s, 82.100 mph/132.128 km/h.
Pole position: Neal.

BRITISH TOURING CAR CHAMPIONSHIP, Brands Hatch Grand Prix Circuit, West Kingsdown, Dartford, Kent, Great Britain, 2 May. 3 x 18 laps of the 2.301-mile/3.703-km circuit.
Round 7 (41.416 miles/66.653 km).
1 Tom Chilton, GB (Ford Focus ST), 33m 15.656s, 74.711 mph/120.236 km/h; **2** Gordon Shedden, GB (Honda Civic), 33m 21.439s; **3** Tom Onslow-Cole, GB (Ford Focus ST), 33m 24.591s; **4** Rob Collard, GB (BMW 320si E90), 33m 30.040s; **5** Matt Neal, GB (Honda Civic), 33m 30.847s; **6** Paul O'Neill, GB (Honda Integra), 33m 32.760s; **7** Alex MacDowall, GB (Chevrolet Cruze), 33m 35.316s; **8** Jason Plato, GB (Chevrolet Cruze), 33m 35.559s; **9** Tom Boardman, GB (SEAT Leon), 33m 37.518s; **10** Mat Jackson, GB (BMW 320si E90), 33m 51.843s.
Fastest race lap: Chilton, 1m 41.919s, 81.272 mph/130.795 km/h.
Pole position: Chilton, 1m 31.604s, 90.424 mph/145.524 km/h.

Round 8 (41.416 miles/66.653 km).
1 Tom Onslow-Cole, GB (Ford Focus ST), 34m 03.212s, 72.972 mph/117.437 km/h; **2** Gordon Shedden, GB (Honda Civic), 34m 03.221s; **3** Alex MacDowall, GB (Chevrolet Cruze), 34m 03.997s; **4** Paul O'Neill, GB (Honda Integra), 34m 04.161s; **5** Andrew Jordan, GB (Vauxhall Vectra), 34m 04.995s; **6** Tom Boardman, GB (SEAT Leon), 34m 07.066s; **7** Steven Kane, GB (BMW 320si E90), 34m 08.294s; **8** David Pinkney, GB (Vauxhall Vectra), 34m 08.464s; **9** Matthew Hamilton, GB (Honda Civic Type-R), 34m 10.733s; **10** James Nash, GB (Vauxhall Vectra), 34m 12.568s.
Disqualified: Chilton (ride height failure).
Fastest race lap: Neal, 1m 42.176s, 81.068 mph/130.466 km/h.
Pole position: Chilton.

Round 9 (41.416 miles/66.653 km).
1 Mat Jackson, GB (BMW 320si E90), 32m 50.721s, 75.656 mph/121.757 km/h; **2** Matt Neal, GB (Honda Civic), 32m 51.190s; **3** Steven Kane, GB (BMW 320si E90), 32m 52.429s; **4** Rob Collard, GB (BMW 320si E90), 32m 55.764s; **5** Andrew Jordan, GB (Vauxhall Vectra), 32m 58.559s; **6** Tom Chilton, GB (Ford Focus ST), 33m 02.018s; **7** James Nash, GB (Vauxhall Vectra), 33m 04.857s; **8** Tom Boardman, GB (SEAT Leon), 33m 09.163s; **9** Gordon Shedden, GB (Honda Civic), 33m 10.100s; **10** Tom Onslow-Cole, GB (Ford Focus ST), 33m 10.105s.
Fastest race lap: Neal, 1m 38.992s, 83.675 mph/134.663 km/h.
Pole position: Kane.

BRITISH TOURING CAR CHAMPIONSHIP, Oulton Park Circuit, Tarporley, Cheshire, Great Britain, 6 June. 17, 15 and 18 laps of the 2.226-mile/3.582-km circuit.
Round 10 (37.842 miles/60.901 km).
1 Tom Onslow-Cole, GB (Ford Focus ST), 26m 23.471s, 86.033 mph/138.457 km/h; **2** Gordon Shedden, GB (Honda Civic), 26m 23.819s; **3** Rob Collard, GB (BMW 320si E90), 26m 24.644s; **4** Mat Jackson, GB (BMW 320si E90), 26m 25.568s; **5** Tom Chilton, GB (Ford Focus ST), 26m 26.333s; **6** Steven Kane, GB (BMW 320si E90), 26m 26.935s; **7** Alex MacDowall, GB (Chevrolet Cruze), 26m 28.591s; **8** Matt Neal, GB (Honda Civic), 26m 29.561s; **9** James Nash, GB (Vauxhall Vectra), 26m 29.801s; **10** Jason Plato, GB (Chevrolet Cruze), 26m 35.100s.
Fastest race lap: Shedden, 1m 27.793s, 91.278 mph/146.898 km/h.
Pole position: Onslow-Cole, 1m 27.330s, 91.762 mph/147.677 km/h.

Round 11 (33.390 miles/53.736 km).
1 Jason Plato, GB (Chevrolet Cruze), 22m 22.567s, 89.532 mph/144.089 km/h; **2** Matt Neal, GB (Honda Civic), 22m 23.316s; **3** Tom Onslow-Cole, GB (Ford Focus ST), 22m 26.050s; **4** Mat Jackson, GB (BMW 320si E90), 22m 27.488s; **5** Steven Kane, GB (BMW 320si E90), 22m 31.945s; **6** Tom Chilton, GB (Ford Focus ST), 22m 34.583s; **7** James Nash, GB (Vauxhall Vectra), 22m 34.895s; **8** Tom Boardman, GB (SEAT Leon), 22m 35.701s; **9** Alex MacDowall, GB (Chevrolet Cruze), 22m 59.751s; **10** David Pinkney, GB (Vauxhall Vectra), 22m 59.794s.
Fastest race lap: Plato, 1m 28.111s, 90.948 mph/146.368 km/h.
Pole position: Onslow-Cole.

Round 12 (40.068 miles/64.483 km).
1 Matt Neal, GB (Honda Civic), 29m 17.935s, 82.053 mph/132.052 km/h; **2** Steven Kane, GB (BMW 320si E90), 29m 18.217s; **3** James Nash, GB (Vauxhall Vectra), 29m 19.256s; **4** Tom Chilton, GB (Ford Focus ST), 29m 20.044s; **5** Tom Onslow-Cole, GB (Ford Focus ST), 29m 20.428s; **6** Jason Plato, GB (Chevrolet Cruze), 29m 21.854s; **7** Mat Jackson, GB (BMW 320si E90), 29m 22.311s; **8** Rob Collard, GB (BMW 320si E90), 29m 23.183s; **9** Paul O'Neill, GB (Honda Integra), 29m 26.081s; **10** Gordon Shedden, GB (Honda Civic), 29m 33.387s.
Fastest race lap: Shedden, 1m 27.979s, 91.085 mph/146.587 km/h.
Pole position: MacDowall.

BRITISH TOURING CAR CHAMPIONSHIP, Croft Racing Circuit, Croft-on-Tees, North Yorkshire, Great Britain, 20 June. 3 x 15 laps of the 2.125-mile/3.420-km circuit.
Round 13 (31.875 miles/51.298 km).
1 Gordon Shedden, GB (Honda Civic), 21m 59.863s, 86.940 mph/139.917 km/h; **2** Rob Collard, GB (BMW 320si E90), 21m 59.898s; **3** Jason Plato, GB (Chevrolet Cruze), 22m 18.218s; **4** Matt Neal, GB (Honda Civic), 22m 19.875s; **5** Paul O'Neill, GB (Honda Integra), 22m 20.128s; **6** James Nash, GB (Vauxhall Vectra), 22m 27.139s; **7** Daniel Lloyd, GB (Vauxhall Vectra), 22m 27.751s; **8** Tom Onslow-Cole, GB (Ford Focus ST), 22m 30.186s; **9** Mat Jackson, GB (BMW 320si E90), 22m 30.417s; **10** Andrew Jordan, GB (Vauxhall Vectra), 22m 30.862s.
Fastest race lap: Shedden, 1m 26.297s, 88.647 mph/142.664 km/h.
Pole position: Chilton, 1m 24.629s, 90.394 mph/145.475 km/h.

Round 14 (31.875 miles/51.298 km).
1 Gordon Shedden, GB (Honda Civic), 22m 16.514s, 85.857 mph/138.174 km/h; **2** Matt Neal, GB (Honda Civic), 22m 17.256s; **3** Jason Plato, GB (Chevrolet Cruze), 22m 22.864s; **4** Paul O'Neill, GB (Honda Integra), 22m 26.472s; **5** Tom Onslow-Cole, GB (Ford Focus ST), 22m 27.423s; **6** Tom Boardman, GB (SEAT Leon), 22m 33.922s; **7** Andrew Jordan, GB (Vauxhall Vectra), 22m 34.113s; **8** Rob Collard, GB (BMW 320si E90), 22m 34.303s; **9** Alex MacDowall, GB (Chevrolet Cruze), 22m 34.857s; **10** Andy Neate, GB (BMW 320si E90), 22m 35.845s.
Fastest race lap: O'Neill, 1m 26.809s, 88.124 mph/141.822 km/h.
Pole position: Shedden.

Round 15 (31.875 miles/51.298 km).
1 Andrew Jordan, GB (Vauxhall Vectra), 22m 14.953s, 85.958 mph/138.336 km/h; **2** Tom Onslow-Cole, GB (Ford Focus ST), 22m 22.838s; **3** Steven Kane, GB (BMW 320si E90), 22m 28.895s; **4** Tom Chilton, GB (Ford Focus ST), 22m 29.891s; **5** Paul O'Neill, GB (Honda Integra), 22m 31.153s; **6** Tom Boardman, GB (SEAT Leon), 22m 31.357s; **7** Mat Jackson, GB (BMW 320si E90), 22m 31.457s; **8** Daniel Lloyd, GB (Vauxhall Vectra), 22m 31.542s; **9** Gordon Shedden, GB (Honda Civic), 22m 36.631s; **10** Alex MacDowall, GB (Chevrolet Cruze), 22m 37.947s.
Fastest race lap: Plato, 1m 26.674s, 88.261 mph/142.043 km/h.
Pole position: Jordan.

BRITISH TOURING CAR CHAMPIONSHIP, Snetterton Circuit, Thetford, Norfolk, Great Britain, 8 August. 18, 21 and 18 laps of the 1.952-mile/3.141-km circuit.
Round 16 (35.136 miles/56.546 km).
1 Jason Plato, GB (Chevrolet Cruze), 21m 58.345s, 95.945 mph/154.409 km/h; **2** Mat Jackson, GB (BMW 320si E90), 22m 00.148s; **3** Tom Chilton, GB (Ford Focus ST), 22m 01.610s; **4** Gordon Shedden, GB (Honda Civic), 22m 07.045s; **5** James Nash, GB (Vauxhall Vectra), 22m 08.801s; **6** Tom Onslow-Cole, GB (Ford Focus ST), 22m 11.442s; **7** Steven Kane, GB (BMW 320si E90), 22m 16.460s; **8** Tom Boardman, GB (SEAT Leon), 22m 17.970s; **9** Andrew Jordan, GB (Vauxhall Vectra), 22m 19.060s; **10** Rob Collard, GB (BMW 320si E90), 22m 19.551s.
Fastest race lap: Plato, 1m 12.512s, 96.910 mph/155.962 km/h.
Pole position: MacDowall, 1m 19.332s, 88.579 mph/142.555 km/h.

Round 17 (40.992 miles/65.970 km).
1 Jason Plato, GB (Chevrolet Cruze), 28m 20.424s, 86.784 mph/139.666 km/h; **2** Tom Chilton, GB (Ford Focus ST), 28m 23.350s; **3** Tom Onslow-Cole, GB (Ford Focus ST), 28m 23.842s; **4** Steven Kane, GB (BMW 320si E90), 28m 31.097s; **5** Mat Jackson, GB (BMW 320si E90), 28m 31.643s; **6** Andrew Jordan, GB (Vauxhall Vectra), 28m 32.231s; **7** Rob Collard, GB (BMW 320si E90), 28m 32.502s; **8** Gordon Shedden, GB (Honda Civic), 28m 32.818s; **9** Matt Neal, GB (Honda Civic), 28m 33.248s; **10** James Nash, GB (Vauxhall Vectra), 28m 34.959s.
Fastest race lap: Plato, 1m 12.378s, 97.090 mph/156.251 km/h.
Pole position: Plato.

Round 18 (35.136 miles/56.546 km).
1 Gordon Shedden, GB (Honda Civic), 22m 01.411s, 95.723 mph/154.051 km/h; **2** Rob Collard, GB (BMW 320si E90), 22m 03.559s; **3** Matt Neal, GB (Honda Civic), 22m 04.252s; **4** Tom Chilton, GB (Ford Focus ST), 22m 05.958s; **5** Jason Plato, GB (Chevrolet Cruze), 22m 06.338s; **6** Steven Kane, GB (BMW 320si E90), 22m 06.596s; **7** Mat Jackson, GB (BMW 320si E90), 22m 14.202s; **8** Paul O'Neill, GB (Honda Integra), 22m 30.962s; **9** David Pinkney, GB (Vauxhall Vectra), 22m 31.767s; **10** Andy Neate, GB (BMW 320si E90), 22m 32.069s.
Fastest race lap: Onslow-Cole, 1m 12.344s, 97.135 mph/156.325 km/h.
Pole position: Nash.

BRITISH TOURING CAR CHAMPIONSHIP, Silverstone Short Circuit, Towcester, Northamptonshire, Great Britain, 22 August. 22, 22 and 25 laps of the 1.639-mile/2.638-km circuit.
Round 19 (36.058 miles/58.030 km).
1 Tom Chilton, GB (Ford Focus ST), 22m 35.870s, 95.738 mph/154.075 km/h; **2** Tom Onslow-Cole, GB (Ford Focus ST), 22m 36.152s; **3** Jason Plato, GB (Chevrolet Cruze), 22m 38.765s; **4** Alex MacDowall, GB (Chevrolet Cruze), 22m 38.941s; **5** Andrew Jordan, GB (Vauxhall Vectra), 22m 39.634s; **6** Rob Collard, GB (BMW 320si E90), 22m 42.343s; **7** Paul O'Neill, GB (Honda Integra), 22m 43.468s; **8** Matt Neal, GB (Honda Civic), 22m 44.643s; **9** Steven Kane, GB (BMW 320si E90), 22m 45.806s; **10** Gordon Shedden, GB (Honda Civic), 22m 46.256s.
Fastest race lap: Onslow-Cole, 1m 00.682s, 97.234 mph/156.484 km/h.
Pole position: Onslow-Cole, 59.659s, 98.902 mph/159.167 km/h.

Round 20 (36.058 miles/58.030 km).
1 Tom Chilton, GB (Ford Focus ST), 22m 44.416s, 95.138 mph/153.110 km/h; **2** Rob Collard, GB (BMW 320si E90), 22m 45.520s; **3** Tom Onslow-Cole, GB (Ford Focus ST), 22m 45.639s; **4** Jason Plato, GB (Chevrolet Cruze), 22m 46.880s; **5** Matt Neal, GB (Honda Civic), 22m 47.533s; **6** Paul O'Neill, GB (Honda Integra), 22m 47.603s; **7** Gordon Shedden, GB (Honda Civic), 22m 47.705s; **8** Steven Kane, GB (BMW 320si E90), 22m 48.311s; **9** Alex MacDowall, GB (Chevrolet Cruze), 22m 48.703s; **10** Mat Jackson, GB (BMW 320si E90), 22m 52.958s.
Fastest race lap: Onslow-Cole, 1m 00.757s, 97.114 mph/156.291 km/h.
Pole position: Chilton.

Round 21 (40.975 miles/65.943 km).
1 Tom Onslow-Cole, GB (Ford Focus ST), 28m 42.835s, 85.620 mph/137.792 km/h; **2** Paul O'Neill, GB (Honda Integra), 28m 45.463s; **3** Mat Jackson, GB (BMW 320si E90), 28m 49.432s; **4** Matt Neal, GB (Honda Civic), 28m 49.660s; **5** Gordon Shedden, GB (Honda Civic), 28m 50.044s; **6** Tom Chilton, GB (Ford Focus ST), 28m 50.542s; **7** Steven Kane, GB (BMW 320si E90), 28m 52.122s; **8** James Nash, GB (Vauxhall Vectra), 28m 59.722s; **9** Jason Plato, GB (Chevrolet Cruze), 28m 59.968s; **10** Alex MacDowall, GB (Chevrolet Cruze), 29m 02.270s.
Fastest race lap: Onslow-Cole, 1m 01.120s, 96.537 mph/155.362 km/h.
Pole position: O'Neill.

BRITISH TOURING CAR CHAMPIONSHIP, Knockhill Racing Circuit, Dunfermline, Fife, Scotland, Great Britain, 5 September. 3 x 27 laps of the 1.271-mile/2.046-km circuit.
Round 22 (34.325 miles/55.241 km).
1 Gordon Shedden, GB (Honda Civic), 25m 26.498s, 80.950 mph/130.276 km/h; **2** Alex MacDowall, GB (Chevrolet Cruze), 25m 28.090s; **3** Steven Kane, GB (BMW 320si E90), 25m 32.128s; **4** Matt Neal, GB (Honda Civic), 25m 32.801s; **5** Tom Chilton, GB (Ford Focus ST), 25m 33.018s; **6** Jason Plato, GB (Chevrolet Cruze), 25m 33.447s; **7** Tom Onslow-Cole, GB (Ford Focus ST), 25m 43.754s; **8** Paul O'Neill, GB (Honda Integra), 25m 43.806s; **9** Andrew Jordan, GB (Vauxhall Vectra), 25m 44.688s; **10** Mat Jackson, GB (BMW 320si E90), 25m 44.827s.
Fastest race lap: MacDowall, 53.313s, 85.845 mph/138.154 km/h.
Pole position: MacDowall, 53.001s, 86.350 mph/138.968 km/h.

Round 23 (34.325 miles/55.241 km).
1 Matt Neal, GB (Honda Civic), 27m 56.927s, 73.688 mph/118.590 km/h; **2** Gordon Shedden, GB (Honda Civic), 27m 57.414s; **3** Jason Plato, GB (Chevrolet Cruze), 28m 00.088s; **4** Tom Chilton, GB (Ford Focus ST), 28m 02.220s; **5** Steven Kane, GB (BMW 320si E90), 28m 05.803s; **6** Mat Jackson, GB (BMW 320si E90), 28m 06.220s; **7** Tom Onslow-Cole, GB (Ford Focus ST), 28m 06.738s; **8** Andrew Jordan, GB (Vauxhall Vectra), 28m 07.169s; **9** Alex MacDowall, GB (Chevrolet Cruze), 28m 07.756s; **10** Paul O'Neill, GB (Honda Integra), 28m 14.411s.
Fastest race lap: Chilton, 53.302s, 85.863 mph/138.183 km/h.
Pole position: Shedden.

Round 24 (34.325 miles/55.241 km).
1 Jason Plato, GB (Chevrolet Cruze), 26m 18.277s, 78.294 mph/126.002 km/h; **2** Tom Onslow-Cole, GB (Ford Focus ST), 26m 19.952s; **3** Matt Neal, GB (Honda Civic), 26m 20.271s; **4** Paul O'Neill, GB (Honda Integra), 26m 23.212s; **5** Mat Jackson, GB (BMW 320si E90), 26m 23.614s; **6** Rob Collard, GB (BMW 320si E90), 26m 24.253s; **7** Alex MacDowall, GB (Chevrolet Cruze), 26m 25.314s; **8** Andrew Jordan, GB (Vauxhall Vectra), 26m 26.459s; **9** Gordon Shedden, GB (Honda Civic), 26m 27.595s; **10** Tom Chilton, GB (Ford Focus ST), 26m 29.193s.
Fastest race lap: O'Neill, 53.788s, 85.087 mph/136.934 km/h.
Pole position: Onslow-Cole.

BRITISH TOURING CAR CHAMPIONSHIP, Donington Park National Circuit, Castle Donington, Great Britain, 19 September. 19, 17 and 16 laps of the 1.979-mile/3.185-km circuit.
Round 25 (37.601 miles/60.513 km).
1 Gordon Shedden, GB (Honda Civic), 26m 45.547s, 84.309 mph/135.683 km/h; **2** Tom Chilton, GB (Ford Focus ST), 26m 45.846s; **3** Mat Jackson, GB (BMW 320si E90), 26m 46.740s; **4** Alex MacDowall, GB (Chevrolet Cruze), 26m 47.105s; **5** Matt Neal, GB (Honda Civic), 26m 48.336s; **6** Steven Kane, GB (BMW 320si E90), 26m 49.754s; **7** Tom Boardman, GB (SEAT Leon), 26m 51.408s; **8** Tom Onslow-Cole, GB (Ford Focus ST), 26m 51.988s; **9** James Kaye, GB (Honda Integra), 26m 52.806s; **10** David Pinkney, GB (Vauxhall Vectra), 26m 53.516s.
Fastest race lap: Chilton, 1m 12.432s, 98.359 mph/158.294 km/h.
Pole position: Chilton, 1m 11.328s, 99.882 mph/160.744 km/h.

Round 26 (33.643 miles/54.143 km).
1 Tom Onslow-Cole, GB (Ford Focus ST), 21m 07.476s, 95.555 mph/153.782 km/h; **2** Gordon Shedden, GB (Honda Civic), 21m 08.411s; **3** Jason Plato, GB (Chevrolet Cruze), 21m 09.018s; **4** Tom Chilton, GB (Ford Focus ST), 21m 15.032s; **5** Mat Jackson, GB (BMW 320si E90), 21m 17.712s; **6** Steven Kane, GB (BMW 320si E90), 21m 18.454s; **7** Rob Collard, GB (BMW 320si E90), 21m 18.523s; **8** Matt Neal, GB (Honda Civic), 21m 19.591s; **9** Andrew Jordan, GB (Vauxhall Vectra), 21m 20.678s; **10** James Nash, GB (Vauxhall Vectra), 21m 21.025s.
Fastest race lap: Plato, 1m 12.126s, 98.777 mph/158.966 km/h.
Pole position: Shedden.

Round 27 (31.664 miles/50.958 km).
1 Matt Neal, GB (Honda Civic), 19m 29.257s, 97.489 mph/156.894 km/h; **2** Rob Collard, GB (BMW 320si E90), 19m 33.372s; **3** Jason Plato, GB (Chevrolet Cruze), 19m 35.659s; **4** Steven Kane, GB (BMW 320si E90), 19m 37.009s; **5** Tom Chilton, GB (Ford Focus ST), 19m 38.240s; **6** Gordon Shedden, GB (Honda Civic), 19m 38.557s; **7** Andrew Jordan, GB (Vauxhall Vectra), 19m 39.463s; **8** Mat Jackson, GB (BMW 320si E90), 19m 44.549s; **9** Tom Onslow-Cole, GB (Ford Focus ST), 19m 49.156s; **10** James Nash, GB (Vauxhall Vectra), 19m 49.203s.
Fastest race lap: Plato, 1m 12.082s, 98.837 mph/159.063 km/h.
Pole position: Jordan.

BRITISH TOURING CAR CHAMPIONSHIP, Brands Hatch Indy Circuit, West Kingsdown, Dartford, Kent, Great Britain, 10 October. 24, 26 and 27 laps of the 1.199-mile/1.929-km circuit.
Round 28 (28.766 miles/46.295 km).
1 Jason Plato, GB (Chevrolet Cruze), 19m 56.707s, 86.536 mph/139.267 km/h; **2** Gordon Shedden, GB (Honda Civic), 19m 58.861s; **3** Matt Neal, GB (Honda Civic), 19m 59.457s; **4** Alex MacDowall, GB (Chevrolet Cruze), 20m 01.333s; **5** Rob Collard, GB (BMW 320si E90), 20m 01.593s; **6** Paul O'Neill, GB (Honda Integra), 20m 07.983s; **7** Tom Chilton, GB (Ford Focus ST), 20m 08.578s; **8** James Nash, GB (Vauxhall Vectra), 20m 09.709s; **9** Andrew Jordan, GB (Vauxhall Vectra), 20m

10.975s; **10** Tom Boardman, GB (SEAT Leon), 20m 12.846s.
Fastest race lap: Plato, 49.021s, 88.022 mph/ 141.658 km/h.
Pole position: Plato, 48.647s, 88.699 mph/ 142.747 km/h.

Round 29 (31.164 miles/50.153 km).
1 Jason Plato, GB (Chevrolet Cruze), 22m 11.749s, 84.241 mph/135.574 km/h; **2** Matt Neal, GB (Honda Civic), 22m 12.636s; **3** Rob Collard, GB (BMW 320si E90), 22m 16.532s; **4** Paul O'Neill, GB (Honda Integra), 22m 17.420s; **5** Tom Chilton, GB (Ford Focus ST), 22m 20.063s; **6** Steven Kane, GB (BMW 320si E90), 22m 21.234s; **7** Andrew Jordan, GB (Vauxhall Vectra), 22m 27.771s; **8** Mat Jackson, GB (BMW 320si E90), 22m 28.082s; **9** James Nash, GB (Vauxhall Vectra), 22m 28.597s; **10** Andy Neate, GB (BMW 320si E90), 22m 31.843s.
Fastest race lap: Collard, 48.898s, 88.244 mph/ 142.015 km/h.
Pole position: Plato.

Round 30 (32.362 miles/52.082 km).
1 Andrew Jordan, GB (Vauxhall Vectra), 23m 37.692s, 82.178 mph/132.253 km/h; **2** Steven Kane, GB (BMW 320si E90), 23m 38.641s; **3** Tom Chilton, GB (Ford Focus ST), 23m 39.034s; **4** Mat Jackson, GB (BMW 320si E90), 23m 39.297s; **5** Paul O'Neill, GB (Honda Integra), 23m 39.665s; **6** Rob Collard, GB (BMW 320si E90), 23m 40.022s; **7** James Nash, GB (Vauxhall Vectra), 23m 40.816s; **8** Gordon Shedden, GB (Honda Civic), 23m 41.162s; **9** Jason Plato, GB (Chevrolet Cruze), 23m 41.838s; **10** Sam Tordoff, GB (Vauxhall Vectra), 23m 43.653s.
Fastest race lap: Jackson, 49.199s, 87.704 mph/ 141.146 km/h.
Pole position: Jordan.

Final championship points
Drivers: 1 Jason Plato, GB, 260; **2** Matt Neal, GB, 229; **3** Gordon Shedden, GB, 218; **4** Tom Onslow-Cole, GB, 200; **5** Tom Chilton, GB, 191; **6** Steven Kane, GB, 169; **7** Mat Jackson, GB, 155; **8** Rob Collard, GB, 144; **9** Paul O'Neill, GB, 136; **10** Andrew Jordan, GB, 101; **11** Alex MacDowall, GB, 83; **12** James Nash, GB, 52; **13** Tom Boardman, GB, 48; **14** Fabrizio Giovanardi, I, 38; **15** David Pinkney, GB, 12; **16** Philip Glew, GB, 9; **17** Daniel Lloyd, GB, 7; **18** Andy Neate, GB, 6; **19** Martin Johnson, GB, 2; **20** John George, GB, 2; **21** Matthew Hamilton, GB, 2; **22** James Kaye, GB, 2; **23** Sam Tordoff, GB, 1.
Teams: 1 Honda Racing Team, 424; **2** Team Aon, 366; **3** Silverline Chevrolet, 322; **4** Airwaves BMW, 321; **5** WSR, 146; **6** Sunshine.co.uk with Tech-Speed Motorsport, 135; **7** Uniq Racing with Triple Eight, 104; **8** Pirtek Racing, 98; **9** Special Tuning UK, 46; **10** Pinkney Motorsport, 12; **11** Boulevard Team Racing, 2; **12** TH Motorsport, 2; **13** WRC Developments, 2.
Manufacturers: 1 Honda, 546; **2** Ford, 522; **3** Chevrolet, 466.
Independent Drivers: 1 Tom Chilton, GB, 249; **2** Steven Kane, GB, 247; **3** Tom Onslowe-Cole, GB, 241.
4 Mat Jackson, GB, 221; **5** Paul O'Neill, GB, 208.
Independent Teams: 1 Team Aon, 342; **2** Airwaves BMW, 311; **3** WSR, 250; **4** Sunshine.co.uk, 249; **5** Triple Eight, 189.

IZOD Indycar Series

All cars are Dallara IR4-Honda HI8R.

SAO PAULO INDY 300, Streets of Sao Paulo, Brazil, 14 March. Round 1. 61 laps of the 2.536-mile/4.081-km circuit, 154.696 miles/248.959 km.
1 Will Power, AUS, 2h 00m 57.7112s, 76.733 mph/ 123.490 km/h; **2** Ryan Hunter-Reay, USA, 2h 00m 59.5693s; **3** Vitor Meira, BR, 2h 01m 07.4206s; **4** Raphael Matos, BR, 2h 01m 08.1347s; **5** Dan Wheldon, GB, 2h 01m 08.5995s; **6** Scott Dixon, NZ, 2h 01m 09.0585s; **7** Dario Franchitti, GB, 2h 01m 09.7691s; **8** Mike Conway, GB, 2h 01m 09.8766s; **9** Hélio Castroneves, BR, 2h 01m 10.4523s; **10** Tony Kanaan, BR, 2h 01m 11.1962s; **11** Justin Wilson, GB, 2h 01m 11.6305s; **12** Ernesto Viso, YV, 2h 01m 14.6151s; **13** Ana Beatriz, BR, 2h 01m 17.3563s; **14** Ryan Briscoe, AUS, 2h 02m 12.6303s; **15** Danica Patrick, USA, 60 laps; **16** Simona de Silvestro, CH, 58; **17** Mario Romancini, BR, 46 (DNF-accident); **18** Alex Lloyd, GB, 30 (DNF-accident); **19** Alex Tagliani, CDN, 28 (DNF-accident); **20** Hideki Mutoh, J, **27** (DNF-accident); **21** Milka Duno, YV, **20** (DNF-accident); **22** Takuma Sato, J, 0 (DNF-accident); **23** Marco Andretti, USA, 0 (DNF-accident); **24** Mário Moraes, BR, 0 (DNF-accident).
Most laps led: Franchitti, 29.
Fastest race lap: Power, 1m 28.1892s, 103.523 mph/ 166.604 km/h.
Pole position: Franchitti, 1m 27.7354s, 104.058 mph/ 167.466 km/h.
Championship points: Drivers: 1 Power, 50; **2** Hunter-Reay, 40; **3** Meira, 35; **4** Matos, 32; **5** Wheldon, 30; **6** Franchitti, 29.

HONDA GRAND PRIX OF ST. PETERSBURG, St. Petersburg Street Circuit, Florida, USA, 29 March. Round 2. 100 laps of the 1.800-mile/2.897-km circuit, 180.000 miles/289.682 km.
1 Will Power, AUS, 2h 07m 05.7968s, 84.975 mph/ 136.754 km/h; **2** Justin Wilson, GB, 2h 07m 06.6212s; **3** Ryan Briscoe, AUS, 2h 07m 10.5258s; **4** Hélio Castroneves, BR, 2h 07m 10.9667s; **5** Dario Franchitti, GB, 2h 07m 28.0140s; **6** Alex Tagliani, CDN, 2h 07m 35.1192s; **7** Danica Patrick, USA, 2h 07m 36.1328s; **8** Raphael Matos, BR, 2h 07m 36.4663s; **9** Graham Rahal, USA, 2h 07m 36.6394s; **10** Tony Kanaan, BR, 2h 07m 37.1476s; **11** Ryan Hunter-Reay, USA, 2h 07m 37.4254s; **12** Marco Andretti, USA, 2h 07m 37.9671s; **13** Mario Romancini, BR, 2h 07m 45.6054s; **14** Hideki Mutoh, J, 2h 07m 45.7917s; **15** Vitor Meira, BR, 2h 08m 01.8561s; **16** Simona de Silvestro, CH, 99 laps; **17** Ernesto Viso, YV, 97; **18** Scott Dixon, NZ, 73 (DNF-accident); **19** Mike Conway, GB, 64 (DNF-accident); **20** Dan Wheldon, GB, 46 (DNF-suspension/accident); **21** Mário Moraes, BR, 45 (DNF-accident); **22** Takuma Sato, J, 24 (DNF-accident); **23** Alex Lloyd, GB, 14 (DNF-accident); **24** Milka Duno, YV, 7 (DNF-handling).
Most laps led: Power, 50.
Fastest race lap: Viso, 1m 03.8605s, 101.471 mph/ 163.302 km/h.
Pole position: Power, 1m 01.6026s, 105.190 mph/ 169.287 km/h.
Championship points: Drivers: 1 Power, 103; **2** Hunter-Reay, 59; **2** Wilson, 59; **4** Franchitti, 59; **5** Matos, 56; **6** Castroneves, 54.

INDY GRAND PRIX OF ALABAMA, Barber Motorsports Park, Birmingham, Alabama, USA, 11 April. Round 3. 90 laps of the 2.300-mile/3.701-km circuit, 207.000 miles/333.134 km.
1 Hélio Castroneves, BR, 1h 56m 41.3928s, 106.436 mph/ 171.292 km/h; **2** Scott Dixon, NZ, 1h 56m 41.9631s; **3** Dario Franchitti, GB, 1h 56m 49.5518s; **4** Will Power, AUS, 1h 56m 50.0567s; **5** Marco Andretti, USA, 1h 56m 51.1338s; **6** Ryan Briscoe, AUS, 1h 56m 52.3539s; **7** Justin Wilson, GB, 1h 56m 52.9406s; **8** Tony Kanaan, BR, 1h 56m 54.2461s; **9** Mike Conway, GB, 1h 56m 54.7090s; **10** Alex Tagliani, CDN, 1h 56m 56.2378s; **11** Dan Wheldon, GB, 1h 56m 56.5935s; **12** Ryan Hunter-Reay, USA, 1h 56m 57.0655s; **13** Mário Moraes, BR, 1h 56m 58.1170s; **14** Raphael Matos, BR, 89 laps; **15** Hideki Mutoh, J, 89; **16** Ernesto Viso, YV, 89; **17** Graham Rahal, USA, 89; **18** Vitor Meira, BR, 89; **19** Danica Patrick, USA, 89; **20** Bertrand Baguette, B, 89; **21** Simona de Silvestro, CH, 89; **22** Mario Romancini, BR, 89; **23** Alex Lloyd, GB, 89; **24** Milka Duno, YV, 86; **25** Takuma Sato, J, 68.
Most laps led: Andretti, 58.
Fastest race lap: Wilson, 1m 12.7853s, 113.759 mph/ 183.078 km/h.
Pole position: Power, 1m 10.1356s, 118.057 mph/ 189.994 km/h.
Championship points: Drivers: 1 Power, 136; **2** Castroneves, 104; **3** Franchitti, 94; **4** Wilson, 85; **5** Dixon, 80; **6** Briscoe, 79.

TOYOTA GRAND PRIX OF LONG BEACH, Long Beach Street Circuit, California, USA, 18 April. Round 4. 85 laps of the 1.968-mile/3.167-km circuit, 167.280 miles/269.211 km.
1 Ryan Hunter-Reay, USA, 1h 47m 12.5404s, 93.619 mph/ 150.665 km/h; **2** Justin Wilson, GB, 1h 47m 18.1435s; **3** Will Power, AUS, 1h 47m 21.1268s; **4** Scott Dixon, NZ, 1h 47m 23.1691s; **5** Tony Kanaan, BR, 1h 47m 24.3136s; **6** Mário Moraes, BR, 1h 47m 29.0575s; **7** Hélio Castroneves, BR, 1h 47m 29.4332s; **8** Ryan Briscoe, AUS, 1h 47m 30.7618s; **9** Dan Wheldon, GB, 1h 47m 31.9979s; **10** Mike Conway, GB, 1h 47m 32.4711s; **11** Vitor Meira, BR, 1h 47m 39.9409s; **12** Dario Franchitti, GB, 1h 47m 40.6756s; **13** Hideki Mutoh, J, 1h 47m 41.1441s; **14** Marco Andretti, USA, 1h 47m 42.5524s; **15** Ernesto Viso, YV, 1h 47m 44.1586s; **16** Danica Patrick, USA, 1h 47m 44.7208s; **17** Simona de Silvestro, CH, 1h 47m 45.7056s; **18** Takuma Sato, J, 84 laps; **19** Alex Lloyd, GB, 84; **20** Raphael Matos, BR, 84; **21** Alex Tagliani, CDN, 65 (DNF-suspension); **22** Graham Rahal, USA, 58 (DNF-accident); **23** Mario Romancini, BR, 58 (DNF-accident); **24** Bertrand Baguette, B, 45 (DNF-suspension); **25** Milka Duno, YV, 10 (DNF-handling).
Most laps led: Hunter-Reay, 64.
Fastest race lap: Hunter-Reay, 1m 10.5537s, 100.417 mph/161.606 km/h.
Pole position: Power, 1m 09.3185s, 102.206 mph/ 164.485 km/h.
Championship points: Drivers: 1 Power, 172; **2** Castroneves, 130; **3** Hunter-Reay, 129; **4** Wilson, 125; **5** Dixon, 112; **6** Franchitti, 112.

ROAD RUNNER TURBO INDY 300, Kansas Speedway, Kansas City, Kansas, USA, 1 May. Round 5. 200 laps of the 1.520-mile/2.446-km circuit, 304.000 miles/ 489.241 km.
1 Scott Dixon, NZ, 1h 50m 43.1410s, 164.741 mph/ 265.125 km/h; **2** Dario Franchitti, GB, 1h 50m 46.1938s; **3** Tony Kanaan, BR, 1h 50m 46.3620s; **4** Hélio Castroneves, BR, 1h 50m 46.9710s; **5** Ryan Hunter-Reay, USA, 1h 50m 49.2543s; **6** Ryan Briscoe, AUS, 1h 50m 49.9361s; **7** Mário Moraes, BR, 199 laps; **8** Alex Tagliani, CDN, 199; **9** John Andretti, USA, 199; **10** Vitor Meira, BR, 199; **11** Danica Patrick, USA, 198; **12** Will Power, AUS, 198; **13** Marco Andretti, USA, 198; **14** Mike Conway, GB, 198; **15** Dan Wheldon, GB, 198; **16** Raphael Matos, BR, 198; **17** Sarah Fisher, USA, 198; **18** Justin Wilson, GB, 197; **19** Alex Lloyd, GB, 197; **20** Bertrand Baguette, B, 197; **21** Simona de Silvestro, CH, 197; **22** Mario Romancini, BR, 196; **23** Hideki Mutoh, J, 186 (DNF-accident); **24** Takuma Sato, J, 186 (DNF-accident); **25** Jay Howard, GB, 172 (DNF-accident); **26** Milka Duno, YV, 84 (DNF-mechanical); **27** Ernesto Viso, YV, 71 (DNF-accident damage).
Most laps led: Dixon, 167.
Fastest race lap: Kanaan, 25.6653s, 213.206 mph/ 343.122 km/h.
Pole position: Briscoe, 1m 43.1747s, 212.145 mph/ 341.414 km/h (over 4 laps).
Championship points: Drivers: 1 Power, 190; **2** Dixon, 164; **3** Castroneves, 162; **4** Hunter-Reay, 159; **5** Franchitti, 152; **6** Wilson, 137.

94th INDIANAPOLIS 500, Indianapolis Motor Speedway, Speedway, Indiana, USA, 30 May. Round 6. 200 laps of the 2.500-mile/4.023-km circuit, 500.000 miles/804.672 km.
1 Dario Franchitti, GB, 3h 05m 37.0131s, 161.623 mph/260.107 km/h; **2** Dan Wheldon, GB, 3h 05m 37.1667s; **3** Marco Andretti, USA, 3h 05m 58.0006s; **4** Alex Lloyd, GB, 3h 05m 58.0007s; **5** Scott Dixon, NZ, 3h 05m 58.5053s; **6** Danica Patrick, USA, 3h 05m 58.7691s; **7** Justin Wilson, GB, 3h 06m 02.9892s; **8** Will Power, AUS, 3h 06m 07.2605s; **9** Hélio Castroneves, BR, 3h 06m 10.0268s; **10** Alex Tagliani, CDN, 3h 06m 11.2613s; **11** Tony Kanaan, BR, 3h 06m 36.6088s; **12** Graham Rahal, USA, 3h 06m 36.9870s; **13** Mario Romancini, BR, 3h 06m 38.6875s; **14** Simona de Silvestro, CH, 3h 06m 38.6876s; **15** Tomas Scheckter, ZA, 199 laps; **16** Townsend Bell, USA, 199; **17** Ed Carpenter, USA, 199; **18** Ryan Hunter-Reay, USA, 198 (DNF-accident); **19** Mike Conway, GB, 198 (DNF-accident); **20** Takuma Sato, J, 198; **21** Ana Beatriz, BR, 196; **22** Bertrand Baguette, B, 183; **23** Sebastian Saavedra, CO, 159 (DNF-accident); **24** Ryan Briscoe, AUS, 147 (DNF-accident); **25** Ernesto Viso, YV, 139 (DNF-handling); **26** Sarah Fisher, USA, 125 (DNF-handling); **27** Vitor Meira, BR, 105 (DNF-accident); **28** Hideki Mutoh, J, 76 (DNF-handling); **29** Raphael Matos, BR, 72 (DNF-accident); **30** John Andretti, USA, 62 (DNF-accident); 31 Mário Moraes, BR, 17 (DNF-accident); **32** Bruno Junqueira, BR, 7 (DNF-accident); **33** Davey Hamilton, USA, 0 (DNF-accident).
Did not qualify: Jaques Lazier, USA; Bryan Herta, USA; Paul Tracy, USA; Milka Duno, YV; AJ Foyt IV, USA; Jay Howard, GB.
Most laps led: Franchitti, 155.
Fastest race lap: Power, 39.9840s, 225.090 mph/ 362.247 km/h.
Pole position: Castroneves, 2m 37.9154s, 227.970 mph/ 366.882 km/h (over 4 laps).
Championship points: Drivers: 1 Power, 227; **2** Franchitti, 216; **3** Dixon, 203; **4** Castroneves, 199; **5** Hunter-Reay, 175; **6** Wilson, 167.

FIRESTONE 550K, Texas Motor Speedway, Fort Worth, Texas, USA, 5 June. Round 7. 228 laps of the 1.455-mile/2.342-km circuit, 331.740 miles/ 533.884 km.
1 Ryan Briscoe, AUS, 2h 04m 47.1555s, 159.508 mph/ 256.704 km/h; **2** Danica Patrick, USA, 2h 04m 48.6184s; **3** Marco Andretti, USA, 2h 04m 49.4717s; **4** Scott Dixon, NZ, 2h 04m 50.2325s; **5** Dario Franchitti, GB, 2h 04m 54.7437s; **6** Tony Kanaan, BR, 2h 04m 55.2219s; **7** Ryan Hunter-Reay, USA, 2h 05m 01.0945s; **8** Alex Lloyd, GB, 2h 05m 01.4639s; **9** Dan Wheldon, GB, 2h 05m 02.2414s; **10** Vitor Meira, BR, 2h 05m 02.9805s; **11** Ernesto Viso, YV, 2h 05m 06.0242s; **12** Hideki Mutoh, J, 2h 05m 10.2004s; **13** Tomas Scheckter, ZA, 227 laps; **14** Will Power, AUS, 227; **15** Sarah Fisher, USA, 227; **16** Raphael Matos, BR, 226; **17** Mario Romancini, BR, 226; **18** Alex Tagliani, CDN, 225; **19** Justin Wilson, GB, 225; **20** Hélio Castroneves, BR, 129 (DNF-accident); **21** Mário Moraes, BR, 129 (DNF-accident); **22** Bertrand Baguette, B, 129 (DNF-accident); **23** Milka Duno, YV, 116 (DNF-radiator); **24** Simona de Silvestro, CH, 97 (DNF-accident); **25** Takuma Sato, J, 56 (DNF-suspension/ accident); **26** Jay Howard, GB, 37 (DNF-fuel pressure).
Most laps led: Briscoe, 102.
Fastest race lap: Hunter-Reay, 24.2854s, 215.685 mph/347.112 km/h.
Pole position: Briscoe, 1m 37.3275s, 215.273 mph/ 346.449 km/h (over 4 laps).
Championship points: Drivers: 1 Franchitti, 246; **2** Power, 243; **3** Dixon, 235; **4** Castroneves, 211; **5** Briscoe, 208; **6** Hunter-Reay, 201.

IOWA CORN INDY 250, Iowa Speedway, Newton, Iowa, USA, 20 June. Round 8. 250 laps of the 0.894-mile/1.439-km circuit, 223.500 miles/ 359.688 km.
1 Tony Kanaan, BR, 1h 42m 12.4036s, 131.205 mph/ 211.153 km/h; **2** Hélio Castroneves, BR, 1h 42m 16.6066s; **3** Ernesto Viso, YV, 1h 42m 17.6574s; **4** Ryan Briscoe, AUS, 1h 42m 21.4572s; **5** Will Power, AUS, 1h 42m 21.9938s; **6** Scott Dixon, NZ, 1h 42m 27.6719s; **7** Vitor Meira, BR, 1h 42m 29.2739s; **8** Ryan Hunter-Reay, USA, 249 laps; **9** Graham Rahal, USA, 249; **10** Danica Patrick, USA, 249; **11** Dan Wheldon, GB, 249; **12** Alex Tagliani, CDN, 248; **13** Alex Lloyd, GB, 248; **14** Raphael Matos, BR, 247; **15** Marco Andretti, USA, 244; **16** Mario Romancini, BR, 244; **17** Bertrand Baguette, B, 237; **18** Dario Franchitti, GB, 212; **19** Takuma Sato, J, 177 (DNF-accident); **20** Hideki Mutoh, J, 131 (DNF-handling); **21** Simona de Silvestro, CH, 128 (DNF-handling); **22** Sarah Fisher, USA, 92 (DNF-accident); **23** Milka Duno, YV, 31 (DNF-handling); **24** Justin Wilson, GB, 0 (DNF-accident); **25** Mário Moraes, BR, 0 (DNF-accident).
Most laps led: Franchitti, 69.
Fastest race lap: Franchitti, 17.9696s, 179.102 mph/ 288.238 km/h.
Pole position: Power, 1m 10.9925s, 181.337 mph/ 291.834 km/h (over 4 laps).
Championship points: Drivers: 1 Power, 274; **2** Dixon, 263; **3** Franchitti, 260; **4** Castroneves, 251; **5** Briscoe, 240; **6** Kanaan, 229.

CAMPING WORLD GRAND PRIX AT THE GLEN, Watkins Glen International, New York, USA, 4 July. Round 9. 60 laps of the 3.370-mile/5.423-km circuit, 202.200 miles/325.409 km.
1 Will Power, AUS, 1h 40m 27.4391s, 120.768 mph/ 194.357 km/h; **2** Ryan Briscoe, AUS, 1h 40m 28.6572s; **3** Dario Franchitti, GB, 1h 40m 30.1145s; **4** Raphael Matos, BR, 1h 40m 35.4599s; **5** Mário Moraes, BR, 1h 40m 36.7620s; **6** Dan Wheldon, GB, 1h 40m 37.1914s; **7** Ryan Hunter-Reay, USA, 1h 40m 37.9394s; **8** Scott Dixon, NZ, 1h 40m 39.4937s; **9** Hélio Castroneves, BR, 1h 40m 40.4225s; **10** Justin Wilson, GB, 1h 40m 41.0026s; **11** Ernesto Viso, YV, 1h 40m 46.1982s; **12** Hideki Mutoh, J, 1h 40m 47.6670s; **13** Marco Andretti, USA, 1h 40m 54.1356s; **14** Paul Tracy, CDN, 1h 40m 55.1701s; **15** Takuma Sato, J, 1h 40m 56.3165s; **16** Adam Carroll, GB, 1h 40m 56.8015s; **17** Alex Tagliani, CDN, 1h 41m 02.8144s; **18** Bertrand Baguette, B, 1h 41m 03.9741s; **19** Vitor Meira, BR, 1h 41m 04.4260s; **20** Danica Patrick, USA, 1h 41m 05.7066s; **21** Tony Kanaan, BR, 1h 41m 06.1091s; **22** Mario Romancini, BR, 59 laps (DNF-out of fuel); **23** Milka Duno, YV, 57; **24** Simona de Silvestro, CH, 38 (DNF-accident); **25** Alex Lloyd, GB, 22 (DNF-steering).
Most laps led: Power, 45.
Fastest race lap: Power, 1m 31.0496s, 133.246 mph/ 214.439 km/h.
Pole position: Power, 1m 29.3164s, 135.832 mph/ 218.600 km/h.
Championship points: Drivers: 1 Power, 327; **2** Franchitti, 295; **3** Dixon, 287; **4** Briscoe, 280; **5** Castroneves, 273; **6** Hunter-Reay, 251.

HONDA INDY TORONTO, Toronto Street Circuit, Ontario, Canada, 18 July. Round 10. 85 laps of the 1.755-mile/2.824-km circuit, 149.175 miles/ 240.074 km.
1 Will Power, AUS, 1h 47m 15.2554s, 83.451 mph/ 134.302 km/h; **2** Dario Franchitti, GB, 1h 47m 16.5311s; **3** Ryan Hunter-Reay, USA, 1h 47m 17.0159s; **4** Tony Kanaan, BR, 1h 47m 18.7936s; **5** Graham Rahal, USA, 1h 47m 24.9903s; **6** Danica Patrick, USA, 1h 47m 27.1993s; **7** Justin Wilson, GB, 1h 47m 27.6337s; **8** Marco Andretti, USA, 1h 47m 31.5914s; **9** Simona de Silvestro, CH, 1h 47m 36.7875s; **10** Dan Wheldon, GB, 1h 47m 38.4091s; **11** Vitor Meira, BR, 1h 47m 41.1514s; **12** Hideki Mutoh, J, 1h 47m 41.5432s; **13** Paul Tracy, CDN, 84 laps; **14** Mário Moraes, BR, 84; **15** Tomas Scheckter, ZA, 84; **16** Bertrand Baguette, B, 84; **17** Alex Tagliani, CDN, 84; **18** Ryan Briscoe, AUS, 83; **19** Ernesto Viso, YV, 82; **20** Scott Dixon, NZ, 71 (DNF-accident); **21** Raphael Matos, BR, 64 (DNF-accident); **22** Mario Romancini, BR, 31 (DNF-accident); **23** Alex Lloyd, GB, 26 (DNF-accident); **24** Hélio Castroneves, BR, 21 (DNF-accident); **25** Takuma Sato, J, 15 (DNF-accident); **26** Milka Duno, YV, 8 (DNF-handling).
Most laps led: Wilson, 32.
Fastest race lap: Power, 1m 01.3934s, 102.910 mph/ 165.618 km/h.
Pole position: Wilson, 1m 00.2710s, 104.827 mph/ 168.702 km/h.
Championship points: Drivers: 1 Power, 377; **2** Franchitti, 335; **3** Dixon, 299; **4** Briscoe, 292; **5** Hunter-Reay, 286; **6** Castroneves, 285.

EDMONTON INDY, Rexall Speedway, Edmonton City Centre Airport, Alberta, Canada, 25 July. Round 11. 95 laps of the 1.973-mile/3.175-km circuit, 187.435 miles/301.647 km.
1 Scott Dixon, NZ, 1h 50m 37.0551s, 101.666 mph/ 163.616 km/h; **2** Will Power, AUS, 1h 50m 39.7239s; **3** Dario Franchitti, GB, 1h 50m 40.3382s; **4** Ryan Briscoe, AUS, 1h 50m 45.9203s; **5** Ryan Hunter-Reay, USA, 1h 50m 48.2033s; **6** Paul Tracy, CDN, 1h 50m 48.9642s; **7** Mário Moraes, BR, 1h 50m 53.9566s; **8** Ernesto Viso, YV, 1h 50m 55.2757s; **9** Takuma Sato, J, 1h 50m 58.6431s; **10** Hélio Castroneves, BR, 1h 51m 39.6562s; **11** Marco Andretti, USA, 94 laps; **12** Tony Kanaan, BR, 94; **13** Raphael Matos, BR, 94; **14** Bertrand Baguette, B, 94; **15** Danica Patrick, USA, 94; **16** Vitor Meira, BR, 93; **17** Hideki Mutoh, J, 93; **18** Alex Lloyd, GB, 92; **19** Tomas Scheckter, ZA, 90; **20** Dan Wheldon, GB, 90; **21** Justin Wilson, GB, 88; **22** Simona de Silvestro, CH, 87 (DNF-spin); **23** Alex Tagliani, CDN, 52 (DNF-accident); **24** Mario Romancini, BR, 52 (DNF-accident); **25** Milka Duno, YV, 4 (DNF-handling).
Most laps led: Power, 76.
Fastest race lap: Dixon, 1m 02.1277s, 114.326 mph/ 183.990 km/h.
Pole position: Power, 1m 00.7126s, 116.991 mph/ 188.278 km/h.
Championship points: Drivers: 1 Power, 420; **2** Franchitti, 370; **3** Dixon, 349; **4** Briscoe, 324; **5** Hunter-Reay, 316; **6** Castroneves, 305.

HONDA INDY 200, Mid-Ohio Sports Car Course, Lexington, Ohio, USA, 8 August. Round 12. 85 laps of the 2.258-mile/3.634-km circuit, 191.930 miles/ 308.881 km.
1 Dario Franchitti, GB, 1h 54m 32.2568s, 100.542 mph/ 161.806 km/h; **2** Will Power, AUS, 1h 54m 32.7802s; **3** Hélio Castroneves, BR, 1h 54m 36.3451s; **4** Alex Tagliani, CDN, 1h 54m 37.8991s; **5** Scott Dixon, NZ, 1h 54m 38.1718s; **6** Ryan Briscoe, AUS, 1h 54m 38.7668s; **7** Raphael Matos, BR, 1h 54m 39.0086s; **8** Simona de Silvestro, CH, 1h 54m 42.4019s; **9** Marco Andretti, USA, 1h 54m 43.2123s; **10** Ryan Hunter-Reay, USA, 1h 54m 45.4912s; **11** Bertrand Baguette, B, 1h 54m 47.0828s; **12** Mário Moraes, BR, 1h 54m 48.3029s; **13** Alex Lloyd, GB, 1h 54m 48.8138s; **14** Dan Wheldon, GB, 1h 54m 51.6086s; **15** Vitor Meira, BR, 1h 54m 52.3350s; **16** J.R. Hildebrand, USA, 1h 54m 52.4737s; **17** Tony Kanaan, BR, 1h 54m 57.6854s; **18** Hideki Mutoh, J, 1h 54m 58.8486s; **19** Adam Carroll, GB, 1h 54m 59.5870s; **20** Graham Rahal, USA, 1h 54m 59.8909s; **21** Danica Patrick, USA, 1h 55m 00.4667s; **22** Francesco Dracone, I, 82 laps; **23** Milka Duno, YV, 81; **24** Jay Howard, GB, 38 (DNF-accident damage); **25** Takuma Sato, J, 28 (DNF-accident); **26** Ernesto Viso, YV, 22 (DNF-accident); **27** Justin Wilson, GB, 22 (DNF-accident).
Most laps led: Tagliani, 30.
Fastest race lap: Briscoe, 1m 08.8148s, 118.126 mph/ 190.105 km/h.
Pole position: Power, 1m 07.1997s, 120.965 mph/ 194.674 km/h.
Championship points: Drivers: 1 Power, 461; **2** Franchitti, 420; **3** Dixon, 379; **4** Briscoe, 352; **5** Castroneves, 340; **6** Hunter-Reay, 336.

INDY GRAND PRIX OF SONOMA, Infineon Raceway, Sears Point, Sonoma, California, USA, 22 August. Round 13. 75 laps of the 2.303-mile/3.706-km circuit, 172.725 miles/277.974 km.
1 Will Power, AUS, 1h 52m 34.1915s, 92.063 mph/ 148.161 km/h; **2** Scott Dixon, NZ, 1h 52m 34.9347s; **3** Dario Franchitti, GB, 1h 52m 40.8047s; **4** Ryan Briscoe, AUS, 1h 52m 42.0522s; **5** Hélio Castroneves, BR, 1h 52m 44.6509s; **6** Justin Wilson, GB, 1h 52m 45.1010s; **7** Tony Kanaan, BR, 1h 52m 45.7161s; **8** Ryan Hunter-Reay, USA, 1h 52m 46.0853s; **9** Graham Rahal, USA, 1h 52m 51.6934s; **10** Alex Lloyd, GB, 1h 52m 52.3984s; **11** Mário Moraes, BR, 1h 52m 54.4326s; **12** Marco Andretti, USA, 1h 52m 54.8674s; **13** Simona de Silvestro, CH, 1h 52m 56.0154s; **14** Alex Tagliani, CDN, 1h 52m 56.6773s; **15** Vitor Meira, BR, 1h 52m 58.4794s; **16** Danica Patrick, USA, 1h 53m 20.3254s; **17** Hideki Mutoh, J, 74 laps; **18** Takuma Sato, J, 74; **19** Ernesto Viso, YV, 74; **20** Francesco Dracone, I, 71 (DNF-accident); **21** Raphael Matos, BR, 67 (DNF-accident); **22** Milka Duno, YV, 67; **23** Bertrand Baguette, B, 65 (DNF-accident damage); **24** J.R. Hildebrand, USA, 38 (DNF-accident); **25** Dan Wheldon, GB, 0 (DNF-accident).
Most laps led: Power, 73.
Fastest race lap: Hildebrand, 1m 19.1564s, 104.739 mph/168.562 km/h.
Pole position: Power, 1m 16.5282s, 108.337 mph/ 174.351 km/h.
Championship points: Drivers: 1 Power, 514; **2** Franchitti, 455; **3** Dixon, 419; **4** Briscoe, 384; **5** Castroneves, 370; **6** Hunter-Reay, 360.

PEAK ANTIFREEZE AND MOTOR OIL INDY 300, Chicagoland Speedway, Chicago, Illinois, USA, 28 August. Round 14. 200 laps of the 1.520-mile/2.446-km circuit, 304.000 miles/489.241 km.
1 Dario Franchitti, GB, 1h 47m 49.5783s, 169.161 mph/272.238 km/h; **2** Dan Wheldon, GB, 1h 47m 49.6206s; **3** Marco Andretti, USA, 1h 47m 49.6834s; **4** Ryan Hunter-Reay, USA, 1h 47m 49.7414s; **5** Tony Kanaan, BR, 1h 47m 49.9191s; **6** Hélio Castroneves, BR, 1h 47m 50.0651s; **7** Justin Wilson, GB, 1h 47m 50.1736s; **8** Scott Dixon, NZ, 1h 47m 50.4920s; **9** Vitor Meira, BR, 1h 47m 50.5371s; **10** Graham Rahal, USA, 1h 47m 50.5624s; **11** Ryan Briscoe, AUS, 1h 47m 50.5968s; **12** Bertrand Baguette, B, 1h 47m 50.6616s; **13** Hideki Mutoh, J, 1h 47m 50.8825s; **14** Danica Patrick, USA, 1h 47m 51.1441s; **15** Sarah Fisher, USA, 199 laps; **16** Will Power, AUS, 199; **17** Mário Moraes, BR, 199; **18** Davey Hamilton, USA, 199; **19** Milka Duno, YV, 197; **20** Ed Carpenter, USA, 179 (DNF-refuelling nozzle); **21** Alex Lloyd, GB, 162 (DNF-accident); **22** Jay Howard, GB, 161 (DNF-gearbox); **23** Simona de Silvestro, CH, 150 (DNF-mechanical); **24** Ana Beatriz, BR, 88 (DNF-suspension); **25** Alex Tagliani, CDN, 85 (DNF-accident damage); **26** Takuma Sato, J, 80 (DNF-accident damage); **27** Ernesto Viso, YV, 80 (DNF-accident damage); **28** Tomas Scheckter, ZA, 4 (DNF-accident); **29** Raphael Matos, BR, 4 (DNF-accident).
Most laps led: Briscoe, 113.
Fastest race lap: Dixon, 25.0486s, 218.455 mph/351.570 km/h.
Pole position: Briscoe, 50.5857s, 216.346 mph/348.175 km/h (over 2 laps).
Championship points: Drivers: 1 Power, 528; **2** Franchitti, 505; **3** Dixon, 443; **4** Briscoe, 406; **5** Castroneves, 398; **6** Hunter-Reay, 392.

KENTUCKY INDY 300, Kentucky Speedway, Fort Mitchell, Kentucky, USA, 4 September. Round 15. 200 laps of the 1.480-mile/2.382-km circuit, 296.000 miles/476.366 km.
1 Hélio Castroneves, BR, 1h 41m 50.0059s, 174.402 mph/280.674 km/h; **2** Ed Carpenter, USA, 1h 42m 03.1656s; **3** Dan Wheldon, GB, 1h 42m 03.9273s; **4** Tony Kanaan, BR, 1h 42m 03.9990s; **5** Dario Franchitti, GB, 1h 42m 04.2027s; **6** Marco Andretti, USA, 1h 42m 04.5728s; **7** Scott Dixon, NZ, 1h 42m 05.1084s; **8** Will Power, AUS, 1h 42m 05.6201s; **9** Danica Patrick, USA, 1h 42m 05.8553s; **10** Bertrand Baguette, B, 199 laps; **11** Justin Wilson, GB, 199; **12** Paul Tracy, CDN, 199; **13** Alex Lloyd, GB, 199; **14** Tomas Scheckter, ZA, 199; **15** Alex Tagliani, CDN, 199; **16** Raphael Matos, BR, 199; **17** Hideki Mutoh, J, 199; **18** Mário Moraes, BR, 198; **19** Milka Duno, YV, 195; **20** Graham Rahal, USA, 195; **21** Ryan Hunter-Reay, USA, 174 (DNF-suspension); **22** Sarah Fisher, USA, 134 (DNF-gearbox); **23** Vitor Meira, BR, 79 (DNF-accident); **24** Ryan Briscoe, AUS, 79 (DNF-accident); **25** Simona de Silvestro, CH, 78 (DNF-accident); **26** Ernesto Viso, YV, 45 (DNF-brakes); **27** Takuma Sato, J, 0 (DNF-accident).
Most laps led: Wheldon, 93.
Fastest race lap: Hunter-Reay, 24.2752s, 219.483 mph/353.224 km/h.
Pole position: Carpenter, 48.8958s, 217.933 mph/350.729 km/h (over 2 laps).
Championship points: Drivers: 1 Power, 552; **2** Franchitti, 535; **3** Dixon, 469; **4** Castroneves, 448; **5** Briscoe, 418; **6** Hunter-Reay, 404.

INDY JAPAN 300, Twin Ring Motegi, Motegi-machi, Haga-gun, Tochigi Prefecture, Japan, 19 September. Round 16. 200 laps of the 1.520-mile/2.446-km circuit, 304.000 miles/489.241 km.
1 Hélio Castroneves, BR, 2h 04m 04.4780s, 147.008 mph/236.587 km/h; **2** Dario Franchitti, GB, 2h 04m 09.0526s; **3** Will Power, AUS, 2h 04m 09.5523s; **4** Ryan Briscoe, AUS, 2h 04m 10.9605s; **5** Danica Patrick, USA, 2h 04m 12.0837s; **6** Scott Dixon, NZ, 2h 04m 12.8421s; **7** Tony Kanaan, BR, 2h 04m 13.8873s; **8** Graham Rahal, USA, 2h 04m 16.1943s; **9** Ryan Hunter-Reay, USA, 2h 04m 16.6905s; **10** Dan Wheldon, GB, 2h 04m 16.9500s; **11** Marco Andretti, USA, 2h 04m 19.9787s; **12** Takuma Sato, J, 2h 04m 20.5473s; **13** Alex Tagliani, CDN, 2h 04m 22.1554s; **14** Hideki Mutoh, J, 2h 04m 22.7591s; **15** Ernesto Viso, YV, 2h 04m 23.2129s; **16** Justin Wilson, GB, 2h 04m 23.9073s; **17** Vitor Meira, BR, 2h 04m 24.5827s; **18** Raphael Matos, BR, 2h 04m 25.7126s; **19** Milka Duno, YV, 197 laps; **20** Roger Yasukawa, USA, 195; **21** Alex Lloyd, GB, 131 (DNF-accident); **22** Paul Tracy, CDN, 114 (DNF-accident); **23** Simona de Silvestro, CH, 85 (DNF-mechanical); **24** Mário Moraes, BR, 66 (DNF-accident); **25** Bertrand Baguette, B, 1 (DNF-accident).
Most laps led: Castroneves, 153.
Fastest race lap: Castroneves, 27.3743s, 199.896 mph/321.701 km/h.
Pole position: Castroneves, 54.1803s, 201.992 mph/325.075 km/h (over 2 laps).
Championship points: Drivers: 1 Power, 587; **2** Franchitti, 575; **3** Castroneves, 501; **4** Dixon, 497; **5** Briscoe, 450; **6** Hunter-Reay, 426.

CAFES DO BRASIL INDY 300, Homestead-Miami Speedway, Florida, USA, 2 October. Round 17. 200 laps of the 1.485-mile/2.390-km circuit, 297.000 miles/477.975 km.
1 Scott Dixon, NZ, 1h 52m 08.5580s, 158.905 mph/255.732 km/h; **2** Danica Patrick, USA, 1h 52m 11.3167s; **3** Tony Kanaan, BR, 1h 52m 11.3278s; **4** Ryan Briscoe, AUS, 1h 52m 12.3407s; **5** Hélio Castroneves, BR, 1h 52m 13.8904s; **6** Vitor Meira, BR, 1h 52m 15.7706s; **7** Marco Andretti, USA, 1h 52m 16.9217s; **8** Dario Franchitti, GB, 1h 52m 19.6981s; **9** Dan Wheldon, GB, 1h 52m 30.8101s; **10** Graham Rahal, USA, 199 laps; **11** Ryan Hunter-Reay, USA, 199; **12** Alex Lloyd, GB, 199; **13** Ed Carpenter, USA, 199; **14** Alex Tagliani, CDN, 199; **15** Bertrand Baguette, B, 199; **16** Sebastian Saavedra, CO, 199; **17** Raphael Matos, BR, 199; **18** Takuma Sato, J, 199; **19** Ernesto Viso, YV, 198; **20** Hideki Mutoh, J, 198; **21** Justin Wilson, GB, 198; **22** Sarah Fisher, USA, 197; **23** Simona de Silvestro, CH, 197; **24** Milka Duno, YV, 170 (DNF-accident); **25** Will Power, AUS, 143 (DNF-accident/suspension); **26** Ana Beatriz, BR, 42 (DNF-accident); **27** Mário Moraes, BR, 25 (DNF-lost power).
Most laps led: Franchitti, 128.
Fastest race lap: Andretti, 25.2248s, 211.934 mph/341.075 km/h.
Pole position: Franchitti, 50.1532s, 213.187 mph/343.091 km/h (over 2 laps).

Final championship points
1 Dario Franchitti, GB, 602; **2** Will Power, AUS, 597; **3** Scott Dixon, NZ, 547; **4** Hélio Castroneves, BR, 531; **5** Ryan Briscoe, AUS, 482; **6** Tony Kanaan, BR, 453; **7** Ryan Hunter-Reay, USA, 445; **8** Marco Andretti, USA, 392; **9** Dan Wheldon, GB, 388; **10** Danica Patrick, USA, 367; **11** Justin Wilson, GB, 361; **12** Vitor Meira, BR, 310; **13** Alex Tagliani, CDN, 302; **14** Raphael Matos, BR, 290; **15** Mário Moraes, BR, 287; **16** Alex Lloyd, GB, 266; **17** Ernesto Viso, YV, 262; **18** Hideki Mutoh, J, 250; **19** Simona de Silvestro, CH, 242; **20** Graham Rahal, USA, 235; **21** Takuma Sato, J, 214; **22** Bertrand Baguette, B, 213; **23** Milka Duno, YV, 184; **24** Mario Romancini, BR, 149; **25** Mike Conway, GB, 110; **26** Sarah Fisher, USA, 92; **27** Paul Tracy, CDN, 91; **28** Ed Carpenter, USA, 90; **29** Tomas Scheckter, ZA, 89; **30** Ana Beatriz, BR, 55; **31** Jay Howard, GB, 44; **32** John Andretti, USA, 35; **33** Sebastian Saavedra, CO, 29; **34** Adam Carroll, GB, 26; **35** J.R. Hildebrand, USA, 26; **36** Davey Hamilton, USA, 26; **37** Francesco Dracone, I, 24; **38** Townsend Bell, USA, 18; **39** Bruno Junqueira, BR, 13; **40** Roger Yasukawa, USA, 12.

NASCAR Sprint Cup Series

Cars are Chevrolet Impala SS, Dodge Charger, Ford Fusion and Toyota Camry.

2009

The following races were run after AUTOCOURSE 2009–2010 went to press.

DICKIES 500, Texas Motor Speedway, Fort Worth, Texas, USA, 8 November. Round 34. 334 laps of the 1.500-mile/2.414-km circuit, 501.000 miles/806.281 km.
1 Kurt Busch, USA (Dodge), 3h 24m 18s, 147.137 mph/236.793 km/h; **2** Denny Hamlin, USA (Toyota), 3h 24m 43.686s; **3** Matt Kenseth, USA (Ford), 334 laps; **4** Mark Martin, USA (Chevrolet), 334; **5** Kevin Harvick, USA (Chevrolet), 334; **6** Tony Stewart, USA (Chevrolet), 334; **7** Clint Bowyer, USA (Chevrolet), 333; **8** Greg Biffle, USA (Ford), 333; **9** Jeff Burton, USA (Chevrolet), 333; **10** A.J. Allmendinger, USA (Ford), 333.
Pole position: Jeff Gordon, USA (Chevrolet), 28.255s, 191.117 mph/307.572 km/h.
Drivers' championship points: 1 Johnson, 6297; **2** Martin, 6224; **3** Gordon, 6185; **4** Busch (Kurt), 6126; **5** Stewart, 6119; **6** Montoya, 6061.

CHECKER O'REILLY AUTO PARTS 500, Phoenix International Raceway, Arizona, USA, 15 November. Round 35. 312 laps of the 1.000-mile/1.609-km circuit, 312.000 miles/502.115 km.
1 Jimmie Johnson, USA (Chevrolet), 2h 49m 26s, 110.486 mph/177.810 km/h; **2** Jeff Burton, USA (Chevrolet), 2h 49m 27.033s; **3** Denny Hamlin, USA (Toyota), 312 laps; **4** Mark Martin, USA (Chevrolet), 312; **5** Martin Truex Jr., USA (Chevrolet), 312; **6** Kurt Busch, USA (Dodge), 312; **7** Clint Bowyer, USA (Chevrolet), 312; **8** Juan Pablo Montoya, CO (Chevrolet), 312; **9** Jeff Gordon, USA (Chevrolet), 312; **10** David Reutimann, USA (Toyota), 312.
Pole position: Truex Jr., 26.643s, 135.120 mph/217.454 km/h.
Drivers' championship points: 1 Johnson, 6492; **2** Martin, 6384; **3** Gordon, 6323; **4** Busch (Kurt), 6281; **5** Stewart, 6207; **6** Montoya, 6203.

FORD 400, Homestead-Miami Speedway, Florida, USA, 22 November. Round 36. 267 laps of the 1.500-mile/2.414-km circuit, 400.500 miles/644.542 km.
1 Denny Hamlin, USA (Toyota), 3h 06m 18s, 128.986 mph/207.582 km/h; **2** Jeff Burton, USA (Chevrolet), 3h 06m 20.632s; **3** Kevin Harvick, USA (Chevrolet), 267 laps; **4** Kurt Busch, USA (Dodge), 267; **5** Jimmie Johnson, USA (Chevrolet), 267; **6** Jeff Gordon, USA (Chevrolet), 267; **7** Carl Edwards, USA (Ford), 267; **8** Kyle Busch, USA (Toyota), 267; **9** Martin Truex Jr., USA (Chevrolet), 267; **10** A.J. Allmendinger, USA (Ford), 267.
Pole position: Johnson, 31.049s, 173.919 mph/279.895 km/h.

Final championship points
Drivers: 1 Jimmie Johnson, USA, 6652; **2** Mark Martin, USA, 6511; **3** Jeff Gordon, USA, 6473; **4** Kurt Busch, USA, 6446; **5** Denny Hamlin, USA, 6335; **6** Tony Stewart, USA, 6309; **7** Greg Biffle, USA, 6292; **8** Juan Pablo Montoya, CO, 6252; **9** Ryan Newman, USA, 6175; **10** Kasey Kahne, USA, 6128; **11** Carl Edwards, USA, 6118; **12** Brian Vickers, USA, 5929; **13** Kyle Busch, USA, 4457; **14** Matt Kenseth, USA, 4389; **15** Clint Bowyer, USA, 4359; **16** David Reutimann, USA, 4221; **17** Jeff Burton, USA, 4022; **18** Marcos Ambrose, AUS, 3830; **19** Kevin Harvick, USA, 3796; **20** Joey Logano, USA, 3791; **21** Casey Mears, USA, 3759; **22** Jamie McMurray, USA, 3604; **23** Martin Truex Jr., USA, 3503; **24** A.J. Allmendinger, USA, 3476; **25** Dale Earnhardt Jr., USA, 3422; **26** Elliott Sadler, USA, 3350; **27** David Ragan, USA, 3252; **28** Sam Hornish Jr., USA, 3203; **29** Reed Sorenson, USA, 3147; **30** Bobby Labonte, USA, 3128.
Raybestos Rookie of the Year: Joey Logano, USA.
Manufacturers: 1 Chevrolet, 265; **2** Toyota, 207; **3** Ford, 164; **4** Dodge, 156.

2010

DAYTONA 500, Daytona International Speedway, Daytona Beach, Florida, USA, 14 February. Round 1. 208 laps of the 2.500-mile/4.023-km circuit, 520.000 miles/836.859 km.
1 Jamie McMurray, USA (Chevrolet), 3h 47m 16s, 137.284 mph/220.937 km/h; **2** Dale Earnhardt Jr., USA (Chevrolet), 3h 47m 16.119s; **3** Greg Biffle, USA (Ford), 208 laps; **4** Clint Bowyer, USA (Chevrolet), 208; **5** David Reutimann, USA (Toyota), 208; **6** Martin Truex Jr., USA (Toyota), 208; **7** Kevin Harvick, USA (Chevrolet), 208; **8** Matt Kenseth, USA (Ford), 208; **9** Carl Edwards, USA (Ford), 208; **10** Juan Pablo Montoya, CO (Chevrolet), 208.
Pole position: Mark Martin, USA (Chevrolet), 47.074s, 191.188 mph/307.688 km/h.
Drivers' championship points: 1 McMurray, 190; **2** Earnhardt Jr., 175; **3** Biffle, 170; **4** Bowyer, 165; **5** Harvick, 156; **6** Reutimann, 155.

AUTO CLUB 500, Auto Club Speedway, Fontana, California, USA, 21 February. Round 2. 250 laps of the 2.000-mile/3.219-km circuit, 500.000 miles/804.672 km.
1 Jimmie Johnson, USA (Chevrolet), 3h 31m 24s, 141.911 mph/228.384 km/h; **2** Kevin Harvick, USA (Chevrolet), 3h 31m 25.523s; **3** Jeff Burton, USA (Chevrolet), 250 laps; **4** Mark Martin, USA (Chevrolet), 250; **5** Joey Logano, USA (Toyota), 250; **6** Kurt Busch, USA (Dodge), 250; **7** Matt Kenseth, USA (Ford), 250; **8** Clint Bowyer, USA (Chevrolet), 250; **9** Tony Stewart, USA (Chevrolet), 250; **10** Greg Biffle, USA (Ford), 250.
Pole position: Jamie McMurray, USA (Chevrolet), 39.185s, 183.744 mph/295.707 km/h.
Drivers' championship points: 1 Harvick, 331; **2** Bowyer, 312; **3** Biffle, 304; **4** McMurray, 302; **5** Burton, 300; **6** Martin, 297.

SHELBY AMERICAN, Las Vegas Motor Speedway, Nevada, USA, 28 February. Round 3. 267 laps of the 1.500-mile/2.414-km circuit, 400.500 miles/644.542 km.
1 Jimmie Johnson, USA (Chevrolet), 2h 49m 53s, 141.450 mph/227.642 km/h; **2** Kevin Harvick, USA (Chevrolet), 2h 49m 54.874s; **3** Jeff Gordon, USA (Chevrolet), 267 laps; **4** Mark Martin, USA (Chevrolet), 267; **5** Matt Kenseth, USA (Ford), 267; **6** Joey Logano, USA (Toyota), 267; **7** Tony Stewart, USA (Chevrolet), 267; **8** Clint Bowyer, USA (Chevrolet), 267; **9** Kasey Kahne, USA (Ford), 267; **10** Greg Biffle, USA (Ford), 267.
Pole position: Kurt Busch, USA (Dodge), 28.614s, 188.719 mph/303.713 km/h.
Drivers' championship points: 1 Harvick, 506; **2** Bowyer, 459; **3** Martin, 457; **4** Kenseth, 448; **5** Johnson, 443; **6** Biffle, 443.

KOBALT TOOLS 500, Atlanta Motor Speedway, Hampton, Georgia, USA, 7 March. Round 4. 341 laps of the 1.540-mile/2.478-km circuit, 525.140 miles/845.131 km.
1 Kurt Busch, USA (Dodge), 3h 59m 59s, 131.294 mph/211.297 km/h; **2** Matt Kenseth, USA (Ford), 3h 59m 59.482s; **3** Juan Pablo Montoya, CO (Chevrolet), 341 laps; **4** Kasey Kahne, USA (Ford), 341; **5** Paul Menard, USA (Ford), 341; **6** A.J. Allmendinger, USA (Ford), 341; **7** Brian Vickers, USA (Toyota), 341; **8** Greg Biffle, USA (Ford), 341; **9** Kevin Harvick, USA (Chevrolet), 341; **10** Scott Speed, USA (Toyota), 341.
Pole position: Dale Earnhardt Jr., USA (Chevrolet), 28.761s, 192.761 mph/310.219 km/h.
Drivers' championship points: 1 Harvick, 644; **2** Kenseth, 618; **3** Biffle, 585; **4** Johnson, 570; **5** Bowyer, 558; **6** Burton, 538.

FOOD CITY 500, Bristol Motor Speedway, Tennessee, USA, 21 March. Round 5. 500 laps of the 0.533-mile/0.858-km circuit, 266.500 miles/428.890 km.
1 Jimmie Johnson, USA (Chevrolet), 3h 20m 50s, 79.618 mph/128.133 km/h; **2** Tony Stewart, USA (Chevrolet), 3h 20m 50.894s; **3** Kurt Busch, USA (Dodge), 500 laps; **4** Greg Biffle, USA (Ford), 500; **5** Matt Kenseth, USA (Ford), 500; **6** Carl Edwards, USA (Ford), 500; **7** Dale Earnhardt Jr., USA (Chevrolet), 500; **8** Jamie McMurray, USA (Chevrolet), 500; **9** Kyle Busch, USA (Toyota), 500; **10** Jeff Burton, USA (Chevrolet), 500.
Pole position: Joey Logano, USA (Toyota), 15.396s, 124.630 mph/200.572 km/h.
Drivers' championship points: 1 Harvick, 774; **2** Kenseth, 773; **3** Johnson, 760; **4** Biffle, 750; **5** Stewart, 685; **6** Busch (Kurt), 677.

GOODY'S FAST PAIN RELIEF 500, Martinsville Speedway, Virginia, USA, 29 March. Round 6. 508 laps of the 0.526-mile/0.847-km circuit, 267.208 miles/430.030 km.
1 Denny Hamlin, USA (Toyota), 3h 39m 05s, 73.180 mph/117.772 km/h; **2** Joey Logano, USA (Toyota), 3h 39m 05.670s; **3** Jeff Gordon, USA (Chevrolet), 508 laps; **4** Ryan Newman, USA (Chevrolet), 508; **5** Martin Truex Jr., USA (Toyota), 508; **6** Brian Vickers, USA (Toyota), 508; **7** Clint Bowyer, USA (Chevrolet), 508; **8** Carl Edwards, USA (Ford), 508; **9** Jimmie Johnson, USA (Chevrolet), 508; **10** Greg Biffle, USA (Ford), 508.
Pole position: Kevin Harvick, USA (Chevrolet).
Drivers' championship points: 1 Johnson, 898; **2** Biffle, 886; **3** Kenseth, 882; **4** Harvick, 837; **5** Burton, 786; **6** Busch (Kurt), 776.

SUBWAY FRESH FIT 600, Phoenix International Raceway, Arizona, USA, 10 April. Round 7. 378 laps of the 1.000-mile/1.609-km circuit, 378.000 miles/608.332 km.
1 Ryan Newman, USA (Chevrolet), 3h 48m 14s, 99.372 mph/159.924 km/h; **2** Jeff Gordon, USA (Chevrolet), 3h 48m 14.130s; **3** Jimmie Johnson, USA (Chevrolet), 378 laps; **4** Mark Martin, USA (Chevrolet), 378; **5** Juan Pablo Montoya, CO (Chevrolet), 378; **6** Matt Kenseth, USA (Ford), 378; **7** Carl Edwards, USA (Ford), 378; **8** Kyle Busch, USA (Toyota), 378; **9** Clint Bowyer, USA (Chevrolet), 378; **10** Joey Logano, USA (Toyota), 378.
Pole position: A.J. Allmendinger, USA (Ford), 26.731s, 134.675 mph/216.739 km/h.
Drivers' championship points: 1 Johnson, 1073; **2** Kenseth, 1037; **3** Biffle, 981; **4** Harvick, 961; **5** Gordon, 948; **6** Bowyer, 885.

SAMSUNG MOBILE 500, Texas Motor Speedway, Fort Worth, Texas, USA, 19 April. Round 8. 334 laps of the 1.500-mile/2.414-km circuit, 501.000 miles/806.281 km.
1 Denny Hamlin, USA (Toyota), 3h 25m 34s, 146.230 mph/235.334 km/h; **2** Jimmie Johnson, USA (Chevrolet), 3h 25m 34.152s; **3** Kyle Busch, USA (Toyota), 334 laps; **4** Kurt Busch, USA (Dodge), 334; **5** Kasey Kahne, USA (Ford), 334; **6** Mark Martin, USA (Chevrolet), 334; **7** Kevin Harvick, USA (Chevrolet), 334; **8** Dale Earnhardt Jr., USA (Chevrolet), 334; **9** Martin Truex Jr., USA (Toyota), 334; **10** Greg Biffle, USA (Ford), 334.
Pole position: Tony Stewart, USA (Chevrolet), 28.224s, 191.327 mph/307.910 km/h.
Drivers' championship points: 1 Johnson, 1248; **2** Kenseth, 1140; **3** Biffle, 1120; **4** Harvick, 1107; **5** Gordon, 1028; **6** Busch (Kyle), 1020.

AARON'S 499, Talladega Superspeedway, Alabama, USA, 25 April. Round 9. 200 laps of the 2.660-mile/4.281-km circuit, 532.000 miles/856.171 km.
1 Kevin Harvick, USA (Chevrolet), 3h 31m 58s, 150.590 mph/242.351 km/h; **2** Jamie McMurray, USA (Chevrolet), 3h 31m 58.011s; **3** Juan Pablo Montoya, CO (Chevrolet), 200 laps; **4** Denny Hamlin, USA (Toyota), 200; **5** Mark Martin, USA (Chevrolet), 200; **6** David Ragan, USA (Ford), 200; **7** Clint Bowyer, USA (Chevrolet), 200; **8** Kurt Busch, USA (Dodge), 200; **9** Kyle Busch, USA (Toyota), 200; **10** Mike Bliss, USA (Chevrolet), 200.
Pole position: Jimmie Johnson, USA (Chevrolet).
Drivers' championship points: 1 Johnson, 1323; **2** Harvick, 1297; **3** Biffle, 1237; **4** Kenseth, 1224; **5** Busch (Kyle), 1163; **6** Martin, 1154.

CROWN ROYAL PRESENTS THE HEATH CALHOUN 400, Richmond International Raceway, Virginia, USA, 1 May. Round 10. 400 laps of the 0.750-mile/1.207-km circuit, 300.000 miles/482.803 km.
1 Kyle Busch, USA (Toyota), 3h 00m 47s, 99.567 mph/160.237 km/h; **2** Jeff Gordon, USA (Chevrolet), 3h 00m 47.755s; **3** Kevin Harvick, USA (Chevrolet), 400 laps; **4** Jeff Burton, USA (Chevrolet), 400; **5** Carl Edwards, USA (Ford), 400; **6** Juan Pablo Montoya, CO (Chevrolet), 400; **7** Martin Truex Jr., USA (Toyota), 400; **8** Ryan Newman, USA (Chevrolet), 400; **9** Marcos Ambrose, AUS (Toyota), 400; **10** Jimmie Johnson, USA (Chevrolet), 400.
Pole position: Busch (Kyle), 21.247s, 127.077 mph/204.510 km/h.
Drivers' championship points: 1 Harvick, 1467; **2** Johnson, 1457; **3** Busch (Kyle), 1358; **4** Kenseth, 1348; **5** Biffle, 1334; **6** Gordon, 1305.

SHOWTIME SOUTHERN 500, Darlington Raceway, South Carolina, USA, 8 May. Round 11. 367 laps of the 1.366-mile/2.198-km circuit, 501.322 miles/806.800 km.
1 Denny Hamlin, USA (Toyota), 3h 57m 35s, 126.605 mph/203.752 km/h; **2** Jamie McMurray, USA (Chevrolet), 3h 57m 36.908s; **3** Kurt Busch, USA (Dodge), 367 laps; **4** Jeff Gordon, USA (Chevrolet), 367; **5** Juan Pablo Montoya, CO (Chevrolet), 367; **6** Kevin Harvick, USA (Chevrolet), 367; **7** Kyle Busch, USA (Toyota), 367; **8** Jeff Burton, USA (Chevrolet), 367; **9** Ryan Newman, USA (Chevrolet), 367; **10** Brian Vickers, USA (Toyota), 367.
Pole position: McMurray, 27.264s, 180.370 mph/290.277 km/h.
Drivers' championship points: 1 Harvick, 1622; **2** Johnson, 1512; **3** Busch (Kyle), 1509; **4** Gordon, 1475; **5** Kenseth, 1472; **6** Hamlin, 1458.

AUTISM SPEAKS 400 PRESENTED BY HERSHEY'S MILK & MILKSHAKES, Dover International Speedway, Delaware, USA, 16 May. Round 12. 400 laps of the 1.000-mile/1.609-km circuit, 400.000 miles/643.738 km.
1 Kyle Busch, USA (Toyota), 3h 06m 21s, 128.790 mph/207.267 km/h; **2** Jeff Burton, USA (Chevrolet), 3h 06m 28.551s; **3** Matt Kenseth, USA (Ford), 400 laps; **4** Denny Hamlin, USA (Toyota), 400; **5** David Reutimann, USA (Toyota), 400; **6** Greg Biffle, USA (Ford), 400; **7** Kevin Harvick, USA (Chevrolet), 400; **8** Carl Edwards, USA (Ford), 400; **9** Tony Stewart, USA (Chevrolet), 400; **10** Joey Logano, USA (Toyota), 400.
Pole position: Martin Truex Jr., USA (Toyota), 22.884s, 157.315 mph/253.174 km/h.
Drivers' championship points: 1 Harvick, 1768; **2** Busch (Kyle), 1699; **3** Kenseth, 1642; **4** Johnson, 1637; **5** Hamlin, 1618; **6** Gordon, 1605.

COCA-COLA 600, Lowe's Motor Speedway, Concord, Charlotte, North Carolina, USA, 30 May. Round 13. 400 laps of the 1.500-mile/2.414-km circuit, 600.000 miles/965.606 km.
1 Kurt Busch, USA (Dodge), 4h 08m 20s, 144.966 mph/233.301 km/h; **2** Jamie McMurray, USA (Chevrolet), 4h 08m 20.737s; **3** Kyle Busch, USA (Toyota), 400 laps; **4** Mark Martin, USA (Chevrolet), 400; **5** David Reutimann, USA (Toyota), 400; **6** Jeff Gordon, USA (Chevrolet), 400; **7** Clint Bowyer, USA (Chevrolet), 400; **8** Paul Menard, USA (Ford), 400; **9** Ryan Newman, USA (Chevrolet), 400; **10** Matt Kenseth, USA (Ford), 400.
Pole position: Newman, 28.793s, 187.546 mph/301.825 km/h.
Drivers' championship points: 1 Harvick, 1898; **2** Busch (Kyle), 1869; **3** Kenseth, 1781; **4** Gordon, 1760; **5** Hamlin, 1732; **6** Busch (Kurt), 1726.

GILLETTE FUSION PROGLIDE 500 PRESENTED BY TARGET, Pocono Raceway, Long Pond, Pennsylvania, USA, 6 June. Round 14. 204 laps of the 2.500-mile/4.023-km circuit, 510.000 miles/820.765 km.
1 Denny Hamlin, USA (Toyota), 3h 44m 30s, 136.303 mph/219.358 km/h; **2** Kyle Busch, USA (Toyota), 204 laps; **3** Tony Stewart, USA (Chevrolet), 204; **4** Kevin Harvick, USA (Chevrolet), 204; **5** Jimmie Johnson, USA (Chevrolet), 204; **6** Kurt Busch, USA (Dodge), 204; **7** Jeff Burton, USA (Chevrolet), 204; **8** Juan Pablo Montoya, CO (Chevrolet), 204; **9** Clint Bowyer, USA (Chevrolet), 204; **10** A.J. Allmendinger, USA (Ford), 204.
Pole position: Busch (Kyle), 53.102s, 169.485 mph/272.760 km/h.
Drivers' championship points: 1 Harvick, 2063; **2** Busch (Kyle), 2044; **3** Hamlin, 1927; **4** Kenseth, 1893; **5** Busch (Kurt), 1881; **6** Johnson, 1849.

HELUVA GOOD! SOUR CREAM DIPS 400, Michigan International Speedway, Brooklyn, Michigan, USA, 13 June. Round 15. 200 laps of the 2.000-mile/3.219-km circuit, 400.000 miles/643.738 km.
1 Denny Hamlin, USA (Toyota), 2h 33m 28s, 156.386 mph/

251.678 km/h; **2** Kasey Kahne, USA (Ford), 2h 33m 29.246s; **3** Kurt Busch, USA (Dodge), 200 laps; **4** Jeff Gordon, USA (Chevrolet), 200; **5** Tony Stewart, USA (Chevrolet), 200; **6** Jimmie Johnson, USA (Chevrolet), 200; **7** Dale Earnhardt Jr., USA (Chevrolet), 200; **8** Jeff Burton, USA (Chevrolet), 200; **9** Greg Biffle, USA (Ford), 200; **10** Joey Logano, USA (Toyota), 200.
Pole position: Busch (Kurt), 37.898s, 189.984 mph/305.749 km/h.
Drivers' championship points: 1 Harvick, 2169; **2** Busch (Kyle), 2147; **3** Hamlin, 2122; **4** Busch (Kurt), 2051; **5** Kenseth, 2019; **6** Johnson, 1999.

TOYOTA/SAVE MART 350, Infineon Raceway, Sears Point, Sonoma, California, USA, 20 June. Round 16. 110 laps of the 1.990-mile/3.203-km circuit, 218.900 miles/352.285 km.
1 Jimmie Johnson, USA (Chevrolet), 2h 56m 38s, 74.357 mph/119.667 km/h; **2** Robby Gordon, USA (Toyota), 2h 56m 41.105s; **3** Kevin Harvick, USA (Chevrolet), 110 laps; **4** Kasey Kahne, USA (Ford), 110; **5** Jeff Gordon, USA (Chevrolet), 110; **6** Marcos Ambrose, AUS (Toyota), 110; **7** Greg Biffle, USA (Ford), 110; **8** Boris Said, USA (Ford), 110; **9** Tony Stewart, USA (Chevrolet), 110; **10** Juan Pablo Montoya, CO (Chevrolet), 110.
Pole position: Kahne, 1m 16.300s, 93.893 mph/151.105 km/h.
Drivers' championship points: 1 Harvick, 2334; **2** Johnson, 2194; **3** Busch (Kyle), 2193; **4** Hamlin, 2183; **5** Gordon, 2142; **6** Busch (Kurt), 2118.

LENOX INDUSTRIAL TOOLS 301, New Hampshire Motor Speedway, Loudon, New Hampshire, USA, 27 June. Round 17. 301 laps of the 1.058-mile/1.703-km circuit, 318.458 miles/512.508 km.
1 Jimmie Johnson, USA (Chevrolet), 2h 48m 38s, 113.308 mph/182.351 km/h; **2** Tony Stewart, USA (Chevrolet), 2h 48m 38.753s; **3** Kurt Busch, USA (Dodge), 301 laps; **4** Jeff Gordon, USA (Chevrolet), 301; **5** Kevin Harvick, USA (Chevrolet), 301; **6** Ryan Newman, USA (Chevrolet), 301; **7** Clint Bowyer, USA (Chevrolet), 301; **8** Dale Earnhardt Jr., USA (Chevrolet), 301; **9** Joey Logano, USA (Toyota), 301; **10** A.J. Allmendinger, USA (Ford), 301.
Pole position: Juan Pablo Montoya, CO (Chevrolet), 28.781s, 132.337 mph/212.976 km/h.
Drivers' championship points: 1 Harvick, 2489; **2** Johnson, 2384; **3** Busch (Kyle), 2328; **4** Hamlin, 2304; **5** Gordon, 2302; **6** Busch (Kurt), 2288.

COKE ZERO 400 POWERED BY COCA-COLA, Daytona International Speedway, Daytona Beach, Florida, USA, 3 July. Round 18. 166 laps of the 2.500-mile/4.023-km circuit, 415.000 miles/667.878 km.
1 Kevin Harvick, USA (Chevrolet), 3h 03m 18s, 135.843 mph/218.618 km/h; **2** Kasey Kahne, USA (Ford), 3h 03m 18.092s; **3** Jeff Gordon, USA (Chevrolet), 166 laps; **4** Dale Earnhardt Jr., USA (Chevrolet), 166; **5** Jeff Burton, USA (Chevrolet), 166; **6** Carl Edwards, USA (Ford), 166; **7** Kurt Busch, USA (Dodge), 166; **8** Reed Sorenson, USA (Toyota), 166; **9** Mike Bliss, USA (Chevrolet), 166; **10** Scott Speed, USA (Toyota), 166.
Pole position: Harvick.
Drivers' championship points: 1 Harvick, 2684; **2** Gordon, 2472; **3** Johnson, 2459; **4** Busch (Kurt), 2439; **5** Hamlin, 2400; **6** Busch (Kyle), 2376.

LIFELOCK.COM 400, Chicagoland Speedway, Chicago, Illinois, USA, 10 July. Round 19. 267 laps of the 1.500-mile/2.414-km circuit, 400.500 miles/644.542 km.
1 David Reutimann, USA (Toyota), 2h 45m 34s, 145.138 mph/233.577 km/h; **2** Carl Edwards, USA (Ford), 2h 45m 34.727s; **3** Jeff Gordon, USA (Chevrolet), 267 laps; **4** Clint Bowyer, USA (Chevrolet), 267; **5** Jamie McMurray, USA (Chevrolet), 267; **6** Kasey Kahne, USA (Ford), 267; **7** Jeff Burton, USA (Chevrolet), 267; **8** Denny Hamlin, USA (Toyota), 267; **9** Tony Stewart, USA (Chevrolet), 267; **10** Paul Menard, USA (Ford), 267.
Pole position: McMurray, 29.421s, 183.542 mph/295.383 km/h.
Drivers' championship points: 1 Harvick, 2745; **2** Gordon, 2642; **3** Johnson, 2557; **4** Hamlin, 2542; **5** Busch (Kurt), 2524; **6** Busch (Kyle), 2488.

BRICKYARD 400, Indianapolis Motor Speedway, Speedway, Indiana, USA, 25 July. Round 20. 160 laps of the 2.500-mile/4.023-km circuit, 400.000 miles/643.738 km.
1 Jamie McMurray, USA (Chevrolet), 2h 56m 24s, 136.054 mph/218.958 km/h; **2** Kevin Harvick, USA (Chevrolet), 2h 56m 25.391s; **3** Greg Biffle, USA (Ford), 160 laps; **4** Clint Bowyer, USA (Chevrolet), 160; **5** Tony Stewart, USA (Chevrolet), 160; **6** Jeff Burton, USA (Chevrolet), 160; **7** Carl Edwards, USA (Ford), 160; **8** Kyle Busch, USA (Toyota), 160; **9** Joey Logano, USA (Toyota), 160; **10** Kurt Busch, USA (Dodge), 160.
Pole position: Juan Montoya, CO (Chevrolet), 49.375s, 182.278 mph/293.349 km/h.
Drivers' championship points: 1 Harvick, 2920; **2** Gordon, 2736; **3** Hamlin, 2660; **4** Johnson, 2659; **5** Busch (Kurt), 2658; **6** Busch (Kyle), 2630.

SUNOCO RED CROSS PENNSYLVANIA 500, Pocono Raceway, Long Pond, Pennsylvania, USA, 1 August. Round 21. 200 laps of the 2.500-mile/4.023-km circuit, 500.000 miles/804.672 km.
1 Greg Biffle, USA (Ford), 3h 46m 51s, 132.246 mph/212.829 km/h; **2** Tony Stewart, USA (Chevrolet), 3h 46m 54.598s; **3** Carl Edwards, USA (Ford), 200 laps; **4** Kevin Harvick, USA (Chevrolet), 200; **5** Denny Hamlin, USA (Toyota), 200; **6** Jeff Gordon, USA (Chevrolet), 200; **7** Mark Martin, USA (Chevrolet), 200; **8** Jeff Burton, USA (Chevrolet), 200; **9** Martin Truex Jr., USA (Toyota), 200; **10** Jimmie Johnson, USA (Chevrolet), 200.
Pole position: Stewart, 52.511s, 171.393 mph/275.830 km/h.
Drivers' championship points: 1 Harvick, 3080; **2** Gordon, 2891; **3** Hamlin, 2820; **4** Johnson, 2803; **5** Burton, 2757; **6** Busch (Kyle), 2724.

HELUVA GOOD! SOUR CREAM DIPS AT THE GLEN, Watkins Glen International, New York, USA, 8 August. Round 22. 90 laps of the 2.450-mile/3.943-km circuit, 220.500 miles/354.860 km.
1 Juan Pablo Montoya, CO (Chevrolet), 2h 23m 52s, 91.960 mph/147.996 km/h; **2** Kurt Busch, USA (Dodge), 2h 23m 56.735s; **3** Marcos Ambrose, AUS (Toyota), 90 laps; **4** A.J. Allmendinger, USA (Ford), 90; **5** Carl Edwards, USA (Ford), 90; **6** Jamie McMurray, USA (Chevrolet), 90; **7** Tony Stewart, USA (Chevrolet), 90; **8** Kyle Busch, USA (Toyota), 90; **9** Jeff Burton, USA (Chevrolet), 90; **10** Jeff Gordon, USA (Chevrolet), 90.
Pole position: Edwards, 1m 10.882s, 124.432 mph/200.254 km/h.
Drivers' championship points: 1 Harvick, 3210; **2** Gordon, 3025; **3** Burton, 2895; **4** Busch (Kurt), 2892; **5** Johnson, 2882; **6** Hamlin, 2872.

CARFAX 400, Michigan International Speedway, Brooklyn, Michigan, USA, 15 August. Round 23. 200 laps of the 2.000-mile/3.219-km circuit, 400.000 miles/643.738 km.
1 Kevin Harvick, USA (Chevrolet), 2h 46m 38s, 144.029 mph/231.792 km/h; **2** Denny Hamlin, USA (Toyota), 2h 46m 39.731s; **3** Carl Edwards, USA (Ford), 200 laps; **4** Greg Biffle, USA (Ford), 200; **5** Matt Kenseth, USA (Ford), 200; **6** Tony Stewart, USA (Chevrolet), 200; **7** Juan Pablo Montoya, CO (Chevrolet), 200; **8** Martin Truex Jr., USA (Toyota), 200; **9** Elliott Sadler, USA (Ford), 200; **10** Joey Logano, USA (Toyota), 200.
Pole position: Kasey Kahne, USA (Ford), 38.465s, 187.183 mph/301.242 km/h.
Drivers' championship points: 1 Harvick, 3400; **2** Gordon, 3107; **3** Hamlin, 3047; **4** Stewart, 3020; **5** Johnson, 3014; **6** Edwards, 2986.

IRWIN TOOLS NIGHT RACE, Bristol Motor Speedway, Tennessee, USA, 21 August. Round 24. 500 laps of the 0.533-mile/0.858-km circuit, 266.500 miles/428.890 km.
1 Kyle Busch, USA (Toyota), 2h 41m 24s, 99.071 mph/159.439 km/h; **2** David Reutimann, USA (Toyota), 2h 41m 24.677s; **3** Jamie McMurray, USA (Chevrolet), 500 laps; **4** Clint Bowyer, USA (Chevrolet), 500; **5** Kasey Kahne, USA (Ford), 500; **6** Ryan Newman, USA (Chevrolet), 500; **7** Juan Pablo Montoya, CO (Chevrolet), 500; **8** Greg Biffle, USA (Ford), 500; **9** Kurt Busch, USA (Dodge), 500; **10** Matt Kenseth, USA (Ford), 500.
Pole position: Jimmie Johnson, USA (Chevrolet), 15.540s, 123.475 mph/198.714 km/h.
Drivers' championship points: 1 Harvick, 3521; **2** Gordon, 3242; **3** Busch (Kyle), 3170; **4** Edwards, 3113; **5** Hamlin, 3108; **6** Stewart, 3107.

EMORY HEALTHCARE 500, Atlanta Motor Speedway, Hampton, Georgia, USA, 5 September. Round 25. 325 laps of the 1.540-mile/2.478-km circuit, 500.500 miles/805.477 km.
1 Tony Stewart, USA (Chevrolet), 3h 52m 43s, 129.041 mph/207.671 km/h; **2** Carl Edwards, USA (Ford), 3h 52m 44.316s; **3** Jimmie Johnson, USA (Chevrolet), 325 laps; **4** Jeff Burton, USA (Chevrolet), 325; **5** Kyle Busch, USA (Toyota), 325; **6** Kurt Busch, USA (Dodge), 325; **7** Clint Bowyer, USA (Chevrolet), 325; **8** Ryan Newman, USA (Chevrolet), 325; **9** Juan Pablo Montoya, CO (Chevrolet), 325; **10** Marcos Ambrose, AUS (Toyota), 325.
Pole position: Denny Hamlin, USA (Toyota), 29.587s, 187.380 mph/301.558 km/h.
Drivers' championship points: 1 Harvick, 3585; **2** Gordon, 3366; **3** Busch (Kyle), 3325; **4** Stewart, 3302; **5** Edwards, 3288; **6** Burton, 3261.

AIR GUARD 400, Richmond International Raceway, Virginia, USA, 11 September. Round 26. 400 laps of the 0.750-mile/1.207-km circuit, 300.000 miles/482.803 km.
1 Denny Hamlin, USA (Toyota), 2h 52m 55s, 104.096 mph/167.527 km/h; **2** Kyle Busch, USA (Toyota), 2h 52m 55.537s; **3** Jimmie Johnson, USA (Chevrolet), 400 laps; **4** Joey Logano, USA (Toyota), 400; **5** Marcos Ambrose, AUS (Toyota), 400; **6** Clint Bowyer, USA (Chevrolet), 400; **7** Juan Pablo Montoya, CO (Chevrolet), 400; **8** A.J. Allmendinger, USA (Ford), 400; **9** Kevin Harvick, USA (Chevrolet), 400; **10** Carl Edwards, USA (Ford), 400.
Pole position: Edwards, 21.133s, 127.762 mph/205.613 km/h.
Drivers' championship points: 1 Hamlin, 5060; **2** Johnson, 5050; **3** Harvick, 5030; **4** Busch (Kyle), 5030; **5** Busch (Kurt), 5020; **6** Stewart, 5010.

SYLVANIA 300, New Hampshire Motor Speedway, Loudon, New Hampshire, USA, 19 September. Round 27. 300 laps of the 1.058-mile/1.703-km circuit, 317.400 miles/510.806 km.
1 Clint Bowyer, USA (Chevrolet), 2h 58m 22s, 106.769 mph/171.828 km/h; **2** Denny Hamlin, USA (Toyota), 2h 58m 22.477s; **3** Jamie McMurray, USA (Chevrolet), 300 laps; **4** Dale Earnhardt Jr., USA (Chevrolet), 300; **5** Kevin Harvick, USA (Chevrolet), 300; **6** Jeff Gordon, USA (Chevrolet), 300; **7** David Reutimann, USA (Toyota), 300; **8** Ryan Newman, USA (Chevrolet), 300; **9** Kyle Busch, USA (Toyota), 300; **10** Sam Hornish Jr., USA (Dodge), 300.
Pole position: Brad Keselowski, USA (Dodge), 28.515s, 133.572 mph/214.963 km/h.
Drivers' championship points: 1 Hamlin, 5230; **2** Harvick, 5185; **3** Busch (Kyle), 5168; **4** Gordon, 5155; **5** Busch (Kurt), 5144; **6** Johnson, 5138.

AAA 400, Dover International Speedway, Delaware, USA, 26 September. Round 28. 400 laps of the 1.000-mile/1.609-km circuit, 400.000 miles/643.738 km.
1 Jimmie Johnson, USA (Chevrolet), 3h 02m 27s, 131.543 mph/211.698 km/h; **2** Jeff Burton, USA (Chevrolet), 3h 02m 29.637s; **3** Joey Logano, USA (Toyota), 400 laps; **4** Kurt Busch, USA (Dodge), 400; **5** Carl Edwards, USA (Ford), 400; **6** Kyle Busch, USA (Toyota), 400; **7** Paul Menard, USA (Ford), 400; **8** Ryan Newman, USA (Chevrolet), 400; **9** Denny Hamlin, USA (Toyota), 400; **10** A.J. Allmendinger, USA (Ford), 400.
Pole position: Johnson, 23.116s, 155.736 mph/250.633 km/h.
Drivers' championship points: 1 Hamlin, 5368; **2** Johnson, 5333; **3** Busch (Kyle), 5323; **4** Busch (Kurt), 5309; **5** Harvick, 5303; **6** Edwards, 5295.

PRICE CHOPPER 400 PRESENTED BY KRAFT FOODS, Kansas Speedway, Kansas City, Kansas, USA, 3 October. Round 29. 267 laps of the 1.500-mile/2.414-km circuit, 400.500 miles/644.542 km.
1 Greg Biffle, USA (Ford), 2h 54m 02s, 138.077 mph/222.213 km/h; **2** Jimmie Johnson, USA (Chevrolet), 2h 54m 09.638s; **3** Kevin Harvick, USA (Chevrolet), 267 laps; **4** Tony Stewart, USA (Chevrolet), 267; **5** Jeff Gordon, USA (Chevrolet), 267; **6** Carl Edwards, USA (Ford), 267; **7** Matt Kenseth, USA (Ford), 267; **8** Paul Menard, USA (Ford), 267; **9** Ryan Newman, USA (Chevrolet), 267; **10** A.J. Allmendinger, USA (Ford), 267.
Pole position: Kasey Kahne, USA (Ford), 30.920s, 174.644 mph/281.063 km/h.
Drivers' championship points: 1 Johnson, 5503; **2** Hamlin, 5495; **3** Harvick, 5473; **4** Edwards, 5450; **5** Gordon, 5445; **6** Busch (Kurt), 5433.

PEPSI MAX 400, Auto Club Speedway, Fontana, California, USA, 10 October. Round 30. 200 laps of the 2.000-mile/3.219-km circuit, 400.000 miles/643.738 km.
1 Tony Stewart, USA (Chevrolet), 3h 01m 53s, 131.953 mph/212.357 km/h; **2** Clint Bowyer, USA (Chevrolet), 3h 01m 53.466s; **3** Jimmie Johnson, USA (Chevrolet), 200 laps; **4** Kasey Kahne, USA (Ford), 200; **5** Ryan Newman, USA (Chevrolet), 200; **6** Mark Martin, USA (Chevrolet), 200; **7** Kevin Harvick, USA (Chevrolet), 200; **8** Denny Hamlin, USA (Toyota), 200; **9** Jeff Gordon, USA (Chevrolet), 200; **10** David Reutimann, USA (Toyota), 200.
Pole position: Jamie McMurray, USA (Chevrolet), 38.859s, 185.285 mph/298.188 km/h.
Drivers' championship points: 1 Johnson, 5673; **2** Hamlin, 5637; **3** Harvick, 5619; **4** Gordon, 5588; **5** Stewart, 5566; **6** Busch (Kurt), 5533.

BANK OF AMERICA 500, Lowe's Motor Speedway, Concord, Charlotte, North Carolina, USA, 16 October. Round 31. 334 laps of the 1.500-mile/2.414-km circuit, 501.000 miles/806.281 km.
1 Jamie McMurray, USA (Chevrolet), 3h 34m 07s, 140.391 mph/225.937 km/h; **2** Kyle Busch, USA (Toyota), 3h 34m 08.866s; **3** Jimmie Johnson, USA (Chevrolet), 334 laps; **4** Denny Hamlin, USA (Toyota), 334; **5** Greg Biffle, USA (Ford), 334; **6** Matt Kenseth, USA (Ford), 334; **7** Joey Logano, USA (Toyota), 334; **8** Kevin Harvick, USA (Chevrolet), 334; **9** David Reutimann, USA (Toyota), 334; **10** David Ragan, USA (Ford), 334.
Pole position: Jeff Gordon, USA (Chevrolet), 28.192s, 191.544 mph/308.260 km/h.
Drivers' championship points: 1 Johnson, 5843; **2** Hamlin, 5802; **3** Harvick, 5766; **4** Gordon, 5687; **5** Busch (Kyle), 5666; **6** Stewart, 5666.

TUMS FAST RELIEF 500, Martinsville Speedway, Virginia, USA, 24 October. Round 32. 500 laps of the 0.526-mile/0.847-km circuit, 263.000 miles/423.257 km.
1 Denny Hamlin, USA (Toyota), 3h 40m 20s, 71.619 mph/115.259 km/h; **2** Mark Martin, USA (Chevrolet), 3h 40m 22.318s; **3** Kevin Harvick, USA (Chevrolet), 500 laps; **4** Kyle Busch, USA (Toyota), 500; **5** Jimmie Johnson, USA (Chevrolet), 500; **6** Joey Logano, USA (Toyota), 500; **7** Dale Earnhardt Jr., USA (Chevrolet), 500; **8** Carl Edwards, USA (Ford), 500; **9** Jeff Burton, USA (Chevrolet), 500; **10** Brad Keselowski, USA (Dodge), 500.
Pole position: Hamlin, 19.518s, 97.018 mph/156.136 km/h.
Drivers' championship points: 1 Johnson, 5998; **2** Hamlin, 5992; **3** Harvick, 5936; **4** Busch (Kyle), 5826; **5** Gordon, 5795; **6** Edwards, 5785.

AMP ENERGY JUICE 500, Talladega Superspeedway, Alabama, USA, 31 October. Round 33. 188 laps of the 2.660-mile/4.281-km circuit, 500.080 miles/804.801 km.
1 Clint Bowyer, USA (Chevrolet), 3h 03m 23s, 163.618 mph/263.318 km/h; **2** Kevin Harvick, USA (Chevrolet), 188 laps; **3** Juan Pablo Montoya, CO (Chevrolet), 188; **4** David Reutimann, USA (Toyota), 188; **5** Joey Logano, USA (Toyota), 188; **6** Martin Truex Jr., USA (Toyota), 188; **7** Jimmie Johnson, USA (Chevrolet), 188; **8** Jeff Gordon, USA (Chevrolet), 188; **9** Denny Hamlin, USA (Toyota), 188; **10** Brad Keselowski, USA (Dodge), 188.
Pole position: Montoya, 51.863s, 184.640 mph/297.150 km/h.
Drivers' championship points: 1 Johnson, 6149; **2** Hamlin, 6135; **3** Harvick, 6111; **4** Gordon, 5942; **5** Busch (Kyle), 5919; **6** Edwards, 5902.

AAA TEXAS 500, Texas Motor Speedway, Fort Worth, Texas, USA, 7 November. Round 34. 334 laps of the 1.500-mile/2.414-km circuit, 501.000 miles/806.281 km.
1 Denny Hamlin, USA (Toyota), 3h 34m 01s, 140.456 mph/226.043 km/h; **2** Matt Kenseth, USA (Ford), 3h 34m 01.488s; **3** Mark Martin, USA (Chevrolet), 334 laps; **4** Joey Logano, USA (Toyota), 334; **5** Greg Biffle, USA (Ford), 334; **6** Kevin Harvick, USA (Chevrolet), 334; **7** Clint Bowyer, USA (Chevrolet), 334; **8** David Ragan, USA (Ford), 334; **9** Jimmie Johnson, USA (Chevrolet), 334; **10** Paul Menard, USA (Ford), 334.
Pole position: Sadler, 27.636s, 195.397 mph/314.461 km/h.
Drivers' championship points: 1 Hamlin, 6325; **2** Johnson, 6292; **3** Harvick, 6266; **4** Edwards, 6008; **5** Kenseth, 6000; **6** Gordon, 5994.

KOBALT TOOLS 500, Phoenix International Raceway, Arizona, USA, 14 November. Round 35. 312 laps of the 1.000-mile/1.609-km circuit, 312.000 miles/502.115 km.
1 Carl Edwards, USA (Ford), 2h 49m 01s, 110.758 mph/178.248 km/h; **2** Ryan Newman, USA (Chevrolet), 2h 49m 05.770s; **3** Joey Logano, USA (Toyota), 312 laps; **4** Greg Biffle, USA (Ford), 312; **5** Jimmie Johnson, USA (Chevrolet), 312; **6** Kevin Harvick, USA (Chevrolet), 312; **7** Matt Kenseth, USA (Ford), 312; **8** Mark Martin, USA (Chevrolet), 312; **9** Kurt Busch, USA (Dodge), 312; **10** Jamie McMurray, USA (Chevrolet), 312.
Pole position: Edwards, 26.395s, 136.389 mph/219.498 km/h.

Provisional Championship points
Drivers: 1 Denny Hamlin, USA, 6462; **2** Jimmie Johnson, USA, 6447; **3** Kevin Harvick, USA, 6416; **4** Carl Edwards, USA, 6198; **5** Matt Kenseth, USA, 6151; **6** Jeff Gordon, USA, 6124; **7** Kyle Busch, USA, 6115; **8** Greg Biffle, USA, 6113; **9** Tony Stewart, USA, 6074; **10** Kurt Busch, USA, 6033; **11** Clint Bowyer, USA, 6028; **12** Jeff Burton, USA, 5958; **13** Mark Martin, USA, 4249; **14** Jamie McMurray, USA, 4225; **15** Ryan Newman, USA, 4156; **16** Joey Logano, USA, 4139; **17** Juan Pablo Montoya, CO, 4060; **18** David Reutimann, USA, 3975; **19** Dale Earnhardt Jr., USA, 3871; **20** A.J. Allmendinger, USA, 3843; **21** Kasey Kahne, USA, 3806; **22** Martin Truex Jr., USA, 3781; **23** Paul Menard, USA, 3670; **24** David Ragan, USA, 3496; **25** Brad Keselowski, USA, 3366; **26** Marcos Ambrose, AUS, 3337; **27** Elliott Sadler, USA, 3155; **28** Sam Hornish Jr., USA, 3123; **29** Regan Smith, USA, 3117; **30** Scott Speed, USA, 3084.
Raybestos Rookie of the Year: Kevin Conway, USA.
Manufacturers: 1 Chevrolet, 255; **2** Toyota, 213; **3** Ford, 167; **4** Dodge, 135.

Result of the Homestead. race will be given in AUTOCOURSE 2011–2012.

Other NASCAR races

BUDWEISER SHOOTOUT, Daytona International Speedway, Daytona Beach, Florida, USA, 6 February. 76 laps of the 2.500-mile/4.023-km circuit, 190.000 miles/ 305.775 km.
1 Kurt Busch, USA (Dodge), 76 laps; **2** Kasey Kahne, USA (Ford), 76; **3** Jamie McMurray, USA (Chevrolet), 76; **4** Kyle Busch, USA (Toyota), 76; **5** Denny Hamlin, USA (Toyota), 76; **6** Jeff Gordon, USA (Chevrolet), 76; **7** Joey Logano, USA (Toyota), 76; **8** Brian Vickers, USA (Chevrolet), 76; **9** Tony Stewart, USA (Chevrolet), 76 (DNF-accident); **10** Juan Pablo Montoya, CO (Chevrolet), 76.
Pole position: Carl Edwards, USA (Ford).

SPRINT ALL-STAR RACE, Lowe's Motor Speedway, Concord, Charlotte, North Carolina, USA, 22 May. 100 laps of the 1.500-mile/2.414-km circuit, 150.000 miles/241.402 km.
1 Kurt Busch, USA (Dodge), 1h 35m 34.0s, 94.175 mph/ 151.560 km/h; **2** Martin Truex, USA (Toyota), 1h 35m 34.358s; **3** Joey Logano, USA (Toyota), 100 laps; **4** Denny Hamlin, USA (Toyota), 100; **5** Tony Stewart, USA (Chevrolet), 100; **6** Kevin Harvick, USA (Chevrolet), 100; **7** Brad Keselowski, USA (Dodge), 100; **8** Matt Kenseth, USA (Ford), 100; **9** Greg Biffle, USA (Ford), 100; **10** Bobby Labonte, USA, 100.
Pole position : Busch (Kurt).

Firestone Indy Lights

All cars are Dallara IPS-Infiniti.

FIRESTONE INDY LIGHTS, St. Petersburg Street Circuit, Florida, USA, 28 March. Round 1. 35 laps of the 1.800-mile/2.897-km circuit, 63.000 miles/101.389 km.
1 Jean-Karl Vernay, F, 1h 02m 02.6848s, 60.924 mph/98.047 km/h; **2** Jan Heylen, B, 1h 02m 13.9186s; **3** Stefan Wilson, GB, 1h 02m 14.2633s; **4** Charlie Kimball, USA, 1h 02m 23.0889s; **5** Gustavo Yacaman, CO, 1h 02m 24.4861s; **6** Martin Plowman, GB, 1h 02m 25.7754s; **7** James Winslow, GB, 1h 02m 27.3584s; **8** Jonathan Summerton, USA, 1h 02m 48.7474s; **9** Rodrigo Barbosa, BR, 34 laps; **10** Junior Strous, NL, 34.
Fastest race lap: Sebastian Saavedra, CO, 1m 19.0338s, 81.990 mph/131.950 km/h.
Pole position: James Hinchcliffe, CDN, 1m 06.3497s, 97.664 mph/157.176 km/h.

FIRESTONE INDY LIGHTS, Barber Motorsports Park, Alabama, USA, 11 April. Round 2. 40 laps of the 2.300-mile/3.701-km circuit, 92.000 miles/148.060 km.
1 Jean-Karl Vernay, F, 57m 07.6033s, 96.627 mph/155.507 km/h; **2** Charlie Kimball, USA, 57m 08.7575s; **3** Sebastian Saavedra, CO, 57m 13.4003s; **4** Martin Plowman, GB, 57m 16.6827s; **5** James Hinchcliffe, CDN, 57m 17.9030s; **6** Stefan Wilson, GB, 57m 20.0135s; **7** Dan Clarke, GB, 57m 20.9011s; **8** Junior Strous, NL, 57m 28.0235s; **9** Gustavo Yacaman, CO, 57m 33.9617s; **10** Philip Major, CDN, 57m 35.1902s.
Fastest race lap: Vernay, 1m 17.9752s, 106.188 mph/170.892 km/h.
Pole position: Vernay, 1m 14.8726s, 110.588 mph/177.974 km/h.

FIRESTONE INDY LIGHTS, Long Beach Street Circuit, California, USA, 18 April. Round 3. 45 laps of the 1.968-mile/3.167-km circuit, 88.560 miles/142.524 km.
1 James Hinchcliffe, CDN, 1h 03m 41.4082s, 83.429 mph/134.266 km/h; **2** Charlie Kimball, USA, 1h 03m 42.2452s; **3** Jean-Karl Vernay, F, 1h 03m 42.6373s; **4** Sebastian Saavedra, CO, 1h 03m 44.3208s; **5** Martin Plowman, GB, 1h 03m 45.8817s; **6** Tonis Kasemets, EST, 1h 03m 52.0840s; **7** Philip Major, CDN, 1h 03m 53.2392s; **8** Pippa Mann, GB, 1h 03m 53.5645s; **9** Niall Quinn, IRL, 1h 03m 59.2481s; **10** Carmen Jordá, E, 1h 04m 01.1283s.
Fastest race lap: Hinchcliffe, 1m 15.3236s, 94.058 mph/151.372 km/h.
Pole position: Hinchcliffe, 1m 14.6261s, 94.937 mph/152.787 km/h.

FIRESTONE FREEDOM 100, Indianapolis Motor Speedway, Speedway, Indiana, USA, 28 May. Round 4. 40 laps of the 2.500-mile/4.023-km circuit, 100.000 miles/160.934 km.
1 Wade Cunningham, NZ, 39m 55.4552s, 150.285 mph/241.860 km/h; **2** Charlie Kimball, USA, 39m 55.8920s; **3** James Hinchcliffe, CDN, 39m 57.8190s; **4** Dan Clarke, GB, 39m 58.1011s; **5** Martin Plowman, GB, 39m 59.1576s; **6** Philip Major, CDN, 40m 01.2809s; **7**

Stefan Wilson, GB, 40m 02.8542s; **8** Brandon Wagner, USA, 40m 05.1587s; **9** Sebastian Saavedra, CO, 40m 05.6811s; **10** Adrián Campos Jr., E, 40m 05.8127s.
Fastest race lap: Jeff Simmons, USA, 47.5608s, 189.231 mph/304.539 km/h.
Pole position: Pippa Mann, GB, 1m 35.7505s, 187.989 mph/302.538 km/h (over 2 laps).

AVOIDTHESTORK.COM 100, Iowa Speedway, Newton, Iowa, USA, 19 June. Round 5. 115 laps of the 0.894-mile/1.439-km circuit, 102.810 miles/165.457 km.
1 Sebastian Saavedra, CO, 46m 10.0471s, 133.614 mph/215.030 km/h; **2** Martin Plowman, GB, 46m 10.5291s; **3** Jean-Karl Vernay, F, 46m 11.4153s; **4** Adrián Campos Jr., E, 46m 15.8939s; **5** James Hinchcliffe, CDN, 46m 17.5446s; **6** Philip Major, CDN, 46m 20.5984s; **7** Stefan Wilson, GB, 46m 23.7772s; **8** Pippa Mann, GB, 46m 30.6738s; **9** Dan Clarke, GB, 114 laps; **10** Rodrigo Barbosa, BR, 112.
Fastest race lap: Major, 20.0876s, 160.218 mph/257.846 km/h.
Pole position: Saavedra, 40.0594s, 160.681 mph/258.592 km/h (over 2 laps).

CORNING 100, Watkins Glen International, New York, USA, 4 July. Round 6. 30 laps of the 3.370-mile/5.423-km circuit, 101.100 miles/162.705 km.
1 Jean-Karl Vernay, F, 58m 48.4946s, 103.149 mph/166.002 km/h; **2** James Hinchcliffe, CDN, 58m 48.7081s; **3** Sebastian Saavedra, CO, 58m 52.4581s; **4** Martin Plowman, GB, 59m 07.5675s; **5** James Winslow, GB, 59m 11.8240s; **6** Philip Major, CDN, 59m 13.2079s; **7** Adrián Campos Jr., E, 59m 13.3183s; **8** Gustavo Yacaman, CO, 59m 19.6273s; **9** Rodrigo Barbosa, BR, 59m 29.4009s; **10** Anders Krohn, N, 59m 34.7258s.
Fastest race lap: Hinchcliffe, 1m 38.5742s, 123.075 mph/198.070 km/h.
Pole position: Hinchcliffe, 1m 37.3594s, 124.610 mph/200.541 km/h.

TORONTO 100, Toronto Street Circuit, Ontario, Canada, 18 July. Round 7. 50 laps of the 1.755-mile/2.824-km circuit, 87.750 miles/141.220 km.
1 Jean-Karl Vernay, F, 58m 52.0083s, 89.439 mph/143.938 km/h; **2** Dan Clarke, GB, 58m 53.7552s; **3** Gustavo Yacaman, CO, 58m 54.7529s; **4** Charlie Kimball, USA, 58m 55.5771s; **5** Stefan Wilson, GB, 58m 56.2750s; **6** Tonis Kasemets, EST, 58m 58.8303s; **7** Martin Plowman, GB, 59m 00.1705s; **8** Pippa Mann, GB, 59m 22.4483s; **9** Rodrigo Barbosa, BR, 59m 38.6562s; **10** James Hinchcliffe, CDN, 49 laps (DNF-accident).
Fastest race lap: Wilson, 1m 05.8173s, 95.993 mph/154.486 km/h.
Pole position: Vernay, 1m 05.2989s, 96.755 mph/155.712 km/h.

EDMONTON 100, Rexall Speedway, Edmonton City Centre Airport, Alberta, Canada, 25 July. Round 8. 50 laps of the 1.973-mile/3.175-km circuit, 98.650 miles/158.762 km.
1 James Hinchcliffe, CDN, 58m 33.2721s, 101.085 mph/162.681 km/h; **2** Jean-Karl Vernay, F, 58m 34.4994s; **3** Martin Plowman, GB, 58m 42.8326s; **4** Charlie Kimball, USA, 58m 44.9712s; **5** Dan Clarke, GB, 58m 45.8041s; **6** Sebastian Saavedra, CO, 58m 57.9493s; **7** Stefan Wilson, GB, 59m 01.9973s; **8** Adrián Campos Jr., E, 59m 14.8388s; **9** Gustavo Yacaman, CO, 59m 21.1397s; **10** Philip Major, CDN, 59m 24.2740s.
Fastest race lap: Hinchcliffe, 1m 06.8782s, 106.205 mph/170.920 km/h.
Pole position: Hinchcliffe, 1m 06.2160s, 107.267 mph/172.630 km/h.

MID-OHIO 100, Mid-Ohio Sports Car Course, Lexington, Ohio, USA, 8 August. Round 9. 40 laps of the 2.258-mile/3.634-km circuit, 90.320 miles/145.356 km.
1 Martin Plowman, GB, 50m 28.5067s, 107.364 mph/172.785 km/h; **2** Dan Clarke, GB, 50m 29.3510s; **3** Charlie Kimball, USA, 50m 32.6801s; **4** Stefan Wilson, GB, 50m 36.1282s; **5** Sebastian Saavedra, CO, 50m 36.3112s; **6** Adrián Campos Jr., E, 50m 36.8247s; **7** James Hinchcliffe, CDN, 50m 40.1827s; **8** Jean-Karl Vernay, F, 50m 44.9842s; **9** James Winslow, GB, 51m 16.6744s; **10** Philip Major, CDN, 51m 18.8753s.
Fastest race lap: Hinchcliffe, 1m 13.9532s, 109.918 mph/176.896 km/h.
Pole position: Plowman, 1m 12.8624s, 111.564 mph/179.544 km/h.

CARNEROS 100, Infineon Raceway, Sears Point, Sonoma, California, USA, 22 August. Round 10. 40 laps of the 2.303-mile/3.706-km circuit, 92.120 miles/148.253 km.
1 Jean-Karl Vernay, F, 1h 02m 21.4252s, 88.638 mph/142.649 km/h; **2** Charlie Kimball, USA, 1h 02m 24.8497s; **3** James Hinchcliffe, CDN, 1h 02m 31.9835s; **4** Gustavo Yacaman, CO, 1h 02m 36.6367s; **5** Pippa Mann, GB, 1h 02m 44.6851s; **6** Juan Pablo García, MEX, 1h 02m 46.2693s; **7** Adrián Campos Jr., E, 1h 02m 47.5239s; **8** David Martínez, MEX, 1h 02m 51.0267s; **9** Joel Miller, USA, 1h 02m 56.3926s; **10** Giancarlo Vilarinho, BR, 1h 02m 58.3533s.
Fastest race lap: Vernay, 1m 24.9443s, 97.603 mph/157.076 km/h.
Pole position: Vernay, 1m 23.5582s, 99.222 mph/159.682 km/h.

CHICAGOLAND 100, Chicagoland Speedway, Chicago, Illinois, USA, 28 August. Round 11. 67 laps of the 1.520-mile/2.446-km circuit, 101.840 miles/163.896 km.
1 James Hinchcliffe, CDN, 42m 30.9080s, 143.723 mph/231.300 km/h; **2** Pippa Mann, GB, 42m 30.9239s; **3** Philip Major, CDN, 42m 30.9637s; **4** Jean-Karl Vernay, F, 42m 31.0351s; **5** Dan Clarke, GB, 42m 31.1141s; **6** Stefan Wilson, GB, 42m 32.1200s; **7** Arie Luyendyk Jr., NL, 42m 32.5614s; **8** Adrián Campos Jr., E, 42m 32.6650s; **9** Dillon Battistini, GB, 42m 34.2435s; **10** Rodrigo Barbosa, BR, 42m 34.5922s.
Fastest race lap: Hinchcliffe, 28.4836s, 192.111 mph/309.172 km/h.
Pole position: Martin Plowman, GB, 57.7510s, 189.503 mph/304.976 km/h (over 2 laps).

DRIVE SMART. BUCKLE-UP KENTUCKY 100, Kentucky Speedway, Fort Mitchell, Kentucky, USA, 4 September. Round 12. 67 laps of the 1.480-mile/2.382-km circuit, 99.160 miles/159.583 km.
1 Pippa Mann, GB, 34m 04.7529s, 174.581 mph/280.962 km/h; **2** James Hinchcliffe, CDN, 34m 11.5901s; **3** Jean-Karl Vernay, F, 34m 14.4666s; **4** Adrián Campos Jr., E, 34m 14.5453s; **5** Gustavo Yacaman, CO, 34m 18.6774s; **6** Charlie Kimball, USA, 34m 18.7264s; **7** Martin Plowman, GB, 34m 19.2067s; **8** Brandon Wagner, USA, 34m 28.2754s; **9** Arie Luyendyk Jr., NL, 34m 29.2413s; **10** Dan Clarke, GB, 66 laps.
Fastest race lap: Adrian Campos Jr., 27.9820s, 190.408 mph/306.432 km/h.
Pole position: Mann, 55.9447s, 190.474 mph/306.538 km/h (over 2 laps).

FUZZY'S ULTRA PREMIUM VODKA 100, Homestead-Miami Speedway, Florida, USA, 2 October. Round 13. 67 laps of the 1.485-mile/2.390-km circuit, 99.495 miles/160.122 km.
1 Brandon Wagner, USA, 40m 38.3036s, 146.898 mph/236.409 km/h; **2** James Hinchcliffe, CDN, 40m 39.0042s; **3** Wade Cunningham, NZ, 40m 47.3872s; **4** Adrián Campos Jr., E, 40m 48.4371s; **5** Pippa Mann, GB, 40m 49.2297s; **6** Martin Plowman, GB, 40m 55.0741s; **7** Daniel Herrington, USA, 40m 56.2955s; **8** Philip Major, CDN, 41m 05.8472s; **9** Dillon Battistini, GB, 41m 07.4638s; **10** Sean Guthrie, USA, 66 laps.
Fastest race lap: Hinchcliffe, 28.7036s, 186.248 mph/299.738 km/h.
Pole position: Mann, 57.2999s, 186.597 mph/300.299 km/h (over 2 laps).

Final championship points
1 Jean-Karl Vernay, F, 494; **2** James Hinchcliffe, CDN, 471; **3** Martin Plowman, GB, 392; **4** Charlie Kimball, USA, 388; **5** Pippa Mann, GB, 313; **6** Adrián Campos Jr., E, 307; **7** Dan Clarke, GB, 304; **8** Sebastian Saavedra, CO, 303; **9** Philip Major, CDN, 299; **10** Gustavo Yacaman, CO, 293; **11** Stefan Wilson, GB, 278; **12** Rodrigo Barbosa, BR, 241; **13** Brandon Wagner, USA, 136; **14** James Winslow, GB, 130; **15** Wade Cunningham, NZ, 87; **16** Carmen Jordá, E, 84; **17** Arie Luyendyk Jr., NL, 82; **18** Tonis Kasemets, EST, 56; **19** Junior Strous, NL, 56; **20** Juan Pablo García, MEX, 47; **21** Daniel Herrington, USA, 44; **22** Dillon Battistini, GB, 44; **23** Joel Miller, USA, 41; **24** Jan Heylen, B, 40; **25** David Martínez, MEX, 40; **26** Niall Quinn, IRL, 38; **27** Giancarlo Vilarinho, BR, 37; **28** Jonathan Summerton, USA, 24; **29** Sean Guthrie, USA, 20; **30** Anders Krohn, N, 20; **31** Henry Clarke, USA, 19; **32** Nic LeDuc, USA, 19; **33** Alex Ellis, CDN, 16; **34** Jeff Simmons, USA, 15.

Superleague Formula By Sonangol

All cars are developed by Élan Motorsports Technologies and powered by a Menard 4.2 litre V8 engine.

SUPERLEAGUE FORMULA BY SONANGOL, Silverstone Grand Prix Circuit, Towcester, Northamptonshire, Great Britain, 4 April. Round 1. 25, 25 and 5 laps of the 3.194-mile/5.141-km circuit.
Race 1 (79.862 miles/128.525 km).
1 Tottenham Hotspur-Craig Dolby, GB, 40m 51.242s, 117.288 mph/188.757 km/h; **2** AC Milan-Yelmer Buurman, NL, 41m 02.540s; **3** Flamengo-Duncan Tappy, GB, 41m 13.580s; **4** FC Porto-Álvaro Parente, P, 41m 13.788s; **5** FC Basel-Maximilian Wissel, D, 41m 26.740s; **6** Sevilla FC-Marcos Martinez, E, 41m 27.769s; **7** Sporting Clube de Portugal-Borja García, E, 41m 28.356s; **8** AS Roma-Julien Jousse, F, 41m 32.991s; **9** RSC Anderlecht-Davide Rigon, I, 41m 44.048s; **10** Atletico de Madrid-John Martin, AUS, 41m 49.612s; **11** Corinthians-Robert Doornbos, NL, 41m 59.749s; **12** PSV Eindhoven-Narain Karthikeyan, IND, 42m 00.976s; **13** Olympiacos-Chris van der Drift, NZ, 42m 08.842s; **14** Galatasaray-Tristan Gommendy, F, 24 laps; **15** Olympique Lyonnais-Sébastien Bourdais, F, 24; **16** Liverpool FC-James Walker, GB, 3 (DNF-spin); **17** Girondins de Bordeaux-Franck Montagny, F, 0 (DNF-driveshaft).
Fastest race lap: FC Porto, 1m 33.982s, 122.364 mph/196.927 km/h.
Pole position: FC Basel, 1m 43.282s, 111.346 mph/179.194 km/h.

Race 2 (79.862 miles/128.525 km).
1 Olympique Lyonnais-Sébastien Bourdais, F, 40m 27.836s, 118.419 mph/190.577 km/h; **2** Olympiacos-Chris van der Drift, NZ, 40m 38.708s; **3** Atletico de Madrid-John Martin, AUS, 40m 42.238s; **4** Tottenham Hotspur-Craig Dolby, GB, 40m 42.939s; **5** FC Porto-Álvaro Parente, P, 40m 44.440s; **6** FC Basel-Maximilian Wissel, D, 40m 45.077s; **7** Corinthians-Robert Doornbos, NL, 40m 48.949s; **8** Girondins de Bordeaux-Franck Montagny, F, 40m 49.917s; **9** Sevilla FC-Marcos Martinez, E, 41m 00.216s; **10** RSC Anderlecht-Davide Rigon, I, 41m 00.901s; **11** Sporting Clube de Portugal-Borja García, E, 41m 01.447s; **12** Flamengo-Duncan Tappy, GB, 41m 04.418s; **13** AS Roma-Julien Jousse, F, 41m 06.047s; **14** Galatasaray-Tristan Gommendy, F, 41m 42.730s; **15** PSV Eindhoven-Narain Karthikeyan, IND, 23 laps (DNF-brakes); **16** AC Milan-Yelmer Buurman, NL, 23 (DNF-clutch); **17** Liverpool FC-James Walker, GB, 13 (DNF-gearbox).
Fastest race lap: Olympique Lyonnais, 1m 32.818s, 123.899 mph/199.396 km/h.
Pole position: Liverpool FC.

Race 3 (15.972 miles/25.705 km).
1 Tottenham Hotspur-Craig Dolby, GB, 7m 55.043s, 121.042 mph/194.799 km/h; **2** FC Basel-Maximilian Wissel, D, 7m 56.817s; **3** Olympiacos-Chris van der Drift, NZ, 7m 57.718s; **4** Olympique Lyonnais-Sébastien Bourdais, F, 7m 58.354s; **5** FC Porto-Álvaro Parente, P, 7m 59.075s; **6** Atletico de Madrid-John Martin, AUS, 8m 00.900s.
Fastest race lap: FC Porto, 1m 34.451s, 121.757 mph/195.949 km/h.
Pole position: Tottenham Hotspur.

SUPERLEAGUE FORMULA BY SONANGOL, Nationale Circuit Assen, Netherlands, 16 May. Round 2. 31, 31 and 5 laps of the 2.830-mile/4.555-km circuit.
Race 1 (87.741 miles/141.205 km).
1 RSC Anderlecht-Davide Rigon, I, 45m 02.776s, 116.867 mph/188.079 km/h; **2** Flamengo-Franck Perera, F, 45m 05.419s; **3** FC Basel-Maximilian Wissel, D, 45m 07.378s; **4** AS Roma-Julien Jousse, F, 45m 11.931s; **5** AC Milan-Yelmer Buurman, NL, 45m 13.850s; **6** Liverpool FC-James Walker, GB, 45m 31.625s; **7** Tottenham Hotspur-Craig Dolby, GB, 45m 37.099s; **8** Galatasaray-Tristan Gommendy, F, 45m 37.464s; **9** Corinthians-Robert Doornbos, NL, 45m 46.871s; **10** Beijing Guoan-John Martin, AUS, 46m 23.105s; **11** FC Porto-Álvaro Parente, P, 29 laps (DNF-engine); **12** Sevilla FC-Marcos Martinez, E, 29; **13** PSV Eindhoven-Narain Karthikeyan, IND, 24 (DNF-clutch); **14** Girondins de Bordeaux-Franck Montagny, F, 14 (DNF-clutch); **15** Olympiacos-Chris van der Drift, NZ, 7 (DNF-gearbox); **16** Atletico de Madrid-Maria de Villota, E, 5 (DNF-spin); **17** Olympique Lyonnais-Sébastien Bourdais, F, 1 (DNF-accident damage); **18** Sporting Clube de Portugal-Borja García, E, 0 (DNF-accident).
Fastest race lap: AC Milan, 1m 23.547s, 121.958 mph/196.272 km/h.
Pole position: RSC Anderlecht, 1m 23.687s, 121.754 mph/195.944 km/h.

Race 2 (87.741 miles/141.205 km).
1 Olympiacos-Chris van der Drift, NZ, 45m 21.763s, 116.052 mph/186.767 km/h; **2** Tottenham Hotspur-Craig Dolby, GB, 45m 24.220s; **3** Girondins de Bordeaux-Franck Montagny, F, 45m 33.158s; **4** Sevilla FC-Marcos Martinez, E, 45m 39.341s; **5** Sporting Clube de Portugal-Borja García, E, 45m 42.093s; **6** Liverpool FC-James Walker, GB, 45m 43.285s; **7** AC Milan-Yelmer Buurman, NL, 45m 46.196s; **8** Galatasaray-Tristan Gommendy, F, 45m 47.036s; **9** PSV Eindhoven-Narain Karthikeyan, IND, 45m 55.446s; **10** RSC Anderlecht-Davide Rigon, I, 45m 59.567s; **11** Flamengo-Franck Perera, F, 46m 00.621s; **12** AS Roma-Julien Jousse, F, 46m 06.677s; **13** FC Basel-Maximilian Wissel, D, 46m 12.477s; **14** Atletico de Madrid-Maria de Villota, E, 30 laps; **15** Corinthians-Robert Doornbos, NL, 0 (DNF-accident); **16** FC Porto-Álvaro Parente, P, 0 (DNF-accident); **17** Beijing Guoan-John Martin, AUS, 0 (DNF-accident).
Did not start: Olympique Lyonnais-Sébastien Bourdais, F (gearbox).
Fastest race lap: Tottenham Hotspur, 1m 25.004s, 119.867 mph/192.908 km/h.
Pole position: Sporting Clube de Portugal.

Race 3 (14.152 miles/22.775 km).
1 RSC Anderlecht-Davide Rigon, I, 7m 16.174s, 116.802 mph/187.975 km/h; **2** Tottenham Hotspur-Craig Dolby, GB, 7m 16.801s; **3** AC Milan-Yelmer Buurman, NL, 7m 17.695s; **4** Liverpool FC-James Walker, GB, 7m 19.327s; **5** FC Basel-Maximilian Wissel, D, 7m 19.916s; **6** Flamengo-Franck Perera, F, 7m 23.673s.
Fastest race lap: RSC Anderlecht, 1m 25.677s, 118.926 mph/191.393 km/h.
Pole position: Tottenham Hotspur.

SUPERLEAGUE FORMULA BY SONANGOL, Circuit de Nevers, Magny-Cours, France, 23 May. Round 3. 31, 29 and 5 laps of the 2.741-mile/4.411-km circuit.
Race 1 (84.967 miles/136.741 km).
1 AC Milan-Yelmer Buurman, NL, 45m 59.226s, 110.857 mph/178.407 km/h; **2** Tottenham Hotspur-Craig Dolby, GB, 46m 12.128s; **3** Olympiacos-Chris van der Drift, NZ, 46m 20.508s; **4** Beijing Guoan-John Martin, AUS, 46m 27.770s; **5** FC Porto-Álvaro Parente, P, 46m 28.504s; **6** Liverpool FC-James Walker, GB, 46m 29.555s; **7** RSC Anderlecht-Davide Rigon, I, 46m 30.357s; **8** Flamengo-Franck Perera, F, 46m 31.238s; **9** Olympique Lyonnais-Sébastien Bourdais, F, 46m 45.809s; **10** Girondins de Bordeaux-Franck Montagny, F, 46m 48.133s; **11** Sporting Clube de Portugal-Borja García, E, 46m 55.541s; **12** Corinthians-Robert Doornbos, NL, 46m 59.234s; **13** AS Roma-Julien Jousse, F, 47m 10.821s; **14** Galatasaray-Tristan Gommendy, F, 47m 16.442s; **15** Atletico de Madrid-Maria de Villota, E, 30 laps; **16** Sevilla FC-Marcos Martinez, E, 30; **17** FC Basel-Maximilian Wissel, D, 0 (DNF-accident damage).
Fastest race lap: AC Milan, 1m 26.722s, 113.778 mph/183.109 km/h.
Pole position: Tottenham Hotspur, 1m 27.029s, 113.377 mph/182.463 km/h.

Race 2 (79.485 miles/127.919 km).
1 FC Basel-Maximilian Wissel, D, 46m 21.647s, 102.869 mph/165.552 km/h; **2** AS Roma-Julien Jousse, F, 46m 42.974s; **3** RSC Anderlecht-Davide Rigon, I, 46m 51.612s; **4** Tottenham Hotspur-Craig Dolby, GB, 47m 03.111s; **5** Sporting Clube de Portugal-Borja García, E, 47m 09.639s; **6** Atletico de Madrid-Maria de Villota, E, 47m 41.934s; **7** AC Milan-Yelmer Buurman, NL, 28 laps; **8** Liverpool FC-James Walker, GB, 28; **9** Galatasaray-Tristan Gommendy, F, 25 (DNF-gearbox); **10** Beijing Guoan-John Martin, AUS, 20 (DNF-clutch); **11** FC Porto-Álvaro Parente, P, 18 (DNF-clutch); **12** Olympiacos-Chris van der Drift, NZ, 7 (DNF-gearbox); **13** Flamengo-Franck Perera, F, 7 (DNF-accident damage); **14** Girondins de Bordeaux-Franck Montagny, F, 6 (DNF-accident); **15** Olympique Lyonnais-Sébastien Bourdais, F, 6 (DNF-accident); **16** Corinthians-Robert Doornbos, NL, 1 (DNF-accident damage); **17** Sevilla FC-Marcos Martinez, E, 0 (DN-accident).
Fastest race lap: FC Basel, 1m 28.142s, 111.945 mph/180.159 km/h.
Pole position: FC Basel.

Race 3 (13.704 miles/22.055 km).
1 AC Milan-Yelmer Buurman, NL, 7m 23.812s, 111.163 mph/178.900 km/h; **2** RSC Anderlecht-Davide Rigon, I, 7m 25.806s; **3** FC Basel-Maximilian Wissel, D, 7m 26.432s; **4** AS Roma-Julien Jousse, F, 7m 31.660s; **5** Liverpool FC-James Walker, GB, 7m 32.202s; **6** Tottenham Hotspur-Craig Dolby, GB, 7m 32.484s.
Fastest race lap: AC Milan, 1m 28.380s, 111.644 mph/179.674 km/h.
Pole position: Tottenham Hotspur.

SUPERLEAGUE FORMULA BY SONANGOL, Circuito Permanente del Jarama, Madrid, Spain, 20 June. Round 4. 33, 33 and 5 laps of the 2.392-mile/3.850-km circuit.
Race 1 (78.945 miles/127.050 km).
1 Beijing Guoan-John Martin, AUS, 45m 47.162s, 103.453 mph/166.491 km/h; **2** AC Milan-Yelmer Buurman, NL, 45m 47.626s; **3** Olympiacos-Chris van der Drift, NZ, 46m 00.181s; **4** FC Basel-Maximilian Wissel, D, 46m 01.708s; **5** Tottenham Hotspur-Craig Dolby, GB, 46m 17.089s; **6** Flamengo-Franck Perera, F, 46m 17.979s; **7** Olympique Lyonnais-Sébastien Bourdais, F, 46m 21.696s; **8** FC Porto-Álvaro Parente, P, 46m 28.001s; **9** Corinthians-Robert Doornbos, NL, 46m 32.561s; **10** RSC Anderlecht-Davide Rigon, I, 46m 41.201s; **11** PSV Eindhoven-Narain Karthikeyan, IND, 46m 52.458s; **12** Galatasaray-Tristan Gommendy, F, 47m 14.258s; **13** AS Roma-Julien Jousse, F, 47m 17.228s; **14** Sevilla FC-Marcos Martinez, E, 31 laps; **15** Liverpool FC-James Walker, GB, 31; **16** Girondins de Bordeaux-Franck Montagny, F, 15 (DNF-throttle); **17** Sporting Clube de Portugal-Borja García, E, 7 (DNF-spin).
Disqualified: Atletico de Madrid-Maria de Villota, E, finished 12th in 47m 08.490s (caused accident).
Fastest race lap: AC Milan, 1m 20.945s, 106.395 mph/171.227 km/h.
Pole position: Beijing Guoan, 1m 21.329s, 105.893 mph/170.418 km/h.

Race 2 (78.945 miles/127.050 km).
1 Girondins de Bordeaux-Franck Montagny, F, 45m 59.602s, 102.986 mph/165.741 km/h; **2** AS Roma-Julien Jousse, F, 46m 03.165s; **3** Tottenham Hotspur-Craig Dolby, GB, 46m 42.534s; **4** Liverpool FC-James Walker, GB, 46m 43.083s; **5** Corinthians-Robert Doornbos, NL, 46m 43.859s; **6** RSC Anderlecht-Davide Rigon, I, 46m 44.865s; **7** FC Basel-Maximilian Wissel, D, 46m 45.157s; **8** Flamengo-Franck Perera, F, 46m 45.906s; **9** Beijing Guoan-John Martin, AUS, 46m 46.238s; **10** AC Milan-Yelmer Buurman, NL, 46m 47.019s; **11** FC Porto-Álvaro Parente, P, 46m 47.178s; **12** Olympiacos-Chris van der Drift, NZ, 46m 47.971s; **13** Sporting Clube de Portugal-Borja García, E, 46m 49.035s; **14** Galatasaray-Tristan Gommendy, F, 47m 10.782s; **15** PSV Eindhoven-Narain Karthikeyan, IND, 19 laps (DNF-throttle); **16** Sevilla FC-Marcos Martinez, E, 4 (DNF-mechanical); **17** Olympique Lyonnais-Sébastien Bourdais, F, 2 (DNF-accident).
Disqualified: Atletico de Madrid-Maria de Villota, E, 2 laps (caused accident in race 1).
Fastest race lap: AS Roma, 1m 20.910s, 106.441 mph/171.301 km/h.
Pole position: Sporting Clube de Portugal.

Race 3 (11.961 miles/19.250 km).
1 Olympiacos-Chris van der Drift, NZ, 6m 48.119s, 105.510 mph/169.803 km/h; **2** Beijing Guoan-John Martin, AUS, 6m 52.708s; **3** AC Milan-Yelmer Buurman, NL, 6m 57.540s; **4** FC Basel-Maximilian Wissel, D, 7m 12.881s; **5** AS Roma-Julien Jousse, F, 7m 15.086s; **6** Tottenham Hotspur-Craig Dolby, GB, 0 laps (DNF-accident).
Fastest race lap: Olympiacos, 1m 21.140s, 106.140 mph/170.815 km/h.
Pole position: Tottenham Hotspur.

SUPERLEAGUE FORMULA BY SONANGOL, Nürburgring, Nürburg/Eifel, Germany, 27 June. Round 5. 26, 25 and 5 laps of the 3.199-mile/5.148-km circuit.
Race 1 (83.169 miles/133.848 km).
1 AC Milan-Yelmer Buurman, NL, 46m 36.469s, 107.066 mph/172.307 km/h; **2** RSC Anderlecht-Davide Rigon, I, 46m 44.193s; **3** Olympiacos-Chris van der Drift, NZ, 46m 48.031s; **4** Flamengo-Franck Perera, F, 46m 50.427s; **5** AS Roma-Julien Jousse, F, 47m 10.235s; **6** Liverpool FC-James Walker, GB, 47m 10.760s; **7** Corinthians-Robert Doornbos, NL, 47m 11.430s; **8** FC Basel-Maximilian Wissel, D, 47m 11.879s; **9** Galatasaray-Tristan Gommendy, F, 47m 12.514s; **10** Tottenham Hotspur-Craig Dolby, GB, 47m 23.484s; **11** Sevilla FC-Marcos Martinez, E, 47m 29.742s; **12** Sporting Clube de Portugal-Borja García, E, 47m 38.782s; **13** PSV Eindhoven-Narain Karthikeyan, IND, 47m 56.037s; **14** Olympique Lyonnais-Sébastien Bourdais, F, 25 laps; **15** Girondins de Bordeaux-Franck Montagny, F, 25; **16** Atletico de Madrid-Maria de Villota, E, 15 (DNF-accident); **17** FC Porto-Álvaro Parente, P, 12 (DNF-misfire).
Did not start: Beijing Guoan-John Martin, AUS (wheel loose)
Fastest race lap: FC Basel, 1m 44.896s, 109.782 mph/176.677 km/h.
Pole position: AS Roma, 1m 44.401s, 110.303 mph/177.515 km/h.

Race 2 (79.970 miles/128.700 km).
1 FC Porto-Álvaro Parente, P, 45m 03.384s, 106.493 mph/171.385 km/h; **2** Girondins de Bordeaux-Franck Montagny, F, 45m 04.210s; **3** Galatasaray-Tristan Gommendy, F, 45m 08.899s; **4** Atletico de Madrid-Maria de Villota, E, 45m 33.259s; **5** FC Basel-Maximilian Wissel, D, 45m 33.901s; **6** Tottenham Hotspur-Craig Dolby, GB, 45m 42.094s; **7** Sporting Clube de Portugal-Borja García, E, 45m 46.040s; **8** AC Milan-Yelmer Buurman, NL, 45m 46.579s; **9** Flamengo-Franck Perera, F, 45m 47.271s; **10** Corinthians-Robert Doornbos, NL, 45m 47.870s; **11** Olympiacos-Chris van der Drift, NZ, 45m 50.920s; **12** RSC Anderlecht-Davide Rigon, I, 45m 54.643s; **13** Sevilla FC-Marcos Martinez, E, 46m 06.810s; **14** AS Roma-Julien Jousse, F, 24 laps; **15** Beijing Guoan-John Martin, AUS, 22; **16** PSV Eindhoven-Narain Karthikeyan, IND, 22; **17** Olympique Lyonnais-Sébastien Bourdais, F, 15 (DNF-gearbox).
Did not start: Liverpool FC-James Walker, GB, **1** (gearbox compressor).
Fastest race lap: Girondins de Bordeaux, 1m 45.414s, 109.243 mph/175.809 km/h.
Pole position: Beijing Guoan.

Race 3 (15.994 miles/25.740 km).
1 Olympiacos-Chris van der Drift, NZ, 8m 57.984s, 107.026 mph/172.243 km/h; **2** RSC Anderlecht-Davide Rigon, I, 9m 03.791s; **3** AC Milan-Yelmer Buurman, NL, 9m 06.446s; **4** FC Basel-Maximilian Wissel, D, 9m 14.472s; **5** Galatasaray-Tristan Gommendy, F, 9m 32.257s.
Did not start: Flamengo-Franck Perera, F (stalled).
Fastest race lap: Olympiacos, 1m 45.522s, 109.131 mph/175.629 km/h.
Pole position: AC Milan.

SUPERLEAGUE FORMULA BY SONANGOL, Circuit Zolder, Heusden-Zolder, Belgium, 18 July. Round 6. 34, 32 and 5 laps of the 2.485-mile/4.000-km circuit.
Race 1 (84.506 miles/136.000 km).
1 Olympiacos-Chris van der Drift, NZ, 46m 07.239s, 109.937 mph/176.927 km/h; **2** RSC Anderlecht-Davide Rigon, I, 46m 09.131s; **3** Corinthians-Robert Doornbos, NL, 46m 11.205s; **4** AC Milan-Yelmer Buurman, NL, 46m 11.758s; **5** Tottenham Hotspur-Craig Dolby, GB, 46m 15.504s; **6** Liverpool FC-James Walker, GB, 46m 16.511s; **7** FC Basel-Maximilian Wissel, D, 46m 19.671s; **8** Sevilla FC-Marcos Martinez, E, 46m 31.554s; **9** Sporting Clube de Portugal-Andy Soucek, E, 46m 32.809s; **10** PSV Eindhoven-Narain Karthikeyan, IND, 47m 07.006s; **11** FC Porto-Álvaro Parente, P, 47m 08.388s; **12** Girondins de Bordeaux-Jaap van Lagen, NL, 47m 09.856s; **13** Beijing Guoan-John Martin, AUS, 47m 12.533s; **14** Galatasaray-Tristan Gommendy, F, 47m 19.236s; **15** AS Roma-Julien Jousse, F, 33 laps; **16** Atletico de Madrid-Maria de Villota, E, 33; **17** Flamengo-Duncan Tappy, GB, 24 (DNF-clutch).
Fastest race lap: RSC Anderlecht, 1m 18.806s, 113.541 mph/182.727 km/h.
Pole position: Olympiacos, 1m 18.721s, 113.664 mph/182.924 km/h.

Race 2 (79.536 miles/128.000 km).
1 AS Roma-Julien Jousse, F, 45m 16.364s, 105.408 mph/169.638 km/h; **2** Flamengo-Duncan Tappy, GB, 45m 26.825s; **3** Galatasaray-Tristan Gommendy, F, 45m 29.173s; **4** FC Basel-Maximilian Wissel, D, 45m 29.741s; **5** AC Milan-Yelmer Buurman, NL, 45m 29.978s; **6** Sporting Clube de Portugal-Andy Soucek, E, 45m 32.333s; **7** Beijing Guoan-John Martin, AUS, 45m 39.303s; **8** Olympiacos-Chris van der Drift, NZ, 45m 45.045s; **9** RSC Anderlecht-Davide Rigon, I, 45m 48.585s; **10** Girondins de Bordeaux-Jaap van Lagen, NL, 45m 51.055s; **11** Atletico de Madrid-Maria de Villota, E, 31 laps; **12** FC Porto-Álvaro Parente, P, 28 (DNF-gearbox); **13** Liverpool FC-James Walker, GB, 20 (DNF-spin); **14** PSV Eindhoven-Narain Karthikeyan, IND, 3 (DNF-accident); **15** Sevilla FC-Marcos Martinez, E, 1 (DNF-accident); **16** Corinthians-Robert Doornbos, NL, 0 (DNF-accident); **17** Tottenham Hotspur-Craig Dolby, GB, 0 (DNF-accident).
Fastest race lap: AC Milan, 1m 19.010s, 113.248 mph/182.255 km/h.
Pole position: Flamengo.

Race 3 (12.427 miles/20.000 km).
1 RSC Anderlecht-Davide Rigon, I, 6m 39.980s, 111.852 mph/180.009 km/h; **2** Olympiacos-Chris van der Drift, NZ, 6m 41.009s; **3** AS Roma-Julien Jousse, F, 6m 47.371s; **4** Galatasaray-Tristan Gommendy, F, 6m 48.325s; **5** AC Milan-Yelmer Buurman, NL, 6m 49.573s; **6** FC Basel-Maximilian Wissel, D, 6m 54.340s.
Fastest race lap: Olympiacos, 1m 18.595s, 113.846 mph/183.217 km/h.
Pole position: Olympiacos.

SUPERLEAGUE FORMULA BY SONANGOL, Brands Hatch Grand Prix Circuit, West Kingsdown, Dartford, Kent, Great Britain, 1 August. Round 7. 36, 29 and 5 laps of the 2.301-mile/3.703-km circuit.
Race 1 (82.834 miles/133.308 km).
1 Beijing Guoan-John Martin, AUS, 45m 20.096s, 109.629 mph/176.430 km/h; **2** Tottenham Hotspur-Craig Dolby, GB, 45m 27.534s; **3** Sporting Clube de Portugal-Andy Soucek, E, 45m 34.862s; **4** AC Milan-Yelmer Buurman, NL, 45m 35.802s; **5** Girondins de Bordeaux-Franck Montagny, F, 45m 37.352s; **6** FC Basel-Maximilian Wissel, D, 46m 02.169s; **7** Olympiacos-Chris van der Drift, NZ, 46m 13.213s; **8** Galatasaray-Tristan Gommendy, F, 46m 13.977s; **9** Flamengo-Duncan Tappy, GB, 46m 17.110s; **10** Liverpool FC-James Walker, GB, 46m 17.767s; **11** FC Porto-Álvaro Parente, P, 46m 18.979s; **12** Olympique Lyonnais-Franck Perera, F, 46m 19.642s; **13** RSC Anderlecht-Davide Rigon, I, 35 laps; **14** Atletico de Madrid-Maria de Villota, E, 35; **15** Corinthians-Robert Doornbos, NL, 34; **16** Sevilla FC-Marcos Martinez, E, 33 (DNF-out of fuel); **17** AS Roma-Julien Jousse, F, 33 (DNF-out of fuel); **18** PSV Eindhoven-Narain Karthikeyan, IND, 5 (DNF-accident).
Fastest race lap: Tottenham Hotspur, 1m 13.460s, 112.760 mph/181.470 km/h.
Pole position: Sevilla FC, 1m 13.856s, 112.155 mph/180.497 km/h.

Race 2 (66.727 miles/107.387 km).
1 PSV Eindhoven-Narain Karthikeyan, IND, 36m 47.240s, 108.831 mph/175.147 km/h; **2** RSC Anderlecht-Davide Rigon, I, 36m 59.976s; **3** Flamengo-Duncan Tappy, GB, 37m 05.188s; **4** FC Porto-Álvaro Parente, P, 37m 08.082s; **5** AS Roma-Julien Jousse, F, 37m 08.901s; **6** Olympiacos-Chris van der Drift, NZ, 37m 09.161s; **7** Atletico de Madrid-Maria de Villota, E, 37m 14.261s; **8** Sevilla FC-Marcos Martinez, E, 37m 18.375s; **9** Olympique Lyonnais-Franck Perera, F, 37m 19.002s; **10** Liverpool FC-James Walker, GB, 37m 19.826s; **11** FC Basel-Maximilian Wissel, D, 37m 20.612s; **12** AC Milan-Yelmer Buurman, NL, 37m 21.522s; **13** Tottenham Hotspur-Craig Dolby, GB, 37m 21.643s; **14** Girondins de Bordeaux-Franck Montagny, F, 37m 22.389s; **15** Sporting Clube de Portugal-Andy Soucek, E, 37m 24.256s; **16** Beijing Guoan-John Martin, AUS, 37m 57.619s; **17** Galatasaray-Tristan Gommendy, F, 20 laps (DNF-clutch); **18** Corinthians-Robert Doornbos, NL, 12 (DNF-gearbox).
Fastest race lap: Flamengo, 1m 14.023s, 111.902 mph/180.089 km/h.
Pole position: PSV Eindhoven.

Race 3 (11.505 miles/18.515 km).
1 Beijing Guoan-John Martin, AUS, 6m 16.188s, 110.096 mph/177.182 km/h; **2** RSC Anderlecht-Davide Rigon, I, 6m 19.411s; **3** Flamengo-Duncan Tappy, GB, 6m 22.881s; **4** AC Milan-Yelmer Buurman, NL, 6m 24.223s; **5** Tottenham Hotspur-Craig Dolby, GB, 6m 24.970s; **6** FC Porto-Álvaro Parente, P, 6m 28.463s.
Fastest race lap: Beijing Guoan, 1m 13.849s, 112.166 mph/180.514 km/h.
Pole position: Flamengo.

SUPERLEAGUE FORMULA BY SONANGOL, Autodromo Adria International Raceway, Adria, Italy, 5 September. Round 8. 40, 40 and 5 laps of the 1.679-mile/2.702-km circuit.
Race 1 (67.158 miles/108.080 km).
1 RSC Anderlecht-Davide Rigon, I, 45m 31.975s, 88.495 mph/142.420 km/h; **2** Beijing Guoan-John Martin, AUS, 45m 35.650s; **3** Olympiacos-Benjamin Hanley, GB, 45m 36.481s; **4** FC Basel-Maximilian Wissel, D, 45m 37.779s; **5** AS Roma-Julien Jousse, F, 45m 52.803s; **6** FC Porto-Álvaro Parente, P, 45m 53.744s; **7** Liverpool FC-Frédéric Vervisch, B, 46m 03.784s; **8** Corinthians-Robert Doornbos, NL, 46m 08.530s; **9** Galatasaray-Tristan Gommendy, F, 46m 08.598s; **10** Flamengo-Duncan Tappy, GB, 46m 21.374s; **11** AC Milan-Yelmer Buurman, NL, 46m 27.179s; **12** PSV Eindhoven-Hywel Lloyd, GB, 46m 35.375s; **13** Tottenham Hotspur-Craig Dolby, GB, 39 laps; **14** Sevilla FC-Marcos Martinez, E, 38; **15** Olympique Lyonnais-Celso Miguez, E, 34 (DNF-gearbox).
Did not start: Atletico de Madrid-Maria de Villota, E (neck injury).
Fastest race lap: FC Basel, 1m 06.580s, 90.781 mph/146.097 km/h.
Pole position: RSC Anderlecht, 1m 06.644s, 90.693 mph/145.957 km/h.

Race 2 (67.158 miles/108.080 km).
1 Sevilla FC-Marcos Martinez, E, 45m 53.970s, 87.788 mph/141.282 km/h; **2** Tottenham Hotspur-Craig Dolby, GB, 45m 59.621s; **3** Flamengo-Duncan Tappy, GB, 46m 03.546s; **4** AC Milan-Yelmer Buurman, NL, 46m 04.016s; **5** Liverpool FC-Frédéric Vervisch, B, 46m 04.537s; **6** Corinthians-Robert Doornbos, NL, 46m 04.991s; **7** FC Basel-Maximilian Wissel, D, 46m 05.945s; **8** RSC Anderlecht-Davide Rigon, I, 46m 06.499s; **9** Beijing Guoan-John Martin, AUS, 46m 07.193s; **10** Olympiacos-Benjamin Hanley, GB, 46m 14.126s; **11** FC Porto-Álvaro Parente, P, 46m 20.576s; **12** PSV Eindhoven-Hywel Lloyd, GB, 46m 29.526s; **13** Galatasaray-Tristan Gommendy, F, 46m 32.243s; **14** AS Roma-Julien Jousse, F, 46m 34.609s; **15** Olympique Lyonnais-Celso Miguez, E, 12 laps (DNF-gearbox).
Fastest race lap: Corinthians, 1m 06.944s, 90.287 mph/145.303 km/h.
Pole position: Olympique Lyonnais.

Race 3 (8.395 miles/13.510 km).
1 RSC Anderlecht-Davide Rigon, I, 5m 36.851s, 89.716 mph/144.384 km/h; **2** FC Basel-Maximilian Wissel, D, 5m 37.876s; **3** Olympiacos-Benjamin Hanley, GB, 5m 38.279s; **4** Beijing Guoan-John Martin, AUS, 5m 40.145s; **5** Sevilla FC-Marcos Martinez, E, 5m 42.395s; **6** Liverpool FC-Frédéric Vervisch, B, 5m 43.633s.
Fastest race lap: Olympiacos, 1m 06.646s, 90.691 mph/145.953 km/h.
Pole position: RSC Anderlecht.

SUPERLEAGUE FORMULA BY SONANGOL, Autódromo Internacional do Algarve, Portimão, Portugal, 19 September. Round 9. 29, 29 and 5 laps of the 2.891-mile/4.652-km circuit.
Race 1 (83.828 miles/134.908 km).
1 Beijing Guoan-John Martin, AUS, 45m 37.236s, 110.250 mph/177.430 km/h; **2** RSC Anderlecht-Davide Rigon, I, 45m 38.410s; **3** FC Porto-Álvaro Parente, P, 45m 56.724s; **4** Liverpool FC-Frédéric Vervisch, B, 45m 59.193s; **5** Tottenham Hotspur-Craig Dolby, GB, 46m 07.180s; **6** Corinthians-Robert Doornbos, NL, 46m 08.448s; **7** FC Basel-Maximilian Wissel, D, 46m 09.357s; **8** Flamengo-Duncan Tappy, GB, 46m 17.049s; **9** Galatasaray-Andy Soucek, E, 46m 18.073s; **10** AC Milan-Yelmer Buurman, NL, 46m 18.327s; **11** Olympique Lyonnais-Tristan Gommendy, F, 46m 21.655s; **12** Sevilla FC-Marcos Martinez, E, 46m 50.173s; **13** AS Roma-Julien Jousse, F, 46m 52.296s; **14** Olympiacos-Neel Jani, CH, 46m 52.554s; **15** Sporting Clube de Portugal-Máximo Cortés, E, 47m 12.715s; **16** PSV Eindhoven-Hywel Lloyd, GB, 26 laps; **17** Atletico de Madrid-Maria de Villota, E, 2 (DNF-accident damage); **18** Girondins de Bordeaux-Celso Miguez, E, 1 (DNF-accident damage).
Fastest race lap: Galatasaray, 1m 31.935s, 113.191 mph/182.163 km/h.
Pole position: Beijing Guoan, 1m 33.149s, 111.715 mph/179.789 km/h.

Race 2 (83.828 miles/134.908 km).
1 Olympiacos-Neel Jani, CH, 46m 00.710s, 109.312 mph/175.921 km/h; **2** Olympique Lyonnais-Tristan Gommendy, F, 46m 10.095s; **3** Corinthians-Robert Doornbos, NL, 46m 12.158s; **4** FC Basel-Maximilian Wissel, D, 46m 14.933s; **5** Galatasaray-Andy Soucek, E, 46m 18.367s; **6** Liverpool FC-Frédéric Vervisch, B, 46m 25.109s; **7** Flamengo-Duncan Tappy, GB, 46m 31.864s; **8** PSV Eindhoven-Hywel Lloyd, GB, 46m 39.820s; **9** RSC Anderlecht-Davide Rigon, I, 46m 41.717s; **10** AS Roma-Julien Jousse, F, 46m 44.608s; **11** Beijing Guoan-John Martin, AUS, 47m 05.372s; **12** Atletico de Madrid-Maria de Villota, E, 47m 09.785s; **13** Tottenham Hotspur-Craig Dolby, GB, 28 laps; **14** Girondins de Bordeaux-Celso Miguez, E, 12 (DNF-gearbox); **15** Sporting Clube de Portugal-Máximo Cortés, E, 9 (DNF-gearbox); **16** AC Milan-Yelmer Buurman, NL, 8 (DNF-gearbox); **17** FC Porto-Álvaro Parente, P, 8 (DNF-wheel lost); **18** Sevilla FC-Marcos Martinez, E, 6 (DNF-gearbox).
Fastest race lap: Olympique Lyonnais, 1m 32.578s, 112.404 mph/180.898 km/h.
Pole position: Girondins de Bordeaux.

Race 3 (14.453 miles/23.260 km).
1 Liverpool FC-Frédéric Vervisch, B, 7m 50.206s, 110.656 mph/178.083 km/h; **2** RSC Anderlecht-Davide Rigon, I, 7m 50.677s; **3** Beijing Guoan-John Martin, AUS, 7m 51.146s; **4** FC Basel-Maximilian Wissel, D, 7m 59.381s; **5** Corinthians-Robert Doornbos, NL, 0 laps (DNF-accident); **6** Olympique Lyonnais-Tristan Gommendy, F, 0 (DNF-accident).
Fastest race lap: RSC Anderlecht, 1m 32.777s, 112.163 mph/180.510 km/h.
Pole position: Corinthians.

SUPERLEAGUE FORMULA BY SONANGOL, Ordos International Circuit, Ordos City, China, 3 October. Round 10. 30, 29 and 5 laps of the 2.331-mile/3.752-km circuit.
Race 1 (69.942 miles/112.560 km).
1 Olympiacos-Benjamin Hanley, GB, 46m 07.003s, 90.997 mph/146.445 km/h; **2** FC Basel-Maximilian Wissel, D, 46m 09.623s; **3** FC Porto-Earl Bamber, NZ, 46m 34.210s; **4** Tottenham Hotspur-Craig Dolby, GB, 46m 37.631s; **5** RSC Anderlecht-Davide Rigon, I, 46m 42.234s; **6** AC Milan-Yelmer Buurman, NL, 46m 45.825s; **7** Girondins de Bordeaux-Franck Perera, F, 46m 48.596s; **8** Sevilla FC-Marcos Martinez, E, 47m 12.359s; **9** Atletico de Madrid-Bruno Méndez, E, 48m 01.530s; **10** PSV Eindhoven-Adderly Fong, HK, 29 laps; **11** AS Roma-Julien Jousse, F, 29; **12** Team China-Qinghua Ma, CN, 29; **13** Galatasaray-Giacomo Ricci, I, 28; **14** Olympique Lyonnais-Tristan Gommendy, F, 25 (DNF-gearbox); **15** Liverpool FC-Frédéric Vervisch, B, 1 (DNF-engine); **16** Sporting Clube de Portugal-Adrián Vallés, E, 1 (DNF-gearbox); **17** Flamengo-Andy Soucek, E, 0 (DNF-accident); **18** Corinthians-Robert Doornbos, NL, 0 (DNF-accident); **19** Beijing Guoan-John Martin, AUS, 0 (DNF-accident).
Fastest race lap: Olympiacos, 1m 30.021s, 93.233 mph/150.044 km/h.
Pole position: Olympiacos, 1m 30.347s, 92.897 mph/149.503 km/h.

Race 2 (67.610 miles/108.808 km).
1 Liverpool FC-Frédéric Vervisch, B, 45m 12.859s, 89.719 mph/144.389 km/h; **2** FC Basel-Maximilian Wissel, D, 45m 20.484s; **3** Flamengo-Andy Soucek, E, 45m 22.296s; **4** Olympiacos-Benjamin Hanley, GB, 45m 31.769s; **5** Sporting Clube de Portugal-Adrián Vallés, E, 45m 34.471s; **6** Girondins de Bordeaux-Franck Perera, F, 45m 55.477s; **7** AC Milan-Yelmer Buurman, NL, 45m 56.184s; **8** RSC Anderlecht-Davide Rigon, I, 45m 59.911s; **9** Sevilla FC-Marcos Martinez, E, 46m 07.845s; **10** Tottenham Hotspur-Craig Dolby, GB, 46m 08.836s; **11** PSV Eindhoven-Adderly Fong, HK, 46m 14.434s; **12** FC Porto-Earl Bamber, NZ, 46m 22.216s; **13** Team China-Qinghua Ma, CN, 28 laps; **14** Atletico de Madrid-Bruno Méndez, E, 17 (DNF-accident); **15** Corinthians-Robert Doornbos, NL, 12 (DNF-puncture); **16** AS Roma-Julien Jousse, F, 0 (DNF-accident); **17** Olympique Lyonnais-Tristan Gommendy, F, 0 (DNF-accident).
Did not start: Galatasaray-Giacomo Ricci, I (gearbox); Beijing Guoan-John Martin, AUS (accident damage).
Fastest race lap: Olympiacos, 1m 30.740s, 92.494 mph/148.856 km/h.
Pole position: Flamengo.

Race 3 (11.657 miles/18.760 km).
1 FC Porto-Earl Bamber, NZ, 7m 52.997s, 88.721 mph/142.783 km/h; **2** Girondins de Bordeaux-Franck Perera, F, 7m 53.157s; **3** RSC Anderlecht-Davide Rigon, I, 7m 54.063s; **4** AC Milan-Yelmer Buurman, NL, 8m 57.282s; **5** Olympiacos-Benjamin Hanley, GB, 0 laps (DNF-accident); **6** FC Basel-Maximilian Wissel, D, 0 (DNF-accident).
Fastest race lap: Girondins de Bordeaux, 1m 31.332s, 91.895 mph/147.891 km/h.
Pole position: FC Basel.

SUPERLEAGUE FORMULA BY SONANGOL, Beijing International Street Circuit, China, 10 October. Round 11. 31, 27 and 0 laps of the 1.691-mile/2.721-km circuit.
Race 1 (52.413 miles/84.351 km).
1 Tottenham Hotspur-Craig Dolby, GB, 40m 05.209s, 78.449 mph/126.252 km/h; **2** Girondins de Bordeaux-Franck Perera, F, 40m 08.256s; **3** Liverpool FC-Frédéric Vervisch, B, 40m 10.100s; **4** Olympique Lyonnais-Tristan Gommendy, F, 40m 16.956s; **5** Sporting Clube de Portugal-Adrián Vallés, E, 40m 19.141s; **6** PSV Eindhoven-Earl Bamber, NZ, 40m 21.308s; **7** AC Milan-Yelmer Buurman, NL, 40m 21.923s; **8** AS Roma-Julien Jousse, F, 40m 24.606s; **9** Olympiacos-Benjamin Hanley, GB, 40m 51.959s; **10** Team China-Adderly Fong, HK, 17 laps; **11** Beijing Guoan-John Martin, AUS, 3; **12** Galatasaray-Giacomo Ricci, I, 2; **13** RSC Anderlecht-Davide Rigon, I, 0; **14** Atletico de Madrid-Paul Meijer, NL, 0; **15** FC Porto-Álvaro Parente, P, 0; **16** Sevilla FC-Marcos Martinez, E, 0.
Fastest race lap: Liverpool FC, 1m 05.058s, 93.558 mph/150.567 km/h.
Pole position: FC Porto, 1m 05.287s, 93.229 mph/150.039 km/h.

Race 2 (45.650 miles/73.467 km).
1 FC Porto-Álvaro Parente, P, 49m 18.621s, 55.546 mph/89.393 km/h; **2** PSV Eindhoven-Earl Bamber, NZ, 49m 19.465s; **3** AC Milan-Yelmer Buurman, NL, 49m 21.254s; **4** Sevilla FC-Marcos Martinez, E, 49m 21.317s; **5** Atletico de Madrid-Paul Meijer, NL, 49m 27.974s; **6** Beijing Guoan-John Martin, AUS, 49m 50.272s; **7** Liverpool FC-Frédéric Vervisch, B, 26 laps; **8** Tottenham Hotspur-Craig Dolby, GB, 26; **9** Sporting Clube de Portugal-Adrián Vallés, E, 26; **10** Girondins de Bordeaux-Franck Perera, F, 26; **11** Olympique Lyonnais-Tristan Gommendy, F, 24; **12** Galatasaray-Giacomo Ricci, I, 23; **13** AS Roma-Julien Jousse, F, 20; **14** Olympiacos-Benjamin Hanley, GB, 5; **15** RSC Anderlecht-Davide Rigon, I, 2.
Fastest race lap: Liverpool FC, 1m 05.719s, 92.617 mph/149.052 km/h.
Pole position: RSC Anderlecht.

Race 3 not run due to dark conditions.

SUPERLEAGUE FORMULA BY SONANGOL, Circuito de Navarra, Los Arcos, Spain, 24 October. Round 12. 26, 22 and 5 laps of the 2.444-mile/3.933-km circuit.
Race 1 (63.540 miles/102.258 km).
1 Beijing Guoan-John Martin, AUS, 41m 02.447s, 92.893 mph/149.497 km/h; **2** RSC Anderlecht-Davide Rigon, I, 41m 08.497s; **3** Tottenham Hotspur-Craig Dolby, GB, 41m 16.703s; **4** Flamengo-Andy Soucek, E, 41m 18.569s; **5** Girondins de Bordeaux-Franck Perera, F, 41m 19.293s; **6** FC Basel-Maximilian Wissel, D, 41m 32.902s; **7** AC Milan-Yelmer Buurman, NL, 41m 33.645s; **8** FC Porto-Álvaro Parente, P, 41m 33.871s; **9** Corinthians-Robert Doornbos, NL, 41m 35.087s; **10** Sporting Clube de Portugal-Adrián Vallés, E, 41m 43.107s; **11** PSV Eindhoven-Esteban Guerrieri, RA, 41m 53.355s; **12** Olympiacos-Benjamin Hanley, GB, 42m 01.307s; **13** Atletico de Madrid-Maria de Villota, E, 42m 12.863s; **14** Olympique Lyonnais-Tristan Gommendy, F, 42m 14.681s; **15** Sevilla FC-Marcos Martinez, E, 42m 22.198s; **16** Liverpool FC-Frédéric Vervisch, B, 25 laps; **17** Galatasaray-Chris van der Drift, NZ, 6 (DNF-spin); **18** AS Roma-Máximo Cortés, E, 2 (DNF-spin).
Fastest race lap: Liverpool FC, 1m 27.348s, 100.722 mph/162.096 km/h.
Pole position: RSC Anderlecht, 1m 26.702s, 101.472 mph/163.304 km/h.

Race 2 (53.765 miles/86.526 km).
1 FC Porto-Álvaro Parente, P, 40m 46.976s, 79.098 mph/127.297 km/h; **2** PSV Eindhoven-Esteban Guerrieri, RA, 40m 48.869s; **3** Sevilla FC-Marcos Martinez, E, 40m 53.657s; **4** Tottenham Hotspur-Craig Dolby, GB, 40m 54.018s; **5** AS Roma-Máximo Cortés, E, 40m 55.185s; **6** Beijing Guoan-John Martin, AUS, 40m 56.147s; **7** Galatasaray-Chris van der Drift, NZ, 40m 58.639s; **8** Olympiacos-Benjamin Hanley, GB, 40m 58.939s; **9** Girondins de Bordeaux-Franck Perera, F, 40m 59.371s; **10** Atletico de Madrid-Maria de Villota, E, 41m 00.435s; **11** RSC Anderlecht-Davide Rigon, I, 41m 01.327s; **12** AC Milan-Yelmer Buurman, NL, 41m 01.824s; **13** Olympique Lyonnais-Tristan Gommendy, F, 41m 02.882s; **14** FC Basel-Maximilian Wissel, D, 41m 06.622s; **15** Corinthians-Robert Doornbos, NL, 6 laps (DNF-accident damage); **16** Sporting Clube de Portugal-Adrián Vallés, E, 5 (DNF-spin); **17** Liverpool FC-Frédéric Vervisch, B, 5 (DNF-gearbox); **18** Flamengo-Andy Soucek, E, 0 (DNF-gearbox).
Fastest race lap: FC Porto, 1m 28.302s, 99.633 mph/160.345 km/h.
Pole position: AS Roma.

Race 3 (12.219 miles/19.665 km).
1 Beijing Guoan-John Martin, AUS, 7m 26.597s, 98.498 mph/158.518 km/h; **2** Tottenham Hotspur-Craig Dolby, GB, 7m 28.549s; **3** PSV Eindhoven-Esteban Guerrieri, RA, 7m 31.752s; **4** RSC Anderlecht-Davide Rigon, I, 7m 32.163s; **5** Girondins de Bordeaux-Franck Perera, F, 7m 34.917s; **6** FC Porto-Álvaro Parente, P, 7m 34.948s.
Fastest race lap: PSV Eindhoven, 1m 27.750s, 100.260 mph/161.353 km/h.
Pole position: Beijing Guoan.

Final championship points
1 RSC Anderlecht, 699; **2** Tottenham Hotspur, 697; **3** FC Basel, 667; **4** Olympiacos, 653; **5** AC Milan, 631; **6** Flamengo, 540; **7** FC Porto, 495; **8** AS Roma, 458; **9** Beijing Guoan, 453; **10** Liverpool FC, 439; **11** Girondins de Bordeaux, 372; **12** Corinthians, 363; **13** Galatasaray, 358; **14** Sevilla FC, 355; **15** Sporting Clube de Portugal, 329; **16** PSV Eindhoven, 288; **17** Atletico de Madrid, 265; **18** Olympique Lyonnais, 235; **19** Team China, 26.